AMERICAN WRITERS

A Collection of Literary Biographies

LEONARD UNGER
Editor in Chief

VOLUME II
Ralph Waldo Emerson
to
Carson McCullers

Charles Scribner's Sons, New York

Acknowledgment is gratefully made to those publishers and individuals who have permitted the use of the following materials in copyright.

"Robert Frost"
from *The Poetry of Robert Frost*, ed. Edward Connery Lathem, copyright 1923, 1928, 1934, © 1969 Holt, Rinehart and Winston, Inc.; copyright 1936, 1942, 1951, © 1956, 1962 Robert Frost; copyright © 1964, 1970 Lesley Frost Ballantine. Reprinted by permission of Holt, Rinehart and Winston, Inc. and Jonathan Cape Ltd.

"Randall Jarrell"
from *The Complete Poems*, by Randall Jarrell, copyright 1935, 1936, 1937, 1940, 1941, 1942, 1944, 1945, 1946, 1947, 1948, 1949, 1950, 1951, 1952, © 1965, 1966, 1967, 1968, 1969 Mrs. Randall Jarrell, copyright renewed 1968, 1969 Mrs. Randall Jarrell. Reprinted by permission of Farrar, Straus & Giroux, Inc. and Faber and Faber Ltd.
from *The Lost World*, by Randall Jarrell, "A Hunt in the Black Forest," copyright 1948 Randall Jarrell. Originally published as "The King's Hunt" in *Poetry* Magazine. By permission of The Macmillan Company and Eyre & Spottiswoode (Publishers) Ltd.
from *The Lost World*, by Randall Jarrell, "A Street off Sunset," copyright © 1963 Randall Jarrell. Originally published in *Poetry Magazine*, by permission of The Macmillan Company and Eyre & Spottiswoode (Publishers) Ltd.

from *The Woman at the Washington Zoo*, by Randall Jarrell, "The Woman at the Washington Zoo," copyright © 1960 Randall Jarrell; "In Those Days," copyright 1952 Curtis Publishing Company; "The Elementary Scene," copyright © 1960 Randall Jarrell; "Windows," copyright 1954 Randall Jarrell, by permission of Atheneum Publishers
from "To a Conscript of 1940," *Collected Poems*, by Sir Herbert Read, copyright 1966, by permission of Horizon Press and Faber and Faber Ltd.

"Ring Lardner"
from *I Gaspiri*, reprinted from *What of It?*, by Ring Lardner, copyright 1925 Charles Scribner's Sons; renewal copyright 1952 Ellis A. Lardner, by permission of Charles Scribner's Sons
from "A Caddy's Diary" (1927), *Round Up*, by permission of Charles Scribner's Sons
from "On Conversation" (1934), *First and Last*, by permission of Charles Scribner's Sons

"Sinclair Lewis"
material drawn from Mark Schorer, *Sinclair Lewis: An American Life*, by permission of Mr. Schorer

"Jack London"
from "Birches," *The Poetry of Robert Frost*, ed. Edward Connery Lathem, copyright 1916, © 1969 Holt, Rinehart and Winston, Inc.; copyright 1944 Robert Frost. Reprinted by permission of Holt, Rinehart and Winston, Inc. and Jonathan Cape Ltd.

AMERICAN WRITERS

AMERICAN WRITERS

Ralph Waldo Emerson

1803-1882

FROM wise men the world inherits a literature of wisdom, characterized less by its programmatic informativeness than by its strength and brevity of statement. *Proverb, aphorism, maxim* are terms for the succinct wise sayings which we have from every language, from Moses and Jesus, from Confucius, Buddha, and Mohammed, from Heraclitus, Martial, and Marcus Aurelius, from Montaigne and Bacon, down the traditions of time to America's man of wisdom, Ralph Waldo Emerson.

To understand Emerson's writing we had best try to follow what he has to say in the way that he says it. First, in three maturely characteristic books, let us look at his setting forth of ideas. Then, in all his writing from youthful speculation to aging reminiscence, let us trace his suiting of thought to event. Finally, let us try to specify, by a closer look at his traits of style, some of the particular individuality of our wisdom-writer in his tradition.

One of his most solidly organized and directly speaking books is *The Conduct of Life,* published along with *Representative Men* and *English Traits* in Emerson's mature years and representing the fullness of his achievement. Before these three, he had made many beginnings in journals, sermons, lectures, poems, and such widely discussed volumes as *Nature*

of 1836 and the two *Essays* series. And in the later years, he continued his writing and lecturing, with special emphasis on the Civil War and the new science. To both beginnings and conclusions, *The Conduct of Life, Representative Men,* and *English Traits* were central. If we look at them first, for Emerson's chief ideas as they concern us, we may then turn to a more historical and a more literary view for further understanding of his purposes and effects.

The Conduct of Life begins with one main question: How shall I live? Not, What is the theory of the age, or What is the spirit of the times, or What can we do to reform men? The question is not *What,* but *How*; the questioner not *we,* but *I*; the problem, *to live.* These characteristics of active and personal process establish the tone and the construction of Emerson's whole book, and of his whole work.

Say that you, as reader, have this book in hand, a gracefully compact volume of two hundred pages, how will you most easily follow its thought? By following Emerson's belief that the parts of an idea are given meaning by the whole, as they in their turn give substance to the whole. The parts in *The Conduct of Life* are nine chapters, derived from nine lectures which Emerson had given in sequence to an audience of Boston townspeople gathered together in the 1850's to hear him because of his great reputation for saying well what they needed to hear. What audiences in the 1970's might hear on the theme "How Shall I Live?" would depend, probably, on the speaker's specialization; they might get a businessman's or a churchman's answer, a scientist's answer, a psychologist's or an artist's answer, an "academic" or a "journalistic" answer. For each specialty, there would be a series of informative topics, say, "Automation," or "Renaissance Humanism," or "Zen." In contrast, how surprising in their speculative generality are Emerson's nine: "Fate," "Power," "Wealth," "Culture," "Behavior," "Worship," "Considerations by the Way," "Beauty," and "Illusions." How, the reader may wonder, can he make a whole of these? And where is the information in them? Our modern habit of information-seeking will probably lead to doubts about such a list of contents. Emerson's own hearers probably felt a different doubt. Bred to churchgoing and sermon-listening, they may have wondered at the nonreligiousness of such titles, their lack of Biblical texts and canons. So this list has a kind of daring to it, for either century, moral yet secular as it is. Few writers except wisdom-writers have the power to span the years by the endurance of their generalities in combination with the immediacy of their references to daily life.

How shall I live? With fate; that is, with the limitations of my inheritance and the natural world. With power, my abilities and energies. With wealth, my gains or losses. With culture, my widest sympathies and affinities. With behavior, my manner of life. With worship, my belief. With considerations, the positive centers for my action. With beauty, the underlying likenesses of the beautiful. And with illusions, the games and masks of my self-deception.

The sequence of answers begins with fate, impersonally and negatively; grows more and more strongly personal through the center in worship; then adds in conclusion a triad of impersonal and negative warnings on the dissonances and consonances of the process of composing a living and a life. The last essay ends as the first ends, with the axiom, the accepted, undemonstrated, intuitive assertion that there is no chance, no anomaly, in the universe; that all is system and gradation; and that the young mortal, the pure in heart, survives with the true, beautiful, and moral gods.

To see more clearly how Emerson established this coherent universe, it is useful to look closely at the form of the first essay, "Fate"; then, to gain a sense of the complementary solidity of individual choice and action, to look at "Wealth"—to relate, that is, life to the living of it. Note the difference from the Christian incarnation, which Emerson had studied to preach and had resigned from preaching. Incarnation draws mind and spirit downward into body, into the crucifixion and redemption of body. For Emerson, the motion is upward, cyclical, opposing and circling into spiral, through the power of every individual soul as it participates in the unifying force of the one soul, the over-soul, which composes all. The positive energy is earthly as well as heavenly.

The essay "Fate" proceeds through a half-dozen steps of four or five pages each. The first step is to make use of the limitations, negations, brute facts, tyrannies of life. The second, in both individual and national inheritance, is to accept the force of such restrictive circumstance. "Nature is, what you may do. There is much you may not. . . . Once we thought, positive power was all. Now we learn, that negative power, or circumstance, is half. Nature is the tyrannous circumstance, the thick skull, the sheathed snake, the ponderous, rock-like jaw; necessitated activity; violent direction; the conditions of a tool, like the locomotive, strong enough on its track, but which can do nothing but mischief off of it; or skates, which are wings on the ice, but fetters on the ground. The book of Nature is the book of Fate." But the third step is to recognize the power of thought in man—"On one side, elemental order, sandstone and granite, rock-ledges, peat-bog, forest, sea and shore; and, on the other part, thought, the spirit which composes and decomposes nature,—here they are, side by side, god and devil, mind and matter, king and conspirator, belt and spasm, riding peacefully together in the eye and brain of every man." The fourth is to see that man's thought not only counters but uses fate, by design, by dream, by will, by moral purpose. "Fate, then, is a name for facts not yet passed under the fire of thought;—for causes which are unpenetrated." The fifth is to see that their inter-relations, fate's and thought's, are manifold. The sixth is to think about the spirit of the age as the interworking of event and person, the advance out of fate into freedom, and their rebalancing. The soul "contains the event that shall befall it, for the event is only the actualization of its thoughts; and what we pray to ourselves for is always granted." So finally, the peroration of the pulpit and lecture hall: "Let us build altars to the Beautiful Necessity" which rudely or softly educates man to the perception that there are no contingencies.

The following essay, "Power," stresses again the potential force of man, especially the strength that comes with concentration and habituation of his abilities, and uses the analogy of the energy and husbandry of a machine, which is constructed by man to exclude follies and hindrances, broken threads and rotten hours, from his production.

Coming then to the essay on production, called "Wealth," we may stop to take note of another of Emerson's characteristics as essayist, his sermonlike use of a verse text not scriptural but his own. We note key lines from the poem that stands at the head of this essay:

And well the primal pioneer
Knew the strong task to it assigned
Patient through Heaven's enormous year
To build in matter home for mind.

The whole poem is a treatise, a history, a four-beat, irregularly rhyming re-creation of past wealth, of wheat, metal ores, coal, and then the binding threads of city and trade, the ties of nature and of law which hold even in the most youthful being.

In the essay itself, the theme is set early: "How does that man get his living? . . . He fails to make his place good in the world, unless he not only pays his debt, but also adds something to the common wealth." "Wealth," says Emerson, "has its source in applications of the mind to nature, from the rudest strokes of spade and axe, up to the last secrets of art." It is "the greatest possible extension to our powers, as if it added feet, and hands, and eyes, and blood, length to the day, and knowledge, and good-will."

By a law of nature, man feeds himself, fills his own needs. "He is the richest man who knows how to draw a benefit from the labors of the greatest number of men, of men in distant countries, and in past times." Economy is moral when it makes for profound, not trivial, independences. No man, in whatever time, is as rich as he ought to be. Property is an intellectual production; commerce, a game of skill; money, the delicate measure of civil, social, and moral changes. "A dollar in a university, is worth more than a dollar in a jail . . . the value of a dollar is social, as it is created by society." Economy has its own inner balances.

In the essay, Emerson makes four main points about economy, that is, about means related to ends: that each man's expense should proceed from his character; that each man should proceed by system; that each should follow the custom of the country; that each will reap what he sows, for "the counting-room maxims liberally expounded are laws of the Universe." Investment is the final significance: from wealth, to money, to value, to expenditure; from bread, to strength, to thought, to courage, invested toward higher goods. Like "Fate," then, "Wealth" is organized by a handful of sections, one moving into the next, with an initial question answered early and then finally raised to a higher power.

The idea of culture tempers the ideas of power and wealth by moderating and expanding them. Books, travels, cities, solitude, with all their difficulties, carry man from focused energy to widening thought, from quadruped to human. Superficially, but no less significantly, the *how* of men's life is the *how* of "Manners." Manners are the best ways of doing things, the gentlest laws and bonds. Their basis lies in self-reliance, in thoughtful choice; their grammar of gesture is clearer than English grammar, a part of both nature and character.

"Worship," in turning back from spirit in body to body in spirit, takes note of criticisms made by hearers of the earlier lectures in this series: that there is too much of body in the lectures; that they grant too much power either to animal man or to negative man. But Emerson says he will persist, against all sanctified airs, in recognizing both, the one for praise, the other for blame. Religious worship is a flowering from bodily stems: it needs the vigor of nature. Vigorless worship, institutionalized, dogmatized, sectarian, as in many of the churches of his day, is weak and wrong; where it exists new forms are needed, new channels for spirit to move in. "In our large cities, the population is godless, materialized,—no bond, no fellow-feeling, no enthusiasm. These are not men, but hungers, thirsts, fevers, and appetites walking. How is it people manage to live on,— so aimless as they are? After their peppercorn aims are gained, it seems as if the lime in their bones alone held them together, and not any worthy purpose." We need not fear, on the other hand, if creeds and sects decline. "The public and the private element, like north and south, like inside and outside, like centrifugal and centripetal, adhere to every soul, and cannot be subdued, except the soul is dissipated. God builds his temple in the heart on the ruins of churches and religions."

Vividly in this climactic chapter, Emerson makes clear the bent of his philosophy. It is not methodology, not logic, not systematic analysis or inquiry that concerns him; it is the creation of a pattern of thought and observation in reasonable harmony with certain accepted axioms of intuited belief. First, "We are born believing. A man bears beliefs, as a tree bears apples." Second, morality and intellect are related in growth. "Every man takes care that his neighbor shall not cheat him. But a day comes when he begins to care that he does not cheat his neighbor. Then all goes well. He has changed his market-cart into a chariot of the sun. What a day dawns, when we have taken to heart the doctrine of faith! to prefer, as a better investment, being to doing . . . the life to the year. . . ." The word *investment*, echoing from the essay on wealth, carries the sense of treasure used, of active commitment, in faith, to present and future. After a number of examples, for those faint in heart, comes the peroration of "Worship," which we may take for as strongly and briefly phrased a conclusion as Emerson ever came to. "And so I think that the last lesson of life, the choral song which rises from all elements and all angels, is, a voluntary obedience, a necessitated freedom. Man is made of the same atoms as the world is, he shares the same impressions, predispositions, and destiny. When his mind is illuminated, when his heart is kind, he throws himself joyfully into the sublime order, and does, with knowledge, what the stones do by structure."

To this larger theme of detail in the sublime order, the last three essays in *The Conduct of Life* devote themselves.

"Considerations" deals with true and false bonds, true and false allegiances and centers, for groups and for individuals. "Our chief want in life, is, somebody who shall make us do what we can. This is the service of a friend." This is the service, too, of a good minority in a government, and of any heroic, obligable nucleus—to loose false ties, to give us the courage to serve and to be what we are.

"Beauty" also stresses such relations of harmony. Like science, beauty extends and deepens us, takes us from surfaces to the foundations of things. That which is beautiful is simple, has no superfluous parts, serves its end, stands related to all things, is the mean of many extremes. Each of these qualities Emerson illustrates further; the structure of this essay is a series of exemplifications moving toward the highest power of beauty—to relate.

He concludes with an essay on deceptive relations, "Illusions," to remind us what we are so conscious of today—false fronts, masks. He will not allow us to rest easy; we must ride a beast of ever-changing form. With the young mortal and the gods together in the realm of pure truth, Emerson ends his advices on the conduct of life, catching up in his last sentences what he had set forth in his first: "If we must accept Fate, we are not less compelled to affirm liberty, the significance of the individual, the grandeur of duty, the power of character." He has harped on each string, as he has said, through nine essays, in order to harmonize them. His compositions have been played on these few main themes. Do we grant

him his premises, his intuitive beliefs? Whether or no, at least we can grant him his questions and therefore follow where he leads in his ever-varying range of effort to answer.

The Conduct of Life was Emerson's last, most coherent, and for many his most admirable book. We may take it as the mature effort of his thought in his fifties, tried out in journal entries and on lecture platforms, and finally published forth in 1860. Even more than the *Conduct,* the other two books of his maturity, *Representative Men* (1850), and *English Traits* (1856), harped on certain strings. The lifelong personal question of *Conduct*—How shall I live?—they asked more historically and descriptively: How do great men and nations live?

We know that one of the much-read books of Emerson's youth was Plutarch's *Lives*—lives of soldiers and statesmen, of men of political action in Greece and Rome. We know that he admired Carlyle's kind of hero, as Divinity, Prophet, Poet, Priest, Man of Letters, King. He might be expected, then, to give us in *Representative Men* American leaders and prophets, like George Washington, Benjamin Franklin, Thomas Jefferson, or one of the men he most admired in his own day, like Daniel Webster. But we perhaps have learned enough from *The Conduct of Life* to know that Emerson's men will not be such models. He believes in aspiring men, of negative as well as positive quality. To be representative, they may be villains as well as heroes. So we find the six of them: Plato the philosopher, Swedenborg the mystic, Montaigne the skeptic, Shakespeare the poet, Napoleon the man of the world, Goethe the writer—no one a hero or even a heroic type, but each representative of a complex of traits of thought in human kind. Note the introductory essay, "Uses of Great Men." *Uses,* indeed! How shall they live? *For us.*

To begin once more with the assumption

of belief: "It is natural to believe in great men. . . . Nature seems to exist for the excellent. The world is upheld by the veracity of good men: they make the earth wholesome. . . . The search after the great man is the dream of youth, and the most serious occupation of manhood." But now when he asks how such men aid us, we see Emerson's surprising yet clearly characteristic point: "Each man seeks those of different quality from his own, and such as are good of their kind; that is, he seeks other men, and the *otherest*." Their service therefore is indirect, not by gift, but by representation, each "connected with some district of nature, whose agent and interpreter he is; as Linnæus, of plants; Huber, of bees . . . Euclid, of lines; Newton, of fluxions." "Every ship that comes to America got its chart from Columbus. Every novel is a debtor to Homer."

One danger is that these men become too much our masters. But change carries them and their kind along. "In some other and quite different field the next man will appear; not Jefferson, not Franklin, but now a great salesman; then a road-contractor; then a student of fishes; then a buffalo-hunting explorer; or a semi-savage western general. . . . With each new mind, a new secret of nature transpires; nor can the Bible be closed until the last great man is born." Nature protects each from every other in his variety; from what varieties can we learn?

From "Plato": "He represents the privilege of the intellect, the power, namely, of carrying up every fact to successive platforms, and so disclosing, in every fact, a germ of expansion." From "Montaigne": "Who shall forbid a wise skepticism, seeing that there is no practical question on which any thing more than an approximate solution can be had?" From "Shakespeare": "The greatest genius is the most indebted man. A poet is . . . a heart in unison with his time and country." From "Na-

poleon": "He had a directness of action never before combined with so much comprehension."

English Traits, the third in his trio of mature volumes, asks How shall I live? by asking it of a country, and, note, a country to which America was only recently opposed, yet from which it was descended. Oppose Goethe, oppose Montaigne, oppose England: and learn from these oppositions. Why is England England?—this is the way Emerson puts the question now. His steps of inquiry proceed via "Land" to "Race," to "Ability," to "Manners," to "Truth," to "Character," to "Cockayne" (Humor), to "Wealth," to "Aristocracy," to "Universities," to "Religion," to "Literature," to "Result." Each general concern is given its specific English location and form: the land locates the race; aristocracy, the wealth; and humor, the character.

Each section has its theme: "England is a garden." "The English composite character betrays a mixed origin. Everything English is a fusion of distant and antagonistic elements." "The Norman has come popularly to represent in England the aristocratic, and the Saxon the democratic principle." "I find the Englishman to be him of all men who stands firmest in his shoes." "The Teutonic tribes have a national singleness of heart, which contrasts with the Latin races." "The English race are reputed morose." "The English are a nation of humorists." "There is no country in which so absolute a homage is paid to wealth." "The feudal character of the English state, now that it is getting obsolete, glares a little, in contrast with the democratic tendencies." "The logical English train a scholar as they train an engineer. Oxford is a Greek factory, as Wilton mills weave carpet and Sheffield grinds steel." "The religion of England is part of good-breeding." "England is the best of actual nations. . . . Broad-fronted, broad-bottomed Teutons, they stand in solid phalanx foursquare to the points of compass; they constitute the modern world, they have earned their vantage ground and held it through ages of adverse possession. . . . They cannot readily see beyond England."

These brief statements of idea, one for almost each section, let us know how much we can learn, in specific documentation, analysis, anecdote, and in the personal experience of the twice-visitor. Together they let us know about the English, that they have gained by opposing, and that we will gain by opposing them.

Emerson has carried his sense of moral unity from person to object, to representative man, to nation and type, and through all of these the active and creating power of inner divinity, of intuition, gives shape to the natural forces of heredity, geography, history. English traits are English fate; within them move man's powers. His study of England puts Emerson's theories to a strong test; to see what Nietzsche and Spengler have since done with them, would, as Philip Nicoloff suggests, put them to a still stronger test. But it is not one Emerson would avoid. Form, change, purpose were organic for him in the classic sense, a part of a pattern, as he said, not a romantic caprice. So England could not but add strength to his beliefs; as his beliefs could not but inform that Saxon substance.

These three main volumes in the decade of his maturity were built upon works already established in the heart of New England readers through the two series of *Essays* and the *Poems* of the 1840's. Together these six collections of his thoughts give us Emerson's most formal and formulated wisdom. The startling assertions of such essays as "Self-Reliance" and "The Over-Soul," the contained force of "Woodnotes" and "Threnody," find their stability of focus in the various forms of the question How shall I live? It may now be

helpful to consider what in Emerson's earlier world and purpose had helped bring the several forms of this question into being.

The events of Emerson's life in brief summary provide a context for his thought—the *why* of his beliefs. He was born on May 25, 1803, in Boston, in a family of merchants and ministers. His father, the Reverend William Emerson, Unitarian minister and chaplain of the state senate, died in 1811, and his mother turned to boardinghouse keeping to support the children. He attended Boston Latin School from 1812 to 1817 and Harvard College from 1817 to 1821, where he kept journals of his reading and thought, and won prizes for his essays. Encouraged by his Aunt Mary Moody, Emerson early began to write poetry, on the victories of 1812, for example. He taught at his brother William's school for young ladies, studied for the ministry at Harvard, went south to Florida to cure a long-threatening tuberculosis, came back to more preaching, and in 1829 was ordained pastor of the Second Church in Boston, in the same year he was married to the young and fragile Ellen Tucker. She died in 1831, and in 1832 Emerson resigned his pastorate, preached a farewell sermon, and went to England to try to recover strength and purpose.

Though he visited the literary men he most admired, Coleridge, Wordsworth, Carlyle, remarkably it was the botanical world of France's Jardin des Plantes which most gave him what he sought. He returned then to begin in Concord in 1834 his years of leadership in thought and expression. He married Lydia Jackson, and of their four children three survived to later life, the while he lost his eldest, his brothers, and later his mother. He met in the next years new friends, Margaret Fuller, Bronson Alcott, Horace Greeley, the elder Henry James, Hawthorne, Thoreau, Whitman. He began to turn his early practice in sermon making to lecture making on the new lecture circuits which were to illuminate the cities, villages, and frontiers of America for the rest of the century. He turned from much-argued-about lectures, like the early "The American Scholar," to much-argued-about publications: *Nature* in 1836, the writings for the *Dial* in 1840–44, the *Essays* of 1841 and 1844, the *Poems* of 1846. He took a number of further trips west and abroad, gave the first of many speeches on problems of slavery, the war, and the nation's leadership, and in the fifties published his three most thematically integrated books—*Representative Men*, *English Traits*, and *The Conduct of Life*—which took their place alongside the other great volumes of that era, Thoreau's *Walden* and Whitman's *Leaves of Grass*. The sixties brought the Civil War, the death of Lincoln, of Thoreau, of Hawthorne, and a gradual slowing for Emerson: the effort to meet honors at Harvard with new explorations of science and intellect, trips as far as California as guest of his son-in-law, loss of his home by fire, final journeyings abroad, final collecting, despite failing memory, of loved work, like *Parnassus*, and death on April 27, 1882, at Concord.

As a boy, Emerson had looked to his family and town and school for his ideas. What wisdom did he seek in these busy and hard-pressed years? Records of reading in his *Journals* and, more indirectly, in the lists of withdrawals he and his mother made from the Boston Library Society, show his early concern with seeking out belief. His step-grandfather, Ezra Ripley, who lived in the Old Manse in Concord, which was later to be Hawthorne's, and his Aunt Mary Moody, devoted spurrer-on of his thought, both helped lead him in the direction of theology and of moral meditation, so that his readings through his twenties ran as follows: the novels of Sir Walter Scott, Mrs. Inchbald, and Mrs. Edgeworth; Thomas Campbell's long poem *The Pleasures of Hope* and Vicesimus Knox's *Elegant Extracts* in prose and verse; works of Benjamin Franklin, Cicero, Shakespeare, the English essayists like Bacon and Addison, and historians like Robertson; translations of Cervantes, Dante, Euripides, Montaigne, Pascal, Plutarch, Rousseau, *Arabian Nights' Entertainments*, and *Selections from the Popular Poetry of the Hindus*. Scott furnished his world of fictive landscape and romance, Cicero his world of oratorical meditation, Plato his world of speculation about what is true; English prose writers gave a solid professional background, and Eastern lore added a spice to the whole. His first poem, *The History of Fortus*, begun when he was ten, was a romance.

His college studies were standard; among them, first year, Greek Livy, Latin Horace, geometry, and Lowth's *Grammar*; second year, Cicero, history, geometry, Blair's *Rhetoric*, Locke's *Human Understanding*; third year, Homer, Juvenal, Hebrew, astronomy, Stewart's *Human Mind*; fourth year, chemistry, political economy, Butler's *Analogy*, and *The Federalist*. The members of his college literary club wrote essays and read them aloud.

There are qualities which can be called Emersonian even in his earliest works, in his two Bowdoin prize essays of 1820 and 1821, when he was not yet twenty, in his first printed essay, his first sermon, his first lecture. Consider his first Bowdoin essay, on the assigned topic "The Character of Socrates." It begins, as his essays were long to do, as his favorite Scott had done, with a poetic epigraph; and note the references: to Plato's academic walk, the Lyceum, which was to be the name for the great American lecture circuit established a decade later; reference also to *pure* and *stream*, terms to be especially characteristic of Emerson's writing; and reference to the needs of his own country:

> Guide my way
> Through fair Lyceum's walk, the green retreats
> Of Academus, and the thymy vale
> Where, oft enchanted with Socratic sounds,
> Ilissus pure devolved his tuneful stream
> In gentler murmurs. From the blooming store
> Of these auspicious fields, may I unblamed
> Transplant some living blossoms to adorn
> My native clime.

Then this on his main topic: "Socrates taught that every soul was an eternal, immutable form of beauty in the divine mind, and that the most beautiful mortals approached nearest to that celestial mould; that it was the honor and delight of human intellect to contemplate this *beau ideal*, and that this was better done through the medium of earthly perfection." How much discussion of Emerson's mysticism would be tempered if it took into account this approbation of idea's form and substance!

How much too the stress on his individualism would be tempered by a reading of his senior essay of 1821. In it he traces "The Present State of Ethical Philosophy" from the limits of moral science set by the Greeks to the church's "obstinacy of ignorance," to Cudworth's and Burke's corrections of Hobbes, and the valuable common sense of the modern philosophers Clark, Price, Butler, Reid, Paley, Smith, and Stewart. Then he makes the important approving distinction that "The moderns have made their ethical writings of a more practical character than the sages of antiquity. . . . The ancients balanced the comparative excellence of two virtues or the badness of two vices; they determined the question whether solitude or society were the better condition for virtue. The moderns have substituted in-

quiries of deep interest for those of only speculative importance. We would ask in passing, what discussion of Aristotle or Socrates can compare, in this respect, with the train of reasoning by which Dr. Price arrives at the conclusion that every wrong act is a step to all that is tremendous in the universe." Democratically, too, modern moral philosophy shows "that a series of humble efforts is more meritorious than solitary miracles of virtue. . . . The plague spot of slavery must be purged thoroughly out. . . . The faith of treaties must be kept inviolate. . . ."

Earlier than most he expressed concern for his country. When he was nineteen, only a decade past the battles of 1812, in which as a boy he had served, reinforcing the barricades on Boston's lines to the sea, he feared the settling down of the national spirit. "In this merry time," he wrote to a classmate, "and with real substantial happiness above any known nation, I think we Yankees have marched on since the Revolution to strength, to honor, and at last to *ennui*. It is most true that the people (of the city, at least) are actually tired of hearing Aristides called the Just, and it demonstrates a sad caprice when they hesitate about putting on their vote such names as Daniel Webster and Sullivan and Prescott, and only distinguish them by a small majority over bad and doubtful men. . . . Will it not be dreadful to discover that this experiment, made by America to ascertain if men can govern themselves, does not succeed; that too much knowledge and too much liberty make them mad?"

In his notes for his first sermon, "Pray without Ceasing," he wrote, "Take care, take care, that your sermon is not a recitation; that it is a sermon to Mr. A. and Mr. B. and Mr. C." The idea for this he, a Unitarian, got not only from Thessalonians but from a Methodist farm laborer, who said to him that men are always praying. "I meditated much on this saying and wrote my first sermon therefrom, of which the divisions were: (1) Men are always praying; (2) All their prayers are granted; (3) We must beware, then, what we ask." Between this first sermon in Waltham in 1826, and his ordination at Boston's Second Church in 1829, he preached two hundred sermons, learning to dread the demands of Sunday, learning to use one sermon in different places and different ways, yet becoming so habituated that long after he had left the pulpit he still continued to make notes on sermon topics.

In the first Sunday of his Boston ministry, speaking of styles of preaching, he said that preaching should apply itself to the good and evil in men. "Men imagine that the end and use of preaching is to expound a text, and forget that Christianity is an infinite and universal law; that it is the revelation of a Deity whose being the soul cannot reject without denying itself, a rule of action which penetrates into every moment and into the smallest duty. If any one hereafter should object to the want of sanctity of my style and the want of solemnity in my illustrations, I shall remind him that the language and the images of Scripture derive all their dignity from their association with divine truth, and that our Lord condescended to explain himself by allusions to every homely fact, and, if he addressed himself to the men of this age, would appeal to those arts and objects by which we are surrounded; to the printing-press and the loom, to the phenomena of steam and of gas, to free institutions and a petulant and vain nation." In sermon after sermon, "The Christian Minister," "Summer," "The Individual and the State," "Trust Yourself," "Hymn Books," "The Genuine Man," he carries out this active relation. The active verbs of his talks are indicative of his manner.

During the three years of his ministry at Boston's Second Church, the old church of Increase and Cotton Mather in its Puritan tradition, Emerson's reading moved toward the specific wisdoms needed to support him against what his journals had referred to as his own "sluggishness," "silliness," "flippancy," even "frigid fear," along with his lack of unction at "funerals, weddings, and ritual ceremonies," his unwilling absorption in sick calls, in swelling of the poor fund, and in other managements. Here he became more philosophically focused. He borrowed from the library again and again in 1830 de Gérando's *Histoire comparée des systèmes de philosophie* (1804), which provided brief views of the pre-Platonists, pointed to their distinguishing of the ideal from the material, and, especially, emphasized God as unity, first cause, harmony, the law of order by abstraction, repulsion, relation. Then Plato abridged by Dacier, a Harvard text, then Thomas Taylor's editions of Plato's *Cratylus*, *Phaedo*, *Parmenides*, and *Timæus*, which he borrowed many times from 1830 to 1845 and finally bought, for their treasurable emphasis on the soul, its motion, being, and becoming. Then work on Neo-Platonism, possibly Cudworth's *The True Intellectual System of the Universe*, with its concept that nature "doth reconcile the contrarieties and enmities of particular things, and bring them into one general harmony in the whole." Then the English philosopher Berkeley, as against his predecessor Hobbes, on the laws of nature as they discipline us, and on "our delight in every exertion of active moral power." And then at last, along with Boehme and Swedenborg, his own contemporary, Coleridge, in whose *Aids to Reflection*, *Friend*, and *Biographia*, he found the distinctions between Reason and Understanding, Imagination and Fancy, which Coleridge had adapted from Kant and the Germans and which amounted to the nineteenth century's scientific "reasonable" renaming of the old pair Faith and Reason—that Faith which seems an inward Reason, a powerful and compelling intuition of validity, of the sort which finally enabled Emerson to write in his journal in 1831 the lines of "Gnothi Seauton," "Know Thyself," and to reason himself after his wife's death into a withdrawal from his career, into a year's journey away from America and his own youth.

When in 1832 he resigned his ministry, spoke against church dogma and the communion ceremony, left behind the sorrows of his wife's death and his family's illnesses, Emerson seemed to be seeking in Europe the strong sources of his bookish admirations, in Coleridge, Wordsworth, Carlyle, and others. But what he discovered was the Jardin des Plantes—in the Old World, its new world of biological and geological science. Finding his men of letters, except for Carlyle, self-centered, withdrawn, or garrulous, he found in zoological gardens and institutes of science the invigoration he sought. When he came back to America his ideas, perhaps under the pressures of a long hard sea voyage, combined youthful literary and religious studies with newly strengthened views of science. In a letter of 1834 he wrote, "Is it not a good symptom for society, this decided and growing taste for natural science which has appeared though yet in its first gropings? . . . I have been writing three lectures on Natural History and of course reading as much geology, chemistry, and physics as I could find." As the editors of his *Early Lectures* say, "The science which Emerson studied and professed was pre-Darwinian and concerned itself more with the classification than with the evolution of natural phenomena. Largely deductive in its theoretical base, it could serve as illustration of divine law and at the same time offer opportunities for observation and experimentation."

Emerson's first lecture to laymen in 1833 began, "It seems to have been designed, if anything was, that men should be students of Natural History." That Lyceum of which his junior essay had spoken was off to its great success. "The beauty of the world is a perpetual invitation to the study of the world." Emerson went on: "While I stand there [in the Jardin] I am impressed with a singular conviction that not a form so grotesque, so savage, or so beautiful, but is an expression of something in man the observer. . . . I am moved by strange sympathies. I say I will listen to this invitation. I will be a naturalist." The advantages of the study: health and useful knowledge, and delight, and improvement of character, and explanation of man to himself. "Nothing is indifferent to the wise. If a man should study the economy of a spire of grass—how it sucks up sap, how it imbibes light, how it resists cold, how it repels excess of moisture, it would show him a design in the form, in the color, in the smell, in the very posture of the blade as it bends before the wind. . . . the whole of Nature is a metaphor or image of the human Mind. The laws of moral nature answer to those of matter as face to face in a glass."

Such scientific titles as "On the Relation of Man to the Globe," "Water," and "The Naturalist" alternated throughout his lecturing career, in Boston, New York, Philadelphia, the Midwest, with those of a more historical and biographical order. The lectures of 1835 lauded Michelangelo, Chaucer, Shakespeare, Bacon, Milton, Jeremy Taylor for their earthiness, and Jonson, Herrick, Herbert for their strong and simple sentences and objects. The 1836 series in Boston on "Philosophy of History," and the later series on "Human Culture," "Human Life," "The Present Age," "The Times," stressed the common interests of men, saying of Michelangelo, as of Martin Luther, "so true was he to the laws of the human mind that his character and his works like Isaac Newton's seem rather a part of Nature than arbitrary productions of the human will."

In publication, Emerson's career began from Concord in 1836, when he was just over thirty years old, with a small, not popular, pamphlet called *Nature*, which stated succinctly in its third sentence: "But if a man would be alone, let him look at the stars." This early individual man of Emerson's is a man alone, apart from his friends and even from his own studies and pursuits, an unmediated part of the universe. By "nature," Emerson says, he means "the integrity of impression made by manifold natural objects. It is this which distinguishes the stick of timber of the wood-cutter from the tree of the poet." A good local example: "Miller owns this field, Locke that, and Manning the woodland beyond. But none of them owns the landscape."

The main parts of his essay rest upon these distinctions. The causes of the world he calls "Commodity," how things are served and used; "Beauty," how their harmony is perceived, in outline, color, motion, grouping; "Language," how they are signified and symbolized; "Discipline," how they are ordered and distinguished—these are his own versions of Aristotle's classical causes, material, effective, formal, and final. Then in three final sections, Emerson treats man's view of "Idealism," "Spirit," and "Prospects": his perspective through intuitive ideas stronger than that through sense or argument; his power, in incarnation, of worship; and his power to speculate, to guess about relations, *whence* and *whereto*. He draws upon *The Tempest*, the Bible's Proverbs, *Comus*, and George Herbert's "Man" to voice his guesses. Both learned and innocent men, he warns, limit their powers and fail to speculate. "The invariable mark of wisdom is to see the miraculous in the common," that is, idea in material, beauty and spirit in commodity and discipline. "What is a day? What is a year? What is summer? What is woman? What is a child? What is sleep? . . . Whilst the abstract question occupies your intellect, nature brings it in the concrete to be solved by your hands. . . . Every spirit builds itself a house, and beyond its house a world, and beyond its world a heaven. . . . Adam called his house, heaven and earth; Cæsar called his house, Rome; you perhaps call yours, a cobbler's trade; a hundred acres of ploughed land; or a scholar's garret. . . . Build, therefore, your own world. As fast as you conform your life to the pure idea in your mind, that will unfold its great proportions. A correspondent revolution in things will attend the influx of the spirit. So fast will disagreeable appearances, swine, spiders, snakes, pests, madhouses, prisons, enemies, vanish; they are temporary and shall no more be seen. . . . so shall the advancing spirit . . . draw beautiful faces, warm hearts, wise discourse, and heroic acts, around its way, until evil is no more seen."

Here in its peroration, the essay "Nature" makes the proposals of Emerson's whole lifetime on the simple questions of life, the range and scope of spirit, the fit of historical past and possible future, the nature of evil, the values of fact and of spirit. Emerson's future style, too, is proposed and exemplified here: the broad speculative generalizations followed by the simplest questions and instances; the speaking to *you*; the quick strides of survey covering miles and centuries; the parallels and dismissals; the earnest recommendations for the life of the universe as for the life of every day.

The poems and the two volumes of essays which follow in the 1840's, as well as some of his most moving lectures, such as "The American Scholar" and the "Divinity School Address," set the fame of Emerson moving into its channels. These accepted works we, too, may accept, to read them all, rather than to explore them here. The *Essays* followed patterns with which we have already learned to be familiar: from time in "History" to more than time in "Art," from art in "Poet" to religion in "Reformers," ending, as in his more loosely collected essays of the sixties and seventies, with transcendences of age and death. The poems, too, move toward "Terminus," "Farewell," and "In Memoriam."

But two fates, laws of his life, carried Emerson's work to less predictable intensities: one, the force of the slavery question and the Civil War; the other, the force of his concern with the "natural history of intellect" in poetry as in prose. In these we see not seasonal pattern and temporal decline, but the late maturing demanded by event and drawn from the aging seer after his chief works, his solidest books, were done. "Emancipation in the British West Indies" (1844), "The Fugitive Slave Law" (1851 and 1854), "John Brown" (1859), "The Emancipation Proclamation" (1862), "Abraham Lincoln" (1865), all carry the weight of a pressing issue.

Thoreau is said to have rung the bell for the public meeting at the Concord Court House in 1844, at which many citizens opposed Emerson's attitudes on emancipation. Emerson began: "Friends and Fellow Citizens: We are met to exchange congratulations on the anniversary of an event singular in the history of civilization; a day of reason; of the clear light; of that which makes us better than a flock of birds and beasts; a day which gave the immense fortification of a fact, of gross history, to ethical abstractions."

How he delights in the fact of the West Indies' final emancipation, in the fact of "the steady gain of truth and right," in the intelligent self-interest despite the voluptuousness of power. So in America in the fifties, the Whig *must*'s, the Liberal *may*'s, need to combine. So we need, like John Brown, to see the facts behind the forms. So, "this heavy load lifted off the national heart, we shall not fear henceforward to show our faces among mankind." And Providence makes its own instruments, "creates the man for the time." In verse, the Concord "Ode," read July 4, 1857:

> United States! the ages plead,—
>   Present and Past in under-song,—
> Go put your creed into your deed,
>   Nor speak with double tongue.

And the "Boston Hymn," read January 1, 1863, in Boston, when the President's Emancipation Proclamation went into effect:

> God said, I am tired of kings,
> I suffer them no more;
> Up to my ear the morning brings
> The outrage of the poor. . . .
>
> To-day unbind the captive,
> So only are ye unbound;
> Lift up a people from the dust,
> Trump of their rescue, sound!
>
> Pay ransom to the owner
> And fill the bag to the brim.
> Who is the owner? The slave is owner.
> And ever was. Pay him.

Emerson has said, "I compared notes with one of my friends who expects everything of the universe and is disappointed when anything is less than the best, and I found that I begin at the other extreme, expecting nothing, and am always full of thanks for moderate goods." Yet his intuition that God need not be so modest could find expression in God's own voice in this hymn and thus raise the responsive shouts of a Boston audience.

The work of his last active years, of the postwar sixties, was the work again of the "natural history of intellect." This theme he still wanted to clarify. "His noun had to wait for its verb or its adjective until he was ready; then his speech would come down upon the word he wanted . . ." as his biographer James Cabot commented. He never spoke impromptu; indeed, in his last years, he sought so long for the right word that he hesitated to appear in public. Part of his reticence was that, as he wrote in his journal of 1859, he wanted no disciples, he spoke to bring men not to him but to themselves. Harvard Phi Beta Kappa speaker in 1867, as in 1837, he took up again for Harvard in 1870 the series which he had projected thirty years before and had given in 1848 and later, in London, Boston, and New York, again in 1858 as a course on the "Natural Method of Mental Philosophy," and again in 1866 as "Philosophy for People." Now for a group of thirty students in 1870 and 1871 he would try to bring together what he had to say. He still was not satisfied. Nevertheless: "If one can say so without arrogance, I might suggest that he who contents himself with dotting only a fragmentary curve, recording only what facts he has observed, without attempting to arrange them within one outline, follows a system also, a system as grand as any other, though he does not interfere with its vast curves by prematurely forcing them into a circle or ellipse, but only draws that arc which he clearly sees, and waits for new opportunity, well assured that these observed arcs consist with each other."

This is the way his speaking seemed to a contemporary, W. C. Brownell: "The public was small, attentive, even reverential. The room was as austere as the chapel of a New England Unitarian church would normally be in those days. The Unitarians were the intellectual sect of those days and, as such, suspect. Even the Unitarians, though, who were the aristocratic as well as the intellectual people of the place,

found the chapel benches rather hard, I fancy, before the lecture was over, and I recall much stirring. There was, too, a decided sprinkling of scoffers among the audience, whose sentiments were disclosed during the decorous exit. Incomprehensibility, at that epoch generally, was the great offence; it was a sort of universal charge against anything uncomprehended, made in complete innocence of any obligation to comprehend. Nevertheless the small audience was manifestly more or less spellbound. Even the dissenters—as in the circumstances the orthodox of the day may be called—were impressed. It might be all over their heads, as they contemptuously acknowledged, or vague, as they charged, or disintegrating, as they—vaguely—felt. But there was before them, placidly, even benignly, uttering incendiarism, an extraordinarily interesting personality. It was evening and the reflection of two little kerosene lamps, one on either side of his lectern, illuminated softly the serenest of conceivable countenances—nobility in its every lineament and a sort of irradiating detachment about the whole presence. . . ."

To think about Emerson not only for himself in his own time and for us in ours, but in the larger context of tradition, we need to think of the qualities which relate him to others, as an author to other authors, as a writer of prose wisdom to other such writers. What place does Emerson hold in the tradition, of his own English literature and of the larger world of wisdom? This question cannot be answered by considering his ideas as if they were separable from his presentation of them. Rather, his presentation of them gives them their special identifiable character. We need to discover the special traits and traditions of this essayist of ours, how he differed from any other we may know—from Cicero and Seneca on old age, from Montaigne on life and friendship, from the Elizabethan essayists whom he read with such pleasure as a boy, from the sermons he heard, from the eighteenth- and nineteenth-century philosophic and journalistic prose which he kept reading in the English reviews, from Carlyle, whom he admired so directly, from his own American contemporaries, from the wisdom-literature of China, Persia, India, from his own Bible.

If we read the beginning of his perhaps most famous essay, "Self-Reliance," which followed "History" in introducing his popular series of *Essays* in the 1840's, we may catch his way of expression. In the atmosphere of three quotations to the effect that "man is his own star," Emerson begins: "I read the other day some verses written by an eminent painter which were original and not conventional. The soul always hears an admonition in such lines, let the subject be what it may. The sentiment they instil is of more value than any thought they may contain. To believe your own thought, to believe that what is true for you in your private heart is true for all men—that is genius. Speak your latent conviction, and it shall be the universal sense; for the inmost in due time becomes the outmost, and our first thought is rendered back to us by the trumpets of the Last Judgment. Familiar as the voice of the mind is to each, the highest merit we ascribe to Moses, Plato and Milton is that they set at naught books and traditions, and spoke not what men, but what *they* thought. A man should learn to detect and watch that gleam of light which flashes across his mind from within, more than the lustre of the firmament of bards and sages."

The tone of this whole beginning is at once particular and personal: "I read . . . your own"; general and confident: "the soul always hears"; evocative: "the trumpets of the Last Judgment"; wide-reaching: "Moses, Plato and Milton"; recommendatory: "speak . . . learn"; figurative: "that gleam of light . . . more than the lustre of the firmament."

In this combination of qualities, Emerson's style is more focused and condensed than Cicero's, say, or Seneca's, or Montaigne's, setting its generalities in specific actions and analogies. It is not what we traditionally call a classic style either in Latin or in English, because it does not carry the tone of a full and logical unfolding of the thought, but rather moves as if by flashes of illumination. This is not to say that it is unlogical, merely that it does not give the effect of explicit stress on logical connections. Nor does it stress the literal qualifications, descriptions, with which classical prose is concerned. Both adjectives and connectives are relatively subordinated to direct active verbs. This is to say that Emerson characteristically in this paragraph and throughout this essay, as still in "Illusions" twenty years later, writes a very active, predicative style, one in which the structure is basically simple statement, for which both modification and connective addition are only minimally necessary, and the sentences are relatively short, the central statements relatively unqualified.

There is scarcely another essayist like this among the famed of English prose. Closest to Emerson are sermon-makers like the pre-Elizabethan Latimer, or Tyndale in his translation of Paul to the Romans, or narrative writers, the Bunyan of *Pilgrim's Progress*, the Joyce of Molly Bloom's soliloquy; and these are styles we do not probably think of as Emersonian. Yet even less so are the styles of classic arguers in the tradition of Hooker, Bacon, and Locke, or of the soaring describers he loved: Sir Thomas Browne, for example, or his own contemporaries like Carlyle, or what he himself called the "mock-turtle nutriment as in Macaulay."

But there is one writer in the tradition with whom he is closely allied, one whose works in prose and poetry were Emerson's own favorite youthful reading: Ben Jonson. Jonson was as singular in his own time as Emerson in his: their sense of the English language as best used in active concise statements, making connections by implication, was a sense shared in its extreme by few others, and therefore especially lively both in its singularity and in its function as bond between them. Even their use of specific connectives and the proportion of relative clauses to causal clauses and locational phrases are striking. Not Plutarch, not Montaigne, not Bacon, but specifically the aphoristic Jonson of *Timber* is Emerson's direct model.

Emerson's critics, and he himself, have often complained of the sentences which seemed to repel rather than to attract one another. But lack of connectives does not necessarily mean lack of connections. The thought moves from general to particular, and from key word to key word. Such thought is logical, even syllogistic: the general, all men are mortal; the particular, a man; the conclusion, a man is mortal; you and I participate in this truth. But the *and*'s and *therefore*'s have been omitted, or have been used with relative infrequency. In other words, the logical relation of all to one is present, but not the explicit links in the steps of relation. Further, Emerson might begin with what we would call an untenable premise: "All men are immortal." He would feel this intuitively, "the blazing evidence of immortality," the "gleam of light which flashes across his mind from within," and so he would base upon it his logical argument for any one man and for us. And still further, he would treat key words like *man* in a special way, including in them all their degrees of evaluative

reference from lowest to highest; so that "man" would mean man in his limitless degree of spirit, as well as in his limiting degree of body, thus supporting by definition, implicit or explicit, the relation between *man* and *immortal* which the syllogism makes. It is as if Emerson were essentially satisfied to say, "All men are men (with all men's limitations and potentialities); a man acts like a man." The connective *therefore*'s and adjectival *immortal*'s are minimal; the subject-predicate *Men are, a man is,* is central.

In the early sermons, according to Kenneth Cameron's index-concordance, key terms are *God, Jesus, man, memory, mind, nature, self, soul, truth.* These suggest three centers, religious, psychological, scientific. Then in *Nature,* key terms are *action, beauty, God, man, mind, nature, poet, soul, spirit, thought, truth, world.* The changes make clear Emerson's motion away from religion in the shape of person toward religion in the sense of creation of beauty, whereby *action, thought,* and *world* are taken up into the forms and purposes of *spirit,* and thus made beautiful by their harmony.

Index terms tend to be nouns; but if we look more closely at the recurrent language of specific prose texts, early and late, we will see how strong and traditional are Emerson's verbs, especially those of feeling, knowing, thinking, how evaluative and discriminating his adjectives, as for example in "Self-Reliance," *divine, good, great, new, own, other, same, strong, such, true,* and in the later "Fate" and "Illusions," *fine, find,* and *hold.* The nouns of those essays also parallel the concordance listings for the whole work: the early *action, being, character, fact, friend, truth, virtue;* the later *circumstance, element, form, fate;* and the shared *God, law, life, man, mind, nature, nothing, power, thought, time, world.* The shift in emphasis from early *action* and *character* to later *circumstance* and *fate* is represented in the structure of the prose, as of the poetry also: an unusually high proportion of verbs and low proportion of connectives in the early work and "Self-Reliance" establishing later a proportion of about ten verbs and fewer adjectives to twenty nouns, achieving the precarious and shifting balance between action and circumstance which he argues for.

Poetry and prose for Emerson are not far apart. In syntax, in vocabulary, in idea, their likenesses are greater than their differences. The main differences are the larger proportion of sensory terms in the poetry, and the framing by meter and rhyme. His first poems appeared not in the volume called *Poems* but as epigraphs for essays. He saw poems as epigraphs, like Biblical verses, texts for sermons. Therefore his poetic allegiances were divided —on the one hand to the succinctness of a Jonson, as in prose, yet on the other to the materials and moods of his own day, which were freer, more natural, more exploratory.

His was a sensorily active and receptive vocabulary like that of the English eighteenth and American nineteenth centuries, its especial impact being in its direct joining of man and nature, a nature *wise* and *good*, an *air, sky, sea, star* related to *joy, form, beauty*. This stylistic joining of human and natural realms as both natural, though differently, is like the metaphysical joining, as in Cowper's "church-going bell," which Wordsworth with his more literal connecting processes disapproved; it made condensations of Emerson's widest extensions.

To this outreaching vocabulary he did at least consider suiting a freer form. Like Carlyle, he wearied of the "Specimens" of English verse he had read. Carlyle had written him in the 1830's, ". . . my view is that now at last we have lived to see all manner of Poetics and Rhetorics and Sermonics . . . as good as broken and abolished . . . and so one leaves the pasteboard coulisses, and three unities, and Blair's

Lectures quite behind; and feels only that there is *nothing sacred*, then, but the *Speech of Man* to believing Men! [which] will one day doubtless anew environ itself with fit modes, with solemnities that are *not* mummeries." Emerson's own *Journals* of this time (1839) expressed his interest not only in Pope's couplets and Scott's quatrains but in freer measures like those characteristic of Wordsworth's "Immortaliy Ode"—"not tinkling rhyme, but grand Pindaric strokes, as firm as the tread of a horse," suggesting not a restraint, "but the wildest freedom." Later he wrote to Herman Grimm concerning his *Life of Michelangelo*, "I hate circular sentences, or echoing sentences, where the last half cunningly repeats the first half,—but you step from stone to stone, and advance ever." And he expressed to Grimm his corollary lack of taste for drama: "Certainly it requires great health and wealth of power to ventriloquize (shall I say?) through so many bodies. . . ." Rather, "The maker of a sentence . . . launches out into the infinite and builds a road into Chaos and old Night, and is followed by those who hear him with something of wild, creative delight." And: "Who can blame men for seeking excitement? They are polar, and would you have them sleep in a dull eternity of equilibrium? Religion, love, ambition, money, war, brandy,—some fierce antagonism must break the round of perfect circulation or no spark, no joy, no event can be."

He is aware, too, of freedom in natural forms. In 1841: "I told Henry Thoreau that his freedom is in the form, but he does not disclose new matter. . . . But now of poetry I would say, that when I go out into the fields in a still sultry day, in a still sultry humor, I do perceive that the finest rhythms and cadences of poetry are yet unfound, and that in that purer state which glimmers before us, rhythms of a faery and dream-like music hall enchant us, compared with which the finest measures of English poetry are psalm-tunes. I think now that the very finest and sweetest closes and falls are not in our metres, but in the measures of eloquence, which have greater variety and richness than verse. . . ." Such freedom he aimed for in his prose and poetry of the sea, and such sense of freedom enabled him in 1855 to hail Whitman's new scope and form.

Yet there is a stronger controlling force for him, his youthful note-taking interest in pithy statements. As far back as 1820 we see his mood: "Have been of late reading patches of Barrow and Ben Jonson; and what the object —not curiosity? no—nor expectation of edification intellectual or moral—but merely because they are authors where vigorous phrases and quaint, peculiar words and expressions may be sought and found, the better 'to rattle out the battle of my thoughts.' " And in 1840, he stated his philosophical reasons for condensation: "yet does the world reproduce itself in miniature in every event that transpires, so that all the laws of nature may be read in the smallest fact."

Then in 1842 he expressed recognition of the power of concentration within scope and range: "This feeling I have respecting Homer and Greek, that in this great, empty continent of ours, stretching enormous almost from pole to pole, with thousands of long rivers and thousands of ranges of mountains, the rare scholar, who, under a farmhouse roof, reads Homer and the Tragedies, adorns the land. He begins to fill it with wit, to counter-balance the enormous disproportion of the unquickened earth."

While his chief substance, then, comes from the protestant naturalism of Sylvester and the eighteenth century, in *air, sea, sky, land, cloud, star,* and its American specifications in *beautiful river, music, morning, snow, rose,* like Whitman's *grass,* the counter, wry, limiting, and constructing tradition was his aphoristic one,

the *good and wise thought, nature, fate, form, time* of the Elizabethans. When, later in life, Emerson published his collection, *Parnassus,* of the poems he had liked best, the most space went to Shakespeare, the next to Jonson and Herrick, Wordsworth and Tennyson. While the nineteenth-century poets gave him his guide to beauty of reference, the seventeenth century, in poetry as in prose, gave him his form. The Jonson he called master of song he represented by lines which sound like his own:

Come on, come on, and where you go
So interweave the curious knot
As even the Observer scarce may know
Which lines are pleasures, and which not . . .
Admire the wisdom of your feet:
For dancing is an exercise
Not only shows the mover's wit,
But maketh the beholder wise,
As he hath power to rise to it.

So Emerson "studied thy motion, took thy form," giving to cosmos the active limitations of man's rhymes and meters in the shape of aphorism and epigraph, combining, from his favorite readings, the gnomic force of translations from the Anglo-Saxon and Persian with the pith of segments from Jonsonian "Old Plays" used as epigraphs in Scott's novels.

In "Permanent Traits of the English National Genius," for example, Emerson quotes and admires the strength of the Anglo-Saxon verse line:

O in how gloomy
And how bottomless
A well laboreth
The darkened mind
When it the strong
Storms beat
Of the world's business. . . .

This is much like Emerson's own "Gnothi Seauton":

He is in thy world,
But thy world knows him not.
He is the mighty Heart
From which life's varied pulses part.
Clouded and shrouded there doth sit.
The Infinite . . .

Such concision he found also when in 1842 he edited the prose and verse of the Persian Saadi's *Gulistan* ("Rose Garden"), a representative collection of wise maxims As he later explained, "The dense writer has yet ample room and choice of phrase and even a gamesome mood often between his valid words."

Emerson's cryptic and summary comment on more extended thought gave it the close form of meter and rhyme which he was concerned with as a part of the structure of the universe—its recurrent tide in season and in man. For him this form was not "organic" in the sense that we sometimes use the term, as Coleridge used the term, in the individual and spontaneous unfoldment of self as a flower. This Emerson called romantic and capricious. Rather, for him "organic" meant structural, necessary, recurrent in a context of use, in material, formal, and direct cause, that is, as he said, classic.

A close look at the form of his poetry in relation to his prose tells us much of the form of the world for him. Its lines, its regular or varied stresses, its coupled or varied rhymes, are part of the body, the law, of nature. With and against them the poet's free spirit works. Similarly, names are part of the categorizing force of nature. With and against them, through metaphor, the seeing of likeness in difference and difference in likeness, the seeing poet's vision of image and symbol, of individual entity, works. Similarly, sentence, generalizations, are part of the law of nature, and with and against them the vital instance works. In structure, in reference, in sound, his poetry gives us, even more closely than his prose, and with the focus in which he believed, the presence of all in one, the interplay of likeness and difference in every entity of art.

Among Emerson's best-liked poems, "Each and All," "Uriel," "Good-Bye," "Woodnotes," "Merlin," "Concord Hymn," "Boston Hymn," "Brahma," "Days," "Terminus," as among his longer descriptions and shorter fragments, condensations and variations appear in all sorts of degrees, from the strictness of "Concord Hymn" to the obliquities of "Merlin." Even some of his choppiest addenda are likable— "Limits," for example, or "The Bohemian Hymn," or "Water" from "Fragments," or "Nature and Life," or

Roomy Eternity
Casts her schemes rarely,
And an æon allows
For each quality and part
Of the multitudinous
And many-chambered heart.

Or, from "The Poet,"

That book is good
Which puts me in a working mood.
    Unless to thought is added Will,
    Apollo is an imbecile.
What parts, what gems, what colors shine,—
Ah, but I miss the grand design.

This was Emerson's steadiest complaint about his style: that he dealt in parts and fragments and could not achieve the whole, which he himself bespoke. Yet his very worry about this achievement, as about his friendship and love, is indicative of their importance to him, their religious center for him. We must not take at face value his fears of coldheartedness, of infinitely repellent particles; these were the recalcitrances of substance in which his spirit worked. "It is very unhappy, but too late to be helped, the discovery we have made that we exist. That discovery is called the Fall of Man." Yet, "we are sure, that, though we know not how, necessity does comport with liberty," and, "a part of Fate is the freedom of man." These are the principles of his life; they are guides, too, to the form of his art. In the speculative turns of "Merlin," as in the steady pace of "Brahma" and "Days," is the strength of freedom joined with measure.

The essay "The Poet" makes specific application of these beliefs. Ideally, the poet is the sayer, the teller of news, utterer of the necessary and causal. "For the Universe has three children, born at one time, which reappear under different names in every system of thought, whether they be called cause, operation and effect; or, more poetically, Jove, Pluto, Neptune; or, theologically, the Father, the Spirit and the Son; but which we will call here the Knower, the Doer and the Sayer. These stand respectively for the love of truth, for the love of good, and for the love of beauty. These three are equal. Each is that which he is, essentially, so that he cannot be surmounted or analyzed, and each of these three has the power of the others latent in him and his own, patent."

The poet, by saying, makes new relations, heals dislocations and detachments, shows defects as exuberances, as in Vulcan's lameness, Cupid's blindness. "Every new relation is a new word." The world is thus "put under the mind for verb and noun" with an explicit connective. It is important to realize what this sense of saying means to Emerson's own poetry. It means that as a poet he is not an imagist, not a symbolist, but specifically a figurist. That is, he accepts image and symbol as vital, from the natural world; and then his contribution as poet is to show them in new relation. "He knows why the plain or meadow of space was strown with these flowers we call suns and moons and stars. . . ." There is the metaphoric

way of speaking. He names now by appearances, now by essences, delighting in the intellect's sense of boundaries, and then in the ascension of things to higher kinds, that is, in both being and becoming, the inebriation of thought moving to fact—even in algebra and definitions, the freedom of trope. Emerson blames mystics, as he would blame modern ritualistic symbolizers, for too many fixities. "The history of hierarchies seems to show that all religious error consisted in making the symbol too stark and solid." "Let us have a little algebra"—a little relation and proportion! "I look in vain for the poet whom I describe. We do not with sufficient plainness or sufficient profoundness address ourselves to life, nor dare we chaunt our own times and social circumstance."

Is Emerson a philosopher? Yes, if we agree with William James (as John Dewey quotes him in a *Southern Review* article of 1937): "Philosophic study means the habit of always seeing an alternative, of not taking the usual for granted, of making conventionalities fluid again, of imagining foreign states of mind." In this way Emerson prepares for James, for Dewey, for Charles Peirce, the great American pragmatists. In this way, too, he prepares metaphysically for Nietzsche's Dionysus. But Emerson was not systematic and Germanic. Critics like René Wellek, writing on Emerson's philosophy, Andrew Schiller on his "gnomic structure," Kathryn McEuen on his rhymes, Frank Thompson on his theories of poetry, Walter Blair and Clarence Faust on his method, Nelson Adkins on his bardic tradition, J. D. Yohannan on his Persian translations, Percy Brown on his aesthetics, Vivian Hopkins and Stephen Whicher on his sense of form, and Frederic Carpenter on his use of Oriental materials, all suggest variations on the theme of his fragmentary illuminations. So did his elder critics like Carlyle, Arnold, Santayana.

So did he. When in 1870 he began his final series "On the excellence of Intellect, its identity with nature, its formations in Instinct and Inspiration, and relation to the existing religion and civility of the present," he warned his hearers that this series would consist of "anecdotes of the intellect; a sort of Farmer's Almanac of mental moods," and even defended this method, as we have noted before, in his metaphor of the dotted line. He had reasons for not filling in the lines, for not always writing a smoothly qualified prose, poetry, or philosophy. "I think that philosophy is still rude and elementary. It will one day be taught by poets. The poet is in the natural attitude; he is believing; the philosopher, after some struggle, having only reasons for believing." "I confess to a little distrust of that completeness of system which metaphysicians are apt to affect. 'Tis the gnat grasping the world."

But in his sense of metaphysics as useful, for daily use, he had a great deal of work to do in the world. To feed the hunger of the young for ideas; to think what simple pattern of being could include man's sense of joy in being as well as his fear and falsification of it; to draw the world as newly understood by scientific thought into the world of common intuition; to combine his feeling that "the beauty of the world is a perpetual invitation to the study of the world" with his explanation of such combination, as to his brother Edward in 1834, that visionary reason and toiling understanding work together, "by mutual reaction of thought and life, to make thought solid and life wise."

A man who has been called monist, dualist, pantheist, transcendentalist, puritan, optimist, pragmatist, mystic may well feel dubious about the validity of labels, of adjectives. His style shows us how all of these terms fit him and how they work together, and over and over he tells us that it is degree he believes in; in degree, the one and the many may work together, god, man, nature may work together; all varieties of difference, from dissimilar to contrasting, will share degrees of likeness. His common term *polarity* referred not to modern positive and negative poles merely, and not to modern negative correlations or annihilations, but to "action and interaction," to differences or counterparts which are unified by a common direction, a North Star, a magnetic field, a spirit in the laws and limits of body, a drawing of body along in the direction of spirit —a golden mean with a lodestar.

Emerson's plan for the *Essays*, early set down in his *Journals*, well summarizes his steadiest concerns:

There is one soul.
It is related to the world.
Art is its action thereon.
Science finds its methods.
Literature is its record.
Religion is the emotion of reverence that it inspires.
Ethics is the soul illustrated in human life.
Society is the finding of this soul by individuals in each other.
Trades are the learning of the soul in nature by labor.
Politics is the activity of the soul illustrated in power.
Manners are silent and mediate expressions of soul.

His plan, his tables of contents, his major vocabulary, his syntax, are all of a piece, seeking and finding, in what he sees to be the major activities of man, that unifying vitality of good, that one essential likeness, which he calls *soul*. He could say, "Within and Above are synonyms"—a metaphor crucial to belief in our day—so that "transcendental" could easily mean "a little beyond"; and he was able to say in another town or on a weekday what he had not felt able to say at home and on Sunday. For as one of his small-town congregations said, "We are very simple people here, and don't understand anybody but Mr. Emerson." And as their Emerson said, "What but thought deepens life, and makes us better than cow or cat?"

It was fortunate that there was enough of an artist in this wise man of America's nineteenth century, that he tried not only to advise but to preserve, not only to tell but to make and give; that the artistic power of Renaissance poets and prose writers gave him a means to hold and shape the fluent continuities of a liberal eighteenth- and nineteenth-century romanticism; that sermon structure, like rhyme and meter, gave him ways of holding fast the free Aeolian strains of sky and sea in their relevance to thought and fate and form.

There is no permanent wise man, Emerson says. Yet, "How does Memory praise? By holding fast the best." This is the work for a wise art, a laborious but joyful understanding.

Selected Bibliography

WORKS OF RALPH WALDO EMERSON

The standard collected edition is *The Complete Works of Ralph Waldo Emerson,* the Centenary Edition, edited by Edward Waldo Emerson and published in 12 volumes by Houghton Mifflin in 1903–04. It has been supplemented by the collections listed at the end of this section.

Nature. Boston: James Munroe, 1836.
Essays [First Series]. Boston: James Munroe, 1841.
Essays: Second Series. Boston: James Munroe, 1844.

Poems. Boston: James Munroe, 1847 [1846].
Nature, Addresses, and Lectures. Boston: James Munroe, 1849.
Representative Men. Boston: Phillips, Sampson, 1850.
English Traits. Boston: Phillips, Sampson, 1856.
The Conduct of Life. Boston: Ticknor and Fields, 1860.
May-Day and Other Pieces. Boston: Ticknor and Fields, 1867.
Society and Solitude. Boston: Fields, Osgood, 1870.
Parnassus, edited by Ralph Waldo Emerson. Boston: Osgood, 1875.
Letters and Social Aims. Boston: Osgood, 1876.
Selected Poems. Boston: Osgood, 1876.
Poems. Boston: Houghton, Osgood, 1876.
Miscellanies. Boston: Houghton Mifflin, 1884.
Lectures and Biographical Sketches. Boston: Houghton Mifflin, 1884.
Natural History of Intellect and Other Papers. Boston: Houghton Mifflin, 1893.
Two Unpublished Essays: The Character of Socrates; The Present State of Ethical Philosophy. Boston: Lamson, Wolffe, 1896.
Uncollected Writings: Essays, Addresses, Poems, Reviews and Letters by Ralph Waldo Emerson, edited by Charles C. Bigelow. New York: Lamb, 1912. (Includes especially work from the *Dial.*)
The Journals of Ralph Waldo Emerson, edited by Edward Waldo Emerson and Waldo Emerson Forbes. 10 vols. Boston: Houghton Mifflin, 1909–14. (Not all-inclusive.)
Young Emerson Speaks: Unpublished Discourses on Many Subjects, edited by Arthur C. McGiffert, Jr. Boston: Houghton Mifflin, 1938.
The Letters of Ralph Waldo Emerson, edited by Ralph L. Rusk. 6 vols. New York: Columbia University Press, 1939. (There are other major collections of letters to Thomas Carlyle, Arthur Clough, William Furness, Herman Grimm, John Sterling, Henry David Thoreau, and Samuel Ward.)
The Early Lectures of Ralph Waldo Emerson. Cambridge, Mass.: Harvard University Press, 1959.
The Journals and Miscellaneous Notebooks, edited by William H. Gilman and others. 8 vols.

Cambridge, Mass.: Harvard University Press, 1960–70.

BIBLIOGRAPHIES

The *Emerson Society Quarterly* (1955 to date), edited by Kenneth W. Cameron, provides bibliographical information on a continuing basis.

Carpenter, Frederic I. *Emerson Handbook.* New York: Hendricks House, 1953. (Invaluable for rich biographical and critical material also.)

Ferguson, Alfred Riggs. *Checklist of Ralph Waldo Emerson.* Columbus, Ohio: Merrill, 1970.

Hubbell, G. S. *A Concordance to the Poems of Ralph Waldo Emerson.* New York: H. W. Wilson, 1932.

Stovall, Floyd, ed. "Emerson," in *Eight American Authors: A Review of Research and Criticism.* New York: Modern Language Association, 1956.

BIOGRAPHIES

Cabot, James. *A Memoir of Ralph Waldo Emerson.* 2 vols. Boston: Houghton Mifflin, 1887.

Cameron, Kenneth. *Emerson the Essayist.* 2 vols. Raleigh, N.C.: Thistle Press, 1945.

Emerson, Edward Waldo. *Emerson in Concord: A Memoir.* Boston: Houghton Mifflin, 1889.

Firkins, Oscar W. *Ralph Waldo Emerson.* Boston: Houghton Mifflin, 1915.

Hoeltje, Hubert. *Sheltering Tree.* Durham, N.C.: Duke University Press, 1943.

Perry, Bliss. *Emerson Today.* Princeton, N.J.: Princeton University Press, 1931.

Rusk, Ralph L. *The Life of Ralph Waldo Emerson.* New York: Scribners, 1949.

Sanborn, F. B., ed. *The Genius and Character of Emerson.* Boston: Osgood, 1885. (Selected early views.)

Woodbury, Charles J. *Talks with Emerson.* New York: Horizon Press, 1970.

CRITICAL STUDIES

Adkins, Nelson F. "Emerson and the Bardic Tradition," *PMLA,* 63:662–77 (June 1948).

Berry, Edmund G. *Emerson's Plutarch.* Cambridge, Mass.: Harvard University Press, 1961.

Blair, Walter, and Clarence Faust. "Emerson's Literary Method," *Modern Philology,* 42:79–95 (November 1944).

Brown, Percy W. "Emerson's Philosophy of Aesthetics," *Journal of Aesthetics and Art Criticism,* 15:350–54 (March 1957).

Carpenter, Frederic I. *Emerson and Asia.* Cambridge, Mass.: Harvard University Press, 1930.

Cowan, Michael H. *City of the West: Emerson, America, and Urban Metaphor.* New Haven, Conn.: Yale University Press, 1967.

Harding, Walter. *Emerson's Library.* Charlottesville: University Press of Virginia, 1967.

Hopkins, Vivian C. *Spires of Form: A Study of Emerson's Aesthetic Theory.* Cambridge, Mass.: Harvard University Press, 1951.

Konvitz, Milton, and Stephen Whicher, eds. *Emerson, A Collection of Critical Essays.* Englewood Cliffs, N.J.: Prentice-Hall, 1962. (Reprints articles by Daniel Aaron, Newton Arvin, John Dewey, Charles Feidelson, Jr., Norman Foerster, Robert Frost, William James, F. O. Matthiessen, Perry Miller, Henry B. Parkes, Sherman Paul, George Santayana, Henry Nash Smith, and Stephen Whicher.)

McEuen, Kathryn A. "Emerson's Rhymes," *American Literature,* 20:31–42 (March 1948).

Nicoloff, Philip L. *Emerson on Race and History: An Examination of English Traits.* New York: Columbia University Press, 1961.

Paul, Sherman. *Emerson's Angle of Vision: Man and Nature in American Experience.* Cambridge, Mass.: Harvard University Press, 1952.

Schiller, Andrew. "Gnomic Structure in Emerson's Poetry," in *Papers of the Michigan Academy of Science, Arts and Letters,* Vol. 40. Ann Arbor: University of Michigan Press, 1955. Pp. 313–20.

Sealts, Merton M., Jr., and Alfred R. Ferguson, eds. *Emerson's "Nature": Origin, Growth, Meaning.* New York: Dodd, Mead, 1969.

Silver, Mildred. "Emerson and the Idea of Progress," *American Literature,* 12:1–19 (March 1940).

Smith, Henry Nash. "Emerson's Problem of Vocation: A Note on 'The American Scholar,'" *New England Quarterly,* 12:52–67 (March 1939).

Thompson, Frank T. "Emerson's Theory and Practice of Poetry," *PMLA,* 43:1170–84 (December 1928).

Wellek, René. "Emerson and German Philosophy," *New England Quarterly,* 16:41–62 (March 1943).

Whicher, Stephen. *Freedom and Fate: An Inner Life of Ralph Waldo Emerson.* Philadelphia: University of Pennsylvania Press, 1953.

Yohannan, J. D. "Emerson's Translations of Per-sian Poetry from German Sources," *American Literature,* 14:407–20 (January 1943).

Young, Charles L. *Emerson's Montaigne.* New York: Macmillan, 1941.

—*JOSEPHINE MILES*

James T. Farrell

1904-

I WOULD say than any genuine artist seeks to give the fullest possible expression to his own psychological life-cycle, and that he seeks to give the best organized form that he can to his own way of seeing the world." James T. Farrell wrote these words in 1948. In a letter to H. L. Mencken two years earlier he had suggested his way of seeing the world and the course his life had taken: "I was, after all, a young man of plebeian origins trying to write. The background from which I came was not one which fostered and affirmed the values of sophisticated literary culture. It was one of spiritual poverty. Through books, I gained something of a vision of possibilities in life. . . . As I went on, this . . . new world of envisioned and acquired values . . . stood in striking contrast to the past. . . ." He knew that one of his major problems as a writer was to draw upon the "social universe" of his various pasts with truth, and still to make them "consistent with a conception of expanded values, a fuller life, a broader range of perspectives."

This problem was implicit in his first two tales of any substance, "Slob" (1929) and "Studs" (1930). The first shows a young man struggling with his drunken aunt. In the second a young man goes to a wake and listens to the crude talk of the dead man's friends. The young man of each tale is deeply dis-turbed at human degradation, even to the point of revulsion. But his feelings betray deep involvement with those concerned, and we observe that the author is full of his subject. "Slob" is a germ of Farrell's autobiographical Danny O'Neill pentalogy—Farrell prefers to call it the O'Neill-O'Flaherty series—and the other story is the well-known origin of the Studs Lonigan trilogy. When he wrote these tales, the "plebeian" writer had found books and "expanded values" at the University of Chicago near his home.

James Thomas Farrell was born February 27, 1904, in Chicago, where he lived until April 1931, except for eight months in New York City during the late 1920's. He was the second oldest of Mary and James Francis Farrell's six children who lived to maturity. Mary Farrell was a native of Chicago. Her parents, John and Julia Brown Daly, had come to America during the Civil War from a background of poverty in County Westmeath, Ireland. John Daly became a teamster in Chicago, and on his meager earnings he and Julia reared five children. James Francis ("Big Jim") Farrell also became a Chicago teamster after he left his parents' home in Kentucky. His father was James Farrell of Tipperary, who had been an overseer of slaves in Louisiana before he became a Confederate foot soldier in—Farrell believes—the Second Louisiana Infantry Battalion, known as the Louisiana Tigers. After the war the ex-soldier settled in Kentucky and married.

Farrell's father was a strong and enterprising man—he once tried to start his own saloon in Chicago—but his wages as a teamster were not adequate to support his growing family. When Farrell was three, he was taken to live permanently with his grandparents, the Dalys, who were then comfortably supported by an unmarried son and daughter. This removal was the most important event of Farrell's youth. Eight years later, eager for companionship and filled with dreams, he moved with his grandmother, his Uncle Tom, and his Aunt Ella into the middle-class neighborhood, immediately west of Washington Park, that was made famous in *Studs Lonigan*. Altogether he attended three of Chicago's parochial schools—once he called his schooling a "mis-education," but later, in 1963, he praised it for having instilled moral values in him. During his high school years (1919–23) he worked summers and after school in the Wagon Call Department of the Amalgamated Express Company and continued there full time after graduation.

Faced with a dreary future of office routine, he enrolled as a pre-law student in De Paul University night school in September 1924. He entered the the University of Chicago in June 1925, and in four years, paying his own way, he completed eight quarters. During 1929 and 1930 while working on his *Studs Lonigan* manuscript, he published fiction in *Blues, Tambour*, and *This Quarter* and articles in *Plain Talk* and the *New Freeman*. After eloping with Dorothy Butler in April 1931, he lived for a year in Paris, where he received substantial encouragement from Ezra Pound and Samuel Putnam, editor of the *New Review*. While he was there, James Henle of the Vanguard Press accepted *Young Lonigan*, an act marking the

beginning of an important editorial association and friendship. Since 1932 Farrell has made New York City his home, although from 1933 to 1936 he lived for long periods at the Yaddo writers' colony, and for many years he has traveled widely in this country and abroad as as a lecturer—his 1956 visit to Israel is related in *It Has Come to Pass* (1958). He has supported himself and his family—he has two sons, Kevin and John—mainly by his writing, at which he works each day wherever he is. In addition he has actively engaged in the public literary and political life of his times, most dramatically, perhaps, in his early and clear-sighted opposition to the Communist literary line during the 1930's. His differences then with Granville Hicks, Michael Gold, Joseph Freeman, Malcolm Cowley, and others led to *A Note on Literary Criticism* and to his later attacks on the Communist-dominated League of American Writers. On behalf of the artist he has fought against commercialism, censorship, political dictation, and dogmatic theory—such as the Marxian doctrine of art as a weapon for proletarian revolution. Economically his course has not been easy, and personal troubles have compounded his problems. In 1935 he and Dorothy Farrell separated. His later marriage to Hortense Alden also ended in divorce and was followed in 1955 by his remarriage to Dorothy Farrell, from whom he is again separated.

At the University of Chicago Farrell began an intellectual development as unpredictably intense as Melville's unfolding eighty years before. Earlier his reading had been casual and undistinguished, although it included *Huckleberry Finn, Tom Sawyer, Silas Marner, Sartor Resartus, Lord Jim, You Know Me, Al*, portions of Dreiser's *Hey Rub-a-Dub-Dub*, and some Shakespeare. In college he concentrated his studies in the social sciences, but in 1927 he decided to be a writer of fiction, come what might. By 1930 he had formed lasting attitudes and, like Melville, had swum through libraries. William James, Dewey, Mead, Nietzsche, Stirner, Russell, Veblen, Freud, Pater, Ibsen, Chekhov, Mencken, Dreiser, Anderson, Lewis, Hemingway, and Joyce are some who were important to him. The ardent Catholic became a naturalist and pragmatist who affirmed the power of reason to improve society, but his greatest strength lay in a new and liberating sense of ego. He liked fiction, he wrote, having "the pressure of reality," the authority of personal experience he found in Anderson's *Tar*. Also by 1930 he had a bulky stack of manuscript tales and was well into *Studs Lonigan*. As early as 1928, in fact, he had begun to develop a life-plan for writing twenty-five volumes of fiction about the character later named Danny O'Neill and others. These books were to be loosely integrated—as he later wrote, "panels of one work." They would picture life in "connected social areas," first and basically in Chicago and then elsewhere.

In 1957 Farrell published his twenty-fifth book of fiction twenty-five years after his first. Behind him were the Studs Lonigan trilogy, the Danny O'Neill pentalogy, the Bernard Carr trilogy, three other novels, a novelette, ten collections of tales, and a play (with Hortense Alden Farrell), as well as six books of essays and criticism. The fiction re-creates "connected social areas" through its range of characterization and its use of cultural details. Its geographical poles are Chicago and New York City, but other parts of America and Europe come in for attention. A surprising number of memorable characters move about in their homes and neighborhoods, in leisure and working hours. They represent four generations and their actions span half a century. They come from a wide variety of social, economic, professional, national, and ethnic groups. Revealing a steadfast purpose and unrelenting en-

deavor, Farrell has explored, with a complexity not generally recognized, a representative segment of America, and in doing this he has established his personal style and his mode of realism. Since 1957 he has added other "panels." *Invisible Swords* (1971) is his twenty-third novel, his thirty-ninth volume of fiction, and his forty-ninth book. His present hope, time permitting, is to expand his lifework to include at least sixty-two books of fiction. Toward that goal he is making steady progress as he continues to bring out portions of his massive new series, *A Universe of Time*.

Farrell's reputation rose rapidly in the early 1930's, those Depression years when proletarian fiction was the vogue. But before the end of the decade his reputation with reviewers began to suffer. He soon saw that the current of critical opinion was running against realism—his own brand, in particular, offended many left-wing reviewers, Catholics, and academic critics. To be sure, he has had sympathetic interpreters, notably Joseph Warren Beach and Blanche Gelfant, and he has contemporary admirers, those whom Leslie Fiedler has called "a few surly defenders." Paperback editions of his books have sold into the millions and still sell when available. Many of his major works have been widely translated. He is sometimes called America's greatest living realist or naturalist, just as years before he was sometimes called proletarian. But often praise is tempered with strong reservations, sometimes very strong indeed. Farrell is still breasting the current.

A typical view writes him off as a pessimistic determinist, negative and unwholesome. The Christian critic Nathan A. Scott, Jr., believes Farrell has nothing to say because he lacks mythical and religious imagination. Others think of him as locked up in his boyhood or as simply an expert on adolescent behavior. Still others find that his style is inadequate.

They see his writing as repetitious and without form or grace. Another group dismisses him as a notebook writer, a photographic realist who literally reports facts or case histories. Those who hold this view believe he specializes unimaginatively and at random in the external. In effect they say of his work, with Mark Schorer, that "really, the thing is dead." His fiction rarely receives close critical attention; yet no recent American writer has been so variously —and confidently—impaled since the 1930's when William Faulkner was pigeonholed as a pornographer, or a regionalist, or a naturalist, or an uneducated primitive whose formless writing was needlessly complicated and lacking in affirmation.

It is important to see the wholeness of Farrell's fiction. His writing is truly a single body of work because it expresses his "psychological life-cycle" through the development of a unified subject. His novels and stories, following one after the other, are like a group of islands in the sea. Each is separate yet all rise out of one land mass below the ocean's surface, and when seen from above they form an impressive pattern. His poetry as well, and *A Universe of Time*—his work in progress since 1958—continue to reflect the unified imagination that lies behind his three completed cycles of novels on Studs Lonigan, Danny O'Neill, and Bernard Carr together with the individual novels and the tales related to them.

The scope of Farrell's fiction and its chain-linked social areas are distinctive features, but a quality more in the grain is its inner continuity of feeling, the shifting yet related clusters of emotions experienced by the characters. The sensitive young man of "Slob" and "Studs" is a simple example. Danny O'Neill in the early story "Helen, I Love You' is a better example. There we see the twelve-year-old boy, new in the neighborhood like Tom Sawyer, hoping that pretty red-haired Helen Scanlan will be his girl. But he makes no headway with her because he is bashful. Lonesome and fearful, he indulges in lush fantasies as he walks at dusk in Washington Park wishing Helen were with him. In this tale of a boy's adoration for a girl, there is a cluster of emotions—the devotion, the romantic yearning, the fear of criticism, the pain and guilt of having lost the girl through timidity, the longing to be understood—comparable to those that stir Studs Lonigan when he thinks of his lost Lucy. In *The Face of Time* seven-year-old Danny O'Neill feels much the same way about his Aunt Louise. With shifting emphases the pattern reappears several times in Danny's later life, helping to define his growth. Rooted in similar feelings are Bernard Carr's fantasies of his childhood sweetheart, a symbol of perfection that works creatively in his imagination.

The early story "Boyhood" yields a related set of emotions that has a long history in Farrell's fiction. Danny is thirteen and wants to be one of the gang, but they think he is a "goof." He recoils into himself. Although he is a little ashamed at being a misfit, he vows to fight the injustice and "show them." He will be a great man. With different coloration these feelings bubble up later in Danny, Studs, and Bernard. Other clusters of emotions, like the one centering in nostalgia for the past, similarly recur.

The continuity of Farrell's writing also is seen in the patterns of action flowing from the insistent emotions. Consider three sequences, one each from the completed major cycles about Danny O'Neill, Studs Lonigan, and Bernard Carr. In the first—actually the second to be written—Danny O'Neill is taken from his hard-pressed family at the age of three to live with his grandparents, the O'Flahertys. They share a comfortable apartment in Chicago with their son Al and two unmarried daughters. Because

Danny's father, Jim O'Neill, is hurt by this loss of a son to his wife's relatives, he brings Danny home two weeks later. The boy will not eat and he screams day and night. Afraid his son will die in convulsions, Jim carries him back to Mrs. O'Flaherty at 2:00 A.M. At her apartment door Danny opens his arms and says, "Mother, put me to bed!" He will often be unhappy and fearful in her home, but he will live with her until, in his middle twenties, he leaves for New York to write.

Toward the close of *Judgment Day* Studs Lonigan is out of work and desperately ill. Painfully he drags himself through Chicago streets to his unhappy parental home, his only refuge. As he enters the apartment he collapses at his mother's feet and says, "Mom, I'm sick. Put me to bed." A few days later, not yet thirty, he dies.

At twenty-nine Bernard Carr is a high-principled writer from Chicago living in New York. In the last chapter of *Yet Other Waters* he and his pregnant wife, Elizabeth, have returned to Chicago to visit her parents, whom Bernard once scorned but now respects. We see them in Jackson Park, an old haunt of his, watching Philip, their two-year-old son, play in the grass. Bernard, happily married, is determined that Philip's boyhood shall not be "lost and betrayed" like his own. In the closing scene Philip sleeps peacefully in his father's arms as the parents return to the grandparents' apartment to put him securely to bed.

These sequences are variations on the theme of family loyalty and estrangement, and they focus on the son's place in the family. Turbulent emotions and actions of critical importance mark the personal relationships. Often the characters are unhappy, and even during happy moments they are likely to sense the sadness time will bring. Beginnings, setbacks, new starts, and endings are examined as though to answer the question "Who am I and where am I headed?" Moral indignation and confident rationalism enter strongly into Farrell's sensibility, especially early in his career. But a deeper strain in his fiction, although not as broodingly apparent as in Dreiser's, is humility: an acceptance, tinged with melancholy, of the mysterious and inevitable transfigurations of time.

This tendency in Farrell's fiction often is expressed in suggestive short passages. There is Studs's plaintive recognition not long before his death that "he had never thought . . . his life would turn out this way," or Bernard's thoughts in *The Road Between*: "Chicago! He had once been a boy there, a frightened and ordinary boy, and somehow that boy had grown into this Bernard Carr, an American writer. . . . How had it happened? How had he found his road and won the confidence he now felt? The seeds of this change were not here in New York. They had been planted back there. . . ." In his fiction Farrell seeks detailed answers to the question "How had it happened?" and also "What happened?" He tries to identify the seeds that flower as qualities of mind and heart. As he fills out his characters' lives, he explores growth, self-discovery, creativity— and their frustration. These are his themes.

The business of Farrell's fiction, then, is to trace the "human destinies"—a favorite phrase —of many characters. Hundreds of his people, to be sure, appear only once or twice and have no proper history. But scores of others do, and these thread their way through separate tales and novels. They include minor characters like Milt Cogswell and Father Doneggan, more important ones like Red Kelly and Ed Lanson who appear time after time, and major ones like Jim O'Neill and Peg O'Flaherty. They prosper or decline, or simply live from day to day busy with their thoughts or with other persons. In the Chicago fiction, for example, their interweaving lives cohere around family, grammar school, boy gang, church, social circle, high school, fraternity, sports team, office or other place of work, poolroom, saloon, bohemian colony, university, political group. These related centers of activity, shown intimately or obliquely, merge to form a colorful neighborhood just as the characters form a spectrum of human possibilities. And as the neighborhood flows into the larger city, so the characters' actions are not contained within neatly plotted sequences. They overflow formal boundaries with the wash of time. The effect is to suggest the novelty and inconclusiveness of life, particularly the surging complexity of city life.

Towering out of this setting is the major dramatic action of Farrell's work to date: the organic story uniting the lives of Studs, Danny, and Bernard, three crucial characters intimately related to each other in the author's imagination. That story affirms love and the creative power of mind and will. It traces the rise of a type of twentieth-century American male—urban, Irish Catholic, aspiring—from a condition of slavish ignorance and appalling human waste (Studs) through a growing awareness and independence (Danny) to a state of useful self-fulfillment (Bernard). The story is one of emergence in which Studs represents the life Danny rejects, and Bernard the life he chooses. It presupposes free will not as an endowment but, in Farrell's words, as "an achievement . . . gained . . . through knowledge and the acquisition of control, both over nature and over self." In Farrell's novel *Boarding House Blues,* Danny writes: "A life is blown by a wind called destiny, and that wind is controlled by the mind as much as by circumstances." Elsewhere Farrell calls Danny a "bridge character." Yet the crossover Danny makes from Studs's world to Bernard's has the decisive effect of a breakthrough. In each world habits of mind and circumstances are

important, but Danny learns that the key to freedom is the creative use of knowledge—the all-important difference. Bernard, who begins where Danny leaves off, gives additional moral content to the newly won freedom. In his personal and professional life Bernard moves toward the integrity appropriate to each.

In 1941 Farrell wrote to Van Wyck Brooks: "In a sense the theme of my fiction is the American way of life." For one thing, he meant that his books counteracted American myths of easy success. In particular he was thinking of those immigrants "from a poor, bitter and oppressed little island" who fail to find their "land of heart's desire" in America. Their sons and grandsons often grow up in a rootless urban culture, and like Studs they may destroy themselves. Farrell wrote to his publisher, Henle, in 1942 that his books show the ways in which America deprived its youth during his formative years; surely many of his characters are badly twisted—some virtually pinioned—by their experience. In its extreme form the human cost of American growth as seen in Farrell's writing includes education for death.

Education for life also is part of his vision, for some characters build successful futures from past deprivations. "The American way of life" in Farrell's writing presupposes the "social making" of *all* the characters—as his friend Meyer Schapiro phrased it in a letter to Farrell. Just as surely Farrell's vision includes individuals making their culture. The poolroom and the brothel are patronized by Slug Mason and his kind. Others, like Jim O'Neill, Al O'Flaherty, or Paddy Lonigan, all idealists in their way, help build workaday America. Then there are those, including the important Danny and Bernard, who overcome—and creatively use—deficiencies in their pasts to become professional men or artists. Whether Farrell's major characters work with their hands or their minds, and whether they fail or succeed, most of them aspire to rise because they have known privation.

Farrell's subject is the unity of personal and national American growth within the "social universe" of his experience. Following that experience closely, his fiction records an urban America—Irish Catholic at the core—growing up; his large cast of characters merges into part of a nation sluggishly groping upward to the light. Plebeian vigor leads toward cultural sophistication, and cultural clichés stimulate intellectual revolt. A crude self-defeating individualism gives ground to mutual trust and accomplishment. The author rarely neglects for long the darkness of Studs's world: man cherishes his delusions and hostile divisions. Farrell once called that strain in his consciousness "an appalling terror, like a grinning and menacing mask." But the promise is also there. Danny O'Neill and Bernard Carr, especially, represent the creative will and secular reason that give Farrell's work its over-all Zarathustrian and Promethean pattern. They turn the feelings of the young man of "Slob" and "Studs" to account.

Studs Lonigan: A Trilogy (1935) is composed of *Young Lonigan* (1932), *The Young Manhood of Studs Lonigan* (1934), and *Judgment Day* (1935). Usually called Farrell's best work, it is a powerful realistic portrayal of the failure of understanding and potential growth in its hero. Studs is the elder son in a well-to-do Irish Catholic family that lives in a respectable neighborhood on Chicago's South Side. Essentially he is an aspiring person who responds too readily to what is malignant in his culture. Chiefly through Studs the trilogy dramatizes man's capacity for self-destruction. Its double condemnation of Studs and his culture is rooted partly in the emotions of Farrell's early faith, for it projects Farrell's Catholic imagination through the mode of secular realism.

The action spans fifteen years, one-half of Studs's life, from June 1916 to his death in August 1931. It goes from World War I to early Depression days; Studs declines from a strong young fighter to an impoverished weakling. The structure of his life is built up in massive, architectural fashion. The first book covers five months in 1916, and the last, six months in 1931. In the first, Studs chooses a way of life: he scorns learning, breaks with Lucy, whom he adores, joins the tough Prairie Avenue gang, becomes "a man" at fifteen with Iris. *Judgment Day* shows the outcome of his choice: he is an insignificant laborer; loses his work, money, and health; gets his girl, Catherine, pregnant but does not really love her; at twenty-nine dies a miserable death. In *Young Lonigan* life seemingly opens up for him. In *Judgment Day* it relentlessly closes in.

The ironically titled middle volume spans twelve and one-half years, from April 1917 to January 1929. Studs tries to join the army, drops out of school, works as a house painter for his father, and graduates from young punk to accredited poolroom barbarian. When Negro families begin filtering into the neighborhood, the Lonigans move to better surroundings, but Studs cannot move away from his impoverished values. Instead, he pursues them with a certain single-mindedness. The physically strong chauvinistic idealist changes to the helpless, bloodied figure, to whom "most things are just plain crap," draped around the fireplug at Fifty-eighth Street and Prairie Avenue. The middle volume, then, gives the stages of Studs's corruption, not neglecting his dense "social universe." The trilogy is fashioned to support Farrell's moralistic view of Studs's life as a darkening progress toward death.

Farrell avoided making Studs a slum-dweller because he wanted to explore the interaction of character and culture in his own middle-class neighborhood. He had come to think of human personality as both social product and social cause. Studs and his friends constantly absorb—and then fairly exude— the values of their milieu. Notice Studs in a moment of guilt: after having inwardly belittled Catherine, "he suddenly asked himself who the hell he was, wanting so damn much, and thinking she wasn't enough for him." But the momentary self-recognition fizzles out in renewed social cliché as he wishes "he were a six-foot handsome bastard, built like a fullback . . ." With equal constancy the story returns to the personal origins of social disorganization, dramatized in episodes showing uncontrolled drinking, rapes and beatings, and racial strife.

Studs's character lies at the heart of the work. As a boy Studs is hopeful, imaginative, aware of his feelings, sensitive to criticism— but outwardly already "hard." He is a leader with a romantic and adventurous flair, and he wants his life to count for something. Morally he is often at odds with himself; his conscience is active. Nor does he lack will. His painful hacking at his humanity is a major point of the action. He wills to be tough because he understands how tricky and unreliable his tender feelings can be, and because he knows, on the other hand, that toughness can be controlled and can get results. The young Studs sometimes reminds us of Huck Finn, who also once tried to make himself feel good by doing the conventional and inhuman thing. But if Studs begins as a truncated Huck, he ends as his opposite. Each boy seeks human intimacy, but Studs learns to value his own miserable isolation. He finds self-assurance in rigidity. So he knows he is "the real stuff" by the very act of denying his best impulses. Huck affirms his best impulses in action but without full under-

standing, and humbly he thinks he acts from the devil. Studs repeatedly wills his own victimization; ironically his environment "takes" on him all too well because he needs to make his life count. Studs is a rather average person who betrays his potentiality for good and descends to disaster. As a spiritually crippled man in *Judgment Day* he condemns himself, although falteringly and darkly, for the self-destruction he has worked.

Farrell wanted to re-create a sense of what life meant to Studs by unfolding the story in Studs's "own words, his own actions, his own patterns of thought and feeling." In this way he hoped to create the vivid illusion of life going on, the very process itself, apparently free from the author's manipulation. This famous and traditional "objective" method is Farrell's convention to get perspective upon personally meaningful material and is not, as some seem to believe, an impossible effort to reveal objective reality as it is, untinged by subjectivity. In practice, Farrell went beyond his description of his method. The writing ranges from the interior monologue, baring Studs's reveries and dreams, to a neutral recording of dialogue, setting, and action— sometimes with Studs not present. Perhaps most typically the external world is shown colored by Studs's awareness, a merging of the inner and outer in varying proportions that helps to determine pace of action, sense of time, and manner of character portrayal.

Standing with "the older guys" in front of the poolroom, Studs at fifteen watches the neighborhood people go by: ". . . they had the same sleepy look his old man always had when he went for a walk. . . . Those dopey-looking guys must envy the gang here, young and free like they were. Old Izzy Hersch, the consumptive, went by. He looked yellow and almost like a ghost; he ran the delicatessen-bakery down next to Morty Ascher's tailor shop near the corner of Calumet, but nobody bought anything from him because he had the con, and anyway you were liable to get cockroaches or mice in anything you bought. Izzy looked like he was going to have a funeral in his honor any one of these days. Studs felt that Izzy must envy these guys. They were young and strong, and they were the real stuff; and it wouldn't be long before he'd be one of them and then he'd be the real stuff."

The author also reveals the external world through the minds of other characters, notably Studs's father and some of Studs's friends. These additional perspectives and the stream of action involving many persons create a strong sense of cultural process. Studs is thereby firmly related to the past and to his contemporaries. He is precisely located in a well-defined historical current.

This method leaves room for ideal and mature elements in Studs's culture. Not all of his friends sink into crime like Weary Reilley or into destitution like Davey Cohen. Many succeed in their business or profession. Other persons like Christy, John Connolly, Danny O'Neill, Mr. Legare, Helen Shires, Catherine Banahan, and Lucy are humane and relatively enlightened. Studs often is in touch with the excellence that might have given him the "something more" he sought. Nor are the issues and institutions of the larger world excluded. Near Lake Michigan Studs overhears two students discuss a Communist demonstration against Japanese imperialism. In this brief episode the reminder of the nearby university and of active world forces underscores his ignorant isolation, while the surging lake in the background suggests the ever-accessible vitality of nature. Farrell's method by no means leaves an impression of Studs as merely a helpless victim. His destiny therefore becomes all the more terrible. Because we feel through Studs and still see him in context, we experi-

ence both the personal tragedy and the full social implications of the flow of his life toward the trivial and shameful.

Farrell handles that flow with skill. The chronological episodes form a series of penetrations into Studs's experience during sixty-five days selected from fifteen years. Studs's egotistic sense of time—first cocky, later nostalgic, and subject to a haunting fear of death—contrasts vividly with our understanding of what is happening. From the first we feel time's shaping passage as well as its repetitive heaviness, a deathlike stagnancy reflected in Studs's boredom. As the action proceeds, we see Studs's past in shifting ironic lights, while simultaneously we feel time moving invincibly toward Studs's future death.

Farrell's images and symbols are drawn from the empirical world and are used incisively to reveal Studs's changing condition. The city and nature provide patterns of imagery related to rigidity and fluidity, light and dark. Social actions like drinking or dancing and entire scenes reverberate with meaning, both forward and backward in time, through the trilogy. On the surface Father Gilhooley's graduation talk, for example, is a rather heavy-handed satire of Catholic religion and education. Yet the fatuous Father is a true prophet; he foretells the judgment day. His talk works in *Studs Lonigan* something like Father Mapple's sermon in *Moby Dick*. On a deep ironic level his dire Catholic admonitions send out vibrations echoing in Studs's moral imagination and also in Farrell's.

Although flaws in *Studs Lonigan* are easy to find, the objective method is a great success. Studs comes fully alive, and lesser characters also stay with us. In the main Farrell faithfully gave us Studs's world as Studs knew it. At the same time he charged it with the meaningful tensions of his personal feelings. He identified partly with Studs, yet the acceptance falls within a larger pattern of rejection. Farrell also re-created Studs's world from the perspectives he gained through his hard-won study and his growing success. His knowledge of Dewey's thought, and Mead's, was a major constructive force in the trilogy; and in *Judgment Day*, written considerably later than the first two volumes, his growing interest in Marxism had its impact. The method also is well suited to Farrell's view of time and experience. The episodic panorama of Studs and his friends constantly bobbing up in an earthly hell that ends in the blackness of death is itself a fitting expression of an imagination both Catholic and naturalistic.

Farrell's insight that "Studs is a consumer who doesn't know how to consume" applies to Studs as he drinks in platitudes or bootleg gin, a living example of the misuse of leisure in a modern city. But the trilogy strikes deeper, for it accurately pictures those basic evils charged against industrial society by the southern Agrarians, who spoke out at the very time Farrell was publishing his work. Their premises and solutions were poles apart from his, yet every evil they attacked is dramatically alive in *Studs Lonigan*. John Crowe Ransom called industrialism the contemporary form of pioneering, "a principle of boundless aggression against nature." Studs, brought up in a great industrial center, waged a personal war against his nature so that he might realize his dream of the tough he-man. Farrell once called Studs "the aftermath in dream of the frontier days."

The trilogy exposes a middle-class morality that arises more ominously from human urges than it does in Sinclair Lewis' Zenith. In his business Paddy Lonigan practices the aggressive individualism that Studs acts out in fantasy or reality as Lonewolf Lonigan, or a hard guy who beats up Jews and Negroes. As David Owen has shown, Studs strips the clothing of respectability from the illiberal ideal of rugged individualism and so clashes with respectability while remaining a son of the culture. The trilogy also extends the range of social conflict found in Upton Sinclair or Theodore Dreiser. Possibly it affects us most as an intimate picture of personal disintegration, of adult corruption fully at work in a representative boy who in turn convincingly becomes father to the man. For here is much of the terror and agony of our modern cities. We feel the ugly power of man's irrational drive toward the brutal and destructive. The failure of family, school, and church seems to lie in the impotence of love and reason themselves. Yet we know that this black picture is the oblique expression of Farrell's idealism.

Farrell's next major work is the Danny O'Neill pentalogy: *A World I Never Made* (1936), *No Star Is Lost* (1938), *Father and Son* (1940), *My Days of Anger* (1943), and *The Face of Time* (1953). The action covers more than eighteen years in Danny's life. It goes from 1909, when he is an insecure child of five, to 1927, when he resolutely leaves home and his college studies to become a writer in New York City. As a college student, Danny had appeared briefly in *The Young Manhood of Studs Lonigan*. There he condemns the ignorance and inhumanity of the city life around him. He considers his former beliefs to be lies and delusions, "so many maggots on the mouldering conception of God dead within his mind." Through his writing he intends to win recognition and to help build a better world. The pentalogy shows the growth of the child into the young man who has found the means to satisfy the deepest needs of his nature.

This series is central in Farrell's imagination and work. As an exploration of Danny's growth, it is the author's most direct adventure in self-understanding. For Danny's development is patterned upon Farrell's, and Danny's feelings approximate the "way it was" with Farrell during his formative years. The series therefore illuminates Farrell's other work and his life. It is rich in memorable characterizations based upon members of his family. Moreover, taken as a unit the five novels are central in the over-all design of his fiction. The rebel Danny emerges out of a long foreground not unlike Studs's in some respects. He wins his freedom and comes to the threshold of accomplishment. Having discarded supernaturalism, he wants to infuse humanitarian values into the existence that becomes "plain crap" to Studs. In these books the imagination that shaped Studs's earthly hell turns to the origins of Danny's dream of "a newer, cleaner world."

Those origins go back to Danny's traumatic removal at three from his own family to the O'Flahertys' home. This experience sets the pattern of his future relations to others. For example, it helps to explain the shame he feels toward his mother, and his later strained relationship with his father. As the son in two families, a kind of double outsider, he is a subject of contention. He feels bewildered and insecure. He knows he is different from other boys whose family life is normal, and naturally he seeks an identity. He searches for understanding and a wholesome directness in his personal relations. When these satisfactions are denied him, his reaction is likely to be sharp. Whatever its form, it is intended to assert his importance and independence, to help him leave the past behind and to move on to the new friend, the new neighborhood, or the new belief.

True to this basic pattern, Danny gradually takes on substance and color: Farrell is as interested in showing processes of growth as the end result. In *The Face of Time* Danny is a dependent, impressionable child overshadowed by adults already set in their ways. Sensitive to others' feelings toward him, confused in his loyalties, reaching out for affection, he is like a chip on a torrent of adult emotions. Already the later Danny who wants to be a free man is dimly visible in the small boy, who is effectively contrasted to his dying grandfather, Tom O'Flaherty. As a seven-year-old in *A World I Never Made*, Danny is still an anxious and sheltered little boy, but his experience broadens rapidly. His increasing interest in baseball is a good example of Farrell's use of common materials to suggest the dynamics of his growth. Broad outlines of his character begin to emerge: his family loyalty, a sense of honor, quick guilt feelings, a childish judiciousness, a capacity for faith. These qualities, together with the blunderings and weaknesses of an unsure child, make a balanced picture. Danny is rarely, if ever, sentimentalized.

As a pre-adolescent in *No Star Is Lost*, Danny lives more in a public world than before. The insecurities arising from family troubles grow more intense, and he reaches out eagerly for acceptance by his classmates. He begins to confront the hierarchy of authority he must eventually reject—the chain of command running from God through parents and relatives, priests and nuns, policemen, other grownups, and older boys. In *Father and Son*, as Danny enters high school, his troubles grow. His efforts to fit the stereotypes of his surroundings build inner pressures that eventually will erupt in the revolt he cannot yet conceive. For he is still the unsuccessful conformist. Yet his very "goofiness" is evidence of an unchanneled creative drive. As the fourth novel ends, Danny still lacks critical awareness, but the ties to his environment are wearing thin and he is beginning to understand the meaning of his father's life and death.

When Danny gets to college in *My Days of Anger*, the old gods tumble rapidly as the tensions of many years find release through knowledge. He develops a naturalistic philosophy with shifting overtones of despair, stoical endurance, confidence, and angry indignation, but he is really not very different from the little boy to whom affection and fair treatment meant the most. Danny's life naturally lacks the gravitational inevitability we feel in Studs's. Yet his reclamation is entirely plausible, for the series elaborately shows the complex interaction of his character and his environment. In the particulars of his daily living we can feel the origin of his sincere aspirations and his emotional needs that eventually lead to the University of Chicago and to New York City. As Danny confronts the nebulous future—the world he wants to make—Farrell ends his series with a sure touch. In the call room of the Express Company we again feel the power of delusion, the sense of people terribly caught in the mechanisms of our civilization, the opposite of what Danny wants. Yet there, too, is the vigorous authority of an established way of life that puts Danny's highfalutin and untested aspirations in a realistic perspective.

Of all Farrell's work, these novels are richest in major characters. Jim O'Neill is the proud, self-reliant workingman, a person of moral force and Danny's true spiritual father. His wife, Lizz, is an aggressive, salty woman, central in the pentalogy as wife, mother, daughter, sister, neighbor. Her father, old Tom O'Flaherty, is fundamentally a gentle, understanding man still not at ease in America after many years. Mary, Tom's wife, is one of Farrell's finest characters, a shrewd, resourceful woman who never loses her zestful will to live and to control. Mary's other children are also exceptional creations, especially the rigid and lonely Al, and the self-tormented Peg who keeps the family in turmoil. These characters, patterned after members of Far-

rell's family, are created out of the mature author's love and understanding. The pentalogy in effect is an act of piety toward his own people, an effort to recapture their feelings, to show how their lives went in the city they helped to build. To be an honest tribute, the picture had to include in all relentlessness their violence and weakness as well as their affection and will to live.

The adult O'Neills and O'Flahertys intimately affect Danny and form a relatively stable human backdrop to his story. We measure his growth against it as he changes from a dependent child among towering adults to the young man whose educated perception reduces them to true scale. Yet they are far more than adjuncts to Danny's growth, for they are seen and created as autonomous characters. Much of the pentalogy traces their lives and faithfully explores their personal feelings. Moreover they add a special blend of comedy and pathos. For example, Al's childlike illusion that the true wise guy achieves cultural status through decorum contrasts effectively with Jim's hardheaded realism. Lizz sprinkles holy water or has a Mass said to shape the future to her desire. We are amused but sympathetic, for her action reflects a naive concept of the power of spirit, and her faith measures the immensity of her need. Particularly through Lizz and Mrs. O'Flaherty, Farrell develops a broad and rich humor, a quality of his writing that often goes unrecognized.

Compared to Danny, whose urgent needs drive him *through* experience, the members of his family show little radical development, except, perhaps, Jim O'Neill. For instance, Al remains loyal to his ideals of business success and self-improvement through a study of Lord Chesterfield's letters and the dictionary. The repetition of such effects, emphasizing the cultural naiveté of the family, heightens our sense of what Danny must overcome before he finds his way. The repeated family quarrels over him or over Peg's affairs, for example, and the adults' occasional harshness toward Danny burn the pattern of shame and fear into him, thereby making his ultimate revolt more certain. Also, while reiteration of Al's pretensions to culture, his brother Ned's New Thought, Peg's vain resolutions to reform, and Mary's verbal onslaughts says a great deal about the deprivation in their lives, it conveys as well their stubborn vitality. Farrell's repetition of these traits simultaneously shows the O'Neills' and O'Flahertys' strong will to live and the cultural stunting that affects them as it does Studs and his friends. As first- or second-generation immigrants struggling in a competitive world, they transmit a heritage that is terribly inadequate, but it has the validity of a bludgeoning weapon forged of necessity in the heat of battle.

Again, as in *Studs Lonigan*, the development of individual character is used to reveal historical process in human life. In love and strife Danny's family act out social forces, seen as individual habits or predispositions. They quarrel but they stick together and help each other. Their loyalty shows the common need of first- and second-generation Americans for support from family and cultural tradition. Their belligerence derives from their violent past. The scheming, the shouting, the blows, the talk of splitting skulls with skillets is deeply ingrained and shows them, in effect, meeting their problems with the habits and language developed from their Irish past. Their actions also reveal the clash of cultural patterns between the generations and between economic classes. Farrell's method spotlights his characters under institutional pressures, typically from the Church and the job. We feel the power of money and dogma in their lives. These books show what it means to have been a big-city Irish-American Catholic, of

modest income, during the first three decades of this century—one reason Farrell is a significant Catholic novelist—and they display the broad human meaning of early twentieth-century capitalism, from its drudgery and harsh competition to its genuine opportunities.

The Danny O'Neill series keeps to the episodic and objective method of *Studs Lonigan*, for it presents life as felt by the characters during selected segments of time. Studs's limited awareness dominates in the trilogy, but in the later work the family members establish many viewpoints. The resulting autonomy of these convincing people strengthens Danny's characterization, for he grows through involvement with other persons. Farrell's procedure in the pentalogy suits the theme of individual growth, just as the method in *Studs Lonigan* dramatizes the substance of lonely spiritual impoverishment.

Farrell again uses the Chicago setting with a sure and revealing touch. But for various reasons neighborhood plays a less crucial role than it did in the trilogy. Instead we feel the confining apartment or job more strongly. Even so, the pentalogy yields a broader spectrum of life than *Studs Lonigan*, which is dominated by the dramatic curve of one meager destiny. It includes more characters, traces more careers, presents several persons with explosive emotional lives, ranges more widely in action, and follows up Danny's drive toward a spacious world. For these reasons the city is more broadly present in the pentalogy but less immediately and fatally than in the trilogy, which makes such effective use of urban imagery. In keeping with its theme of emergence, the Danny O'Neill cycle, unlike *Studs Lonigan*, leaves a sense of an open society despite the limitations of individual characters.

The 2500 pages of the loosely jointed Danny O'Neill books show little formal plotting, although causal relationships are everywhere and narrative strands, like the story of Peg and Lorry Robinson, hold some suspense. The episodes are most easily seen as a panorama, a vast succession of scenes leading to many climaxes and to a fitting conclusion for Danny. It would indeed be difficult to justify formally all the episodes; yet when the five books are examined as a unit they reveal a unique structure with its own logic. This structure is appropriate to Danny's position as a son in two families, to the slowly rising curve of his personal development, to the three-generation process which transforms immigrant stock from laborer to intellectual American, and to the large rhythms of life flowing through the books: birth and death, growth and decay, regeneration and sterility. The result is not as intensely dramatic as *Studs Lonigan* but it is more inclusive, for here Farrell significantly extends his story of the making of Americans. He broadens the implicit indictment of reigning values and urban conditions, and in Danny he presents the emerging artist—his awakening identity and sources of courage.

Farrell rounded out his basic story with the Bernard Carr trilogy: *Bernard Clare* (1946)—(after a libel suit brought by a man of that name, *Clare* was changed to *Carr* in the second novel)—*The Road Between* (1949), and *Yet Other Waters* (1952). The over-all movement in the three major series is this: Studs goes under, Danny discovers his true calling and escapes from Chicago, and after considerable floundering Bernard succeeds as a writer in New York City. The action occurs between 1927 and 1936, overlapping Studs's later years and in effect taking up the thread where Danny dropped it. The work fulfilled Farrell's long-standing ambition to write of New York literary life and radical political groups.

The trilogy brings together several matters of importance to Farrell. He wanted to indicate what happened, spiritually and artistically, to a generation of New York writers and intellectuals who were either Communists or fellow travelers. (In this respect *The Road Between* and *Yet Other Waters* approximate *romans à clef.*) He felt that their relatively sophisticated story also would enrich his picture of contrasting values and milieus in America. Moreover, he intended his hero to mirror the economic and spiritual struggles he had known. From a working-class family, Bernard illustrates Chekhov's statement used as the epigraph to *Bernard Clare*: "What writers belonging to the upper class have received from nature for nothing, plebeians acquire at the cost of their youth." As Farrell wrote to Henle in 1944, Bernard wrestles with "the problem of sincerity" and seeks his identity. Eventually he defines himself vis-à-vis his boyhood past, the economic order, his lovers and wife, and especially the American Communist party, which tries to use him for its political ends. In this work Farrell returned to familiar themes, and like James, Dreiser, Anderson, and others before him, he took up the artist's relation to society—a special case of his general interest in the social making of Americans. Bernard's life, somewhat like Farrell's, becomes a search for integrity, the struggle to be himself through serious writing.

Farrell used the Communist theme to underscore the continuity of his three major cycles. Ironically, the party brings Bernard to himself. In effect he learns that Communists are moral cousins to Studs: absolutists whose idealism—or fanatic faith—sanctions their efforts to be strong and tough and the real stuff in politics and art; or, less kindly, hooligans with a philosophy. But they pay the price of a shattered integrity and a withered inner life. Whereas they behave like Studs on a higher level, Bernard becomes more and more like a mature version of Danny. Three crowd scenes show his progression. In 1927 on the night

Sacco and Vanzetti were executed the rebellious Bernard, although no Communist, is strong for social justice and as capable of "solidarity" with Communist-manipulated demonstrators as Studs is with his gang. In 1932 with some reservations he marches in the Communist May Day parade. Finally in 1936 he watches the May Day marchers from the curb, aloof, seeing them as both dupes and deceivers, Stalin's "local boys," corruptors of the Revolution. He thinks: "He was alone here, as he had been in Chicago in his boyhood." But his is the isolation of integrity and not that arising from aggressive hostility toward others as in Studs, or from rejection by others as in Danny. Like Danny he is a stranger in a world he never made and has a tough endurance Studs never really had, but he has outgrown Danny's frustration and rage. Instead of feeling Danny's early insecurity—*A Legacy of Fear* was Farrell's first choice of title for *The Face of Time*—he knows he can "walk the streets with confidence." Like Farrell, he becomes more aware of the evil flowing straight out of men's hearts and minds, as distinct from the evil of social injustice. In *Judgment Day* the Communist parade held out hope for the deceived, the "prisoners of starvation" like the Lonigans, but in *Yet Other Waters* the Communist marchers are themselves prisoners of the deceit they practice.

As in the Danny O'Neill series, the central story is the hero's growth. At twenty-one Bernard is an immature, confused romantic who spends half of 1927 in New York City trying to write. His view of life as a drab affair and a race with Time in which Death is the ultimate winner masks his angry determination to expose life's shame and injustice through his writing. He publishes nothing, but he grows in self-understanding and compassion. His identification with the executed Sacco and Vanzetti and his affair with Eva, a young married woman, enable him to define his aims with greater certainty. His menial jobs teach him the plight of misfits in a society all out for money and progress. He begins to see his chosen craft and the flaws in his writing more clearly. As *Bernard Clare* ends, he is still relatively immature, a parochial Nietzschean who can be disagreeably egotistical; but at the core of his personality is a strong will to fight tenaciously for what he wants—and he knows that he is a "collection of somebodies wanting to be a synthesis of somebodies" through his art.

The Road Between opens in 1932 with Bernard, newly married to his Chicago sweetheart, Elizabeth Whelan, receiving recognition for his first novel. He still feels a Zarathustrian defiance and loneliness, yet his art permits him to harness much of his inner torment. Emerging from the 1920's into the 1930's, he is well along on the road between his conventional Chicago past—reflected in chapters about his and Elizabeth's families—and his radically different New York life. His growing understanding of each world is the measure of his development. With increasing flexibility he comes to understand his crude father's sexual and cultural frustrations and his own similarity to his pious Catholic mother, who seeks immortality not through art but through religion. He sees that, to the faithful, the Church he has rejected clothes life with meaning and dignity—as he tries to do in his writing—and he begins to see significant differences between Communist theory and practice. The road between that he travels thus leads from mind to heart. Eventually the journey will enable him to heal a split in his consciousness between the rational and the emotional. His earlier condemnation of his past and his acceptance of Marxism were steps toward freedom, but his heart now feels the tug of loyalty to family and to native traditions as part of the truth he will affirm in his writing. *The Road Between* ends in 1933: Bernard publishes his second novel, he wins a Loewenthal Fellowship, and Elizabeth's baby is born dead.

Yet Other Waters traces Bernard's life for a year and a half beginning in the spring of 1935; and as before, interspersed Chicago scenes take us back to his origins. Now fairly well off, the Carrs have a son, Philip, and Bernard has written a third novel. He pickets in a strike directed by the party, and he speaks at the 1935 American Writers Congress, where he sees Communist intrigue from the inside. He successfully resists inducements to make his fiction and his criticism follow the party line, explaining that he seeks "to rediscover and put down . . . some of my own continuity." Before long he publicly denounces the party for its disruptive tactics and its deceit. As the trilogy ends, Bernard's mother dies and Elizabeth is expecting their second child.

The third volume makes clear that the triology, like much of Farrell's work, sets up an opposition between forces of life and death in modern America and shows the growth of life out of death. Bernard believes that death is life's framework and end, the extinction of awareness, and that whatever diminishes awareness, whether because of rigid attitudes or cultural sterility, is a form of death-in-life. It may be said, then, that absolutisms like the Church and the party, although meeting deep human needs, are blinders to help fearful men cope with the fact of death. Bernard regards his writing as an opposite method of outwitting death: a splurge of consciousness, a sustained effort to intensify awareness and understanding. He learns that to write with truth he must constantly return to the flux of experience—to *his* feelings and thoughts—and must distrust all systems claiming perfection and finality; "for other and yet other waters are ever flowing on." This Heraclitean,

pragmatic theme is restated through a parallel set of symbols, the women in Bernard's life. The vision of Elsie that haunts his imagination is a boyhood ideal of perfection like the Church, and Alice is his seductive Communist mistress who would like him to knuckle under. Elizabeth, one of Farrell's best women characters, is intuitive, warm, sensible, and loyal to Bernard and to the needs of her family—a good example of feminine "realism" in contrast to masculine "idealism." Bernard's renewed affection for her is a return to a love which, like a heightened consciousness, is a creative breach of death's power and one that gives added point to Bernard's—and Danny's —earlier angers and hates. Bernard grows through his ability to perceive and reject the disembodied ideal, the seductive Absolute, in his emotional life and in his thinking. His final wisdom is to seek the attainable ideal in the ever-changing present reality and not to locate it in a fantasy of the past or future, as Studs does, or in a Utopia of this world or a heaven of the next. It is the wisdom, strangely echoing Hawthorne, of Saint-Just's phrase, "Happiness is a new idea." For Bernard, this saying sums up a way of life embracing a democratic social philosophy, a pragmatic trust in experience, a naturalistic metaphysics, and an ethics of self-fulfillment in one's personal and occupational lives.

Judged as fiction, the trilogy is weaker than the two earlier series—unfortunately so, for its climactic position calls for strength. At the heart of the difficulty lies Farrell's uncertain conception of Bernard's character and fate. The original intention to have Bernard return to Mother Church or Stalinism—as some of the characters in Bernard's fiction do—did not square with Farrell's compelling need to have Bernard become triumphantly self-sustaining. The cloudiness in Bernard's character cannot be entirely accounted for by the effort to highlight the problem of identity or to avoid the "giganticism" of "Wolfeism," as Farrell explained to F. O. Matthiessen in 1946.

Nor do the Bernard Carr books flow from the visceral knowledge of environment and manners evident in Farrell's Chicago novels. Bernard does not really know his world; he is homeless in a way Studs and Danny never are. Although this quality is not inappropriate to a seeker, Farrell's method, as Blanche Gelfant has shown, fails to convey the density of Bernard's inner life—that very flux he learned to trust. Moreover, for a fertile writer, he is shown too seldom in creative interplay with ideas, and too often, perhaps, in merely hostile relationship to his environment. Farrell justified his plebeian hero's character to James Henle in 1946: he had tried to place Bernard "on the same plane as the other characters," and he did not want to have "culture . . . conceal reality in the books." Yet we miss a compelling sense in Bernard that human culture, in its broader sense, *is* his reality, his very livelihood as a writer. The autonomous "social universe," the seething background Farrell wished to catch, is clouded over by Bernard's narrow self-absorption. To be sure, the Chicago scenes, some of the Chicago characters —notably Mr. Whelan and Mrs. Carr—and a number of objective New York sequences show much of Farrell's earlier power. Some of the Communists, especially Jake, Sam, and Sophie, come alive at intervals, but by and large the New York writers and radicals are ghostly figures who inadequately project social realities of magnitude. Although Bernard succeeds in his significant quest, the world he moves in lacks the solidity and meaningful implication of that other rejected world in *Studs Lonigan*, and Bernard himself insufficiently represents the positive ideal made real.

Nevertheless, with a brilliance of conception, the trilogy rounds out the organic story begun in *Young Lonigan*, for Bernard's hard-won wisdom and freedom are ultimately a triumph over spiritual rigidity, seen in rudimentary form in Studs. In its concern with the artist's entanglement with modern society, the work is unusually ambitious and partly successful. Unquestionably it extends and enriches Farrell's picture of America.

Farrell's other novels and his short stories interlace with his three major series through characters, settings, and themes. They help to round out his fictional world.

In Paris during the fall of 1931, he wrote *Gas-House McGinty* (1933), a novel whose composition influenced the last two volumes of *Studs Lonigan*. The new work was the first book of a projected trilogy on the Amalgamated Express Company in Chicago. Originally called *The Madhouse* and intended as "a Romance of Commerce and Service," it focuses on the hectic Wagon Call Department presided over by Chief Dispatcher Ambrose J. McGinty during the summer of 1920. The slight narrative centers on the frustrated McGinty and his demotion to route inspector, paralleling the "fall" of the old song, but in a real sense the office itself is the protagonist (the anonymous, blaring telephone conversations of the clerks and the incessant sadistic banter create a nightmarish collective personality), and Farrell constructed his work accordingly. He explained to Henle, probably in July 1931, that his new work would be "something in which the characters are massed" to give a "composite picture . . . a sense of them squirming inside this large institution." Scenes of McGinty at home or on the street, interchapters about the outside route men, and echoes of current events in the men's talk and in McGinty's thoughts add perspective; but the crowded, claustrophobic office remains the central stage. Farrell accurately wrote to Henle in September 1931 that his characters "bring everything down to the Call Department, and, so to speak, dump it."

Awake or dreaming, McGinty is a small triumph of characterization, and his co-workers, including Jim and Danny O'Neill, are created deftly and surely. Dialogue used for narration is overworked (Farrell cut the Vanguard text for the Avon reprint edition), yet the men's frantic talk, functioning as release from devitalizing routine, makes its point and shows Farrell at his best in handling a robust vernacular. Despite the evident influence of Joyce's *Ulysses* in particular, the novel remains fresh and meaningful. It vividly dramatizes the shaping—and scarring—of character through occupation and thus complements the stories of Studs and Danny, which constantly return to the effect of leisure activity and family relationships upon personal growth. It vigorously re-creates the human significance of the commercial purgatory Danny fled.

This Man and This Woman (1951), a successful minor novel, returns to the milieu of the Express Company almost incidentally in relating the domestic catastrophe of the aging Walt and Peg Callahan. Farrell's theme is "biological tragedy," earlier developed in the stories of Jim O'Neill, Tom O'Flaherty, and Bernard's parents. It is the erosion of human life through physical and psychological causes, and is seen here particularly in Peg's aberration. The action is limited to a few days during the 1940's and builds upon Peg's growing paranoia that suffocates her former buoyant spirit. The novel's strength lies in the convincing and sympathetic portrayal of her change into the very thing she thinks she sees in the likable Walt. Appropriately minimizing the social background, the story explores seemingly unbridgeable differences between the sexes with an intensity suitable to Peg's obsessional character.

Ellen Rogers (1941) also is a story of blighted love in Chicago, this time an affair in 1925 between Edmond Lanson and Ellen, just out of high school. Begun as a novelette, the work developed into a full-length chronicle whose mounting climax, as Mencken wrote to Farrell in September 1941, was managed with impressive effect. Because Farrell believed he had established the middle-class social context of his characters in earlier books, he played down the background and concentrated on his lovers' personal relationships. The story thus lacks the massive impact of *Studs Lonigan*, and the origins of Ed Lanson's destructive egotism are left in obscurity; its specific quality is suggested by Thomas Mann's judgment that it "is one of the best love-stories I know, of unusual truthfulness and simplicity."

Mann believed that Ellen's agony and humiliation following her abandonment by Ed were brilliantly portrayed. She is, indeed, Farrell's far lesser Anna Karenina, the female in the grip of passion. Once she is in love, her calculating worldliness and her self-sufficiency fall away. Depths of devotion, suffering, and fury open up, and her superficial life takes on meaning. Although Ellen is the source of emotional strength in this novel, her destroyer, Ed Lanson, interests us more as an individual and as a symbolic figure of the 1920's. Farrell imagined him as a mixture of a middle-class Sanine, a shallow Raskolnikov, and an eighteenth-century rogue transplanted to the 1920's; in short, a vulgarized product of "the Ben Hecht, Bodenheim, Cabell, Nietzsche influence." Ed is a character of calculated ambiguity. He is not merely morally starved or conventional, but a man who directs his charm, his courage, and his intelligence toward wicked ends. A rebel in the cause of romantic, selfish egotism, he is more dangerous than Studs because he is aware—an accomplished technician in evil. Like Studs, he is a foil to Danny (significantly *Ellen Rogers* came just before *My Days of Anger*), for he grows toward irresponsibility and ill will. He takes a road more deathlike than Studs's; he is incapable of true love even in dream. *Ellen Rogers* is remarkable as a love story and as a study of the deceitful heart that awakens love for the pleasure of strangling it.

Ed Lanson and Danny O'Neill are key figures in *Boarding House Blues* (1961), Farrell's fifteenth published novel. The action of this uneven but haunting work takes place in 1929 while Danny is back in Chicago trying to get his career started by writing "about the 58th Street boys in the old neighborhood." The surface story is the tawdry conflict between Ed and Bridget O'Dair, a nymphomaniac grandmother, over a disintegrating rooming house for bohemians on Chicago's near North Side. But the deeper concern is with Danny's new-found maturity that is set against a background of triviality and moral irresponsibility symbolized by the house. The theme is man's use of his brief lifetime—Farrell's old concern with the mysterious alternatives and rhythms of human life. As the moralist Danny writes in his notebook: "The question is which 'to be' before we are 'not to be.' There are no Hamlets today who are of Hamlet's quality."

Closely connected with *Boarding House Blues*, Farrell's *New Year's Eve/1929* (1967) is a short novel that places Danny—now an ex-student immersed in his writing—and his girl Anna once again in bohemian circles, but this time on Chicago's South Side near the University of Chicago. They attend a New Year's Eve party, where one of the revelers is Beatrice Burns, the only character of the novel deeply explored by Farrell. Knowing that she is dying of tuberculosis but romantically "gay and game" with every cigarette she smokes, Bea finds her only reason for living in gossip and in meddling in the affairs of others. Danny understands Bea's inner torment because he thinks of his own future, which is now closely identified with an ambitious program of writing fiction, as she thinks of hers: as a race against time. But while Bea turns to the trivia of personal intrigue and to sentimental thoughts of the past, Danny, equally haunted by the sense of fleeting time, looks to the uncertain future and to his writing. He resolutely pursues his proper work. Farrell's chief triumph in this novel is to portray the banal busybody Bea with merciless clarity and yet to sustain the reader's sympathy for her as "a frightened little girl" who still "wanted to . . . dream when there was no use in dreaming."

Farrell's approximately two hundred and thirty published short stories, most of them collected in thirteen volumes—and many others in manuscript as well—provide ample evidence, if more is needed, of his expressed intention to shake reality like a sack until it is empty. A few of them, to use Robert Morss Lovett's phrase, literally are chips off the blocks of his novels: preliminary experiments, deletions, or parts of abandoned works. The great majority were written as independent pieces, yet many of these mesh with the novels and among themselves. All the stories remain faithful to his version of reality while reflecting his continuing experience. Thus they reinforce our impression of his writing as a loosely organized, expanding work-in-progress. Danny O'Neill or his near equivalent turns up in over fifty stories, often at a new time and place like Italy in the mid-1950's. Familiars like Red Kelly and Willie Collins carry on through several tales. The stories tighten the personal relationships among Farrell's vast body of characters, yet leave his "social universe" open and permit quick probings of unexplored regions. They add significantly to Farrell's picture of youth and age, family life and marriage, the Church and clergy, education up through the university, unions and the laboring man, the politics of the ward heeler and the radical, bohemian and literary circles, organized urban violence and organized sports, and the every-day life of city people from the down-and-outer to the chain-store magnate. Working outward from numerous Chicago communities —not confined to what is loosely called Far-rell's "South Side"—the stories eventually reach to New York, Paris, and Europe at large. Their relentless pursuit of a fallible humanity is tempered by rare understanding, whether the quarry is a sheik "looking 'em over" on a Chicago beach in the twenties or a contemporary writer sardonically aware of his self-deception.

The stories range from mere scraps of experience to *Tommy Gallagher's Crusade* (1939), a novelette about a Studs-like char-acter of the 1930's who gives his floundering life direction through fascism. Farrell has written that an experience may call for trans-lation into anecdote, sketch, tale, novelette, or novel. Regardless of the genre, what mat-ters most in the re-created experience is "the sense of life" arising with "internal conviction" when character is not sacrificed to ideology or to frozen form. To this end Farrell has most often, but not invariably, used the "plotless short story," the artifice of an intentionally primitive method. Not surprisingly his tales have been profoundly affected by Chekhov's short fiction, which also emphasizes character over plot and portrays the ordinary experience of common people. In Chekhov's prodigal out-put Farrell found strong support for his view of short stories as "doors of understanding and awareness opening outward into an entire world." About the time he read the Russian realist Farrell learned from Anderson ("Mary O'Reilley"), Hemingway ("A Casual Inci-

dent"), Dreiser ("The Open Road"), and prob-ably Lardner. Severely controlling a preference for descriptive and metaphorical language to be seen in his earliest fiction, he rapidly de-veloped his manner of "letting life speak" by presenting characters through their own con-sciousness or their own language:

" 'Jesus, we sure get paper on the floor here, don't we?' Jim said, seeing the paper stacked and piled under the dining-room table as he came into the room, wearing his work clothes.

'Well, Jim, I always think this. When the children are playing, I think to myself that if they got their health, it's good, and the paper they throw on the floor don't hurt the floor, not this floor full of slivers. You couldn't hurt a floor in this dump,' Lizz said, standing in the door.

'The floor's sometimes so covered with pa-pers that we can't even see it,' Jim said.

'Our Lord was born in a stable. It isn't what the outside looks like. It's what the in-side looks like. If your soul is clean, that counts more than if your house is. Many there are in the world with clean houses and dirty souls. And this morning, the souls in this house are clean. This morning, everyone who's old enough to in my house received the Body and Blood of our Blessed Lord,' Lizz said, her voice rising in pride as she drew to the end of her declamation.

'Well, it isn't necessary to have a dirty house in order to have a clean soul,' Jim said." (From *No Star Is Lost.*)

This style has its limitations, as critics have freely shown. Yet it permits effective and color-ful contrasts of idiom and it achieves dramatic immediacy, for character is directly exposed through the interplay of dialogue and through the free association of interior monologues. At its best the style *is* the character-in-action.

Experimenting in his new manner during

the prolific years between 1928 and 1932, Farrell quickly came to his lyrical vein of boyhood loves and sorrows in early stories like "Autumn Afternoon" and "Helen, I Love You," and to his fiercely ironic style in stories like "The Scarecrow" and "Two Sisters." He progressively opened up the broader world of his Chicago youth in such tales as "A Jazz Age Clerk," "Spring Evening," and, somewhat later, "Comedy Cop" and "The Fastest Runner on Sixty-first Street." "They Ain't the Men They Used to Be," "The Girls at the Sphinx," and "An American Student in Paris" are examples of superior stories, completed later, that take us outside Chicago. During the past two decades, as Farrell has gone farther afield in his settings, he also has increasingly experimented with different styles in his tales. He has tried the monologue, the stream of consciousness, and other variants of the first-person point of view. In many of the late tales he has moved away from the vocally dramatic method of dialogue and from other methods that yield a direct impression of particularized experience, relying instead upon a generalized narrative manner somewhat like the summary of a rather detached chronicler of human events.

Farrell's stories can be heavy-handed and verbose ("Honey, We'll Be Brave"), tendentious ("Reverend Father Gilhooley"), synthetic ("Just Boys"), more skilled in portraying belching and banalities ("Thanksgiving Spirit") than nuances of feeling or thought ("The Philosopher"). Perhaps they are most moving when he gives the illusion of dramatic objectivity to simple, compact action known from the inside. Then, most likely, truth to individual character becomes social revelation, and we feel the story as a self-sufficient unit. At the same time we seem to be confronted not by a discrete and packaged experience but by an on-going actuality momentarily spotlighted in the stream of time. We might say with Danny O'Neill in *Boarding House Blues*: "It is not a story at all. It is an account of . . . that which has happened, has come to pass and has passed to become part of the welter of all that has happened." Although Farrell has succeeded best in his novels, which impressively embody his concern with time and human emergence, his tales are an integral part of his work, and a surprising number of them are individually memorable.

With few exceptions, Farrell's other imaginative writing also has been in the form of prose fiction. In 1940 he and Hortense Alden wrote the three-act drama "The Mowbray Family" (included in *When Boyhood Dreams Come True* [1946]), a mediocre domestic comedy of "penthouse Bolshevism" in New York City. A selection of Farrell's poems appeared in 1965 as *The Collected Poems of James T. Farrell*. Almost half of the forty-four poems in the volume date from Farrell's sustained creative period of the late 1920's and early 1930's, and the remainder were written after 1960 while Farrell was launching, during his "second career," as he called it, his new multicycled series of novels entitled *A Universe of Time*. In general the earlier poems, expressing a wide range of Farrell's youthful emotional turmoil, are more successful than the later. "Nostalgic Mood" (1929–30), for example, captures the poet's helpless yet willful attachment to a past love:

These slight spring winds
Form a frail and trembling bridge
To yesterday.
Across their precarious stretch
I move
Delicate sentiments
That shudder

With the swinging bridge
And their own shaking weakness.
Yet they move relentlessly—
At my command—
Back to you.

Whatever the deficiencies of Farrell's poetry, many of his verses hold up exceptionally well. Moreover, his poetry intimately exposes the sensibility that has created important fiction in our time. In it may be seen the author's zealous dedication to his work, his romantic temperament, and his susceptibility to beauty and love—sources of the equally evident hatred of all that is vulgar and defiling in his "ugly and hideous corner" of the world. Here too is expressed his broad understanding of humanity and the enduring will and the hardy optimism which has sustained him in the face of his naturalistic philosophy.

Farrell considers *A Universe of Time*, his current cycle of novels, tales, and poems, to be the culmination of his lifework. Based upon a reassessment of his experience, it aims to present "a relativistic panorama of our times." At present, Farrell believes the entire project should run to about thirty volumes, to be organized into four divisions:

I. When Time Was Young (1924–31)
II. Paris Was Another Time (1931–32)
III. When Time Was Running Red (1932–37)
IV. A Universe of Time (1937 to the present)

Occasionally the action of the series will dip backwards in time to the mid-nineteenth century, thus creating a countermovement to the over-all forward progression.

Much of the action of *A Universe of Time* will relate to Eddie Ryan (roughly Danny O'Neill's equivalent), whom Farrell thinks of as the integrating image of the total work. Yet, as the author has remarked, "The world is bigger than Eddie. Through a pattern of associations, many characters are introduced, and many paths are traced. From book to book, the past shall grow, and change, and grow and swell." Farrell intends *A Universe of Time* to interlock with his earlier work but to yield a more comprehensive view of experience than do any of his other series. Presumably, if Farrell realizes his purpose, the interpretation of modern life emerging from the new cycle will reinforce the large patterns of meaning implicit in the interrelated series on Studs Lonigan, Danny O'Neill, and Bernard Carr. For the author has maintained that the basic themes of his current cycle will be "man's creativity and his courageous acceptance of impermanence."

Through mid–1972, in addition to various related tales and poems, Farrell has published seven volumes in *A Universe of Time: The Silence of History* (1963), *What Time Collects* (1964), *When Time Was Born* (1966), *Lonely for the Future* (1966), *A Brand New Life* (1968), *Judith* (1969), and *Invisible Swords* (1971). These works do not compose a continuous narrative, and in most instances the positions they ultimately will assume in the vast cycle are open to conjecture.

Farrell has asserted about *The Silence of History*, however, that it was planned to "carry and predicate" the entire series. Its essential action, covering a year in the mid–1920's, explores Eddie Ryan's spiritual growth, which climaxes in his fateful decision to give up the job that financed his university education. Eddie tends to see his problem as one pitting artistic destiny against business success. His decision in favor of the former demands personal sacrifice and risk, but he sees it as "an assertion, an irrevocable step toward freedom" —his way of saying "No" to the sacred values of an acquisitive society that he increasingly mistrusts. Eddie knows that through education he can gain a valuable training and also establish a relationship to a wider and nobler reality than any his impoverished past has offered. Nevertheless, his decision to drop out is an existential affirmation of uniqueness that he hopes will nullify, in his life, the anonymity that befalls most men—the silence of history. The novel, therefore, is a study of the individual growth of an incipient artist at a crucial stage in his development. To point up the theme, Farrell makes extensive excursions into the past history and the psychology of numerous other characters—ranging from professors to commercial flunkies—whose directions in life are at variance with the course Eddie takes.

Lonely for the Future continues the exploration of Eddie Ryan's past. The action opens in Chicago in March 1927, some eight months after Eddie's decision to give up his job. It closes in mid-July as Eddie and his friend George Raymond (the equivalent of Ed Lanson) hitchhike to New York. Eddie, George, and their close friend Alec McGonigle become implicated in the affairs of the Bohemian Forum, a night spot near Eddie's South Side Chicago home. This discotheque of the prohibition 1920's is the setting in which each of the three friends comes to understand better the values he wishes to live by. Alec will return to law school and eventually to the conventional commonplaces of Chicago politics and law. George, the pseudo-Nietzschean, travels farther down the self-destructive road of the "superman beyond good and evil." Eddie, already a naturalist, finds that in practice he can not approve of George's callous use of other people. Furthermore, Eddie's awareness that men are caught in a trap of time and nothingness intensifies his need to find order and meaning through art, while life may last.

Major themes of *The Silence of History* and *Lonely for the Future* permeate *When Time Was Born*, a prose poem of several thousand words. This brief work is Farrell's celebration of the creation and creativity, of "the undying wonder of the world," the incessant surge of existence toward more complex states of awareness and being as the self interacts with others and with the world as experienced. Farrell's use of the Adam and Eve theme presents man's creativity as springing from his weakness and his need for another person. Love in all its forms is linked to the growth of personal awareness—the strengthening of "the inner wind of consciousness"—and to the beat and pace of time itself.

What Time Collects is an important, ambitious addition to Farrell's canon. In this novel the present time is approximately 1924 to 1925, but long stretches of the action look to the past, as far back as the 1870's, to explore the antecedents of Anne and Zeke Daniels of Valley City (Indianapolis). None of the characters of *The Silence of History* or *Lonely for the Future* enters this novel—the connections will come in later books—but *What Time Collects* parallels Eddie Ryan's story in its concern with a "decision to make some kind of leap into life" in pursuit of self-liberation. Anne Duncan Daniels, a girl in her early twenties, focuses this theme. What time collects in Anne is precisely the strength to break out of her degrading marriage to Zeke Daniels and to reject her past. She belongs with seekers like Danny O'Neill and Eddie Ryan, who develop the self-knowledge and the courage that permit them to act decisively in response to individual needs. What time has collected for Zeke is a spiritually crippled self, the end result of "the whole loveless heritage" of the Daniels family over several generations. Zeke is a victim as well as a monster of crudity and aggression. Like Studs, he symbolizes a spiritual malady in his society. He is an excrescence of the solid, middle-class Protestants of Valley City, who are smug, materialistic, and puritanical to the core. *What Time Collects* projects Farrell's exceptional understanding of the many characters in three generations of the Duncan and Daniels families. It effectively adds a new panel to Farrell's picture of America.

In *A Brand New Life* Anne Duncan Daniels, newly divorced from Zeke, is living in Chicago seeking "the real Anne" through love, first with Roger Raymond and then with his brother George, two friends of Eddie Ryan. Thus she moves close to the periphery of Eddie's life, although Eddie enters the book only indirectly through the conversation of Anne's lovers. They recognize Eddie's strength of purpose, his compassion, and his obsession with time and impermanence—qualities commenting on the frantic and passion-bound interests of Anne and her lovers. But the story is Anne's, her search to overcome loneliness. Her tragedy is that neither of her lovers really wants her or anyone else to breach the spiritual walls behind which he feels secure; and, by herself, Anne is inadequate to the task. At the moment when she believes she has found genuine oneness with George, he already has discarded her in his thoughts. Presumably, in later novels, Anne's search for a satisfying, truly mutual love will continue.

Judith, an excellent short novel, brings Eddie Ryan to the center of the stage as narrator and chief actor. The tale is his first-person retrospective account of his on-and-off affair with Judith, an internationally known concert pianist of New York City, during the years 1951 to 1954. Eddie, now in his early fifties, is an established professional writer. He and Judith are both hard-driving, successful artists in mid-career. Eddie recognizes that "we had both hemmed ourselves within our separate loneliness," inevitable for the artist, and that each craved a liberating love. But the ever-present obstacle to a stable relationship that will satisfy the craving is the inescapable contradiction, felt by each, between the demands of art and the demands of love. The emotional see-saw tossing them up and down is effectively comic. But ultimately each of these artists must go his own way. As Farrell has written in a private letter, the theme of *Judith* appears to be "Artists and Egos go on." Much of the excellence of this novella lies in the ability of Eddie as narrator, for he is factual, accurate, honest, and sensitive. Through Eddie, Farrell has provided a terse, swiftly moving first-person narrative of remembered experience, including generous passages of dialogue that provide still another level of dramatic immediacy. Presumably *Judith* fits into the final division of Farrell's plan for *A Universe of Time*.

Invisible Swords, Farrell's latest novel, makes a strong cumulative impact. With *Judith* it belongs in the fourth part of *A Universe of Time*. It is the story of a child's congenital retardation and its effect upon the parents, Bill Martin, a New York City editor, and his wife, Ethel; and as such it reflects the experience of Farrell and Hortense Alden with their child John. In addition, the important character Tod Johnson, a writer somewhat similar in his honesty to Eddie Ryan of *Judith*, reflects important aspects of Farrell the mature novelist. The story, set in New York City from 1946 to 1949, simultaneously relates the growth of the Martins' harrowing realization of what the hopeless retardation of their beautiful child Billy means, the consequent damaging strain upon their marriage, and the connection between the overpowering despair of such "biological tragedy" as Billy's idiocy to the creation of art that earnestly explores the meaning of the most searing events. The lingering death from cancer of Tod Johnson's wife, an ordeal he honestly faces in his novel *Caroline's Destiny*, parallels the experience of the Martins with Billy. But Bill Martin, Johnson's editor, blocks the publication of the novel because its honesty forces him to face up to personal realities he can not handle. In the concluding pages of *Invisible Swords*, Bill Martin's evasiveness and Tod Johnson's tormented grappling with his experience effectively suggest two ways of meeting the horror that lurks behind the beauty of little Billy.

At present *A Universe of Time* is too incomplete to judge as a cohesive work. Evidently as it grows, it will continue to be compatible in themes and patterns of experience with Farrell's earlier work; but also it may develop new techniques suitable to its own purpose, and it may give fresh emphases to Farrell's interpretation of the past. For the novelist has long believed that the emergence of novelty in the present means that "new pasts are always rising behind us." Whatever may be the potential of *A Universe of Time*, its published portions do not as yet make the strong and unified impact of either *Studs Lonigan* or the O'Neill-O'Flaherty series.

" 'You live badly, my friends. It is shameful to live like that.' " Maxim Gorki's words express the sad indictment of humanity he found implied in Chekhov's fiction. They suggest the reproach in Farrell's writing, although the American's attitude is more yeasty with indignation. Like Chekhov in his way, Farrell makes us aware of life as it might be by showing life as he often found it: riddled with contempt for mind and fear of affection. But his critical realism recognizes man's idealism as well as his shabbiness, and its constant assumption is man's capacity for reason and dignity. His humanism is friendly to reformist social thought and to modern pragmatism. His fiction says to us that the only real ends are earthly consequences and that in human society consequences are men and women, affected for better or worse by their culture. Also it says that elemental emotions impel men and women toward self-fulfillment or self-deception. At the heart of his fiction is an ethics of self-development more basic than his rationalism and displayed in his rise from "plebeian" origins and in his stubborn independence of mind. This ethics is a kind of Emersonian individualism without the supernatural aura. It asserts the possibility of radical self-improvement through the right and the will to grow. As he has written: "Man is my concern. Freedom is my concern. . . . the dream that each and all have the opportunity to rise to the full stature of their potential humanity." Farrell is a philosophic naturalist who simultaneously sees life in the context of death and affirms with utter seriousness the values of the Enlightenment. A cantankerous Irishman with a zest for living, he never sees life as "absurd." Nor does he reject modern civilization as an irreclaimable wasteland. Nostalgia in a Farrell character is not a sign of abhorrence for the bases of modern society. Instead it is a technique of character revelation, a sign of one man's failure to live the good life.

The same values are alive in his historical and critical writing: *A Note on Literary Criticism* (1936), *The League of Frightened Philistines* (1945), *Literature and Morality* (1947), *Reflections at Fifty* (1954), and even the sly mouthings of Jonathan Titulescu Fogarty in *The Name Is Fogarty: Private Papers on Public Matters* (1950). These values may be seen in his political development through various stages of anti-Stalinist socialism to the liberal internationalism of Stevenson and Kennedy. His social criticism, often joyously pugnacious but sometimes shrill, employs touchstones of human freedom and of growth toward excellence. It identifies shoddy cultural products of the profit system ("The Fate of Writing in America") and of political orthodoxy ("The Literary Popular Front before the War"). It condemns what he believes is intellectually regressive ("The Faith of Lewis Mumford") or morally insensitive ("Moral Censorship and the Ten Commandments"). Because it attacks sources of cultural stagnancy and personal frustration, his social criticism is blood brother to his fiction and demonstrates anew the unity of his work.

So does his thinking about literature. Books freed him (Bernard links *library* and *liberty*) and helped him to grow. The unforgettable lesson was that literature intensifies awareness, expands what George H. Mead called "the sense of the other," so narrowly developed in Studs. By assuring the cultural continuity that crowns life with meaning, literature "humanizes the world." It brings men back to the essence of all "destinies": "the struggles, aspirations, joys, and sorrows of human beings." The writer works at "shaping . . . life itself into literary form" in order to convey his vision through "the structure of events, the quality of the characterization, the complex impact of the work itself." The critic's role is to illuminate the work. He should explore its internal relationships and patterns, then relate these to social processes. Farrell's criticism of Joyce, Tolstoi, and others takes this approach, in keeping with his idea of the two uses of literature, aesthetic and functional, elaborated in *A Note on Literary Criticism*.

Farrell's initial advantage as a writer was his thorough possession of an urban, Irish Catholic world. As a child in two families he sought acceptance and identity, and as a talented boy in culturally illiterate surroundings he groped to find himself. His need charged his youthful experience with unforgettable tensions and burned it into his consciousness. His fiction, an extension of his search for himself, brings his Chicago experience into focus. It creates the larger self—his famous "South Side" in its spatial, temporal, cultural, and emotional dimensions—by opening out to include family, society, and cultural process extending over half a century. It explores this past with great objective validity, employing a method and style appropriate to his view of life and drawing upon a constructive imagination both informed and savage. The writing remains intensely personal—and this is a deep strength—if only because its subjects, the education of Americans, is rooted in his early predicament and in his accomplishment, just as many of his characters are imagined versions of the possibilities and actualities of his experience.

This personal and ultimately self-centered quality of his art helps to explain its limitations. His shaking the sack of reality—his intimate reality—until it is empty shows his unqualified desire to master what is genuinely his own and to get it all down, and critics have responded according to their disposition: he is truthful, honest, thorough, stubborn, or repetitious. Surely this quality sometimes hampers control and selectivity, and it may make for writing that lacks sufficient aesthetic distance in spite of the objective method. Moreover his imagination is most vitally engaged with his pre-University of Chicago life, that experience of the nerve ends and the emotions that absorbed him for years before he found the essential intellectual tools to shape it into clarity. So he best creates the wounded and confused boy, the aspiring or rebellious young man, the adult grotesque, in short, those very human personalities in his fiction who are defined by deep involvement with their family and their severely limited culture. Yet the dynamics of his social philosophy and the grand design of his fiction call for an equally convincing picture of men and women who have emerged into larger worlds—social, intellectual, and psychological. As Robert Gorham Davis has cogently argued (in the *New York Times Book Review* for November 2, 1947), his fiction does not do complete justice to what is rich and creative in human consciousness, Farrell's included.

This is to say that Farrell has not realized the full potential in his vision. But his vision is large and single, and step by step he has created a single world of ample proportions. His cycles of novels with his other fiction approximate a sequence, a rarity in our literature. At its best, the American past he creates is deeply authentic, like Cather's Nebraska or Faulkner's South. It is especially meaningful to us because, through its rich details of urban manners, it shows the heavy cost exacted of people and institutions by the modern city. His characters' lives expose social process; time slowly brings change, and the making of personality and the formation of society merge. His Lonigans, O'Flahertys, and O'Neills are deeply immersed in their time and place—interesting contrasts to Hemingway's disengaged Americans—and his work is exceptional in our fiction for the number of its living characters. The contrast between their often blind groping for a better future and the grimness of their present, flowing inevitably out of their past, is a subject with tragic power.

Selected Bibliography

WORKS OF JAMES T. FARRELL

NOVELS

Young Lonigan: A Boyhood in Chicago Streets. New York: Vanguard Press, 1932.

Gas-House McGinty. New York: Vanguard Press, 1933.

The Young Manhood of Studs Lonigan. New York: Vanguard Press, 1934.

Judgment Day. New York: Vanguard Press, 1935.

Studs Lonigan: A Trilogy. New York: Vanguard Press, 1935. (Includes *Young Lonigan, The Young Manhood of Studs Lonigan, Judgment Day.*)

A World I Never Made. New York: Vanguard Press, 1936.

No Star Is Lost. New York: Vanguard Press, 1938.

Father and Son. New York: Vanguard Press, 1940.

Ellen Rogers. New York: Vanguard Press, 1941.

My Days of Anger. New York: Vanguard Press, 1943.

Bernard Clare. New York: Vanguard Press, 1946.

The Road Between. New York: Vanguard Press, 1949.

This Man and This Woman. New York: Vanguard Press, 1951.

Yet Other Waters. New York: Vanguard Press, 1952.

The Face of Time. New York: Vanguard Press, 1953.

Boarding House Blues. New York: Paperback Library, 1961.

The Silence of History. New York: Doubleday, 1963.

What Time Collects. New York: Doubleday, 1964.

Lonely for the Future. New York: Doubleday, 1966.

New Year's Eve/1929. New York: Horizon Press, 1967.

A Brand New Life. New York: Doubleday, 1968.

Judith. Athens, Ohio: Duane Schneider Press, 1969.

Invisible Swords. New York: Doubleday, 1971.

SHORT STORIES AND NOVELLAS

Calico Shoes and Other Stories. New York: Vanguard Press, 1934.

Guillotine Party and Other Stories. New York: Vanguard Press, 1935.

Can All This Grandeur Perish? and Other Stories. New York: Vanguard Press, 1937.

The Short Stories of James T. Farrell. New York:

Vanguard Press, 1937. (Includes the three volumes above.)

Tommy Gallagher's Crusade. New York: Vanguard Press, 1939. (Reprinted in *To Whom It May Concern and Other Stories*, 1944.)

$1,000 a Week and Other Stories. New York: Vanguard Press, 1942.

To Whom It May Concern and Other Stories. New York: Vanguard Press, 1944.

When Boyhood Dreams Come True. New York: Vanguard Press, 1946.

The Life Adventurous and Other Stories. New York: Vanguard Press, 1947.

A Misunderstanding. New York: House of Books, 1949. (A limited edition of 300 copies; reprinted in *An American Dream Girl*, 1950.)

An American Dream Girl. New York: Vanguard Press, 1950.

French Girls Are Vicious and Other Stories. New York: Vanguard Press, 1955.

An Omnibus of Short Stories. New York: Vanguard Press, 1957. (Reprints *$1,000 a Week and Other Stories, To Whom It May Concern and Other Stories, The Life Adventurous and Other Stories.*)

A Dangerous Woman and Other Stories. New York: New American Library, Signet edition, 1957. (Followed by Vanguard Press photolithograph edition.)

Side Street and Other Stories. New York: Paperback Library, 1961.

Sound of a City. New York: Paperback Library, 1962.

Childhood Is Not Forever. New York: Doubleday, 1969.

POETRY AND PROSE POEM

The Collected Poems of James T. Farrell. New York: Fleet, 1965.

When Time Was Born. New York: Horizon Press, 1966.

OTHER PROSE

A Note on Literary Criticism. New York: Vanguard Press, 1936.

The League of Frightened Philistines and Other Papers. New York: Vanguard Press, 1945.

Literature and Morality. New York: Vanguard Press, 1947.

The Name Is Fogarty: Private Papers on Public Matters. (Pseudonym Jonathan Titulescu Fogarty, Esq.), New York: Vanguard Press, 1950.

Reflections at Fifty and Other Essays. New York: Vanguard Press, 1954.

My Baseball Diary. New York: A. S. Barnes, 1957.

It Has Come to Pass. New York: Theodor Herzl Press, 1958.

Dialogue on John Dewey, edited by Corliss Lamont. New York: Horizon Press, 1959. (Farrell was one of eleven persons who contributed to this transcription of an evening of reminiscences and personal impressions of Dewey.)

BIBLIOGRAPHIES

Branch, Edgar M. *A Bibliography of James T. Farrell's Writings, 1921-1957.* Philadelphia: University of Pennsylvania Press, 1959.

————. "A Supplement to the Bibliography of James T. Farrell's Writings," *American Book Collector,* 11:42–48 (June 1961).

————. "Bibliography of James T. Farrell: A Supplement," *American Book Collector,* 17:9–19 (May 1967).

————. "Bibliography of James T. Farrell: A Supplement, 1967–August, 1970," *American Book Collector,* 21:13–18 (March–April 1971).

CRITICAL AND BIOGRAPHICAL STUDIES

Aldridge, John W. "The Education of James T. Farrell," in *In Search of Heresy: American Literature in an Age of Conformity.* New York: McGraw-Hill, 1956.

Beach, Joseph Warren. "James T. Farrell: Tragedy of the Poolroom Loafer" and "James T. Farrell: The Plight of the Children," in *American Fiction, 1920–1940.* New York: Macmillan, 1941.

Branch, Edgar M. "American Writer in the Twenties: James T. Farrell and University of Chicago," *American Book Collector,* 11:25–32 (June 1961).

————. "Freedom and Determinism in James T. Farrell's Fiction," in *Essays on Determinism in*

American Literature, Kent Studies in English, Number 1, edited by Sydney J. Krause. Kent, Ohio: Kent State University Press, 1964.

————. *James T. Farrell*. New York: Twayne, 1971.

————. "James T. Farrell's Studs Lonigan," *American Book Collector*, 11:9–19 (June 1961).

————. "The 1930's in James T. Farrell's Fiction," *American Book Collector*, 21:9–12 (March–April 1971).

Curley, Thomas F. "Catholic Novels and American Culture," *Commentary*, 36:34–42 (July 1963).

Dyer, Henry Hopper. "James T. Farrell's Studs Lonigan and Danny O'Neill Novels." Unpublished dissertation, University of Pennsylvania, 1965.

Frohock, Wilbur M. "James T. Farrell: The Precise Content," in *The Novel of Violence in America*. 2nd ed. Dallas: Southern Methodist University Press, 1958.

Gelfant, Blanche H. "James T. Farrell: The Ecological Novel," in *The American City Novel*. Norman: University of Oklahoma Press, 1954.

Glicksberg, Charles I. "The Criticism of James T. Farrell," *Southwest Review*, 35:189–96 (Summer 1950).

Grattan, C. Hartley. "James T. Farrell: Moralist," *Harper's*, 209:93–94, 96, 98 (October 1954).

Gregory, Horace. "James T. Farrell: Beyond the Provinces of Art," in *New World Writing: Fifth Mentor Selection*. New York: New American Library, 1954.

Hatfield, Ruth. "The Intellectual Honesty of James T. Farrell," *College English*, 3:337–46 (January 1942).

Howe, Irving. "James T. Farrell—The Critic Calcified," *Partisan Review*, 14:545–46, 548, 550, 552 (September–October 1947).

Kazin, Alfred. *On Native Grounds: An Interpretation of Modern American Prose Literature*. New York: Reynal and Hitchcock, 1942. Pp. 380–85.

Lovett, Robert Morss. "James T. Farrell," *English Journal*, 26:347–54 (May 1937). (Reprinted as the introduction to *The Short Stories of James T. Farrell*.)

Lynch, William James. "The Theory and Practice of the Literary Criticism of James T. Farrell." Unpublished dissertation, University of Pennsylvania, 1966.

Mitchell, Richard. "*Studs Lonigan*: Research in Morality," *Centennial Review*, 6:202–14 (Spring 1962).

O'Malley, Frank. "James T. Farrell: Two Twilight Images," in *Fifty Years of the American Novel: A Christian Appraisal*, edited by Harold C. Gardiner. New York: Scribners, 1951.

Owen, David H. "A Pattern of Pseudo-Naturalism: Lynd, Mead, and Farrell." Unpublished dissertation, University of Iowa, 1950.

Reiter, Irene Morris. "A Study of James T. Farrell's Short Stories and Their Relation to His Longer Fiction." Unpublished dissertation, University of Pennsylvania, 1964.

Walcutt, Charles C. "James T. Farrell: Aspects of Telling the Whole Truth," in *American Literary Naturalism, A Divided Stream*. Minneapolis: University of Minnesota Press, 1956.

—EDGAR M. BRANCH

William Faulkner

1897-1962

WILLIAM FAULKNER'S Yoknapatawpha County, Mississippi, with Jefferson as the county seat, is both a mythical and an actual region. Reality and myth are difficult to separate because Faulkner has transcribed the geography, the history, and the people of northern Mississippi, and he has also transmuted them. Clearly it is more sensible to see Yoknapatawpha County and its people as a little self-contained world of the imagination than as an accurate history, from the time of the Chickasaw Indians down to the present, of northern Mississippi.

Yoknapatawpha County is an area of 2400 square miles, with a population of 15,611 persons. There is the rich delta land of the hunt; there is the sand and brush country; there is Jefferson, with its jail, the town square, and the old houses emanating decay; there is Beat Four, and there is the Old Frenchman's Place; there are dusty roads, swamps, cemeteries, a railroad, and there is the great river, sometimes smooth and deep but when in flood wild, turbulent, and destructive. More than several generations inhabit Yoknapatawpha County: Indians, slaves, plantation owners, Civil War soldiers, bushwackers, genteel old ladies, veterans, first of the Civil War, then of World War I, and finally of World War II, exploiters, servants, peddlers, preachers, lawyers, doctors,

farmers, college students, and many others. The pigeons in a church belfry, the scent of honeysuckle, a sultry July afternoon, the drugstore on Sunday afternoon, the rancid smells of a Negro cabin, the clop-clop of a horse's hoofs in the town square—these and a hundred other scenes have, thanks to Faulkner's descriptive powers, become part of a timeless panorama.

And perhaps one should add that this mythical country, as a part of the South, is seen as being very different from the rest of the United States—the West, the East, and the North. The southerner, the resident of Yoknapatawpha County, carries his burden of guilt, his part in the troubled and painful heritage that began with slavery, and he responds to it in his individual way.

Northern Mississippi—especially the town of Oxford ("Jefferson") and Lafayette County ("Yoknapatawpha County")—was Faulkner's own territory. His family had lived there since before the Civil War. As a family they had moments of high achievement, and they saw days when the family and its future seemed menaced. Faulkner pondered the family history and his own personal history—and he used both in writing his stories.

William Faulkner was born in New Albany, Mississippi, in 1897. In 1902 his family moved to Oxford, the seat of the University of Mississippi, where his father, Murray C. Falkner, ran a livery stable and a hardware store, and later was business manager of the university. (The *u* was added to the family name by the printer who set up William's first book, *The Marble Faun*.) Faulkner's mother was Maud Butler. There were four children: William, Murray, John, and Dean.

William C. Falkner, William's great-grandfather, was born in 1825. He has been a legendary figure in northern Mississippi. The details in his life, many of which turn up in his great-grandson's books, read like episodes in a picaresque novel. Twice he was acquitted of murder charges. He was a severe disciplinarian and a dashing soldier as the colonel of a group of raiders in the Civil War. He had begun as a poor youngster trying to earn enough money to help his widowed mother, but he ended his career as the owner of a railroad and a member of the state legislature. He was killed by his former railroad partner shortly after he had defeated the latter for a seat in the legislature. Appropriately, there is a statue of William C. Falkner facing his railroad.

William C. Falkner's son, J. W. T. Falkner, the novelist's grandfather, was a lawyer, a banker, and an assistant United States attorney. He was active in the "rise of the 'rednecks,'" the political movement that gave greater suffrage to tenant farmers. Those residents of Oxford who can remember him say he was a man of stiff dignity, deaf, and with a testy, explosive temper.

The great-grandfather and the grandfather are obviously the originals for Colonel Sartoris and Bayard Sartoris in *Sartoris, The Unvanquished*, and many other stories. They are a part of the legend of the Old South, and they play an important part in Faulkner's Yoknapatawpha saga. Faulkner's immediate family seem, in a more indirect fashion, to be the originals for the Compson family. They are central in *The Sound and the Fury*, but they appear also in other stories.

William Faulkner was a poor student, and left high school after the tenth grade for a job in his grandfather's bank. He read widely, and wrote poetry. He also tried his hand at painting. He was a moody young man and a puzzle to the townspeople of Oxford. In 1914 he began a friendship with Phil Stone, a young lawyer, which gave him a chance for literary discussions and helped acquaint him with such rising reputations as Conrad Aiken, Robert Frost, Ezra Pound, and Sherwood Anderson.

Because he was underweight and only five feet five in height, Faulkner was turned down by the United States Army. He succeeded, however, in joining the Royal Flying Corps in Toronto, Canada, as a cadet. On December 22, 1918, the date of demobilization, he became an honorary second lieutenant. Like most other writers of his age, Faulkner has often been preoccupied with both the events and the implications of World War I. His early books deal with it, as does one of his later, *A Fable*.

As a veteran he was allowed to enroll at the University of Mississippi, where he studied English, Spanish, and French, but he was in residence for only one full academic year. Some of his contributions to student publications suggest that he was a witty and sardonic young man who was having difficulty in finding himself either as an artist or professionally. He took a job in a bookstore in New York City, but this did not last long and he was soon back in Oxford. For two years he did odd jobs, as a carpenter and house painter, then became postmaster at the university. He soon resigned, saying in his letter of resignation, "I will be damned if I propose to be at the beck and call of every itinerant scoundrel who has two cents to invest in a postage stamp." This same year, 1924, saw the publication of *The Marble Faun*, an imitative book of poems. Stone had subsidized its publication.

Faulkner decided to go to Europe, by way of New Orleans. Once in New Orleans, however, he stayed for six months. He wrote a few sketches for the *Times-Picayune* entitled "Mirrors of Chartres Street," contributed to the *Double-Dealer*, an important "little magazine," and became friends with Sherwood Anderson, at that time one of the most admired of American writers. He also wrote his first novel, *Soldiers' Pay*, which Anderson helped him get published. He and Anderson remained friends despite differences in temperament which occasioned quarrels and despite Faulkner's having written a parody of Anderson's style in *Sherwood Anderson and Other Famous Creoles*, a volume of drawings by William Spratling, one of his New Orleans friends. In this book there is a drawing by Spratling of Faulkner and himself sitting at a table painting, writing, and drinking. On the wall there is a sign reading "Viva Art." Beneath Faulkner's chair are three gallons of corn liquor. In June 1925, Faulkner and Spratling shipped on a freighter for Italy and a walking trip through France and Germany.

Faulkner was back in New York for the publication, in March 1926, of *Soldiers' Pay*, a self-consciously elegant novel about the "lost generation." Its style is indebted to Swinburne and Beardsley, or, more generally, to the *fin de siècle* tradition. This is an example: "They had another drink. The music beat on among youthful leaves, into the darkness, beneath the gold and mute cacophony of stars. The light from the veranda was lost, the house loomed huge against the sky: a rock against which waves of trees broke, and breaking were forever arrested: and stars were golden unicorns neighing unheard through blue meadows, spurning them with hooves sharp and scintillant as ice. The sky, so remote, so sad, spurned by the unicorns of gold, that, neighing soundlessly from dusk to dawn had seen them, had seen her—her taut body prone and naked as a narrow pool . . . " The *fin de siècle* tradition never matured in the United States, unless it can be said to have matured in the poetry of Wallace Stevens, but in the young Faulkner America had a writer greatly attracted to it. Thematically the novel comes to very little, but clearly the young man who wrote it had talent. *Soldiers' Pay* received favorable reviews, and its publisher signed a contract for a second novel. Faulkner went off to Pascagoula, Mississippi, to write it.

Mosquitoes, published in 1927, used New Orleans as a setting. Insofar as it has a theme *Mosquitoes* says that actions are more important than words and doers more important than talkers. It is a satirical novel, but most of the satire is heavy-handed. One of the characters, Dawson Fairchild, is based on Anderson, and one of the more interesting parts of the book is a series of "tall tales" which Faulkner later said he and Anderson had worked up together. *Mosquitoes* was less well received than *Soldiers' Pay*.

Sartoris (1929) helped Faulkner find himself as a writer. Doing it, he "discovered that writing is a mighty fine thing; it enabled you to make men stand on their hind legs and cast a long shadow." *Sartoris* is an uncritical account of the Sartoris (or Falkner) family legend, brought down to Faulkner's own generation and centered in young Bayard, a war veteran. He is one of the young men Gertrude Stein called the "lost generation," but he is also preoccupied with his southern heritage. *Sartoris* is a source book for many later stories, and in writing it Faulkner began to see and feel the dignity and pathos of what was to become his most persistent subject matter.

While writing *Sartoris* Faulkner had also

been working on *The Sound and the Fury*. They were published within a few months of each other. *Sartoris* marks the end of an apprenticeship. *The Sound and the Fury* is the work of a major writer.

In June 1929 Faulkner married Estelle Oldham and settled down to a career as a writer. Within a ten-year span he wrote and published most of what has come to be regarded as his major work. There were trips to Hollywood, where he worked on movie scripts, and trips to New York City, but mostly he remained in Oxford. *Sanctuary* brought him notoriety. Critical acclaim, however, came more slowly. Oddly, the French recognized Faulkner's power more quickly and more widely than Americans did. André Malraux wrote a preface for *Sanctuary*, and Jean-Paul Sartre wrote a long critical essay on Faulkner's work. In 1946, when Malcolm Cowley published his influential *Portable Faulkner*, all of Faulkner's books were out of print, and there had been very little serious criticism devoted to Faulkner. But valuable studies began in 1946, and now there is hardly a critical or scholarly journal that has failed to devote article after article to Faulkner. The Nobel Prize was awarded to him in 1950. Faulkner, accompanied by his daughter, went to Sweden, and delivered an address that has been widely aclaimed. Many other awards followed, including Pulitzer prizes for *The Town* and, posthumously, *The Reivers*. Faulkner visited European countries, especially France, spent some weeks in Japan in 1955, and made occasional public appearances in the United States. In 1957 he was a writer in residence at the University of Virginia. Three weeks after being thrown from a horse, he died, from a heart attack, in Oxford, Mississippi, July 6, 1962.

Many editions of Faulkner's books continue to appear, especially in inexpensive reprints; versions of some of them are done for television and the movies; and *Requiem for a Nun* had a run as a Broadway play, was performed in many European countries, and in France was adapted by Albert Camus. Faulkner has been accepted as a great American writer, despite occasional cries of dissent from readers and sometimes from critics who feel he is overvalued, is wildly rhetorical or merely obscure and difficult to read. The admirers of Faulkner sometimes claim that his detractors disparage him because they fail to understand the nature of his genius, and his detractors sometimes say Faulkner's admirers are bemused by his rhetoric. The truth lies in between.

Robert Penn Warren, in an article first published in 1946, says this: "William Faulkner has written nineteen books which for range of effect, philosophical weight, originality of style, variety of characterization, humor, and tragic intensity, are without equal in our time and country. Let us grant, even so, that there are grave defects in Faulkner's work. Sometimes the tragic intensity becomes mere emotionalism, the technical virtuosity mere complication, the philosophical weight mere confusion of mind. Let us grant that much, for Faulkner is a very uneven writer. The unevenness is, in a way, an index to his vitality, his willingness to take risks, to try for new effects, to make new explorations of material and method." Mr. Warren implies that Faulkner's admirers do him no service when they refuse to recognize that his limitations are sometimes inextricably intertwined with his great achievements.

A few of Faulkner's critics have also tried to schematize his themes, saying, for example, that he favors the antebellum "aristocrats" and their descendants over other groups in southern society, or that he is anti-modern and sees only evils in twentieth-century industrialization and mechanization. Anyone who takes Faulkner's novels in chronological order, summarizing their plots and analyzing their themes, as is done here, can see that no such schematic account really works.

The critic of, say, Robert Frost, Wallace Stevens, or Ernest Hemingway can write a long essay tracing persistent themes. In each of these writers there is a homogeneity of subject and point of view from the first book to the last. This is not the case with Faulkner. Nor is there a large "philosophical" subject, as there is in Henry James or Robert Penn Warren, that is being investigated and enlarged in each succeeding book. One can say that Faulkner lived in a section of the country where nineteenth-century pieties are more alive than they are in other regions of the United States and that these pieties sometimes conflicted with the assumptions that Faulkner as a product of the twentieth century tended to hold. But again this conflict is not the controlling or central theme in any particular novel. Perhaps the best way of generalizing about Faulkner's themes is to say that he accepts the elementary Christian virtues, providing one adds at once that certain of the forms of conduct Faulkner seems to advocate in certain novels would be seen as perverse or as evil by most orthodox Christians. A fair and just method in writing about his career—the method attempted in this essay—is to take the major works one at a time, summarizing the action, sorting out the themes, and describing, since Faulkner is an important innovator, the method of narration.

Faulkner once said he had "written his guts" into *The Sound and the Fury*. Many of his admirers believe it is his best novel, and one of the greatest novels written in the twentieth century. Without doubt it is a work of great virtuosity, even genius, but there is some critical disagreement about what Faulkner was trying to say in it.

The Sound and the Fury is clearly a "modern" novel. It is in the impressionistic tradition of James, Conrad, Crane, Ford Madox Ford, and Joyce—the tradition that said "Life does not narrate but makes impressions on our brains." And that said the novelist allows, or seems to allow, the story to tell itself; he does not intrude. (To Joyce in particular Faulkner owes the interior monologue, the stream of consciousness, and portmanteau words.) Occasionally, however, Faulkner does intrude, but in a special sense: he lends his own rhetorical voice, a kind of chorus, to a character. For example, Quentin Compson, who ordinarily is shown thinking in a disordered, disturbed, even mad fashion, suddenly remembers in a quite different sort of language a train trip during which he had seen, from the window, an old Negro astride a small mule. This is the passage:

"Then the train began to move. I leaned out the window, into the cold air, looking back. He stood there beside the gaunt rabbit of a mule, the two of them shabby and motionless and unimpatient. The train swung around the curve, the engine puffing with short, heavy blasts, and they passed smoothly from sight that way, with that quality about them of shabby and timeless patience, of static serenity: that blending of childlike and ready incompetence and paradoxical reliability that tends and protects them it loves out of all reason and robs them steadily and evades responsibility and obligations by means too barefaced to be called subterfuge even and is taken in theft or evasion with only that frank and spontaneous admiration for the victor which a gentleman feels for anyone who beats him in a fair contest, and withal a fond and unflagging tolerance for whitefolks' vagaries like that of a grandparent for unpredictable and troublesome children which I had forgotten."

The passage is very similar to *Sartoris*, in which Faulkner himself is doing the narrating. Faulkner's rhetorical voice intrudes in this fashion in all the books subsequent to *The*

Sound and the Fury. But primarily the characters think and speak in their own peculiar fashion. Thus Benjy, the idiot, watching a golfing match: "Through the fence, between the curling flower spaces, I could see them hitting. They were coming toward where the flag was and I went along the fence. Luster was hunting in the grass by the flower tree. They took the flag out, and they were hitting." All of Benjy's thoughts have to do with sensations, with smells, eating, going to bed, or tones of voice. Time past and time present merge and interflow in his mind. He never speculates or plans—he feels. Jason Compson's thoughts and speech are invariably ironic, expressing his bitter humor and frustration: "I told Mother good night and went on to my room and got the box out and counted it again. I could hear the Great American Gelding snoring away like a planing mill. I read somewhere they'd fix men that way to give them women's voices. But maybe he didn't know what they'd done to him. I dont reckon he even knew what he had been trying to do or why Mr. Burgess knocked him out with the fence picket." Everywhere in *The Sound and the Fury* the reader sees, hears, and experiences, whether it is the young Compson children getting ready for bed, the tone of the genteel and whining Mrs. Compson, the decency and patience of Dilsey, the magnificently rendered Negro sermon, or the sound of Queenie's hoofs in the town square.

The primary story being told in *The Sound and the Fury* is the decline of a family. The family has had generals, a governor, and wealthy planters. They had owned the Compson Mile. In a chronology of the Compsons, done for Malcolm Cowley's *Portable Faulkner*, Faulkner traces the family history from 1699 to 1945. But the novel proper is limited from June 2, 1910, to April 8, 1928, and it tells what happens to the last generation of Compsons. Mr. Compson is a witty but alcoholic lawyer, and Mrs. Compson is preoccupied with her honor, faded glories, and present indignities, such as her idiot son and ineffectual brother Maury. Candace, Quentin, Jason, and Benjy are seen as children and as adults.

Quentin is seen in Cambridge, Massachusetts, readying himself for suicide: he contemplates his family but particularly Candace's fornication with Dalton Ames and her marriage to Sydney Herbert Head. His experiences during that day (June 2, 1910) impinge in a shadowy way on his memories, more especially his frustrated desire to free himself and Candace from time's meaningless roar. Behind his desire to commit incest with Candace was the hope that this would cause Jehovah to cast them into hell for eternity. But his father had told him that virginity was an ideal invented by men, and that his talk of incest was merely a way of giving himself a significance neither he nor anyone else can have. Except for Candace, Quentin also feels unloved. Once he says, *"I have no mother."*

As an adult, Jason IV, Quentin's brother, works in a hardware store, plays the stock market, and systematically steals the money Candace sends for the board and room of her illegitimate daughter, named Quentin. The girl, to whom Jason is always mean and sometimes cruel, steals the money from him and runs off with a fellow employed by a carnival. Jason is unable either to find them or to recover the money—and his frustrations are nearly unbearable. Jason is scornful of tradition, of principle and honor.

It is Dilsey, the old Negress, decent, sympathetic, and responsible, who provides the coherence and moral principles against which the Compsons are, by implication, judged. She is one of Faulkner's most memorable characters.

Faulkner has said *The Sound and the Fury*

is a story of "lost innocence." It is also the history of an inward-turning family living for the most part in the past. As such, it is reminiscent of Hawthorne's *The House of the Seven Gables*. It is also reminiscent of Dostoevski's *The Brothers Karamazov*. One critic has said that Quentin has some kinship with Raskolnikov in *Crime and Punishment*. If *The Sound and the Fury* is seen as essentially Quentin's story (certainly a partial and lopsided emphasis) it becomes the search of the modern protagonist, usually a sensitive aesthete, for a sense of radical significance. It can also be read as a failure of love within a family, an absence of self-respect and of mutual respect. It is a southern story. It is a twentieth-century story. And as the fall of a house it is akin to some of the most ancient stories in Western literature.

As I Lay Dying (1930) is both a simple and a puzzling book. Structurally and stylistically it exhibits Faulkner's amazing virtuosity. Concentrating on a character at a time, fifteen of them in all, the action breaks into sixty sections. Each character, simultaneously refracting and participating in the forward movement of the story, cuts into the substance and suggests meanings to the degree possible to his consciousness and perception. The technique makes for what Henry James called the "highest possible degree of saturation." But it also makes for some confusion. Is it Addie's story? Or Darl's or Cash's, or the story of all of them and that of the other participants as well? A further complication is that *As I Lay Dying* exists on two levels, as a ritualistic and symbolic journey and as a naturalistic and psychological story. For, although it is set in Mississippi and is about a "redneck" family, *As I Lay Dying* evokes memories of ancient times and places far away. Neither *As I Lay Dying* nor any other Faulkner novel should be read as having a one-to-one relationship with north-

ern Mississippi. They are highly stylized stories—and their geography is more of the soul than of Mississippi.

The funeral journey could suggest the Mosaic trek out of Egypt, the crossing of the river Jordan, the difficult journey of the dead across the river Styx, the long caravans on sacred journeys to Mecca or to some sanctuary within Mongolia or Tibet. Addie Bundren's funeral journey has an epic tone. It is a ritual, the fulfilling of a promise. Each member of the family is given an opportunity to ponder his relationship to the others, especially to Addie. But Addie herself is not a simple or absolute symbol of virtue and wisdom, although she is an amazingly vital and in some ways an admirable person. *As I Lay Dying* does not minimize selfishness, aggrandizement, obsessions, or plain human stupidity. In tone it can be quiet, grim, wild, bizarre, or sublime. Faulkner does not pretend that at the journey's end each character has had his opportunity to drink from the cup of wisdom and go home fully renewed. Darl goes mad, little Vardaman is as bemused as ever, Dewey Dell is simply frustrated, and Anse has used the burial journey as a way of getting a new wife.

Essentially this is the action: Addie Bundren is dying. Cash, the eldest son, is building a coffin for her. Anse, her husband, allows others to carry his burdens and is given to easy self-justification. Darl, the second son, rejected by Addie, has what is sometimes called "second sight." Jewel is Addie's illegitimate son, fathered by Whitfield, a self-justifying preacher. Dewey Dell, the fourth child, is pregnant by Lafe, a neighbor boy. Darl knows, without being told, that Jewel is Addie's illegitimate, as well as best loved, son, and he knows Dewey Dell wants to get to Jefferson to buy abortion pills. The youngest child, Vardaman, who sometimes seems moronic, thinks Dr. Peabody has killed his mother, and confuses a dead fish with his dead mother. (Dr. Peabody, entering the action from outside the family, provides a way of evaluating them.) Addie wants to be buried in Jefferson, where her family are buried. Exacting a promise from Anse, she feels, will involve him, and possibly allow her life to enter his in a way it never had before. After her death, the family set out for Jefferson. The journey is a nightmare. The coffin is upset in a stream. Cash's leg is broken and Anse, to save money, coats it with cement. Darl sets fire to a barn to destroy Addie's corpse, but she is saved by Jewel. Buzzards follow them. A druggist refuses to sell pills to Dewey Dell, and a soda clerk seduces her. Anse borrows a spade and shovel to dig Addie's grave. Darl is taken off to the asylum in Jackson, and Anse, having taken Dewey Dell's money, buys new teeth and gets himself a new wife.

Addie's belief is that one should violate one's aloneness, should not allow words like *sin* or *love* to serve in lieu of violation and involvement. And she has tried to live this way—getting ready to be dead. This doctrine is sometimes said to be the theme of the novel. But Addie also has curious rationalizations: Cash is her true son, she says, because while carrying him she had not yet realized that Anse's life did not violate hers nor her life violate his. Her second child, Darl, seemed a betrayal, and she rejects him. Then she had Jewel—but Whitfield is like Anse, so she feels Jewel is solely hers. She had Dewey Dell and Vardaman to make up for her having had Jewel. The two sons she accepts, Cash and Jewel, make great sacrifices to get her to Jefferson. Darl hates Jewel because Addie loved him, and he tries to prevent her getting there. He says: "I have no mother." Dewey Dell is indifferent to her mother and Vardaman is incapable of a moral decision.

There are several themes. According to Addie, one has an obligation to be involved, and to accept the accompanying and inevitable violence and suffering. Cash and Jewel apparently accept her doctrine, and live by it. Anse and the remaining children, for various reasons, do not. The three children are also victims of the lack of love between Anse and Addie. Addie, while faithful to her belief in the need for violation, is not faithful to Darl, Dewey Dell, or Vardaman, the children of her flesh though not of her doctrine. She rejects them. And in Darl, as a poetic, speculative type ("sicklied o'er with the pale cast of thought"), there is a third theme. He is not unlike Quentin Compson (both see themselves as motherless) in his preoccupation with man as a lost creature in the universe. He gives himself to speculations and searches into the dark corners of other people's minds. Cash holds fast to the physical world, and so does Jewel. But Darl, like Quentin Compson, loses his hold and goes mad.

These, then, are the major themes—Addie's doctrine of involvement, the consequences that follow the breakdown of family love, and the dangers in turning away from action and giving oneself to endless speculation. And if one wanted to concentrate attention on Anse or certain other characters, undoubtedly still further themes could be pointed up. The fifteen characters in their relationships with each other, especially with Addie, and in the way they illuminate the several themes seem a part of the world's mystery and irreducible complexity.

Sanctuary (1931) made Faulkner famous. In the preface to the Modern Library edition, he says he once asked himself what would sell at least 10,000 copies. He hit upon the horrific story of the rape of a coed by a perverted gangster, wrote it in three weeks, and sent it off. His publisher, Harrison Smith, answered almost at once, "Good God, I can't publish this. We'd both be in jail." This was before

Faulkner had written either *The Sound and the Fury* or *As I Lay Dying*. He says he had forgotten about it when the galleys arrived. Harrison Smith had obviously changed his mind. At the cost of several hundred dollars to himself Faulkner made extensive revisions.

Sanctuary is a "thriller," or, in its own way, what another writer, Graham Greene, calls an "entertainment." It is not Faulkner's fiction at its serious best. At least one of the themes—the attack on modernism—is stated too insistently and without qualification. And the image of the world as a "cooling ball in space," borrowed from *fin de siècle* writers, is self-consciously "literary." But *Sanctuary* is obviously the work of a skillful and highly inventive novelist.

The sexual evils in *Sanctuary* are identified with the oldness and the decay of the world, with the grape and honeysuckle, and the changing seasons; there is "a conspiracy of female flesh and female season." Sex "writhes like cold smoke." Throughout the book descriptions and characterizations are made in terms of nature and flower imagery. There are also descriptions and characterizations made in terms of metallic and mechanical images. Both serve to suggest a society for whom sex is only lust and human relationships merely amoral engagement.

Sanctuary opens as a Gothic story, then moves toward and merges into a double vision, as though in montage, of amoral modernism and the world as ripe and overripe. The Gothic beginnings include the remote Old Frenchman's Place, a decayed plantation house, surrounded by a foreboding woods. The sky is dark, there are dimly perceived movements, and strange sounds. There is a blind man whose "cataracted eyes looked like two clots of phlegm." The maiden-heroine is Temple Drake, the hero is the ineffectual and alcoholic Gowan Stevens; they are parodies of the usual Gothic heroine and hero. Temple flees from Lee Goodwin, who plans to seduce her, and escapes, with the aid of the moron Tommy, to a rat-infested corncrib. She is discovered there by Popeye, who shoots Tommy and rapes her with a corncob, a scene that outdoes any of the sexual crimes found in Gothic fiction. Popeye sets her up in a Memphis whorehouse. He arranges for a young man named Red to be her lover, and he, Popeye, is present during their lovemaking. Temple becomes thoroughly depraved, a fact upon which much of the subsequent action depends.

Popeye is sometimes said to represent amoral modernism. He is impotent, but with the aid of Natural Lust (Red), he corrupts Southern Womanhood (Temple), and she becomes his ally. Formalized Tradition (Horace Benbow, the lawyer) tries to defend Goodwin, who is accused of the murder of Tommy, but the Amoral Modernists (the politicians, the townspeople, and Eustace Graham, the district attorney) see to it that Goodwin is lynched. Faulkner himself said that Popeye was "all allegory." Oddly, near the end of the story, Faulkner attempts to account for him psychologically and naturalistically, by recounting Popeye's childhood, thereby destroying some of his effectiveness as a symbol of amoral modernism.

Much of the humor of *Sanctuary*—the scenes with the three madams, Miss Reba's sense of propriety, Uncle Bud's getting drunk, and the escapades of Virgil and Fonzo Snopes—is folk humor. Some of the satire on the townspeople of Jefferson is in the realistic tradition. And there are the characters carried over from *Sartoris*. That the humor, satire, and predefined characterizations (Narcissa's character is different in the two books) do not destroy but, rather, merge into the nightmarish quality of the book is a tribute to Faulkner's ability to control his materials. But their complexity may also suggest that Faulkner was more concerned with telling a sensational, grim, and sometimes funny story than he was with investigating its significances.

Light in August (1932) is a novel about the spirit of righteousness. Possibly it is in this book that Faulkner is closest to Hawthorne. A source of the spirit of persecution, as developed by both writers, is puritanical righteousness, the inability or refusal to forgive human frailty, the placing of duty above charity. Protestantism, as treated in *Light in August*, is grim, demanding, "stern and implacable." Gail Hightower, the old minister, says that this spirit is behind the lynching of Joe Christmas, the culmination of the novel's action. Of the community he says: "Pleasure, ecstasy they cannot seem to bear. Their escape from it is in violence, in drinking and fighting and praying; catastrophe too, the violence identical and apparently inescapable. *And so why should not their religion drive them to crucifixion of themselves and one another?* And they will do it gladly, gladly. . . . Since to pity him would be to admit self-doubt and to hope for and need pity themselves. They will do it gladly, gladly. That's what is so terrible, terrible."

Faulkner chose to make the community of Jefferson Presbyterian or Calvinist. The United States Census figures show that the Baptists are by far the largest Protestant group in Mississippi, the Methodists the second largest, and the Presbyterians a small minority. Faulkner's reasons for doing this presumably were literary or dramatic. It allowed him to introduce the doctrines of predestination and of man's terrible depravity. (He also attributes such doctrines to the family of Calvin Burden, from New England, even though he says they were Unitarian.) A second reason possibly is that he wanted to stress the Scotch-Irish origins of the majority of the townspeople. (In one of the interviews in *Faulkner at Nagano*, Faulkner is quoted as saying his townspeople are of "Scottish descent." He should have said that many of them are also of Scotch-Irish descent.) Eupheus Hines, the mad grandfather of Joe Christmas, is forever talking about predestination and depravity; Joanna Burden, Joe's guilt-ridden lover, believes that God did not intend that the Negro's plight be ameliorated; and Simon McEachern, Joe's foster father, is a stern Presbyterian elder and on one occasion "the representative of a wrathful and retributive Throne."

But *Light in August* is not wholly an attack on Protestant excesses. Percy Grimm, the town's instrument in killing Joe, does not act in the name of Deity. He sees himself as the agent of patriotism—and Faulkner seems to be saying, through Grimm, whom he once called a Nazi, that patriotism can also generate the sort of righteousness that leads to persecution. Lena Grove and Byron Bunch believe in that peace which, as Hightower describes it, results from sinning and being forgiven. Both of them are fallible, and both are capable of guile. But they are also kindly and sympathetic, and they are able to accept as well as extend charity.

Light in August can also be read in more strictly psychological terms. The child, Joe, is the illegitimate son of Eupheus Hines's daughter. Joe's father is never seen, but he may (only *may*) have been a Negro. Hines refuses to call a doctor for his daughter and she dies in childbirth. On Christmas Day (thus the name, Joe Christmas) Hines puts the child into an orphanage, where he is treated impersonally and coldly. On one occasion, while eating stolen toothpaste, he uncomprehendingly witnesses the lovemaking of the dietitian and an intern. He expects to be punished, but the dietitian tries to buy his silence. His mad grandfather hovers at the edge of his life, something after the manner of Chillingworth in *The Scarlet Letter*. Later, McEachern, on whose farm he lives and works, disciplines him severely. There is no affection in their relationship. Mrs. McEachern tries to scheme with Joe to outwit McEachern, but the boy refuses her help, her sympathy, and her affection. Thus Joe is denied a system of rules and sanctions administered with love. For the rest of his life he refuses to give affection or to receive it. Even though he could pass as a white man, Joe chooses to present himself as a Negro; he wants to be rejected. On the other hand, he refuses to accept Negro status in a white society—and in the end this, in part, causes his break with Joanna, which leads to his killing her and to his being lynched.

Hightower also is the product of a too strict upbringing. And his weak constitution is the result of his father's refusal of charity for his wife and child. The young Hightower escapes, by fantasy, into the life his grandfather had lived as a Confederate raider. Hightower enters the church for two reasons, as a shelter from the world and as a means of joining his grandfather's ghost in Jefferson. He meets and marries a girl, the daughter of one of the seminary teachers, who wants desperately to escape from the seminary. He fails her as a husband and after several affairs she kills herself. His parishioners reject him, and even try to make him leave Jefferson, but he stays on in the town. Only Byron Bunch befriends him. Late in his life Hightower realizes the nature of his own failures, as well as the failure of the church. He makes a futile effort to save Christmas, and befriends Lena and her child.

Light in August can be interpreted religiously or psychologically—the interpretations come to the same point, that men should treat each other charitably and be tolerant of human weaknesses. If they fail to do so they invite the persecutions, the perversions, and the violence of which the novel is largely composed.

Light in August is very skillfully done. There are three story strands, and each is narrated in a way that illuminates the theme and creates a sense of great variety and multiplicity of life. Although *Light in August* seems to have come out of Faulkner's visceral life, and to exist as a breathing, throbbing, tormented community of human beings, it exhibits a greater intellectual play and resonance than any of his other novels. It may be his highest achievement as a novelist.

Pylon (1935) is a failure, at least when seen in relation to the several books published immediately before it and to *Absalom, Absalom!*, published the year following it. The setting is New Valois, or New Orleans, and the central characters are a reporter, his editor, and a "family" of stunt fliers. Faulkner is not writing about Yoknapatawpha, but he did know New Orleans well, and he knew the newspaper world and stunt flying. The failure does not derive from a limited knowledge of his subject; it derives from a failure in conception.

Faulkner apparently set out to explain the curious "family"—Laverne and her two bed companions, Jack Holmes, a parachute jumper, and Roger Shumann, who races the planes. Laverne does not know which man is the father of her six-year-old boy. The reporter gets involved with the "family" during their stay in New Valois. Early in the novel, he says to his editor, Hagood: "Because they ain't human like us; they couldn't turn those pylons like they do if they had had human blood and senses and they wouldn't want to or dare to if they just had human brains. Burn them like this one tonight and they don't even holler in the fire; crash and it ain't even blood when you haul him out: It's cylinder oil the same as in the crankcase." These people, as Faulkner saw them, belonged to the then new world of machines and speed, which was totally different from anything man had previously known. But when he tries to explain them, to show how and why they are a diffrent breed of human beings, his imagination fails him.

There are no interior monologues, and one never learns what goes on in Roger Shumann's head as he races a plane, finally crashing to his death, or what Jack or Laverne feels during a race or when jumping. Nor is there any attempt to explain their intense sexuality in relation to speed and to jumping, although such a relationship is clearly implied. The explanations for the conduct of Laverne, Roger, Jack, and the mechanic Jiggs are sociological accounts of their childhoods. None of this illuminates their being a different breed.

In *Faulkner at Nagano*, Faulkner says, "My characters, luckily for me, name themselves. I never have to hunt for their names. Suddenly they tell me who they are. In the conception, quite often, but never very long after I have conceived that character, does he name himself. When he doesn't name himself, I never do. I have written about characters whose names I never did know. Because they didn't tell me. There was one in *Pylon*, for instance, he was the central character in the book, he never did tell me who he was." This is a very revealing comment—and if one considers the names of characters in *Light in August*, for example, one realizes that a character's name in Faulkner's fiction is usually an important part of the characterization itself. The reporter in *Pylon* did not reveal his name because he does not wholly exist. He is borrowed from the dramatis personae of T. S. Eliot. In one chapter his lament is called "Lovesong of J. Alfred Prufrock." Hagood, his editor, is borrowed from Hollywood's conception of newspaper editors, loud, tough, but with hearts of gold.

The whole background of the book, New Orleans, the population, the newspaper office,

and the airport, is described as a wasteland. This is a not untypical passage: "She looked at him now: the pale stare without curiosity, perfectly grave, perfectly blank, as he rose, moved, dry loose weightless and sudden and longer than a lath, the disreputable suit ballooning even in this windless conditioned air as he went toward the candy counter. Above the shuffle and murmur of feet in the lobby and above the clash and clutter of crockery in the restaurant the amplified voice still spoke, profound and effortless, as though it were the voice of the steel-and-chromium mausoleum itself, talking of creatures imbued with motion though not with life. . . ."

It is as though Faulkner had borrowed, from Eliot, the backdrop of the wasteland and put in front of it his strange "family." The background is painted skillfully enough, but it does not really help to explain the fliers. As always in Faulkner's fiction, there are excellent scenes and striking characters (Jiggs is an example), but the failure of *Pylon* is a failure of its inner life. Faulkner had the *idée,* or germ, for a novel, but it did not develop or mature. The characterization of the reporter wavers because Faulkner does not understand him, the fliers are seen only from the outside, and finally the reader is left with a suspicion or the conviction that the *idée* for *Pylon* was not a good one, or if it was that Faulkner did not know how to make it expand and reveal itself. Interesting too is the fact that *Pylon*, almost alone among Faulkner's novels, shows no advance in or interest in developing the techniques of fiction.

Absalom, Absalom! (1936) is a pivotal story in Yoknapatawpha stories, and for it Faulkner drew his now famous map with this legend: "Jefferson Co., Mississippi, Area, 2400 Square Miles—Population, Whites, 6298; Negroes, 9313, William Faulkner, Sole Owner and Proprietor." Quentin Compson, soon to go to

Harvard, is asked by Miss Rosa Coldfield to tell the story of Thomas Sutpen, her brother-in-law, whom she sees as a "demon," a man so possessed by an ambition to build an impressive plantation and to found a line that he destroys everyone close to him. At Harvard, Quentin is asked by Shreve McCannon to tell him about the South: "Tell me about the South. What's it like there. What do they do there. Why do they live there. . . ." In response Quentin tells the story of Thomas Sutpen and Sutpen's family, aided by letters from his father, and with Shreve's shrewd guesses and inferences thrown in. And at the end, Shreve says, " 'Now I want you to tell me just one thing more. Why do you hate the South?' 'I dont hate it,' Quentin said, quickly, at once, immediately; 'I dont hate it,' he said. *I dont hate it* he thought, panting in the cold air, the iron New England dark; *I dont. I dont! I dont hate it! I dont hate it.*" Sutpen's story, told in a series of anecdotes, guesses, and inferences, represents the South to Quentin. His investigation of Sutpen's rise and fall and the family's subsequent destruction is also an investigation of his own heritage.

Thomas Sutpen's ambition had first been kindled when as a child of a very poor family he had been turned away from the front door of a plantation house, turned away by a liveried Negro. In his early teens he had run away to the West Indies, where he later married Eulalia Bon, and fathered a child, Charles. Learning his wife had a small amount of Negro blood, he had left her and the child. In Mississippi, he bought land from the Indians, built a plantation house, Sutpen's Hundred, married Ellen Coldfield, the daughter of a poor but highly respectable shopkeeper, and fathered two children, Henry and Judith. At the university, Henry met Charles Bon, who was there at his mother's instigation. Thomas Sutpen soon learned the identity of

Charles. Sutpen's wife, Ellen, not knowing who Charles was, wanted to see Judith marry him. Thomas Sutpen refused his permission, and Henry quarreled with his father and went off to New Orleans with Charles. Soon they were all caught up in the Civil War, but Thomas Sutpen continued to refuse any sign of recognition or affection toward Charles. Henry learned that Charles was his brother, but, despite this, was willing to condone Charles's marriage with Judith, believing that this perverse relationship would be an appropriate badge of the family's and the South's defeat. It was only when he learned that Charles had Negro blood that he refused to allow it. Charles persisted and Henry killed him. Sutpen himself was finally killed by Wash Jones, the father of Milly Jones, upon whom Sutpen had begot a child. Sutpen had repudiated her because the child was a girl. Sutpen's flaw—he is forever asking what went wrong in his "design"—was not merely his flaw, it was Henry's flaw, and the South's flaw: the inability to accept the Negro as human equal. It was over this that the war was fought and because of this that the Sutpen family was ruined. For example, Charles Etienne St. Valery Bon, the son of Charles Bon, flailed out at the white world much in the way Joe Christmas did. In Thomas Sutpen's case there is a terrifying innocence or literalness in his pursuit of his ambition to found a family. His adherence to his region's attitude toward the Negro is a part of this innocence.

The above is a sketchy account of a story that is heavy with mythic overtones and told in a baroque and frequently tortured prose. Occasionally a character speaks in his or her own voice, but usually the narration is in Faulkner's rhetorical "voice." This passage is Quentin's account of Henry and Charles riding up to the old house:

"(It seemed to Quentin that he could actually see them, facing one another at the gate. Inside the gate what was once a park now spread, unkempt, in shaggy desolation, with an air dreamy, remote and aghast like the unshaven face of a man just waking from ether, up to a huge house where a young girl waited in a wedding dress made from stolen scraps, the house partaking too of that air of scaling desolation, not having suffered from invasion but a shell marooned and forgotten in a backwater of catastrophe—a skeleton giving of itself in slow driblets of furniture and carpet, linen and silver, to help to die torn and anguished men who knew, even while dying, that for months now the sacrifice and the anguish were in vain. They faced one another on the two gaunt horses, two men, young, not yet in the world, not yet breathed over long enough, to be old but with old eyes, with unkempt hair and faces gaunt and weathered as if cast by some spartan and even niggard hand from bronze, in worn and patched gray weathered now to the color of dead leaves, the one with the tarnished braid of an officer, the other plain of cuff, the pistol lying yet across the saddle bow unaimed, the two faces calm, the voices not even raised: *Dont you pass the shadow of this post, this branch, Charles*; and *I am going to pass it Henry*) '—and then Wash Jones sitting that saddleless mule before Miss Rosa's gate, shouting her name into the sunny and peaceful quiet of the street, saying "Air you Rosie Coldfield? Then you better come on out yon. Henry has don shot that durn French feller. Kilt him dead as beef." ' "

Frequently the sentences, sometimes a page long, are impressions, seemingly collected piecemeal—inside parentheses or dashes, or in series of phrases and clauses—until a whole scene is dramatically rendered. The elements described within the sentence exist as in a continuum, in living relationships. The total action of the novel also has that quality of seeming to be always in motion, moving forward and backward in time, and constantly adding meanings. Something said in the first chapter is more fully understood chapters later when a relevant detail is added, but is not wholly understood until even a later chapter. *Absalom, Absalom!* is a kind of vortex, with characters and events ever in motion, but finally the reader is able to see that there is a still point at the bottom of the cone, the point in relation to which the characters and events have meaning.

The Unvanquished (1938) is composed of five fairly long stories, each involving Bayard Sartoris' experiences of the Civil War. He and Ringo, his Negro companion, have a number of Tom Sawyerish adventures. In the earlier stories they are boys, in the final story Bayard is a law student at the university, and the war is over. Some of the critics, such as George Marion O'Donnell, who see Faulkner as an apologist for the "aristocrat" of the Old South say this is a novel about the conflict between the Sartorises, who act "traditionally," and the Snopeses, who have no ethical code and employ low cunning. This interpretation of *The Unvanquished* is surely wrong. Some of the stories were published in "slick" magazines and have a minimum of inner life. One sees the boys firing on a troop of Yankees, then scooting for the house and being hid under the wide skirts of Bayard's grandmother, Rosa Millard, while the Yankees search for them, or sees John Sartoris outwitting a Yankee patrol. In one of the stories, "Skirmish at Sartoris," Aunt Louisa insists that Drusilla marry John Sartoris because Drusilla, dressed as a man, has ridden with his raiders. The marriage ceremony is interrupted long enough for John Sartoris to ride to town and shoot two men, thus disenfranchising the Negroes. Then the ceremony is performed. There is almost no attempt to explore the meaning of John Sartoris' action. The only story with thematic force is "Odor of Verbena," in which Bayard, now grown, refuses to engage in a duel with Redlaw, who has shot John Sartoris. Bayard has come to see that John Sartoris' loyalty to a former way of life invited not merely heroics but wanton killing. He sees Drusilla as "voracious," wholly indifferent to killing if done in the name of "honor." And he sees that George Wyatt and other gentlemen who want Redlaw killed are playing parts in a theatrical game.

Insofar as *The Unvanquished* is about the "southern code" it is a criticism of that code. But for the most part, the actions in *The Unvanquished* are romantic episodes, the adventures of the two boys and the dashing exploits of John Sartoris. There are many Yoknapatawpha characters brought into the stories, but none of them lives intensely or very meaningfully.

During his stay in New Orleans, Faulkner undoubtedly heard Sherwood Anderson talk about Hemingway. Anderson and Hemingway had known each other since the winter of 1920–21. In 1923 the *Little Review* carried several of Hemingway's stories. That same year the Contact Publishing Company in Dijon published his *Three Stories and Ten Poems*. Other stories appeared in the *Transatlantic*. *In Our Time* appeared in 1925. One may assume that Faulkner knew the Hemingway stance and the Hemingway dramatis personae. *Soldiers' Pay*, in large part, reads like a pastiche of *The Sun Also Rises*. Joe Gilligan and Margaret Powers are ineffective variations on Jake Barnes and Lady Brett. Bayard Sartoris is a kind of Hemingway "initiate," except that he does not really understand the Hemingway code; he feels empty, bleak, hopeless—and seeks his own death.

When he came to write *The Wild Palms* (1939), Faulkner was fully aware of the dif-

ferences between his vision of the world and Hemingway's vision. Yet there are many parallels with Hemingway's *A Farewell to Arms* in the part of Faulkner's book called "The Wild Palms," which is a love story; "Old Man," the second story in the book, is about a convict and his experiences during a great Mississippi flood.

In "The Wild Palms" Henry Wilbourne, a young intern, falls in love with Charlotte, married and the mother of two children. Charlotte, the more dedicated of the two, urges their absolute commitment to love. She believes that society destroys love. They live in Chicago, on a lake in northern Wisconsin, at a mine in Utah. They know cold and poverty, but nothing is allowed to interfere with their love. Charlotte becomes pregnant and urges Wilbourne to perform an abortion. For a time he refuses but then does as she asks. They return to the Gulf Coast. Charlotte hemorrhages and dies. Wilbourne is arrested, tried, and sent to prison.

In *A Farewell to Arms* Lt. Frederic Henry and Catherine Barkley also resign from society. Like Faulkner's couple, Henry and Catherine feel the world is blind to the needs of lovers. The idyll enjoyed by Hemingway's characters is more peaceful than the "idyll" of Faulkner's lovers, but both women die, one from abortion, the other after childbirth. In both stories the men say that if society catches you "but off step once" (Wilbourne) or "off base" (Henry) it destroys you. When near death both women are on fire from pain, and say "Don't touch me!" In both stories the men are reluctantly allowed to see the corpses of their lovers. In "The Wild Palms" defeat is symbolized by palms jeering and risible in the wind. In *A Farewell to Arms* it is the rain.

During the Chicago interlude Faulkner's lovers meet a character named McCord, who says, "Yah . . . Set, ye armourous sons, in a sea of hemingwaves." McCord is a bluff newspaperman, and sounds like a Hemingway character or like Hemingway himself. Outdoorsy, he belongs to the country associated with Nick Adams' fishing and hunting and adventures in Michigan. At one point Wilbourne says he has learned something about love from McCord and asks his blessing. " 'Take my curse,' McCord said."

Most commentaries on *The Wild Palms* and *A Farewell to Arms* say that Hemingway's love story is more poignant and touching than Faulkner's—and it is. But Faulkner's all-for-love is not "loaded" to the extent Hemingway's is. Charlotte's love is at the expense of her husband, her children, her own life, and Wilbourne's career and peace of mind. She is not in love with Wilbourne, she is in love with love. Like Hemingway initiates she finds the *meaning* in sex and love. In a sense, Wilbourne is her victim. Faulkner is not saying he accepts the doctrine that society destroys love. On the contrary, he is saying that an excessive commitment to love is itself destructive.

In commenting about the two story lines in *The Wild Palms* Faulkner said that when he finished the first chapter of the love story he felt something was missing. "So I wrote on the Old Man story until *The Wild Palms* rose back to pitch." On yet another occasion, he said he put the two strories together because neither story alone was long enough for book publication. The former explanation makes better sense.

"Old Man" is a criticism of the love story. The Tall Convict, the principal character, accepts his obligations, and goes to almost ridiculous lengths to satisfy his sense of duty. He fights the river in flood, subdues snakes and alligators, avoids bullets intended for him, and voluntarily returns to prison after anguish-ing adventures. In his bunk, he enjoys watching the smoke from his cigar curl upward in the twilight. He asks only "permission to endure to buy air, to feel sun," and to feel the earth under his feet. Like Dilsey and Byron Bunch, the Tall Convict is one of Faulkner's accepters. Like the character in *As I Lay Dying*, he does not believe "life is supposed to be easy on folks." He knows, although he would not know how to say it, "that love no more exists just at one spot and in one moment and in one body out of all the earth and all time . . . than sunlight does."

The convict does little or no theorizing about his lot. He is courageous and dedicated because he feels compelled to be. He accepts the lot fate has cast him for, and he is happy in it. He is truly free. The lovers refuse to let their love confront limitations or restraints —and in the struggle they are completely, or almost completely, destroyed.

The dramatics personae of *The Hamlet* (1940) are "rednecks," poor farmers. Faulkner describes them as being descendants of non-slaveholders. They have Welsh, Scotch, and English names. "They supported their own churches and schools, they married and committed infrequent adulteries and more frequent homicides among themselves. . . . They were Protestants and Democrats and prolific." Faulkner treats most of them with respect, and there is no indication that he is contemptuous or entertains feelings of superiority toward them because of their nonaristocratic heritage.

Essentially *The Hamlet* is the story of the Snopes family, especially Flem, moving into Frenchman's Bend, twenty miles from Jefferson, and systematically defrauding the community. Neither Flem's face nor voice ever indicates emotion and he doesn't even entertain the possibility of acting decently or respecting the rules of fair play. He takes advantage of every gesture of good will made toward him. This is a description of an early encounter between him and Jody Varner, who has heard that Ab Snopes, Flem's father, is a barn burner, and is rightfully fearful:

" 'Howdy,' he said. 'You're Flem, ain't you? I'm Varner.'

" 'That so?' The other said. He spat. He had a broad flat face. His eyes were the color of stagnant water. He was soft in appearance like Varner himself, though a head shorter, in a soiled white shirt and cheap gray trousers.

" 'I was hoping to see you,' Varner said. 'I hear your father has had a little trouble once or twice with landlords. Trouble that might have been serious.' The other chewed. 'Maybe they never treated him right; I dont know about that and I dont care. What I'm talking about is a mistake, any mistake can be straightened out so that a man can still stay friends with the fellow he aint satisfied with. Dont you agree to that?' The other chewed steadily. His face was as blank as a pan of uncooked dough. 'So he wont have to feel that the only thing that can prove his rights is something that will make him have to pick up and leave the country the next day,' Varner said. 'So there wont come a time some day when he will look around and find out he has run out of new country to move to.' Varner ceased. He waited so long this time that the other finally spoke, though Varner was never certain whether this was the reason or not:

" 'There's a right smart of country.' "

Flem victimizes the Varners, who are the largest landowners in Frenchman's Bend, marries Eula Varner, a symbol of fertility, of the pagan ripening of spring and summer, dupes most of the townspeople, outwitting even the wily Ratliff, and at the book's end is headed for Jefferson.

The Hamlet is episodic, part of it incorporating earlier short stories. And although the parts dealing with Flem are told mostly in a folk idiom, there are many highly rhetorical and lyrical passages, some of them running for many pages. These passages are mostly devoted to descriptions of Eula and to the idiot Ike Snopes's grotesque love for a cow. There are four story strands dealing with love—there is the marriage of Houston, a farmer, Mink Snopes's marriage, the amours of Eula and her loveless marriage to Flem, and Ike's love for the cow. Ironically Ike's love is a purer form of affirmation and of respect than any of the seemingly "normal" loves. Whether or not the courtly and romantic language in which it is described is an effective device is another question. The writing itself is both dazzling and beautiful. It contrasts sharply with the folk language of the other sections.

Discussions of "native American prose" are usually related to the "tall tale" tradition of the frontier, especially the Southwest. Among the best known of the tall tales are A. B. Longstreet's *Georgia Scenes* (1835) and George W. Harris' *Sut Lovingood's Yarns* (1867). It was Mark Twain who first elevated or transformed this sort of humor into literature. In idiom the tall tale is invariably folksy and ungrammatical, and the manner of narration includes both understatement and wild exaggeration. With *The Hamlet*, Faulkner made a major contribution to this "native" strain in American writing. (Ratliff, the sewing machine agent, who is both a participant in and an interpreter of much of the action, belongs to a similar tradition, the Yankee peddler of nineteenth-century literature. Like Ratliff, the peddler was practical, shrewd, witty, and sometimes caustic.) At least three major scenes in *The Hamlet*—the story of horse swapping, Flem Snopes's outwitting the devil, and the wild charging of a horse through a house—are borrowed from the tall-tale tradition.

The Hamlet is a comic novel. It participates in the ancient tradition of man satirizing his own weaknesses. Flem is personal aggrandizement incarnate, and Ratliff is his shrewd, witty, but fallible opponent. The humor of *The Hamlet* is grim, but even so it is humor of a more comforting sort than is to be found in any of the earlier books.

Go Down, Moses (1942) resembles *The Unvanquished* to the extent that both books are composed of interrelated stories. The comparison ends there, however, because *Go Down, Moses* is a serious and moving examination of the shame and pathos of white and black relationships. Undoubtedly the best of the seven stories is the frequently anthologized "The Bear." Properly enough, it is to "The Bear" that many critics turn when trying to explain Faulkner's social and moral doctrines —for in it Faulkner says that a right attitude toward nature should lead one to the right attitude toward human beings, white and black.

Old Ben, the bear, is more than a bear to be hunted—it is a symbol of the wilderness, of freedom, courage, and of the fruitful earth. Sam Fathers, son of a Chickasaw chief and a Negro slave, understands the wilderness and teaches its lessons to Isaac (Ike) McCaslin. From Sam Fathers Ike learns endurance, humility, and courage. No one owns or should own nature—and no one should exploit it. In the first version, published as a short story, Faulkner presents a sacramental view of the world, not unlike that of Coleridge's Ancient Mariner. In the second, revised, version which appears in *Go Down, Moses*, other elements are introduced: the exploitations of civilization and the evils of slavery.

There are two story strands in *Go Down, Moses*, the history of Ike and the history of mulatto "heirs" of old Carothers McCaslin, Ike's grandfather. Ike learns that these heirs usually suffered greatly, mostly from the humiliation of being treated as chattel, as objects, rather than as persons. A partial exception to this is Lucas Beauchamp, who was to become a central figure in *Intruder in the Dust* and who refused to accept the role of inferior being. The antecedents to *Intruder in the Dust* are in "The Fire and the Hearth," the second section of *Go Down, Moses*. Roughly half of the stories in *Go Down, Moses* are about Ike and the wilderness, and half are about the Negroes.

The two story lines meet in the revised "The Bear." Old Ben turns on those who exploit the wilderness, and he is destroyed. And in the long fourth section, Ike and his cousin McCaslin Edmonds discuss the heritage of Carothers McCaslin's Negro heirs. Faulkner's point is that a proper attitude toward the wilderness would, or should, lead to a proper attitude toward the Negro. The point is repeated in "Delta Autumn," in which Ike is an old man close to eighty.

Much of the writing in *Go Down, Moses*, especially in "The Bear," has an hallucinatory beauty, especially those scenes describing Old Ben and the virgin fields and forests. Possibly the second-best story is "Pantaloon in Black," a marvelous rendering of the actions of a young grief-crazed Negro. However, not all the stories are so successful, nor do all of them fall easily into place in the intended over-all pattern. "Was" is a humorous account of Uncle Buddy and Uncle Buck, and of the latter's being trapped into a marriage he was far from desiring. The three chapters entitled "The Fire and the Hearth" have the appearance of incidents that Faulkner intended to work up into a novel. "The Old People" seems largely a preparation for "The Bear," and "Go Down, Moses," interesting in some of its characterizations, a tacked-on story that adds little or nothing to the themes developed in "The Bear." At its best, however, *Go Down, Moses* provides images of piety, justice, and decency more moving than any similar passages in American literature.

All the novels published after *Go Down, Moses* exhibit Faulkner's virtues, especially his willingness to try new forms, and his wit, but they also suggest a weakening of his powers. Much of the former hypnotic quality in the rhetoric is diminished, and Faulkner seems less concerned to dramatize his stories. Also he became self-consciously didactic. Social problems invite solutions, and as an eminent writer, and a Nobel Prize winner, he was expected to provide them. Whether he assumed this new role willingly, or out of a sense of duty, does not matter. It was not a role suited to his peculiar genius.

Intruder in the Dust (1948), the first of the late novels, is a moving account of the relationships between young Charles Mallison and Lucas Beauchamp—the slow process of the boy's learning to accept the old Negro as an equal. It is reminiscent of Huck Finn and Nigger Jim. And the rather bizarre incidents— the boy and an elderly lady digging up a corpse, one body being substituted for another, a burial in quicksand, and the actions of the tough Gowrie family from Beat Four—are also reminiscent of the melodrama of *Huckleberry Finn*. On this level *Intruder in the Dust* is a fine story, but Faulkner was not satisfied to let well enough alone. He introduced Gavin Stevens, Charles's uncle, and Lucas' lawyer, and put into Stevens' mouth garrulous and often extraneous speeches about the South versus the North, and the methods that should be followed to bring about better race rela-

tions. Unfortunately Stevens' theories are not always convincing, and they seriously interfere with the pace of what would otherwise be a simple and possibly a graceful story.

Knight's Gambit (1949) is a series of detective stories, but Faulkner was unwilling to stay within the conventions of that genre. He employs the usual detective story gimmicks, but adds to them the sort of psychological probing and characterizations that are peculiar to the short story or the novel. The contrasting conventions almost cancel each other out.

In 1950 Faulkner published *Collected Stories*, a drawing together of *These Thirteen* (1931) and *Doctor Martino* (1934), plus additional stories. There are a few rather run-of-the-mill stories as there would be in any such collection, but there are enough good ones to make it clear that Faulkner is among the masters. None of his contemporaries who are acclaimed as short-story writers has either his intensity or range. Possibly the best of the stories are "Red Leaves," about the death of the Old Indian chief, Issetibbeha, "Wash," the basis for *Absalom, Absalom!*, "That Evening Sun," "Dry September," "A Rose for Emily," and "Barn Burning." The world of Faulkner's short fiction is Shakespearean in its multiplicity of characters and its variety of nuance, gesture, time, and place.

Requiem for a Nun (1951), a sequel to *Sanctuary*, is a strange morality play involving Temple Drake and Gowan Stevens, as well as Nancy Mannigoe and Gavin Stevens. The acts of the play, reminiscent of Jacobean drama, are interlarded with long historical chapters on Jefferson and the state of Mississippi. Temple and Gowan, young students in *Sanctuary*, are here a good deal older, and the parents of a young child. Both of them are restless and unhappy. The action, which includes the murder of the child by Nancy

Mannigoe, carries them to a point where they believe in purification by suffering and are ready to accept their burdens. The chapters, involving Temple and Gowan in history, are more convincingly done, but they do not keep *Requiem for a Nun* from being a poor performance for a writer of William Faulkner's stature.

A Fable (1954), set in France, is also a strange book, not so much a novel as an allegory about man's search for peace. Unfortunately the message or doctrine Faulkner put into it is either confused and badly worked out or is expressed in such a vague manner that it is extremely difficult to comprehend. There are occasional descriptive passages of great brilliance, but few if any entire scenes are so rendered that they come alive in the reader's imagination. *A Fable* seems to have been conceived as a speech, or an extended piece of rhetoric, rather than as a novel.

The Town (1957), the second of a promised series on the Snopes clan, is an improvement on *A Fable* but a lesser work than *The Hamlet.* Many of the old characters are in it, but Faulkner, having telescoped time, has also included Charles Mallison and Gavin Stevens. Eula and Flem are not as vividly realized as they are in *The Hamlet,* and the action as a whole is less sharply rendered. But with *The Mansion* (1959), a novel devoted mostly to Mink Snopes, Faulkner shows much of his former power.

The Reivers (1962), published shortly before his death, is Faulkner's most autobiographical novel, a nostalgic reliving of his boyhood in Oxford, when the automobile was new, and wet roads could be all but impassable quagmires. Characters include Boon Hogganbeck, from "The Bear," and Miss Reba, her husband, and the Memphis cathouse, earlier described in *Sanctuary.* The humor has little of the grimness of Faulkner's earlier comedy, but many of the episodes are amusing, and the world of his own childhood is skillfully evoked.

The themes in Faulkner's novels and short stories have to do with the elementary Christian virtues of self-respect and mutual respect, forgiveness of others as well as oneself, fortitude, a proper balance between humility and pride, and charity. Although he disavows any particular orthodoxy, Faulkner obviously accepts the Christian moral code. He is not, however, wholly admiring of practicing Christians. Some of his bitterest satire is at the expense of self-assured piety. He despises stiff-necked and literal-minded righteousness, whether it is in the service of the southern mores or of Christian doctrines. Since so many of his stories have southern settings, these virtues and vices are frequently presented in a context of white and black relationships. And sometimes his concern with them leads him to study the southern heritage and the "southern code."

Faulkner is a great writer, possibly the finest American novelist, but an essential simplicity of mind is a part of his genius. He is not a sophisticated writer in the sense that Henry James or Joseph Conrad or James Joyce is sophisticated. When he undertakes subjects of a certain magnitude and order, as he did with *Pylon* and *A Fable,* he flounders badly. But when he is treating subjects and themes that he feels in his bones—the frustration of the Negro in "Dry September," the decency of Dilsey in *The Sound and the Fury,* the self-preoccupation of Anse Bundren in *As I Lay Dying,* or the anguish of young Sarty Snopes in "Barn Burning"—Faulkner is magnificent. Faulkner's themes are as simple and as complicated, and persistent, as those in the Bible.

Fortunately, his powers of inventiveness

were very great, and he contributed to the theory of the novel as an art form. No other American novelist has created so many memorable characters, and possibly none of them has been his equal as a creator of multiple and varied sorts and levels of life within a novel, as in, say, *Light in August* or *The Hamlet.* Faulkner did not suffer from a lack of imagination.

He was also a master of style, of a "high rhetoric" and of a "folk rhetoric." One of his critics has said, "Faulkner's prose has an archaic sound, like a hunter's horn." This is a good characterization. Faulkner's language and his fictional world evoke the past, or, better, relate the past to the present. Reading Faulkner one feels involved in a long history, of torment, suffering, and anguish but also of endurance, dedication, and love.

When Faulkner was writing and publishing the works of his middle and greatest period, most of his contemporaries, for example Theodore Dreiser, Sinclair Lewis, and John Dos Passos, were writing a more "realistic" fiction. It was more realistic in the sense that they were less likely to create allegorical characters, to invent highly symbolic actions, or to write a poetic or richly rhetorical prose. Their kind of realism was an effort to reflect everyday experience or "ordinary reality." It was a period when many Americans were suspicious of rhetoric, elegance, style, even literary conventions. They would have denied that the "realism" of Dreiser or Lewis or Dos Passos was itself a literary convention. Fiction was held to have documentary value in the sense that Lewis' Main Street was precisely Main Street, Sauk Centre, Minnesota, where the author had grown up. There was some bewilderment therefore when readers confronted *Sanctuary* or *As I Lay Dying* or *The Hamlet.* Either Faulkner was showing Mississippi as it actually was, or he was exaggerating, and in

the latter case he was not telling the truth. More recent criticism has helped to clarify the fact that the literary conventions employed by Faulkner were not those, at least not exclusively those, of the "new realism."

In retrospect we can see that Faulkner's fiction in some ways is closer to earlier literary conventions than it is to the "new realism." The sensational and eerie imaginings of Charles Brockden Brown, Edgar Allan Poe, and even Ambrose Bierce, those specialists in the *frisson,* are clearly a part of Faulkner's heritage. Present too are Hawthorne's allegory and Gothic romance, both employed in a detached explication of a people of grim righteousness. Cooper's protagonists of innocence are there, and so too is the tall tale. And in at least one respect, Faulkner is reminiscent of Melville: both writers, out of an inherited tradition of hope and expectation, can create a vision of pure innocence, and they can create, out of a personal skepticism of profound depths, a vision of nightmarish horror. Faulkner was also aware of the Elizabethan and Jacobean drama, the Russian novel, and the "modern" novel as it was created by James, Conrad, and Joyce. Faulkner's dual heritage, American and European, is not uncomplicated—and he was conscious of its variety.

Selected Bibliography

WORKS OF WILLIAM FAULKNER

The Marble Faun, with a preface by Phil Stone. Boston: The Four Seas Company, 1924. (Reissued with *A Green Bough.* New York: Random House, 1965.)
Soldiers' Pay. New York: Boni and Liveright, 1926.
Mosquitoes. New York: Boni and Liveright, 1927.

Sartoris. New York: Harcourt, Brace, 1929.

The Sound and the Fury. New York: Jonathan Cape and Harrison Smith, 1929.

As I Lay Dying. New York: Jonathan Cape and Harrison Smith, 1930.

Sanctuary. New York: Jonathan Cape and Harrison Smith, 1931.

These Thirteen. New York: Jonathan Cape and Harrison Smith, 1931. (Contains "Victory," "All the Dead Pilots," "Crevasse," "A Justice," "Mistral," "Ad Astra," "Red Leaves," "Divorce in Naples," "Carcassone," "A Rose for Emily," "Hair," "That Evening Sun," and "Dry September.")

Idyll in the Desert. New York: Random House, 1931. (A limited edition of 400 copies; never reprinted.)

Miss Zilphia Gant. The Book Club of Texas, 1932. (A limited edition of 300 copies; never reprinted.)

Light in August. New York: Harrison Smith and Robert Haas, 1932.

Salmagundi. Milwaukee: The Casanova Press, 1932. (Contains early essays and poems, mostly from the *Double-Dealer.)*

A Green Bough. New York: Harrison Smith and Robert Haas, 1933.

Doctor Martino and Other Stories. New York: Harrison Smith and Robert Haas, 1934. (Contains "Black Music," "Leg," "Doctor Martino," "Fox Hunt," "Death Drag," "There Was a Queen," "Smoke," "Turn About," "Beyond," "Wash," "Elly," "Mountain Victory," "Honor.")

Pylon. New York: Harrison Smith and Robert Haas, 1935.

Absalom, Absalom! New York: Random House, 1936.

The Unvanquished. New York: Random House, 1938.

The Wild Palms. New York: Random House, 1939.

The Hamlet. New York: Random House, 1940.

Go Down, Moses and Other Stories. New York: Random House, 1942. (In subsequent printings and other editions, "and Other Stories" was omitted from the title, thus emphasizing the unity of the collection.)

Intruder in the Dust. New York: Random House, 1948.

Knight's Gambit. New York: Random House, 1949. (Contains "Smoke," reprinted from *Doctor Martino,* "Monk," "Hand upon the Waters," "Tomorrow," "An Error in Chemistry," and "Knight's Gambit.")

Collected Stories of William Faulkner. New York: Random House, 1950. (Reprints all the stories from *These Thirteen* and *Doctor Martino* as well as "Artist' at Home," "The Brooch," "Centaur in Brass," "A Courtship," "Golden Land," "Lo!" "Mule in the Yard," "My Grandmother Millard and General Bedford Forrest and the Battle of Harrykin Creek," "Pennsylvania Station," "Shall Not Perish," "Shingles for the Lord," "The Tall Men," "That Will Be Fine," "Two Soldiers," and "Uncle Willy.")

Notes on a Horsethief. Greenville, Miss.: The Levee Press, 1951.

Requiem for a Nun. New York: Random House, 1951.

A Fable. New York: Random House, 1954.

Big Woods. New York: Random House, 1955. (A collection of earlier stories plus "Race at Morning.")

New Orleans Sketches by William Faulkner. Tokyo: The Hokuseido Press, 1955. (Contains the "Mirrors of Chartres Street" sketches which appeared originally in the *Times-Picayune.)* Revised edition, edited by Carvel Collins, New York: Random House, 1968. (Includes new preface and critical essay "Sherwood Anderson.")

Faulkner at Nagano, edited by Robert A. Jelliffe. Tokyo: The Kenkyusha Press, 1956. (Contains interviews Faulkner gave during his visit to Japan, plus statements and speeches.)

Faulkner in the University, edited by Frederick L. Gwynn and Joseph Blotner. Charlottesville: University Press of Virginia, 1959. (Contains questions put to Faulkner by students and faculty and his replies.)

The Town. New York: Random House, 1957.

The Mansion. New York: Random House, 1959.

The Reivers. New York: Random House, 1962.

William Faulkner: Early Prose and Poetry, edited by Carvel Collins. Boston: Little, Brown, 1962.

The Wishing Tree, illustrated by Don Bolognese. New York: Random House, 1967. (The author's only children's story. Version previously existed in a single typescript copy dated February 5, 1927.)

Essays, Speeches and Public Letters of William Faulkner, edited by James B. Meriwether. New York: Random House, 1965.

Lion in the Garden: Interviews with William Faulkner, 1926–1962, edited by James B. Meriwether and Michael Millgate. New York: Random House, 1968.

BIBLIOGRAPHIES

Beebe, Maurice. "Criticism of William Faulkner: A Selected Checklist with an Index to Studies of Separate Works," *Modern Fiction Studies,* 2:150–64 (Autumn 1956). (Published at Purdue University, Lafayette, Indiana.)

Daniel, Robert W. *A Catalogue of the Writings of William Faulkner.* New Haven, Conn.: Yale University Library, 1942.

Massey, Linton R. *William Faulkner: "Man Working," 1919-1962: A Catalogue of the William Faulkner Collections at the University of Virginia.* Charlottesville: Bibliographical Society of Virginia, 1968.

Meriwether, James B. "William Faulkner: A Checklist," *Princeton Library Chronicle,* 18: 136–58 (Spring 1957).

CRITICAL AND BIOGRAPHICAL STUDIES

Backman, Melvin. *Faulkner: The Major Years.* Bloomington: Indiana: University Press, 1966.

Beck, Warren. *Man in Motion.* Madison: University of Wisconsin Press, 1961.

Brooks, Cleanth. *William Faulkner: The Yoknapatawpha Country.* New Haven, Conn.: Yale University Press, 1963.

Brylowski, Walter. *Faulkner's Olympian Laugh: Myth in the Novels.* Detroit: Wayne State University Press, 1968.

Campbell, Harry M., and Ruel E. Foster. *William Faulkner: A Critical Appraisal.* Norman: University of Oklahoma Press, 1951.

Cowley, Malcolm. *The Faulkner-Cowley File: Letters and memories, 1944–1962.* New York: Viking Press, 1966.

Cullen, John B. *Old Times in the Faulkner Country.* Chapel Hill: University of North Carolina Press, 1961.

Falkner, Murry C. *The Faulkners of Mississippi: A Memoir.* Baton Rouge: Louisiana State University Press, 1967.

Hoffman, Frederick J. *William Faulkner.* New York: Twayne, 1961.

——— and Olga Vickery, eds. *William Faulkner: Three Decades of Criticism.* East Lansing: Michigan State University Press, 1960.

Howe, Irving. *William Faulkner: A Critical Study.* New York: Random House, 1952; revised edition, 1962.

Millgate, Michael. *The Achievement of William Faulkner.* London: Constable, 1966.

Miner, Ward L. *The World of William Faulkner.* Durham, N.C.: Duke University Press, 1952.

O'Connor, William Van. *The Tangled Fire of William Faulkner.* Minneapolis: University of Minnesota Press, 1954.

Runyan, Harry. *A Faulkner Glossary.* New York: Citadel Press, 1965.

Thompson, Lawrance. *William Faulkner.* New York: Barnes and Noble, 1963.

Vickery, Olga W. *The Novels of William Faulkner: A Critical Interpretation.* Baton Rouge: Louisiana State University Press, 1959; revised edition, 1964.

Volpe, Edmond L. *A Reader's Guide to William Faulkner.* New York: Farrar, Straus, 1964.

Warren, Robert Penn, ed. *Faulkner: A Collection of Critical Essays.* Englewood Cliffs, N.J.: Prentice-Hall, 1966.

Webb, James W., and A. Wigfall Green, eds. *William Faulkner of Oxford.* Baton Rouge: Louisiana State University Press, 1965.

—WILLIAM VAN O'CONNOR

F. Scott Fitzgerald
1896-1940

THE general acceptance of Scott Fitzgerald into the ranks of serious and ambitious American novelists had to wait until his death in 1940. He was forty-four when he died and the story of the early rise and abrupt fall of his literary reputation—as well as his personal fortunes—can be fitted with neat symmetry into those two dramatic decades of the American twentieth century, the twenties and the thirties. The twenties were less than three months old when Fitzgerald's first novel, *This Side of Paradise*, arrived and immediately became a famous American book. Within weeks of this first success a second brand-new, post-war product, his stories of the flapper and her boy friends, made it clear that the twenties would be his oyster and that he, handsome, clever, and lucky Scott Fitzgerald, would be one of the brightest figures of the new age. The climax of his fortunes arrived, we can see now, very rapidly. In 1925 came the splendid artistic success of *The Great Gatsby*, and then in the second half of the twenties the days and months of his private world began to descend into tragedy. He could not bring the order into his life that would allow him to write his next novel. By the end of the twenties he was living too high and drinking too much. In April 1930 Zelda Fitzgerald had the mental breakdown that ended the romantic life they had built together over the preceding ten years. During the thirties, his last decade, Fitzgerald's life encompassed enough pathos, irony, and final agony to make his biography by Arthur Mizener one of the saddest records of an American literary life since Edgar Allan Poe. Before he died he was dead as a writer. No one was buying his books though seven were still in print. What has become clearer since his death in 1940 is a final irony, at the expense not of Fitzgerald but of American literary culture: the neglect he suffered during the 1930's was hugely undeserved. It took two posthumously published works to reveal to America how much serious work he had accomplished against great odds during the last ten years of his life.

The critical neglect of Fitzgerald had of course the effect of making the popular neglect seem deserved. That he shortened his own life by dissipation and wasted his fine talent all along the way was the judgment passed by most of the critics at the time of his death. The severity of their judgments may have been justified, but this did not excuse the failure to see how hard Fitzgerald had written all his life, or the failure to distinguish his best work from the rest and to recognize how much good work there was. It will perhaps become less of a temptation as the decades pass to be preoccupied with Fitzgerald as a person, and with his life as a cautionary tale, at the expense of a close concentration on his stories and novels. He used himself so mercilessly in his fiction, there is often such a complete fusion between his life and his stories, that conscientious criticism will always have to remember D. H. Lawrence's warning to biographically-minded critics: don't trust the artist, trust the tale. There is, however, another order of difficulty in appreciating Fitzgerald's best work. His attitude toward money and moneyed people has been much misunderstood.

One way to begin a consideration of Fitzgerald's attraction to the American rich as the prime subject matter of his fiction is to look at the most famous Fitzgerald literary anecdote. As Ernest Hemingway originally wrote it into his story "The Snows of Kilimanjaro," published in *Esquire* in 1936, it went this way. Hemingway's writer-hero is musing on his own life among the American rich. "He remembered poor Scott Fitzgerald and his romantic awe of them and how he had started a story once that began, 'The very rich are different from you and me.' And how someone had said to Scott, Yes they have more money. But that was not humorous to Scott."

Although the exchange never actually took place it has become part of the story of our two most legendary modern novelists. The moral implications of the anecdote, political, personal, and artistic, have usually been chalked up to Hemingway's score. It is significant for understanding the distance that separated the two men at this point in their friendship that Hemingway could make such demeaning use of Fitzgerald as a character in a piece of magazine fiction. The anecdote concludes with this comment, "He thought they were a special glamorous race and when he found they weren't it wrecked him just as much as any other thing that wrecked him." This was the public burial of a has-been writer, and Fitzgerald was deeply offended.

Hemingway's rebuke belongs to the general charge against Fitzgerald made frequently in the thirties that he was captivated by the rich and their expensive manners, and forgot that too much money in America is always supposed to be a sign of vulgarity and wickedness. Applied to Fitzgerald's fiction this moralism is simple-minded. To disprove it there is exhibited in the novels and stories all the moral energy that Fitzgerald spent "fixing" the rich. Since we read Fitzgerald's stories of the rich in a more affluent American society, in which the rich have become less shocking because they are now less removed from middle-class mores, we should more easily detect the moral and cultural confusions in Fitzgerald's fiction if they are really there. Most Americans can no longer feel superior to Fitzgerald's interest in the American greed for fine cars, the right clothes, and the pleasures of the best hotels and off-beat entertainment. The American people now seem to be less embarrassed than they once were at the snobbery of large parts of their social system. Contemporary social analysis has shown them how far ahead of his times Fitzgerald was in describing the rigorous systems of status that underlie that rather contradictory American term, the Open Society.

We may in fact be today more responsive readers of Fitzgerald's stories of money and display and expensive charm than many of his contemporaries were. He wrote during two decades when an American social revolution seemed more probable to thoughtful people than it does today. Nowadays we may be more ready to accept as he did the final complexity of our society and to recognize that we create a large part of our moral selves as we become engaged in that society. This is the theme that runs through his fiction—and through his life. We do him an injustice if we assume at the start that in order to understand the dreadful sanctions of social prestige—that is, money—Fitzgerald had to make a fatal submission of himself to the glamorous rich.

The story of the legendary Fitzgerald of the twenties usually begins with the picture of newly married, handsome Zelda and Scott Fitzgerald dancing around or jumping into the fountain of the Plaza Hotel. This pastoral scene may be useful in reminding us that the Fitzgeralds were not native New Yorkers. She was from the deep South, from Montgomery, Alabama. He was a midwestener. Edmund Wilson, one of Fitzgerald's closest literary friends, insisted on the important influence of St. Paul, Minnesota, in forming Fitzgerald's literary personality. In 1922 when Wilson did a literary profile of Fitzgerald he wrote, "Fitzgerald is as much of the middle west of large cities and country clubs as Lewis is of the middle west of the prairies and little towns." The culture that formed him, Wilson went on in a superior eastern manner, was characterized at its best by "sensitivity and eagerness for life without a sound base of culture and taste; a brilliant structure of hotels and exhilarating social activities built not on the eighteenth century but simply on the prairie." Wilson then took the occasion to advise Fitzgerald—his friends were always giving him advice in public—to exploit the "vigorous social atmosphere" of his native state, "to do for Summit Avenue what Lewis has done for Main Street." Fitzgerald never followed Wilson's suggestion to write a midwestern novel—despite all that public advice one of Fitzgerald's most surprising attributes was a capacity for making up his mind in private—but he made his own kind of use of his Minnesota background. It was not at all like Sinclair Lewis' exploitation of that same territory.

Francis Scott Key Fitzgerald was born in St. Paul on September 24, 1896. On his mother's side he was the grandson of an Irish immigrant who did well in the wholesale grocery business. His grandfather's estate was worth three to four hundred thousand dollars when he died at the age of forty-four. This McQuillan money gave young Scott Fitzgerald the advantageous background of his grandmother's large house on Summit Avenue, the most aristocratic street in St. Paul, and it gave him eventually his expensive education in private schools and at Princeton. But he was always sensitive to the McQuillan beginnings as being what he called "straight 1850 potato famine Irish." The other half of his inheritance was much more pleasing to his keen sense of himself. His admiration for his gentlemanly but ineffectual father, who was descended from a seventeenth-century Maryland family, he put into both *The Great Gatsby* and *Tender Is the Night*. He was named for Francis Scott Key, a distant cousin of his paternal grandmother's. In the thirties he wrote that he had early developed an inferiority complex in the midst of a family where the "black Irish half . . . had the money and looked down upon the Maryland side of the family who had, and really had, that . . . series of reticences and obligations that go under the poor old shattered word 'breeding.' "

Fitzgerald's Catholic background was also oppressive to him as a boy. He wrote in his notebook later in his life that when he was young "the boys in my street still thought that Catholics drilled in the cellar every night with the idea of making Pius the Ninth autocrat of this republic." But Fitzgerald never wrote these feelings of social displacement directly into his fiction or into the confessional essays of the mid-thirties. None of his important protagonists is noticeably Irish or Catholic and none of the agonies they suffer is religious. He was not, apparently, a very devout schoolboy, even in a Catholic boarding school and under the influence of a sophisticated and cultivated priest, Monsignor Fay, who was devoted to him and to whom he dedicated his first novel. (*This Side of Paradise* is not at all a Catholic novel.) In 1919 at the end of his college career at Princeton and his war service he wrote to Edmund Wilson that his Catholicism was scarcely more than a memory. The autobiographical essays in *The Crack-Up* tell us a great deal about Fitzgerald's sense of sinning against himself, against his gift of life and his gift of talent, but none of the sources of his despair take us directly back to his early years in the midst of a dubiously genteel Irish Catholic family in St. Paul.

His loyalty to his father may have been partly a way of defending his father against failure in business. As a boy of eleven Fitzgerald shared intensely the embarrassment of his father's being fired as a salesman for Proctor and Gamble in Buffalo and the family's subsequent return to St. Paul to live under the protection of the McQuillan money. As if his family were restive under the pressures of feeling dependent, they moved from one house to another in the Summit Avenue neighborhood, circling the social strongholds but never able to afford more than "a house below the average/Of a street above the average" as Fitzgerald once put it. One of his best-known stories, "Winter Dreams," a Jazz Age version of the Horatio Alger fable, is based on St. Paul and its summertime suburb White Bear Lake. The hero at fourteen is a grocer's son who must earn his spending money as a caddy at the country club to which many of Fitzgerald's Summit Avenue friends belonged. Fitzgerald was never a caddy, but it was easy for him to project a poor boy's social insecurity. His mother was a further embarrassment. She dressed oddly and sometimes behaved oddly in public. He was always aware that she had spoiled him and helped him to be the little show-off who could easily get on

the nerves of his teachers and contemporaries. But the young Fitzgerald is also remembered in St. Paul as an imaginative, vital, and attractive boy. Plenty of social success came his way before he was sent off to boarding school in New Jersey at the age of fourteen.

Fitzgerald mined his boyhood years, as he did every stage of his life, for story material. The *Saturday Evening Post* stories of his youth in St. Paul and at Newman School that he wrote at the end of the twenties are delightful and show what a competent writer of magazine fiction he was by this time. But the moments in the stories that distinguish them as Fitzgerald's are those that show how exactly he could recall a moment of a boy's deep feeling about a person, or a place, or "the way it was." One of the safest generalizations that can be made about Fitzgerald is that he is America's most sentient novelist of manners. He was deeply interested in recording the history of his own sensibility at the same time that he wanted to describe a typical American boyhood. The *Post* stories of his young hero Basil Duke Lee are full of events that have their meaning in social distinctions, envious comparisons, and the important implications for young Americans of manners and possessions. But as Basil moves from one emotional crisis to another in his search for who he really is and who he wants to be, Fitzgerald would have us believe that Basil deliberately penetrates each moment of passion for its absolute emotional significance, and then passes on. On one magical late summer afternoon in a St. Paul backyard—the story is called "The Scandal Detectives"—fourteen-year-old Basil really looked into a girl's beautiful, "gnome-like" face for the first time. He had scarcely begun to drink his fill of his response to her, "a warm chill of mingled pleasure and pain," when, Fitzgerald writes, he realized it was "a definite experience and he was immediately conscious of it." Then, as the swift moment of excitement filled him to the brim the boy consciously let it go, "incapable of exploiting it until he had digested it alone." The emotional plot of the story is about a writer-to-be, as well as, we are almost persuaded, a typical American boy.

Fitzgerald's first boyish successes were literary and they were important to both his emotional and his social life. In an autobiographical essay written in the mid-thirties he recalled a piece of schoolboy writing and remembered how necessary it had been to his ability to meet the world. At Newman School the football coach had taken him out of a game unfairly, according to Fitzgerald. The coach thought he had been afraid of an opposing player and had let the team down. Fitzgerald was able to dominate the whole situation, the coach, his lack of success at football, and probably his own cowardice by writing a poem about the experience that made his father proud of him. "So when I went home that Christmas vacation it was in my mind that if you weren't able to function in action you might at least be able to tell about it, because you felt the same intensity—it was a back door way out of facing reality." The need to feel the same intensity of social success that more popular, better-balanced schoolboys felt kept Fitzgerald writing stories, poems, and plays. His academic record always suffered, but as a young poet, editor, and playwright he could express his considerable ego and win the kind of public acclaim that was necessary to him. By the age of sixteen he had written and produced two melodramas that had public performances in St. Paul and earned over two hundred dollars for a local charity. He was learning to depend on his literary talent very early in his life. When it came time to choose a college he chose Princeton because he learned that you could be a big man at Princeton if you could provide librettos for its musical comedy organization,

the Triangle Club. He entered college in the fall of 1913, when he was still sixteen years old.

Princeton's contribution to Fitzgerald's education as an American writer can be best discovered in his autobiographical first novel, *This Side of Paradise*. For the writer as a person it was, from the first moment, a lovely place, an atmosphere full of poignant emotions. ". . . the sense of all the gorgeous youth that has rioted through here in two hundred years" —that was one of the feelings written into the novel, and as Fitzgerald's young men left Princeton for the army camps of World War I they wept for their own lost youth. Through most of the pages of the novel Princeton is primarily a richly complex American social order with very attractive possibilities for a bright young man on the make. The world you aspired to, as soon as you learned your way around, was composed of admirable, even glamorous men, in the classes above you, who could be envied and imitated both for themselves and for their functions in this specialized society. They were the athletes, writers, campus politicians, or just the Men with an Aura. As a freshman you chose your models, entered the intense but secret social competition, and with good luck and much clever management you would be accepted, by the middle of your second year when you joined an eating club, as one of the best of your generation. This was the Princeton that first consumed Fitzgerald's imagination.

What Fitzgerald as an educated man owed to Princeton is harder to discern. Arthur Mizener believes that the group of literary friends that he was lucky to find there—Edmund Wilson and John Peale Bishop were two of them —gave him "the only education he ever got, and, above all, they gave him a respect for literature which was more responsible than anything else for making him a serious man."

The narrowness of his educated mind, in one sense the failure of his Princeton education, can be fairly deduced from letters he wrote to his daughter studying at Vassar during the last year of his life.

Twenty-five years after his Princeton career he still recommends what were evidently his own college practices to his daughter. To form a prose style she must read the poets over and over. If she has anything of an ear she will soon hear the difference between poetry and non-poetry and thus have an advantage over most English professors. She must have "some politeness toward ideas," but about adjectives, ". . . all fine prose is based upon the verbs carrying the sentences. . . . Probably the finest technical poem in English is Keats' *Eve of Saint Agnes.* . . . Would you read that poem for me, and report?" Looking back at his own beginnings in college, he identifies himself as a poetic talent. It is the prose talents, he believes, who need the benefits of a formal education; they depend upon "other factors—assimilation of material and careful selection of it, or, more bluntly: having something to say and an interesting, highly developed way of saying it." As for the education of poets, if she will try to give ". . . not the merely *reported* but the *profound* essence of what happened at a prom or after it, perhaps that honesty will come to you—and then you will understand how it is possible to make even a forlorn Laplander *feel* the importance of a trip to Cartier's!"

It was one of the great blows of Fitzgerald's life that his formal Princeton career as he had carefully plotted it and at first began to achieve it was in the end a failure. By the close of his second year he seemed to be well on his way to the first public display of his personality. He had made the right club, had written the book for a Triangle show, and was an editor of a magazine called *The Tiger.* The aura was

beginning to form. But he had overextended himself. Too many academic deficiencies piled up, and under cover of an illness he left college at the beginning of his third year. A year's absence meant forfeiting all the tangible prizes he had aimed for, and he could still relive the pangs of his disappointment twenty years later. When he returned to college in the fall of 1916 he had improved his notion of the superior Princeton type. He began to see more of "literary" men and to fill the literary magazine with his poems and stories. This was the only year of serious education for him at Princeton, and what he learned came chiefly through private reading. He read especially Shaw and Butler and Wells, and read and then imitated Tennyson, Swinburne, and Rupert Brooke. He discovered the prototype for his first hero and novel when he read Compton Mackenzie's *Sinister Street.* Then between his third and fourth years he applied for a commission in the army. What should have been Fitzgerald's last year at Princeton was only two months long and on November 20 he left the campus for Fort Leavenworth.

Before Fitzgerald left Princeton for what was to be fifteen months of service in American training camps—he was never sent overseas— he finished the first of three versions of *This Side of Paradise.* Professor Christian Gauss read the manuscript and returned it saying that it was not ready for publication. During Fitzgerald's first six months as an officer in training he struggled not with army manuals and training exercises but with his manuscript. In the summer of 1918 *The Romantic Egotist,* as he first called the novel, was sent to Scribners, and in the fall that house rejected it by a vote of two editors to one. Meanwhile he had been transferred to Camp Sheridan near Montgomery, Alabama, and there, on the seventh of September, as he noted precisely in his journal, he fell in love. The girl, barely eighteen, was Zelda Sayre, the daughter of a judge.

The close resemblance between Zelda Sayre —who was going to become Zelda Fitzgerald after a courtship of a year and a half—and the heroines of Fitzgerald's fiction makes its important to try to see her clearly as a person. It is not a simple thing to do. Since her death she has always been referred to unceremoniously as Zelda, even in formal literary essays. But this informality is really a continuing acknowledgment that the combined destinies of Zelda and Scott Fitzgerald are finally one and indivisible. Nancy Milford's biography of Zelda (1970) makes use for the first time of her intimate journals and correspondence. Most of Miss Milford's book concentrates on the years after 1925 and tells a poignant story of two competitive and finally tattered lives held together at the deep center by a remarkable human devotion.

When Fitgerald first met Zelda Sayre he was just recovering from the collapse of a college love affair, the central story of his novel in manuscript. The romantic egotist of his novel was free to make another absolute commitment, to invest another beautiful young lady with the aura of "the top girl." (He wrote later into his notebook, "I didn't have the two top things: great animal magnetism or money. I had the two second things, though: good looks and intelligence. So I always got the top girl.") Zelda was beautiful and desirable for herself, but she was also a prize to be won against very worthy competition, all the other presentable young officers in the two army camps near Montgomery. At the moment of triumph when at last he made her his girl we must assume that he felt the same ecstatic joy that filled Jay Gatsby's ineffable moment in the love scene he was going to write five years later. The persons of the drama were the same: the anonymous young lieutenant from the North and the belle of a southern city. The language of the Gatsby passage is as florid and brilliant as anything in modern fiction since Meredith's early novels. "He knew that when he kissed this girl, and forever wed his unutterable visions to her perishable breath, his mind would never romp again like the mind of God. . . . At his lips' touch she blossomed for him like a flower and the incarnation was complete." In *The Great Gatsby* Fitzgerald was in full control of the language of the religion of love spoken by a modern but strangely old-fashioned courtly lover. None of the ironies visited upon Gatsby in the novel is allowed to tarnish his first response to Daisy. The lack of self-consciousness, the commitment to such pure feelings of sexual tenderness and compassion, distinguish Fitzgerald's romantic attitude toward women from any other modern novelist's.

The demands of feeling that Zelda Sayre brought to the courtship and marriage appear to have been as grand in their terms as Fitzgerald's. If we can trust his early descriptions of her in his fiction, she was above all ambitious, like the southern girl in "The Ice Palace" who was planning to live "where things happen on a big scale." And like the flappers in the early stories who baited their elders and showed in all their responses to life that they valued spontaneity and self-expression before those duller virtues that required self-control, Zelda Sayre was daring and had a local reputation for recklessness and unconventionality. She did what she wanted to, and her parents discovered that they belonged to that generation upon whom, as Fitzgerald one wrote in a story, "the great revolution in American family life was to be visited." Her youthful beauty gave her great confidence. The men in her life were expected on the one hand to make gallant gestures, and of these Fitzgerald was quite capable;

on the other hand they were expected to promise her a solid and glittering background—here Fitzgerald's lack of expectations after he was discharged from the army in February 1919 sent them both into agonies of frustration.

For four months he struggled in New York to support himself by writing advertising copy by day and to make the fortune that would convince the girl by writing short stories at night. He sold just one story for thirty dollars, and by June he had lost the girl. Zelda broke the engagement. His response to her decision in the summer of 1919 was to chuck his New York job, return to St. Paul, and rewrite his novel. By early September he had finished *This Side of Paradise*, by the middle of the month Scribners had accepted it, and by early November he had earned over five hundred dollars from three recently written short stories. With the confidence of a real capitalist and the conviction that he had written a best-selling novel, Fitzgerald returned to Montgomery, and there Zelda promised to marry him in the spring when his novel was published.

Fitzgerald did not hold Zelda Sayre morally responsible for the mercenary views she took of their engagement. They both felt poor, and they were both eager to participate in the moneyed society around them. In the United States in 1919, they agreed, the purpose of money was to realize the promises of life. When Gatsby says, in his famous remark, that Daisy's voice sounds like money, we should read him sympathetically enough to understand, as Arthur Mizener has pointed out, that he is not saying that he loves money or that he loves both Daisy and money, but that he loves what the possession of money has done for Daisy's charming voice. And yet after we have said this, we must also say that Daisy Buchanan, because of her money, is seen at last as a false woman and Gatsby as a simple boy from the provinces who has not been able to tell gilt from real gold. The

circumstances of the Fitzgeralds' courtship and marriage seem fabulous—in the narrow sense of that word—because they often seem to suggest for us in outline the complex stories of women and marriage and money that Fitzgerald kept returning to in his fiction.

Fitzgerald was as fully aware of the power of women over men as D. H. Lawrence was, but in a different way. In his journal he once made a note that "Men get to be a mixture of the charming mannerisms of the women they have known." In Fitzgerald's fiction the villain has "animal magnetism" and masculinity but in the end he is stupid about women and treats them like whores. The Fitzgerald hero has softer qualities. "His mannerisms were all girls' mannerisms," he noted in plans for what sounds like a characteristic Fitzgerald hero, "rather gentle considerations got from [—] girls, or restrained and made masculine, a trait that, far from being effeminate, gave him a sort of Olympian stature that, in its all-kindness and consideration, was masculine and feminine alike." The men in his fiction are often, as he was, astonished by the fearlessness and recklessness of women. They are also finally made aware of the deceitfulness and moral complacency of many women. Jordan Baker in *The Great Gatsby* and Baby Warren in *Tender Is the Night*, for example, are studies of mercenary American women as dangerous to men as classical sorceresses. Daisy Buchanan and Nicole Warren are fatally irresponsible human beings. All his critics have noticed Fitzgerald's ability to project himself into women's lives. Near the end of his life, when he had decided to see the story of *The Last Tycoon* through the eyes of Cecilia Brady, age twenty-five, he wrote to his editor, "Cecilia is the narrator because I think I know exactly how such a person would react to my story."

To understand Fitzgerald's life and his stories of love and marriage we must be prepared to accept the tragic love plot strongly implied in his biography: he so built himself into Zelda Fitzgerald's life that when in 1930 her life went down, her fall brought him down as well. From Rome during the winter of 1924-25 at the peak of his pleasure over having written *The Great Gatsby,* he wrote to John Peale Bishop: "The cheerfulest things in my life are first Zelda and second the hope that my book has something extraordinary about it. I want to be extravagantly admired again. Zelda and I sometimes indulge in terrible four day rows that always start with a drinking party but we're still enormously in love and about the only truly happily married people I know." This was the Fitzgerald marriage at the height of its turbulent career. In 1933 after Zelda's first severe illness and while they were living quietly and Scott Fitzgerald was making a valiant stand against alcoholism, he characterized their life together in far different terms. "We have a good way of living, basically, for us; we got through a lot and have some way to go; our united front is less a romance than a categorical imperative and when you criticize it in terms of a bum world . . . [it] seems to negate on purpose both past effort and future hope. . . ." The more knowledge we have of the Fitzgeralds' marriage, the less his choice of those strong words "categorical imperative" surprises us. Their married life was a continual source of both the "romance" and the moral education out of which his best fiction came.

The novel with which Fitzgerald won Zelda, *This Side of Paradise,* is usually praised for qualities that pin it closely to an exact moment in American life. Later readers are apt to come to it with the anticipation of an archaeologist approaching an interesting ruin. Its publication is always considered to be the event that ushered in the Jazz Age. Glenway Wescott, writing for his and Fitzgerald's generation, said that it had "haunted the decade like a song, popular but perfect." Social historians have pointed out that the college boys of the early twenties really read it. There have been public arguments as to whether or not the petting part first occurred when Fitzgerald's novel said it did or two years earlier. Anyone reading the novel with such interests will not be entirely disappointed. One of the responsibilities it assumes, especially in its first half, is to make the hero, Amory Blaine, report like a cultural spy from inside his generation. "None of the Victorian mothers—and most of the mothers were Victorian—had any idea how casually their daughters were accustomed to be kissed." "The 'belle' had become the 'flirt,' the 'flirt' had become the 'baby vamp.'" "Amory saw girls doing things that even in his memory would have been impossible: eating three-o'clock, after-dance suppers in impossible cafés, talking of every side of life with an air half of earnestness, half of mockery, yet with a furtive excitement that Amory considered stood for a real moral let-down." The "moral let-down" enjoyed by the postwar generation has given the work its reputation for scandal as well as for social realism.

Today, the novel's young libertines, both male and female, would not shock a schoolgirl. Amory Blaine turns out to be a conspicuous moralist who takes the responsibility of kissing very seriously and disapproves of affairs with chorus girls. (He has no scruples, it must be said, against going on a three-week drunk when his girl breaks off their engagement.) At the end of the story he is ennobled by an act of self-sacrifice in an Atlantic City bedroom that no one would admire more than a Victorian mother. For modern readers it is probably better to take for granted the usefulness of *This Side of Paradise* for social historians and to admire from the distance of another age the obviously wholesome morality of the hero. Neither of these is the quality that saves the novel for a later time. What Fitzgerald is really showing is how a young American of his generation discovers what sort of figure he wants to cut, what modes of conduct, gotten out of books as well as out of a keen sense of his contemporaries, he wants to imitate. The flapper and her boy friend do not actually pet behind the closed doors of the smoking room. They talk, and each one says to the other, unconvincingly, "Tell me about yourself. What do you feel?" Meaning, "Tell me about myself. How do I feel?" The real story of *This Side of Paradise* is a report on a young man's emotional readiness for life.

The only interesting morality it presents is the implied morality that comes as a part of his feelings when the hero distinguishes, or fails to distinguish, between an honest and a dishonest emotion. The highly self-conscious purpose of telling Amory Blaine's story was, one suspects, to help Fitzgerald to discover who he really was by looking into the eyes of a girl— there are four girls—or into the mirror of himself that his college contemporaries made. And the wonder of it is that such a self-conscious piece of autobiography could be imagined, presented, and composed as a best-selling novel by a young man of twenty-three.

The novel is very uneven, and full of solemn attempts at abstract thought on literature, war, and socialism. It has vitality and freshness only in moments, and these are always moments of feeling. Fitzgerald said of this first novel many years later, "A lot of people thought it was a fake, and perhaps it was, and a lot of others thought it was a lie, which it was not." It offers the first evidence of Fitzgerald's possession of the gift necessary for a novelist who, like him, writes from so near his own bones, the talent that John Peale Bishop has described as "the rare faculty of being able to experience romantic and ingenuous emotions and a half hour later regard them with satiric detachment." The ingenuous emotions most necessary to the success of *This Side of Paradise* are vanity and all the self-regarding sentiments experienced during first love and the first trials of pride. The satire visited upon them is often as delicate and humorous as in this picture of Amory at a moment of triumphant egoism: "As he put in his studs he realized that he was enjoying life as he would probably never enjoy it again. Everything was hallowed by the haze of his own youth. He had arrived, abreast of the best of his generation at Princeton. He was in love and his love was returned. Turning on all the lights, he looked at himself in the mirror, trying to find in his own face the qualities that made him see more clearly than the great crowd of people, that made him decide firmly, and able to influence and follow his own will. There was little in his life now that he would have changed. . . . Oxford might have been a bigger field."

The ideas in the novel, unlike the tributes paid to a life of feeling, have the foreign country of origin and the importer's labels still on them. Edmund Wilson said *This Side of Paradise* was not really about anything. "Intellectually it amounts to little more than a gesture —a gesture of indefinite revolt." Toward the end of the novel Fitzgerald's normally graceful sentences begin to thicken and "sword-like pioneering personalities, Samuel Butler, Renan and Voltaire," are called in to add the weight of their names to Amory's reflections on the hypocrisy of his elders. The best pages of the novel come early, where Fitzgerald was remembering in marvelous detail the scenes at Newman School and Princeton. Later in his life he would always find it easy to return to those adolescent years, when feelings were all in all. Bishop once accused him of taking seventeen as his norm and believing that after that year life began to fall away from perfection. Fitzgerald replied, "If you make it fifteen I will agree with you."

The Fitzgerald novel, then, began in his acute awareness of a current American style of young life and in his complete willingness to use his own experience as if it were typical. The charm of his first stories and novels is simply the charm of shared vanity and enthusiasm for oneself as an exceptional person. Fitzgerald often persuades us that he was the one sensitive person there—on the country club porch or in a New York street—the first time something happened, or at the very height of the season. And when this ability to exploit his life began to succeed beyond his dreams, the only next step he could think of was to use it harder.

His success arrived almost overnight: 1920 was the *annus mirabilis.* In that year, the *Saturday Evening Post* published six of his stories, *Smart Set* five, and *Scribner's* two. In 1919 he had made $879 by writing; in 1920 he made $18,850 from his novel, from magazine stories and essays, and from the rights to two stories sold to the movies. His success with the *Saturday Evening Post* and the movies suggests how quickly he had discovered the formulas for popular fiction and the big money. Within fifteen years between 1919 and 1934 Fitzgerald earned, he estimated, four hundred thousand dollars, most of it writing for magazines and the movies. From the beginning of his success Fitzgerald was quite aware of the temptations of commercial writing and how well adapted he was to succumb to them. The question as to whether the conflict between the use and misuse of his talent opened the crack in Fitzgerald's self-respect that at last killed him as a novelist has been argued by many of his friends. Dos Passos spoke at his death for those who thought it did. Fitzgerald had invented for

their generation, he said, the writing career based on the popular magazines and he was "tragically destroyed by his own invention."

Fitzgerald's struggle with his literary conscience is often apparent in his letters and journals. He wrote Maxwell Perkins, his editor at Scribners, that he knew he had "a faculty for being cheap, if I want to indulge that." When in the winter of 1923–24 he needed money, concentrated on producing commercial stories for *Hearst's International,* and made $17,000, he wrote Edmund Wilson that "it was all trash, and it nearly broke my heart." But he also had another way of imagining himself: "I'm a workman of letters, a professional," he would say in this mood, "I know when to write and when to stop writing." He wanted to be both a good writer and a popular one. His high living, he knew, depended on magazine money and it is significant that he devoted most of his time to short fiction during those years between 1926 and 1931 when his life became most disordered and the completion of a new novel came hard. Yet he thought of himself most proudly as a novelist. His most poignant confession of a failure to be true to his talent he expressed to his daughter six months before he died: "Doubt and worry—you are as crippled by them as I am by my inability to handle money or my self-indulgences of the past. . . . What little I've accomplished has been by the most laborious and uphill work, and I wish now I'd *never* relaxed or looked back—but said at the end of *The Great Gatsby*: 'I've found my line—from now on this comes first. This is my immediate duty—without this I am nothing.' "

But the final record shows that he wrote four complete novels and more than 150 short stories. Forty-six of them he chose to print in four separate collections. In an ambitious set of plans for future productions that he once projected, there were to be in his collected works seven novels and also seven volumes of short stories. He was quite aware of his achievements as a short-story writer, and twentieth-century American writing would be much poorer if it lacked six, at least, of Fitzgerald's stories which are brilliant, and perhaps thirty to forty more which are full of finely observed life.

The first collection of Fitzgerald's stories in 1921 was timed by Scribners to profit from the vogue of *This Side of Paradise*. It was called *Flappers and Philosophers*. A second collection, *Tales of the Jazz Age*, was published a year later in the wake of his second novel, *The Beautiful and Damned*. The nineteen stories in the two collections represent with more variety and perhaps more immediacy than the two first novels the manners and morals that have come to compose, at least in the minds of later historians, the Jazz Age. In 1922 we catch a glimpse of Fitzgerald imagining his relation to his Jazz Age public when he writes his editor about the second book of stories: "It will be bought by *my own personal public*, that is by the countless flappers and college kids who think I am a sort of oracle." The various mysteries that the young oracle was making known to his followers may be observed in two slight, early stories, "The Jelly-Bean" and "Bernice Bobs Her Hair." They both follow conventional formulas of popular fiction, but the young people in the stories act out a new version of the American pastoral. The man known as the Jelly-Bean is a good-natured garage mechanic in a sleepy Georgia town, a son of one of the town's first families now fallen on evil days. He has been awakened to his true responsibilities by the kiss of a young flapper and Belle Dame sans Merci named Nancy Lamar. "With the awakening of his emotions, his first perception was a sense of futility, a dull ache at the utter grayness of his life." With this Keatsian strain life deepens for an American Jelly-Bean. Nancy is the story's chief excitement. She

drinks corn liquor, shoots craps with the men after a country club dance, and, in the story's best scene, wades through a pool of gasoline tapped from a car to remove a wad of chewing gum from the sole of her dancing slipper. Nancy lives with her dream of Lady Diana Manners. "Like to have boat. Like to sail out on a silver lake, say the Thames, for instance. Have champagne and caviare sandwiches along. Have about eight people." Bernice, who bobbed her hair on a dare, comes from another American Forest of Arden, Eau Claire, Wisconsin. She is an innocent who has to learn by rote a "line" for attracting boys—the same line that Fitzgerald taught his sister Annabel once when he despaired of her chances of becoming Lady Diana Manners of St. Paul. Fitzgerald had observed two provincial societies in Montgomery, Alabama, and St. Paul, and we can watch him exploiting like a veteran novelist details of types and manners in these two stories and in "The Ice Palace." Zelda Sayre posed as the model for a southern flapper in "The Ice Palace" and Fitzgerald used their own situation to imagine the shocks that might be in store for a lively southern girl among the likeable Babbitts of Minnesota. All these stories, as well as that Hollywood natural "The Off-Shore Pirate," were imagined from a young girl's dreams of a glamorous life. "Dalyrimple Goes Wrong" examines from a young ex-soldier's point of view the deceits of the world of business and politics as it is being run by a hypocritical older generation. "The Lees of Happiness" and "The Cut-Glass Bowl" imagine American domestic tragedies, lives that go down in "the flight of time and the end of beauty and unfulfilled desire." There is more pathos in these Jazz Age stories than one might expect.

Two of the stories in the first collections are important, "May Day" for what it attempts and "The Diamond as Big as the Ritz" for what it achieves. "May Day" was probably a discarded beginning to a novel about New York. May Day 1919 was the exact day, Fitzgerald said later, when the Jazz Age began. The story is planned to carry more weight than the usual early Fitzgerald story. Using three plots with intertwining action, like a Dos Passos chronicle novel, it opens with an economic motif, the Manhattan crowds staring greedily at the glowing contents of shopwindows, and in other ways gives evidence of Fitzgerald's willingness to steal some pages from the American naturalists. The mob scenes and the two "primitives," the foot-loose soldiers looking for whiskey, may have come not from Fitzgerald's observation but from the novels of Norris and Dreiser. But if these are the story's weak spots they are also marks of its ambition. Fitzgerald wanted to use the whole loud and anarchic world of Manhattan as the background of his forlorn state in the spring of 1919 when he was an ex-lieutenant writing advertising copy, broke, and heartsick at the loss of his girl. The portrait he draws of Gordon Sterrett, in the midst of the big money, desperately poor and depending on alcohol, shows how intensely he could project fears for his own failures—and perhaps how fascinated he would always be with the drama of failure. "I can't stand being poor," Gordon says. "You seem sort of bankrupt—morally as well as financially," says his rich Yale classmate. "Don't they usually go together?" Gordon asks. At the big dance at Delmonico's Gordon gets drunk and tells a girl how it feels to go to pieces. "Things have been snapping inside of me for four months like little hooks on a dress, and it's about to come off when a few more hooks go." Metaphors of bankruptcy and of coming unhooked are going to turn up later when Fitzgerald contemplates his own sense of failure.

"The Diamond as Big as the Ritz" is a satirical American fantasy that comes as squarely out of the bedazzled daydreams of the twenties as Hawthorne's wry fables came out of the 1840's when an earlier American generation had Utopian dreams of human nature. The young visitor to the diamond mountain kingdom, John T. Unger, from a little midwestern town named Hades, watches his host, Mr. Braddock Washington, the richest man in the world, turn at last into a madman who believes he can bribe God with his money. But young Unger has not learned much. After the diamond mountain has blown up he hates to return to his middle-class Hades with an heiress and no money. ". . . turn out your pocket and let's see what jewels you brought along. If you made a good selection we three ought to live comfortably all the rest of our lives." At the age of twenty-five Fitzgerald had written a highly imaginative folk tale of modern American life.

The Beautiful and Damned was an attempt to write a dramatic novel about a promising American life that never got anywhere; *The Flight of the Rocket,* it was once called. It was the first and least convincing of what were going to be three studies of American failures. As he started the novel in August 1920, Fitzgerald wrote to his publisher that his subject was ". . . the life of Anthony Patch between his 25th and 33rd years (1913–1921). He is one of those many with the tastes and weaknesses of an artist but with no actual creative inspiration. How he and his beautiful young wife are wrecked on the shoals of dissipation is told in the story." Anthony Patch, unlike Amory Blaine, was to be placed at some distance from Fitzgerald's life. He is an American aristocrat, the only heir of a multimillionaire grandfather, "Cross" Patch, whose money goes back to the Gilded Age but whose hypocritic Puritanism is of the kind that Mencken was excoriating. Anthony's story opens as if he were going to be offered up on the smoking altars of

American vulgarity and commercialism. After Harvard he spends an aesthetic year in Rome, then returns to a comfortable apartment on 52nd Street, to his small society of bachelor friends and an income of seven thousand a year left him by his mother. Anthony is not a spoiled rich boy. He is certainly not American Youth in revolt. He is simply a graceful outsider with no ambitions but to be a beleaguered gentleman, to despise his grandfather, and, he hopes, to stay unmarried.

It is hard to see where Fitzgerald is going to go with Anthony except into amiable eccentricity. He has no character except his vague cynicism, a smarting sensibility, and the seven thousand a year. But then he falls in love with Gloria Gilbert and Fitzgerald's novel begins to deepen. As a lover and a husband, and soon as a failure, inexplicable but pathetic, Anthony Patch becomes a genuine fictional character, if not a very clear one. His reality comes, as the reality of all Fitzgerald's unhappy heroes will come, out of the expression of a strong romantic will. All he has he invests in his life with Gloria. The final clue to their failure is never given us. It is not just the eternal enmity between their aspirations to beauty and the hungry generations that tread them down, though this is part of it. They live too high, waste their money, and burn themselves out. That they are simply lost from the start is almost assumed. The morning after one of their desperately drunken parties, they decide never again to give a damn, "Not to be sorry, not to loose one cry of regret, to live according to a clear code of honor toward each other, and to seek the moment's happiness as feverishly and persistently as possible." But Gloria is not enough of a Hemingway character, and Anthony is not at all one, and the code does not work. Gloria, whose conception owes something to Fitzgerald's admiration for Mencken's

book on Nietzsche, begins to develop ". . . her ancient abhorrence, a conscience."

The Beautiful and Damned is a novel of mood rather than a novel of character. The misfortunes of Anthony and Gloria are forced in the plot, but the mood in places is desperate. Fitzgerald does not know what to do with his hero and heroine in the end but make them suffer. The novel will place no blame, either on the nature of things or on the injustices of society. Anthony and Gloria are finally willing to accept all the unhappy consequences as if they had earned them, but the reader has stopped believing in the logic of consequences in this novel long before. The failure of *The Beautiful and Damned* suggests where the soft spots are going to occur in Fitzgerald's art of the novel, in the presentation of character and motivation. With Anthony Patch, Fitzgerald assumes that if he has displayed a man's sensibility in some detail he has achieved the study of a tragic character. The "tragedies" suffered by Anthony and Gloria, Fitzgerald's members of the lost generation, lack a moral context as the characters in *The Sun Also Rises* do not. Fitzgerald's fears of his own weaknesses and the excesses that, according to his troubled conscience, he and Zelda were learning to like too easily, endowed the parable of the Patches with moral weight and urgency for its author; but the reader had to invent the worth of the moral struggle for himself.

The Beautiful and Damned was a commercially successful novel, despite a mixed reception from reviewers. It sold 43,000 copies the first year after its serialization in the *Metropolitan Magazine*. Its success to some extent was due to well-circulated rumors that it was autobiographical, as indeed it was in many places. Zelda Fitzgerald, in a review of the novel for the *New York Tribune*, confessed she recognized parts of her diary and some personal letters in the book. "In fact, Mr. Fitzgerald—I believe that is how he spells his name —seems to believe that plagiarism begins at home." Recognizable portraits of the Fitzgeralds appeared on the book's dust jacket. In June 1922 an essay on contemporary life in the *New York Times* recommended that remarkable book, *The Beautiful and Damned*, to anyone who wanted to understand what went on during a typical drunken party in prohibition America.

Most of Anthony and Gloria's parties occur in a cottage in Connecticut like the one the Fitzgeralds rented in Westport in May 1920 soon after their marriage. But they were too restless for suburban Connecticut and moved back to New York. In the summer of 1921 they were in England and France, and by August they had settled in St. Paul, where their only child, a daughter, was born in October. They lived in St. Paul for a year after that and Fitzgerald wrote stories, began and discarded a novel with a Catholic and midwestern hero, and finished a first version of his comedy, *The Vegetable*. (It is a pretty bad play which failed on its tryout, two years later.) St. Paul was too provincial for more than a short residence and by October 1922 they were living in their most memorable house, a large one in Great Neck, Long Island. One powerful image of their life on Long Island has entered American folk history through the pages in *The Great Gatsby* which describe Gatsby's parties and the people who came to them. In the Great Neck house the Fitzgeralds' life reached its expensive culmination. They spent $36,000 during their first year and then Fitzgerald wrote an essay for the *Saturday Evening Post* to show how they had done it. They entertained their literary set, which included Edmund Wilson, Ring Lardner, H. L. Mencken, and George Jean Nathan, and

periodically Fitzgerald tried to stop drinking and get on with his new novel. In the spring of 1924 they decided that they must begin to save money and that the south of France was the place to do it. By June they were established in a villa at St. Raphaël, on the Riviera, and in November Fitzgerald sent the manuscript of *The Great Gatsby* off to New York. It was published in April 1925.

The Great Gatsby has been discussed and admired as much as any twentieth-century American novel, probably to the disadvantage of Fitzgerald's other fiction. None of its admirers finds it easy to explain why Fitzgerald at this point in his career should have written a novel of such perfect art—though it is usually conceded that he never reached such heights again. His discovery of Conrad and James is sometimes given credit for teaching him a new sense of proportion and control over form. But *The Great Gatsby* does so many things well that "influences" will not explain them all. The real mystery of how the novel was conceived and written may have to do with how the undisciplined life of a Long Island and St. Raphaël playboy could yield such moments of detachment and impersonality as this novel required. If we can trust Fitzgerald's backward glance from 1934 when he was writing an introduction to the Modern Library edition of *Gatsby*, it was a matter of keeping his "artistic conscience" "pure." "I had just re-read Conrad's preface to *The Nigger*, and I had recently been kidded half haywire by critics who felt that my material was such as to preclude all dealing with mature persons in a mature world." Also in 1934 he wrote his friend Bishop that he thought of *Gatsby* as his *Henry Esmond* and *Tender Is the Night* as his *Vanity Fair*: "The dramatic novel has cannons [Fitzgerald's spelling was notoriously unreliable] quite different from the philosophical, now called the psychological novel. One is a kind of *tour de force* and the other a confession of faith. It would be like comparing a sonnet sequence with an epic." Fitzgerald's language of literary sources and literary analysis always has an innocent ring. It is probably best to remember the language he used when he wrote his editor his plans for a new novel. " I want to write something *new*, something extraordinary and beautiful and simple and intricately patterned."

The Great Gatsby is worthy of all these adjectives. It was new for Fitzgerald to succeed in placing a novel of contemporary manners at such a distance from himself. Telling the story through a Conradian narrator, who was half inside and half outside the action, prevented the errors of self-identification he had fallen into with Anthony Patch. And Gatsby is not allowed to be a character who invites questions about his credibility as Anthony did. He is a figure from a romance who has wandered into a novel, the archetypal young man from the provinces who wants to become Lord Mayor, and to wake the sleeping beauty with a kiss. "Also you are right about Gatsby being blurred and patchy. I never at any one time saw him clear myself," Fitzgerald wrote a friend. But in a tour de force it is the power behind the conception that matters, and Fitzgerald was himself so sure of Gatsby's essential and primitive springs of action that he has required us to share his belief in Gatsby or reject the whole affair. "That's the whole burden of this novel," he wrote in a letter, "—the loss of those illusions that give such color to the world so that you don't care whether things are true or false as long as they partake of the magical glory."

The short novel tells the story of how James Gatz, a poor farm boy from North Dakota, imitates the example of Benjamin Franklin and other proven American moralists and rises at last to be a rich and powerful criminal named Jay Gatsby. Along the way, when he is an anonymous young lieutenant in a Kentucky training camp, when American "society" is open to him for the first time, he meets and marries in his mind, in an act of absolute commitment, a lovely southern girl named Daisy Fay. But he has to leave Daisy behind when he goes to France; and he loses her to a rich American from Chicago, Yale, and Wall Street. The only course conceivable to him when he returns is to pursue Daisy and in the American way to convince her of her error, to show he is worthy of her by the only symbols available to them both, a large house with a swimming pool, dozens of silk shirts, and elaborate parties. But Daisy believes in the symbols themselves, and not in the purer reality which (for Jay Gatsby) they only faintly embody. She loses her nerve and sacrifices her lover to the world.

Gatsby's mingled dream of love and money, and the iron strength of his romantic will, make up the essence of the fable, but the art of its telling is full of astonishing tricks. To make the rise and fall of a gentleman gangster an image for the modern history of the Emersonian spirit of America was an audacious thing to attempt, but Fitzgerald got away with it. His own romantic spirit felt deeply what an Englishman has called the "myth-hunger" of Americans, our modern need to "create a manageable past out of an immense present." The poignant effect of the final, highly complex image of the novel, when Gatsby's dream and the American dream are identified, shows how deeply saturated with feeling Fitzgerald's historical imagination was. From his own American life he knew that with his generation the midwesterner had become the typical American and had returned from the old frontier to the East with a new set of dreams—about money. No reader needs to worry about Fitzgerald's complicated attraction to the glamorous rich in this novel if he puts his trust in the midwestern narrator, Nick Carraway. Nick guides us safely through all the moral confusions of the wealthy East and leads us in the end back to the provinces where the fundamental decencies depend upon a social order of families who have lived in the same house for three generations.

The success of Nick as a device for controlling the tone of the narrative is remarkable. It is the quality of his response to Gatsby that at crucial moments compels our suspension of disbelief. The tranquil tone of his recollected feelings gives the story its serenity and tempts some of its admirers to compare it to a pastoral poem. Nick is everywhere he is needed, but he never intrudes on a presented scene. He is the butt of our ironies and his own. The range of the story's ironic intentions is very wide. They encompass the wonderfully comic vulgarity of Myrtle Wilson, Tom Buchanan's mistress, as well as Daisy's almost irresistible charm. Fitzgerald's imagination plays with wit and perfect taste over the suggestive details of the story's surface: cuff buttons, a supper of cold chicken and two bottles of ale, Gatsby's shirts, and the names of the people who came to his parties. The whole novel is an imaginative feat that managed to get down the sensational display of postwar America's big money, and to include moral instructions on how to count the cost of it all. *The Great Gatsby* has by this time entered into the national literary mind as only some seemingly effortless works of the imagination can. We can see better now than even some of Fitzgerald's appreciative first reviewers that he had seized upon an important set of symbols for showing that time had run out for one image of the American ego. Poor Gatsby had been, in the novel's terms, deceived into an ignorance of his real greatness by the American world that had for its great men Tom Buchanan and Meyer Wolfsheim, the Wall Street millionaire and his colleague the racket-

eer. The story does not pretend to know more than this, that Americans will all be the poorer for the profanation and the loss of Gatsby's deluded imagination.

The principal fact in Fitzgerald's life between his twenty-eighth and thirty-fourth year was his inability to write a new novel. He seems to have known all along the kind of novel he wanted to write: in his terms it was to be the "philosophical, now called the psychological novel." He began a novel called *The World's Fair*, and in 1929 when he abandoned it he had written over twenty thousand words in the history of a failed life quite different from Gatsby's. The new hero was to be a bright young movie-maker named Francis Melarky who comes to the Riviera on a vacation from Hollywood and there in a fit of anger murders his possessive mother. "In a certain sense my plot is not unlike Dreiser's in the American Tragedy," he told his editor Perkins. In 1929 he dropped the matricide plot, and changed his title to *The Drunkard's Holiday*. Then after Zelda became psychotic in 1930 he had a different kind of American tragedy to put at the center. The new novel, like *The Beautiful and Damned*, was to arise out of his own life. The pathos inherent in these years is that he seemed fated to create his own agony, and study it as if it wasn't his, before he could use it in the confessional novel he felt driven to write. Looking back on his life near the end of it, he saw what he had done and wrote to his daughter, then a freshman at Vassar, the coolest summation of the Fitzgerald legend ever made: "I am not a great man but sometimes I think the impersonal and objective quality of my talent and the sacrifices of it, in pieces, to preserve its essential value has some sort of epic grandeur. Anyhow after hours I nurse myself with delusions of that sort."

If we can accept Fitzgerald's self-analysis it

only remains to be astonished at the terrible cost of preserving the "essential value" of his literary talent. Between the publication of *Gatsby* and the final return to America in 1931 the Fitzgeralds moved between Europe and America as if they could not find a home anywhere. In the south of France or in Paris Fitzgerald had even less control over his extravagance than he had in America. The sales of *Gatsby* were not up to the sales of his first two novels, but stage and screen rights brought him over $30,000. Despite yearly incomes that were always over $20,000 and often nearly $30,000, Fitzgerald came home in 1931 with hardly any money. These are the years of the steady production of magazine fiction and articles. Between 1925 and 1932 he published fifty-six stories, most of them in the *Saturday Evening Post*. But, as Malcolm Cowley has said, the critics did not read the *Post*, and Fitzgerald's reputation began the decline from which it never recovered in his lifetime.

The best stories of those years he selected for two collections, *All the Sad Young Men* (1926) and *Taps at Reveille* (1935). Two recently published collections, *The Stories of F. Scott Fitzgerald*, edited by Malcolm Cowley, and *Afternoon of an Author*, edited by Arthur Mizener, have assured the modern availability of all the good magazine fiction of Fitzgerald's last fifteen years. One of the best stories in *All the Sad Young Men* is "Winter Dreams," a Jay Gatsby-Daisy Buchanan story set in St. Paul and told as if this time Gatsby had wisely given up the enchantress and learned to settle for less. But Dexter Green's dreams, like Gatsby's, are more powerful than he knows. With their loss he has lost his capacity to love anything, or even to feel anything strongly again. "Absolution" is another early story which owes its strength to the conception of Gatsby. It is a provocative sketch of the boyhood days of

James Gatz in the Red River Valley of North Dakota. Fitzgerald published it as a separate story after he decided to preserve the mystery of Gatsby's early years. "The Rich Boy," written in 1926, is by common consent one of the half-dozen best Fitzgerald stories. Anson Hunter's privileged New York world is solidly established because Fitzgerald seems so intent on understanding it. The concentration of good American material in this thirty-page story might have provided a lesser novelist—provided he could have understood Anson Hunter—with the substance of a full-length fiction. The story's success seems to justify Fitzgerald's interest in the lives of the rich. He once underlined for his Hollywood friend, Sheilah Graham, a sentence from an Arnold essay, "The question, *how to live*, is itself a moral idea," and in the margin he commented, "This is Arnold at his best, absolutely without preachment." It is entirely appropriate to associate Arnold's Victorian moral seriousness with the quality of Fitzgerald's mind when he wrote "The Rich Boy."

During three years beginning in 1928 he sent the *Saturday Evening Post* a series of fourteen stories out of his boyhood and young manhood. The first eight were based on a portrait of himself as Basil Duke Lee. The last six were built around Josephine, the portrait of the magnetic seventeen-year-old girl of his first love affair. It was characteristic of Fitzgerald to relive his youth during the frustrated and unhappy days of his early thirties. His characters always know how much of their most private emotional life depends upon what Anson Hunter calls the "brightest, freshest, rarest hours" which protect "that superiority he cherished in his heart." Fitzgerald was becoming acquainted with real despondency. His inability to write serious fiction sent him into desperate moods and touched off public acts of violence that ended in nights in jail. In 1928 he wrote Perkins from France, "If you see anyone I know tell 'em I hate 'em all, him especially. Never want to see 'em again. Why shouldn't I go crazy? My father is a moron and my mother is a neurotic, half insane with pathological nervous worry. Between them they haven't and never have had the brains of Calvin Coolidge. If I knew anything I'd be the best writer in America."

What he knew was his own divided life, and after Zelda's breakdown he began to write the stories of self-appraisal and self-accusation that led up to *Tender Is the Night*. In the autumn of 1930 the *Post* published the first of them, "One Trip Abroad," a Jamesian fable of the deterioration of two American innocents in Europe. Fitzgerald once wrote in his notebook, "France was a land, England was a people, but America . . . was a willingness of the heart." Nelson and Nicole Kelly come to Europe with money, a pair of small talents, his for painting, hers for singing, and the naive hope that they will find somewhere the good life. But willingness of the heart is not enough. They are not serious and self-sufficient, their American vitality makes them restless, and they become dependent on people, parties, and alcohol. Their first sensitiveness to each other hardens into occasional violence, and they end up in the sanatoriums and rest hotels of Switzerland, " a country where very few things begin, but many things end." A better story, "Babylon Revisited" is a compassionate but morally strict portrait of a reformed American drunk who has to confront his complicity in his wife's death during a quarrel in Paris some years before. He wants desperately to get back his young daughter from her aunt and uncle's care, and he would give anything to "jump back a whole generation and trust in character again. . . ." But Charlie Wales cannot escape the furies from his past. He can only learn to face them with personal dignity.

Fitzgerald's big novel *Tender Is the Night* was written in its final form while Fitzgerald was living very close to his wife's illness. She was being treated by doctors in Baltimore—and writing her novel, *Save Me the Waltz*, to tell her version of their lives—and Fitzgerald and their daughter were making a home for her to return to in the countryside nearby. During 1932 and 1933 her health seemed to improve and he finished the manuscript. Then, early in 1934 when he was reading proofs of the novel, she had her most severe breakdown, and for the next six years, except for short periods of stability, she lived her life in hospitals. Their life together was over. It is astonishing that, written under such emotional pressures, *Tender Is the Night* is such a wise and objective novel as it is.

On the simplest level, it is the story of an American marriage. Dr. Richard Diver, a young American psychiatrist, practicing in Switzerland in 1919, falls in love with his patient, Nicole Warren of Chicago, knowing quite well that her transference to him is part of the pattern of her schizophrenia. By consecrating—to use Fitzgerald's word—himself to their marriage, she is finally cured but he is ruined. To imagine Nicole, Fitzgerald could start from Zelda in her illness and partial recovery. But his heroine is also depicted as a beautiful princess of a reigning American family, whose wealth is the source of a monstrous arrogance: Nicole's trauma was the result of her father's incestuous attack on her. Dick Diver is stigmatized with Fitzgerald's understanding of his own weaknesses. He suffers a kind of moral schizophrenia, for his precarious balance comes to depend on Nicole's need for him. After his morale has cracked he still tries to play the role of a confident man, and out of sheer emotional exhaustion he fades at last into the tender night, where he hopes nothing will ever be required of him again.

A weakness charged against the novel by some readers is that the causes of Dick Diver's deterioration are left unclear. Was it the careless, rich Nicole Warren who destroyed him, or his own bad judgment in choosing her? The only explanation the novel offers is Dick's willful self-sacrifice: he gave more generously of himself than any man could afford to. One of the reasons Dick is not coherent is that the quality of his devotion to Nicole—"a wild submergence of the soul, a dipping of all colors into an obscuring dye," it is called—is of the same degree of abandonment as Gatsby's devotion to Daisy. But Dick's romantic soul must be understood "psychologically" as Gatsby's did not need to be; the complexity of the task Fitzgerald set himself is one source of the novel's weakness. Another is Fitzgerald's use of the young movie star, Rosemary Hoyt, as the novel's Nick Carraway. Through her impressionable eyes we first see the Divers and their circle on the summer Riviera before we know the history of the marriage. To begin this long novel dramatically, as he had *Gatsby*, yields some exciting results, but Fitzgerald came to believe it was a mistake not to tell the events of the story chronologically. *Tender Is the Night* has had recent printings in both versions. Fitzgerald's readers can decide for themselves.

Notwithstanding these faults, *Tender Is the Night* is Fitzgerald's weightiest novel. It is full of scenes that stay alive with each rereading, the cast of characters is the largest he ever collected, and the awareness of human variety in the novel's middle distance gives it a place among those American novels which attempt the full narrative mode. Arnold's assumption that how to live is itself a moral idea provides the central substance of the novel. The society

Dick has chosen is a lost one, but Dick must function as if he is not lost. To bring happiness to people, including his wife, is to help them fight selfishness and egotism, to allow their human imaginations to function. To fill in the background of a leisured class with human dignity does not seem a futile mission to Dr. Diver until he fails. For Fitzgerald's hero "charm always had an independent existence"; he calls it "courageous grace." A life of vital response is the only version of the moral life Fitzgerald could imagine, and when Dr. Diver hears the "interior laughter" begin at the expense of his human decency he walks away. He returns to America and his life fades away in small towns in upstate New York as he tries unsuccessfully to practice medicine again.

Dick Diver is Fitzgerald's imagination of himself bereft of vitality, but also without his one strength of purpose, his devotion to literature. The poor reception of *Tender Is the Night* was a stiff blow to his confidence in himself as a writer when that confidence was about all he had left. Nearly all the influential critics discovered the same fault in the novel, that Fitzgerald was uncertain, and in the end unconvincing, about why Dick Diver fell to pieces. Fitzgerald could only fight back in letters to his friends by asking for a closer reading of his complex story. The novel sold 13,000 copies. His short stories in *Taps at Reveille,* the next year, were greeted by even more hostile reviews and the volume sold only a few thousand. For a writer who in 1925 had received letters of congratulation from Edith Wharton, T. S. Eliot, and Willa Cather, it was depressing to realize that during 1932 and 1933, while he was writing *Tender Is the Night,* the royalties paid for all his previous writing had totaled only fifty dollars. His indebtedness to his agent and his publisher began to grow as the prices paid for his stories went down.

And between 1934 and 1937 his daily life declined into the crippled state that is now known after his own description of it as "the crack-up." He first fell ill with tuberculosis, and then began to give in more frequently than ever before to alcohol and despondency. Twice before his fortieth birthday he attempted suicide. By 1937 at the age of forty-one he had recovered control sufficiently to accept a writing contract in Hollywood, where he could begin to pay off his debts, which by this time had grown to $40,000.

Fitzgerald's public analysis of his desperate condition, published in three essays in *Esquire* in the spring of 1936, will be read differently by different people. But some kind of public penance was probably a necessary part of the pattern of Fitzgerald's life. "You've got to sell your heart," he advised a young writer in 1938, and he had—from his first college writing to *Tender Is the Night*. "Forget your personal tragedy . . ." Hemingway wrote him in 1934 after reading *Tender Is the Night*. "You see, Bo, you're not a tragic character. Neither am I. All we are is writers and what we should do is write." Hemingway and Edmund Wilson both disapproved of Fitzgerald's confessions as bad strategy for a writer. The only explanation one can imagine Fitzgerald making to them is Gatsby's explanation, that it was only personal.

The crack-up essays have become classics, as well known as the best of Fitzgerald's short fiction. The spiritual lassitude they describe is attributed to the same "lesion of vitality" and "emotional bankruptcy" that Dick Diver and Anthony Patch and all Fitzgerald's sad young men suffer. Fitzgerald calls it becoming "identified with the objects of my horror and compassion." As Fitzgerald describes it here it closely resembles what in Coleridge's ode "Dejection" is called simply the loss of joy. The

process of its withdrawal from Coleridge as a power which he had drawn on too often he describes as stealing "From my own nature all the natural man." Fitzgerald was conscious of his relation to the English Romantics in his confession. He calls up the examples of Wordsworth and Keats to represent good writers who fought their way through the horrors of their lives. The loss of his natural human pieties that Fitzgerald felt he associated with a memory of "the beady-eyed men I used to see on the commuting train from Great Neck fifteen years back—men who didn't care whether the world tumbled into chaos tomorrow if it spared their houses." Fitzgerald's style was never more gracefully colloquial or his metaphors more natural and easy than in these *Esquire* pieces. "I was impelled to think. God, was it difficult! The moving about of great secret trunks." The grace of the prose has made some readers suspect that Fitzgerald is withholding the real ugliness of the experience, that he is simply imitating the gracefully guilty man in order to avoid the deeper confrontation of horror. But his language often rises above sentiment and pathos to the pure candor of a generous man who decided "There was to be no more giving of myself" and then, in writing it down, tried to give once more.

Once settled in Hollywood and in love with Miss Graham, Fitzgerald returned to the East only occasionally—and usually disastrously. He needed any strength he could muster to try to stay away from drinking and hold on to his contract as a movie writer. For a year and a half he commanded a salary of over a thousand dollars a week, and, given the breaks, he said, he could double that within two years. One of his breaks was Miss Graham, who helped him to live a quiet productive life for almost a year after they met. But late in 1938 his contract was not renewed and in February

1939 he drank himself out of a movie job in Hanover, New Hampshire, a disaster that Budd Schulberg has turned into a novel and a play, *The Disenchanted.* For several months in 1939 he was in a New York hospital but by July he was writing short stories again for *Esquire.* He wrote in all twenty-two stories in the eighteen months remaining to him, seventeen of them neat and comic little stories about a corrupt movie writer named Pat Hobby, and one little masterpiece, "The Lost Decade," a sardonic picture of a talented man who had been drunk for ten years.

During the last year of his life Fitzgerald wrote as hard as his depleted capacities allowed him on the novel he left half-finished at his death, *The Last Tycoon.* It is an impressive fragment. When it was published in 1941 many of Fitzgerald's literary contemporaries, including John Dos Passos and Edmund Wilson, called it the mature fulfillment of Fitzgerald's great talent, and a belated revaluation of Fitzgerald as a writer began.

The Last Tycoon had the mark of the thirties on it as surely as his early novels had the American boom as their principal theme. The subject was Hollywood as an industry and a society, but also as an American microcosm. Instead of drawing a deft impression of American society as he had in his earlier fiction, Fitzgerald now wanted to record it. The first hundred pages of the novel take us behind the doors of studios and executive offices in Hollywood with the authority of first-rate history. The history fastens on the last of the American barons, Hollywood's top producer, Monroe Stahr, and we watch him rule a complex industry and produce a powerful popular art form with such a dedication of intelligence and will that he becomes a symbol for a vanishing American grandeur of character and role. "Unlike *Tender Is the Night,*" Fitzgerald explained, "it is not the story of deterioration—

it is not depressing and not morbid in spite of the tragic ending. If one book could ever be 'like' another, I should say it is more 'like' *The Great Gatsby. . . .*" The plot was to show Stahr's fight for the cause of the powerful and responsible individual against Hollywood's labor gangsters and Communist writers. Violent action and melodrama were to carry the story, like a Dickens novel, to seats of power in Washington and New York. "Action is character," Fitzgerald reminded himself in one of his last notes on his novel's progress. The action is brilliantly conceived and economically executed. Fitzgerald's style is lean and clear. His power of letting his meanings emerge from incident was never more sharply displayed. At the center of his hero's last two years of life is an ill-starred love affair, like Fitzgerald's own, that comes too late and only reminds him of his lost first wife. But Fitzgerald kept his romantic ego in check in imagining Stahr. What obviously fascinated him was the creation of an American type upon whom responsibility and power had descended and who was committed to building something with his power, something that would last, even though it was only a brief scene in a movie.

It was an ironic and courageous image for Fitzgerald to cherish in the last days of his crippled life. He had not written order into his life, though he once noted wryly that he sometimes read his own books for advice. But his devotion to his writing up to the end shows how much his work flowed from his character as well as from his talent. It is hard in coming to terms with Fitzgerald to follow Lawrence's advice and learn to trust the tale, not the author. But if we succeed we shall learn that the aspects of himself that he continually made into the characters in his fiction are imaginatively re-created American lives. He often wrote that high order of self-revelation that reveals humanity.

Selected Bibliography

WORKS OF
F. SCOTT FITZGERALD

This Side of Paradise. New York: Scribners, 1920.

Flappers and Philosophers. New York: Scribners, 1921. (Contains "The Off-Shore Pirate," "The Ice Palace," "Head and Shoulders," "The Cut-Glass Bowl," "Bernice Bobs Her Hair," "Benediction," "Dalyrimple Goes Wrong," and "The Four Fists.")

The Beautiful and Damned. New York: Scribners, 1922.

Tales of the Jazz Age. New York: Scribners, 1922. (Contains "The Jelly-Bean," "The Camel's Back," "May Day," "Porcelain and Pink," "The Diamond as Big as the Ritz," "The Curious Case of Benjamin Button," "Tarquin of Cheapside," "O Russet Witch!" "The Lees of Happiness," "Mr. Icky," and "Jemina.")

The Vegetable, or From President to Postman. New York: Scribners, 1923.

The Great Gatsby. New York: Scribners, 1925.

All the Sad Young Men. New York: Scribners, 1926. (Contains "The Rich Boy," "Winter Dreams." "The Baby Party," "Absolution," "Rags Martin-Jones and the Pr-nce of W-les," "The Adjuster," "Hot and Cold Blood," "The Sensible Thing," and "Gretchen's Forty Winks.")

Tender Is The Night. New York: Scribners, 1934. 1934.

Taps at Reveille. New York: Scribners, 1935. (Contains Basil: 1. "The Scandal Detectives," 2. "The Freshest Boy," 3. "He Thinks He's Wonderful," 4. "The Captured Shadow," 5. "The Perfect Life"; Josephine: 1. "First Blood," 2. "A Nice Quiet Place," 3. "A Woman with a Past"; and "Crazy Sunday," "Two Wrongs," "The Night of Chancellorsville," "The Last of the Belles," "Majesty," "Family in the Wind," "A Short Trip Home," "One Interne," "The Fiend," and "Babylon Revisited.")

The Last Tycoon, edited by Edmund Wilson. New York: Scribners, 1941.

The Crack-Up, edited by Edmund Wilson. New York: New Directions, 1945. (Contains "Echoes of the Jazz Age," "My Lost City," "Ring" " 'Show Mr. and Mrs. F. to Number ——,' " "Auction—Model 1934," "Sleeping and Waking," "The Crack-Up," "Handle with Care," "Pasting It Together," "Early Success," "The Note-Books," Letters.)

The Stories of F. Scott Fitzgerald, a selection of 28 stories with an introduction by Malcolm Cowley. New York: Scribners, 1951. (Contains eighteen stories from the four earlier volumes and "Magnetism," "The Rough Crossing," "The Bridal Party," "An Alcoholic Case," "The Long Way Out," "Financing Finnegan," "Pat Hobby Himself: A Patriotic Short, Two Old Timers," "Three Hours between Planes," and "The Lost Decade," all previously uncollected.)

Afternoon of an Author; A Selection of Uncollected Stories and Essays, with an introduction and notes by Arthur Mizener. New York: Scribners, 1958. (Contains twelve stories and eight essays: "A Night at the Fair," "Forging Ahead," "Basil and Cleopatra," "Outside the Cabinet-Maker's," "One Trip Abroad," "I Didn't Get Over," "Afternoon of an Author," "Design in Plaster," Pat Hobby: 1. "Boil Some Water—Lots of It," 2. "Teamed with Genius," 3. "No Harm Trying," "News of Paris—Fifteen Years Ago," "Princeton," "Who's Who—and Why," "How to Live on $36,000 a Year," "How to Live on Practically Nothing a Year," "How to Waste Material: A Note on My Generation," "Ten Years in the Advertising Business," "One Hundred False Starts," and "Author's House.")

The Pat Hobby Stories, with an introduction by Arnold Gingrich. New York: Scribners, 1962. Contains "Pat Hobby's Christmas Wish," "A Man in the Way," "Boil Some Water—Lots of It," "Teamed with Genius," "Pat Hobby and Orson Welles," "Pat Hobby's Secret," "Pat Hobby, Putative Father," "The Homes of the Stars," "Pat Hobby Does His Bit," "Pat Hobby's Preview," "No Harm Trying," "A Patriotic Short," "On the Trail of Pat Hobby," "Fun in an Artist's Studio," "Two Old-Timers," "Mightier Than the Sword," "Pat Hobby's College Days.")

Thoughtbook of Francis Scott Key Fitzgerald. Princeton, N.J.: Princeton University Library, 1965.

The Apprentice Fiction of F. Scott Fitzgerald, 1909–1917, edited by John Kuehl. New Brunswick, N.J.: Rutgers University Press, 1965.

F. Scott Fitzgerald in His Own Time. A Miscellany, edited by Matthew J. Bruccoli and Jackson R. Bryer. Kent, Ohio: Kent State University Press, 1971.

The Letters of F. Scott Fitzgerald, edited by Andrew Turnbull. New York: Scribners, 1963.

Dear Scott/Dear Max. The Fitzgerald-Perkins Correspondence, edited by John Kuehl and Jackson R. Bryer. New York: Scribners, 1971.

As Ever, Scott Fitz–, Letters between F. Scott Fitzgerald and His Literary Agent, Harold Ober, 1919-1940, edited by Matthew J. Bruccoli. Philadelphia: Lippincott, 1972.

BIBLIOGRAPHY

Bryer, Jackson R. *The Critical Reputation of F. Scott Fitzgerald: A Bibliographical Study.* New York: Archon Books, 1967.

CRITICAL AND BIOGRAPHICAL STUDIES

Bruccoli, Matthew J. *The Composition of Tender Is the Night.* Pittsburgh: University of Pittsburgh Press, 1963.

Callaghan, Morley E. *That Summer in Paris; Memories of Tangled Friendships with Hemingway, Fitzgerald, and Some Others.* New York: Coward-McCann, 1963

Eble, Kenneth E. *F. Scott Fitzgerald,* New York: Twayne, 1963.

Goldhurst, William. *F. Scott Fitzgerald and His Contemporaries.* Cleveland: World, 1963.

Graham, Sheilah, and Gerold Frank. *Beloved Infidel.* New York: Henry Holt, 1958.

———. *The Rest of the Story.* New York: Coward-McCann, 1964.

Hemingway, Ernest. *A Moveable Feast.* New York: Scribners, 1964.

Hoffman, Frederick J., ed. *"The Great Gatsby": A Study.* New York: Scribners, 1962.

Kazin, Alfred, ed. *F. Scott Fitzgerald: The Man and His Work.* Cleveland: World, 1951.

La Hood, Marvin J., ed. *Tender Is the Night: Essays in Criticism.* Bloomington: Indiana University Press, 1969.

Latham, Aaron. *Crazy Sundays: F. Scott Fitzgerald in Hollywood.* New York: Viking Press, 1971.

Lehan, Richard D. *F. Scott Fitzgerald and the Craft of Fiction.* Carbondale: Southern Illinois University Press, 1966.

Lockridge, Ernest H., ed. *Twentieth Century Interpretations of "The Great Gatsby."* Englewood Cliffs, N.J.: Prentice-Hall, 1968.

Milford, Nancy. *Zelda: A Biography.* New York: Harper and Row, 1970.

Miller, James E., Jr. *F. Scott Fitzgerald—His Art and His Technique.* New York: New York University Press, 1964.

Mizener, Arthur. *The Far Side of Paradise.* Rev. ed. Boston: Houghton Mifflin, 1965.

Morris, Wright. "The Function of Nostalgia—F. Scott Fitzgerald," in *The Territory Ahead.* New York: Harcourt, Brace, 1958.

Perosa, Sergio. *The Art of F. Scott Fitzgerald.* Ann Arbor: University of Michigan Press, 1965.

Piper, Henry Dan. *F. Scott Fitzgerald, A Critical Portrait.* New York: Holt, Rinehart and Winston, 1965.

Schulberg, Budd. "Old Scott: The Mask, the Myth, and the Man," *Esquire,* 55:96-101 (January 1961).

Sklar, Robert. *F. Scott Fitzgerald, The Last Laocoön.* New York: Oxford University Press, 1967.

Stern, Milton R. *The Golden Moment: The Novels of F. Scott Fitzgerald.* Urbana: University of Illinois Press, 1970.

Tomkins, Calvin. *Living Well Is the Best Revenge.* New York: Viking Press, 1971.

Turnbull, Andrew. *Scott Fitzgerald.* New York: Scribners, 1962.

—CHARLES E. SHAIN

Benjamin Franklin

1706-1790

NOTHING goes by luck in composition," Thoreau remarked in his journal in 1841. "It allows of no tricks. The best you can write will be the best you are. Every sentence is the result of a long probation. The author's character is read from title-page to end."

The Comte de Buffon is supposed to have meant much the same thing by his statement that the style is the man, and the concept is held in general esteem. It presents some difficulties, however, when applied to Benjamin Franklin, a man whose character remains mysterious and whose voluminous writing are full of what he himself regarded as tricks of his trade.

Many readers may indeed be surprised to find Franklin discussed in a series devoted to American authors. His fame rests less upon authorship than upon other things. Printer, scientist, statesman, and promoter of schools, libraries, hospitals, insurance companies, savings banks, and the post office, he would be conspicuous among American notables if he had never written a line.

Nevertheless, when in 1771 he began to compose his widely read autobiography, he put "My writing" at the head of the topics to be treated and proceeded to give careful attention to his experience in mastering English composition, which he thought had contributed greatly to his success in the various roles he had been called upon to play. He unquestionably fancied himself as a writer, and it is no more than fair to take him at his word.

Anyone who admires Franklin is likely to wish occasionally that he had written rather less than he did. Two pieces in particular—and they happen to be his best-known works—have provided much ammunition to his detractors and are likely to diminish his stature even among his friends.

The first is *The Way to Wealth*, originally the preface to *Poor Richard's Almanac* for 1758. It strung together into a connected narrative the pithy sayings relating to industry, frugality, and prudence from twenty-four earlier issues of Franklin's almanac, adding some new ones for good measure. Later separately published, *The Way to Wealth* is known in more than 150 editions, many of them translations into languages other than English. To its enormous audience Franklin and Poor Richard were indistinguishable, and hence arose the widespread impression that Franklin's basic faith was that "God helps them that help themselves" and his gospel that of acquisitiveness:

Get what you can, and what you get hold;
'Tis the Stone that will turn all year lead into
    gold.

Those who think of Franklin as materialistic, cautious, and prudent to a fault can feel with some justice that like David Harum, the shrewd protagonist of Edward N. Westcott's novel of 1898, Franklin read the Golden Rule as "Do unto the other feller the way he'd like to do unto you an' do it fust."

One can argue that *The Way to Wealth* does not fairly represent either Poor Richard or his creator, but no such excuse can be offered for the worldliness of the *Autobiography*. In it Franklin candidly undertook to explain how he had risen in the world and his explanation is not a wholly pretty story. Advancement, he implied, is a matter of keeping an eye on the main chance. It requires calculation and may even mean using one's friends, flattering one's superiors, and suppressing one's opinions if they seem likely to offend influential people. The good life, according to the *Autobiography*, is not the pursuit of simple saintliness or spiritual serenity but the attainment of economic independence and social position. The aura of finagling and of elasticity of conviction which surrounds the *Autobiography* offends many sensitve readers and is the justification for the castigation of Franklin by such critics as D. H. Lawrence. In his *Studies in Classic American Literature* Lawrence referred to Franklin as "snuff-coloured" and as wishing to confine the "dark vast forest" of the soul of man in a barbed-wire paddock, there to grow "potatoes or Chicagoes." The judgment is severe, but not a gross misrepresentation of Franklin as he explained himself in the *Autobiography*.

Neither his most popular writings nor his detractors, however, have utterly destroyed Franklin as a national hero. He was lionized during his lifetime and visitors still toss pennies on his grave in Christ Church Burying Ground in Philadelphia. How can this be, if his ideals were so pint-sized and mundane?

One answer is that the masses are always worldly in their aspirations and, since like appeals to like, commonplace people create commonplace heroes. Another is that the crowd is readily captured by showmanship, a quality which Franklin possessed as richly as any man of his time. A third answer, and perhaps the best one, is that no man really understands himself, Franklin not excepted. His practice did not always follow his precepts and he often acted upon rasher impulses and nobler principles than those which he publicly avowed. Many discrepancies between theory and practice can be demonstrated in his life and, as will appear, in his writing as well. He was not as uncomplicated a man as he thought he was, nor was his literary style as simple as he believed it to be.

His life can be quickly disposed of, since it is in its main outlines common knowledge.

The son of a candlemaker, he was born in Boston in 1706. After meager schooling he was apprenticed, at the age of twelve, to an older brother who was a printer. Five years later he ran away from home. Following some disillusioning adventures, including an eighteen-month residence in London, he settled in Philadelphia in 1726 and proceeded to make a modest fortune. By 1748 he was financially independent and freed himself from business to turn his abundant energy to science and public affairs. Within a few years he was internationally famous as the author of *Experiments and Observations on Electricity* (1751), a book which assured him a warm welcome when his political activities took him back to England in 1757. At this point the *Autobiography* ends.

Twenty-five of the remaining years of his life were spent in Europe. He was in London first (1757–62) as a representative of the Pennsylvania elected assembly and again (1764–75) as semiofficial ambassador of most of the British American colonies during the series of disputes about taxation which culminated in the Revolution. Finally (1776–85) he was in Paris, where he helped to secure desperately needed naval and military assistance for the armed struggle for independence and to negotiate the peace treaty which recognized the sovereignty of the United States. Suffering from a painful stone in the bladder, he returned at seventy-nine to Philadelphia, where he died in 1790, soon after taking part in the convention which drafted the Constitution. Of this long period of distinguished public service the *Autobiography* says almost nothing.

Europe first knew Franklin as a scientist, and remembered him as the man who rashly flew a kite in a thunderstorm to prove that lightning is an electrical phenomenon. To this dramatic picture others were added as his later life unfolded. One was that of the mild-mannered colonial agent, facing the House of Commons at the height of the Stamp Act crisis to answer 174 questions from friends and critics of the colonies with such directness as to astonish the House and enchant large sections of the British public. Another was of an old man in a fur cap and spectacles, who among the powdered wigs of Paris seemed the incarnation of the simple virtues of the New World, so that when he and Voltaire met at the Academy of Sciences the audience was not satisfied until the two *philosophes* hugged one another and exchanged kisses on both cheeks. Snuff-colored as his ideals may have been, the eighteenth century adored him. "He snatched the lightning from the sky and the sceptre from tyrants," Turgot the economist proclaimed in a famous epigram. He was more renowned, wrote his envious compatriot, John Adams, than Leibniz, Sir Isaac Newton, Frederick the Great, or Voltaire, and "more beloved and esteemed than any or all of them."

Franklin, then, was something more than "Poor Richard, the Boy Who Made Good," as Dixon Wecter labeled him in *The Hero in America*. The books on Franklin the "amazing" and the "many-sided" are not wholly in the wrong, nor are the biographers who have called him "the first civilized American," "the apostle of modern times," and, as Carl Van Doren happily phrased it, "a harmonious human multitude." For versatility, wide-ranging intellectual curiosity, and political acumen, Benjamin Franklin has had few peers. His *Autobiography* does him far less than justice.

With his writing as with his life one must begin with the *Autobiography*, but with the awareness that it does not tell the whole story. When he began to write it he was a man of sixty-five, generalizing about English composition as he was generalizing about worldly success, and interpreting his early experience in terms of maturity and mellowed memories.

By his own account Franklin was a precocious, bookish child, and his family naturally thought that he might become an ornament to the ministry, then the most honored profession in the Boston Puritan community. At eight, therefore, he was sent to Latin grammar school as a first step toward Harvard College and a Congregational pulpit. His father, however, thinking of the expense of a college education and the size of ministerial salaries, soon had a change of heart. After less than a year's exposure to Latin syntax he was withdrawn and enrolled in a private school which advertised, in the *Boston News-Letter*, instruction in "Writing, Cyphering, Treble Violin, Flute, Spinet, &c. Also English and French Quilting, Imbroidery, Florishing, Plain Work, Marking in several sorts of Stitches and several other works." In this evidently busy and co-educational establishment, he mastered penmanship but little else, failing, he recalled, in arithmetic. This took a year or so; at the age of ten his school-days were over.

Home study was another matter. He could not remember when he learned to read, but at an early age was devouring what few books his father had accumulated. Among them were a number of works of theological controversy; he regretted later that more suitable material was not at hand when he was so eager for knowledge. He remembered three other books: Plutarch's *Lives*, Defoe's *Essay on Projects*, and Cotton Mather's *Essays to Do Good*. The time spent on Plutarch was not, he thought, wasted, and it may have had something to do with his lifelong taste for history and his delight in the delineation of character. From Defoe and Mather he derived, he said, a turn of thought which influenced some of the chief events of his later life, by which he no doubt meant his use of some of their ideas on education and mutual association for "good works." His first systematic purchases out of his spending money were works by John Bunyan. "Honest John," he wrote, "was the first that I know of who mix'd Narration & Dialogue, a Method of Writing very engaging to the Reader, who in the most interesting Parts finds himself as it were brought into the Company, & present at the Discourse. De foe in his Cruso, his Moll Flanders, Religious Courtship, Family Instructor, & other Pieces, has imitated it with Success. And Richardson has done the same in his Pamela, &c." Like Bunyan, Franklin was to make effective use of dialogue and allegory.

More books became available in his brother's print shop. The office stock was supplemented by loans from a friendly merchant. At night and early in the morning and whenever on Sunday he could get out of going to church, Franklin read and studied.

In 1718 he ventured into print with a topical ballad about a shipwreck, which sold well enough to make any twelve-year-old vain. An-other on Blackbeard the pirate followed; then his father discouraged him "by ridiculing my Performances, and telling me Versemakers were always Beggars; so I escap'd being a Poet, most probably a very bad one." Thereafter he showed only a mild interest in poetry. He composed verses occasionally, but "approv'd the amusing one's Self with Poetry now & then, so far as to improve one's Language, but no farther."

The father's influence on his son's prose was rather happier. Among the boy's friends was another booklover, John Collins, with whom he was fond of arguing—a liking for argument, Franklin believed, had been one result of reading theological works. He and Collins debated the mental capacities of women and whether or not girls should be educated. Franklin, already on the side of the ladies, felt himself overpowered, not so much by Collins' logic as by his fluency. To present his own case effectively he wrote out his arguments in the form of letters and exchanged them with his friend. His father found this correspondence, made a point of discussing it, and observed that though Benjamin with his print-shop training had an advantage in spelling and punctuation he "fell far short in elegance of Expression, in Method and in Perspicuity, of which he convinc'd me by several Instances. I saw the Justice of his Remarks, & thence grew more attentive to the *Manner* in Writing, and determin'd to endeavour at Improvement." Franklin never deviated from his father's standards: elegance, in the sense of ingenious simplicity; method, or careful organization; and perspicuity, or complete clarity.

To improve his style Franklin adopted a device which other would-be writers have found effective. He undertook to imitate the writing then most fashionable and admired, that of *The Specator*. "I took some of the Papers," he tells us, "& making short Hints of the Sentiment in each Sentence, laid them by a few Days, and then without looking at the Book, try'd to compleat the Papers again, by expressing each hinted Sentiment at length & as fully as it had been express'd before, in any suitable Words, that should come to hand.

"Then I compar'd my Spectator with the Original, discover'd some of my Faults & corrected them. But I found I wanted a Stock of words or a Readiness in recollecting & using them, which I thought I should have acquir'd before that time, if I had gone on making Verses, since the continual Occasion for Words of the same Import but of different Length, to suit the Measure, or of different Sound for the Rhyme, would have laid me under a constant Necessity of searching for Variety, and also have tended to fix that Variety in my Mind, & make me Master of it. Therefore I took some of the Tales & turn'd them into Verse: And after a time, when I had pretty well forgotten the Prose, turn'd them back again. I also sometimes jumbled my Collections of Hints into Confusion, and after some Weeks, endeavour'd to reduce them into the best Order, before I began to form the full Sentences, & compleat the Paper. This was to teach me Method in the Arrangement of Thoughts. By comparing my work afterwards with the original, I discover'd many faults and amended them; but I sometimes had the Pleasure of Fancying that in certain Particulars of small Import, I had been lucky enough to improve the Method or the Language and this encourag'd me to think I might possibly in time come to be a tolerable English Writer, of which I was extreamly ambitious."

Those who cherish originality or believe in "inspiration" are sure to scorn Franklin's imitative methods. Fresh perception and wide reading are perhaps more valuable in the long run than laborious exercises such as his. On the other hand, there are few better ways of building a vocabulary and mastering the elements of logical organization. Compared to learning ten new words a day or outlining modern essays, Franklin's technique stands up well, and in his own case undoubtedly produced the results he sought.

To a modern eye the prose of Addison and Steele and the expository writing of Defoe seem overly contrived. They rely upon numerous parallelisms and contrasts, upon balance, antithesis, and climax. All good prose shows careful pruning, but eighteenth-century prose-writers, like eighteenth-century gardeners, were fond of the espalier method, patiently laboring to achieve a careful and instantly impressive structure rather than simply to cut out the dead wood and to increase the productiveness of the bearing branches. Some of Franklin's early prose was espaliered, but working against that tendency were other influences: his father's standards, the example of the Puritan sermon which he never mentions but to which he was exposed at an impressionable age, and his newspaper experience, which encouraged both conciseness and a conservatism about language.

His early fondness for contradiction, shared with his friend Collins, seemed to him later a bad habit. He claimed to have abandoned it after encountering the Socratic method of disputation, in which a point of view is established by a sequence of leading questions rather than by direct argument. His curiosity led him to Xenophon's *Memorabilia*; in emulation of Socrates he dropped "abrupt Contradiction, and positive Argumentation, and put on the humble Enquirer & Doubter." Finding the pose safe and successful, "I took a Delight in it, practis'd it continually & grew very artful & expert in drawing People even of superior Knowledge into Concessions the Consequences of which they did not foresee, entangling them in Difficulties out of which they could not extricate themselves, and so obtaining Victories that neither my self nor my Cause always deserved." This device, more useful in face-to-face oral discourse than in writing, became a part of his bag of tricks. As will appear, he often sought to assume the mask or persona of the humble inquirer and, keenly aware of the importance of his audience in determining his strategy, led his readers into unwary concessions.

As Franklin realized, the Socratic method contains an element of sophistry, in that there is some intentional deception. He said that he gradually gave it up, "retaining only the Habit of expressing my self in Terms of modest Diffidence, never using when I advance any thing that may possibly be disputed, the Words, *Certainly, undoubtedly,* or any others that give the Air of Positiveness to an Opinion; but rather say, *I conceive, or I apprehend* a Thing to be so and so, *It appears to me, or I should think it so and so for such & such Reasons,* or *I imagine* it to be so, or *it is so if I am not mistaken.* This Habit I believe has been of great Advantage to me, when I have had occasion to inculcate my Opinions & persuade Men into Measures that I have been from time to time engag'd in promoting. And as the chief Ends of Conversation are to *inform,* or to be *informed,* to *please* or to *persuade,* I wish well-meaning sensible Men would not lessen their Power of doing Good by a Positive assuming Manner that seldom fails to disgust, tends to create Opposition, and to defeat every one of those Purposes for which Speech was given us, to wit, giving or receiving Information, or Pleasure." As a politician Franklin was remarkably faithful to this theory of oral discourse, of which the practicality is self-evident to anyone who has ever attended a public meeting or legislative assembly.

He also applied the strategy of the humble inquirer to writing. Good writing, he observed, "ought to have a tendency to benefit the reader, by improving his virtue or his knowledge. . . . an ill man may write an ill thing well; that is, having an ill design, he may use the properest style and arguments (considering who are to be readers) to attain his ends. In this sense, that is best wrote, which is best adapted for obtaining the end of the writer." He who would write to please good judges, Franklin said in 1733, should attend to three things: "That his Performance be *smooth, clear,* and *short*: For the contrary Qualities are apt to offend, either the Ear, the Understanding, or the Patience." The audience, then, was always uppermost with Franklin the writer as well as the speaker.

His training and his theory, in short, gave Franklin some confidence in tricks. An examination of his writings will show how he used them and will also demonstrate, I hope, that he wrote with more variety, color, temper, and whimsey than he himself realized.

Aside from his ballads, neither of which has been certainly identified, Franklin's earliest literary efforts were the Silence Dogood papers, a series of fourteen essays printed in 1722 in the *New England Courant,* his brother's newspaper. The *Courant* had invited its readers to contribute suitable compositions. "I was excited," Franklin tell us, "to try my Hand among them. But being still a Boy, & suspecting that my Brother would object to printing any Thing of mine in his Paper if he knew it to be mine, I contriv'd to disguise my Hand, & writing an anonymous Paper I put it at Night under the Door of the Printing House." He was then sixteen.

The imitation of *The Spectator* is direct and immediate, as Elizabeth C. Cook has neatly shown. "I have observed," Addison began, "that a reader seldom peruses a book with pleasure till he knows whether the writer of it be a black or a fair man, of a mild or choleric disposition, married or a bachelor, with other particulars of the like nature, that conduce very much to the right understanding of an author." Franklin's second sentence was: "And since it is observed, that the Generality of People, now a days, are unwilling either to commend or dispraise what they read, until they are in some measure informed who or what the Author of it is, whether he be *poor* or *rich, old* or *young*, a *Scollar* or a *Leather Apron Man*, &c. and give their Opinion of the Performance, according to the Knowledge which they have of the Author's Circumstances, it may not be amiss to begin with a short Account of my past Life and present Condition, that the Reader may not be at a Loss to judge whether or no my Lucubrations are worth his reading." The idiom the boy so much admired is slightly localized by such invention as "Leather Apron Man," and conciseness is not yet a passion.

Franklin also shows himself a devotee of Addison and Steele in his persona and in his perception of his audience. Silence Dogood tells us that she was born en route from London to New England. "My Entrance into this troublesome World was attended with the Death of my Father, a Misfortune, which tho' I was not then capable of knowing, I shall never be able to forget; for as he, poor Man, stood upon the Deck rejoycing at my Birth, a merciless Wave entred the Ship, and in one Moment carry'd him beyond Reprieve. Thus was the *first* Day which I saw, the *last* that was seen by my Father; and thus was my disconsolate Mother at once made both a *Parent* and a *Widow*." (One can still feel the pride of the boy who polished off that last sentence, with its antithesis and ingeniously paradoxical climax.) Silence bears some resemblances to her creator. Her education was informal, picked up in the library of a bachelor country minister to whom she was bound at an early age, and who saw that she learned needlework, writing, and arithmetic before he at length married

her. Their seven years of "conjugal Love and mutual Endearments" ended with his death, and left her with two likely girls, a boy, and her native common sense. She now enjoys the conversation of an honest neighbor, Rusticus, and an "ingenious" clergyman who boards with her, "and by whose Assistance I intend now and then to beautify my Writings with a Sentence or two in the learned Languages, which will not only be fashionable, and pleasing to those who do not understand it, but will likewise be very ornamental." (Franklin's flair for irony thus appears at the very beginning of his writing life.) Silence has, she admits, a "natural Inclination to observe and reprove the Faults of others," and in her third communication she reveals her calculation of her audience. "I am very sensible," she says, "that it is impossible for me, or indeed any *one* Writer to please *all* Readers at once. Various Persons have different Sentiments; and that which is pleasant and delightful to one, gives another a Disgust. He that would (in this Way of Writing) please all, is under a Necessity to make his Themes almost as numerous as his Letters. He must one while be merry and diverting, then more solid and serious; one while sharp and satyrical, then (to mollify that) be sober and religious; at *one* Time let the Subject be Politicks, then let the next Theme be Love. Thus will every one, one Time or another, find some thing agreeable to his own Fancy, and in his Turn be delighted."

For all his theory, Franklin was not yet a skillful writer. The Dogood papers lack plan, fail to sustain the point of view of the persona, and indeed permit that creation to fade gradually into limbo. Of the fourteen essays, the best are a dream allegory on education at Harvard College (No. 4) and a satire on the New England funeral elegy, with a hilarious recipe for writing one (No. 7). These two essays are the first revelation of Franklin the rebel, whose real feelings break through the mask.

They attracted attention of a kind which in his more cautious moments Franklin sought to avoid. He gives as one of his reasons for leaving Boston "that I had already made myself a little obnoxious to the governing Party." The pose of the bland inquirer did not go well with satire.

Nor did the delight in logic and contradiction die as early a death as an unwary reading of the *Autobiography* may lead one to think. In 1725, working in Palmer's printing shop in London, Franklin helped set in type an edition of William Wollaston's *The Religion of Nature Delineated*. Finding himself questioning some of Wollaston's arguments, he wrote and had printed a brief, closely reasoned essay, the gist of which is that God is all-wise, all-good, and all-powerful, and that therefore neither evil nor free will actually exist. Whatever is, is right, Franklin asserted, and the principle which governs human behavior is not the ill-founded distinction between virtue and vice but the inexorable balancing out of pleasure and pain. In other words, *A Dissertation on Liberty and Necessity, Pleasure and Pain* reduces moral conduct to a matter of sound judgment, in which religious considerations are conspicuously absent. He tells us that his employer found the principles of his pamphlet "abominable," and he himself decided quickly that they were at the least injudicious. He destroyed most of the hundred copies that were printed and fifty years later told his friend Benjamin Vaughan that his views had changed.

The *Dissertation* is the only elaborate example of formal syllogistic reasoning among Franklin's works of persuasion. Its content and method go back to his early reading in theology, most probably to Samuel Clarke's Boyle Lecture sermons on the attributes of God (1704–05). That reading, said Franklin, "wrought an Effect on me quite contrary to what was intended by them: For the Arguments of the Deists which were quoted to be refuted, appeared to me much Stronger than the Refutations. In short I soon became a thorough Deist." A Deist he remained, writing to Ezra Stiles only five weeks before he died in terms parallel to those in the *Autobiography* and to the classic statement of Deistic principles in Lord Herbert of Cherbury's *De Veritate* (1624): "Here is my creed. I believe in one God, the creator of the universe. That he governs it by his Providence. That he ought to be worshipped. That the most acceptable service we render to him is doing good to his other children. That the soul of man is immortal, and will be treated with justice in another life respecting its conduct in this. These I take to be the fundamental points in all sound religion, and I regard them as you do in whatever sect I meet with them." Reason, not the Bible, was Franklin's standard for religious faith.

Franklin's exploration of the processes of persuasion was continued in two other early works: *A Modest Enquiry into the Nature and Necessity of a Paper-Currency* (1729) and *Poor Richard's Almanac*, of which the first issue was that for 1733. Both were intimately connected with his main concern in the decade after his final settlement in Philadelphia in 1726—to establish himself in his trade as a printer.

A Modest Enquiry appeared in the same year in which he acquired his newspaper, the *Pennsylvania Gazette*. His first venture into the realm of economic theory, it resembles neither the Addisonian essay nor the theological polemic, although it is a carefully structured argument. I suggest that its model was the Puritan sermon. No Biblical text heads it, to be sure, but in place of that authority is a truism to which no reader was likely to object: to carry on trade requires a "certain proportionate quantity of money . . . more than which would be of no advantage in trade, and less, if much less, exceedingly detrimental to it."

From this Franklin draws four axioms, roughly parallel to the "doctrines" which the Puritan preacher customarily derived from his text: (1) great scarcity of money means high interest rates; (2) great scarcity of money reduces prices; (3) great scarcity of money discourages the settlement of workmen and leads to the exodus of those already in the country; and (4) great scarcity of money, in such a country as America, leads to greater consumption of imported goods. Plentiful money of course produces exactly the opposite effects: low interest, good prices, encouragement of settlement and of home production.

What persons, he then asks, will be for or against the emission of a large additional amount of paper currency? Opposing it, he replies, in a passage with many emotional overtones, will be money-lenders, land speculators, lawyers, and the dependents of these classes. "On the other Hand, those who are Lovers of Trade, and delight to see Manufactures encouraged, will be for having a large Addition to our Currency." Furthermore, Franklin asserts, plenty of money will make land values rise, and will be to the advantage of England; a currency issue, therefore, will not be against the interest of either the proprietors (the Penn family) or the homeland.

He next turns to the question of whether or not the issue of more currency would lead to depreciation of its value. This demanded his consideration of the nature and value of money in general. To such theoretical discussion, in which he anticipates at some points Adam Smith's *The Wealth of Nations*, he devotes about half his entire space. A number of possible objections are then disposed of and the essay concludes with a paragraph in the persona of the humble inquirer, who had previously been conspicuously absent. "As this Essay is wrote and published in Haste, and the Subject in itself intricate, I hope I shall be censured with Candour, if, for want of Time carefully to revise what I have written, in some Places I should appear to have express'd my self too obscurely, and in others am liable to Objections I did not foresee."

Despite its final gesture of humility, *A Modest Enquiry* is basically an appeal to the self-interest of the masses, in which their prejudices against moneylenders, speculators, and lawyers were skillfully brought to bear upon a political issue. The piece was Franklin's first real success in persuasion. It was, he said, "well receiv'd by the common People in general; but the Rich Men dislik'd it; for it increas'd and strengthen'd the Clamour for more Money; and they happening to have no Writers among them that were able to answer it, their Opposition slacken'd, & the Point was carried by a Majority in the House. My Friends there, who conceiv'd I had been of some Service, thought fit to reward me, by employing me in printing the Money, a very profitable Jobb, and a great Help to me. This was another Advantage gain'd by my being able to write." The next year, one may add, he was appointed public printer of the province and his business success was thereafter never in doubt.

His decision to publish an almanac was natural for a young printer. Almost everyone needed an almanac. It was a calendar, a record of historical anniversaries, a guide to the times of the rising and setting of the sun and of the phases of the moon. Farming and medical practice were still widely governed by folk belief in the influence of the heavenly bodies. Firewood, to burn well, had presumably to be cut while the moon was waxing, fruit gathered for the winter when it was on the wane. Horoscopes were cast to settle the proper moment to swallow medicine or wean babies. Moreover, since the aspect of the heavens varied with the latitude and longitude, it was not much use to have an almanac unless it was locally prepared. The almanac, consequently, had been a staple money-maker since the invention of printing and there were dozens in America, beginning with one for 1639 which is believed to have been the second imprint of the pioneer press at Cambridge.

In 1732 seven almanacs, one of them in German, were being printed in Philadelphia. The most successful was probably the *American Almanac*, begun by Daniel Leeds in 1686 and continued in Franklin's time by Leeds's son Titan. Despite this competition *Poor Richard's Almanac* was immediately successful. Three printings of the first issue were needed, and by the middle 1760's nearly 10,000 copies were being printed annually.

Franklin's triumph owed much to his creation of another persona: Richard Saunders, Philomath (i.e., astrologer). Richard confesses in his first preface that he is "excessive poor" and his wife "excessive proud." She cannot bear "to sit spinning in her Shift of Tow, while I do nothing but gaze at the Stars, and has threatned more than once to burn all my Books and Rattling-Traps (as she calls my Instruments) if I do not make some profitable Use of them for the Good of my Family. The Printer has offer'd me some considerable share of the Profits, and I have thus begun to comply with my Dame's Desire." The purchaser of his almanac, concludes Poor Richard, will get a useful utensil and also perform an act of charity.

A seventeenth-century English astrologer and almanac-maker had been named Richard Saunders and a popular eighteenth-century London almanac was called *Poor Robin's*. Poor Richard, nevertheless, is an imaginative al-

though short-lived creation. At first he is an improvident and henpecked dreamer, not unlike Rip Van Winkle except for his interest in extracting pennies from the public. Within a few years he turns moralist, and in *The Way to Wealth* he is little more than a handy reference for the venerable Father Abraham, who inserts "as Poor Richard says" now and then to punctuate his sermon on the homely virtues. John F. Ross has suggested that like some later American comic creations Poor Richard gradually faded as his creator assumed the role of philosopher and oracle. The persona, in short, was neither developed nor long maintained.

The first few issues of Franklin's almanac are even more remarkable for his experiment with the hoax, a form of joke wherein he pushed the strategy of extracting unconscious concessions from an unsuspecting reader to its limit. A number of his finest pieces are hoaxes, presenting absurdities with such a poker-faced manner than even ordinarily perceptive readers were taken in. The classic example is his "Proposed New Version of the Bible," an ironic paraphrase of Job 1:6–11, which no less a reader than Matthew Arnold interpreted as a lapse of Franklin's customary good sense, failing to recognize it as an attack on the English king and his ministers.

The hoax which launched *Poor Richard's Almanac* was borrowed directly from Jonathan Swift, who in 1707–08 had attacked the pretensions of a London astrologer, John Partridge, in a series of papers purportedly written by Isaac Bickerstaff. Franklin adopted Swift's strategy and many of his details. Poor Richard asserts, in the preface which has been quoted, that he would have issued an almanac many years earlier had he not been "overpowered" by regard for Titan Leeds. This obstacle, he observes, is "soon to be removed, since inexorable Death, who was never known to respect Merit, has already prepared the mortal

Dart, the fatal Sister has already extended her destroying Shears, and that ingenious Man must soon be taken from us." Leeds will die, predicts Poor Richard, on October 17, 1733. By Leeds's own calculation "he will survive till the 26th of the same Month. . . . Which of us is most exact, a little Time will now determine."

Leeds, like John Partridge, saw nothing funny in this macabre joke, and wrote the next year of the folly and ignorance of Poor Richard, who had not only lied about the date of his rival's death but had also perpetrated "another gross Falsehood in his said Almanack, viz.—*That by my own Calculation, I shall survive until the 26th of the said month* (October) which is as untrue as the former." To this Poor Richard replied, as Bickerstaff had to Partridge: "I convince him in his own Words, that he is dead . . . for in his Preface to his Almanack for 1734, he says, '*Saunders adds . . . that by my own Calculation I shall survive until the 26th of the said Month October 1733, which is as untrue as the former.*' Now if it be, as Leeds says, *untrue* and a *gross Falsehood* that he surviv'd till the 26th of October 1733, then it is certainly *true* that he died *before* that Time . . . anything he may say to the contrary notwithstanding." In dealing with a satirist it is well to look to the precision of one's language.

Its opening gambit, however, is not what made *Poor Richard's Almanac* a continuing success. Its popularity grew along with Franklin's ingenuity in filling the spaces above, below, and beside his tables of dates and astronomical data with more readable material than his competitors could find. Little of it was original, but not much was borrowed without artful revision to make it more attractive to his audience. Perhaps the transformation of the dreamy astrologer into the moralist was determined by his largely rural audience, which

honored hard work and saving more than jokes or sophisticated wit. At any rate, the "sayings" of Poor Richard eventually came close to being gospel to the country folk, and they still find a market in such little books as *Ben Franklin's Wit and Wisdom*.

Robert Newcomb, who has made the most extensive of the many studies of their origins, finds two major types of sources. In the early issues of his almanac, Franklin tended to rely on such collections of proverbs as James Howell's *Lexicon Tetraglotton* (1659) and Thomas Fuller's *Gnomologia* (1732). These were not all in a moral vein; as Van Doren has said, Poor Richard's early period was distinctly "gamy." As time went on, however, Franklin turned more often to literary and moralistic aphorisms, which he found in books such as Fuller's *Introductio ad Prudentiam* (1727), Charles Palmer's *Collection of Select Aphorisms and Maxims* (1748), Lord Halifax's *Thoughts and Reflections* (1750), and Samuel Richardson's appendix to *Clarissa* (1751). Other sources were *Wits Recreations* (1640) by John Mennes and James Smith and an anonymous *Collection of Epigrams* (1735–37). For short poems he plundered John Gay's *Fables* (1727–38), Edward Young's *Universal Passion* (1725–28), Pope's *Essay on Man* (1733), and James Savage's *Public Spirit* (1747). Rabelais, Francis Bacon, La Rochefoucauld, John Ray, John Dryden, Matthew Prior, and George Lillo he knew at first or second hand. He was an expert in the literature of the concise and succinct statement. All his life, in fact, he loved to quote proverbial and well-turned phrases. On one occasion he wrote of his own life as an epigram which, although some of its lines were barely tolerable, he hoped to conclude with a bright point.

Franklin's revisions of his borrowed materials, particularly the prose, were sometimes extensive. His admiration for conciseness was perhaps the determining factor, but he experimented with metaphor, occasional rhyme, and of course the familiar rhetorical devices, particularly balance and climax. Van Doren and Charles W. Meister give many examples, of which a few must suffice here.

Franklin's skill in compression is well illustrated by "Fish and visitors smell in three days," thought to derive from John Ray's "Fresh fish and new come guests smell, by that they are three days old." His sharpening of metaphor may be seen in "Neither a fortress nor a maid will hold out long after they begin to parley," from a Scottish proverb, "A listening damsel and a speaking castle shall never end with honor," and by "Time is an herb that cures all diseases," from Lillo's "Time and reflection cure all ills." His fondness for balance may explain the transformation of Fuller's "The fox is grey before he's good" into "Many foxes grow gray, but few grow good." The mastery of climax, or anticlimax, is evident in "Let thy maidservant be faithful, strong, and homely" and "None preaches better than the ant, and she says nothing."

In one extended borrowing, noted by Van Doren, Franklin deliberately Americanized his material. At the end of *Pantagruel* Rabelais has a book on prognostications, with a chapter on eclipses. This year, he says, "Saturn will be retrograde, Venus direct, Mercury as unfix'd as quicksilver. . . . For this reason the crabs will go side-long, and the rope-makers backward . . . bacon will run away from pease in lent; the belly will waddle before; the a— will sit down first; there won't be a bean left in a twelfth-cake, nor an ace in a flush; the dice won't run as you wish, tho' you cog them, and the chance that you desire will seldom come; brutes shall speak in several places . . . and there will be above twenty and seven irregular verbs made this year, if Priscian doesn't hold them in." In the almanac for 1739 Frank-

lin reworks the passage as follows: "During the first visible Eclipse *Saturn* is retrograde: For which Reason the Crabs will go sidelong, and the Ropemakers backward. The Belly will wag before, and the A— shall sit down first. *Mercury* will have his share in these Affairs, and so confound the Speech of People, that when a *Pensilvanian* would say PANTHER he shall say PAINTER. When a New Yorker thinks to say (THIS) he shall say (DISS) and the People in *New England* and *Cape-May* will not be able to say (COW) for their Lives, but will be forc'd to say (KEOW) by a certain involuntary Twist in the Root of their Tongues. No *Connecticut-Man* nor *Marylander* will be able to open his Mouth this Year, but (SIR) shall be the first or last Syllable he pronounces, and sometimes both. Brutes shall speak in many Places, and there will be above seven and twenty irregular Verbs made this Year, if Grammar don't interpose." Franklin is not at his best here, but his eye is obviously on his audience and his ear attuned to the vernacular, as it was in many of Poor Richard's more sucessful borrowings.

By the time he was thirty, Franklin had a prospering printing house, a successful newspaper, and a popular almanac. He had too active a mind, however, to be content with business. Temperamentally disposed toward the improvement of the society of which he was a part, he looked at the world about him with a critical but optimistic eye. His disappointments and his failures he was able to write off quickly, turning to new projects with undiminished enthusiasm. Apathy he appears never to have experienced, and only rarely was he cynical. These qualities, which acount for much of his personal charm, appear consistently in the writings of his middle years. For convenience they may be treated under three themes—promotion, science, and politics.

Because he thought a newspaper should be

informative and entertaining rather than an instrument for influencing public opinion, he rarely used the *Pennsylvania Gazette* for promotion. His early schemes, such as that which resulted in the first American subscription library, were urged by word of mouth, and indeed he always seems to have done some talking before resorting to print. For a larger audience, however, he turned to the broadside and pamphlet, the customary promotion devices of his day. The most important of his promotional tracts is probably *Proposals Relating to the Education of Youth in Pensilvania* (1749). The scheme it proposed had been in his mind for at least six years, and for once he laid some groundwork for it by reprinting in the *Gazette* a letter from the younger Pliny to Tacitus on the subject of education. His pamphlet, a month later, did not get Franklin what he wanted, but it remains a thought-provoking example of his literary strategy.

What he wanted was an academy with a curriculum better adapted to the needs of Pennsylvania youth than that of the traditional Latin grammar school. He hoped to get it by obtaining the financial support of wealthy citizens, most of whom were conservatives and saw little wrong with the central place of Latin and Greek in the training of young gentlemen. Franklin, who a quarter century earlier had satirized the classical tradition at Harvard College, was convinced that it was time for reform, for a new emphasis upon training in English and in practical subjects.

His preface is therefore designed to conciliate a possibly hostile audience. Some public-spirited gentlemen have already approved the plan; he now puts it into print in order "to obtain the Sentiments and Advice of Men of Learning, Understanding, and Experience in these Matters." With their help it can perhaps be carried into execution. If so, they will have "the hearty Concurrence and Assistance of many who are Wellwishers to their Country." Those who incline "to favour the Design with their Advice, either as to the Parts of Learning to be taught, the Order of Study, the Method of Teaching, the Oeconomy of the School, or any other Matter of Importance to the Success of the Undertaking, are desired to communicate their Sentiments as soon as may be, by Letter directed to *B. Franklin*, Printer, in *Philadelphia*."

The pose of the humble seeker of advice is belied, however, by the pamphlet itself. Before he begins Franklin lists the authors to be quoted: "The famous *Milton*," "the great Mr. *Locke*," "the ingenious Mr. *Hutcheson*" (actually David Fordyce), "the learned Mr. *Obadiah Walker*," "the much admired Mons. *Rollin*," and "the learned and ingenious Dr. *George Turnbull*." The steel hand beneath the velvet glove is clear: only a vain and provincial Philadelphian will oppose such champions. Then comes the scheme, in which the only concession to the classicists in the actual text is that the rector of the academy should be "learn'd in the Languages and Sciences," a combination which at that date would have required something of a paragon. The crux of the argument (which in differing forms is still with us) lies in six brief paragraphs:

"As to their STUDIES, it would be well if they could be taught *every Thing* that is useful, and *every Thing* that is ornamental: But Art is long, and their Time is short. It is therefore propos'd that they learn those Things that are likely to be *most useful* and *most ornamental*. Regard being had to the several Professions for which they are intended.

"All should be taught to write a *fair Hand*, and swift, as that is useful to All. And with it may be learnt something of *Drawing*, by Imitation of Prints, and some of the first Principles of Perspective.

"*Arithmetick, Accounts*, and some of the

first Principles of *Geometry* and *Astronomy*.

"The *English* Language might be taught by Grammar; in which some of our best Writers, as *Tillotson, Addison, Pope, Algernoon Sidney, Cato's Letters*, &c., should be Classicks; the *Stiles* principally to be cultivated, being the *clear* and the *concise*. Reading should also be taught, and pronouncing, properly, distinctly, emphatically; not with an even Tone, which *under-does*, nor a theatrical, which *over-does* Nature.

"To form their Stile they should be put on Writing Letters to each other, making Abstracts of what they read; or writing the same Things, in their own Words; telling or writing Stories lately read, in their own Expressions. All to be revis'd and corrected by the Tutor, who should give his Reasons, and explain the Force and Import of Words, &c.

"To form their Pronunciation, they may be put on making Declamations, repeating Speeches, delivering Orations, &c., the Tutor assisting at the Rehearsals, teaching, advising, correcting their Accent, &c."

Here, in little more than 250 words, is the summation of Franklin's conviction, obviously based upon his own experience and making use of some of the learning processes which he himself had found profitable. That he knew it to be unpopular with his audience is clear from the elaborate support of it by authority. For these 250-odd words he provided more than 3000 words of footnotes, largely direct quotations, with the great Mr. Locke most prominent among those who had argued for training youth in their native language.

The academy was formed, and later a college, with some provisions for instruction such as Franklin wanted. He himself chose the first provost, the Reverend William Smith, a man well disposed toward the sciences. Smith, however, compromised with the classicists and later became Franklin's bitter political enemy.

The pose of the humble inquirer and the marshaling of authorities both failed. Franklin did not take that defeat philosophically, and in 1789, the year before his death, charged in his "Observations Relative to the Intentions of the Original Founders of the Academy in Philadelphia" that the English program had been injudiciously starved while favors were showered upon the Latin part. There is in mankind, he said, "an unaccountable prejudice in favor of ancient customs and habitudes, which inclines to a continuance of them after the circumstances, which formerly made them useful, cease to exist." He illustrated the point by a characteristic story of how hats, once generally worn, had been replaced by wigs and umbrellas. Yet, because of fashion, men still carried them under their arms, "though the utility of such a mode . . . is by no means apparent, and it is attended not only with some expense, but with a degree of constant trouble."

The writing which made Franklin world-famous was of course that related to science. Although he was interested in natural phenomena throughout his life, his chief contributions to the knowledge of electricity were made between 1746 and 1752. The subject was fashionable from 1745, when articles on it by William Watson appeared in the *Philosophical Transactions* of the Royal Society of London. Franklin heard some lecture-demonstrations, read Watson's papers, and when a few pieces of apparatus were sent to the Library Company he and some of his friends began to explore electrical phenomena. Their discoveries were reported by Franklin in letters to Peter Collinson, a Quaker merchant of London, who read some of them before the Royal Society and arranged for others to be printed in the *Gentleman's Magazine*. Collinson was also responsible in part for the publication of a collection, *Experiments and Observations on Electricity*, in 1751. Before 1769 four additional English editions, with new letters, had been printed. French translations appeared in 1752 and 1756, a German one in 1758, and an Italian in 1774.

Science brought into play all of Franklin's best qualities as a writer. It demanded clarity and conciseness. The persona of the humble inquirer fitted perfectly, for in science there is little respect for dogmatism. Yet there was room for imagination, since from the phenomena observed hypotheses had to be constructed, and for persuasion, because those hypotheses had to be supported. For once the writer and his audience were in complete accord. Franklin's literary skill is attested by the general acceptance of some of the terms he invented—*positive, negative, battery,* and *conductor.* His passion for doing good was satisfied, moreover, in his invention of the lightning rod for protecting property from one of the more destructive forces of the natural world.

Many letters in the *Experiments and Observations* are models of reporting and evaluating scientific investigation. The best, perhaps, and certainly the most famous, is the paper proposing the grounded lightning rod (the general theory had been previously stated) and the experimental demonstration of the hypothesis of the identity of electricity and lightning. To illustrate requires a long quotation, but no better example of Franklin's clarity or of the high order of his scientific imagination can readily be found.

After some remarks on the nature of the electrical fluid or element, Franklin notes that the charge in an electrified body can be drawn off by the point of a pin from a foot's distance, while if the head of the pin is the attracting agent it must be moved to within a few inches of the electrified body before a charge is drawn off. Points apparently draw off the electrical atmosphere more readily than blunt bodies do; "as in the plucking the hairs from the horse's tail, a degree of strength insufficient to pull away a handful at once, could yet easily strip it hair by hair; so a blunt body presented cannot draw off a number of particles at once; but a pointed one, with no greater force, takes them away easily, particle by particle." Franklin is not sure of the true reasons for this phenomenon, but it is not of much importance, he says, "to know the manner in which nature exercises her laws; 'tis enough if we know the laws themselves. 'Tis of real use to know, that china left in the air unsupported will fall and break; but *how* it comes to fall, and *why* it breaks, are matters of speculation. 'Tis a pleasure indeed to know them, but we can preserve our china without it." He goes on:

"Thus in the present case, to know this power of points, may possibly be of some use to mankind, tho' we should never be able to explain it. The following experiments . . . show this power. I have a large prime conductor made of several thin sheets of Fuller's pasteboard form'd into a tube, near 10 feet long and a foot diameter. It is covered with *Dutch* emboss'd paper, almost totally gilt. This large metallic surface supports a much greater electrical atmosphere than a rod of iron of 50 times the weight would do. It is suspended by silk lines, and when charg'd will strike at near two inches distance, a pretty hard stroke so as to make ones knuckle ach. Let a person standing on the floor present the point of a needle, at 12 or more inches distance from it, and while the needle is so presented, the conductor cannot be charged, the point drawing off the fire as fast as it is thrown on by the electrical globe. Let it be charged, and then present the point at the same distance, and it will suddenly be discharged. In the dark you may see a light on the point, when the experiment is made. And if the person holding the point stands upon wax, he will be electrified by receiving the fire at that distance. Attempt to draw off the electricity with a blunt body, as a bolt of iron round at the end and smooth (a silversmith's iron punch, inch-thick, is what I use) and you must bring it within the distance of three inches before you can do it, and then it is done with a stroke and crack. As the pasteboard tube hangs loose on silk lines, when you approach it with the punch iron, it likewise will move towards the punch, being attracted while it is charged; but if at the same instant a point be presented as before, it retires again, for the point discharges it. Take a pair of large brass scales, of two or more feet beam, the cords of the scales being silk. Suspend the beam by a packthread from the ceiling, so that the bottom of the scales may be about a foot from the floor: the scales will move round in a circle by the untwisting of the packthread. Set the iron punch on the end upon the floor, in such a place as that the scales may pass over it in making their circle: Then electrify one scale by applying the wire of a charged phial to it. As they move round, you see that scale draw nigher to the floor, and dip more when it comes over the punch; and if that be placed at a proper distance, the scale will snap and discharge its fire into it. But if a needle be stuck on the end of the punch, its point upwards, the scale, instead of drawing nigh to the punch and snapping, discharges its fire silently, through the point, and rises higher from the punch. Nay, even if the needle be placed upon the floor, near the punch, its point upwards, the end of the punch, tho' so much higher than the needle, will not attract the scale and receive its fire, for the needle will get it and convey it away, before it comes nigh enough for the punch to act. And this is constantly observable in these experiments, that the greater quantity of electricity on the pasteboard tube, the farther it strikes or discharges its fire, and the point likewise will draw it off at a still greater distance.

"Now if the fire of electricity and that of lightening be the same . . . this pasteboard tube and these scales may represent electrified clouds. If a tube of only 10 feet long will strike and discharge its fire on the punch at two or three inches distance, an electrified cloud of perhaps 10,000 acres may strike and discharge on the earth at a proportionably greater distance. The horizontal motion of the scales over the floor, may represent the motion of the clouds over the earth; and the erect iron punch a hill or high building; and then we see how electrified clouds passing over hills or high buildings at too great a height to strike, may be attracted lower till within their striking distance. And lastly, if a needle fix'd on the punch with its point upright, or even on the floor, below the punch, will draw the fire from the scale silently at a much greater than the striking distance, and so prevent its descending towards the punch; or if in its course it would have come nigh enough to strike, yet being first deprived of its fire it cannot, and the punch is thereby secured from the stroke. I say, if these things are so, may not the knowledge of this power of points be of use to mankind, in preserving houses, churches, ships &c. from the stroke of lightning, by directing us to fix on the highest parts of those edifices, upright rods of iron, made sharp as a needle, and gilt to prevent rusting, and from the foot of these rods a wire down the outside of the building into the ground; or down round one of the shrouds of a ship and down her side till it reaches the water? Would not these pointed rods probably draw the electrical fire silently out of a cloud before it came nigh enough to strike, and thereby secure us from the most sudden and terrible mischief?

"To determine the question, whether the clouds that contain lightning are electrified or not, I would propose an experiment to be try'd where it may be done conveniently. On the top of some high tower or steeple, place a kind of sentry-box . . . big enough to contain a man and an electrical stand. From the middle of the stand let an iron rod rise and pass bending out of the door, and then upright 20 or 30 feet, pointed very sharp at the end. If the electrical stand be kept clean and dry, a man standing on it when such clouds are passing low, might be electrified and afford sparks, the rod drawing fire to him from a cloud. If any danger to the man should be apprehended (tho' I think there would be none) let him stand on the floor of his box, and now and then bring near to the rod, the loop of a wire that has one end fastened to the leads, he holding it by a wax handle; so the sparks, if the rod is electrified, will strike from the rod to the wire, and not affect him"

Franklin constructs his hypothesis, with its usefulness firmly in mind, from careful observation of experiments with simple apparatus easily obtainable by anyone. His description is clear and factual, although the analogies of the horse's tail and the falling china are valuable aids to understanding. His conclusions are the earliest written suggestions of their kind, and they quickly came to fruition. Lightning rods were erected and found to work, and on May 13, 1752, Thomas-François Dalibard reported to the Academy of Sciences in Paris on his successful performance of the proposed experiment with a tall pointed rod and an electrical stand. "En suivant la route que M. Franklin nous a tracée," he began, "j'ai obtenu une satisfaction complète." With that sentence the triumph of Franklin the natural philosopher was assured. It was to be some weeks before he was to fly his famous kite, in a simpler but much more dangerous experiment.

Franklin's first skirmish with power politics on the international level, where the ravages of war as a means of settling conflicts of interest are an ever-present risk, came at about the same time that he was beginning his exploration of electricity, in 1747. England had been at war with Spain since 1739 and with France since 1740, which meant that the British colonies had enemies to the south in the Spanish Main and to the north in French Canada. To the west, moreover, were the Indians, with whom the French could make alliances. If English sea power failed, the colonies would be encircled. It took some time for this fact to disturb Pennsylvanians. Their geographical location seemed to promise safety; the powerful Quaker leaders were conscientiously opposed to all things military, including preparation against attack; and the numerous German farmers and artisans cared nothing for British supremacy. Then, in the spring and summer of 1747, Spanish and French privateers appeared in the Delaware River, one of them raiding a settlement less than sixty miles from Philadelphia. The War of the Austrian Succession was suddenly something that had to be reckoned with.

Franklin's *Plain Truth: Or, Serious Considerations on the Present State of the City of Philadelphia, and Province of Pennsylvania,* which appeared in November, is his most effective piece of propaganda. Its purpose was to arouse a divided community to the desperate necessity of unity and action. Like Thomas Paine's *Common Sense* it is an appeal to emotion rather than to reason, directed to almost every special interest which might suffer if the worst should happen and the city and province be attacked. Like Paine, too, Franklin offered a specific course of action, one quickly followed.

Plain Truth has upon its title page a long Latin quotation from Cato, not for ornament but to satisfy the learned that military preparedness had classical precedent. Its first paragraph ends with a proverb, "When the Steed is stolen, you shut the Stable Door," a warning the most illiterate could understand. Every other British colony has taken measures for its defense, Franklin notes. The wealth of Pennsylvania, unprotected, must certainly be a temptation to an enemy which has been exploring the river approaches, is known to have spies everywhere, and very probably has subverted unscrupulous men within the province itself. Remember, Franklin says, the eighth chapter of Judges, which he quotes at length. The French Catholics have converted many Indians, and it may not be long before the scalping parties which have already raided New York will be ravaging the back country of Pennsylvania. City and country are alike in being threatened, and their interests are the same. Trade is in dire danger, and if trade declines bad debts will multiply and land values decrease. The enemy may count upon Quaker pacifism, although Franklin thinks some Quakers will fight in self-defense. Preparedness will cost money, but think of the loss from plundering and burning. Well-to-do Philadelphians may be granted time to flee to the country, but what if there is a sudden attack, "perhaps in the Night! Confined to your Houses, you will have nothing to trust to but the Enemy's Mercy. Your best Fortune will be, to fall under the Power of Commanders of King's Ships, able to controul the Mariners; and not into the Hands of *licentious Privateers*. Who can, without the utmost Horror, conceive the Miseries of the Latter! when your Persons, Fortunes, Wives and Daughters, shall be subject to the wanton and unbridled Rage, Rapine, and Lust, of *Negroes*, *Molattoes*, and others, the vilest and most abandoned of Mankind." The governing party, not even "Friends" to the people (he is here playing on the formal name for the Quakers), will not permit the appropriation of the funds necessary for defense, nor is anything to be hoped for from the opposition, who will not lay out their wealth to protect the trade of their Quaker adversaries. " 'Till of late I could scarce believe the Story of him who refused to pump in a sinking Ship, because one on board, whom he hated, would be saved by it as well as himself. But such, it seems, is the Unhappiness of human Nature, that our Passions, when violent, often are too hard for the united Force of *Reason, Duty,* and *Religion.*" What must be done, therefore, will have to be done by the "middling People"—farmers, shopkeepers, and tradesmen. They are strong enough to muster 60,000 men, exclusive of the Quakers, and all of them are acquainted with the use of firearms. Englishmen have shown before that they can fight, and there are thousands of "*brave* and *steady*" Germans. If the hints of the author, "A Tradesman of Philadelphia," are well received, he will within a few days lay before the people the form of an association, "together with a practicable Scheme for raising the Money necessary for the Defence of our Trade, City, and Country, without laying a Burthen on any Man." The tract then concludes with a prayer.

Here Franklin addressed himself to selfish interests, fear, and prejudice—national, social, racial, and religious. The humble inquirer is forgotten, together with caution other than that which might conciliate the more militant Quakers. *Plain Truth* made him enemies in high places, chief among them Thomas Penn, the proprietor, but it got results. The extralegal association for defense which he proposed was organized almost immediately, despite the objection that it constituted a private army which might be a potential source of danger to government. The money was raised by a lottery which Franklin showed the "middling" people how to run. Arms were procured and the province readied for a battle which fortunately never came, the exhausted great powers of Europe signing the Treaty of Aix-la-Chapelle in 1748. The association thereafter languished, but Franklin was now a man of political influence. He exerted himself again in large affairs in 1754, during the Albany Congress, at which he proposed a plan of colonial union and editorialized in the *Gazette* for that cause, printing the first American newspaper cartoon: a segmented snake, representing the several colonies, above a caption reading "Join, or die." He also took a leading part in the American phase of the Seven Years' War, but never again did he display the sustained passion of the propagandist which *Plain Truth* reveals.

During his two long stays in London Franklin's tasks were essentially diplomatic. His first assignment was to get some settlement of a dispute about taxes which had soured the relations between the Pennsylvania assembly and the Penn family, who retained immense proprietary rights in provincial lands. Later his job was to represent the colonial interests to the British ministry, increasingly hostile as its measures for taxation were opposed by the Americans, and to the British public, which tended to be indifferent to issues so remote. Because of these responsibilities, Franklin's writing between 1757 and 1775 was predominantly political, although he did not neglect science and occasionally found time for such *jeux d'esprits* as the "Craven Street Gazette" of 1770, a fictitious newspaper prepared for the Stevenson family, with whom he lodged for many years.

Over 125 anonymous contributions to English newspapers between 1765 and 1775 have been identified as Franklin's. In addition he had a hand in a number of important pamphlets and sometimes appeared in public to testify, as an expert witness, on American opinion. Facing a hostile or apathetic audience, he was usually ingratiating and conciliatory, appealing to the British concern for national interests and fair play. Only at the end did he despair

of settling the quarrel without separation and bloodshed.

Of his pamphlets the most considerable was *The Interest of Great Britain Considered, with Regard to Her Colonies and the Acquisition of Canada and Guadaloupe* (1760). Written toward the end of the Seven Years' War, it strongly urged the annexation of Canada as a condition of peace. Strange as it may now seem, there were some Englishmen who preferred to acquire Guadaloupe, an island group in the West Indies where sugar was already being produced in large quantity. One of their arguments for leaving Canada to the French was that British America was already large enough, since if it grew stronger it might become dangerous to Great Britain. In preparing his answer to this line of reasoning Franklin had the help of an English lawyer-friend, Richard Jackson, and the tone of the piece is largely legalistic. Here and there, however, Franklin's feelings enliven things, as in his suggestion that the growth of the colonies could be checked less cruelly if Parliament should emulate the Egyptian treatment of the Israelites and pass a law requiring midwives to stifle every third or fourth child at birth.

In February 1766, Franklin appeared before the House of Commons in the course of a debate on the repeal of the Stamp Act. He made an impressive showing, not that he was an accomplished orator but because of his talent as a face-to-face persuader. His answers to questions, stenographically reported, reveal a well-planned strategy for dealing with an audience partly friendly and partly hostile. Usually he replied in a sentence or two, but he added more when he saw the chance to appeal to British self-interest or patriotism, and on three or four occasions he spoke at length. Again and again he stood firm on the main point, that the colonies were right in their distinction between external taxes, properly levied for the regulation of commerce, and internal taxes, which they insisted should be imposed only by their own legislatures.

Typical of the many newspaper contributions is "The Causes of American Discontents before 1768," an even-tempered explanation of colonial grievances as they might appear to a disinterested Englishman. In this and many other letters Franklin's role was to inform rather than to argue; he was what we would now call a public relations man. By 1773, however, he was understandably discouraged, and his two best-known newspaper articles are satires: "Rules by Which a Great Empire May Be Reduced to a Small One" and "An Edict by the King of Prussia." He himself said they were "designed to expose the conduct of this country towards the colonies in a short, comprehensive, and striking view, and stated therefore in out-of-the-way forms, as most likely to take the general attention."

The "Rules," one of his most ironic pieces, indirectly but clearly suggests rebellion, and reviews American complaints in highly emotional language. One paragraph will illustrate its method and feeling: "However peaceably your colonies have submitted to your government, shown their affection to your interests, and patiently borne their grievances; you are to suppose them *always inclined to revolt*, and treat them accordingly. Quarter troops among them, who by their insolence may provoke the rising of mobs, and by their bullets and bayonets suppress them. By this means, like the husband who uses his wife ill from suspicion, you may in time convert your suspicions into realities."

The "Edict" is the most effective of what Paul Baender has called Franklin's "duplicative" satires, in which the strategy was to demand that the reader put himself in someone else's place, so that he may feel more keenly feelings which he might otherwise misunder-

stand. It is also a hoax, whose success greatly pleased its joke-loving author. What Franklin did was to use the very words of the Parliamentary statutes restricting American commerce and manufactures, ranging from the reign of Charles II to that of George III, as if they were enacted by Prussia, a nation with some claim to being Britain's mother country from the time of the Angles and the Saxons. The "Edict" makes clearer than any lengthy argument how shipping and manufacturing interests had "lobbied" for their own advantage over the shipowners, ironmakers, and hatters of the colonies. But by this time, no literary skill could long postpone the appeal to arms.

Having failed to avert the rebellion he dreaded, Franklin returned to Philadelphia long enough to serve on the committee which drafted the Declaration of Independence. By the end of 1776, however, he was back in Europe, this time in Paris, to plead the cause of a new nation and to deal with still another public, this time a most admiring one.

One of his first acts, apparently, was to compose still another hoax. "The Sale of the Hessians" attacks the British employment of German mercenaries in the American war. It is a letter in French, ostensibly written in Rome by the Count de Schaumbergh, to the commander of the German soldiers for whose services the British were paying large subsidies, including lump sums for men killed. Nearly 30,000 Germans were thus hired out by their princes, and in one case the agreement was to count three wounded men as one dead one in reckoning up the account. Franklin's matter-of-fact assumption of the Count's desire to have as many casualties as possible leads to cutting irony.

"I am about to send to you some new recruits. Don't economize them. Remember glory before all things. Glory is true wealth. There is nothing degrades the soldier like the love of money. He must care only for honour and reputation, but this reputation must be acquired in the midst of dangers. A battle gained without costing the conqueror any blood is an inglorious success, while the conquered cover themselves with glory by perishing with their arms in their hands. Do you remember that of the 300 Lacedæmonians who defended the defile of Thermopylæ, not one returned? How happy should I be could I say the same of my brave Hessians!

"It is true that their king, Leonidas, perished with them: but things have changed, and it is no longer the custom for princes of the empire to go and fight in America for a cause with which they have no concern. And besides, to whom should they pay the thirty guineas per man if I did not stay in Europe to receive them? Then, it is necessary also that I be ready to send recruits to replace the men you lose. For this purpose I must return to Hesse. It is true, grown men are becoming scarce there, but I will send you boys. Besides, the scarcer the commodity the higher the price. I am assured that the women and little girls have begun to till our lands, and they get on not badly. You did right to send back to Europe that Dr. Crumerus who was so successful in curing dysentery. Don't bother with a man who is subject to looseness of the bowels. That disease makes bad soldiers. One coward will do more mischief in an engagement than ten brave men will do good. Better that they burst in their barracks than fly in a battle, and tarnish the glory of our arms. Besides, you know that they pay me as killed for all who die from disease, and I don't get a farthing for runaways."

Franklin's busy life in France, where he received the adulation usually reserved for matinee idols, was not all grimly political. Living at Passy, then a Paris suburb, he became the center of a group of admirers, many of them women. For their amusement and his own

he set up a printing press in his house, upon which were printed, from time to time, short light essays of a sort sometimes known as *bijoux*. These are usually referred to as the "bagatelles," and there are nineteen of them altogether. The best-known are "Dialogue between Franklin and the Gout," "The Whistle," "The Ephemera," and "The Morals of Chess." All exploit an old man's personality or hobbies and, since they were written for a French audience, they have an unusual flavor for English writing—a Gallic delight in the well-turned phrase and the expression of delicate feeling. They are carefully structured, with the tone sustained just long enough for their effect. There is some moralizing, to be sure; that had become a habit of Franklin's.

Every reader has his favorite bagatelle, and few fail to be charmed by one of them or another. My favorite is "The Ephemera," addressed to Madame Brillon, a woman many years Franklin's junior whom he called by the pet name of "Brillante." It is an allegory, "an emblem of human life," which compares men and women to a species of small flies. One white-haired philosopher fly, seven hours old, reflects upon his lot, now that he cannot hope to live more than seven or eight minutes longer. What to him are politics, or scientific investigations, or a name to leave behind him? "For me," he concludes, "after all my eager pursuits, no solid pleasures now remain, but the reflection of a long life spent in meaning well, the sensible conversations of a few good lady ephemeræ, and now and then a kind smile and a tune from the ever amiable *Brillante*." In that gallant commentary on fame and old age Franklin comes alive more fully than he ever does in the *Autobiography*.

Autobiography is, indeed, an imperfect instrument at best. Memory, whether conscious or unconscious, is tricky and mysterious, and a biographer is sometimes able to get the facts more accurately than he who seeks to explain himself. What the autobiographer does not tell us is sometimes more significant than what he does.

Franklin's autobiography, for example, omits consideration of a vast area of his early life which must have had important psychological effects. He recounts some of his sexual adventures and admits that in his first years in Philadelphia he was resorting to "low Women" to allay "that hard-to-be-govern'd Passion of Youth," but he does not say that a son was born to him in the winter of 1730–31 by a woman who has never been satisfactorily identified. She may have been Deborah Read, whom he took as his common-law wife in September of 1730, regular marriage being impossible because her runaway husband might still have been alive. Deborah was his faithful companion until her death in 1774, but of their life together we know little other than that she brought up William, the illegitimate son, as well as their daughter Sarah, and that she did not have the capacity to share the intellectual growth and social success of her printer husband. It is hard to escape the conviction that the Franklins were always on the wrong side of the tracks, and that some of Benjamin's pleasures in his diplomatic triumphs (he was, some have thought, a bit of a snob in later life) may be explained by his domestic situation.

The *Autobiography* was begun as a letter to William, who had already given Franklin an illegitimate grandson, and for whom some moralizing was no doubt appropriate. (William was later, as the last royal governor of New Jersey, to break with his father over politics.) Franklin wrote eighty-six pages of it in England in 1771; other parts were added later (seventeen pages in 1784 and 117 pages in 1788, all written in France, and a final seven and a half pages in 1790, in Philadelphia). Its piecemeal composition was followed by piecemeal publication, in which Franklin of course had no hand, so that until very recently no reliable text has been available. These circumstances, together with its coverage of only the first part of Franklin's life, make it a remarkably imperfect book.

One much-discussed question about the *Autobiography* has been its style. In the late nineteenth century it was believed that Temple Franklin, editor of the first "official" version in 1818, had systematically susbstituted Latin words for his grandfather's more vigorous Anglo-Saxon expressions. He was accused of changing "guzzlers of beer" to "drinkers of beer," "Keimer stared like a pig poisoned" to "Keimer stared with astonishment," and making other similar concessions to false gentility. Max Farrand's lengthy examination of the original manuscript, however, has shown that many changes of this kind were probably Franklin's own. In the last months of his life he was apparently much less admiring of a colloquial style than he was in 1771. He seems, indeed, to have grown conservative about language as he grew older, expressing opposition to innovations which he feared might hamper communication between Englishmen and Americans. One wonders what would have been the result had he lived to see the *Autobiography* through the press himself. Or, what is even more frightening, had he edited his own collected works.

For these and various other reasons Franklin is probably best and most fully revealed in those writings with which he had no opportunity to tamper, and particularly in his letters. Of these there are hundreds, to his family (including a lively and favorite sister in Boston, Mrs. Jane Mecom), to his scientific and philosophical friends, and to correspondents who, like Ezra Stiles, invaded his privacy with a slight touch of malice. The majority of his letters date from the latter part of his life. They show his warm feelings for his friends, which were ordinarily warmly reciprocated, the extraordinary range of his interests, and the play of a lively and imaginative mind. That he had a long life of "meaning well" is clear enough.

It should be evident by this time that I believe Franklin was right in thinking of himself as a writer and that he was seldom as calculating and unemotional a writer as he thought he was. He had a purpose in almost everything he wrote, usually persuasion. He believed written persuasion to be distinct from oral, and he always came back to clarity, brevity, and purpose. An essay of 1733, discovered by Whitfield J. Bell, Jr., contains a passage which sums up his conception of the difference between writing and speech. "*Amplification*, or the Art of saying Little in Much," it reads, "should only be allowed to Speakers. If they preach, a Discourse of considerable Length is expected from them, upon every Subject they undertake, and perhaps they are not stock'd with naked Thought sufficient to furnish it out. If they plead in the Courts, it is of Use to speak abundance, tho' they reason little; for the Ignorant in a Jury, can scarcely believe it possible that a Man can talk so much and so long without being in the Right. Let them have the Liberty then, of repeating the same Sentences in other Words; let them put an Adjective to every Substantive, and double every Substantive with a Synonima; for this is more agreeable than hauking, spitting, taking Snuff, or any other means of concealing Hesitation. Let them multiply Definitions, Comparisons, Similitudes and Examples. Permit them to make a Detail of Causes and Effects, enumerate all the Consequences, and express one Half by Metaphor and Circumlocution: Nay, allow the Preacher to tell us whatever a Thing is nega-

tively, before he begins to tell us what it is affirmatively; and suffer him to divide and subdivide as far as *Two and fiftieth*. All this is not intolerable while it is not written. But when a Discourse is to be bound down upon Paper, and subjected to the calm leisurely Examination of nice Judgment, every Thing that is needless gives Offence; and therefore all should be retrenched, that does not directly conduce to the End design'd."

The final judgment upon the question of whether or not Franklin was a great writer rests upon the evaluation of his purposes. If the advancement of science and the resolution of political differences are of major importance, he was. If the exploration of the depths of human psychology is the primary purpose of literature, he was not. If the great thing for the writer to do is to present a thought-provoking or satisfying philosophy of life, the question is debatable. Purpose aside, however, and greatness left to individual opinion, Franklin has one telling advantage over most American writers who must be read in the context of their time. People do read him.

Selected Bibliography

WORKS OF BENJAMIN FRANKLIN

COLLECTED WORKS

The Works of Benjamin Franklin, edited by Jared Sparks. 10 vols. Boston: Hilliard, Gray, 1840.

The Writings of Benjamin Franklin, edited by Albert Henry Smyth. 10 vols. New York: Macmillan, 1905–07.

The Papers of Benjamin Franklin, edited by Leonard Labaree and others. 15 vols. to date (January 6, 1706, to December 31, 1768). New Haven, Conn.: Yale University Press, 1959–72. (A joint project of the Yale University Press and the American Philosophical Society, expected to run to 40 or more volumes, when completed.)

PRINCIPAL SEPARATE WORKS AND
PERIODICAL PUBLICATIONS

Franklin wrote only a few books. Many of his best-known pieces were circulated in manuscript; others were printed anonymously and without title in newspapers. The following list is selective, with emphasis on items available in modern or facsimile editions. Those marked with an asterisk were originally untitled; a dagger indicates anonymous publication.

*†The Silence Dogood Papers, *New England Courant,* April 2–October 8, 1722.

†*A Dissertation on Liberty and Necessity, Pleasure and Pain.* London: n.p., 1725. Edited in facsimile by Lawrence C. Wroth, New York: Facsimile Text Society, 1930.

†*A Modest Enquiry into the Nature and Necessity of a Paper-Currency.* Philadephia: n.p., 1729.

Poor Richard, 1733. An Almanack for the Year of Christ 1733. Philadelphia: B. Franklin, [1732]. (First of twenty-five annual issues for which Franklin prepared the literary content. All of this material is now readily available in the *Papers.* There are many selective reprints, such as *Poor Richard's Almanack,* with a foreword by Phillips Russell [Garden City, N.Y.: Doubleday, Doran, 1928], which prints the 1733, 1749, 1756, 1757, and 1758 issues in facsimile.)

†*Plain Truth: Or, Serious Considerations on the Present State of the City of Philadelphia, and Province of Pennsylvania.* N.p., 1747.

†*Proposals Relating to the Education of Youth in Pensilvania.* N.p., 1749. Edited in facsimile by Randolph G. Adams, Ann Arbor, Mich.: William L. Clements Library, 1927, and by William Pepper, Philadelphia: University of Pennsylvania Press, 1931.

Experiments and Observations on Electricity. London: E. Cave, 1751. (Later editions in 1754, 1760, and 1769. Translations into French [1752 and 1756], German [1758], and Italian [1774].) Edited by I. Bernard Cohen, Cambridge, Mass.: Harvard University Press, 1941.

*Father Abraham's Speech, or "The Way to Wealth," or "Bonhomme Richard," in *Poor Richard Improved: Being an Almanack . . . For the Year of Our Lord 1758.* Philadelphia: Franklin and Hall, 1757. (Separately printed, it is known in more than 150 editions.)

†*The Interest of Great Britain Considered, with Regard to Her Colonies and the Acquisition of Canada and Guadaloupe.* London: T. Becket, 1760. (The best example of a large body of material on British colonial policies; cf. Verner W. Crane, ed., *Benjamin Franklin's Letters to the Press, 1758–1775* [Chapel Hill: University of North Carolina Press, for the Institute of Early American History and Culture, 1950].)

The Examination of Doctor Benjamin Franklin. N.p., n.d. [London: J. Almon, 1766?]

*†"The Causes of American Discontents before 1768," *London Chronicle,* January 7, 1768.

†"Rules by Which a Great Empire May Be Reduced to a Small One," *Public Advertiser* (London), September 1773.

†"An Edict by the King of Prussia," *Public Advertiser,* September 1773.

*Bagatelles. Passy: Privately printed, 1779–84? (Most of them are extant in their original form only in a unique volume in the Yale University Library. See Richard E. Amacher, *Franklin's Wit & Folly: The Bagatelles* [New Brunswick, N.J.: Rutgers University Press, 1953].)

Mémoires de la vie privée de Benjamin Franklin, écrites par lui-même. Paris: Chez Buisson, 1791. (First printing of the first part of the *Autobiography.* For the intricate history of that work's writing and publication, see *Benjamin Franklin's Memoirs,* Parallel Text Edition edited by Max Farrand [Berkeley and Los Angeles: University of California Press, 1949].)

BIBLIOGRAPHIES AND SURVEYS OF SCHOLARSHIP

Ford, Paul Leicester. *Franklin Bibliography: A List of Books Written by, or Relating to Benjamin Franklin.* Brooklyn, N.Y.: Privately printed, 1889.

Granger, Bruce. "Benjamin Franklin," in *Fifteen American Authors before 1900: Bibliographic*

Essays on Research and Criticism, edited by Robert A. Rees and Earl N. Harbert. Madison: University of Wisconsin Press, 1971. Pp. 185–206.

Lemay, J. A. Leo. "Franklin and the *Autobiography*: An Essay on Recent Scholarship," *Eighteenth-Century Studies*, 1:185–211 (1967).

Miller, C. William. "Franklin's *Poor Richard Almanacs*: Their Printing and Publication," *Studies in Bibliography*, 14:97–115 (1961).

Spiller, Robert E., and others, eds. *Literary History of the United States*. 3rd ed., revised. 2 vols. New York: Macmillan, 1963. (The selective bibliography, 2:507–15, was originally compiled by Thomas H. Johnson; it has been supplemented by Richard M. Ludwig.)

BIOGRAPHICAL INTERPRETATIONS

Aldridge, Alfred Owen. *Franklin and His French Contemporaries*. New York: New York University Press, 1957.

————. *Benjamin Franklin, Philosopher and Man*. Philadelphia and New York: Lippincott, 1965.

Conner, Paul W. *Poor Richard's Politicks: Benjamin Franklin and His New American Order*. New York: Oxford University Press, 1965.

Crane, Verner W. *Benjamin Franklin and a Rising People*. Boston: Little, Brown, 1954.

Fleming, Thomas. *The Man Who Dared the Lightning: A New Look at Benjamin Franklin*. New York: Morrow, 1971.

Miles, Richard D. "The American Image of Benjamin Franklin," *American Quarterly*, 9:117–43 (Summer 1957).

Van Doren, Carl. *Benjamin Franklin*. New York: Viking Press, 1938.

BOOKS AND ARTICLES RELATING TO FRANKLIN AS A WRITER

Amacher, Richard E. *Benjamin Franklin*. New York: Twayne, 1962.

Baender, Paul. "The Basis of Franklin's Duplicative Satires," *American Literature*, 32:267–79 (November 1960).

Cook, Elizabeth Christine. *Literary Influences in Colonial Newspapers, 1704–1750*. Columbia University Studies in English and Comparative Literature. New York, 1912.

Davy, Francis X. "Benjamin Franklin, Satirist: The Satire of Franklin and Its Rhetoric," *Dissertation Abstracts*, 19:317 (1958).

Granger, Bruce Insham. *Benjamin Franklin, an American Man of Letters*. Ithaca, N.Y.: Cornell University Press, 1964.

Hall, Max. *Benjamin Franklin & Polly Baker: The History of a Literary Deception*. Chapel Hill: University of North Carolina Press, 1960.

Horner, George F. "Franklin's *Dogood Papers* Reexamined," *Studies in Philology*, 37:501–23 (July 1940).

Lynen, John. *The Design of the Present: Essays on Time and Form in American Literature*. New Haven, Conn., and London: Yale University Press, 1969.

MacLaurin, Lois Margaret. *Franklin's Vocabulary*. Garden City, N.Y.: Doubleday, Doran, 1928.

McMaster, John Bach. *Benjamin Franklin as a Man of Letters*. American Men of Letters Series. Boston: Houghton, 1887.

Meister, Charles W. "Franklin as a Proverb Stylist," *American Literature*, 24:157–66 (May 1952).

Newcomb, Robert. "The Sources of Benjamin Franklin's Sayings of Poor Richard," *Dissertation Abstracts*, 17:2584–85 (1957).

Ross, John F. "The Character of Poor Richard: Its Source and Alteration," *PMLA*, 35:785–94 (September 1940).

Sayre, Robert F. *The Examined Self: Benjamin Franklin, Henry Adams, Henry James*. Princeton, N.J.: Princeton University Press, 1964.

—THEODORE HORNBERGER

Harold Frederic

1856-1898

*I*N EARLY 1883, Harold Frederic wrote a eulogy to a young poet who had died before the promise of his career could be fulfilled. At the time Frederic was preocupied with thoughts of fame which might transcend death. "Worse than the terrors of dissolution itself is the fear that death may bring forgetfulness. The oldest graven records of the race are barriers raised to stop this dread oblivion,—at once a protest against the effacing march of generations and a plea for posterity's attention, pitiful in its helplessness. 'Let his name be forgotten,' was the sternest and most merciless form of ancient condemnation." Though referring to another, the words, written at a time when Frederic himself was preparing for a literary career, say far more about the novelist than about the forgotten poet.

For Frederic was ambitious to earn a place among the greatest of those whose names were recorded in the "graven records of the race." And, judging from the evidence then available to him, there was every reason to anticipate that he would. Only twenty-six years old, he was already a successful newspaper editor for the second time. A brilliant, articulate, forceful man, he had served apprenticeships as a novice painter and as an author of modest but publishable short stories, and had in progress a novel which, he hoped, would bring him fame. As an editor, he had already influenced a significant segment of New York State political opinion and been instrumental in the election of Grover Cleveland as governor. Many well-remembered men had done far less at Frederic's age.

Nor did he fail to recognize much of his promise. As a journalist, he has been given much of the credit for developing the *New York Times* into an international newspaper. His columns were distinguished by aggressive reporting and luminous insight into events. Most important, he succeeded in fulfilling much of his potential as a literary artist. After a painful trial period, he produced a small body of distinguished novels and novellas, one of which ranks very high among American works of the century. Yet in fifteen years he was dead, and soon thereafter his name was forgotten with that of the poet he eulogized, his works scarcely read, and it is only in recent years that scholars have revived interest in him and made tentative beginnings toward an evaluation of his achievement. Surely literary fortune has rarely rebuffed so summarily a man who, with good reason, expected so much of it.

Harold Frederic committed himself to a literary career in 1884. It was mid-June when he sailed from New York City to London aboard the steamer *Queen* as London correspondent of the *New York Times*, and thus became a member of that earlier, more innocent pre-Hemingway wave of American expatriates who crossed the Atlantic, not to escape America, but to rediscover Europe. Frederic was not a runaway, but a confident American in the tradition of Ralph Waldo Emerson and Walt Whitman, optimistic, self-reliant, burly, robust, democratic. From Whitman and Emerson, and more remotely Ben Franklin, he had inherited a typically American understanding of the nature of reality: that the universe proceeds according to a dependable cosmic timetable along an undeviating track, leading not to Hawthorne's chill waters but to a secular Celestial City filled with gaudy rewards for the diligent whose actions harmonize with that order. Accordingly, the freedom and unlimited opportunity of America permit the vigorous to rise to eminence according to their merit and industry. Rising from poverty to affluence, discovering the nature of lightning, writing a great book widely read and applauded, all these result from the same harmony with the spheres. Like many another American of his time, though more tentatively, Frederic accepted this as a working principle of life.

Yet Frederic was not without Hawthorne-like doubts. There had been moments of disharmony in his life when the principle had failed, when with the best of intentions he had mistaken the main chance, and certain self-destructive temptations had proved irresistible—to his disgust. He was after all not formed in an amiable Unitarian tradition, like Emerson, or in an atmosphere of Quaker calm and light, like Whitman, but in the sterner Methodist discipline. Unlike them, he retained an intuitive sense of the sinfulness of man's nature, although he rejected sin conceptually. Further-

more, as a young reporter along the Erie Canal he had witnessed scenes of cruelty and degradation for which his democratic idealism failed to account.

Because of this ambivalence in Frederic's personality, close acquaintances often erred seriously in estimating his qualities. They saw his veneer of rough force, heard his quick repartee and tireless joviality. But they failed to see the complex mind, the depth of introspection, and the refinement of sensibility beneath; it was from this deeper level of apprehension that fiction of lasting importance eventually came.

But when he left for England he had as yet written no significant fiction. His juvenile stories were slight inventions, about a starving waif rescued from the snow by a rich man who proves to be her father, about a girl disguised as a monk in a French monastery, and about symbolic brothers with opposing loyalties in the American Revolution. His present ambitions were far grander. For seven years he had worked fitfully on a historical romance of the Revolutionary period, and he saw in the independence of his life in England an opportunity to complete it. In addition, he had half-formed plans for a trilogy of novels of contemporary upstate New York, patterned after Disraeli's Young England novels and beginning, as in *Coningsby*, with a study of American politics.

He envisioned a far different return to America. "I dream," he had written, "of the day when I can command a living by honest work in good humane literature, as the anchorite dreams of the day when he shall exchange his hair-shirt for the white robe." Two or three years of work and the white robe would be his, and he could cast aside the hair shirt of journalism. He would then return triumphantly to America to take his place on Parnassus with

Emerson, Hawthorne, and Howells. Much later, when his dreams of immediate success had proved overly sanguine, he could still write, "I'm not a Hawthorne, but as the small Charleston darkey said to the old one, who insisted on God's superiority over the black Congressmen from the Sixth District—'Yes, but don' you fohget—Bob Smalls he young man yet!'"

Frederic was born on August 19, 1856, in the Mohawk Valley city of Utica, New York. Left a widow when her son was only eighteen months old, his mother assumed the roles of both parents. Even after her remarriage, the family remained a matriarchy. It was "Frank" the woman-man who superintended the family enterprises, who dominated her home and set its tone in egalitarian politics and fundamentalist religion. She came to symbolize for Frederic the plain-featured, sturdy pioneer women of America, and as such she frequently appears thinly disguised in his works—in which there are seldom fathers.

A lively, sensitive boy, Frederic received the usual limited education of his modest circumstances. He had a natural talent for pencil sketching and scribbling stories and poems, and after his schooling was completed he experimented with the freedom of an artist's life, traveling to Boston to paint and write. For a brief time in 1873 he lived irregularly with a pack of bohemian starvelings, then found regular work as a photo retoucher. The pay was good, and he was enabled to satisfy his love of books and dandified clothes. Undoubtedly, his ambitions were stimulated by Boston. The schoolroom poets and decaying Brahmins were nearby, and he read the "classic" English authors there. Perhaps because of this inspiration he decided that his future lay in writing rather than painting, and in 1875 he returned to Utica.

There Frederic set about his new career energetically, joining the staff of the Utica *Observer*, and before long the *Observer* was publishing his stories. However, he concentrated on his journalistic duties rather than fiction. He performed most of the routine tasks of the editorial loft, gathering daily news and reviewing traveling art exhibits and road company performances. Success, personal and professional, came fast; by 1880, just twenty-four years old, he was married, a father, managing editor of the *Observer,* and *enfant terrible* of Utica. All social doors were open to him, and he shared the confidences of nationally influential men. He was particularly attracted to the Irish Catholic community and its good-natured men and beautiful women. Among them he met Edward A. Terry, a priest, who was for the rest of Frederic's life his closest and most faithful friend. Terry was a brilliant theologian whose liberal views antagonized more dogmatic Catholic clerics, and as a result he was banished to the diocesan headquarters in Albany. After a short interval, Frederic followed him.

In 1882, the young editor was sought out to revivify the ailing Albany *Evening Journal,* an influential Republican newspaper. He told the owners that despite his former Democratic allegiance he had become an independent with Republican leanings. Truth or not, he was hired and, leaving his family in Utica, moved into bachelor quarters with Father Terry. Then in the 1882 campaign for the governorship he threw the support of the *Journal* behind the Democratic nominee, Grover Cleveland. He thereby became an intimate of Cleveland, and soon the *Journal's* columns were demanding Cleveland for President. Frederic was a resourceful editor who stimulated the wilting paper to new life, but after it was purchased by a more scrupulous Republican in 1884 Frederic resigned rather than support the high-tariff policy of the new owner.

Was Frederic the victim of a political purge by the new owner? Or was his resignation motivated by other reasons, his growing discontent with journalism and his impatience with the tempo of his rise in the world? There is some evidence of journalistic suicide. For one thing, the complimentary publicity resulting from his resignation brought offers of important editorships. He refused them, as well as Cleveland's suggestion that he enter politics, and accepted the subordinate *Times* position in London instead. Also, not long before he resigned he had described journalism as a "vile and hollow fool-rink," and the journalist as a "fakir." Finally, he made it abundantly clear in letter after letter from London that he regarded the *Times* post as no more than a temporary haven which he intended to abandon after a year or two. It appears therefore that he left his editorial career purposefully and with some relief. Certainly the *Times* position was ideal for a restless young man of affairs who had survived the rough-and-tumble of American public life and was ready to challenge Europe, to analyze and probe it, and add it to his growing store of world knowledge.

This was the Harold Frederic who, armed with charm, wit, energy, and a handsome introductory letter from Cleveland, disembarked from the *Queen* in England in mid-1884. He moved rapidly to establish himself in London. He infiltrated the city's club world, where the news and news makers were to be found. The bohemian Savage Club and the politically important National Liberal Club were restricted to an exclusive membership, but Cleveland's letter opened the forbidding doors easily. Soon he was intimate with many of the most influential men in England, at ease with Parliamentarians, with periodical publishers, and in the parlors, the studios, and the theaters of London.

He had also to establish a reputation as an international journalist. Immediately after his arrival, a cholera epidemic infected southern Europe, slaughtering thousands and terrifying the entire Western world. Alone among European correspondents, he visited the area and cabled a clearheaded analysis of the causes of the plague, reassuring his readers that communities which took ordinary sanitary precautions would be in no danger. His dispatches were widely reprinted, his heroism extravagantly praised, and with this single adventure his reputation as a correspondent was secured.

In politics he championed Irish home rule. He met T. P. O'Connor, Tim Healy, and Charles Stewart Parnell soon after his arrival in England, and for a number of years he was on dining and conspiratorial terms with all three. Gradually he became personally involved with the cause of Irish independence, touring the island and absorbing its customs, history, and geography. His cables became increasingly pro-Irish and he published as his own an essay which was in fact a disguised statement of policy written by the Irish leaders. By 1886 he was acting as their envoy; on a visit to America he presented the Utica Irish with a scroll signed by the Irish members of Parliament and delivered a stirring oration about the imminence of home-rule victory.

At the time of this visit, two years of Frederic's expatriation had passed and his success had continued uninterrupted. Preeminence and fortune seemed within reach. One great desire had been fulfilled already, the birth of his first son and namesake who, he said, "represents all my hopes and aspirations." Now a second was fulfilled, a leisurely, sentimental journey to Washington with Father Terry for an intimate White House dinner with Cleveland and his new bride. And a third, literary prominence, was in sight. He had sold the first novel of his trilogy, which, Scribners informed him, was a remarkably strong performance. Already he was at work on a stage adaptation. The Revolutionary War romance was nearly finished, needing only "pointing up" to become the American *Henry Esmond*, and Frederic confided to friends that he intended to spend no more than one additional year in Europe. Just before the sale of the novel he had asked Cleveland for the new post of consular inspector for Great Britain. But now his future seemed assured, and neither the *Times* position nor a foreign service appointment would be needed. As he banqueted with his friends in the presidential mansion he felt confident that his term in journalism was nearly at an end, and that he had arrived at the beginning of a great career in "good, humane literature."

During these first years in England, Frederic was also searching for a usable aesthetic technique. He realized that his earlier sentimentalism was inadequate to his present intentions, and that more useful literary tools were needed. His impulses had by now become strongly didactic. His years as an editor, as a confidant of reform politicians, such as Cleveland and Theodore Roosevelt, and more recently as a co-conspirator of the Irish, had encouraged a conception of fiction as an instrument for political and sociological polemic. The Victorian novelists and his native American predecessors failed to provide him with models for this purpose. The witty, formally rhetorical prose structures and the characters and situations related to the comedy of manners of the former, and the brooding darkness of the latter, were equally unsuited to the ambience of Gilded Age expansiveness and Zolaesque scientific empiricism.

Although he was a natural raconteur, Frederic was at this time wholly incapable of devising aesthetic principles of his own. Largely self-educated in the course of a busy public life, he had no critical apparatus or vocabulary. He thought in terms of accidentals rather than essentials: sufficient room in which to "turn around," the truth or mendacity of incident, and marketability. For his philosophy of fiction, he turned to principles of realism articulated by William Dean Howells. These included the utmost fidelity to the actual scenes, actions, and language of everyday life, and the "dramatic method" of plotting, in which "real" people are set at liberty in a "real" environment to work out "real" problems without authorial interference. Optimistic assumptions underlay this method. Granted a benign cosmic order, a plot so produced should conform to an essentially comic pattern by demonstrating in its inevitable resolution the potential of the unfettered democratic man to rise to new degrees of human achievement and happiness in the American Eden. Yet Frederic also groped instinctively for a means of expressing the more complex suspicions and perceptions which could not be wholly suppressed by his Emersonian assumptions. From the first, his discipleship to Howells was qualified by the knowledge that there were disruptive elements in American life as well as those "smiling" aspects which Howells insisted upon.

"The Editor and the Schoolma'am" (1888), part short story and part essay, throws some light on his confusion. A young, vain editor of a city newspaper quarrels with a pretty schoolteacher over an essay she has submitted on "The True Place of Milton Among the English Poets." His knowledge of Milton is scant, but he nevertheless arrogantly advises her to abandon such abstract themes (Frederic himself had written comparable essays). Read Dostoevski's *Crime and Punishment*, he tells her, and write "articles" from real life on "the butcher, the baker, the candlestick maker." After reading the novel she concludes, like Howells, that a vicious murder is foreign to the placid realities of America. The subdued editor protests that there is an element of violence in the American character, only to be answered with the feminine argument that "there oughtn't to be." The two marry, leaving the central question undecided. The equally matched characters speak for the two elements of Frederic's uncertainty; he is both the doubter and the doubt.

In spite of this ambivalence, Frederic had for the time sufficient faith to write two novels in the Howells mode. But his duplicity of attitude mars his otherwise strong first novel, *Seth's Brother's Wife* (1887), and its sequel. Both are set in a fictitious congressional district of upstate New York, a re-creation of his Mohawk Valley home. As in Faulkner's Yoknapatawpha County, the area contains cities and towns, individuals and families, which reappear from work to work. An entire community is created in which Frederic tests his attitudes toward American life, and, ultimately, toward the human condition.

Seth appears to be conceived as a kind of fictionalized newspaper editorial, an attempt, in the words of Thomas F. O'Donnell and Hoyt C. Franchere, to "demonstrate, in a tone of restrained optimism, that in spite of a certain drabness and apparent moral and spiritual laxity of life in upstate New York, the region could still produce from its own citizenry honest and devoted leaders who were capable of arousing the moral vigor of the public when such vigor was needed." The main concerns are journalistic: the decay of New York State agriculture under the pressure of competition from the midwestern granaries, the operation and influence of a regional newspaper, and the power structure of a district political caucus. Frederic's style is similarly journalistic. Though tinged with Addisonian rhetoric, it is essentially colloquial and descriptive, substituting for elegance and wit a muscular, often crude prose. To readers who preferred the former, it appeared that Frederic was the victim of "jour-

nalistic standards." Yet his painter's eye, his reporter's knack of getting directly to the point, and his raconteur's ability to create striking vignettes give vividness and pungency to his first novel.

The three principal concerns intersect in Seth Fairchild. Seth is threatened with a life of ignorance and despair on the ramshackle and dismembered Fairchild farm; he gains, almost loses, and then prospers in a newspaper career; and he opposes his brother Albert's cynical scheme to seize the district congressional nomination by bribery. Had Frederic had less insight into the weaknesses of men, had he not tested Seth's responses against suspicions about his own character, *Seth* might have gained in coherence while losing in significance and interest. But Frederic was unwilling to grant his protagonist the unqualified virtue which his heroic role demands.

Much of the vigor of the novel comes from its autobiographical nature; characters, incidents, and scenes are flooded with vitality as they emerge from Frederic's memory. Seth becomes Frederic's surrogate, reliving the author's youthful experiences in editorial offices and in the caucus. Even Seth's marriage to Annie Warren, arranged at the bedside of Annie's dying mother, is a re-enactment of Frederic's courtship.

But as his surrogate, Seth bears the consequences of Frederic's deep-rooted sense of insufficiency and guilt. His dissipation nearly ruins his newspaper career, and his sexual irresponsibility very nearly results in adultery with Albert's flirtatious wife, Isabel. Nor is he able to conquer either of these weaknesses through self-correction. His waning journalistic fortunes are rescued at the last minute by the intervention of Richard Ansdell, an indistinct figure who appears only occasionally, though following this Seth rises unaided to the editorship. Similarly, he is saved from committing adultery only because Albert returns home unexpectedly just as Seth is responding to Isabel's coquetry. Because of this he forfeits his moment of intended heroism; his intention of announcing his paper's opposition to Albert's corrupt candidacy shrivels in the heat of the husband's justified wrath: "You set yourself up to judge *me;* you arrogate to yourself airs of moral superiority, and assume to regulate affairs of State by the light of your virtue and wisdom—and you have not brains enough meanwhile to take care of yourself against the cheapest wiles of a silly woman, who amuses herself with young simpletons just to kill time." This humiliation disqualifies Seth as hero; his moral triumph is stillborn and he agrees to become Albert's political tool.

At this point Frederic's divided attitudes reach a fictional crisis. Is the democratic system capable of self-regulation through the virtues of its citizens and institutions, of frustrating the ambitions of the power-hungry who threaten to subvert it, or is the model Democratic Man naïve and self-indulgent, powerless in his insufficiency? To put it another way, are the natural forces of probity capable of overcoming the forces of corruption, of evil, or are they themselves blighted by natural depravity? Seth, the instrument of Frederic's optimism, fatally disqualifies himself from action.

Yet Frederic is unwilling to accept the implications of Seth's failure. With the presumptive hero discredited, he moves outside of the social machinery he has created to salvage a positive resolution. A villain is made of an otherwise ineffectual farmhand, who preserves the integrity of the political process by murdering Albert, and an unexpected hero is made of a previously obscure third brother, John. John plays Fortinbras, reassembling the scattered plot pieces by occupying the farm which is the family patrimony and demonstrating an integrity as editor of his weekly newspaper

which Seth could not sustain. Thus the "moral and spiritual laxity" are embodied in Seth, and the "honest and devoted leaders" are peripheral and dramatically neutral figures.

Frederic attempted to rectify the defects of *Seth* in the sequel, *The Lawton Girl* (1890). Following the apparent plan for the trilogy, he shifted his attention from politics to economics and treated urban problems. His working notes called for a single protagonist, but, warned by Seth's unreliability and not yet aware of the confusion of attitude which Seth has embodied, he divided the original protagonist into two. Reuben Tracy receives all of Seth's admirable traits, while Horace Boyce receives his cupidity. Reuben is honest, sober, hard-working, and a bloodless prig; Horace is a self-deceiving lecher, a dilettante, a cheat, and at last a scoundrel. Yet it is Horace who wins the reader's interest and sympathy, again frustrating Frederic's intended optimism.

The story is built on two plot lines, Jessica Lawton's rehabilitation after her seduction by Horace and subsequent brothel degradation, and the rescue of the Minster Iron Works from a shadowy cartel, which, using Horace as an instrument, plans to seize it. With adequate materials for an energetic novel, *The Lawton Girl* nevertheless fails. Jessica's reclamation proceeds to the point of decent employment as a milliner, then founders on Frederic's unwillingness to allow her to marry the seducer she still loves. Furthermore, the economic bandits deserve more success in stealing the Minster factory than Frederic allows them. They are unconvincingly defeated in a dishonestly melodramatic climax: at the moment of crisis Reuben discovers documents which incriminate the gang, thereby earning him the hand and fortune of heiress Kate Minster.

"It was a false and cowardly thing to do," Frederic later wrote of his decision to kill Jessica rather than to allow her to marry Horace.

But this self-criticism applies equally to his decision to employ twin protagonists. Reuben's perfection makes him incredible. He is qualified through natural gifts and unassailable character to restore community equilibrium, to the benefit of owner and worker alike, as the manless Minsters are not. In contrast, the selfishness and vanity of Horace are disruptive of the cosmic order and his every action threatens the communal well-being. Order and the "smiling" aspects of life triumph, but it is a triumph without dramatic validity. Reuben is never more than an animated fabrication, an artifact in the worst sense of the word, transmitted inert from Frederic's imagination to the printed page. Tellingly, most of the vitality emanates from the disreputable and unscrupulous figures. The dialogue, schemes, and actions of these figures are vital and fictionally engaging; those of their honest and decent counterparts are not. In a valid resolution of conflicts, order is not restored through the aseptic law-school oratory with which Reuben pacifies the rioting workers. As Frederic was writing, the meretriciousness of this climax was being demonstrated by riots in Chicago's Haymarket.

In 1890 Frederic also published his Revolutionary War romance, *In the Valley*. The appearance of a study of the origins of the nation at this time is suggestive. When the national character on which his "dramatic method" depended demonstrated moral instability, it was necessary to turn to the causative events which had produced that character, as Hart Crane and William Carlos Williams were later to do. Thus his impulses were epic, a search for cultural roots related to those of Homer, Virgil, and Camões, and it is as epic that Frederic's American historical fiction can most usefully be read.

In the Valley was actually completed sometime before *The Lawton Girl*, yet, with the Civil War tales which followed, it is a response to Frederic's philosophical and fictional dilemma. Frederic sought the symbols of the past which might explain the present, and although *In the Valley* is scrupulously faithful to historical and geographical fact, it is nevertheless the most completely symbolic of Frederic's works. Many of the characters represent factions of the Valley population: Douw Mauverensen, the hero, the early European colonists; Philip Cross, his enemy, the arrogant English aristocrats. Daisy, the girl of indeterminate origin, is a symbol of the land itself for which the two groups compete. Even the geography is symbolic: the Mohawk Valley which divides the colonies culturally and strategically in two, and the gorge which separates Douw's home from Philip's, both represent the divisions between the settlers and between the Old World and the New, which resulted in warfare and were healed at last by brotherly reconciliation.

Its dimensions are epic as well. In time it reaches back through the allusions and recollections of Douw to precolonial days, and forward through its dramatic events, from 1757 to 1777, to the time of narration, about 1815. Further, it is spatially immense, sweeping from Europe (in the recalled background of Douw's patron) to the fur-trading encampments of the Midwest, and from the early battles at Boston to the siege of Quebec. The cast of characters is enormous, literally an army, a roll call of the German, Dutch, and English settlers whose differences and doggedness precipitate and sustain the action. The events often correspond with those of the traditional epic: the journey of the hero into the wilderness to prepare him for his mature mission, the premonitory vision given the hero of the final crucial battle, the muster of the warriors, and the single combat between the hero and his personal adversary within the larger framework of battle.

Frederic deftly navigates between the Scylla and Charybdis which endanger the writer of historical fiction, the gratuitous introduction of famous men for fictional effect and the tendency to sentimentalize or glorify the "forefathers." The hero is no paladin, but a stubborn Dutchman whose occasional petulance humanizes him and prevents him from becoming a Reuben Tracy stereotype; although the villain is unpleasant, his arrogance and rascality result from the incompatibility of his aristocratic manners and assumptions with egalitarian frontier life. And Daisy comes to Douw not an immaculate virgin but the abused widow of his enemy, ravaged like the land by the struggle in which she is won.

America, Frederic concluded, is not simply a consequence of grafting an ideal system to a new unspoiled continent in which latter-day Adams and Eves started afresh under a new covenant. It is, in addition, a result of the melding of barely miscible ethnic elements on blood-tempered soil, and the necessary catalyst is mutual tolerance. It is on this realistic foundation that the qualified promise of America stands. The implied danger, which tempts Douw, is that there may arise a new arrogance and intolerance which will invalidate the original victory. What is required, then, is manliness and unselfish responsibility which combine the best qualities of individualism with mutual understanding and respect between men. It is his inhumane treatment of a helpless slave which leads to the death of Philip Cross.

In the Valley is not wholly successful. Though the scenic elements and dramatic passages are technically excellent, the total effect is of events and places seen through a remote haze, and except for Douw the main characters seldom attain more than symbolic life. Frederic admitted that "their personalities always remained shadowy in my own mind." His style, elevated to meet the demands of an epic, loses force and stability in the process. Still, the novel is conceived with originality and de-serves a prominent place in American historical fiction.

Following this Frederic traced the effects of independence during the period between Douw's growth to manly tolerance and Seth Fairchild's reversion to paralyzing self-indulgence. At precisely what point had the national experiment failed, if it had, and what could be learned from the subsequent experiences which might illuminate and suggest remedies for the ills of the present? The Civil War had left vivid images of community apprehension and suffering on Frederic as a child, and to the maturing artist it attained a significance analogous to that of the War of Independence. Between these wars the nation had tested diverse political and social postures, had experienced waves of immigration and, disturbingly, had begun to reorganize class distinctions. Great questions had remained unresolved: the relative supremacy of national and regional interests, and the willingness or unwillingness of individuals to suppress self-interest and tolerate divergent attitudes and ways in others.

The Copperhead (1893) begins at the point where *In the Valley* ended, tracing its protagonist's ideas back to the age of "Matty" Van Buren and to Jefferson. Opening on the outbreak of the war, it dramatizes the philosophical divisions which tore the nation, North and South alike. The copperhead (or sympathizer with the South) is Abner Beech, a states' rights individualist who, though he does not support slavery, cannot accept self-righteous interference with southern affairs. His ideological opponent is an evangelical abolitionist named "Jee" Hagadorn. Their children are in love, a hopeful new generation capable of transcending the narrow attitudes which make enemies of their parents.

The theme of intolerance is repeated in *The Copperhead*. States' rights and abolitionist attitudes lead to persecution rather than dialogue.

Although he has been a farsighted "natural aristocrat" among the community farmers, Abner is now despised, banished from the co-operative dairy which he was instrumental in founding, and deserted by his hired men. But Abner returns intolerance for intolerance: after his son joins the Union army, he reads the story of Absalom and David at family prayers and disinherits the boy. Mutual intolerance grows until, in an orgy of patriotic enthusiasm, his neighbors burn Abner's house unintentionally, to the horror of both sides. Local and national tragedy meet when Abner's son returns to the ashes of his home maimed by battle, and the implications of the formerly abstract dispute are made manifest in human suffering. Copperhead and abolitionist alike are chastened, and in a gesture of reconciliation the two children marry.

Marsena (1894 in serial form) anatomizes a form of seemingly innocent folly, the viciousness of which is revealed in the context of war, the egotism of a beautiful woman who gratifies herself by playing sexual roulette with human destiny. Marsena is an ironic self-portrait created in a tone lying somewhere between sharp self-criticism and tolerant whimsy. Affecting melancholy Byronic poses, he is impossibly romantic, as the young Frederic just returned from Boston may have been. His romanticism is soon focused on the aristocratic town flirt who is the ideal of the young men of the town, Julia Parmalee.

The comedy of the first scenes is rich as the gallants contest for Julia's attentions and as she lures them one by one into the militia as testimony of their devotion to her, dropping each at the conscript train. "If you only give her time, she'll have the whole male unmarried population of Octavius, between the ages of sixteen and sixty, down there wallerin' around in the Virginny swamps, feedin' the musketeers and makin' a bid for glory," says

the local philosopher. And that is exactly what happens when the comic-opera skirmishes of Lincoln's ninety-day army give way to the bitter struggle between heavily gunned opponents and all too real casualty lists begin to sum up the cost of Julia's flirtatious recruiting. The awkward chivalry of the town hopefuls and the mischievous arrogance of a town flirt take on a horrifying new significance in the vicious fighting; what begins as ironic comedy turns inexorably to bitter revulsion.

At this point the tone of an otherwise brilliant novella disintegrates. Perhaps lacking sufficient artistic detachment from its autobiographical protagonist, Frederic allows his outrage to take command. "It was one of the occasions on which Man had expended all his powers to prove his superiority to Nature. The elements in their wildest and most savage mood could never have wrought such butchery as this. . . . the broad, sloping hillside and the valley bottom lay literally hidden under ridge upon ridge of smashed and riddled human forms, and the heaped débris of human battle. The clouds hung thick and close above, as if to keep the stars from beholding this repellent sample of earth's titanic beast, Man, at his worst." Finally, in uncontrolled anger, Frederic provides an impossible ending, the callous Julia, now a socialite nurse at the front, ministering to a slightly scratched staff officer as Marsena dies clutching the hem of her skirt.

The epic cycle is concluded by "The War Widow" (1893), the last (in internal chronology) and the greatest of Frederic's historical fiction. It is a powerful novella which looks ahead from the tragedy of war into the coming Gilded Age to suggest, perhaps regretfully, a road not taken, the recapture from the experience of death and suffering of certain important human values.

Two living characters dominate the action along with two others about whom, though they are dead when the story begins, the action turns. Old Arphaxed Turnbull is an earthy Valley patriarch whose fathers cleared the land, made it say crops instead of briars, and built the prosperous farm which he has inherited and increased. Aunt Em, his daughter, is a taciturn, kindly woman, like her pioneer ancestors a vigorous household drudge without the slightest glamour, so plain that it is assumed that she will never marry. Nevertheless, one day she brings home a good-natured ne'er-do-well she has taken to husband. Although Abel Jones is hardly received as an ornament to the successful family, he is everything to Em. The fourth figure is Em's half-brother Alva, a brilliant, educated man whose early distinction promises fulfillment of Arphaxed's dynastic dreams; through Alva, Arphaxed glimpses a world of gentility he himself can never enter. When a local regiment is raised, it is natural that Alva ride away in command, sword at side, while Abel joins the rear rank as a private soldier.

The bereavement of war exposes Arphaxed's vanity: he has begun to revert to the repudiated European aristocratic ideals. His grief at the death of Alva is nearly unbearable, perhaps more because of the death of his dynastic ambitions than because of that of his son, while the death of Abel, though equally tragic, he ignores.

When Alva's casket is opened for a last time before he is to be buried in a hillside grave overlooking the Valley he might one day have ruled, Arphaxed is horrified to find that war profiteers have substituted the body of an anonymous enlisted man. The wives of the sons have experienced a real loss much greater than the frustration of Arphaxed's vision of family eminence, as have those who loved the soldier in the coffin. But in his unthinking rage Arphaxed orders the body sent to the county authorities for a pauper's burial. At this, Em angrily confronts her father. "On Resurrection Day, do you think them with shoulder-straps 'll be called fust an' given all the front places? I reckon the men that carried a musket are every whit as good, there in the trench, as them that wore swords. They gave their lives as much as the others did, an' the best man that ever stepped couldn't do no more." Chastened by Em's angry dignity and intimidated by the intercession of Alva's wife, Arphaxed buries the stranger in Alva's grave, in acknowledgment of the democracy of suffering of the living and the awful equality of the dead.

Frederic thus concluded that by the time of the Civil War there had been a rebirth of foreign vanities and illusions which the plain-featured and direct-spoken men and women of *In the Valley* had attempted to extirpate from the new democratic society, a rebirth which threatened corruption to the great ideal. However bigoted Abner Beech and Jee Hagedorn may have been, each still cherished individual human rights and unadorned virtues, and neither could have given Arphaxed's order to send away the symbolic coffin. Yet "The War Widow" suggests that amid the seemingly senseless slaughter and the unworthy ambitions of a newer kind of American, a rebirth of democratic brotherhood for the future American and an exorcism of the vanity which threatened to corrupt the "smiling" aspects of American life were possible.

That there had been a further transmission of Arphaxed's vanity to Seth Fairchild and Horace Boyce suggests that Frederic's suppressed fears would yet have to be accounted for. By the time of *Marsena*, the last published of the cycle, they had reached the surface, and the center of his Howellsian optimism was no longer able to hold. Death, the awful absolute which purges and chastens in "The War Widow," has by the time of *Marsena* lost its nobility, has become frivolous, a ghastly queen who scarcely notices as victims gasp at her feet.

Vanity, not heroism, leads men to their deaths, and the society they die defending is not a community of dignified creatures but "earth's titanic beast, Man." Frederic saw that "an Egyptian blackness was over it all" in one of his last glances back over the American past.

In other ways aside from his shaken idealism 1890 was a watershed in Frederic's life, followed by a gradually increasing "Egyptian" darkness. The momentum of his success had begun to falter as early as 1887, when the baby Harold Frederic, who had been the focus of all his father's "hopes and aspirations," died. The following year his political hero, Cleveland, was denied re-election, challenging Frederic's faith that a democratic electorate would recognize integrity in its leaders. In addition, literary success proved elusive. Although critics like Howells praised *Seth* and fellow realists wrote their congratulations, the novel was foreign to the expectations of the mass of readers, who preferred their fiction perfumed with elegance, romance, and sentiment. It was alternately deplored and ignored by influential reviewers in the popular magazines, and sales were poor. Far from achieving the financial independence which he was already anticipating in his standard of living, he was forced to continue indefinitely with the *Times*. He was settling into a nearly permanent pattern of high living and low sales which frustrated permanently his hope of abandoning the "fool-rink" of journalism for the life of a literary aristocrat.

He was still sanguine about *In the Valley*, however. Even if the public failed to respond to it, he expected a more favorable reaction from the perceptive few. But the most important of these failed him. Through an oversight, Howells had ignored Frederic completely until 1890, when, in a combined review of the first three novels, he buried praise for the others under condemnation of the intended master-piece, calling it a "fresh instance of the fatuity of the historical novel." During a visit to Boston that year Frederic appealed his case in person and they parted on friendly terms. But Howells always remained aloof from Frederic and, for Frederic, Howells ceased to be the supreme trail-breaker and arbiter, though he always remained important as a leader in the search for literary truth.

In other areas Frederic experienced disappointments. In his favorite retreat, the Savage Club, a nasty quarrel broke out with a London editor. Frederic was finally sued for libel, of which he was probably guilty. When he lost the suit, his estrangement from the Savages became permanent and this outlet for his ambitions and good spirits was closed. A similar catastrophe occurred in his relations with the Irish leaders. As a result of the scandal surrounding Parnell's marriage to the divorced Kitty O'Shea, Tim Healy contested his leadership. Frederic followed Healy's example, using his *Times* cable to repudiate the "lost leader." But Parnell's charisma with the Irish people remained and was abruptly transformed into martyrdom when he died tragically in 1891. Frederic found himself on the wrong side, a rational voice drowned in keening Irish emotionalism. He was never again influential among the Irish, and resentment against him ran high among the Irish in America. Whether for this reason or not, Frederic never returned to the United States.

Before 1890 Frederic hoped to attain eminence and affluence by marching to the Howells drum and conforming to the Horatio Alger Junior success pattern; thereafter he realized that he must create a compensating social and artistic world of his own. Increasingly, he sought out private friendships among writers and artists to substitute for the salon society of the Philistines, and aspired to success in the perfection of his artistry rather than in the reviewers' columns. Remarkable changes occurred beneath his hearty exterior, alterations in his ambitions, his loyalties, his habits, and, ultimately, his art. The bankrupt thrust toward public eminence was replaced by an ideal of inner growth and personal fulfillment.

It was in 1890 that Kate Lyon became his mistress. There was a certain idealism about the alliance, which accorded with his radical views of sexual relationships in the age of the New Woman. It was a genuine attempt to substitute a vital and joyous love for the hypocritical and sterile, though unseverable, bond which his marriage had become. There were both good and bad effects of the new liaison. He found purity in his relationship with Kate, who, George Gissing claimed, was his "real wife"; she "saved him and enabled him to do admirable things." On the other hand, it may have been his heterodox love life that disqualified him from the Liverpool consulship, which, in a last effort to salvage his failing dream, he requested soon after Cleveland returned to the presidency in 1893.

Aside from his historical cycle, the years from 1890 to 1896 constitute a chaotic second "period" in Frederic's literary development. They were years filled with anguish and vexations, in which his adopted sociological realism was of little use to him, he had developed no substitute technique or philosophy, and the demands on his income were doubled by the needs of his two families. He was forced by poverty and aesthetic uncertainty to a broad range of literary experiments which produced some trivial work and some interesting results as well. Although this was a perplexing and uncomfortable time for him, it had one invaluable result. Along with the insights he was gaining into his own attitudes in his Civil War tales, the experience of dabbling in a variety of styles and subjects enabled him to perfect the craftsmanship which characterized the fiction of his last years.

This dabbling is imposing in its range. Infected with the theatrical fever which was endemic among his contemporaries Twain, Howells, and James, he worked both singly and in collaboration with Brandon Thomas (*Charley's Aunt*) on a number of plays. Few were completed, however, and of those which were, only one was cast and rehearsed. He wrote journalistic books as well, an effective and influential study of contemporary anti-Semitism in Russia and a gossipy, unscholarly biography of the German Kaiser. In another vein, he wrote two inferior tales of the War of the Roses, which, though he attempted verisimilitude and historical accuracy, are unmistakably juvenile fiction. One further experiment, unsuccessful but suggestive of the direction which his later fiction would take, is the frankly Hawthornesque "The Song of the Swamp-Robin" (1891). Though Frederic misunderstood Hawthorne's genius and patterned the story after his worst rather than his best tales, it is significant that this early he was glancing away from the Howells imperatives toward the unfashionable moral romance.

There are two genuine achievements among these experiments, a social satire and a series of Irish tales. The first is a series of sketches of English middle-class society written for magazine publication in 1892 and collected as *Mrs. Albert Grundy: Observations in Philistia* (1896). Loosely linked by the scantest of courtship plots, they allowed Frederic to meander brightly and skillfully among whatever topics attracted him at the moment: self-portrait, character sketches, the English courts, middle-class prudery, and so forth. With deft control of tone he comments on matters as slight as the social consequences of shaving one's beard and as serious as the plight of a genteel woman thrown unprepared into the economic labyrinth of sexually unequal London. The style is nimble and urbane, the humor precise and delightfully understated; the reader coming to this book from the rough force of Frederic's early work is forced to reassess his versatility and recognize a finer sensibility than he is often said to have had. But there is a further dimension which underlies the surface delicacy. The sketches provided Frederic with an emotional release through which he could rid himself of some of the multiplying frustrations and disappointments of his daily life. Through the vertiginous Miss Timby-Hucks he was able to discharge his animosity toward women journalists, particularly a certain Miss Stevens who was employed by the *Times* to write feature letters about the Royal Academy art exhibitions despite Frederic's superior qualifications, and to strike back at the English courts following his conviction for libel. And in the reactions of the American outsider to English society he was enabled to comment on the British character and on the fate of being an American innocent confronted with old Europe.

It was natural that after Frederic's alienation from Irish affairs and after hope for Irish self-rule diminished he would turn to fiction to express his responses to the islanders whom he never ceased to love. After a false beginning with an abortive novel he produced an apparently uncompleted series of haunting tales of the O'Mahony septs, which, despite their small bulk, relate him to the Irish literary renaissance. The setting is his adopted area of southern Ireland, the Ivehagh peninsula, and the time is the last half of the sixteenth century, the period during which Ireland fell gradually under the domination of Elizabeth's generals. Alternately tragic and comic, they dramatize what Frederic conceived to be the salient qualities of the rich and contrary Irish character: bravery and treachery, seismic loves and hatreds, piety and superstition, and, pervading all, the fierce Irish pride. In execution they reveal Frederic at a new plateau of achievement, in full command of a supple style which ranges from lush lyricism to sparse tragedy.

There are four tales in all, begun and ended by stories concerned with the chieftainship of Turlogh of the Two Minds. He is an Irish Hamlet whose character, deficient in the passion and self-assertiveness which make other overlords feared warriors and unquestioned leaders, is reflective and gentle. He affords his kerns a wise rule which, if it disappoints their combative natures, echoes the great scholarly tradition of medieval Ireland and offers a hope, not to be realized in Turlogh's time, of a future of peaceful prosperity.

"In the Shadow of Gabriel" (1895) tells of the coming of age of Turlogh, in which it is the studious youth rather than his terrified warriors who doggedly pursues the devil haunting his lands, and the "devil" who saves him from death at the hands of a supposed holy man. Through a topsy-turvy inversion of good and evil, wit and witlessness, bravery and cowardice, Turlogh wins the right to his fiefdom in a conclusion both comical and brutal. Ironic comedy is counterpointed in the second tale by the legendary tragedy of Murtogh and his unfaithful wife; the third returns to another coming-of-age rite, this one farcical, in which Teige, a boastful, lustful young chieftain, is gulled into a remarkably rewarding marriage by the lies of a cringing bard.

In the climaxing tale, "The Truce of the Bishop" (1895), the burial of a magnificently vain bishop is combined with the ritualistic death of Turlogh and his warriors in combat with the invading English. Turlogh is now an old man, his lands laid waste. The end of free Ireland is at hand; the only choice left to the now single-minded Turlogh is to submit or to perish on his own terms. Seizing control of the black fate of his sept, Turlogh conducts the bishop's last rites with all the magnificence left to him, then provokes a battle to the end with the astonished English. As he stands over their bodies, the English commander pronounces their epitaph: "Has ever there been such a land of madmen and saints?" He speaks as well for Frederic, who, looking back over the long history of Irish repression and self-destructiveness, was similarly perplexed by their heroic grandeur and suicidal passions.

At precisely this point Frederic's period of consolidation ended, his literary maturity complete. He had tested a broad spectrum of styles, subjects, and modes, and had refined his implements, rendering them responsive to subtle variations of thought and mood. He was, in addition, uniquely qualified for the important work ahead, the critical re-examination of the Whitmanic democratic man. He had struggled to sustain his own faith, and when his optimism was suborned by the flawed character of his representative protagonists, he had probed the American past diagnostically, hoping in the process to discover some hope for future melioration. But the heroism he discovered was confined to the remote past. As his fiction approached the present, he confronted the truth that men had not improved under egalitarian conditions; if anything, they had degenerated. Frederic's last measure of nineteenth-century optimism died on the battlefield with Marsena, clutching the skirts of a seductive ideal with which he had flirted.

Nor was this a purely literary discovery. In his rise from a modest background to international stature as a journalist, his life had approximated the American Dream. Yet for all of his high principles and dedication to the truth, his deepest impulses were undependable

and self-defeating. His enemies could, after all, without departing wholly from the truth describe him as a gross man, a liar, a financial irresponsible, and an adulterer. As this self-knowledge grew, he sensed that the flaws of his protagonists were reflections of flaws within himself. He realized in the most personal way that the New World Adam was really post-lapsarian, his innocence confined to his manners and to his ideal conception of himself. Beneath was an uncharted subterranean cavern of id—or original sin, to vary the terminology—where obscene monsters might and too often did exist. As long as the innocence was imperfectly tested by experience, its surface might hold. But once it was shattered, the true nature of the democratic man was exposed.

Not even Henry James could perform this anatomization with his remarkably delicate scalpel; his imagination was confined to a social stratum above the Whitmanic quotidian and he was unable to deal with humdrum reality. Mark Twain had insufficient intellectual discipline and sense of form. Howells lacked brilliance of perception. Only Frederic could. His experience, his perception, his darkened vision, and his perfected talent made it possible. In his final phase of innocent turned cynic he asked himself inevitable questions. What was the fate of the American to be in the new, complex century about to arrive? And what was to be the fate of the world should its destiny fall into his hands? Frederic's answer was embodied in some of the most significant fiction of the era.

The Damnation of Theron Ware (1896) is a study of a new kind of American not-so-innocent, whose ancestors include both Huckleberry Finn and Faust. It is the story of a likable, talented, but ignorant young Methodist minister whose superficial religion and deficient character are challenged in the microcosmic

Mohawk Valley city of Octavius. A teacup dilettante, he is thrust into a primitive parish to face a religious and cultural ugliness which he has heretofore been able to avoid. His good-natured weakness is inadequate to the challenge, and in revulsion he accepts offers of intellectual companionship from three figures whose philosophies offer sophisticated alternatives to the narrow fundamentalism of his parishioners: Father Forbes, a Catholic philosophical skeptic modeled on Father Terry; Doctor Ledsmar, an atheistic scientist; and, most attractive to Theron, Celia Madden, a beautiful and wealthy young woman who, though a Catholic, offers him aesthetic epicureanism. It is a classic instance of egocentric innocence confronted with the allure of exotic philosophies it fails to comprehend—indeed, is prevented from comprehending by an inherent voluptuousness concealed beneath a surface of affable charm. As Theron accepts their friendship, the terms of which he never bothers to ascertain, he turns his back on his parish, losing control over its affairs to the elders of the church. Just in time (for Theron's damnation) two pragmatic confidence men turned evangelists, Brother and Sister Soulsby, arrive for a "debt-raising." Taking his affairs into their hands, they reconcile minister and congregation. Thus the necessary forces are deployed for the paradigmatic loss of innocence of a tawdry American Adam. He must choose among them, and his choice leads to his damnation (the English edition of the book was ironically titled *Illumination*). But his fall is a peculiarly modern one, preordained by the conditions of the modern world, and reworked by Frederic into a pratfall into the twentieth century.

Theron Ware is one of the most widely misread novels in American literature, though in spite of Frederic's narrative subtlety and a certain ambiguity its meaning seems relatively clear. The conflicting values are those of his earlier fiction: goodheartedness and sincerity set against hypocrisy and self-seeking. Although the "European" triumvirate are occasionally associated with diabolical imagery (they have a diabolical *effect* on Theron) they are genuinely, if unwisely, anxious to help him rise to knowledge, each according to his own beliefs. Ledsmar lends him atheistic books, keeps reptiles, and experiments on the narcotics tolerance of his Chinese servant. Celia has flaming red hair and has converted her rooms to an exotic palace of pleasure where she promises to show Theron "that which is my very own." Forbes scoffs at literal interpretation of the Scriptures, has ominously white skin and a plush, phallus-like body, and lives a sumptuously nonclerical life in the privacy of his pastorate. They must share some of the blame for destroying his innocence by their proselyting. Certainly they are careless, but each is genuinely concerned with his intellectual and spiritual growth. Such innocence as Theron's cannot endure in the modern world; how he reacts to their ministries is a function of his honesty.

The same cannot be said of Sister Soulsby, the true Mephistopheles of the morality. Although through pure fictional vitality she is an engaging figure, she is a shape-changer, a disarmingly frank and earthy woman who at the same time darts her eyes at Theron like a bird of prey, advises him to have some of the "wisdom of the serpent," and bargains his church away from him with a Faustian handshake. It is she who touches Theron's weakest point, immobilizing his moral faculties with a vision of petty illusions disguising the sordid "reality" of the world. "Did you ever see a play? In a theatre, I mean. I supposed not. But you'll understand when I say that the performance looks one way from where the audience sit, and quite a different way when you are behind the scenes. *There you see that the trees and houses are cloth, and the moon is tissue paper, and the flying fairy is a middle-aged woman strung up on a rope . . . everything in this world is produced by machinery—by organization.*"

With this "common sense" appeal she wins a permanent convert to the cynical philosophy of sharp practices and self-indulgent rationalizations. Ware sees his ministry now as no more than a theatrical illusion which he must stage-manage from the pulpit. Father Forbes's traditional attacks on Protestant literalism he now interprets as atheism and Celia's sincere commitment to beauty he interprets as an invitation to petty vice. Ledsmar's philosophical battles with Celia he supposes to be personally vindictive and he crudely attempts to use Ledsmar as an informant against the other two. Under Sister Soulsby's pernicious tutelage he believes that he is onstage where the machinery may be seen, gaining every moment in moral stature and enlightenment, penetrating to the sordid motives behind human activity known only to the favored few. But Celia's brother, with the insight of the dying, knows better. "You are much changed, Mr. Ware, since you came to Octavius, and it is not a change for the good. . . . Only half a year has gone by, and you have another face on you entirely. . . . If it seemed to me like the face of a saint before, it is more like the face of a bar-keeper now!"

In technique the novel is Hawthornesque, except for Frederic's deceptively realistic prose. Most of the proper names are heavily allusive and the passage of the seasons symbolizes a reversal of the regeneration of *Walden*. It moves from emblem to emblem, embodying meaning in those still-life pictures which have been characteristic of classic American fiction

from its beginnings—Leatherstocking silhouetted against the sky, Dimmesdale standing bare-chested on a Boston scaffold, Bulkington glimpsed frozen to the *Pequod*'s tiller. The decay of the modern ministry is displayed in the hierarchical arrangement of the assembly of the Methodist Conference; Theron's revulsion from the fundamentalists and his attraction to the sophisticates are repeated in his reactions to the squalor of his parsonage yard and the lush foliage next door; the foreign allure of Celia's paganized Christianity is reflected in the décor of her apartment; and Theron's youthful prejudice against Catholics is remembered in a Nast-like cartoon of sinister priests.

When Theron meets Celia in a remote wood, halfway between the austere frenzy of a Methodist camp meeting and the Dionysian revelry of a Catholic picnic, they discover the novel's central emblem. "The path they followed had grown indefinite among the grass and creepers of the forest carpet; now it seemed to end altogether in a little copse of young birches, the delicately graceful stems of which were clustered about a parent stump, long since decayed and overgrown with lichens and layers of thick moss." The path lost and the solid beliefs of the past rotted away, tentative alternatives compete for dominance, though none now dominates. Theron is free to choose, but his choice must be sincere, positive, creative, rather than nihilistic. Above all, he must recognize that the new shoots are real and alive, not, as Sister Soulsby insists, illusory. When he does not, his damnation is assured.

Furthermore, it is a damnation against which Frederic himself struggled. For the qualities which animate the central characters are fractions of his own complex personality. Within, the same alternatives were at war: the hopeful, opportunistic Theron is the young reporter ar-

riving in London; the Darwinian horticultural-
ist Ledsmar is Frederic; the epicurean Celia is
Frederic; and the glib charlatan Sister Soulsby
is Frederic. Alice Ware, the simple wife abandoned by the upward-seeking Theron is Grace
Frederic, that tragic woman left behind in isolation and bitterness by her ambitious husband.
The city of Octavius is more than a microcosm
of innocent America at last confronting the
complexities of Europe and the coming century; it is an allegory of the spirit of a diverse
and troubled man who fatally senses the centrifugal drama being enacted within him.

Whatever doubts he may have had about
his own character, Frederic had none about
Theron's. When he elects Sister Soulsby's bad
faith, the rest is downward spiral. Succumbing
to the logic of his degeneration, he becomes
successively a would-be adulterer, an embezzler, a Peeping Tom, and a near murderer
and suicide before returning to Sister Soulsby,
now her creature. Not recognizing his new allegiance to the Prince of Darkness, he claims
that God has forsaken him. Alice, more empirical, claims that "it was all that miserable, contemptible Octavius that did the mischief." But
Sister Soulsby, who should know, replies that
"if there hadn't been a screw loose somewhere
. . . Octavius wouldn't have hurt him." At the
end Theron is stuffed with straw and set on
his feet again, now ambitious for the one career which, since Albert Fairchild, has always
meant damnation in Frederic's fiction: seeking political power for his own profit and for
the satisfaction of his damaged ego.

Theron Ware is a powerful masterpiece. It
presents not only a brilliantly conceived and
psychologically fascinating protagonist but a
representative if unpromising man at the end
of an era of confidence and simple faith and
the beginning of a darker era of complexity and
doubt. It is only from the perspective of the
present that we can see the full significance of
what Frederic discerned at the end of the nineteenth century. The era to come—our era—
would demand an inner strength much greater
than had been required of men before. Deprived of the comforting assurance of the past,
the modern man would be forced back upon
the resources of his own character, his virtues,
to use a nearly outmoded term, in order to
make his way among the tangle of often questionable choices of the world-maze. To look
for stage machinery instead of truth is to invite
degeneration, to confuse darkness with illumination, to strike a bargain with Satan, to lose
what weed-grown Paradise is left in a diminished world.

Frederic's own slight version of Paradise,
the solace he found in his mistress, Kate Lyon,
is the subject of a small, graceful novel written
in reaction to the darkness of *Theron Ware*.
Perhaps beauty in this world *is* stage illusion.
In that case, a temporary stay against despair
may be had by preserving the illusion. *March
Hares* (1896) is the story of such protective
self-deception, of failure and emptiness eluded
by an escape into an artificial fairyland, embraced and substituted for distasteful truth.

The story opens on the September reality of
London. David Mosscrop, a brilliant time-
server in a meaningless sinecure, has wasted
his life in stale dissipation with oafish companions, and stands on Westminster Bridge, unshaven, groggy with drink, contemplating suicide. There he meets a despondent young
woman who, without money or friends, also
considers suicide or prostitution. What follows
was known as "cat-fiction" at the time. The
two band together, fall in love, and on David's
modest resources command that September dissolve and that the freshness of March return.
They eat and drink, buy new clothes, disappear
and reappear, and finally, in a minuet of mis-

taken identities, are reunited. The reality of September is only precariously suppressed, awaiting a moment of depression or misunderstanding to reassert itself, but as long as both agree to the mutual enchantment it is March.

Perhaps his life with Kate was necessary to save Frederic from destruction, as the story suggests. Nevertheless, the novel is unfulfilled, ending in irresolution. The basic failure of David's life, his wasted brilliance and the meaningful squirrel cage of his profession, is in the end unchanged. It is disguised but present, to reappear again when the illusion of March can no longer be sustained. Kate Lyon may have been a defense against despair, but in story and life alike the fates remained unplacated behind the make-believe of happiness.

With the popular success of *Theron Ware,* Frederic at last gained acceptance as a man of letters, though on far different terms from the Bostonian dignity he had sought. He was in demand as a reviewer, accepted in important intellectual circles, and acquainted with Shaw, Gissing, James, Conrad, Wells, and Ford Madox Ford. Yet it was with a fellow American journalist that he had his only intimate literary association. Stephen Crane, who praised his Civil War fiction and was praised by him in turn, met Frederic in London on his way to the war in Greece, and on his return moved into a suburban house Frederic had secured. The two novelists and their mistresses were companions, frequenting each other's homes and vacationing together in Ireland. The relationship was occasionally stormy, and the two added little or nothing to each other's art. Nevertheless, it was the kind of alliance Frederic had long sought to substitute for the neglects and disappointments of his later life, and he threw himself into it with enthusiasm.

But the idyll ended when Crane departed abruptly for the Spanish-American War. Frederic's heart was failing just when his intellec-tual and artistic powers were at their peak. Doctors were called, but with fatalistic independence he lived his last days on his own terms, refusing all advice and care. As his body declined he punished it contemptuously, driving furiously across the country, smoking cigars, and drinking. When this was no longer possible, Kate sent for a Christian Science healer, and the two women attempted to substitute faith for the medicine he refused. On October 19, 1898, Frederic died, leaving a heavy legacy of debt and recrimination to his two families. A vindictive trial followed, in which Kate and the healer were spared imprisonment only because of a judicial determination that, despite Frederic's difficult personality, he was sane at the time of his illness and capable of seeking medical aid had he desired it. Thus the man who aspired to dignified eminence ended his life in the midst of scandal and vituperation.

Following the trial, Frederic's two posthumous novels enjoyed wide circulation among the curious. It was a surprise to his readers and a disappointment to reviewers to find that both were set in England. The subject matter, paralleling in many ways that of *Seth* and *The Lawton Girl,* makes it appear that he had in mind another trilogy, this one "studying" English life. That this was the case is strongly suggested by the combined historical allegory and political-sociological didacticism of *Gloria Mundi* (1898), an unfortunately artificial and weak novel. It yokes a shadowy recapitulation of the origins and development of the English people to a yet-unraveled *roman à clef* of contemporary English society. In the peregrinations of the French-born protagonist, whose prospective inheritance of an impoverished English barony provides the primary plot thread, the book wanders over a lot of territory, solves no problems, and ends in irresolution.

The novel suggests that the cosmic order exists as Frederic had earlier supposed, but now indifferent to men, who can no longer prosper by harmonizing with it. After considering the various uses to which he may put his titled prerogatives, Christian Tower decides at the end that it is useless to adopt any program at all. His dukedom is "all a great organized machine, like some big business." "A man is only a man after all. He did not make this world, and he cannot do with it what he likes. It is a bigger thing, when you come to think of it, than he is. At the end there is only a little hole in it for him to be buried in and forgotten." Perhaps a premonition of Frederic's death can be read into this passage. If so, Christian's stoicism contrasts sharply with the vision of immortality which had been before Frederic in Albany fifteen years earlier.

Frederic returned to the force of *Theron Ware* in his remarkable last novel, *The Market-Place* (1899). In a sinewy narrative he utilizes the world of London finance to develop the central theme of his last years, the implications of the chaotic century which was about to arrive for the directionless people who must live in it. For this purpose he unleashed a selfish, brutal speculator (developed from Sister Soulsby) named Joel Stormont Thorpe on a decayed society which, seeking a hero, invites a dictator. Representative figures of the mordant English ruling class surround him: a marquis of ancient family, a newer aristocrat, a retired general, all impecunious and prepared to sacrifice principle for cash. The degeneracy of these atrophied remains of traditional European authority is manifest; the question raised is, after them what?

The inevitable answer is that with the erosion of the hereditary estates of rule, the power vacuum will be filled with or without the intelligent assent of the governed. To the illuminated, troubled author the future seemed clouded and ambiguous, potential leaders grasping and amoral, and the citizenry apathetic. Power seemed within the reach of greedy, arrogant men, and this danger was amplified by the seeming sanction given to the domineering ego by some of the more alarming implications of the philosophies of Carlyle and Nietzsche. Good and evil, they suggested to some readers, at least, are defined by the whims of the new aristocrat, the barbarian whose lust for power and efficiency in gaining it provide a new pragmatic standard of conduct. If this were true, then it invalidated Frederic's remaining belief in the commonwealth of humanity; if it were false, then the very currency of the concept lent an appearance of respectability to demagoguery, social vandalism, and megalomania.

While literary naturalists assented to the new philosophy, Frederic offered an example whose strength, will, and amorality approximate those of the superman, but who is at the same time human, originating within the social structure rather than above it. Thorpe is fallible, lacking the ability to crush his victims at will. In dozens of earlier escapades this middle-aged fortune hunter has been balked by bad luck, traitorous associates, or perhaps his own bungling. It is only in his present stock-market swindle that circumstances combine to allow him success, and now only because of the arrogant miscalculations of the financiers who oppose him.

With success, Thorpe demonstrates prophetically the implications of Nietzsche's abstractions when twisted to suit the purposes of the demagogue. His swindle assumes an anti-Semitic character; boasting of his power, he says, " 'I used to watch those Jews' hands, a year ago, when I was dining and wining them. They're all thin and wiry and full of veins. Their fingers are never still; they twist round and keep stirring like a lobster's feelers. But there aint any real strength in 'em. They get hold of most things that are going, because they're eternally on the move. It's their hellish industry and activity that gives them such a pull, and makes most people afraid of them. But when a hand like that takes them by the throat'—he held up his right hand as he spoke, with the thick uncouth fingers and massive thumb arched menacingly in a powerful muscular tension—'when *that* tightens round their neck, and they feel that the grip means business—my God! what good are they?' He laughed contemptuously." His pillage becomes murderous when an old derelict endangers his scheme and is quietly eliminated in a final solution. Thorpe's appearance changes into that of an Adolf Hitler, as he trims his mustache to military size and becomes jowly. "It was palpably the visage of a dictator."

Thorpe's scheme prospers, partly because his greed is shared by his victims, and partly because of the failure of the moral resources of decency. Both are embodied in the woman he marries. There is an element of masochistic sexual aberration in Edith Cressage, whose blood has run thin and whose normal responsiveness has been vitiated by her marriage to a degenerate aristocrat, forced upon her by her corrupt father. Now she is willing to submit to Thorpe's crude force, seeing in it a stimulant to her exhausted feminine appetites and a mastery to which she can sublimate her disappointed need for personal fulfillment.

After Thorpe has made his fortune, married, and retired to a country manor, the final warning is given. He is dissatisfied with the opulent life which had earlier been his goal, for there is no satisfaction for the power seeker except in the pursuit of power. Therefore, in a much-misread ending, Thorpe returns to London to spend his money charitably among the poor —except that his largess will be bartered for a seat in Parliament, and ultimately for power over all England. One of the judges who voted to behead Charles I was a Thorpe, he reminds us.

Frederic's deft manipulation of point of view makes severe demands on the reader's discrimination; one must be attentive to his road markers. Tension builds as the financial scheme alternates between apparent success and the constant danger of collapse, and as Thorpe's courtship is alternately frustrated and successful. The temptation to sympathize with an energetic figure who is also a scoundrel makes Thorpe's success all the more insidious. Evil appearing as evil is dangerous; evil masquerading as gumption, individualism, shrewdness, the American Dream, is a transcendent danger which can only be evaluated by the most exacting attention to humane principle. That is precisely Frederic's point. It is only by listening to the voice of principle, here that of Celia Madden (carried over from *Theron Ware*) and Thorpe's sister, that gross misreadings of the novel, such as attributing Thorpe's anti-Semitism to Frederic, can be avoided. There are numerous other pitfalls for the unwary, such as believing Thorpe's self-characterization at the end as a new man with new ideas. There is no new, humanized Thorpe; he is still a "man gathering within himself, to expend upon his fellows, the appetites, energies, insensibilities, audacities of a beast of prey." He is a twentieth-century political pirate, seizing power with stolen money. Celia's last analysis of him is accurate. "I shall always insist . . . that crime was his true vocation."

Recognition came to Frederic late, and then for the wrong reasons. *Theron Ware* was read because of its scandalous impiety; *The Market-Place* because of the scandal surrounding his death. Soon thereafter, interest in his work subsided, and he has been a victim of the "effacing march of generations" which he dreaded. To a certain extent this neglect has been justified. Beginning with a journalistic conception of literature, and lacking Henry James's ability to theorize about the nature of fiction and to translate theory into practice, Frederic tended on occasion to write dramatized essays rather than novels. Not only that, but he was curiously inept with essay materials and in these novels he was often betrayed by the unresolved conflict between his ideology and the dramatic reality which embodied most faithfully his deepest understanding of the nature of men. It was only in his last three years that this conflict was resolved and his mature genius found expression. When it did, his achievement was too far in advance of current attitudes to be comprehensible to his public.

Nor has subsequent criticism been notably perceptive. Readers have classified him as a regionalist, as a realist, and as a naturalist, whereas his true descent from Hawthorne and Melville has largely gone unnoticed. Many sense the depth and power of *Theron Ware*, but find the source of his creative energy elusive.

Frederic's achievement lies in the sensitivity and power with which he probed the naiveté and inconsistency of the American Dream and announced its inevitable collapse in the face of the new order of complexity of the twentieth century. In this he surpassed all his contemporaries in his ability to dramatize, allegorize, and mythicize the coming fall from innocence. In addition, testing his vision against his own experience, he understood that a loss of innocence might not bring a dignified, saddened wisdom, but might transform youthful egotism into debased cynicism, and ultimately into predatory rapacity. Thus Frederic wrote for the twentieth century, not his own, and in his greatest works achieved a vigorous and alarming vision of the civilization to come which has, as we can now see, verified his worst fears and proved him to be one of the most perceptive and important novelists of his time.

Selected Bibliography

WORKS OF HAROLD FREDERIC

NOVELS

Seth's Brother's Wife: A Study of Life in the Greater New York. New York: Scribners, 1887.

In the Valley. New York: Scribners, 1890.

The Lawton Girl. New York: Scribners, 1890.

The Return of the O'Mahony. New York: Bonner's, 1892.

The Copperhead. New York: Scribners, 1893.

Mrs. Albert Grundy: Observations in Philistia. London: Lane, 1896.

The Damnation of Theron Ware. Chicago: Stone and Kimball, 1896. (Published in England with a few textual variations as *Illumination*. London: Heinemann, 1896.)

March Hares. London: Lane, 1896. (Initially issued under the pseudonym "George Forth.")

Marsena. London: Unwin, 1896. (Serialized in 1894.)

Gloria Mundi: A Novel. Chicago and New York: Stone, 1898.

The Market-Place. New York: Stokes, 1899.

COLLECTIONS OF FICTION

The Copperhead and Other Stories of the North during the American War. London: Heinemann, 1894. (Contains "My Aunt Susan," *The Copperhead*, "The Eve of the Fourth," and "The War Widow.")

Marsena and Other Stories of the Wartime. New York: Scribners, 1894. (Contains "My Aunt Susan," "The Eve of the Fourth," "The War Widow," and *Marsena*.)

In the Sixties. New York: Scribners, 1897. (Contains a preface which is Frederic's only systematic discussion of his work, as well as all of the fiction in the preceding two items.)

The Deserter and Other Stories: A Book of Two Wars. Boston: Lothrop, 1898. (Contains "Where Avon into Severn Flows," "How Dickon Came by His Name," "The Deserter," and "A Day in the Wilderness.")

MAJOR UNCOLLECTED SHORT STORIES

"Brother Angelan," *Harper's*, 73:517–28 (September 1886).

"The Editor and the Schoolma'am," *New York Times*, September 9, 1888, p. 14.

"The Martyrdom of Maev," *New York Ledger*, 46:1–3 (March 22, 1890) and 46:–3 (March 29, 1890).

"The Song of the Swamp-Robin," *Independent*, 43:394–95, 430–32 (March 12 and 19, 1891).

"Cordelia and the Moon," in Liber *Scriptorum.* New York: Author's Club, 1893. Pp. 241–52.

"The Path of Murtogh," *Idler* (London), 7:455–79 (May 1895).

"The Truce of the Bishop," *Yellow Book*, 7:84–111 (October 1895).

"In the Shadow of Gabriel. A.D. 1550," *New York Ledger*, 51:12–13 (December 21, 1895); *Black and White*, 10:21–26 (Christmas 1895).

"The Wooing of Teige," *Pall Mall Magazine*, 10:418–26 (November 1896).

"The Connoisseur," *Saturday Review* (London), 82:18–21 (Christmas 1896); *New York Ledger*, 52:8–9 (January 2, 1897).

NONFICTION BOOKS

The Young Emperor, William II of Germany: A Study in Character Development on a Throne. New York: Putnam's, 1891.

The New Exodus: A Study of Israel in Russia. New York: Putnam's, 1892.

STANDARD EDITION

A definitive edition of Frederic's literary works, produced at The University of Texas at Arlington and published by The Texas Christian University Press, is in progress.

BIBLIOGRAPHY

American Literary Realism, 1870–1910, 1:1–89 (Spring 1968) and 3:95–147. (Secondary and some primary bibliography, largely by Robert H. Woodward.)

Blanck, Jacob. *Bibliography of American Literature*, Vol. III. New Haven, Conn.: Yale University Press, 1959.

Woodward, Robert H. "Harold Frederic: A Bibliography," *Studies in Bibliography*, 13:247–57 (1960).

BIOGRAPHICAL AND CRITICAL STUDIES

Berryman, John. *Stephen Crane.* New York: William Sloane Associates, 1950.

Blackall, Jean Frantz. "Frederic's *Gloria Mundi* as a Novel of Education," *The Markham Review*, 3:41–46 (May 1972).

————. "Perspectives on Harold Frederic's *Market-Place*," *PMLA*, 86:388–405 (May 1971).

Briggs, Austin. *The Novels of Harold Frederic.* Ithaca, N.Y.: Cornell University Press, 1969.

Carter, Everett. "Introduction," *The Damnation of Theron Ware.* Cambridge, Mass.: Harvard University Press, 1960.

Crane, Stephen. "Harold Frederic," *Chap-Book*, 8:358–59 (March 15, 1898).

Earnest, Ernest. *Expatriates and Patriots.* Durham, N.C.: Duke University Press, 1968.

Garmon, Gerald M. "Naturalism and *The Damnation of Theron Ware*," *West Georgia College Review*, 2:44–51 (November 1969).

Garner, Stanton. "Some Notes on Harold Frederic in Ireland," *American Literature*, 39:60–74 (March 1967).

Gilkes, Lillian. *Cora Crane.* Bloomington: Indiana University Press, 1960.

Haines, Paul. "Harold Frederic." Unpublished dissertation New York University, 1945. (Still the standard biography.)

Johnson, George W. "Harold Frederic's Young Goodman Ware: The Ambiguities of a Realistic Romance," *Modern Fiction Studies*, 8:361–74 (Winter 1962–63).

Kane, Patricia. "Lest Darkness Come upon You:

An Interpretation of *The Damnation of Theron Ware*," *Iowa English Yearbook*, 10:55–59 (Fall 1965).

Lovett, Robert Morss. "Introduction," *The Damnation of Theron Ware*. New York: Boni, 1924.

McWilliams, Carey. "Harold Frederic: 'A Country Boy of Genius,' " *University of California Chronicle*, 35:21–34 (1933).

O'Donnell, Thomas F. "Editor's Foreword," *Harold Frederic's Stories of New York State*. Syracuse: Syracuse University Press, 1966.

————, and Hoyt C. Franchere. *Harold Frederic*. New York: Twayne, 1961. (A fundamental study, with information not in Haines.)

Raleigh, John Henry. *"The Damnation of Theron Ware*," *American Literature*, 30:210–27 (May 1958).

Ravitz, Abe C. "Harold Frederic's Venerable Copperhead," *New York History*, 41:35–48 (January 1960).

Sage, Howard. "Harold Frederic's Narrative Essays: A Realistic-Journalistic Genre," *American Literary Realism, 1870–1910*, 3:388–92 (Fall 1970).

Stein, Allen F. "Evasions of An American Adam: Structure and Theme in *The Damnation of Theron Ware*," *American Literary Realism, 1870–1910*, 5:23–36 (Winter 1972).

Suderman, Elmer F. *"The Damnation of Theron Ware* as a Criticism of American Religious Thought," *Huntington Library Quarterly*, 33:61–75 (November 1969).

Towers, Tom H. "The Problem of Determinism in Frederic's First Novel," *College English*, 26:361–66 (February 1965).

Walcutt, Charles Child. *American Literary Naturalism, a Divided Stream*. Minneapolis: University of Minnesota Press, 1956.

Williams, David. "The Nature of the Damnation of Theron Ware," *Massachusetts Studies in English*, 2:41–48 (Fall 1969).

Wilson, Edmund. "Introduction," *Harold Frederic's Stories of New York State*. Syracuse: Syracuse University Press, 1966.

————. "Two Neglected American Novelists: II —Harold Frederic, the Expanding Upstater," *New Yorker*, 46:112–34 (June 6, 1970).

Woodward Robert H. "Illusion and Moral Ambivalence in *Seth's Brother's Wife*," *American Literary Realism, 1870–1910*, 2:279–82 (Fall 1969).

————. "The Political Background of Harold Frederic's Novel *Seth's Brother's Wife*," *New York History*, 43:239–48 (July 1962).

————. "Some Sources for Harold Frederic's *The Damnation of Theron Ware*," *American Literature*, 32:46–51 (March 1961).

Ziff, Larzer. *The American 1890's; Life and Times of a Lost Generation*. New York: Viking Press, 1966.

—STANTON GARNER

Robert Frost

1874-1963

IN ROBERT FROST's dramatic dialogue entitled "West-running Brook" a farmer and his wife are represented as admiring the contrary direction of a small New England stream which must turn eastward, somewhere, to flow into the Atlantic. As they talk, they notice how the black water, catching on a sunken rock, flings a white wave backward, against the current. The husband says,

"Speaking of contraries, see how the brook
In that white wave runs counter to itself."

Within the poem, various "contraries" are interlocked to illuminate one of the poet's major and recurrent themes; yet no harm is done the poem if that wave image is borrowed, temporarily, for use in another sense. It can serve to suggest a possible approach to an interpretation of Robert Frost's life and art, in terms of elements which there run counter to themselves.

Start with a few "contraries" implicit in the story of his life. Widely celebrated as a New England poet, Robert Frost was actually born in San Francisco, California, on March 26, 1874. Although his father was a native of New England, his mother was a true Scotswoman, an emigrant from Edinburgh. She had been well educated in Columbus, Ohio, had become

a schoolteacher, and had met her future husband while both of them were teaching school in Lewistown, Pennsylvania. Because Isabelle Moodie Frost was fond of writing verse, it would not have been surprising if she had named her son after Robert Burns; but as it happened the father chose to name the child after the South's most distinguished general, Robert E. Lee.

Further contraries are suggested by the motives for that naming. The poet's father, William Prescott Frost, was descended from a puritanic line of Maine and New Hampshire farmers, public servants, and Revolutionary War soldiers. Yet William had developed such a violent hatred for his native New England that he had remained only long enough to be graduated with honors from Harvard College, in the class of 1872. Thereupon he had started west, pausing for one year of teaching at Lewistown to acquire funds, and then, with his new wife at his side, moving on to seek his fortune in the Golden Gate city. Part of his hatred for New England had been engendered by the Civil War, which had interrupted the flow of raw cotton from the South to factories in New England. William's father, having abandoned farming in his native New Hampshire in order to try his luck as a worker in the cotton and woolen mills along the Merrimack River at Lawrence, Massachusetts, had become a foreman in one of those mills. But when local economies were upset by the Civil War and by the shortage of raw cotton, he and many other New Englanders had found their sympathies thus bound up with the southern cause.

Raised as a city boy, in San Francisco, until he was eleven years old, Robert Lee Frost found his life uprooted when his father died there of tuberculosis, in 1885, leaving as his only will the seemingly inconsistent request that his remains be taken back to his native and hated New England for burial. Thus it happened that the boy crossed the continent with his mother and his younger sister, Jeanie. Because funds were not available for the return trip to California, the widow and her children settled in the village of Salem, New Hampshire, where Mrs. Frost earned a precarious living for a few years teaching in the grammar school which her children attended.

Robert Frost often said that when first he came to New England he prided himself so much on being a Californian that he felt a decided hostility toward those reticent Yankees whose idiom he later honored in his poetry. Perhaps it was the shock of newness which sharpened his various responses to those peculiar New England speech-ways, images, scenes, characters, and attitudes.

Disliking study, and refusing to read any book by himself until he was twelve, the boy suddenly developed an intense pleasure in learning, during his four years in the Lawrence High School. After he was graduated as valedictorian, and class poet, in 1892, he enrolled as a freshman at Dartmouth College, but soon left, insisting that he had had enough of scholarship. During the next few years, seemingly without any worldly ambition, he tried his hand at various ways of earning a living. At different times, he worked in mills in Lawrence, dabbled in newspaper reporting, taught school. Meanwhile, his fondness for writing poetry occupied his leisure hours. In 1894, to celebrate his first sale of a poem, "My Butterfly," to a prominent literary magazine, the *New York Independent*, he arranged to have five of his lyrics privately printed in a booklet entitled *Twilight*. The edition was limited to only two copies, one for his affianced, Elinor White, and one for himself.

After his marriage in 1895, he tried to settle into the routine of schoolteaching. For more than two years he helped his mother manage a small private school in Lawrence, then spent two years as a special student at Harvard College, hoping to prepare himself for college teaching. But again he decided that the academic atmosphere was not congenial to him. For reasons of health, in 1899, he turned to an outdoor occupation and tried to make a successful business enterprise out of raising hens and selling eggs. In 1900, after his doctor had warned him that his recurrent illnesses (largely nervous) might indicate tuberculosis, he moved with his growing family to a small farm in Derry, New Hampshire, and there continued his poultry business.

Nothing went well for him, and he seemed to have a gift for failure only. During the winter of 1906, he came so near to death from pneumonia that both he and his doctor were surprised when he recovered. Thus reduced to the verge of nothingness, and feeling completely without prospects, he turned more and more to his almost furtive writing of poetry, as a kind of consolation. Occasionally he sold a poem or two. But when he was forced to admit that he could not make ends meet, financially, as either poet or farmer, he turned again to schoolteaching, this time at Pinkerton Academy in Derry. Subsequently, he taught psychology for one year at the New Hampshire State Normal School in Plymouth.

Having grown accustomed to gambling with his own life, he decided, in 1912, to bet all on poetry. After selling his farm in Derry, Frost took his wife and four children to England, rented a house in Beaconsfield, Buckinghamshire, and settled in, to write. The gamble was very successful. Much to his relief, his first book of lyrics, *A Boy's Will* (1913), was accepted by the first publisher to whom it was offered. His book of dramatic dialogues, *North of Boston* (1914), attracted so much attention that by the time the Frost family returned to the United States, early in 1915, both books were being reissued there. *North of Boston* soon became a best seller.

Success embarrassed him. Extremely shy, painfully sensitive, inwardly tortured by crowds, Frost bought a small farm in Franconia, New Hampshire, hoping to escape from public adulation. For reasons of economics and pride, however, he could not long refuse invitations to give public lectures and readings. In less than a year after his return from England he had publicly performed in various parts of the United States, literally from Maine to Texas. Then in spite of his asserted distaste for all things academic, he became one of the first American poets to make arrangements with various institutions to live on campus as poet-in-residence, for a few months or years. While his major relationships of this sort were with Amherst College in Massachusetts, he also spent intermittent years in residence at the University of Michigan, at Harvard College, and at Dartmouth.

Throughout these various sojourns as troubadour Frost managed to indulge his liking for the life of a farmer, particularly during vacation months of seedtime, growth, and harvest. He left New Hampshire for Vermont when he moved with his family from Franconia to South Shaftsbury and bought a farm there in 1919. After his children had grown, and after Mrs. Frost had died, he changed his legal residence from South Shaftsbury to an upland farm which he purchased in Ripton, Vermont. On doctor's orders he began spending the most severe winter months in Florida, starting in 1936; then in 1940 he bought a two-acre palmetto patch outside Coral Gables, Florida, cleared the land, set out citrus trees, and erected a pair of small New England cottages. His feeling for the soil and for growing things remained a passion with him, long after that kind of life ceased to be a necessity.

Having survived without any public recognition until his fortieth year, Frost thereafter received more honors than any other contemporary literary figure in America. He was elected to membership in the National Institute of Arts and Letters in 1916, to membership in the American Academy in 1930. Four times he was awarded the Pulitzer Prize for Poetry. On the occasion of his seventy-fifth birthday, and again on his eighty-fifth, the United States Senate adopted a formal resolution extending felicitations to him. In spite of his resistance to earning even the lowliest college diploma, he was given honorary degrees by forty-four colleges and universities. One phase of his career came full circle in the spring of 1957, when he returned to England (where he had gone as a complete stranger in 1912) to receive honorary degrees from Oxford and Cambridge.

Near the end of his life, Frost dramatized additional contraries by accepting incongruous honors. Strongly conservative in his political views, and outspokenly isolationist, he nevertheless accepted an invitation to participate in the inauguration ceremonies of President-elect John F. Kennedy. On that occasion, he read his poem entitled "The Gift Outright." In August 1962, President Kennedy sent him to Russia on a "good-will mission." Robert Frost died at the age of eighty-eight, on January 29, 1963, from the aftereffects of an operation for cancer.

Further patterns of contraries may be found within and between Frost's eleven separate volumes of poems. In the lyrics of *A Boy's Will*, he was content to use traditional forms; but even in the earliest of these lyrics he had already begun to displace "musicality" by emphasizing dramatic intonations and cadences of everyday conversational speech, together with a simple vocabulary which heightened the typical Yankee understatements.

The consciously arranged pattern of lyrics in *A Boy's Will* was designed to represent the poet's youthful growth, in a wavering progression of subjective moods. Independent searchings, questionings, doubtings, affirmings, cherishings are dramatically and poetically realized. The sequence begins with the poet's acknowledged need for separateness and isolation ("Into My Own"), progresses through a group of subtly intense love-and-courtship lyrics ("A Late Walk," "Flower-gathering," and "A Dream Pang"), turns to a newly perceived sense of the brotherhood of men "whether they work together or apart" (in "The Tuft of Flowers"), and finally circles back to a mood of isolation which has become wistful ("Reluctance").

That circular or spiral pattern of complementary moods, in *A Boy's Will*, is enriched by arranging a related progression of responses to the seasonal cycle of nature, starting with a subdued enjoyment of the autumnal mood, moving through deeds and images of winter, spring, summer, and finally returning "with a difference" to the autumnal settings. In these variations of attitudes toward nature, the young and maturing poet's moods entertain different values at different times. If nature, at one moment, seems indifferent and blind toward man's "faltering few steps" between birth and death

(as in "Stars"), or if nature at another moment seems malevolent, hostile, bestial (as in "Storm Fear"), it can and does sometimes reflect a benevolently divine plan or design (as in "A Prayer in Spring"). These contradictions of mood are permitted to remain unresolved; but the structural arrangement itself implies a progression toward a maturing solution. For Frost, this pattern of arranging his poems, within a single volume, became a matrix. It recurs in several of his books, all the way from *A Boy's Will* to *In the Clearing*.

By contrast, *North of Boston* is "a book of people," wherein the prevailing mode is dramatic narrative and dialogue. The poet's attention is primarily directed outward, rather than inward, as he portrays a variety of rural New England responses to the human predicament, not for purposes of recording "local color" but rather to evoke universal extensions of meaning. The kinship of these poems with the idylls of Theocritus is not accidental. Predominantly, these blank-verse narratives of rural manners and ways focus attention on psychological characterizations which represent a tragicomic blend of human failures and triumphs. The poet's own contemplative reveries, thus oriented, are frequently handled in terms of both implicit and explicit dialogue. For example, in the familiar poem entitled "Mending Wall," the brief narrative represents two opposed attitudes toward tradition, in that the poet imaginatively challenges the literal and therefore meaningless rituals, symbolized by repairing a wall at a point where there is no need for a wall. While the opposed views of the two neighbors are presented with playful seriousness as foils, the conclusion resolves the conflict in favor of the poet's view, as he characterizes his neighbor's typical blindness:

He moves in darkness as it seems to me,
Not of woods only and the shade of trees.

He will not go behind his father's saying,
And he likes having thought of it so well
He says again, "Good fences make good
     neighbors."

Thus in these dramatic dialogues, another kind of Frostian matrix is provided through his poetic representation of thought, in various forms of inner and outer dialogue, to provide counterbalanced ways of looking at one and the same thing.

Mountain Interval (1916) takes its title from the side-hill New Hampshire farm above the intervale where the Frost family lived, after returning from England in 1915. The poems in this volume combined the two previously separated modes of the inner lyric vision and the outer narrative contemplation, in ways which reveal increasing poetic subtlety and versatility. For example, while all of Frost's lyrics partake of the dramatic, five lyrics are gathered under the title "The Hill Wife" to provide a miniature drama in five moods rather than acts: obliquely, an isolated woman's cumulative sense of fear, loneliness, and marital estrangement is represented as being so completely misunderstood by her husband that he is baffled when she disappears, irrevocably and without warning. Another foreshadowing of a subsequently favorite Frostian mode occurs in a farm fable entitled "The Cow in Apple Time," a genre portrait which (adapting the tradition of Aesop and La Fontaine) implies with mingled amusement and sadness that the wayward creature's self-injurious action personifies one kind of headstrong and ill-considered human rebellion. Still another indication of Frost's increasing versatility is reflected in his handling of the initial poem entitled "The Road Not Taken." With dramatic irony, the soliloquizing speaker is permitted to characterize himself, of course unintentionally, as one who habitually wastes energy in regret-

ting any choice made: belatedly but wistfully he sighs over the attractive alternative rejected. (When this poem was teasingly sent without comment to Frost's English friend the poet Edward Thomas, who provided the initial inspiration for it, Thomas shamefacedly acknowledged it a good portrait of himself, but not of Frost.) This volume also contains the familiar favorite entitled "Birches."

New Hampshire: A Poem with Notes and Grace Notes (1923) constitutes another kind of new departure for Frost, this time a venture into the humorous, witty, relaxed realm of gentle social satire, particularly aimed at the American glorification of big business, commercialism, materialism. Taking his inspiration from the *Sermones* of Horace, the poet here sings New Hampshire by praising it for having nothing to sell—just "one each of everything as in a showcase"—and thus being a safe retreat or pleasant contrast to the mercenary drift of other regions. The flat and relaxed conversational tone of the blank-verse lines deliberately risks and largely avoids the prosaic.

The "notes and grace notes" which follow the title poem are lyrics and dramatic narratives which serve as oblique commentaries on the initial text, oblique in that no attempt is made at explicit correlation. The more compressed, terse, clipped lines of the lyrics are strikingly contrasted with the mode of the title poem. Some of the memorable lyrics in *New Hampshire* include "Fire and Ice," "Stopping by Woods," "Dust of Snow," "To Earthward," and "The Need of Being Versed in Country Things."

Of the dramatic narratives and dialogues in this volume, perhaps Frost's most successful one is "The Witch of Coös" (the Biblical place-name is also the name of the northernmost county in New Hampshire). This narrative takes the form of a little drama, beginning with comic overtones and ending with decidedly tragic implications. It begins as an outrageously impossible ghost-story, told collaboratively to the stranger-narrator of the poem by an isolated back-country widow and her grown son; but it accumulates their accidental hints that perhaps their fiction has been used by them for years to let them talk symbolically about a gruesome crime they have otherwise concealed. Psychologically, one gathers, they need to relieve a gnawing sense of guilt by means of the fiction. When the mother concludes her story, she reveals that the intolerable burden of concealment has gradually driven her to the verge of insanity, and she nows sees no reason why she ever made a secret of the truth—the "bones" of the "ghost" were those of her former lover:

> "They were a man's his father killed for me.
> I mean a man he killed instead of me."

None of Frost's dramatic psychological characterizations goes more deeply or more subtly into the tragedy of self-betrayal than "The Witch of Coös."

West-running Brook (1928) is particularly important because of the title poem which has already been mentioned and which will be considered in more detail later. Some of Frost's best lyrics are also contained in this volume, as for example "Spring Pools," "A Peck of Gold," "Once by the Pacific," "Tree at My Window," "Acquainted with the Night," and "The Soldier."

A Further Range (1936), *A Witness Tree* (1942), and *Steeple Bush* (1947), while adding some excellent lyrics, are volumes too heavily padded with relatively unimpressive and inartistic "editorials." They provide some pointed satirical thrusts at the American scene without adding much to Frost's poetic stature.

Two complementary volumes of verse drama, *A Masque of Reason* (1945) and *A Masque of Mercy* (1947), were eventually and significantly placed together at the end of the collected works which Frost chose to call *Complete Poems* (1949). These two masques paved the way for metaphysical and religious considerations which provide a thematic center for his last book, *In the Clearing* (1962). Artistically considered, this final volume is disappointing; but most of the poems in it were written while Frost was in his eighties.

Now that we have completed a superficial survey of Robert Frost's separate volumes, in order to gain a comprehensive view, we can come to grips with problems of interpretation which might be phrased in questions such as these: What gains in our understanding of Frost's idiom can be achieved by noticing how some of Frost's dominant and recurrent poetic themes run counter to each other? What essential elements of Frost's poetic theory can be deduced from his poetic practice?

One way to start finding answers to such questions might be taken by remembering that, even though Frost is extremely gifted in his ability to make even the least lyric poem dramatic, he is primarily a subjective lyric poet, at his best in his apparently contradictory moods of response to experience and in his figurative ways of defining differences. As already noticed the matrix-pattern of *A Boy's Will* foreshadows his persistent pleasure in employing the lyric mode as an expression of self-discovery, even of psychological self-education, concerning his own ties to his beloved, to strangers, to nature, to the universe, to God. If it might be argued that these are the familiar concerns of most lyric poets, one differentiation may be suggested. For Frost, the ultimate and ulterior preoccupation is with a poetic view of life which he can consider complete, in the sense that it encompasses and integrates all these relationships figuratively, and yet not systematically. His ulterior concern is always with psychic and spiritual salvation. Frost's awareness of his differences from conventional attitudes, in his defense of the unsystematic, is at least implied in such a confession as this:

And were an epitaph to be my story
I'd have a short one ready for my own.
I would have written of me on my stone:
I had a lover's quarrel with the world.

Once again, the contraries implicit in that phrase "lover's quarrel" do not imply either physical or metaphysical rebellion against the human condition. His poem entitled "Not Quite Social" contains assurance on that point, an assurance expressed as though he were fearful of being misunderstood:

You may taunt me with not being able to flee
the earth.
You have me there, but loosely as I would be
held.
The way of understanding is partly mirth.
I would not be taken as ever having rebelled.

His "lover's quarrel with the world" may have begun through his wanting and trying to discover or define his own sense of simultaneous separateness and integration. More than that, a large part of his poetic pleasure would seem to be derived from his finding verse not only an end in itself but also a means to the end of making each poem a "clarification of life," at least a clarification of his own attitude toward life. Presumably there was a time in his youth when he felt relatively comfortable within the framework of inherited and conventional assumptions or beliefs. Yet his poem entitled "The Door in the Dark" develops, with characteristically amusing seriousness, a crucial experience of disillusionment:

In going from room to room in the dark
I reached out blindly to save my face,
But neglected, however lightly, to lace

My fingers and close my arms in an arc.
A slim door got in past my guard,
And hit me a blow in the head so hard
I had my native simile jarred.
So people and things don't pair any more
With what they used to pair with before.

This figurative dramatization of disillusionment may serve as a reminder that such a plight always heightens the sense of discrepancy between two contrasting ways of looking at anything. Repeatedly, in Frost's lyrics, the playful seriousness evokes ironies and ambiguities which imply that some of the poet's representations of his outward quarrels with the world may also be taken as either conscious or unconscious projections of inward conflicts. At times, some of his poems achieve an extra dimension of meaning if viewed as constructed around his conscious and yet unstated realization of his own divided awareness. His taunts and counter-taunts thus pick up enrichments of meaning if the poet is viewed as contending, at one and the same time with enemies inside and outside his own heart and mind. Take, for example, Frost's classical use of hendecasyllabics in his unrhymed and yet sonnet-like poem "For Once, Then, Something." At first glance, the central image of an action represents only the familiar rural pastime of trying to look down through the water, in a well, to see to the bottom, or to see how deep the well is. Yet the metaphorical undertones and metaphysical overtones are cunningly interwoven:

Others taunt me with having knelt at well-curbs
Always wrong to the light, so never seeing
Deeper down in the well than where the water
Gives me back in a shining surface picture
Me myself in the summer heaven, godlike,
Looking out of a wreath of fern and cloud
puffs.
Once, when trying with chin against a well-
curb,

I discerned, as I thought, beyond the picture,
Through the picture, a something white,
          uncertain
Something more of the depths—and then I
          lost it.
Water came to rebuke the too clear water.
One drop fell from a fern, and lo, a ripple
Shook whatever it was lay there at bottom,
Blurred it, blotted it out. What was that
          whiteness?
Truth? A pebble of quartz? For once, then,
          something.

Such a tantalizing poem may serve to remind us that the ultimate mysteries always provide Frost with his favorite topic for serious play. Although the reader is being gently teased by this ingeniously "metaphysical" development of images, the overt appearance of the question "Truth?" at the beginning of the last line points up the metaphorical concern, here, in terms of two opposed ways of searching for truth. It may even recall an echo of that aphorism attributed to Democritus: "Of truth we know nothing, for truth lies at the bottom of a well." With Frost, as with Democritus, the immediate emphasis is obviously on ultimate truth. But the figurative overtones of the opening lines imply that the speaker has previously acknowledged to "others" (perhaps even to himself) his own limitations of perception, in regard to ultimate truth. That acknowledgment seems to have evoked a taunting kind of criticism. More than that, the choice of words, at the very start of the poem, figuratively identifies ultimate truth with a form of worship: the speaker has been taunted because he "knelt" —"always wrong to the light . . ." It would seem that his faultfinders (again perhaps inner and outer) have claimed that, Narcissus-like, his own failure of vision has caused him to let his own image get between him and the ulterior object of his quest, so that instead of

worshiping God he contemplates only "Me myself in the summer heaven godlike . . ." This complaint apparently provides the taunters with self-justification. But, as this inverted sonnet pattern reaches the conclusion of the single sentence which constitutes the sestet, the speaker moves on into the octave (plus one line) to defend himself with a quiet kind of countertaunt: perhaps the fault of his failure has not been entirely his own, else how explain the implicitly mysterious rebuke which interrupted his figuratively epistemological search?

If the poem is taken in that sense, the entire tone reflects the poet's rather sly and teasing pleasure in establishing an implied antithesis between the smug certainties of some orthodox views and the tentativeness of the poet's own ambiguous viewpoint, which includes his almost boastfully heretical (and yet not really unorthodox) tendency to approach truth by cautiously accepting and accentuating the limitations of human knowledge. At precisely such a moment the reader should postpone conclusions in order to make room for subsequent modifications which occur within the Frostian manipulations of contraries.

If one is hot on the trail of actual evidences concerning Frost's heretical views, of course some of his brief epigrams will tentatively serve:

They say the truth will make you free.
My truth will bind you slave to me.

Here again the serious play of wit involves antithetically opposed points of view. The initial assertion directly quotes from the familiar words of Jesus in John 8:32. But the covering assertion implicitly inverts the meaning of those familiar words by suggesting that the acceptance of any so-called ultimate "truth" can be viewed as a limiting action and therefore as a form of enslavement. It would seem that, for Frost, the ultimate truth does indeed lie at the bottom of a very deep well; that he refuses to find that kind of truth subsumed within the dogma of Christian belief. Nevertheless, Frost was well aware that orthodox Christian teaching has always agreed with Job that the truth is mysterious, concerning the ways of God, and past finding out.

A remark pertinent here was plaintively made by T. S. Eliot while lecturing at the University of Virginia in 1933: ". . the chief clue to the understanding of most contemporary Anglo-Saxon literature is to be found in the decay of Protestantism. . . . I mean that amongst writers the rejection of Christianity— Protestant Christianity—is the rule rather than the exception. . . ." That postulate is provocative and helpful for anyone trying to understand Frost's chronic tendency to tease the orthodox Christian believer; but again no quick conclusions can be reached. Eliot's remark may further remind us of the often noticed fact that Protestantism has unintentionally encouraged the individual seeker to formulate his own beliefs quite apart from any established sect or creed. In America, the Puritan nonconformists who had fled from Archbishop Laud to indulge their own rigorous beliefs very soon discovered other kinds of nonconformity developing to plague them, even in their midst. Frost, who boasted of his Puritan descent, and who was decidedly puritanical in many of his sympathies, might be viewed as a nonconforming Puritan nonconformist.

For the sake of poetry, there would seem to be a kind of convenience or luxury or at least artistic usefulness in the very posture of heresy. It provides the artist not only with greater freedom to manipulate his raw materials but also with the added chance to indulge varying moods of belief and unbelief. He can say with Horatio, in *Hamlet*, "So have I heard and do in part believe it." But in Frost's case it would seem more accurate to suggest that his poetic

flaunting of heresies largely stems from his inability to derive adequate intellectual-emotional-spiritual satisfaction from any systematic dogma which imposes intolerable limitations on a temperament which delights to seek truth through questions and dialogue.

Before considering Frost's thematic affirmations, we may profitably stay with his doubts and negations a bit longer. For various and complicated reasons, his fluctuating and ambiguous viewpoint mocks, at times, any complacent notions concerning a benevolent design in nature. One of his sonnets which has occasionally been singled out for particular praise is a dark study-in-white, ambiguously entitled "Design":

I found a dimpled spider, fat and white,
On a white heal-all, holding up a moth
Like a white piece of rigid satin cloth—
Assorted characters of death and blight
Mixed ready to begin the morning right,
Like the ingredients of a witches' broth—
A snow-drop spider, a flower like froth,
And dead wings carried like a paper kite.

What had that flower to do with being white,
The wayside blue and innocent heal-all?
What brought the kindred spider to that height,
Then steered the white moth thither in the
    night?
What but design of darkness to appall?—
If design govern in a thing so small.

Taken out of context, that sonnet might seem to carry overtones more ominous than the context of Frost's other poems actually permits. By contrast, if this sonnet is considered in a relation to the other poems, it suggests not so much a mood of depressed brooding over "the design of darkness to appall" but rather a grim pleasure in using such a peculiar *exemplum* for challenging and upsetting the smug assurance of complacent orthodox belief concerning Who steers what where, and how. Yet this sonnet resists even that much reduction. For Frost, the attempt to see clearly, and from all sides, requires a willingness to confront the frightening and the appalling in even its darkest forms.

Any careful reader of Frost's poems notices how frequently "fear" provides different kinds of premises for him. If nature and human nature have the power to reduce man to a fearful sense of his own smallness, his own lostness, in a seemingly indifferent or even malicious universe, then one suggested way to confront such fear is to imagine life stripped down to a minimum; to decide whether enough is left to go on with; then to consider the question whether the possible gains are worth the necessary cost. As already hinted, the structural pattern of moods in *A Boy's Will* may be viewed in this light. But many of the later poems even more closely represent the confrontations of fear, lostness, alienation, not so much for purposes of shuddering as for purposes of overcoming fright, first through individual and then through social ingenuity, courage, daring, and action.

In 1936, when Frost was asked to name some of his favorite books, he mentioned Defoe's *Robinson Crusoe* and Thoreau's *Walden* as thematically rhyming for him: *"Robinson Crusoe is never quite out of my mind. I never tire of being shown how the limited can make snug in the limitless. Walden has something of the same fascination. Crusoe was cast away; Thoreau was self-cast away. Both found themselves sufficient. No prose writer has ever been more fortunate in subject than these two."* By implication, no subject matter has ever made stronger appeal to Frost, for poetry, than that same question as to how the limited man can make snug in the limitless. As it happens, many of his poems talk back and forth to each other as though calculated to answer something like

Pascal's old-new observation, "When I consider the brief span of my life, swallowed up in the eternity before and behind me, the small space that I fill, or even see, engulfed in the infinite immensity of spaces which I know not, and which know not me, I am afraid." Understanding that kind of fear, Frost expresses much the same mood, with a twist, in his poem entitled "Desert Places." But he more often prefers to answer the existential problem of "what to make of a diminished thing" by representing characters who confront the excruciations by means of order-giving actions. For example, in the dramatic monologue entitled "An Empty Threat," the speaker is a fur trader who has chosen to work out his purposes almost alone, on the frozen shore of Hudson Bay. Although he recognizes all the symbols of defeat and death in the bleak landscape, the speaker is represented as uttering his flat rejoinder, "I stay," in the first line of the poem. What can a man make of such expansive diminishment? He considers the extremes of contradictory possibility:

> Give a head shake
> Over so much bay
> Thrown away
> In snow and mist
> That doesn't exist,
> I was going to say,
> For God, man or beast's sake,
> Yet does perhaps for all three.

The question of plan or design thus obliquely raised suggests answers not so much in terms of the known or unknown but rather in terms of the possible. The poem concludes with the suggestion that if man is given his choice of succumbing to paralyzing doubts and fear or of translating even limited faith into possibly constructive action, then the choice ought to be made with ease.

An amusing yet serious variant on that same

theme occurs in the ambiguous animal fable entitled "A Drumlin Woodchuck," wherein the creature which makes his home in the sand-bank left by the ice-age glacier explains to his mate in tones of snug-and-smug pride that he has adequately constructed their home as a defense against at least the foreseeable forms of destruction. Poetically considered, the wood-chuck's boast symbolizes a process of asserting a creative design which is valid, even "though small, as measured against the All." Viewed in that sense, the poet's own creation of order in verse forms takes on a doubly symbolic meaning. Frost has said as much in his highly poetic prose:

"We people are thrust forward out of the suggestions of form in the rolling clouds of nature. In us nature reaches its height of form and through us exceeds itself. When in doubt there is always form for us to go on with. Anyone who has achieved the least form to be sure of it, is lost to the larger excruciations. I think it must stroke faith the right way. The artist, the poet, might be expected to be the more aware of such assurance. But it is really everybody's sanity to feel it and live by it. . . . The background is hugeness and confusion shading away from where we stand into black and utter chaos; and against the background any small man-made figure of order and concentration. What pleasanter than that this should be so. . . . To me, any little form I assert on it is velvet, as the saying is, and to be considered for how much more it is than nothing. If I were a Platonist I should have to consider it, I suppose, for how much less it is than everything."

There again, not-knowing is balanced off against knowing-at-least-enough, and doing-at-least-enough, to provide different kinds of formal defense against different kinds of chaos. But notice the cautious observation, "I think it must stroke faith the right way." Faith in what? If man finds himself encompassed merely by hugeness and confusion which shades away into black and utter chaos, then faith in self might seem to be inadequate. But if the rolling clouds of nature suggest form, and if nature reaches its heights of form in man, then Frost implies that another possibility may exist in some ulterior form-giving Power back of nature, no matter how much is left in doubt. Even though he likes to indulge at least the posture of not-knowing, Frost sooner or later makes it clear that not too much is left in doubt, for him. If there are times when he seems to take particular pleasure in defining his beliefs in terms of his heresies, he cannot play metaphorical hide-and-seek too long without trailing clouds of puritanic certainty. For example, one of his most paradoxical and most metaphysical poems begins by tantalizing the reader with ambiguities, and even continues with various forms of teasing provocation through the last line:

A head thrusts in as for the view,
But where it is it thrusts in from
Or what it is it thrusts into
By that Cyb'laean avenue,
And what can of its coming come,

And whither it will be withdrawn,
And what take hence or leave behind,
These things the mind has pondered on
A moment and still asking gone.
Strange apparition of the mind!

But the impervious geode
Was entered, and its inner crust
Of crystals with a ray cathode
At every point and facet glowed
In answer to the mental thrust.

Eyes seeking the response of eyes
Bring out the stars, bring out the flowers,
Thus concentrating earth and skies
So none need be afraid of size.
All revelation has been ours.

Enigmatic as the opening lines of "All Revelation" are, on first reading, they may have been so designed for the deliberate purpose of requiring us initially to act out an important part of Frost's theme, here. A "mental thrust" is required of us; we may find that it is necessary to read the whole poem through, more than once, before it begins to acquire coherence, even in a literal sense. Originally, this poem was entitled "Geode," and the central image is that impervious—but only seemingly impervious—geode. Some readers may not even know that a geode is a round stone, rarely as big as a baseball, with an ordinary exterior and a hollow interior which is extraordinarily lined with crystals. These crystals, when exposed to a cathode ray, glow with all the colors of the rainbow.

In the poem, the literal meaning lends itself to a paraphrase which can be given a quality of narrative: Once upon a time, someone had enough thrust of mind to look beneath the surface of a geode (as though it were a poem) and to find the crystals; once upon another time, someone had enough thrust of mind to see what would happen if the crystals were exposed to a cathode ray; once upon still another time, someone placed on exhibition, perhaps for the first time in a geology museum, a geode with crystals which could be hit by a cathode ray whenever the current might be turned on. People came to see this marvelous phenomenon; but what they took away from the geode depended partly on how much they brought to the geode.

In the dramatic arrangement of characters and "props," as provided by "All Revelation," the action begins when the speaker is standing and watching and describing someone who has come as a spectator to "view" a geode. The speaker, making his own "thrust of mind," asks psychological questions concerning the spectator: What mental-emotional-spiritual preparation may or may not have been brought to focus, for the spectator who looks along the "Cyb'laean avenue" provided by this mystery? (Cybele: the ancient stone-statued earth-mother-goddess.) And what mental-emotional-spiritual rewards may or may not be taken away from here, as a consequence of the spectator's own thrust of mind?

The first two stanzas indicate that the poet chose to start *in medias res*; the geode is not even mentioned until the third stanza, where the speaker hints at all the other thrusts of mind which had to take place before this experience could be made available for the spectator. In the concluding stanza, figurative analogies and extensions give reminders that similar thrusts of mind are always required before any process of human revelation achieves fulfillment—even the process of writing and showing poems. The speaker adds that the individual who asserts his capacities will find that he had within him enough power to overcome various kinds of fear which are based on not-knowing; to that degree, man finds himself adequate to cope with all he needs to know of the unknown.

The last line of "All Revelation" makes a use of hyperbole which ought to be challenged by any thoughtful reader. "All revelation has been ours" is a bold assertion. It might suggest that man endows nature with whatever order and meaning it has. But if that way of interpreting this last line may be attractive to some readers, it is not congenial to the controls provided by Frost's larger context of poetic utterances. On reconsideration, we might notice that the someone who discovered, beneath the plain surface of the geode, the underlying order and wonder of those inner crystals, did not create either the outer or the inner surface, so wonderfully ordered. For Frost, whatever kind of revelation man here makes or achieves, through the uses of sense and skill, implies at least some kind of precedence of order and of design in nature. So the word "revelation," as poetically operative here, would seem to pick up its Frostian meaning only if it is viewed as representing a two-way process: an act of collaboration. (As we shall see, the same theme, with its religious overtones of meaning, is developed further by Frost in *A Masque of Reason*.)

The counterbalancing of contrary attitudes or viewpoints, in "All Revelation," further suggests the poet's distaste for lingering too long in moods which merely accentuate the apparent design of darkness to appall, in the structure of the universe; his distaste for stressing too heavily the fright which can be and is derived from too much contemplation of inner and outer desert places. Yet he never lets us forget the limitations. At times, he editorializes or even preaches, poetically, with unabashed and strongly puritanical tones of warning and corrective, against the sin of indulging too much concern for the imponderables, in or beyond nature. In his poem entitled "Too Anxious for Rivers," the basic arrangement of imagery represents a landscape vista where a stream flowing through the foreground would seem to be blocked off by a mountain in the background. If so, what happens to the river in its attempt to reach the sea? Taken symbolically, or (in this extremely puritanical poem) taken allegorically, the river is life, the mountain is death, the sea is life-beyond-death, and the rebuked questioner implicitly may be any descendant of Adam who has a tendency to ask too many questions about life and death:

The truth is the river flows into the canyon
Of Ceasing to Question What Doesn't Concern
    Us,
As sooner or later we have to cease somewhere.
No place to get lost like too far in the distance.

It may be a mercy the dark closes round us
So broodingly soon in every direction.

That regrettable lapse into an allegorical abstraction may seem to reinforce only Puritan elements of theme. But the poem develops thereafter in such a way as to mock the attempts of both science and religion to explain first causes and last effects; then the last stanza blends the ambiguous and the didactic:

Time was we were molten, time was we were
    vapor.
What set us on fire and what set us revolving
Lucretius the Epicurean might tell us
'Twas something we knew all about to begin
    with
And needn't have fared into space like his
    master
To find 'twas the effort, the essay of love.

The allusion is enough to remind us that, at the beginning of *De Rerum Natura*, Venus or love as the great creative force in nature is invoked for purposes of attacking and dismissing the fear of death, the fear of the gods. Lucretius goes on to plead for an unsystematic enjoyment of life and nature, free from superstition. In Frost's poem, this pagan appeal to Lucretius would seem to constitute a deliberate and calculated displacement or substitution for Christian notions as to just how love provides divine motivation for the creation and the salvation of man. Further extensions may occur if we recall that life is viewed by Lucretius as a river or stream or flux of everything that runs away to spend itself in death and nothingness except as somehow resisted by the spirit of human beings.

In that sense, "Too Anxious for Rivers" is related to Frost's most revealing poetic statement of continuity: "West-running Brook." There he implicitly invokes images drawn from Lucretius and would seem to blend them with

Heraclitan metaphors such as these: the death of the earth gives life to fire, the death of fire gives life to air, the death of air gives life to water, and the death of water gives life to earth, thus figuratively suggesting the endless cycle of birth and death and rebirth and continuity in nature. In "West-running Brook," Frost further suggests his awareness that Henri Bergson, in his highly poetic theories of "creative evolution," adapts many figures and images from both Lucretius and Heraclitus. Additional kinship between the poetry of Bergson and of Frost may be found in our remembering Bergson's insistence that all dogmas, systems, and logical constructions are so rigid that they interfere with man's direct or intuitive awareness; that the effort of intuition is needed to reverse intellectual straining and to provide a more creative, a more poetic, approach to knowledge.

Frost may have found Bergson's habit of mind even further congenial to his own because of Bergson's Lucretian insistence that life or spirit is a movement which runs counter to the dead flux of matter, "a reality which is making itself in a reality which is unmaking itself." The stream image occurs and recurs, throughout Bergson, together with the image of man's vital and creative and spiritual resistance to the flow of mere matter: "Life as a whole, from the initial impulse that thrust it into the world, will appear as a wave which rises, and which is opposed by the descending movement of matter." If we keep in mind these images and views of Lucretius, Heraclitus, and Bergson, then Frost's literal and symbolic and even metaphysical meanings in "West-running Brook" may be more easily understood. After the husband and wife have compared thoughts, in dialogue, concerning the symbolism of the black stream, catching on a sunken rock, and thus flung backward on

itself in the white wave, the husband is permitted to make this interpretation of that symbol:

"Here we, in our impatience of the steps,
Get back to the beginning of beginnings,
The stream of everything that runs away.
Some say existence like a Pirouot
And Pirouette, forever in one place,
Stands still and dances, but it runs away,
It seriously, sadly, runs away
To fill the abyss' void with emptiness.
It flows beside us in this water brook,
But it flows over us. It flows between us
To separate us for a panic moment.
It flows between us, over us, and *with* us.
And it is time, strength, tone, light, life, and
    love—
And even substance lapsing unsubstantial;
The universal cataract of death
That spends to nothingness—and unresisted,
Save by some strange resistance in itself,
Not just a swerving, but a throwing back,
As if regret were in it and were sacred.
It has this throwing backward on itself
So that the fall of most of it is always
Raising a little, sending up a little.
Our life runs down in sending up the clock.
The brook runs down in sending up our life.
The sun runs down in sending up the brook.
And there is something sending up the sun.
It is this backward motion toward the source,
Against the stream, that most we see ourselves
    in,
The tribute of the current to the source.
It is from this in nature we are from.
It is most us."

Here we, in our attempt to understand the art and thought of Robert Frost, would seem to have arrived at a philosophic mood diametrically opposed to that which we found expressed in the sonnet entitled "Design." Notice that the evident design which Frost finds symbolized in that wave image lends itself to the creative process in human life, thought, art, action: that which runs counter to itself establishes a closely interlocked continuity between man and even that in nature which is hostile or indifferent to man. Moreover, that which runs counter establishes a symbolic relationship of both man and nature to the source.

If Frost seems cautiously hesitant to define the source, one implicit corollary is that the Creator's revelations, through nature, as viewed by Frost, are equally indirect, emblematic, contradictory, even discontinuous, and highly symbolic. Moreover, while much of Frost's poetry suggests that he cannot resist figurative utterances concerning his wavering and yet centered spiritual preoccupations, we have at least seen that he often prefers to reveal-conceal some of his most intimate and personal beliefs through poetic indications which grow more meaningful because they do contain and maintain elements of self-contradiction.

Yet it can be demonstrated that from his early lyrics in *A Boy's Will* (such as, for example, "A Prayer in Spring") to his last major poem, "Kitty Hawk" (which is thematically central to his last book, *In the Clearing*), Frost makes representations of the venture of spirit into matter, in ways best understood if interpreted as expressions of worship, even as expressions of prayer. His basic point of departure (and return) is a firmly rooted belief in both nature and human nature as at least poetically relatable within a design which has its ultimate source in a divine plan, a plan with which man collaborates to the best of his limited ability. Remember the concluding quatrain of "A Prayer in Spring":

For this is love and nothing else is love,
The which it is reserved for God above

To sanctify to what far ends He will,
But which it only needs that we fulfill.

That recurrent theme of collaboration is perhaps given its most explicit statement at the conclusion of the poem entitled "Two Tramps in Mudtime." The initial action there represents the poet as engaged in the ritualistic routine of splitting firewood in his farmyard, and as enjoying the play of such work until he is embarrassed by the passing presence of two expert lumberjacks. Their mocking comment suggests that they need, and could better perform, the work he is doing. The poet is aware that if his own motive is more love than need and if their motive is more need than love, perhaps he should relinquish the task to them, for pay. Nevertheless, he concludes with puritanical assertiveness, there are other factors to consider:

But yield who will to their separation,
My object in living is to unite
My avocation and my vocation
As my two eyes make one in sight.
Only where love and need are one,
And the work is play for mortal stakes,
Is the deed ever really done
For Heaven and the future's sakes.

What has happened, then, to Frost's recurrent elements of theme involving fear, isolation, lostness, not-knowing, and discontinuity? They remain operative in the poems, side by side with these recurrent elements of faith and love and continuity. His juxtaposition of contrary and yet ultimately complementary images and themes finds its most elaborately paradoxical expression in those two masques which Frost chose to place in a significant summary position, at the conclusion to his volume which he also chose to entitle, with figurative overtones, *Complete Poems*.

As the titles suggest, *A Masque of Reason* and *A Masque of Mercy* explore contrary themes; yet once again they are contraries which permit us to view the two masques as complementary. More than that, they provide an epitome, or a gathering metaphor, of many major themes developed by Frost in the poems which precede and succeed them. Relationships are again explored in each of the masques; man's ultimate relationships to self, to society, to nature, to the universe, to God. Or, to say it another way, the two masques further extend themes involving man's perennial sense of isolation and communion, of fear and courage, of ignorance and knowledge, of discontinuity and continuity.

In *A Masque of Reason*, Frost anticipated what Archibald MacLeish has more recently and more artistically done in building a modern philosophical drama out of the Biblical story of Job for purposes of exploring possible meanings within and behind man's agony. The answers offered by MacLeish, in *J.B.*, primarily emphasize humanistic values, in that the conclusion of the action finds human love the best justification and the best defense. By contrast, the answers offered by Frost are attempts to justify the ways of God to men, thus making Frost's emphasis ultimately metaphysical and theistic. Significantly, earth provides the setting for MacLeish's drama, while heaven provides an ambiguous setting for Frost's masque.

In the initial action, Frost represents Job, his wife, and God as conducting an intimate postmortem concerning the strengths and weaknesses of human reason in trying to understand the divine plan or design. Intimacy permits Job to ask his questions with all the ardor, boldness, even insolence of one participating in a family quarrel. If the orthodox reader should find himself offended by such apparent irreverence, or should find God represented in terms contrary to trite conventional concepts, the implicit mockery of accepted notions is again not accidental.

Because the action begins some two thousand years after the death of Job, all the characters have the advantage of encompassing modern knowledge and attitudes, so that the seeming anachronisms of reference suggest continuity in time and space. Job's concern is to ask God's "reason" for inflicting torture on innocent human beings. After preliminary hesitancy and sparring, God takes occasion to thank Job for his collaboration in an epoch-making action:

I've had you on my mind a thousand years
To thank you someday for the way you helped
    me
Establish once for all the principle
There's no connection man can reason out
Between his just deserts and what he gets.

That phrase "the way you helped me" may recall notions advanced by William James and others concerning a suffering God, limited and thwarted in his plan to realize his divine purpose so long as man is indifferent and uncooperative. Also echoed throughout the masque is the related Bergsonian concept of a continuously creative process which develops the universe. But as Frost adapts these assumptions to his own sympathetic uses, he combines them with his favorite puritanic emphasis on the limitations of reason as it affects the relationship between man and God: "there's no connection man can *reason* out. . . ." God is represented as continuing his explanation to Job:

Virtue may fail and wickedness succeed.
'Twas a great demonstration we put on. . . .
Too long I've owed you this apology
For the apparently unmeaning sorrow

You were afflicted with in those old days.
But it was of the essence of the trial
You shouldn't understand it at the time.
It had to seem unmeaning to have meaning.

The phrase "it was of the essence of the trial" may permit a further reminder here that Frost's earlier poems can be taken as notes and grace notes to these two masques. He had previously honored the conventional puritanic tendency to heap a heavy burden of meaning on the word "trial." In *A Boy's Will*, the poem entitled "The Trial by Existence" creates a mythic view of Heaven to dramatize metaphysical mysteries. The central action of the poem represents the moment when certain souls among the angelic hosts daringly choose earthly existence as a form of collaborative trial, even though "the pure fate to which you go/Admits no memory of choice,/Or the woe were not earthly woe/To which you give the assenting voice." That early poem concludes with an equally puritanical notion that "life has for us on the wrack/Nothing but what we somehow chose," even though we cannot remember that initial choice. In *A Masque of Reason*, these various views are again invoked and now mingled with Jamesian-Bergsonian notions, as God reviews the changing or evolving attitude of man toward God, achieved with the help of Job and others. The passage continues:

And it came out all right. I have no doubt
You realize by now the part you played
To stultify the Deuteronomist
And change the tenor of religious thought.

By implication, the Book of Deuteronomy, containing the laws of Moses, asserted certain incorrect notions as to the extent of God's being under obligation to reward all for doing good, and to punish all for doing ill, notions which implied that if man follows the commandments, he prospers, that if man does not, he fails. Because Job had helped correct these misunderstandings, God is wryly grateful to Job:

My thanks are to you for releasing me
From moral bondage to the human race.
The only free will there at first was man's,
Who could do good or evil as he chose.
I had no choice but I must follow him
With forfeits and rewards he understood—
Unless I liked to suffer loss of worship
I had to prosper good and punish evil
You changed all that. You set me free to reign.
You are the Emancipator of your God,
And as such I promote you to a saint.

If viewed in these historical and evolutionary terms, the prophets of the Old Testament might also be considered as related emancipators because they advanced new concepts of God. Amos revealed him as a God of justice, Hosea revealed him as a God of love. ("All revelation has been ours.") Later in the action of the masque, God is represented as saying to Job, "I'm a great stickler for the author's name./By proper names I find I do my thinking." By extension, that concept is congenial to Frost's way of viewing thought as a form of dialogue. Here Job is represented as having been a prophet, without previously realizing it.

But Job, not yet satisfied with God's explanation of suffering, says at one point, "Such devilish ingenuity of torture/Did seem unlike You. . . ." God has already admitted to Job that even as Job had been one of his helpers, so Satan had been another, with all his originality of sin. Job's wife helps by describing Satan as "God's best inspiration." In other words, good needs evil to complement it, else each would be meaningless. The conclusion of the masque represents God as confessing his motive had initially been that simple: "I was just showing off to the Devil, Job." To complete the symbolic grouping of collaborators, the Devil is invited on stage, and Job's wife quickly grasps her camera to take an emblematic picture of God and Satan, with Job standing precariously between them.

Considered as a work of art, *A Masque of Reason* is too largely composed of talk-talk, and too little dependent on action, to give it dramatic merit. But if considered as poetry, it can at least serve to clarify and unify many of the contrary meanings in the earlier and later poems. Notice that Frost's mockery of conventional religious concepts is here once again counterbalanced by sympathetic representations of theological views which, however fragmentary, are quite in accord with certain elements of Calvinistic Puritan doctrine. The masque thus provides further evidence that no matter how much Frost may have thought he rejected the received assumptions of his religious heritage, he indulged that posture of rejection, through his art and thought, to realize a difference which was never too pronounced.

Similarly, in Frost's artistic manipulation of *A Masque of Mercy*, while the inspiration is provided by the Biblical story of Jonah as prophet, and while the heretical flavor or tone of the handling is quite obvious, the action eventually resolves into notions congenial to a fairly conventional viewpoint. The setting, this time, is a small bookstore in New York City. This action begins just at closing time, when a conversation between the owner of the bookstore (named Keeper) and his wife (named Jesse Bel) and a lingering friend and customer (named Paul) is interrupted by the frenzied entrance of a Jonah-possessed fugitive who announces fearfully, "God's after me!" (and a moment later) "[To] make me prophesy . . .

This is the seventh time I have been sent/To prophesy against the city evil." The other characters quickly discover his motivation for flight:

I've lost my faith in God to carry out
The threats He makes against the city evil.
I can't trust God to be unmerciful.

The customer, Paul, takes charge and assures the fugitive Jonah that he is a self-deceived escapist,

. . . though you are not
Running away from Him you think you are
But from His mercy-justice contradiction.
. . . I'm going to make you see
How relatively little justice matters.

Thus the central theme of the masque becomes overtly established, and is elaborated through a dramatic clash of the four opposed points of view, expressed largely in dialogue, not in action. The basic resolution involves the gradual surrender of certain Old Testament attitudes toward the primacy of justice, in favor of the New Testament emphasis on the primacy of mercy. Eventually Jonah is led to confess, "I think I may have got God wrong entirely . . . Mercy on me for having thought I knew." Jesse Bel, true to her Biblical name, assumes the posture of a modern false-prophetess who would corrupt mankind into immorality and idolatry, and who is thus beyond redemption. Keeper, motivated by socialistic concerns for his brother man, as his name suggests, initially ridicules the attitudes of the other three characters; then gradually he discovers and expresses a sympathetic agreement with the Pauline attitude.

Taken in a slightly different sense, the dominant thematic concern of *A Masque of Mercy* may be said to pivot once again on the limitations of human knowledge as it involves different responses to various kinds of fear, starting and ending with the wisdom-unwisdom of man's fearing God. Indirectly, these notions are related to the convictions of Job, in the earlier masque, that no matter what "progress" may be, it cannot mean that the earth has become an easier place for man to save his soul; that unless earth can serve as a difficult trial-ground, the hardships of existence become meaningless.

Here once again, in the attitudes of both Jonah and Paul, the puritanical views dominate. At one moment Paul is permitted to fall back on Book Three of *Paradise Lost* to make his meaning clear:

. . . After doing Justice justice,
Milton's pentameters go on to say,
But Mercy first and last shall brightest shine,
Not only last, but first, you will observe.

As the fugitive Jonah begins to understand Paul, he in turn is permitted to make his own adjustment to Paul's brand of puritanism by invoking a celebrated passage in *Pilgrim's Progress*:

You ask if I see yonder shining gate,
And I reply I almost think I do . . .

But in the denouement of the action, fear again provides the center of attention. Paul concludes by answering Keeper's remarks about the fear of death and judgment, thus:

We have to stay afraid deep in our souls
Our sacrifice, the best we have to offer,
And not our worst nor second best, our best,
Our very best, our lives laid down like Jonah's
Our lives laid down in war and peace, may not
Be found acceptable in Heaven's sight.
And that they may be is the only prayer
Worth praying. May my sacrifice
Be found acceptable in Heaven's sight.

Paul is closely paraphrasing a familiar passage in Psalm 19:14: "Let the words of my mouth, and the meditations of my heart, be acceptable in thy sight, O Lord, my strength and my redeemer." This prayer and this preachment, so central to the current didacticism and puritanism throughout Frost's poems, reinforce the significance of his emphasis on settling for limited knowledge, provided sufficient courage and resourcefulness can be mustered for translating man's predicament into an act of collaboration. In *A Masque of Reason*, Job was permitted to set up and then to attack an opposed view of life in these lines:

We don't know where we are, or who we are.
We don't know one another; don't know You;
Don't know what time it is. We don't know,
    don't we?
Who says we don't? Who got up these misgivings?
Oh, we know well enough to go ahead with.
I mean we seem to know enough to act on.

So we return to where we started in considering the positive affirmations within Frost's poems: action, in the living present, is recurrently represented as providing different forms of human redemption, atonement, salvation, if only such action is viewed as collaborative with whatever little man can understand of the divine design.

Robert Frost did not bother to articulate more than fragments of his poetic theory, and yet certain essentials of it can be deduced from his poetic practice. If we remember that his wide acclaim has been earned during an era of artistic innovation and experiment, we may marvel at his having achieved such distinction merely by letting his idiom discover old ways to be new, within the traditional conventions of lyric and dramatic and thematic modes. While Yeats, Eliot, Pound, and others invoked or invented elaborate mythic frames of reference which have enriched and complicated artistic strategies, Frost would seem to have risked successfully the purification of poetic utterance, in complicating simple forms. As we have seen, however, he quite consciously assimilates to his own New England idiom such varieties of classical conventions as the relaxed modes of the Theocritan idylls, the terse epigrammatic brevity of Martial, the contemplative serenity of Horace, the sharply satirical intensity of Juvenal, the homely didacticism of Aesop. Yet his treasured firsthand familiarity with and admiration for the classics have not been displayed in ways which make his meanings depend on esoteric scholarship. Quite clearly, he has deliberately chosen to address himself to the common reader.

But if the majority of Frost's admirers would seem content to share the poet's delight in cherishing the humble beauties of nature, recorded by him with such precision of response to images of experience among New England fields, farms, roadsides, and forests, those readers have been willing to settle for too little, when so many other and deeper levels of meaning are available in his poems. It has frequently and correctly been pointed out that Frost's poetic concerns are akin to those which led Wordsworth to choose incidents and situations from common life and then to present them in a language actually used by the common man whose heartfelt passions are not restrained. Like Wordsworth, and like many poets before and after Wordsworth, Frost has particularly emphasized his concern for catching within the lines of his poems the rhythms and cadences and tones of human speech. Among modern poets, he has been one of the many who have advocated a capturing of what he has repeatedly referred to as "the sound of sense" or "sound posturing" to provide a complicating enrichment of the underlying metrical rhythm.

Perhaps without his realizing it, Frost's own Puritan heritage has made him find congenial the related theories of Coleridge, Wordsworth, and Emerson, particularly in matters related to the organic growth of a poem and the organic relationship between imagery and symbol. "When I see birches bend to left and right," says Frost, "I like to *think*. . . ." There it is. His primary artistic achievement, which is an enviable one, in spite of shortcomings, rests on his blending of thought and emotion and symbolic imagery within the confines of the lyric. It would seem to be an essential part of both his theory and practice to start with a single image, or to start with an image of an action, and then to endow either or both with a figurativeness of meaning, which is not fully understood by the reader until the extensions of meaning are found to transcend the physical.

While no one could correctly call Frost a transcendentalist, his kinship with Emerson goes deeper than might at first be noticed. One approach to this relationship, as it involves a basic element of both poetic theory and practice, may be found through Frost's early sonnet entitled "Mowing":

There was never a sound beside the wood but
    one,
And that was my long scythe whispering to the
    ground.
What was it it whispered? I knew not well
    myself;
Perhaps it was something about the heat of the
    sun,
Sometimes, perhaps, about the lack of sound—
And that was why it whispered and did not
    speak.
It was no dream of the gift of idle hours,
Or easy gold at the hand of fay or elf:
Anything more than the truth would have
    seemed too weak

To the earnest love that laid the swale in rows,
Not without feeble-pointed spikes of flowers
(Pale orchises), and scared a bright green
   snake.
The fact is the sweetest dream that labor
   knows.
My long scythe whispered and left the hay to
   make.

The initial effect of that sonnet is one of mood, in which the reverie of the worker picks up for contemplation the tactile and visual and audial images in terms of action and of cherishing. The sensuous response is heightened and enriched not only by the speaking tones and modulations and rhythms struck across the underlying metrical pattern of iambics but also by the intricate and irregular sonnet rhyme scheme: a-b-c-a-b-d-e-c d-f-e-g-f-g. Although the mood of the reverie is not interrupted by the somewhat paradoxical generalization in the thirteenth line, the reader is likely to return to that line, puzzling over it and feeling slightly teased by the possible ambiguities. If the fact-as-dream is interpreted as indicating that the entire reverie reflects an intensely sensuous joy in the immediate human experience, that such pleasurable experience constitutes an end in itself, the poem obviously makes sense in those terms. Taken thus, the sonnet clearly is related to that fundamental theme of love and cherishing which runs throughout Frost's poetry. Any other meaning found ought not to displace or cancel that. But if the fact-as-dream might also be interpreted to represent the act of mowing as a means to an end as well as an end in itself, it could serve to symbolize not only a process of being but also a process of becoming, within the farmer-poet's life. The grass is cut and the hay is left to make, for an ulterior purpose.

The context of other poems within which "Mowing" occurs invites and encourages deeper reading. We have noticed that in Frost's poetic theory and practice he likes to endow images and actions with implicitly metaphorical and symbolic meanings until they repeatedly suggest a continuity between his vision of the human "fact" and the divine "fact." We have also noticed that he likes the tension between two ways of looking at such thought-felt moods; that his own moments of doubts, in these matters, seem to afford him the luxury of reaffirmation. In such a context, a poem like "Mowing" reveals further kinships between Frost and Emerson. In his essay on "The Poet" Emerson writes, "I find that the fascination resides in the symbol." Frost would agree. Emerson goes on to say that the response of the farmer to nature is a sympathetic form of worship: "No imitation or playing of these things would content him; he loves the earnest of the north wind, of rain, of stone and wood and iron. A beauty not explicable is dearer than a beauty which we can see to the end of. It is nature the symbol, nature certifying the supernatural, body overflowered by life which he worships with coarse but sincere rites." Again Frost would agree, at least in part; but it must be pointed out that Frost's view of nature-as-symbol does not coincide with the Emersonian view. Neither does it coincide with the New England puritanical view of nature-as-symbol. Nevertheless, to those Puritan forefathers against whom both Emerson and Frost partially rebelled, self-reliance was God-reliance. Even those Puritan forefathers also insisted that *laborare est orare*. Whatever the differences in the three positions, the likenesses are significant.

"Prayer," says Emerson, with almost puritanical exultation, "is the contemplation of the facts of life from the highest point of view. It is the soliloquy of a beholding and jubilant soul." Frost would have been embarrassed to speak out that frankly in open meeting; but his poems obliquely imply his own assent to the notion. The core of his poetic theory, as of his poetic practice, is to be found in his uses of the sensuous responses of loving and cherishing, first as important poetic images of human actions; then, simultaneously, as even more important symbols of divine worship and even of prayer: "May my sacrifice be found acceptable in Heaven's sight."

In conclusion it should be said that the approach here used, in an attempt to increase our appreciation and understanding of Robert Frost's life and art, is only one of many possible approaches. It is calculated to suggest that many elements run counter to themselves, therein, without any ultimate contradictions. It also provides a means of noticing that Frost's entire work is deeply rooted in the American, even in the most vital Puritan, idiom. It is "native to the grain," and yet thoroughly original. No wonder, then, that Robert Frost has earned a place of distinction, at home and abroad, as a major American poet.

Selected Bibliography

WORKS OF ROBERT FROST

SEPARATE WORKS
A Boy's Will. London: David Nutt, 1913; New York: Holt, 1915.
North of Boston. London: David Nutt, 1914; New York: Holt, 1914.
Mountain Interval. New York: Holt, 1916.
New Hampshire: A Poem with Notes and Grace Notes. New York: Holt, 1923.
West-running Brook. New York: Holt, 1928.
A Further Range. New York: Holt, 1936.
A Witness Tree. New York: Holt, 1942.
A Masque of Reason. New York: Holt, 1945.
Steeple Bush. New York: Holt, 1947.
A Masque of Mercy. New York: Holt, 1947.

In the Clearing. New York: Holt, Rinehart and Winston, 1962.

SELECTED AND COLLECTED EDITIONS
The first four editions below are of particular importance because they represent Robert Frost's own winnowings and arrangements.
Selected Poems. New York: Holt, 1923. (Contains 43 poems.) Revised, 1928. (Contains 57 poems.) Again revised, 1934. (Contains 73 poems.) English edition, London: Jonathan Cape, 1936. (Contains 62 poems chosen and significantly rearranged by the author; this edition also contains introductory essays by W. H. Auden, C. Day Lewis, Paul Engle, and Edwin Muir.)
Collected Poems. New York: Holt, 1930. (Contains 163 poems.) Reissued, 1939. (Contains 163 poems and Frost's prose preface entitled "The Figure a Poem Makes.")
Complete Poems. New York: Holt, 1949. (Contains 304 poems and "The Figure a Poem Makes.")
Selected Poems. London: Penguin Books, 1955. (In the Penguin Poets series. Contains 186 poems and a preface by C. Day Lewis.)
Selected Poems of Robert Frost, with an introduction by Robert Graves. New York: Holt, Rinehart and Winston, 1963.

LETTERS
Robert Frost and John Bartlett: The Record of a Friendship, by Margaret Bartlett Anderson. New York: Holt, Rinehart and Winston, 1963.
The Letters of Robert Frost to Louis Untermeyer, edited by Louis Untermeyer. New York: Holt, Rinehart and Winston, 1963.
Selected Letters of Robert Frost, edited by Lawrance Thompson. New York: Holt, Rinehart and Winston, 1964.

BIBLIOGRAPHY
Clymer, W. B., and Charles R. Green. *Robert Frost: A Bibliography.* Amherst, Mass.: The Jones Library, 1937.

BIOGRAPHICAL STUDIES
Cox, Sidney. *A Swinger of Birches: A Portrait of*

Robert Frost. New York: New York University Press, 1957.

Mertins, Louis. *Robert Frost: Life and Talks-Walking.* Norman: University of Oklahoma Press, 1965.

Sergeant, Elizabeth Shepley. *Robert Frost: The Trial by Existence.* New York: Holt, Rinehart and Winston, 1960.

Thompson, Lawrance. *Robert Frost: The Early Years.* New York: Holt, Rinehart and Winston, 1966.

CRITICAL STUDIES

Brower, Reuben A. *The Poetry of Robert Frost: Constellations of Intention.* New York: Oxford University Press, 1963.

Nitchie, George W. *Human Values in the Poetry of Robert Frost.* Durham, N.C.: Duke University Press, 1960.

Thompson, Lawrance. *Fire and Ice: The Art and Thought of Robert Frost.* New York: Holt, 1942.

—*LAWRANCE THOMPSON*

Ellen Glasgow
1873-1945

*E*LLEN GLASGOW's parents combined the qualities that gave to both antebellum and reconstructed Virginia its stubborn romanticism and its peculiar strength. Her father, of Valley stock, was an ironworks executive and a Scotch Presbyterian in every nerve and sinew; he gave his children all the things they needed but love, and in eighty-six years never "committed a pleasure." The best his daughter could say of him was that he had not hurt anyone for the mere satisfaction of hurting. Her mother, on the other hand, descended from Randolphs and Yateses, was a flower of the old Tidewater, who, smiling in the constant sadness of her tribulations, would have divided "her last crust with a suffering stranger." Miss Glasgow attributed the lingering, undiagnosed malady of which her mother ultimately died to the exhaustion of bearing ten children and the hardships of war and reconstruction, but it was more probably the result of the same nervous temperament that her daughter inherited. "Born without a skin," the young Ellen's Negro mammy, shaking her head, used to say of her charge.

But in 1873, the year of her birth, the worst, at least financially, was over. The Glasgows had, in addition to a town house in Richmond, the farm of Jerdone Castle where their daughter could range over wide fields, the greater part of which were left to run wild in broom sedge and scrub pine and life everlasting, and cultivate the love of natural things and the sense of kinship with birds and animals that were never to leave her. Too nervous to go regularly to any school, she educated herself by reading all the books in the family library, science and history as well as fiction and poetry. An older sister's husband, a scholar, made her study *The Origin of Species* till she knew "its every page." According to her posthumous and by no means modest memoirs, she seems as a young woman to have had her cake and swallowed it, for she "won all the admiration, and felt all the glorified sensations, of a Southern belle" while at the same time making acquaintance with the squalor of Richmond slums as a worker for the City Mission and becoming a "Fabian Socialist." One can assume, at least, that she was no ordinary debutante.

When her mother died in 1893 she was so prostrated with grief that she tore up the uncompleted manuscript of her first novel, *The Descendant,* and a year passed before she was able to turn back to writing. Something of the same paralyzing prostration was to follow, in later years, the deaths of her sister Cary and of the man described in her memoirs as "Gerald B———." Miss Glasgow always regarded herself as a uniquely sensitive and unhappy

173

person. Answering in 1934 the question of how she had liked her life, she replied: "not one day, not one hour, not one moment—or perhaps, *only one* hour and one day." It was true that on top of the nervous headaches and attacks of her youth was loaded the burden of increasing deafness, but she was given the compensations of looks, wit, charm, gaiety (she was never one to wear her melancholy on her sleeve), friends innumerable, and a talent that was to grow in power through a long life almost to the end. She never married, but this was for no lack of opportunity. She broke two engagements and recorded that the maternal instinct, sacred or profane, had been left out of her nature.

Nor was she neglected by the reading public. Again and again she was a best seller. But the delay in the serious critical recognition to which she regarded herself as entitled rankled deeply. Believing that she was leading a literary crusade away from a sterile romantic tradition toward the presentation of the South in a realist manner, lightened by irony, she found it hard to be crossed off as a sentimental regionalist. That she obviously loved her native state and that her books sold by the thousands were perhaps enough to make her seem to the casual eye like the very thing that she abominated. And when she did break through the literary barriers with *Barren Ground* in 1925, she was already in her fifties and beginning to have a nostalgic eye for the old state of society against which she had rebelled. If she shuddered at Thomas Nelson Page, she shuddered more at *Sanctuary*. She might almost have said at the end, like that disillusioned Victorian, Rhoda Broughton: "I began life as Zola; I finish it as Miss Charlotte Yonge."

From the beginning she never wavered in her conviction that her role in life was to write novels—important novels. She kept a sharp eye on every development of her career, including all steps of publication, to ensure the unhampered growth of her reputation as a major novelist. She left Harper, which had published her first two novels, without a qualm (so far as appears in her correspondence) when she decided that Walter Hines Page at Doubleday would do a better job on the third, and after Doubleday had published sixteen of her titles (including a volume of poetry and another of short stories) she left it for Harcourt, Brace because she concluded that much of the Doubleday promotion which had helped to make her famous was "cheap." Similarly, although never rich, she did not hesitate, in the depths of the Depression, to turn down an offer by *Good Housekeeping* of $30,000 to serialize *The Sheltered Life*, and she made a habit of seeking out critics to have the chance to present her literary case personally and to make perfectly clear what her books were about. In short, she was Ellen Glasgow's own best agent, as Amy Lowell had been Amy Lowell's.

Her first two novels, *The Descendant* (1897) and *Phases of an Inferior Planet* (1898), bristle with the young liberal's determination to be shockingly realistic and seem a bit jejune to modern eyes, but it should not be forgotten what a determined step away from romantic fiction, particularly on the part of a young woman gently bred, they must have represented to her contemporaries. If a southern lady produced novels at all, they were expected to deal with plantation life, either in its antebellum splendor or in heroic and picturesque decay. Miss Glasgow's first two tales may seem as far from Faulkner as the sentimental tosh to which they were a reaction, and she herself in later years came to regard the so-called "honest" school of southern literature as a combination of everything that was "too vile and too degenerate to exist anywhere else," but there was nonetheless a strong historical link between the two.

It is a pity that she chose to lay the scene of

both of these novels in New York, which she knew then only as an occasional visitor. Even later, when she had lived in the city for several years in succession, she never caught its flavor as she caught that of Williamsburg, Petersburg, and Richmond. She objected to being labeled a Virginia writer, and, indeed, her truths were universal, but it was still the case that they were better seen against a Virginia background. This, however, was to be no serious limitation, for hers was a diverse state, and she knew it thoroughly, its cities and its rural areas, its aristocrats and its businessmen, its politicians and its farmers. If she was a regionalist, she was a regionalist on a Trollopian scale.

The style of these early books combines the epigrammatic with the sentimental in a way that suggests a mixture of Meredith and Charlotte Brontë. Clever sentences like "Conscience represents a fetish to which good people sacrifice their own happiness, bad people their neighbors'" are to be found with such others as "It was the old, old expiation that Nature had demanded and woman paid since the day upon which woman and desire met and knew each other." Even more awkward is the intrusion into the supposedly free and easy life of the young bohemian characters of certain undiscarded standards of the author's Richmond upbringing. The radical hero of *The Descendant*, who preaches against marriage, is nonetheless still chaste when he meets and falls in love with an emancipated virgin to whom he protests: "I am not worthy to touch the hem of your garment." And Algarcife in *Phases of an Inferior Planet*, who loses his job in a women's college because of his articles on the "origin of sex," can still condemn his wife to bitter need rather than let her supplement the family income by taking a role in light opera. In bitter need, too, be it noted, they still have a "slipshod maid of work."

The important thing, however, to be observed about these forgotten little books is that, for all their crudeness, they demonstrate a flow of narrative power and a vitality that show a young writer bound to make her mark. *The Descendant*, published anonymously, was by many attributed to Harold Frederic, which seems a greater compliment today than Miss Glasgow thought it at the time. In her middle twenties she was already established and could write Mr. Page about her third novel: "If the gods will it to be my last I don't want people to say 'she might have done big things,' because I am writing this book not to amuse, or to sell, but to *live*, and if it does so I shall be content not to—after it is finished."

The Voice of the People (1900), indeed, marks the real beginning of her career as a novelist. She had already conceived her master plan of writing "in the more freely interpretative form of fiction" a social history of Virginia from the decade before the Confederacy. Possibly using a bit of hindsight and showing that passion to see a lifework as centralized that characterizes the great French novelists, she later classified her fiction as fitting into the following categories and covering the following chronological periods:

History: *The Battle-Ground,* 1850–65; *The Deliverance,* 1878–90; *The Voice of the People,* 1870–98; *The Romance of a Plain Man,* 1875–1910; *Virginia,* 1884–1912; *Life and Gabriella,* 1894–1912.

Novels of the country: *The Miller of Old Church,* 1898–1902; *Barren Ground,* 1894–1924; *Vein of Iron,* 1901–33.

Novels of the city: *The Sheltered Life,* 1910–17; *The Romantic Comedians,* 1923; *They Stooped to Folly,* 1924; *In This Our Life,* 1938–39.

Actually, the only common denominator of all these novels is the Commonwealth of Virginia, as the only one that links the masterpieces of Zola's *Rougon-Macquart* is France in the Second Empire, but at least Miss Glasgow had the wisdom to rest her case on geography and did not try to connect her characters through the branches of an immense and exotic family tree.

The Voice of the People, although third in the history series, was the first to be published, because, unlike *The Battle-Ground* and *The Deliverance*, it required no research. Battle Hall might have been the Jerdone Castle of Ellen Glasgow's own childhood, and we meet her for the first time as a writer in full possession of her native materials. She was to make Virginia the setting of all her subsequent novels but two: *The Wheel of Life* and *Life and Gabriella*. The first takes place totally in New York and is a total failure; the second takes place partly in New York and is in that part a failure. Without the Virginia that Miss Glasgow knew as a historian and felt as a poet, her characters never become fully alive.

As one first begins to succumb to the fascination of Battle Hall, with the visiting aunt who comes for a week and stays for years, with the miraculous reorganizing domestic powers of Miss Chris, with the friendly darkies and the long, succulent meals, with the rumbling memories in sleepy afternoons of more heroic days, one may start up and ask: How is all this so different from the romantic tradition? Isn't this more of Thomas Nelson Page? Perhaps. Miss Glasgow had a deeply ingrained sympathy for the antebellum aristocracy, but at the same time one begins to perceive the parts of the picture that her realist eye picks out: General Tom sinking into sloth and fantasy and the rigid standards of Mrs. Webb operating to depress and freeze people in their born stations. Nicholas Burr, the hero, of the poor white class, may educate himself, like Akershem in *The Descendant*, and may even rise to become governor of Virginia, and die a martyr's death holding off a lynching mob, but he fails to win Eugenia Battle, and his failure has been foreordained by the blind prejudice of her family.

Miss Glasgow's resolution of the class problem, however, is a bit muddied by her own preconceptions. One is willing to accept the fact that Nicholas Burr, like Akershem, is subject to violent fits of rage, and even to accept his rages as attributes of the uncivilized barbarian lurking in all of us, but one cannot as easily accept Miss Glasgow's complacent assumption that such violence lurks more insidiously in the lower orders. Why would not *any* man explode against a heroine who, without a hearing, blandly condemns him for the seduction of a farm girl who has in fact been seduced by the heroine's own brother? Yet Eugenia appears to have the author's sympathy when she finds in Nicholas' fury a "sinister" reminder of his father. And why sinister? Is his father an evil man? No, simply a vulgar one. Certainly there is here a tendency to equate violence with low birth and sex appeal, for the heroes of these early novels, however ugly of temper, have also some of the attributes of supermen. Later on, after she had had a disillusioning personal experience, the men with whom Miss Glasgow's heroines become involved (no longer heroes by any stretch of the term) are weak, self-indulgent, and faithless. The confusion that exists in *The Voice of the People* was ultimately cleared up, but at the expense of the male sex.

Throughout this initial period of her literary career, Ellen Glasgow's hearing was steadily failing. As her income increased she began pilgrimages all over the world "more hopeless than the pilgrimages to shrines of saints in the Dark Ages," for there was no cure for the hardening in the Eustachian tube and the middle ear. Science had failed her body, she complained, as ruinously as religion had failed her soul, and she had to fall back on a humane stoicism and—ultimately—on golf. Deliberately she built "a wall of deceptive gaiety" around herself and cultivated the "ironic mood, the smiling pose." There was a surer refuge in mockery, she found, than in too grave a sincerity.

Romanticism, however, was still evident in *The Battle-Ground* (1902), which Alfred Kazin has called a "superior sword and cape romance based on the legend that the Civil War was fought between gentlemen and bounders." It is the only Glasgow novel where the action takes place before and during the Civil War and consequently before the author's own memory, which may explain why the early chapters are so filled with frothy chatter and gallantry, with toasts and boasts ("To Virginia, the home of brave men and of angels"), with loving, loyal slaves and proud, high-tempered colonels. Of course, Miss Glasgow may have been deliberately intensifying the cavalier atmosphere in order to heighten the drama of the coming conflict that would sweep it all away. It has become the classic method of handling the opening of the Civil War, as seen in Margaret Mitchell's *Gone with the Wind* (a book which Miss Glasgow admired) and in Stephen Vincent Benét's *John Brown's Body*. It is, indeed, almost a literary convention to show the Confederacy dancing its way into disaster.

She did better, however, in the war chapters. Here she kept away as much as possible from battle scenes, for she never liked to write about things that she had not seen with her own eyes, and she concentrated on pictures, such as that of wartime Richmond, where her own hard research and contemporary knowledge could combine to give a proper focus. The novel ends where her real work in fiction begins: at the end of the war when the South faces the future in defeat. It is here that she establishes herself as totally distinct from those novelists who could only lament what had passed away and sigh over characters who did the same. Dan Montjoy, coming back to the ruins of his an-

cestral home, wounded and half-starved, can yet reflect that the memory of a beaten slave which used to haunt him need bother him now no more. And his grandfather, Major Lightfoot, who is unable mentally to take in the fact of Appomattox, augurs the postwar southern mental evasiveness about which Miss Glasgow was to have so much to say and to the exposure of which she was to devote her ironic art.

The Deliverance (1904) is her first fully mature work. It is a well-organized centripetal novel about impoverished aristocrats and unscrupulous parvenus in the era of reconstruction. For the first time Miss Glasgow was able to make effective use of the Virgina soil; and the tobacco fields which bring a fortune to Bill Fletcher, the embezzler who has robbed the Blake family of the plantation where he was once overseer, make a perfect setting for the bloody conflict between the still vigorous old order and the already decadent new, and for the terrible revenge of Christopher Blake, who deliberately corrupts and destroys the ex-overseer's grandson. Miss Glasgow was to be outdone only by Willa Cather in her handling of rural atmosphere.

In her affection for the Blakes there is still a bit of nostalgia for antebellum days, but the bleak and closely observed present gives the twist of irony to all the memories and stories of that glorious era. The blind Mrs. Blake, whose family and servants together conspire to create in her sickroom the illusion of a victorious South, going so far as to invent names for the Confederate presidents of two postwar decades, is, of course, the symbol of the old South that rejected reality. Her son Christopher, on the other hand, who works in the tobacco fields to support the family, is an example of the aristocrat who has the courage to face and defeat poverty, even though born with the love of ease and the weakness to temptation in his blood, "with the love, too, of delicate food, of rare wines and of beautiful women." Did Miss Glasgow actually believe in the physical transmission of aristocratic characteristics? Evidently so, for Christopher, without education or other advantages, stands out among his fellow farmers as a natural leader. He is another of Miss Glasgow's supermen—he risks smallpox to bury the children of a former family slave—but he is even more irresistible to women than Nicholas Burr because of his noble birth, and when Maria Fletcher sees him, her creator's style slumps suddenly to the level of the lowest potboiler: "All the natural womanhood within her responded to the appeal of his superb manhood."

Maxwell Geismar has pointed out that Ellen Glasgow's novels are among our best sources of information on the southern mind because we can see in them the persistent imprint of primary cultural myths on even a perceptive and sophisticated talent. Miss Glasgow, he feels, for all her compassion and liberalism, could never quite free herself from her admiration of the old aristocracy with all its narrowness and prejudice. It is true. Negroes in her fiction are apt to appear as a carefree, feckless, lovable servant class whose peccadilloes and promiscuities are to be laughed at rather than condemned. In *One Man in His Time* she was actually able to write a whole book on the social problems facing a liberal governor of Virginia without mentioning the Negroes. She belonged, of course, to a generation that was taught to duck the problem in its cradle. But all this does not mean that she was unaware that it existed. Dan Montjoy in *The Battle-Ground* helps an escaped slave; Mrs. Pendleton in *Virginia* forces herself not to see the slave market; Dorinda Oakley in *Barren Ground* is a true friend of her Negro servant; Asa Timberlake in *In This Our Life* defies his family in order to protect a Negro boy from being framed for a crime. In this last episode Miss Glasgow does, if only for a few pages, face up to the fact that otherwise respectable white people may be willing to sacrifice an innocent colored boy to protect a vicious member of their own race. By and large, however, she did not choose to be overly concerned with the problem. She was one who felt that the modern Negro had lost the "spiritual" quality of his forebears, and she evaded the connection between such spirituality and bondage. She had her loves and her loyalties, and even at her most ironical there were certain boats that she was not going to rock.

In 1900 Ellen Glasgow met the man whom she describes as "Gerald B———" in her memoirs, and until his death seven years later she lived "in an arrested pause between dreaming and waking." As with "Harold S———," the other great love of her life, it was a case of opposites attracting. Gerald was a financier and a married man; they could meet only fleetingly and only on her visits to New York. One infers that the relationship was not happy, but it must have had its wonderful moments, and when he died of an inoperable ailment she was completely overwhelmed. If we are to take the relationship of Laura Wilde and Arnold Kemper in *The Wheel of Life*, a novel which she admittedly wrote as an antidote to her sorrow and later confessed to be in part autobiographical, as a picture of herself and Gerald, we thresh up an interesting speculation. Why was this woman, so dedicated to the mind and spirit, twice to fall in love with egocentric and hedonistic philistines? Was *this* what she meant by the indignities of the spirit to which she was relentlessly subjected? It is difficult to imagine greater ones.

After receiving the news that Gerald was doomed, she records that she went up on a hillside in Switzerland and lay down on the grass where a high wind was blowing. There she had a mystical experience. "Lying there, in that golden August light, I knew, or felt, or beheld, a union deeper than knowledge, deeper than sense, deeper than vision. Light streamed through me, after anguish, and for one instant of awareness, if but for that one instant, I felt pure ecstasy. In a single blinding flash of illumination, I knew blessedness. I was a part of the spirit that moved in the light and the wind and the grass. I was—or felt I was—in communion with reality, with ultimate being. . . ." Something very like this experience was to go into the making of *Barren Ground* and *The Sheltered Life.*

In the terrible years that followed Gerald's death she became engaged to a man with whom she was never in love, but who offered her everything that her love for Gerald missed: "intellectual congeniality, poetic sympathy, and companionship which was natural and easy, without the slightest sting of suspicion or selfishness." Everything, in short, but delight and joy. His letters, those of a poet, stirred in her no greater emotion than gratitude. She asked herself if she had failed because she had preferred the second best in emotion, just as her fellow countrymen so often preferred the second best in literature. Perhaps she had, but the fact that she could see the irony of her situation was the rock on which she would later build her Queenborough trilogy.

In *The Wheel of Life* (1906), conceived in a mystical mood, poet Laura Wilde and her mentor Roger Adams struggle toward the recognition that man's only valid purpose is to identify himself with God and to lose his ego. The pursuit of happiness, even in love—love, in Laura's case, for a man, Arnold Kemper, who, however inconstant, sincerely offers marriage—is simply an invitation to disillusionment and betrayal. This is a theme that will constantly be met again in Ellen Glasgow's work. The most that a woman can expect from love is the opportunity to develop her character by facing inevitable abandonment with fortitude. It is a dreary credo, and enveloped in the somber atmosphere of *The Wheel of Life*, it makes for dreary reading. Laura's collapse into a living death when she discovers that she no longer loves Kemper is so humorlessly described that it engenders no sympathy. And worst of all, this quiet little drama of the soul is played out in New York, with none of the powerfully evoked landscapes of the Virginia novels. Miss Glasgow could never seem to get interested in describing Manhattan. It is always a cold, shadowy island seen only in terms of directions, "east along Sixty-sixth Street," "west to Fifth Avenue." Nor are even the minor characters indigenous. Angela Wilde, who never leaves her house, hovering upstairs like a wraith because she was compromised in her youth, is more Richmond than New York (we will meet her in later Glasgow fiction), and her senile brother who likes to play the flute seems a faded descendant from the gentle family of Dickensian lunatics.

A Virginia setting makes *The Ancient Law* (1908) better reading, but it is again the inferior product of a depressed period. Novels about saints are apt to be tedious, and Daniel Ordway, born in the arid tradition of those austere heroes of George Eliot, Felix Holt and Daniel Deronda, is not made more credible by having been, like another library model, a convict. The end of the book seems almost designed as a parody of nineteenth-century fictional saints. Ordway, having taken upon his own shoulders the guilt of his daughter's forgery, leaves his home a second time in disgrace and travels back to Tappahannock, the town which under an alias he has redeemed and made prosperous (compare *Les Misérables*), just in time to purchase the steel mills from the villain and save them from destruction by a mob of furious strikers to whom he promises fair hours and wages and by whom he is hailed in a final apotheosis. There was a curious streak of the preacher in Ellen Glasgow, quite at odds with her natural skepticism and ironical humor, that tended to seize upon her in her low moments.

The Romance of a Plain Man (1909) finds her happily back on the main avenue of a career which, almost uniquely among those of American writers, was to improve in quality (except for two long hiatuses caused by mental depression) until her old age. For the first and last time in a novel she adopted the stratagem of the hero narrator, which disembarrassed the author of all problems as to points of view. She violated, however, the literary principle attached to its use: that everything to be told can be naturally told by the narrator. One does not believe, for example, that Ben Starr, who is announced in the title itself as a "plain man" and who has had to make his way up a rough business ladder from lower-middle-class rags to upper-middle-class riches, would describe breezes as being "fragrant with jessamine" or air as "heavy with the perfume of fading roses." Nor does one believe that Miss Glasgow ever intended him to sound as fatuous as he does when he notes that "I, the man of action, the embodiment of worldly success, was awed by the very intensity of my love."

Yet Ben's conquest of Sally Mickleborough's world is well described, and the best thing about it is that he can never make himself realize that he *has* conquered it. He feels that he must go on making money for Sally even when he suspects—or ought to suspect—that she wants only his love. But that, of course, is just Miss Glasgow's point: that he isn't really making money for her, but only to prove to himself that he is as good as her aunts and even as good as the great General Bolingbroke. He has been made to feel too deeply his own social inferiority as a child to imagine that it could ever

be hidden by anything but a wall of gold. It is thus that materialism engenders materialism; in the end, when there is almost no hope left for the Starrs' happiness, Ben at last sees that the real division between himself and Sally has come "not from the accident of our different beginnings but from the choice that had committed us to opposite ends." It is Ben who ultimately insists on the importance of class as rigidly as Sally's Aunt Mitty Bland, who has contemptuously remarked, when urged to concede the physical strength and stature of her proposed nephew-in-law: "What are six feet, two inches without a grandfather?"

Miss Glasgow was very sensitive to social changes; she saw and took it on herself to record that all over the South, as the industrial system displaced the agrarian aristocracy, men like Ben Starr were forging their way into prominence. She was perfectly willing to welcome them and to give them their due, perhaps even more, for she endows Ben with a touch of her old supermen when he knocks down a man whom he finds beating a horse. But she was handicapped in the business scenes by her ignorance of financial matters. Ben's money dealings are misty, which is again the fault of the narrator technique. He cannot talk about things that his creator did not understand, yet one knows that such a man would never stop talking about his big deals. Perhaps if one saw him through the eyes of Sally, who hated business, this part of the book would be more convincing. Edith Wharton, by showing her tycoons only at parties in *The House of Mirth*, was able to conceal from her reader an ignorance of stock exchange matters as deep as, if not deeper than, Miss Glasgow's. The latter should have done some of the research that Theodore Dreiser did for his Cowperwood novels before letting Ben Starr tell his own story.

If Ben Starr has risen, however, the old

order has by no means collapsed. Ben's greatest ambition is to rise only as high as General Bolingbroke, a Civil War hero and aristocrat who has turned in his later years to business to lead the South out of defeat. The General, one of Miss Glasgow's most vivid characters (he cannot allow Miss Matoaca Bland to criticize a politician's immoral life because he cannot allow that she should know that it existed), achieves independence from his own caste by sheer success. Having been exalted in war as well as in peace, having been a leader in the old plantation days as well as the smoky industrial new ones, he, alone of the characters, can see how fluctuating and passable are class lines. He can see what Sally's aunts can never see, that Ben Starr will ultimately change his class with his clothes and that only a few old maids will oppose him to the end.

The Miller of Old Church (1911) marks Ellen Glasgow's coming of age, her advent as a major talent in American fiction. It dramatizes the same rise of the lower middle class as *The Romance of a Plain Man*, but it does so more effectively because the scene is laid in a rural area. Miss Glasgow knew a lot more about millers than she knew about financiers. The drama, too, is intensified by the fact that the upper class here is declining. Ben Starr and General Bolingbroke go forward, so to speak, hand in hand, but the Revercombs on the way up meet and clash with the declining Gays. This makes for a better story, though on a more fundamental level it is the soil, as opposed to the cobblestones of Richmond, that gives the deeper interest. The Revercombs triumph over the Gays because they have stronger roots. We have already seen that rural aristocrats can hold their position only, like Christopher Blake in *The Deliverance*, by turning to the land. In making her point Miss Glasgow occasionally allows us a glimpse of George Eliot and Thomas Hardy looking over

her shoulder, and Jonathan Gay's seduction of Blossom Revercomb is a little too reminiscent of both *Adam Bede* and *Tess of the d'Urbervilles*. She was to assimilate more entirely the bleak morality of her great predecessors when she brought her own to its most effective expression in *Barren Ground*.

The Miller of Old Church shows some of the bluntness of style of Miss Glasgow's earlier days, and the omniscient author continues from time to time to obtrude a bit clumsily on the scene. One feels oneself back in the author's workshop on learning, of Abel Revercomb, that "essentially an idealist, his character was the result of a veneering of insufficient culture on a groundwork of raw impulse," or of Molly that "a passing impulse was crystallized by the coldness of her manner into a permanent desire." But in the delineation of Mrs. Gay, Ellen Glasgow was writing as well as she would ever write. It is the revenge of her aristocrats that even slipping they dominate the scene. Mrs. Gay is everything that old Virginia wanted a woman to be—lovely, helpless, indolent, and ignorant, and she conceals behind these qualities an inner force that enchains and destroys all those around her: her brother-in-law, his mistress, her sister Kesiah (a magnificent portrait of an ugly old maid rejected by a world that idolizes beauty), and finally her own son. The last chapter, where after the catastrophe of Jonathan's murder the characters raise their arms in a paean of praise to the wonder of his mother's fortitude, the same mother whose selfishness and prejudice have caused the tragedy, is the first great triumph in Miss Glasgow's use of irony.

The Mrs. Gays of Virginia, however, were not always destructive. Sometimes they were heroic, in which case, poor creatures, they found themselves, by the turn of the century, harmless anachronisms. Such a one is the heroine of *Virginia* (1913), the first of Ellen Glasgow's great tragicomedies. The amazing thing about the character of Virginia Pendleton is that, loyal, sweet, brave, unimaginative, and uncomplaining, she bores everybody but the reader. In this she surpasses Thackeray's Amelia, who bores everybody but Dobbin. She is brought up to be the model wife that every southern gentleman was supposed to desire, and may have desired—twenty years before her birth. She admires her husband without comprehending him or without even trying to. She is gentle when a lady should be gentle but capable of a pioneer woman's strength in adversity. Like her old schoolmistress, the embattled spinster Priscilla Batte, she is capable "of dying for an idea but not of conceiving one." She is ignorant, pure, and beautiful, a rose of the Tidewater, but fascinating to meet —in a novel.

From the very beginning of this admirable book, Virginia's parents and teachers are perfectly united in their unconscious aim of turning her into a creature bound to be blighted by the world in which she must live. Her only hope would have been to find a husband (and there were such) who had been in his turn educated to appreciate her type. But, ironically enough, it is old Priscilla Batte herself who, incapable of envisaging any nice young man who would not cherish Virginia, deliberately stimulates the interest of Oliver Treadwell in this finest flower of her educational garden. From the moment she does so the novel moves as relentlessly to its conclusion as if it had been conceived by Flaubert or Zola. Virginia's undiscriminating adoration ends by driving her husband to New York and another woman, and when he has gone she has nothing to fall back on but the same commodious attic of fortitude that sustained her mother through the dreary years of war and reconstruction. But military defeat is easier to bear than de-sertion, and Virginia's cup is bitterer than her parents'.

She does, however, have one consolation, her son Harry, who in the last paragraph of the book telegraphs that he is coming back from Europe to be with her. One does not feel it is quite fair of Miss Glasgow to leave us on this enigmatic note. Might Virginia not become a worse fiend than Mrs. Gay and ruin Harry's life by a possessiveness disguised as unselfishness? Would that not be just the revenge that her type might unconsciously take on a world and a sex that had let her down?

Virginia is addressed to a social problem that had largely been solved at the time of its publication, for Miss Priscilla Batte and her academy for preserving the natural ignorance of young ladies belonged to an earlier generation. Yet it is hard to imagine a more effective illustration of the romanticism and intransigency of the South, which had certainly not disappeared in 1913. When asked what the South needed Miss Glasgow once quipped: "blood and irony." The latter she was to supply in increasing doses, but first was to come the second of those hiatuses in her literary development.

The death of her sister Cary in 1911 was followed by a period of depression in which much of *Virginia* was written. Fortunately for that book it had been conceived and commenced before the final blow, and the writing of it acted as a kind of therapy for her grief. But *Life and Gabriella* (1916), having its birth in a time of desolation, is the arid product of a preoccupied imagination. It is as if Ellen Glasgow were saying over and over again with an almost psychotic monotony: "It does not matter what happens to one, so long as one has fortitude, so long as one is not crushed by life." If Mrs. Gay is the weak and selfish Virginia woman and if Virginia Pendleton is the good and crushed one, Gabriella is the Virginia woman triumphant over all obstacles. The obstacles, indeed, bend like rushes before the storm of her resolution.

Her story reads like the outline of a novel with all the author's notes unerased. The very subtitle, *The Story of a Woman's Courage*, suggests a juvenile. Gabriella Carr, after a few vivid chapters describing the desperate life of decayed gentlewomen in Richmond, is captured by the charms of a New Yorker, George Fowler, marries him, and goes to live in his native city. His charms must be accepted because Miss Glasgow insists upon them. They are not otherwise apparent, though his magnetism is faintly suggestive of Arnold Kemper's in *The Wheel of Life* and may have the same source. When we first see Gabriella and George together we are told in the heaviest of asides that "In his eyes, which said enchanting things, she could not read the trivial and commonplace quality of his soul." George, in the now habitual way of Glasgow men, deserts her, and Gabriella, with serene faith in her own capacities, takes over the management of a flourishing dress shop and, after a brief struggle with her old Dominion blood, marries Ben O'Hara, another lowly born superman who has passed the hero's test by rescuing an asphyxiated woman and her small children from a burning house.

Another unfortunate thing about this novel is that the author's snobbishness is among the notes that she failed to erase. Gabriella's difficulties in bringing herself to accept the Irishman are understandable in a woman of her background, but her attitude toward the newly rich whom she meets at Mrs. Fowler's dinners is based on a pride of birth that the author seems to find quite acceptable. To Miss Glasgow as well as to her heroine it is inconceivable that Mrs. Fowler, "with the bluest blood of Virginia in her veins, should regard with such artless reverence the social activities of the granddaughter of a tavern-keeper." If Mrs. Fowler is going to be a snob, in other words, she should go about it in a larger spirit!

American involvement in World War I and Miss Glasgow's infatuation with the "Harold S——" of the memoirs came at the same time, and neither event helped to get her out of the slump of this period. It was obviously humiliating for the possessor of an eye so keen to irony to have to turn it on herself and her lover, but turn it she did in the pages of her memoirs. There is nothing sharper or more devastating in all her fiction than the picture of Harold in *The Woman Within*. Everything that she despised most in life—trivial honors, notoriety, social prominence, wealth, fashion, ladies with titles, the empty show of the world—he adored, and she loved him in spite of it for nothing more than a "defiant gaiety" that piqued her interest. Only when, on a Red Cross mission to the Balkans, he had acted out against a background of war horrors his grotesque parody of a Graustarkian romance with Queen Marie of Romania, was she partially cured of her infatuation. But in the despair that followed this episode she took an overdose of sleeping pills, not caring if she lived or died.

She lived, and there was left the war. Even worse for her fiction than her passion for the "pluperfect snob" was her vicarious suffering over distant carnage. This produced her worst novel—if a political tract full of Wilsonian idealism can be called a novel at all. *The Builders* (1919) grew out of the same shrill war feeling that produced Edith Wharton's *A Son at the Front*. David Blackburn, a waxwork Rochester, harangues his child's nurse, Caroline Meade, a rather testy Jane Eyre, on the sad state of the solid South, the evils of the one-party system, and the need for a league of nations. "The future of our democracy," he writes her in his first love letter, "rests not in the halls of Congress but in the cradle, and to build for permanency we must build, not on theory, but on personal rectitude." Angelica Blackburn's wickedness and her success in playing the injured wife provide what little story there is, but even this is spoiled by the clumsy device of having the reader see her first through Caroline's eyes as a noble, suffering creature. It is so manifest that she is not this that we brand Caroline as a ninny, and the central point of view of the novel is hopelessly discredited.

The almost immediate disillusionment that came to so many after the Armistice came to Ellen Glasgow, and one suspects that she was soon a bit ashamed of *The Builders*. Certainly there is no trace of David Blackburn's exalted idealism in *One Man in His Time* (1922). It is not a good novel, but it is at least a novel, and there must have been those who wondered, after its predecessor, if she would ever write one again. Gideon Vetch, the poor white who has risen to be governor of Virginia, is a man who believes that the end justifies the means, but at least he believes in an end, and he dies, assassinated, the victim of the rising under-dogs and the static "haves," the second Glasgow hero to suffer a violent end in this high but evidently dangerous office. For the first time in her fiction Miss Glasgow paid serious attention to her points of view and handled them with some degree of subtlety. Vetch is never seen directly, but always through the eyes of others, hostile or admiring, which lends a needed suspense to his story.

Other than Vetch, however, the characters in this book, as in *Gabriella* and *The Builders*, are thin. One feels that Miss Glasgow shares Corinna Page's feeling about the hero: "She

had a sincere though not very deep affection for Stephen." Stephen Culpeper is too much under the influence of his vapid mother to have been the war hero he is reputed. One does not believe that it took such valiance in 1920 for a young man to marry the daughter of the governor of Virginia simply because Patty Vetch's mother had reportedly been a circus rider. And his awakening to human misery after a single tour of the slums of Richmond is a turgid interruption of the story, as is the melodramatic episode when Patty, who does not know she is adopted and thinks her mother dead, visits her "aunt," actually her mother, now a drug addict. But at least one feels in the pulse of the novel that Ellen Glasgow was emerging from the second period of despondency in which she had been so long engulfed.

The best thing about her life was that the best part of it came after the age of fifty. As she wrote herself: "After those intolerable years, all my best work was to come." Her parents were dead, as were Cary and Gerald, and she was largely cured of Harold. She was alone now in the old gray Georgian house with the great tulip poplars at One West Main Street, except for her companion, Anne Virginia Bennett, who had come as a trained nurse and stayed to be a secretary. She regretted the absence of literary life in Richmond, but it was the world in which she had grown up and from which she drew much of her inspiration. It was home, and a home, too, where she was increasingly admired and respected. When she went out to parties, she talked, as she described it, of "Tom, Dick, and Harry," but why not? The real life was within. And what did Tom, Dick, and Harry matter when she was entering the finest part of her career?

Barren Ground (1925) shows the influence of Hardy at last assimilated. Egdon Heath is no more part of the lives of the characters of

The Return of the Native, than is the Piedmont countryside part of the lives of the Oakleys. Its flatness creates the illusion of immensity, and the broom sedge spreads in smothered fire over the melancholy brown landscape to a bleak horizon. The colors are fall colors from autumnal flowers: the crimson sumach, the wine-colored sassafras, the silvery life everlasting. The Oakleys themselves are "products of the soil as surely as were the scant crops." Joshua looks heavy and earthbound even in his Sunday clothes; for all his scrubbing the smell of manure clings to him; and when Dorinda walks in the October countryside she feels her surroundings so sensitively that "the wall dividing her individual consciousness from the consciousness of nature vanished with the thin drift of woodsmoke over the fields." The inanimate character of the horizon becomes as personal, reserved, and inscrutable as her own mind.

Even the morality springs from the soil, or, rather, from man's battle with it. The broom sedge is the eternal enemy, always ready to engulf every new farm and field, and men are graded by how they fight it. "For it was not sin that was punished in this world or the next; it was failure. Good failure or bad failure, it made no difference, for nature abhorred both." Jason Greylock, Dorinda's lover in her youth, is weak, and he is broken and finally in dying becomes a lesser thing than the soil; he is identified with a thistle. Dorinda in her fortitude, a Glasgow fortitude built on Jason's desertion, triumphs over the land and builds a dairy farm where the broom sedge was. After the death of her husband, Nathan Pedlar, married for convenience, and of Jason, Dorinda embraces the land anew. Perhaps Miss Glasgow is a bit carried away by her theme here: "The storm and the hag-ridden dreams of the night were over, and the land which she had forgotten was waiting to take her back to its heart. Endurance. Fortitude. The spirit of the land was flowing into her, and her own spirit, strengthened and refreshed, was flowing out again toward life."

Aside, however, from a few such overladen passages and the old habit of dwelling at too great length on her heroine's suffering in abandonment, *Barren Ground* is her finest work. She achieves a greater unity than in the earlier books by strictly limiting the points of view. The central struggle in the story is between Dorinda and the soil, and we see it entirely through Dorinda's mind except when the author intervenes to supplement our picture of the countryside and Pedlar's Mill. In this the technique is not unlike Flaubert's in *Madame Bovary*, where, as Percy Lubbock has pointed out, we have to see only two things: Yonville as it looks to Emma Bovary and Yonville as it looks to Flaubert. Actually, there is much less of the author in *Barren Ground* because Dorinda, unlike Emma, is a woman of enough perception to give us most of the necessary impressions herself.

Miss Glasgow maintained that the Abernethys (Dorinda's mother was an Abernethy), the Greylocks, and the Pedlars were representative of a special rural class, not "poor whites" but "good people" and descendants of English yeomen, who had never before been treated in fiction. She gains greatly in the vividness of her portrayal by not mixing them with characters of other backgrounds. Everyone we see in Pedlar's Mill belongs in Pedlar's Mill like the broom sedge, and the only chapters that mar the otherwise perfect unity of mood in this beautifully conceived novel are those where Dorinda goes to New York to work for a doctor. Manhattan, which provides the only important non-Virginian settings in Miss Glasgow's fiction, is, as usual, fatal to it.

She now embarked on her great trilogy of Richmond, or "Queenborough": *The Romantic Comedians* (1926), *They Stooped to Folly* (1929), and *The Sheltered Life* (1932). The three books do not constitute a trilogy in the sense that they have a continuous plot or even characters in common, but they share a common setting and class, the latter being the old but still prosperous Richmond families, and a spirit of ironic high comedy. They also share— and this is a fault if they are read consecutively —a hero, at least to the extent that the elderly man who is the principal observer in each has a melancholy sense of having missed the real fun in life. It is confusing that they are so alike yet not the same. Miss Glasgow never hesitated to plagiarize herself.

Turning from *Barren Ground* to *The Romantic Comedians* is like turning from Hardy to Meredith, from *The Return of the Native* to *The Egoist*. It is one of the great tours de force of American literature. "After I had finished *Barren Ground*," she wrote in her preface, "which for three years had steeped my mind in the sense of tragic life, the comic spirit, always restless when it is confined, began struggling against the bars of its cage." Never was it to escape to greater advantage. Judge Honeywell, surrounded and tormented by women, is surely one of the most amusing studies in southern fiction. His outrageous twin sister, Edmonia Bredalbane, who wears her scarlet letter as if it were a decoration, his old sweetheart, Amanda Lightfoot, the eternally brave and sweet "good" woman, whose life is a ruin because she could never face a fact, and his dead wife, whose image wears a halo of oppressive rectitude, would all keep him from the folly of turning to a girl forty years his junior, but the benighted old fool has had enough of them (who wouldn't?) and wants one joy, one real joy of his own, before the end. The reader knows, everyone knows, even the judge, deep down, knows that this joy will turn to brambles, but he *will* have his way and does. The young wife, Annabel, is just right, too, for she has all the selfishness of youth and all its charm, and we expect her to find her marriage impossible. There is a tragic tone to the book, but it is never allowed to become heavy. The laughter, even when muted almost to a compassionate silence, is still there.

Ellen Glasgow was now in her early fifties and beginning prematurely to suffer from the tendency of so many older people to find youth without standards and to deplore the loss of disciplines in the world about her. It was the same tendency that spoiled so much of the later fiction of Edith Wharton. Miss Glasgow's correspondence is now increasingly full of complaints about the sloppiness and sordidness of modern living and modern literature. She came to look back on her own past, which she had found so stultifying as a girl, with increased nostalgia as she saw the effects of the new liberty of deportment and the new realism of expression that she had herself espoused. Once the note of shrillness, even of petulance, had entered her fiction it could only be lost when, as in *The Sheltered Life* and in the early chapters of *Vein of Iron*, she moved her setting back prior to those ills with which she now saw the world inundated.

They Stooped to Folly is the first of her books to suffer from this lack of sympathy with young people. The youthful characters are hard, angular, and unconvincing. Millie Burden, with the monotony of a minor character in Dickens, repeats over and over that she is "entitled to her life." Mary Victoria is so repellently fatuous and egocentric that she has to be kept off the scene if we are to believe, as the author insists that we shall, in her great influence over other people. And Martin Welding is too weak and self-pitying to cause the havoc he is supposed to cause in female hearts.

The novel as a whole seems like a compilation of discarded sketches from the atelier that produced its happier predecessor. Virginius Littlepage is a small, stuffy version of Judge Honeywell, and nothing happens to him except that he loses his unloved but superior spouse during and not before his chronicle. There is no Annabel for him, only a flirtation with a gay widow that makes him ridiculous but never pathetic. It is impossible to believe in his great love for his daughter Mary Victoria, whose meanness he sees as clearly as does the reader, or in his great sorrow over her obviously doomed marriage to a man whom she has ruthlessly torn from another woman. It is difficult, in fact, for the reader not to feel that all of the Littlepages deserve anything they get.

So what is left? Nothing but epigrams, and even these are repetitive. The characters cannot seem to make their points too often. Millie Burden talks only of her "rights," and her mother only of Millie's need for punishment. Mrs. Littlepage keeps insisting that she has never known her husband to be sarcastic, whereas the reader has never known him to be anything else. And what is the theme of it all? That a woman should not be punished all her life for having lived with a man out of wedlock! What can Miss Glasgow have thought she was up to? Nobody *is* so punished in the book, except Aunt Agatha, and that was in the ancient past. And nobody in the book thinks anyone *should* be so punished except Mrs. Burden, and she is represented as an absurd anachronism. Why then, in 1929, did the author keep flogging so dead a horse? Is it possible that she was beginning to feel that the age of prejudices had at least had standards? That one could only have ladies if one burned witches?

They Stooped to Folly cleared out the author's atelier of all these rag ends, for the last volume of the trilogy, *The Sheltered Life*, is a masterpiece. "In *Barren Ground*, as in *The Sheltered Life*," she wrote, "I have worked, I felt, with an added dimension, with a universal rhythm deeper than any material surface. Beneath the lights and shadows there is the brooding spirit of place, but, deeper still, beneath the spirit of place there is the whole movement of life." It is not a modest statement, but Miss Glasgow felt that she had worked too hard to have time for modesty, and certainly these two novels have a vibration different from all her others.

Into the double, battered stronghold of the Archbalds and Birdsongs on Washington Street, now all commercial but for them, creeps the fetid smell of the neighboring chemical plant. The smell is more than the modern world that threatens them from without; it is the smell of decadence that attacks them from within. The sheltered life is also the life of willful blindness; the two families resist change and resist facts. Eve Birdsong, keeping up the queenly front of a Richmond beauty, tries not to see that her husband is a hopeless philanderer. General Archbald, dreaming of a past which he understands, avoids the duty of facing a present which he does not, while his daughter-in-law brings up little Jenny Blair to be a debutante of the antebellum era. Etta, the hypochondriac, lives in a fantasy world of cheap novels and heroes, and Birdsong, in the arms of his Negro mistress, imagines that he still loves his wife. The rumbles of a world war are heard from very far off. Like the smell down the street they do not yet seem to threaten the sheltered lives of the Archbalds and Birdsongs.

The terrible story that follows is seen from two points of view, General Archbald's and

Jenny Blair's, those of age and youth. The General's long reverie into his own youth, "The Deep Past," is probably the finest piece of prose that Miss Glasgow ever wrote. The picture of a nauseated child being "blooded" by his sporty old grandfather on a fox hunt is for once without sentiment for the great Virginia days. Like Judge Honeywell and Virginius Littlepage, General Archbald has missed the high moments of life and has been married, like all elderly Glasgow gentlemen, to a good woman whom he did not love. He has been a gentleman and done his civic duty because, in the last analysis, nothing else seemed any better or certainly any finer, but he has a much deeper sense of what is wrong with his world than the other two heroes of the trilogy and a mystic sense that in death he may yet find the ecstasy that he has lost without ever possessing. Under the prosperous attorney and the member in good standing of the Episcopal church is a poet. If he were not quite so old, he might have saved his granddaughter.

But nobody is going to do that. Jenny Blair, brought up in innocence by her gallant widowed mother, cannot believe herself capable of doing anything that is not quite nice. She is drawn into an entanglement with Mr. Birdsong because she will not see that adultery is something that could happen to her. She is a little girl, even at eighteen, a bright, innocent, enchanting little girl, and the subtlest thing in this subtle book is that even while we keep seeing the small events of Washington Street from her point of view, we gradually become aware that others are beginning to see her differently, that John Welch, the Birdsongs' ward, suspects what she's up to, that Birdsong is aware that she's tempting him, that even her mother and grandfather begin to sense a change. The warnings proliferate, and the tempo of the book suddenly accelerates until the vision of Jenny Blair as a sharp-toothed little animal, free of all rules and restraints, reaching out to snatch the husband of her desperately ill friend, bursts upon us in its full horror, just before the final tragedy. Eva Birdsong shoots her husband, and his body slumps in the hall amid the carcasses of the ducks that he has killed. It is the ultimate dramatization of the divorce between the Virginian myth and the Virginian fact, the climax of the novel and of Ellen Glasgow's fiction.

John Welch is the best of youth, as Miss Glasgow was coming to see youth, but he is a dry young man, tough and belligerently unsentimental. In assessing Eva Birdsong's chances of surviving her operation he mentions to General Archbald that her kidneys are sound. It is not, of course, agreeable to this gentleman of the old school to hear a lady's vital organs spoken of as plainly as if they were blocks of wood, but he reflects that perhaps such bluntness is the better way, that "wherever there is softness, life is certain to leave its scar." In this he is certainly the spokesman for his creator, who felt that all her life she had been constantly soft and constantly wounded, but there is no question of where her sympathies lay. For all her expressed tolerance of Welch and his contemporaries, they lay with the General, and with her sympathies went the conviction that the suffering life was the richer one.

Two more novels were to follow *The Sheltered Life*, but they show an attenuation of powers. *Vein of Iron* (1935) seems a hollow echo of *Barren Ground*. It starts well enough, for it starts in the past, where as an older woman Miss Glasgow was increasingly at home, and deals with people whom she had not treated before, the descendants of the Scotch-Irish settlers in the southern part of the Virginia Valley. This was where her father's people had come from, and she was able effectively to evoke in the early chapters the bare, grim

Presbyterian elements of the Fincastle family and their village, called, with a labored appropriateness, Ironside. The characters who are hard are very hard, and those who are stoical are very stoical, and even the names of the surrounding geographical features suggest the somber spiritual atmosphere in which these joyless people live: God's Mountain, Thunder Mountain, Shut-in Valley. Mobs of shrieking children cast pebbles at idiots and unmarried mothers alike, though there are few of the latter, as a girl need only point to the man actually, or allegedly, responsible to have him dragged to the altar by her fellow villagers. It seems possible that Miss Glasgow may have written a bit too much of her father's character into Ironside, but the result is very much alive. Such cannot be said of the second part of the novel, where the characters move to Queenborough and to the present. Ada Fincastle becomes a serial heroine, a soap-opera queen.

Consider the list of her wrongs. Ralph McBride is wrested from her by an unscrupulous girl friend and returns, a married man, to make her pregnant. Ironside spits at her, and her grandmother dies of the disgrace. Ralph eventually marries her, but war neuroses have made him moody and unfaithful, and in Queenborough, during the Depression, they are reduced to desperate want. Ralph, out driving with the girl next door, is nearly paralyzed in an automobile accident. Yet Ada is always superb; her vein of iron sees her through. The reader must take it on faith. One does not see her, as one sees Dorinda in *Barren Ground*, working on her farm, milking cows, supervising the help, purchasing new fields. Even in *Life and Gabriella* one sees what Gabriella does in her shop, so that one has a sense of the therapy which she applies to her sorrow. But Ada relies simply on her inheritance of character.

The book ends on a harsh note of denunciation of the formlessness and aimlessness of life in the 1930's, a theme that is picked up and enlarged upon in Miss Glasgow's final novel, *In This Our Life* (1941), where the amoralism in which she believed Richmond to have been engulfed seems to have affected not only the young but the old and—one almost suspects—the author herself. For how else can one explain Asa Timberlake?

At first blush he seems in the tradition of Honeywell, Littlepage, and Archbald, those elderly, nostalgic gentlemen who have missed the thrills as well as the substance of life, and like them he has his creator's sympathy. "For the sake of a past tradition he had spent nearly thirty years doing things that he hated and not doing things that he liked; and at the end of that long self-discipline, when he was too old to begin over again, he had seen his code of conduct flatten out and shrivel up as utterly as a balloon that is pricked." But *was* it self-discipline? Asa's life has simply gone by default; he is that commonest of American fictional heroes, the husband dominated by a strong-minded hypochondriac wife. But Asa has none of the dignity of his predecessors in the Queenborough trilogy; he is plotting, with the author's apparent approval, a weak man's escape. As soon as his wife shall have inherited the fortune of a rich uncle, he will quietly decamp with the widow of an old friend. Surely he is as bad as the young folk.

Well, not quite, for they are monsters. Roy, the heroine, and Peter have married with the understanding that either may have back her or his liberty on request. Incidentally, there is a similar bargain between the young couple in Mrs. Wharton's equally disapproving novel, *The Glimpses of the Moon*. Roy's sister, Stanley, ditches her fiancé, Craig, in order to take Peter from Roy, and then, having driven Peter to suicide, she returns to rob her sister a second time, of Craig, with whom poor Roy has been consoling herself. During all of these goings-on the four characters, like Asa, are saturated with self-pity. One feels that Miss Glasgow's conviction that men are doomed to weakness and that women can rise above their destiny of betrayal only by stoicism has now reached the pitch of an obsession. Yet she works her plot around the gravely offered thesis that love is vital to the young because it is "the only reality left," though it cannot save them because they treat each other "as if they were careless fellow-travellers, to be picked up and dropped, either by accident or by design, on a very brief journey." But that is not necessarily one's own experience of America in 1938, when the action of the novel takes place.

There are, however, moments. There are always moments, even in the least estimable of Ellen Glasgow's books. When Stanley tries to put the blame of her hit-and-run accident on a Negro boy, and the family prepare to back her up, the novel suddenly soars in stature. Here, at last, is a problem that is real and competently handled, the only time, too, in nineteen novels where Miss Glasgow faces, however briefly, what the South has done to its colored people. And Uncle William Fitzroy, the tycoon whose millions have vulgarized him, despite his genteel background, into the likeness of a noisy parvenu, the forerunner of "Big Daddy" in *Cat on a Hot Tin Roof*, seems to bring Tennessee Williams and Ellen Glasgow into brief but entrancing partnership.

Mention should be made of Miss Glasgow's twelve short stories assembled in a volume by Richard K. Meeker. It was not a medium that she much liked or in which she enjoyed much success. She was a discursive writer and needed space to appear to her best advantage. Almost half of the stories deal, as might be anticipated, with the struggle of women with men who are not worthy of them, the theme that underlies so much of her "social history" of the South. As Mr. Meeker amusingly sums

it up: "Her typical plot sequence runs: girl meets boy; girl is taken advantage of by boy; then girl learns to get along without boy, or girl gets back at boy."

Best of the tales are four ghost stories, all told in the first person, a method adopted in only one of her novels, but a useful one in helping the reader suspend his disbelief. "Dare's Gift" and "Whispering Leaves" are most effective because of their atmosphere of old Virginia mansions which she knew so well how to evoke; but because in her earlier writing she had no interest in keeping things back, because she seemed, on the contrary, to have almost a compulsion to let her reader know what was on her mind at each moment, she had to remain an amateur in the fiction of the supernatural.

In 1954, nine years after Ellen Glasgow's death of heart disease, her literary executors published under the title *The Woman Within* the memoirs that had been confided to their discretion. There were those who were distressed by this posthumous revelation of the author's self-pity and vanity and who claimed that the memoirs gave a wrong impression of a woman who had always seemed in life so gay and bright and full of sympathy for others. But so long as one bears in mind that this is only Ellen Glasgow as Ellen Glasgow saw her, *The Woman Within* is filled with valuable insights.

It also contains some of her best writing. The pages about "Harold S——," the snob and name-dropper, are as good as anything in *The Romantic Comedians*, and the irony is supplied by the memoirist herself who was in love with the man she despised. How could one get a better glimpse of an author at work than in her description of her meeting with Harold: "I observed him for an instant over my cocktail, wondering whether he could be used effectively in a comedy of manners. My curiosity flagged. What on earth could I find to talk about to a person like that?" What indeed? Yet the association that began that night was to last twenty-one years. So we see the novelist looking for a story and finding one—as ironical as any she wrote—happening to herself. Why, she asks herself in despair, was Harold fated to meet every crisis with a spectacular gesture? "Afterwards, when I read in the 'Life Story' of a Balkan Queen, that, as she said farewell to a Southern Colonel, he had fallen on his knees before her and kissed the hem of her skirt, I recognized the last act of chivalry. So Harold had parted from me when he sailed for the Balkans."

The most valuable thing in the memoirs, however, is the picture of a woman's dedication to her art. From the beginning she had wanted to be a writer above everything, and not just a writer, but specifically a novelist. After the publication of her first book she realized that she needed a steadier control over her ideas and material, a philosophy of fiction, a prose style so pure and flexible that it could bend without breaking. From Maupassant she gained a great deal, but not until, by accident, she happened to read *War and Peace* did she know what she needed. "Life must use art; art must use life. . . . One might select realities, but one could not impose on Reality. Not if one were honest in one's interpretation, not if one possessed artistic integrity. For truth to art became in the end simple fidelity to one's own inner vision." She summed up her artistic credo as follows: "I had always wished to escape from the particular into the general, from the provincial into the universal. Never from my earliest blind gropings after truth in art and truth in life had I felt an impulse to write of a single locality or of regional characteristics. From the beginning I had resolved to write of the South, not, in elegy, as a conquered province, but, vitally, as a part of the larger world. Tolstoy made me see clearly what I had realized dimly, that the ordinary is simply the universal observed from the surface, that the direct approach to reality is not without, but within."

It puts one off a bit that Ellen Glasgow struck, again and again, so high a note for herself. As she conceived of her personal sufferings as more intense than anyone else's, so did she conceive of herself as a novelist on a Tolstoian scale. She did not hesitate, in the preface to *Barren Ground*, to nominate it as the one of her books best qualified for immortality, and in her memoirs she described it further, together with the Queenborough trilogy and *Vein of Iron*, as representing "not only the best that was in me, but some of the best work that has been done in American fiction." In her personal philosophy, and despite a sensitive mind that "would always remain an exile on earth," she believed that she had found a code of living that was sufficient for life or for death. And in her later years she loved to play the queen in the New York publishing world, dangling the possibility of her largess, half in jest, half in earnest, before the different editors who bid for her books. John Farrar relates that when she made her ultimate decision to go to Alfred Harcourt, the latter went down on his knees before her in her hotel suite like Harold S—— before Marie of Romania. But one can see through the boasting and the jesting, with its aspect of essentially southern horseplay, to her never joking resolution and determination to be a great novelist. One can look back at the young Ellen Glasgow like the young Victoria (to evoke another queen), affirming solemnly her will to be good.

The advantages that she brought to her task and ambition were indeed considerable. Out of her wide reading she selected the mightiest and probably the best models to guide her in her re-creation of the Virginia scene. She used

Hardy as her master in rustic atmosphere, George Eliot as her guide in morality, Maupassant for plot, and Tolstoi for everything. She had the richest source material that any author could wish, consisting simply of a whole state and its whole history, a state, too, that occupies the center of our eastern geography and of our history and that not coincidentally has produced more Presidents than any other. And the social range among Miss Glasgow's characters is far greater than that of most twentieth-century novelists, suggesting that of such Victorians as Trollope, Dickens, Elizabeth Gaskell, and, again, George Eliot.

She not only considered every social group, but she also covered wide varieties within each. In the top ranks of the old hierarchy she showed aristocrats in their glory, such as Major Lightfoot, and aristocrats in their decay, such as Beverly Brooke (in *The Ancient Law*). She showed them turning to the new world of business and dominating it, such as General Bolingbroke, and turning to the same world to be dominated and ultimately vulgarized by it, such as William Fitzroy. She showed aristocrats surviving into our own time, such as Judge Honeywell and Virginius Littlepage, having made the necessary adjustments and compromises, respectable, prosperous, but curiously unsatisfied, and she showed aristocrats like Asa Timberlake, who have been beaten into mediocrity and have failed in life without even the consolation and romance of a picturesque decay. Among the women of this world she created such magnificent anachronisms as Mrs. Blake, such noble, docile, and submissive wives as Virginia Pendleton, such apparently submissive but actually dominating mothers as Mrs. Gay, and such a reconstructed success in the North as Gabriella Carr.

In the middle ranks we find the rising businessman, Ben Starr, the risen politician, Gideon Vetch, the corrupt overseer, Bill Fletcher, the poor philosopher, John Fincastle, the "yeoman" farmers, Dorinda Oakley and Nathan Pedlar, the thriving miller, Abel Revercomb, and, among the lower orders, the "poor white" Burr family, the Starrs from whose midst Ben rises, the victims of the Richmond slums whom Stephen Culpeper is made to visit, the village prostitute and her idiot son in *Vein of Iron*, and, of course, all the Negro servants. Despite what has already been said about the limitations of Miss Glasgow's characterization of Negroes, the servants in her novels are absolutely alive and convincing. In at least one instance, that of the maid and companion to Dorinda in *Barren Ground*, the characterization is as successful as of any of the author's other women.

Miss Glasgow had the same range in scenery that she had in human beings, and she could make the transfer without difficulty from the grim mountains and valleys of *Vein of Iron* to the interminable fields of broom sedge in *Barren Ground* and thence to the comfortable mansions of Richmond and to the smaller gentility of Petersburg and Williamsburg. Highly individual in American letters is her ability to pass with equal authority from country to city, from rusticity to sophistication, from the tobacco field to the drawing room, from irony to tragedy.

Yet for all her gifts and advantages she does not stand in the very first rank of American novelists. She was unable sufficiently to pull the tapestry of fiction over her personal grievances and approbations. The latter are always peeping out at the oddest times and in the oddest places. It is strange that a novelist of such cultivation and such fecundity and one who was also such a student of her craft should not have seen her own glaring faults. How is it possible that the woman who could imagine the brilliant repartee of Edmonia Bredalbane, which annihilates every vestige of pretentiousness in Queenborough, should not have torn up the dreary sermon that is called *The Builders*? How could the author of prose which conveys all the beauty and mystery of the desolate countryside in *Barren Ground* have written the tired purple passages in earlier novels which describe the animal charm of handsome men and women in terms that might have been lifted from the very women's magazines that she so violently despised? How, moreover, could she have failed to see that her own bitterness on the subject of men was reflected in her heroines to the point of warping the whole picture of their lives? The mystery of Ellen Glasgow is not so much how she could be so good a writer as how she could on occasion be so bad a one.

Like Edith Wharton, she will be remembered for her women, not her men. The course of her heroes is a curious one. They start, romantically enough, as men of fierce ideals and raging passions, Byronic in their excesses, impatient of injustice and burning to remake the world. Akershem and Burr are men of the people; the lowness of their origin contributes to their strength, their violence, and their sex appeal. They are a bit lurid, but there will come a time in Miss Glasgow's fiction when we would be glad enough to see them again. With Dan Montjoy in *The Battle-Ground* she inaugurated a period of more respectable, conventional heroes. He is followed by Christopher Blake, Ben Starr, and Abel Revercomb, all of them men of considerable strength and power. But in *Virginia* the weak, selfish, deserting male makes his appearance, and he is to stay through to the end of her fiction. Oliver Treadwell, George Fowler, Jason Greylock, George Birdsong, Peter Kingsmill, Martin Welding, Ralph McBride, and Craig Fleming

are all faithless to good women who love them and are all faithless more from the weakness of their characters than the force of their passions. What is most appalling in Miss Glasgow's indictment is that the only ground of redemption that she can find in those of them whom she regards as redeemable, i.e., the last three of the list, is a groveling, lachrymose self-pity. Listen to Martin Welding as his father-in-law interrogates him about the unhappiness of his marriage to Mary Victoria:

" 'Why don't you tell me about it and let me help you?' the older man asked with all the sympathy that he could summon.

"The merest flicker of gratitude shone in the sullen misery of Martin's look. 'The trouble is that I have come to the end of my rope. I am wondering how much longer I shall be able to stand it.'

" 'Stand what, my boy?'

" 'Stand the whole thing. Stand life, stand marriage, stand women.'

"Mr. Littlepage frowned. 'But this isn't normal,' he said sternly. 'This isn't rational.'

" 'Well, what am I to do?'

" 'You should see a physician.'

" 'I've seen dozens of them since I met Mary Victoria.'

" 'And what do they say?'

" 'That I'm not normal, I'm not rational.'

" 'Then, it seems to me, you will have to believe it.'

" 'I do believe it, but that doesn't make it easier. I am still that way no matter what I believe.' "

Then men would not matter so much if they were not taken quite so seriously by the women. Lawrence Selden in Edith Wharton's *The House of Mirth* is a passive spectator hero, but Lily Bart suffers little enough from his preference for the sidelines. Miss Glasgow's heroines, on the other hand, are devastated by her worthless men, and it is just here that her fiction is pulled most seriously out of line. Acceptance of Dorinda Oakley and Gabriella Carr as the towers of strength that they must be to accomplish what they do is difficult to reconcile with the long, tortured passages in which they dwell with the lovingness of hypochondriacs upon their grief. One wonders if their kind of women would not have thrown off disappointment and disillusionment with more dispatch and if Miss Glasgow was not attributing her own sensitivity to natures that had, by definition, to possess tougher fibers. In the final novel the question is reduced to absurdity by Roy Timberlake, who succeeds in being abandoned by *two* men and suffers equally at the hands of each.

For all her faults, however, it is hard to get away from the fact that without Ellen Glasgow there would be a great gap in our fiction, particularly where it concerns the South. She was determined to reproduce the South as it was, and although we are conscious today of things added and things omitted, we search in vain for any contemporary or predecessor of hers who even approached her accomplishment. Furthermore, it is astonishing to consider how different in style and mood were her three principal works. *Virginia* might not be worthy of Flaubert, but one suspects that Zola would not have disowned it, nor would Hardy have been ashamed of *Barren Ground*. And any novelist of manners would have been delighted to have produced *The Romantic Comedians*.

Frederick P. W. McDowell has astutely pointed out that Ellen Glasgow's accomplishments and limitations as a writer are best suggested in her own judgment of another southern writer, Edgar Allan Poe: "Poe is, to a large extent, a distillation of the Southern. The formalism of his tone, the classical element in his poetry and in many of his stories, the drift toward rhetoric, the aloof and elusive intensity,

—all these qualities are Southern. And in his more serious faults of overwriting, sentimental exaggeration, and lapses, now and then, into a pompous or florid style, he belongs to his epoch and even more to his South."

When Ellen Glasgow began her career, there was almost no serious literature in the South. The pioneer element in her work today is obscured by the fact that the romantic school of southern fiction against which she reacted not only has disappeared but has hardly left a trace. Similarly, the modern school has gone so far beyond her in exploration of the freakish and the decadent that she seems as mild in comparison as Mary Johnston or Amélie Rives. She herself enlarged the distance between her work and that of the southern novelists who were becoming popular in her later years by deriding them. "One may admit that the Southern States have more than an equal share of degeneracy and deterioration; but the multitude of half-wits, and whole idiots, and nymphomaniacs, and paranoiacs, and rakehells in general, that populate the modern literary South could flourish nowhere but in the weird pages of melodrama." Yet she herself is the bridge, and the necessary bridge, between the world of Thomas Nelson Page and the world of William Faulkner, Katherine Anne Porter, Eudora Welty, and Tennessee Williams.

She will probably not be remembered as the historian of Virginia that she wished to be. This ambition may have been too great for the fiction that she produced. Only four of her nineteen novels, *Virginia*, *Barren Ground*, *The Romantic Comedians*, and *The Sheltered Life*, have won more than a temporary place in American letters. But her picture of the South emerging from defeat and reconstruction with all its old legends intact and all its old energy preserved and managing to adapt itself, almost without admitting it, to the industrial exigencies of a new age—like the Bourbons in that it had forgotten nothing, but unlike them in that it had learned a lot—is one that has passed into our sense of American history.

Selected Bibliography

WORKS OF ELLEN GLASGOW

There are two collected editions of Ellen Glasgow's work: the Old Dominion Edition (Garden City, N.Y.: Doubleday, Doran, 1929, 1933) and the Virginia Edition (New York: Scribners, 1938). Both collected editions include Miss Glasgow's prefaces.

NOVELS AND COLLECTIONS OF SHORT STORIES
The Descendant. New York: Harper, 1897.
Phases of an Inferior Planet. New York: Harper, 1898.
The Voice of the People. New York: Doubleday, Page, 1900.
The Battle-Ground. New York: Doubleday, Page, 1902.
The Deliverance. New York: Doubleday, Page, 1904.
The Wheel of Life. New York: Doubleday, Page, 1906.
The Ancient Law. New York: Doubleday, Page, 1908.
The Romance of a Plain Man. New York: Macmillan, 1909.
The Miller of Old Church. Garden City, N.Y.: Doubleday, Page, 1911.
Virginia. Garden City, N.Y.: Doubleday, Page, 1913.
Life and Gabriella. Garden City, N.Y.: Doubleday, Page, 1916.
The Builders. Garden City, N.Y.: Doubleday, Page, 1919.
One Man in His Time. Garden City, N.Y.: Doubleday, Page, 1922.
The Shadowy Third and Other Stories. Garden City, N.Y.: Doubleday, Page, 1923.
Barren Ground. Garden City, N.Y.: Doubleday, Page, 1925.
The Romantic Comedians. Garden City, N.Y.: Doubleday, Page, 1926.
They Stooped to Folly. Garden City, N.Y.: Doubleday, Doran, 1929.
The Sheltered Life. Garden City, N.Y.: Doubleday, Doran, 1932.
Vein of Iron. New York: Harcourt, Brace, 1935.
In This Our Life. New York: Harcourt, Brace, 1941.
The Collected Stories of Ellen Glasgow, edited by Richard K. Meeker. Baton Rouge: Louisiana State University Press, 1963.

POETRY
The Freeman and Other Poems. New York: Doubleday, Page, 1902.

NONFICTION
A Certain Measure. New York: Harcourt, Brace, 1943.
The Woman Within. New York: Harcourt, Brace, 1954.
Letters of Ellen Glasgow, edited by Blair Rouse. New York: Harcourt, Brace, 1958.

CRITICAL STUDIES

Brooks, Van Wyck. *The Confident Years.* New York: Dutton, 1952.
Geismar, Maxwell. *Rebels and Ancestors.* Boston: Houghton Mifflin, 1953.
Giles, Barbara. "Character and Fate: The Novels of Ellen Glasgow," *Mainstream,* 9:20–31 (September 1956).
Hoffman, Frederick J. *The Modern Novel in America.* Chicago: Regnery, 1951.
Kazin, Alfred. *On Native Grounds.* New York: Reynal and Hitchcock, 1942.
McDowell, Frederick P. W. *Ellen Glasgow and the Ironic Art of Fiction.* Madison: University of Wisconsin Press, 1960. (The only thorough survey of Ellen Glasgow's work, containing an exhaustive bibliography.)
Monroe, N. Elizabeth. *Fifty Years of the American Novel.* New York: Scribners, 1951.
Rubin, Louis D., Jr. *No Place on Earth: Ellen Glasgow, James Branch Cabell, and Richmond-in-Virginia.* Austin: University of Texas Press, 1959. (Supplement to *Texas Quarterly,* Vol. 2.)

—LOUIS AUCHINCLOSS

Caroline Gordon

1895-

CAROLINE GORDON'S work is more impressive in its totality than each book seemed to be on publication. The result has been that only recently have critics felt the full impact of her work and been able to see its unity. Her fiction is beginning, however, to receive some of the recognition that is its due, now that the literary history of the twentieth century can be seen in clearer perspective.

Caroline Gordon was born October 6, 1895, at Merry Mont farm near Trenton in Todd County, Kentucky, close to the Tennessee border. Here "Black Patch" tobacco is the main crop, so called because it needs to be fired to darkness in curing. This region forms the setting for many of Miss Gordon's short stories and all her novels except *Green Centuries* and *The Malefactors*. *The Garden of Adonis* and "Her Quaint Honour," for example, contain many details of tobacco growing, and references to local agriculture abound in her work. Her early writing reflects many of the same beliefs held by the group of writers known as the "Agrarians," who declared their principles in *I'll Take My Stand* (1931). She felt, as they did, that the hierarchical society of the early South was preferable to the social disintegration she saw in North and South alike. Modern chaos, the Agrarians contended,

resulted from the prevalence of a scientific cast of mind and a mechanized culture, from the decay of a feudal relationship between landowners and workers on the soil, and from the loss of spiritual certitude. In tendency Miss Gordon was Agrarian as she began her career, and she tried through her fiction to offset the empiricism, skepticism, and impersonal aspects of an industrial society.

Directly or by implication she has always celebrated the stability to be found in the southern past and the dynamic quality of personal relationships at their best. Her earlier novels, which stressed the need for both social hierarchy and individual responsibility, are Christian "in hope," in the same sense that she once used this term to describe the fiction of the unorthodox Henry James. More recently, she has turned to Christianity as a redemptive force in a fissured age. In *The Strange Children* (1951) and *The Malefactors* (1956), however, she continued to value an ordered social existence and a sympathetic understanding between human beings even while she became increasingly Christian in emphasis. In *The Glory of Hera* (1972) she went back to Greek legend, away from an interest in the psychological problems of human beings to consider, through the means of myth and its allegorical significance, the destiny of gods and men and the importance of the hero for people in all ages of history. The Christian emphasis is strong but implicit in this philosophical parable. Christ was also a hero and is often, I assume, an unstated later analogue for Heracles, toward whom Miss Gordon is admiring and reverent. The relationship between Greek and modern civilizations, between the Greek hero and the Christian savior, may become clearer as Miss Gordon goes on to the second part of this double novel and writes *A Narrow Heart: The Portrait of a Woman.*

Her own heritage encouraged respect for the southern tradition. Her mother's ancestors, the Meriwethers, came to Kentucky from Virginia in the eighteenth century; the early phase of this migration forms the subject of *Green Centuries.* Her father, James Morris Gordon, arrived in the 1880's as a tutor for the Meriwethers. From his love of the classics and his passion for sport, Miss Gordon was to derive her complete knowledge of these two facets of southern culture. Recollections of her father form the animating source of *Aleck Maury Sportsman.* Like Aleck Maury, James Gordon conducted a boys' school—in Clarksville, Tennessee—which emphasized the classics, history, and mathematics; and for some years Miss Gordon attended this school. Only later, in her teens, did she regularly attend public schools. In 1916 she graduated from Bethany College, which thirty years later awarded her an honorary degree.

After she completed college, Miss Gordon taught for three years in high school and then turned to journalism. As a reporter for the *Chattanooga News* from 1920 to 1924, she reviewed the Fugitive poets and got to know many of the Agrarians. She became the wife of one of them, Allen Tate, in November 1924. The marriage was a happy and understanding relationship, although it ended in divorce in 1959. Association with Tate enabled Miss Gordon to define her theory of fiction and the kind of novel she wanted to write. This relationship resulted in the joint editorship of *The House of Fiction* with its incisive discussions of literary theory and, more important, she was encouraged to devote herself, without dissipation of her energies, to the artist's career.

The Tates went to live in Paris in 1928 when he was awarded a Guggenheim Fellowship, and they stayed abroad until 1930. In Paris Miss Gordon wrote and gave final form to *Penhally.* In 1932 she herself received a Guggenheim award and was enabled to compose *Aleck Maury Sportsman* and the short stories which have Maury as their protagonist. After 1930 the Tates settled for some years at Benfolly farm, a colonial house on a bluff overlooking the Cumberland River near Clarksville, Tennessee, where their daughter Nancy grew up. The farm and the life there—they had many visitors—were later to serve as background for *The Strange Children.* Here Caroline Gordon perfected her art, publishing a number of short stories and novels. Though few in number, the short stories gained for Miss Gordon her initial recognition, and she was awarded the second O. Henry Prize in 1934 for "Old Red." She did not collect her stories, however, until 1945 with *The Forest of the South* and 1963 with *Old Red and Other Stories.* The Tates were in Princeton from 1939 to 1942, and in Washington from September 1943 to June 1944 where Tate was poetry consultant at the Library of Congress.

Between 1946 and 1951 Miss Gordon lived partly in Sewanee, Tennessee, where Tate edited the *Sewanee Review,* and partly in Princeton where her daughter resides. During these years she taught a workshop in techniques of fiction at the Department of General

Studies, Columbia University; she has taught there several times since. In 1951, Tate went to the University of Minnesota; and the Tates lived in Minneapolis much of each year. Since the early 1950's, Miss Gordon has taught courses in fiction and creative writing at Minnesota colleges and at universities throughout the country.

A very important event in her life in the 1940's was her conversion to Roman Catholicism. Her celebration of an ordered past in her early fiction led her inevitably to explore the possibilities for an ordered present which Christianity extends to the believer. She has even been able to trace analogies between the writing of fiction and the practice of religion: both forms of the spiritual life require, she maintains, an imitation of "the patience of Christ" and a display of faith. It has taken Miss Gordon sixteen years to complete her latest novel, *The Glory of Hera*, in which Heracles also reveals, as a forerunner to Christ, this same patience and faith.

The House of Fiction (1950; second edition, 1960) and *How to Read a Novel* (1957) are both invaluable for defining the kind of fiction which Miss Gordon writes. That she evolved her theory of fiction over a period of years is evident in her practice and in her pronouncements, which have come late. Flaubert, Chekhov, James, Crane, Ford Madox Ford, and Joyce, her admired forebears, confirmed her belief that fiction must embody a heightened psychological reality. As these writers did, she maintains that narrative art must be concerned with the conduct of life, especially with the relationships of people to one another and with the changes in these relationships. Aware of Aristotle and the example of Greek drama, the novelist will be sensitive to the "complications" arising among individuals which follow upon the "discovery" of crucial knowledge. Like the

Greek dramatists, he next devotes his skill to the "resolving" of these complications, a process that depends upon the "peripety," the decisive change from one state to another.

In his analysis of personal relationships, the novelist must attempt to convey every nuance in the values and every shade in the feelings embodied in his characters. "A direct impression of life" will be the result, especially if he uses with a craftsman's skill the vivid detail and the vivid image to evoke his characters, their situations, and their emotions. In sum, the modern writer of fiction will control his energies in order to secure the greatest immediacy for the impressions he wishes to record. He will appreciate the resources provided by tone and style in attaining unity, precision, and consistency of effect. One characteristic of fiction since Hawthorne, Flaubert, and James, Miss Gordon asserts, has been the writer's recourse to vivid metaphors to render his vision; the more evocative of such metaphors function organically as symbols. The intensity of the artist's vision can also endow character, incident, and speech with more than ordinary import. So the artist will succeed to the extent that he gives his experience significance through the use of symbolically rich situations, characters, and images. So also, according to Miss Gordon, "the most characteristic literary trend of our time is a fusion of Naturalism and Symbolism."

With her study of James, Miss Gordon further refined her views on the technique of fiction. He it was who taught her the virtues of a restricted point of view and its importance for determining both form and spiritual authority in the novel. Nineteenth-century writers had made most frequent use of the "omniscient" or "panoramic" point of view which they alternated with a restricted or dramatized point of view when they focused on the individual scene. With Flaubert resort was had to a "concealed narrator" who interprets the action by inhabiting the minds of several characters, at the same time that he does not obtrude as spokesman for the author. It is therefore possible for the character to react directly to his experience as in a first-person narrative but to have these reactions interpreted implicitly by the author's superior intelligence which not only inhabits the character's consciousness but ranges above it.

The "central intelligence" that organizes a late James novel is an even more sophisticated interpreter of the action than is the concealed narrator. In this method the mind of one person constitutes an organizing medium as it develops his impressions, his evaluations of experience, and his growth in moral awareness. In this method we have the immediacy of the first-person mode, the flexibility of the omniscient mode, and the penetrativeness of the mode of the concealed narrator. The method of the central intelligence goes furthest in the dramatizing of the interior life.

As for Miss Gordon's own fiction, such a central intelligence is at its purest in *The Strange Children* and *The Malefactors*. In her novel *The Glory of Hera*, Miss Gordon reverted to the panoramic, omniscient technique that she had used in *Penhally*; and she left behind, in large degree, the naturalistic component of her "symbolic naturalism," the mode she had used most often in her previous fiction, to concentrate on symbol, myth, and allegory. In *The Strange Children* and *The Malefactors*, however, the moral sensibilities of the leading characters organize the action as these protagonists reflect upon it and assimilate its implications. In her earlier books, Miss Gordon used the Flaubertian concealed narrator, since she did not confine the psychological drama to one person's mind. At the same time, she approached in them the method of the central intelligence because there is more exhaus-

tive analysis of the mind of Catherine Chapman, for example, in *The Women on the Porch* than we find in novels not written in the Jamesean tradition. In any event, the main formal problem for Miss Gordon has been the securing of maximum "organic" authority for her presentation of life. This she has endeavored to achieve by an ever sharper demarcation, and an ever more sophisticated manipulation, of the mind which interprets the experiences dramatized in her novels.

Miss Gordon's use of symbolic naturalism is most clearly seen in her short stories. "The Brilliant Leaves," "The Presence," "Old Red," "Her Quaint Honour," "The Petrified Woman," and "The Forest of the South" are some of her best and some of the best written in the present century. By their limited scope they have kept Miss Gordon confined to a single point of view. The short stories pre-eminently reveal her use of the vivid detail for establishing mood, for conveying subtleties of psychological shading, and for achieving the expansiveness of meaning that in literature we associate with symbolism.

Almost any of the stories illustrates Miss Gordon's method and accomplishment. "The Brilliant Leaves" is typical. It charts the disillusionment and frustration when ardent love disintegrates. The situation is complicated because the girl realizes that a change in the relationship has occurred while the boy does not. The superficiality of the boy's relatives in their neat houses; the disaster to his Aunt Sally when her father met her spineless lover with a shotgun; the brilliant, but soon to be decaying, leaves of autumn in contrast to the verdant glade in the woods to which the lovers retreat in order to recapture their passion; the beautiful waterfall there and the cliff that must be climbed to get the best view of it; the restive girl's impulse to climb the cliff and her falling to her death, whether by accident or by a subconscious drag toward death; the boy's panic and the girl's revulsion from him before her death—all comment implicitly upon the entanglements presented in the tale and give it a density of substance that eludes paraphrase.

Another story that treats realistically yet symbolically the contemporary scene is "Her Quaint Honour." Bud Asbury's lust for the Negro wife of a hired man leads to the spoiling of a fine tobacco crop for the first-person narrator who had hired Bud to supervise the firing. Not only do the characters and their conflicts embody the symbolism developed in the tale but so do nature and the agricultural life. Accordingly, the whole significance of the story is concentered in the image of the barn filled with prime tobacco, irreparably spoiled because the fires are damped as a result of Bud's irresponsibility and his yielding to momentary passion. And there is much irony in the narrator's having made his grandmother's fallow land blossom, only to witness the destruction of the wealth it produces because men do not love the land enough to work for it devotedly. More generally, the story points to the horror of a world in which lust takes the place of love and the cruelty of a caste system in which the Negro has few resources to withstand the depredations of a stronger race.

Some of the stories that are nearly contemporary in concern use Aleck Maury as first-person narrator or third-person controlling intelligence. His memoirs form the subject of *Aleck Maury Sportsman*; and all the Maury stories can be regarded as its spiritual appendages. "One More Time" and "The Last Day in the Field" follow the novel in using a first-person narrator. The former takes place in Florida where a friend of Maury's comes for one more fishing trip despite illness and an unsympathetic wife who little realizes that she has driven her husband to suicide. Nostalgic fervor pervades "The Last Day in the Field,"

as Maury, succumbing to age and failing physical powers, pays a ritual farewell to the chase that has sustained him for so long.

Excellent stories which use as method a central intelligence are "Old Red" and "The Presence." In "Old Red" Maury experiences some alienation from the members of his family, because they do not understand the frenetic nature of his devotion to sport. Social obligations and the conventions of society mean little to a man who is driven to compensate for the few years allotted him by his desire to fathom all the secrets of nature he can. Symbolically, Maury becomes the one who is persecuted by the conventions his relatives represent as he feels his own identity merge with that of "Old Red," the hunted fox. Just as "Old Red" barely escapes destruction by heroic effort, so Maury knows that, old as he is, he must struggle to the end against restrictive pressures. "The Presence" finds Maury in a mood of deep concern for others. Jim Mowbray is the best dog trainer and Jenny, Jim's wife, the best cook and kindest woman Maury has ever known. The loss is catastrophic to Alec when Jim is unfaithful to Jenny; his friends have been more than friends, they have become symbols for him of a harmony rarely found among human beings. At seventy-five Maury finds that his stable world is about to dissolve and that he will again be homeless. He thinks of his orthodox Aunt Vic on her deathbed and his murmuring of the Angelic Salutation as a boy; he knows that he also needs the Holy Mary to pray for him at this moment which represents for him a spiritual death.

The stories dealing with the Civil War again illustrate Miss Gordon's recourse to symbolic naturalism as an artistic method. In these tales the situations and the details are realistic even while they convey a more than literal, an almost indefinable, intent. An individual image or metaphor often conveys the essence of a story, although other details elaborate further the significance of the work.

In "The Forest of the South" several such images coalesce to establish the impact of this tale: the madness of Mrs. Mazereau, the mistress of the Villa Rose plantation; the intensification of her daughter's disorders during the narrative; the Yankee killing, half by accident and half by design, of the returning Colonel Mazereau; the blowing up of the nearby estate, Clifton, because of a Yankee engineer's injured pride; the deserted Macrae mansion with its mute fountain as an emblem of lost greatness; the arrest there as a spy of Eugénie Mazereau's former lover by her Yankee fiancé, Lieutenant John Munford; the lover's subtle confirmation to Munford of Eugénie's insanity; and the comparison by Munford of Eugénie's eyelids to a magnolia blossom he had seen not long before: "When he had first come into the country he had gathered one of those creamy blossoms only to see it turn brown in his grasp." His love for Eugénie too will wither as the flower once did, for he proposes to her without knowing that she is mad. Once he knows, he is bound in honor to marry her, but he divines that his future with her will be torture for both of them. In this unpredictable world the conquered girl becomes the conqueror of her suitor; the madness of the invader's enterprise recoils on Munford when he innocently allies himself to a girl whose degeneration has been caused by those who have fought like himself for an ideal without being able to foresee the consequences of their actions. In "Hear the Nightingale Sing" a mentally unstable girl and a stubborn mule defeat a homeward-bound Yankee when he stifles his humane instincts and attempts to steal the mule, only to be thrown and killed by the animal's brute force. And a bizarre humor lightens the horror of "The Ice House" wherein two southern boys dig up Yankee skeletons for a federal contrac-

tor who fraudulently and haphazardly places the bones among the coffins he has brought with him. Such an entrepreneur is a favorite Agrarian symbol, the capitalist who without conscience pursues his own gain.

In *Penhally* (1931) Miss Gordon developed at still greater length the theme of the grandeur of the southern past compared to the diminished present. The novel has for central presence a place rather than a person; and Penhally, in its flourishing state before the Civil War and in its fall from power after the Reconstruction, is a symbol for the South, the antebellum way of life, and the attenuated survival of southern traditions into the present. In its heyday Penhally irradiated the security and the sense of purpose present in southern civilization before the war. Part I of the novel ends appropriately with some account of the Llewellyn men during the war. Penhally endures the depredations of war; and the stoic force of the house is inseparable from that of its owner, Nicholas Llewellyn.

As a psychological novel, *Penhally* dramatizes the division between Nicholas and his half-brother Ralph and the parallel conflict between Nick and Chance Llewellyn in the fourth generation of the family. Nicholas, traditional in point of view and tenacious of the land, believes in primogeniture and dispossesses Ralph. He is opposed to the war, for he regards land as a responsibility and does not want to participate in a venture that threatens his property. He does provide admirably for his dependents, including his slaves, during the war; and, symbolically perhaps, he dies in 1866, when the South is conquered and Penhally's greatness is declining, though he is richer than at the war's beginning.

Ralph is improvident and less responsible than his brother in everyday affairs; and he lacks Nicholas' determination to hold his property at all costs. Yet there is much to admire in Ralph, since he despoils himself to support the Confederacy. Miss Gordon respects his devotion to principle, country, and heritage as much as she respects Nicholas' devotion to the soil. Ralph gives that his country may have life; Nicholas refuses to give so that he can keep life in the land. Some of the war sequences which end Part I are forceful—those concerned with the courtship by Charles Llewellyn of Alice Blair, his marriage to her, and his death as a cavalry officer. Other of these episodes relate loosely to the society and the characters presented in the novel and contribute little to its forward motion. Still, the impression registers that at no time was the South so great as in the hour of defeat.

Part II develops, at the Reconstruction, the first stage of the decline of Penhally and is the most moving section of the novel. John Llewellyn, who survived the war, inherits the estate but lacks the energy of his uncle Nicholas. Lassitude prevents him from functioning effectively, although he, too, loves the land and guards it jealously. His fatigue is matched by the instability of the cousin he marries, Lucy, the daughter of Ralph. She turns against John as a result of her misplaced energies and neurotic indisposition; but she survives into the 1920's as a twisted representative of tradition. The inability of John and Lucy to achieve a sympathetic relationship emphasizes the hopelessness of these years. The suicide of their son Frank, who had alienated Lucy by marrying a promiscuous cousin, adds to the oppressiveness of this part of the novel. Defeat in the war has been total, material and spiritual, local and national; and it goes beyond the conquered to infect the conquerors. John's decline is in part the result of inner debility, and this debility has its parallel in a nation weakened by a materialistic ethic. Thus John perceives "his own personal misfortunes monstrously shadowed in those of the nation."

In Part II Penhally remains, in the 1920's, a covert influence and a monument to a culture. The land has been entailed to Nick, grandson of John, although his brother Chance has the ancestral passion for the soil and Penhally house. Nick has, as it were, defected and uses his intelligence not to improve his inheritance but to establish himself in banking. The elder Nicholas splits in two in his twentieth-century descendants; Chance has his forebears' love of the farm and Nick his practical sense. Since Chance is a passionate man and since he is on the defensive about his values, he looms as a figure destined for involvement in tragic violence.

In the twentieth century harmonious human relationships are more possible than they were for the boys' grandparents, since war-induced trials of the spirit are now over. But in a deeper sense, a greater disunity prevails. Chance and Nick have strong affection for each other, yet Nick, because he has aligned himself with an aggressive materialism, is his brother's antagonist. The infection which had begun in Reconstruction has now reached the substratum of American life. Eastern millionaires overrun the region. Nick and his wife, Phyllis, cater to them; and he sells Penhally to Joan Parrish, who organizes a hunt club to take in the most fertile farms. The agrarian economy disintegrates as a new wealth, based on industrialism, takes over.

In general *Penhally* reveals little development in the characters and little intensification of conflict. The impressionistic technique, which allowed Miss Gordon to etch her characters brilliantly and to present individual scenes with much precision and evocativeness, led to excessive fragmentation as supernumerary personages and detachable incidents crowd the pages of the novel. It is in some respects, then, more tenuous than it ought to be. In certain others, it possesses an imaginative fullness that Miss Gordon was to control for notable results as her novels grew away from an episodic organization.

Aleck Maury Sportsman (1934) is Miss Gordon's only novel with a first-person narrator; and like *Penhally* it consists of a number of episodes arranged in linear time sequence. The elderly Maury recalls the main incidents of a life outwardly uneventful but for him rich with significance. Despite all pressures, especially the need to win worldly success and the demands of family upon him, Aleck Maury has had the strength of purpose to make his avocation—hunting and fishing—his vocation. Always he proceeds according to well-worked-out rituals and reads a sacramental significance into his ventures. His single-mindedness is epical in quality. Maury is a Ulysses figure, always seeking the new and untried, or an Aeneas figure, remaining constant to his aims through many wanderings. Reviewing his life since he was a boy, Maury realizes that he has brought all his resources of skill, caution, and patience to bear upon the chase and that he has succeeded as few men ever have. He has been as devoted to the techniques of sport as any true artist must be to the techniques of his calling. As a man of imagination himself, he pays tribute in "Old Red" to this quality in a friend of his by noting how rare it is: "He's a man of imagination. There ain't many in this world." His total involvement in his pursuits generates interest in the details of sporting lore that fill the novel and a nostalgic atmosphere as he recalls his ventures.

The quest is both inspiriting and sad. Whereas Maury attempts the impossible, the attempt gives him dignity. He knows that time will slip away and age overtake him before he has gone far in his explorations of nature. For a sportsman, as Maury says, "no day is ever long enough" and no effort is too great to make in the pursuit of his pleasures. In the sequences laid in Gloversville the tone is idyllic. The landscape induces an elation in Maury similar, he conjectures, to that known by the pioneers as they first came upon this country. The pool at West Fork sums up not only the joy he feels in nature but also his satisfactions with her, since the pool is all that a fisherman could ever hope to find.

The idyllic tone makes for a book in which the element of human conflict is muted. Except for his involvement with Molly, his wife, Maury's relationships with other people count for little. But he always regards his wife and children with the affection of a large-souled man, and he remains friendly with his associates unless they try to interfere with his vocation. Miss Gordon does exhibit much delicacy and subtlety in depicting Maury's life with Molly. In this instance, he is moved by the fate of someone external to himself. After his son drowns by accident, Maury divines that Molly thinks herself betrayed because he appears less grief-stricken than she does, and he is disturbed by this suggestion of division between them. If Maury's life is a personal search for the truth, the sincerity of his quest mitigates any hint of egotism in it. His dedication to some aspects of antebellum culture proves, moreover, that he is sensitive to ranges of value often disregarded in post-Civil War America.

The mood of the book is also elegiac. The "fatality tinged with sadness" which surrounds the death of Maury's Uncle James and the resignation implicit in the quoted last lines of *Oedipus Tyrannus* suffuse Maury's whole saga. Although he maintains that with "the halcyon days" at Gloversville and West Fork stream the melancholy of his childhood disappears forever, his very zest for life accentuates for him its evanescence. There are tragic aspects to Maury's career as well as rich fulfillments. The restless seeker learns that all aspiration is limited by the very nature of the human situation. The brutal aspects of nature are, upon occasion, disconcerting: see the quail that kill in his uncle's barn by tearing out each other's jugular veins. Some parts of life seem gratuitously senseless to Maury. The drowning of his son and the unlooked-for death of Molly are clouds on his existence almost impossible to dispel. Not only Dick's death but his birth had led to sober meditation instead of great joy: "I had never realized before with what reluctance a human soul faces this world." The autumnal sadness of age confers upon the pageantry of life as Maury has known it the bittersweet consistency of tone so prevalent in the book. The sustaining of this double-edged view of life as both exhilarating and poignant is the final measure of Miss Gordon's artistry in this novel.

In one segment of *The Garden of Adonis* (1937) Miss Gordon depicts agricultural life in the South, now devitalized as it was at the end of *Penhally* but containing within it sources for renewal if they can only be discovered by those who work the soil. The farm recession of the 1920's and the depression of the 1930's have caused much poverty; but men have also been careless of their agrarian heritage and have listened to the false gods of a mechanized culture. For all these reasons, a mode of existence which sustained men in the past can no longer do so.

The poverty of those who till the soil is equaled by the shiftlessness or the futility of their lives. Under the best circumstances the Sheelers would always have been failures. But even for admirable individuals life on the soil is rigorous, and rewards for the deserving Ote Mortimer and the conscientious Ben Allard are meager. Just as in *Penhally* affection ends in violence, so in this novel Ote turns upon his symbolic father, Ben. When Ben is unable to lend Ote money to marry the pregnant Idelle Sheeler and objects to his cutting the shared

timothy and clover crop early, Ote in a fit of rage attacks with a single-tree from his mower the man who loves him. The assault presumably results in Ben's death, and demonstrates how even well-disposed individuals, motivated by affection and by passion for the earth, survive precariously, if at all, in a hostile age.

The passion and insight present in these scenes occur only fitfully in the other segment of the novel, the long middle section which devolves about Jim Carter and his frustrations. He derives from a genteel but poverty-stricken family; and like Ote and Ben, he is a victim. If anything, he has suffered more than they have from the defeat of aspiration. His rigorous, conventional mother has sacrificed him for her other children and has prevented him from following his bent as dog trainer. He is defeated in his marriage to Sara Camp by a certain lack of imagination but also by her rootlessness and selfishness. And given his situation, his subsequent love for Ben's daughter, Letty, is hopeless. Jim and Sara are interesting characters, but Miss Gordon's analysis of them is sketchy. Nor do the members of Sara's family emerge clearly as individuals. They are rather her too patent subjects for satire as invading plutocrats, come to Alabama to exploit cheap labor.

The title indicates that Miss Gordon has made use of mythology to give her novel added ramifications of meaning. When the two strands of the story are viewed together, the epigraph of the novel, from Frazer's *The Golden Bough*, assumes a complex significance. The men are Adonis figures whose fates are determined, in part, by women who act irrationally when motivated by sexual passion: Sara disorganizes Jim, Idelle is false to Ote, and Letty betrays her father. Through myth Miss Gordon underlines her agrarian theme and bridges the two strands of her book. Ben Allard is a much less firm link between them. As a character he lacks centrality in the action and is convincing only as an ineffectual farmer and the victim of forces over which he has little control. In any case, the distinctive art that re-creates the lives and psychology of the poor white characters compensates for whatever impression we form of the novel as divided in structure and conception.

None Shall Look Back (1937) has the massive proportions associated with the epic; and in fact, Miss Gordon's model throughout seems to have been Tolstoi's epical *War and Peace*. Like Tolstoi she begins by presenting the aristocratic culture which war disrupts; and when war comes close, she adopts Tolstoi's technique of alternating panoramic battle scenes with nearer views of the main characters as they participate in the war or suffer behind the lines.

An epical hero, General Nathan Bedford Forrest, dominates activity in the field much as General Kutuzov does in Tolstoi's book. At all times, Forrest is the commanding presence in Miss Gordon's book from the time he is seen worrying about supplies in the early days of the conflict until his last days on the field as still a formidable antagonist in the months of southern defeat. When Rives Allard, the fictional hero and one of Forrest's scouts, retires from action because of a wound, Miss Gordon takes advantage of his absence to enter Forrest's mind directly and to record one of the chief battles through his consciousness. Largely because he is seen so completely from within and without, he is not only a great historical figure but also a novelistic character who appeals with aesthetic authority to our emotions and imaginations. In short, we are involved in the drama of his life. We identify with him when he opposes Generals Pillow and Floyd who counsel the disastrous surrender of Fort Donelson; when he engages in angry parley at Chickamauga with the indecisive Bragg; when he

holds his dying brother in his arms at Okolona; and when, at Franklin, thinking of the deaths of his brother and General Cleburne, he perceives that death had always been at his side and he now understands, without endorsing it, the prudence of his superiors who had wanted to keep death at a distance. Like Kutuzov, Forrest possesses the preternatural insight which gives him greatness. Like the Russian, Forrest intuitively appraises a situation which neither he nor any other man can clearly define. Unlike Kutuzov, Forrest is sometimes ineffective because his intuitions are countermanded by his superiors who can only proceed according to rule and who are always cautious, never bold.

Some of the battle scenes are not organically part of the novel and reveal the weakness of the panoramic method. When Miss Gordon uses the Flaubertian concealed narrator and records action or psychology through the minds of her central characters, she much more successfully creates a universe possessing imaginative immediacy. Principally, she views the action through the eyes of Rives Allard and of Lucy Churchill, successively distant relative, sweetheart, wartime wife, and, finally, widow of Rives. Occasionally, some of the other characters reflect the action and their emotions, since Miss Gordon's extended canvas requires a roving narrator. Sometimes she even enters the minds of military figures who are peripheral to the main line of the novel. Still the impression remains that this is the story of Rives Allard and Lucy Churchill and, at another level, that of General Forrest.

Throughout, Miss Gordon contrasts the assertive forces of life, which also informed the gracious antebellum culture, with the negative forces of death and destruction as they overwhelm, with Götterdämmerung finality, this culture and its advocates. The woman Lucy is seen as the life-affirming individual, while the warrior Rives becomes aligned in part with the destructive forces that he struggles against. Man, the pioneer and protector of the hearth, is juxtaposed with woman who renews the life of the race and elaborates the arts of peace. The warrior who protects has no protection himself. This Lucy realizes when a skirmish is fought outside the home of the Georgia Allards and a Confederate captain is brought inside to die. Lucy now perceives that Rives, being human, may also die, and she can hardly bear the weight of this knowledge.

The two most powerful scenes in the novel dramatize the confrontation between the powers of life and death as they may be associated with Lucy and Rives respectively. On the field at Chickamauga, not far from his home, Rives searches through the multitude of the dead to find the body of his school friend George Rowan. After a sickening search Rives finds George's body and buries it. On such a battlefield as this, the mop-up is a gruesome process from which even seasoned soldiers recoil; and Rives reacts with the same fascinated horror that suffuses Hemingway's nightmarish "Natural History of the Dead." It is here that Rives, a potentially dead man among the dead, fortuitously meets Lucy, who walks among the dead and dying, asserting by her very presence a defiance of the death which surrounds her on every side. Lucy is helping Rives's mother, who has engineered a volunteer operation to remove the wounded men from the field to an improvised hospital in the closest home and grove of trees. Amid this desolating scene, Rives responds to Lucy's presence and is able to withdraw from his preoccupation with war and death to the point of loving his wife in the few moments they can snatch from war and caring for the wounded.

The second sequence occurs near the end of the novel when Rives is on leave in Georgia to recover from a wound. Lucy is unprepared for his gradual withdrawal from her, as though he has business elsewhere which does not involve her. The lines and hollows of his face and its deathlike pall oppress her as she gazes at the sleeping man beside her. His brutal talk in his sleep horrifies her, and she recalls with involuntary revulsion that her husband is, actually, a spy. She hardly recognizes the man she loves, and she can hardly endure the changes that war has caused in him. Something more central than domestic life or love of woman has laid hold of him; war and imminent death make the purely personal gratifications seem irrelevant. The dance which Susan Allard arranges, with depleted resources, is a melancholy rather than a joyous affair. It becomes, in effect, a ritual farewell to the soldiers about to leave for the field, a preliminary dance of death in parallel sequence to the dance at the Rowans' early in the novel when the soldiers first go off to war. Then the dance was an expression of expectant triumph and a life-inciting rite, a fertility ritual.

The incompetence of the Confederate generals in the West increases the fatality which pervades the central characters and their land. The ability and discernment of the generals are incommensurate with the moral and spiritual qualities of the people they are defending. Death is associated with the Confederate cause from the time those in command fail to exploit their victories. The generals lack both the absolute selflessness and the realistic insight that would have brought victory. Only the subordinate generals Hill and Forrest possessed both ranges of qualities. Even Lee, dedicated as he was, lacked the realism that might have saved the situation in the West; and Jefferson Davis was foolishly loyal to all those to whom he had once entrusted power. Part of the trouble with the South, too, was the very fervor of its idealism. Thus George Rowan, like Lucy, feels revulsion at Rives for being a spy. Yet without accurate intelligence of Federal movements, Forrest could not have achieved his victories; and part of Bragg's failure was his inability to use information once he was supplied with it.

War not only produces actual death but death-in-life as well. War brutalizes a good man, when Rives, for example, becomes proficient in the conscript guard. War makes an old man of Ned Allard after his three years at Johnson's Island prison camp: a man from whom all energy has gone, a man whose eye seems no longer to see. Fontaine Allard, whose birthday celebration opens the book on an idyllic note, is unable to recover from the burning of his house and the despoiling of his property. Not only the great house goes, but so does the original structure of the first cabin which is outlined in the flames before the whole structure collapses. War burns and destroys, then, to the very roots of a culture. And death sears the living. With Rives's death, Lucy knows that she will see the Kentucky landscape in an alien light. But the fact that she can think at all of "the green fields of Kentucky" argues for something indestructible in Lucy, in the human spirit itself.

The artistry of the novel resides in Miss Gordon's skilled intertwining of her central characters with the fortunes of the South. As individuals involved in the basic experiences of love, war, and death Rives, Lucy, and General Forrest are capacious enough to objectify Miss Gordon's mythic vision. Their emotions and conflicts stretch beyond their immediate situations and attain a significance that is universal. In a very real sense, then, her characters speak for all human beings who become involved in a cataclysmic war.

In the image of the westward road on the first page of *Green Centuries* (1941) and its attractiveness for Rion Outlaw, the protagonist, there is established a central motive of this novel which portrays the life of southern colonials as they push beyond the Blue Ridge. Always, however, practical necessity tempers romantic impulse. Rion Outlaw would like to go with Daniel Boone in the early pages of the book, but he cannot afford a horse. Later, he does not go beyond the Watauga region in western North Carolina though fabulous Kentucky lures him and Boone again invites him to go. If Rion feels the wilderness call him, he is aware that he is settling a family on the frontier and cannot abandon his responsibilities as citizen, husband, and father.

Rion is a complex person who wishes to subdue the wilderness to the order of civilization at the same time that the innovative spirit of the pioneer calls him away from a settled existence. He is the romantic who eternally seeks and who is perpetually disappointed. He is to some degree a spiritual outlaw, regarding himself as beyond the ordinary constraints laid upon mankind, and he resists the advent of law in the new community. Rather, he works in accord with the basic laws of his own being which enable him at times to achieve notable, if inadequate, results. If Rion is complacent about his own powers, he is industrious and draws satisfaction from his wife, Cassy, the land he cultivates, and his children. In 1776, at the end of five years in the wilderness, he has a farm of twenty acres and feels just pride in the fruits of his labors. His devotion to the land, in fact, anticipates the rapport that men felt for it, according to Miss Gordon, in the antebellum civilization of the South. His most reprehensible aspect is a willingness to regard the Indians as subhuman. And the hatred with which he fights them after Cassy leaves him to visit a sick neighbor brings its own nemesis, as he unknowingly shoots his brother and his Indian wife on land that the Indians have recently settled.

Rion and Cassy are the victims of forces that reach beyond them. External catastrophe and the inability of the psyche to withstand great shock defeat them. There is nothing dishonorable in Rion's aligning himself with the Regulators and his rebellion against British tyranny. But after defying British soldiers, he flees his native region for the frontier to escape being hanged. Then as settler in a new land, there is nothing dishonorable in his alliance with those who stand against British authority. The view that Rion is the prideful, self-sufficient, godless man, and as such typical of the pioneers, is true to a point. But it is this outlaw element that also gives him decisiveness and creative force.

Cassy Dawson becomes the selfless wife and mother, and has more power than Rion to analyze her situation. Her introspective temperament is sometimes a liability as it fosters an undue sense of alienation. She is happy for five years with Rion on the Holston; but, when the two oldest children are scalped, she succumbs to morbid guilt. In her misery she refuses the only anodyne, her husband's devotion, which is sexual as well as spiritual. In recoil from him, she drives him to the infidelity which only intensifies her bitterness and brings her to neurotic collapse. Earlier, she had loved Rion for himself more than for the security he could give her. Even after the death of her children she thinks first of her husband and not of herself as she counsels him to cry no more. But soon her self-command vanishes, and her own gaze turns inward and destroys her. In the last sequences she withholds love and irrationally expects Rion's feeling for her to remain the same. At Cassy's death both Rion and Cassy are apologetic, and each confesses the wrong done the other. In essence, each has in life's journey turned aside from the true way of mutual affection.

Miss Gordon throughout stresses the difficulties in establishing order in a strange environment. Simply, they are often too great to be borne. This truth reaches Rion when in his concluding reverie he thinks of the significance of his name and now learns the cost in human terms of the westward venture: "Did Orion will any longer the westward chase? No more than himself. Like the mighty hunter he had lost himself in the turning. Before him lay the empty west, behind him the loved things of which he was made. . . . Were not men raised into the westward turning stars only after they had destroyed themselves?"

Ironically, one form of order, that represented by the culture of the Indians, is fated to disappear. Although he is in a vital relationship to nature, the Indian is not able to adjust to alien modes of social existence and the white man's callousness. The Indians have values and rituals which unite them into an organic society; and they possess a poise and serenity often absent from the white man. But they are cruel and vindictive and reveal few compunctions in their treatment of captives. Miss Gordon appreciates the stamina and courage of the Indian, but does not regard him as a moral exemplar. She is skeptical of the noble-savage view and knows that European civilization brings possibilities for ranges of insight and order unknown to the Indian. At the same time it brings disease, firearms, and unsuspected depths of perfidy.

In the main characters we have the partial failure of qualities which sustained the characters in *None Shall Look Back*. The failure of creative masculinity and conservative feminism to keep intact a harmonious existence under frontier conditions is one chief theme in *Green Centuries*. Miss Gordon's increased emphasis on human limitation would argue that she was now moving toward a Christian orientation. From the beginning she had recognized candor and generosity as essential qualities in human relationships; what she began to recognize now was the precariousness of such relationships in the absence of a divine sanction.

In the green woods of America at any rate, Eden cannot be recaptured, at best only glimpsed. The paradisal wilderness is only superficially a paradise and more truly a wilderness as the epigraph, by John Peale Bishop, would indicate: "The long man strode apart./ In green no soul was found,/ In that green savage clime/ Such ignorance of time." Rion's observing the swans that tear each other apart persuades him and us of the brutality of nature; the brutality of men is implicit in another image, of Negroes being taken westward and chained together in the straw of covered wagons as if they were chattel goods.

One of the virtues of the novel resides in the characters who are complex without being sophisticated. This complexity and their basic reality make them timeless. The novel also extends toward universality because of Miss Gordon's recourse to myth; thereby the personae achieve added dimensions without themselves having to articulate them. So Rion learns from the Apollo figure (Cassy's brother, Frank) that he has been named for the Greek giant and hunter Orion. Rion possesses the grandeur and strength, some of the moral force, too, associated with a god, something, moreover, of the restlessness of the prototypic hunter. Cassy as a Diana figure (in the legend she kills Orion by accident) has at first the stature of a goddess, and then loses authority as she succumbs to morbid thoughts. The name Cassy suggests affinity with the pathetic and forsaken Cassandra, a woman unfairly overcome by fate. Cassy's formal name, Jocasta, recalls to us the heroine of the Oedipus legends whose end was as tragic as it was unexpected.

In many ways *Green Centuries* is an expressive novel, successful within the limitations Miss Gordon imposed on herself. Her style is careful and exact, her ear for speech is un-

erring, and her eye for the precise detail is sure. The novel builds impact slowly and is more powerful in retrospect than as we read it first. The middle sections go on at too great length; and Archy Outlaw lacks force and development for a crucial character. As a result he cannot sustain interest in the chapters depicting the culture of the Indians. The earlier chapters are excellent, particularly as they describe the troubled love between Rion and Cassy and his involvement with the Regulators. But the best sequences are those at the end which treat the growing rift between Rion and Cassy. As the tenderly built harmony of their lives is destroyed, we become aware that time and process erode even the most conscientious and loving relationships.

The Women on the Porch (1944) is the last of Miss Gordon's books in her earlier manner and the first of her books in her later manner. The technique is that of the Flaubertian narrator, in which the author enters the minds of many people. A more explicit use of the Joycean stream of consciousness prevails here than in her preceding books; and these explorations into the unconscious possess much lyrical intensity. Many of the details have symbolical value: as in *The Garden of Adonis* and *Green Centuries*, mythology enlarges the meaning of character and incident.

The central drama concerns Catherine Chapman, scion of a decaying family of Tennessee aristocrats, and her husband, Jim, a history professor in New York. He is unfaithful to Catherine, inexplicably even to himself, after several years of placid marriage. As in *Green Centuries*, Miss Gordon knows the difficulty of maintaining human relationships in a world in which meaningful values exist precariously. The city, for example, is a kind of queen bee in wild flight which leads all her inhabitants to destruction so long as they remain passive, careless, and uncritical in their personal lives.

Both Catherine and Jim must experience hell and be rescued therefrom before they appreciate each other. New York is hell, an inferno, wherein values that ought to be esteemed are lightly discounted. Jim has lost the dedication that led him to compose a history of Venice; and he gets no sustenance from friends, less even from Edith Ross, the superficial intellectual who becomes his mistress. He realizes his loss only after Catherine has been gone a few weeks; by the time he leaves in pursuit of her, the intensity of his feeling reminds us of Orpheus' plaints for Eurydice in the early scenes of *Orfeo ed Euridice*. In a letter to me Miss Gordon states that when she was writing this novel, "I was haunted by Gluck's opera. . . . Both by the music and by his version of the Orpheus story . . . it was chiefly the form of the opera which impressed me. At any rate, I was conscious of parallels between the form of the opera and that of my novel."

Jim has never identified himself with anything, person, or place: "I do not belong anywhere. There is no place anywhere that is a part of me." In his relationship with Catherine he had known a steadiness and strength that nothing else has ever given him. The portrait in the Chapman apartment of Catherine caressing a unicorn hints at her unusual nature, her purity (the unicorn is a symbol of chastity), and her reserves of spirit. Jim's reading Dante emphasizes the inferno-like nature of his surroundings and brings him to a new awareness, for he perceives that he has indeed departed from "the straight way" "in the middle" of his life. He perceives, moreover, that sexual intimacy gives knowledge of another person impossible to come by in any other way: "Did the woman who once truly received a man become the repository of his real being and thenceforward, witch-like, carry it with her wherever she went?" He has never before realized the sanctity of marriage as a relationship built on sex but going far beyond it.

Catherine has gone to her family homestead, Swan Quarter, hoping to find, in tradition and in proximity to the land, values that will steady her. Since the death of her Uncle Jack in a fall from a horse, Swan Quarter has been the home of three elderly relatives who remind us of the Fates or Norns. As frustrated and barren women, they are the presiding powers at her journey's end. In poignant sequences Catherine's grandmother and Aunt Daphne Passavant relive their tragedies. Catherine Fearson remembers the anguish of the war and her lover's wound; he lost the power of speech and lived apart from others while Catherine, feeling she may have betrayed him, married his brother. Aunt Daphne recalls how her lover had jilted her on her honeymoon night; a friend of hers had arranged this match as a joke, leading the man to think that Daphne had a fortune. The admirable Aunt Willy Lewis has learned to live without delight and refuses love simply because she has become accustomed to doing without it.

Instead of being a refuge for Catherine, Swan Quarter becomes a more disheartening hell than the city had been. Like Eurydice, Catherine will be rescued by a determined mate who has learned her true worth. The atmosphere in these sequences is close to that of Gluck's opera. Most often house and grounds are seen at night or in an autumnal setting. For Catherine, the house contains ghostly presences which seem to prophesy evil and force her into Tom Manigault's company the night after Aunt Willy leaves for the fair to exhibit Red, her fine stallion. Close to the end, Jim comes from New York through a desolate September landscape; he arrives at dusk, feels his passion for Catherine revive, and knows uncontrollable jealousy when Catherine confesses to an affair with Tom. As the shadows lengthen, like an infuriated Othello he virtually strangles her and is only saved by her insistence that he cease. While Jim's fingers had been about his wife's neck, he had seemed to look into an abyss; and this abyss still yawns before him until his reconciliation with her. Husband and wife prepare for a new life after the terrors of this long night. They decide to leave just as light is about to scatter the darkness and the shadows clouding their souls. Aunt Willy's homecoming with her report of Red's accidental electrocution hastens their departure. In Red's death we see that the unassisted life energies are not so strong as they appear to be; their power is limited, and they fail to provide in themselves any durable basis, moral or metaphysical, for existence.

Catherine is not only a Eurydice figure, but like Cassy Outlaw she brings to mind such forsaken women in legend as Ariadne or Iphigenia; in her patient overcoming of suffering she is like Saint Catherine, her namesake; and she seems also a Persephone figure who has retreated for a season into Hades. Jim brings Catherine out of hell away from the darkness of decaying Swan Quarter; yet in some sense Catherine also rescues him from his own spiritual hell. Her dream of a dead man's spirit for whose safety she is responsible would seem to indicate that she stands in this vital relationship to Jim. As in Gluck's opera, the characters experience both the pangs and the delights, and then the transcendent power, of love. Jim and Catherine now know the truth that their mythological prototypes learned before them, that the claims of love are overpowering and cannot be lightly foregone: "For Love's every captive humble rejoices;/ None would go free that ever wore his chain!"

The Strange Children (1951) presents through the central intelligence of the nine-year-old Lucy Lewis a view of the adult world which surrounds her as she attempts to relate herself to it. The most remarkable facet of the novel is the consistency with which Miss Gordon maintains point of view and the thoroughness with which she charts the development in Lucy of moral and religious awareness. Kevin Reardon, a visiting friend of the family, explains that she is named after Saint Lucy whose name means light: one so named should be able to experience an accession of light, as Lucy in fact does.

Miss Gordon depicts with subtlety the tensions between Lucy and the adults about her, "the strange children" of the title "whose mouth speaketh vanity." If Lucy is a "changeling" to her mother, Sarah Lewis is, for the girl, an object of pity as she drudges for the guests, of bewilderment as she suffers from a hangover, and of antagonism as she tries to prevent Lucy from going with Uncle Tubby and Isabel Reardon for a swim. Tubby MacCollum is a "successful" poet whose work about the Civil War, *If It Takes All Summer*, has been immensely popular; he has visited the Reardons in France recently, and Isabel has telegraphed him to meet her at the Lewises'. Stephen Lewis, Lucy's father, is a lapsed poet and an amateur historian, too intellectual to be capable of spontaneity. Lucy notes her parents' tendency to disparage their friends; and in her mind's eye, she sees the dismembered bodies of these people lying about the lawn when her parents are done with their gossiping.

Throughout, Lucy thus modulates her sensations and thoughts from the conscious plane to the unconscious, passing from articulate utterance to the half-formed impressions and the psychic fluctuations of the stream of consciousness. In addition, she frequently juxtaposes the perceptions of the moment with dim recollections of her past in France and elsewhere. She is shaken by the discovery of Tubby and Isabel embracing in the woods, intuitively understanding what is happening though she is unable to define her reactions precisely. Evil thus disturbs her before she knows enough about it to come to terms with it.

Lucy Lewis continually learns about her elders and is able to use some of this knowledge for her own enlightenment. Her own imaginativeness and spontaneity are symbolized through her involvement with the characters in the romantic tale of *Undine*, which she constantly ponders. And like Undine, Lucy acquires a soul and learns of both the sufferings and the satisfactions which knowledge brings. She regards the world of pretentious intellectuals with the asperity of Aleck Maury, her grandfather; the old man regards his daughter, her husband, and their friends as fools who bore him. Lucy would agree with her grandfather that unspoiled nature is more vital than the "civilized" life of her parents and their circle. She experiences a peace in contemplating the waterfall, for instance, which she finds nowhere else at Benfolly.

Lucy illustrates in her own actions the basic truth that evil impulses divide human nature. She cannot retain an unsoiled virtue in the decadence that surrounds her. She steals a crucifix from Reardon. When she returns it, she confesses her theft in a kind of penance rite. The eyes of the crucifix have fascinated her, and they will undoubtedly have a renovative effect upon her in the future. She finds the same depths of understanding in Reardon's eyes, and she feels especial remorse at her theft when she learns that he is buying her a pony. The eyes of the crucifix and Reardon's awaken in her a sense of moral perspective, but she is reluctant to face the implications of inner change. But Reardon's spiritual presence is so compelling that she cannot evade the man who acts upon her like a "hound of heaven."

Lucy has gotten further in moral enlargement than most of the other characters have. But in the last two pages, light breaks into the soul of Stephen Lewis and the point of view shifts to him. Born under Scorpio he realizes now the true meaning of this zodiacal sign, "The House of Death—unless a man be reborn." He sees that he and all men have desert places to cross and that life is a pilgrimage involving both a progression and an unknown goal. Stephen at last surmounts his intellectual pretensions and his arid way of discounting spiritual experience.

No longer will he be able to do as he had done when he belittled Reardon's vision of the the saint who succored him after an accident in France. Sarah had been impressed with Reardon's recital and had complained of her husband's callow comments upon it. She asserts, in fact, that Stephen's intellect inhibits his feelings and prevents them both from being able to grasp life's ineffable dimensions. But at the end Stephen is ready to admit that transcendental values may exist.

The coda at the end is in sequence with an earlier high point when Lucy in a dream had seen all the Benfolly adults now journeying through a dark wood; her father and mother separate to go each his own way. From another path comes Isabel carrying a trencher with a man's head on it, that of a Captain Green murdered by his personal servant in the Civil War. Isabel scares away her husband and Tubby, her admirer; and we have intimations that she is a sinister person. The people are traversing not a forest but a wasteland on the edge of a chasm; and they can only be saved from death by turning back to the arduous path they had come by. Lucy thus sees modern man as both a victim of spiritual paralysis and a wanderer in a wasteland; her perceptions are essentially those of Stephen when he views his own plight and that of his family and friends. The visions are so closely connected that the modulation in point of view in the last two paragraphs from Lucy's to Stephen's represents no violation of aesthetic probability.

In *The Strange Children*, Miss Gordon is fascinated with the subject of religion. Lucy represents the receptive mind, the person who has not lost the ability to feel. Unless one becomes as a little child, Miss Gordon implies, he will never be able to see God. Stephen Lewis and his friend Tubby are agnostics by intellectual preference, temperamental dryness, and excessive pride; Sarah Lewis' Uncle Fill voices a militant, unsophisticated skepticism. Sarah possesses the religious temperament without religious conviction; the Holy Rollers, who hold their meetings on the Lewis farm, possess religious conviction but are wayward, extreme, and mindless. Kevin Reardon is a Roman Catholic and a source of truth. As a result of his accident, his vision then, and his devotion to his wife, he has achieved humility, grace, and religious knowledge. He had, as a young man, spurned the religious devotions of his father; his conversion is one way whereby he makes peace with a parent he had only seen that one time since childhood. Reardon in acknowledging his Heavenly Father has acknowledged his earthly father as well. Reardon is distressed by the irreligion of his friends, particularly as that reaches sacrilege when, in charades, Tubby impersonates a priest, acting out the name Parnell, which, according to Tubby, means "priest's mistress." The Lewises perceive finally that their patronizing judgments of Reardon as drifter and religious pretender are mistaken. The madness of his wife also seems to mirror the madness of a world that does not appreciate Reardon's values.

Madness in Isabel is paralled by the frenzy let loose in the meeting of the Holy Rollers. They follow the teachings of Arnold Watkins, whom God had commanded to follow the text "They shall take up serpents; and if they drink any deadly thing, it shall not hurt them." So they tempt providence by charming rattlesnakes; as a result, Terence MacDonough, Lewis' tenant, is bitten and barely escapes death. A more genuine faith than theirs can actually subdue savage beasts. Thus Saint Marthe tamed a wild dragon with her girdle; and Reardon, born on her day, has lived to subdue the beast in himself through a life of discipline which neither the evangelical Rollers nor his agnostic associates attain.

The conflicts of the characters within the self and with each other are genuine; in retrospect the situations the people are in, their spiritual dilemmas, interest us most. The tone is, if anything, neutral and understated, and the characters are seen with perhaps excessive objectivity. For Miss Gordon's characters, heroic action is not quite possible. As for her one heroic person, Reardon, we do not see the truth about him soon enough for the novel to center upon him as well as upon Lucy Lewis. In *The Malefactors* (1956), Miss Gordon solved this problem by making Catherine Pollard spiritually central to the novel from the first time she appears in it, even though the skeptical poet Tom Claiborne is the central intelligence.

Claiborne is, like Stephen Lewis, a lapsed middle-aged poet, who has lost the capacity to relate freshly to life. He is restless and sensitive, because his creativity is thwarted. Vera, his wife, makes his life an easy but a barren one on her Pennsylvania estate. One of his shallow associates describes, in a moment of insight, Claiborne's failing, his never having "been aware of the existence of another human being." When he and Vera separate over his affair with her cousin Cynthia Vail, he attacks Vera in order to defend himself, accusing her of his own preoccupation with the self. Claiborne later sees the truth, how he has described a circle about himself and struck away any living things springing up in it. How then, he wonders, can he now expect Vera to breathe willingly "the impoverished air" which envelops him?

Claiborne is a misguided son of the world instead of a son of light. His secular values extinguish the poetic inspiration which had once been genuine; and the "cold determination to write more verses" which followed upon his early creativity has been stultifying. With creativity gone and nothing left to arouse him to loyalty or action, it is not surprising that he envies Keats his early death. Nor is it surprising, once the prop of marriage is gone, that Vera tries to gain release from her empty life through suicide. When his affair with Cynthia goes flat, Claiborne realizes that Vera had been searching for darkness and that he, too, has been seeking such oblivion all his life. The death wish grows powerful, then, as he contemplates jumping from his apartment house window.

Miss Gordon's notable achievement is to keep us interested in the culpable Claiborne. We are immediately immersed in his situation and in his evaluations of his contemporaries and his own past life. They are often perceptive, for he knows the weaknesses of the people in his set; and he can see clearly, within limits, his own acts. He has intelligence and talent in desuetude to offset his failures in sympathy, imagination, and purposiveness. The fact, too, that he can learn from experience elevates him over most of the other people in the novel who are satisfied with life in a secular and hedonistic wasteland. His associates are the malefactors, so named because they do wrong and recall the criminals crucified with Christ, one of whom resisted salvation even while he was dying. Claiborne at least retains the poet's re-

ceptivity toward experience even if he has lost the power to interpret it meaningfully.

Before long he perceives the worth of Vera, whom he has abandoned for life with the literary Cynthia. Cynthia has green, vixen-like eyes in contrast to Vera's blue, steady gaze. Cynthia's beauty and talent blind him to her shallow, calculating nature; and it is not until after they give a large party that he sees her for what she is, a self-centered person even more guilty than he has been of a failure to "know how other people feel." As for Vera, we at first see her through Claiborne's eyes and judge her with his good-natured indulgence and latent dissatisfaction. Her activities as a lady farmer do not channel her energies effectively and, in fact, make her seem faintly ridiculous. Her involvement with Bud, the prize Red Poll bull, reveals a connoisseur's fussiness more than the Christian's love for a form of created life. The fete which she stages in honor of the bull is in part a thanksgiving rite, in part a Saturnalia; and the bull itself suggests a priapic deity. The bull is not only a sexual but a reality symbol. After the party is over, Claiborne feels there is more truth in the bull's vitality than he or his friends will ever express. The revulsion with which both Claiborne and Vera receive the propaganda of the inseminator at the fete reveals them both as opposed to the coarser manifestations of a secular culture. They regard this man's manipulations of nature as unnatural and contrary to the way that things were meant to be.

Gradually, Vera's strengths emerge. Her love for Claiborne is unquestioned if too protective. For one thing she wants him to return to her after he has begun the affair with Cynthia; for another, she knows such excess of feeling that she attempts suicide. When her latent Catholicism awakes, however, she finds completion in tending Joseph Tardieu (the now senile author of *The Green Revolution*) and a physically deprived little boy, while she works on one of Catherine Pollard's farms. Claiborne accuses her of interested motives in not granting him a divorce so that she can more readily retain the child.

But he sees how baseless this accusation is when he looks directly into her blue eyes. Hitherto he had evaded her glance because it made him uncomfortable; her innocence was an affront, and he hated her momentarily because of her scrutiny of his face when she found him in Cynthia's apartment. Her eyes "are the mirror of the soul" and symbolize the spiritual realities basic to her nature, though her life with Claiborne for a while overshadows them; and her eyes have an intensity comparable in their effects to Beatrice's in *The Divine Comedy*. Claiborne also overcomes his aversion to his dead father especially after a friend, the psychiatrist George Crenfew, interprets one of his dreams. George explains how, in the dream, the elder Claiborne had tried to protect his son from the excesses of his nature, especially the tendency to blunt his emotions by intellectualizing his experiences. The epigraph from Maritain, "It is for Adam to interpret the voices that Eve hears," comments upon Claiborne's failure until the end to bring his mind into a fruitful relationship with intuition.

In his course toward enlightenment, two Roman Catholics help him. Sister Immaculata is writing a study of the dead homosexual poet Horne Watts, who had been a friend of the Claibornes in their expatriate years and who gains some of his force through his resemblances to Hart Crane. She instructs Claiborne that the heart of man is wicked but that no man need yield to all his impulses. There is hope, too, for fallen man, since "the Humanity of the Word," as Watts perceived, is the bridge between earth and heaven. She regards God as the Hound of Heaven who tracks us down when we would avoid him. Claiborne is impressed by her in spite of his agnosticism.

Catherine Pollard is modeled in part on Dorothy Day, a Catholic well known for her philanthropy in the 1930's and later in behalf of New York City outcasts. Catherine is the other agent in Claiborne's renovation, a beautiful woman who has turned from a frivolous life to saintlike effacement. She now runs a shelter in New York and some farms in outlying regions for the homeless. For her these outcasts are not "offal" but "Christ," and "we must be Christ to them." For all his skepticism, Claiborne recognizes unusual sensations in Catherine's presence: ease and a sense of relaxation, a sense of being plunged into an unknown element, a sense that he and she may be going toward a common goal. She also asserts that Horne Watts, through all the disorders of his life, was trying to find love, that "the love of love" sustained him through his sufferings. In Claiborne's last dream, Horne Watts guides him to a praying woman who resembles Catherine before she fades from sight. This is a sign to him that he should seek her out in his own extremity; and he finds her in Saint Eustace's chapel adjoining her shelter. She encourages him to seek Vera again although Vera has just rejected his overtures. Vera is a Catholic, Catherine asserts, and recognizes the sacramental aspect of marriage and will be subject to her husband as the Church is subject to Christ. Through Catherine, Claiborne learns that human relationships must be cherished and made firm through love, and he discovers the authority of a spiritual reality that transcends the self.

The book abounds in Christian images, particularly those connected with the saints featured in it, Catherine of Siena, Saint Ciannic, whose statue is in the Claiborne garden, and Saint Eustace. The latter's miraculous powers and ultimate failure indicate that the Christian faith can move mountains and yet be ineffectual in many worldly contingencies. Eustace was a Roman general converted to Christianity when he saw the sign of the Cross poised between the horns of a deer. He and his family tamed the lions to which they were exposed but succumbed when they were thrust into a brazen bull and burned to death. Insofar as Bud's animalism is destructive, he may be linked with the bull in the Eustace legend or with minotaur figure of the classics. The fete in honor of the bull at Vera's farm takes place in 1946 on the feast day of Saint Eustace, September 22. This has been through no design on Vera's part, despite her own fondness for the saint, at least for his church in Rome.

Most effective in extending the perspectives of the book are Claiborne's dreams. These primarily concern caves and have some basis in his experience. He had explored much in caves when a boy. In a cave similar to one which he and George had found long ago, he and Cynthia have their first carnal contact. Claiborne's recurring dream is of a broad river that opens into a cavern. In the dream the current swirls him along until he sees the cavern yawning for him at the end of a tributary stream. The dream always ends here until the affair with Cynthia gains momentum. Then he is swept into the cavern itself. The cavern represents the chaos and the flux of the unconscious life, which can be terrifying without some clue how one is to travel through it. He wishes to begin a new life with Cynthia, even if this means consulting like Saul the Witch of Endor or descending like Odysseus to Orcus to gain intelligence from the dead. In Cynthia's company he seems to be wandering in a vast cavern while she casts a new (but not necessarily valid) light on the figures of all the people he has known. In another dream a woman guards the stairs leading to a vast hall below. Once there, he sits at a table with others, only to find that their robes cover figures without flesh; and he knows then that he is in hell. In Cynthia's presence, we can infer, he sees things falsely and he yields to dark, mindless, corrosive, evil instincts. She is no reliable guide in exploring the deepest facets of the self, although at first he experiences with her a release of powers that have long been submerged within him.

The caves of the unconscious may illuminate as well as obscure; and they allow us to confront, for what they are, the elemental realities of the self. In a dream that has for locale the cave that he and George once found, his father prevents him from throwing himself over a cliff and destroying himself as Horne Watts and Carlo Vincent (the mad painter who was Vera's father) do in the dream (they were suicides in life as well). Another dream with a cave as locale allows Claiborne again to confront reality, the dream already discussed in which Catherine Pollard helps him to see the truth about himself and Vera. He finds her praying in Saint Eustace's chapel, just as he had seen her in the cave of his dream. This chapel is the cavern toward which his essential being had been bearing him, in spite of his being detained in other caves along his pilgrim's way. Here he receives from Catherine the kiss of Christ. In her counsel to him, moreover, the structural lines of the novel converge. The uneasy marriage of Claiborne and Vera yielded to division; but now, with Catherine's blessing, Claiborne wishes a firmer union with Vera than he has known before.

In this novel as in her others, Caroline Gordon reaches a just balance between the idea and the fact, the abstract and the concrete, the metaphysical and the physical. Her novels and short stories take us in a speculative direction and enlarge upon issues that are intellectual and spiritual. But always the abstraction has its basis in the people and the circumstances of the world as she has known it. In her mind and art she has weighed dispassionately the claims of intuition and intelligence, and has been her own best interpreter of the voices that she has heard. In her work sensibility and intellect reach that dynamic equilibrium in which the one faculty strengthens the other. This constantly controlled inspiration of hers accounts, too, for the even quality and the consistent excellence of her books.

Qualities that we associate with the southern mind dominate Miss Gordon as they do writers as various as William Faulkner, Eudora Welty, and Robert Penn Warren. Like these distinguished contemporaries, she has embodied in her fiction the aborted aspirations of most human beings, the sense of evil infecting the good and true, the glories and burdens of a legendary past, the sense of cultures and individuals in conflict, a rich feeling for place, a passion for the heroic, and an abiding sense of the tragic dimensions of human life.

It is the strength of Miss Gordon's work to suggest continually new facets of significance as one lives through the books in his mind. The characters and the incidents form new configurations with the result that the significance of any one of her books enlarges constantly as one reviews it. Her purpose has been from the beginning to suggest that reality is spiritual as well as empiric, immaterial as well as material. Accordingly, she has presented the experience of her characters in time and then again as it reaches beyond time. The ineffable dimensions of her materials she suggests through a discerning use of myth; and in her later books Christianity reinforces their universal implications. In the first instance, however, her books are faithful to the requirements of art, no matter where they lead philosophically. Only in the most general sense, then, are the books doctrinal. As a writer Miss Gordon is the inquiring moralist even before

she is the religious writer. Because of her passionate concern with the way life should be, her books are rooted in social realities even as they look toward the visionary. Intelligence, compassion, psychological insight, depth of vision, and stylistic distinction inform a canon of work that impresses always by its comprehensiveness and strength.

Some of the conclusions expressed above, which are valid for all Miss Gordon's other work, have to be modified for *The Glory of Hera* (1972), in which she recounts the Greek legends surrounding Heracles. The mythic aspect is still strong, but she is much less "the inquiring moralist" and the psychological novelist than she had formerly been. Social realities, moreover, are incidental to her vision in this novel rather than basic to it. But we observe in *The Glory of Hera* the same intelligence, compassion, depth of vision, and stylistic distinction that we find in her other books. Her earlier moral and psychic predilections may also come more directly to the fore in *A Narrow Heart: The Portrait of a Woman*, the second part of the double novel which she is composing (*The Glory of Hera* is the first part). As she has explained in a letter to Donald E. Stanford, *The Glory of Hera* traces the "lower pattern" of human experience, "the archetypal world which the present day Jungians and the archaic Greeks inform us lies at the very bottom of every human consciousness." The "upper pattern" will emerge in *The Narrow Heart* as Miss Gordon re-creates, in a fictionalized autobiography, the archetypal aspects of those figures in her own family who have most excited her imagination, many of whom had connections with such heroic figures as Dr. Joseph Hunter, Thomas Jefferson, Meriwether Lewis, Sir Walter Scott, and others.

Many of the implications in *The Glory of Hera* are Christian, although no direct mention is made of Christianity. At the least, knowing the strength of Miss Gordon's religious belief, we cannot ignore Christian values in interpreting her latest book. The incidents connected with Heracles suggest, in Miss Gordon's version, parallels to those connected with Christ. Sometimes the Heraclean myths will contrast ironically with the events in which Christ was involved or with his personal qualities. But such disparities between pagan and Christian values are implicit, not directly expressed. The book remains essentially an unembellished transcription of Greek myth, though Miss Gordon brings out those features in it which have counterparts in later myths, religions, or cultures. She implies that human civilization runs in cyclic patterns. Thus Greek history, culture, and myth introduce (or repeat) universal human interests and forms that will recur in later ages. Those ages, for example, that are not blessed with a hero-savior can with assurance look forward to the appearance of such a godlike man.

In *The Glory of Hera* Zeus, the Father of Gods and Men, is uneasy because men are unprotected from malignant cosmic forces and from themselves; and he feels responsible for them, even though they are "envious, treacherous, willful, cruel to each other and ungrateful to the gods." He has had (like the Jehovah of Judaeo-Christian tradition or, for that matter, the Wotan of Scandinavian legend) the inspiration to conceive a heroic son to help vulnerable mankind, to provide for its redemption. Some of the most effective sequences in the book are those in heaven as Zeus ponders his past history, his present difficulties with gods and men, and his plan to engender the newest and the greatest of his sons. He decides to descend to the mortal Alcmene, who has just become the bride of Amphitryon; he assumes the guise of Amphitryon and causes time to stop for the equivalent of three days and nights of dalliance. As a result of this "annun-

ciation" twin sons are born, Iphicles and Alcides. Amphitryon seems as bewildered by his wife's aspect after this visitation as Joseph was said to be by Mary's. Alcides, at the behest of Teiresias, is given the name of Heracles, "the glory of Hera," an ironical designation in view of Hera's enmity toward him as the chosen favorite of Zeus. In a sense he does eventually become Hera's greatest glory when she overcomes her aversion to him and, at the time of his translation to Olympus, recognizes his greatness of nature.

Heracles, throughout his troubled life, is the victim of forces over which he has no control: Hera's unbridled antagonism, Zeus's exalted expectations, and his own fallible nature which impulsively leads him, at times, to crime and acts of cruelty. He is in part an untamed savage, guilty of peremptory egotism and inflammable pride, but also capable of much gentleness and courtly behavior to women and those dependent on him. His pride, moreover, is of the pardonable sort, that of the hero contemplating his exploits, not an intellectual arrogance. Even when he sets himself up as a god, Palemon, he does so out of a naive sense that he is worthy of such homage, not out of calculation. If he is partly a barbarous man, he is also a man exalted by his love for wife and children, by his agony at their death, by his sense of honor and fair play, and by his determination to outlast the hardships and afflictions visited upon him by the gods, by his adumbration of "the patience of Christ." To the degree that his misery is intense, so is his satisfaction with the task accomplished. The ambiguity which was always to surround him Alcmene once expressed by prophesying for him "the most toilsome and at the same time happiest life of any mortal."

Zeus's messianic design as it materializes has more flaws than he had anticipated, partly because of Hera's malignance and partly because of Heracles' earlier insensitivity and inhumanity. But the design also succeeds more fully than he could have known. Like Christ, Heracles assumes many of the burdens of humanity: as a result of his activities he brings life to men. So King Eurystheus' physician perceives the significance of Heracles and the labors he performs for the King: "he is promising his fellow mortals deliverance from that which formerly threatened death." Heracles has a sense of mission and dedication; at one point he says that he cannot waste time but must return to Thebes, to "go about my father's business." Like Christ he descends into the lower world (before his death rather than after, however) and is changed forever as a result of this experience. Here he is reconciled with his former rival, Meleager. His death, like Christ's, is the result of the machinations of a smaller-natured individual. Deineira, his second wife, is not analogous precisely to Judas, but her function is the same: to encompass the death of a potential savior, half-man, half-divine. In a fit of pique she tries to regain his love; she lines the robe which he wears at a sacrifice with the poisoned blood of the centaur Nessus from whose embrace he had once rescued her by mortally wounding the would-be ravisher.

Heracles, the hero, is killed as the result of irrational forces incommensurate with the largeness of his nature. But he has partly delivered humanity by lightening its burdens, by "purging the seas and lands of monsters so that men might live in peace." He has devoted his life, as Caroline Gordon in "Cock-Crow" says that a hero should devote it, to "the confrontation of the supernatural in one or other of those forms which men of every age have labelled 'monstrous.'" Heracles climaxes Miss Gordon's preoccupation with the hero, the individual who as questing man (or woman) or renouncing saint (sometimes as both) exerts spiritual authority over those less gifted. Aleck Maury, General Forrest, Rives Allard, Rion and Archy Outlaw, Catherine Chapman, Kevin Reardon, and Catherine Pollard all have these magical resources of nature which make of them, if sometimes fallible persons, indubitable creative powers in the worlds in which they are placed.

Heracles, it is not surprising, becomes a dynamic force for good as his moral nature matures. When he is brought to Olympus he reconciles those at enmity, Zeus and Hera; we are to understand that the senseless rivalry between the two will yield to harmony and understanding. Truly the son surpasses the father, as Christ morally surpasses the tribal, vengeful Jehovah of the Old Testament. Not only does Heracles deliver mankind as Zeus had intended, but he changes the tone of existence among the gods. Not only is Hera softened, but Zeus is mellowed. Zeus loses the vindictiveness which had allowed him to exult, for example, in the punishment of his large-souled enemy, Prometheus, whom he may not really have understood. Heracles liberates in Prometheus, moreover, a force that works for the secular betterment of mankind. Heracles and Prometheus are both mythic savior figures though neither one quite perceives at the time his exalted destiny or recognizes in the other a kindred nature. Nor does Zeus quite clearly see the affinity between the two.

Much in the book is admirable. Miss Gordon actualizes ancient Greece and captures the essence of a civilization in transition from a barbaric, cattle-tending tribal sort to one that is more cosmopolitan and intellectual. At the opposite extreme the scenes in heaven are related with an impressive economy, compression, and authority: see, for example, the convocation of the gods when Teiresias expounds upon the quality of sexual pleasure which the two sexes may experience, or the conferences between Zeus and Athena, who acts in part as his conscience, in part as his wise adviser. Many of the scenes on earth also linger in the memory: Heracles relieving the siege of Thebes, his slaying of his first wife and three sons as a result of a madness induced by Hera, his appearing before King Eurystheus (for whom he labors) in the hide of the Nemean lion, his killing of the hydra with the help of his nephew, his adventures in Egypt and the appearance of Zeus to him there at the temple of Zeus-Ammon, his outwitting of Atlas, and his freeing of Prometheus, to mention some. Yet the method of narration used in the book yields little insight into the internal lives of the characters. We are always on the outside of Heracles, too much involved, perhaps, in learning the innumerable incidents in his career: we are never in his inmost self. An excessively analytic approach would have been inappropriate for a man who claims to be "slow of wit"; but still, as a psychic entity, Heracles is pallid. Nor do the other characters exist much more than in name. They do not develop nor do they reveal themselves to us incrementally. Texture is thin, the narrative line is excessively simple for a writer with Caroline Gordon's impressive knowledge of human motives. Variety is lacking; and the central figures are too remote from our immediate concerns to generate in themselves much pressure upon our imaginations.

Actually, we are close to the medieval romance or the saga in *The Glory of Hera*; in such forms the artist also focuses upon event and its general import rather than on the actors. In *The Glory of Hera* Miss Gordon's art is narrative and pictorial. The chief interest is in the fable, and in the metaphysical, allegorical implications of that fable. The book exerts its hold, finally, upon the intellect, rather than upon the emotions. Within such limits, it has weight, authority, and philosophical cogency. It is a challenging work that marks the zenith of a career notable for its originality, vitality, variety, and breadth.

Selected Bibliography

WORKS OF CAROLINE GORDON

NOVELS, COLLECTIONS OF SHORT STORIES, AND FICTION IN PROGRESS

Penhally. New York: Scribners, 1931.

Aleck Maury Sportsman. New York: Scribners, 1934.

The Garden of Adonis. New York: Scribners, 1937.

None Shall Look Back. New York: Scribners, 1937.

Green Centuries. New York: Scribners, 1941.

The Women on the Porch. New York: Scribners, 1944.

The Forest of the South. New York: Scribners, 1945. (Contains "The Captive," "Hear the Nightingale Sing," "The Forest of the South," "The Ice House," "The Burning Eyes," "To Thy Chamber Window, Sweet," "One More Time," "The Last Day in the Field," "Old Red," "Tom Rivers," "The Long Day," "Summer Dust," "Mr. Powers," "Her Quaint Honour," "The Enemies," "The Brilliant Leaves," and "All Lovers Love the Spring.")

The Strange Children. New York: Scribners, 1951.

The Malefactors. New York: Scribners, 1956.

Old Red and Other Stories. New York: Scribners, 1963. (Contains "One Against Thebes," "Emmanuele! Emmanuele!," "The Brilliant Leaves," "All Lovers Love the Spring," "Tom Rivers," "The Petrified Woman," "Old Red," "One More Time," "The Last Day in the Field," "The Presence," "The Ice House," "Hear the Nightingale Sing," and "The Captive.")

"Cock-Crow," *Southern Review*, n.s., 1:554–69 (July 1965); and "Always Summer," *ibid.*, n.s.,

7:430–46 (April 1971). (Excerpts from novel in progress, *A Narrow Heart: The Portrait of a Woman;* "Cock-Crow" important for interpretation of *The Glory of Hera.*)

The Glory of Hera. Garden City, N.Y.: Doubleday, 1972. (First part of double novel, to be followed by second novel, *A Narrow Heart: The Portrait of a Woman.*)

NONFICTION

The House of Fiction: An Anthology of the Short Story, with commentary by Caroline Gordon and Allen Tate. New York: Scribners, 1950; second edition, 1960. (Incorporates much of the material in Miss Gordon's previously published critical articles.)

"Some Readings and Misreadings," *Sewanee Review,* 61:384–407 (1953).

"The Art and Mystery of Faith," *Newman Annual,* 1953, pp. 55–62.

"Mr. Verver, Our National Hero," *Sewanee Review,* 63:29–47 (1955). (On Henry James's *The Golden Bowl.*)

How to Read a Novel. New York: Viking Press, 1957.

"Flannery O'Connor's *Wise Blood,*" *Critique,* 2:3–10 (1958).

"The Novels of Brainard Cheney," *Sewanee Review,* 67:322–30 (1959).

A Good Soldier: A Key to the Novels of Ford Madox Ford. Davis: University of California Library, 1963.

"The Elephant," *Sewanee Review,* 74:856–71 (October–December 1966). (On Ford Madox Ford.)

"Flies in Their Eyes? A Note on Joseph Heller's *Catch-22,*" *Southern Review,* n.s., 3:96–105 (January 1967) [with Jeanne Richardson, co-author].

"Heresy in Dixie," *Sewanee Review,* 76:263–97 (Spring 1968). (On Flannery O'Connor and Flaubert.)

"Caroline Gordon and 'The Captive': An Interview," by Catherine B. Baum and Floyd C. Watkins, *Southern Review,* n.s., 7:447–62 (April 1971).

"Foreword," *Flannery O'Connor: Voice of the Peacock,* by Sister Kathleen Feeley. New Brunswick, N.J.: Rutgers University Press, 1972. Pp. ix–xii.

BIBLIOGRAPHY

Brown, Ashley. "Caroline Gordon," in *A Bibliographical Guide to the Study of Southern Literature,* edited by Louis D. Rubin, Jr. Baton Rouge: Louisiana State University Press, 1969. Pp. 206–07.

Griscom, Joan. "Bibliography of Caroline Gordon," *Critique,* 1:74–78 (Winter 1956).

CRITICAL AND BIOGRAPHICAL STUDIES

Blum, Morgan. "The Shifting Point of View: Joyce's 'The Dead' and Gordon's 'Old Red,' *Critique,* 1:45–66 (Winter 1956).

Bradbury, John M. *Renaissance in the South: A Critical History of the Literature, 1920–1960.* Chapel Hill: University of North Carolina Press, 1964.

Brown, Ashley. "The Achievement of Caroline Gordon," *Southern Humanities Review,* 2:279–90 (Summer 1968).

————. *"None Shall Look Back:* The Novel as History," *Southern Review,* n.s., 7:480–94 (April 1971).

————. "The Novel as Christian Comedy," in *Reality and Myth: Essays in American Literature in Honor of Richard Croom Beatty,* edited by William E. Walker and Robert L. Welker. Nashville, Tenn.: Vanderbilt University Press, 1964.

Cheney, Brainard. "Caroline Gordon's Ontological Quest," *Renascence,* 16:3–12 (Fall 1963).

————. "Caroline Gordon's *The Malefactors,*" *Sewanee Review,* 79:360–72 (July–September 1971). (Reprinted in *Rediscoveries,* edited by David Madden. New York: Crown, 1971.)

Cowan, Louise. "Nature and Grace in Caroline Gordon," *Critique,* 1:11–27 (Winter 1956).

Eisinger, Chester. *Fiction in the Forties.* Chicago: University of Chicago Press, 1964.

Fletcher, Marie. "The Fate of Women in a Changing South: A Persistent Theme in the Fiction of Caroline Gordon," *Mississippi Quarterly,* 21:17–28 (Winter 1967–68).

Ford, Ford Madox. "A Stage in American Literature," *Bookman,* 74:371–76 (December 1931).

Hartman, Carl. "Charades at Benfolly," *Western Review*, 16:322–24 (Summer 1951). (On *The Strange Children*.)

Heilman, Robert B. "School for Girls," *Sewanee Review*, 60:293–304 (April–June 1952). (On *The Strange Children*.)

Hoffman, Frederick J. "Caroline Gordon: The Special Yield," *Critique*, 1:29–35 (Winter 1956). (Reprinted in revised form in *The Art of Southern Fiction*. Carbondale: Southern Illinois University Press, 1967.)

King, Lawrence T. "The Novels of Caroline Gordon," *Catholic World*, 181:274–79 (July 1955).

Koch, Vivienne. "Companions in the Blood," *Sewanee Review*, 64:645 (Autumn 1956). (On *The Malefactors*.)

————. "The Conservatism of Caroline Gordon," in *Southern Renascence*, edited by Louis D. Rubin and Robert D. Jacobs. Baltimore: Johns Hopkins Press, 1953.

————. "The Forest of the South," *Sewanee Review*, 54:543–47 (July–September 1946).

Landess, Thomas H. "The Function of Ritual in Caroline Gordon's *Green Centuries*," *Southern Review*, n.s., 7:495–508 (April 1971).

————, ed. *The Short Fiction of Caroline Gordon: A Survey*. Dallas: University of Dallas Press, 1972.

Lytle, Andrew N. "Caroline Gordon and the Historic Image," *Sewanee Review*, 57:560–86 (Autumn 1949). (Reprinted in *The Hero with the Private Parts*. Baton Rouge: Louisiana State University Press, 1966.)

————. "The Forest of the South," *Critique*, 1:3–9 (Winter 1956).

McShane, Frank. *The Life and Work of Ford Madox Ford*. New York: Horizon Press, 1965.

Mizener, Arthur. *The Saddest Story: A Biography of Ford Madox Ford*. New York and Cleveland: World Publishing Co., 1971.

O'Connor, Mary. "On Caroline Gordon," *Southern Review*, n.s., 7:463–66 (April 1971).

O'Connor, William Van. "Art and Miss Gordon," in *The Grotesque: An American Genre and Other Essays*. Carbondale: Southern Illinois University Press, 1962.

Rocks, James E. "The Christian Myth as Salvation: Caroline Gordon's *The Strange Children*," *Tulane Studies in English*, 16:149–60 (1968).

————. "The Mind and Art of Caroline Gordon," *Mississippi Quarterly*, 21:1–16 (Winter 1967–68).

————. "The Short Fiction of Caroline Gordon," *Tulane Studies in English*, 18:15–35 (1970).

Ross, Danforth. "Caroline Gordon's Golden Ball," *Critique*, 1:67–73 (Winter 1956).

Rubin, Larry. "Christian Allegory in Caroline Gordon's 'The Captive,'" *Studies in Short Fiction*, 5:283–89 (Spring 1968).

Squires, Radcliffe. "The Underground Stream: A Note on Caroline Gordon's Fiction," *Southern Review*, n.s., 7:467–79 (April 1971).

Stanford, Donald E. "Caroline Gordon: From *Penhally* to *A Narrow Heart*," *Southern Review*, n.s., 7:xv–xx (April 1971).

Stewart, John L. *The Burden of Time: The Fugitives and Agrarians*. Princeton, N.J.: Princeton University Press, 1965.

Sullivan, Walter. "Southern Novelists and the Civil War," in *Southern Renascence*, edited by Louis D. Rubin and Robert D. Jacobs. Baltimore, Md.: Johns Hopkins Press, 1953.

Thorp, Willard. "The Way Back and the Way Up: The Novels of Caroline Gordon," *Bucknell Review*, 6:1–15 (December 1956).

—FREDERICK P. W. McDOWELL

Nathaniel Hawthorne
1804-1864

WHEN Hawthorne was born in Salem, Massachusetts, in 1804 the town was already very old by American standards. The Hathornes had been there from the beginning. (Hawthorne added the *w* to the family name when he began to sign his stories.) By the 1690's one of them was prominent enough to be a judge in the witchcraft trials. His descendant's remarks on him in "The Custom House" introduction to *The Scarlet Letter* mix pride in his prominence and a sense of inherited guilt for his deeds as judge.

Hawthorne is being a little whimsical in "The Custom House," protectively light in his tone, when he takes the judge's guilt on himself and offers to do penance that the family curse may be removed. But there is an undercurrent of seriousness. Salem is a part of him, for good and for ill. The "mere sensuous sympathy of dust for dust" is perhaps all that is needed to bind town and man together. Like William Faulkner in a later century, like Quentin remembering the tales out of the past in *Absalom, Absalom!* Hawthorne admits to being haunted by the figure of the prominent but guilty ancestor who "was present to my boyish imagination, as far back as I can remember."

Later Hathornes were neither so prominent nor so conspicuously guilty. While Salem grew and prospered, they sank into that "dreary and unprosperous condition" Hawthorne hopes, in "The Custom House," may be alleviated by his public assumption of the family guilt. When Captain Nathaniel Hathorne, a shipmaster, died on one of his voyages the year that young Nathaniel was four, the family decline was complete. Left without resources, Elizabeth Manning Hathorne moved with her three children into the nearby home of her brother.

As he grew up, Hawthorne watched Salem decline. The Embargo of 1807 struck the town a heavy blow, and when the end of the War of 1812 made shipping possible again, Salem did not recover its importance as a seaport. The town was repeating the family history, it seemed. It was perhaps too late for both town and family. In his first work of fiction, which Hawthorne compounded of about equal portions of undigested, undistanced personal feelings and experience, and the conventions of the Gothic novel, the central figure, Fanshawe, thinks of himself as nobility in decline. He anticipates, and experiences, an early death. Late in life Hawthorne tried repeatedly to write a romance about an American claimant to a lost great English estate. With a part of himself at least, he was that claimant, as he was also Fanshawe.

When he graduated from Bowdoin in 1825, with *Fanshawe* (1828) already complete or nearly so, Hawthorne was determined to become a writer of fiction. Composition was the only subject in which he had excelled in college, or in which he had showed any great interest, and now he proposed to teach himself to write by writing. He spent the next dozen years in the now famous third-floor chamber of his uncle's house on Herbert Street in Salem, reading, writing, projecting volumes of tales refused by publishers, and, during the latter part of the period, published regularly in magazines and Christmas gift books or annuals. But the rate of pay for the stories was very low, and though he had increasing success in placing his work, he found himself unable to make even a modest living as a writer of tales.

In 1837 a friend secretly paid for the publication of *Twice-Told Tales*. This brought him a little group of admiring readers but no income. As an expedient, he undertook editorial work in Boston, then got a job in the Boston Custom House, and finally joined the Brook Farm community, hoping, apparently, that in that socialist society he would be able to combine the practical and the creative. But hard daily labor and social evenings left him neither energy nor time for writing, and after little more than a year there he left without regret and poorer than when he had joined.

At the age of thirty-eight Hawthorne married Sophia Peabody of the famous Salem family, and the next several years, spent in the Old Manse in Concord, were the happiest in his life. Here he partly wrote and partly collected from magazines which had published his work earlier the tales and sketches to make a second volume, *Mosses from an Old Manse* (1846). Emerson, Thoreau, and Ellery Channing were friendly neighbors. With Channing Hawthorne boated on the river that flowed beside the house, as he tells us in "The Old Manse." It seemed, for a while, not unfitting to play with the notion that he and Sophia were a "New Adam and Eve."

But he was haunted from the beginning by a sense that this idyll could not last, and his fears, as was so often the case, proved to be well founded. With unpaid bills mounting steadily, and the owner giving notice that he wanted the Old Manse back for his own use, the family was forced to return to Salem, where Hawthorne took the job in the Custom House described in the introduction to *The Scarlet Letter*. Fired from this position for political reasons, he turned back to his craft and wrote his greatest romance. As he worked on it, anxiety about money was still severe and grief at the death of his mother was intense, but he never again wrote so rapidly or so surely, or so much from the depths of his sensibility.

In this tale set in Puritan Boston, Hawthorne created four unforgettable characters of American fiction: Hester Prynne, condemned to wear a scarlet *A* on her breast in token of her sin of adultery; the Reverend Arthur Dimmesdale, revered as saintly by his parishioners but torn by hidden guilt; their child, the " 'Pearl' . . . of great price"; and Roger Chillingworth, Hester's husband, who as he probes into the hearts of those who have wronged him, becomes the greatest sinner of them all. The identity of Hester's lover, a secret her ministerial inquisitors cannot force her to reveal, is at last made public in a way the community could not have foreseen and would not have wished.

The Scarlet Letter (1850) established Hawthorne's reputation and made it possible, it seemed, for him to devote himself entirely to his writing. Settling in Lenox in the Berkshires, he quickly wrote *The House of the Seven Gables* (1851) and several works for children, a type of writing he found pleasant, easy, and comparatively profitable. Here he became a friend of Herman Melville, who was at work nearby on *Moby Dick*, which he later dedicated to Hawthorne. The cursed Hathornes became the cursed Pyncheons in *The House of the Seven Gables*, declining from wealth and prominence to poverty and eccentricity. Their claim to a great estate cannot be established, for the deed has been lost, as the actual deed to land in Maine was lost to Hawthorne's branch of his family. The many-gabled mansion images the family history: since it will not yield up its secrets for the guilt to be purged, it must be left behind by the new generation.

Mountain scenery and the simple life in the "little red farmhouse" finally palled, and the Hawthornes—there were now three children, Una, Julian, and Rose—returned to Concord to buy The Wayside from Amos Bronson Alcott. Then, when *The Blithedale Romance* (1852), in temper and theme an antiutopian reflection of the Brook Farm experience, failed to please Hawthorne's newly won public, and when the election of his college classmate and friend Franklin Pierce to the presidency opened the opportunity for a really remunerative political job, he accepted the consulship in Liverpool. The following half-dozen years were uncreative ones. Though he worked sporadically at his writing, it was not until the end of the period that, by a sustained effort, he was able to write his last completed romance, *The Marble Faun* (1860), in which an innocent young man falls into sin and rises into maturity.

When the family returned to America in 1860, Hawthorne had just four troubled years left. The European experience had proved valuable and pleasant, but it had not, as he had hoped it would, made him financially secure. Further, he found himself disliking the American climate and missing his English friends. Settling in Concord was, he began to think, a mistake. The Wayside—and Concord itself—

did not seem like home to him, and as he thought of the many places the family had lived, he wondered if he could truthfully be said ever to have had a "home."

Working harder and more steadily on his writing now than he ever had for any extended period before, he was unable to bring any work of fiction to completion. Familiar scenes and symbolic images were reused, but in the margins of his manuscripts he wrote himself notes asking "What meaning?" His health began to fail and, haunted by a premonition of early death, he drove himself to write that he might at least leave his family provided for. Though the romances refused to take shape, the sketches of English life that came out as *Our Old Home* (1863) showed that he could still write trenchantly and beautifully on subjects that did not demand exploration of the depths of his imagination.

Provincial Salem and the secluded years of the long apprenticeship were now far in the past, and he had almost succeeded in becoming the "man of society" he had always wanted to be. His publishers pressed him for new work, and recognition of his achievement was widespread and gratifying. Now at least there was no outward reason for his recurrent dream of failure. But his ambivalence of mood increased until everything was Janus faced. Much that we should like to know about these last years must remain speculative. We do not even know, for instance, what disease he was suffering from, whether physical or psychophysical. Oliver Wendell Holmes examined him but could arrive at no sure diagnosis. The evidence for any conclusion is largely missing, but what there is of it seems to me to point to psychosomatic changes.

One thing seems clear, though, if not the disease that aged him so suddenly and brought death at the age of sixty. The manuscripts of the romances he could not complete suggest that the convictions that had once sustained him, providing a tolerable margin of clarity and meaning in a dark and ambiguous world, were now no longer operative, even if, in some sense, still held. "What meaning?"

When he died in 1864 in Plymouth, New Hampshire, on a trip with former President Pierce intended to benefit his health, he was far from home both literally and symbolically —far, in those days, from The Wayside in Concord, and farther still from that home of the heart's desire, that Eden that had been lost so long ago.

Hawthorne has remained an enigma to his biographers. Those who concentrate on the facts of the outward life tend to present a thoroughly normal and well-adjusted Hawthorne. They show us a man who liked to smoke cigars and drink brandy while playing cards. This Hawthorne may have seemed shy to Emerson but he enjoyed an easy friendship with less intellectual friends like Horatio Bridge and Franklin Pierce. It is quite true that to most of those whose impressions have come down to us he seemed reserved but not unusually withdrawn, thoughtful but certainly not depressed or melancholy. Indeed a good part of the record suggests that many found him ordinarily cheerful and sociable.

But this picture begins to waver and blur as soon as we turn from the remarks of observers to the inner life as revealed in the writing. The well-adjusted Hawthorne, we begin to suspect, is the man he would have liked to be, and no doubt partly succeeded in being, but it is not the man he knew from within. The letters, the *Notebooks*, and the more personal sketches all reveal a quite different man behind the social mask.

With varying degrees of disguise and aesthetic distance from his personal situation, the sketches in particular can take us into the imagination of the man who wrote the major works. "The Devil in Manuscript" is almost autobiography, while Hawthorne appears in "Earth's Holocaust" only as a naive young man who needs to be guided into an understanding of life's complexities. "The Journal of a Solitary Man," which is neither so literally informative as "The Devil in Manuscript" nor so distanced as "Earth's Holocaust," reveals a good deal of the inner Hawthorne whose existence casual observers did not often guess.

The sketch of the "solitary man" reveals not facts so much as attitudes. The years of Hawthorne's "solitary" apprenticeship, after his graduation from college and before his marriage, were not nearly so solitary as they seemed, both at the time and in retrospect. But the important thing is precisely how they *seemed* to the man who wrote so often of alienation. They seemed years of imprisonment in the solitude of self.

Hawthorne pictures the solitary man as "walking in the sunshine . . . yet cold as death." The young unfortunate suffers often from a "deep gloom sometimes thrown over his mind by his reflections on death." He longs to break out of his isolation by travel: perhaps thus he will find something more real than his shadowy existence. But he gets no further from his native village than Hawthorne had gone at the time of writing the sketch. Instead, he spends much of his time looking at himself in the mirror and trying to understand the "pale beauty" he sees there.

There is some aesthetic distance here, to be sure. In part, Hawthorne is contributing to the tradition of the romantic hero as sad clown. But there is also self-revelation. The Hawthorne revealed is not the one family and friends thought they knew but a melancholy young Narcissus who often felt alone even in the midst of company and who was gravely dissatisfied with what he saw in the looking glass. He thought much of death, felt cold and guilty, and wrote "Alice Doane's Appeal."

This Hawthorne blamed himself for his detachment and wrote "The Christmas Banquet." He wished that he could relate to others more easily, that he were not so coldly rational and appraising: he cast cold-hearted scientists in the roles of villains. He worried often about whether being an artist might not have the effect of increasing his alienation. Certainly it required him to study people as objects to be manipulated on his fictional canvas. Might he not come to feel that they were as much *his* creatures as the characters in his book? Should art be thought of as a kind of black magic and the artist as a sort of magician, like the witch of old and the mesmerist of the present? "The Prophetic Pictures" and "The Old Apple Dealer" express his concern with the problem.

This Hawthorne felt guilty about being an artist and determined not to become a mesmerist. Though he toyed, at least once, with the thought that he might enjoy, for a while, being "a spiritualized Paul Pry, hovering invisible round man and woman, witnessing their deeds, searching into their hearts," he countered the temptation by writing so often of the hearth as a redemptive symbol that reference to it became a hallmark of his style. The hearth suggested all that the solitary man and the cold observer of Christmas festivities lacked: warmth and hope and fellow-feeling and the love that held together the family circle. Reunion after isolation came in his works to be both a symbol of and the literal means to salvation. No writer has ever placed a higher value on communion and community.

But he continued to note in himself, and to disapprove, feelings and attitudes he projected in Chillingworth and Rappaccini and Goodman Brown. He noted his tendency not only to study others with cold objectivity but to study himself with almost obsessive interest. He looked into the glass too often and searched too curiously the hearts of others: he wrote "Egotism, or the Bosom Sergent" and "Ethan Brand," condemning both protagonists, the first for his self-concern, the second for treating people as objects of study. Hawthorne had no admiration for detached observers, but he knew one well enough from within to be able to write about the type with authority.

"No human effort, on a grand scale, has ever yet resulted according to the purpose of its projectors. The advantages are always incidental. Man's accidents are God's purposes." Thus Hawthorne dismissed the moral significance of the Civil War. "Chiefly about War Matters," in which these aphorisms occur, is one of his last completed pieces of writing, done when his health was already failing and he was deeply distressed about the war itself. His political position as a Democrat, too, must have made it peculiarly difficult for him to clarify his feelings. We may be tempted to attribute the coldness of the remark, its implied disengagement from the human effort, to conditions of the moment.

But the idea was not new to Hawthorne. Years before, writing his campaign biography of Franklin Pierce, he had said the same thing: "There is no instance, in all history, of the human will and intellect having perfected any great moral reform by methods which it adapted to that end. . . ." The idea was obviously a useful one in a defense of Pierce, a New Hampshire Democrat who needed the support of the South to be elected, but Hawthorne felt no need to invent it for the occasion. He found himself predisposed toward it by feelings that recurred throughout his life, whenever his supply of hope ran low.

The background of the idea is lighted up by a passage in *The English Notebooks* discussing his reluctance to give the advice his position as American consul in Liverpool seemed to require him to give. "For myself," he wrote, "I had never been in the habit of feeling that I could sufficiently comprehend any particular conjunction of circumstances with human character, to justify me in thrusting in my awkward agency among the intricate and unintelligible machinery of Providence. . . . It is only one-eyed people who love to advise, or have any spontaneous promptitude of action."

Hawthorne believed in Providence even while he found it unintelligible. Confronted with the problem of evil in the form of diseased and suffering English children, he concluded a *Notebook* entry with "Ah, what a mystery!" But he trusted there was a higher purpose, a final meaning in a dark and bewildering world, even if we could not clearly *know* it. "Man's accidents are God's purposes."

Hawthorne in short was a theist who thought of himself as a Christian, but he was skeptical of all claims, whether Puritan or Roman Catholic, to know the details of the divine will. Brought up a Unitarian, he associated himself with no church at all, yet preferred Bunyan to the religious liberals of his day and impressed family and friends as a religious man. He and Melville talked often, and with full mutual understanding, of "final things," but where Melville, like his own Ahab, was compelled to try to strike through the mask of appearance, Hawthorne could better abide the not knowing.

Hawthorne's special mixture of skepticism and faith had much to do with the form of his art as well as his choice of themes. His clearest convictions tended to get expressed in allegory; his dimmer intimations, his hopes and fears, on the other hand, often found expression in tales more mythopoetic than allegorical, closer to modern symbolic fiction than to Bunyan. No

less honest and courageous than Melville, he had a different temperament. He found he could live in the darkness with only a little light. Whatever else Hawthorne was, he was not one-eyed. Out of his ironic vision and his sense of paradox came most of his finest work.

Since ours is an age that has found irony, ambiguity, and paradox to be central not only in literature but in life as well, it is not surprising that Hawthorne has seemed to us one of the most *modern* of nineteenth-century American writers. The bulk and general excellence of the great outburst of Hawthorne criticism of the past decades attest to his relevance for us. It requires no distortion of him to see him not only as foreshadowing Henry James in his concern for "the deeper psychology" but also as first cousin to Faulkner and Robert Penn Warren. In all the essentials, "My Kinsman, Major Molineux" is as "modern" a story as "The Bear." Hawthorne's themes, especially, link him with the writing and sensibility of our time.

Alienation is perhaps the theme he handles with greatest power. "Insulation," he sometimes called it—which suggests not only isolation but imperviousness. It is the opposite of that "osmosis of being" that Warren has written of, that ability to respond and relate to others and the world. Its causes are many and complex, its results simple: it puts one outside the "magic circle" or the "magnetic chain" of humanity, where there is neither love nor reality. It is Hawthorne's image of damnation. Reunion, often imaged by the hearth, is his redemptive cure. Anticipating Archibald MacLeish of *J.B.*, he would have his characters "blow on the coal of the heart." Not "knowing" or "using" but "meeting" others—to borrow Martin Buber's terms—would offer a way back into the magic circle to alienated Chillingworth, Ethan Brand, or Rappaccini.

Contemporary critics have shown an even greater interest in Hawthorne's treatment of initiation. Though he wrote only a few stories directly concerned with it, several of them are among his greatest and a number of others touch it tangentially. Stories as rich, yet controlled, in meaning as "My Kinsman" are rare in this or any language. Initiated into life's complexity in a dreamlike evening in a strange city, the young man of the story achieves a difficult maturity. But the protagonist of "Young Goodman Brown" is unable to understand or accept the evil revealed to him in the forest of the soul, loses faith in the reality of the good, and lives the rest of his long life in gloomy alienation. The young couple in "The Maypole of Merrymount" are granted a happier outcome, but Giovanni in "Rappaccini's Daughter" is, like Goodman Brown, unable to accept life's ambiguous mixture of good and evil and so cannot understand his Beatrice or gain the salvation her love would grant.

When such initiations as these have happy outcomes, as in "My Kinsman," we are tempted to see them primarily in psychological terms, as dramatizing the process of maturation. When the results are less happy, so that we have a sense chiefly of the cost of losing innocence, we are likely to read them as versions of the Fall, the myth of the expulsion from the Garden. The psychological and the theological readings are perhaps just different ways of looking at the same archetypal story.

Hawthorne at any rate refused to simplify guilt by reducing it either to merely subjective and irrational "guilt feeling" or to wholly objective and external "sin." He concerned himself instead with guilt feelings that have personal and social causes and cures that are objectively real, not merely subjective or irrational, and that imply the reality of moral obligation. His special way of maintaining the ambiguous connection between the psychological, the moral, and the religious is one of the principal reasons why his works seem to relevant to us.

Moral and religious concerns, in short, are almost always central in Hawthorne's work, but Hawthorne's interest in them is primarily subjective and psychological. But his subjectivism is never solipsistic and his psychologism never reductive. Rather, they are signs that his concern with matters moral and religious is existential. Like the Existentialist philosophers who articulate the sensibility of our time, Hawthorne is more concerned with the experienced toothache than with orthodontic theory. Like them he explores the nature of existential guilt, relating it to alienation, reunion, and commitment. Like them, too, he distrusts the claim of objective reason to be able to arrive at humanly relevant truth: his rationalistic "empiricists" all end unhappily.

We may call such attitudes romantic rather than existential if we wish. Existential philosophy begins with Kierkegaard, in the romantic movement; but Kierkegaard seems more relevant to many today than John Dewey. Romanticism at this depth is still with us, and perhaps always will be, now that unquestioning certainty about life's "essences" seems unlikely ever to return. Not to be existential in the sense in which Hawthorne was is either to be content with positivism or to assume as unquestionable a fixed and absolute order of truth.

But if the first thing we should notice about Hawthorne is his "modernity," his immediate relevance to us and our concerns, the second thing, if we are to avoid the distortion of seeing in him only our own image, is the way in which he is *not* one of us. It has been said that he was an eighteenth-century gentleman living in the nineteenth century, and the remark has enough truth in it to be useful to us at this point.

His style, for instance, though at its best a wonderfully effective instrument for the expression of his sensibility, is likely to strike us as not nearly so modern as Thoreau's. It was slightly old-fashioned even when he wrote it. It is very deliberate, with measured rhythms, marked by formal decorum. It is a public style and, as we might say, a "rhetorical" one—though of course all styles are rhetorical in one sense or another. It often prefers the abstract or generalized to the concrete or specific word. Compared to what the writers of handbooks, under the influence of modernist literature, have taught us to prefer—the private, informal, concrete, colloquial, imagistic—Hawthorne's style can only be called pre-modern.

But it is not only style in this narrow sense that marks Hawthorne as a nineteenth-century writer. Apart from that aspect of his writing that we may summarize under the general heading of his symbolism, his whole procedure as a fictionist is pre-modern—which is to say, pre-Flaubert and pre-James. He is one of the most regularly intrusive of intrusive authors. The basic rule of post-Jamesian fiction, reduced by handbook writers to a simple inviolable formula, has been "Don't tell, show!" Hawthorne both tells and shows—tells not simply in his characteristic final moral comment but all the way through.

Ethan Brand, for instance, seeing the absurdity of his situation, bursts into laughter. Hawthorne, having presented the image, then comments: "Laughter, when out of place, mistimed, or bursting forth from a disordered state of feeling, may be the most terrible modulation of the human voice." Hawthorne has lost something in immediacy, and gained something in meaning. Later in the story, in his summary of Brand's career, he does not "show" at all, he merely tells: "Thus Ethan Brand became a fiend. He began to be so from the moment that his moral nature had ceased to keep the pace of improvement with his intellect." "He had lost his hold of the magnetic chain of humanity."

In its insistence that the author never appear in his own pages, that the image alone do all the work, recent fiction has paralleled Imagist poetry. Hawthorne knows nothing of this. For him, fiction was a way of exploring life to find meaning. Not being post-Jamesian, he thought he had a right to bring out and underline the meanings his images revealed. The classic forms of fiction had always permitted this.

If Hawthorne had thought he needed any excuse for his intrusive comments, he might well have said what Faulkner once said of *his* writing, that he wrote "to uplift men's hearts . . . [to] say No to death." Hawthorne wants to strengthen and encourage man, to help him to live in a world in which the ways of Providence are mostly unintelligible.

Since Melville first detected the darkness in Hawthorne's work and praised him for saying No in thunder, a great many sensitive readers have found the dark Hawthorne more impressive than the light. But this is not the way Hawthorne wanted to be, these not the meanings he intended.

The problem is a complex one, but in part it may be somewhat simplified by making two distinctions, the first between the artist and the man, the second between two types of meaning in the art. Except in the sketches, Hawthorne the artist usually did his best writing when he wrote not of what he "believed," or wanted to believe, or thought he should believe, but of the "phantoms" that came unsought and "haunted" him. "The Haunted Mind" can give us the clue here. To the "passive sensibility" halfway between sleep and waking the spectral shapes of shame and death appear: when we get fully awake and the conscious mind takes control, they vanish. Much of Hawthorne's best writing comes out of the haunted mind.

But it is not pleasant or comfortable to be visited by such specters. Hawthorne had to live as a man as well as survive as an artist, and it may well be that one of the reasons he gave up writing short fiction after he had established himself as a writer is that so many of his best early tales *had* come from the depths of the mind—by a process he had no wish to repeat. Hawthorne's desire to be a well-adjusted "man of society" and his disinclination to reveal his inner life in public were in some degree in conflict with his desire to be an artist.

The distinction between the two types of meaning in his art takes us into an area somewhat less conjectural. The distinction I have in mind is that between intended and achieved meaning. Hawthorne hoped that *The Scarlet Letter* might have a happy ending, but the hope he expressed in his first chapter in connection with the rose blooming on the bush beside the prison—that it might lighten his dark tale—did not materialize, even for him. He resolved that his next novel would be a happier one.

The conflict here is only between the hope (or intention?—how consciously had Hawthorne thought out *The Scarlet Letter* before writing it?) of the man and the achievement of the artist. There is no conflict in the novel, of the type that weakens a work, between intended and achieved meanings. The novel is all of a piece, with a magnificent unity of meaning that emerges equally from what it says and what it shows. But *The House of the Seven Gables* is perhaps not so perfect, for this reason among others. It is almost equally difficult to suppose that the ending was intended to be ironic and for the modern reader to take it any other way. And *The Blithedale Romance* was probably intended to mean only that utopian communities will not succeed unless their members have a change of heart and that frosty old

bachelors like Coverdale need girls like Priscilla (or Sophia) to warm their hearts and give them hope. But what it actually means as a work of art is not so simply said, or so hopeful.

We may often, as we have seen, go to the sketches to find out the meanings Hawthorne *intended* to express in the fiction. In the sketches *belief* is generally in control, the phantoms that haunt the mind mostly absent; and Hawthorne's belief maintains a nice balance between the light and the dark. "Earth's Holocaust," for instance, tells us what Hawthorne must have intended to say on his theme of social reform in *Blithedale*. The sketch is one of Hawthorne's finest, and its structure is dramatic, so its meaning is not easily reduced to a brief summary. But a part of its meaning is this: reform is perennially needed, and we may well be grateful for many of the reforms of the past, but reform is superficial and impermanent unless it is accompanied by a change of heart. The source of evil is in the heart of man, not primarily in institutions. The devil laughs when man supposes that lasting progress toward the good can be brought about by merely external and social changes.

But if man's misguided efforts cause laughter in Hell, there is still hope, for if man will look deeper for the source of the evil he may find it. There is at any rate a guide for his efforts which he may use if he will. The attempt of the reformers to destroy the Bible as the climax of their enlightened reforms is unavailing. The fire, Hawthorne tells us, is powerless to consume it. Its pages even "assumed a more dazzling whiteness as the finger marks of human imperfection were purified away."

"Sunday at Home" maintains the same kind of balance between the light and the dark, negation and affirmation, that we find in "Earth's Holocaust." But since the language in which Hawthorne defines himself in the sketch as at once gentle skeptic and firm believer seems more dated than the language of the greater sketch, and since the meanings are less solidly embodied in dramatic images, "Sunday at Home" may reveal the balance Hawthorne intended to express better than the greater works do. It is more interesting as a piece of self-revelation than as a work of art.

Hawthorne begins by dissociating himself from the committed believers among his fellow townsmen. While they go to church, he stays at home and peeps at them through the window. He hears the bells but misses the sermon—and feels no loss. He finds aids to faith everywhere, not only in the sound of the bells. Even the sunshine seems to have a special "sabbath" quality about it. This last is no doubt an illusion, but such illusions, he believes, are often "shadows of great truths": Doubts may flit around me, or seem to close their evil wings, and settle down; but, so long as I imagine that the earth is hallowed, and the light of heaven retains its sanctity, on the Sabbath—while that blessed sunshine lives within me—never can my soul have lost the instinct of its faith. If it have gone astray, it will return again."

The ideas being expressed here may strike us at first as just as archaic as the language. Nineteenth-century "religion of the heart" offers as little appeal today to the orthodox as to the skeptical. But if we look again and note the meaning in the idea of a "hallowed" earth, we may find the notion not simply sentimental. To find the earth itself holy is to find the sources of religious faith in experience. The General Revelation—Nature—will then complement and reinforce the special, unique Revelation of Scripture. The idea is, we are likely to say too quickly, a romantic one; too quickly, because it is not only romantic but also Scriptural, as we may see in the Psalms.

The sketch is light in tone and does not pretend to any profundity, but it seems fair to say that Hawthorne is groping here toward a sacramental view of nature. He is no primitivist. He does not suppose that going "back to nature" will cure man's ills or automatically dispel all "evil" doubts. But he does think nature, as the handiwork of God, contains a general revelation of God's purposes and life's meaning, if we will only read it aright.

Religious faith, then, in this sketch, rests on our ability to experience the world in a certain way. And that way of experiencing is dependent on the imagination. When Hawthorne says "so long as I imagine that the earth is hallowed," he does not mean "so long as I pretend" or "so long as I make believe." He means that religion, like art, is visionary. This is the complement to his acknowledgment, in "Earth's Holocaust" and elsewhere, of the authority of a "purified" Scriptural revelation.

"Sunday at Home" maintains the kind of balance Hawthorne always wanted to keep and affirms the light in a way quite typical of him. It reveals a side of Hawthorne that Melville missed—or was not interested in—when he hailed the nay-sayer.

Writing in 1842 to the editor of *Sargent's New Monthly Magazine* about a sketch he hoped to place there, Hawthorne made a statement that, while it applies directly to the piece he had in mind, applies also, less directly and not intentionally, to all his fiction. "Whether it have any interest," he wrote, "must depend entirely on the sort of view taken by the writer, and the mode of execution."

As an artist, Hawthorne knew that in art the question is less *what* than *how*, that in a very important, though probably not absolute and exclusive sense, manner is more important than matter, the "fact" unimportant until transformed by "vision." Though he did not normally choose to exercise his talent or test his vision on trifles, he always insisted that the artist's *way of seeing* his subject was the important thing.

This insistence was, of course, both a permanent truth in art and a reflection of the romantic aesthetic, in which the artist is always peculiarly central. Just as clearly, it reflects an idealistic metaphysic. Not the thing known but the knowing, not matter but mind, is the locus of reality for idealism. Here Hawthorne and Emerson agreed. Whether or not Hawthorne should be called a "transcendentalist" depends on how one uses the term—broadly, to point to all varieties of transcendental philosophy, or narrowly, to designate the Concord New Thought. If broadly, then Plato was one of the first transcendentalists, and perhaps the most important; and Hawthorne was a somewhat uneasy and qualified one, too. If narrowly, then Hawthorne was still in some respects a transcendentalist *malgré lui*, but it is important to remember that he thought of himself as not "tinged" with that radicalism.

In any case, however much he may have minimized, or been unaware of, his agreements with his neighbor Emerson, Hawthorne believed that not only the finished work of art but reality itself depended on "the sort of view taken" by artist or man. The best sort of view would, he thought, be that which provided *distance*—in time or space—so that the raw fact as such could not dominate, so that irrelevant multiplicity would be dimmed and softened by distance to allow the pattern, the meaning, to emerge. Long views were best, just *because* the viewer could not see the details so well.

In view of this conviction, it is not hard to see why the past was so useful to him. The past was not only his South Seas, where romance was, but his relevant truth. We may see the consequences of such an aesthetic credo clearly enough in *The Scarlet Letter*. It is not the fact of adultery itself that engages Hawthorne's interest. Adultery might mean anything or nothing. Let it occur before the novel opens and explore its consequences. In Hawthorne's view it was personal guilt, not sin abstractly defined, that was interesting. This was one of the differences between him and his Puritan ancestors.

Writing the novel, Hawthorne took pains to supply just enough verisimilitude to make it credible. But for the most part he was simply not deeply concerned with merely external reality—except as that reality, perceived as symbol, could take us into the interiors of hearts and minds. That is why writing that must be classified as expository and descriptive (as compared with narrative) bulks so large in the work.

"The Old Apple Dealer" does not have even *The Scarlet Letter*'s minimum of action, but it illuminates what Hawthorne was about in his greatest novel. As a sketch rather than a tale, it is purely descriptive and expository: in it nothing happens except to the speaker, who gains a recognition which alters his point of view. There is even a sense in which the sketch is not "about" anything—or rather, in which it is about "nothing." It is for this reason that any interest it may have must come, as Hawthorne explained to the editor of *Sargent's*, from something other than the intrinsic interest of the subject itself.

For the old apple dealer who will be described is, Hawthorne says in the sketch, a purely negative character, featureless, colorless, inactive, hardly alive apparently. He seems an embodiment of torpor, an instance of nonentity. Such a subject is a challenge to the artist, and Hawthorne opens his sketch with a confession of his difficulty. How could one make interesting, or even imaginatively real, a subject intrinsically colorless and featureless?

Hawthorne is not sure he can succeed, but he will try, for the very insignificance of the old man gives him a special kind of interest. "The lover of the moral picturesque may sometimes find what he seeks in a character which is nevertheless of too negative a description to be seized upon and represented to the imaginative vision by word painting."

That Hawthorne had indeed found in the old apple dealer what he sought as a lover of the "moral picturesque" is attested by the success of the sketch. For the subject allows Hawthorne to do several things at once. From one point of view, the sketch is about man's nothingness, and the significant qualification of that nothingness. From another, it is about the difficulties, opportunities, and dangers of the artist.

By the end, the difficulties have become opportunities—though Hawthorne does not claim so much—but the dangers remain. Against them Hawthorne issues a final warning that unites the two "subjects" of the sketch, art and life—issues it to himself most clearly, but to all artists by implication. The language of the ending is explicitly religious, but the aesthetic implications of it are clear enough.

Hawthorne had begun his sketch by telling us that without his subject's being aware of his scrutiny, he has "studied the old apple dealer until he has become a naturalized citizen of my inner world." Since what interests one in this "featureless" man is the perfection of his insignificance, if he is to come alive for readers, the artist will have to give him life. By what James would later call "the alchemy of art" he will be brought into being.

Power so great as this brings with it great danger. Hawthorne's metaphor for art in the sketch is witchcraft. Was art a kind of black magic? If the artist can legitimately claim his literary creations as entirely his own, may he not as man similarly conceive of other people

as created—and perhaps controlled—by his knowing them? But if we think of other people as objects to be studied and manipulated, as Chillingworth thought of Dimmesdale and Ethan Brand thought of the subjects of his moral experiment, we shall be totally shut out from the saving realities of life. The fate to which the artist, like the scientist, Hawthorne felt, was peculiarly liable was alienation.

The assumption of Godlike knowledge could destroy artist and man equally. Knowledge brings with it the possibility of control, and the artist must achieve control of his subject by controlling his medium; but he will falsify reality if he omits the element of mystery and assumes that he knows the unknowable. One error, then, to which the artist is peculiarly liable, threatens both artist and man. But to see how Hawthorne prepares us to accept his conclusion, which tests art by life's standards and sees life through the eyes of the artist, we must return to Hawthorne's way of bringing the old apple dealer to life in his pages.

Early in the sketch Hawthorne decides that with so negative a subject the only way to describe him is to use negative comparisons, to tell us what he is *not* like. Perhaps in this way he will be able to get at the paradox of a man who seemed completely inactive and stationary, yet whose immobility was composed of continuous minor, almost undetectible, movements. (So "stationary" a man will never "go ahead," never join in "the world's exulting progress.") Then the inspiration comes: what he is most of all *not* like is the steam engine that roars at intervals through the station where the old man sits so quietly. "I have him now. He and the steam fiend are each other's antipodes. . . ."

"I have him now." By using contrast the artist has succeeded in conveying to us what he had almost despaired of conveying, the reality of a person who is almost nothing. But as soon as it is made, the claim seems excessive: Hawthorne does not finally "know" the old man at all, nor do we. For he has omitted something from his description, something all-important that he has no way of getting at—the soul. In a superficial sense he has succeeded: insofar as the old man is merely viewed, merely scrutinized, he is a torpid machine in perfect contrast to the active, "progressive" machine. But there is a deeper contrast involved than mere activity or lack of it, and here the artist must confess the limits of his art. "Could I read but a tithe of what is written . . . [in the old man's "mind and heart"] it would be a volume of deeper and more comprehensive import than all that the wisest mortals have given to the world; for the soundless depths of the human soul and of eternity have an opening through your breast. God be praised. . . ."

So in the end Hawthorne makes his last confession: whatever his success in describing the old man behavioristically, he did *not* "have" him when he compared him, the stationary machine, to the steam engine, the active machine. Man cannot be fully known in the way we know a machine. This is the deeper sense in which the old man is the antipodes of the engine. To confuse the two is the ultimate error, for both artist and man.

"The Old Apple Dealer" emphasizes the creativity of the artist and the danger such creativity brings with it. The danger is partly that the artist will suppose that he *knows* more than he can possibly know. "Night Sketches: Beneath an Umbrella" dramatizes the danger of the artist's becoming so isolated from reality that his art will be a sort of daydream. Considered together, the two pieces imply that art is both a kind of knowledge—which must never pretend to finality, never lose its sense of mys-

tery—and a kind of dream—which must keep in touch with reality. Art is more like myth than like document, but there are true myths and false myths, and art had better be true.

"Beneath an Umbrella" opens with a long paragraph devoted to describing the pleasures of the unrestricted imagination as it takes one on imaginary travels to exotic lands. "Pleasant is a rainy winter's day, within doors!" the speaker exclaims at the beginning, going on to explain that the "sombre" condition of the world outside the chamber window makes the exercise of unrestrained fancy all the more delightful by contrast. The warm, well-lighted chamber contains the whole world, so long as imagination is active.

Nevertheless, pleasant as daydreaming is, reality *will* break in: "the rain-drops will occasionally be heard to patter against my window panes. . . ." As nightfall approaches, "the visions vanish, and will not come again at my bidding." Irresponsible dreaming, it would seem, finally ceases to be even pleasurable: "Then, it being nightfall, a gloomy sense of unreality depresses my spirits, and impels me to venture out, before the clock shall strike bedtime, to satisfy myself that the world is not entirely made up of such shadowy materials as have busied me throughout the day. A dreamer may dwell so long among fantasies, that the things without him will seem as unreal as those within."

About to step outside, the speaker pauses to "contrast the warmth and cheerfulness of my deserted fireside with the drear obscurity and chill discomfort" into which he is about to "plunge." The contrast contains, it becomes clear as the sketch goes on, nearly all of Hawthorne's favorite antinomies: the light and the dark; warmth and coldness, in the human heart as well as externally; faith and doubt; even, implicitly, the heart and the head, if we see here the meanings Hawthorne constantly implies elsewhere when he uses hearth and chamber as heart images. The sketch is rich in meaning. It contains, indeed, in epitome nearly all the central issues of Hawthorne's moral and religious thought, and it significantly illuminates a side of his aesthetic thinking it is easy to overlook.

On the doorstep now, the speaker asks the reader to pardon him if he has "a few misgivings." He is, he thinks, entitled to them, our "poor human nature" being what it is. And in view of what is about to be revealed about reality outside the chamber, the world of fact, as contrasted with the world of feeling and dream he is leaving, we find the misgivings justified. For once he is really outside, he finds himself confronted by "a black, impenetrable nothingness, as though heaven and all its lights were blotted from the system of the universe. It is as if Nature were dead. . . ."

A "dead" Nature was, of course, the specter conjured up by nineteenth-century naturalism, the conception of a purposeless, valueless, colorless world, a "charnel house" world, faced by Ishmael at the end of the chapter on the whiteness of the whale in *Moby Dick*. Melville, we have long known, stared in fascinated horror at this vision of an "alien universe," stared at it more fixedly and with greater philosophic rigor than Hawthorne did. But one of the uses of this sketch is to remind us that Hawthorne was very much aware of what Melville was looking at, even though both his way of looking and what he finally saw were different from Melville's.

Here, for instance, the speaker, though at first plunged into a Slough of Despond, soon finds that there are various kinds of lights in what had at first seemed an unbroken darkness. Some of the lights are deceptive or illusory, especially if they are so bright that they seem utterly to dispel the darkness, but others are real and trustworthy. As the speaker continues his "plunge into the night," he discovers a way of distinguishing the false lights from the true: any light which makes men "forget the impenetrable obscurity that hems them in, and that can be dispelled only by radiance from above," is certain to be illusory.

Like Wallace Stevens a century later, who proposed to create a "skeptical music," Hawthorne is talking here at once about art and about life. He is proposing a life test for art's truth, without at all suggesting that the artist should abdicate, leaving "fact" and Nature in control. The internal world, the chamber of the heart where imagination operates freely, the world of dream, is the peculiar realm of the artist, and Hawthorne returns to it after his excursion into an apparently meaningless external reality has served its purpose. But the internal world is embedded in an external world, which it may ignore only at its peril. The imagination must remain responsible, even while it guards its freedom. No mere daydreaming will do. The romancer, Hawthorne wrote of himself elsewhere, need not aim at "a very minute fidelity" to history and nature, but he "sins unpardonably" if he violates "the truth of the human heart."

Irresponsible daydream, responsible imagination, fact without meaning, or even destructive of meaning—all are present and played against each other in this sketch. The center of Hawthorne's interest is, to be sure, elsewhere, in the moral and religious meanings which, with his usual emphasis, he makes explicit at the end. (Having encountered a figure with a lantern that casts its light in a "circular pattern," Hawthorne concludes, "This figure shall supply me with a moral . . . thus we, night wanderers through a stormy and dismal world, if we bear the lamp of Faith, enkindled at a celestial fire, it will surely lead us home to that heaven whence its radiance was borrowed.")

But the aesthetic meanings are here, too, implicitly. No overreading is required to see them. It was as a "dreamer," with insufficient experience of the world, Hawthorne says several times elsewhere, that he produced his tales and sketches during his apprentice years. But even while he dreamed and created, he was dissatisfied with dreaming. He wanted to test his dreams against a reality he could not control, to determine their truth.

When, in the preface to *The House of the Seven Gables*, Hawthorne made his famous distinction between the novel and the romance, he was not at all intending to assign "truth" to the novel and mere "fantasy," or escapist dreaming, to the romance. He was distinguishing between "fact" (which the novel deals with) and "truth" (which is the province of the romance), and at the same time suggesting an orientation in which "fact" is external and "truth" internal. So far as he was defending, implicitly, the validity of his own practice as a romancer, he was implying a "mere" before "fact." (He was ambivalent about this, as he so often was on other matters, to be sure. He thought Emerson *too* idealistic, and he greatly admired the "beef and ale" realism of Trollope.)

The romantic artist creates, Hawthorne thought, by transforming fact into symbol, that is, into *meaningful* fact. Facts that he cannot see as meaningful may be disregarded. He is at liberty to manipulate his materials, to shape them freely into meaningful patterns, so long as he does not violate the truth of the human heart. Hawthorne felt that he himself could pursue his desired truth best by a combination of looking within and exercising the kind of imaginative sympathy that had been both his subject and his method in "The Old Apple Dealer." In a very suggestive metaphor in the preface to *The Snow-Image and Other Twice-Told Tales* in 1851, he defined his role as artist as that of "a person, who has been burrowing, to his utmost ability, into the depths of our common nature, for the purposes of psychological romance—and who pursues his researches in that dusky region, as he needs must, as well by the tact of sympathy as by the light of observation. . . ."

After 1850 Hawthorne wrote no more tales or sketches and consistently belittled the ones he had written. He wondered, once, what he had ever meant by these "blasted allegories." Yet several of his earliest tales are among his best. "My Kinsman, Major Molineux," first printed in 1832, is surely one of the finest short stories in the language. Again and again in recent years critics have turned back to it and found new meanings—and no wonder, for its images are archetypal.

The vehicle for its themes is the journey from country to city, from simplicity and innocence to complexity and experience. Young Robin makes the journey to enlist the aid of a powerful kinsman, who will, he hopes, help him to "rise in the world." Armed only with a club, his innocence, and his native shrewdness, he is mysteriously baffled in his search for Major Molineux. He finds the city a bewildering and threatening place. Everything is ambiguous. Cruelty appears in the guise of patriotism and lust calls out in a "sweet voice" that seems to speak "Gospel truth." Symbols of authority have no power and epiphanies of meaning go unrecognized. To those already initiated, he is the object of ridicule, but he cannot discover the reason for the laughter that follows him through the streets as though he were having a bad dream.

When he finally rests beside a church after his long "evening of ambiguity and weariness," he sees, inside, a Bible illuminated by a ray of moonlight. He has remembered his father in their country home "holding the Scriptures in the golden light that fell from the western clouds." Nature and Scripture, General and Special Revelation, are united here, Hawthorne suggests, in presenting a way out of Robin's impasse. But Robin himself does not make the connection. Fortunately, a kindly stranger appears at this point, offers helpful advice, and finally tells Robin that "perhaps, as you are a shrewd youth, you may rise in the world without the help of your kinsman, Major Molineux." But this hope is offered only after Robin has taken his place in mankind's brotherhood in guilt by joining in the mob's ridicule of his Tory kinsman, thus repudiating the father-figure.

The reader feels that Robin may indeed rise, though not by means of his club, his innocence, or his shrewdness. His club has of course only made him ridiculous: one does not force one's way through moral and psychological initiations. His innocence is more fancied than real. Of it one might say what Hawthorne wrote in "Fancy's Show Box," that "Man must not disclaim his brotherhood, even with the guiltiest. . . . Penitence must kneel." His shrewdness, if it is without love, can only alienate him, as a merely intellectual development made Ethan Brand lose his hold of "the magnetic chain of humanity." The kindly stranger is being gently ironic when he refers to Robin's shrewdness.

The ultimate reason why Robin's shrewdness is not enough for him to rely on is that man, as Hawthorne made clear in "The Old Apple Dealer," is not a machine. He has a soul. He therefore cannot be understood, Hawthorne believes, by empirical reason or observation alone. At the very center of his being there is a mystery, which will always remain a mystery, never be "solved," for, in Gabriel Marcel's terms, it is a mystery and not a problem. In the last analysis, what baffled Robin in his quest, before the kindly stranger came to his aid, is the same thing that made Hawthorne confess failure in his effort wholly to capture in words the essence of the old apple dealer.

The moonlit Bible in the church in "My Kinsman" may be related to the man with the lantern and to the "radiance from above" in "Beneath an Umbrella." The tin lantern is an analogue of the "lamp of Faith" which will lead us home to heaven just because its radiance is not of our creation but "borrowed" from heaven itself. There are two tests, apparently, for the validity of the various lights that appear in a dark world, their source and their effect. About the test by effect, Hawthorne is explicit: if a light is bright enough to seem to make the darkness disappear entirely, it is false—its effect depends upon a bedazzling of the eyes. The test by source he leaves to implication in his conclusion, but the implication is clear enough. The stranger's light will lead him home to his fireside because it was kindled there. "Just so" our faith will lead us back to its source. The light cast by the fire on the family hearth is our best analogue of the supernatural light that must guide us to an ultimate home. It images the light that art cannot picture more directly.

The sketch and the story reinforce each other on this matter. If Robin is not to become another Goodman Brown, overwhelmed by the discovery of evil, he must salvage something of his childhood faith. The vision of the moonlit Bible in the church and the appearance of the stranger who comes to his aid combine to suggest that he will do so once he ceases to rely solely on himself to save himself—on his innocence, his strength, and his shrewdness. Justification by faith, not by works, is implied —by a mature faith, a tested and tried faith that does not deny the darkness or ignore the complexity of the world.

If Robin's adventures in town had ended before he arrived at the church and met the friendly stranger, his story would have been one of simple loss with no compensating gain —a fall with no rise, an initiation into evil with no accompanying redefinition of the good. But Robin at the end has not been destroyed by the loss of his innocence. Indeed, he seems to be better for it.

Could his case be taken as a paradigm for mankind? Could the Fall of Man be conceived as fortunate? On the whole, most of the time, Hawthorne thought so; or at least hoped so. But part of the time he could not summon so much hope. And he was aware of dangers involved in pursuing a line of thought that might seem to suggest that sin was beneficial. Taking as instructive myth what his ancestors had taken as literary history, he turned the subject around and around, examining it from every angle.

Of his four completed novels, only the last treats the subject directly. *The Marble Faun* is Hawthorne's theological novel. But *The Blithedale Romance* explicitly examines the possibility of undoing the Fall, and *The House of the Seven Gables* retells the story as enacted by a family over generations. Only *The Scarlet Letter* is not concerned with it. It simply assumes it. But even it adumbrates the familiar pattern: a clear fall into sin, followed by an ambiguous rise.

The Scarlet Letter is the perfect expression of what Roy Male has called "Hawthorne's tragic vision." There is light in this story as well as darkness, clarity as well as ambiguity —a symbolic rose in the first chapter as well as a cemetery and a prison. But the "radiance from above" never reaches the center of the action to save, to rescue, to guide home. The saintly Mr. Wilson walks by the scaffold carrying a lantern like that carried by the man of faith in "Beneath an Umbrella," but the light he sheds about him has no such effect on Dimmesdale as the stranger's light has on the

speaker in the sketch. Hester's dark glossy hair shines in the sunlight as though it were surmounted by a halo, making her almost an image of "the divine maternity"; but the Puritans look at her only as an adulteress, and the reader is likely to feel that she is only a suffering woman. Though the novel shows us good coming out of evil, it shows it coming only at a tragic cost.

Hester, the "woman taken in adultery," rises to saintliness as she becomes an "angel of mercy" to the community, but her dreams of a new order of society can find no expression in her life and resignation is all she has to take the place of happiness. Few of us would envy her "rise." Or Dimmesdale's. In a novel constructed of ironic reversals, the apparently saintly minister first falls into a life of utter falsehood, then finally—too late, too late— rises toward integrity and truth until, in the final scaffold scene, the allusions to the death of Christ on the cross seem not wholly ironic. But there is no joy for Dimmesdale either, any more than there is for Hester. And though his faith is always assumed, it seems to have as its only consequence an intensification of his feeling of guilt. He is first cousin to Roderick Elliston in "Egotism," the man with the snake in his stomach, so tormented by his morbid symptoms that he cannot forget himself.

The novel ends in a kind of gloomy Good Friday. The minister accepts the justice of his crucifixion, blesses his persecutors, and warns Hester not to expect fulfillment of their love in another life. The faith that earlier had chiefly served to increase his torment, now seems to afford him little basis for hope that his life has not been wasted. The light that feebly penetrates the gloom of the ending is of uncertain source—not from the hearth, certainly, and only obscurely "from above." The tombstone that serves the two graves of lovers separated in death as they were in life is lit "only by one ever-glowing point of light gloomier than the shadow." And what the dark light reveals as it strikes the words on the stone is the ambiguity not only of Hester's symbolic *A* (adulteress? angel?) but of the still dominant colors, red and black.

The red has been associated with nature and life and beauty—the rose beside the prison, Hester's vivid coloring, her beautiful needlework—but also with sin. Black has been associated with both sin and death—the prison and the cemetery. Hester and Arthur have not been able to escape the consequences of their past. There is very little here to relieve what Hawthorne calls in his first chapter "the darkening close of a tale of human frailty and sorrow." No wonder he resolved to make his next novel a happier one.

The chief problem facing the critic of *The House of the Seven Gables* today is presented precisely by his happy ending. Almost all modern readers have found it unconvincing, for a number of reasons. Phoebe and Holgrave fall in love, for one thing, rather abruptly. We see too little of them as lovers to believe fully in the reality of their love, and so in its redemptive power, as we must if we are to find Hawthorne's theme fully achieved. Then, too, we may have trouble believing in their love because we have trouble believing in *them*. The portrayal of Phoebe is likely to strike us as a little sentimental: she moves too quickly from being an attractive country girl to being a symbol of Grace. Holgrave is better. Certainly he is very interesting theoretically as a portrait of the young American, pragmatic, oriented toward the future, full of energy and boundless hope, confident that he can control his destiny, a self-reliant secular utopian in effect. Yet for most readers he seems to have proved more interesting as a symbol than convincing as a character.

The marriage of Phoebe and Holgrave is the symbolic union of heart and head. Hawthorne associates the conservatism of the heart not only with the feminine but with both Nature and Grace. The ringlets of Phoebe's shining hair and the curves of her figure are related to the cycles of Nature's annual death and renewal exhibited in the elm that overshadows the house. The radicalism of the head, of reason, that leads Holgrave to expect uninterrupted progress, is associated equally with the fact of decline and the dream of easy progress without suffering. Rejecting the paradox of life through death suggested by the flowers growing in an angle of the rotting roof, rationalism oversimplifies history in its reading of both past and future. For all his "futurism," Holgrave is in a sense more closely linked to the past than Phoebe is, for without her influence he would perpetuate the very errors that led to the long Pyncheon decline.

The Pyncheons have lived by the merely reasonable standards of a secular morality. For the sake of the world's goods, power and money, they have violated the heart's higher laws. The result has been self-defeating. Living by reason alone, they have planned and schemed shrewdly, but time and nature have defeated them. Clifford's mind is ruined and the dead judge sitting in the dark chamber will never execute his plans. Though he is at first morally neutral, Holgrave falsifies history, which is better expressed by images of circles than by straight lines, whether the lines are pictured as pointing downward or upward, suggesting uninterrupted decline or uninterrupted progress. He might have learned his lesson from the ancient elm, if he had been more sensitive to its meanings, as earlier Pyncheons might have learned the same lesson from "Alice's posies," but it takes his love for Phoebe to teach him what Clifford intuitively knows, that history neither endlessly repeats itself nor marches straight onward from novelty to novelty, but moves in an "ascending spiral curve."

But the heart can read such revelations, provided equally by Nature and Scripture, better than the mind, so it is not surprising that this first cousin to idealistic Aylmer and empirical Giovanni should need Phoebe to teach him. That he is so quickly taught is the surprising thing. One of the reasons the ending strikes the reader as unconvincing is that Holgrave puts up so little resistance to Phoebe's truths. The escape from the house and what it has stood for seems at last too easy.

What Hawthorne *meant* to suggest by his ending, though, is pretty clear, whether it works with us or not. The basic pattern is one of life, death, and resurrection or renewal. Within this cyclical pattern love acts redemptively, but not in the sense of removing one from the downward phase of the cycle. If love has its way, the inherited fortune and the fine new house in the suburbs will not bring about a pointless repetition of tragic Pyncheon history. We may legitimately hope that the circles of history include an upward movement to form a "spiral curve."

Just how difficult Hawthorne found it to maintain even so chastened a hope becomes apparent in his next novel. *The Blithedale Romance* assumes the Fall of Man and examines the hope of undoing it, of returning to an unspoiled Eden or Arcadia by creating a pilot model of a better world. Blithedale is a socialistic colony in which the conditions that have prevailed since the Fall should prevail no more. It aspires to be a true community in which men will work together for the common good. The law of love will be put into effect in a practical way for perhaps the first time in human history. Man will no longer be shut in the prison of self.

But the project does not work out that way. This is Hawthorne's most hopeless novel. *The Scarlet Letter* was tragic, but this is simply cold. Coverdale, the narrator, is glad that he *once* hoped for a better world, but since experience has destroyed the hope, in effect he is saying that innocence is a happy state while it lasts, before the plunge into experience destroys it. The colonists at Blithedale were not united for the common good. Instead, each used the project for his own selfish purposes. Furthermore, the group as a whole found itself in a state of competition with the surrounding larger community. Not love and sharing and truth were dominant here but competition, mutual distrust, and masquerading.

Two patterns of imagery carry a great burden of the meaning in the novel, and both have the same effect thematically. Fire images suggest that warmth of the heart, that mutuality of hope that, if it could have been maintained (if indeed it was ever as real as it once seemed), *might* have made the venture succeed. But the great blazing fire on the hearth that warmed the hearts as well as the bodies of the colonists on the first night of Coverdale's stay burned out quickly: it was built merely of brushwood. Only ashes remain now, as Coverdale looks back at the experience, to remind him of generous hopes once entertained.

The other chief line of the dual image pattern is made up of various types of veils and disguises. As Hawthorne had said of Dimmesdale in *The Scarlet Letter* that at least one clear truth emerged from his complex and tragic story, "Be true! Be true!" so here he feels that if the colonists cannot "be true" with one another, cannot take off their several veils and disguises, there can be no real community. From the "Veiled Lady" of the opening chapter, who would *like* to take off her veil; to Coverdale, whose name suggests covering the valley of the heart and who spends much of his time observing people from behind a screen of leaves or window curtains; to Old Moodie, with the patch over his eye and his false name; to Westervelt, with his false teeth, and Zenobia, with her artificial flowers—all the chief characters are in some way masked. Until they take off their masks, revealing themselves to each other in love and truth, no such venture as theirs can succeed, Hawthorne implies. Since instead of unveiling themselves they masquerade throughout the novel, there is no real hope in their enterprise, generous and idealistic though it once seemed.

But of course if, as Hawthorne was to write later about the Civil War, "No human effort . . . has ever yet resulted according to the purpose of its projectors," then the venture was doomed from the start, whether or not the reformers managed to take off their veils. Hawthorne does not resolve this ambiguity, and it is one of the sources of our sense that this is his most hopeless novel. If we take the veils to mean only that which hides man from man, then there may be hope that a sufficient number of personal conversions may ultimately result in a better world: what no merely external changes can do, an inner change may effect. Utopianism may be mistaken, but individuals do change, and if enough of them change . . .

With this reading, the final meaning of the novel is not far from the meaning of "Earth's Holocaust." A better world required better people, a change in the *heart*: "unless they hit upon some method of purifying that foul cavern, forth from it will reissue all the shapes of wrong and misery—the same old shapes or worse ones—which they have taken such a vast deal of trouble to consume to ashes."

But perhaps what is ultimately veiled is an intolerable reality. If so, this "exploded scheme for beginning the life of Paradise anew," this

effort to reverse man's mythic history and undo the Fall, was doomed before it began, before Coverdale "plunged into the heart of the pitiless snow-storm, in quest of a better life." At times the "wintry snow-storm roaring in the chimney" at Blithedale seems more real to Coverdale than the "chill mockery of a fire" that is all his memory retains to keep hope alive. The outside darkness and cold may *be* reality, the brushwood fire itself a kind of veiling delusion, necessary if we are to have hope but nonetheless false.

Such a reading would make the meaning of the novel equivalent to what the meaning of "Beneath an Umbrella" would have been if the speaker had stopped just outside his door, with the discovery of a Nature seemingly dead, and had not gone on through the dark to find at last a true light. Dream and reality, the light and the darkness were, finally, not utterly at odds in the sketch. In the novel they may be. Neither Coverdale, at any rate, nor the reader, can quite dispose of the suspicion that they are.

By the time Hawthorne came, a few years later, to write his last completed novel, he was ready to confront directly the subject he had treated implicitly so often before. *The Marble Faun* is, as the dark mysterious Miriam says, "the story of the fall of man." In it Donatello, who has grown up in innocence in a kind of rural Eden or Arcadia, is, like Robin before him, introduced to sin in the city. Like Robin, too, who had joined in the cruel laughter of the mob, Donatello is corrupted by what he encounters among art students in Rome. He commits a murder, though his intentions are obscure and his provocation great. Like Robin, finally, he is matured by the experience, brought from an innocence that was only half human at best to a condition in which he shares mankind's nature and lot.

Was the fall, then, "fortunate"? Miriam poses the question and implies a hopeful answer:

" 'The story of the fall of man! Is it not repeated in our romance of Monte Beni? And may we follow the analogy yet further? Was that very sin—into which Adam precipitated himself and all his race,—was it the destined means by which, over a long pathway of toil and sorrow, we are to attain a higher, brighter, and profounder happiness, than our lost birthright gave?' "

We must suppose, I think, that Hawthorne intended his reader to answer Miriam's question in the affirmative and that he further intended this answer to be the largest meaning of his novel. But if this was his intention, he was only partially successful in embodying it. Hilda, the blond New England maiden, comes down from the tower of her spotless innocence, to be sure, to marry the coolly detached sculptor Kenyon, and he is presumably humanized by his love for her. But this union of heart and head is not much more convincing as a symbol of redemptive possibilities than the similar marriage of Phoebe and Holgrave in *The House of the Seven Gables*; and for the two chief actors in the plot—Kenyon and Hilda are onlookers, affected by what they see—there is no promise of happiness. Donatello, the archetypal man, ends in prison, isolated not only from Miriam but also from mankind by his sin. Only in some figurative or purely spiritual sense has he been drawn into Hawthorne's *brotherhood* of sin. And for Miriam, the most thoroughly created and felt character in the novel, there is even less assurance of happiness than Hawthorne granted Hester.

In short, though the intended meaning of the novel may be reasonably clear—a qualified affirmation, of the kind consistent with a tragic but not hopeless view of life—the achieved meaning is obscure. We end convinced of the loss of innocence, and of the present reality of the "long pathway of toil and sorrow," but the evidence that this pathway may lead to "a higher, brighter, and profounder happiness" falls far short of being convincing—to us, and, I suspect, to Hawthorne himself at this stage in his life.

The qualified happy ending of "My Kinsman" was much more convincing, and the ending of "Roger Malvin's Burial" is clearer. The meaning of the latter tale is comparable to what we may take to be the intended meaning in the novel, that suffering and sacrifice are the only means to redemptive reunion with God and man, but there is nothing in the tale, as there is in the novel, to make us doubt the validity of that meaning. In *The Marble Faun* Hawthorne leaned principally upon Hilda with her spotless heart to provide hope. She proved a weak reed.

Hawthorne has never been wholly out of favor since the publication of *The Scarlet Letter*, but in the half century following his death he seemed much more old-fashioned than he does now. In a period of literary realism his symbolic and allegorical fiction seemed to need defense: it was not clear that it was a valid way of writing. Even James patronized him and could generally think of no better way of praising the pieces he liked best than to call them "charming."

Both literary and philosophical and religious changes since James's day have made it quite unnecessary to apologize for or defend either Hawthorne's mode of writing or his vision. When he failed, as of course he often did, it was sometimes because he had, for the time being, succeeded too well in becoming the "man of society" he always wanted to be— had too successfully adjusted himself to his age, come to share both its mode of feeling and its opinions too uncritically. His blond maidens are a case in point. Reflecting the mid-century idealization of woman and wholly inconsistent with his own otherwise persistent and consistent idea of mankind's brotherhood in guilt, they remain, fortunately, on the fringes of the action in *The Scarlet Letter* but weaken *The House of the Seven Gables* when they move into center in the person of Phoebe.

But even his failures are more interesting than most writers' successes. His probings into the nature and consequences of guilt and alienation sometimes struck earlier generations as morbid, but we have been prepared to understand them by Camus and Sartre and Kafka. His explorations of the possibilities of redemptive reunion need no defense in an age when philosophers have popularized the term *engagement*.

The scene in *The House of the Seven Gables* when Clifford attempts to join the procession in the street by jumping through the arched window suggests both Existential philosophy and antirealist fictional practice. Hawthorne's terms *head* and *heart* may sound a little old-fashioned, but his constant implication that the realities they stand for must interpenetrate and balance each other is as modern as psychoanalysis. His characteristic way of treating moral matters with the kind of ambiguity that makes both the psychological and the moral or religious perspectives on them relevant, the two perspectives quite distinct yet neither canceling the other, is likely to seem a major virtue to an age determined to assert the reality of man's freedom and responsibility, yet almost overwhelmingly conscious of the mechanisms of conditioning.

We are prepared today even for his special blend and alternation of light and darkness. Tillich and the religious Existentialists have taught us enough about the dynamics of faith to enable us to respond naturally to a writer who explored the darkness to the very limits of the town searching for a trustworthy light. Few nineteenth-century American writers today seem so likely to reward rereading as Hawthorne.

Selected Bibliography

WORKS OF NATHANIEL HAWTHORNE

Hawthorne's novels are available in the Scholarly Centenary Edition being brought out by the Ohio State University Press, edited by William Charvat, Roy H. Pearce, and others. The standard complete editions are the Riverside Edition, 12 vols. (Boston: Houghton Mifflin, 1883), and the Old Manse Edition, 22 vols. (1904).

Fanshawe. Boston: Marsh and Capen, 1828.
Twice-Told Tales. Boston: American Stationers Co., 1837. (Second series, Boston: James Monroe, 1842).
Mosses from an Old Manse. New York: Wiley and Putnam, 1846.
The Scarlet Letter. Boston: Ticknor, Reed and Fields, 1850.
The House of the Seven Gables. Boston: Ticknor, Reed and Fields, 1851.
The Snow-Image and Other Twice-Told Tales. Boston: Ticknor, Reed and Fields, 1851.
The Blithedale Romance. Boston: Ticknor, Reed and Fields, 1852.
The Life of Franklin Pierce. Boston: Ticknor, Reed and Fields, 1852.
A Wonder-Book for Girls and Boys. Boston: Ticknor, Reed and Fields, 1852.
Tanglewood Tales for Girls and Boys. Boston: Ticknor, Reed and Fields, 1853.
The Marble Faun. Boston: Ticknor and Fields, 1860.
Our Old Home. Boston: Ticknor and Fields, 1863.
Passages from the American Note-Books, edited by Sophia Hawthorne. Boston: Ticknor and Fields, 1868. (*The American Notebooks,* edited by Randall Stewart. New Haven: Yale University Press, 1932.)

Passages from the English Note-Books, edited by Sophia Hawthorne. Boston: Fields, Osgood, 1870. (*The English Notebooks*, edited by Randall Stewart. New York: Modern Language Association, 1941.)

Dr. Grimshawe's Secret, edited by Julian Hawthorne. Boston: Osgood, 1883. (*Hawthorne's Dr. Grimshawe's Secret*, edited by Edward H. Davidson. Cambridge, Mass.: Harvard University Press, 1954.)

Hawthorne as Editor: Selections from His Writings in the American Magazine of Useful and Entertaining Knowledge, edited by Arlin Turner. Baton Rouge: Louisiana State University Press, 1941.

BIBLIOGRAPHIES

American Literary Scholarship: An Annual, edited by James Woodress, 1962–68; edited by J. Albert Robbins, 1969—. Durham, N.C.: Duke University Press.

Browne, Nina E. *A Bibliography of Nathaniel Hawthorne*. Boston: Houghton, Mifflin, 1905.

Cathcart, Wallace H. *Bibliography of the Works of Nathaniel Hawthorne*. Cleveland: Rowfant Club, 1905.

Fogle, R. H. Bibliography in *Hawthorne's Fiction: The Light and the Dark*. Norman: University of Oklahoma Press, 1952. (The bibliography at the back of this book is the best available for literary critical purposes.)

Gross, Seymour L. *A "Scarlet Letter" Handbook*. San Francisco: Wadsworth, 1960. (A full and well-selected bibliography on this novel.)

Woodress, James, ed. *Eight American Authors*. Rev. ed. New York: Norton, 1971.

CRITICAL AND BIOGRAPHICAL STUDIES

Arvin, Newton. *Hawthorne*. Boston: Little, Brown, 1929.

Bridge, Horatio. *Personal Recollections of Nathaniel Hawthorne*. New York: Harper, 1893.

Crews, Frederick C. *The Sins of the Fathers: Hawthorne's Psychological Themes*. New York: Oxford University Press, 1966.

Fogle, Richard H. *Hawthorne's Fiction: The Light and the Dark*. Norman: University of Oklahoma Press, 1952

Hawthorne, Julian. *Nathaniel Hawthorne and His Wife*. Boston: Osgood, 1885.

————. *Hawthorne and His Circle*. New York: Harper, 1903.

Hoeltje, Hubert H. *Inward Sky: The Mind and Heart of Nathaniel Hawthorne*. Durham, N.C.: Duke University Press, 1962.

James, Henry. *Hawthorne*. London: Macmillan, 1879.

Lathrop, G. P. *A Study of Hawthorne*. Boston: Osgood, 1876.

Lathrop, Rose Hawthorne. *Memories of Hawthorne*. Boston: Houghton Mifflin, 1897.

Loggins, Vernon. *The Hawthornes: The Story of Seven Generations of an American Family*. New York: Columbia University Press, 1951.

Male, Roy R. *Hawthorne's Tragic Vision*. Austin: University of Texas Press, 1957.

Pearce, R. H., ed. *Hawthorne Centenary Essays*. Columbus: Ohio State University Press, 1964.

Stewart, Randall. *Nathaniel Hawthorne: A Biography*. New Haven: Yale University Press, 1948.

Turner, Arlin. *Nathaniel Hawthorne: An Introduction and Interpretation*. New York: Barnes and Noble, 1961.

Van Doren, Mark. *Nathaniel Hawthorne: A Critical Biography*. New York: William Sloane Associates, 1949.

Wagenknecht, Edward. *Nathaniel Hawthorne: Man and Writer*. New York: Oxford University Press, 1961.

Waggoner, Hyatt H. *Hawthorne: A Critical Study*. Cambridge, Mass.: Harvard University Press, 1955.

BOOKS CONTAINING CHAPTERS ON HAWTHORNE

Bewley, Marius. *The Complex Fate*. London: Chatto and Windus, 1952.

————. *The Eccentric Design: Form in the Classic American Novel*. New York: Columbia University Press, 1959.

Feidelson, Charles, Jr. *Symbolism and American Literature*. Chicago: University of Chicago Press, 1953.

Hoffman, Daniel G. *Form and Fable in American Fiction*. New York: Oxford University Press, 1961.

Levin, Harry. *The Power of Blackness: Hawthorne, Poe, Melville*. New York: Knopf, 1958.

Lewis, R. W. B. *The American Adam: Innocence, Tragedy, and Tradition in the Nineteenth Century*. Chicago: University of Chicago Press, 1955.

Matthiessen, F. O. *American Renaissance*. New York: Oxford University Press, 1941.

Stewart, Randall. *American Literature and Christian Doctrine*. Baton Rouge: Louisana State University Press, 1958.

Warren, Austin. *Rage for Order*. Chicago: University of Chicago Press, 1948.

Winters, Yvor. *In Defense of Reason*. New York: Swallow Press and Morrow, 1947.

—*HYATT H. WAGGONER*

Ernest Hemingway

1899-1961

DURING his lifetime Ernest Hemingway was very probably America's most famous writer. His style, his "hero" (that is to say, the protagonists of many of his works, who so resemble each other that we have come to speak of them in the singular), his manner and attitudes have been very widely recognized—not just in the English-speaking world but wherever books are widely read. It may be that no other novelist has had an equivalent influence on the prose of modern fiction, for where his work is known it has been used: imitated, reworked, or assimilated. In addition he had an extraordinary reputation as a colorful human being, and for over thirty years his every escapade was duly reported in the press. But for a long time neither he nor his work was well understood, and despite a considerable growth in understanding during the last decade, neither is yet understood as well as it might be.

There is never a simple key to any writer worth much attention, but in the case of Hemingway there is something that looks so like a key—even conceivably a master key—that it cannot escape any informed and thoughtful reader's notice. It lies waiting, curiously (a few might say fatefully), in the very first story in his first book of short stories, which was his first significant book of any kind.

The book appeared in Paris in 1924, was expanded in its American publication in 1925, and is called *In Our Time*. Very probably the author intended his title as a sardonic allusion to a well-known phrase from the Church of England's Book of Common Prayer: "Give peace in our time, O Lord." At any rate the most striking thing about the volume is that there is no peace at all in the stories. The next most striking thing about them (long unremarked, since it was not clear to readers that he was the central figure in the stories in which he appears) is that half of the stories are devoted to the spotty but careful development of a crucial character—a boy, then a young man—named Nick Adams. These stories are roughly arranged in the chronological order of Nick's boyhood and early manhood, and are intimately related, one to another. Indeed in this aspect the book is almost a "novel," for some of the stories are incomprehensible if one does not see the point, and it is often subtle, of some earlier piece.

The most significant and interesting of these stories, however, is that first one. It is called "Indian Camp," and it reveals a great deal about what its author was up to for some thirty-five years of his writing career. It tells about a doctor, Nick's father, who delivers an Indian woman's baby by Caesarean section, with a jackknife and without anesthesia. The woman's invalid husband lies in a bunk above his screaming wife; Nick, a young boy, holds a basin for his father; four men hold the mother down until the child is born. When it is over the doctor looks in the bunk above and discovers that the husband, who has listened to the screaming for two days, has cut his head nearly off with a razor.

A careful reading of this story will show that Hemingway is not primarily interested, here, in these shocking events: he is interested in their effect on the little boy who witnessed them. For the moment the events do not seem to *have* any great effect on the boy. But it is very important that he is later on a badly scarred and nervous young man, and here Hemingway is relating to us the first reason he gives why that is so.

The story has already provided, then, a striking insight into the nature of his work. But it has, in addition, a notable conclusion, as Nick and his father discuss death—and death specifically by one's own hand:

" 'Why did he kill himself, Daddy?'

" 'I don't know, Nick. He couldn't stand things, I guess.'

" 'Do many men kill themselves, Daddy?'

" 'Not very many, Nick.' . . .

"They were seated in the boat, Nick in the stern, his father rowing. . . . In the early morning on the lake sitting in the stern of the boat with his father rowing, he felt quite sure that he would never die."

Now from a purely aesthetic point of view it is perfectly irrelevant, but from a human and biographical point of view perfectly unavoidable, to remark the uncanny fact that the originals of both these characters, making their first appearances here as doctor and son, were destined to destroy themselves. Clarence Edmonds Hemingway, M.D., the prototype for Dr. Adams, while in ill-health committed suicide with a pistol (a relic of the Civil War which the

writer's mother later sent him) in 1928; the son, the prototype for Nick Adams, Ernest (Miller) Hemingway, blew most of his head off, with a favorite shotgun, in 1961. "He couldn't stand things, I guess."

As closely as this are many of the key events in the life of the hero tied to the life of the writer. Nearly as simple as this was his preoccupation with violence, and above all the fact of violent death. And seldom in the whole history of literature can there have been a more unlikely focusing on things-to-come as in this first little story.

The six following stories from *In Our Time* concerning Nick Adams are not so violent as "Indian Camp," but each one of them is unpleasant or upsetting in some way or other. In one, "The Doctor and the Doctor's Wife," Nick discovers that he is unsure about his father's courage and is completely dissatisfied with his mother's way of looking at things. Two others, "The End of Something" and "The Three-Day Blow," detail among other matters the disturbing end of an adolescent love affair. In "The Battler" Nick is knocked off a moving freight train by a brakeman, and encounters a crazy ex-prizefighter who nearly beats him up, along with an extremely polite Negro hobo who in his own way is even more sinister. One should suspect that Nick is being exposed to more than may be entirely good for him.

Immediately following "The Battler" comes a little sketch, less than a page long, which serves to confirm this suspicion. It tells us that Nick is in World War I, that he has been wounded, and that he has made a "separate peace" with the enemy—is not fighting for his country, or any other, any more. It would be quite impossible to exaggerate the importance of this short scene in any understanding of Hemingway and his work. It will be duplicated at more length by another protagonist, named Frederic Henry, in *A Farewell to Arms*, and it will serve as a climax in the lives of all of Hemingway's heroes, in one way or another, for at least the next quarter-century.

The fact that Nick is seriously injured is significant in two important ways. First, the wound intensifies and epitomizes the wounds he has been getting as a boy growing up in the American Middle West. From here on the Hemingway hero will appear to us as a wounded man—wounded not only physically but, as soon becomes clear, psychologically as well. Second, the fact that Nick and his friend, also wounded, have made a "separate peace," are "Not patriots," marks the beginning of the long break with organized society as a whole that stays with Hemingway and his hero through several books to come, and into the late 1930's. Indeed the last story in this first volume, called "Big Two-Hearted River," is a kind of forecast of these things. It is obscure until one sees the point, and almost completely so; its author complained in 1950 that the tale was twenty-five years old and still had not been understood by anyone. But it is really a very simple "story." It is a study of a young man who has been hurt in the war, who is all by himself on a fishing trip, escaping everyone. He is suffering from what used to be called "shell shock"; he is trying desperately to keep from going out of his mind.

In his next two collections of short stories, *Men without Women* (1927) and *Winner Take Nothing* (1933), Hemingway included several more stories about Nick Adams. They do not change anything, but they fill in some of the gaps in his sketchy career. In one, an eternally reprinted tale called "The Killers," he is exposed to a sickening situation in which a man refuses to run any more from some gangsters who are clearly going to murder him. In another, "The Light of the World," he is somewhat prematurely introduced into the seamy realms of prostitution and homosexuality. In a

third, "Fathers and Sons," he is deeply troubled by thoughts of his father's death. (At the time we cannot know exactly why, and do not know until many years later when the hero, now under the name of Robert Jordan, in *For Whom the Bell Tolls*, returns to this situation and explains; *his* father committed suicide.) And in a fourth, "A Way You'll Never Be," Nick meets the fate he was trying desperately to avoid in "Big Two-Hearted River" and, as a direct result of his war experiences, goes entirely out of his mind.

Further gaps in the picture we should have of Nick are filled by several stories Hemingway wrote in the first person. It is abundantly clear that the narrator of them is Nick, and in one of the tales, a war story called "Now I Lay Me," he is called by that name. This one is a story about insomnia, which Nick suffered for a long time following his wounding; he cannot sleep "for thinking," and several things that occupy his mind while he lies awake relate closely to scenes and events in stories already mentioned. "In Another Country" extends the range of Hemingway's essential interest from Nick to another individual casualty of the war, and thus points toward *The Sun Also Rises,* where a whole "lost generation" has been damaged in the same disaster. A further development occurs in "An Alpine Idyll," which returns us to a postwar skiing trip Nick took in a tale called "Cross Country Snow"; here the interest focuses on the responses of Nick and others to a particularly shocking situation, as it did in the more famous "Killers." But whereas in the earlier story Nick was so upset by the thought of the man who was passively waiting to be murdered that he wanted to get clean out of the town where the violence impended, healthy tissue is now growing over his wounds, and one feature of the story is the development of his defenses.

By now it is perfectly clear what kind of boy,

then man, this Adams is. He is certainly not the simple primitive he is often mistaken for. He is honest, virile, but—clearest of all—very sensitive. He is an outdoor male, and he has a lot of nerve, but he is also very nervous. It is important to understand this Nick, for soon, under other names in other books, he is going to be known half the world over as the "Hemingway hero": every single one of these men has had, or has had the exact equivalent of, Nick's childhood, adolescence, and young manhood. This man will die a thousand times before his death, and although he would learn how to live with some of his troubles, and how to overcome others, he would never completely recover from his wounds as long as Hemingway lived and recorded his adventures.

Now it is also clear that something was needed to bind these wounds, and there is in Hemingway a consistent character who performs that function. This figure is not Hemingway himself in disguise (which to some hard-to-measure extent the Hemingway hero was). Indeed he is to be sharply distinguished from the hero, for he comes to balance the hero's deficiencies, to correct his stance. We generally, though unfelicitously, call this man the "code hero"—this because he represents a code according to which the hero, if he could attain it, would be able to live properly in the world of violence, disorder, and misery to which he has been introduced and which he inhabits. The code hero, then, offers up and exemplifies certain principles of honor, courage, and endurance which in a life of tension and pain make a man, as we say, and enable him to conduct himself well in the losing battle that is life. He shows, in the author's famous phrase for it, "grace under pressure."

This man also makes his first appearance in the short stories. He is Jack, the prizefighter of "Fifty Grand," who through a superhuman effort manages to lose the fight he has promised to lose. He is Manuel, "The Undefeated" bullfighter who, old and wounded, simply will not give up when he is beaten. He is Wilson, the British hunting guide of "The Short Happy Life of Francis Macomber," who teaches his employer the shooting standards that make him, for a brief period preceding his death, a happy man. And, to distinguish him most clearly from the Hemingway hero, he is Cayetano, the gambler of "The Gambler, the Nun and the Radio," who with two bullets in his stomach will not show a single sign of suffering, while the generic Nick, here called Mr. Frazer, is shamed to suffer less but visibly. The finest and best known of these code heroes appears, however, in a famous novel. He is old Santiago of *The Old Man and the Sea*. The chief point about him is that he behaves perfectly—honorably, with great courage and endurance—while losing to the sharks the giant fish he has caught. This, to epitomize the message the code hero always brings, is life: you lose, of course; what counts is how you conduct yourself while you are being destroyed.

The three matters already introduced—the wound, the break from society, the code (and a working adjustment of these things)—are the subjects of all of Hemingway's significant work outside as well as inside the short stories. This work comes to fourteen book-length pieces: seven novels, a burlesque, a book on big-game hunting, one on bullfighting, another of reminiscence, a journalistic collection, a play, and a collection of new Nick Adams material. The pattern already set up will, it is hoped, help to place these works and to clarify their meanings.

It will not help much with the first of them, however, for this is an anomaly: the burlesque, a "satirical novel," *The Torrents of Spring*. It appeared in 1926, and is a parody of Sherwood Anderson's novels in general, and of his *Dark*

Laughter (1925) in particular. It is a moderately amusing performance, especially if one will first take the trouble to read or reread the specific object of attack; there were ridiculous elements even in Anderson's "better" novels, and Hemingway goes unerringly to them. But this book, dashed off in a great hurry, has never had as many readers as Hemingway's other books, and it has no relation to anything else he has written—except that in it he was declaring himself free of certain egregious weaknesses in a man who had at one time influenced him. It is said that he was also breaking his contract with his publishers, Boni and Liveright, who would feel that they must reject this satire on one of their leading writers; thus Hemingway would be free to take his work to Scribners, whom he much preferred.

It is very doubtful that Hemingway intended his book primarily as a means whereby he might change publishers. But Liveright did reject it, Scribners did bring it out, and thus Scribners have been able to publish the rest of his work. Nor did they have to wait long to prove the wisdom of their acceptance of Hemingway, for his first true novel, *The Sun Also Rises*, came into their hands the same year. This book in time became a best seller and made its author's reputation. *The Sun Also Rises* reintroduces us to the hero, here called Jake Barnes. His wound, again with both literal and symbolic meanings, is transferred from the spine (where Nick was hit) to the genitals: Jake was emasculated in the war. His wound, then, has undergone a significant transformation, but he is still the hero, still the man who cannot sleep when his head starts to work, and who cries in the night. He has also parted with society and the usual middle-class ways; he lives in Paris with an international group of expatriates, a dissolute collection of amusing but aimless people—all of them, in one way or another, blown out of the paths of ordinary life by the war. This was, as Gertrude Stein had remarked to Hemingway, the "lost generation," and in this book Hemingway made it famous.

Although it is not highly developed yet, Jake and the few people he likes have a code. There are certain things that are "done," and many that are "not done," and one of the characters distinguishes people as belonging or not belonging according to whether they understand or not. The whole trouble with Robert Cohn, a would-be writer, for instance, is that he does not understand, and he is sharply juxtaposed to a young bullfighter named Romero (an early code hero) who, in the way he conducts himself both personally and professionally, does understand.

The action of the novel is taken up with drinking, fishing, and going to the bullfights, as well as with the promiscuous affairs of a young lady named Brett Ashley. Brett is in love with Jake, and he with her, but since he is wounded as he is there is not much they can do about it. Brett, although engaged to a man who like herself and Jake is a casualty of the war, passes from Cohn to Romero and then —because she has principles too—she leaves him and in the end is back, hopelessly, with Jake. Nothing leads anywhere in the book, and that is perhaps the real point of it. The action comes full circle—imitates, that is, the sun of the title, which also rises, only to hasten to the place where it arose (the title is, of course, a quotation from Ecclesiastes). For the most part the novel is a delightful one. The style is fresh and sparkling, the dialogue is fun to read, and the book is beautifully and meaningfully constructed. But its message is that for these people at least (and one gets the distinct impression that other people do not matter very much), life is futile.

It happens that this is not precisely the message Hemingway intended to give. He once said that he regarded the line "you are all a lost generation," which he used as an epigraph, as a piece of "splendid bombast," and that he included the passage from Ecclesiastes, also quoted as an epigraph, to correct the remark attributed to Miss Stein. As far as he was concerned, he wrote his editor Maxwell Perkins, the point of his novel is, as the Biblical lines say in part, that "the earth abideth forever."

To be sure, some support for these contentions can be found in the novel itself. Not quite all the characters are "lost"—Romero is not—and the beauty of the eternal earth is now and again richly invoked. But most of the characters do seem lost indeed, a great deal of the time, and few readers have taken the passage from Ecclesiastes as Hemingway did. The strongest feeling in it is not that the earth abides forever, but that all motion is endless, circular, and unavailing; and for all who know what the Preacher said, the echo of "Vanity of vanities; all is vanity" is nearly as strong. For once Hemingway's purpose and accomplishment are here two things, but the result is nonetheless impressive, and *The Sun Also Rises* remains one of the two best novels he wrote.

The other is his next book, *A Farewell to Arms* (1929), and one thing it does is to explain how the characters of *The Sun Also Rises*, and the hero in particular, got the way they are. In the course of the novel Lt. Frederic Henry is wounded in the war as was Nick Adams (although now the most serious of his injuries is to his knee, which is where Hemingway himself was hardest hit). Henry shows clearly the results of this misfortune; again he cannot sleep at night unless he stops thinking; again, when he does sleep he has nightmares. While recuperating in Milan, he falls in love with an English nurse, but when he is returned to the front he is forced to desert the army in which he has been fighting in order to save his life. He escapes to Switzerland with the nurse,

a compliant young woman named Catherine Barkley who is now pregnant with his child, and there she dies in childbirth. Henry is left, at the end, with nothing. A man is trapped, Hemingway seems to be saying. He is trapped biologically and he is trapped socially; either way it can only end badly, and there are no other ways.

Once again this is a beautifully written book. The prose is hard and clean, the people come to life instantly and ring true. The novel is built with scrupulous care. A short introductory scene at the very start presents an ominous conjunction of images—of rain, pregnancy, and death—which set the mood for, and prefigure, all that is to follow. Then the action is tied into a perfect and permanent knot by the skill with which the two themes are brought together. As the intentionally ambiguous title suggests, the two themes are, of course love and war. (They are developments, incidentally, from two early fragments: the sketch, "Chapter VI," in which Nick was wounded, and the "love story," called "A Very Short Story," that immediately followed it in *In Our Time*.)

Despite the frequency of their appearance in the same books, love and war are—to judge from the frequency with which writers fail to wed them—an unlikely mixture. But in this novel their courses ran exactly, though subtly, parallel, so that in the end we feel we have read one story, not two. In his affair with the war Henry goes through six phases: from desultory participation to serious action and a wound, and then through his recuperation in Milan to a retreat which leads to his desertion. Carefully interwoven with all this is his relationship with Catherine, which undergoes six precisely corresponding stages: from a trifling sexual affair to actual love and her conception, and then through her confinement in the Alps to a trip to the hospital which leads to her death. By the time the last farewell is taken, the stories are as one in the point, lest there be any sentimental doubt about it, that life, both personal and social, is a struggle in which the Loser Takes Nothing, either.

But like all of Hemingway's better books this one is bigger than any short account of it can indicate. For one thing there is the stature of Frederic Henry, and it is never more clear than here that he is the Hemingway "hero" in more senses than are suggested by the term "protagonist." Henry stands for many men; he stands for the experience of his country: in his evolution from complicity in the war to bitterness to escape, the whole of America could read its recent history in a crucial period, Wilson to Harding. When he expressed his disillusionment with the ideals the war claimed to promote, and jumped in a river and deserted, Henry's action epitomized the contemporary feeling of a whole nation. Not that the book is without positive values, however—as is often alleged, and as Robert Penn Warren, for one, has disproved. Henry progresses from the messiness represented by the brothel to the order that is love; he distinguishes sharply between the disciplined and competent people he is involved with and the disorderly and incompetent ones: the moral value of these virtues is not incidental to the action but a foundation on which the book is built. Despite such foundations, however, the final effect of this mixture of pessimism and ideals is one of tragedy and despair.

The connection between Hemingway and his hero was always intimate, and in view of the pessimism of these last two books it is perhaps not surprising that his next two books, which were works of nonfiction, find the hero—Hemingway himself, now, without disguise—pretty much at the end of his rope, and in complete escape from the society he had renounced in *A Farewell to Arms*. The books are *Death in the Afternoon* (1932) and *Green Hills of Africa*

(1935). Neither of them is of primary importance. The first is a book about bullfighting, one of a surprising number of subjects in which the author was learned; the second is a book on big-game hunting, about which he also knew a great deal. But the books are really about death—the death of bulls, bullfighters, horses, and big game; death is a subject which by his own admission obsessed Hemingway for a long time. Both books are also a little hysterical, as if written under great nervous tension. To be sure the bullfighter is a good example of the man with the code. As he acts out his role as high priest of a ceremonial in which men pit themselves against violent death, and, with a behavior that formalizes the code, administers what men seek to avoid, he is the very personification of "grace under pressure." And both volumes contain long passages—on writing, Spain, Africa, and other subjects— that are well worth reading. But more clearly than anything else the books present the picture of a man who had, since that separate peace, cut himself off so completely from the roots that nourish that he was starving. The feeling is strong that he would have to find new roots, or re-establish old ones, if he were going to write any more good novels.

This process was not a painless one, and Hemingway's next book, *To Have and Have Not* (1937), amply betrays that fact. This is a novel, though not a good one—at least not for this novelist. But it is one in which its author clearly showed that he had learned something that would become very important to him before he was done writing. As often before, and later too, it is the code hero, piratically named Harry Morgan, who teaches the lesson. The novel tells the story of this man who is forced, since he cannot support his wife and children through honest work, to go his own way: he becomes an outlaw who smuggles rum and people into the United States from Cuba. In the end he is killed, but before he dies he has learned the lesson that Hemingway himself must recently have learned: alone, a man has no chance.

It is regrettable that this pronouncement, articulating a deathbed conversion, does not grow with any sense of inevitability out of the action of the book. A contrast between the Haves and the Have Nots of the story is meant to be structure and support for the novel and its message, but the whole affair is unconvincing. The superiority of the Nots is apparently based on the superiority of the sex life of the Morgans, on some savage disgust aimed at a successful writer in the book, and on some callow explanations of how the Haves got their money. Just how all these things lead to Harry's final pronouncement was Hemingway's business, and it was not skillfully transacted.

But the novel itself is of minor significance. What it represents in Hemingway is important. Here is the end of the long exile that began with Nick Adams' separate peace, the end of Hemingway's ideological separation from the world: a man has no chance alone. As a matter of fact, by 1937, the year of this novel, Hemingway had come close to embracing the society he had deserted some twenty years before, and was back in another "war for democracy."

More than any other single thing, it seems to have been the civil war in Spain that returned Hemingway to the world of other people. He was informally involved in that war, on the Loyalist side, and his next full-length work was a play, called *The Fifth Column* (1938), which praises the fighters with whom he was associated and declares his faith in their cause. The play is distinguished by some excellent talk, and marred by a kind of cops-and-robbers action. The Hemingway hero, now called simply Philip, is immediately recognizable. He is still afflicted with his memories, and

with insomnia and horrors in the night. A kind of Scarlet Pimpernel dressed as an American reporter, Philip appears to be a charming but dissolute wastrel, a newsman who never files any stories. But actually, and unknown to his mistress, Dorothy, he is up to his neck in the Loyalist fight. The most striking thing about him, however, is the distance he has come from the hero, so like him in every other way, who decided in *A Farewell to Arms* that such faiths and causes were "obscene."

But it is almost no distance at all from the notion that a man has no chance alone to the thought that "No man is an *Iland*, intire of it selfe. . . ." These words, from a devotion by John Donne, are part of an epigraph to Hemingway's next novel, whose title, *For Whom the Bell Tolls* (1940), comes from the same source. The bell referred to is a funeral bell: "And therefore never send to know for whom the *bell* tolls; It tolls for *thee*."

This time the novel is true to its controlling concept. It deals with three days in the life of the Hemingway hero, now named Robert Jordan, who is fighting as an American volunteer in the Spanish civil war. He is sent to join a guerrilla band in the mountains near Segovia to blow up a strategic bridge, thus facilitating a Loyalist advance. He spends three days and nights in the guerrillas' cave, while he awaits what he expects will be his own destruction, and he falls in love with Maria, the daughter of a Republican mayor who has been murdered—as she herself has been raped—by the Falangists. Jordan believes the attack will fail, but the generals will not cancel it until it is too late. He successfully destroys the bridge, is wounded in the retreat, and is left to die. But he has come to see the wisdom of such a sacrifice, and the book ends without bitterness.

This is not a flawless novel. For one thing the love story, if not sentimental, is at any rate idealized and very romantic; for another, there are a good many passages in which Jordan appears more to be struggling for the faith on which he acts than to have achieved it. The hero is still the wounded man, and new incidents from his past are supplied to explain why this is so; two of the characters remark pointedly that he was too young to experience the things he tells them of having experienced. But Jordan has learned a lot, since the old days, about how to live and function with his wounds, and he behaves well. He dies, but he has done his job, and the manner of his dying convinced many readers of what his thinking had failed to do: that life is worth living and that there are causes worth dying for.

The skill with which this novel was for the most part written demonstrated that Hemingway's talent was once again intact and formidable. None of his books had evoked more richly the life of the senses, had shown a surer sense of plotting, or provided more fully living secondary characters, or livelier dialogue. But following this success (this was the most successful of all his books so far as sales are concerned), he lapsed into a silence that lasted a whole decade—chiefly because of nonliterary activities in connection with World War II. And when he broke this silence in 1950 with his next book, a novel called *Across the River and into the Trees*, the death of his once-great gifts was very widely advertised by the critics and reviewers.

To be sure, this is a poor performance. It is the story of a peacetime army colonel (but almost an exact self-portrait) who comes on leave to Venice to go duck-shooting, to see his very young girl friend, and to die, all of which he does. The colonel is the hero again, this time called Richard Cantwell, and he has all the old scars, including the specific ones he received as Frederic Henry in *A Farewell to Arms*. Again there is the "Hemingway heroine," a title that designates the British nurse

Catherine of that novel, the Spanish girl Maria of *For Whom the Bell Tolls*, and now the young Italian countess Renata of this novel. (They are all pretty much the same girl, though for some reason their nationality keeps changing, as the hero's never does, and they grow younger as the hero ages.) There are also many signs of the "code." But the code in this book has become a sort of joke; the hero has become a good deal of a bore, and the heroine has become a wispy dream. The distance that Hemingway once maintained between himself and his protagonist has disappeared, to leave us with a self-indulgent chronicling of the author's every opinion; he acts as though he were being interviewed. The novel reads like a parody of the earlier works.

But there is one interesting thing about it. Exactly one hundred years before the appearance of this novel Nathaniel Hawthorne published *The Scarlet Letter*, in which he wrote: "There is a fatality, a feeling so irresistible and inevitable that it has the force of doom, which almost invariably compels human beings to linger around and haunt, ghostlike, the spot where some great and marked event has given the color to their lifetime; and still the more irresistibly, the darker the tinge that saddens it." From Hawthorne himself and Poe, from Hawthorne's Hester Prynne and Melville's Ahab right down to J. D. Salinger's "Zooey," who is unwilling to leave New York ("I've been *run over* here—twice, and on the same damn *street*")—no one in the history of American letters has demonstrated Hawthorne's insight with as much force and clarity as have Hemingway and his hero. And nowhere in Hemingway is the demonstration more clear than in *Across the River and into the Trees*, for it is here that Colonel Cantwell makes a sort of pilgrimage to the place where he—and where Nick Adams, and Frederic Henry (and Hemingway himself)—was first wounded. He takes instruments, and locates by survey the exact place on the ground where he had been struck. Then, in an act of piercing, dazzling identification, he builds a very personal if ironic sort of monument to the spot, acknowledges and confronts the great, marked event that colored his lifetime—and Hemingway's writing-time—and comes to the end of his journey (or the end so far), not at the place where he first lived, but where first he died.

The critics who professed to see in this book the death of Hemingway's talent, as well as of his hero, happily proved to be mistaken, for they were forced almost unanimously to accept his next book, called *The Old Man and the Sea* (1952), as a triumph. This very short novel, which some insist on calling rather a long short story (and it was for some time rumored to be part of a longer work-in-progress), concerns an old Cuban fisherman. After eighty-four days without a fish Santiago ventures far out to sea alone, and hooks a giant marlin in the Gulf Stream. For two days and two nights the old man holds on while he is towed farther out to sea; finally he brings the fish alongside, harpoons it, and lashes it to his skiff. Almost at once the sharks begin to take his prize away from him. He kills them until he has only his broken tiller to fight with. Then they eat all but the skeleton, and he tows that home, half-dead with exhaustion, and makes his way to bed to sleep and dream of other days.

The thing that chiefly keeps *The Old Man and the Sea* from greatness is the sense one has that the author was imitating instead of creating the style that made him famous. But this reservation is almost made up for by the book's abundance of meaning. As always the code hero, here Santiago, comes with a message, and it is essentially that while a man may grow old, and be wholly down on his luck, he can still dare, stick to the rules, persist when he is licked, and thus by the manner of his losing win his victory. On another level the story can be read as an allegory entirely personal to its author, as an account of his own struggle, his determination, and his literary vicissitudes. Like Hemingway, Santiago is a master who sets out his lines with more care and precision than his competitors, but he has not had any luck in a long time. Once he was very strong, the champion, yet his whole reputation is imperiled now, and he is growing old. Still he feels that he has strength enough; he knows the tricks of his trade; he is resolute, and he is still out for the really big success. It means nothing that he has proved his strength before; he has got to prove it again, and he does. After he has caught his prize the sharks come and take it all away from him, as they will always try to do. But he caught it, he fought it well, he did all he could and it was a lot, and at the end he is happy.

To take the broadest view, however, the novel is a representation of life as a struggle against unconquerable natural forces in which a kind of victory is possible. It is an epic metaphor for life, a contest in which even the problem of right and wrong seems paltry before the great thing that is the struggle. It is also something like Greek tragedy, in that as the hero falls and fails, the audience may get a memorable glimpse of what stature a man may have. And it is Christian tragedy as well, especially in the several marked allusions to Christian symbolism, particularly of the crucifixion—a development in Hemingway's novels that begins apparently without much importance, in the early ones, gathers strength in *Across the River and into the Trees*, and comes to a kind of climax in this book.

Although the view of life in this novel had a long evolution from the days of total despair, it represents nonetheless an extraordinary change in its author. A reverence for life's struggle, and for mankind, seems to have descended on Hemingway like the gift of grace on the religious. The knowledge that a simple man is capable of the decency, the dignity, and even the heroism that Santiago possesses, and that his battle can be seen in heroic terms, is itself, technical considerations for the moment aside, perhaps the greatest victory that Hemingway won. Very likely this is the sort of thing he had in mind when he remarked to someone, shortly after finishing the book, that he had got, finally, what he had been working for all of his life.

Although he is known to have left a good deal of manuscript behind him—fiction, poems, reminiscence—Hemingway brought out nothing really significant during the last nine years of his life. One reason for this silence was surely ill health; among other things the author seems never to have entirely recovered from grievous injuries suffered during his last trip to Africa. Another explanation is even simpler: taxes, for Hemingway was in that not altogether unenviable position where a substantial part of the profit from new work went to the government. If, however, he could leave his estate a couple of vintage books and some stories (the profits from a single short story, "The Snows of Kilimanjaro," must by now be approaching two hundred thousand dollars), then his widow would be fairly well off.

That there was sense in such a scheme (if scheme it was) is indicated by the success of his first posthumous publication, *A Moveable Feast*, which appeared in 1964 and soon established tenure at the top of the best-seller lists. It deserved to, for despite sensationally harsh (but astonishingly deft) treatments of old friends and rivals—Ford Madox Ford, Gertrude Stein, and Scott Fitzgerald—this little collection of sketches dealing with the apprentice days in Paris is a minor work of art. The mean, wary streak in a fierce competitor

who himself manages to look marvelous all the while is clearly revealed, and some of the book must indeed, as the author remarks, "be regarded as fiction." But the rest of it is easily the best nonfiction he ever wrote.

The achievement is chiefly stylistic; it is largely the shock of immediacy, the sense of our own presence on Paris streets and in Paris cafés, that makes the book. Some of the dialogue with the first Mrs. Hemingway is a little embarrassing, and occasionally the borders of sentimentality are at least skirted. But for the most part the prose glitters, warms, delights— or is witty, or is as hard-hitting as ever. It moves and evokes, as the author looks back on the time of innocence, poverty, and spring, so soon to pass. The book is interesting on the subject of writing as well, and reveals a "secret theory" the young man had about omitting things from stories so as "to make people feel something more than they understood." There are special rewards, too, for those who remember "The Snows of Kilimanjaro" well enough to realize that they are vicariously experiencing precisely that Paris which the writer Harry, Hemingway's momentary persona in the story, died regretting he had not lived to write about. And so fresh and quick do the sketches seem that readers can sense how good it must have been—now and then, anyway, during the last unhappy years—to have so successfully recaptured the heady, ordered days when fame was just around a corner from the Place Contrescarpe.

A Moveable Feast contained a large amount of what vintage Hemingway the author left behind him; in the more than 3,000 pages of manuscript not published at the time of his death there was unfortunately not a great deal of similar quality. Nor have posthumous issues or re-issues of his work done much to enhance his reputation. *By-Line: Ernest Hemingway* (1967), a generous collection of his journalism that begins when he was a cub reporter in Toronto and moves spottily across three and a half decades through wars, travels, and hunting and fishing, among other things, to end in Cuba, makes generally available some extremely fine, highly distinctive writing. Had Hemingway made the work of a reporter his life's own, he could have ranked with the very best. But though some of it is not very different from fiction, the book is indeed journalism. And one notes a drift to the volume in which the author begins by interviewing certain notables and finishes by interviewing himself, by then among the chiefest of them. A similar tendency is clear in a 1969 re-issue of *The Fifth Column* together with four previously uncollected *Stories of the Spanish Civil War*—fiction tinged with autobiography.

But for many the greatest disappointment was *Islands in the Stream* (1970), the big "sea novel" that Hemingway when alive had pinned such hopes on and made such claims for. It is not really a "novel" at all, but three related novellas (*The Old Man and the Sea* was originally a fourth) which the author had optimistically planned to weld into one. And the three parts are of very unequal value. The first section, "Bimini," is much the best, an account of Thomas Hudson's vacation with his three sons, which has a few superb passages, comic and otherwise. Part Two, "Cuba," is the worst —uncomical high jinks in and around Havana on Hudson's leave from chasing U-boats. "At Sea" is straight but unexciting adventure— pursuit of a Nazi submarine crew in the Keys —which ends with Hudson's probable death, an outcome less disturbing than all the preparation for it. Clearly Hemingway was not done with the job, unless with the last section. It is not only that he had not drawn the parts together and finished revising them, but also that in relating all the experience the book deals with he had simply not discovered its

meaning. Indeed he did not even provide a reason for the central fact about the protagonist, his stoicism—not, that is, beyond a desperation-shot at one, which misfires: the sudden deaths of the two younger boys, later of the oldest, all manufactured to stand in for what is not understood.

It is never more obvious than in this work that self-dramatization was the origin of Hemingway's work. As long as the raw material is disciplined and transmuted there is nothing disqualifying about that. But increasingly as his career moved toward its close, Hemingway was less and less willing or able to turn himself into a protagonist who is anything different from or more than Hemingway. One result in *Islands in the Stream* is that the unaccountable adulation of Hudson—by his sons, women, servants, friends, and cats—produces the most damaging of all critical responses, embarrassment. And self-adulation mingles with self-pity, the unloveliest form of charity.

It was when he put on a mask which was a true disguise that the autobiographical method worked, and the bank vault after his death did contain a little more fiction involving Nick Adams. Much of this was material which Hemingway had discarded as misguided or trivial, but two pieces, "The Last Good Country" and "Summer People" are neither. All of this, together with all previously published fiction in which Nick appears, arranged for the first time in the chronological order of his advancing age, child to parent, was published in 1972 as *The Nick Adams Stories*. "The Last Good Country," which is actually the start of what might have been a long novel about Nick and his kid sister taking off into a Michigan forest in escape from some game wardens, becomes Hemingway's only pastoral: idyllic, sentimental, mythic. Its difference from all other Nick stories can be attributed in part to the fact that, written in the 1950's, it is much the latest of them. So "Summer People" is apparently the earliest, a cheerful, deft piece about Nick with his friends (especially a girl, Kate, to whom he makes love) on a summer night at Walloon Lake, during which Nick senses something in him that is special, and ends praying to be a "great writer."

There is more unpublished Hemingway: a long novel called *Garden of Eden*, a very sizable "African Book" (which *Sports Illustrated* printed excerpts from in 1971), several short stories, and quite a few poems, early and late. But it is doubtful that publication of any of this would add to our appreciation of a writer who, to judge him by his best, became quite sufficiently "great." Publish or no, the general interest in that work, and in him, remains intense. In the academy, indeed, it has grown to the point where he is now—with Hawthorne, Melville, James, and Faulkner—one of the five American authors "most written about." There is a truly *Comprehensive Bibliography* by Audre Hanneman (1967), and his *Life Story*, Carlos Baker's authorized biography (1969), which is crammed with accurate data if intentionally empty of interpretation, became a considerable best seller. Even publication of an inventory of his manuscripts was thought to call for front-page stories in the world's great newspapers. As the most publicized American writer in history, Hemingway eventually surpassed Mark Twain.

Thus his life, which is so hard to separate from his work, itself attracted extraordinary attention, and it was colorful. Ernest Miller Hemingway was born on July 21, 1899, in the middle-class suburb of Chicago, Illinois, called Oak Park. His father was a doctor of medicine, devoted to hunting and fishing; his mother was a religious woman, talented in music and painting. The doctor seems to have had the greater influence on the child. The parts of his boyhood that meant most to him were spent on summer vacations in Michigan, and are reflected in the Nick Adams stories—as, for the most part, his life-long rebellion against the intense Victorianism of Oak Park and both parents is not.

As a boy he learned to box and he played high school football. He was not much pleased with the latter activity, however, partly because he was already more interested in writing. Working for his English classes and the school paper, he composed light verse, wrote a good many columns in imitation of Ring Lardner (a practice at which he became very adept), and tried his hand at some short stories. Although it looked for many years as though he was cut out to be a humorist, he also turned his hand to more serious fiction, and this is really the most impressive part of his juvenilia; already he was choosing to write about northern Michigan, and many of the features of his later style—especially some of the earmarks of his famous dialogue—are discernible in this early prose.

Half-seriously, doubtless, Hemingway once remarked that the best training for a writer is an unhappy boyhood. He himself, however, appears to have been reasonably happy a good part of the time. But he seems also to have been on occasion deeply dissatisfied with his home life and with Oak Park, and no sooner did he graduate from high school than he was off for Kansas City, never really to return home. If it had not been for parental objections that he was too young (seventeen), and if not for a bad eye, he would have gone much farther away, for he was desperately eager to get into the war. Repeatedly rejected by the army, he went instead to the Kansas City *Star*, then one of the country's best newspapers, lied about his age (which accounts for the fact that his birth date was long given as 1898), and partly on the strength of his high school newspaper experience landed a job as a reporter. Here he was known for his energy and eagerness, and for the fact that, in the line of duty, he always wanted to ride the ambulances. Finally able to get into the war as an honorary lieutenant in the Red Cross, he went overseas, in a state of very great excitement, as an ambulance driver. He was severely wounded, while passing out chocolate to the troops in Italy, at Fossalta di Piave, on July 8, 1918, and was decorated by the Italians for subsequent heroism. A dozen operations were performed on his knee, and during his recuperation in Milan he unavailingly fell in love with a nurse.

After the war, "literally shot to pieces," according to a friend, he returned to the United States, his riddled uniform with him. Heading for northern Michigan again, he spent a time reading, writing, and fishing. Then he worked for a while in Canada for the Toronto *Star*, moved temporarily to Chicago, found himself unhappy with America, married, and took off for Paris as a foreign correspondent, employed again by the Toronto *Star*. He served in this role for some time, and then settled down in Paris to become once and for all, under the guidance of Gertrude Stein and others, a writer. Though it brought little in the way of money, his work soon began to attract attention, and *The Sun Also Rises* made him famous while he was still in his twenties. After that time he had no serious extended financial troubles, and with both critics and the general public commanded a very wide following.

From other standpoints, Hemingway's story was one of mixed success and failure. His first three marriages—to Hadley Richardson, the mother of his first son, to Pauline Pfeiffer, the mother of his second two boys, and to Martha Gellhorn, the novelist—all ended in divorce. (His widow is the former Mary Welsh of Minnesota—all the other wives came from St. Louis—whom he met in England in 1944.) For a long time, the whole span of the thirties during which he lived mostly in Key West, Florida, his work did more to advance his reputation as sportsman and athlete than as a writer of memorable fiction. During the forties his nonliterary activities were even more spectacular, and though he published only one book in this period he was very much alive. There is subject matter for several romantic novels in his World War II adventures alone.

In 1942 he volunteered himself and his fishing boat, the *Pilar*, for various projects to the United States Navy, was accepted, and for two years cruised off the coast of Cuba with a somewhat suicidal plan for the destruction of U-boats in the area. In 1944 he was in England, and as an accredited correspondent went on several missions with the RAF. Shortly before the invasion of France he was in an auto wreck which necessitated the taking of fifty-seven stitches in his head. But he pulled the stitches out on D Day, and after the breakthrough in Normandy attached himself to the division of his choice, the Fourth of the First Army, with which he saw considerable action at Schnee Eifel, in Luxembourg, and in the disaster at Hürtgen Forest. At one point in a battle, according to the commanding officer of the division ("I always keep a pin in the map for old Ernie Hemingway"), he was sixty miles in front of anything else in the First Army. Ostensibly a correspondent he was by now running his own small, informal, but effective army—motorized, equipped with "every imaginable" German and American weapon, and nearly weighed down with bottles and explosives. Less exuberant and better-qualified testimony records the fact that he had genuine expertise in military matters, especially with regard to guerrilla activities and the collection of intelligence, and that he was extremely brave under fire.

But on other counts Hemingway as a man appears to have been complicated to the point of contradictions that have not yet been resolved. He was by turns witty, cheerful, and irascible, generous and selfish, expansive and self-centered as a tornado. This was a hedonist who worked, a stoic who suffered, a lover of life obsessed with death, a life-long student and sportsman, a powerful, damaged man who basked and perspired in the limelight he alternately sought and shunned.

He was a gifted, strong personality, and at times eccentric. In *Across the River and into the Trees* Cantwell's driver speculates that some of the colonel's eccentricities are the result of his having been so often injured. Although this diagnosis may seem both offhand and indirect, one of the consequences of Hemingway's physical adventures was that he, like Cantwell, physically long retained the record of about as many blows as a man may take and live. Understandably he did not wish to go down in history for this fact. But there seems little or no danger of that, and a list of his major injuries is certainly impressive and possibly significant. His skull was fractured at least once; he sustained at least a dozen brain concussions, several of them serious ones; he was in three bad automobile accidents; and several years prior to his death he was in two airplane accidents in the space of two days in the African jungle, during which time he suffered severe internal injuries, "jammed" his spine, and received a concussion so violent that his eyesight was impaired for some time. (It was on this occasion that quite a few newspapers printed obituaries, which he read, after his recovery, with great pleasure; the notices were favorable.) In warfare alone he was shot through nine parts of the body, and sustained six head wounds. When he was blown up in Italy at the age of eighteen, and was left, for a time, for dead, the doctors removed all of the 227 steel fragments which had penetrated him that they could get at.

Some amount of such gossip is relevant to any discussion of Hemingway's work if only because it confirms and informs the picture of him which the work has given us. Our view of that work is in turn informed and confirmed by modern psychology, which offers an account of how many of the things to be found in Hemingway come to be there. This is no place to go into the niceties and vagaries of contemporary psychoanalytic theory, much of it post-Freudian, but it is perhaps not out of place to remark that such theory does give an explanation of the preoccupations Hemingway's books and life reflect. His hero's nightmares and insomnia (attendant on his first serious wounding), his preoccupation with death, and with the scene of what was nearly his own premature end, his devotion to hunting and fishing, his intellectual limitations—all these things and several others may be accounted for in psychoanalytic terms. They used to be called symptoms of "shell shock"; now it is called "traumatic neurosis." The name matters very little. The point is that our understanding of Hemingway has medical backing, if such is desired. The point is further that his work so faithfully and accurately documented how this kind of illness conducts itself that it in turn lends considerable credence to the medical theory.

And his end, his own death, reconfirms the view. Retreating very quietly from Castro's Cuba, where he had lived for many years outside Havana, to Franco's Spain, where he was not bothered despite *For Whom the Bell Tolls*, and where he could follow the bullfights again, he did produce "The Dangerous Summer," a somewhat abortive account of these fights. Then he returned to the States, and bought a house in Ketchum, Idaho. He was not at all well. In addition to damages already noted he was suffering from high blood pressure and an enlarged liver—perhaps from diabetes and (most serious) from hemochromatosis as well.

Even more disturbing was the fact that visitors reported him shockingly frail, withdrawn, and in a state of acute anxiety and deep depression, for which he had undergone a total of twenty-five electroshock treatments while twice hospitalized at the Mayo Clinic. Soon the world, which knew little or nothing of the seriousness of his condition, was to be stunned on July 2, 1961, by the violent end that his first really important story had, by hindsight, so unwittingly and obscurely pointed toward. (Death, thinks Thomas Hudson: "all your life is just pointed toward it.")

There should be no inference here that psychological hypothesis or ill-health in any way detracts from or qualifies Hemingway's accomplishment. Emphatically the contrary. "The world breaks everyone and afterward many are strong at the broken places," as he remarked in *A Farewell to Arms*. His own life and career were for a long time an extraordinary illustration of that notion. At his very best he became one of those Nietzsche wrote of, "who see all the strengths and weaknesses of their own natures and then comprehend them in an artistic plan until everything appears as art and reason and even weakness delights the eye."

But primary attention should go of course to Hemingway the writer, not the man—and still less the case history—and there is little doubt that his technical achievement has been great. Indeed in the view of many people it is his simple, fresh, and clean prose style that is his true claim to renown and permanence. Those responsible for bestowing the Nobel Prize for Literature seemed to reflect this view, for in 1954 when he was awarded it they cited "his powerful style-forming mastery of the art of modern narration. . . ."

It is of course not true, as has been alleged, that this style sprang from nowhere. Actually it had a long evolution, which may be said to have begun when Mark Twain wrote the first paragraph of his *Adventures of Huckleberry Finn* (1884). What Twain was trying to do in this novel is very clear. He was trying to write as an American boy might speak—write, that is, not a "literary" English style, but a natural spoken English. Or rather a natural spoken American, for Twain was the first man to "write American," at least to do it really well. He found a freshness and a poetry in that speech which have not diminished one particle with the passing of the years. It is far too much to say, as Hemingway himself once said, that "all modern American literature" comes from that one book, but the book does indeed represent the true beginning of a widespread contemporary American style.

Other writers came between Twain and Hemingway in this evolution. It would be possible to draw up an extraordinary list of parallels between the lives and personalities of Hemingway and an intervening writer: Stephen Crane. Both men began their careers very young as reporters, then foreign correspondents. Both journeyed widely to wars. Each was profoundly shocked by the death of his father; each childhood was marred by the experience of violence; each man found in warfare an absorbing formalization of violence and an essential metaphor for life. Each tested himself against violence and in the end was cited for courage—and so on and on. Perhaps all this helps to account for the fact that a great many of the characteristics of Hemingway's prose— its intensity, its terse, unliterary tone, and many of the features of the dialogue, for instances— can be found first, when he is at his best, in Crane. (This is a debt which Hemingway also, obliquely, acknowledged.)

Any effort to write a simple, spare, concise, and yet repetitive prose—clean, free of cliché and "artful" synonyms and all but the smallest and simplest of words—could and did benefit as well from the efforts of Gertrude Stein. In addition, Hemingway's early stories show a debt to Sherwood Anderson, and a good many other writers seem also to have had at least a small hand in the forming of him. The names F. Scott Fitzgerald, Ezra Pound, Ring Lardner, Joseph Conrad, Ford Madox Ford, and Ivan Turgenev should appear, among others, on any list that pretended to be complete.

Almost all writers show their chief debts in their earliest work. In Hemingway's case, however, the situation is complicated by the fact that eighteen of his earliest stories, and the first draft of a first novel—the better part of his production for four years—were in a suitcase that was stolen from his first wife on a train to Lausanne. Thus the material that almost certainly recorded the most imitative and faltering steps of a person learning a new skill is missing, and almost certainly for good. Not missing, however, are a few copies of a pamphlet called *Three Stories and Ten Poems* which he published at Dijon in 1923, and we must settle for this. As the title suggests, Hemingway made his debut, a sort of a false start, as a poet. Most of the verse in this volume brings to mind the poetry either of Stephen Crane or of Vachel Lindsay, and is without other real interest. The three stories—"Up in Michigan," "Out of Season," and "My Old Man"—are on the other hand already accomplished performances, and as such were reprinted in *In Our Time*. But they still reveal something of the influences of other writers on this one, and include as well Hemingway's first attempt to work at what became his major theme.

The clearest direct obligation is to Sherwood Anderson, for "My Old Man" seems transparently Hemingway's version of Anderson's widely reprinted "I Want to Know Why," which had appeared two years earlier. Both stories are about horse racing, told by boys in their own vernacular; in each case the boy has to con-

front mature problems while undergoing a painful disillusionment with an older man he had been strongly attached to. (Hemingway claimed that he had not read any Anderson when he wrote "My Old Man," but if this is so the coincidences are very remarkable indeed.) "Out of Season," a tale of lovers under the spell of disenchantment, has reminded a few of Scott Fitzgerald's *The Beautiful and Damned* (1922). But "Up in Michigan" is much the most important of the *Three Stories*; it is a tale of initiation, precisely parallel to the stories of Nick Adams soon to be written. It takes place in the locale of "Indian Camp," and just as Nick in that episode was first exposed to violence, brutality, and pain, so in this story a girl named Liz learns a similar lesson, but for girls. The dogged simplicity of "Up in Michigan" suggests both Anderson and Gertrude Stein, but it is too hardheaded for the former, and cut off by its subject matter from the latter. All Hemingway had to do, once he had written it, was to take up a protagonist in whom he could see himself more directly, and he would have the adventures of Nick Adams.

The influence of other writers on even so distinctive a writer as Hemingway is sometimes perceptible even in work that is completely mature. Good cases in point are two of his best and best-known stories, "The Snows of Kilimanjaro" and "The Short Happy Life of Francis Macomber." Both are unmistakably Hemingway, and both are substantially dependent on, or allied to, earlier fiction. "The Short Happy Life" is among other things a detailed description of the process of learning the code, and its value. Macomber, a coward, learns the code from Wilson, his professional hunting guide, and becomes in the process, for a short happy lifetime, a man. He confronts danger at first with a terrible fear, and when it comes he bolts and flies in a panic. But on the next occasion he is awakened from a kind of fighting trance to discover that his fear is gone, his manhood attained, and his life (for a moment) begun.

The story is authentic, vintage Hemingway. But insofar as it deals with Macomber's warlike relations with his wife, Margot, it is a very close development and intensification of some notions about the relationship of the sexes in America as put down by D. H. Lawrence in an essay he once wrote on Hawthorne's *Scarlet Letter*. And to the much larger extent that it deals with fear and manhood, it is an almost exact reworking of the story Stephen Crane told in *The Red Badge of Courage*, a novel for which Hemingway long ago expressed his great —possibly excessive—admiration.

Similarly "The Snows of Kilimanjaro" is a story whose technique has been, deservedly, much praised; again few could mistake it for the work of another writer. But several of its basic ingredients are strongly reminiscent of other writers, and its most unusual structure has an exact precedent in an experimental tale published in 1891 by Ambrose Bierce and called "An Occurrence at Owl Creek Bridge," a story Hemingway was also known to admire. Both stories deal with a man at the point of death who imaginatively experiences his escape in such a realistic fashion that the reader is fooled into believing that it has been made. Both stories open with the situation of impending death, then flash back to explain how the situation came about, and then flash "forward" with the imaginary escape, only to conclude with the objective information that the death has indeed occurred.

Some of Hemingway's longer pieces have similar affiliations. If, for instance, *To Have and Have Not* does not owe a good deal to such an unlikely combination of books as James Joyce's *Ulysses* and Frank Norris' *Moran of the Lady Letty* (and Jack London's *Sea-Wolf*), then we have on our hands a set of impossible coincidences. It is not, however, that Hemingway's work seems derived. Gertrude Stein thought it did: "he looks like a modern and he smells of the museums," she said. Edmund Wilson disagreed: "Hemingway should perhaps more than anyone else be allowed to escape the common literary fate of being derived from other people." And Alfred Kazin concurred, writing that he "had no basic relation to any prewar culture."

It seems entirely possible that all of these judgments are wrong. Hemingway took a good deal from other writers, but if he smells of the museums Miss Stein's nose was one of the few to detect the odor. Like most writers, he went to those who preceded him for what his experience and taste made meaningful and attractive to him. With the force of his personality and the skill of his craft he made what he borrowed distinctly and undeniably his own.

More striking, however, is the extent to which, once Hemingway got started, other writers began to make it all theirs. There is probably no country in which American books are read whose literature has been entirely unaffected by Hemingway's work; in his own country we are so conditioned to his influence that we hardly ever notice it any more. On the positive side he taught the values of objectivity and honesty, helped to purify our writing of sentimentality, literary embellishment, padding, and a superficial artfulness. Almost singlehanded he revitalized the writing of dialogue. His influence has extended even more pervasively, however, to the realms of the subliterary, and here the results, through no direct fault of his, have been much less appealing. Many writers, of the "tough-detective school" in particular, demonstrate what happens when the attitudes and mannerisms which have meaning in one novelist are taken over by others, for whom they have rather different meanings, or none. Violence is the meaningful core of

Hemingway, but the host of novelists and short-story and script writers who have come to trade on him have seized a bag of tricks—usually a mixture of toughness and sex, with protagonists based on crude misunderstandings of one or the other—or both—of the heroes. In their hands the meanings either are cheap and sordid, or have departed altogether.

It is Hemingway's prose style, however, that has been most imitated, and it is as a stylist that he commands the most respect. His prose is easily recognized. For the most part it is colloquial, characterized chiefly by a conscientious simplicity of diction and sentence structure. The words are normally short and common ones and there is a severe economy, and also a curious freshness, in their use. As Ford Madox Ford remarked some time ago, in a line that is often quoted, the words "strike you, each one, as if they were pebbles fetched fresh from a brook." The typical sentence is a simple declarative one, or a couple of these joined by a conjunction. The effect is of crispness, cleanness, clarity, and a scrupulous care. (And a scrupulous care went into the composition; Hemingway worked very slowly. He claimed to have rewritten the last page of *A Farewell to Arms* thirty-nine times and to have read through the manuscript of *The Old Man and the Sea* some two hundred times before he was finished with it.)

It is a remarkably unintellectual style. Events are described strictly in the sequence in which they occurred; no mind reorders or analyzes them, and perceptions come to the reader unmixed with comment from the author. The impression, therefore, is of intense objectivity; the writer provides nothing but stimuli. Since violence and pain are so often the subject matter, it follows that a characteristic effect is one of irony or understatement. The vision is narrow, and sharply focused.

The dialogue is equally striking, for Heming-way had an ear like a trap for the accents and mannerisms of human speech; this is chiefly why he was able to bring a character swiftly to life. The conversation is far from a simple transcription, however, of the way people talk. Instead the dialogue strips speech to an essential pattern of mannerisms and responses characteristic of the speaker, and gives an illusion of reality that reality itself would not give.

Nothing in this brief account of the "Hemingway style" should seem very surprising, but the purposes, implications, and ultimate meanings of this manner of writing are less well recognized. A style has its own content, and the manner of a distinctive prose style has its own meanings. The things that Hemingway's style most conveys are the very things he says outright. His style is as communicative of the content as the content itself, and is a large and inextricable part of the content. The strictly disciplined controls exerted over the hero and his nervous system are precise parallels to the strictly disciplined sentences. The "mindlessness" of the style is a reflection and expression of the need to "stop thinking" when thought means remembering the things that upset. The intense simplicity of the prose is a means of saying that things must be *made* simple, or the hero is lost, and in "a way you'll never be." The economy and narrow focus of the prose controls the little that can be absolutely mastered. The prose is tense because the atmosphere in which the struggle for control takes place is tense, and the tension in the style expresses that fact.

These notions are scarcely weakened by the reminder that the style was developed and perfected in the same period when the author was reorganizing his personality after the scattering of his forces in Italy. These efforts were two sides of one effort. Hemingway once said, in a story called "Fathers and Sons," that if he wrote some things he could get rid of them; it is equally to the point that he wrote them in the style that would get rid of them. The discipline that made the new personality made the prose style that bespoke the personality. The style is the clear voice of the content. It was the end, or aim, of the man, and a goal marvelously won. It was the means of being the man. An old commonplace never had more force than here: the style *is* the man.

One of the most common criticisms of Hemingway used to be that he had wandered too far from his roots, his traditions, and had gotten lost. People who made this criticism usually said that the author should find a way home to some such tradition as is to be found in a novel like Mark Twain's *Huckleberry Finn*—this one, presumably, because it seems to be by almost unanimous consent the most American of all novels. This is of course the book that Hemingway said all modern American writing comes from; the suspicion is forced on us that someone is confused.

It was the critics who were confused, partly because they missed some of the depths and subtleties in both writers. The curious truth is that if the pattern in Hemingway's work discussed here—the pattern of violence, psychological wounding, escape, and death—has any validity, then Hemingway never got very far from *Huckleberry Finn*. A careful reading of that novel will show precisely that pattern. The adventures of Huckleberry Finn and of Nick Adams are remarkably of a piece. "It made me so sick I most fell out of the tree," says Huck of his exposure to the Grangerford-Shepherdson feud. "I ain't a-going to tell *all* that happened. . . . I wished I hadn't ever come ashore that night to see such things—lots of times I dream about them."

There is so much either hilarious or idyllic in the novel about this boy that we are easily but mistakenly diverted from the spill of blood that gives the book a large part of its meaning and deeply affects Huck. Life on the Mississippi around 1845 could be gory, and Twain based his novel largely on experiences he himself had undergone as a boy, or had known intimately of, and had never quite got over. (We know, for instance, that he witnessed four murders.) A lot of this experience found its way into the book, and it is impossible to understand the novel completely without seeing what all this violence results in. But the results are clear: Huck's overexposure to violence finally wounds him. Each episode makes a mark, and each mark leaves a scar. Every major episode in the novel, with the exceptions only of the rather irrelevant Tom Sawyer scenes at the beginning and conclusion, ends in violence, in physical brutality, and usually in death. All along the way are bloodshed and pain, and there are thirteen separate corpses. The effect of all this, and the only effect that is relevant to the main plot, is that it serves to wound Huck Finn. Either tortured with nightmares or unable to sleep at all ("I couldn't, somehow, for thinking"), he is "made sick" by —among other things—the thought of a man left alone to drown, by the sale of some colored servants, and by the departure of the Duke and the King, tarred, feathered, and astraddle a rail. In addition he is becoming disgusted with mankind in general. Exposed to more bloodshed, drowning, and sudden death than he can handle, he is himself their casualty. And from his own experience Mark Twain could make the prediction: Huck isn't ever going to get over them.

Here, transparently, is the pattern of violence and psychological wounding we have been reading in Hemingway. The rest of it, the elements of escape and death, though in part submerged in symbolism, is also demonstrable in the same book. Huck's whole journey is of course made up of a series of escapes—escapes for the most part down a mighty and deeply mysterious river. His strange journey down the glamorous Mississippi, blurred, mythic, and wondrously suggestive, becomes in the end a supremely effortless flight into a dark and silent unknown. Symbolically Huck escapes more than he is aware of, and into something which—if this were literal and not metaphorical—he could not return from. Over and over again his silent, effortless, night-time departures down the black and mighty stream compel us. In the end they transport us from a noisy, painful, and difficult life to the safety of the last escape of all. In the end as well, Twain is forced to drop Huck and to turn the story over to Tom Sawyer. The reason is not hard to find: Huck had grown too hot to handle. A damaged boy, tortured by the terror he has witnessed and been through, afflicted with insomnia and bad dreams, and voluntarily divorced from the society in which he had grown up, Huck could no longer be managed by a man who had not resolved his own complications, many of which he had invested in the boy. What the author did not realize was that in his journey by water he had been hinting at a solution all along: an excessive exposure to violence and death produces first a compulsive fascination with dying, and finally an ideal symbol for it.

The parallel is complete. In both Huck and Nick, Hemingway's generic hero, we have a sensitive, rather passive but courageous and masculine boy, solitary and out of doors, who is dissatisfied with respectability, chiefly as represented by a Bible-quoting woman of the house. Each runs away from home. "Home" in both cases—St. Petersburg or northern Michigan—was a place of violence and pain, but though it was easy to flee the respectability, off on their own both boys came up against brutality harder than ever. Both were hurt by it and both ended by rebelling utterly against

a society that sponsored, or permitted, such horror. Nick decides that he is not a patriot, and makes his own peace with the enemy; Huck decides that he will take up wickedness, and go to hell. He lights out for the territory, the hero for foreign lands. Huck and Nick are very nearly twins. Two of our most prominent heroes, Huck and the Hemingway hero, are casualties whom the "knowledge of evil," which Americans are commonly said to lack, has made sick.

This theme of the boy shattered by the world he grows up in is a variation on one of the most ancient of all stories, and one of the greatest of all American stories, which relates the meeting of innocence and experience. It was a primary theme of our first professional man of letters, Charles Brockden Brown, and it has run through our literature ever since. In the latter half of the nineteenth century it was related at what might be called the very poles of our national experience—on the frontier and in Europe—and with the steady flow of travelers abroad it was primarily in Europe that the drama of the meeting of youth and age was enacted. Here developments of the theme ranged all the way from comic and crude accounts of innocents abroad to the subtleties of Hawthorne and James, with their pictures of American visitors under the impact of the European social order.

The story is a great American story not only because it is based on the experience of every man as he grows up, but also on the particular and peculiar history of the country. Once we were fully discovered, established, and unified we began to rediscover the world, and this adventure resulted in our defining ourselves in the light of people who did not seem, to us or to them, quite like us.

The stories of Huck Finn and the Hemingway hero share this general theme, for they tell again what happens when innocence, or a spontaneous virtue, meets with something not at all itself. But they are variations on the theme. The traveling comedians in Europe made spectacles of their ignorance, but usually had the last laugh. The more serious pilgrims were usually enriched at their pain, but showed up well in the process, often displaying a kind of power that comes from purity. But there is nothing subtle about the force that confronts the natural goodness of Huck and Nick. It is violence, an essential experience of the frontier, and also in our time—which is a wartime—of the American in Europe. And there is nothing triumphant about the beating which innocence takes, or about what happens to it after it is beaten.

The repetition of Twain's story by Hemingway establishes a continuity of American experience from one century to another, and reinforces the meaning of either story taken separately. The narrative begins to take on overtones that are larger than the facts themselves would seem to warrant. Indeed we might, conscious that we employ an abused term loosely, call it a "myth." At any rate it is a highly suggestive tale that falls, not surprisingly, within the Christian system and relates once more the fall of man, the loss of paradise. But it is an American myth, and it reveals us in a way that no historical, social, or philosophical treatise can do. It speaks to the people of the country from which it springs, and to the world, if it cares to hear, in such a way as to say: We start out smiling and well disposed to the world and our fellowmen. We see ourselves in the image of a naturally good, innocent, and simple boy, eager and expectant. But in the process of our going out into the world we get struck down, somehow, and after that it is hard for us to put ourselves all the way back together again.

This myth seems to bespeak in Americans an innocent desire for a decent life on the one hand and a sense of betrayal on the other. It says that we would do justly and be kind, that we wished no evil to anyone. But it also says that as we grew up evil was everywhere, and our expectations were sold out. The myth is one attempt to explain us, to ourselves and to the world. It also tries to explain why it is that despite all our other, opposing myths—of success, progress, the certain beneficence of technical advance, and the like—we are neither completely happy nor whole. It says, rather wistfully, we would have been, we could have been, but we were wounded before we were grown by the world we were given to grow in. The original beauty of a new country, the anticipation of the possibilities of life in what seemed the most promising world since Eden, were part of a seduction that went bad and should have ended at the doctor's. This is not a story that we believe literally, of course. No myth is to be taken literally or we would not, nowadays, call it a myth. But in a figurative way, on a metaphorical level, one suspects that we believe something of this sort about our experience in the world.

It remains to say something about Hemingway's world—the world his experience caused his imagination to create in books. It is, of course, a very limited world that we are exposed to through him. It is, ultimately, a world at war—war either literally as armed and calculated conflict, or figuratively as marked everywhere with violence, potential or present, and a general hostility. The people of this world operate under such conditions—of apprehension, emergency, stiff-lipped fear, and pleasure seized in haste—as are imposed by war. Restricted grimly by the urgencies of war, they are limited in their pleasures pretty much to those the sense can communicate, and their morality is a harshly pragmatic affair; what's moral is what you feel good after. Related to this is the code, summarizing the virtues of the soldier, the ethic of wartime. The activities of escape go according to the rules of sport, which make up the code of the armistice, the temporary, peacetime modification of the rules of war.

Hemingway's world is one in which things do not grow and bear fruit, but explode, break, decompose, or are eaten away. It is saved from total misery by visions of endurance, competence, and courage, by what happiness the body can give when it is not in pain, by interludes of love that cannot outlast the furlough, by a pleasure in the countries one can visit, or fish and hunt in, and the cafés one can sit in, and by very little else. Hemingway's characters do not "mature" in the ordinary sense, do not become "adult." It is impossible to picture them in a family circle, going to the polls to vote, or making out their income tax returns. It is a very narrow world. It is a world seen through a crack in the wall by a man pinned down by gunfire. The vision is obsessed by violence, and insists that we honor a stubborn preoccupation with the profound significance of violence in our time.

We may argue the utter inadequacy of the world Hemingway refracted and re-created; indeed we should protest against it. It is not the world we wish to live in, and we usually believe that actually we do not live in it. But if we choose to look back over our time, what essential facts can stack against the facts of violence, evil, and death? We remember countless "minor" wars, and two tremendous ones, and prepare for the day when we may be engaged in a holocaust beyond which we cannot see anything. We may argue against Hemingway's world, but we should not find it easy to prove that it is not the world we have been living in.

It is still too early to know which of all the worlds our writers offer will be the one we shall turn out to have lived in. It all depends on what happens, and you never know at the time. "Peace in our time," however, was Hemingway's obscure and ironic prophecy, stated at the start and stuck to. From the beginning his eyes were focused on what may turn out decades hence to have been the main show. With all his obvious limitations, it is possible that he said many of the truest things of our age truly, and this is such stuff as immortalities are made on.

Selected Bibliography

WORKS OF ERNEST HEMINGWAY

Three Stories and Ten Poems. Paris and Dijon: Contact Publishing Co., 1923.

In Our Time. New York: Boni and Liveright, 1925.

The Torrents of Spring. New York: Scribners, 1926.

The Sun Also Rises. New York: Scribners, 1926.

Men without Women. New York: Scribners, 1927.

A Farewell to Arms. New York: Scribners, 1929.

Death in the Afternoon. New York: Scribners, 1932.

Winner Take Nothing. New York: Scribners, 1933.

Green Hills of Africa. New York: Scribners, 1935.

To Have and Have Not. New York: Scribners, 1937.

The Fifth Column and the First Forty-nine Stories. New York: Scribners, 1938.

For Whom the Bell Tolls. New York: Scribners, 1940.

Across the River and into the Trees. New York: Scribners, 1950.

The Old Man and the Sea. New York: Scribners, 1952.

A Moveable Feast. New York: Scribners, 1964.

By-Line: Ernest Hemingway, edited by William White. New York: Scribners, 1967.

The Fifth Column and Four Stories of the Spanish Civil War. New York: Scribners, 1969.

Islands in the Stream. New York: Scribners, 1970.

The Nick Adams Stories. New York: Scribners, 1972.

BIBLIOGRAPHIES

Hanneman, Audre. *Ernest Hemingway: A Comprehensive Bibliography.* Princeton, N.J.: Princeton University Press, 1967.

White, William. *Checklist of Ernest Hemingway.* Columbus, Ohio: Charles E. Merrill, 1970.

Young, Philip, and Charles W. Mann. *The Hemingway Manuscripts: An Inventory.* University Park: Pennsylvania State University Press, 1969.

BIOGRAPHIES

Baker, Carlos. *Ernest Hemingway: A Life Story.* New York: Scribners, 1969.

Hemingway, Leicester. *My Brother, Ernest Hemingway.* Cleveland: World, 1962.

Montgomery, Constance Cappel. *Hemingway in Michigan.* New York: Fleet, 1966.

Ross, Lillian. *Portrait of Hemingway.* New York: Simon and Schuster, 1961.

Sanford, Marcelline Hemingway. *At the Hemingways: A Family Portrait.* Boston: Little, Brown, 1962.

CRITICAL STUDIES

Baker, Carlos. *Hemingway: The Writer as Artist.* 3rd ed. Princeton, N.J.: Princeton University Press, 1963.

Baker, Sheridan. *Ernest Hemingway: An Introduction and Interpretation.* New York: Holt, Rinehart and Winston, 1967.

Benson, Jackson J. *Hemingway: The Writer's Art of Self-Defense.* Minneapolis: University of Minnesota Press, 1969.

Fenton, Charles A. *The Apprenticeship of Ernest Hemingway.* New York: Farrar, Straus and Young, 1954.

Hovey, Richard B. *Hemingway: The Inward Terrain.* Seattle: University of Washington Press, 1968.

Rovit, Earl. *Ernest Hemingway.* New York: Twayne, 1963.

Stephens, Robert O. *Hemingway's Nonfiction: The Public Voice.* Chapel Hill: University of North Carolina Press, 1968.

Waldhorn, Arthur. *A Reader's Guide to Ernest Hemingway.* New York: Farrar, Straus and Giroux, 1972.

Watts, Emily Stipes. *Ernest Hemingway and the Arts.* Urbana: University of Illinois Press, 1971.

Young, Philip. *Ernest Hemingway: A Reconsideration.* University Park: Pennsylvania State University Press, 1966.

—PHILIP YOUNG

William Dean Howells

1837-1920

As a journalist, poet, travel writer, critic, and novelist, W. D. Howells wrote professionally for nearly seventy years. In 1852, when *The Blithedale Romance* appeared, Howells at the age of fifteen published his first poem; he was still writing a column for *Harper's* in the year of his death, 1920, when *Main Street* burst upon the literary world. Achieving editorial power and a name before he was thirty, he came to know, or to interpret, justly on the whole, every American writer of four generations, the forgotten Melville excepted. He introduced to American readers a host of Continental novelists, at first noticing their fiction in the French, Italian, and Spanish editions. He was the first advocate and editor and became the warm friend of Henry James and Mark Twain. For forty years he made his literary convictions strongly felt, first as editor-reviewer and then as conductor of critical departments in influential magazines.

From 1875 to 1895 he was at his most imaginative and productive. His work earned the praise of Turgenev, Tolstoi, Taine, Verga, Hardy, Shaw, and Kipling. At the same time, certain English reviewers attacked Howells for maligning Dickens and Thackeray while lesser American critics accused him of vulgarity and lack of idealism. Ambrose Bierce sneered at "Miss Nancy Howells and Miss Nancy James" for their gentility. But the effect of this criticism on the reading public was negligible. Howells' fiction and travel volumes continued throughout these years to sell steadily (if never spectacularly). By the turn of the century, however, the tide had shifted. Thereafter, his creative power waning, he was still often praised but less frequently read. As the "Dean of American Letters," he became in effect a dean without faculty or students. Late in life he noted wryly his loss of popularity, saying his statues were cut down, "the grass growing over them in the pale moonlight."

Then, when Mencken in 1919 charged Howells "has nothing to say"; when Van Wyck Brooks a year later persuaded many readers, even Sherwood Anderson, that Howells had clipped Mark Twain's wings by censorship—Lewis Mumford renewing the charge; and when Sinclair Lewis on winning the Nobel Prize in 1930 identified Howells with "Victorian" restrictive codes, Howells had reached the limbo of being subject rather than object. Certain readers might take pleasure in D. G. Cooke's and O. W. Firkins' critical studies (1922, 1924), or find the letters edited by his daughter Mildred (1928) full of life and intelligence. But the bright spirits of the second American literary renaissance took Mencken and Lewis and especially Brooks at their word.

Beyond the usual American whirligig of taste, one reason for their revulsion seems clear. These leaders in a decade dominated by Freudian doctrine were chiefly familiar with Howells' latest, least vigorous writing. Determined to break through the literary conventions governing sexual morality of earlier decades—conventions which they identified with Howells—they convicted Howells of prudery and optimism and condemned him forthwith.

The depression years of the 1930's saw Howells regain some of his lost stature. As Fitzgerald vanished and Steinbeck appeared, the liberal and radical critics, dismayed and protesting, looked to the American past for present comfort and rediscovered Howells as a Christian socialist. In the succeeding decades a group of scholar-critics have further redressed the balance. His life has been well outlined, his best novels have been distinguished from the worst and partially explicated. But his boldness and subtlety as a critic are scarcely recognized even now, and the full breadth and depth of his work need to be understood. To that end the reader must bring something like Howells' own sensibility—an appreciation of irony, social comedy, and style, and a taste for both James and Twain, Jane Austen and Tolstoi, Emily Dickinson and Thorstein Veblen. Howells' "beautiful time," as James envisioned it, and a just valuation of his work are yet to come.

In the meantime a new reading of Howells' life, encompassing yet going beyond Edwin H. Cady's solid, full, pioneer biography, ought to be made, and certain of its emphases may be suggested here. One obvious justification for such a new reading is that sketches of his life before Cady's were rendered impossibly gray by adulation, indifference, or ignorance. Another reason, challenging in nature, is that Howells, though willing enough to write of literary acquaintance and literary passions, spoke of his own life infrequently and guardedly. "Cursed with self-consciousness to the core," he hated, he said, to write of his early life "because it's so damned humiliating." His mood of reserve is curiously like Melville's or Hawthorne's when late in life he told Twain: "I'd like immensely to read your autobiography. You always rather bewildered me by your veracity, and I fancy you may well tell the truth about yourself. But *all* of it? The black truth, which we all know of ourselves in our hearts, or only the whity-brown truth of the pericardium, or the nice, whitened truth of the shirt-front? Even you won't tell the black heart's-truth. The man who would do it would be famed to the last day the sun shone on." The inner life, in short, of "William Dean Howells"—he disliked his full name heartily—and its intellectual and emotional crises remain only half explored.

Howells began life with a difference. His boyhood and early manhood in post-frontier Ohio (1837–60), typical in many respects, were still such as to make him both proud and self-conscious about the differences between his family and their neighbors in the villages of Hamilton and Jefferson. Jefferson was no more a cultural waste for a lively printer's apprentice, it is true, than the Hannibal, Missouri, of Sam Clemens, "Mark Twain." But the complex of circumstance and temperament was already marking young Howells with inchoate desires for life in city-centers of culture such as Columbus, Boston, or New York, for experience of the countries of Heine and Cervantes, and for literary fame. Unable to recall a time when he could not set type, the boy grew up with hard work and poverty in a large and close-knit family whose goal was to own a printing plant, a newspaper, and a home. His earliest neighbors had been largely southerners, yet even after the family moved to northern Ohio, their antislavery, Quaker, and Swedenborgian principles set them and him off from others. The backwoods communal experiment which his father and uncle undertook for a year in the country, near Xenia, at "New Leaf Mills," was unusual, if not unique. Other boys shared many of his childhood fears, but few or none of his young friends suffered until marriage and maturity from a private "demon" created by fears of hydrophobia, the ghosts of contemporary spiritualism, the world's coming to an end, and early death. These fears culminated in a recurrent nightmare of fire and alarmed cries of "Arms, Poe, Arms, Poe," induced by his reading of *Tales of the Grotesque and Arabesque*; eventually, in Howells' mid-teens, they led to hypochondria and nervous breakdown. William C. Howells' reassuring his son that he too had suffered from fears when young afforded some release; the rest came for Howells in constant reading, venturing into the classical languages, studying German, Spanish, and French, and writing poetry.

How much of Howells' later writing is fitfully illuminated by his childhood! His portrayal of ineffectual, warmhearted characters, with a touch of Colonel Sellers, like his father. His profound distrust of the Puritan tradition and Quaker dislike of violence, comparable to Whitman's. His ineradicable memories of hard work and bone-deep fatigue balanced against strong contempt for the scrambling life of self-made men. His lifelong preoccupation with communal experiments and with dream analysis. His devotion to principle in the face of popular disapproval. His taste for the "cleanly respectabilities." And withal, his establishing a pantheon of culture heroes and cultivating from the beginning the humors and ironies of Cervantes and Heine.

When Howells became news and literary editor of the *Ohio State Journal* at Columbus (1857–61), he began to breathe the air of a larger world, in spite of bouts of homesickness. Dickens, Tennyson, and the New England poets joined the pantheon of Heine, Cervantes, Goldsmith, and Shakespeare. James Russell Lowell accepted five of his poems for the *Atlantic* for 1860. He published *Poems of Two Friends* with J. J. Piatt, presumably thinking of Wordsworth and Coleridge. He wrote a good campaign biography of Lincoln. And he danced and talked literature and made friends and courted a visiting New England girl, Elinor Mead, in the deep-lawned homes of the state capital's simple, open society. The royalties from his campaign biography and a contract for newspaper letters made possible a pilgrimage through Canada to eastern publishing centers. In Boston, Lowell introduced him by letter to Hawthorne, and he met Holmes, Emerson, and Thoreau as well. In New York he encountered the *Saturday Press* bohemians and Walt Whitman at Pfaff's beer parlor. A year after his return to Ohio, his biography and his family's political devotion won for him a long-hoped-for opportunity, a position as American consul in Venice. A familiar cycle in American letters was once again to repeat itself.

The four years in Venice (1861–65), which included his marriage to Elinor Mead in Paris and the birth of Winifred, their first child, in Venice, completed an education begun at the type case in Hamilton, Ohio. Witty, loquacious, something of a blue-stocking, talented in art and letters, this girl from an idiosyncratic Vermont family remains a shadow in Howells' biography. Yet in these first years of marriage, Howells was liberated from the fears and the provinciality of his youth and he acquired professional skills as a writer. Though it remains largely undefined, Elinor Howells' influence upon her husband was subtle and strong, and along with his rich experience of Italian life and letters, it prepared him for the central role he would play for over four decades in American literature. Passing a turning point in his life, he had discovered that his gift was analysis of character, both national and individual, in simple, finely wrought prose. He had read Italian history, Dante, contemporary poetry and drama, and he had immersed himself in the stream of vulgar Italian life. Above all he had read (and witnessed in the Teatro Malibran) the plays of Carlo Goldoni and the *commedia dell'arte* which reflected the same life. Thus, having translated Goldoni's memoirs (published in 1877) and produced fresh travel sketches and criticism, the slender, diffident journalist came home stouter and stronger in his craft, an Italianate American.

But it was not to Ohio that Howells returned, for American publishing centers were in the East. Acutely aware that he might be trailing behind in the post-Civil War procession, Howells fell back on literary journalism in New York City for a temporary "basis" and a livelihood. Writing free-lance reviews and editorials quickly led to his conducting a department, "Minor Topics," for E. L. Godkin's *Nation,* and in his column he turned easily from reviews of Dickens, Whitman, and the Longfellow translation of Dante to murder, scandal, divorce, criminal insanity, New York politics, defense of the liberated Negro, the consular service, and the troubles of the Fenian brotherhood.

Boston was still his goal, nonetheless, and when in 1866 James T. Fields, Lowell's successor, offered him the assistant editorship of the *Atlantic,* Howells fulfilled the dream of his mature life (as he then thought), conceived when he first visited New England before the war. Though not officially editor-in-chief until 1871, Howells was soon actually in charge and responsible for a change in character in this avant-garde monthly. Over a fifteen-year period, he made it a national magazine, accepting contributions from the South and the West, introducing new features (music, political comment), and favoring a fresh, colloquial style. He met deadlines, read proof closely, wrote lead reviews, searched out new talent, and made many friends and certain enemies as he rose in these years from the status of minor poet and skilled journalist to that of new novelist and nationally known editor.

Perhaps the chief effects upon Howells of the editorial burden and of established editorial policies were delay in his development as a writer of fiction and limitation, in a degree, of what he might choose to represent in his fiction. The great success of *Venetian Life* (1866), a book which he had fashioned from his travel letters to the *Boston Advertiser,* and of *Italian Journeys* (1867) persuaded him to apply his skill in observing Italian characters and manners to the American scene. But *Atlantic* subscribers demanded reserve in the treatment of love and courtship in the pages of the magazine, and Howells therefore had to fit his treatment of sexual mores, in his first stories and novels, to *Atlantic* conventions. "Scene," for example, which depicts a Boston prostitute's suicide by drowning, is the only one of the *Suburban Sketches* which did not first appear in the magazine. Similarly, Howells could not easily forget that his approving Harriet Beecher Stowe's essay in defense of Lady Byron and Fields's publishing it lost the *Atlantic* some thousands of subscribers. Yet another consequence of Howells' editorship was his tendency to overvalue certain of the founders of the *Atlantic*: he had read them in the West, and and now they made him—almost—one of them. He knew Emerson and Thoreau and Hawthorne chiefly in their work, and their work encouraged him in the direction of his own talents. But his adulation of Lowell, Longfellow, and Holmes was for many years restrictive and even stultifying, as his reaction to Mark Twain's speech burlesquing the New

England worthies at a birthday dinner for Whittier suggests—clearly he overreacted.

If editing the *Atlantic* cramped Howells' talent in certain respects, however, it freed it in others, for the audience was intelligent and critical; certainly it made possible the flowering of other writers' genius. In the postwar years, Howells met Henry James, Jr., in Cambridge, published his early stories, and talked with him about the art of fiction for hours on end. Subsequently he competed with James for subjects, and with him invented the "American girl" and the international novel; he placed James's late novels; and he elucidated James's fiction discriminatingly for four decades. Howells' friendship with Mark Twain, which was even closer, was of prime consequence. It began with praise of *Innocents Abroad* (1869) in the *Atlantic*—an act comparably free and bold with Emerson's letter praising Whitman in that Howells was approving in print a "subscription book," that is, vulgar "non-literature." Thereafter Howells guided Clemens, so far as a friend and editor might, away from burlesque and failures in *vraisemblance* and mere buffoonery in the direction of his true capacities: an entire spectrum of satire, humor ranging from black to bright, true pathos touched with the tears of things, speech in the mouth, epic action, and living characterization. Howells was the first and most sensitive of Twain's critics, who never touched his copy when it was right and who was midwife to most of the work by which Twain is now known.

Finally, despite the restraining influence of the "counting house" and the limited sensibilities of feminine readers, Howells was able to use his editorial power on the *Atlantic* to extend the horizons of American fiction by selecting what to publish and by the great weight attached to his reviews. He gave short shrift to sentimental-domestic-melodramatic tales, and devoted his attention to stories that were au-

tochthonous in setting and probable in action, whose characters possessed "God-given complexity of motive." Thus, early in his editorial career, he detected realistic traits and qualities in certain novels of Elizabeth Stoddard, Bayard Taylor, and Henry Ward Beecher, but praised with greater enthusiasm the work of Björnson, George Eliot, and J. W. De Forest as he discovered it. Later, he discovered realism full-blown in the dramatic method and the sensibility of Ivan Turgenev, the directness and humor of Mark Twain, and the analytic subtlety and moral discrimination of James. And he drew upon each of these three masters as he wrote his own fiction at the time.

During his last years as editor of the *Atlantic*, Howells grew "miserably tired of editing" and correspondingly eager to write plays and fiction full time. The breaking up of the firm of Houghton and Osgood, which had published the *Atlantic*, a severe illness, and Winifred Howells' nervous prostration led him to resign the editorship in 1881 and take his wife and children abroad again for a year. Howells reached the peak of his power as a novelist in the decade that followed and as a critic took the leading role in a violent intercontinental war over realism. In the decade he wrote his best dramatic and international novels, *A Modern Instance* and *Indian Summer*; the transitional novel *The Rise of Silas Lapham*; and the major novels of social criticism *Annie Kilburn* and *A Hazard of New Fortunes*. In it he wrote telling criticism of the comparative and rhetorical kind, much of it in "The Editor's Study" column of *Harper's*, on Tolstoi, Dostoevski, Zola, Verga, Galdós, Hardy, James, and Twain. In it too he suffered a painful revolution in his mode of thinking and feeling, a revulsion from self and self-interest comparable to the "vastation" that Henry James, Sr., had undergone more than forty years earlier.

The change began, probably, in his growing

uneasiness over the widening social and economic chasm in America, and in his reading of Tolstoi and the American socialists Gronlund, George, and Bellamy. The change grew at a bound when he chose deliberately to risk his career and livelihood by declaring publicly that the Chicago anarchists, in 1887, had been unfairly tried—this from the writer who sought to be regarded as he himself regarded Cervantes. His altered viewpoint made his success taste of ashes. Then, when his daughter Winifred died, after a long, obscure illness, it deepened to the conviction that personal happiness can bear no part in the legitimate goals of a man's life. James had written of Winifred, "To be young and gentle, and do no harm, and pay for it as if it were a crime"—and Howells added, "That is the whole history of our dear girl's life." Howells' last major move, from Boston to New York and a new publisher, Harper and Brothers, took place in these years and has traditionally marked this profound change in his life. The change was scarcely unique: *The Princess Casamassima, A Connecticut Yankee,* and *Looking Backward* attest to the same deep unease. But Howells' "vastation" has not yet been full understood in its nature and its consequences.

After 1892 as a novelist Howells entered upon a plateau inclining gradually downward. *A Hazard of New Fortunes* was followed by many novels on a smaller scale, but only two of them, *The Landlord at Lion's Head* and *The Leatherwood God,* are of comparable quality. The social criticism becomes direct and overt in a series of articles, or is imperfectly integrated into the Altrurian romances. More significantly, Howells began his series of literary recollections and reminiscences, and after a time returned to literary journalism. Yet his practical criticism of this period, of plays and fiction, is distinguished, and his lecture on "Novel-Writing and Novel-Reading" represents

his critical theory at its comprehensive and penetrating best. The criticism becomes less tendentious than it was in "The Editor's Study," is extraordinarily sensitive to the currents of impressionism and naturalism among new writers, and treats the mature realists' work in a deeper perspective. Between ages fifty-five and sixty-five Howells first revealed the special qualities, lesser and greater, of Emily Dickinson, Crane, Garland, Fuller, Frederic, Norris, and Veblen, and of Herne, Harrigan, Ibsen, and Shaw. At the same time, novelists so different as Dreiser and Kate Chopin were reading and profiting from his fiction. Howells was also working, at the century's turn, to syndicate in newspapers the work of a group of novelists, including James, and to gain for them a wider audience and larger royalties; but he had to give up the scheme when he found that its backer was a former book pirate. He largely failed, as well, opposing national policy in the Philippine phase of the Spanish-American War. Even so, his anti-imperialist rhetoric, like that of Mark Twain and William James, is vigorous and memorable.

Until his death at eighty-three, Howells continued to review books and events in the "Editor's Easy Chair" of *Harper's.* He still wrote well when he was stirred by Ibsen or Brand Whitlock or Wells or Zola or Havelock Ellis, or the Irish executions in 1916, and he was still open to such new works as the poetry of Frost, Masters, and Lindsay and the *Education of Henry Adams.* The autobiographical *Years of My Youth* (1916), and *My Mark Twain* (1910), which Edmund Wilson calls the "best character" of Twain we have, bear comparison with the best earlier writings. Howells took keen pleasure in a variety of activities in his green old age: in serving as the first and continuing president of the American Academy of Arts and Letters and in preventing the

Academy from accepting endowments; in cultivating his garden at Kittery Point, Maine; in talking about the movies with his admirer and denigrator, Sinclair Lewis. He was writing about Henry James when he died.

Cooper, Melville, and Mark Twain wrote their first novels on a bet or at the urging of friends, turning from active lives to the writer's study. Hawthorne, Emily Dickinson, and James on the other hand became engaged in the craft of literature at an early age, and Howells is one with them in this matter of conscious literary intention. His first ambition was to become a lyric and narrative poet like Longfellow, sustaining himself by literary journalism until poetry would support him. But the popular failure of *Poems of Two Friends* (1860) and of *No Love Lost, a Romance of Travel* (1869) became the "turning point" of Howells' life, as he later explained, especially in the light of the high critical success of *Venetian Life* (1866). In this new kind of travel book, the first of many, Howells had contrasted the high art and the deep past of Venice with people and incidents in the shabby-picturesque present. The point of view is distinctly American, the tone is ironic in the manner of Heine, the style is finished. His "fatal gift of observation" already apparent, the young ex-consul and *Atlantic* editor turned to fiction.

From "The Independent Candidate, a Story of Today" (1854–55, never collected) to *The Leatherwood God* (1916) Howells wrote thirty-five novels—and more than forty tales and sketches. Apart from the juvenile "Candidate" story, *Suburban Sketches* (1871) is Howells' first tentative venture into fiction. With an eye educated by the Italian experience, Howells drew Irish and Italian and Negro figures in the Cambridge background, and expanded his scenes from the serving girl at home and doorstep acquaintance, through horsecar vignettes,

to Boston and Nahant. Two scenes, however, are very largely imagined. The first depicts recovering from the Charles River the body of a drowned prostitute, the second an ex-convict's "romantic" yarns about his past. "If the public will stand this," Howells wrote to James, "I shall consider my fortune made." The public response was favorable, and Howells took a long step toward the novel in his next book.

"I wrote 'Their Wedding Journey,'" Howells remarked to an interviewer long afterwards, "without intending to make it a piece of fiction. . . . It was simply a book of American travel, which I hoped to make attractive by a sugar coating of romance." Howells' distrust of his "fitness for a sustained or involved narration," however—he admitted it in the first page of his book—was quickly dissipated. A family friend whom he had asked to mark passages embodying real incidents marked instead "passages which were purely invention," and Howells was elated: he had proved his fictive art. He was also gratified when the first edition of 1500 copies sold out in a day.

The biographical elements in *Their Wedding Journey* (1872) are apparent in Howells' letters of the time and in the manuscript. Howells framed his narrative on his summer's travel with his wife, in 1870, from Boston to New York and Albany, Buffalo, Montreal, and Quebec. He also used descriptive bits and thumbnail character sketches which he had already printed in the travel columns written for Ohio newspapers in 1860, when he had made his literary pilgrimage to New England by way of Canada. Within this framework, nonetheless, *Their Wedding Journey* is fiction. Rapidly limned characters encountered along the route come to life as Basil and Isabel March, delayed honeymooners, talk with them and react to them. The Marches, in fact, provide such action as there is by humorous persiflage and frequent clashes of opinion and occasional quarreling. They also lend depth to the travelogue by recalling Francis Parkman's interpretations of the French-Canadian past, and by comparing Canadian to European sights. Howells provided a rationale for his story thus: "As in literature the true artist will shun the use even of real events if they are of an improbable character, so the sincere observer of man will not desire to look upon his heroic or occasional phases, but will seek him in his habitual moods of vacancy and tiresomeness." More positively, Howells has March tell his wife the story of Sam Patch, who invented the saying "Some things can be done as well as others" and tested it by jumping over Niagara Falls twice. From this tall tale, March then infers that Americans will never have a poetry of their own "till we get over this absurd reluctance from facts . . . till we consent to face the music in our simple common names, and put Smith into a lyric and Jones into a tragedy." *Their Wedding Journey,* which Henry Adams called "a pleasing and faithful picture of American existence," thus exemplifies Howells' early, anti-romantic, Emersonian theory of realism, a tradition that led to Eugene O'Neill's *The Emperor Jones.*

The Saguenay-Quebec travel scene again forms the background for *A Chance Acquaintance* (1873)—"There's nothing like having railroads and steamboats transact your plot for you," said Howells to a friend in 1871. But Kitty Ellison, who had appeared briefly in *Their Wedding Journey,* is a real creation. She is a girl from the West, brought up to revere John Brown and the abolitionists of Boston, bright and witty and unconventional, with natural good manners and taste. She finds the Canadian scene and character as rich and strange as Miles Arbuton of Boston thinks them dull, especially by comparison with European counterparts. Howells probably found his idea for the clash of such differing temperaments in Jane Austen, but his characteri-

zation is original—and so is his conclusion. Kitty in the end rejects Arbuton's suit, wholly in accord with Howells' and James's shared determination, at this time, to avoid the "everlasting young man and young woman" as a subject for serious fiction. Howells' satire, moreover, on one kind of Boston manners—the stiffness, coldness, and extreme self-regard of Arbuton—is pointed and amusing. James considered Kitty too pert, in the early serial chapters, and also wondered whether Arbuton's proposal might not have been dramatically rendered. But, he wrote his friend, he delighted in a figure "so real and complete, so true and charming." It is no wonder, for Kitty is the older sister of James' Daisy Miller, the first fictional portrait of the "American girl" who would make for Howells and James a linked reputation.

Howells' first "true novel," *A Foregone Conclusion* (1875), was also his first international novel. He was now prepared to venture beyond Canadian-American or native East-West contrasts, and by juxtaposing characters of the New World in the Old, to dramatize a tragic *donnée.* "The hero is a Venetian priest in love with an American girl," he wrote James. "There's richness!" The idea for the novel he had presumably been recurring to since 1866, when he thought of beginning "a romance—the scene of it to be laid in Italy, or Venice, rather" and composed an editorial for the *New York Times* on the celibacy of the priesthood as a cause of corruption in Italian society. He argued further that the current advocacy for clerical marriages was "the most natural and consequent growth from present conditions." Howells drew certain touches in the career of his skeptical inventor-priest from the life of Padre Libera, with whom he had read Dante a decade earlier, and introduced his friend Padre Giacomo, of the Armenian convent, very briefly as Padre Girolamo, a character who serves as a foil to Don Ippolito. But these, along with details of setting repeated from *Venetian Life*, are borrowings at the surface. *The Tragedy of Don Ippolito*, as Howells first titled the novel, gains its depth from four fully imagined characters, a tragic action that develops from their relationships, and a highly functional setting.

In the development of his American consul, Ferris, Howells breathes life into the anti-romantic convention that people rarely fall in love at first sight: for all his intelligence, Ferris is inwardly diffident and slow to recognize that he has become jealous of Don Ippolito, a priest. Howells' Mrs. Vervain, the wealthy widow of a choleric American army officer, is as addlepated as she is amiable. She is thus unable to perceive that Don Ippolito is falling in love with her daughter while he tutors her in Italian, and she is even capable of leading the young priest to believe that he might make his way in the then dis-United States. The moody seventeen-year-old "heroine," Florida Vervain, wavers between sharp-tongued outbursts and remorseful self-abasement. After humiliating Don Ippolito, she promises misguidedly to help him leave the church in which he has never truly believed and find a career in America as an inventor. With these three portraits, Howells' grasp of character matured. But the relationship of the Americans, all of them types of innocence, to the dreamy Italian cleric who has turned his oratory into a forge marks an even greater advance of the novelist in his craft, for it is Don Ippolito's character and the breakup of his illusions that count most. Into this figure Howells dissolves faint aromas of Don Quixote, of Arthur Dimmesdale, of Shylock, in order to show him a divided man, inwardly tormented by "a black and deadly lie." Don Ippolito is both unbelieving priest and impractical inventor, "under sentence of death to the natural ties between himself and the human race" and increasingly

deluded in the belief that Florida may love him. Howells had thus firmly prepared his actors, his entangling action, and his setting for the climactic chapter. In the moonlit, walled garden of Casa Vervain, the priest declares his love to Florida, who first repels him in unconscious shock and distaste—and then embraces him in pity and understanding before she runs out of his presence. The unobtrusive symbolism and symbolic reference made in earlier chapters now reach their height simultaneously, as the garden fountain that Don Ippolito had repaired to run briefly every day from its limited supply of water, "capering and babbling on," "all at once, now, as a flame flashes up and then expires . . . leaped and dropped extinct at the foot of the statue."

Howells marred the perfect verity of this ending, under pressure from James T. Fields, by adding a foreshortened epilogue in which he shifted his setting, reported the death of Don Ippolito, and concluded with the marriage of Florida to Ferris. "If I had been perfectly my own master . . ." Howells admitted to C. E. Norton, "the story would have ended with Don Ippolito's rejection." As it was, he kept the final action credible and somber enough. Ferris and Florida speculate fleetingly about Don Ippolito's feelings and motives; and in their consciousness finally he "ceased to be even the memory of a man with a passionate love and a mortal sorrow."

Howells' development as a novelist cannot always be neatly periodized. After completing a major work, he frequently lapsed into an earlier accustomed manner before venturing further—or continued to satisfy the taste of his public for psychologized tales of courtship. So, although it comes after *A Modern Instance* (1882) and *The Rise of Silas Lapham* (1885), both works of more scope, *Indian Summer* (1886) may be said to culminate Howells' first period of small-scale novels of manners, and is probably the best of them. Two interim works preceding *Indian Summer* are "Private Theatricals" *(Atlantic,* 1875) and *The Lady of the Aroostook (*1879). The first is a brilliant comic account of Belle Farrell's destroying the friendship of two young men who both become her suitors. A master of feminine psychology, Howells surpassed himself in delineating Mrs. Farrell, a New England Hedda Gabler before Ibsen. Like De Forest's Mrs. La Rue, she is beautiful and clever and irresponsible and yet somehow sympathetic, because she is driven by passions she does not fully understand. The second is a once very popular but much slighter work. In Howells' own words, it is the story of a girl who, by a series of misunderstandings, "finds herself the only woman on board a vessel going to Italy with three young men" who "do everything they can to keep her from embarrassment or even consciousness," one of whom marries her when they get to Venice.

Howells took especial pleasure in writing *Indian Summer,* chiefly because the realistic comedy of manners (one surmises) was the form most congenial to his temperament in his first period. The story grew out of his revisiting Italy in 1882–83 with his family, and duplicates certain pictures and episodes from Florentine history in *Tuscan Cities* (1886), a travel book that overlapped the novel in serial parts. The runaway carriage episode, the artist Inglehart (Duveneck), and the wish of the point-of-view character, Colville, to write a cultural history of Florence stem from Howells' recent direct experience. Understanding of the pervasive tone of the novel, however, its color and flavor, must be sought in his ambivalent attitude toward Italy revisited and in his response to the values of melancholy and nostalgia in Turgenev's fiction. The sense of loss was all the more clearly defined for him by the rapturous encounter of his daughter Wini-

fred, then eighteen, with the country of her birth.

Indian Summer, Howells told Mark Twain, "is all a variation on the one theme" of January and May, of youth and age. The variations are amusing and complex. Effie Bowen, whom De Forest considered "the most perfectly painted child in fiction," appears to be twelve. Her mother, Lina Bowen, is a charming widow of thirty-eight. Imogene Graham, their guest in Italy, twenty, a happier Florida Vervain, is counterpointed against mother and daughter. And the forty-one-year-old Colville, involving himself with all three, creates discords among them and multiplies the bemuddlement and the humor before final harmony is attained. Two memorable "confidants" help to spin the plot and clarify the theme. Elderly, curious Mrs. Amsden is always one stage behind in tracing the changes within the triangle and thus maintains the comic note. The Reverend Mr. Waters, aged seventy, who has cheerfully left Haddam East Village for Florence, forever, considers Mrs. Bowen and Colville young and provides Howells perspective.

The narrative method of *Indian Summer* is dramatic. The mood is nostalgia for lost youthful love and the Italian past, in the manner of Turgenev, well tempered by irony and wit. The characters, as noted, are Americans in Italy, of all ages. The action is single, culminating in Colville's marriage to Mrs. Bowen, after his engagement to the girl, Imogene, breaks of its own sentimental weight. But Howells' transforming into fictional life his leading ideas—that longing for youth when youth is past results only in the waste of human energy and devotion, and that the notion of self-sacrifice may prove a pure mischief—is achieved only by close attention to motive and characterization. When Imogene strikes youthful attitudes, or confides her delusions to her astonishing diary, or teeters happily at the edge of a mis-marriage, she errs foolishly and openly. Mrs. Bowen's faults are more subtly, though quite as clearly, indicated. The older woman's repressed jealousy and her wish to conform to European codes of behavior lead her to bewilder Colville and to torture Imogene and herself. Colville, though he often acts like a proto-Prufrock, is a paragon of common sense compared to the women of the novel. As for the carriage accident that reveals Colville's love for Mrs. Bowen, or Effie's appeal at the last moment to prevent Colville's leaving, these are acceptable *coups de théâtre*, because Colville now recognizes Imogene's immaturity, and Imogene has weighed Colville's social ineptitudes and found him wanting. The tone is high comedy. Only the dullest reader would expect disaster in *Indian Summer*.

Colville's sentimental dream of recapturing his lost love, reembodied in Imogene, thus ends happily in the "clear light of common day" and an uncommonly happy marriage. Colville's inner conflict, however, the tug of war within him between American present and European past, remains unresolved, to profounder but equally satisfying effect. Howells' skill as a novelist is well displayed in the natural symbolism by which he represents this wavering equilibrium. At key points in the action, scene, and internal dialogue, he enriches the theme of Indian summer by contrasts in age, in weather, in season, in history, in country. To name only three: When Colville first glances out on the piazza where he is lodging, it seems full of snow, until he discovers that "it was the white Italian moonlight." Further, Howells manages a most delicate and natural allegory of Florentine flowers to illuminate Colville's varying relations with Effie, Imogene, and Mrs. Bowen—the flowers he gives or forgets to give and the flowers they prefer. (The reference is as unforced in *Indian Summer* as it is exotic and artificial, for example, in Melville's *Mardi*.) And again, at Etruscan Fiesole, the mild Italian spring and the ancient landscape with "history written all over it" are set in Colville's consciousness against the raw country around Buffalo, New York, bursting impatient and lavish with "blossoms and flowers and young leaves and birds." In short, *Indian Summer* embodies the international theme in high comedy, and Colville is an earlier, more fortunate Lewis Lambert Strether. On finishing the work, Howells consciously abandoned the international field to James, and turned his full attention to the American scene.

In Howells' first period, therefore, he began by adapting his formula of travel and observation to fiction, with the sanction of the picaresque novel and perhaps of Heine's *Pictures of Travel*. The methods of Hawthorne and Turgenev and maturing concepts of motive and character led to the comedies of manners and courtship—with the Howellsian difference. Toward the end of the period Howells considered himself a "built-in novelist" because he was competent to begin serializing a work before he had finished it. Yet, despite increasing intensity in plot, the early books are alike in their depending on intersectional and international clash and contrast and on dramatic encounter between "two persons only, or three or four at the most."

In the second period, 1880–86, Howells turned to the American scene and to certain large problems of contemporary life. His characters increased in number and variety; his novels grew longer, from six to eight or ten magazine installments. He found justification first in Zola and then in Tolstoi for his matter and his motives. Most strikingly, he had come to the decision to excise those humorous or reflective comments on which he had heretofore leaned heavily in order to win approval for a character or an action—asides which formed for many readers a signature of his style and manner. Thus, the manner of Goldsmith or Thackeray or Heine is much diminished in *A Foregone Conclusion*, and by the time of *Indian Summer*, it has either vanished or become an element of the speech of Colville, a created character.

The second period opens with *The Undiscovered Country* (1880), "a serious work" Howells called it, which ventures into an area that he would explore again and again: the channels into which the will to believe was flowing in contemporary America, as religious convictions decayed and religious sanctions weakened. In this novel Howells sets the delusions of spiritualism in New England against Shaker belief and practice. Dr. Boynton's long decline as a spiritualist parallels the growing liberation of his daughter and medium, Egeria, and reaches its climax in his discovery that his spiritualism has been only a grosser kind of materialism. Apart from its intrinsic interest and its treatment of the father-daughter relation, the novel forms an interesting link between Hawthorne's *Blithedale Romance* and James's *The Bostonians*.

Doctor Breen's Practice (1881) also explores the growing feminist mood of the decade, but the author's stance is at least as masculine and satirical as it is sympathetic. Though Dr. Grace Breen, a homeopathist fresh from medical school, is first humbled by and then humbles the allopathist Dr. Mulbridge, her marriage to the man she loves cannot alter her bottom nature. She is a belated Puritan, a devotee of New England "dutiolatry."

A Modern Instance (1882) is a very different story. It was born in Howells' mind as "The New Medea" when he conceived an In-diana divorce case as a commonplace example of the dire ancient conflict in Euripides' drama. It grew with Howells' experience of the quarrels between his summer landlord and landlady in 1875 and 1876—a "tragedy, dreary and squalid beyond conception," he called it. It was written under the stimulus of reading Zola, "everything . . . I can get my hands on," and displayed a powerful motive and a firm grasp of the characters. Ostensibly the novel treats divorce and the failure of belief; less obviously but more truly it probes the mystery of love turned to hatred.

Marcia Gaylord is a most intensely imagined and realized character—pretty, self-centered, full-blooded, bewildered, hotly jealous. She is the child of parents who are as attached to her as they are cold to each other. Her marriage to Bartley Hubbard ends disastrously, partly because her uncontrolled temper and tendency to self-indulgence find counter-traits in her good-humored but amoral husband. Squire Gaylord, the agnostic lawyer of Equity, Maine, and his reproachful self-effacing wife habitually allow Marcia her way but do not give her a sustaining standard of conduct or belief. Hubbard, an orphan who has made his own way through college into small-town journalism, achieves his majority like Marcia with few convictions and grows increasingly sure that only those of his acts that the world sees can be of any account. Given a chance at the bar, enough money, a few friends, Hubbard might have prospered and lived out his life, however stormily, with his wife and child— so Howells seems to imply. But the virus of countinghouse journalism and Marcia's loss of faith in him lead to his cheating Kinney, a devoted friend, for money. This using of a friend brings on, in turn, the break with Ricker, his friend and conscience, the losing of his editorial job, and a final violent quarrel with Marcia over his encounter with a former Equity girl turned prostitute. When Hubbard leaves Boston and loses his pocketbook, return seems impossible. He perjures himself seeking an Indiana divorce, again runs away when confronted in court by the enraged Squire Gaylord, and dies—so it is reported—in Whited Sepulchre, Arizona.

James's well-known charge that the American scene too meagerly nourished the novelist's needs is refuted in this novel. As Howells wrote his publisher, J. R. Osgood, his story was to be on "no mean scale geographically." He was fully aware how the background, East and West, might add life to his characters and clarify his theme. So tight-fisted Equity, where the rats smell in the wainscoting, prefigures Boston as the Hubbards know it, a city of high rents and mean streets and sharp social cleavages, and the raw town of easy divorce, Tecumseh, Indiana, as well.

The Tecumseh courthouse and its tobacco-chewing idlers form the backdrop for Howells' most intense scene. There Squire Gaylord, accipitrine in feature and in his hatred of Bartley, defends his daughter's conduct and proves his son-in-law a liar, only to be brought down in the midst of the trial with a stroke. Howells does not end *A Modern Instance* at this point, however. True to his realistic tenets he returns to half-crippled Ben Halleck's futile struggle between his conscience and his long-indulged love for the widowed Marcia, and to the debate, still further removed from reality, of Clara Kingsbury and her wealthy lawyer-husband, Atherton, as to Ben's proper course. But the issue is no issue. Bartley is dead. Halleck regresses to Calvinist orthodoxy and self-punishment. In Marcia the spring of tenderness is broken, and she will, surely, return to the narrow life of Equity and "stiffen into the old man's aridity." Though the ending of the novel is open, it is not indeterminate.

When *A Modern Instance* appeared, Robert Louis Stevenson (who married a divorcée) withdrew an invitation to Howells to visit him because he thought Howells was condemning divorce. Much later Edith Wharton accused Howells of "moral timidity" that had checked him from arriving at a logical conclusion, even as she acknowledged his pioneer treatment of "the tragic potentialities of life in the drab American small town." Neither writer had followed the long logic of the tale or understood Howells' view that "the novel ends well that ends faithfully." No second marriage could ever redeem the past for either Halleck or Marcia Hubbard. Despite the weakened dramatic tension in the last chapters, Howells achieved his "strongest" work, as he himself believed, in *A Modern Instance*. It is a moving representation of moral ignorance and moral decay, unmatched until Dreiser imagined Hurstwood and Fitzgerald created Dr. Diver.

The Rise of Silas Lapham (1885) opens dramatically with an interview between Bartley Hubbard, still a struggling reporter, and the newly rich paint-king of Boston, on the perennially fascinating subject of how he had made his million. The novel has always been popular, partly because it presents Lapham's financial and social failure as "consciously and deliberately chosen" when he has to decide whether he shall cheat and stay on top in business, or tell the truth and fail irrecoverably. Lapham's true rise is therefore moral, and all the more dramatic in the context of the elastic business codes of the Gilded Age and his own business failure.

How much the novelist had learned of his art by the age of forty-eight appears in the complexities of the plot. Lapham's physical strength and bulk and country speech indicate that he is still the son of a hard-scrabble Vermont farmer. He is vigorous, raw, naive, uneducated, and socially ambitious for his wife and two daughters—a man who had risen fast as a competent soldier and officer in the Civil War. In sharp contrast, Bromfield Corey is physically slight and well educated, once fought under Garibaldi and has lived much abroad, lives moderately on family money, and plays at painting. In wit and ancestry he represents the Boston Brahmin type par excellence. Howells' device for bringing the two families into contact and conflict is chiefly the confused triangle of Tom Corey, the son, and Irene and Penelope Lapham, the daughters. Tom's polite attention to both girls and Irene's charming but nitwit egotism lead the Lapham's to believe that he loves Irene, so that Tom's eventual proposal to witty, reserved Penelope precipitates a period of harsh learning of "the economy of pain," as the Reverend Mr. Sewell calls it, before Tom and Penelope marry—and leave for Mexico.

But the heart motive of the novel, as Howells' original synopsis shows, is Lapham's determination to emulate Boston society and to make his family a part of it. The first clear sign that he will fail occurs in the dinner party scene at the Coreys', midway in the novel, when Lapham becomes boastfully tipsy—the result of his being unused to wine and of Corey's lapse of tact as he fails to note this fact. The vividest symbolic indication of Lapham's determination is Silas' "letting out" his mare and cutter one winter afternoon on the Longwood road. Driving with iron control and unmolested by the mounted policemen, he passes a "hundred rival sledges" with little apparent risk. The effective symbol of Lapham's desire is his building a new house on the Back Bay—a handsome, airy structure, with library and music room, to be decorated in white and gold. It is the product of an architect's taste, chiefly: Lapham contributes only money. The impression of this new house is strengthened by contrast to the ugly farmhouse of Lap-

ham's childhood; the dark, overheated, over-finished house in Nankeen Square; Mrs. Corey's "old-fashioned" house with a classic portico and "bare" interior; and Bromfield Corey's "ancestral halls" in Salem, presumably of the seventeenth century. When the new house burns to the ground, the insurance on it lapsed, Lapham must confess that he had set it on fire himself, carelessly, trying out his new fireplace. In the end, Lapham wrestles, like Jacob, with an angel and achieves an unhappy victory with his conscience; he tells Sewell that if "the thing was to do over again, right in the same way, I guess I should have to do it." Howells presents the larger conflict of Laphams and Coreys more stringently, however, and despite the marriage of the most businesslike Corey and the most cultured Lapham, the couple cannot remain in Boston. Of this conflict, Howells says: "It is certain that our manners and customs go for more in life than our qualities. The price that we pay for civilisation is the fine yet impassable differentiation of these. Perhaps we pay too much; but it will not be possible to persuade those who have the difference in their favour that this is so."

The Rise of Silas Lapham is more finely proportioned at the beginning than in the last third. This may be owing to Howells' need to foreshorten Lapham's slow business decline; but it also stems from his inability to make business loss as interesting as social climbing, or even as Irene's error in love and her hardening into maturity. James's comment on his *Roderick Hudson*, that its head was too big for its body, applies equally here. But in terms of style, the novel deserves its reputation. Bromfield Corey's wit and Penelope's tartness gain from contrast with Colonel Lapham's boastful speech, in the idioms and rhythms of his New England vernacular. Howells' narrative prose is equally functional, concrete, and clear. This was the style that both James and Twain, themselves stylists, found so distinctive and took so much pleasure in.

The serious motive and the large impression of occupations and professions that Howells sought in the fiction of his second period gave way to profound concern with social and economic questions in the third period, the decade from 1887 to 1894. In these years he suffered his profound spiritual and psychological crisis. The ground shifted under his feet when he stood, almost alone, in a glare of publicity after he asserted the rights of the Chicago anarchists. His daughter's death brought sharp suffering: perhaps he had sought the wrong treatment. He experienced a sense of alienation, as well as excitement, in moving to New York. In 1886, almost inadvertently he became involved in a sharp, often bad-tempered, running battle concerning the new realism with a host of critics because of his "monthly ministrations of gall and wormwood" in "The Editor's Study" of *Harper's*.

Howells plunged into this storm of change, weathered it, and emerged from it largely by learning the "transcendent vision" of Leo Tolstoi and adopting Christian socialism. Most of his novels in the period have been characterized as "economic" novels, and it is true that they share certain characteristics of the *Tendenz-roman* or propaganda novel, a form Howells scorned. Ideologically they culminate in *A Traveler from Altruria* (1894), a Utopian romance that brings together Howells' ideas in defense of liberty, equality, and fraternity in that altruistic "other land" which America only partially shadowed forth. But "novels of complicity" is a more accurate tag than "economic" novels, because complicity is the dominant concept in them; and a "panoramic theory of fiction"—Howells' own phrase as Van Wyck Brooks later reported it—is equally useful since it fits these works concerned with the lives of many rather than few characters. These definitions, however, apply only to the main stream in the third period; they will not account for *April Hopes* (1888) or *The Shadow of a Dream* (1890)—both substantial novels and each different in form and motive.

In *The Minister's Charge, or The Apprenticeship of Lemuel Barker* (1887) Howells first fully stated his doctrine of complicity, combining it with that major motif of the nineteenth-century novel, the provincial in the city. The minister, Sewell, has unintentionally encouraged Lemuel to come to Boston from his home in the country by politely dishonest praise of the boy's poems. Lemuel becomes his "charge." And in a sermon he is driven to conclude that "no one for good or for evil, for sorrow or joy, for sickness or health, stood apart from his fellows, but each was bound to the highest and the lowest by ties that centred in the hand of God. . . . If a community was corrupt, if an age was immoral, it was not because of the vicious, but the virtuous who fancied themselves indifferent spectators." Sewell's rhetoric is heightened by echoes from the marriage ceremony, and takes on additional ironic force in the context of Barker's fortunate escape later from marriage to a factory worker, "poor, sick, flimsy little Statira" Dudley. The reason for Barker's escape is striking. Just as sexual passion turning to hatred and the persistent tie between father and daughter had spun the plot of *A Modern Instance,* so masculine, "whopper-jawed" 'Manda Grier retains her hold, implicitly sexual, upon Statira, against Barker's sense of obligation to the girl. Thus "The Country Boy in Boston"—this was Howells' first title for the novel—fails and returns to the country; and thus Howells stands the American drama of the self-made man on its head. The work is suffused with other and subtler ironies that delighted Mark Twain, for example, which make up for the blurred double focus on Sewell and Barker. To suggest only two: Sewell preaches complicity but is unable to conceive of Barker's torment when he falls in love with the gentle Jessie Carver while he is still pledged to Statira. (One thinks of Clyde Griffiths.) The society girl Sibyl Vane treats Barker as her inferior with cutting arrogance, even as she finds time to bestow "a jacqueminot rosebud on a Chinaman dying of cancer" in a charity hospital.

The naked issue of charity versus justice becomes, in fact, the central issue of *Annie Kilburn* (1889), though Howells keeps his actors in this Tolstoian novel thoroughly limited and human. For all his social passion, Peck, the egalitarian minister of Hatboro, Massachusetts, cares little for his motherless child. Putney, the lawyer who defends the mill workers in labor disputes, is a periodic drunkard. And Annie Kilburn, Lady Bountiful with a conscience, fails utterly in her efforts to help the working poor of her company town, marries the apolitical doctor, and "waits, and mostly forgets, and is mostly happy."

Between March 1889 and October 1891, Howells published in serial form three extraordinary books: *A Hazard of New Fortunes* (1890), *The Shadow of a Dream* (1890), and *An Imperative Duty* (1892). The third is an intensely imagined study of miscegenation. The second, taking its title from *The Scarlet Letter*, explores the morbid psychology of jealous delusion; it is an experimental novel rendered from three points of view, anticipating rather than following James. The first is very simply Howells' biggest novel. It sets forth panoramically, as *Manhattan Transfer* would later, the struggles of fifteen major characters and a host of minor figures to establish a national magazine in New York City and to enter into its "vast, gay, shapeless life." The execution of

the Chicago anarchists and the Brooklyn trolley-car strike of 1889 provided Howells with a "strenuous action" and an "impressive catastrophe." A "moment of great psychological import" both national and private added tensions. And his theme, the American scramble for success with the inner revulsions bred by that struggle, lent the whole fable "dignity," as Howells himself later claimed.

A Hazard of New Fortunes envisions the city as a magnet and a microcosm. In social terms it contrasts Margaret Vance, the sensitive girl of old New York society, with the Dryfoos daughters, Christine and Mela, whose aim is to break into society under the guidance of the well-paid Mrs. Mandel. The elegant but unsure Beaton wavers in the middle, courting independent Alma Leighton and flirtatious Christine. At the bottom are Lindau and a prostitute pursued by the police, slum-dwellers, the one by choice and the other by necessity. In political-economic terms, the novel presents Dryfoos as the coldest of newly rich entrepreneur-speculators, with Fulkerson as his prophet, in contrast to Conrad Dryfoos, the son, who turns from his father and his father's life to passive resistance and Christian socialism. Similarly, Colonel Woodburn, whose private integrity matches his admiration for the feudal institutions of the prewar South, is set against Lindau, a German revolutionary who has lost his forearm fighting slavery in the Civil War. Still another kind of contrast appears in the characters' attitudes toward art: Beaton's great talent, Alma Leighton's aspirations, the barbarous taste of the Dryfoos family. In moral worth as well, Howells sets his characters in a kind of hierarchy, as George Arms has argued, from lowest to highest: Beaton, Dryfoos, Fulkerson, March, Woodburn, Lindau, and Conrad Dryfoos.

The measure of Howells' skill in representing "God-given complexity of motive" within these characters is that they act out their roles credibly. Beaton fails in a half-comic attempt at suicide. Lindau, a new John Brown, fights with the police in the strike and, his arm again shattered, dies of injuries. Conrad attempts conciliation in the strike and is shot in the heart. Dryfoos suffers, and takes his half-savage daughters off to Europe. Margaret Vance becomes a nun in a charitable sisterhood. March, the witness and chorus-character, is now able to buy the magazine that originally brought the group together. Yet at the moment of his success, March says to his wife, ". . . so we go on, pushing and pulling, climbing and crawling, thrusting aside and trampling underfoot; lying, cheating, stealing . . . to a palace of our own, or the poorhouse," blind to the principle that "if a man will work he shall both rest and eat." "And so we go on," March cries, "trembling before Dryfooses and living in gimcrackeries."

Howells had looked at Boston society from the bottom in *The Minister's Charge.* He had surveyed a Massachusetts mill town from the top in *Annie Kilburn.* Now in *A Hazard* he consciously employed the "historical" form, anatomizing New York City through many eyes. Though James thought the "composition" weak, he found the novel as a whole "simply prodigious," just as Twain considered it "a great book" wrought with "high art." One may not dismiss these appraisals as friendly prejudice: the novel singularly combines the wit of Jane Austen and the elaborate irony of Thorstein Veblen, before Veblen. It is a broad, vital comedy, as provocative in its implications as it is entertaining in its fable, in which Howells artfully and unobtrusively colored the public dream of success with private awareness of complicity.

Following the period of novels of complicity, which ended in the romance *A Traveler from Altruria,* Howells, reverted to smaller canvases

in his fiction, now persuaded that the great social questions must be represented from within rather than from without. Characteristic and perhaps best of the novels between 1894 and 1908 is *The Landlord at Lion's Head* (1897). Here Howells' idea was to bring a true New England rustic type into conflict with Cambridge and Harvard society, and his bottom motive was to realize "that anti-Puritan quality which was always vexing the heart of Puritanism." The great ambition of his hero, Jeff Durgin, is to build a fashionable summer hotel on the shoulder of his native mountain, Lion's Head. In the course of realizing it, the aggressive Durgin hardens from the contempt he suffers as a "jay" at college, and from his experience with three young women. Genevieve Vostrand refuses Jeff's offer of marriage, preferring a titled Italian, but at the last after separation from her husband and her husband's death, accepts the successful "landlord." Bessie Lynde, a Cambridge society girl, flirts and has a tentative affair with Jeff before her alcoholic brother horsewhips him. Cynthia, the country girl with whom he has grown up, who loves him, is reluctantly forced to give him up. With all three girls, but especially with Bessie, Jeff gets a dark glimpse into "the innate enmity between the sexes" in the game of courtship and passion—"passion lived" and "passion played." As the novel ends, Durgin is thoroughly successful on his own terms, taking for his motto, "You pay, or you don't pay, just as it happens." His career has borne him out. He might have succumbed to drink, except for his will and his constitution. He might have formed a dangerous liaison with Bessie Lynde, but her brother whipped him. He might have murdered Alan Lynde, but circumstance and obscure impulse spared him. He might have committed arson and been caught, but the old hotel burned by accident. Clearly, Howells created this new Bartley Hubbard, the successful failure who suffers from an incapacity for good, with special sympathy and entire aesthetic control. More nearly naturalistic than any other story by Howells, it is as Delmar Cooke judged it "a master novel."

Finally, *The Leatherwood God* (1916) represents a late, fine flowering of Howells' talent and his one punitive tragedy. It re-creates the rise of an actual Ohio backwoodsman of the 1840's, who deluded others and even himself momentarily into believing that he was God. Dylks's power arises from his stallionlike sexuality and from the will to believe of spiritually starved women of the frontier. His fall is necessary, but it is moving because it carries so many with him.

Turning from Howells' fiction to his critical theory, one may observe that interpretation of his fiction is further advanced than elucidation of his critical principles or his practical criticism in their full range. Three reasons for this condition may be suggested. First, the mass of Howells' critical writing remains uncollected and it is therefore difficult to view it in sequence or as a whole. Second, Howells' usual critical stance implies that criticism is a secondary form of discourse. Third, the body of critical writing by which he has usually been judged, *Criticism and Fiction* (1891), is argumentative, rhetorical, for the moment, and not wholly representative. It is well to recall that the novel came to be treated seriously, as "literature," only within Howells' lifetime, and that much contemporary criticism was vitiated by irresponsible anonymity or puffery or exhibitionism or ignorance. Howells wrote reviews and critical essays in every year from 1859 to 1920, as a journalist. But he loved literary art, especially the art of fiction. His best criticism is reasoned, reflected, distilled. He was a critic in spite of himself.

Despite his low opinion of the critical office,

then, Howells formed a theory of fiction that was subtler and more eclectic than literary history has allowed. Certainly its effect was and has been far-reaching. (It is possible that he is one of those masters "who are more accepted through those they have influenced than in themselves," but this is not the view taken here.) Hackwork and journalism aside, few critics of his day are comparable to him in breadth, in subtlety when he is engaged, and in clairvoyance.

The first element, at once apparent, in Howell's early theory of the realistic novel is his dislike for *"Slop, Silly Slop,"* as Nanny Corey characterizes a popular novel. The generic sloppiness of such fiction, Howells believed, derived from sentimental thought, melodramatic action, and poorly motivated character. Of course, James, Twain, De Forest, and many lesser realists shared Howells' revulsion and strengthened him in his view. Very early, Howells' and James decided to ignore or play down, so far as they could, simple-minded courtships in favor of other significant relations —of mother and son, father and daughter, husband and wife—and of other passions than love, such as avarice, ambitions, hatred, envy, devotion, friendship.

Conversely, Howells early developed a positive concept of form from the example of Turgenev and by reaction against the method of his early idols, Dickens and Thackeray. If readers were to take the novel seriously, then the novelist himself must take his craft seriously, and without intruding or commenting or appealing to the reader, learn to represent, to describe, and to dramatize. That is, if the illusion of life was worth creating, it was worth preserving unbroken. "Everything necessary to the reader's intelligence should be quietly and artfully supplied," Howells maintains, "and nothing else should be added." In these early years Howells distrusted the French writers for the moral vacuity or the obsessive sexuality in their tales, but he accepted as law Flaubert's dictum that the writer must be everywhere present in his work and everywhere invisible. A corollary of this dramatic ideal of Howells was that a strong motive and a firm, long-brooded-over grasp of character were equally necessary for the aspiring realist. It was character that counted, and not the "moving accidents" and thrilling adventures of earlier or popular contemporary tale-telling. In short, Howells' first concept of the novel was that the writer ought to begin by imagining several characters in the round, then bring them together to work out a credible dramatic action. He accepted the ideal of the novel of character the more readily because biography and autobiography fascinated him, both their form and their matter, and he was already writing and translating plays. Howells stated this double principle clearly in his essay on "Henry James, Jr.," in the *Century* (1882).

Plot, then, in the sense of continual gross or overt actions, Howells found less interesting than the slower pace of life as he observed it, "interiorly" and "exteriorly." It followed that a novel might end inconclusively, in the view of readers accustomed to the usual marriages, prosperity, and tying up of loose ends, and yet end faithfully and "well." Howells' youthful passion for Cervantes, his fondness for the episodic "memoirs" of Tom Sawyer and Huckleberry Finn, and his pleasure in the moral logic of Isabel Archer's final decision all confirmed him in his approving the open or ironic ending. To cite only one example, from his fictional practice, he brought *April Hopes*, a sardonic story of courtship, to this conclusion: "If he had been different she would not have asked him to be frank and open; if she had been different, he might have been frank and open. This was the beginning of their married life."

As the vehicle for the "new fiction," Howells advocated, published, and practiced a new, supple, colloquial English, taking as his authority writers so diverse as Dante and Emerson, James Russell Lowell and Artemus Ward, Mark Twain and Henry James. The "language of the street" in many regional varieties functions vitally in his own fiction, and he praised it as it appeared in the "local color" stories of Harte, De Forest, Cable, Frederic, Garland, and even Norris and Crane. He even taught it with some success to his Norwegian protégé, H. H. Boyesen. Mark Twain chiefly created a revolution in the language of fiction; Howells was the architect of the revolution. For many years Howells effectively and persistently advocated the use in fiction of native backgrounds, manners, and speech, often in the light of national difference. Hence it is no wonder that he pioneered, with James, in the international novel, and invented a new kind of city-novel. H. L. Mencken, who cites Howells frequently in *The American Language,* brackets him only a little grudgingly with Twain and Whitman as a chief proponent of American English. Thus, the language line from Emerson through Howells, Twain, and Whitman to Stephen Crane, Robert Frost, Gertrude Stein, Sherwood Anderson, and Ernest Hemingway is a line of direct descent.

These, in sum, are the major propositions of Howells' earlier theory of fiction, and most of them persist in his later theory. He modified his views in several respects during the free-lance years, 1881–86, and the period of novels of complicity and argumentative criticism, 1886–94. Most obviously, he wrote panoramic novels with larger casts of characters under a compulsion to treat the "social question" in an economic chance-world. A less apparent but equally significant change was his creating chorus characters, to serve as centers of consciousness or to focus upon ethical issues implicit in the action. Atherton, Evans, Sewell, the March couple, and others create the illusion of an ongoing society by their reappearance; but their prime reason for being is to debate moral questions more lucidly than less conscious or less dispassionate characters can. But, despite the success of *A Hazard of New Fortunes*, Howells never lost his interest in the psychological "novelette." Both *The Shadow of a Dream* (1890) and his liking for Stephen Crane's economical, effective stories suggest this persisting interest. In fact, Howells came in the end to believe that "the phenomena of our enormous enterprise" were not truly the "best material for fiction," except as such wonders of the "outer world" could be related to the "miracles of the inner world."

Defining Howells' key terms, especially as they are used in his later essays on major writers and in his lecture "Novel-Writing and Novel-Reading" (delivered 1899, published 1958), will serve to round out this sketch of his fictional theory, and to suggest his view of the ends of literature. Howells conceived of three ways of representing life in fiction: the novel, the romance, and the romanticistic novel. The novel, which comes from the sincere endeavor "to picture life just as it is," deals with character and incidents that "grow out of character." It is the "supreme form" of fiction, exemplified in *Pride and Prejudice*, *Middlemarch*, *Anna Karenina*, *Fathers and Sons*, *Doña Perfecta*, and *Marta y Maria*. The romance, Howells says, deals with life "allegorically," in terms of the ideal, of types, and of the passions broadly treated. *The Scarlet Letter* and *The Marble Faun*, Sylvester Judd's *Margaret*, and Stevenson's *Dr. Jekyll and Mr. Hyde* exemplify the form. Romances, he adds, partake of the nature of poems and are not to be judged by "the rules of criticism that apply to the novel." But the romanticistic novel seeks effect rather than truth, according to Howells: its motives are false, it is excessive in coloring

and drawing, and it revels in "the extravagant, the unusual, and the bizarre." Two very great men, Dickens and Hugo, wrote books of this kind. Their success is due to readers, prevailing in number, who have childish imaginations and no self-knowledge.

As to the "outward shape of the inward life of the novel," Howells contends, the three principal kinds are the autobiographical, the biographical, and the historical. The first he holds to be the most perfect literary form after the drama, because the tale-teller is master of the situation and can report his first-person narrator's mind with authority. But the "I" narrator cannot go outside his own observations, the range of the form is narrow, and none of the greatest novels have been written in it except *Gil Blas*, though it is the form of *The Luck of Barry Lyndon*, *The Blithedale Romance*, and *David Copperfield*. (One wonders if Howells exempted, or forgot, *The Adventures of Huckleberry Finn*.) The biographical novel, as Howells defines it, is the form in which the author's central figure, who must be of "paramount importance," reflects all the facts and feelings involved. Though he considers it "nearly as cramping as the autobiographical," he asserts that Henry James had used it in *Roderick Hudson* and has lately cast in it "work of really unimpeachable perfection." Here Howells is in effect predicting James's work of "the major phase." But the "great form," however impure and imperfect, he declares with much force and eloquence, is the "historical" form—the novel as if it were history. In it the novelist enters into the minds and hearts of his characters, invents speeches for them, gives their innermost thoughts and desires, and has their confidence in hours of passion or of remorse or even of death itself. He is a "universal intelligence" in this world. In spite of the contradictions, absurdities, improbabilities, and impossibilities inherent in the historical form,

Howells prizes it as the "primal form of fiction" and a form of the future. "Think," he says, "of *Don Quixote*, of *Wilhelm Meister*, of *The Bride of Lammermoor*, of *I Promessi Sposi*, of *War and Peace*, of *Fathers and Sons*, of *Middlemarch*, of *Pendennis*, of *Bleak House*, of *Uncle Tom's Cabin*, of *The Scarlet Letter*, of *l'Assommoir*, of the *Grandissimes*, of *Princess Casamassima*, of *Far from the Madding Crowd*," all masterpieces. The historical form may be "sprawling, splay-footed, gangling, proportionless and inchoate," he concludes, "but if it is true to the life which it can give no authority for seeming to know, it is full of beauty and symmetry."

The term "symmetry," drawn from Howells' study of art and architecture, introduces related ideas in his terms "perspective," "relation," and "proportion." All of them stem from his fondness for eighteenth-century English thought: concepts of rationality and control, measure and balance. The novel, he explained to Stephen Crane in an interview (1894), is "a perspective made for the benefit of people who have no true use of their eyes. The novel . . . adjusts the proportions. It preserves the balances." And again, it is "the business of the novel to picture the daily life . . . with an absolute and clear sense of proportion." What Howells means by these terms is presumably formal skill in representing norms of experience within the "microcosm" of the novel. Thus a storyteller like Maupassant, in Howells' view, often fails because he is "obsessed" with his own rather than with universal experience. Like Arnold, quoting Sophocles, Howells' goal is to "see life steadily and see it whole."

The effect that a novelist may achieve by representing his characters and their actions in "relation and proportion" is beauty and repose—terms not ordinarily associated with Howells' theory but central to his deepest intent. Repose, he explains (even as he admits he cannot define it), may arise from squalor or grief or agony in a piece of fiction; yet it is the quality that charms readers in every age, it is "the soul of beauty in all its forms." By repose, Howells may mean catharsis, "all passion spent," or he may mean the reader's rational pleasure in the inevitable working out of fictional logic. Perhaps he means both. As for truth, from truth to beauty is scarcely a step in Howells' theory of fiction. Realism is but the "truthful treatment of material," or the "truest possible picture of life." Truth, which is the only beauty, is "truth to human experience and human experience is so manifold and so recondite, that no scheme can be too remote, too airy for the test."

If Howells seems vague in this definition of truth in the novel, he is far more precise in asserting what the business of the novelist is and what effect the masterwork of fiction has on its audience. The novelist, he asserts, had "better not aim to please," and he "had still better not aim to instruct." His story must be a work of art, outside the realms of polemics and ethics, and if his story does not tell, nothing in it tells. What, then, he asks, is the purpose of the novel, the chief intellectual stimulus and influence of the day, this "supreme literary form, the fine flower of the human story"? His answer is both shrewd and penetrating. Though *The Scarlet Letter* or *Romola* may at once instill the dread of falsehood, he says, the novel can affect readers only so far as it shall "charm their minds and win their hearts." It can do no good directly. "It shall not be the bread," Howells urges, "but the grain of wheat which must sprout and grow in the reader's soul and be harvested in his experience, and in the mills of the gods ground slowly perhaps many years before it shall duly nourish him." In his essay on Ibsen (1906), Howells restated his resolution of the ancient dispute over literature's instructing or pleasing. He said: "The great and dreadful delight of Ibsen is from his power of dispersing the conventional acceptations by which men live on easy terms with themselves, and obliging them to examine the grounds of their social and moral opinions." In the end of ends, Howells made this slow-working indirect power the prime tenet of his critical theory. He sought it in his own fiction. He achieved it in his best novels.

Selected Bibliography

WORKS OF WILLIAM D. HOWELLS

Titles given below are first editions; revised texts are not noted, nor are translations. Much of Howells' writing has been out of print, but *A Selected Edition of W. D. Howells* in 40 volumes is filling this gap. Edwin H. Cady was the first general editor, succeeded by Don L. Cook; Indiana University Press is the publisher. "IE" followed by the name of individual editors and date of publication in the list below signifies "Indiana Edition." The fullest list of criticism of Howells is *A W. D. Howells Bibliography*, special number (1969) of *American Literary Realism*, compiled by James Woodress and Stanley P. Anderson.

TRAVEL AND PLACE

Venetian Life. London: Trubner, 1866.
Italian Journeys. New York: Hurd and Houghton, 1867.
Three Villages. Boston: Osgood, 1884.
Tuscan Cities. Boston: Ticknor, 1886.
A Little Swiss Sojourn. New York: Harper, 1892.
London Films. New York: Harper, 1906.
Certain Delightful English Towns. New York: Harper, 1906.
Roman Holidays and Others. New York: Harper, 1908.
Seven English Cities. New York: Harper, 1909.
Familiar Spanish Travels. New York: Harper, 1913.

NOVELS

Their Wedding Journey. Boston: Osgood, 1872. IE, John K. Reeves, 1968.
A Chance Acquaintance. Boston: Osgood, 1873. IE, Jonathan Thomas and David J. Nordloli, 1970.
A Foregone Conclusion. Boston: Osgood, 1875.
The Lady of the Aroostook. Boston: Houghton, Osgood, 1879.
The Undiscovered Country. Boston: Houghton, Mifflin, 1880.
Doctor Breen's Practice, a Novel. Boston: Osgood, 1881.
A Modern Instance, a Novel. Boston: Osgood, 1882. IE, 1973.
A Woman's Reason, a Novel. Boston: Osgood, 1883.
The Rise of Silas Lapham. Boston: Ticknor, 1885. IE, Walter J. Meserve, 1971.
Indian Summer. Boston: Ticknor, 1886. IE, Scott Bennett, 1972.
The Minister's Charge, or The Apprenticeship of Lemuel Barker. Boston: Ticknor, 1887.
April Hopes. New York: Harper, 1888. IE, 1972.
Annie Kilburn, a Novel. New York: Harper, 1889.
A Hazard of New Fortunes, a Novel. New York: Harper, 1890. IE, 1973.
The Shadow of a Dream, a Story. New York: Harper, 1890. IE, Martha Banta, 1970.
An Imperative Duty, a Novel. New York: Harper, 1892. IE, Martha Banta, 1970.
The Quality of Mercy, a Novel. New York: Harper, 1892. IE, 1973.
The World of Chance, a Novel. New York: Harper, 1893.
The Coast of Bohemia, a Novel. New York: Harper, 1893.
A Traveler from Altruria, Romance. New York: Harper, 1894. IE, Clara and Rudolf Kirk, 1969.
The Day of Their Wedding, a Novel. New York: Harper, 1896.
The Landlord at Lion's Head, a Novel. New York: Harper, 1897.
An Open-Eyed Conspiracy, an Idyl of Saratoga. New York: Harper, 1897.
The Story of a Play, a Novel. New York: Harper, 1898.
Ragged Lady, a Novel. New York: Harper, 1899.

Their Silver Wedding Journey. New York: Harper, 1899.

The Kentons, a Novel. New York: Harper, 1902. IE, George C. Carrington, Jr., 1970.

Letters Home. New York: Harper, 1903.

The Son of Royal Langbrith, a Novel. New York: Harper, 1904. IE, David Burrows, 1970.

Miss Bellard's Inspiration, a Novel. New York: Harper, 1905.

Through the Eye of the Needle, a Romance. New York: Harper, 1907. IE, Clara and Rudolf Kirk, 1969.

Fennel and Rue, a Novel. New York: Harper, 1908.

The Leatherwood God. New York: Century, 1916. IE, 1973.

The Vacation of the Kelwyns, an Idyl of the Middle Eighteen-Seventies. New York: Harper, [1920].

Mrs. Farrell, a Novel. New York: Harper, [1921]. First serialized as "Private Theatricals" in the *Atlantic*, November 1875 to May 1876.

STORIES

Suburban Sketches. New York: Hurd and Houghton, 1871.

A Fearful Responsibility and Other Stories. Boston: Osgood, 1881.

A Day's Pleasure and Other Sketches. Boston: Houghton, Mifflin, 1881.

A Parting and a Meeting. New York: Harper, 1896.

A Pair of Patient Lovers. New York: Harper, 1901.

Questionable Shapes. New York: Harper, 1903.

Between the Dark and the Daylight, Romances. New York: Harper, 1907.

The Daughter of the Storage and Other Things in Prose and Verse. New York: Harper, [1916].

POEMS AND PLAYS

Poems of Two Friends, with John J. Piatt. Columbus. Ohio: Follett, 1860.

No Love Lost, a Romance of Travel. New York: Putnam, 1869.

Poems. Boston: Osgood, 1873; enlarged edition, Boston: Ticknor, 1886.

Stops of Various Quills. New York: Harper, 1895.

The Complete Plays of W. D. Howells, edited by Walter J. Meserve. New York: New York University Press, 1960. (Brings together all 36 plays.)

IE, *Complete Poetry*, 1974.

CRITICISM

Modern Italian Poets, Essays and Versions. New York: Harper, 1887.

Criticism and Fiction. New York: Harper, 1891.

My Literary Passions. New York:, Harper, 1895.

Impressions and Experiences. New York: Harper, 1896.

"Novel-Writing and Novel-Reading, an Impersonal Explanation," in *Howells and James: A Double Billing,* edited by William M. Gibson and Leon Edel. New York: New York Public Library, 1958. (A lecture delivered in 1899.)

Heroines of Fiction. New York: Harper, 1901.

Literature and Life, Studies. New York: Harper, 1902.

Imaginary Interviews. New York: Harper, 1910.

The Seen and Unseen at Stratford-on-Avon, a Fantasy. New York: Harper, 1914.

IE, *Criticism 1898–1920,* Vol. III, 1973.

CRITICAL INTRODUCTIONS

Prefaces to Contemporaries, edited by George Arms, William M. Gibson, and Frederic C. Marston, Jr. Gainesville, Fla.: Scholars' Facsimiles and Reprints, 1957. (Collects 34 of Howells' introductions.)

BIOGRAPHY

Lives and Speeches of Abraham Lincoln and Hannibal Hamlin. Columbus, Ohio: Follett, Foster, 1860.

The Life and Character of Rutherford B. Hayes. Boston: Houghton, 1876.

"Meetings with King," in *Clarence King Memoirs.* New York: Putnam, 1904.

My Mark Twain, Reminiscences and Criticisms. New York: Harper, 1910.

AUTOBIOGRAPHY AND REMINISCENCE

A Boy's Town. New York: Harper, 1890.

My Year in a Log Cabin. New York: Harper, 1893.

Literary Friends and Acquaintance, a Personal Retrospect of American Authorship. New

York: Harper, 1900. IE, David F. Hiatt and
Edwin H. Cady, 1968.

New Leaf Mills, a Chronicle. New York: Harper,
1913.

Years of My Youth. New York: Harper, [1916].
IE, 1973.

LETTERS

Life in Letters of William Dean Howells, edited
by Mildred Howells. New York: Doubleday,
Doran, 1928.

Mark Twain–Howells Letters . . . 1872–1910,
edited by Henry Nash Smith and William M.
Gibson. Cambridge, Mass.: Harvard Universi-
sity Press, 1960.

IE, *Letters*, Vol. I (of five), 1974.

A Bibliography of William Dean Howells, by William M. Gibson and George Arms (New York:
New York Public Library, 1948; reprinted by
Arno Press in 1971), lists Howells' primary
writings. Jacob Blanck's *Bibliography of American Literature* (Vol. IV) adds certain contributions to books and pamphlets and refines upon
issues.

CRITICAL AND
BIOGRAPHICAL STUDIES

Bennett, George N. *William Dean Howells, the
Development of a Novelist.* Norman: University of Oklahoma Press, 1959.

Brooks, Van Wyck. *Howells, His Life and World.*
New York: Dutton, 1959.

Cady, Edwin H. *The Road to Realism, the Early
Years, 1837–1885, of William Dean Howells.*
Syracuse, N.Y.: Syracuse University Press,
1956.

————. *The Realist at War, the Mature Years,
1883–1920, of William Dean Howells.*

————, and David L. Frazier, eds. *The War
of the Critics over William Dean Howells.*

Evanston, Ill.: Row, Peterson, 1962. (Sixty
pieces, from excerpts to full articles, from
1860 to 1960.)

Carrington, George C., Jr. *The Immense Complex Drama: The World and Art of the Howells
Novel.* Columbus: Ohio State University Press,
[1966].

Carter, Everett. *Howells and the Age of Realism.*
Philadelphia: Lippincott, [1954].

Cooke, Delmar G. *William Dean Howells.* New
York: Dutton, 1922.

Eble, Kenneth E., ed. *Howells, a Century of
Criticism.* Dallas, Texas: Southern Methodist
University Press, 1962. (Twenty-eight essays.)

Firkins, Oscar W. *William Dean Howells.* Cambridge, Mass.: Harvard University Press,
1924.

Fryckstedt, Olov W. *In Quest of America, a
Study of Howells' Early Development as a
Novelist.* Cambridge, Mass.: Harvard Univer-
sity Press, 1958.

Hough, Robert L. *The Quiet Rebel, William
Dean Howells as Social Commentator.* Lincoln:
University of Nebraska Press, 1959.

Kirk, Clara M. *W. D. Howells, Traveler from
Altruria, 1889–1894.* New Brunswick, N.J.:
Rutgers University Press, 1962.

————. *W. D. Howells and Art in His Time.*
New Brunswick, N.J.: Rutgers University Press,
1965.

————. and Rudolf Kirk. *William Dean Howells.*
New York: Twayne, 1962.

Lynn, Kenneth S. *William Dean Howells. An
American Life.* New York: Harcourt Brace
Jovanovich, 1971.

McMurray, William. *The Literary Realism of
William Dean Howells.* Carbondale: Southern
Illinois University Press, 1967.

Woodress, James L., Jr. *Howells and Italy.* Durham, N.C.: Duke University Press, 1952.

—WILLIAM M. GIBSON

Washington Irving

1783-1859

FEW writers have successfully stretched a small talent farther than Washington Irving. He was an alert, ingenuous man who liked to be liked, and who tried to write what other people expected of him. His success was at once the measure of his own placid adaptability and of assurance among most of his contemporaries that literary excursions should be pleasantly trivial, skipping over surfaces without disturbing deeper matters of trade or politics, the opening of the West, or decisions on what democracy should be. People who spoke their minds sharply, like Philip Freneau or Fenimore Cooper, held Irving in great scorn, but almost everyone else admired him. He was comfortable to have around, for he seldom raised his voice, and he flattered his countrymen's assumption that they were, in truth, gentlefolk who could sip appreciatively on Old World culture at the same time that they built new traditions of strength and hardihood.

Irving spoke out at a time when his country needed someone like him. No longer was quizzical Ben Franklin, sage but uncouth, to represent the best in native accomplishment. People had already begun to talk of him as a despoiler of polite language and cultivated taste. His influence made for penny-pinching vulgarities, so that even poetry from the New World often spoke of commerce as a be-all and end-all. Many Englishmen of discrimination seemed to agree with Dr. Samuel Johnson that there was something degenerate about most Americans. Few were surprised at the scorn in Sydney Smith's tone as he asked in 1820, "Who reads an American book?"

When Washington Irving's *The Sketch Book* appeared at just that time, as if to provide by its popularity an answer to the question, literature of the United States gave first promise of eventual maturity. It had lived through a difficult, war-torn childhood, and for years was to struggle through an awkward adolescence. Clothed often in castoff garments, pampered, and praised for the wrong things, nurtured more often in parlor or library than in its spacious backyard, it nonetheless grew, its voice wavering and cracking, until finally, by the time of Irving's death in 1859, it had learned to communicate with authenticity and persuasion. During the years between, when Emerson and Hawthorne spoke most clearly, when Thoreau was thought strange and Poe shocking, when Melville and Whitman wrote of matters beyond the experience of many men, then Irving was more famous and respected than any of these, the dean indeed of American letters, envied by Cooper, admired by Longfellow, whose deft extensions of Irving's moods made him seem his logical successor.

Neither Irving nor Longfellow is esteemed so highly now, but neither is forgotten. The latter's songs still occasionally gladden or gently lull, and Irving, at the very least, has presented his country with the inestimable gift of two characters and a name. Either Rip Van Winkle or Ichabod Crane would be recognized at once if he walked down almost any American street. Their adventures have become as much a part of native lore as Captain Smith's rescue by Pocahontas, Tom Sawyer's slick whitewashing deal, or Paul Bunyan's gargantuan strength and appetite. In much the same sense, the word *knickerbocker* has become, through Irving's use of it, more than a designation for a baggy Dutch garment: it describes a period in the history of native culture, and an attitude toward literature and life; it appears today almost one hundred times in the Manhattan directory, to identify, among others, a fashionable corps of cadets, a brewery, a bookshop, a professional basketball team, and a manufacturer of plastics.

But Irving's reputation during his lifetime rested on greatly more than this, and a candid revaluation of his writing today suggests more also. He had two effective voices. As Diedrich Knickerbocker, he spoke of native themes, with crusty vigor—almost everything of Irving's which is most affectionately remembered is put in the words of that unpretentious and sometimes impolite old gentleman. As Geoffrey Crayon, he was decorous and superbly polished, beloved as an ambassador of good will between the New World and the Old, who lifted the literary embargo on both sides by disproving "the old notion that it is impossible for an *American to write decent English."* Praised by Scott and Byron and Moore, Irving became a solid, cheerful, adaptable symbol of

what a proper man of letters might be. As much as Franklin, he studied the way toward success.

Like Franklin also, he was the last child born in a large family, but without forebears deeply rooted in colonial America, as Franklin's had been. Irving's dour Presbyterian father had come to New York from Scotland only two decades before the birth of his youngest son on April 3, 1783, just as the Revolution drew to a close. In spite of wartime troubles, William Irving had prospered, and was assisted now by his oldest son and namesake, already at seventeen active in the family wine, sugar, hardware, and auctioneering business. The next son, Peter, was two years away from entrance to Columbia College, where he would receive preliminary training toward a medical degree which he was never to use. Seven-year-old Ebenezer was musical, but already promised to be the steadiest of them all, destined for a career in trade. John Treat, five years older than the youngest Irving, would also attend Columbia, to prepare in law. The three sisters married early and moved away, but wrote affectionate letters home which testify to close-knit family ties.

As the youngest, Washington Irving seems to have been a spoiled child, precocious, moody, and sensitive, and subject to alarming bronchial attacks. "When I was very young," he remembered, "I had an impossible flow of spirits that went beyond my strength. Every thing was fairy land to me." From the age of six to fifteen, he was doomed, he said, "to be mewed up the lifelong day in that purgatory of boyhood, a schoolroom." Thereafter, instead of entering college, he read haphazardly in whatever books came to hand, and explored nooks and crannies of little New York: "I knew every spot," he said, "where a murder or robbery had been committed, or a ghost seen."

More often, he wandered about the country-side, seeking health, it was explained, in the open air. Sometimes he adventured along the banks of the Hudson River, even above Spuyten Duyvil and Yonkers, through Dutch villages to Tarrytown, where his brother William's wife's family, the Pauldings, lived, "adding greatly to my stock of knowledge," he said, by noting rural habits and customs, and conversing with country people. Passing through Sleepy Hollow to the Pocantico Hills, he could look across the river to the legend-haunted headlands of the lower Catskills.

Between excursions, after 1799, he read law intermittently, finally with Josiah Ogden Hoffman, who had two attractive daughters. During the summer of 1803, he made a long journey with the Hoffmans, by boat and oxcart into Canada, squiring the girls, playing his flute, reciting Shakespeare, and filling notebooks with impressions of moonlight over the Hudson, of trading with Dutch farmers for milk and cheese, of squalid frontier lodgings and overland travel through deep-rutted forest roads, alert for whatever was comic or picturesque or appealed to sentiment.

For he had already, at nineteen, become known to contemporaries as a person of "extraordinary . . . literary accomplishments," deserving of the best "admiration and esteem." When the previous autumn his brother Peter had become editor of the new *Morning Chronicle* in New York, Irving contributed a series of nine sportive letters, from November 15, 1802, to April 23, 1803, over the signature of "Jonathan Oldstyle, Gent." They played with grave pleasantry over the state of manners, dress, and marriage in New York, but with greatest enthusiasm over the state of the theater. The jingoistic drama of the time—brave American sailors in love and at war—was lampooned; actors were caricatured, and mu-

sicians who with "solemn and important phizes" produced discordant noise; the managers were chided for not keeping the playhouse clean or the playgoers quiet; and critics were taunted as "pests of society," who attended performances only to "lounge away an idle hour."

Jonathan Oldstyle was so merry and vulgar an old gentleman that a more sedate Irving was later to be ashamed of him, but he spoke zestfully, and colloquially well. He disliked candle-grease dripping on his jacket from the theater chandeliers, and he became tired of dodging apple cores thrown by rowdies in the gallery. Jonathan discreetly ogled the belles who smiled flirtatiously from the boxes, their charms set off to most alluring advantage— here an arched look, there a simper, everywhere bewitching languish. He was sorry that spyglasses were no longer used to observe them more closely. And the critics—"ha! ha!"— how foolish and subversive: "they reduce feelings to a state of miserable refinement, and destroy entirely all the enjoyments in which our coarser sentiments delighted."

Much of what Irving would do best is foreshadowed in these juvenile essays: the physical caricature, which Dickens would admire and imitate—the dapper Frenchman, the persnickety spinster, the talkative old gentleman, the suave but foolish gallant, and the honest countryman "gazing in gaping wonder"; the pose of nostalgia—"Nothing is more intolerable . . . than innovation"; the rich delight in describing food and feasting—"the hissing of frying pans, winding the savory steams of roast or boiled." Most predictive, however, are the style and manner: the tailored sentences, well buttoned with adjectives; the jocular good humor, vulgar sometimes, but seldom ribald; the quip and the laugh and the quick retreat before feelings are deeply hurt; and through all the sense that Irving liked the people at whom he flicked his whimsically bantering wit—"that quiet, shrewd, good-humored sense of the ridiculous" which contemporaries recognized as setting Irving apart "from every other writer in our language," but which never of itself was enough to ensure him place as a major writer.

Perhaps because they did prick republican pretensions and looked shrewdly down their nose on native manners, the Oldstyle essays established young Irving as a kind of social arbiter for young America. Charles Brockden Brown, fresh from minor triumphs as a novelist, invited him to contribute to his *Philadelphia Literary Magazine*. Joseph Dennie, who conducted the *Port Folio* as "Oliver Oldschool," recognized and applauded the literary kinship implied by his choice of pseudonym. During the spring of 1804, Irving probably contributed to Peter's short-lived, astringent *Corrector*, and he continued his precocious career as a wit among men and a favorite with the ladies. His health, however, did not withstand even such pleasantly diversified pastimes, and he was packed off in May for a recuperative voyage to Europe.

The traveling did him good, in health and spirit. He made new friends and learned new manners, and filled notebook after notebook with careful records of what he saw and did, whether reverently viewing castles and cathedrals or in hairbrained escapades with his companions. He endured pirate attacks, excursions through bandit-infested hills, rough rides, bad lodgings, and poor food, picking up smatterings of French, Spanish, and Italian, reading volume after volume of travel adventures written by other men, and flirting with exotic women, now with novices in a convent, at another time with country damsels at a wayside tavern. Even the Italians, he wrote his father, "stared at us in surprise and called us the *wild Americans*."

In Rome, he met Madame de Staël, and was astonished that any woman could talk so much and so well. In Genoa, he met Washington Allston, the American artist, who almost persuaded him to remain in Italy to study painting. In Paris, he visited the tailors and the theater, and was thrilled to be accosted on the street by handsome, predatory young women. In London, he saw Mrs. Siddons at Covent Garden—in fact, he saw every play he could, and wrote home about them enthusiastically in detail. By the end of twenty-three months, however, Irving admitted that "one gets tired of travelling, even in the gay and polished countries of Europe. Curiosity cannot be kept ever on the stretch; like the sensual appetites, it in time becomes sated." He was happy therefore "once more [to] return to my friends, and sink again into tranquil domestic life."

Back in New York, he entered a scattered round of activities, reserving just enough time for the study of law to allow him to pass his bar examinations late in 1806. He helped Peter translate a travel book from the French; he contributed to the *Literary Picture Gallery*, a periodical dedicated to activities of visitors at Ballston Spa; he wrote occasional verse, including doggerel lines for the opening of the New Park Theater. Perhaps it was of himself that he spoke when later he allowed a character to confess: "I had too much genius for study . . . so I fell into bad company, and took to bad habits. Do not mistake me. I mean that I fell into the company of village literati, and village blues, and took to writing village poetry. It was quite the fashion in the village to be literary."

They were gay blades, those "lads of Kilkenny"—Peter and Gouverneur Kemble, Henry Brevoort, Henry Ogden, James Kirke Paulding, the Irving brothers, Peter and Washington and sometimes William—the "worthies" who met for literary powwows at Dyde's tavern, and for "blackguard suppers" at a porterhouse on Nassau Street: "sad dogs" indeed, fond of conscientious drinking and good fun. Among their favorite haunts was the old Kemble mansion on the Passaic River, about a mile above Newark, which they renamed Cockloft Hall; they transferred to it much of the fictitious adventure set forth in *Salmagundi*, a periodical which, when it appeared in twenty numbers irregularly from January 24, 1807, to January 25, 1808, became the talk and wonder of the town. "If we moralize," they promised, "it shall be but seldom, and on all occasions, we shall be more solicitous to make our readers laugh than cry; for we are laughing philosophers, and truly of the opinion that wisdom, true wisdom, is a plump, jolly dame, who sits in her arm-chair, laughs right merrily at the farce of life—and takes the world as it comes."

Who wrote it was soon suspected—the Irvings, Washington and William and perhaps Peter, and William's brother-in-law, James Kirke Paulding; but who wrote what has never been determined, so mixed and various but unified in temper was the matter set forth as "the whim-whams and opinions of Launcelot Langstaff, Esq., and others." Usually "Anthony Evergreen, Gent.," commented on fashionable society; "William Wizard, Esq.," handled theatrical and literary criticism; "Pindar Cockloft" contributed verse; and Launcelot Langstaff, as proprietor, roamed at will over all subjects. "In hoc est hoax, cum quiz et jokesez. Et smokem, toastem, roastem folksez, Fee, faw fum," they asserted on the title page in a cryptic motto, which was obligingly translated as "With baked and broiled, stew'd and toasted, and fried, boil'd, smok'd and roasted, we treat the town."

"As everybody knows, or ought to know," the first issue began, "what a SALMAGUND is, we shall spare ourselves the trouble of an explanation; besides we despise trouble as we do everything low and mean, and hold the man who would incur it unnecessarily as an object worthy of our highest pity and contempt." Most people, however, have been tempted to look up the word, to discover that it describes an appetizer made of chopped meat (raw), pickled herring, and onions, liberally seasoned with olive oil, vinegar, and cayenne pepper— excellent, some find, with cocktails or beer. No less savory were the elements compounded in *Salmagundi*, expertly mixed to encourage "genuine honest American tastes" rather than fashionable "French slops and fricasseed sentiment." For the convenience of readers, it was printed "on hot-pressed vellum paper, as that is held in highest estimation for buckling up young ladies' hair," in size just right for fitting "old ladies' pockets and young ladies' work bags."

The ladies came in for a great share of attention as the young men from Cockloft Hall labored to "instruct the young, reform the old, correct the town, and castigate the age." The ladies of New York were "the fairest, the finest, the most accomplished, the most ineffable things that walk, creep, crawl, swim, float, or vegetate in any or all of the four elements," but how alarmingly they dressed—in flesh-colored stockings and off-the-shoulder gowns: "*nudity* being all the rage." Actors and critics received sharp flicks, and fashionable upstarts like "Ding Dong," "Ichabod Fungus," and "Dick Paddle." Open war was declared against local folly and stupidity, especially in the letters of "Mustapha Rub-a-Dub Khan," written unashamedly in imitation of Oliver Goldsmith's "Citizen of the World" essays. Boorish English travelers and foppish French dancing masters were laughingly derided; even so popular a favorite as Thomas Moore, recently a visitor to America, was reproved for having "hopp'd and skipp'd our country o'er,"

. . . sipped our tea and lived on sops,
Revel'd on syllabubs and slops,
And when his brain, of cob-web fine,
Was fuddled with five drops of wine,
Would all his puny loves rehearse,
And many a maid debauch—in verse.

All was good humor, laughingly sustained, even when the satire turned political, like that directed against Thomas Jefferson, his embargo, his red riding breeches, and his scientific interest in "impaling butterflies and pickling tadpoles." More bitter invective was reserved for literary rivals, like Thomas Green Fessenden, an outlander, recently from New England, who in his *Weekly Spectator* dared criticize *Salmagundi* as a frothy imitation of Addison and Steele. "From one end of the town to another," he complained, "all is nonsense and 'Salmagund.' America has never produced great literature—her products have been scrub oaks, at best. We should, then, encourage every native sapling; but when, like *Salmagundi*, it turns out to be a *bramble*, and pricks and scratches everything within its reach, we naturally ask, why it encumbereth the ground."

Quarreling which turned bitter was not to the taste of the lads from Cockloft Hall; it was certainly not to Irving's, who for all his wit, was shy, more fond of conciliation than argument. *Salmagundi* was intended only as "pleasant morning or after-dinner reading, never taking too much of a gentleman's time from his business or pleasures." It was calculated for the mood of New York, "where the people—heaven help them—are the most irregular, crazy-headed, quick-silver, eccentric, whim-whamsical set of mortals that were ever jumbled together." Though frivolous and derivative *Salmagundi* was expertly done. If it were possible to know what parts of it Washington Irving wrote, they would probably be recognized as almost as good as anything he ever did.

Not only did *Salmagundi* hurt feelings; it was also not profitable—or so the young men claimed when they suspended publication after a year. Footloose again, Irving enjoyed his friends in Washington, Philadelphia, and New York, where he played lightly in chaste drawing-room flirtations with lovely ladies in the highest society and, with gentlemanly disdain, in politics. At Richmond, he helped Josiah Hoffman defend Aaron Burr in his trial for treason. He wrote occasional verse and squibs, and perhaps contributed political commentary to the newspapers, composing what was expected of him—usually at someone else's request. But ever since the decease of *Salmagundi*, he had been casually at work on a book of his own.

He and Peter had started it together, as a parody of a guidebook to New York, but when Peter was called abroad as manager of the family business in Europe, Washington Irving completed it alone—in grief, it has been said, and sadness. For on April 26, 1809—a date which he never forgot—young Matilda Hoffman died, she on whom Washington Irving's errant attentions had at length settled. His heartbreak was so great, and finally so well known, that it has become a commonplace to suppose that Irving remained all his life a bachelor because of loyalty to Matilda Hoffman's memory: "her image was continually with me, and I dreamt of her incessantly."

But, however sorrowful the months through which Irving brought it to completion, *A History of New York, from the Beginning of the World to the End of the Dutch Dynasty*, which appeared in December 1809, remains his first unified and his most joyous book. He wished it thought to have been written by a strange, inquisitive little gentleman named Diedrich Knickerbocker, who had disappeared, leaving behind him the manuscript of this "only authentic history of the times that hath been or ever will be published." Fact was jumbled with fiction, some dates were wrong, some footnotes spurious, but it was a gay, mirth-filled book. The "unutterable ponderings of Walter the Doubter, the disastrous projects of William the Testy, and the chivalric achievements of Peter the Headstrong" had New York in an uproar; when they reached England, they made Walter Scott's sides, he said, "absolutely sore with laughter." But many people of Dutch descent resented it: horsewhipping was spoken of, and ostracism. Emerson was later to disapprove of Knickerbocker's "deplorable Dutch wit," and Whitman of his "shallow burlesque." More feelings were hurt than Irving had intended.

Yet Knickerbocker's *History* continues light-heartedly to beguile readers of later generations, who enjoy its lovely comic pose—its "Münchausen vein of exaggeration run mad" —without being bothered by attempts to identify every victim of Irving's satire. John Adams may be recognized, and perhaps James Madison; no one will miss Thomas Jefferson, who is ridiculed for his "cocked hat and corduroy small clothes," and his eccentric, democratic manners. What lives, however, are not these things, any more than what lives in *Gulliver's Travels* are the political allusions which scholars discover there. Byron prized Knickerbocker's *History* for its copious style; Dickens is said to have worn out his copy with eager reading and Coleridge to have stayed up all one night to finish his. Not every modern reader will respond as heartily, but none will find Irving more consistently pleasant to be with than in this boisterous book which he completed at the age of twenty-six.

His laughter is directed at historians, explorers, plump Dutch matrons, and robust Connecticut girls, at Yankee skinflints and parsons, cock-fighting Virginians, the cozy pleasures of bundling and overeating (in luscious detail). As a resident of "the beloved isle of Manna-hata," Knickerbocker looked with suspicion on New Englanders as "pumpkin-eating, molasses-daubing, shingle-splitting, cider-watering, horse-jockeying, notion-pedling" creatures. Colonists to the south "lived on hoe-cakes and bacon, drank mint julips and brandy toddy," and amused themselves with "slave-driving, tavern-haunting, Sabbath-breaking, and mulatto-breeding." Frontiersmen were "a gigantic, gunpowder race of men . . . exceedingly expert at boxing, biting, gouging, tar and feathering"—"half man," they were, "half horse, half alligator."

The extravagance, mock gravity, and massive irreverence which was to characterize American humor from Sam Slick through Mark Twain to Faulkner are anticipated as Irving describes a sunbeam falling on the giant red nose of Antony the Trumpeter as he leaned over the side of a ship plying the Hudson, then bouncing off, "hissing hot," into the water "to kill a mighty sturgeon that was sporting beside the vessel." Wouter van Twiller, "exactly five feet six inches in height and six feet five inches in circumference," was a man of such extraordinary wisdom that he avoided disturbances of the world by closing his eyes for hours at a time, his active intelligence producing all the while "certain guttural sounds, which his admirers declared were merely the noise of conflict made by his contending doubts and opinions."

Irving's weapon was less often the rapier than what Stanley Williams has described as a "true Dutch blunderbuss, shooting off in all directions." More often than not, the humor is broad, sometimes mirthfully vulgar, as when brave Peter Stuyvesant, harassed in a duel, falls backward "on his seat of honor," to land kerplunk on a meadow "cushion, softer than velvet, which providence or Minerva, or St. Nicholas, or some kindly cow, had benevolently prepared for his reception." No wonder his countrymen were scandalized when Irving compared a Dutch ship to a maiden from New York: "both full in the bows, with a pair of enormous cat-heads, a copper bottom, and a most prodigious poop!"

Legend is created and local legend is utilized as Irving shaped from whatever came to his quick-moving hands a mirage of tradition, through which characters moved in quixotic grandeur, their noble pretensions made absurd, though no less noble, because of the provincial background against which they suffered inevitable, comic defeat. His reading was ransacked for archetypal patterns against which native heroes could be measured: at the Battle of Fort Christina, "immortal deities, who whilom had seen service at the 'affair' of Troy —now mounted their feather-bed clouds and sailed over the plain," until "victory in the likeness of a gigantic ox-fly, sat perched upon the cocked hat of the gallant Stuyvesant." How ludicrously small the deeds of warriors in this New World "when contrasted with the semi-mythic grandeur with which we have clothed them, as we look backward from the crowned result, to fancy a cause as majestic as our conception of the effect." With these words, James Russell Lowell was perhaps the first to recognize that Irving, as much as Cooper, though with lighter touch, produced a "homespun and plebeian mythos"—in Fielding's terms a "comic epic"—in which gallant protagonists tested ideals of the Old World against the frontier requirements of the New.

There was theme and scheme behind the "coarse caricature" of Knickerbocker's *History*. The *Monthly Anthology* of Boston greeted it as a book "certainly the wittiest our press has ever produced." In Philadelphia, the *Port Folio* praised its "drollery and quaintness," its "copious and natural style." Neither recognized it, as did the *Athenaeum* in Lon-

don a few years later, as "an honest and manly attempt to found an American literature. Those who read it must have exclaimed involuntarily, 'Yes, this is the work which was wanted. The umbilical cord is severed. America is indeed independent.' " For not even Irving quite knew what he had done; when he revised the *History* a few years later, he cleansed it of much colloquial coarseness, and of caricature which might wound, apparently so intent on being liked that he failed to realize that he had written the first American book capable of outliving the man who made it. Only Franklin's *Autobiography* claims precedence, for reasons quite different.

Irving's book is more irresponsible, more fun, and more literary. Source hunters have searched libraries to discover every influence on it, and none has done the job to another's satisfaction. Sterne and Fielding were certainly on Irving's mind, imitated or parodied; Swift, Cervantes, Shakespeare, Rabelais, the King James Bible, Aesop, Homer, Thomas Malory, and Thomas Paine are all present, in allusion or idiom; Arthurian legend, Greek myth, and the ponderous supposings of Cotton Mather's *Magnalia Christi Americana* jostle one another in exuberant disarray. Historians have derided or defended his adaptation of fact to fancy, sometimes locating in some half-forgotten volume in Latin, French, or Dutch the phrase or incident which Irving wove into a fabric not quite like any other.

Knickerbocker's *History* brought some profit (two thousand dollars) and more renown: "I was noticed, caressed, and for a time elated by the popularity I had gained"; but "this career of gayety and notoriety soon palled on me. I seemed to drift without aim or object." A second edition was called for in 1812, another in 1819; it was translated to French and German, and adapted for the stage. But it marked the end of one phase, the most carefree and lavish, of Irving's literary career. Not again would he write with such abandon; seldom would he write so spontaneously well. Grief or circumspection, or the enervating deceleration of spirits called growing up, sobered Irving.

In 1810, he became a partner in the family hardware business, but was apparently expected to devote little time to its routine affairs. Instead, he went to Washington as a lobbyist against restrictions in trade, and there he spent many hours in seeing the town with Paulding, and attending official balls, where he became a favorite of Washington's favorite hostess, Dolly Madison. Back in New York, he prepared a brief biographical introduction for an American edition of the poems of Thomas Campbell, declaring that in "an age when we are overwhelmed by an abundance of eccentric poetry, it is really cheering and consolatory to behold a writer . . . studiously aiming to please."

Irving's consistent demand of literature was that it should please, and more by familiarity than strangeness. As editor for two years beginning in January 1813 of the *Analectic Magazine*, he warned readers against Wordsworth's "new and corrupt fashion of writing," preferring instead the comfortable rhythms of Scott and Byron, the "warm sensibilities and lively fancies" of Thomas Moore. Friends complimented him for having "sacrificed his elegant leisure" thus to contribute to the literary advancement of his country, but Irving was bored and restless. He grumbled about the routine of editorial work and the quality of materials he found to print: "I really stagger under the trash." Paulding contributed an occasional short story, and joined the editor in a series of sketches of naval heroes. Irving himself conducted a column of "literary intelligence," wrote undiscriminating reviews, and

published a handful of sketches, among them the "Traits of Indian Character" and "Philip of Pokanoket," which he would later resurrect to fill out the pages of *The Sketch Book*.

Finally, in 1815, "weary of everything and myself," he set out again for Europe, determined "to break off . . . from idle habits and idle associates and fashionable dissipation." There he hoped to "pursue a plan I had some time contemplated, of studying for a while, and then travelling about the country for the purpose of observing the manners and characters of various parts of it, with a view to writing a work which, if I have any acquaintance with my talents, will be far more . . . reputable than anything I have yet written."

In England, he visited with relatives and old friends, explored romantic byways of London, called on Campbell and Moore, breakfasted with Samuel Rogers, went on literary pilgrimages to Kenilworth, Warwick, and Stratford, but most reverently to Abbotsford, where Scott welcomed him cordially. He studied German so that he could read legends which Scott admired. He wrote some tales of his own and assiduously noted impressions, in words or deftly sketched drawings, of each new scene. He helped whenever necessary with the family business, filling in as he could for Peter who was increasingly unwell. When, toward the end of 1817, the commercial enterprises of the Irving brothers faced bankruptcy, William, now in Congress, tried to get government positions for the two brothers stranded in England, and did manage an appointment for Washington, who turned it down, because, he said, "My talents are purely literary. . . . I do not wish to undertake any situation that must involve me in routine duties."

Faced now, in his mid-thirties, for the first time with the necessity of depending on himself for support, Irving took stock of his literary wares: he reworked Knickerbocker's *History* for new publication, thumbed through his journals for usable materials, and reminisced with friends about incidents which might be turned to account. He feared, however, that his mind had lost "much of its cheerfulness and some of its activity." When early in March 1819 he sent home a packet of manuscript, he apologized, "I have attempted no lofty theme, nor sought to look wise and learned. I have preferred addressing myself to the feeling and fancy of the reader rather than to his judgment. My writing, therefore, may seem light and trifling."

But with the appearance in New York two months later of the first number of *The Sketch Book of Geoffrey Crayon, Gent.*, Irving's reputation rose at once to a level from which nothing he had done before or would do again would budge it. A pamphlet of ninety-three pages, in gray-brown paper covers, it contained five sketches, the first four skillfully done but commonplace, and the fifth, "Rip Van Winkle," the slender, indestructible peg on which much of his fame has ever since been hung. Six more numbers were issued in New York, irregularly over the next sixteen months, until September 1820, each greeted with applause and admiration.

When parts of *The Sketch Book* began to appear, without permission or profit, in English periodicals, Irving early in 1820 arranged for a London edition of the whole, first done at his own expense; but soon—thanks to assistance from Scott, to whom in gratitude (or perhaps to set right those readers who supposed Scott had written the pseudonymous work) the edition was dedicated—it was issued by John Murray in two attractive volumes which sold prodigiously well in printing after printing. Of its thirty-two essays and sketches, twenty-six were about England, six of them descriptive of London scenes and five celebrating old-time Christmas festivities at an English country house; two were asides—"The Voyage" and "The Spectre Bridegroom"; and four were on American themes, two of these the Indian sketches from the *Analectic* which had not appeared in the periodical publication of *The Sketch Book* in New York.

Scott thought the book delightful, not so "exclusively American" as Knickerbocker's *History* and *Salmagundi*; William Godwin admitted that he hardly knew an Englishman who could write so well. Few contemporary readers seemed to agree with Wordsworth that *The Sketch Book*, "though a work of talent, is disfigured by an abundance of affectations"; more thought Irving, as Southey did, "a remarkably agreeable writer," with touch light enough "to conciliate any reader." These pleasantly diverting samples from Geoffrey Crayon's portfolio were shaded with humor and delicately colored with sentiment, not studied "with the eye of a philosopher; but rather with the sauntering gaze with which humble lovers of the picturesque stroll from one shop window of a print shop to another; caught sometimes by the distortions of caricature, and sometimes by the loveliness of landscape."

Familiarity added to the charm of the sketches. Scott's influence was plain throughout, his fastidious archaizing and untidy eloquence, later so distasteful to Mark Twain. Strokes learned from Addison were clearly discernible, and moods borrowed from Goldsmith's *The Deserted Village*, Thomson's *The Seasons*, Cowper's *The Task*, and Crabbe's somber rustic vignettes. So soft and adroitly accommodating was his touch that Irving was constantly compared to someone else, as if he had not manner or substance of his own—to Sir Thomas Browne, Fielding, Smollett, Sterne (never Swift, though sometimes Defoe), but especially to the ruminative and moralizing essayists of the eighteenth century. As an artist, he seemed copyist rather than creator: his literary offspring, said one unkind commentator, "resemble a family of sickly, but pretty children,—tall, feeble, and delicately slender, with white hair and white eyes,—dressed in jaconet muslin, trimmed with pink ribbon."

In England, his "eye dwelt with delight on neat cottages, with their trim shrubberies and green grass plots," on "the mouldering abbey overgrown with ivy, with the taper spire of a village church rising from the brow of a neighboring hill." His landscapes were stylized in the manner of the Flemish colorists whom he admired. Broad, traditionally evocative strokes pictured "vast lawns that extend like sheets of vivid green, and here and there clumps of gigantic trees, heaping up rich piles of foliage: the solemn pomp of groves and woodland glades, with deer trooping in silent herds across them; the hare bounding away to the covert; or the pheasant, suddenly bursting upon the wing; the brook, taught to wind in natural meanderings, or expand into a glassy lake: the sequestered pool, reflecting the quivering trees, with the yellow leaf sleeping on its bosom, the trout roaming fearlessly about its limpid waters; while some rustic temple or sylvan statue grown green and dank with age, gives an air of classic sanctity to the seclusion."

More important than the scene was the mood which it called forth, of serenity—"classic sanctity," wherein each once free-flowing brook is *taught* to wind in what are made to seem, but which are not, "natural meanderings"; or made to "expand into a glassy lake" which calmly reflects the lethargic quiescence which the scene suggests. Geoffrey Crayon's still waters have little depth; the irrepressible bright flow of language with which Diedrich Knickerbocker spoke of old New York had been taught to conform to London manners. Though he admired, Irving said, the

elegance and strength, robustness, manliness, and simplicity of the English gentleman, these were not traits which he easily transferred to his laboriously correct, embellished prose. He was not, it can be said, to the manor born.

Even the portraiture which as Geoffrey Crayon he now contrived was less vibrant, and the humor more timidly mannered. A line or two, whimsically suggestive because stylized, was often enough to represent a person—"the little swarthy Frenchman," for example, "with a dry weazen face, and large whiskers." Sometimes the portrait is briefly elaborated, like that of the angler in "broad-skirted fustian coat perplexed with half a hundred pockets; a pair of stout shoes, and leathern gaiters; a basket slung one side for fish; a patent landing net, and a score of other inconveniences." What people looked like was more important than what they were. Even in detailed "characters," like that of "John Bull," Irving assiduously balanced every blemish with some appealing trait.

Careful now that feelings should not be hurt, his comic pose was altered. "Wit, after all," he explained, "is a mighty tart, pungent ingredient, and much too acid for some stomachs; but honest good-humor is the oil and wine of a merry meeting." In a world so roiled, who was he to venture a disturbing idea? "If, however, I can by some lucky chance, rub out one wrinkle from the brow of care, or beguile the heavy heart of one moment of sorrow . . . I shall not have written in vain."

Exactly what happened to Irving's comic sense has not been adequately explained. Perhaps it was caution—once burned, twice shy; or perhaps it was maturity, which may be the same thing, or a desire to be liked, which is not. Always dependent on crutches made of other men's literary manner, Irving once had agility enough sometimes to dance a little jig of his own, using the rubber-tipped supports to beat out a muffled accompanying rhythm; or, like some temporarily crippled athlete, had swung from them a breath-taking two steps at a time up some hazardous stairway of ridicule. Now he learned to use them more sedately, careful that his own feet, once bruised by criticism, should touch the ground no more often than necessary, but with his gait so well adjusted to other people's that they hardly noticed his using crutches at all. Some even remarked that he got on very well without them when he adventured in American themes.

But even when he spoke as Diedrich Knickerbocker, Irving was accused of plagiarism. The plot of "Rip Van Winkle" was shamelessly stolen. Passages from the old German tale of "Peter Klaus" have been placed side by side with passages from Irving's narrative, to reveal imitation so blatant that much of Rip's unhappy experience seems little more than direct translation. But such bookish detective work may miss much of Irving's intention. "I wish in every thing I do," he once declared, "to write in such a manner that my productions may have something more than mere interest in narrative to recommend them, which is very evanescent; something, if I may use the phrase, of classic merit, i.e. depending on style . . . which gives a production some chance for duration beyond the whim and fashion of the day."

Something more than style, however, has kept Rip Van Winkle alive, on stage, on screen, and in the hearts of his countrymen. He has become their "muse of memory," Hart Crane once said, their "guardian angel of a trip to the past," and he remains their conscience, accusing and amusing at the same time. As Irving gave local habitation to a myth, perhaps as old as any which has beguiled the mind of man—that of Epimenides, Endymion, Sleeping Beauty, and the seven sleepers of Ephesus —he added such other familiar elements of

popular lore as the thunder of the gods, birds of ill omen, a magic potion, man's canine best companion, and dwarfs who are spectral spirits, transporting Valhalla and the Brocken to the Catskills, where Rip still triumphantly postures as the man-boy American (Huck Finn and Anse Bundren) who never grows up, the New World innocent who yearns to return to prelapsarian freedom from work and responsibility, to retire like Franklin at forty and fly a kite. "A child playing with children," he has been called, "a kid with a dog."

Before Fenimore Cooper or Mark Twain, Henry James, Sinclair Lewis, or William Faulkner, Irving created—it may be thought inadvertently—a symbol of the mythic American, presenting, as Philip Young has pointed out, "a near-perfect image of the way a large part of the world looks at us: likeable enough, up to a point and at times, but essentially immature, self-centered, careless and above all— and perhaps dangerously—innocent. Even more pointedly Rip is a stereotype of the American male as seen from abroad, or in some jaundiced quarters at home: he is perfectly the jolly overgrown child, abysmally ignorant of his own wife and the whole world of adult men—perpetually 'one of the boys' " —a Lazarus come back from the dead, as if to warn his countrymen, and yet a comic figure, in spite of the tragedy of a life slept away. His son is like him, and his grandson is another Rip.

Irving himself was surely not consciously so devious a contriver—it is the critics who have found him out. When in "The Legend of Sleepy Hollow," he adapted parts of Bürger's *Der Wilde Jäger*, and perhaps Robert Burns's "Tam O'Shanter" also, Irving admitted the tale "a random thing, suggested by scenes and stories about Tarrytown"; its borrowed plot was "a mere whimsical band to connect descriptions of scenery, customs, manners." Yet in creating

Brom Bones and Ichabod Crane, and the contest between them, he has been recognized as "the first important American author to put to literary use the comic mythology and popular traditions of American character which, by the early nineteenth century, had proliferated widely in oral tradition," demonstrating that "Dutch rowdies of the upper Hudson Valley were frontiersmen of the same stamp as the Ohio riverboatmen and Missouri trappers."

The Dutch of "The Legend of Sleepy Hollow" are indeed different from the chuckle-headed, indolent, pipe-smoking, stoop-sitting Dutch burghers of Irving's earlier writings. Brom is a frontier braggart, burly and roistering, "a Catskill Mike Fink, a ring-tailed roarer from Kinderhook." He is the sturdy backwoodsman who tricks the tenderfoot, acting out for the first time in our literature, says Daniel G. Hoffman, a theme which "has proliferated ever since: in Davy Crockett, in Mark Twain, in thousands of dime novels and popular magazines in which the yokel gets the best of the city slicker." Ichabod, a jack of many trades—schoolmaster, singing teacher, farmer, and eventually a successful lawyer—is rightly designated as Irving's Connecticut Yankee, a comic and less spectacular ancestor of Mark Twain's mechanic, a more optimistic witness to the common man's fate than Melville's Israel Potter. Obtrusively pious, this psalm-singing son of New England, naive and superstitious, but shrewdly ambitious, his head filled with daydreams of quick wealth through union with the "blooming Katrina" and setting out with her toward riches of the frontier, "for Kentucky, Tennessee, or the Lord knows where"—bloodless Ichabod is father to many confident, untrained, blundering, successful native heroes, and is the American cousin certainly of Dickens' Uriah Heep.

Almost all of Irving's better-remembered tales thus celebrate victory for the practical man, defeat for the dreamer—as if they were modest or masochistic sardonic parables of his own career. Men like Brom, who understand or defy superstition and know that visions are illusory, come out well. Fancy must be replaced by common sense as one grows older: tales of goblins, or even of high adventure and romance, are for children or childish men. What an ironic twinkle must have accompanied Irving's postscript notification to readers that even an ungainly visionary like Ichabod Crane turned out well, when he left daydreaming, as Irving had not, and turned to law.

As Diedrich Knickerbocker rather than Geoffrey Crayon speaks, the technique of broadly sketched caricature is managed with surer touch: readers do not forget Ichabod Crane astride his bony nag, the short stirrups bringing "his knees nearly up to the pommel of the saddle; his sharp elbows stuck out like grasshoppers'; he carried his whip perpendicularly in his hand, like a sceptre, and, as his horse jogged on, the motion of his arms was not unlike the flapping of a pair of wings." Dickens seldom displayed more gustatory fervor than Irving when he described "the ample charms of a genuine Dutch country tea-table" —the "doughty doughnut, the tenderer oly koek, and the crisp and crumbling cruller," the abundance of pies and meats and poultry, and "delectable dishes of preserved plums, and peaches, and pears, and quinces . . . all mingled higgledy-piggledy."

Not Hawthorne or Balzac or Frank Norris at his descriptive best could better have presented Mynheer Van Tassel's spacious farmhouse, over which "a great elm tree spread its broad branches . . . at the foot of which bubbled up a spring of the softest and sweetest water in a little well formed of a barrel; and then stole sparkling away through the grass to a neighboring brook that bubbled along among alders and dwarf willows." Beneath its low-projecting eaves were "flails, harness, various utensils of husbandry, and nets for fishing"; inside the house were "rows of resplendent pewter, ranged on a long dresser."

"In one corner stood a huge bag of wool ready to be spun; in another a quantity of linsey-woolsey just from the loom; ears of Indian corn, and strings of dried apples and peaches, hung in gay festoons along the walls, mingled with the gaud of red peppers . . . claw-footed chairs and dark mahogany tables shone like mirrors; and irons with their accompanying shovel and tongs, glistened from their covert of asparagus tops; mock-oranges and conch-shells decorated the mantel-piece; strings of various colored birds' eggs were suspended above it; a great ostrich egg was hung from the centre of the room, and a corner cupboard, knowingly left open, displayed immense treasures of old silver and well-mended china."

Without Rip Van Winkle and Ichabod Crane, and Diedrich Knickerbocker to tell their stories, *The Sketch Book* would still be a pleasantly diverting, but an undistinguished, collection. The Christmas sketches, the observations on country customs, the descriptions of Westminster Abbey, Stratford-on-Avon, and Boar's Head Tavern contain painstakingly colored vignettes of people and of venerable scenes. "The Art of Bookmaking" is a good-natured spoof of the manner in which Irving culled from writers of the past. His remarks on "The Mutability of Literature" are engaging rephrasings of melancholy certainties about there being no end to the making of books, or to mute, inglorious authors who are fated to write unknown. In his mild rebuke to "English Writers on America," Irving comes perilously close to expressing ideas which might offend.

From this time on, the spirit of Geoffrey Crayon almost completely took charge, and manner became increasingly more important than matter. "I consider the story," Irving repeated a few years later, "merely as a frame on which to spread my materials. It is the play of thought, and sentiment, and language; the weaving in and out of characters lightly, yet expressively delineated; the familiar and faithful presentation of scenes of common life; and the half-concealed vein of humor that is often playing through the whole;—these are what I aim at." But his aim was uncertain: when friends advised him to try longer fiction, he objected that anyone could write a novel—"the mere interest of story . . . carries the reader through pages and pages of careless writing, and the author may be dull for half a volume at a time, if he has some striking scene at the end of it." In composition such as he preferred, the "author must be continuously piquant; woe to him if he makes an awkward sentence or writes a stupid page."

Yet like Poe, who also disputed the effectiveness of longer fiction, Irving did not turn aside from the novel until he had tried to write one and discovered that he did not do it well. Though *Bracebridge Hall, or, The Humorists* was offered in 1822 as a "medley" of fifty-one sketches centered about an English country house, it is in fact a novel-*manqué*, faintly derisive and winsomely derivative. Squire Bracebridge may have been modeled, as Irving once suggested, on Walter Scott, but General Hardbottle, Lady Lillycraft, the village antiquary, and the faithful family retainers come direct from memories of characters better drawn by Goldsmith and Sterne. Ghost stories, bits of village gossip, essays on falconry, fortunetelling, and love-charms are strung almost haphazardly on a slender thread of romance, which ends with the wedding of Fair Julia, a shy, exemplary English girl, adroitly a caricature of heroines of sentimental fiction.

But most endearing of the sketches in *Bracebridge Hall* are not the village tales which form its substance but the fillers, the stories told as evening pastime at the ancient country house. Suspense is artfully created in "The Stout Gentleman," and exotic charm in "The Student of Salmanaca," but not as successfully as in "Dolph Heyliger" and "The Storm Ship," both re-creations of Hudson River lore drawn "from the MSS. of the late Diedrich Knickerbocker." Once again, however, these native tales were exceptions, for the New World offered little of appeal comparable to that of Europe. In America, Irving explained, all was "new and progressive, and pointed to the future rather than to the past"; there all "works of man gave no ideas but of young existence," without historical associations such as Irving found in England, where he wandered happily, "a grown-up child," he said, "delighted with every object."

"Never need an American look beyond his own country for the sublime and beautiful of natural scenery," he had said in *The Sketch Book*. "But Europe held forth charms of storied and poetical association. There were to be seen the masterpieces of art, the refinements of highly-cultivated society, the quaint peculiarities of ancient and local custom. My native country was full of youthful promise: Europe was rich in the accumulated treasures of age. Her very ruins told the history of times gone by, and every mouldering stone was a chronicle. I longed to wander over the scenes of renowned achievement—to tread, as it were, in the footsteps of antiquity,—to loiter about the ruined castle,—to meditate on the falling tower,—to escape, in short, from the commonplace realities of the present, and lose myself among the shadowy grandeurs of the past." Irving meant what Cooper, Hawthorne, Henry James, and Van Wyck Brooks later were to mean when they spoke of what America lacked which Europe had—the sustaining sense of history, and a decorum bred by tradition; but, perhaps because he said it first, he did not say it as clearly as they.

He searched through Europe now for more tales to retell, in a series of new collections—a German sketch book, an Italian, a Spanish, a French. "There are," he observed, "such quantities of these legendary and romantic tales now littering the press," needing only, as he had said, the polish of style to improve them. So he set out for the Continent in 1823, filling more notebooks with observations on quaint ceremonials, boar hunts, old castles, and bright national costumes—anything calculated to delight the eye or excite the imagination. But he worked by fits and starts, for he was not well, and he was forty: "My sunny days of youth are over." In Dresden, he puttered over translations, entertained himself and his friends with amateur theatricals, and courted young Emily Foster, who thought him too old. In Paris, where French editions of his writings made him seem a man of importance, he collaborated with John Howard Payne on plays, none of which was successful; he considered a book on Napoleon, worked over a series of American tales, and planned an edition of English classics and a play based on the life of Shakespeare.

After two dilatory years, hounded by his publisher for new materials but unable to collect enough of any one kind for a new book, in the summer of 1824 Irving threw together what he had into *Tales of a Traveller*—a mélange of German stories, tales of Italian banditti, an abortive novelette, and more American sketches found among the papers of the late Diedrich Knickerbocker." Though containing some of the liveliest writing which Irving had done since leaving America, and presenting in "The Devil and Tom Walker" his third-best native tale, the collection was not well received. We have heard these stories all before, said *Blackwood's*: the characters are corpses in clumsy new clothing. Irving was called "indisputably feeble, unoriginal and timorous; a mere adjective of a man, who had neither vigor nor courage to stand alone."

If it were to bring such dubious returns, further travel seemed a wearisome prospect. Irving considered writing a life of Byron, of Cervantes—tempted now to suspect that he was by nature a biographer, which he was; and he worked long hours over a projected American sketch book—and then either destroyed or lost the manuscript. His talent, he thought, was blighted, the romance of life past. When early in 1826 he was invited to join the staff of the American Legation at Madrid, he welcomed the opportunity to settle in one place. He vowed again to work assiduously, and for three years he did.

Irving was wanted in Spain, not as a diplomat, but as a writer, to translate Don Martín de Navarette's recently published collection of documents relating to Columbus. The work was congenial and appealingly sedentary: Irving rummaged with such zeal through old libraries for collateral materials that when Longfellow called on him that spring he was astonished at the older man's energy—up at six, at his desk through the day. Incidents from Navarette's book were elaborated with bits and pieces from other chronicles, and the whole was polished until it shone attractively as a straightforward narrative of exotic color and maritime adventure. But by the time the four volumes of *A History of the Life and Voyages of Christopher Columbus* were issued in the summer of 1828, Irving was excitedly involved with another book, more surely his own, which he hoped might recapture, though with

circumspection, something of the ironic tone of Knickerbocker's *History*.

Assuming the pseudonym of Fray Antonio Agapida, a zealot monk who distorted history, "marring the chivalry of the camp by the bigotry of the cloister," Irving presented the *Chronicle of the Conquest of Granada* in 1829 as "something of an experiment": a book made "out of old chronicles, embellished, as I am able, by the imagination, and adapted to the romantic taste of the day—something that was . . . between a history and a romance." William H. Prescott and Francis Parkman were to do this kind of thing better; but Irving did it first, mingling "romance and satire with grave historical details" as he told the story of Baobdil, last Moorish king of Granada, a dashing man in love or battle. But irony filters only dimly through these corpse-strewn fields lighted by flashes of sunlight on the "exterminating scimitar"; as halls resound with shrieks and fountains run red with blood, the spirit of old romance so illuminates each of its one hundred brief and chiseled chapters that Prescott declared Irving's *Granada* was permeated with such "dramatic brilliancy denied to sober history" that it "superseded all further necessity for poetry."

The *Voyages and Discoveries of the Companions of Columbus*, in 1831, was another modified translation, expertly done and well received. Meanwhile, however, Irving had been traveling again—through the "rugged valleys and long, naked, sweeping plains" of southern Spain, where he was captivated by the "proud, hardy, frugal, and abstemious" country people, and by the stories they told and the songs they sang; and he had settled in the old Moorish castle of the Alhambra. Through most of the spring and into the summer of 1829, Irving threw all his energies into a Spanish sketch book which, when published in 1832 as *The Alhambra*, would revive his reputation as "the first English prose-writer of the day," an artist with a true and tender eye for the unusual or picturesque, with feeling for scene at once precise and emotionally expansive.

The luxuriant southern sun, quiet countryside, and remains of Oriental splendor in the ancient Moorish stronghold seemed "too beautiful to be real": "As I loiter through these oriental chambers, and hear the murmur of fountains and the song of the nightingale; as I inhale the odor of the rose and feel the influence of the balmy climate, I am almost tempted to fancy myself in the paradise of Mahomet." He admired the refinement of those Moorish "princes of a departed and almost forgotten race, who reigned in elegance and splendor in Andalusia, when Europe was in complete barbarism," their achievements in art and education, their benevolent administration of justice. How splendid was this past, when "lovers of the gay sciences resorted to Cordova and Granada, to imbibe the poetry and music of the east; and the steel-clad warriors of the north hastened thither, to accomplish themselves in the grateful exercises and courteous usages of chivalry."

Irving's love of ancient lore, his feeling for scenery, his sentiment for people as simple, tranquilly suffering, but well-meaning and ultimately good, seldom had been better exercised than in *The Alhambra*, which for generations has vied with *The Sketch Book* as the most popular of his works, anticipating Flaubert, Pierre Loti, Stevenson, and Lafcadio Hearn in luxuriant sensuality. If all seems surface polish and prettiness; if dark areas are lighted with too soft a glow; if "manly defiance of hardships, and contempt of effeminate indulgence" again seem traits inappropriately honored by a person of Irving's haphazard sensibility, *The Al-*

hambra nonetheless does present him at his burnished best and at his wayward worst. The story of Peregil, the water carrier, in the "Legend of the Moor's Legacy" combines pathos and humor with narrative skill, to produce another minor masterwork; the rest of *The Alhambra* blends to a deliquescent glow which is remembered as pleasant long after details are forgotten.

Fame now completely engulfed Washington Irving, celebrated in the press of two continents as a purveyor of culture from the Old World to the New, and as the good-natured explainer of American idiosyncrasies to Europe: his writings went through half a hundred editions, and were translated into a dozen languages. On leaving the Alhambra in the later summer of 1829, Irving returned to London as secretary to the American Legation there. The next year, he received a medal from the Royal Society of Literature, and he edited Bryant's *Poems* for publication in England, changing some of the words to make them conform to British taste. The year after that, he was awarded an honorary doctorate at Oxford. Then, following a final tour to Stratford and Kenilworth, he set out for home, something he had contemplated doing every year, he said, for the past seventeen years.

His return was triumphant, but his effective literary career was over. He had succeeded for more than two decades in presenting himself to the world, as William L. Hedges has so well explained, as a "somewhat puzzled and alienated observer," beset by whimsey and beguiled by grotesquerie of the kind which during the next twenty years would find more complete expression in the writings of Nathaniel Hawthorne, Herman Melville, and Edgar Allan Poe. The essential characteristic of Irving's early, and better, tales and sketches is, says Mr. Hedges, "that they are told by a man who is not altogether sure of himself"; his fiction "is a fiction of dream, fantastic symbolic projections; it is heavily loaded with imagery functioning as metaphor. . . . It alternately sympathizes with, laughs at, and turns in fear from the stranger, the homeless or orphaned young man, the provincial abroad, the recluse, the eccentric scholar, the teller of tales." Irving had confessed himself "a poor devil of an author," torn by tensions he never completely understood. But he had discovered a style and a manner. From this time on he would be able to achieve something of composure by capitalizing on his reputation and repeating tested formulas. He would become less harried, more at ease with himself, and less consistently successful.

On May 23, 1832, he once again saw "the bright city" of his birth. New York provided him a hero's welcome, with a ceremonious dinner at the City Hotel, where the halls "rang with bravos, handkerchiefs were waved on every side, three cheers given again and again," as Irving, tears in his eyes, announced that he was home to stay, and that, above all, he loved America: "It was the home of the heart." He visited Saratoga Springs and Niagara Falls, and as the result of a chance meeting with a commissioner to the Indians, made a four-month trip into the Pawnee country of the Southwest, recording excitedly in his journal each new scene of picturesque interest.

Back in New York that winter, among friends now as sedate but not nearly so famous as he had become, plaudits continued to be showered on him. He declined nomination to Congress, as he would later decline nomination by Tammany Hall as candidate for mayor of New York, and appointment by President Van Buren as secretary of the navy. Instead he engaged himself to John Jacob Astor—for a tremendous sum, it was rumored—for the

purpose of going over that self-made millionaire's papers, to make a book from them about the opening of the West and the fur trade. In 1836, he moved to an old Dutch farmhouse below Tarrytown, which he first named "Wolfert's Roost," and then "Sunnyside," a "little, old-fashioned, stone mansion, all made up of gabled ends, as full of angles and corners as an old cocked hat."

The Crayon Miscellany had appeared in 1835, most of it taken up with the lively *A Tour on the Prairies*, but pieced out with memorials of Abbotsford and Newstead Abbey to make it of book length. Often reprinted as another "minor American classic," a book to be placed beside Parkman's *The Oregon Trail* or even Mark Twain's *Roughing It*, Irving's *Tour* has gone through more than thirty editions in English and twenty in translation. Because, in Irving's words, it is "a simple narrative of everyday occurrence," with "no wonders to describe, nor any moving accidents by flood or field to narrate," it represents to readers with little patience for whimsy or sentimental humor the crown of Irving's work. It offers them a rugged Irving, with trousers tucked inside his boots, gun in hand, fording streams, sprawled (elegantly perhaps) beside a campfire.

Unlike *Astoria*, in 1836 ("Not even WASHINGTON IRVING," said one reviewer, "can beat furs into eloquence"), or *Adventures of Captain Bonneville*, in 1837, both of them, like the Spanish histories, suavely adapted from other men's accounts, *A Tour on the Prairies* recounted Irving's own discovery of the frontier West. He noted the "gypsy fondness" of Creek Indians for brilliant color and gay decorations, the proud independence of the Pawnee ("sons of Ishmael, their hand is against everyone"), and the fine, Roman features of the Osages; their manly independence reminded him, almost twenty years before Thoreau expressed the same thought in *Walden*, that "we in society are slaves, not so much to others as to ourselves; our superfluities are the chains that bind us." Some forecast of the tone of Lambert Strether, who also learned in his middle years that he had never really lived, creeps into Irving's voice when, over fifty, he admits, "We send our youths abroad to grow luxurious and effeminate in Europe; it appears to me that a previous tour of the prairies would be more likely to produce that manliness, and self-dependence, most in unison with our political institutions."

But, though he spoke of trappers as a "rabble rout of nondescript beings" who hover like bats "about the frontiers between civilized and savage life"; though he described his half-breed guide as "one of the worthless brood engendered and brought up among the missions," who "fancied himself highly connected, his sister being concubine to an opulent white trader"; and though he sometimes caught in dialogue the clipped colloquialism of the native woodsman ("Next to my rifle, I'd as leave lend you my wife"), Irving's old manner of piquant phrase and romantic extension crept often into his record of these frontier experiences, especially when he retold at second hand the stories of hunting and Indian warfare, tall tales recounted by trappers, and Indian legends which had "a wild romantic interest heard from the lips of half-savage narrators." His brief chapter on "The Bee Hunt" may deserve comparison with William Bartram's account of Florida alligators or Thoreau's description of the battle of the ants; but the brief vignette of forest rangers in bivouac, in a "wild bandit" or "Robin Hood" atmosphere, is another set piece of the kind at which Geoffrey Crayon had always excelled—an assemblage of particularized notations, memoranda in an artist's field book: "Some were cooking at large fires made at the feet of trees; some were stretching

and dressing deer skins; some were shooting at a mark, and some were lying about in the grass. Venison jerked and hung on frames, was drying over embers in one place; in another lay carcasses recently brought in by the hunters. Stacks of rifles were leaning against the trunks of trees, and saddles, bridles, and powder-horns hanging above them, while the horses were grazing here and there among the thickets."

But pictures like this, carefully drawn from observation, seldom appeared in what Irving now considered his more important work. He grumbled about imitators who climbed toward fame with sketch books of their own, none quite done in his painstaking manner, not even Longfellow's *Outre-Mer* in 1834, which spoke of Europe and its legends. John Pendleton Kennedy's *Swallow Barn* in 1832 seemed simply a Virginian adaptation of *Bracebridge Hall*, not to speak of Cooper's *The Pioneers* nine years earlier, which told of an old family mansion on the frontier, and James Hall's *Legends of the West*, which skimmed most of the good stories from that region. Nathaniel Parker Willis had done a *Pencillings by the Way*, and Augustus Longstreet a boisterous *Georgia Scenes*, both in 1835. Irving had no heart for continuing in competition with any of these, or with the younger men like Hawthorne, who admired him, or Poe, who thought him pallid, or Emerson, whose remarks on self-reliance and throwing off shackles of the past may have seemed a rebuke.

Instead, at Sunnyside from 1837 to 1842, Irving rummaged through old notebooks for materials capable of being reworked, "writing away *like fury*," said Longfellow, on "remnants—odds and ends,—about Sleepy Hollow, and Granada. What a pity!" Another Spanish book was on his mind, a history of the conquest of Mexico, but he gave that up when he learned that Prescott was engaged with the subject, turning instead to an even more "American" theme—a life of George Washington which, like the *Columbus*, might examine roots of New World tradition, providing indisputable evidence that strength and resolution and solid sense and gallantry had been from their beginning characteristic of the best of his countrymen.

To the *Knickerbocker Magazine* in New York he contributed sketches and tales—"a hodgepodge of his experiences from the age of eighteen to fifty-eight," which were to be collected in *Wolfert's Roost* in 1855 and in the posthumous volume of *Spanish Papers*. "Mount-Joy: or Some Passages Out of the Life of a Castle-Builder" made good-natured fun of Transcendentalists "who render many of our young men verbose and declamatory, and prone to mistake aberrations of their fancy for inspirations of divine philosophy," and both "The Great Mississippi Bubble" and "The Early Adventures of Ralph Ringwood" are sprawling narratives of frontier life which look tentatively toward the lustier ironic realism of Mark Twain.

These better things were few, however, and not greatly different from other contributions by younger Americans who now vaunted their devotion to native scene and theme; but the Irving stamp was on them, certifying their authenticity by a style which shaped whatever subject to his familiar moods. He reworked his biography of Campbell and the sketch of Goldsmith which he had first done in Paris fifteen years before. Few books written during these decorous years were more popularly applauded than his sentimental *Biography and Poetical Remains of the Late Margaret Miller Davidson* of 1841, in which Irving spoke tenderly about the yearnings and aspiring verse of a tremulous, tubercular girl who had died at the age of sixteen, only a year younger than Matilda Hoffman had been when she died.

Early in 1842, Irving accepted appointment as minister plenipotentiary to the court of Spain, a position which came to him as the result of an apparent political about-face which had Fenimore Cooper—just then caged about by legal controversies with Whig opponents—growling in disgust. During the next few years, briefly in England and then in Madrid, Irving played a modestly important role as a diplomat, lending his prestige and suave good humor to negotiations over Cuba, the Oregon boundary dispute, and defense of his country's attitude in the Mexican War, "though I regret to say my endeavors have occasionally been counteracted by the derangement of my health." By the late summer of 1846, he was happy to be back once more at Sunnyside, which he would not leave for long again.

"In the early part of my literary career," he remembered, "I used to think I would take warning by the fate of writers who kept on writing until they 'wrote themselves down,' and that I would retire while still in the freshness of my powers—but . . . circumstances have obliged me to change my plan, and I am likely to write until the pen drops from my hand." Day after day at Sunnyside, he tinkered over old writings and projected new. In 1849 he arranged with George P. Putnam for a revised edition of his works, which would finally grow from fifteen to twenty-one, to twenty-seven volumes. *Mahomet and His Successors*, over which he had been worrying for almost a quarter of a century, appeared in 1850, to be followed by the miscellaneous *Wolfert's Roost* five years later, a book which it pleased him to find praised in the London *Spectator* as filled with "as much elegance of diction, as graceful a description of natural scenery, as grotesque an earnestness in diablerie, and as quiet but telling a satiric humor, as when Geoffrey Crayon came before the English world, nearly forty years ago."

Meant as praise, these words describe much of Irving's literary fortune, and foretell the inevitable decline of his reputation. For forty years there had been no change. This man of limpid style was without a subject, except as he could find it ready-made, available for transforming to language adroitly adapted to popular taste. Adventures as revealed in old tales or old documents, nostalgic recollection of bygone scenes, and the fallible, lovable, admirable characteristics of people—these were the themes which brought Geoffrey Crayon fame. Diedrich Knickerbocker could do better, and did, slipping into each miscellaneous volume a tale or two which gives it body, usually through the creation of characters indelibly drawn.

For it was finally people who interested Washington Irving most—whimsical people, droll manifestations of popular whim-whams; people who drifted as he had drifted, from one project to another, searching the key to success; or successful people, the heroes of whom Carlyle had written, and the representative men of whom Emerson spoke. Irving's life had been checkered with plans for biographies never completed, of Byron, Napoleon, Cervantes. The lives of English poets which he had supplied as hackwork introductions spurred his ambition to do something larger. The popular success of the little book about Margaret Davidson made him think he could do even better.

He did do greatly better with *Oliver Goldsmith*, one of the most appealing literary biographies of the first half of the nineteenth century. It was "a labor of love," said Irving, "a tribute of gratitude to the memory of an author whose writings were the delight of my childhood, and have been a source of enjoyment to me throughout life." Done in three versions, first in Paris in 1825 as an introduction to the Goldsmith volume in Galignani's

series of English Classics, expanded in 1840 as *The Life of Oliver Goldsmith, with Selections from His Writings* in Harper's Family Library, it was published in final form as *Oliver Goldsmith: A Biography* by Putnam in 1849. Though much of its material is drawn from Sir James Prior's and John Forster's more complete studies, Irving's *Oliver Goldsmith* outlives either, partly because, as Hazlitt recognized, its author "binds up his own portrait with Goldsmith's."

Irving admired "the artless benevolence" of Goldsmith, the "whimsical, yet amiable views of human life and nature; the unforced humor, blending so happily with good feeling and good sense, and singularly dashed at times with a pleasing melancholy"—all characteristics which readers for so many years had been accustomed to associate with Irving's own writing. Each, it has been said, looks "at human nature from the same generous point of view, with the same kindly sympathies, and the same tolerant philosophy"; each has "the same quick perception of the ludicrous, and the same tender simplicity in the pathetic"; in each runs "the same quiet vein of humor, and the same cheerful spirit of hopefulness." Irving defended his own literary intentions when he praised Goldsmith's writings because they "sweeten our tempers, and harmonize our thoughts; they put us in a good humor with the world, and in so doing they make us happier and better men."

Veneration and a sense of responsibility got in the way, however, as Irving devoted his final, failing energies to the *Life of George Washington*, the first volume of which appeared in 1855. Planned for three volumes, the work dragged on, filled with fact and anecdote and with massive descriptions of military events; too seldom graced even with vestiges of Irving's former easy prose, it moves by fits and starts, as if pushing desperately toward completion. "The shadows of departed years," he confided to a friend, "are gathering over me." But, he said, "I must get through with the work which I have cut out for myself. I must weave my web, and then die."

Scarcely six months after seeing the fifth and last volume of the *Life of George Washington* through the press, on November 28, 1859, Washington Irving died. At his funeral "thousands from far and near silently looked for the last time on his genial face, and mourned his loss as that of a personal friend and national benefactor." His grave in Sleepy Hollow Cemetery is still carefully attended, and flowers are placed in Christ Episcopal Church in Tarrytown each year on the anniversary of his death. The old house at Sunnyside has been restored, and schoolchildren make pilgrimages there to see the room where Washington Irving wrote.

For his reputation does live on, not perhaps among somber critics, for Irving was not in their sense a dedicated or committed person. But for those who accept in literature what they find there, and who are experienced enough not to expect too much, refreshing discoveries are to be made in reviewing his writings. It will not do to think of Irving as a complicated man. With quick eye, ready tongue, and alert recognition of absurdities, he sits quietly at both ends of the American literary spectrum—an expatriate seeking reverently in Europe for sources of culture, but, like James and Eliot and Pound, most effective in realizing American characters enmeshed in American ideals; and at the same time a native mythmaker who wove indigenous lore into comic tales which become fables. His country's first, but not her best, romantic historian; an early, but unsatisfying, impressionistic biographer; an exotic local colorist before Flaubert popularized the term; a mildly boisterous, thigh-slapping, sidesplitting rural humorist, a comic realist before Thackeray, a caricaturist before Dickens—Irving was tentatively all of these. He writes better than anyone who has written of him, in praise or condemnation; and he shares with each critic the handicap of having little of final importance to write about.

Selected Bibliography

WORKS OF WASHINGTON IRVING

Irving's collected writings have appeared in more than forty editions, one not greatly different from another; most often available is the Author's Uniform Revised Edition: *The Works of Washington Irving* (New York: G. P. Putnam's Sons, 1860–61), in 21 volumes. See Stanley T. Williams and Mary E. Edge, *A Bibliography of the Writings of Washington Irving* (New York: Oxford University Press, 1936).

"Letters of Jonathan Oldstyle, Gent," New York *Morning Chronicle,* 1802–03. (Reprinted, New York: William H. Clayton, 1824.)
Salmagundi; or, The Whim-Whams and Opinions of Launcelot Langstaff, Esq., and Others. New York: David Longworth, 1807–08.
A History of New York, from the Beginning of the World to the End of the Dutch Dynasty. New York: Inskeep and Bradford, 1809.
The Sketch Book of Geoffrey Crayon, Gent. New York: C. S. Van Winkle, 1819–20; London: John Miller, 1820.
Bracebridge Hall, or, The Humorists. A Medley. New York: C. S. Van Winkle, 1822; London: John Murray, 1822.
Tales of a Traveller. Philadelphia: H. C. Carey and I. Lea, 1824; London: John Murray, 1824.
A History of the Life and Voyages of Christopher Columbus. New York: G. and C. Carvill, 1828; London: John Murray, 1828.
A Chronicle of the Conquest of Granada. Phil-

adelphia: Carey, Lea, and Carey, 1829; London: John Murray, 1829.

Voyages and Discoveries of the Companions of Columbus. Philadelphia: Carey and Lea, 1831; London: John Murray, 1831.

The Alhambra. Philadelphia: Carey and Lea, 1832; London: Henry Colburn and Richard Bentley, 1832.

The Crayon Miscellany. Philadelphia: Carey and Lea, 1835. As *Miscellanies*, London: John Murray, 1835. *(A Tour on the Prairies*, separately published, London: John Murray, 1835; Paris: Galignani, 1835.)

Astoria, or, Anecdotes of an Enterprise beyond the Rocky Mountains. Philadelphia: Carey, Lea and Blanchard, 1836.

The Rocky Mountains: or, Scenes, Incidents, and Adventures in the Far West; Digested from the Journal of Captain B. L. E. Bonneville, of the Army of the United States, and Illustrated from Various Other Sources. Philadelphia: Lea and Blanchard, 1837. As *Adventures of Captain Bonneville*, London: Richard Bentley, 1837; Paris: Galignani, 1837.

Oliver Goldsmith: A Biography. New York: G. P. Putnam, 1849.

A Book of the Hudson. New York: G. P. Putnam, 1849.

Mahomet and His Successors. New York: G. P. Putnam, 1850.

Wolfert's Roost. New York: G. P. Putnam, 1855.

Life of George Washington. New York: G. P. Putnam, 1855–59.

Spanish Papers and Other Miscellanies. New York: G. P. Putnam, 1866.

The Wild Huntsman. Boston: Bibliophile Society, 1924.

Abu Hassan. Boston: Bibliophile Society, 1924.

JOURNALS

Journal of Washington Irving, 1803, edited by Stanley T. Williams. New York: Oxford University Press, 1934.

Washington Irving: Journals and Notebooks, 1803–1806, edited by Nathalia Wright. Madison: University of Wisconsin Press, 1969.

Washington Irving: Notes and Journal of Travel in Europe, 1804–1805, edited by William P. Trent. 3 vols. New York: Grolier Club, 1921.

"Washington Irving's Notebook of 1810," edited by Barbara D. Simison, *Yale University Library Gazette*, 24:1–16, 74–94 (Winter, Spring 1949).

The Journals of Washington Irving [1815–42], edited by William P. Trent and George S. Hellman. 3 vols. Boston: Bibliophile Society, 1919.

Tour in Scotland, 1817, and Other Manuscript Notes, edited by Stanley T. Williams. New Haven: Yale University Press, 1927.

Washington Irving: Notes while Preparing a Sketch Book, etc. 1817, edited by Stanley T. Williams. New Haven: Yale University Press, 1927.

Washington Irving: Journals and Notebooks, 1819–1827, edited by Walter A. Reichart. Madison: University of Wisconsin Press, 1970.

Journal of Washington Irving (1823–1824), edited by Stanley T. Williams. Cambridge, Mass.: Harvard University Press, 1931.

"Washington Irving's Madrid Journal, 1827–1828," edited by Andrew B. Myers, *Bulletin of the New York Public Library*, 62:217–27, 300–11, 407–19, 463–71 (1958).

Washington Irving Diary, Spain, 1828–1829, edited by Clara Louisa Penney. New York: Hispanic Society of America, 1930.

The Western Journals of Washington Irving, edited by John Francis McDermott. Norman: University of Oklahoma Press, 1944.

BIOGRAPHIES

Bowers, Claude G. *The Spanish Adventures of Washington Irving.* Boston: Houghton Mifflin, 1940.

Cater, Harold Dean. *Washington Irving at Sunnyside.* Tarrytown: Sleepy Hollow Restorations, 1957.

Hellman, George S. *Washington Irving Esquire, Ambassador at Large from the New World to the Old.* New York: Knopf, 1925.

Irving, Pierre M. *The Life and Letters of Washington Irving.* 4 vols. New York: G. P. Putnam, 1862–64.

Reichart, Walter A. *Washington Irving and Germany.* Ann Arbor: University of Michigan Press, 1957.

Wagenknecht, Edward. *Washington Irving: Moderation Displayed.* New York: Oxford University Press, 1962.

Williams, Stanley T. *The Life of Washington Irving*. 2 vols. New York: Oxford University Press, 1935.

CRITICAL STUDIES

Beach, Leonard. "Washington Irving: The Artist in a Changing World," *University of Kansas City Review*, 14:259–66 (Summer 1948).

Brooks, Van Wyck. *The World of Washington Irving*. New York: Doubleday, 1944.

Hedges, William L. "Irving's *Columbus:* The Problem of Romantic Biography," *The Americas*, 13:127–40 (1956).

————. *Washington Irving: As American Study, 1802–1832*. Baltimore, Md.: Johns Hopkins Press, 1965.

Hoffman, Daniel G. "Irving's Use of American Folklore in 'The Legend of Sleepy Hollow,' " *PMLA*, 68:425–35 (June 1953).

Hoffman, Louise M. "Irving's Use of Spanish Sources in *The Conquest of Granada*," *Hispania*, 28:483–98 (November 1945).

Laird, C. G. "Tragedy and Irony in *Knickerbocker's History*," *American Literature*, 12:157–72 (May 1940).

LeFevre, Louis. "Paul Bunyan and Rip Van Winkle," *Yale Review*, 36:66–76 (Autumn 1946).

Leisy, E. E. "Irving and the Genteel Tradition," *Sewanee Review*, 21:223–27 (September 1946).

Lloyd, F. V. "Irving's *Rip Van Winkle*," *Explicator*, 4:26 (February 1946).

Martin, Terrence. "Rip, Ichabod, and the American Imagination," *American Literature*, 31:137–49 (May 1959).

Pochmann, Henry A. "Irving's German Sources in *The Sketch Book*," *Studies in Philology*, 27:477–507 (July 1930).

Snell, George. "Washington Irving: A Revaluation," *Modern Language Quarterly*, 7:303–10 (September 1946).

Webster, C. M. "Irving's Expurgation of the 1809 *A History of New York*," *American Literature*, 4:293–95 (November 1932).

Wegelin, Christopher. "Dickens and Irving: The Problem of Influence," *Modern Language Quarterly*, 7:83–91 (November 1932).

Young, Philip. "Fallen from Time: The Mythic Rip Van Winkle," *Kenyon Review*, 22:547–73 (Autumn 1960).

—LEWIS LEARY

Henry James
1843-1916

Henry James was the "largest" literary figure to come out of America during the nineteenth and early twentieth centuries. He was not "large" as Melville is large; he did not have Melville's global vision, nor did he dream of epical landscapes. His largeness stemmed, rather, from the literary territories he annexed to the New World and the career he fashioned in two hemispheres. At a time when American literature was still young and certain of its writers were still sharpening their pens, Henry James crossed from the New World to the Old and was able to take his seat at the table of fiction beside George Eliot and Turgenev, Flaubert and Zola. He found the novel in English still the easy undisciplined and relaxed form it had been from its early days, and he refashioned it into a complex work of literary art. If he was junior to the fellow craftsmen whom he joined in Europe, he achieved, in the fullness of time, a status equal to them, and in some instances he surpassed them. For he was not only a practitioner of fiction; he was also one of its finest critics and theorists. It was he who gave us the terminology most useful in our time for the criticism of the novel.

Henry James wrote for fifty years; he was a prolific writer and several times glutted his own market in the magazines. Never a "best seller," as we know best sellers today, he never-

theless earned an honorable living by his pen. He was fortunate in being born into an affluent family; but from his early twenties he began to earn his own way and wholly by literary work. He was alone among major American writers in never seeking any other employment. He was devoted to his art; and his productivity did not influence his meticulous style—that style by which he believed a writer gains his passport to posterity. At first his prose was fresh and clear; later it became magnificently weighted and complex in its allusiveness and imagery—and accordingly in its evocative power. His goals remained always aesthetic. He believed from the first that the artist in fiction is a historian of that part of life never found in history books: the private life that goes on behind the walls of dwellings, but which is also a part of the society in which it is lived. Literature for him was the great repository of life; and he believed that if the novel is a mirror in a roadway, it reflects not only the panorama of existence, but also the countenance of the artist in the very act of experiencing the world around him.

During his five decades of creation he brought into being some twenty novels and one hundred and twelve tales, some of them almost of novel length. He was the first of the great psychological realists in our time, on a much more complicated and more subtly subjective level than his Russian predecessors Turgenev, Tolstoi, and Dostoevski. In his productivity and the high level of his writing, in his insight into human motivation, and in his possession of the architectonics of fiction, he was a remarkable innovator, constantly fertile, bold, and independent—and a man with a style. R. P. Blackmur has imaged him as a sort of Shakespeare of the novel, in the power with which he brought into being, at the century's turn, with extraordinary rapidity, his three magisterial works—*The Ambassadors*, *The Wings of the Dove*, and *The Golden Bowl*—as Shakespeare set down in fast succession his three great tragedies at the turn of another century. René Wellek has spoken of James as a kind of American Goethe, Olympian in his view of literature and life, certainly in his capacity to hold both at arm's length as he analyzed and reflected upon them—upon poetry and truth, man and reality.

Criticism indeed has never done sufficient justice to Henry James's uniqueness in fiction. He alone created the cosmopolitan novel in English and made of it a rich study of men, manners, and morals on two continents. More significant still, he was able to treat both as comedy and as tragedy his transatlantic vision of the New World's relations to the Old. In doing this he anticipated the central fact of the twentieth century—America's assumption, among the nations of the world, of those international responsibilities from which it once isolated itself. James early recognized the drama of the confrontation of the New World and the Old—at a time when the Americans were too busy on their own expanding continent to be aware of it, and when Europe considered itself sufficiently distant to be able to ignore its transatlantic offspring, or to be interested in it essentially as the land of Fenimore Cooper's Indians to be viewed with that

"certain condescension" of which Lowell complained.

In James's fiction Americans are often treated as if they still possess the innocence of Eden; and in their unawareness of evil they are shown as highly vulnerable once they venture outside their American paradise. This large drama James projected, during his later phase, as a drama of consciousness, for he had a profound sense of man's inner life. All his virtuosity was addressed, in his fiction, to discovering how to capture in words the subjective, and reflective, and even the phantasmagorial side of man.

It is because Henry James wrote so much and experimented so widely, was so complex a literary "case," that criticism has found it difficult to see him whole. However, his authority and his vision have increasingly imposed themselves, and certain of his formulations have entered into the very texture of twentieth-century literary thought. As one of the first modern psychological analysts in the novel has had a pervasive influence. Joseph Conrad, James Joyce, Virginia Woolf, Graham Greene, Dorothy Richardson are among the many novelists who derived technique or aesthetic ideas from the fount of Henry James. It was no accident that even during his lifetime certain of his fellow novelists abroad addressed this American in their midst as "Master."

The literary career of Henry James extended from the last days of the American Civil War to the middle of World War I. He was born on April 15, 1843, in New York City and belongs, in America's literary annals, with two other sturdy children of Manhattan, Herman Melville and Walt Whitman. The three can now be seen as distinctly urban artists: their vision was of the sea-girt city and of the ocean; of ferries and teeming commerce, and a city-community—as distinct from the vision of the rooted children of the orchards and woods of Concord. Thus, where the New England writers were more abstract and philosophical—their works still linked to the pulpit and the sermon in spite of a disengagement from them—the writings of the New Yorkers dealt with things more concrete and palpable. Melville's glimpse of faraway life in the Pacific made him forever a great cosmopolite of the spirit; and Henry James's transatlantic life made him a cosmopolite of fact. Walt Whitman, for all his "cosmos," dealt in concretions. All three paid their respects to a "flowering" New England, but they represented on their side a great urban "flowering"—a great urban impulse—in the new American literature.

It is not surprising that James, in later years, was to speak of his Concord predecessors as "exquisite provincials," and indeed, of Thoreau, as being "worse than provincial—he was parochial." He said this not in an altogether derogatory sense: he was simply describing their limited untraveled state, their adherence to the homely, the worldly wisdom that came out of reflection on native ground rather than out of action and life abroad. James spoke of them as would a cosmopolite for whom the Old World and the New had figured as a kind of double landscape from the very first. For, although he was born just off Broadway, at Number 21 Washington Place, he was taken abroad when he was less than six months old. He opened his eyes of childhood upon European lawns and gardens; and one of his earliest memories was of the Napoleonic column in the Place Vendôme. Nevertheless he was returned to Manhattan when he was just learning to walk. If his eyes had first observed Europe, his feet planted themselves firmly upon American soil—that of Washington Square, within a stone's throw of where he had been born and the Square that would furnish him

with the title of one of his most popular short novels. He spent a boyhood in the streets of what was then "uptown" but what is today the lower part of Fifth Avenue. With summers in Staten Island, and trips up the Hudson, with the familiar teeming scenes of Broadway, and in a New York of muddy streets with chickens on the sidewalks and pigs rooting in the gutters, James reached the age of twelve a thorough little Manhattanite.

His grandfather had been an Irish immigrant who amassed a large fortune in Albany. His father was a religious visionary who embraced the exalted dreams of Swendenborg and Blake. His elder brother, William James, grew up to found at Harvard the first psychological laboratory in America, to write the *Principles of Psychology*, and to become America's philosopher of pragmatism. The senior Henry James had a comfortable income and was a restless wanderer. Twice during his adolescence Henry was taken to Europe, from twelve until sixteen, and again during his seventeenth year. The father gave his sons tutors and governesses, and Henry attended an assortment of schools, but his education was erratic. Much of it was carried on in European museums, galleries, and parks. From the first, the future novelist had before him the two worlds: the early-forming America, in all of its indigenous rawness and with its European borrowings—and the European scene, as a series of cities, Geneva, Paris, London, the Boulogne-sur-Mer of Thackeray, as well as the suburbs of the British metropolis.

Henry was a sensitive and shy boy; he tended to assume a quiet observer's role beside his active elder brother. He was an inveterate reader of novels; indeed it might be said that no novelist before James had had so thorough a saturation in the fiction of both sides of the Atlantic. Having learned French in his childhood, he read through shelvesful of French novels as well as the great English novelists from Richardson to the then-serialized Dickens and Thackeray. His father spoke of him as a "devourer of libraries"; for a while the parent worried about this and attempted to make his son attend a preparatory school for engineers. Henry resisted this experience as he was to resist the study of law two or three years later. He wanted to be simply "literary" and he realized this goal more rapidly than might have been expected.

On the eve of the Civil War the family returned from the third of their European journeys and settled at Newport in Rhode Island. The seventeen-year-old Henry here formed a friendship with John La Farge, the painter, his senior by several years, who guided him in his reading of French works and encouraged him to begin writing. During the early weeks of the war Henry suffered a strained back while helping to put out a fire, and this "obscure hurt," as he called it in his memoirs, kept him from military service. In 1862 he registered at the Harvard Law School but soon withdrew, for he was already writing short stories and book reviews.

The earliest identified piece of fiction is an unsigned tale, "A Tragedy of Error," published in the *Continental Monthly*, a New York magazine, in February 1864. It is a precocious tale, lurid and melodramatic, yet strangely talented. It reveals that James, at the threshold of his manhood, already possessed a vigorous grasp of certain storytelling techniques which were to guide him in all his work and culminate in the remarkable architecture of his final novels. His second tale dealt with life on the civilian front of the Civil War and was accepted by the *Atlantic Monthly* in 1865 when he was twenty-two. From then on the pages of this magazine were open to him. The *North American Review* and the newly founded *Nation* accepted his book reviews, and when William Dean Howells began to work for the *Atlantic* he gave James encouragement and editorial support, recognizing at once that he had to do with a young man of extraordinary talent. Indeed by the time James had published half a dozen short stories a reviewer in the *Nation* spoke of him as one of the most skillful writers of fiction in America. However, from the first, the critics complained that his heroes did not lead a life of action; they tended to be self-absorbed and reflective, and the tales themselves took as their subjects problems in human behavior. The stories of this early period deal entirely with the American scene and show the leisurely existence of the well-to-do in Newport, Boston, and New York. James's models were largely French: Balzac, Mérimée, George Sand. But his writing at this time shows also an attentive reading of Hawthorne.

There is a touch of Hawthorne in "The Romance of Certain Old Clothes" (1868), first of the many ghostly tales James was to write. His most ambitious story of this period was "Poor Richard" (1867), which described a young man's helplessness in courtship when faced with rather vigorous rivals. James republished a few of these tales, much revised, in England in a series of volumes called *Stories Revived* (1885), among them "A Landscape Painter" and "A Day of Days" of 1866, "A Most Extraordinary Case" (1868), and "A Light Man" (1869). Later he disavowed all his early stories and chose to date his literary debut from the appearance of "A Passionate Pilgrim" in the *Atlantic Monthly* during 1871.

During 1869 and 1870 Henry James went abroad on his first adult journey. He was twenty-six and the experience was unforgettable. For the first time he crossed the Alps into Italy, but before doing this he renewed his old boyhood impressions of London. Here he found Charles Eliot Norton, the Harvard professor of fine arts who had published him in the *North*

American Review, and through Norton met William Morris, Rossetti, and Ruskin. He also paid a call on Darwin. As he traveled, he gradually became aware of the theme that was to be central to his writings: he observed his journeying fellow Americans in hotels and pensions, captured their sense of dislocation while trying to imbibe foreign culture; he studied particularly the itinerant American families with passive mothers and undisciplined children, and noted the absence from their lives of any standard of culture and behavior. These were the shortcomings of American innocence. On the other hand James was not blind to certain other aspects of life abroad; it is striking how often the adjective "corrupt" precedes the word "Europe" in his writings. He found in the old countries, nevertheless, a continuing spectacle of life and art. The Italian towns on their hillsides, the spires of the churches gleaming in the landscape, customs and manners bearing witness to time and tradition, served as a constant stimulus to his imagination. The galleries of Europe provided a feast for his eyes. His complaint on returning home was at one with Hawthorne: in America there was only raw nature, the forest primeval, and a broad, daylight prosperity. Eden would have been a dull place for a novelist.

While he was in England the news reached him that his beloved cousin, Minnie Temple, to whom he had formed a deep if unvoiced attachment, had died. This was the climax of his "passionate pilgrimage"; and it was to be remembered in *The Portrait of a Lady* and years later in *The Wings of the Dove*. The twelve-month of wandering in England, France, and Italy—the countries in which he was to travel for the rest of his life—had set the scene for all his future. He was to remain satisfied with this terrain; he traveled neither to Spain nor to the Isles of Greece; he only briefly visited the Low Countries, and on two trips cast a hurried glance at Munich. The capitals in Jamesian geography, extending from the New World to the Old, were Boston and New York, London, Paris, and Rome. Florence and Venice were way stations. And occasionally James explored the rural scenery of these countries. But his particular landscape was that of the affluent and civilized humans who peopled or visited these places and whose lives he dealt with as a part of a continuing Americano-European *comédie humaine*.

Before Henry James recognized that this was his fundamental theme, he made a serious attempt to discover what he could accomplish as a writer within the United States. Twice between 1870 and 1875—first in Boston and then in New York—he sought systematically to gain a livelihood by the writing of fugitive journalism and fiction within the American scene. In Boston he wrote a short novel entitled *Watch and Ward*. For a brief moment he entertained the common fantasy of novitiates in fiction that this would be a Great American Novel: even the supersubtle James allowed himself this cliché-dream of overnight fame and power. Set in Boston and its suburbs, the novel told of a wealthy young man who adopts an orphan and rears her in the hope she will someday become his wife. The strange thing about this novel was James's failure to paint any background; he became fascinated by the relationships between the orphan, her guardian, her suitors; but the story might have taken place anywhere. Nevertheless in the book may be found an early sketching out of some of the material he would use with finished art in *The Portrait of a Lady*.

More important, at this time, was James's writing of "A Passionate Pilgrim." In it there is the rhapsodic note of his rediscovery of Europe. The tale has all the ingredients of James's later "international" stories: the narrator, discovering Europe, infatuated with the things of the Old World; the contrast of American cultural bareness with the old traditions and manners of Europe and at the same time the awareness of the New World's egalitarianism, for if the American protagonist dies in England, there is an Englishman at the end of the story who goes forth with new hope to replace him in America.

During his stay in Boston James continued to write book reviews; and he tried his hand at art criticism. Early in 1875 he went to New York, spending the winter there, but found it artistically—and financially—unremunerative. Between these brief "sieges" of Boston and New York he made another journey to Europe, spending in particular a winter in Rome (1872–73) where he met many American artists and closely observed the life of the long-established American colony on the banks of the Tiber. Out of this experience came his first important novel: *Roderick Hudson*. In substance and setting it seems to take up where Hawthorne left off in *The Marble Faun*. Hawthorne attempted a characteristic "romance," reworking, in terms of the real and the mystical, the Puritan struggle between guilt and goodness in a Roman setting. James, on the other hand, wrote a novel romantic in theme—that of an American artist destroyed by his passion for a beautiful woman—yet realistic in its painting of the American art expatriates in the Holy City. On a deeper level *Roderick Hudson* reflects the conflicts that were experienced by James during his search to discover what it meant to be an American, and an artist, at this moment of history. If the novel did not find the answer, it at any rate stated the problem and weighed the possibilities. Written in a clear and highly readable style, it suffered from the excesses of first novels: the author was trying to say too much, to cram too many future novels into this one. Yet it is a work of great charm and

feeling; compared with the novels being published in America at the time, it is indeed an extraordinary performance.

The novel was completed in New York in 1875 and ran through twelve installments in the *Atlantic Monthly*. With it James established the pattern by which he was to earn his living for the next forty years—that of publishing a serial in a magazine and thereby assuring himself of a steady monthly income, and augmenting this by the writing of articles, reviews, and tales. It was clear to him now that he could expatriate himself without difficulty. He could live more cheaply in Europe and make money by his travel articles; he would find the material for his fiction and have the leisure in which to write it. By 1875 Henry had devoted a full decade to periodical publication; and now he made a substantial debut between book covers: in that year appeared *A Passionate Pilgrim and Other Tales*; a collection of travel articles, *Transatlantic Sketches*; and the novel *Roderick Hudson*. From this time on he was to publish a book or more every year—drawing upon the great backlog of his periodical writings, which he never exhausted, to make up the volumes of tales, criticism, and travel that came out at the same time as his novels.

In the autumn of 1875 he settled in Paris, and one of his first acts was to call upon the Russian novelist Ivan Turgenev. James had greatly admired his work and he found in this older writer a congenial mentor. If from Balzac James had learned how to set a scene and launch a drama, and from Hawthorne how to suffuse the drama with charm, and from George Eliot the value of endowing his story with intellectual illumination, he learned his most important lesson of all from Turgenev. This was to make his novel flow from his personages. The Russian writer provided James with the concept of the "organic" novel; he helped James to see that the novel need not be a haphazard story, but one in which characters live out their natures. This might be called "psychological determinism," and James was to become perhaps the greatest (and often misunderstood) exponent of it in his work. He was one of the rare writers of fiction to grasp the psychological truth that an action properly derives from a character, that a novel creates the greatest illusion of truth when it grows out of a personage's observations and perceptions. This is why, in James, we find an insistence upon the fundamental truths of human behavior, rather than the cheerful coloring of these truths indulged in by so many of his contemporaries. Like Turgenev and the other Russian novelists—but at an opposite emotional pole—James concerned himself with character above all else, and with people in relation to one another. Unlike the characters in Russian novels, James's personages tended to subordinate their emotions and passions to their intellect; but with extraordinary subtlety James could show the force of passion and emotion beneath the intellectual façade.

Turgenev took James to meet Flaubert; and in Flaubert's apartment, high in the rue du Faubourg St. Honoré, the American made friends with Zola, Edmond de Goncourt, Daudet, Maupassant. Later he was to know Loti, Coppée, and Bourget, who became a particularly close friend. If he had found the men of Concord to be "exquisite provincials," he felt that these Parisians lived also within narrow horizons. He felt indeed, and understandably, that he was more cosmopolitan and possessed wider experience of the world than they did, if less experience of an immediate physical environment. He ruefully remarked in a letter home that he could talk French to them but they, in their insularity, knew not a word of English.

A year in Paris sufficed. In December of 1876 Henry James crossed the channel and settled in the heart of London, a few blocks from Piccadilly Circus; and little more than a twelvemonth later he was famous both in America and in England as the author of "Daisy Miller."

The career of Henry James has been divided, for convenience, by most critics into three "periods" and these once humorously characterized by a British writer as falling (by dynastic arrangement) into those of "James I, James II, and the Old Pretender." The "Old Pretender" was an allusion to James's elaborate manner in his old age, his involuted sentences, his search for precision of statement at the expense of the patience of his listeners. A closer examination of the sequence of his works gives to his first period a distinctive unity; it is the period of his apprenticeship and his success, his discovery of his great cosmopolitan subject and his exploitation of it. It may be said to end with the triumphant writing of *The Portrait of a Lady*, long planned—and brought to completion according to plan. The second period has often been spoken of as the period of James's "social" novels; but it would be more exact to see this period as falling, in itself, into three acts: the abandoning for the time being of the "international" theme and the writing of three long novels in the naturalist mode; then the abandoning of fiction for five years of writing for the stage; in 1895 the return to the novel, followed by half a dozen years of experimental writing in which James assimilated the techniques derived from the theater. Out of these experiments emerged the third period, which—far from being that of an Old Pretender—has been more accurately described as "the major phase," certainly "major" in terms of its influence upon the twentieth-century novel. During this final phase James wrote, within a four-year period, the three novels by which he makes his greatest claim on posterity.

The first period extended from 1865 to 1882, and it is symbolized by the tale of "Daisy Miller"—the "ultimately most prosperous child of my invention," James called her many years later. During his lifetime his reputation was to rest largely upon his "studies" of young American girls encountering Europe, and Daisy was their prototype. His stories of American families touring in the Old World as if it were a painful duty rather than a civilized pleasure were famous and much discussed. Like Hawthorne's young heroes, these Americans have to discover that the world is not as innocent as it seems, and that behind the smiling façades of castles and picturesque ruins lurk centuries of wrongdoing and the dark and evil things of the human spirit. "Daisy Miller" dramatized this on a level of comedy and pathos: the tale of the young and radiant Daisy, with the dew of her homeland still freshly sprinkled over her, arriving in Rome and never realizing for a moment that European life and European standards may be different from those she has known in Schenectady, New York. What she deems to be a pleasant flirtation with a friendly Italian is viewed by Europeans, and even more by Europeanized Americans, with deadly seriousness. Daisy knows no evil and is unable to think it; she cannot comprehend why her behavior, which seems harmless enough to her, should be the cause of so much social anxiety. As James himself put it: "The whole idea of the story is the little tragedy of a light, thin, natural, unsuspecting creature being sacrificed as it were to a social rumpus that went on quite over her head and to which she stood in no measurable relation. To deepen the effect, I have made it go over her mother's head as well."

The story indeed gained its power from the portraits of the wholly passive mother and the undisciplined young brother; the picture of an upper-middle-class family, the permissive and indulgent parents wholly subjugated by their children, transported to a foreign environment where the parents are helpless and ignorant and the children run wild. The drama is heightened by the skill with which James shows this family through the sophisticated eyes of an American expatriate who feels he has lost touch with his native land. His failure to understand the "new" American girl, represented by Daisy, in the end only accentuates her sense of isolation; in Europe the transplanted American Daisy can only wither and die.

In *Roderick Hudson* James had portrayed the American artist, going abroad to find the schooling and traditions of art not available to him in his homeland. In *The American* of two years later, his "easiest" and most romantic novel, he had drawn a picture of a businessman possessing great charm of character and the candor of a trusting and innocent nature, seeking to win for himself a wife in the French aristocracy. The novel is a mixture of melodrama and romance, yet it dramatizes most clearly the irony James was seeking to express to his readers. For Christopher Newman, bearing the name of Columbus, represents one type of new man from the New World, who has strayed among the nobles of the Old. They are corrupt. They want to make use of him and his wealth. They also have complete contempt for him. The American has his chance for revenge. But he throws it away with the remark that two wrongs do not make a right; he thereby reveals himself more noble than the nobles, and more the Christian gentleman. James has shown him, equally however, in all his crudity, his curious self-assurance, his predilection for strenuous action without thought, and his ignorance of the ways of the civilized world. The novel ends in a splendid passage of muted emotion as Newman walks away from the bleak Paris street in which his love is immured in her convent, and hears the "far-away bells chiming off into space at long intervals, the big bronze syllables of the Word." Revenge, he meditates, is not his "game."

With the success of "Daisy Miller" James promptly recognized that the public liked his Americano-European stories and particularly his tales of international marriages and of bright young American girls discovering Europe. "The Last of the Valerii," "Madame de Mauves," "Four Meetings," and "Daisy Miller" itself had fully attested to this. And now he began to play out his themes in all their variations—stories of the self-made girl, who arranges life for her fiancé so she may make a splendid marriage; stories of English noblewomen who marry Americans but despise them; and of Americans unable to grasp the guile and duplicity of certain kinds of Europeans. His tales were clever, witty, charming; he was in all the magazines and editors asked for more—which he always gave them; it seems now, when one looks over the long list of his "international" productions, as if he wrote with both hands. When London laughed too heartily over Daisy and her young brother, James replied by writing a tale in which Americans could laugh at the smugness and fatuity of Britons visiting America ("An International Episode"). But he was playing upon national sensitivities: the Americans and English enjoyed laughing at each other; they did not care to laugh at themselves.

In his late prefaces James spoke of his "Americano-European legend," and showed how clearly he had envisaged his international dramas. What his stories had represented, he said, was a record of the American "state of innocence," that of the Americans being "almost incredibly *unaware of life*—as the old European order expressed life," and what he

had studied was "their more or less stranded helplessness" abroad. And he went on; "Conscious of so few things in the world, these unprecedented creatures were least of all conscious of deficiencies and dangers; so that, the grace of youth and innocence and freshness aiding, their negatives were converted and became in certain relations lively positives and values." Out of their experience he fashioned the comedy and pathos and beauty of their state. His long observation of traveling Americans, his thorough knowledge of the American character, his saturation in European life, had given him his data. He was artist enough to make of it splendid literary capital. But if he treated it in his shorter tales on a level of wit and comedy—and in a comic spirit which has never been sufficiently praised—he found in it also larger and more tragic implications. These he embodied in the novel which marked the end of this phase—*The Portrait of a Lady*.

It was planned for almost a decade. To write it, James produced in fast succession three short novels and a nonfictional work—his *Hawthorne*—earning in this way the funds needed to pursue his big novel at leisure. During the next fifteen months his works literally tumbled from the presses in England and America. *The Europeans* came out in October 1878; "Daisy Miller" and two other tales, in a two-volume edition, appeared in February 1879; in October of the same year he issued another collection of tales, and in December there appeared, within two days of each other, the short novel *Confidence* and the *Hawthorne*. By this time James hal also completed the last of this group, *Washington Square,* which was published during 1880 while he was preparing the first installments of *The Portrait of a Lady*.

The *Hawthorne* was written for the *English Men of Letters* series. It is a finished piece of work, the tribute of one American genius to another. The argument of the book was that America had been bare of society and history when Hawthorne came upon the scene; having no rich social fabric such as English novelists could draw upon, he tissued his work out of the haunted Puritan history of New England. In depicting the America of Hawthorne's time, and in describing certain institutions "absent" from American life, James touched American editorial sensitivities. "In the United States, in those days, there were no great things to look out at (save forests and rivers); life was not in the least spectacular; society was not brilliant; the country was given up to a great material prosperity, a homely bourgeois activity, a diffusion of primary education and the common luxuries." Sentences such as this one, while accurate enough, seemed to certain of his readers depreciatory. Perhaps James used the word "provincial" too many times. His easy cosmopolitanism was interpreted as condescension. A remark such as "in the light, fresh American air, unthickened by customs and institutions" invited challenge. And when James described the materials available to the English novelist of manners—court, church, society, peerage, and so forth—he was held to be making invidious and undemocratic comparisons. His book set off a sharp flurry in the American press, and from this time on there was formed the legend that James was an expatriate who mocked his countrymen and exalted Europe at the expense of America.

Today we can see the *Hawthorne* for what it is: a finely sketched picture of Hawthorne's Salem and Concord, and a profoundly accurate critique of his work. The tone and the style of the book is felicitous at every turn. It contains a large measure of devotion to New England and its traditions, and its picture of Brook Farm and the Transcendentalists is drawn with affection and from intimate sources. But there

was no denying that the book served equally to veil James's defense of his own work, and the shortcomings of *his* America—for the kind of novelist he was and sought to be.

The three short novels were thrown off in a happy and spontaneous vein. They represent James at his most gifted "professionalism." The least important was a novel called *Confidence,* which is talented hack work, a minor comedy of manners. The most important, *Washington Square,* set in New York, was the story of a plain girl who lived in a big house in the Square with her wealthy father, but who was prevented by him from having the shoddy lover she wanted to marry. This novel, written as if it were a piece of naturalism by the Goncourts or a neo-Balzacian *Eugénie Grandet,* has long been a favorite with readers of James and won him wide popularity long after his death when it was dramatized and cinematized as *The Heiress.* James always regarded it as a trifling work, stale and flat and without the richer experimental values of his best narratives. It is nevertheless a vigorous drama of parental misunderstanding and cruelty. His third potboiler was *The Europeans,* written in response to an appeal from William Dean Howells that he give the *Atlantic Monthly* a story less sober and tragic than *Roderick* and more cheerful than *The American.* To accomplish this James reversed his "international" situation; instead of showing Americans abroad, he brought back to Boston two Americans who had lived in Europe for so long that they had little knowledge of their own country. How they fare among a group of rigid New Englanders was the situation out of which James's comedy of *The Europeans* grew. Boston readers were not amused. Today, however, the story reads as one of the brightest and most humorous of the novelist's inventions.

Now he could finally set to work on *The*

Portrait of a Lady. He took a vacation in Italy and got the book under way, carefully revising each section. He had succeeded in selling it to *Macmillan's* magazine in London as well as to the *Atlantic* and this brought him a substantial income during the period of serialization. More important still, it firmly established him before a public on both sides of the ocean. The novel was his largest and most carefully wrought canvas to date; and if his career had ended after producing it he would still rank as a major figure in the history of American fiction.

The Portrait of a Lady was the third in James's group of fictional American expatriations; he had "done" the artist in Rome and the businessman in Paris. Now he brought Isabel Archer, the young girl from Albany, to England, and placed her among her suitors in the Old World. She, too, is an heiress; she is given the freedom for which she romantically strives. She is an idealistic and intelligent girl, not the flirtatious hunting-for-a-husband girl James had pictured in Daisy Miller or Pandora Day. And the drama in which she becomes involved resides in the choice which she thinks she "freely" makes. Having the opportunity to marry a British lord, she shrinks from being drawn into the life of the nobility, with its rituals and its responsibilities; she shrinks equally from marrying an intense and over-insistent, but upright, American. Neither marriage, she feels, would leave her free. When she makes her choice, it is to marry the one man who in the end limits her freedom most—an American dilettante, fastidious and fussy, who "collects" her—and her money—as he collects his *objets d'art*. But if Isabel has been the victim of her romantic illusions and her self-absorption, she has also been the victim of a carefully laid plot: the man she marries has a daughter by a former mistress, Madame Merle, who has become Isabel's best friend; and it is

through Madame Merle's connivance that the heiress has been steered into the orbit of the dilettante that she may assure, by her fortune, the future of the child.

The melodramatic underpinning of the story is handled with the novelist's characteristic realism. He knew that he could make the reader accept almost any story if his people were truly drawn; and the series of portraits of the characters surrounding Isabel—no less than Isabel herself—give the novel its remarkable force and intensity. Few "psychological" villains have ever been sketched with greater power than Gilbert Osmond, the pretentious and cynical husband; and his scheming yet sympathetic mistress, Madame Merle, is one of James's most completely realized characters. The novel shows step by step how the unconventional and "free" Isabel is "ground in the very mill of the conventional." The "portrait" of the lady—her private history, her illusions and her disillusionment—is in essence a psychological portrait. Isabel confronts her destiny with courage and determination: but James shows us that behind this egotistical boldness there are fears and uncertainties. What is dramatized in the novel is New World ignorance foundering upon hard realities long known to the Old World. The novel's success lies in its brilliant projection of the American girl, the delineation of her character, and the establishment of *tone*: this is achieved in great part by a remarkable narrative rhythm, an unfailing sense of narrative movement.

When the novel was nearing its end in the magazines, Henry returned to America. He was received in Boston, New York, and Washington as the successful if often criticized author who had made a reputation for himself abroad. His mother died during his stay in America; and he had barely returned to England when he was summoned back to Boston, to the deathbed of his father. He was named executor, and after arranging for the division of the family property, he once more crossed the Atlantic. This time he was to remain abroad for twenty years. He inherited a modest income, but he was making his way so successfully that he turned this over to his sister, and continued to live by his pen.

The novelist now entered upon the second period of his writings. It was marked by his decision to attempt new subjects. He was tired of the "international" theme and he felt that he had exhausted it. With extraordinary energy he wrote two long novels during the next three years—*The Bostonians* and *The Princess Casamassima.* The American novel dealt with New England reformers; the *Princess* with another and more dangerous kind of reformer, the European anarchist. These novels are, in a sense, tales of two cities—Boston and London. They are brilliantly "social" in their painting of certain scenes of urban life and they are a calculated attempt by James to write a "naturalistic" novel. A visit to Paris in 1884 and long talks with Zola, Edmond de Goncourt, and Daudet had deeply impressed him. James failed this time, however, to take the measure of his public: it was awaiting more tales from him about helpless and bright Americans in Europe, and wandering foreigners in the United States (such as those described in "A Bundle of Letters"). Instead James offered his readers a realistic and minutely painted picture of Bostonian suffragettes and another of London radicals; this was the kind of novel which was not to gain a firm hold until the Edwardian period, and which in America would have as its foremost exponents Norris and later Dreiser. *The Princess Casamassima* anticipated by five decades the major theme of the twentieth century —the young man who seeks to overthrow the very society in which he in reality also seeks

acceptance. It is a valuable study of individuals who seek to rise to power by exploiting working-class causes. James's picture of the British laboring class in its pre-Fabian confusion, while sympathetic, tended to be too generalized and impressionistic; and his plea for the grandeur of art at the expense of human suffering could not convince his readers. In attempting to place the American novel into the stream of the Zolaesque Continental fiction, James alienated his limited but appreciative public. The novels were flat failures.

He made one more attempt. This time he wrote of the world of art and tried to record the problems confronting a young politician-painter and an actress. *The Tragic Muse* ran for many months in the *Atlantic Monthly,* yet it had small success with its readers for all the high craft of its writing. James, with his experimental attitude toward the novel, had done more than switch from his main theme: he had tried "naturalism" but he was an incomplete "naturalist"—naturalism relying on literalism and the portrayal of primitive passion and violence. What James created was a series of subtle studies of individuals caught in forces and movements beyond their control, undone by conflicts between their temperaments and their environment. James's "determinism" was essentially psychological, where Zola's was physical.

While he was writing these novels he continued to turn out a brilliant series of tales; some of them were of such length that by current measurement they are counted as short novels. During a sojourn in Italy in 1886–87 and immediately after, he created a group of short masterpieces of which the best known is "The Aspern Papers"—with its evocation of a dying Venice and a dying old lady trying to keep from a privacy-invading age the love letters written to her more than half a century before by a great poet. He based the tale on a brief anecdote of a Boston collector who had taken rooms in the Florentine home of Claire Clairmont, Byron's mistress, in the hope of finding Shelley and Byron relics. The story moves with the rhythmic pace and tension of a mystery story; and the double climax—the unmasking of the "publishing scoundrel" and the proposal made to him by the middle-aged niece, that he marry her and receive the Aspern papers as a "dowry"—give this tale the high drama reflected in the extraordinary success of the play version. Between the lines of "The Aspern Papers" James is saying that an artist's life should be preserved from prying hands, that he should be read in his work alone. Yet James is also, ambivalently, on the side of the biographer who seeks the human elements in the artist's work.

In 1889 Henry James faced the fact that if he had had great success a decade earlier, he was now a distinguished man of letters with several distinct public failures on his hands. He knew that he was a finer artist than ever; he had, as always, a sense of his destiny; but he had written three big novels which we now know were destined for posterity rather than for his time. He sought to revive his fortunes by turning to the theater. During the next five years, from 1890 to 1895, he wrote seven plays. Two of them reached the stage: a dramatization of *The American*, which had a modest run, and *Guy Domville,* a carefully written costume play, produced in 1895 by the popular London manager George Alexander. This was booed by an ill-tempered audience which vented its anger on James himself, when he came out to take a bow on his first night. Repudiated once again by his public, and this time in an open and violent fashion, James turned his back on the theater and resumed his writing of fiction.

In a sense he turned his back on his public altogether. He withdrew from London, after

years of city life, living first in a rented house, and later purchasing Lamb House, in Rye, Sussex, at the top of a winding cobbled street in that picturesque coastal town. It was an old house, and had a walled garden. This became his permanent abode, although he later kept rooms at the Reform Club and in the end had a flat in Cheyne Walk. It was in Lamb House that his final works were written, and here that he partially resolved the deep feeling of frustration and failure engendered by public indifference to his art. He had been writing shorter tales on the margin of his unsuccessful novels and during his nervous adventures in the theater. He was at the top of his narrative power just before plunging into the theater, as "The Aspern Papers" of 1887 and the delicately conceived "The Pupil" of 1891 show. Now he wrote a series of tales which are patently autobiographical, dealing in ironic fashion with writers who know they have greatness in their pen but who cannot somehow meet the simple and unsubtle requirements of readers and critics. Between the failure of *Guy Domville* and the turn of the century the fictions of Henry James show him experimenting at every turn, but also selecting themes reflecting the crisis of his career: the troubled sense that he was a "lost" author, unwanted by an indifferent and illiterate world.

When he was not writing his parables about unsuccessful writers he wrote ghostly tales; indeed most of his tales in this form belong to this haunted period. And it was between 1895 and 1900 that he set down his series of stories of ravaged childhood and adolescence, in reality a reworking of his theme of innocence in a corrupting world.

The most celebrated in this group, which combines both the theme of tormented childhood and the ghostly element, is "The Turn of the Screw." James himself dismissed it as trivial: he told Howells it was a "down-on-all-fours pot-boiler." Nevertheless it promptly captured the imagination of his readers and has held it ever since. No work of James's has, indeed, stirred up more argument or provoked more insistent claims by critics, each insisting on his particular interpretation. The truth is that every reader can supply his own reading. James revealed on more than one occasion how he deliberately sought ambiguity so that his reader would imagine his own "horror"—on the theory that a nightmare is most frightening to the person who dreams it. In this fashion he established the ground for an unusual collaboration between author and reader. The haunted governess is the narrator, but she supplies few tangible "facts," and the reader is placed in the difficult position of having to determine, from the story she tells—and the way she tells it—how reliable a witness she is. James called this "a trap for the unwary." Most readers, caught up in the movement of the narrative, understandably take the governess's account in good faith. But if the reader begins to study her testimony he notices that it does not always hang together, and that the very language she uses is filled with imagery which reveals her own terror in the midst of her apparent composure.

By the governess's own account the children never see the ghosts which are haunting her. The reader, on his side, consciously or unconsciously, is sensitized to one of two horrors, or indeed to both: he may participate in the governess's terror that the children are exposed to damnation, or be terrified himself at the children's being exposed to such an anxiety-ridden governess. Out of such shadowings, such "gleams and glooms," as James called them, the novelist created one of the most profoundly evocative stories ever written. "The Turn of the Screw" illustrates James's matured theory of the ghostly tale. Awe and mystery, he held, do not hinge on the crime and the cadaver, the

dark castle, chains, blood, secret trapdoors, and frankensteins walking at midnight. James's ghosts walk mostly in broad daylight. He creates his eerie atmosphere by having the unusual occur on the margin of the usual. In this way the horror is greatly intensified. What James added to the ghostly tale, in reality, were a series of acute studies of forms of human anxiety—of the capacity of humans to scare themselves with phantoms of their own creation.

Among his other stories of troubled childhood were *What Maisie Knew,* the story of a little girl who lives alternately with each of her divorced parents and is flung from one to the other as if she were a tennis ball, and how she tries, in the process, to fathom the strange moral world in which she sees them living; "In the Cage," the tale of a girl in late adolescence, who works in a branch post office and seeks to construct in her imagination the fashionable world whose telegrams pass through her hands; and *The Awkward Age,* a novel concerned with the female adolescent who reaches the time when she can put up her hair and join her elders in the drawing room. A kind of childish curiosity is at the center of these stories, curiosity about sex and manners and the ways of the adult world. And James conveys in them the bewilderment—and often the terror—of the young plastic consciousness trying to come to terms with a world that it can experience but cannot wholly comprehend. If the themes of these stories reflect a regression by James to his own bewildered early state when *he* had tried to fathom the adult world (and was now trying again, since it had rejected him), they also show the delicate probing by a subtle artist of the sexual mores of Victorian England. These works have greater interest for the student of fiction than the general reader, for whom they must be accounted as failures. And the novel which completed the decade, *The*

Sacred Fount, is a complex tour de force in which James seems to ask himself whether anything he has seen as artist has validity and reality, or whether he has been living in an unreal fantasy-world.

The technical innovations in these tales are perhaps even more important than their themes: for James was led to explore methods of storytelling which would accurately render the consciousness of childhood *in terms of its own unawareness.* To do this he resorted increasingly to the lessons he had learned in the theater: revelation of action through scene, use of dialogue as narration, removal of the omniscient author from his role as informer and commentator. This meant also imposing upon the reader the burden of ferreting out for himself what is happening in the story. In a sense it converts the reader into a spectator, it places him at the author's window in the "house of fiction." Few readers were willing during James's lifetime to accept the responsibility he asked them to assume, or yield that "attention of perusal" which he demanded. His discovery of the possibilities of merging stagecraft with fictional method is one of the great moments of revelation in his notebooks, in which he recorded *"the singular value for a narrative plan of the . . . divine principle of the Scenario."*

That James fully discovered this "singular value" may be discerned in the final period of his career, those years from 1900 to World War I which are now spoken of as constituting his "major phase." The three large novels which Henry James wrote between 1900 and 1904—in which he returned to his "international" subjects and this time on a grandiose scale—can be understood only in the light of the techniques of James's maturity. At the end, form and substance coalesced to give us the psychological drama of James's highest comedy, *The Ambassadors,* the brooding tragedy of *The Wings of the Dove,* and what might be called James's supreme novel of manners, *The Golden Bowl.* He had sought to be a naturalist: he became in the end a symbolist.

The Ambassadors, published in 1903 but written between 1899 and 1901, exemplified both James's use of "point of view" (that is, the telling of the story through various angles of vision) and his method of alternation of scene. By the "point of view" method James was able to make the reader feel himself at one with the given character, and impart to him only as much of the story as that character perceives at any given moment; by alternating scenic action with his narrative of the reflective and analytic side of his personages, James created a novel unique in the history of fiction. His "ambassador" is a middle-aged New Englander who discovers how little he has been emotionally awake, because of the inhibitions of his youth and those of his environment; he finds himself balancing the rigidities of New England against the laxities of Paris, without altogether being able to shake off his own New England conscience. But he at least has been opened up to experience and has gained insight into himself. The "envoys" of *The Ambassadors* are sent out at various times to bring home the American lingerers in Paris, including the original "ambassador" himself. At the core of the novel is James's mature belief that life is a process of *seeing,* and through awareness the attaining of understanding; that if man is a creature with a predetermined heredity and a molding environment, he still can cherish the "illusion of freedom." He should, therefore, James holds, make the most of this illusion.

Written in the high style of James's late years, *The Ambassadors* represents the novel form carried to a level of extraordinary "art": mere storytelling has given way to intricate effects, as on a stage. There is no scene in James more brilliantly realized than that in which

Lambert Strether, thinking of an old painting of the French countryside he had once looked at in Boston, wanders into the Parisian suburbs and finds himself, as it were, inside the frame of that painting, walking about in its landscape.

Technique is also the key to *The Wings of the Dove*, published a year before *The Ambassadors* although written immediately after that novel. It clearly exemplifies the way in which James insisted that his subject dictate structure and why he believed he could achieve an "organic" novel. Wishing to write the story of a doomed girl (the disease is not specified), he told himself that fiction cannot concern itself with dying, but is concerned wholly with the act of living; and so he arranged the scenic structure of the book to keep the picture of Milly Theale's dying state from the reader save at certain moments when she affirms her will to live. The novel focuses, rather, on the personages around her, and on the cruel plot of her friends to supply her with a "lover" who will inherit her money and thus be free, after her death, to make the marriage he wishes. This is one of the strangest variants ever introduced into the old love triangle and James rigorously adhered to his plan: the "big" scenes, those in which the dying heroine is involved, are never written. They would have turned the novel into mere pathos. The characters hear about the events afterwards; these have occurred off-stage, as in classical tragedies. And James realizes the artistic unity of his work not only in his study of a passive young man in the hands of a fascinating and power-driven woman, but also in the way in which, in the end, the dead Milly, "the dove," has changed the course of the lives of all his characters.

In a remarkable way *The Ambassadors* and *The Wings of the Dove* were an elaborate rewriting, in terms of his late maturity, of *The American* and *The Portrait of a Lady,* a weaving out of old materials of a new and complex fabric within the large vision the novelist had finally achieved of the Western world—its greatness and its glory, its corruption and its decay. James wrote out of a charged consciousness and, as he said of Shakespeare, "out of the history of his soul and the direct exposure of his sensibility." In doing this he bethought himself of "our towering idol"—the man who had tried to write the history of the world into the France of his day, Balzac, saluted by James as "the master of us all."

Balzac had tried to create certain novels which would serve also as "philosophical studies" within the frame of his "human comedy." They had been rather poor novels, but James had looked at them attentively. And there is an implied homage to them, or to their intention, in these late works. Thus James named the hero of *The Ambassadors* Lewis Lambert Strether, after Balzac's *Louis Lambert*. Strether himself remarks that Balzac's novel "is an awfully bad one"—but James nevertheless makes his, like Balzac's, the story of an education. There is perhaps a more profound relationship between *The Wings of the Dove* and another of the *études philosophiques,* Balzac's Swedenborgian novel *Séraphita* (which, in our time, fascinated Yeats). A great Christian awareness pervades both the *Wings* and *Séraphita;* and both tell of a young woman who enacts the sacrifice of Christ. Séraphita says "there are two ways of dying—to some death means victory, to some it is defeat"—and Milly's great moral triumph is in making of her death a victory and a sacrifice. Balzac's work is, however, mystical whereas James's is grounded in the human stuff of nobility and betrayal, grandeur and defeat. To Balzac James may be said to be indebted for the symbolism of his novel—in both works we seem to hear a beating of great angelic wings, and the heroines are found perched on the edge of great abysses, surveying the precipices and terrors of the life they are to leave. Séraphita wishes she had "wings to cover you withal" and "the wings of the dove" in James's book in the end enfold those who sought to betray her. In these novels James created human dramas, within the large social organisms man has shaped for himself, and within the ideas by which he reared his churches and his civilization. Perhaps for this reason, certain critics have tried to read allegories into them, overlooking the fact that James rejected this form of writing and held himself a realist concerned with things visible and palpable. His tradition was not that of the *Divine Comedy*, but of the *comédie humaine*.

If these two major works of the final phase reached back to earlier fictions, James's ultimate novel, *The Golden Bowl*, reveals him breaking new ground and finding a resolution to questions left unresolved in his other novels. He chooses a triangle—husband, wife, mistress —but the twist this time is that he marries off the mistress to the father of the wife, makes her the stepmother of the betrayed heroine. A subject as "adulterine" as this James had wanted to treat for many years, complaining that the American "family" magazines made him write at the level of adolescents. But *The Golden Bowl* was not serialized, and he was free to handle his subject without any reservations. The novel is the record of an innocent American girl who really does grow up: in the end she has not only won back her husband, but has also emerged from her all-but-fatal attachment to her father. She sends the father back to America with his young wife and remains in Europe to work out her own future; her marriage is restored and her relationship with her husband "reconstructed" on the firm foundation of maturity: the immaturities had been her own. This time in James, the marriages are not failures: the alliance between Europe and America is consummated and made strong and

durable, and possessed of a future. To say this is but to give the bald elements of a remarkable work, rich in James's most elaborate metaphors. His exploration of the consciousness of the Italian Prince and his American Princess is subtle—she at first as innocent and as ignorant as Isabel Archer; he an aristocrat, taking life as it comes, and ready to ignore his wife if she fails to live up to his high sophistication. She learns actively to *see*; and through this awareness triumphs.

These three novels would seem to be accomplishment enough for any writer; but James, asserting always that he was a slow and poor "producer," also put forth during this time the series of brilliant stories contained in volumes titled *The Soft Side, The Better Sort*, and *The Finer Grain*. Perhaps the most famous of these tales, certainly the most widely read in recent years, is "The Beast in the Jungle," whose forty-odd pages encompass the entire life of an individual—an individual so wrapped in his own egotism that his eyes are sealed to the real experiences of life. He knows only the dark jungle of his own existence. The beast that waits to spring upon him is the emptiness of his life, his failure to understand and to love.

If, at the end of *The Golden Bowl*, Henry James sent Adam Verver and Charlotte, his wife, back to America, it was perhaps because he was about to return himself. He had been away during all his middle years—from his fortieth to his sixtieth year. He was curious, he wanted to take a look at his past. America received him with enthusiasm; he was invited to lecture and to write his impressions; he traveled to the south for the first time and he realized a long-cherished dream when he crossed the continent and saw California. Although he returned to England with a sigh of relief, after a strenuous year, it was with the sense that he had captured the whole new aspect of the United States. His book *The Amer-*

ican Scene is one of his great prose works: with the brush of an impressionist painter he relentlessly analyzes things as they were, and as they had become; he had known old New York and now confronted the skyscrapers; he had known a tight parochial Boston; he now saw a sprawling city. Only Concord seemed much the same, and he wondered whether it had not been in its time a sort of "American Weimar." He revisited it with warm memory of Emerson. He revisited also the family plot in the Cambridge cemetery and wrote into his notebook a lyrical passage that expressed all the felt intensity of that experience. What bothered him about America was that so booming a civilization, capable of the greatest things, was addressed so markedly to material and ephemeral ends. This is the repeated refrain of *The American Scene.*

While in the United States he reached an agreement with his publisher to assemble his novels and tales into a definitive edition. For three years after his return to Lamb House he labored on this task, thinking of Balzac and the way in which the French novelist had harmonized his stories and novels and created categories for them in his *comédie humaine.* The "New York Edition," as James titled it, was rigorously selective. It emphasized the cosmopolitan character of his work, and he selected for inclusion his "international" and psychological stories. He left out those novels and tales which had America for a setting, apparently planning to add these, as a separate group, at some later time. All his early works were carefully revised. The changes he made in his text were substantive; he sought to "point up" the prose, to create a richer verbal texture, to give the edition a uniform polish and maturity. At times old simplicities were sacrificed to the over-ornate; nevertheless the revisions invariably result in more explicit statement and strengthening of character.

To each novel, and each collection of tales, James affixed a long and tightly written preface—again after the manner of Balzac. These are of a piece with the novelist's critical writings —the reviews, portraits, and essays he had written for periodicals and newspapers during his entire career. His criticism had reflected from the first the clearly formulated canons of his novelist's art. The collections he put forth himself during his lifetime testify to this— *French Poets and Novelists, Partial Portraits, Essays in London,* and *Notes on Novelists.* As a critic, James is eclectic and classical in his mode of thought: he insists upon form, on style, on integration of form and substance. He unerringly selects the very writers we today consider to have been "major" in his time; and he reads them for what they may teach him of his own process, and for the "quality of mind" he may find in their work. He believes that the artist is to be discovered in his work, but that the work must be created as an "invulnerable granite" to the seeker.

The late prefaces, since collected in a single volume, are composed of three elements: there is the author's interest in his creative process, the "story of the story," how he came to write it and the personal memories and associations aroused by the rereading of his own work; there is the discussion of the technical problems involved in each case; and, with all this, there are James's generalizations on the art of novel writing which form the heart of these essays and give them remarkable force as critical documents. The pages are crowded with critical ideas; they show the creative and analytical vision of an artist who meditates on his career and on old artistic problems long since resolved in his workshop. He felt, as he wrote the prefaces, that they would someday be a great manifesto on the art of the novel and would serve as a guide for writers of fiction. His belief was well founded; the prefaces gave to criticism for the first time a valuable terminology for the discussion of the novel. The craft of novel writing had been discussed on many occasions during the nineteenth century, but James, in some measure, codified this discussion in these last and most personal of his critical essays, gave it system and authority in the light of his half-century of practice.

Although he wrote no more novels, James's productivity during his final years was remarkable. Following the pattern of the New York Edition, he revised his travel writings and consolidated them; thus *English Hours* appeared, and then *Italian Hours*, which, with his *Little Tour in France*, commemorated the pathways James had taken during his lifetime on the Continent. He issued a final collection of essays on the eve of the war, *Notes on Novelists*, containing magisterial studies of Flaubert, Zola, and Balzac and his protest against the forms naturalism had taken in the new English novel, particularly as exemplified in the realistic fiction of H. G. Wells and Arnold Bennett. In addition he wrote two remarkable volumes of reminiscence—*A Small Boy and Others* and *Notes of a Son and Brother*, looking back on his own past with the same search for the truths of the emotions which Proust was to show in his novel *A la recherche du temps perdu*. His *Notes* embodied also his memories of his brother William, who had recently died, and those of his father. A third volume of reminiscence, destined to deal with his years in London and Paris, was left a mere fragment, and was published as *The Middle Years* after James's death.

The English-speaking world honored him on his seventieth birthday; and while efforts to obtain the Nobel Prize for him failed, James was given a golden bowl by 250 friends and admirers who also asked him to sit for his portrait to John Singer Sargent. That portrait is now in the National Portrait Gallery in London.

With the outbreak of the war James threw himself into various activities: he visited hospitals, aided refugees, and wrote on behalf of the American volunteer motor ambulance corps in France. Ill and suffering, he decided in 1915 to yield the American citizenship he had retained during his forty years' residence in England, and throw in his lot with the British cause. A stroke three or four months later was followed by pneumonia, and although he survived into 1916, and was given the Order of Merit by King George V, it was clear that there would be no recovery. He died on February 28. His ashes were brought to America and interred in the family plot in Cambridge. An inscription on his grave describes him as the interpreter of his generation on both sides of the sea.

At first, after James's death, there was a period during which his works were dismissed as thin and lifeless by a generation that had read only a few of his books and had lost sight of the total structure of his literary edifice. For a decade or more the view put forth by Van Wyck Brooks, that James, in uprooting himself from his native land, had produced a rootless art, prevailed. Moreover the publication of James's letters in 1920 tended to establish for posterity the "Old Pretender" James, the heavy long-winded figure of Rye and Chelsea, rather than the robust bearded creative James of the turn of the century. This was due to the fact that much of the earlier correspondence was not available to Percy Lubbock, the editor of the letters, who in particular did not have James's "working" letters, his correspondence with editors and publishers; he assembled two volumes which show James the social being and "theorist" of fiction, but not the Balzacian "professional."

The only posthumous works published were the two unfinished novels, *The Sense of the Past* and *The Ivory Tower*, and the fragment of autobiography, *The Middle Years*. James's other papers were allowed to remain in the trunk in which they had been packed and sent back to America. They ultimately passed into the possession of Harvard University, at the time of the James centenary in 1943, when it became clear that there was still much of James to be given to the world. Most important of all were certain of his working notebooks, which when published in 1947 showed the source material out of which the prefaces had been written. These notebooks constitute one of the most remarkable records of an artist-life ever preserved. Written often in the full blaze of creation, they demonstrate James's way of reimagining his materials and the strange, often calculating intellectual force he brought to bear upon his work.

James had been a constant letter-writer from the first. His letters are the surplus production of a writer who, having done his day's work, is unable to stop, and writes on with a free flow and an easy play of imagination. More than ten thousand letters survive, the majority unpublished, and his professional letters, no less than those written in friendship, are filled with remarkable observation of the people and places of his time.

His friendships were numerous. He moved everywhere in the literary and art world and crossed the path of nearly all the leading writers of his day. He knew more intimately, among writers, critics, painters, Robert Browning, Robert Louis Stevenson, Edmund Gosse, Alphonse Daudet, Ivan Turgenev, Paul Bourget, George du Maurier, John Singer Sargent, John La Farge, Emile Zola, Jules Jusserand, Mrs. Humphry Ward and later Joseph Conrad, H. G. Wells, Rudyard Kipling, Edith Wharton. He had met Matthew Arnold in Rome and later in London, chatted in London drawing rooms with Pater, and had encountered Tennyson and George Eliot, William Morris and John Ruskin. If we add the earlier friendship with Emerson, and his close ties with Norton and Howells, it can be seen that James was far from being the recluse of Rye, as he has sometimes been pictured. He touched his age largely during his half-century in the creative world. He tends increasingly to dominate the literature of America because the ramifications of his career are considerable—and complex—beside the simpler lives and simpler works of other American novelists. His achievement resides in his fertility and inventiveness, his grasp of the New World myth in its relation to the Old; and the skill with which he exploits his often modest materials. His shortcomings reside in the narrowness of his actual world and sometimes in the triviality of his social comedies, as well as in the more tortured effects of certain pages of his late style. Some readers find him, in this phase, subtle to the point of exasperation. Yet in all that he wrote he represented the old civilized world at its most questioning and searching. For the didactic or "proletarian" critic, James can have little meaning; his is the stuff of human nerves and mind rather than the body's muscles; his concern is with emotional relations rather than with human physicality. He writes above all about men and women for whom the myths of civilization alone preserve and hold them from regression to savagery. The so-called "revival" of James has in reality been the discovery of him as a world literary figure, a bridge from the romantic movement to all that is "modern" in the literary art of the twentieth cenury.

Selected Bibliography

For a complete listing of Henry James's writings see *A Bibliography of Henry James*, by Leon Edel and Dan H. Laurence (London: Hart-Davis, 1957), which establishes the priority of editions as between America and England, and also lists foreign translations of James's writings. The rather considerable reprinting of James in recent years has tended to be haphazard, with repetition of well-known titles. The present selection lists his books under the titles they bore on original appearance and gives first place of publication.

COLLECTED EDITIONS

Collected Novels and Tales. 14 vols. London: Macmillan, 1883.

The Novels and Tales of Henry James ("New York Edition"). 24 vols. New York: Scribners, 1907–09. (Two volumes were added posthumously.) Reprinted 1961–65.

Uniform Edition of the Tales. 14 vols. London: Secker, 1915–19. (There was one tale in each volume—that is, 14 tales in all were published, of the more than 100 written by James.)

The Novels and Stories of Henry James. 36 vols. London: Macmillan, 1921–23.

The Complete Tales of Henry James. 12 vols. Philadelphia: Lippincott, 1962–65.

NOVELS

Roderick Hudson. Boston: Osgood, 1876.

The American. Boston: Osgood, 1877.

Watch and Ward. Boston: Houghton, Osgood, 1878.

The Europeans. London: Macmillan, 1878.

Confidence. London: Chatto and Windus, 1880.

Washington Square. New York: Harper, 1881 [1880].

The Portrait of a Lady. London: Macmillan, 1881.

The Bostonians. London: Macmillan, 1886.

The Princess Casamassima. London: Macmillan, 1886.

The Reverberator. London: Macmillan, 1888.

The Tragic Muse. Boston: Houghton, Mifflin, 1890.

The Other House. London: Heinemann, 1896.

The Spoils of Poynton. London: Heinemann, 1897.

What Maisie Knew. London: Heinemann, 1897.

The Awkward Age. London: Heinemann, 1899.

The Sacred Fount. New York: Scribners, 1901.

The Wings of the Dove. New York: Scribners, 1902.

The Ambassadors. London: Methuen, 1903.

The Golden Bowl. New York: Scribners, 1904.

The Outcry. London: Methuen, 1911.

POSTHUMOUS NOVELS

The Ivory Tower. London: Collins, 1917. (Uncompleted.)

The Sense of the Past. London: Collins, 1917. (Uncompleted.)

TALES

Titles marked with an asterisk are special titles assigned by James to books containing his tales. All other titles are actual tale titles, often used as title of the book. Where the title is not italicized, the tale was published alone.

A Passionate Pilgrim and Other Tales. Boston: Osgood, 1875.

"Daisy Miller." New York: Harper, 1879 [1878].

"An International Episode." New York: Harper, 1879.

The Madonna of the Future and Other Tales. London: Macmillan, 1879.

"The Diary of a Man of Fifty." New York: Harper, 1880.

The Siege of London and Other Tales. Boston: Osgood, 1883.

Tales of Three Cities. Boston: Osgood, 1884.

The Author of Beltraffio and Other Tales. Boston: Osgood, 1885.

Stories Revived. 3 vols. London: Macmillan, 1885.

The Aspern Papers. London: Macmillan, 1888.

A London Life. London: Macmillan, 1889.

The Lesson of the Master. New York: Macmillan, 1892.

The Real Thing and Other Tales. New York: Macmillan, 1893.

The Private Life. London: Osgood, McIlvaine, 1893.

The Wheel of Time. New York: Harper, 1893.

* *Terminations.* London: Heinemann, 1895.

* *Embarrassments.* London: Heinemann, 1896.

In the Cage. London: Duckworth, 1898.

* *The Two Magics.* London: Heinemann, 1898.

* *The Soft Side.* London: Methuen, 1900.

* *The Better Sort.* London: Methuen, 1903.

"Julia Bride." New York: Harper, 1909.
* *The Finer Grain.* New York: Scribners, 1910.

POSTHUMOUS COLLECTIONS OF TALES

"Gabrielle de Bergerac." New York: Boni and Liveright, 1918.

Travelling Companions, edited by Albert Mordell. New York: Boni and Liveright, 1919.

A Landscape Painter, edited by Albert Mordell. New York: Scott and Seltzer, 1919 [1920].

Master Eustace, edited by Albert Mordell. New York: Seltzer, 1920.

The American Novels and Stories, edited by F. O. Matthiessen. New York: Knopf, 1948.

The Ghostly Tales of Henry James, edited by Leon Edel. New Brunswick, N.J.: Rutgers University Press, 1948 [1949].

Eight Uncollected Tales, edited by Edna Kenton. New Brunswick, N.J.: Rutgers University Press, 1950.

AUTOBIOGRAPHIES

William Wetmore Story and His Friends. Edinburgh: Blackwood, 1903. (Biographical memoir.)

A Small Boy and Others. New York: Scribners, 1913.

Notes of a Son and Brother. New York: Scribners, 1914.

The Middle Years. London: Collins, 1917. (Uncompleted.)

LETTERS

The Letters of Henry James, edited by Percy Lubbock. 2 vols. London: Macmillan, 1920.

Letters of Henry James to A. C. Benson. New York: Scribners, 1930.

Theatre and Friendship. London: Cape, 1932. (Letters of James to Elizabeth Robins.)

Henry James and Robert Louis Stevenson, edited by Janet A. Smith. London: Hart-Davis, 1948.

Selected Letters of Henry James, edited by Leon Edel. New York: Farrar, Straus, 1955.

Henry James and H. G. Wells, edited by Leon Edel and Gordon N. Ray. London: Hart-Davis, 1958.

PLAYS

Daisy Miller, a Comedy. Boston: Osgood, 1883.
Theatricals. London: Osgood, McIlvaine, 1894.

Theatricals; Second Series. London: Osgood, McIlvaine, 1895.

The Complete Plays of Henry James, edited by Leon Edel. Philadelphia: Lippincott, 1949.

ESSAYS, CRITICISM, AND
MISCELLANEOUS WRITINGS

French Poets and Novelists. London: Macmillan, 1878.

Hawthorne. London: Macmillan, 1879.

Partial Portraits. London: Macmillan, 1888.

Essays in London and Elsewhere. London: Osgood, McIlvaine, 1893.

Picture and Text. New York: Harper, 1893.

The Question of Our Speech. Boston: Houghton, Mifflin, 1905.

Views and Reviews, collected by Le Roy Phillips. Boston: Ball, 1908.

Notes on Novelists. London: Dent, 1914.

POSTHUMOUS COLLECTIONS OF ESSAYS, CRITICISM,
AND MISCELLANEOUS WRITINGS

Within the Rim. London: Collins, 1919.

Notes and Reviews, edited by Pierre la Rose. Cambridge, Mass.: Dunster House, 1921.

The Art of the Novel, edited by R. P. Blackmur. New York: Scribners, 1934.

The Notebooks of Henry James, edited by F. O. Matthiessen and Kenneth B. Murdock. New York: Oxford University Press, 1947.

The Scenic Art, edited by Allan Wade. New Brunswick, N.J.: Rutgers University Press, 1948.

The American Essays of Henry James, edited by Leon Edel. New York: Knopf (Vintage), 1956.

The Future of the Novel, edited by Leon Edel. New York: Knopf (Vintage). 1956.

The Painter's Eye, edited by John L. Sweeney. London: Hart-Davis, 1956.

The House of Fiction, edited by Leon Edel. London: Hart-Davis, 1957.

Literary Reviews and Essays, edited by Albert Mordell. New York: Grove, 1957.

TRAVEL

Transatlantic Sketches. Boston: Osgood, 1875. (Titled *Foreign Parts* in Tauchnitz Edition, 1884.)

Portraits of Places. London: Macmillan, 1883.

A Little Tour in France. Boston: Osgood, 1885 [1884].

English Hours. London: Heinemann, 1905.

The American Scene. London: Chapman and Hall, 1907.

Italian Hours. London: Heinemann, 1909.

POSTHUMOUS TRAVEL COLLECTIONS

Parisian Sketches, edited by Leon Edel and Ilse Lind. New York: New York University Press, 1957.

The Art of Travel, edited by Morton D. Zabel. New York: Doubleday, 1958.

BIOGRAPHICAL AND CRITICAL STUDIES

Beach, Joseph Warren. *The Method of Henry James*. New Haven, Conn.: Yale University Press, 1918.

Brooks, Van Wyck. *The Pilgrimage of Henry James*. New York: Dutton, 1925.

Dupee, F. W. *Henry James*. New York: William Sloane Associates, 1951.

————, ed. *The Question of Henry James*. New York: Holt, 1945.

Edel, Leon. *Henry James. The Untried Years: 1843–1870*. Philadelphia: Lippincott, 1953.

————. *Henry James. The Conquest of London: 1870–1881*. Philadelphia: Lippincott, 1962.

————. *Henry James. The Middle Years: 1882–1895*. Philadelphia: Lippincott, 1962.

————. *Henry James. The Treacherous Years: 1895–1901*. Philadelphia: Lippincott, 1969.

————. *Henry James. The Master: 1901–1916*. Philadelphia: Lippincott, 1972.

Grattan, C. H. *The Three Jameses*. New York: Longmans, Green, 1932.

Lubbock, Percy. *The Craft of Fiction*. New York: Scribners, 1921.

Matthiesson, F. O. *Henry James: The Major Phase*. New York: Oxford University Press, 1944.

————. *The James Family*. New York: Knopf, 1947.

Nowell-Smith, Simon, ed. *The Legend of the Master*. London: Constable, 1948 [1947].

Wilson, Edmund. *The Triple Thinkers*. New York: Harcourt, Brace, 1938.

—LEON EDEL

William James

1842-1910

In *A Pluralistic Universe* William James declares that "a philosophy is the expression of a man's intimate character, and all definitions of the universe are but the deliberately adopted reactions of human characters upon it." Whether or not this opinion holds true for the whole history of philosophy, it was profoundly true in the life and character of William James himself, and is a suggestive clue to his contributions to both psychology and philosophy. His own somatic problems led him to study psychology, and his personal concern with the relations of his mind and body underlay all his philosophical speculations.

The first and deepest influence on William James was his father, Henry James, usually called "senior" to distinguish him from his son Henry the novelist. He was the son of William James of Albany, a self-made millionaire and pious Presbyterian. He rebelled not only against his father's theology but also against his compelling drive to acquire property and money. After he received an inheritance from his father's estate which made him independent, he devoted himself to studying and writing books on theology.

The quarrel of Henry James, Sr., with Calvinism was that it taught a natural estrangement between himself and God. But he also came to believe that all evil in the world was the result of men's overvaluation of their selfhood, and especially their pride in moral uprightness. Inverting Calvin, he declared that men are born innocent, but "fall" individually through selfish egotism, and are saved by subordinating their individual wills to the collective good of society. In early manhood Henry, Sr., had come under the influence of the French socialist Charles Fourier and later the Swedish mystic Emanuel Swedenborg. Fourier taught that man's natural instincts are of divine origin and that social ills are caused by institutions which thwart and corrupt them. If people could live in complete freedom—possible, he thought, in small communities or "phalanges"—they would follow their divine impulses and attain social harmony and personal happiness in this world. Swedenborg taught that God incarnated Himself in mankind, not one man, and that His church was not an institution but humanity. Henry, Sr., combined and adapted Fourier and Swedenborg in his theory of the origin of the world: God created the world by a prolonged and continuous exertion of His energy, first in a "formative" stage now nearing completion, and second in a "redemptive" stage ready to begin. As William James summarized his father's doctrine: "To speak very oracularly, *Nature* is for Mr. James the movement of formation, the first quickening of the void into being, and *Society* is the movement of redemption, or finished spiritual work of God."

William James (born in 1842 in New York City) received a novel but erratic education as a consequence of his father's social and religious theories, which inculcated the need for freedom, spontaneity, and innocence. The innocence of the infant should be protected as long as possible to give his innate divine creativity a chance to grow strong enough to resist the corruptions of society and institutions. In *The Nature of Evil* Henry James, Sr., declared: "I desire my child to become an upright man, in whom goodness shall be induced not by mercenary motives as brute goodness is induced, but by love for it or a sympathetic delight in it. And inasmuch as I know that this character or disposition cannot be forcibly imposed upon him, but must be freely assumed, I surround him as far as possible with an atmosphere of freedom."

However, William James's education was not as free and spontaneous as that of Rousseau's Emile. He attended private schools, had a succession of tutors, and in his father's educational experiments was shifted back and forth between Europe and America—and in America between New York City, Albany, and Newport, Rhode Island. He received a smattering of scientific training in France and Switzerland, and acquired fluency in French and German. His father did not want him to specialize or choose a profession too soon, with the result that he was late in choosing at all. He studied painting with William Hunt for a year, gave that up for chemistry in the Scientific School at Harvard, shifted to anatomy and comparative zoology, and finally entered the Harvard Medical School in 1864, only to withdraw for a year to accompany Louis Agassiz to Brazil on a zoological collecting expedition. A few months after returning from Brazil and re-entering Medical School, he withdrew again for a year, ostensibly to study physiology in Germany, but partly to seek a cure for the mysterious pains in his back. Illness prevented him from doing laboratory work at Leipzig or Heidelberg, but he did attend a few lectures at the University of Berlin, acquired a command of scientific German, read the latest books in German on physiology and "psychophysics," and became deeply interested in the possibility of a "real science of psychology." The year in Germany greatly stimulated his intellectual development.

James's poor health had begun in his nineteenth year while he was trying to decide between careers in science and art. Uncertainty, shame over his vacillation, and regret over his inability to understand or reconcile himself to his father's ideas, seemingly so tolerant but maintained with dogmatic vehemence, all these problems combined to undermine the young man's self-confidence and reduce him to nervous prostration, at times so strong that he contemplated suicide. In his youth and early manhood William was his father's favorite of his four sons, and Henry, Sr., wanted him to pursue science instead of art, although, paradoxically, he had a low opinion of scientists because he thought they held "a giant superstition we call Nature." In an article on "Faith and Science" he explained: "Nature, when philosophically regarded, expresses the lowest form of the human intelligence. . . . It is a mere hallucination of nascent intelligence. . . . It has no existence save to a finite intelligence, an intelligence whose knowledge is derived through the senses." To attain real knowledge, therefore, man must emancipate himself from nature and become a spiritual being, but this emancipation tempts him to assert his own individualism and self-expression, his own selfhood instead of acquiescing in the Selfhood of God. This paradox in Henry James's adaptation of

Swedenborg—what might be called Henry James's substitute for the doctrine of "original sin"—was very difficult for William to understand. In *Substance and Shadow* his father wrote: "For we being absolute creatures of God are without any substance in ourselves, and hence are what we are . . . only by virtue of His infinite tenderness imparting, or, as Swedenborg phrases it, *communicating*, Himself to us; permitting us, if we please, to put His love to the basest uses, in order that at last we may through sheer disgust of our own loathsome performances, turn ourselves freely to Him and demand . . . at last the guidance of His unerring laws. . . . For the power by which all this deviltry is enacted is literally God in us."

To a friend William James wrote in 1868: "I have grown up, partly from education and the example of my Dad, partly, I think, from a natural tendency, in a very non-optimistic view of nature, going so far as to have some years ago a perfectly passionate aversion to all moral praise, etc.—an antinomian tendency, in short. I have regarded the affairs of human life to be only a phantasmagoria, which had to be *interpreted* elsewhere in the kosmos into its real significance." Fortunately, about this time William found in Goethe's "realism" a palliative for his father's unhealthy (for William) antinomaianism. In his diary he wrote: "[Goethe's] endless delight in facts & details seems to be no longer the painstaking literalness of a mind which, having no inspiration or intuition of its own, and yet fearing to lose the valuable in anything, gathers the accidental & arbitrary up with the essential in one sheaf; but rather the naif delight of an incessantly active mind & healthy sense in their own operations." However, this conflict between the spiritual determinism of Henry James, Sr., and the "realism" of Goethe would continue

throughout William James's life in his mind and conscience.

James finally received his M.D. degree in 1869, but had no desire to practice medicine, and saw no way opening to a scientific career. Naturally his neurotic symptoms increased, and he worried about his weak will power, which he strongly suspected to be responsible for his physical illness. Frequent debates with a friend and neighbor, the brilliant but unknown determinist Chauncey Wright, and reading the German psycho-physicist Gustav Fechner, who claimed to have measured sensation and reduced it to a mathematical formula, aggravated James's depression. He felt "swamped in an empirical [materialistic] philosophy," his will paralyzed by forces beyond his control or comprehension. He was haunted by an image of an epileptic patient frozen in a cataleptic posture whom he had seen on a visit to a mental hospital. *"That shape am I*, I felt, potentially," he later confessed in the guise of a case history in *The Varieties of Religious Experience.*

Fortunately, two experiences helped James recover hope and a measure of self-control. One was the death of an adored cousin, Minnie Temple, in the spring of 1870. Her death shocked him into a realization of "the nothingness of all our egotistic fury." He attained a kind of existential stoicism, or what Emerson called "fatal courage," and wrote in his diary: "The inevitable release is sure; wherefore take our turn kindly whatever it contain. Ascend to some sort of partnership with fate, & since tragedy is at the heart of us, go to meet it, work it in to our ends, instead of dodging it all our days, and being run down by it at last. Use your death (or your life, it's all one meaning)."

The other experience was reading a book James had brought back from Europe, *Essais* on a "théorie phénoméniste," by Charles

Renouvier, an empiricist who stressed voluntarism and fideism. James recorded in his diary on April 30, 1870: "I think yesterday was a crisis in my life. I finished the first part of Renouvier's 2nd Essay and saw no reason why his definition of free will—'the sustaining of a thought *because I choose to* when I might have other thoughts'—need be the definition of an illusion. At any rate I will assume for the present . . . that it is no illusion. My first act of free will shall be to believe in free will." He resolved also, as an experiment, to indulge less in speculation and to pay more attention to his conduct, or as he expressed it, "the *form* of my action." Very soon he observed a decrease in his morbid tendencies and a diminishing of the pains in his back. The success of this self-therapy might be called William James's first psychological discovery, and it would influence his later philosophical thinking.

William James never found a cure for his neuroses, but he learned to live with them. He was greatly assisted by the sympathy and understanding of his former chemistry teacher, Charles W. Eliot, who became president of Harvard University in 1869. He appointed James to give undergraduate instruction in anatomy and physiology in Harvard College in 1873, and two years later James began giving a course in psychology on the physiological approach he had learned from the *Psychophysik* of the Germans. This was a new departure in America, and in 1876, James was also the first to establish a psychological laboratory, three years before Wundt opened his epochal Institute at Leipzig. James, like the Germans, worked on the Darwinian assumption that there is a continuity between animals and human beings, and though it was an accident that he began his teaching in physiology and comparative anatomy, this was a logical approach to

the "new" psychology. And though his preparation had been somewhat haphazard, actually no one else in his own country was as well prepared in the field. His medical courses had given him sound basic knowledge of the structure and functions of the human body, and he had extended this knowledge in preparing lectures for his courses—also for several years he was in charge of a Museum in Comparative Anatomy at Harvard. Furthermore, his command of languages enabled him to keep abreast of the latest discoveries and theories in Europe.

James's earliest writings on psychology were reviews for magazines, mainly the *Nation*, the *Atlantic Monthly*, and the *North American Review*, and consequently were written in a popular style, which he soon perfected and never lost. Almost at the start of his career he began to question the materialistic bias of the laboratory psychologists. His first contribution to a professional journal was "Remarks on Spencer's *Definition of Mind as Correspondence*," published in the *Journal of Speculative Philosophy* in 1878. Here he advanced an idea which would become the foundation of his later psychological and philosophical theories, namely, that the mind is motivated by interest and preference. Nearly twenty years later in "Reflex Action and Theism" he declared: "I am not sure that all physiologists see that it [the reflex theory of mind] commits them to regarding the mind as an essentially teleological mechanism. I mean by this that the conceiving or theorizing faculty . . . functions *exclusively for the sake of ends* that do not exist at all in the world of impressions we receive by way of our senses, but are set by our emotional and practical subjectivity altogether."

By 1878 *subjectivity* had become a term of opprobrium in physiological psychology, and in his second important contribution of that year, an essay on "Quelques Considérations sur la méthode subjective," which his friend Renouvier published in *Critique Philosophique*, James pointed out that "the whole theory of different local habitations in the brain for different classes of ideas with fibres connecting the localities together—so that when one locality is excited the excitement may travel along the fibres and waken up the other locality—this whole theory, I say, was originally derived from our introspective knowledge of the way in which our feelings awaken each other."

In this same important year (1878) James gave a lecture at Johns Hopkins University and at Lowell Institute in Boston on "The Brain and the Mind," in which he traced the development of scientific theories on the nature and function of the brain and the nervous system, but pointed out that no one had yet been able to explain *consciousness*. He did not question the "reflex arc," and he agreed that many of the responses in the brain to nerve-end stimuli were unconscious and seemingly automatic (as in breathing, digestion, circulation of the blood, etc.), but other conscious responses were decidedly not automatic or scientifically predictable, including the concept of "automatism": "The truth is that science and all these other functions of the human mind are alike the results of man's thinking about the phenomena life offers him. . . . I, for one, as a scientific man and a practical man alike, deny utterly that science compels me to believe that my conscience is an *ignis fatuus* or outcast, and I trust that you too . . . will go away strengthened in the natural faith that your delights and sorrows, your loves and hates, your aspirations and efforts are real combatants in life's arena, and not impotent, paralytic spectators of the game."

In "The Sentiment of Rationality" (1879) James argued strongly for the primacy of *feeling* even in the most "rational" conceptions of the philosopher. As far back as Plato (and perhaps beyond) philosophers had shown distrust of human emotions, regarding them as hindrances to the attainment of rational thought. But James asks how the philosopher knows that he has attained a rational conception, and replies that he recognizes it "as he recognizes everything else, by certain subjective marks with which it affects him. . . . A strong feeling of ease, peace, rest, is one of them. The transition from a state of puzzle and perplexity to rational comprehension is full of lively relief and pleasure." This may sound rather negative, "the absence of any feeling of irrationality," but "all feeling whatever, in the light of certain recent psychological speculations, seems to depend for its physical condition not on simple discharge of nerve-currents, but on their discharge under arrest, impediment or resistance." Just as we are unaware of breathing until there is some interference with respiration, so with cogitation; a perfectly "fluent course of thought awakens but little feeling." But "when the thought meets with difficulties, we experience a distress," which yields to a feeling of pleasure as fast as the obstacle is overcome.

Why we are so made that we are unhappy without this fluency of thought James says is an ethical question; he is concerned here with psychology, and it is "an empirical fact that we strive to formulate rationally a tangled mass of fact by a propensity as natural and invincible as that which makes us exchange a hard high stool for an arm-chair." The formulation, or *conception*, "is a *teleological instrument*" used "to satisfy the sentiment of rationality." In forming a concept, a partial aspect of a thing is seized upon to represent the entire thing, ignoring other qualities and properties which for a given purpose do not seem essential. Both in this essay and elsewhere James regards concepts as thus limited, though the conceiver tends to regard them as all-inclusive and universal. James also detects two kinds of mental dispositions, those which have a "passion for simplification," and others, probably a minority, which have a "passion for distinguishing . . . the impulse to be *acquainted* with the parts rather than to comprehend the whole." Later he calls these different responses "the two great aesthetic needs of our logical nature, the need for unity and the need for clearness." James himself prefers the clearness of "concrete reality" in all its fullness and eccentricity of details, and this preference will lead to his philosophy of "pluralism" and "radical empiricism."

James also preferred concrete reality in its rich diversity to an abstract, simplified unity because it left more room for chance and indeterminism. In 1884 he gave an address at the Harvard Divinity School (and the audience is significant) on "The Dilemma of Determinism," in which he argued for indeterminism on psychological rather than metaphysical grounds— a foreshadowing of his later "pragmatism." At the outset he admitted that "evidence of an external kind to decide between determinism and indeterminism is . . . strictly impossible to find." In a later lecture ("Great Men and Their Environment") he amplified this impossibility: Only an infinite mind able to see all parts of the universe simultaneously could know the ultimate cause and effect of any one action or event in the universe; since it is obviously impossible for a finite mind to attain to such knowledge, the argument must be settled on other grounds than cause and effect—that is, it can never be settled.

But if we cannot *know*, we can at least see the effects of accepting one doctrine over the other. Determinism "professes that those parts of the universe already laid down absolutely appoint and decree what the other parts shall be. The future has no ambiguous possibilities hidden in its womb: the part we call the present is compatible with only one totality. Any other future complement than the one fixed from eternity is impossible." This is an "iron block" universe. "Indeterminism, on the contrary, says that the parts have a certain amount of loose play on one another. . . . It admits that possibilities may be in excess of actualities, and that things not yet revealed to our knowledge may really in themselves be ambiguous. Of two alternative futures which we conceive, both may now be really possible; and the one become impossible only at the very moment when the other excludes it by becoming real. Indeterminism thus denies the world to be one unbending unit of fact. It says there is a certain ultimate pluralism in it; and, so saying, it corroborates our ordinary unsophisticated view of things. To that view, actualities seem to float in a wider sea of possibilities from out of which they are chosen; and, *somewhere*, indeterminism says, such possibilities exist, and form a part of truth."

The real "dilemma," James told the theological students, was the inability of determinism to give a satisfactory explanation of evil in the world. "If God be good, how came he to create—or, if he did not create, how comes he to permit—the devil? The evil facts must be explained as seeming; the devil must be whitewashed, the universe be disinfected, if neither God's goodness nor his unity and power are to remain unimpugned." The determinist can make no distinctions between good and bad; things simply are, and distinctions are merely fantasies. "Calling a thing bad means, if it mean anything at all, that the thing ought not to be, that something else ought to be in its stead. Determinism, in denying that anything else can be in its stead, virtually defines the universe as a place in which what ought to be is impossible—in other words, as an organism whose constitution is afflicted with an incurable taint, an irremediable flaw." The only escape is utter indifference, or cynicism.

In an unfinished universe, bristling with chance and possibilities, both good and bad are real, and eternally at war. Not only did James see hope in such a universe, he also found it immensely stimulating. "Regarded as a stable finality, every outward good becomes a mere weariness to the flesh. It must be menaced, be occasionally lost, for its goodness to be fully felt as such. Nay, more than occasionally lost. No one knows the worth of innocence till he knows it is gone forever, and that money cannot buy it back. Not the saint, but the sinner that repenteth, is he to whom the full length and breadth, and height and depth, of life's meaning is revealed. Not the absence of vice, but vice there, and virtue holding her by the throat, seems the ideal human state. And there seems no reason to suppose it is not a permanent human state."

To the expected question from the divinity students, "Does not the admission of such an unguaranteed chance or freedom preclude utterly the notion of a Providence governing the world?" James replied by an analogy of a chess game between an expert and a novice. The expert will surely win in the end, and he knows all the possible moves, but he cannot foresee every actual move the novice will make. Even this analogy may seem rather gloomy for the novice, but James replied that "it is entirely immaterial . . . whether the creator leave the absolute chance-possibilities to be decided by himself, each when its proper moment arrrives, or whether, on the contrary, he alienate this power from himself, and leave the decision out and out to finite creatures such as we men are. The great point is that the possibilities are

really *here*." Later, in *A Pluralistic Universe*, he would find more encouragement for human effort by speculating that God is not all-powerful, is Himself struggling against obstacles, and needs help, even from finite human beings.

During the 1880's James was trying desperately to get started on writing a textbook in psychology, for which he had signed a contract with Henry Holt in 1878. All the publisher wanted was an elementary exposition of basic principles, though of course he wished it to be as up-to-date as possible. James had thought it would be a simple matter to synthesize the recent discoveries in Germany, France, and England and write the book in a couple of years. But as he began to survey the field, he became convinced that nothing was settled, and scarcely the rudiments of a "science" had yet been formulated. Moreover, he found himself questioning the widely held theories of "associationism" which dominated British psychology and was still accepted by some of the leading German exponents of a psychology based on biological principles.

Associationism began with Locke's *Essay Concerning Human Understanding*, in which he argued that experience gives two sources for ideas (images or representations in the mind), sensation and reflection. Ideas of qualities (color, heat, sound, taste, etc.) come from sensation; thinking, willing, believing, doubting, etc., are the products of reflection. All ideas are simple or complex, the simple being a single sense impression, like the smell of a rose; the complex, a combination of two or more simple ideas, such as green (a mixture of yellow and blue). Some ideas come from two or more senses, such as sight and touch in the experience of space, figure, motion. Others, like ideas of pleasure and pain, come both from sensation and from reflection. Ideas which Locke thought to reside in the objects themselves, the basic ingredients of Newtonian physics, such as solidity, extension, motion, figure, and number, he called *primary qualities*. Qualities existing only in the senses, though produced by the effect of primary qualities in objects, he called *secondary qualities,* such as sights, sounds, tastes. Knowledge of primary qualities Locke regarded as more certain and dependable than knowledge of secondary qualities, which might vary with the state of the senses or individual differences. Berkeley tried to find a way out of Locke's dualism in pure idealism, and Hume ended his inquiry in complete skepticism, but British empiricists did not give up the atomic suppositions of Locke. They still tried to account for certan kinds of knowledge by combining or associating sensations by mental processes.

To William James, however, it seemed that "All our mind's contents are alike empirical," and he began conducting experiments to test this hypothesis. In "The Space Quale," published in the *Journal of Speculative Philosophy* in 1879, he summarized and evaluated the results of his laboratory investigations of sense perception of space. He agreed with the earlier theorizers that man has no special space sense, but he found that several senses give sensations of weight, intensity, interval, muscular stress, etc., which constitute primordial experience of space. In other experiments he proved that the sense of balance is controlled by the semicircular canals of the inner ear, the conclusive evidence being that deaf-mutes whose semicircular canals have been paralyzed by injury or have atrophied cannot experience dizziness or motion sickness. In this field James did important pioneer work. The perception of time he found also to be a function of various senses, including muscular tensions.

James's first publication on the will was a thirty-two-page essay in 1880 on "The Feeling of Effort," in which he argued that the incoming currents in sensory nerves are felt in consciousness (i.e., one is aware that something out there is being seen or heard or touched); but that after the brain has received the "message" and dispatched a reply, there is no feeling of the efferent discharge. If some choice needs to be made for a practical end, the mind is aware of directing the impulse to the right muscle, but "consciousness seems to desert all processes where it can no longer be of any use." Here James was close to discovering the "conditional reflex," and perhaps missed it only because he was more interested in evidence of choice and free will in the processes. He points out that in learning to perform an unfamiliar act, conscious effort has to be exerted, but with practice the act can be performed with less and less conscious attention: "The marksman thinks only of the exact position of the goal, the singer only of the perfect sound, the balancer only of the point in space whose oscillations he must counteract by movement. The associated mechanism has become so perfect in all these persons, that each variation in the thought of the end, is functionally correlated with the one movement fitted to bring the latter about."

Because of this "principle of parsimony in consciousness," James says, "the motor discharge *ought* to be devoid of sentience. The essentials of a voluntary movement are: 1, a preliminary idea of the end we wish to attain; 2, a '*fiat*'; 3, an appropriate muscular contraction; 4, the end felt as actually accomplished. . . . The end conceived will, when these associations are formed, always awaken its own proper motor idea."

Closely akin to this view of the volition process was James's theory of emotions as "indubitably physiological," a process occurring in the motor and sensory centers. There is therefore no such thing as *an emotion*, only these combined motor processes. In an essay on "What Is an Emotion" (1884), he admits, however, that he is speaking only of "emotions . . . that have a distinct bodily expression." There are perhaps others (feelings of pleasure or displeasure, interest or boredom, etc.) which may be "mental operations," though they may be accompanied by involuntary or unconscious physical movements, as in thinking of food, one may move his tongue, moisten his lips, and involuntarily salivate.

James's thesis is "that *the bodily changes follow directly the* PERCEPTION *of the exciting fact, and that our feeling of the same changes as they occur* IS *the emotion*." We might paraphrase this by saying that perception plus bodily manifestation equals emotional feeling. When he published this essay James was not aware that a Danish psychologist named Lange had proposed the same theory, and when this fact was called to his attention he readily agreed to having it called the "James-Lange theory of apperception." In popular parlance, one does not run from a bear because he feels fear; he feels fear because he runs. This simplification sounds more paradoxical than the theory actually is: the point is that bodily activity, not an abstraction, causes the feeling of emotion. The James-Lange theory occupies a major position in James's psychology. James was not trying to reduce all psychological functions to physiological processes, but seeking to show how inseparable and interdependent the mind and body are.

These contributions to physiological psychology were first recognized and appreciated in France, where they were published in translation in *Critique Philosophique*. These early essays are also important because they led James to his most important discovery, for which he became world-famous after publishing his *The Principles of Psychology* in 1890. The German psychologist Franz Brentano had compared consciousness to a stream, but it was James who discovered the "fringe" of consciousness, which gave new meaning to the stream concept. He found that consciousness was not, as the epistemologists who talked of simple and complex ideas believed, awareness of separate objects in procession which the mind somehow connects by association. Instead consciousness was like a flowing river carrying all sorts of detritus, undifferentiated objects until some personal interest causes the consciousness to focus on some part of the flux. And always just beyond consciousness there is a blurry periphery of objects which contribute to the flow, the continuity, some of which never come into focus. One object leads the mind's attention to others, and we ought, James says, to speak of association of objects, not of ideas.

The mind becomes aware of many things without effort, and consciousness is never a blank; there is always a flux of something, or somethings, in it. Although this process takes place even when the will is passive, as in reverie, or in weak, halfhearted action, it is not fortuitous or haphazard. In the first place, consciousness came into existence on strictly Darwinian principles, to aid the organism to adapt itself to its environment and survive. In James's words: "Every actually existing consciousness seems to itself at any rate to be a *fighter for ends*, of which many, but for its presence, would not be ends at all. Its powers of cognition are mainly subservient to these ends, discerning which facts further them and which do not." The more attention needed, the greater the volition, but holding the object in consciousness unlocks the proper motor energy and the flow takes place. If the chosen response is no action, or delayed action, more attention is needed—more volition—and the motor energy is held in reserve, though this, too, is accomplished by switching nerve currents to appropriate circuits.

James has often been accused of inconsistencies and contradictions, and consistency was not a virtue which he cherished; nevertheless there is such a close relationship between his theories of the will, the stream of consciousness with its "fringe," habit, the self, and the nature of reality (to name major subjects) that one theory almost implies the other.

The chapter of his *Principles* which received most popular (unprofessional) approval was "Habit." James begins with the assumption that all organic matter is plastic, nerve tissue especially. Once a particular stimulus has traveled through nerve tissue to a certain center of the brain and activated an ideo-motor response, a similar stimulus will follow the same path unless it is blocked or rerouted by conscious volition, that is, energy generated by attention with effort. Habits are, therefore, the result of "pathways through the nerve-centres," and the more often the same path is used, the deeper and more fixed it becomes.

Habits can be beneficial or harmful, James stressed, and it is very important to start and preserve the helpful habit. The practical benefit is that "habit simplifies our movements, makes them accurate, and diminishes fatigue," because each repetition demands less and less conscious effort. A great difference between man and other animals is that he "is born with a tendency to do more things than he has ready-made arrangements for in his nerve-centres. Most of the performances of other animals are automatic. But in him the number of them is so enormous, that most of them must be the fruit of painful study. If practice did not make perfect, nor habit economize the expense of nervous and muscular energy, he would therefore be in a sorry plight." This theory, like James's "stream of consciousness," emphasizes plasticity, flux, the need for choice in adjusting to new experiences, and the importance of *feeling* in the process of ideo-motor responses.

James's exposition of the "Self" makes great use of the flux of consciousness and the malleability of habits. In the first place, he finds not one self but several, all of course interrelated and interdependent. There is "the empirical self or me," and all that the "me" possesses, including not only his body and his physical possessions, but also his reputation, and his social relations. Then there is the "spiritual me," the "core and nucleus" of the self, which some call the "soul." James wishes to dispense with "mind-substance" and soul, but this controlling center serves the same purpose as the older concepts of a Soul uniting mind and body. James's "self" has consciousness of a consistent personal identity, connecting states of consciousness of the past with the present state, or, as he says, "each successive mental state appropriate[s] the same past Me." Just who the *knower* is James leaves to metaphysics. He accepts the common-sense view that we have *"direct* knowledge of the existence of our states of consciousness'" without the hypothesis of a transcendental Soul or World Spirit "which thinks through us." He concludes provisionally that "the thoughts themselves are the thinkers."

James himself was far from satisfied that thoughts think themselves, but he was trying desperately to keep psychology within the realm of pure empiricism. That it was not yet a "natural science" he ruefully confessed in a Conclusion he wrote for the one-volume edition of his *Principles* which he called *Psychology, Briefer Course* (1892): "When, then, we talk of 'psychology as a natural science,' we must not assume that that means a sort of psychology that stands at last on solid ground. It means just the reverse; it means a psychology particularly fragile, and into which the waters of metaphysical criticism leak at every joint . . . a strong prejudice that we *have* states of mind, and that our brain conditions them: but not a single law in the sense in which physics shows us laws. . . . This is no science, it is only the hope of a science."

The great success of James's *The Principles of Psychology* and his *Psychology, Briefer Course* made him one of the most famous men in the field of American education, and he accepted the opportunity to become a widely acclaimed popular lecturer. He had always addressed himself as much to a nonprofessional audience as to a professional one, and he now became in actual fact a popular psychologist, with a permanent effect on both his writing and thinking. Although he delivered his address on "The Will to Believe" to philosophy clubs at Yale and Brown universities in 1896, it was one of these "popular" lectures. He even called it "something like a sermon on justification by faith."

Scientists had become increasingly agnostic because part of the concept of a scientific method is suspension of belief (or conclusion) until all the evidence is in. But James had decided as early as his "The Dilemma of Determinism" that seldom, if ever, is the evidence all in, and meanwhile *some* decision often needs to be made, both for practical necessity and because prolonged indecision may be deleterious to the nervous system. His thesis in "The Will to Believe" is this: "*Our passional nature not only lawfully may, but must, decide an option between propositions, whenever it is a genuine option that cannot by its nature be decided on intellectual grounds; for to say, under such circumstances, 'Do not decide, but leave the question open,' is itself a passional decision,—just like deciding yes or no,—and is attended with*

the same risk of losing the truth." James was immediately accused of advocating "wishful thinking," but he was advocating a willful entertaining of belief only when there is a "genuine option"; further, not all optional choices need be final. All he was saying was that sometimes it is better to take a chance on a decision than wait indefinitely for elusive evidence. He also believed that at times decisive action may change the circumstances; that, to anticipate "pragmatism," *truth* can sometimes be *made*, and a man's world changed by his own efforts. If this were not so, social reform would be impossible.

The doctrine of pragmatism is almost an extension of "The Will to Believe." James first used the term in a lecture at the University of California in 1898 on "Philosophical Concepts and Practical Results." He borrowed the word from his friend Charles Peirce, who had coined it twenty years earlier in an article on "How to Make Our Ideas Clear." Peirce did not intend to present a theory of truth, only a method of using language so as to avoid ambiguity. In James's version of this method "our beliefs are really rules for action," and "to develop a thought's meaning, we need only determine what conduct it is fitted to produce; that conduct is for us its sole significance"—in *Pragmatism* he would later say its *truth*. "To attain perfect clearness in our thoughts of an object, then, we need only consider what effects of a conceivable practical kind the object may involve—what sensations we are to expect from it, and what reactions we must prepare. Our conception of these effects, then, is for us the whole of our conception of the object, so far as that conception has positive significance at all."

Peirce had strongly objected to James's "The Will to Believe" because this emphasis upon conduct was too subjective for him. He was interested more in the *method* of thinking,

James in *purpose and effect,* though he also called pragmatism a method for attaining truth (*answers* might have been less controversial), and subtitled his book *Pragmatism* "A New Name for Some Old Ways of Thinking." By "old way" James evidently meant that the dependability of an assumption can only be tested by experience. An assumption that proves reliable is a "truth," but only provisionally, for no truth is universal. This rules out "absolutes" of all kinds and makes truth relative, a concept which most philosophers of the past would have called a contradiction of terms. But James claimed that most metaphysical assumptions, such as determinism, as we have seen, can never be settled by objective proof one way or the other. Yet if a man believes he has at least some control over his destiny, he is more likely to make an effort to help out the desired result. The effort itself is good for his character and morale, and it may succeed also on the physical level of practicality. Believing in one's own strength and will power, therefore, has pragmatic value, and the assumption is true because it works.

In *Pragmatism* James says: " 'Grant an idea or belief to be true . . . what concrete difference will its being true make in any one's actual life?' . . . The moment pragmatism asks this question, it sees the answer: *True ideas are those that we can assimilate, validate, corroborate and verify. False ideas are those that we can not.* . . . We live in a world of realities that can be infinitely useful or infinitely harmful. Ideas that tell us which of them to expect count as the true ideas in all this primary sphere of verification, and the pursuit of such ideas is a primary human duty."

Though the book entitled *Pragmatism* was not published until 1907, five years earlier James had used the pragmatic approach in his epoch-making *The Varieties of Religious Experience.* In this work he is not concerned with

the validity of any particular religion, only with the *life of religion,* which "consists of the belief that there is an unseen order, and that our supreme good lies in harmoniously adjusting ourselves thereto." James himself maintains a neutral position regarding these "varieties," but he does not doubt the reality of the experiences to the people who have had them and feel that they have been in a personal relation with "unseen power" of some sort. To the charge that many of the experiences he reports may have been caused by a condition of the person's nervous system, James replies that even if this is true, the experience is no less an empirical fact. He grants that religious ecstasy and insanity may be difficult, or impossible, to differentiate, but who knows what power may be working through human nerves and brains? The religious experience is phenomenally *real.*

In spite of his attempts to be scientifically objective in writing his *The Principles of Psychology,* and his rejection of a Soul or transcendental world or cosmic spirit to account for the phenomenon of consciousness, James had all along harbored a suspicion—perhaps even a secret wish—that a transcendental consciousness might exist. This hypothesis colored his empiricism and made it at times almost an eccentric variety of idealism. For example, in 1898 he had given a lecture on "Human Immortality," in which he had suggested as a hypothesis, not a personal conviction, that the human brain does not *produce* thoughts, as a dynamo produces electricity, but only *transmits* thoughts, as wire conducts electric current. This idea not only contradicts James's "scientific" psychology, but is also ambiguous in his expression of it.

Because he had never found a satisfactory or consistent theory of cognition, James now suggests that we imagine the brain to be a thin membrane separating the world of mind and matter, and that sometimes (why not always?)

spiritual energy flows through it. Then, shifting his metaphor, he speaks of the human threshold of consciousness being lowered, so that a consciousness from a higher than human level flows into it. Something like this seems to take place in religious "conversion" and a "mystical experience." The physiological-psychological explanation that consciousness is in the brain had always been to James an "absolute world-enigma—something so paradoxical and abnormal as to be a stumbling block to Nature, and almost a self-contradiction." So, as a possible way out, James suggests that "we need only suppose the continuity of our consciousness with a mother sea, to allow for exceptional waves occasionally pouring over the dam. Of course the causes of these odd lowerings of the brain's threshold still remain a mystery on any terms."

The enigma of consciousness had led James to become interested in "psychical research" while still a medical student, and he helped found the American Society for Psychical Research in 1884. Before writing his *Principles* he had attended séances, and he spent many years trying to find objective (scientific) evidence of telepathy, clairvoyance, and survival of consciousness after the death of the body. His professed motive was that claims for such phenomena should not be dismissed as fraudulent without scientific investigation, but his continued effort in the field indicated, by his own psychology, a strong passional interest. His acquaintance with hypnotism, with which he experimented, with split personality, which he observed on many field trips to insane asylums, with hallucinatory visions (both he and his very religious father had each had one almost traumatic experience of this kind)—these phenomena made him wonder whether an individual consciousness might somehow be a part of a larger consciousness (or consciousnesses) under certain conditions. He never

found any scientific proof of telepathy, clairvoyance, or survival of consciousness after death; nor did he ever come to believe sufficiently in an Infinite Consciousness encompassing all finite consciousnesses to cause him to renounce pluralism for monism. He entertained this idea in various writings, but he continued to have a strong intuitive feeling that the phenomenon of consciousness was also pluralistic.

This digression is necessary for understanding the kind of book *The Varieties of Religious Experience* is. James began by collecting every record he could find of a religious nature, and it is significant that he subtitled his work "A Study in Human Nature." His procedure was as follows: first description, then comparison, classification, analysis, and finally some tentative conclusions. He wanted first of all to find out the nature of a religious experience, and whether the mass of such experiences had anything in common. His approach was, therefore, psychological, and he soon became convinced that *feeling* and not intellect or reason was the doorway to the religious life. Dogmas and systematic theologies were only the fossils of religion, sometimes surviving centuries after the life had passed out of them. If a person had to prove the existence of God by logic, that person had never had intimate knowledge of God. The only virtue James could find in theology and a church was an aesthetic one, like the symmetry of scholasticism or the beautiful architecture of a medieval church. But why had men built the cathedral, and what function did it serve in their lives? James was never more pragmatic than in his search for answers to such questions.

The one belief James found in all examples of the religious confessions was that the worshiper *felt* that he had been in communication or some sort of contact with spiritual power (singular or plural), from which he derived a charge of new energy. In all religions there seemed to be three similar techniques for tapping this psychic energy: sacrifice (of objects, self, or pleasures), confession (a "general system of purgation and cleansing"), and prayer (every kind of inward communication or conversation with the power recognized as divine"). Of these three techniques James found prayer to be "the very soul and essence of religion." Through prayer the devotee finds purpose, guidance, and strength to endure the accidents and hardships of life, and "at all stages of the prayerful life we find the persuasion that in the process of communion energy from on high flows in to meet demand, and becomes operative within the phenomenal world. So long as this operativeness is admitted to be real, it makes no essential difference whether its immediate effects be subjective or objective. The fundamental religious point is that in prayer, spiritual energy, which otherwise would slumber, does become active, and spiritual work of some kind is effected really." And of course the "spiritual work" may also in turn stimulate the person affected to perform physical work.

The test of a religious experience, therefore, is pragmatic, and it does not matter, James says, where the energy comes from, or that science cannot account for it. "Religion, in short, is a monumental chapter in the history of human egotism. The gods believed in—whether by crude savages or by men disciplined intellectually—agree with each other in recognizing personal calls. Religious thought is carried on in terms of personality," whether by the "healthy-minded" who take their world for granted, or the "sick-minded" oppressed by a sense of guilt and inadequacy: "the religious individual tells you that the divine meets him on the basis of his personal concerns."

James himself suspected that this mysterious psychic energy might come from the person's own subconscious. But this did not, for him,

rule out the possibility of contact with some sort of supernatural—or supranatural—consciousness. The subconscious might be the doorway to the supernatural—a doorway also between a science of religion and the living experience of religion, for science accepts the existence of the *subconscious*, and certain objective techniques can be used to demonstrate the flow of energy from the subconscious to the conscious mind. Of course the assumption that the subconscious is a doorway to a world of nonphysical energy is only an assumption (for James this was Fechnerian, pre-Freudian speculation), but the effects are real, and James could find no other hypothesis for their source. He admits, too, that to experience this flow of energy from the mysterious fountain in the subconscious one must have confidence in its existence, what the church calls "faith" and James an "over-belief."

Although all the transcendental metaphysicians opposed this "thoroughly 'pragmatic' view of religion," James found it to be a common view in the vast confessional literature he had collected, and he saw no reason to interpolate "divine miracles" or build an imaginary "heaven" to make religion more divine or more spiritual. "I believe," he says, "the pragmatic way of taking religion to be the deeper way. It gives it body as well as soul, it makes it claim, as everything real must claim, some characteristic realm of fact as its very own. What the more characteristically divine facts are, apart from the actual inflow of energy in the faith-state and the prayer-state, I know not."

James now held as an over-belief, perhaps influenced by his association with psychical research, the notion that "the world of our present consciousness is only one out of many worlds of consciousness that exist, and that those other worlds must contain experiences which have a meaning for our life also; and that although in the main their experiences and those of this world keep discrete, yet the two become continuous at certain points, and higher energies filter in." He was well aware of the contempt of scientists for such an over-belief, but he also now held the view of his father that "the real world is of a different temperament,—more intricately built than physical science allows. So my objective and my subjective conscience both hold me to the over-belief which I express. Who knows whether the faithfulness of individuals here below to their own poor over-beliefs may not actually help God in turn to be more effectively faithful to his own greater tasks?"

In spite of James's talk of different levels of consciousness, he never wavered in his doctrine (or "philosophical attitude," he preferred to call it) of "radical empiricism," which opposed monism, idealism, and was pluralistic. He defined the terms as early as 1897 in his Preface to *The Will to Believe*: "I say 'empiricism,' because it is contented to regard its most assured conclusions concerning matters of fact as hypotheses liable to modification in the course of future experience; and I say 'radical,' because it treats the doctrine of monism itself as an hypothesis, and, unlike so much of the halfway empiricism that is current under the name of positivism or agnosticism or scientific naturalism, it does not dogmatically affirm monism as something with which all experience has got to square."

Thus by *empiricism* James means that nothing can be known except by human experience, and he postulates that *"the only things that shall be debatable among philosophers shall be things definable in terms drawn from experience.* (Things of an unexperienceable nature may exist ad libitum, but they form no part of the material for philosophic debate.)" This limitation James calls "a methodical postulate" (quoted by Ralph Barton Perry in his preface

to *Essays in Radical Empiricism*). Elsewhere he says that pragmatism and radical empiricism have no necessary logical connection, but actually they use the same method for finding answers to questions, and both look for answers in particular experiences rather than general ones or in abstractions about experiences.

In 1907 James collected and placed in an envelope twelve articles, most of which he had published in philosophical journals from 1904 through 1906, which he intended to republish in a book, but *Essays in Radical Empiricism* was not published until 1912, two years after his death. Though this posthumous volume is in the nature of an anthology, it has a unifying theme in the attempt of the various essays to define the basic concepts of "radical empiricism." In the first essay ("Does 'Consciousness' Exist?") James suggests abandoning the term *consciousness*, though he means "only to deny that the word stands for an entity" and to assert "that it does stand for a function." For "consciousness" he substitutes "pure experience," which is "made of *that*, of just what appears, of space, of intensity, of flatness, brownness, heaviness, or what not." He wants to avoid the dualism of *thought* and *thing*, for *"thoughts* in the concrete are made of the same stuff as things are." This does not mean, for instance, that the thought of a chair can be measured with a tape measure, but the very thought of a chair includes all the physical qualities which make it known as a chair. James answers the old metaphysical riddle of how one object can exist in two minds at the same time by the contention that the two (or more) minds meet in the object which they experience together, just as two lines can pass through one point if they intersect at the point.

In the essay on "A World of Pure Experience" James says: "To be radical, an empiricism must neither admit into its constructions any element that is not directly experienced, nor exclude from them any element that is directly experienced. For such a philosophy, *the relations that connect experiences must themselves be experienced relations, and any kind of relation experienced must be accounted as 'real' as anything else in the system.* Elements may indeed be redistributed, the original placing of things getting corrected, but a real place must be found for every kind of thing experienced, whether term or relation, in the final philosophical arrangement." Berkeley, Hume, James Mill, and other associationists had argued that the relations or connections of things experienced are supplied by the mind.

Although at any given moment experiences may seem unrelated or chaotic, they do not come singly or detached from the stream of experience (what James had called "consciousness" and its "fringe" in his *Principles*). He calls the contents of this stream, "taken all together, a quasi-chaos." Yet, as he argues in "The Thing and Its Relations," in its immediacy, experience "seems perfectly fluent." It is only after intellectual reflection that we distinguish elements and parts, give them separate names, and discover contradictions and incomprehensibilities. " 'Pure experience' is the name which I gave to the immediate flux of life which furnishes the material to our later reflection with its conceptual categories. . . . Pure experience . . . is but another name for feeling or sensation. But the flux of it no sooner comes than it tends to fill itself with emphases, and these salient parts become identified and fixed and abstracted; so that experience now flows as if shot through with adjectives and nouns and prepositions and conjunctions. Its purity is only a relative term, meaning the proportional amount of unverbalized sensation which it still embodies."

James himself admits one difficulty in his theory of "pure experience." Experience can be "pure" only to the newborn babe or some-one in a semicoma from sickness, intoxication, or injury—sensation without reflection of any kind. Normal people tend to verbalize their sensations as soon as they "think" of them. The postulation of "pure experience" is, therefore, hypothetical; we must look (or feel) quickly to get a glimpse of it before it is adulterated by thought.

In a book which he published himself the year before his death, *A Pluralistic Universe* (1909), James continued his quarrel with monistic idealism, a quarrel which he always admitted to be partly a conflict of temperaments, between those who want a tidy, safe universe with divine decisions already made and engraved on eternal tablets and those who prefer an unfinished, imperfect, precarious universe with the final outcome still hanging in the balance. This temperamental difference in types of thinkers was the subject of his first discourse in the Gifford Lectures at Oxford University, published as *A Pluralistic Universe*—and it is worth noting that the article "a" is more tentative and modest than "the" would have been; he does not say dogmatically that this *is* the way the universe is, but here is one man's theory of the way it is.

In his second lecture James also confesses that he prefers some variety of pantheism to a dualistic theism because it allows a greater degree of intimacy with "the creative principle": "we are substantially one with it, and . . . the divine is therefore the most intimate of all our possessions, heart of our heart, in fact," whereas dualistic theism makes man "a secondary order of substances created by God." But pantheism can be of two forms, one absolute or monistic and the other pluralistic. In the monistic form "the divine exists authentically only when the world is experienced all at once in its absolute totality, whereas radical empiricism allows that the absolute sum-total of things may never be actually experienced or realized in that shape at all, and that a disseminated, distributed, or incompletely unified appearance is the only form that reality may yet have achieved."

In Lecture III James calls Hegel an idealistic pantheist and says that "in no philosophy is the fact that a philosopher's vision and the technique he uses in proof of it are two different things more palpably evident than in Hegel. The vision in his case was that of a world in which reason holds all things in solution and accounts for all the irrationality that superficially appears by taking it up as a 'moment' into itself."

Hegel's vision was in two parts: "The first part was that reason is all-inclusive, the second was that things are 'dialectic.'" The dialectic process admits that things are in a flux, and they are often experienced as off-balance and working at cross-purposes. With this James of course agrees. But Hegel finds the equilibrium and symmetry restored in a "higher synthesis" in which opposites merge and become a perfect unity. James calls this synthesis a "treaty," and says that "Hegel's originality lay in transporting the process from the sphere of percepts to that of concepts and treating it as the universal method by which every kind of life, logical, physical, or psychological, is mediated. Not to the sensible facts as such, then, did Hegel point for the secret of what keeps existence going, but rather to the conceptual way of treating them." Even though "concepts were not in his eyes the static self-contained things that previous logicians had supposed, but were germinative, and passed beyond themselves into each other by what he called their immanent dialectic," nevertheless the "absolute" which his logic establishes transcends human experience. The arguments by which James finds Hegel's rationalism irrational are too complicated for brief summary, but regardless of the logic by which he finds Hegel illogical, his main objection is that Hegel's reasoning leads away from the "strung-along unfinished world in time" in which men actually live.

"But if we drop the absolute out of the world," James asks, "must we then conclude that the world contains nothing better in the way of consciousness than our consciousness?" His answer is that "logically it is possible to believe in superhuman beings without identifying them with the absolute at all." As an example of such a belief he turns to the panpsychism of Gustav Fechner, whose earlier *Psychophysiks* had not favorably impressed him; but recently he had read Fechner's *Zend-Avesta* and *Uber die Seelenfrage* and been fascinated by the German's theory of pyramiding souls, which James calls a "republic of semi-detached consciousness," presided over by a God whose limited power absolves Him from responsibility for evil in the world. Fechner's philosophy can be called panpsychic because it finds a hierarchy of souls in all existing things, rising from plants and animals to human beings, planets, and still higher souls ascending to a Supreme Soul. (Query: Wouldn't this make Fechner's soul-empire a monarchy instead of a republic?) James admits that this Supreme Soul or God provides the possibility for an absolutist philosophy, but he insists that Fechner develops his details pluralistically.

James had struggled for many years to escape solipsism without postulating an absolute mind or soul in which all finite consciousnesses could exist. As he confessed in his Hibbert lecture on "Compounding of Consciousness": "Sincerely, and patiently as I could, I struggled with the problem for years, covering hundreds of sheets of paper with notes and memoranda and discussions with myself over the difficulty. How can many consciousnesses be at the same time one consciousness? How can one and the same identical fact experience itself so diversely? [He had attempted to answer this question in *Radical Empiricism*—see above, page 356.] The struggle was vain; I found myself in an *impasse*. I saw that I must either forswear that 'psychology without a soul' to which my whole psychological and kantian education had committed me,—I must, in short, bring back distinct spiritual agents to know the mental states, now singly and now in combination, in a word bring back scholasticism and common sense—or else I must squarely confess the solution of the problem impossible, and then either give up my intellectualistic logic . . . or, finally, face the fact that life is logically irrational."

In Fechner (encouraged, too, by Bergson's attack on logic) James saw a possible way out, a way also suggested by the accumulated data of psychiatry regarding hypnotism, split personality or plural selves, "mystical experiences," etc., which he had studied both for his lectures in *The Varieties of Religious Experience* and as an active member of the Society for Psychical Research. "For my own part," he confesses, "I find in some of these abnormal or super-normal facts the strongest suggestions in favor of a superior consciousness being possible. I doubt whether we shall ever understand some of them without using the very letter of Fechner's conception of a great reservoir in which the memories of earth's inhabitants are pooled and preserved, and from which, when the threshold lowers or the valve opens, information ordinarily shut out leaks into the mind of exceptional individuals among us. But those regions of inquiry are perhaps too spook-haunted to interest an academic audience, and the only evidence I feel it now decorous to bring to the support of Fechner is drawn from ordinary religious experience. I think it may be asserted that there *are* religious experiences of a specific nature, not deducible by analogy or psychological reasoning from our other sorts of experience. I think that they point with reasonable probability to the continuity of our consciousness with a wider spiritual environment from which the ordinary prudential man (who is the only man that scientific psychology, so called, takes cognizance of) is shut off."

James, a scientist in spite of his sympathy with mystics and mental healers, cautiously says he finds *suggestions*—not proof—"in favor of a superior consciousness." This view appeals to him because the believer in it "finds that the tenderer parts of his personal life are continuous with a *more* of the same quality which is operative in the universe outside of him and which he can keep in working touch with, and in a fashion get on board of and save himself, when all his lower being has gone to pieces in the wreck. In a word, the believer is continuous, to his own consciousness, at any rate, with a wider self from which saving experiences flow in."

Such evidence is, of course, purely subjective, but to James it has pragmatic value. And to him personally Fechner's polytheism has advantages over monotheism because it is a way of "escape from the paradoxes and perplexities that a consistently thought-out monistic universe suffers from as from a species of auto-intoxication—the mystery of the 'fall' namely, of reality lapsing into appearance, truth into error, perfection into imperfection; of evil, in short; the mystery of universal determinism, of the block-universe eternal and without a history, etc.;—the only way of escape, I say, from all this is to be frankly pluralistic and assume that the superhuman consciousness, however vast it may be, has itself an external environment, and consequently is finite." At the end of *The Varieties of Religious Experience* James had used the argument for a limited God to restore man's sense of importance and give him an incentive for effort: God needs us as much as we need Him.

In his study of religious experiences James had found so much psychological and human value in them that he wanted to restore religion to intellectual respectability. So he now suggests: "Let empiricism once become associated with religion, as hitherto, through some strange misunderstanding, it thas been associated with irreligion, and I believe that a new era of religion as well as of philosophy will be ready to begin. . . . I fully believe that such an empiricism is a more natural ally than dialectics ever were, or can be, of the religious life. It is true that superstitions and wild-growing over-beliefs of all sorts will undoubtedly begin to abound if the notion of higher consciousnesses enveloping ours, of fechnerian earthsouls and the like, grows orthodox and fashionable; still more will they superabound if science ever puts her approval stamp on the phenomena . . of psychic research so-called—and I myself firmly believe that most of these phenomena are rooted in reality." This *firm belief* was an over-belief, for in his final report on psychical research (1909) James has to admit that after twenty years of reading the literature of the researchers, talking and corresponding with them, and spending many hours "in witnessing (or trying to witness)" psychic phenomena, "Yet I am theoretically no 'further' than I was at the beginning; and I confess that at times I have been tempted to believe that the Creator has eternally intended this department of nature to remain *baffling*."

This candor, however, did not save James from attacks by his scientific colleagues, and his tolerance for the "wild beasts of philosophy," to use his own phrase, was responsible to a considerable extent for a decline in his reputation even before his death in 1910. He was well aware of this decline and dissatisfied with himself for never having completed an integrated philosophical system. At the time of his death James was working on an introduction to metaphysics which he had hoped would complete his "unfinished arch," but he was discouraged by this effort, too, and left a note with the manuscript asking his editor (his son Henry) to call it "a beginning of an introduction to philosophy." The book was published in 1911 as *Some Problems of Philosophy.* It is indeed elementary, but it is the most systematic and organized of all James's books, and in some respects makes a fitting ending for his philosophical writings.

"Philosophy in the full sense is only *man thinking*, thinking about generalities rather than about particulars," he says in his first chapter, "Philosophy and Its Critics." James very concisely and clearly defines the kinds of philosophy (mainly rational and empirical), the kinds of philosophers (for he still thinks that a man's temperament determines his philosophical preferences), and in Chapter Two neatly outlines the major problems and theories of metaphysics. In "The Problem of Being," or ontology, he says that "the orthodox opinion is that the quantity of reality must at all costs be conserved, and the waxing and waning of our phenomenal experiences must be treated as surface appearances which leave the deeps untouched." He admits, however, that "the question of being is the darkest in all philosophy."

The balance and impartiality of *Some Problems* is most evident in James's treatment of *percept* and *concept.* While arguing for his "radical empiricism" and "pluralism" he invariably showed a partiality for perception, which seemed to him nearer to "pure experience." But he now admits: "Had we no concepts we should live simply 'getting' each successive moment of experience, as the sessile sea-anemone on its rock receives whatever nourishment the wash of the waves may bring. With concepts we go in quest of the absent, meet the remote, actively turn this way or that, bend our experience, and make it tell us whither it is bound." This is essentially, again, a Darwinian theory (though James does not say so), an explanation of how human beings have adapted themselves to environment and changes. James does say, "We *harness* perceptual reality in concepts in order to drive it better to our ends."

In mathematics, the sciences, and the branches of philosophy such as aesthetics and ethics, the sense order is transformed into a symbolical rational order. "We may well call this a theoretic conquest over the order in which nature originally comes. The conceptual order into which we translate our experience seems not only a means of practical adaptation, but the revelation of a deeper level of reality in things. . . . Concepts not only guide us over the map of life, but we *revalue* life by their use." Yet if we lose ourselves in abstractions, we lose a feeling for the novelty, the variety, the excitement, and the adventure of the sensual world of experience.

In science, "The notion of eternal elements and their mixture serves us in so many ways, that we adopt unhesitatingly the theory that primordial being is inalterable in its attributes as well as in its quantity, and that the laws by which we describe its habits are uniform in the strictest mathematical sense. These are the absolute conceptual foundations, we think, spread beneath the surface of perceptual variety. It is when we come to human lives, that our point of view changes. It is hard to imagine that 'really' our own subjective experiences are only molecular arrangements, even though the molecules be conceived as beings of a psychic kind. . . . Psychologically considered, our experiences resist conceptual reduction, and our fields of consciousness, taken simply as such, remain just what they appear, even though facts of a molecular order should prove to be the signals of the appearance. Biography is the concrete form in which all that is is immediately given; the perceptual flux is the authentic stuff of each of our biographies, and yields a perfect effervescence of novelty all the time. New men and women, books, accidents, events, inventions, enterprises, burst unceasingly upon the world. It is vain to resolve these into ancient elements, or to say that they belong to ancient kinds, so long as no one of them in its full individuality ever was here before or will ever come again."

Some critics have said that William James was not a philosopher but a literary man, and it is true that in his feeling for and intuition about the infinite variety of the world he had the sensibility of a poet, and his unflagging interest in the unpredictable responses of human beings to their experiences was that of a novelist in his plots and resolutions. His deep sympathies and great imagination gave him the command of a prose style unequaled in vigor, clarity, and colloquial spontaneity by any other philosopher writing in English. His literary reputation kept his name alive long after his psychology and philosophy had faded in popularity. One of his public lectures on "The Moral Equivalent of War" was circulated in several million copies by the American Association for International Conciliation. John Dewey further popularized the term *pragmatism*, but his pragmatic philosophy was strictly functional and social—adaptation of an organism to its environment—and not directly concerned with the problems of James's pluralism. It was Dewey's, not James's, pragmatism which became a world influence in education during the first half of the twentieth century. The rise of J. B. Watson's behaviorism also further eroded James's influence, for Watson scornfully dismissed James's psychology as "introspective," which it was in part, but his theory of emotion might be regarded as the beginning of behaviorism.

James's *The Varieties of Religious Experience* continued to be widely read, and both his *Letters* edited by his son Henry (1920) and the monumental *The Thought and Character of William James* by Ralph Barton Perry (1935) created personal interest in the life and personality of James. But American psychologists found the *Principles* old-fashioned and moralistic, and the contradictions and lack of order in his philosophical writings were regarded by most professional philosophers as fatal defects.

It is hardly surprising that rediscovery of James had to take place in Europe, where he was first appreciated and had never been as forgotten as in his own country. It is difficult to say exactly when this rediscovery began, though the books that show it have been published only recently, the most important being Hans Linschoten's *On the Way toward a Phenomenological Psychology: The Psychology of William James*, 1968 (translated from a German version, 1961); Bruce Wilshire's *William James and Phenomenology: A Study of the "Principles of Psychology,"* 1968; and John Wild's *The Radical Empiricism of William James*, 1969.

As two of these titles indicate (and the other author would agree) what is *new* in James is the discovery that he was a forerunner of the "phenomenology" of Edmund Husserl and the existentialism of Martin Heidegger. Wilshire explains the meaning of the term: "The central thesis of phenomenology is that the world is comprehensible only in terms of its modes of appearance to mind, and that mind cannot be conceived independently of the world which appears to it. Hence, despite Edmund Husserl's aversion to the word metaphysics, the phenomenological thesis generates implications concerning the structure of reality, and must be considered an outgrowth in the broadest sense of Kant's new metaphysics of experience.

It is not that the world exists only in the mind, but that the world can be specified only in terms of what it appears to be to mind. Hence, as well, the phenomenological thesis generates a philosophy of mind. Truths about the relationship are necessary and nonempirical and the discipline which discovers them is a nonempirical one. Mind cannot conceive independently of the world which appears to it. Any phenomenological psychology derives from this fundamental philosophical background."

In 1900 Husserl wrote that he had read James's *Principles of Psychology* in the 1890's: "Although I was able to read only a few things and too little of James' Psychology, it brought some lightning flashes. I saw how a courageous and original man did not let himself be shackled by any tradition but endeavored effectively to hold on to and describe what he saw. This influence was not unimportant to me." Husserl was especially grateful to James for showing him a way out of "psychologism," the view that, since thought is a psychical activity, the object of thought is subject to psychological laws. Alhough James started out to write his *Principles* on the common-sense, dualistic principle that he need not settle the question of the relation of the external object to a mental image of it, and could simply assume that it was *there* where it seemed to be, he soon found himself entangled in the problem of cognition.

Another definition by Wilshire will help to clarify James's predicament: "The central thesis of a phenomenological psychology is that mind and thoughts cannot be conceived independently of the world which appears to mind, and that this phenomenal world can be conceived only through a philosophical investigation of the world's own structures (in Husserl's parlance, essences [in James's, *concepts*]) as revealed to mind. For example, material objects and formal objects like numbers fall into different regional ontologies; if thought's objects are numbers, say, then at some point in the elucidation of the *thought* a mathematician will have to be called in, not just a psychologist. Although the object belongs to thought and thought is psychical, still the object of thought cannot be given an elucidation that is exclusively psychological. Hence psychology is derivative, not ultimate."

Time and again, and especially in his later writings, James stated the impossibility of separating mind and world, and he tentatively resorted to transcendental conjectures, such as Fechner's panpsychism, but he was not able to find a way to elucidate "the world's own structures," or to see that they might have different ontologies. Thus he stopped short of a phenomenological psychology—or philosophy. As Linschoten says, "James confronts us with a doctrine of experience of the body that in many essential points was anticipation of phenomenological psychology."

Instead of regretting James's lack of a consistent system, Linschoten regards it as one of his virtues. He saw that no systematic or rational conception of the whole of reality is possible; it is too large and human experience too limited. "The real world as it is given objectively at this moment," James points out in "Reflex Action and Theism," "is the sum total of all its beings and events now. But can we think of such a sum? Can we realize for an instant what a cross-section of all existence at a definite point of time would be? While I talk and the flies buzz, a sea-gull catches a fish at the mouth of the Amazon, a tree falls in the Adirondack wilderness, a man sneezes in Germany, a horse dies in Tartary, and twins are born in France. What does that mean? Does the contemporaneity of these events with one another and with a million others as disjointed, form a rational bond between them, and unite them into anything that means for us a world?"

Linschoten comments: "A system, if it wants to be a system, must be a *closed* system. And why should all those events form one system? The world is a multiversum, not a universum; a pluralistic 'whole' of infinite diversity; a kaleidoscopic stream of varieties. No system can reduce it to one single principle." In other words, *"Diverse viewpoints lead to diverse formulations."*

James was in search of the sources of the stream of reality, which he believed to be discoverable only in perceptual experience. His "seemingly unsystematic approach," says Linschoten, "is an attempt to reach a more comprehensive system. . . . James' psychology at first shows a methodological pluralism and hence a seeming confusion of heterogeneous viewpoints and explanations. But the idea hidden behind it is the principle of complementarity." Psychology had got divided into a "mental science" and a "natural science." James desired to preserve their mutual connection. This presupposes a theory about that connection and coherence, a phenomenology of the life-world, that was at least implicitly aimed at by James. Hence his seeming lack of a systematic view. It is this which caused him to say: "It is not that we are all nature but some point which is reason, but that all is nature and all is reason too. We shall see, damn it, we shall see."

Professor Wild, a native American and at present a professor of philosophy at Yale, explains in his preface to *The Radical Empiricism of William James* that he had supposed phenomenology and existential philosophy to be exclusively European until he came to know Husserl in 1931 and studied with Heidegger at the University of Freiburg. Then he learned of Husserl's reading of James and began also to see some of the origins of existentialism in James's theories of empiricism. A friend of Wild's at Harvard, Gordon Allport, also told him that if James's *The Principles of Psychology* had been fully understood, it "might have inaugurated a native phenomenological movement in the United States." Professor Wild's intention in writing his book was to "confirm a historical fact that others have suspected, namely that around the turn of the century, a native American philosopher began to think in an existential manner, and made important contributions to the phenomenological movement, in that broader sense which we are now beginning to recognize is required to understand it as a whole. But this is a relatively minor point. In my more optimistic moments I sometimes hope that by trying to see through the conventional tags and labels which have buried a great man of our past, I may have made some of his insights more accessible, and may thus indirectly help some of those who really read him not merely to think, but to think empirically in relation to our existence in the world, and thus to take philosophy seriously again."

This rediscovery of James by the phenomenologists has come about mainly by a more understanding reading of *The Principles of Psychology*. Thus it is James the psychologist (which of course also includes much of his radical empiricism and pluralism) who, in the twentieth century, has become a stronger seminal influence in philosophy than he ever was during his lifetime.

Selected Bibliography

The most complete checklist of William James's publications is Ralph Barton Perry's *Annotated Bibliography of the Writings of William James* (New York: Longmans, Green, 1920), reprinted with additions by John J. McDermott in *The Writings of William James: A Comprehensive Edition* (New York: Random House, 1967), pp. 811-58. The books by Linschoten, Wilshire, and Wild, listed below, also contain titles of critical studies and books relating to the study of James.

WORKS OF WILLIAM JAMES

Introduction to *The Literary Remains of the Late Henry James*, edited by William James. Boston: Houghton Mifflin, 1884.

Introduction to *The Foundations of Ethics*, by John Edward Maude, edited by William James. New York: Holt, 1887.

The Principles of Psychology. 2 vols. New York: Holt, 1890.

Psychology, Briefer Course. New York: Holt, 1892.

The Will to Believe, and Other Essays in Popular Philosophy. New York and London: Longmans, Green, 1897.

Human Immortality: Two Supposed Objections to the Doctrine. Boston and New York: Houghton Mifflin, 1898.

Introduction to *The Psychology of Suggestion*, by Boris Sidis. New York: Appleton, 1899.

The Varieties of Religious Experience: A Study in Human Nature. New York and London: Longmans, Green, 1902.

Introduction to *Little Book of Life after Death*, by G. T. Fechner, translated by M. C. Wadsworth. Boston: Little, Brown, 1904.

Preface to *The Problems of Philosophy*, by Harold Höffding, translated by G. M. Fisher. New York: Macmillan, 1906.

Pragmatism: A New Name for Some Old Ways of Thinking. New York and London: Longmans, Green, 1907.

A Pluralistic Universe. (Hibbert Lectures at Manchester College on the Present Situation in Philosophy.) London: Longmans, Green, 1909.

The Meaning of Truth: A Sequel to "Pragmatism." New York and London: Longmans, Green, 1909.

Some Problems of Philosophy: A Beginning of an Introduction to Philosophy. New York and London: Longmans, Green, 1911.

Essays in Radical Empiricism. New York and London: Longmans, Green, 1912.

SELECTED WRITINGS

Letters of William James, edited by Henry James. 2 vols. Boston: Atlantic Monthly Press, 1920; London: Longmans, Green, 1920.

Collected Essays and Reviews, edited by Ralph Barton Perry. New York and London: Longmans, Green, 1920. (Thirty-nine articles.)

The Philosophy of William James, selected with an introduction by Horace M. Kallen. New York: Modern Library, [1925].

The James Family: Including Selections from the Writings of Henry James, Senior, William, Henry & Alice James, by F. O. Matthiessen. New York: Knopf, 1948.

William James on Psychical Research, compiled and edited by Gardner Murphy and Robert O. Ballou. New York: Viking Press, 1960.

The Selected Letters of William James, edited with an Introduction, by Elizabeth Hardwick. New York: Farrar, Straus and Cudahy, 1961.

The Letters of William James and Théodore Flournoy, edited by Robert C. Le Clair. Madison: University of Wisconsin Press, 1966.

The Writings of William James: A Comprehensive Edition, edited with an introduction by John J. McDermott. New York: Random House, 1967. (Includes "Annotated Bibliography of the Writings of William James.")

The Moral Philosophy of William James, edited by John K. Roth. New York: Crowell, 1969.

James Jackson Putnam and Psychoanalysis: Letters between Putnam, Sigmund Freud, Ernest Jones, William James, Sandor Ferenczi, and Morton Prince, 1877–1917, edited with introductory essay by Nathan G. Hale, Jr. Cambridge, Mass.: Harvard University Press, 1971.

A William James Reader, selected and edited with an introduction by Gay Wilson Allen. Boston: Houghton Mifflin, 1971.

BIOGRAPHIES

Allen, Gay Wilson. *William James, a Biography.* New York: Viking Press, 1967.

Perry, Ralph Barton. *The Thought and Character of William James.* 2 vols. Boston: Little, Brown, 1935.

CRITICAL STUDIES

Allen, Gay Wilson. "Pragmatism: A New Name for Some Old Ways of Thinking," in *Landmarks in American Writing,* edited by Hennig Cohen. New York: Basic Books, 1969.

———. "William James," in *The Horizon Book of Makers of Modern Thought.* New York: American Heritage, 1972. Pp. 356-67.

Allport, G. W. "The Productive Paradoxes of William James," *Psychological Review,* 50:95-120 (1943).

Boutroux, Emile. *William James,* translated from the second edition by Archibald and Barbara Henderson. London: Longmans, Green, 1912.

Capek, Millic. "The Reappearance of the Self in the Last Philosophy of William James," *Philosophical Review,* 62:526-44 (October 1953).

Chapman, Harmon M. "Realism and Phenomenology," in *The Return of Reason,* edited by John Wild. Chicago: Regnery, 1953.

Dewey, John. "The Vanishing Subject in the Psychology of William James," *Journal of Philosophy,* 37:589-99 (1940). (Reprinted in *The Problems of Men.* New York: Philosophical Library, 1946.)

Flournoy, Théodore. *The Philosophy of William James,* translated by Edwin B. Holt and William James, Jr. New York: Holt, 1917.

Hook, Sidney. *The Metaphysics of Pragmatism.* Chicago: Open Court, 1927.

Linschoten, Hans. *On the Way toward a Phenomenological Psychology: The Psychology of William James,* translated from the Dutch by Amedeo Giorgi. Pittsburgh: Duquesne University Press, 1968.

Lovejoy, A. O. *The Thirteen Pragmatisms.* Baltimore: Johns Hopkins Press, 1963.

Metzger, Arnold. "William James and the Crisis in Philosophy," in *In Commemoration of William James.* New York: Columbia University Press, 1942.

Otto, Max. "The Distinctive Psychology of William James," in *William James: Man and Thinker.* Madison: University of Wisconsin Press, 1942.

Perry, Ralph Barton. *In the Spirit of William James*. New Haven, Conn.: Yale University Press, 1938; Bloomington: Indiana University Press, 1958.

Roth, John F. *Freedom and the Moral Life: The Ethics of William James*. Philadelphia: Westminster Press, 1969.

Santayana, George. *William James: Philosopher and Man*, edited by C. H. Compton. New York: Scarecrow Press, 1957.

Schuetz, Alfred. "William James's Concept of the Stream of Thought Phenomenologically Interpreted," *Philosophy and Phenomenological Research*, 1:442-52 (June 1941).

Spiegelberg, Herbert. "What William James Knew about Edmund Husserl: On the Credibility of Pitkin's Testimony," in *Life-World and Consciousness*, essays for Aron Gurwitsch edited by Lester E. Embree. Evanston, Ill.: Northwestern University Press, 1972.

Wahl, Jean. *The Pluralistic Philosophies of England and America*, translated by Fred Rothwell. London: Open Court, 1925.

Wild, John. *The Radical Empiricism of William James*. New York: Doubleday, 1969.

Wilshire, Bruce. *William James and Phenomenology: A Study of the "Principles of Psychology."* Bloomington: University of Indiana Press, 1968.

—*GAY WILSON ALLEN*

Randall Jarrell
1914-1965

ALTHOUGH Randall Jarrell wrote a very witty novel and a good deal of lively criticism as well, his most enduring interest as a writer lies in his poems. Between the appearance of an early group in the New Directions anthology *Five Young American Poets* in 1940 and his death at fifty-one in 1965, he prepared seven books of verse. Their usually melancholy titles suggest the desolation with which he constantly contended and which seems to have won out in the breakdown he finally suffered.

To review very briefly the curve of this psychological struggle as it manifests itself in the succeeding volumes: The first book, *Blood for a Stranger* (1942), reveals amid its many echoes of Auden and others certain underlying motifs of loss and confused focus. The next volumes, *Little Friend, Little Friend* (1945) and *Losses* (1948), take their main strength from a number of elegiac war poems. In these poems Jarrell was often able, because of their concreteness and directness, to objectify the motifs that had knotted up so much of his previous work. Also, he learned a good deal about immediacy from such poets of World War I as Siegfried Sassoon and Wilfred Owen. A period of broadening perspectives followed, marked by the appearance in 1951 of *The Seven-League Crutches*, in 1954 of the novel *Pictures from an Institution*, and in 1955 of

Selected Poems. This last-named volume, containing only two new pieces, was the result of careful reconsideration and, often, revision of past work.

It was not until 1960, actually, that Jarrell published his first book of new poems since *The Seven-League Crutches*. But in the decade and a half after the war he had had a varied experience. He had been literary editor of the *Nation*, poetry consultant at the Library of Congress, visiting lecturer in American colleges and abroad, and, with occasional interruptions, a professor in the Woman's College of the University of North Carolina. He had established himself as one of a small, elite group of poets, protégés originally of Allen Tate and John Crowe Ransom. But Jarrell's outward successes did not anesthetize him against his painful need to gain inward clarification, which finally led him to write the autobiographical poems of *The Woman at the Washington Zoo* (1960) and *The Lost World* (1965).

In a sense, Jarrell tried to make a European of himself, to change over from a bright young American southerner to a sort of German-Austrian-Jewish refugee of the spirit. His interest in Rilke, in the German *Märchen*, and in the neglected European heritage of Americans seems in part an effort to repossess for himself a nourishment denied him in his childhood. Yet this effort, by a process analogous with that described in Keats's "Nightingale" ode, eventually "tolled him back to his sole self."

The word *fey*, meaning both *intensely excited or gay* and *doomed*, is perhaps too grim for Jarrell's poetic personality. Yet it is useful when we think of that side of him which is at once high-spiritedly brilliant and superciliously overinsistent, engaging yet irritating, and which assorts so ill with his capacity for gentleness and for an almost sentimental love of the quieter and more pedestrian virtues—and with the absorption of his imagination by bleakness and horror. The impact on others of this complex of qualities comes through strikingly in the collection of affectionate essays and reminiscences, *Randall Jarrell, 1914–1965*, that appeared in 1967 as a memorial volume. An unusually valuable piece in this excellent collection is "A Group of Two," written by his widow. It is a lovingly drawn portrait of a baffling man: his varied enthusiasms, his childlike ebullience and depressions, his sparkling if somewhat shrill spirit. Mrs. Jarrell is straightforward but protective. She never spells out the nature of his psychic disturbance or the exact circumstances of his death while walking on a highway. She does nevertheless suggest that he carried about with him throughout his life the burden of childhood insecurity, both psychological and financial. His parents were divorced, and for a while he lived happily with his paternal grandparents and great-grandmother, working-class people, in Hollywood, California, before his reluctant return to his mother in Nashville, Tennessee. The gifted, volatile child never "grew up" entirely. The intensity, the traumatic moments, and the accumulated guilt and resentment behind these experiences were never resolved.

He returns to the Hollywood period a number of times in his poetry, most notably in the title sequence of *The Lost World*. The confusion and displacement of that period are crucial, though many of their implications are suppressed. "Mama" and "Pop" in Jarrell's poems are the *grandparents*, while his mother is "Anna." The sense of universal sadness, betrayed vulnerability, and emptiness at the center of the self in Jarrell's work is rooted in these childhood events and relationships, and doubtless helps account for this strong attraction to European literature of tragic consciousness.

In his poems there is at times a false current of sentimental condescension toward his subjects, especially when they are female. But more often another current carries us toward a realization of the ineradicable innocence and pity of the common life in all its alienating reality. This current did not really show itself, as a directive element in Jarrell's art, until the war poems of his second volume. In the first, *Blood for a Stranger*, some of his major themes were visible but neither voice nor tone was yet quite his own. One hears a sort of Auden-static everywhere, with other voices cutting in every so often. In the most accomplished poem of the book, "The Skaters," the voice seems a duet of Hart Crane and Edwin Muir:

> I stood among my sheep
> As silent as my staff;
> Up the sea's massy floor
> I saw the skaters pass.
>
> Long like the wind, as light
> I flowed upon their track
> Until at evening's edge
> I marked their breathless flocks.
>
> I sped among them then
> Like light along its lands—
> Love wreathed their lips, and speed
> Stiffened their tissue limbs. . . .

Half vision, half nightmare, the poem closes in on a note of lost personal focus. The speaker discerns in the stars the image of "one obsessing face," with which he comes into a precarious sympathy or relationship while caught up in the swirling skaters' movement that controls the curve of the poem. But finally, abandoned and abandoning, he is whirled into "the abyss":

> But the iron's dazzling ring, the roar
> Of the starred ice black below
> Whirl our dazed and headlong strides
> Through the whirling night into
>
> The abyss where my dead limbs forget
> The cold mouth's dumb assent;
> The skaters like swallows flicker
> Around us in the long descent.

These motifs of coldness and distance, and of a fantasy realm that is only a heightening of desolate reality, persist throughout Jarrell's career. It is hard not to see "The Skaters" as a suicidal projection of the symbolic search for the irretrievably lost mother:

> The million faces flecked
> Upon my flickering gaze
> Bent to me in the stars
> Of one obsessing face . . .

A hopeless distance, a bewildering cosmos. Another poem in the volume, "The Bad Music," is addressed to "Anna" and uses the same pattern of symbolic imagery as "The Skaters" without reaching the glitteringly impersonal final set of that poem. Here the speaker sits by a window watching students as they return home from caroling. They carry candles that "wink out and on and out, like mixed-up stars," and

I sit here like a mixed-up star:
Where can I shine? What use is it to shine?
I say; and see, all the miles north inside my
    head,
You looking down across the city, puzzling. . . .

High over the millions who breathe and wait
    and sparkle . . .

"The Bad Music" makes almost embarrassingly explicit the buried reference, which is not the literal meaning, of "The Skaters." In its first stanza, the speaker blurts out his accusation of abandonment to Anna:

The breast opening for me, the breaths gasped
From the mouth pressed helplessly against my
    wrist
Were lies you too believed; but what you
    wanted
And possessed was, really, nothing but
    yourself:
A joy private as a grave, the song of death. . . .

Poetically, what is interesting in the relation of the two poems is the similarity of their *process.* Each starts in a state of passive melancholy and moves into active despair. Under surface differences of tone and theme, they share a configuration of feeling and imagery. The "mixed-up star" symbolism in both poems projects the speaker's relation to the elusive object of his love. Faces appear as part of a subjective constellation in which confusion reigns, and it is all but impossible to sort out lover from beloved (son from mother) or either one from the shifting mass of other people or, indeed, from the whole objective universe. The pattern of movement is characteristic of Jarrell: a static initial state of sadness; then a phase of confusion that lets deeper depression flood into the poem; and then a final bitter thrust. We see it working in the famous five-line war poem "The Death of the Ball Turret Gunner":

From my mother's sleep I fell into the State,
And I hunched in its belly till my wet fur froze.
Six miles from earth, loosed from its dream of
    life,
I woke to black flak and the nightmare fighters.

When I died they washed me out of the turret
  with a hose.

This poem is "impersonal." The speaker is not the poet himself but a dramatic character, a soldier who has been killed in the war. Yet the ironic womb imagery recalls the earlier mother theme, as of course the word *mother* itself does. We begin with the abstract yet unhappy assertion in the first line, an assertion that the young man received into the military world from the dreaming family world of childhood has hardly had time to emerge from fetal unconsciousness before he is in a new womb, that of war. Attention shifts in the next line to the chill, metallic character of that new womb. Suddenly then, the next two lines transport us to the gunner's moment of "waking" into nightmarish vision, at the moment his plane is hit by flak in the sky. The image is fetal; a note by Jarrell in *Selected Poems* stresses the fact that, "hunched upside-down in his little sphere," the gunner "looked like the foetus in the womb." The scene itself here is close to the confused cosmos of the two poems already discussed. Life is seen as only a "dream," whereas death is the reality into which the protagonist is born. In the harshly distorted womb images of this poem, we have once again the motif of love betrayed.

What Jarrell forces on our imaginations through his grotesque symbolism is the obscenity of war, its total subversion of human values. In highly compressed form, he has summoned up his subconscious preoccupations and the dynamics of poetic association they generate to make a poem that gets outside his own skin. The conversion process was not simple, though the result is emphatically clear in its narrative movement and in its succession of tones and intensities. Instead of the anapests that launch the first two lines, a suddenly lurching hovering-accent gets the third line off

to a wobbling start that helps shake the poem open to let in wider ranges of felt meaning. (Effects of confusion and ambiguity, in rhythmic shifts as in the literal suggestions of language, often have this function in poems.) The brutal nastiness of the closing line refocuses the poem sharply, yet the final effect is not abrupt. The line is in hexameter, longer by a foot than any of the preceding lines. It has the impact of a final "proof" of war's nature as a mockery of all that is life-giving.

It is easy to see how such a poem was prefigured in *Blood for a Stranger*. If we think of that book as comprising a definite unit of sensibility, we shall perceive it as, in large part, a complaint against loss of the world of childhood. (Jarrell specialized in psychology as an undergraduate at Vanderbilt University and was, in his omnivorous way, a reader of Freud; he is very likely to have "psychoanalyzed" himself to some degree at least.) The unresolved discontents of childhood are certainly present, but the real complaint is against separation, against initiation into adulthood, against the loss of an insufficiently discovered and savored life of innocence. "What we leave," mourns the opening poem ("On the Railway Platform"), "we leave forever." Another poem, "90 North," makes explicit the contrast between the secure childhood where

At home, in my flannel gown, like a bear to its
  floe,
I clambered to bed,

and the present, "meaningless" moment where

all lines, all winds
End in the whirlpool I at last discover.

True enough, a bear climbing onto its floe is not the most secure of beasts; but the nightmares of childhood, in Jarrell's poem, do end in "rest" and a "warm world" of dependable certainties where "I reached my North and it had meaning." Of the poems in *Blood for a Stranger* specifically about childhood and separation, the most poignant is "A Story," a monologue by a boy sent away to school. It has none of the portentous phrasing that mars "90 North" and other poems of this volume. Its thoughts are always appropriate to the speaker. "I liked home better, I don't like these boys" is more to the point than the generalizations in "90 North" about "wisdom" and "pain."

Not to linger overlong with this first book, it has other, though related, points of interest besides this central one of the child soul's vulnerability. In "Children Selecting Books in a Library," for instance, Jarrell meditates charmingly, if slightly pedantically, on the value of reading fairy tales. Another piece, "The Cow Wandering in the Bare Field," has been praised by Allen Tate, who remembers seeing it when Jarrell, then a freshman at Vanderbilt, was seventeen. Its beginning at least is slightly reminiscent of Hart Crane's "Black Tambourine," the details at once starkly literal and accusatory:

> The cow wandering in the bare field,
> Her chain dangling, aimless,—
> The Negro sitting in the ashes,
> Staring, humming to the cat . . .

Jarrell rarely again tried this kind of distanced yet incisive presentation. Indeed, he loses track of it later on in this very poem; he was after a faint modulation toward a theme of social protest, perhaps, and he did think of himself as a "radical" in his youth. But that side of him is seen in poems strongly indebted to Auden and Spender, with such titles as "The Machine-Gun," "The Refugees," "A Poem for Someone Killed in Spain," and "For an Emigrant." Part I of the last-named poem, with its final stanza greatly altered, was salvaged for the *Selected Poems* and retitled there as "To

the New World." It was interesting as showing special sympathy for the victims of the Nazis and for its insight into the life of exiles:

> Free—to be homeless, to be friendless, to be nameless,
> To stammer the hard words in the foreign night . . .

"For an Emigrant" shows, also, Jarrell's early realization that, ultimately, the refugee condition is universal; the balm of America is only a salve.

> You escaped from nothing; the westering soul
> Finds Europe waiting for it over every sea. . . .

"For an Emigrant," despite its political clichés and its sermonizing, meant something for Jarrell's future development. Much of it has to do with the effect of anti-Semitism and fascism on a *child's* life in Europe, and it attempts to assimilate the political lessons of the thirties in such a way as to bring the poet's childhood-obsession into a wider, more adult context of awareness. The poem anticipates, as well, Jarrell's later tendency to assume a European consciousness and graft it onto his American personality—a tendency for which Pound and Eliot had doubtless provided models. Jarrell, however, differed from them by playing the role of an exile in his own land, if far more modestly than they and with a lesser genius though a real, and kindred, sense of cultural mission.

Jarrell served in the Army Air Force between 1942 and 1946. "In the first months of the War," Robert Lowell writes in an "appreciation" appended to the 1966 paperback edition of *The Lost World*, "Jarrell became a pilot. He was rather old for a beginner, and soon 'washed out,' and spent the remaining war years as an aviation instructor. Even earlier, he had an expert's knowledge. . . . Nine-tenths of his war poems are air force poems, and are about planes and their personnel, the flyers, crews, and mechanics who attended them. No other imaginative writer had his precise knowledge of aviation, or knew so well how to draw inspiration from this knowledge." His mind was similar to Hardy's and to Owen's in its fusion of informed objectivity with a compassion as close to sentimentality as intelligence and taste would allow. Of course, the world of which he wrote was very far from Hardy's, and he lacked Owen's combat experience. But in his war poetry he was like Hardy in bringing to bear on it his whole, extraordinarily literate intelligence—an intelligence of the kind that feels imaginative literature as the distillation of considered experience, the usable treasure of a contemplative mind. And he was like Owen in the way the pressure of his empathy with the pilots he knew made him envision their war experience in a vivid, accurate manner unmatched by most of his writing having to do with civilian life. The poetry of their condition lay for him, as for Owen, "in the Pity." For both poets this is a sort of passionately apprehended disproportion between the young soldiers' ultimate innocence and the terror they both suffer and inflict. It is realized not in sentiment but in action.

Jarrell's war poems are found mainly in his *Little Friend, Little Friend* and *Losses* volumes, which came directly out of the war years, and there are a few more in *The Seven-League Crutches*. His vision of the soldier as betrayed child is clearly epitomized in "The Death of the Ball Turret Gunner," a poem strategically placed at the end of *Little Friend, Little Friend*. As with most American and British poets of the second world war, the ultimate implied attitude is an ambiguous, or at any rate a tentative, one. The shock, horror, and questioning that mark the poetry of the first world war were the discovery of a generation, a discovery crystallized on the run, in the midst of death—the discovery that war *was* the trenches, the barbed wire, the humanly pointless slaughter while, in Owen's words, "God seems not to care." Jarrell and his contemporaries had been teethed on that earlier work; for them it was the definition of war experience. All later war poetry is in an important sense informed by the World War I "tradition." However, there are at least two significant differences for Jarrell's generation. First, they felt a far greater initial detachment from official rhetoric and from the assumptions of the social system. And second, though there was a good deal of old-fashioned combat in the later war, the over-all organization and the far greater importance of the air forces and long-range technology and communication made the involvement of most soldier-poets far less immediate than before.

These differences may be overstressed, but I am trying to suggest that the poetry of Jarrell's generation feels the impact of war with a double awareness. It is still in touch with the original shock of World War I, but is further away from the almost tribal sense of participation in a ritual gone wrong. Herbert Read's poem "To a Conscript of 1940" is a bridge between the two positions in time. The ghost of a soldier of 1914–18 speaks to the poet, a survivor who now faces the new war situation:

We think we gave in vain. The world was not
    renewed.
There was hope in the homestead and anger in
    the streets
But the old world was restored and we returned
To the dreary field and workshop, and the im-
    memorial feud

Of rich and poor. Our victory was our defeat.
Power was retained where power had been mis-
    used
And youth was left to sweep away

The ashes that the first had strewn beneath our
    feet.

But one thing we learned: there is no glory in
    the deed
Until the soldier wears a badge of tarnish'd
    braid;
There are heroes who have heard the rally and
    have seen
The glitter of a garland round their head.

Theirs is the hollow victory. They are deceived.
But you, my brother and my ghost, if you can
    go
Knowing that there is no reward, no certain use
In all your sacrifice, then honour is reprieved.

To fight without hope is to fight with grace,
The self reconstructed, the false heart re-
    paired. . . .

Basically, this is the position—acceptance of
the war (presumably because of the policies and
aggression of the Nazi government) but without any chivalric or apocalyptic illusions. The
history of the between-wars governments was
too well known; certain Marxian and pacifist
conceptions, admittedly contradictory, had irrevocably entered Western sensibility; and the
fact that military victory would not solve the
great social problems of the age was widely
understood. Jarrell's way of encompassing all
this was, on the whole, to adopt an existential
approach. Here were men—*child*-men, really
—in circumstances beyond their control or
even their comprehension. It was not existential*ist*—neither a revolutionary perspective,
nor a challenge to men to be as fully and heroically human as possible in the circumstances
of limited choice open to them, is implied. Jarrell's emphasis is on the saving innocence of
those whom these circumstances have after all
made, as he says in "Eighth Air Force"
(*Losses*), "murderers." That is a bitter word,
yet Jarrell uses it a bit lightly and ironically.

Because the young American airmen also run
the risk of death, as he himself does not, he
compares them with Christ. The comparison
has some validity. Whitman, in "A Sight in
Camp in the Daybreak Gray and Dim," had
used it for the soldier as *victim;* and even when
the soldier is constrained to kill he is in some
sense still a victim. Pressed too hard, though,
the argument is obviously forced and sentimental. Could one have put the case otherwise
about young German soldiers in the same situation? Hardly. And if not, must not one say also
that the most hardened killer is ultimately an
innocent victim, a Christ crucified on the cross
of his particular fate? But Jarrell did not follow
the logic through:

The other murderers troop in yawning;
Three of them play Pitch, one sleeps, and one
Lies counting missions, lies there sweating
Till even his heart beats: One; One; One.
O murderers! . . . Still, this is how it's done:

This is a war . . . But since these play, before
    they die,
Like puppies with their puppy; since, a man,
I did as these have done, but did not die—
I will content the people as I can
And give up these to them: Behold the man!

I have suffered, in a dream, because of him,
Many things; for this last saviour, man,
I have lied as I lie now. But what is lying?
Men wash their hands, in blood, as best they
    can:
I find no fault in this just man.

In these lines Jarrell makes explicit the prevailing social assumption about war: that men
cannot be held responsible for what history
compels them to do, especially when they are
on the "just" side of the struggle. But he tries,
too, to make a subtly paradoxical argument to
get past the objections to this assumption, and
his style turns to putty in the process because

the thought is too contrived. The reality of the situation requires the most relentless intellectual toughness and unwillingness to be an apologist for war mentality. Otherwise, the paradoxical fact that one can, in a sense, be good and innocent while behaving murderously becomes merely another sophistical argument for further mass murder. Jarrell himself recognizes this problem by his play on the word *lie*, but self-irony does not always purge a speaker of the error he confesses by it. Indeed, Jarrell's note on this poem, given in his introduction to *Selected Poems*, has no self-irony at all: " 'Eighth Air Force' is a poem about the air force which bombed the Continent from England. The man who lies counting missions has one to go before being sent home. The phrases from the Gospels compare such criminals and scapegoats as these with that earlier criminal and scapegoat about whom the Gospels were written."

The limitation in Jarrell's war poetry is not, however, political or intellectual. It is a matter of energy. He focuses on the literal data of war —their irreversible actuality, and the pity of the human predicament implicit in that actuality. The poems stop short of anger, of programs, of anything that would constitute a challenge to soldiers or to their commanders or to the statesmen who make policy. Letting the facts of war experience speak for themselves, Jarrell sank all his real poetic imagination into primary acts of empathy; ordinarily he resisted any obvious political rhetoric. In "Eighth Air Force" we have a rare instance of his swinging out of his usual orbit to deal with the moral issues of mass bombing. His failure to handle the problem poetically lay in inadequate resources of emotional complexity and intellectual power.

But within the narrower limits of its engagement, Jarrell's war poetry is often superb. In poems like "A Front," "A Pilot from the Car-rier," "Pilots, Man Your Planes," and "The Dead Wingman"—the last of these a dream poem, but one that presents the essence of a familiar situation: a pilot searching for a sign of a shot-down wingman—the poet's entire effort is to project the sense of men and machines in action, from the viewpoint of a participant. In all the poems just named, Jarrell has a double aim. First, he wishes to get the technical and atmospheric details in coherent order (a bombing plane whose radio has gone bad, so that the pilot cannot be diverted from a closed landing field to another still open and therefore crashes; a plane that has been hit and is burning, from which the pilot parachutes; a carrier under attack from a Japanese torpedo plane; the situation of the airman hunting for a lost comrade). And second, he desires to make the perspective that of a living, suffering man. "A Pilot from the Carrier" and "A Front" are in the same volume, *Little Friend, Little Friend*, as "The Death of the Ball Turret Gunner." They carry a kindred birth-death motif, though less explicitly. The pilot in the plane from the carrier, "strapped at the center of his blazing wheel," tears himself loose from that womb of death and is reborn via parachute

In the sunlight of the upper sky—
And falls, a quiet bundle in the sky,
The miles to warmth, to air, to waking:
To the great flowering of his life. . . .

The pilot in "A Front" cannot be wrenched free in time, and perishes. In *Losses*, the men on the carrier in "Pilots, Man Your Planes" are sleeping "hunched in the punk of Death" until awakened into their own literal deaths unless they escape in time. The pilot in "The Dead Wingman" searches in his dream over that same amniotic sea into which so many figures of "Pilots, Man Your Planes" have disappeared, but he never finds the dreadful evidence of the birth into death that he seems to need for deep inward confirmation of his own reality:

The plane circles stubbornly: the eyes distend-
    ing
With hatred and misery and longing, stare
Over the blackening Ocean for a corpse. . . .

I have not really meant to labor this womb referent, which appears and disappears, usually very fleetingly, in Jarrell's shifting float of associations His creation of an ambience of confused details, a dream of total self-loss, before a final note of profound sadness is equally important in all the poems I have just mentioned. What gives them more authority than the poems of *Blood for a Stranger* is not only the precision within the confusion, but also the definiteness of the military setting within which the lost, childlike psyche of Jarrell's soldiers (with the poet's standing in for them, as it were) speaks its pain. Several times in the two "war" books the persons spoken for are women or children. The title of *Little Friend, Little Friend*, which evokes just the childlike psyche to which I have referred, is taken from a phrase used in the book's opening poem, "2nd Air Force." Here, as Jarrell's note tells us, a "woman visiting her son remembers what she has read on the front page of her newspaper the week before, a conversation between a bomber, in flames over Germany, and one of the fighters protecting it: 'Then I heard the bomber call me in: "Little Friend, Little Friend, I got two engines on fire. Can you see me, Little Friend?" I said, "I'm crossing right over you. Let's go home." ' "

The woman of this poem might just as well have been the mother of the ball turret gunner in the closing poem. Her son—this is the whole burden of the poem—has indeed fallen from her womb into that of the state. The barren and dangerous world of the air base appears amid "buses and weariness and loss," with its "sand roads, tar-paper barracks," and "bubbling asphalt of the runways." A specific womb image dramatizes what has happened to her transplanted son: "The head withdraws into its hatch (a boy's)." This alien world—"The years meant *this?*"—is her and our bleak introduction to what the war means for the soldiers as Jarrell understands them. Between "2nd Air Force" and "The Death of the Ball Turret Gunner," then, the volume makes its journey through a wasteland of deadly machinery and pathetic soldiers who "pass like beasts, unquestioning," through their new life where "the bombers answer everything."

Both *Little Friend, Little Friend* and *Losses* contain many closeups and vignettes of soldiers: men being classified, a soldier whose leg has been amputated, prisoners, a soldier being visited in the hospital by his wife and baby, men being discharged from service, a field hospital. Politically and historically, the war may have been unavoidable, but for Jarrell this is more an existential than a moral reality. Despite his recognition of the monstrousness of the Nazis in "A Camp in the Prussian Forest" (*Losses*)—

Here men were drunk like water, burnt like
    wood.
The fat of good
And evil, the breast's star of hope
Were rendered into soap—

it is the pointlessness and cruelty of the war that emerges as the poet's repeated insight. Each soldier, as the mother sees in "2nd Air Force," is "heavy with someone else's death" and a "cold carrier" of "someone else's victory." The poem "Losses," in the earlier book but clearly the source of the later one's title, utters a complaint on behalf of all the young *and* of their victims. Although its speaker does not explore the moral dilemma involved, he does raise an ultimate question:

In bombers named for girls, we burned
The cities we had learned about in school—
Till our lives wore out; our bodies lay among
The people we had killed and never seen.
When we lasted long enough they gave us
    medals;
When we died they said, "Our casualties were
    low."
They said, "Here are the maps"; we burned the
    cities.

It was not dying—no, not ever dying;
But the night I died I dreamed that I was dead,
And the cities said to me: "Why are you dying?
We are satisfied, if you are; but why did I die?"

It is interesting that World War II produced no great poem at once absolutely ruthless in its fidelity to the realities of human experience in the war and encompassing in its understanding of all their complex contradictions: particularly, the crushing choice seemingly thrust on the most advanced spirits between pure pacifism and accepting the need to destroy the Nazi power. The rhetorical questions at the end of "Losses"—slightly confused because of the ambiguous use of the word "I" in the closing line —suggest the epic psychological exploration needed, but not furnished, to give body to their meaning. At a pragmatic and popular level the questions were certainly answerable by reference to recent history. The answers were both moral and practical, involving the fate of nations and of ethnic groups as well as of political and economic systems. The contradiction lay, as Malraux perceived in an only slightly different context, the Spanish Civil War, in the fact that the methods of war compel imitation of the enemy and indeed outstripping him in his own methods. It is indeed possible to present the voice of an innocent and ignorant soldier asking "Why?" Yet even the boys Jarrell wrote about had more of a sense, however inarticu-

lately they might express themselves, of "why" than he quite gives them credit for. As for the poet himself, a number of the pieces show the usual intellectual's grasp of the economic and historical aspects of modern war. Of the American poets who emerged immediately after the war, only Robert Lowell was keyed to the demands of the materials, but on the other hand he had neither the literal experience nor the inclination to work on *the* war poem. Perhaps Pound and Eliot, by their keen location of the inner contradictions of Western culture, had rendered a large effort of this sort redundant for later poets.

That Jarrell wanted to suggest large historical and mythological considerations is clear from "The Wide Prospect," which comes just before "The Death of the Ball Turret Gunner" at the end of *Little Friend, Little Friend*, and from the two poems that close *Losses*: "In the Ward: The Sacred Wood" and "Orestes at Tauris." The influence of Marx via Auden is obvious in the opening stanza of "The Wide Prospect":

Who could have figured, when the harnesses
    improved
And men pumped kobolds from the coal's
    young seams
There to the west, on Asia's unrewarding
    cape—
The interest on that first raw capital?
The hegemony only the corpses have escaped?

The poem ends, after a determinedly sustained exposition along these lines, with an imagery of ritual sacrifice that links Marxian, Freudian, and myth-and-ritual-oriented motifs:

    the man-eaters die
Under the cross of their long-eaten Kin.

All die for all. And the planes rise from the
    years . . .

When men see men once more the food of
    Man
And their bare lives His last commodity.

The poems at the end of *Losses* are superior in being free of the long, expository sections, with a forced liveliness of imagery but without driving energy, of "The Wide Prospect." "Orestes at Tauris," the closing poem, was according to Jarrell an early composition written before any of the poems from *Blood for a Stranger* included in the *Selected Poems*. Very different in character from anything else in the war books, it shows Orestes arriving in Tauris after being pursued relentlessly by the Furies, under compulsion, "in expiation for his crime, to bring back to Greece that image of Artemis to which the Tauri sacrificed the strangers cast up on their shores" (Jarrell's note in *Losses*). This long, partially surrealist narrative poem imagines the sacrificial beheading of Orestes by his sister Iphigenia, now a priestess, instead of their triumphant escape. Jarrell's recasting of the myth, in a well-sustained unrhymed pattern of four- and five-stress lines that focuses on the succession of impressions, states of feeling, and sensations that Orestes experiences, makes for an effect of terror amidst psychological confusion and barbaric splendors. The condition of Orestes and Iphigenia at the end then becomes a perfect mythic embodiment of Jarrell's vision of war as the sacrifice of driven innocents for the sake of a savage, mindless determinism inherent in our natures:

The people, silent, watching with grave faces
Their priestess, who stands there
Holding out her hands, staring at her hands
With her brother's blood drenching her hands.

"In the Ward: The Sacred Wood," which precedes "Orestes at Tauris," is perhaps Jarrell's most determined effort to give mythic dimensions to his theme of the sacrificed innocent in war. His own description of the poem, in his introduction to *Selected Poems*, goes: "The wounded man has cut trees from paper, and made for himself a sacred wood; with these, the bed-clothes, the nurse, the doctor, he works his own way through the Garden of Eden, the dove and its olive-leaf, the years in the wilderness, the burning bush, the wars of God and the rebel angels, the birth and death and resurrection of Christ." This account, and the style of the poem, somewhat recall the symbolic distortions of thought and syntax of Lowell's early poems—

Is the nurse damned who looked on my
    nakedness?
The sheets stretch like the wilderness
Up which my fingers wander, the sick tribes,
To a match's flare, a rain or bush of fire. . . .

But Jarrell's movement does not rip free into Lowell's frenzied piling up of associations and allusions. In this poem, however, he surpasses Lowell in one important respect though he does not achieve that state of passionate intensity of speech which makes the whole language an electric field of highly charged, crackling movements of realization. At each point along the way, as the wounded soldier ponders the symbolic analogies with Christ implicit in his condition, he nevertheless at the same time maintains a basic simplicity and a distance from the mental game he is playing. Unlike "Eighth Air Force," this poem does not press an identity between the dying soldier and Christ. The dominant tone is one of a real man, without hope, letting go though aware of a dream of divinity incarnate—a tone corresponding to the progress of negative heroism in Read's "To a Conscript of 1940." Negation is accepted quietly; this is one of Jarrell's most touching and thoughtful poems:

And beneath the coverlet
My limbs are swaddled in their sleep, and
      shade
Flows from the cave beyond the olives, falls
Into the garden where no messenger
Comes to gesture, "Go"—to whisper, "He is
      gone."

The trees rise to me from the world
That made me, I call to the grove
That stretches inch on inch without one God:
"I have unmade you, now; but I must die."

Earlier, in discussing "The Death of the Ball Turret Gunner," I ventured a description of the characteristic structural dynamics of Jarrell's poems as involving a static initial state of sadness, then a phase of confusion that lets deeper depression flood into the poem, and then a final bitter thrust. Most lyric-contemplative poetry since the early Romantics has, in fact, a comparable structure. That is, an initial state of unease or depressed feeling is followed by the introduction of complicating matter for contemplation: any of a number of contexts of awareness that enlarge and, very likely, confuse the original perspective. The final "resolution" of the poem is a reorientation of the speaker's initial attitude in the light of the intervening complication. It may take the form of acceptance or reconciliation though at the same time what is being "affirmed" is defeat of a sort—what we might call "depressive transcendence." Needless to add that shifts of style, rhythm, intensity, and level of diction are as important as the literal statements.

Without forcing the point, we can say that Jarrell's whole poetic career follows a similar pattern of movement. After the early poems of childhood desolation, the speaking psyche confronts three bodies of material external to itself: war experience, the world of myth and folk legend (to which are added, often, the associations of music, painting, and literature), and individual human suffering. In the final phase of his career, the poet objectifies himself, in relation to his childhood life, as one of the sufferers over whom his attention has hovered with such empathy. That is, he has brought back his earliest preoccupations into the center of his work, but in a focus altered by the discipline through which he has passed and the knowledge he has accumulated. He has learned to isolate the pity of the irrecoverable and, therefore, of the irredeemable in existence and is free to present sharp, concrete memories and to play with them in a number of ways.

In *Losses*, we see the three bodies of "external" material (war, myth and legend, and suffering individual people) already present. War is, of course, the overwhelming major subject. But there are other myth-involved poems besides the two we have already examined, among them "The Märchen" and "The Child of Courts"; Jarrell's fascination with the German *Märchen* (folk tales, in this case those of the brothers Grimm) is at this point related to the historical fatalism induced by his response to the war. The dreams and terrors of primitive life foreshadowed those of the modern age with its discovery of the limitations of man's hopes and prospects:

Listening, listening; it is never still.
This is the forest: long ago the lives
Edged armed into its tides (the axes were its
      stone
Lashed with the skins of dwellers to its
      boughs);
We felled our islands there, at last, with iron.
The sunlight fell to them, according to our
      wish,
And we believed, till nightfall, in that wish;
And we believed, till nightfall, in our lives.

These are the open, and on the whole the

best, lines of "The Märchen," a somewhat preciously proliferative poem which nevertheless shows Jarrell's characteristic wit, ingenuity, and sympathy with the common lot. He had learned, in his war poems, how to write with economy, but there is no economy in this poem of over a hundred lines of moderately roughened blank verse. Jarrell luxuriates in the way the *Märchen* bring folk motifs and folk wisdom, simple and often comic materials related to the life of peasants, together with the symbolic and archetypal motifs of religious or mythical tradition: Christ and the old gods, Hell, "the Scapegoat," "Paradise," and "the Cross, the Ark, the Tree." The perspective he introduces has to do with primitive man's desire, never fulfilled but never forgotten or relinquished either, even in our time, to make reality conform to his wish. Herein, for Jarrell, lies the inescapable pathos of the human condition, of which the vulnerable innocence of children is the most obvious embodiment. The *Märchen* show that it is not so much our inability to make wishes come true as the paltriness of the wishes themselves that is defeating. In Romantic tradition generally, it is the disparity between desire and reality, between subjective and objective "truths," with which the poet is obsessed—ultimately, the pity that we cannot stamp our own images on nature. In Jarrell there is a curious turn of emphasis: the inadequacy of imagination, driven as it is already by conditions imposed on it by nature, is the heart of the problem—

> Poor Hänsel, once too powerless
> To shelter your own children from the cold
> Or quiet their bellies with the thinnest gruel,
> It was not power that you lacked, but wishes.
> Had you not learned—have we not learned, from tales
> Neither of beasts nor kingdoms nor their Lord,

But of our own hearts, the realm of death—
Neither to rule nor die? to change! to change!

"The Child of Courts" (reprinted in *Selected Poems* as "The Prince") presents the ambivalent night-terror of a child who fears that the ghost of a buried man has come up out of the grave toward him but who then is disappointed: "I start to weep because—because there are no ghosts." The poem at first ambiguously suggests a prison atmosphere. But the child calls out "Mother?"—in an equally ambiguous context, however—and thus there is a suggestion not so much of a prison as of a castle or palace in which there is intrigue and insecurity. One thinks of young Prince Edward after Henry's death, a thought mildly encouraged by the two titles. The situation of this brief and simple poem suggests, at one and the same time, the well-known situations of Edward and other English princes, the grisly circumstances of certain folk legends, and the excited imagination of any sensitive child at certain times.

> After the door shuts, and the footsteps die,
> I call out, "Mother?" No one answers.
> I chafe my numb feet with my quaking hands
> And hunch beneath the covers, in my curled
> Red ball of darkness; but the floor creaks,
>   someone stirs
> In the other darkness—and the hairs all rise
> Along my neck, I whisper: "It is he!"

Many years after *Losses*, in his 1965 volume *The Lost World*, Jarrell published "A Hunt in the Black Forest," which begins exactly as "The Child of Courts" does, except for a shift to the third person that heralds a new, or at least a redirected, point of view toward the same situation:

> After the door shuts and the footsteps die,
> He calls out: "Mother?"

The speaker now, however, is not the child but an omniscient narrator. The circumstances, like the title, suggest the world of the *Märchen*, projected in a Freudian nightmare fantasy. A king, out hunting, comes to a hut in the forest where a deaf-mute feeds him a stew that poisons him while a red dwarf watches through the window. At the end of this poem, whose every stage is brilliantly and dramatically clear and sinister, there is a blending of supernatural and psychologically pointed details that brings us all the way over from the climax of the king's death to the further, greater climax of the child's sensibility underlying the entire story.

Then a bubbled, gobbling sound begins,
The sound of the pot laughing on the fire.
—The pot, overturned among the ashes,
Is cold as death.

Something is scratching, panting. A little voice
Says, "Let *me*! Let *me*!" The mute
Puts his arms around the dwarf and raises him.

The pane is clouded with their soft slow
    breaths,
The mute's arms tire; but they gaze on and on,
Like children watching something wrong.
Their blurred faces, caught up in one wish,
Are blurred into one face: a child's set face.

The mute, the dwarf, and the child thus share horrified, guilty fascination; they are three facets of innocence, despite their involvement in a primal tragic scene. It would not be difficult to "interpret" the story as one in which the child (into whose face the other faces blend at the very end of the poem) is both the victim—the stew that the king, his father, ate—and the killer who destroys his father through the very act of being devoured by him. If we put "The Child of Courts" and "A Hunt in the Black Forest" side by side and consider each a gloss on the other, it becomes clear that the addition of the third-person narrator enabled Jarrell to fill out the symbolic context of the original poem's conception. But he added to it the distanced understanding of an adult voice presenting the unresolved anguish of one kind of disturbed childhood. "A Hunt in the Black Forest" brings both its psychological and its archetypal motives directly to bear on the tale it has been telling by a final refocusing of elements present in the story from the start. It represents, as do the more literally autobiographical poems of the final volume, an achieved objectification of the speaking self and an achieved clarity as well. Thought is presented experientially, with sharply sketched action and description that leave room for shadows, depths, and implied complexities.

One poem in *Losses*, "Lady Bates," especially foreshadows Jarrell's turn, after the war period, to poems centered on suffering individual persons, often women. The Lady Bates of the title is, says Jarrell in his notes to *Selected Poems*, "a little Negro girl whose Christian name is *Lady*." The child has died, and the poem is addressed to her as an epitome of everything helpless and betrayed in human existence. Viewed unsympathetically, the poem is an example of sophisticated sentimentality, a humanitarian southerner's attempt to speak to his knowledge of the hurt done to Negroes in a language appropriate to both. "Lady Bates," significantly, comes first in *Losses*, the only poem quite of its kind in this book, preceding all the war pieces. A certain oversimplification of the meaning of ordinary people's lives, comparable to what we have seen in the war poems, comes through in "Lady Bates" despite its genuinely touching aspects. The worst of Jarrell is concentrated into parts of this poem that mercilessly expose both his condescension and the presumptuousness of his spokesmanship for the girl:

Poor black trash,
The wind has blown you away forever
By mistake; and they sent the wind to the
    chain-gang
And it worked in the governor's kitchen, a
    trusty for life;
And it was all written in the Book of Life;
Day and Night met in the twilight by your tomb
And shot craps for you; and Day said, pointing
    to your soul,
"This *bad* young colored lady,"
And Night said, "Poor little nigger girl."

"Lady Bates," with its weaknesses, continues Jarrell's development toward the objectification of the speaking self that I have suggested is the chief triumph of *The Lost World*. Like the many soldiers who are his subjects in the war volumes, the little black girl in this poem serves two functions in this development. First and most obviously, she is one of the many figures in his poems whose reality he seeks to repossess as persons outside himself. Secondly, though, she and the other figures are the beneficiaries (or victims) of an empathy that enables him to project onto them certain basic features of the child psyche familiar in his earlier poems—its confusion, innocence, and betrayal by life. It would be accurate to say that each of these figures is at once himself or herself *and* Randall Jarrell; not, of course, Jarrell the wit, translator of Rilke, and edgily competitive poet, but the essential Jarrell whose sensibility defines itself in his poems in the way we have been tracing.

This essential sensibility enters many of the speaking voices in Jarrell's next volume, *The Seven-League Crutches*. In fact, reading through this volume, one is pierced by the realization of how completely possessed by it his writing is and what a chilling desolateness he coped with. It is not only the specific *child*

minds he presents that make the realization so forcible, though indeed this volume gives us several such characterizations to add to "Lady Bates." The one closest to "Lady Bates" in tone is "The Truth," in which, Jarrell explains in *Selected Poems*, "the little boy who speaks . . . has had his father, his sister, and his dog killed in one of the early fire-raids on London, and has been taken to the country, to a sort of mental institution for children." This poem has none of the cultural overlay of "Lady Bates," the treacherous sense of "understanding" the black child's world that cuts across Jarrell's finer sense of her as one abandoned by life in her own idiosyncratic way. "The Truth" is stripped down to the essential anguish and bewilderment:

When I was four my father went to Scotland.
They *said* he went to Scotland.

When I woke up I think I thought that I was
    dreaming—
I was so little then that I thought dreams
Are in the room with you, like the cinema.
That's why you don't dream when it's still
    light—

They pull the shades down when it is, so you can
    sleep.
I thought that then, but that's not right.
Really it's in your head.

And it was light then—light at *night*. . . .

And yet, as with the play of thought in "Lady Bates," one can well ask of this poem whether the anguish and bewilderment are really the little boy's or Jarrell's. All that charming talk about a child's notion of what dreams are is really in Jarrell's grown-up voice, reminiscing about his own memories. Naturally, these thoughts about dreams being like the cinema might occur to any child, and my only point is that Jarrell is using this kind of situation, so close to his own constant preoccupation, as a suitable instrument on which to play. He is a virtuoso of pity, and the form his virtuosity takes is to work his own voice into his materials so as to bring out their intrinsic pathos and his active insight simultaneously.

In "The Black Swan," a poem about another child, this fusion of sensibilities works superbly. The preface to *Selected Poems* tells us that this poem was "said, long ago, by a girl whose sister is buried under the white stones of the green churchyard." "The Black Swan" and a number of other poems in *The Seven-League Crutches* mark a considerable advance in the artistic isolation and redirection of Jarrell's deepest motifs. The loneliness, the sense of a chaotic universe, and the lost focus of identity (expressed as a shared or confused identity) of his best later work are all present at the very start of "The Black Swan":

When the swans turned my sister into a swan
　　I would go to the lake, at night, from
　　　　milking:
The sun would look out through the reeds like
　　a swan,
　　A swan's red beak; and the beak would
　　　　open
And inside there was darkness, the stars and
　　the moon. . . .

This beginning, a decisive act of empathic imagination, opens up a world of associations to the end of recovering the stab of primal pathos. The swan images proliferate, and the mad or nightmare-ridden speaker becomes a swan herself as, out of the realm of heartless nature and death, her sister responds to her call. This poem alone would make it clear that Jarrell's poetic control had grown enormously by 1951. He could now deal purely and forcefully with psychological and mythic or archetypal materials and could write his own thoughts directly without overintellectualizing and without superciliousness. "The Orient Express" opens *The Seven-League Crutches* on a note of unpretentious intimacy that combines his ever-present child-mindedness with his adult intelligence:

One looks from the train
Almost as one looked as a child. In the sunlight
What I see still seems to me plain,
I am safe; but at evening
As the lands darken, a questioning
Precariousness comes over everything. . . .

All of Jarrell is there, as simply apparent as possible. But the form itself has a new sort of interest when compared to much of Jarrell's earlier work. The ease and grace of movement, the sustained clarity of speech, and the engaging, concrete thoughtfulness keep the reader listening and moving along with the speaker. The lines of this passage, as in the poem as a whole, tend toward a three-stress unit but often —here in the two opening lines—depart from it. Rhyming effects (an exact rhyme in lines one and three, the echoing of *-ing* in lines four, five, and six, the repetitions of "look" and "one," and the sequence of the monosyllabic verbs "look" and "looked" and "see" and "seems" and "comes") are introduced lightly yet saturate the sound structure as in the even richer "The Black Swan." One finds a similar felicity and immediacy in the two poems that close the book, "The Venetian Blind" and "Seele im Raum"—poems which both recall— the former in its literal theme and the latter in its title—a poem of Rilke's. "The Venetian Blind" does indeed present its protagonist as a "Seele im Raum" or "soul in space."

He is lost in himself forever.

And the Angel he makes from the sunlight
Says in mocking tenderness:

"Poor stateless one, wert thou the world?" . . .

The bars of the sunlight fall to his face.

And yet something calls, as it has called:
"But where am *I*? But where am *I*?"

Rilke's "Seele im Raum," written in 1917, has as its literal subject the condition of a soul torn from its body and suddenly become pure potentiality in a realm of pure being. The soul feels stripped of comforts, exposed, and tremulously fearful in its ignorance of its own destiny. Jarrell's "Seele im Raum" has in part the same theme, but the central situation of his poem is that of a woman who once had the grotesque illusion that an eland was present wherever she was. The woman's pathetic obsession would be hilariously absurd were it not, as her monologue shows, symptomatic of her sense of being a lost self despite the fact that she was a wife and mother. Her period of madness is now over; but in an important way she misses the eland, which was so tangibly and oppressively present to her and yet was the only thing that was hers alone: her soul's embodiment of its own misery.

Today, in a German dictionary, I saw *elend*
And the heart in my breast turned over, it was—

It was a word one translates wretched. . . .

—It was worse than impossible, it was a joke.

And yet when it was, I *was*—
Even to think that I once thought
That I could see it is to feel the sweat
Like needles at my hair-roots, I am blind

—It was not even a joke, not even a joke.

Yet how can I believe it? Or believe that I
Owned it, a husband, children? Is my voice the
       voice
Of that skin of being—of what owns, is owned
In honor or dishonor, that is borne and bears—

Or of that raw thing, the being inside it
That has neither a wife, a husband, nor a child
But goes at last as naked from this world
As it was born into it—

And the eland comes and grazes on its
       grave. . . .

The passage I have just quoted takes us from the punning proof that the eland had been for the speaker a projection of her soul's *elend* condition, its misery, to the bitter sense she has now of all that she has lost and then, finally, to that sense of being stripped of a human past and utterly out in space of which Rilke writes. Jarrell's absorption in Rilke was one of his great passions; it must have been of tremendous importance to him in the progress of his art that I have described. He immersed himself in the greater poet, whose themes were so close to his own. The sensibilities of children and of women dominate the attention of both poets. Both are in search of points of directive contact with chaotic reality —both are "souls in space." Both, incidentally, had noncombatant military service involving a certain disillusionment, and there were temperamental affinities as well (as in their mixture of endearing traits with ruthless critical attitudes).

Rilke's essential influence on Jarrell seems to have been to encourage him to widen his poetic thought and to reach for a more concentrated and evocative imagery, a more personal and vital poetic speech and rhythmic movement, and a style both natural to him and in touch with European cultural tradition. It is interesting that *The Seven-League Crutches* begins with a section called "Europe"—poems with European settings to which Jarrell attaches his American awareness. The displacement of context enables him to convert old sets of thought into deepened historical and philosophical musings. Looking out from the Orient Express, he can see that the whole world (not just his own empirical life) is unassimilable to the soul in space and yet has its own aesthetic magnetism we cannot avoid:

It is like any other work of art.
It is and never can be changed.
Behind everything there is always
The unknown unwanted life.

One could conceivably make the same observation looking from an American train, but just that kind of consideration is involved in the implied comparison. It is just the sensed history behind the fields, people, houses, and villages that makes the feeling of an essential changelessness of existence such a powerful one. In "A Game at Salzburg," the same principle is at work. Jarrell's explanation in *Selected Poems* shows how much he relishes the knowledgeableness behind the poem, the kind of Europeanized wit its subject enables him to cultivate: "I put into 'A Game at Salzburg' a little game that Germans and Austrians play with very young children. The child says to the grown-up, *Here I am*, and the grown-up answers, *There you are*; the children use the same little rising tune, and the grown-ups the same resolving, conclusive one. It seemed to me that if there could be a conversation between the world and God, this would be it." And so, in the poem, the whole style is delightfully relaxed until the very end. The poet (during the year in which he was a participant in the Salzburg Seminar in American Civilization) is seen passing lazy, happy days amid the innumerable tokens not only of an old civilization but also of the recent war. One notices with some surprise and interest that his juxtapositions of a modern American intelligence like his own with all these surrounding signs and symbols, under circumstances at once so congenial and so poignantly and volatilely suggestive, have

led him into a tone and rhythm that must have influenced Robert Lowell's style in *Life Studies*:

A little ragged girl, our ball-boy;
A partner—ex-Afrika-Korps—
In khaki shorts, P. W. illegible.
(He said: "To have been a prisoner of war
In Colorado iss a *privilege*.")
The evergreens, concessions, carrousels,
And D. P. camp at Franz Joseph Park;
A gray-green river, evergreen-dark hills.
Last, a long way off in the sky,
Snow-mountains.

These are the social and political and historical realities, all within the unchanged ancient landscape. When, later on, the poet finds himself playing the little game of *Hier bin i'—Da bist du*, with a three-year-old, there is an inevitably ironic echo from that opening scene. Reality is intractably itself, and the fact is softly underlined in the persistence of a language and a ritual even in a tiny girl "licking sherbet from a wooden spoon" as she engages the poet in the game. Later still, he moves "past Maria Theresa's sleigh" and the statues, mostly broken, in the garden where "the nymphs look down with the faces of Negroes." The two worlds suddenly related in this image are one world after all, as is the prewar world that became the one at war and then the postwar one. At the end, Jarrell's old, persistent insight is thrust into the foreground, but the voice adopted is a European one recalling the "dreamy" American to the imponderable:

In anguish, in expectant acceptance
The world whispers: *Hier bin i'*.

We cannot pursue all the examples of Jarrell's "Europeanization" in *The Seven-League Crutches*. One further instance is the translation of Corbière's "Le Poète contumace." Corbière's tough-mindedness and scathing but funny self-characterizations show up the sentimental limits of Jarrell's own work. Nevertheless, Jarrell admired Corbière and aspired to his kind of mentality.

Jarrell's one novel, *Pictures from an Institution*, bears extended analysis because so much that was important to him is packed into it, and also because it is an extremely clever work of satire as well as a humanely intelligent book. It is set in a progressive women's college not altogether unlike Sarah Lawrence College, and its pictures of the academic and personal life of all concerned remain extremely amusing. I shall discuss it only very briefly, in relation to Jarrell's poetic development. It represents, I think, a completion of his attempt to assimilate his own frame of thought to that of cultivated and sensitive Europeans. The novel is written in the first person, from the viewpoint of a poet who has been teaching at Benton College for a number of years. The real hero, though, is an Austrian-Jewish composer named Gottfried Rosenbaum through whose eyes the provincialism, complacency, and emptiness of much of American education is made, somewhat lovingly, clear, while certain genuine American strengths and potentialities are seen as goods after all. Dr. Rosenbaum's mind is razor-keen, though he does not ordinarily use it to slash people. That role is taken by a visiting novelist, Gertrude Johnson, whose analytical savagery has no kindness in it and who is often malignantly inventive in her sizing up of people, all grist for her novels. She is going to do a novel about the college, and it will be merciless—presumably far more so than *Pictures from an Institution* itself. Yet this necessary comparison gives one to think. Gertrude, as it were, discharges the hostile and supercilious side of Jarrell's critical intelligence, while Gottfried represents a more genial ideal. John Crowe Ransom, in his contribution to *Randall Jarrell, 1914–1965*, notes the indications that Gertrude undergoes something like a "conversion" to a more humane attitude in the course of the novel, and I would suggest that the improvement of Gertrude is something in the nature of a purgation for Jarrell himself. The "I" of the novel, the poet who is ready to leave the limited campus scene at the end of the year, has been close to both Gertrude and Gottfried. Gottfried, with his elderly Russian wife who shares his cultivation and his sense of tragic history, will remain after the writers have left. With them will stay the talented and loyal Constance Morgan, who in her life embodies the best of American openness and possibility as Gottfried and Irene embody the living tradition of European art with which we must remain in vital touch. Constance, an orphan, is thus one of four figures who represent ideals or characteristics of Jarrell himself. The book reaches a certain serenity and insight into the best qualities of each of the characters, despite the fun at the expense of most of them along the way.

What an injustice I have done to this novel, with its marvelously amusing passages that Jarrell wrote in an ecstasy of acerbic release. It is his most balanced work, done not long after his marriage to Mary von Schrader in 1952, and it helped him gain a precarious personal balance. It was also a self-deceptive balance, a standoff between barely repressed total revulsion and sentimental voting for the triumph, in any one person, of decency over stupidity and mean-spirited worldliness. A variety of sexual repression is involved as well. In the novel, as in Jarrell's poetry, sexuality in itself seems hardly present as a factor in his own thought and emotions or in those of his characters. His attitude toward women is a little like his attitude toward unhappy children and a little like Sophocles' toward "the Mothers": awe, mystification, and, sometimes, a cozy sympathy with a bitter edge nevertheless.

The sense of a life ridden by despair that comes through in his last two books of poems is linked with that bitter sympathy. The balanced feeling of control of the mid-1950's dissolves into something harsher, more convincing finally, and at its best more brilliant.

The three poems that open the 1960 volume, *The Woman at the Washington Zoo*, are rather precise examples of Jarrell's feeling for women. He thinks about them a great deal, and passionately, but in the ways I have suggested. The title poem is one of a number written from the point of view of a woman, usually aging, who feels that, as she says, "The world goes by my cage and never sees me." (Jarrell discusses the composition of this poem brilliantly in one of his essays in *A Sad Heart at the Supermarket*, 1962.) The poem begins with a tone of quiet desperation and in a sometimes banal cadence of a sort occasionally cultivated by Eliot, but rises to a hysterical pitch at the end—an accusation against fate and an appeal to be transformed. The woman's outcry is directed toward a vulture, both real and symbolic. She wants to be devoured and transformed, and her language suggests that the bird of prey to which her protest and prayer are addressed embodies the male principle:

> Vulture,
> When you come for the white rat that the foxes
>   left,
> Take off the red helmet of your head, the black
> Wings that have shadowed me, and step to me
>   as man:
> The wild brother at whose feet the white wolves
>   fawn,
> To whose hand of power the great lioness
> Stalks, purring. . . .
>   You know what I was,
> You see what I am: change me, change me!

It is the first time in his poems that Jarrell speaks so fiercely through a woman's voice. In the next poem, "Cinderella," he does so again, but here, for once, female toughness—and even hardness—of spirit comes through. Both Cinderella and her fairy godmother are presented as coolly anti-male. Cinderella, on her very wedding day, under the "pulsating marble" of her wedding lace, "wished it all a widow's coal-black weeds." Later she became "a sullen wife and a reluctant mother." The godmother is sophisticated into an archetypal "God's Mother" who comes into her own whenever her son is away. At these times she invites Cinderella into the "gold-gauzed door" of her Heaven that exists only in the flames of the male-created Hell, and they gossip comfortably apart from male ideas, ideals, and laws. This poem is far more effective than the long, rather involved, and precious one that follows: "The End of the Rainbow." In this latter poem, about a woman "old enough to be invisible," Jarrell's proliferating details carry a certain pathos but, even more, suggest the poet's extraordinary identification with his protagonist.

After these opening poems of human sensibility gratingly out of phase come the four most striking pieces of the book—poems that, together with those in the title sequence of *The Lost World*, complete Jarrell's work by closing in on intimate realities of his own actual life and memory. Again we have an interesting parallel to Lowell, for both poets were moving into their confessional period at the same time. Lowell's *Life Studies* had appeared the year before, an enormous gathering of concentrated neurotic energy centered on his childhood and the personalities of his parents as somehow symptomatic of America's and the world's malaise. Although Jarrell's confessional poems are less ambitious formally and symbolically than Lowell's, they are in many ways closer to the anomie and the disturbances that mark the common life in our day.

Jarrell is in his own way as much an exotic as Lowell. The strains of his boyhood are as atypical as those of the privileged Bostonian, and the adult lives of both men have been atypical too. But often in these poems he summons up the world of plain-living, laboring souls and the hardships and pleasures of ordinary life. The confusing images of his beloved grandmother wringing a chicken's neck and of the already dead bird still running about in circles recur, for instance, in a number of the poems. Each is an image of the brutal nature of existence and cannot be separated out from the meaning of love. Millions of ordinary folk know the experience described in "A Street off Sunset" (in *The Lost World*):

Mama comes out and takes in the clothes
From the clothesline. She looks with righteous
    love
At all of us, her spare face half a girl's.
She enters a chicken coop, and the hens shove
And flap and squawk, in fear; the whole flock
    whirls
Into the farthest corner. She chooses one,
Comes out, and wrings its neck. The body hurls
Itself out—lunging, reeling, it begins to run
Away from Something, to fly away from Some-
    thing
In great flopping circles. Mama stands like a
    nun
In the center of each awful, anguished ring.
The thudding and scrambling go on, go on—
    then they fade,
I open my eyes, it's over . . . Could such a thing
Happen to anything? It could to a rabbit, I'm
    afraid;
It could to . . .

The details here are as plain, and as hideous, as, say, those in John Clare's "Badger." Where Jarrell differs from a true *naïf*, though, is in his superimposed notes of observation, themselves simple in tone but implying medi-tative and informed intelligence: "righteous love" (a note of psychological insight, for the woman's look is a gesture both of self-encouragement and of apology and self-justification); "away from Something" (a note to underline the presence of universal terror); "like a nun" (again, the note of reaffirmed innocence, which is yet "the center of each awful, anguished ring"); and at last the deliberate pointing up of the child's reactions. The easily colloquial iambic pentameter lines run on quite naturally; one hardly notices the alternating rhymes that help rock the movement into hysteria—that is, into the child's momentarily traumatized hypnosis by the impossible thing that is happening. Jarrell uses this pattern throughout the "Lost World" sequence. It makes for a slightly relaxed, anecdotal tone that drags boringly at times but provides a frame at others for effects such as this one. This weakness, in itself, is a reflection of Jarrell's desire to keep his form open to common speech and common psychology—something he much admired in Robert Frost's work.

Returning to *The Woman in the Washington Zoo* and the four poems there that I have noted, we can see that "In Those Days" and "The Elementary Scene" are both exceedingly simple in form. "In Those Days" consists of four quatrains with the simplest of rhyme schemes, *abcb*, and is in a basic iambic tetrameter with much variation for naturalness and dramatic immediacy. It reads, except for the deliberate avoidance of smoothness of meter, like an afterbeat from Heine, particularly in the last stanza:

How poor and miserable we were,
How seldom together!
And yet after so long one thinks:
In those days everything was better.

Almost doggerel—but this ending shrugs off a painful nostalgia for a past love, the whole adolescent atmosphere of which has been evoked, with all its bittersweet frustration and sense of wintry isolation of the two young people, in the preceding stanzas. The poem strikes a new personal key for Jarrell, and serves as an overture to the further exploration of the speaker's lost past. Then come "The Elementary Scene" and "Windows," still quite simple in their diction and the scenes they envision: the first a rural elementary school at Hallowe'en, the second the home of dead elders who once loved and cherished the speaker. Jarrell's ability to suggest, with utmost economy, a milieu at once provincial and inarticulate and yet full of unmet challenge—the reality of an irretrievable folk past that might have led to a far different life for the speaker, less to be regretted, perhaps—is his greatest strength.

The thin grass by the girls' door,
Trodden on, straggling, yellow and rotten,
And the gaunt field with its one tied cow . . .

—the lines recall his very early "The Cow Wandering in the Bare Field" and the curious persistence of images demanding clarification again and again during a poet's lifetime. The self-reproach at the end of "The Elementary Scene"—"I, I, the future that mends everything"—is the final evidence that this is one of his purest poems, a poem of unearned but heavily felt depression, in which the speaker takes upon himself the guilt of time's passing. So also in "Windows," it is the unbearable irrevocability of the past that the speaker lives with and endures (in this respect a true heir to Frost and E. A. Robinson). The beloved dead, imagined alive in their time, are compared in their vivid presence to "dead actors, on a rainy afternoon," who "move in a darkened living-room" on a television screen.

These actors, surely, have known nothing of
      today,

That time of troubles and of me. . . .
They move along in peace. . . . If only I were
      they!
Could act out, in longing, the impossibility
That haunts me like happiness!

Sentimentality is held at a distance in this poem by the sheer force of illusion: the construction of a moment of the recaptured past so keenly present to the speaker's desire that it goes beyond imagination—

It blurs, and there is drawn across my face
As my eyes close, a hand's slow fire-warmed
      flesh.

It moves so slowly that it does not move.

The poem "Aging," which follows, does not have the fine sensuous conviction of "Windows" and does lapse into sentimentality. When, in the "Lost World" sequence and in "Remembering the Lost World," literal memory again picks up these motifs, the intensity and concentration are sacrificed for the anecdotal colloquialism we have seen. These are poems banking on total rather than on selected recall and striving to hold their recovered, or reimagined, reality intact against the poisonous fact of elapsed time. Theirs is an opposite method, allowing room for something like a novelistic play of mind over bizarre contradictions of a child's life in Hollywood, a life at once disciplined by good gray work and indulged by an almost sensually remembered aunt and her friends, one of whom owned the MGM lion. It is a bath of charming, touching, and heartbreaking memory in the new open mode that Jarrell had discovered. The new mode seems to have freed him from a vision too sharp to be endured, and to have taken him over the line of belief in the present reality of the past. "Thinking of the Lost World" ends:

LOST—NOTHING. STRAYED FROM NOWHERE.
    NO REWARD.
I hold in my own hands, in happiness,
Nothing: the nothing for which there's no re-
    ward.

"I felt at first," writes John Crowe Ransom in the essay I quoted from earlier, "that this was a tragic ending. But I have studied it till I give up that notion. The NOTHING is the fiction, the transformation; to which both boy and man are given. That World is not Lost because it never existed; but it is as precious now as ever. I have come to think that Randall was announcing the beginning of his 'second childhood.' There is nothing wrong about that, to the best of my knowledge." Perhaps, but what Mr. Ransom is describing is the letdown, or failure of nerve, in the face of the issues (which Jarrell nevertheless did to a certain important extent face) that often takes the form of a paradoxically melancholy complacency in writers just below the energy level of genius. Jarrell himself approaches the issue wryly in the quoted lines, and also in the self-ironically named poem "Hope," which takes us into the poet's grown-up life with all its gaiety, fears, and gallant playing of roles. It is almost as though he had given the tragic its due in "The Elementary Scene," "Windows," and the very dark-spirited Rilke translations of *The Woman at the Washington Zoo* and then turned his back on the discipline of greatness.

But this would be too harsh a judgment. At fifty-one, Jarrell was still expanding his range of technique and of personal sympathies. He might well have reversed his direction once more and made another fresh start as he had done in the war poems and again in *The Seven-League Crutches* and the last books. With all the intelligence and openness to varied literary influences reflected in his criticism and his translations during the two post-war decades,

he was surely capable of a great deal of further development despite a deep formal conservatism. Our poetry—and it is Jarrell's *poetry* almost exclusively that we have been concerned with—is today struggling in a new way with the question of the role of an active, many-sided intellectuality in essential poetic structure. Jarrell might conceivably have contributed something of interest to this exploration. Meanwhile, he remains a force among us as a poet of defeat and loneliness who nevertheless does not allow himself to become less spirited. He is like that ex-P.W. in his poem "A Game at Salzburg" who says, "To have been a prisoner of war in Colorado is a *privilege*."

Selected Bibliography

WORKS OF RANDALL JARRELL

NOTE: The quotations in the foregoing text are all taken from the original volumes rather than from the revised versions in *Selected Poems* and in *The Complete Poems*.

POETRY
"The Rage for the Lost Penny," in *Five Young American Poets*. Norfolk, Conn.: New Directions, 1940.
Blood for a Stranger. New York: Harcourt, Brace, 1942.
Little Friend, Little Friend. New York: Dial, 1945.
Losses. New York: Harcourt, Brace, 1948.
The Seven-League Crutches. New York: Harcourt, Brace, 1951.
Selected Poems. 1st ed., New York: Knopf, 1955; 2nd ed., including *The Woman at the Washington Zoo*, New York: Atheneum, 1964.
The Woman at the Washington Zoo. New York: Atheneum, 1960.

The Lost World. New York: Macmillan, 1965. (Paperback reprint with Robert Lowell's essay "Randall Jarrell, 1914-1965: An Appreciation" appended, New York: Collier, 1966.)

The Complete Poems. New York: Farrar, Straus and Giroux, 1969. Includes *Selected Poems,* poems omitted from *Selected Poems,* and sections of "Uncollected Poems (1934-1965)" and "Unpublished Poems (1935-1965)."

NOVEL

Pictures from an Institution, a Comedy. New York: Knopf, 1954.

CRITICISM

Poetry and the Age. New York: Knopf, 1953.

A Sad Heart at the Supermarket. New York: Atheneum, 1962.

The Third Book of Criticism. New York: Farrar, Straus and Giroux, 1965.

BIBLIOGRAPHIES

Adams, Charles M. *Randall Jarrell: A Bibliography.* Chapel Hill: University of North Carolina Press, 1958. (A supplement to this bibliography appears in *Analects,* 1:49-56 [Spring 1961].)

Gillikin, Dure J. "A Check-List of Criticism on Randall Jarrell, 1941-1970, with an Introduction and a List of His Major Works," *Bulletin of the New York Public Library,* 74:176-94 (April 1971).

Kisslinger, Margaret V. "A Bibliography of Randall Jarrell," *Bulletin of Bibliography,* 24:243-47 (May-August 1966).

Shapiro, Karl. *Randall Jarrell.* Washington, D.C.: Library of Congress, 1967. (Includes a bibliography of primary works and a list of Jarrell materials in the collections of the Library of Congress: manuscripts, phonodiscs, magnetic tapes, and motion pictures as well as books and uncollected poems and prose.)

CRITICAL AND BIOGRAPHICAL STUDIES

Fein, Richard. "Major American Poetry of World War II." Unpublished dissertation, New York University, 1960.

Lowell, Robert, Peter Taylor, and Robert Penn Warren, eds. *Randall Jarrell, 1914-1965.* New York: Farrar, Straus and Giroux, 1967. (Essays by Hannah Arendt, John Berryman, Elizabeth Bishop, Philip Booth, Cleanth Brooks, James Dickey, Denis Donoghue, Leslie A. Fiedler, Robert Fitzgerald, R. W. Flint, Alfred Kazin, Stanley Kunitz, Robert Lowell, William Meredith, Marianne Moore, Robert Phelps, Sister M. Bernetta Quinn, John Crowe Ransom, Adrienne Rich, Delmore Schwartz, Maurice Sendak, Karl Shapiro, Allen Tate, Eleanor Ross Taylor, Peter Taylor, P. L. Travers, Robert Watson, and Mrs. Randall Jarrell. Pages xi-xii list all of Jarrell's books, including editions in preparation, as of the volume's date of publication.)

Mazzaro, Jerome. "Between Two Worlds: The Post-Modernism of Randall Jarrell," *Salmagundi,* Fall 1971, pp. 93-113.

Rideout, Walter B. " 'To Change! to Change!' " in *Poets in Progress,* edited by Edward Hungerford. Evanston, Ill.: Northwestern University Press, 1967.

Rosenthal, M. L. *The Modern Poets: A Critical Introduction.* New York: Oxford University Press, 1960.

—*M. L. ROSENTHAL*

Sarah Orne Jewett

1849-1909

ANYONE from another part of the United States, anyone from another part of the world, who wants to understand New England might do well to begin with the stories of Sarah Orne Jewett. These subtle "sketches," as she called them, do not contain the whole of New England but they distill its essence. Here are the qualities which made New England great, which spread its influence across the continent, which had so much to do with the shaping of those midwesterners who, Miss Jewett herself thought, would be the typical Americans of the future.

Miss Jewett was an integral part of the society she described. Her father was a country doctor, her grandfather a sea captain and an owner of merchant ships. The Jewett family was important in the community of South Berwick, Maine. Among her relatives Sarah Jewett could study most of the New England traits she liked to dwell on: a sense of duty (writing she came to think was her duty), independence, courage, endurance, an enjoyment of work, an imperious conscience.

Her sketches set these qualities in many different lights though she does not deliberately begin with a characteristic and build her story on that. She starts with a character or a place and the virtue, sometimes not even named, appears along the way. In "The Hiltons' Holi-

day," for instance, "the magnitude of the plan for taking a whole day of pleasure confronted [John Hilton] seriously." Again, in "An Autumn Holiday" the narrator (Miss Jewett herself) makes an unexpected call on two elderly sisters and finds them walking back and forth at their spinning wheels. They insist on stopping so that they may talk more comfortably with their guest but each as she sits down takes up her knitting for "neither of them were ever known to be idle."

The humorous side of these serious virtues Miss Jewett often enjoyed pointing out and she was well aware also that they have their unlovely aspects. She does not dwell on these, or on the hidden passions in New England life, but she knew that they were there. When the title character of her *Country Doctor* tells a medical friend from the city a curious story about his ward's mother, the visitor exclaims, "I tell you, Leslie, that for intense, self-centred, smouldering volcanoes of humanity, New England cannot be matched the world over." Miss Jewett had often seen the volcanoes of which Robinson, Frost, O'Neill, and some of her other successors would write at length, but these were not the phenomena she wished to study.

What she did want to accomplish in her sketches she liked to explain by a dictum of

Plato's: that the best thing one can do for the people of a state is to make them acquainted with one another. She wrote her first book because she wanted to do this for her own state of Maine, to explain its natives to the summer visitors from other parts of the country who disturbed her by the way they misunderstood her neighbors. She did not like to hear people laugh at eccentricities which she knew were, more often than not, indications of admirable qualities. She found that she had the power to elucidate her neighbors and to make people like them; and doing this in writing she enjoyed. She understood her world more deeply than most of her contemporaries because her responses to it were more delicate and subtle. One is constantly struck by this as one reads her; what she sets down are not the observations of a reporter but impressions recollected in tranquillity. Her memory is very sure and strong for details of appearance, of voice, of manner. She may not have been able to trace back to its source each trait with which she built up a character but she knew that each was true.

With an equal fidelity she remembered vividly all sorts of sense impressions: the color of marsh rosemary—"the grey primness of the plant is made up from a hundred colors"; the quality of a song sparrow's note; the mingled scents of balsam, fir, and bayberry coming over salt water. Her sense of smell was particularly keen. She did not describe a landscape; she created it from remembered pieces so that many of her readers were sure they knew exactly which village or stretch of seacoast she had in mind—and were always wrong. It is this power of re-creating impressions which make Sarah Jewett something a little larger than a local colorist, which makes one want to read her for other reasons besides the desire to comprehend New England. Her Maine people are not simply authentic Down Easters; they are kin to people of other times and places. The funeral procession in *A Country Doctor* might have been "a company of Druid worshipers." Mrs. Hight in "A Dunnet Shepherdess" has "the features of a warlike Roman emperor. . . . Her scepter was a palm-leaf fan." In *The Country of the Pointed Firs,* which contains more of the essence of New England than any of her other books, one comes often on allusions of this kind. Mrs. Todd, the herbwoman, who is the narrator's guide to Dunnet Landing, is spoken of as a "huge sibyl," a caryatid, an "Antigone alone on the Theban plain." At the annual reunion of the Bowden family, the guests, as they walk from the dinner table to the church "ought to be carrying green branches and singing" as they went.

There was another idea Miss Jewett wanted her stories to demonstrate: the importance of the commonplace. She wanted to write about ordinary life as though she were writing history. "Écrire la vie ordinaire comme on écrit l'histoire." When she came on this maxim of Flaubert's she greeted it at once as a precise statement of what she was trying to do, copied it out, and pinned it over her writing desk. She took deep pleasure in the commonplaces of her own daily existence but she was discriminating in what she enjoyed and this taught her to distinguish in her writing between the significant and the merely precise detail, another point at which she differs from many of the local colorists.

One reason why Sarah Jewett was able to describe New England characteristics accurately was that she had many of them herself. Consider, for instance, the sense of duty, that trait so often puzzling to the outlander who calls it the New England conscience. There is a particularly effective presentation of this in "A Dunnet Shepherdess." The narrator—who comes from Boston to Dunnet Landing—meets Esther Hight, the shepherdess, and learns something of her history.

Esther has been in love for years with William Blackett, a fisherman who lives on one of the outer islands, but she cannot marry him because she must take care of her paralyzed mother. Mrs. Hight, a very energetic woman, had a stroke in middle life which left her almost helpless, except for her left hand. At about the same time her husband died, leaving her a rocky and heavily mortgaged farm. Esther, her only child, was sure that the best use that could be made of the land was sheep farming and set herself to find ways of making that profitable. Her neighbors in the high country above the Landing had been discouraged because so many of their sheep were killed by dogs, and Esther became convinced that what was needed was shepherding. Instead of leaving the sheep to shift for themselves in the stony pastures, she determined, hard though it might be, to watch over them by day and even on moonlight nights when the dogs were likely to roam about. She had physical as well as moral stamina and her sheep prospered. There was a good route to the Boston market for the wool, and her flocks became locally famous, so that sheep breeders paid well for her lambs. She worked off the mortgage on the farm and began to put money in the bank. The teller of the story learns these facts when William, the fisherman, takes her on a trout-fishing expedition into the high country, and she guesses at the romance though neither of the lovers mentions it.

While Esther and William spend a happy afternoon together the narrator has a long talk with the old mother, who puts the situation to her simply: "It has been stubborn work, day and night, summer and winter, an' now she's beginnin' to get along in years. . . . She's tended me 'long o' the sheep, an' she's been a good girl right along, but she ought to have been a teacher." This is the way a Maine woman talks of duty. Later there is a revelatory word from Esther herself, speaking to her visitor. " 'I hope you ain't goin' to feel too tired, mother's so deaf; no, I hope you won't be tired,' she said kindly, speaking as if she well knew what tiredness was."

A portrait of courage, endurance, and self-respect is "Going to Shrewsbury." This is chiefly a monologue by old Mrs. Peet who meets on the train a good friend she has not seen for a long while and details all her present circumstances and the reason for her journey. A hard-dealing nephew persuaded her husband, just before his death, to make over the farm to him in payment for a loan. Mrs. Peet will not stay there and be dependent on the hypocritical young man, so she is seeking asylum with some nieces in Shrewsbury, but she has no intention of being a burden on anyone. "I've got more work in me now than folks expects at my age." (She is seventy-six.) "I ain't goin' to sag on to nobody."

Another trait frequently puzzling to the outsider, especially if he comes from the South, is the New England capacity, even preference, for solitude. Misanthropy has nothing to do with this state of mind. Most of the solitaries like to mix with people and like to talk, but there are other things they value more, independence, the pleasure of being surrounded by their own possessions, freedom to order their lives and do things in their own way. Miss Jewett presents this effectively in "Aunt Cynthy Dallett."

The old widowed aunt lives on a steep hill, many miles above a seaport village. Her spinster niece lives in the village and so is not isolated like her aunt, though much of her daily life is spent without company. Each of them is lonely, but neither can quite bear to give up her independent way of life. Finally the niece agrees to come up the hill and spend the winter. "I'm beat by age at last," Aunt Cynthy says, "but I've had my own way for eighty-five years, come the month o' March."

Sarah Jewett herself never lived completely alone, but many of her greatest pleasures were solitary. She walked alone; she rode alone; she made boating excursions alone on the Piscataqua River. She has left records of many of these expeditions in her essays, and some of the stories have their source in an autobiographical journey. But for all her delight in solitude and admiration for many of those who practiced it, Sarah Jewett could sympathize with the opposite state of mind. She watched it with affectionate amusement among the Irish immigrants who were beginning to flock into Maine in large numbers. One of her Irish stories, "Bold Words at the Bridge," tells of two neighbors whose violent disagreements brought them almost to blows and who once became so angry with each other that for weeks they refused to speak. Finally they made up because neither of them could endure spending another day in silence.

Of the unhealthy extremes to which the endurance of solitude can go Miss Jewett was aware too. She tells, for instance, the story of "Poor Joanna," the recluse of Shell-heap Island. Joanna was crossed in love and came to believe that her anger with God over her cruel fate was an unpardonable sin. She was not fit, she felt, to live among men, so she rowed herself out to a small deserted island where her father had once built a little shack to use on fishing excursions. There for the rest of her life she lived quite alone, receiving only a very occasional visitor.

Worse than this, because of its effect on his family, is the cruelty of the solitary "King of Folly Island." While a young man, he quarreled so fiercely with his neighbors on political issues that he swore he would never again set foot on any land but his own. He bought an island far out in the bay and lived there alone with his wife and daughter. For twenty-six years he carried on his necessary business with his enemies, the John's Islanders, only by boat. His wife pined and died of loneliness and his daughter weakened with tuberculosis, but he would not take her to the mainland and she would not go without him.

Sarah Jewett's preparation for chronicling these people of Maine and their ways began, one might say, with her birth. That event took place on September 3, 1849, in South Berwick, Maine, a strategic little village for her purposes. It is situated on the Piscataqua River, one of those noble tidal rivers so characteristic of Maine which carry the sea inland for many miles. The Piscataqua forms the lower border between Maine and New Hampshire. Just below Berwick it is joined by the Salmon River and the two flow down, some twenty miles, to Portsmouth and the sea.

Berwick was settled in 1627 by Englishmen attracted by the Indians' great salmon fishery and by the fine water power. Above tidewater there is a long succession of falls. Gradually the village grew into an important shipbuilding center which flourished until the Civil War. After that the life of the community altered sharply. Manufacturing began to replace shipping. Factories were built by the falls, wool and cotton mills first, then a cannery. Irish and French-Canadians came in to work them and a new society began to grow up on the New England foundations. Sarah Jewett saw the whole transformation at intimate range. The old ways seemed to her better, and she wanted to record them as standards.

The house in which she was born and lived

for much of her childhood left a strong influence on her tastes. Her grandfather had purchased about 1820 the Haggens house, one of the finest in Berwick. It was built in 1774, admirably built by ship's carpenters. The rooms were well-proportioned, with some fine paneling. To carve the banisters and newel posts of the handsome staircase and the fluted columns of the arch in the hall had occupied, so the story ran, three men for one hundred days. Much of the furnishings Captain Jewett brought from England. There were Sheraton and Chippendale chairs and tables, Adam mirrors, Lowestoft china. Sarah Jewett grew up in contact with excellence.

The beneficent Providence which set her childhood in precisely the environment which would be of most use to her later, provided her with relatives who furnished the little girl with experiences peculiarly helpful to the future writer. Particularly important in this respect was Grandfather Jewett, the patriarch of the family, in whose house Sarah was born.

Theodore Furber Jewett ran away to sea when he was a boy and found that seamanship was his true vocation. He learned fast and at twenty-four became an able captain, a daring one, too. During the War of 1812 he tried to run a cargo to the Caribbean, was captured by the English and held prisoner for many months.

When he retired from the sea Captain Jewett turned shipowner and merchant—a very successful merchant who built up a substantial fortune to the comfort of his descendants and the benefit of American fiction. It was her share of Grandfather Jewett's legacy which enabled Sarah Jewett to write at leisure and as she pleased. The Captain was a fine teller of tales of adventure to which Sarah listened avidly. She knew all his ships and where they were bound on each voyage. She was full of excitement when one was coming up the river, and

when the ship's master came to dine and make his report to her grandfather she took care to be sitting in a quiet corner of the room. She gleaned in this way not only sea stories of all kinds but an intimate knowledge of sea terms and sea speech which her writer's memory registered unconsciously for future use. A general store which Captain Jewett opened in South Berwick provided the future storyteller with another rich mine of Maine speech. The farmers who brought down great logs for the shipyard liked to gather round the stove. They paid small attention to the little girl who sat listening quietly to their talk.

Her grandmother, the Captain's first wife, for whom she was named, Sarah knew only as a legend. The lovely Sarah Orne of Portsmouth married the Captain when she was eighteen, bore him two sons, and died in her twenty-fifth year. The grandmother little Sarah knew was the Captain's third wife, a solemn, formal person who disapproved of her granddaughter's manners. There were uncles and aunts, too, with strongly individual New England characters.

Sarah's maternal grandfather was also an influence, though he lived in Exeter, New Hampshire. Dr. William Perry had a high medical reputation and not a little fame as the inventor of a process for making starch from potatoes. Both he and his lively wife sent Sarah constant instruction on what books to read and made her report to them in letters her impressions and criticism.

Sarah's mother, daughter of the Exeter doctor, had, it would seem, that good New England gift called "faculty," which means that everything she turned her hand to she did well: her cakes were always light, her biscuits delicately browned, her rooms well swept and garnished with flowers from her own garden. She seems, too, to have had "faculty" as a mother:

her three daughters enjoyed her company and confided in her all through her life. She was well-educated and well-read. She taught her girls to enjoy reading aloud and gave them literary as well as domestic standards.

With her two sisters Sarah Jewett's relations were warm and close. Mary was her elder by two years, Caroline six years younger. Of Mary, Laura E. Richards has left, in her *Stepping Westward*, a pleasant portrait. Mary never married but was an indispensable power in her family and in the community. She was not only an excellent housekeeper but also an admirable manager of all the business affairs of the family and, in addition to that, knew so much about South Berwick and had such sound judgment in civic matters that the selectmen consulted her on all sorts of problems from the naming of a street to the purchase of fire-fighting apparatus. Sarah Jewett's *A White Heron*, published in 1886, is dedicated to "My dear sister Mary." To her younger sister, Caroline, Sarah Jewett dedicated in 1893 *A Native of Winby*. "I have had many pleasures," the inscription runs, "that were doubled because you shared them and so I write your name at the beginning of this book."

Another strong influence came into Sarah Jewett's life when she was twenty. At Wells she met Theophilus Parsons, emeritus professor of law at Harvard, who became at once a sustaining friend. As an ardent Swedenborgian he helped her own faith and for many years she poured out to him in letters her troubles and problems as well as her joys. He developed a deep affection for her and helped her in every way he could.

But the person whom Sarah Jewett loved best and whose influence on her was strongest was her father, the Captain's second son, Dr. Theodore Herman Jewett. Theodore Jewett graduated from Bowdoin, studied medicine in Exeter under Dr. Perry and at Jefferson Medical College in Philadelphia where he took his degree. When he had married Dr. Perry's daughter and was ready to establish a practice of his own, he would have preferred to live in some large city where he might keep in touch with the new developments in medicine which interested him greatly but, to please his father, he settled in Berwick and became a country doctor. He never regretted the decision. He enjoyed all phases of his work and performed them with extraordinary diligence and skill. He was tireless in his devotion to his patients, answering calls at any hour and in any weather and serving not only as physician but as psychiatrist, family counselor, and confidential friend. His intellectual interest in his profession never slackened; he taught obstetrics at Bowdoin, was president of the Maine Medical Association, wrote frequently for the medical journals, and often made journeys to Boston to talk with colleagues and inform himself on the newest practices in his art. His daughter's portrait of him in *A Country Doctor* may be accepted as accurate, quite without exaggeration.

Sarah's close friendship with her father was a happy product of her serious physical weakness, the arthritis which troubled her all through life. It was diagnosed then as rheumatism and one of the best remedies for it seemed to be fresh air. At any rate since the little girl began to droop whenever she was long indoors, Dr. Jewett encouraged her again and again to take a day off from school and drive about with him on his country visits. Nothing could have been better for her education than her observation of her father's proceedings and her long talks with that wise and compassionate man.

Not unnaturally Sarah came to think that she would like to be a doctor. She was convinced very early that she would never marry. She had all through her life many excellent male friends of all ages but there is no record of even the faintest shadow of a love affair. This state of mind was easily explained by the pre-Freudian nineteenth century. Miss Jewett's *Country Doctor* says of his ward while she is still quite young: "I see plainly that Nan is not the sort of girl who will be likely to marry. When a man or woman has that sort of self-dependence and unnatural self-reliance, it shows itself very early. I believe that it is a mistake for such a woman to marry . . . and if I make sure by and by, the law of her nature is that she must live alone and work alone, I shall help her to keep it instead of break it, by providing something else than the business of housekeeping and what is called a woman's natural work, for her activity and capacity to spend itself upon."

It seems quite safe to take this as an autobiographical statement. Sarah Jewett thought at first that she could best fulfill the law of her nature by following her father's profession. The obloquy sure to fall on any female who attempted to practice medicine she was quite ready to accept, but it soon became apparent to her that she did not have the physical stamina a doctor requires. She had such frequent bouts of illness that she could not be sure of meeting her patients' needs at any hour of the day or night as her father did. Her New England conscience instructed her that she must make herself of real use in the world, but it took her some time to realize that writing was what she was "meant" to do. For many years she thought of it merely as a pleasant avocation.

When she was still a small girl she began to put down on paper the things she was thinking about and the stories she continually told herself when she was alone. She wrote at first in verse because prose frightened her but gradually she found the cadences of prose "more and more enticing" and took that as her true medium.

It was her father, one might say, who really taught her to write, for it was he who taught her to see. As they drove together on his country visits he constantly called her attention to trees, to birds, to flowers, making her look at them until she was familiar with all their details and could thereafter identify them quickly. He made her study houses and people in the same way, and he convinced her that nothing in this world is uninteresting if you only look at it long enough. Little Sarah caught his enthusiasm and looked with interest all her life.

Sarah Jewett's first appearance in print was made in 1868 when she was eighteen. For *The Flag of Our Union*, published in Boston, she wrote a story called "Jenny Garrow's Lovers." This is a fervid melodrama, a form she never tried again. She composed next a simpler, more realistic tale which she sent boldly to the *Atlantic Monthly*. It was rejected but with so encouraging a letter from the editors that she tried again, and was again rejected. Her third attempt was successful. "Mr. Bruce," published in December 1869, is an amusing little story about a very pretty young girl who helps her mother out of an awkward social situation by masquerading as the second-maid and serving the dinner. Romantic complications ensue.

Encouraged by this success Sarah Jewett began to send a stream of stories and poems for children to the juvenile magazines, which printed them and asked for more. She contributed to *Our Young Folks, Merry's Museum, Riverside Magazine for Young People, St. Nicholas, The Independent*, which liked to present some reading for children, and, later, *The Youth's Companion*. In 1873 the *Atlantic* published the first of her Maine stories, "The Shore House," and Sarah Jewett began to feel that writing was her "duty." She kept at it steadily.

Her first book was published in 1877 when she was twenty-eight. It was William Dean Howells who suggested to Miss Jewett that she collect the Maine stories the *Atlantic* had published, rearrange and add to them, and issue them as a book. They were all set in Deephaven, a seaport town which, she was careful to explain in her preface, she had invented. Both Roberts Brothers and James R. Osgood and Company were ready to publish *Deephaven*. She decided finally on the Osgood firm, which was soon absorbed by the firm now known as Houghton Mifflin. They published most of her other books.

Deephaven does not have a plot in the usual sense of the term. It is a series of impressions of a little Maine coastal town and its inhabitants, as they are received by two lively girls in their early twenties who decide to spend the summer there because one of them has at her disposal the house of a great-aunt who has recently died. Miss Brandon was so much respected in Deephaven that everyone welcomes her niece as an old friend. It seems to the young people that the society and way of life of the town are just what they were fifty years ago when it ceased to be an important seaport, but they find this a good way of life, full of interest and devoted to high standards.

The niece's friend, who tells the story, describes first "The Brandon House" (which resembles in many ways the Jewett house in Berwick), its furnishings, its treasures, its memories. Then she gives accounts of the various kinds of people she and her friend come to know in the town: "My Lady Brandon and the Widow Jim," "Deephaven Society," "The Captains." The sketches present individuals of different types and the girls' relations with them. We listen to their conversation and hear the stories they tell, ranging from the history of their neighbors to adventures at sea, to tales of second sight. There are Miss Brandon's aristocratic friends; there are old sailors—each must be addressed as Captain; there are fishermen; there are housewives of various degrees of social importance. The men are full of wisdom

and salty talk, but they tend to blur a little into one another. The women are more distinctive. There is the lady of the old school, Miss Honora. There is the Widow Jim who has "an uncommon facility of speech" but has endured, courageously, hard years with a drunken husband and is known as "a willin' woman," always respected. There is Mrs. Bonny who comes down from the hills in the summertime riding on her rough-coated old horse with bags and baskets of "rosbries" tied to the saddle. There is old Miss Chauncey, her mind so dim that she thinks herself still rich and elegant as she lives in her denuded, neglected old house, sustained by the charity of her neighbors. There is Mrs. Kew, the lighthouse keeper's wife, with a fine original gift of wit and speech.

There are lively accounts, too, of "Cunner-Fishing," of sailing and cross-country walking, of going to church, attending a lecture, driving to "The Circus at Denby" where the girls hear an illuminating conversation between the Kentucky Giantess and the lighthouse keeper's wife, who had gone to school together.

There seems to be no particular order in the telling of events or in the presentation of characters—that was an art Miss Jewett learned much later—but the young women's enthusiasm for their new friends and new experiences is refreshing and contagious. The tempo and tone of the town become very clear.

The device by which she held these people and events together Miss Jewett was to use again and again. It bears some resemblance, though it is less subtle, to Henry James's central intelligence. A visitor—usually a woman—from Boston or some other part of the outside world comes to Maine and settles for a time in Deephaven, or Grafton, or Dunnet Landing. She meets the most interesting inhabitants of the village, learns their histories, and often makes them into friends. She delights in the old houses she visits and is captivated by the beauty of the austere fields, woods, and sea, so that she presents both narrative and background.

In *Deephaven*, unfortunately, the actual narrator, who is fairly self-effacing, is concerned not only to tell her stories but to make us love her companion, Kate, and admire the way in which she endears herself to different types of people. This puts, from time to time, more emphasis on the double central intelligence than is good for it, but the device of an observer slightly detached but interested is admirable. The weakness is that this central intelligence cannot really function alone; too many of the episodes to be related occurred long before her arrival. It becomes necessary to add an assistant intelligence, an older relative or some long-time resident of the community who knows all the history and legend and can impart them to an eager newcomer.

As a variant on the summer visitor Miss Jewett liked to send back to Maine someone who had roots there but had not lived in the state for a long time. Important among these is the "Native of Winby," now senator from Kansota, who makes a surprise visit to his old school and then to an elderly widow whom he might once have married.

Nineteen years later, when she was writing *The Country of the Pointed Firs* (1896), Miss Jewett was using her visitor device with real skill. The intelligence there is a woman from Boston who has settled in Dunnet Landing as a quiet place to write during the summer. Her response to the people and the stories she encounters is swift and warm but this is not insisted on, as it is in *Deephaven*; it is only implied, so that she does not intrude upon the tale she is telling. Involvement and detachment are beautifully balanced. The assistant narrator, the local herbwoman, is the most interesting of all the narrator assistants, one of the best characters, in fact, Miss Jewett ever drew.

Another literary instrument for which she was to be much admired Miss Jewett used first in *Deephaven*: her accurate and effective employment of Maine speech. Her ear and her memory had been recording it unconsciously ever since she was a little girl and when she came to reproduce it on the printed page she devised a simple method of presenting it to the reader without the cumbersome misspellings so frequently resorted to by the local colorists, even sometimes by a writer as accomplished as Harriet Beecher Stowe.

Miss Jewett's chief tool is the apostrophe, to indicate a dropped final *g* (goin'), or a blurred *a* (same's I always do), or the pronunciation of a word like v'y'ge. She uses it, too, to indicate the shortened vowel sound so characteristic of Maine: co't, bo't, flo't. In addition to this she has a rich knowledge of characteristic words and phrases, some of them very old: "They beseeched me after supper till I let 'em go;" "bespoke;" "master hard;" "master pretty;" "a power of china;" "I'd rather tough it out alone;" "There she goes now, do let's pray her by;" "It allays creeps me cold all over;" "You're gettin' to be as lean as a meetin'-house fly."

One is impressed often by the subtle variation her dialect presents, differences in education and culture, between the young and the very old, between men and women. Sometimes Miss Jewett remarks on the relative social position of two characters she is presenting and this distinction within democracy is reflected by differences in speech.

In the handful of Irish stories the language is not nearly so convincing. Miss Jewett had heard the brogue all her life, chiefly from family servants, but she did not think in it or even, apparently, take an interest in it. As she sets it down it seems correct enough but contrived, not overheard. She records it with a fair amount of restraint but it seems always a little thicker than it ought to be, as though the personages were moving on a stage, not along a country road.

With the occasional French-Canadian characters at whom she tried her hand she is very timid. The Canadians were beginning to come across the border into Maine but not yet to settle, simply to make some money and go home, so that they were not a real part of state life. Of French-Canadian villages Miss Jewett knew something, for she made several trips to Quebec and observed with all her good curiosity the St. Laurent countryside and community life so different from the American. But she did not know it, of course, and what she writes is tentative and generalized. In "Little French Mary," a very slight sketch of a six-year-old daughter of French-Canadians whose pretty affectionate ways charm the old men who sit about the post-office stove in a Maine village, the child has French manners and features but she speaks scarcely two sentences. In "Mère Pochette," set in a French-Canadian village, there is very little dialogue though a good deal of direct report of the dominant character's thinking. The phraseology falls too often into the tiresome form of English translation of the French idiom: "She will be incapable . . . to bring up an infant of no gifts." The story is an uninteresting one, anyway, of a grandmother who finally repents her mistake in breaking up a true love affair.

These dialects never became a serious problem, for Miss Jewett wrote only a few stories about the Irish and the Canadians. What mattered in *Deephaven* and in the later stories was the Maine speech, and her use of that, as I have said, delighted both her readers and the editors who were interested in her literary development. The three particularly concerned to help her were Horace Scudder, at that time editor of the *Riverside*, Howells, the novelist-editor, and Thomas Bailey Aldrich, poet, story writer, and editor of the *Atlantic*, who gave her all the guidance and assistance they could. She asked them many questions and listened with respect to their advice though she did not always follow it. She was quite accurately aware of her own abilities and limitations. One of the points on which she differed with her advisers most strongly was the matter of plot. They urged her to enlarge her sketches to something more nearly resembling the currently popular magazine story and she knew that at that kind of invention she had no skill at all. "I have no dramatic talent," she wrote to Scudder in 1873. "It seems to me I can furnish the theater, and show you the actors and the scenery, but there never is any play." When she tried to make a "play" the result was either sentimental or melodramatic. She contrived sudden inheritances, unfaithful lovers, missing young men who return suddenly rich, wayward daughters who come home to die. There are even thieves and drunkards.

Yet sometimes a preposterous situation produces a convincing story. In "A Lost Lover" all the town of Longfield knows that Miss Horatia had a lover who was lost at sea. The young cousin who comes to visit her one summer is full of curiosity about the romance but Miss Horatia is thoroughly reserved and only a few facts are to be gleaned from Melissa, the devoted family servant. The affair, if it was a real love affair, took place very rapidly many years before when Miss Horatia was on a visit to Salem. The young man went off to sea and his ship was never heard from again.

One morning during the young cousin's visit a tramp comes by asking for food. While he eats he talks freely with Miss Horatia about himself, his bad luck, shipwrecks, craving for drink, and general discouragement. He does not recognize her but she gradually becomes aware who he is. When he leaves she faints, but tells her cousin it is the heat. "God forgive him," she says to herself and takes up her lonely life again.

"A Lost Lover" is an exception. The components of a Jewett story are usually much simpler. The incidents evolve perhaps from two characters in conversation or from a character in relation to an old house or a community. A typical plot is "Miss Tempy's Watchers," in which two elderly women keep the traditional guard, the night before the funeral, over the body of a mutual friend. They install themselves in the kitchen, work at their knitting, and talk about Miss Tempy, to whom both of them had been devoted. The circumstances make them speak more openly than they normally would. Nothing happens, but from the conversation emerge three definite and interesting New England characters and some illuminating information on the qualities of generosity and "closeness."

This construction from everyday materials makes the Jewett stories seem more durable than the, in many ways comparable, tales of Mary E. Wilkins Freeman and Rose Terry Cooke. The plots these writers contrive are ingeniously interesting or amusing, but the joints of their manufacture are too often evident. They are made; they do not grow. Miss Jewett's plots seem inevitable, not something she has invented but something she has seen or overheard or been told of by a friend. It is because she had to manufacture the plots of her Irish and French-Canadian stories that they lack the authenticity of her tales of Maine.

The way in which her Maine stories seemed to grow of themselves never ceased to astonish her. "What a wonderful kind of chemistry it is," she wrote to her close friend Mrs. James T. Fields, "that evolves all the details of a story and writes them presently in one flash of time! For two weeks I have been noticing a certain string of things and having hints of character, etc., and day before yesterday the plan of the story comes into my mind, and in half an hour I have put all the little words and ways into their places and can read it off to myself like print. Who does it? for I grow more and more sure that I don't!"

Her plan of work was to devote her mornings to her large correspondence. She believed firmly that friendships, literary and personal, must be nourished by letters, and friendships were an important element in her life. The afternoons were given to the stories. She wrote swiftly and easily, turning out usually two thousand words in an afternoon, sometimes as many as six or seven thousand. A story took form rapidly, but after it had got itself down on paper there was still much work to be done. Almost always the first draft was too long; there was an unnecessary amount of detail. She was, as she wrote Scudder, "disposed to longwindedness," but as the years went by she became adept at cutting. It was her French ancestry, she told Mrs. Fields, which made her "nibble all round her stories like a mouse. They used to be as long as yardsticks, they are now as long as spools, and they will soon be the size of old-fashioned peppermints, and have neither beginning or end, but shape and flavor may still be left them." After the cutting Miss Jewett tried to tone down exuberances and push sentimentalities out of sight and, like her admired Flaubert, she labored to find the precise word for every effect she wanted to produce.

The success of *Deephaven* attracted the attention of editors, so that soon Miss Jewett was contributing not only to the *Atlantic* but to a number of other magazines, notably *Harper's* and the *Independent*. Her publisher, too, was encouraged to make a collection of her children's stories, *Play Days* (1878), and then began to bring out every few years a volume of selections from her most recent magazine stories. The first of these, *Old Friends and New* (1879), includes "A Lost Lover." Then came *Country By-Ways* (1881) which contains, in addition to stories, several long informal essays. In this genre, which so delighted the nineteenth century and is almost unknown today, Miss Jewett enjoyed working. It gave her opportunity for descriptions of nature, for comment on society and manners, for bits of history and legend, for sketches of good Maine characters. The connecting thread might be as slight as she wished, a horseback ride, a walk, a row on the Piscataqua River, but whatever she treats she treats with skill. What the modern reader enjoys is the vivid picture she gives him of a countryside and a community quite different, probably, from any thing he has ever lived in but unquestionably authentically described. The disadvantage of the form, so far as Sarah Jewett is concerned, was the temptation it offered to indulge two of her weaknesses: sentimentality and overuse of the pathetic fallacy.

No female writer of the nineteenth century could wholly escape the impulse to sentimentalize, but Sarah Jewett, as she grew more mature and more skillful, learned to subdue her sentimentalism effectively. Her overindulgence in the pathetic fallacy was a more personal matter. "The oaks and maples dress themselves as they please, as if they were tired of wearing plain green, like everybody else." The cardinal flowers "keep royal state in the shade, and one imagines that the other flowers and all the weeds at the water's edge take care to bow to them as often as the wind comes by." She wrote that way because trees and flowers and bushes were to her not types and specimens but individual friends. She looked at them as she looked at people. She speaks, for instance, of a row of poplars which she always thought of as cousins.

Country By-Ways is dedicated to "My dear father; my dear friend; the best and wisest man I ever knew." Dr. Jewett had died in 1878 at the age of sixty-three. His heart had been troubling him for a long time but the fatal attack came suddenly and unexpectedly. This was the greatest sorrow Sarah Jewett was ever to know. It was a loss she never ceased to mourn, but she was destined, fortunately for her work, to enjoy all through her life the serenity which comes from constant intercourse with a perfectly sympathetic companion. Only a few years after her father's death her horizons were widened and her knowledge increased by her deepening friendship with Mrs. Fields.

Annie Adams at nineteen had married James Fields, seventeen years her senior and already a prominent member of the firm which would later bear his name, Ticknor and Fields. The marriage was a happy one for American letters; Annie Fields had not only beauty and charm but distinguished gifts as a hostess. Number 148 Charles Street, the Fields's Boston home, began at once to flourish as a kind of informal salon, supplemented by the cottage at Manchester-by-the-Sea where they spent their summers. Longfellow, Emerson, Hawthorne, Lowell, Holmes were close friends, but the Fields's circle was by no means exclusively literary. It included painters, actors, musicians, and men in public life. Many of those who enjoyed the Fields's hospitality have set down their impressions of the rich combination of material comforts with good talk.

Fields, who started as an office boy in a Boston bookstore, had risen swiftly to power in the book publishing world. In addition to that, from 1861 to 1870, he edited the *Atlantic Monthly* so that he knew, and knew well, most of the established and the rising literary figures of the day in the United States, in England, and in France. The life in the Charles Street house was a full and happy one until Fields's death in 1881.

Not long after she was left alone Mrs. Fields invited Sarah Jewett to make her an extended visit. Miss Jewett was her junior by fifteen years but they had many tastes and sympathies in common and had already laid the basis for an excellent relationship. Now each found in the other the consolation and companionship she needed and their friendship became rich and sustaining.

Before long it was established that Miss Jewett would spend about three months with Mrs. Fields each winter in the Charles Street house and three in the summer cottage at Manchester, going back to Berwick in between. This kept her in touch with her family and with her country and gave her longer stretches for writing than could be managed in the busy life of Boston. She and Mrs. Fields were assiduous attendants at lectures, plays, and concerts, and Mrs. Fields was a pioneer in Boston charitable work in which Miss Jewett often shared. They liked so much to exchange impressions on everything they read or did that when they were separated they wrote each other little journal notes almost daily. Many of these, included in Mrs. Fields's edition of Miss Jewett's letters, are interesting and illuminating.

The literary hospitality of Charles Street and Manchester continued as in James Fields's lifetime. There were the regular Saturday Afternoons in Boston to which a dozen or so old friends always came as well as new or visiting luminaries. There were small informal lunches and dinners with such friends and neighbors as Dr. Oliver Wendell Holmes, the Lowells, the Aldriches. There were many guests in the seaside cottage.

Mrs. Fields's friends found Miss Jewett a happy addition to the Charles Street circle. She had grown into a distinguished-looking young woman, tall and well proportioned, with features many people described as beautiful. Elegance is another word which was often applied to her, and Mrs. Fields spoke of her "sweet dignity." Sometimes on first sight people thought her formidable but, as she once said, "I seem impressive but actually I only come up to my own shoulder." One was conscious of a point of reserve but she was always straightforward and friendly. She read widely, and her opinions about what she read were fresh and interesting.

The division of time between Boston and Berwick was an excellent arrangement for a writer. Sarah Jewett was able to nibble at and perfect her work to her heart's content because she worked under almost ideal conditions. Few women writers in the nineteenth century found themselves in a comparable situation. She did not need to write for money, so the only pressures to hurry or to do too much came from admiring editors who wanted more of her stories. She had no domestic responsibilities. In Boston and Manchester Mrs. Fields had plenty of servants and was accustomed, of course, to direct the household. In Berwick sister Mary did the housekeeping. Sarah was an enthusiastic gardener, she assumed certain household tasks, and she shared for years in the care of her invalid mother, but none of this was very difficult or confining. She could spend, if she liked, the better part of the day at her desk. In neither Boston nor Berwick were there children to disrupt the household. One thinks of Mrs. Stowe, as her son describes her, sitting at the kitchen table trying to dictate to a friend a romantic dialogue for her next installment while she alternately tells a new cook how to season the baked beans and tries to still the clamor of her youngest offspring.

That Mrs. Fields was also engaged in literary work, journals, biographical sketches, and the editing of letters, was an incentive to mutual labor and criticism. Sarah Jewett could write as she wanted to, when she wanted to, and between the bouts of work there was stimulating companionship, good talk, reading aloud, and travel.

In 1882 she made her first trip to Europe, with Mrs. Fields. There was another two years later and two more after that. Their routes were for the most part the conventional ones in England, France, and Italy, but they were both enthusiastic travelers and made other excursions—into Ireland, Norway, and even Turkey and Greece. What they enjoyed most were the visits to literary friends, old and new. Most exciting of all these were two to Tennyson, whom Sarah Jewett thought the greatest man she ever had the privilege of meeting. They both took great pleasure also in the Arnolds and the Du Mauriers, in a day with Kipling at Rottingdean and one with Henry James at Rye. Kipling thought Miss Jewett's pictures of New England landscape and New England people corresponded precisely with his own impressions gained in Vermont. James delighted Mrs. Fields by his warm admiration for Miss Jewett's writing.

In the Western hemisphere the two friends did some pioneering in places which have since become standard ground for tourists. They found St. Augustine a delightful town in which to spend part of the winter, and in 1896 they joined the Aldriches for a cruise on a friend's yacht in the Caribbean.

The influence of her travel on Miss Jewett's thinking was strong. "You must know the world before you can know the village," she said once to Willa Cather and one is conscious again and again of the light this wider knowledge shed on her view of Maine, but she never attempted a travel book and only occasionally a story without a New England background. There is one not very interesting tale set in St. Augustine, where the local details are carefully accurate, and there are a few unconvincing attempts at pictures of Virginia after the Civil War, too imaginary to be effective. Miss Jewett wrote letters, of course, to friends while she was traveling but, except for some references to people, they are not particularly interesting. Her first impressions of a scene were never so good as those which came after she had thought about it at length.

With her routine thus established Miss Jewett worked happily and well and volumes of collected stories appeared steadily. Eventually there were twelve of them. After the fourth, *The Mate of the Daylight* (1884), she attempted her first novel. She did not suppose that she had developed any skill in plotting but she wanted to make a portrait of her father and the sketch did not give her scope enough. The portrait is interesting and fairly successful; the story is not.

The family setting invented for Dr. Leslie in *A Country Doctor* (1884) is quite different from Dr. Jewett's—Dr. Leslie is a lonely widower, cared for by a faithful servant—but otherwise Sarah Jewett makes him as like her father as she can. We see him comparing experiences with a much-traveled professional friend, with a charming aged lady he has known from childhood, with patients who desperately need his sympathy and his encouragement as well as his skill, and with others who simply enjoy the importance of being sick. His compassion, adaptability, and quick wit in handling a situation are attractive. His young ward has much the same relation to him that Sarah had to her father but Nan is not an attempt at a self-portrait though she expresses many of Miss Jewett's ideas.

Te novel is not well-proportioned. The first half, which pictures Nan's early life in the village of Oldfields, is much longer than it needs to be, though it is the best part of the book with its skillful Jewett sketches of country friends and neighbors. There is some of the charm of the later *Country of the Pointed Firs*. The real plot, the choice the heroine makes between marriage and a medical career, at a time when few people thought it possible to combine the two, has the substance for a good novel of the day but the conflict is never made sharp enough to be exciting. Nan realizes very early that she is not the sort of woman intended for matrimony (Sarah Jewett states her own case here, as we have seen) and the young man who would like to dissuade her is too pale a character to seem much of a loss. Other difficulties are not strong enough to be very interesting.

The possibilities she neglected here indicate quite clearly that, though she had vigorous and sometimes radical opinions, Sarah Jewett was not a reformer or a propagandist. She did not want her writing to plead a cause but to explore the relationship between an individual and the life in which he found himself. She did believe, in advance of her time, that a woman had as much right as a man to follow a true vocation but she did not expound this theory often. Her own situation was simple enough, for fiction writing, kept within reasonable limits, was a perfectly proper female occupation.

It was its theme as well as its picture of New England life which made *A Country Doctor* the first of Miss Jewett's books to attract attention abroad. The *Revue des Deux Mondes* (February 1, 1885) published a long review-article by Mme. Thérèse Blanc-Bentzon (she signed herself Th. Bentzon). She thought the book gave, as it does, an excellent picture of New England family life, and one of her special concerns was the interpretation of American life to the French. Later, in 1893, she published, with a long preface, a translation of the novel and of nine of Miss Jewett's stories. The correspondence which grew up between them led to a genuine friendship and each eventu-

ally had the pleasure of visiting the other in her home.

Immediately after *A Country Doctor* Miss Jewett tried another novel, *A Marsh Island* (1885). Its proportion and structure are much better than the first novel's, and it moves along quite smoothly, but neither the story nor the characters are very interesting. The plot is trite. A well-to-do dilettante landscape painter boards for part of the summer at the marsh island farm. He almost falls in love with the farmer's daughter and enjoys imagining how she would blossom in a richer cultural environment. He almost alienates her from her real lover, a fine metalworker-farmer, whose jealousy is aroused by Doris' interest in the painter. The situation is saved when Doris hears at the last moment that Dan, in his unhappiness, has signed on for a long voyage. She makes a dangerous trip across the marshes in the early morning before the ship leaves to assure him of her true feelings. He does not sail and marries her soon after.

The best thing about the novel is its picture of the marsh island farm, isolated and quite different from the others in the neighborhood. The farmer and his wife are estimable hard-working people whom the young painter grows to like and admire but they have little of the savor Miss Jewett usually manages to get into her secondary characters. The contrast between the marsh people and the painter's rich relatives, who are spending the summer farther along the coast, has comparatively little force.

Sarah Jewett's only other attempt at a novel was made sixteen years later under the urging of Charles Dudley Warner, the essayist-novelist, who was at that time editing the Hartford *Courant*. He was eager to have her try a story of Berwick in the days of the Revolution and the idea fascinated her because she always wanted to know more about her community's past. As a little girl she had liked to visit the elderly Miss Cushing whose mother had entertained Lafayette and she knew that John Paul Jones had enlisted many Berwick men in the crew of the *Revenge. The Tory Lover* (1901), she said, was the hardest year's work she ever did and the year's work she enjoyed most.

The *Atlantic* ran the novel in serial form before its publication as a book and many people liked it despite its faults. The rather violent action—fighting, imprisonments, escapes—was quite beyond Miss Jewett's scope nor was she successful in her attempt to present the complex character of Jones, but the book has two virtues which have not been sufficiently noticed: the talk of the sailors, which Miss Jewett made, probably quite correctly, like the talk of the seafaring men she knew; and the hero, the most lively and attractive young man she ever drew. She sympathized with the conservatism which attached him to the mother country— he enlists with Jones finally to please his lady love—and the exposition of his Tory inclinations is unusual and interesting. The novel was translated not only into French but into Italian and Spanish as well.

The novels and the hundred or so sketches —her own term is perhaps the best for them— are the most important part of Sarah Jewett's thirty years of literary labor, particularly the sketches, about seventy of which were reprinted in the collections issued during her lifetime. Interspersed among these were many stories and poems for children and two agreeable books for girls, *Betty Leicester* (1890) and *Betty Leicester's Christmas* (1899). The stories for the very young would probably still amuse the very young of today, but Betty Leicester is too unsophisticated for the modern schoolgirl and the moral sentiments in the book are too pointed.

Miss Jewett undertook also, for a series Putnam was publishing for young people, *The Story of the Normans* (1887). She enjoyed the reading she had to do and was apparently unaware how little experience she had in the organization of historical material. There are interesting bits and pieces, but it is not a successful book.

Both the juvenile and the adult magazines were happy to print Miss Jewett's verse. She never thought of herself as a poet but sometimes she liked to express ideas in verse rather than through a fictional personality. Most of the adult poems are concerned with the relation of the individual to nature or with some phase of death. In "Top of the Hill," for instance, she is rejoicing in an autumn landscape, observing with pleasure the kind of detail most people would overlook.

> The hedge-rows wear a veil
>   Of glistening spider threads,
> And in the trees along the brook
> The clematis, like whiffs of smoke,
>   Its faded garland spreads.

The rhymes for children were numerous, but not more than a score of adult poems appeared in print during her lifetime. There were others which she sent in letters to her friends. Mrs. Fields, for instance, received one day a sonnet about a busy, noisy section of Boston where

> I met great Emerson, serene, remote,
> Like one adventuring on seas of thought.

Some years after Miss Jewett's death M. A. De Wolfe Howe arranged a collection of her *Verses* (1916) which were "printed for her friends" by the Merrymount Press in Boston. There are nineteen poems in all here, a few intended for the young, most of the others collected from the *Atlantic, Harper's,* and other journals which had originally printed them. There are also a few which had never been published, notably two on the death of her father, who had taught her to look at the world.

And I must watch the spring this year,
alone.

But it was at the perfection of her prose that Sarah Jewett really labored. Some of the devices by which she taught herself to write more effectively we can deduce from her letters to young aspirants who asked her for guidance. If they seemed serious in their work she was generously helpful. "I think," ran one dictum, "we must know what good work is, before we can do good work of our own," and she suggested reading half a dozen really good stories over and over to see *why* they are good. This she did frequently herself, studying with admiration Tolstoi and Turgenev as well as the more usual French and British models. She advised also that if an idea comes into a writer's mind he should try it, see what he can do with it and if it has any value. But chiefly she insisted that "the only way is to keep at work," and this she herself consistently did.

In the successive collections of her stories it is interesting to see how often she improves a later handling of a certain type of subject. One thing she learned, for instance, was that the more she omitted comments of her own and let the humor or poignance of a situation be presented by one of the actors in the story, the more surely she achieved the effect she wanted. There are some good examples of this among the humorous stories.

One of these particularly enjoyed by her readers is "The Dulham Ladies" (*Atlantic*, April 1886), which has probably been more often reprinted in anthologies than anything else she ever wrote. This is a simple incident concerned with gentility, a quality important to the nineteenth century. Two aging sisters, the Miss Dobins (with one *b*), are unable to realize how much times have changed in their village. They suppose themselves still leaders in the community as they were in the days of

their minister father. They become aware, one day, that with the years their hair has become very thin and they decide that it is their duty to society to supplement it with false fronts. Those imposed upon them by an amused salesman give them great pride and comfort. The idea that they might be ridiculous never occurs to them.

The two old ladies with their high intentions and innocent inability to comprehend reality are full of charm, and their mistakes and miscalculations are really amusing, but the story is somewhat less effective than it might be because the author is too obviously present pointing out the humor of their errors.

About two years after this, Miss Jewett, with admirable effect, tried letting the protagonist of a long story tell the major part of it. "Law Lane" (*Scribners*, December 1887) has perhaps the neatest plot she ever succeeded in making. It is a story of neighboring families who have carried on a feud through several generations over a certain strip of property. (New England feuds are less likely to explode into physical violence than those of the West and South but they can be full of stubbornness and venom.) A Romeo and Juliet love springs up between a son and daughter of the present generation which is finally brought to a happy conclusion by the principal teller of the tale, Mrs. Harriet Powder. She is a famous nurse and is called in to help when the boy's mother has a dangerous fall in her cellar. The shock is so great that the patient is sure she is going to die, a notion which Mrs. Powder skillfully encourages until the suffering woman has remorsefully repented of the long quarrel and forgiven everybody—her neighbors and her son. Both sides are thankful to have the feud over and have no suspicions concerning Mrs. Powder, whose lively speech makes the story of her intrigue thoroughly entertaining.

Six years after "Law Lane" Miss Jewett

tried another device which worked even better. She is telling a story which, like "The Dulham Ladies," is about two elderly women. She lets them make the humorous nature of their situation clear as they talk to one another. "The Guests of Mrs. Timms" (*Century*, February 1894) have met, at a church conference, an old acquaintance who is so friendly and hospitable in pressing them to spend a day with her soon that they decide to go the next week. But they discover, after the long bus ride, that they are neither expected nor wanted, as their hostess makes politely clear by her formal reception, taking it for granted that they have come to town on other business and are merely making her a morning call.

In the stories of autumn courtships which Miss Jewett liked to write there are some significant advances from sentimentality to humor and even irony. In one particularly successful story she carries the romantic sentiments of maturity further still. "The Only Rose" (*Atlantic*, January 1894) is one of the best stories Sarah Jewett wrote. It describes not the humor or the volcanoes under the New England crust but some of the buried romance and sentiment which seldom gets put into words.

Mrs. Bickford, presented by a gardening sister with a great mass of flowers, decides to make them into three "bo'quets" to place on the graves of her three husbands. She would go by the cemetery tomorrow when her favorite nephew comes to drive her over to spend the day with his family. An early flowering plant of her own has just produced a single rose and her great moral problem is to which of the three bouquets it should be added. To a neighbor so self-effacing that talking to her is like thinking aloud, she details the characteristics of the three men, trying, like a good New Englander, to do them each justice. To her last husband, Mr. B, she is grateful for leaving her so comfortably provided for, but he "done everything by rule an' measure" and he "used 'most always to sleep in the evenin's." With Mr. Wallis, her second husband, living was often precarious because he was an unsuccessful inventor. He had all sorts of ingenious ideas which he never managed to bring to practical shape, but he was a fluent talker and "splendid company for winter evenings." Albert she had married when they were both very young, but "we was dreadful happy." Even overnight Mrs. Bickford cannot solve her problem.

It was settled for her the next day by the nephew who carried the bouquets up the steep hillside and placed them on the graves. Suddenly Mrs. Bickford's heart felt lighter. "I know," she said to herself, "who I do hope's got the right one." The boy comes back with the red rose in his buttonhole. This fell out, he says, "an' I kept it. . . . I can give it to Lizzie." He has been telling his aunt of his engagement. "My first husband was just such a tall, straight young man as you be," she says to him. "The flower he first give me was a rose."

With the far more difficult problem of handling a subject somewhat beyond the confines of everyday life Sarah Jewett tried many interesting experiments. Not all of them are successful, but it is fascinating to watch how her skill increased as she made one trial after another, as she matured and her literary ability improved.

One of the early attempts in this kind, "The Landscape Chamber" (*Atlantic*, November 1887), suggests more definitely than anything else she wrote a desire to do something in the manner of Hawthorne. It is the story of a curse.

The narrator is refreshing herself after a tiresome summer by a long horseback journey into country she has never visited before. One afternoon her horse is lamed by a small accident and she asks for lodging at a lonely, handsome, old house which seems to be disintegrating from poverty and neglect. The inhabitants are an aging father, whose manner suggests that he is a miser, and a pathetically agreeing daughter who accepts his penuriousness but covers it a little with immaculate housekeeping and a lovingly tended flower bed. Both seem solitary and without hope but rouse the narrator's interest and compassion. The father finally tells her of the curse which fell upon the family when an ancestor sold his soul for wealth. Since that day "we cannot part with what we have, even for common comfort."

Using the bright autumn landscape as contrast Miss Jewett succeeds in conveying the air of mystery and doom about the old house and its inhabitants. She weakens her effect somewhat by having the narrator admit that she thinks the father "not quite sane," but the daughter's last words restore the tone: "I think we shall all disappear some night in a winter storm, and the world will be rid of us,—father and the house and I, all three."

Far more complex and difficult was the problem Sarah Jewett posed for herself in "A White Heron" (1886). This is a story for which she herself cared greatly but which the *Atlantic* refused to print. The editor's reason, one supposes, was that though it has passages of excellent writing, the story as a whole—this happened rarely with Miss Jewett—is better than the telling of it.

"A White Heron" is one of the earliest conservation stories, but it is conservation based not on practical twentieth-century arguments but on the sense of a mystical kinship between Man and Nature, a kinship which Miss Jewett felt very strongly herself. The heroine of the story is a lonely little girl who lives with her grandmother on an isolated farm. Having no other playmates she has made friends with all sorts of birds and small animals.

A handsome young ornithologist, hunting in the woods, spends a few days with them and Sylvy takes a romantic delight in his company despite his shooting of her bird friends. He wants especially to find a great white heron. Sylvy thinks she knows where his nest is. She gets up very early one morning, takes a long walk, and makes a difficult and dangerous climb of a tall pine tree from which she can see the sun rising over the glistening sea. Then from the marsh far below a great white heron "like a single floating feather comes up from the dead hemlock and grows larger, and rises, and comes close at last, and goes by the landmark pine with steady sweep of wing and outstretched slender neck and crested head." Sylvy feels that she has shared with him the experience of that wonderful sunrise.

Soberly she makes her way home, her young mind struggling with ideas and emotions she has never experienced before. The handsome young man says that he must leave that afternoon but Sylvy cannot tell him what she has discovered, she cannot violate her mystic moment of communion with the great white bird and bring him to his death. Miss Jewett when she tries to express these emotions finds herself bereft of her usual quiet skill. She uses the false self-conscious rhetoric all too common among her contemporaries. She even resorts to that disastrous device of addressing her character directly: "And wait! wait! do not move a foot or a finger, little girl, do not send an arrow of light and consciousness from your two eager eyes, for the heron has perched on a pine bough not far beyond yours."

Fifteen years later Sarah Jewett was handling a not dissimilar theme with simplicity and skill. This time it is a matter of communication with the dead, a possibility in which she firmly believed. Her faith in personal immortality was sure. She was certain, too, that the souls of the departed watch over those they have loved on earth. The story of "The Foreigner" (*Atlantic*, August 1900) is told by Mrs. Almira Todd, the herbwoman of Dunnet Landing who is the chief character in *The Country of the Pointed Firs.*

When Cap'n Tolland brought home from the West Indies a young French wife who found it difficult to adapt to New England ways, Almira Todd, then a young woman, was one of the few in the village who tried to be a friend to her. When the Captain was lost at sea the poor little wife sank into a decline and Mrs. Todd helped to nurse and sustain her through her last days. Not long before her death her dead mother appears to her. "All of a sudden," says Mrs. Todd, "she set right up in bed with her eyes wide open. . . . And she reached out both her arms toward the door, an' I looked the way she was lookin', an' I see some one was standin' there against the dark. . . . 't was a woman's dark face lookin' right at us; 't wa'n't but an instant I could see. I felt dreadful cold, and my head begun to swim; I thought the light went out; 't wa'n't but an instant, as I say, an' when my sight come back I could n't see nothing there."

The solution here is much like that by which Sarah Jewett had improved the telling of her humorous sketches, entrusting the description of strange events and strong emotions to one of the actors in the story. The same solution helped in the suppression of sentimentality, over which she finally achieved full control. In *The Country of the Pointed Firs* which is always, and correctly, spoken of as her finest work, she is able to make her pronouncements in either the assistant narrator's voice or in the narrator's, that is her own, without overstepping any bounds.

The Country of the Pointed Firs (1896) is not a novel and not much seems to be gained by calling it, as some modern critics are inclined to do, a para-novel, but it does have a definite and effective unity. This is achieved by methods reminiscent of *Deephaven* but employed with far more sophistication so that the community of Dunnet Landing is not only a definite seacoast village but an epitome of the whole state of Maine. Between the covers of this remarkable little book one can find, indeed, almost the whole of New England, its landscape, its social changes, its people and their special qualities. Sarah Jewett did not deliberately set out to do anything of the kind but it was at this moment that her long observation and study of her country, her long practice in writing of everyday life as though it were history, came to its climax. It is with *The Country of the Pointed Firs* that one should begin to read the work of Sarah Orne Jewett.

Henry James, who admired the book, once asked Miss Jewett whether Dunnet Landing was a real place, and when she replied that she had invented it, he nodded in approval, murmuring, "I thought so." To less discerning inquirers she said that "it must be somewhere 'along shore' between the region of Tenants Harbor and Boothbay." The sketches which make up the book were published in four installments in the *Atlantic Monthly*. Each of these groups can stand alone, but they seem to have been composed on a definite connecting pattern. Four later sketches set in Dunnet Landing, which were added to the book in posthumous editions, are perfectly consistent in tone but fall outside the time sequence of the pattern, which runs from June to September. One is always conscious of the background—the firs, the balsams, the rocks, the birds and bushes, the constantly changing aspects of the sea—but it is never overemphasized.

The narrator is played down so that she provides only the necessary curiosity, questions, and responses. The important figure is the assistant narrator, one of the best characters, as I have said, Miss Jewett ever drew. She is the narrator's landlady, Mrs. Almira

Todd, herbwoman of the village, and much of the book is told in her distinctive and effective speech. As she and the narrator come to know each other well they develop a real friendship, so that Mrs. Todd reveals something of her inner life. There is no volcano beneath her granite but a deep accepted grief. She had loved above her station. "He come of a high family, an' my lot was plain an' hard-workin'." "His mother didn't favor the match, an' done everything she could to part us; and folks thought we both married well, but 't wa'n't what either one of us wanted most."

The man Almira married, though she could never give him her heart, was lost at sea not long after their wedding. She took to herb-doctoring, at which she was skilled, and made herself a good living and an important position in the community. She knows its history and the details of the lives of most of her neighbors and is agreeably outspoken about their faults and virtues.

As the narrator has been made less conspicuous than she is in *Deephaven* and the language of the book has been made simpler and more precise, so the number of subsidiary characters has been reduced to a few of real significance. In all these characters Miss Jewett is presenting the New England qualities she has been describing in her other stories: endurance, courage, independence, industry, conscientiousness, and her own belief in the happy interest to be found in the commonplaces of day-to-day living.

The clearest exponent of Dunnet Landing's decline since it ceased to be a seaport is Captain Littlepage, long retired but full of pregnant ideas as well as strange, fanciful thoughts. According to Mrs. Todd his mind has been unhinged by too much reading. He is devoted to Milton and Shakespeare. A curious experience in an Arctic shipwreck has left him with the conviction that he knows the location of a strange city, the waiting place for spirits between earth and heaven, but about the changes in the Landing he is quite lucid. "In the old days a good part o' the best men here knew a hundred ports and something of the way folks lived in them. They saw the world for themselves, and like's not their wives and children saw it with them. . . . they got some sense o' proportion."

Mr. Tilley, once a fisherman, keeps his balance by cherishing the memory of his lovable and capable wife who died eight years ago. He keeps everything in his neat little house as nearly as possible in the way "poor dear" liked to have it. There is also the curious tale of Poor Joanna of Shell-heap Island, one of the solitaries already mentioned. She became a hermit but maintained her dignity and her personality. Significant also is the way in which the community respects her way of life without prying or making unjustified attempts to dissuade her.

Most important of all is Mrs. Todd's octogenarian mother, Mrs. Blackett, who lives with her shy fisherman son on one of the outer islands. Its name, Green Island, suggests that it is a kind of little paradise. Mrs. Blackett enjoys nature and her daily life so thoroughly that she refreshes every friend with whom she comes in contact.

The Country of the Pointed Firs brought Miss Jewett enthusiastic approval both from the critics and from her friends. The most precise assessment of all came in a letter from William James. The book, he said, has "that incommunicable cleanness of the salt air when one first leaves town," and this is a quality one is refreshed by in most of Miss Jewett's work.

Agreeable as she found it to have this kind of written and spoken praise and to find herself treated as a distinguished literary lady of Boston, what Sarah Jewett enjoyed most all through her professional life were the tributes from her own state of Maine. She was much pleased when from time to time on May 30 South Berwick included in its official exercises a reading of her "Decoration Day." This is a simple tale of how, some twenty-five years after the war, the nine Union soldiers who are still alive in the little village of Barlow Plains decide that the community, small as it is, ought to honor its soldier dead, of their brave procession through the countryside, planting a flag on each grave, and of how the people of Barlow rise to the occasion.

But the distinction Miss Jewett cared for most of all was the honorary Litt.D., the first the college ever conferred upon a woman, which Bowdoin granted her in 1901. "You can't think," she wrote Mrs. Fields, "how nice it was to be the single sister of so many brothers."

In 1902 Miss Jewett had a serious accident, a fall from a carriage which severely injured her neck and spine and left her with greatly depleted energy. She kept up her friendships and her correspondence vigorously. A particularly happy note here was the acquaintance, which grew into a real friendship, with the young Willa Cather who had, she thought, great promise. But though letters were possible Sarah Jewett was never able to write another story.

In March 1909 she had a stroke while staying with Mrs. Fields and asked to be taken home to Berwick. Her death occurred on June 24, 1909. Some years before she had said in speaking of the old house: "I was born here and I hope to die here, leaving the lilac bushes still green and growing and all the chairs in their places." She could not have made herself a better epitaph; this was an exposition not only of the way she liked to order her life but of the literary creed by which she tried to order her writing.

Selected Bibliography

WORKS OF SARAH ORNE JEWETT

COLLECTIONS OF SHORT STORIES

Deephaven. Boston: James R. Osgood, 1877. (Reissued by Houghton, Mifflin in 1894, with a new preface by the author.)

Old Friends and New. Boston: Houghton, Osgood, 1879.

Country By-Ways. Boston: Houghton, Mifflin, 1881.

The Mate of the Daylight, and Friends Ashore. Boston and New York: Houghton, Mifflin, 1884.

A White Heron and Other Stories. Boston and New York: Houghton, Mifflin, 1886.

The King of Folly Island and Other People. Boston and New York: Houghton, Mifflin, 1888.

Strangers and Wayfarers. Boston and New York: Houghton, Mifflin, 1890.

Tales of New England. Boston and New York: Houghton, Mifflin, 1890. (Collected from the preceding volumes.)

A Native of Winby and Other Tales. Boston and New York: Houghton, Mifflin, 1893.

The Life of Nancy. Boston and New York: Houghton, Mifflin, 1895.

The Country of the Pointed Firs. Boston and New York: Houghton, Mifflin, 1896.

The Queen's Twin and Other Stories. Boston and New York: Houghton, Mifflin, 1899.

Stories and Tales. 7 vols. Boston: Houghton, Mifflin, 1910.

The Best Stories of Sarah Orne Jewett, edited with a preface by Willa Cather. 2 vols. Boston: Houghton Mifflin, 1925. (Vol. 1 contains *The Country of the Pointed Firs.*)

The Only Rose and Other Tales, edited with an introduction by Rebecca West. London: Jonathan Cape, 1937.

NOVELS

A Country Doctor. Boston and New York: Houghton, Mifflin, 1884.

A Marsh Island. Boston and New York: Houghton, Mifflin, 1885.

The Tory Lover. Boston and New York: Houghton, Mifflin, 1901.

STORIES FOR CHILDREN

Play Days: A Book of Stories for Children. Boston: Houghton, Osgood, 1878.

The Story of the Normans, Told Chiefly in Relation to Their Conquest of England. New York and London: G. P. Putnam's Sons, 1887.

Betty Leicester: A Story for Girls. Boston and New York: Houghton, Mifflin, 1890.

Betty Leicester's Christmas. Boston and New York: Houghton, Mifflin, 1899.

VERSE

Verses, Printed for Her Friends. Boston: Merrymount Press, 1916.

LETTERS

Letters of Sarah Orne Jewett, edited by Annie Fields. Boston and New York: Houghton, Mifflin, 1911.

Sarah Orne Jewett Letters, edited by Richard Cary. Waterville, Maine: Colby College Press, 1956. (Revised and enlarged edition, Waterville, Maine: Colby College Press, 1967.)

BIBLIOGRAPHIES

Eichelberger, Clayton. "Sarah Orne Jewett (1849-1909): A Critical Bibliography of Secondary Comment," *American Literary Realism, 1897-1910,* 2:189-262 (1969).

Frost, John Eldridge. "Sarah Orne Jewett Bibliography: 1949-1963," *Colby Library Quarterly,* Sers. 6, 10: 405-17 (June 1964).

Spiller, Robert E., and others, eds. *Literary History of the United States: Bibliography.* 3rd ed., revised. New York: Macmillan, 1963. Pp. 602-04; *Supplement,* pp. 152-53.

Weber, Clara Carter, and Carl J. Weber. *A Bibliography of the Published Writings of Sarah Orne Jewett.* Waterville, Maine: Colby College Press, 1949.

CRITICAL AND BIOGRAPHICAL STUDIES

Auchincloss, Louis. "Sarah Orne Jewett," in *Pio-*

neers and Caretakers. Minneapolis: University of Minnesota Press, 1965.

Berthoff, Warner. "The Art of Jewett's *Pointed Firs,*" *New England Quarterly,* 32:31-53 (March 1959).

Bishop, Ferman. "Henry James Criticizes *The Tory Lover,*" *American Literature,* 27:262-64 (May 1955).

————. "Sarah Orne Jewett's Idea of Race," *New England Quarterly,* 30:243-49 (June 1957).

Buchan, A. M. *"Our Dear Sarah": An Essay on Sarah Orne Jewett.* Washington University Studies, No. 24. St. Louis, Mo.: Washington University Press, 1953.

Cary, Richard. *Sarah Orne Jewett* (United States Authors Series). New York: Twayne, 1962.

Cather, Willa. "Miss Jewett," in *Not under Forty.* New York: Knopf, 1936.

Chapman, Edward M. "The New England of Sarah Orne Jewett," *Yale Review,* n.s., 3:157-72 (October 1913).

Chase, Mary Ellen. "Sarah Orne Jewett as a Social Historian," in *The World of Dunnet Landing,* edited by David Bonnell Green. Lincoln: University of Nebraska Press, 1962.

Frost, John Eldridge. *Sarah Orne Jewett.* Kittery Point, Maine: Gundalow Club, 1960.

Green, David Bonnell. "The World of Dunnet Landing," *New England Quarterly,* 34:514-17 (December 1961).

Howe, M. A. De Wolfe. "Sarah Orne Jewett," in *Memories of a Hostess.* Boston: Atlantic Monthly Press, 1922. (Drawn chiefly from the diaries of Mrs. James T. Fields.)

Jewett, Sarah Orne. "Looking Back on Girlhood," *Youth's Companion,* 65:5-6 (January 7, 1892).

Magowan, Robin. "Pastoral and the Art of Landscape in *The Country of the Pointed Firs,*" *New England Quarterly,* 32:229-40 (June 1963).

Matthiessen, F. O. *Sarah Orne Jewett.* Boston and New York: Houghton, Mifflin, 1929. (Matthiessen also contributed the biographical sketch to the *Dictionary of American Biography,* 1933).

Shackford, Martha Hale. "Sarah Orne Jewett," *Sewanee Review,* 30:20-26 (January 1922).

Short, Clarice. "Studies in Gentleness," *Western*

Humanities Review, 11:387-93 (Autumn 1957).

Smith, Eleanor M. "The Literary Relationship of Sarah Orne Jewett and Willa Sibert Cather," *New England Quarterly,* 29:472-92 (December 1956).

Thompson, Charles M. "The Art of Miss Jewett," *Atlantic Monthly,* 94:485-97 (October 1904).

Waggoner, Hyatt H. "The Unity of *The Country of the Pointed Firs,*" *Twentieth Century Literature,* 5:67-73 (July 1959).

Weber, Carl J. "Whittier and Sarah Orne Jewett," *New England Quarterly,* 18:401-7 (September 1945).

—*MARGARET FARRAND THORP*

Ring Lardner

1885-1933

"**Y**OU could of did better if you had of went at it in a different way." This, when it first appeared in 1914, was the sound of a new voice in American fiction. It was still an age when such masters as Henry James and William Dean Howells were writing their stately periods. The masters had dealt occasionally with the uneducated proletariat, and dialect had traditionally been used as a provincial form of humor. But Ring Lardner's Jack Keefe, hero of the stories that became *You Know Me Al*, represented not only a new and realistic rhythm of speech but a new social caste, a lower class that didn't know it was lower class. Lardner's illiterates, his baseball players and salesmen and barbers and nurses, thought of themselves as clever and prospering, and so did the nation that applauded their creator.

Unlike most American writers, who have traditionally written about themselves and people like themselves, Lardner wrote about the strangers inhabiting the crass and rapacious America that he saw around him. Even when he spoke in the first person, he assumed a disguise and spoke in the prevailing language of the time. The man who came from a wealthy and cultivated family, which originally hoped he would enter the ministry, pretended that he was a yokel. The man whom Scott Fitzgerald described as "proud, shy, solemn, shrewd, po-

lite, brave, kind, merciful, honorable" pretended that he was a bumptious extrovert. And a nation that never really recognized either Lardner's Puritan personality or his Puritan portrait of America nonetheless poured fame and wealth on the young sportswriter as one of the greatest literary folk heroes since Mark Twain. At the height of his success in the middle twenties, he was earning about fifty thousand dollars a year, and issuing folksy pronouncements on everything from disarmament to the emancipation of women. Beyond the national frontiers, Virginia Woolf took mournful pleasure in the fact that Lardner had achieved eminence by ignoring England and its literary traditions. Aside from writing "the best prose that has come our way," she said, ". . . it is no coincidence that the best of Mr. Lardner's stories are about games, for . . . [games have] given him a clue, a centre, a meeting place for the divers activities of people whom a vast continent isolates, whom no tradition controls."

In writing about sports, Lardner had struck a hidden nerve in many Americans, at least in many men, for he described a new kind of American mythology, a mythology that more elegant writers had not observed. In the half-century before Lardner's appearance, the nation had reached and conquered its old frontiers. It had become stabilized, both economically and socially. Neither boys nor men could so easily dream of discovering gold and making millions. Since it was a fairly comfortable time, people began turning to the question that still haunts the affluent society: What shall we do with ourselves? The rich might amuse themselves in collecting bibelots or titled husbands, and the poor still struggled for survival, but the increasingly large and prosperous middle classes were more interested in the simple pursuit of leisure. And so they began to take up sports. Baseball, adapted from the English game of rounders during the 1840's, did not become seriously organized until 1876. Football, once largely confined to the "Big Three" of the Ivy League, exploded into a national sport shortly after the turn of the century and eventually became a hundred-million-dollar industry. Boxing was legalized in the nineties and changed from a system of barroom brawls into the snob-appeal sport it has remained since the days of Gentleman Jim Corbett. Such traditional pastimes as horse racing and such novelties as basketball all became "big time." And the boys of the period often dreamed less of making a million dollars than of being another Eddie Collins or another Red Grange. James T. Farrell, for example, wanted to become a professional baseball player long before he ever considered writing. "We American men are a nation of frustrated baseball players," he wrote. Scott Fitzgerald was prey to a similar fantasy. For twenty years, he recalled, he put himself to sleep by imagining that "Once upon a time . . . they needed a quarterback at Princeton, and they had nobody and were in despair. The head coach noticed me kicking and passing on the side of the field, and he cried: 'Who is *that* man—why haven't we noticed *him* before?' "

Running and fighting have been international sports since classic times, but the major

American sports have American peculiarities. The common denominator in baseball, football, basketball, and hockey is that they are highly organized, highly competitive, and that most people take part in them solely by watching them. The active pursuit of leisure does exercise a certain attraction on Americans. Some twenty-five million of them take out fishing licenses every year, according to one recent estimate, and about twenty million acquire hunting licenses, and the equipment that they take along on their domestic safaris helps to raise the business of sports to an estimated total of more than fifty billion dollars a year. Most of these activities are not sports in any sense of competition or excellence, however, but rather a matter of relaxation and self-indulgence. When it comes to the major sports events that attract the attention of millions of Americans—the World Series or the Kentucky Derby or the Rose Bowl game—the American sportsman is nothing more than a distant spectator.

Yet there is something more than entertainment in sports, some magical quality that has never quite been trapped in words. Perhaps the most perceptive effort to understand this magic was that of the Dutch historian Johan Huizinga, who presumably never got within miles of Yankee Stadium. In *Homo Ludens*, he attempted to study the whole subject of "play," not as a skill that divided men from animals but as one that men shared with their Darwinian ancestors. Play, to Huizinga, was not just baseball or football, but hopscotch and darts—and even war. He found that all play is an attempt to create order. "Into an imperfect world and into the confusion of life it brings a temporary, a limited perfection." He found that it satisfies a human need for aesthetic order. "It is invested with the noblest qualities we are capable of perceiving in things: rhythm and harmony." He found that play has no intrinsic morality but "the element of tension imparts to it a certain ethical value in so far as it means a testing of the player's prowess: his courage, tenacity, resources and last, but not least, his spiritual powers." In all its ritual, in fact, its priests in special clothing, its confinement within a consecrated area, its suspension of normal reasoning, and its insistence on arbitrary values, Huizinga found that "play" was much the same as religion— it antedates religion but fulfills much the same need.

Ring Lardner would naturally have scoffed at such theories. He would have insisted that he couldn't understand them. And yet this is the magic that surrounds sports. We pay hundreds of thousands of dollars to a Cassius Clay, for example, to commit assaults that would normally make us call the police. And we treat the chroniclers of such sports—the Heywood Brouns, the John Kierans, the Red Smiths, and the Ring Lardners—with a special adulation that we reserve for the magicians who know the secrets of the ultimate mystery.

There is something prophetic about the fact that America's most celebrated sportswriter was born a cripple. Ringgold Wilmer Lardner had a deformed foot that was corrected by surgery, but he had to wear a metal brace on his left leg until he was eleven years old. At an age when sports seemed a natural route to celebrity, he knew he would never be an All-American football player or a major league baseball star. It is this kind of handicap, however, that often drives the victim to compete in the very area that appears closed to him.

He was born on March 6, 1885, in Niles, Michigan, the youngest of nine children, and privately educated until he entered high school. During his last year there his father suffered heavy financial losses that wiped out the bulk of the family's fortunes. After a desultory at-

tempt at higher education—Lardner's father had insisted that he become an engineer, but he flunked out during his first year at the Armour Institute in Chicago in 1902—Lardner spent a year loafing around his home in Niles, Michigan, then worked for a year as a bookkeeper for the local gas company, and finally drifted into a job at twelve dollars a week on the *South Bend Times.* "I had a lovely time on that paper," he recalled in an interview recounted in Donald Elder's biography. "In the morning I covered the police stations and courts. Then I would drop over to the Circuit Court to get the divorce news. In the afternoon I went to the ball park."

From South Bend, the young author duly progressed to Chicago in 1907, working successively for the *Inter-Ocean,* the *Examiner,* and, finally, the *Tribune,* where he took over the celebrated column called "In the Wake of the News." His reports still used the traditional language—"Purtell poled a base hit over Lather's bean and Kelly counted . . ."—but they became increasingly fanciful. Each game was a new drama, which Lardner often described from some unusual perspective. One story, for example, concentrated entirely on a hole in the outfield fence, another on a dialogue in the bleachers. Lardner elaborated all this with a kind of lazy amiability, for he loved the game of baseball, loved to spend his afternoons watching its leisurely and methodical progress, loved to spend his evenings talking about it. For a half-dozen years, this tall, reticent, and idealistic man traveled with the Chicago Cubs and White Sox, slowly crisscrossing the country in an atmosphere of card-playing, practical jokes, and the monotonous rhythm of the clacking Pullman coach wheels.

"During those years, when most men of promise receive an adult education . . ." Scott Fitzgerald complained in an obituary essay, "Ring moved in the company of a few dozen illiterates playing a boy's game. A boy's game, with no more possibilities in it than a boy could master, a game bounded by walls which kept out novelty or danger, change or adventure. . . . However deeply Ring might cut into it, his cake had exactly the diameter of Frank Chance's diamond." This is a common view of Lardner, that his training limited him to writing about illiterate men playing a boy's game. But even if Lardner had written only about sports, which is far from the truth, there would be little justification for this commonplace condemnation. For one thing, as Huizinga has shown, the world of sports is no more limited by the diameter of a diamond than a religion is limited by the nave of its church. For another, a writer usually gains rather than loses by a deep experience of one limited field of human life. In contrast to Fitzgerald, who actually was crippled by his inability to shake off the "education" of being a Princeton boy, Melville was proud to say that a whaling ship had been his Harvard and his Yale. One might even cite the statement of the classics scholar John H. Finley that "The very limitation . . . of Thucydides' perspective, while in one sense it led him to generalize on insufficient data, in another sense enabled him to transcend those data because it prompted him to discover their most inward, most essential causes."

But the most important falsity in the common view of Lardner's training as a sportswriter is that it ignores his real nature and personality. Lardner entered the world of professional sports as an outsider. Far from being a character in his own stories, he was the product of a family that staged private theatricals and provided each child with its own Irish nursemaid. It was Lardner's natural kindness and integrity that won him the slightly baffled respect of the baseball players and enabled him to wear the mask of the genial good fellow. Perhaps it appealed to Lardner's strange sense

of humor—he was a professional humorist who sometimes smiled but almost never laughed—that the outside world should consider him a yokel. But since the mask had worked in the dugout, he retained it all his life, a lonely man of genius pretending to be ordinary and sociable, a man of great perception pretending not to understand things that he understood only too well.

The first of Lardner's stories was rejected by the *Saturday Evening Post*, but a scout for the magazine persuaded him to try again. In March of 1914, Jack Keefe was introduced to the world in "A Busher's Letters Home": "Well, Al old pal I suppose you seen in the paper when I been sold to the White Sox. . . ." This was perhaps the most successful dialect narrative since *Huckleberry Finn*, and for many of the same reasons. The dialect is funny, but the humor is incidental to the creation of an immediately real character. Even the failures in the narrative flow are failures because the writer breaks up his story into a series of incidents used to illustrate the character. Most important of all, Huck and Keefe both talk of themselves in a way which contradicts the reality that any reader can see. Like Huck, who shows his moral nature by defying the Puritan morality that he accepts as true, Jack Keefe accepts the considerably corrupted morality of a half-century later, the Puritan preaching of hard work combined with the post-frontier virtues of success at any price and "I would of busted his jaw if they hadn't stopped me." But while Huck reveals a morality higher than the convention he is defying, Keefe invariably reveals a morality lower than the conventions he accepts. In his first letter to Al, when he announces his rise from Terre Haute to the Chicago White Sox, he modestly declares that "You could of knocked me over with a feather," then adds that "though I did more than my share I always felt that my work was appreciated." Soon he is laying waste to the training table but defending himself on the ground that "it's all solid bone and muscle." And when the coach, Gleason, retorts that he is "all solid bone from the neck up," Keefe confides to Al that he will "let them kid me."

This kidding, in fact, is the basic language of *You Know Me Al,* and of most of Lardner's works, just as it is the basic language of the society that Lardner dramatizes. In theory, it is a humorous language, but this is an ill-tempered humor, for the language of kidding represents a compromise between Americans' conflicting demands of aggressiveness and friendliness. In kidding, one can not only disguise the embarrassment of trying to be friendly, but one can say unpleasant things by pretending one doesn't mean them. Lardner himself used the language all his life as a means of softening his harsh judgments, and he ascribed the same charitable instincts to his baseball managers and umpires and coaches, all the figures of authority who had to deal with people like Keefe. Keefe himself, however, was too stupid and too vain to master the language—he couldn't hide his rudeness in speaking it, and he couldn't believe that anyone else might want to be rude to him. "Manager Callahan is a funny guy and I don't understand him sometimes," Keefe complains. "I can't figure out if he is kidding or in ernest. . . . He says . . . if you wind up like that with Cobb on base he will steal your watch and chain. I says Maybe Cobb can't get on base when I work against him. He says That's right and maybe San Francisco Bay is made of grapejuice. Then he walks away from me. He give one of the youngsters a awful bawling out for something he done in the game at supper last night. If he ever talks to me like he done to him I will take a punch at him. You know me Al."

"A Busher's Letters Home," this first story in the Keefe series, could have turned into an easy burlesque of a fraudulent baseball player. To many of Lardner's readers, it would have been warmly satisfying to see the established authorities of "the national pastime" cast out such a braggart and maintain the Puritan principle of virtue rewarded. In other words, he could have "debunked" a player without debunking the game. It would have been even easier for Lardner to make his hero reform and accept the teachings of the establishment. But Lardner saved Keefe, as a creation, by two more interesting methods. One was to endow him with a genuine talent. Despite all his lying and laziness, Keefe is basically a good pitcher, and the establishment needs him because of his talent. The other method was to inflict on Keefe such humiliation that one's sympathies suddenly shift toward the scapegrace yokel. On his first pitching assignment in Chicago, when Keefe has invited all his hometown friends to see him play, he makes all his old mistakes and Callahan makes him keep pitching through one disastrous inning after another. "I had a sore arm when I was warming up," he begins his post-mortem, "and Callahan should never ought to of sent me in there." In the very first inning, Crawford triples—"Collins ought to of catched the ball"—Cobb singles him home—"Weaver . . . never made a move for the ball"—and the disaster goes on and on until the score reaches sixteen to two. "I was looking at the bench all the time expecting Callahan to call me in but he kept hollering Go on and pitch. Your friends wants to see you pitch." It comes as an anticlimax, but an inevitable ending, when the White Sox send Keefe back to the minor leagues. "I ain't had no fair deal Al," he complains, "and I ain't going to no Frisco. I will quit the game first. . . ."

Despite Lardner's reputation for folksy humor, there was nothing accidental about the fact that his first story was a story of defeat, humiliation, and failure. The *Post* requested a sequel, and Lardner dutifully poured out sequels for four more years, but his second published story was another narrative of disaster, a narrative that bordered on the Gothic. One of Lardner's less-known stories, but one of his best, "My Roomy," introduces a baseball player named Elliott, who can hit anything but won't even try to catch the ball in the field. Besides that, he hovers on the brink of insanity. "He always insisted on havin' the water run in the bathtub all night, because he said it reminded him of the sound of the dam near his home," says the narrator. At one point, Elliott seizes control of a hotel elevator and runs it up and down. Another time, he throws a pitcher of ice water out of the window. "That's my business—bustin' things," he says, a remark that ominously anticipates Scott Fitzgerald's portrait of Lardner himself in *Tender Is the Night*. "I am a woman and my business is to hold things together," Nicole Diver tells the alcoholic Abe North. "My business is to tear them apart," North replies.

Part of Elliott's madness is his complete indifference to the outside world—he not only ignores the narrator and the manager but he tears up letters from the girl he plans to marry (if he ever gets "five hundred at once") because "she can't tell me nothin' I don't know already." When he is finally fired, he "goes up to the lookin'-glass and stares at himself for five minutes. Then, all of a sudden, he hauls off and takes a wallop at his reflection in the glass. Naturally he smashed the glass all to pieces and he cut his hand somethin' awful. Without lookin' at it he come over to me and says: 'Well, good-by sport!'—and holds out his other hand to shake. When I starts to shake with him he smears his bloody hand all over my map. Then he laughed like a wild man and run out o' the room and out o' the hotel."

Despite this pseudo-murder, or even because of it, the narrator still feels the establishment's sense of responsibility toward the gifted wild man. He argues his teammates into voting Elliott a share of the city series profits and then he gets the money sent to Elliott's home, not without some anxiety. "I didn't know if I was doin' right by the girl to give him the chance to marry her. . . . I thought to myself: 'If she's all right she'll take acid in a month—and it'll be my fault; but if she's really stuck on him they must be somethin' wrong with her too, so what's the diff'rence?' "

The narrator is rescued from this dilemma by a letter from Elliott's home, disclosing that the girl had already married another man. "She had wrote to him about it but he did not read her letters. The news drove him crazy—poor boy—and he went to the place where they was livin' with a baseball bat and very near killed 'em both. Then he marched down the street singin' 'Silver Threads Among the Gold' at the top of his voice. They was goin' to send him to prison . . . but the jury decided he was crazy." From Elliott, there is only a short postscript: "They tell me they are both alive yet, which I did not mean 'em to be."

If this is Lardner's portrait of the losers in the world of competition, his portrait of the winners is scarcely any more admiring. Turning to a sport where victory goes to a man rather than a team, he began his account of "Champion" by declaring that "Midge Kelly scored his first knockout when he was seventeen. The knockee was his brother Connie, three years his junior and a cripple. The purse was a half dollar given to the younger Kelly by a lady whose electric had just missed bumping his soul from his frail little body."

"Champion," written in 1916, was Lardner's first effort to escape the trap of dialect stories, and his uncertain command of formal English immediately becomes clear in expressions like "knockee" and "frail little body." By the conventional standards of literature, it is a mediocre story, for Midge Kelly is less a human being than a symbol of evil, as black as Fedallah or Aaron the Moor. It lacks the humor of the "Busher's Letters" or the dark complexity of "My Roomy." But if there is still any merit to Edgar Allan Poe's theory that the purpose of a short story is to achieve one concentrated emotional effect, then "Champion" successfully achieves its effect by describing the world champion as a bully, liar, and fraud. This is naturally a judgment that many Americans refuse to accept. It may please them to hear that a boxing champion keeps a mistress, or cheats at cards, but they refuse to believe that he is a monster. A remarkable demonstration of this capacity for disbelief came in the Hollywood adaptation of the story, one of Stanley Kramer's first big successes. In contrast to the usual Hollywood production, which falsifies by oversimplifying, Kramer's *Champion* falsified by overcomplicating, by the normally admirable step of giving greater dimension to a character. The movie ended with a melodramatic scene of Kirk Douglas sobbing in pain and exhaustion as he listened to the far-off applause and realized that he had finally won acclaim and love. In terms of the movie, it was a very effective scene. In terms of Lardner's story, it was a complete lie, for Lardner's whole point was that Midge Kelly represented a lie, and even that the myth of the heroic prizefighter represented a lie. Midge Kelly not only attacked and abandoned his family and wife and children, he not only betrayed friends and managers, but his championship was a triumph over the idea of truth. "Just a kid; that's all he is; a regular boy," Manager Wallie Adams tells a reporter from the *News*. "Get what I mean? Don't know the meanin' o' bad

habits. . . . Clean livin' put him up where he's at. Get what I mean?"

So America saluted the winners and exiled the losers, and tried to convince itself that the best men won. Lardner could have argued that the worst men won, but that would have meant accepting the relevance of virtue to victory, and Lardner didn't accept it. He was neither an apologist for the system nor a rebel against it. Some frauds won and some frauds lost, that was all. Lardner made his point most frankly six years later in a story that belongs in the border area between Lardner's sports stories and his social stories, "A Caddy's Diary":

"Joe I said what do these people mean when they talk about Crane selling his soul?

Why you know what they mean said Joe, they mean that a person that does something dishonest for a bunch of money or a gal or any kind of a reward why the person that does it is selling his soul.

All right I said and it dont make no difference does it if the reward is big or little?

Why no said Joe only the bigger it is the less of a sucker the person is that goes after it.

Well I said here is Mr Thomas who is vice president of a big bank and worth a bbl. of money and it is just a few days ago when he lied about his golf score in order so as he would win 9 golf balls instead of a ½ dozen. . . .

Well said Joe what of it?

Well I said it seems to me like these people have got a lot of nerve to pan Mr Crane and call him a sucker for doing what he done, it seems to me like $8000 and a swell dame is a pretty fair reward compared with what some of these other people sells their soul for, and I would like to tell them about it.

Well said Joe go ahead and tell them but maybe they will tell you something right back. . . . they might tell you this, that when Mr

Thomas asks you how many shots he has had and you say 4 when you know he has had 5, why you are selling your soul for a $1.00 tip. And when you move Mrs Doanes ball out of a rut and give it a good lie, what are you selling your soul for? Just a smile.

O keep your mouth shut I said to him."

This was the truth about American competition that nobody else reported and nobody else would believe, but Lardner went on writing about America in terms of its games. Less than three months after Jack Keefe was sold to San Francisco, the *Saturday Evening Post* published the next installment, entitled "The Busher Comes Back." Jack Keefe was working hard in San Francisco, winning games, dismissing such past failures as the unfaithfulness of the blond Violet ("Good riddance is rubbish as they say"), and courting a new girl called Hazel ("she is some queen, Al—a great big stropping girl that must weigh one hundred and sixty lbs.").

Keefe's romantic and domestic problems almost necessarily come to dominate the rest of the six stories that make up *You Know Me Al*, for there is not too much that even Lardner can create out of the long grind of a baseball season. The returning busher has learned nothing—"Honest Al," he reports home about the legendary Walter Johnson, "he ain't as fast as me"—and there is little drama in Keefe's purely professional life. His career is simply a long series of games, mostly victories, all following the prescribed pattern of the game itself. But Keefe's stumbling pursuit of love is a much more varied sport for Lardner to write about.

Keefe's marriage to Florrie, like his preliminary skirmishes with Violet and Hazel, has the awesome inevitability that is common to classic tragedy and vaudeville jokes. Instead of spending the winter in Keefe's town of Bedford, Florrie wants to stay in a forty-dollar Chicago apartment, but Keefe indignantly de-clares that "I guess they think they must be lots of suckers running round loose." In the next letter, he has taken the apartment but "we got a bargain because it is all furnished and everything." In the next, "Florrie would not stand for no . . . oak chairs . . . and we went downtown to buy some mohoggeny." Step by preposterous step, Florrie leads him to bankruptcy and even into a quarrel with the White Sox owner, Charles Comiskey—"I was scared I would forget myself and call him some name and he is a old man."

Eventually, he is reduced to borrowing money from Al. This Al is a wonderful comic character, the silent man whose answers to Keefe are never disclosed, who endures insults and lies without complaint. Yet despite all of Keefe's foolishness and fraud, we grow fond of him because he remains more the victim than the villain. He does usually try his best at his work—"and if I lose who's fault is it. Not mine Al"—a job at which he is ridiculed and relatively underpaid. Though he borrows money from Al, and repeatedly promises to "pay up all my dedts incluseive," he does finally pay. And in his marriage, he has bound himself to a woman far worse than he, a woman completely indifferent to the baby whom Keefe genuinely loves.

Once Lardner created his folk hero, there were limits to the ordeals he could inflict on Keefe. After the two baseball seasons covered in *You Know Me Al*, as well as a marriage and a birth, Lardner stretched out his final chapter with a series of arguments about Keefe's going on an exhibition tour of Japan. Yet the demand for Keefe stories appeared inexhaustible, and Lardner was too much a journeyman journalist to ignore such a steady source of income. Keefe patriotically entered the army in 1917 and became the hero of an endless series of training-camp jokes, remorselessly collected in *Treat 'Em Rough* (1918); in due time, he went to

France for similar burlesque adventures collected in *The Real Dope* (1919). During 1923 and 1924, Lardner was even writing continuity for a daily comic strip called *You Know Me Al*. It earned him twenty thousand dollars a year before he abandoned it.

In the general diffusion of the Jack Keefe story, the most striking thing is the increasing absence of baseball. Lardner himself had left Chicago in 1919 and moved to New York, where he began to write a syndicated weekly column that dealt less with sports than with Lardner's conventionally whimsical approach to the world in general. "Well, I don't suppose it will surprise nobody to find out that I am in Washington for the disarmament conference," he wrote in 1921, "as it is getting so that they can't put on no event of worldwide interest without they have me there. . . ." That same year, he declared his weariness with the whole subject of baseball:

"I got a letter the other day asking why I didn't write about baseball no more as I usen't to write about nothing else, you might say. Well, friends, I may as well admit that I have kind of lost interest in the old game, or rather it ain't the old game which I have lost interest in it, but it is the game which the magnates has fixed up to please the public with their usual good judgment.

A couple yrs. ago a ball player named Baby Ruth that was a pitcher by birth was made into an outfielder on acct. of how he could bust them . . . and the master minds that controls baseball says to themselfs that if it is home runs that the public wants to see, why leave us give them home runs. . . .

Another result is that I stay home and read a book.

But statistics shows that about 7 people out of every 100 is ½ cuckoo so they's still some that is still interested in the national pastime so for their benefit I will write a little about it

as long as I don't half to set through a game of it to get the material."

Ring Lardner's stories naturally helped to bring a deep change in American views of sports—and of America itself. The extent of that change is clear enough when one looks at the kind of sports writing that preceded Lardner. In 1899, for instance, Walter Camp picked his first All-American football team—three men from Harvard and Pennsylvania, two from Yale and Princeton, and one lonely midwesterner from the University of Chicago—and prefaced his account with this quatrain:

> Who misses or who wins the prize,
>   Go lose or conquer as you can;
> But if you fail or if you rise
>   Be each, pray God, a gentleman!

Perhaps the best illustration of the pre-Lardner tradition is an all-but-forgotten man named Gilbert Patten, who used the all-but-forgotten pseudonym of Burt L. Standish, and who was more widely read than any other American writer during the first years of the century. An estimated one hundred and twenty-five million copies of Patten's books about Frank Merriwell circulated to a generation of wide-eyed youths, and none of them had a more picturesque period charm than the classic *Frank Merriwell at Yale*. "That was great work, Merriwell," says the coach. "Keep it up! Keep it up!" But Merriwell disdains such praises. "That kind of work will not win the game . . ." he says. "Some batting must be done, and there must be some score getting." The coach agrees, and exhorts his team: "Never mind if it does kill you. We are after scores, and a life or two is of small consequence."

The creation of Jack Keefe and Midge Kelly and the maniacal Elliott was a near-fatal blow to the myth of the Frank Merriwell hero. At first, it was hard to accept, but the Black Sox scandal of 1919 virtually proved Lardner's case, and we have gradually come to take it for granted that many prizefights are fixed, that amateur track stars don't live on gold medals, and that many college football players get "scholarships" amounting to a salary for playing. Oddly enough, the "debunking" of sports has scarcely weakened the appeal of the star athlete, for our resilient society responded by admiring the tough professionalism of the debunked. Boxing, for example, is not less but more attractive because of the common knowledge that gangsters dominate it. Its very corruption gives it the new glamour of wickedness. As in our politics and business, we have come to admire the smart operator and the tough success far more than we despise the corrupt and their corruption.

Among the sportswriters who still write for the boy hidden within every man, there is some confusion about how to cope with the new skepticism about sports. Some of the most celebrated writers —a Jimmy Cannon or a Bob Considine—still follow the old traditions of Frank Merriwell. But there is a contrasting newer tradition best illustrated by Red Smith. "Certainly it seems desirable," he remarked in the *New York Herald Tribune*, "that those of us who write about these pastimes should pause now and then in the search for purple adjectives and remind ourselves that we're not watching Armageddon but only a game that little boys can play." One of the masters of this newer manner of sports writing was Lardner's own son. John Lardner never came to dislike sports with the Puritan fervor of his father, but he rarely treated them very seriously. Like Smith, he observed that "this game they play with horses' skins and ash twigs can be indulged in pleasurably, and without public mortification and atonement." He loved prizefights and apparently remained fond of the industry's most dishonest participants. "Gritting his cost-

ly new hand-carved teeth," he remarked of one, "the promoter went right on gamely selling second-rate fights at high prices just as though his heart were not breaking within him."

The development of such stylish skepticism has finally improved not only the reporting of sports but also the quality of fiction based on sports. From the level of Frank Merriwell, there was little improvement in the work of James T. Farrell. It was already 1936 when Farrell wrote *A World I Never Made* and sent his hero to Comiskey Park to see Ed Walsh pitch a no-hit game: "God wasn't going to let Boston get any hits. . . . The last inning. God was going to help Walsh. God was! God, please!" The best of these hero-worshipers was Ernest Hemingway, who dealt with everything from hunting and skiing to bicycle racing, baseball, and, of course, the bullfight. In one of his finest short stories, "Fifty Grand," he wrote about the world of boxing, and, inevitably, he wrote about it in terms of an inverted Frank Merriwell. The hero is both tough and dishonest, the champion in spirit, determined not to win bravely but to lose bravely, not with a smile but with a stoical grimace. "It was nothing," he says.

In the years after Lardner, it became almost axiomatic that nothing of any real merit could be written about baseball. Then, during the fifties, a stream of baseball books began appearing—Eliot Asinof's *Man on Spikes,* Bernard Malamud's *The Natural,* Jim Brosnan's *The Long Season,* and three novels by Mark Harris, *The Southpaw, A Ticket for a Seamstitch,* and *Bang the Drum Slowly.* The ghost of Ring Lardner haunts all such books, particularly those of Harris, who has appropriated many of Lardner's methods without Lardner's sharpness or humor. His hero, Henry Wiggen, and Wiggen's real-life counterpart, Jim Brosnan, both end not as struggling heroes but as slightly freakish entertainers, terribly conscious of money and taxes and the false-idol role they have been hired to play. The world they dramatize is the debased dream-world of the circus in Leonid Andreyev's *He Who Gets Slapped*, a world of sweat and shin-pads and neurotic applause. And though the arena of professional sports contains far more possibilities than Scott Fitzgerald saw in it, a narrative limited to a baseball pennant race inevitably produces the tedium inherent in Brosnan's title, *The Long Season*.

The writer who solved this problem most successfully was Bernard Malamud, and he did it simply by treating baseball's mythology as mythology. *The Natural* follows the traditional narrative of the baseball novel, the feverish pennant race led by the new star. Yet all of it is deliberately kept slightly unreal, out of focus, for the whole drama is vaguely Wagnerian. Though the career of Roy Hobbs slightly resembles that of Lefty O'Doul, and though his team is reminiscent of the Brooklyn Dodgers of the thirties, Malamud names them after the men of the round table, the New York Knights, and their aged and sickly manager is named Pop Fisher, a closer approximation of the Fisher King than Wagner used in naming Amfortas. The knights of Amfortas were guarding the Holy Grail and Spear, weapon made of ash wood, and Malamud tells us that the Parsifalian Roy (King?) Hobbs had cut his own bat from an ash tree that had been split by lightning. But while one can draw innumerable parallels between Malamud's nightmare and Wagner's fantasies, the important fact is the existence of the parallel itself, for it corroborates the view not only that baseball is part of the American mythology but also that sports are themselves mythological or pseudo-religious in their appeal and their importance. "The apparently quite simple question of what play really is, leads us deep into the problem of the nature and origin of religious concepts," as Huizinga put it in *Homo Ludens*. ". . . In this sphere of sacred play, the child and the poet are at home with the savage."

"Standing six foot three in what was left of his stockings," Lardner wrote of a young rookie pitcher with the absurd name of Hurry Kane, "he was wearing a suit of Arizona store clothes that would have been a fair fit for Singer's youngest Midget and looked like he had pressed it with a tractor that had been parked on a river bottom."

This was the scene in Florida every spring as the yokels straggled in, itinerant entertainers in a society that was itself alive with restless motion. They were fighting for a chance at success and fame and the kind of identity which America grants to the successful. The baseball camp that received them was not just a baseball camp but a miniature of America's hostile metropolis. Professional eyes watched the stumbling rookies to assess their value. Ridicule was the price of every failure. The yokels were ridiculed not only for their mistakes but also for their red necks and their ill-fitting clothes and their belligerent vanity, until Hurry Kane cried out: "This is my last day on this ball club. . . . I'm going home where my gal is, where they ain't no smart Alecks kidding me all the while." On such occasions, the authorities, the managers and coaches, moved in to restore order, assuring the newcomers that they were wanted and needed, for the wandering yokels possessed the talent that supported the authorities.

Lardner was just such a newcomer when he arrived in New York in 1919 with his wife and four young sons, arriving in a city which cared little for the celebrity of a Chicago sports columnist and which still considers the rest of the world provincial. Lardner was relatively well known, and the new syndication of his column provided him with ample money, but he always remained an outsider, deliberately maintaining the pose of a midwestern innocent in the big town, and the theme of the alien wanderer repeatedly appeared in his work.

Lardner had already described the misfortunes of the wandering yokel in *Gullible's Travels* (1917), the sad social climbing of a man who enjoys "wearin' the soup and fish and minglin' amongst the high polloi and pretendin' we really was somebody." In Palm Beach, Gullible spends most of his time trying to combat the steady drain on his finances while his wife pursues the high polloi. "She picked out some o' the E-light o' Chicago and tried every trick she could think up. She told 'em their noses was shiny and offered 'em her powder. She stepped on their white shoes just so's to get a chance to beg their pardon." Finally, she encounters *the* Mrs. Potter" in the hotel corridor, and Mrs. Potter stops to address her. " 'Please see that they's some towels put in 559,' says *the* Mrs. Potter from Chicago."

Once established in New York, after a trip he tried to describe by a rather clumsy parody of Daisy Ashford called *The Young Immigrunts* (1920), Lardner started to tell the story of the middle-class midwestern migrant all over again, this time in a cycle of stories called *The Big Town* (1921). The yokel narrator is on a slightly higher level than Gullible, and he seems to have more money, but he is still complaining about expenses and still making wisecracks, most of them despairing rather than funny. The cycle begins, rather like *Gullible*, with the narrator and his wife and sister-in-law vainly searching for society, or at least a place "where they's Life and fun; where we can meet real live people," but it gradually turns into a pursuit of a husband for the sister-in-law. Of all the disastrous possibilities, including a married chauffeur, a dishonest jockey, and an incompetent aviator, the worst of all seems to be the alcoholic actor who talks the sister out of fifteen thousand dollars and finally marries her to avoid further trouble. The cycle ends, inevitably, with the narrator suggesting to his wife that they "mosey back to South Bend."

But Lardner stayed on, abandoning not only his native region but his original career as well. Despite the popular theory that Lardner was a man who wrote sports stories in dialect, most of the stories collected in *Round Up* (1929) are not written in dialect at all but in a very flexible and realistic lower-middle-class idiom. Scarcely one-quarter of them deal with sports, and "Hurry Kane" is the only sports story published after 1922. Instead, Lardner turned to the world of middle-class society, its bridge games and wedding anniversaries and Florida vacations, its boredom and unhappiness and pointlessness. He disliked almost all of it, even hated it, and yet he was not a rebel. He accepted every social institution from marriage to the rules of etiquette, and the whole social turmoil of his time appeared to leave him quite indifferent. "On the subject of the war he refrained from any writing that could be called political . . ." Elder reports in his biography. "The actions of Congress seemed to him amusing at best, contemptible at their worst. . . . He found the Teapot Dome scandals fascinating and deplorable, but not very surprising. When the Sacco-Vanzetti case enlisted the passionate sympathy of almost all the writers in the country, many of them Ring's closest friends, he kept still. He did not think it was his place to take any public stand."

Lardner simply did not see life in terms of politics and economics and sociology but in terms of games. Even after he stopped writing about organized sports, his characters kept using the language of sports and they played games like bridge and horseshoes, mainly to kill time and to kill their endless boredom.

The games have elaborate rules, but most people break them, not out of any inherent dishonesty but because victory and defeat are equally futile. "Mrs. Taylor shuffled a worn pack of cards and began her evening session at solitaire," Lardner started a story called "Anniversary." "She would probably play forty games before she went to bed, and she would win thirty of them. What harm if she cheated a little? . . . Mrs. Taylor shuffled her cards and tried to listen when Louis read aloud from the Milton Daily Star. . . ."

As a writer, Lardner was determined to succeed in the most gamelike form of literature. Like Henry James and Scott Fitzgerald and countless other deluded non-playwrights, he wanted to be a playwright. The disease had infected him since childhood, when he and his family staged little theatricals for the benefit of the servants. In the early twenties, Lardner collaborated with Gene Buck on a show for Fanny Brice. Ziegfeld rejected it. He and Buck then wrote a play called *Going South*, based on *Gullible's Travels*. Ziegfeld first rejected it, then wanted it turned into a musical. Lardner obliged. The play was never produced. At the same time, Lardner wrote to Fitzgerald that he was "Americanizing Offenbach's 'Orpheus in the Underworld.' " The Americanization, which turned Orpheus into a Tin Pan Alley songwriter, was never produced. Then Lardner began a project to collaborate on a musical with Jerome Kern, and a producer agreed to stage it if W. C. Fields would agree to star in it. Fields did agree, but he had also agreed to star in three other projects, and, according to Lardner, "He's going to spend the winter in court."

Then there was a musical based on Cinderella, with the Prince of Wales as the Prince. It was not produced. There was a musical called *All at Sea*, which got as far as having a score written by Paul Lannin. It was not produced. In all of this gloomy chronicle of wasted work, in fact, only two Lardner plays did get produced. One was based on the story called "Hurry Kane," which interested George M. Cohan. Under his aegis, the story of a moronic pitcher, who tries to throw the World Series at the instigation of his money-hungry girl, somehow changed into the story of a fine young man who only pretends to throw the series so that he can catch the gamblers. *Elmer the Great* ran a modest forty performances on Broadway but was turned into a movie twice. The other production was *June Moon*, a success story of a young songwriter, for which Lardner depended heavily on the professional craftsmanship of George S. Kaufman. Once it was established, he got drunk and telephoned Kaufman to ask whether it would damage the play's success if he committed suicide.

The absurdity of the search for theatrical success is that it is the most ephemeral kind of success. With the exception of O'Neill, no American playwright has lasted beyond his own generation. *June Moon* today is probably less known than the short story on which it was based, "Some Like Them Cold." And, as with Henry James, the main importance of Lardner's theatrical experience was its influence on his fiction. Not only did his work become more succinct but it also acquired such characters as Conrad Green, a savage portrait of Ziegfeld, and Mrs. Lou Gregg, the former movie actress who serves as the heroine of "The Love Nest." These were the winners, whom Lardner now knew even better than the defeated. They were stereotypes, but it was one of Lardner's virtues to create stereotypes who illustrate their period, just as he molded slang and clichés into the language of the period. And in the letters of Chas. F. Lewis, the hero of "Some Like Them Cold," Lardner combined the clichés and stereotype into a marvelous portrait of the wandering yokel on his way to triumph.

"My whole future is in the big town," Lewis writes in his first letter to Mabelle Gillespie, whom he had met at the Lasalle Street Station in Chicago. "N.Y. is the only spot and specially for a man that expects to make my living in the song writing game as here is the Mecca for that line of work and no matter how good a man may be they don't get no recognition unless they live in N.Y." Mabelle soon becomes "Dear Girlie," and the Girlie responds with letters to "Dear Mr. Man." Mr. Man repeatedly reports new attempts on his virtue but says he doesn't want to end with "a wife on your hands that don't know a dish rag from a waffle iron." Girlie recognizes her cue to begin reciting her domestic gifts. Aside from her cooking and sewing, she observes that she always looks "cool and unruffled . . . when everybody else is perspiring." Mr. Man ignores this bait because he is too busy describing his new song, "When They're Like You," which his lyric-writer promises "will clean up as much as $25000 apiece which is pretty fair for one song but this one is not like the most of them." Mr. Man also notes that the lyric-writer has a sister, "but she don't hardly count as she has not got no use for the boys." Girlie happily babbles on about being "born to be a home body," and adds a few hints that her sick mother may soon bequeath her a lot of furniture. Mr. Man's next letter is suddenly casual, offering condolences because "I believe you said your father was sick," which prompts Girlie to apologize "if there was something I said in my last letter that offended you." But it is too late, for Mr. Man announces his engagement to the lyric-writer's sister, adding that he "would hate to think of marrying a girl and then have them spend their lives in druggery." As a parting blow, he urges Girlie: "don't never speak to strange men who you don't know nothing about as they may get you wrong and think you are trying to make them."

It is hard not to sympathize with the battered Mabelle, so solemn and so silly, but to sympathize with either her or Lewis is equally hard. Would either of them be any happier if they did marry and shared their vanity and self-delusion? Lardner had stated the problem more extremely in "My Roomy," when the narrator remarks that "if she's really stuck on him they must be somethin' wrong with her too, so what's the diff'rence?"

Yet the image of theatrical success fascinated Lardner, partly because of his own failures, partly because he saw in the type, as Theodore Dreiser saw in all millionaires, an image of America's own values. Dreiser, in an essay called "The American Financier," was awed: "The financial type is the coldest, the most selfish, and the most useful of all living phenomena . . . a highly specialized machine for the accomplishment of some end which Nature has in view." Long after many other industries had been put under government regulation, Lardner saw, the entertainment industry still permitted and rewarded every kind of coercion and deceit.

His account of Florenz Ziegfeld, in "A Day with Conrad Green," is rather like "Champion," less a short story than an indictment, a series of accusations fitted into the framework of a conventional short story plot. In the course of just ten pages, Lardner creates a character whom he accuses of: (1) flirting with another man's wife, (2) cheating the paper boy out of seven months' worth of newspapers ("Tell him to sue us"), (3) browbeating his new private secretary, (4) being unable to read "where words of over two syllables were concerned," (5) cursing his host of the previous night for not having him included on the official guest list, (6) trying to send a threatening telegram to all newspapers for not listing his presence at the dinner party, (7) welcoming a free-lance writer named Robert Blair and turning down his idea for a sketch, (8) paying blackmail to a weekly newspaper that threatens to accuse him of failing to pay his gambling debts, (9) stealing the last week's pay of forty-five dollars due to his late private secretary, (10) calling in his own writer and outlining Blair's idea as his own, and then getting furious when the writer says the sketch was stolen from another show, (11) begging off from his late secretary's funeral because it's too depressing, (12) forgetting his wife's birthday and then, when she enters his office just before the funeral, giving her an unpaid-for string of pearls he had bought for his mistress, (13) promising his mistress another set of pearls. By the time the new secretary returns from the funeral and says the widow "wished you had been there," Conrad Green can only reply: "Good God! So do I!"

Lardner is a bit more graceful in "The Love Nest." Instead of denouncing his characters, he lets them denounce themselves and each other. Lou Gregg, president of Modern Pictures, Inc., begins to accuse himself as soon as he starts talking to the visiting reporter. "We'll start now so as to get there before the kiddies are put away for the night. I mean I want you to be sure and see the kiddies. I've got three. . . . Yes, sir; three girls. I wouldn't have a boy. I mean I always wanted girls. I mean girls have got a lot more zip to them. I mean they're a lot zippier. But let's go!" Gregg's wife, Celia, plays her part in the charade. "I call it our love nest," she tells the reporter, Bartlett. "Quite a big nest, don't you think? . . . But I always say a place is whatever one makes of it."

As soon as Gregg goes off on an appointment and Celia Gregg absorbs enough bourbon, she begins to tell what she has made of the love nest. "Listen, Barker—I'd give anything in the world to be out of this. . . . He was a director then and he got stuck on me and I thought he'd make me a star. See, Barker? I married him to get myself a chance. And now

look at me! . . . I'd change places with the scum of the earth just to be free! See, Barker? And I could have been a star without any help if I'd only realized it. . . . I could be a Swanson and get myself a marquis; maybe a prince!" In that pitiful ambition, Lardner again plays his favorite trick of asking us to pity someone who is pitiable and yet cannot be pitied. When the next morning comes, and the Greggs are again saying, "Good-by, sweetheart!" Lardner again forces us to the question of life as a game: What's the difference?

There was finally only one victory, and that was the victory over life itself, the victory of the French aristocrat who described his achievements during the Revolution by saying: "I survived." This is the victory of Charley, the narrator of "The Golden Honeymoon," who begins his tale by remarking to his wife that " 'they ain't nobody else lived with me as long as you have.' So she says: 'You can bet they ain't, as they couldn't nobody else stand you that long.' . . . You can't get ahead of Mother."

In that opening exchange, Lardner uses the language of monologue not only to establish the relationship between Charley and "Mother" but to establish the whole character of Charley, a character dominated by age. The wisecracks of *The Big Town* have become small and cautious, and many of them revolve around the all-important question of health. The man not only repeats old jokes—always adding that "Mother laughed"—but clings to the boring details of his life. "We reached North Philadelphia at 4.03 p.m. and we reached West Philadelphia at 4.14, but did not go into Broad Street," he reports. The crisis of "The Golden Honeymoon" is equally narrow and querulous with age. Charley and his wife encounter the wife's old suitor and the two lonely couples begin a crabbed but supposedly friendly rivalry at cards, checkers, and horseshoes. When Charley loses at horseshoes—"I oughtn't to of never tried it, as I hadn't pitched a shoe in sixteen years"—he picks a quarrel with the other couple and then with his own wife. But after the others move on to Orlando, Charley and his wife end their quarrel by joining in denunciation of the departed.

" 'Good gracious!' I said. 'Imagine being married to a woman that plays five hundred like she does and drops her teeth on the roque court!'

" 'Well,' said Mother, 'it wouldn't be no worse than being married to a man that expectorates towards ladies and is such a fool in a checker game.'

"So I put my arm around her shoulder and she stroked my hand and I guess we got kind of spoony."

The reactions to "The Golden Honeymoon" were typical of the reactions to much of Lardner's best work. George Horace Lorimer of the *Saturday Evening Post*, which had been publishing most of Lardner's stories, rejected it as too unorthodox. Ray Long of *Cosmopolitan* promptly seized it as "a fine piece of sympathetic human interest writing." He paid fifteen hundred dollars for it—and asked for sequels about the old couple. Clifton Fadiman, apparently a critic of some perception in those days, denounced the idea that the story was "touching" and described it as "one of the most smashing indictments of a 'happy marriage' ever written, composed with a fury so gelid as to hide completely the bitter passion seething beneath every line."

By this time, Scott Fitzgerald was determined that Lardner's stories should be published in book form. He provided a publisher, Scribners, and a title, *How to Write Short Stories*. Scribners was somewhat dubious, and so was Lardner—"my God, he hadn't even saved them," Fitzgerald recalled with awe, "—the material of *How to Write Short Stories*

was obtained by photographing old issues in the public library!" Lardner revised an old newspaper column to serve as a preface, one of his more inane works. "A little group of our deeper drinkers has suggested that maybe boys and gals who wants to take up writing as their life work would be benefited if some person like I was to give them a few hints. . . . The first thing I generally always do is try and get hold of a catchy title, like for instance, 'Basil Hargrave's Vermifuge,' or 'Fun at the Incinerating Plant.' " This kind of thing stirred the solemn Edmund Wilson, then writing for the *Dial*, to exasperation. "The nonsense of his introductions is so far below his usual level that one suspects him of a guilty conscience in attempting to disguise his talent for social observation and satire. . . . Will Ring Lardner, then, go on to his *Huckleberry Finn* or has he already told all he knows?"

Neither alternative was the truth. Lardner never tried to write another *Huckleberry Finn*—who could?—but the best stories in *How to Write Short Stories* (1924), such as "My Roomy," "Champion," "The Golden Honeymoon," and "Some Like Them Cold," were soon matched by the appearance of another collection called *The Love Nest and Other Stories* (1926), containing "A Day with Conrad Green" and "Haircut" as well as the title story. Just three years later—by now Lardner and Scribners were grinding out a book a year—his best thirty-five stories were collected in a volume called *Round Up*. The critics of the day were duly impressed. H. L. Mencken saluted Lardner in *The American Language* for a mastery of the idiom that revealed "not a single error in the whole canon of his writings." T. S. Matthews, then a book reviewer for the *New Republic* and later the editor of *Time*, produced a symptomatic essay entitled "Lardner, Shakespeare and Chekhov."

Lardner was pleased by the praises. He was

mildly amused when the *New York Times* treated his "posthumous" preface to *The Love Nest* as the literal truth, and, as he wrote Fitzgerald, "played up the introduction strong, saying it was too bad I had died so young, etc." But he knew that much of the praise was routine, as were many of the stories. Fitzgerald listed the sum of Lardner's real creations quite accurately when he cited *You Know Me Al,* "about a dozen wonderful short stories," and "some of the most uproarious and inspired nonsense since Lewis Carroll. Most of the rest is mediocre stuff, with flashes." Mediocre is a kind word for some of the rubbish that occupies a place in Lardner's story collections. *How to Write Short Stories,* for example, includes a tale called "The Facts," which is based on nothing more than a man buying insulting presents for in-laws while drunk. *The Love Nest* includes a story called "Mr. and Mrs. Fix-It," which describes the nuisance of having interfering friends. And some of the lesser entries in *Round Up* are even lesser.

Even the best stories like "The Golden Honeymoon" and "Some Like Them Cold" neither approach nor attempt the depth and subtlety of the best contemporary stories by Hemingway, Faulkner, and Fitzgerald. They are comparatively contrived in plot, narrow in judgment, and frigid in tone. Lardner was an extremely interesting and perceptive writer, but he never even tried to be a great one. Indeed, he was only too quick to announce his own shortcomings. "I just start writing about somebody I think I know something about . . ." he declared. "The other characters seem to walk into the story naturally enough. . . . I write three thousand words about nothing; that is a terrible struggle. Then I come to, and say to myself, 'I must get a punch in this.' I stop and figure out the punch, and then sail through to the finish." Despite this characteristically apologetic self-portrait, however, and despite all

the limitations in even the best of Lardner's stories, there is a great deal of truth in Maxwell Geismar's observation: "In the total view of a writer's work, the whole may be greater than the parts, and that of which he is but imperfectly aware may dominate his conscious articulation. It was thus, bit by bit, that our Ring Lardner surrounded the American life of '29 with a barrier of suspicion, enmity, and at last, hatred."

The question of Lardner's value always returns to this question of hatred. Friends and biographers portray him as a kindhearted and compassionate man, and yet the best of Lardner's stories repeatedly express a deep hatred for the whole world in which he lived. The most extreme account of Lardner's view was an essay in the *Nation* by Clifton Fadiman, who almost accusingly described him as expressing "perfectly clear simon-pure, deliberate misanthropy . . . The world he shows us— and it is one in which we feel not the slightest exaggeration or lack of balance—is a world of mental sadists, four-flushers, intolerable gossipers, meal-ticket females, interfering morons, brainless flirts, liars, brutes, spiteful snobs, vulgar climbers, dishonest jockeys, selfish children, dipsomaniacal chorus girls, senile chatterers, idiotically complacent husbands, mean arrrivistes, drunks, snoopers, poseurs. . . ." Fadiman quoted a remark of Lardner's about a police dog which "was like the most of them and hated everybody," and went on to describe Lardner as "the police dog of American fiction." A newspaper version of this duly reached Lardner in California in 1933, and he sent it off to a friend with a characteristically disingenuous comment. He said the clipping "will tell you the latest news of me—and *to* me. The writer is evidently a fellow from whom you simply can't keep a secret. But I do resent being called a police dog, or dog of any kind." Lardner's admirers, throughout the years, have reacted with similar embarrassment. One recent collection of his works, an anthology called *Shut Up, He Explained*, contains introductory pieces by the two editors, Babette Rosmond and Henry Morgan, which conclude on a note of complete absurdity from Morgan: "You may know that Ring drank a lot and played poker. I never heard of anybody who drank *and* played poker who didn't like people."

It seems that nobody can accept the idea that an admirable writer could not "like people." Yet misanthropy is based not on a negative or nihilistic philosophy but on idealism and perfectionism, and on the realization that the world invariably betrays its ideals. Misanthropy is puritanical, and, inevitably, deterministic. It accepts the idea that the essence of free will is to be free to do whatever you want to do, but the American Puritan, from Jonathan Edwards to Ring Lardner, knows that the free soul will choose to be self-serving and dishonest and cruel. Although Puritanism proclaims judgment by faith, the Puritan usually clings faithfully to the idea of judgment by merit, for merit is supposed to triumph not only in baseball but in all the competitions of life. But if men were judged by merit, according to the puritanical Hamlet, who should escape whipping? So the Puritan, seeing evil, whips out in all directions—until, turning misanthropic, he sees that his whipping does no good. Then, like a true determinist, the misanthrope gives up and accepts the triumph of evil in human nature as the triumph of human nature itself. Because he believes in the impossible, he cannot believe in anything at all. "When you have lived with it a while you don't mind," Lardner said. "Which is just as well because they ain't a wk. passes when you wouldn't get touched on the raw if they was any raw left."

This is the acceptance that drives a writer to silence, or to meaningless hack writing, and accounts for what Fitzgerald called "the impenetrable despair that dogged him for a dozen years to his death." It is the acceptance that prompted Lardner to heavy drinking and talk of suicide—but to refrain from committing suicide. He had not only a family that depended on him but also an audience that expected him to provide laughter.

The reputation of most American humorists seems to depend on some early success that the public never forgets or forgives. Mark Twain was the man who wrote about scapegrace boys, Finley Peter Dunne was the one who wrote in Irish dialect, and James Thurber became the proprietor of dogs, word games, and the war between the sexes. As often as not, the humorist accepts the albatross of his early success and wears it all his life. Twain was planning more sequels to Tom Sawyer when he died, and Thurber continued playing word games to the end. In much the same way, Ring Lardner's first fame came as a sportswriter of humorous dialect, whose characters "could or did better" in "the city serious." In all his years of hack writing, Lardner remembered the money-producing formula. Rambling on about subjects like marriage, he called it "the connubial yokel" and declared that "the marital twain should ought to be opp. sex if possible." Covering the Democratic Convention in 1924, he proposed his own list of dark horses: "Man o' War . . . Old Dobbin . . . Black Beauty." And many of his later short stories are little more than newspaper sketches still commemorating the smart yokel who doesn't like antiques ("Ex Parte") or bridge fanatics ("Contract").

Reading such hack work after more than thirty years have passed, one forgets that hacks are still producing similar things in newspapers and magazines, and one wonders how or why anyone ever laughed at such labored and essentially meaningless writing. Then, among all of Lardner's routine "humor," one discovers a fragment like this dialogue on a train:

" 'How long since you been back in Lansing?'

'Me?' replied Butler. 'I ain't been back there for 12 years.'

'I ain't been back there either myself for ten years. How long since you been back there?'

'I ain't been back there for twelve years.'

'I ain't been back there myself for ten years Where are you headed for?'

'New York,' replied Butler. 'I have got to get there about once a year. Where are you going?'

'Me?' asked Hawkes. 'I am going to New York too. I have to go down there every little wile for the firm.'

'Do you have to go there very often?'

'Me? Every litle wile. How often do you have to go there?'

'About once a year. How often do you get back to Lansing?'

'Last time I was there was ten years ago. How long since you was back?'

'About twelve years ago. Lots of changes there since we left there. . . .' "

This is not really "humor," in the way that Lardner and his readers generally understood the word. It is a statement of the fact that nobody really listens to anyone else, or cares what anyone else has to say, but there is something almost metaphysical about this dramatization of the two travelers trying to establish contact. And while most people associated Lardner with the mildly comical anecdote and the mildly comical dialect, the habitually solemn humorist showed a lifelong distaste for such jokes. "Ring hates funny stories, sincerely and deeply," John Wheeler reported in *Collier's* in 1928. "If you make the mistake of saying to him, 'Did you hear the one about—' he will reply, 'yes,' at that point. It generally stops the story. . . . 'Why,' I asked, 'do you detest funny stories?' And he came back with: 'Because most of them are so old and most of them aren't funny and most people are rotten story-tellers.' " Lardner's personal form of humor was much more ethereal. When he went golfing with President Harding, he declared that he wanted to be appointed ambassador to Greece, an ambition that prompted the President to ask why. "Because my wife doesn't like Great Neck," Lardner said.

Lardner's audiences—as defined by his editors—preferred the traditional Lardner, however, the traditional bumbling sketches about middle-class domestication. Lardner, apart from his lifelong desire to tailor his work for his audience, had good practical reasons for supplying his customary market. He had always worried about supporting his four children, and he was stricken with tuberculosis just at the time when he faced the financial climacteric of putting his sons through college. The only solution was to grind out "humor," and still more "humor." The list of his works during these later years shows all the signs of the exhaustion of the imagination: "Jersey City Gendarmerie, Je T'aime;" "Me, Boy Scout;" and "Stop Me If You've Heard This One."

Probably the weariest of all Lardner's efforts at humor was his supposed autobiography, *The Story of a Wonder Man* (1927). It contains no trace of genuine autobiography, for Lardner had long ago acquired what Fitzgerald called "the habit of silence," the habit of describing himself and his family in terms of a grotesque "comic" image that provided him with the anonymity of total disguise. Not only is there no autobiography in *The Story of a Wonder Man* but there is no humor either. Instead, it consists of sophomoric jokes about Lardner becoming an after-dinner speaker at the age of three, "when Taylor and Presser were running for President and Vice President against Polk and Beans," about Lardner going to college at "Michigan, which needed a half back with a sextuple threat," until "the Spanish war broke out and I enlisted as a general." As though the text weren't repellent enough in itself, Lardner decorates every page with "humorous" footnotes, in which the "editor" corrects mistakes, and the author adds rejoinders to the corrections. And so it goes for about one hundred and fifty pages, illustrated.

In such a manufacturing process, Lardner again recalls Mark Twain, another "humorist" who was at his best when writing seriously, who acknowledged that "if the humor came of its own accord and uninvited, I have allowed it a place in my sermon, but I was not writing the sermon for the sake of the humor." Twain wrote hack journalism from the beginning, and the difference between Lardner's early sports writing and *The Story of a Wonder Man* repeats the decline from the young Twain's craftsmanlike pandering in *The Innocents Abroad* to his weary word-production in *Following the Equator*. In Twain's case, the reasons were obvious. He had gone bankrupt in misguided business ventures and he was working off his debts for his own honor and the honor of his family. Lardner never really lacked money, and yet he suffered from what Fitzgerald had diagnosed in himself as emotional bankruptcy, "drawing on resources that I did not possess . . . mortgaging myself physically and spiritually up to the hilt." The theory of emotional bankruptcy is basically unrealistic, and in Fitzgerald's case it was more self-pity than self-analysis, and yet Lardner did suffer from a kind of emotional impoverishment. He could not enjoy even the few things he found worthy of enjoyment. He could not really express even the few things he found worth expressing. And of all the frustrations, this is the bitterest and the most embittering.

Yet Lardner was condemned—like the Twain who wrote but did not dare publish *What Is Man?*—to his reputation as a humorist. Every editor promised him money as long as he would be funny, just as the crowds came to hear the angry old Mark Twain make jokes, and it is scarcely surprising that Lardner expressed a dislike of Twain's work because "some of his fun is spontaneous, but a great deal of it is not." This was exactly the criticism that Fitzgerald had made in saying that Lardner "was a faithful and conscientious workman to the end, but he stopped finding any fun in his work ten years before he died." And it was the same criticism that Lardner made of himself when he wrote, in *Symptoms of Being 35* (1921), that "Laughter is supposed to keep a man young but if its forced laughter it works the opp."

In theory, humor is supposed to serve as a cathartic for both the humorist and his audience, but its cathartic possibilities are really very limited. Despite the popular phrase about *Don Quixote* having ridiculed feudalism out of existence, humor is a feeble force against the monstrosities of the world. If anybody ever made a joke about Auschwitz, its effect remains to be proved. It is only harmless humor that prompts a society to laughter, humor that fits society's own prejudices. The most acceptable forms of humor have always been those which make fun of objects that everyone accepts as harmlessly comic—fat people, henpecked husbands, and so on. Or, if the humorist is determined to be ruthlessly topical, he makes fun of Castro and the John Birch Society. But it is never truly acceptable to laugh at the truly acceptable. And the humorist, whose vocation consists of his lack of conventional perspective, his unusual juxtaposition of realities that other people see only in the usual sequence, ends by declaring the whole world absurd.

In recent years, the New York theater has

been plagued by a series of querulous plays that labor under the burdensome title of "The Theater of the Absurd," and yet none of these ventures achieves the gaiety that Lardner somehow expressed in a series of totally meaningless little dramas. Perhaps the most notable single section is Act I of *I Gaspiri* ("The Upholsterers"):

A public street in a bathroom. A man named Tupper has evidently just taken a bath. A man named Brindle is now taking a bath. A man named Newburn comes out of the faucet which has been left running. He exits through the exhaust. Two strangers to each other meet on the bath mat.

FIRST STRANGER: Where was you born?

SECOND STRANGER: Out of wedlock.

FIRST STRANGER: That's a mighty pretty country around there.

SECOND STRANGER: Are you married?

FIRST STRANGER: I don't know. There's a woman living with me but I can't place her.

(*Three outsiders named Klein go across the stage three times. They think they are in a public library. A woman's cough is heard off-stage left.*)

A NEW CHARACTER: Who is that cough?

TWO MOORS: That is my cousin. She died a little while ago in a haphazard way.

A GREEK: And what a woman she was!

(*The curtain is lowered for seven days to denote the lapse of a week.*)

Contemporary admirers spoke reverently in terms of Dada and Surrealism—*I Gaspiri* was published in Paris in 1924 in the *Transatlantic Review*—but Donald Elder aptly cites a letter from Lardner to Mrs. Grantland Rice in which he reports a conversation with a woman on a bus. "She said: 'What time is it?' I said: 'It is half past three.' She said: 'Oh, I thought you were a Mexican.'" This, like the dialogue between the two old acquaintances on the train,

is not surrealism but realism. Over and over again, Lardner saw people unable to understand what other people were saying, unable to understand even what they were saying themselves. And out of that perception came some of Lardner's most inspired dialogue. In *Dinner Bridge*—which was not only published but performed in 1927 by a cast that included Robert Benchley, George Kaufman, and Robert Sherwood—Lardner populates the Fifty-ninth Street bridge with a group of laborers who "talk in correct Crowninshield dinner English, except that occasionally, say every fourth or fifth speech, whoever is talking suddenly bursts into dialect, either his own or Jewish or Chinese or what you will."

HANSEN: Did you quarrel much?

AMOROSI: Only when we were together.

TAYLOR: I was a newspaperman once myself.

Toward the end, Taylor begins to imitate birdcalls, and Amorosi reaches a kind of climax by announcing that Italians engage in the more subtle "pastime of mimicking public buildings. For example (*he gives a cry*). The American Express Company's office at Rome. (*He gives another cry.*) The Vatican. (*He gives another cry.*) Hotel McAlpin . . ."

It is all very jolly, if one can just accept the idea that humor is meaningless because life is meaningless, or if one can cling to the idea that humor is cathartic. According to Eugene Ionesco, whose plays re-create Lardner's sense of the absurd, "I feel that life is nightmarish, painful, and unbearable. . . . Have we not the impression that the real is unreal . . . ?" But Lardner could not accept the mild role of humorous commentator, for, like Twain, he was "not writing the sermon for the sake of the humor." And there comes a time when the humorist realizes that humor itself is an enemy. Laughter confuses and corrupts everything he is trying to say—Mort Sahl once complained that liberals liked to laugh at jokes about injustice because then they didn't have to do anything about it. Humor cures nothing except people's consciences, and therefore ends by worsening the world's brutalities. Nobody can become indignant when he is told that something is "just a joke." But Lardner did, and he attacked the whole idea of American folk humor in the savage story called "Haircut."

At the very start, the narrating barber tells his silent customer about the late Jim Kendall, who "certainly was a card." One "great trick that he used to play w'ile he was travelin'" consisted of picking out stores in strange towns and writing anonymous postcards to the proprietors, with messages like "Ask your Missus who kept her from gettin' lonesome the last time you was in Carterville." The barber admits that Jim never knew what happened afterwards, "but he could picture what *probably* happened and that was enough."A feeble-minded boy is a natural victim for such a prankster, and "You can imagine that Jim used to have all kinds of fun with Paul. He'd send him to the White Front Garage for a left-handed monkey wrench. Of course they ain't no such thing as a left-handed monkey wrench."

The story is a fairly well-known melodrama—a timid love affair between a new doctor in town, Ralph Stair, and a girl called Julie Gregg, threatened by the villainous Jim Kendall and guarded by the innocent Paul Dickson. Kendall, who once tried to attack Julie, humiliates her by luring her to the office of the absent doctor and then marshaling a bunch of louts who "chased her all the way home, hollerin', 'Is that you, Ralph?' and 'Oh, Ralphie, dear, is that you?'" The feeble-minded Paul gets Kendall to take him on a duck-hunting expedition and shoots him dead in what Coroner Stair calls "a plain case of accidental shootin'." The plot, as usual with Lardner, is far less impressive than the almost flawless narration of

the barber. But perhaps the most important aspect of "Haircut" is the angry sarcasm with which Lardner quotes the barber's defense of Kendall's jokes: "I said it had been a kind of a raw thing, but Jim just couldn't resist no kind of a joke, no matter how raw. I said I thought he was all right at heart, but just bubblin' over with mischief."

Laughter, in other words, does not fulfill the orthodox prescription—it is not the remedy for human evil. In classical humorists, such as Ben Jonson, the fools learn their lesson, but in Lardner, the fools remain fools, and their humor is foolishness. And in a situation of predominant evil, laughter is the ally of evil. Popular mythology illustrates this in the image of the Devil as a laughing figure, while, as Mark Twain put it, "there is no laughter in Heaven." Nathanael West came to a similar conclusion at the very beginning of *Miss Lonelyhearts* when he declared that the absurd letters to the lovelorn "were no longer funny. He could not go on finding the same joke funny thirty times a day for months on end."

For Lardner, who was too decorous and too conventional to become a noisy misanthrope, the hatred eventually turned inward. To anyone with any perception of life, the difference between the costs and the benefits often seems terribly small—smart men play close to the line because they have to, Fitzgerald had said—and Lardner gradually began to see his own life, and life in general, as both painful and ridiculous. And so he ridiculed his own pain. The supposedly posthumous preface to *The Love Nest*—attributed to a Sarah E. Spooldripper, who "lived with the Lardners for years and took care of their wolf"—concludes by saying: "The Master is gone and the next question is who will succeed him? Perhaps some writer still unborn. Perhaps one who will never be born. That is what I hope." Lardner couldn't resist adding a footnote to explain that "the joke is on Miss Spooldripper, for she is gone too. Two months ago she was found dead in the garage, her body covered with wolf bites left there by her former ward, who has probably forgotten where he left them."

Lardner went even further in describing his own death in a morbid sketch called "Large Coffee": "The body of a Mr. Lardner was found in a New York hotel room by a house officer who had broken in after the chambermaids had reported that they had rapped on the door every day for over a fortnight and had received no response, and were disposed to believe that the occupant of the room would need a clean towel if living, and perhaps two of them if dead. The occupant was in the last-named condition or worse. Dressed as usual in pajamas, he was sprawled out on the floor, his head crushed in by a blow from some blunt instrument, probably another hotel."

This was published in the *New Yorker* fully three years before Lardner died in 1933 at the age of forty-eight, but death was never far from him in these last years. His tuberculosis was apparently hopeless, and he spent most of his last seven years in hospitals, writing a constant stream of sketches and radio reviews to support his family, and maintaining an incredibly light-hearted correspondence with the sons who were beginning their studies at Harvard. It was only in the spotlighted communal life of the hospital, according to Elder's biography, that Lardner was sometimes seen "alone, with his face in his hands, sobbing. Whether it was *lacrimae rerum* or only sheer exhaustion that broke him down it is impossible to know. . . . He had more than once thought of death as the means of escape. He had said that the way he wanted to die was to pass by a street fight and get a stray bullet in his back. The final irony of his life was seven years of tormenting illness."

This overwhelming presence of a slow and

inevitable death darkened all of Lardner's last years, but the darkness had been there from the beginning. By all the American standards that Lardner himself appeared to accept, the darkness remains a mystery. His life fitted perfectly into the pattern for which American society dictates unrelieved happiness. His parents treated him with love and indulgence. He chose his own profession and was enormously successful in it. He married happily and remained devoted to his family. And despite all his caustic comments about the society of his time, he was deeply part of it, and even enjoyed being part of it.

And yet he knew in himself a hollowness that was part of the hollowness of the world he lived in. He lived much of his life in what Fitzgerald called the "real dark night of the soul," when "it is always three o'clock in the morning, day after day." This was not a personal sickness but a sickness of the America that Lardner didn't even try to transcend, an America he could only describe with cruel realism. It was an America that spent its time playing games to pass the insufferable time, and Lardner was the supreme chronicler of all the games in its pursuit of leisure. What Jefferson had called the God-given right to the pursuit of happiness was really a pursuit of the self, and that, as Lardner saw it, was the pursuit of nothingness.

Selected Bibliography

WORKS OF RING LARDNER

You Know Me Al. New York: George H. Doran, 1916. (Reprinted, with introduction by John Lardner, New York: Scribners, 1960.)
Gullible's Travels. Indianapolis: Bobbs-Merrill, 1917.

Treat 'Em Rough. Indianapolis: Bobbs-Merrill, 1918.

My Four Weeks in France. Indianapolis: Bobbs-Merrill, 1918.

Own Your Own Home. Indianapolis: Bobbs-Merrill, 1919.

The Real Dope. Indianapolis: Bobbs-Merrill, 1919.

The Young Immigrunts. Indianapolis: Bobbs-Merrill, 1920.

The Big Town. Indianapolis: Bobbs-Merrill, 1921.

Symptoms of Being 35. Indianapolis: Bobbs-Merrill, 1921.

How to Write Short Stories. New York: Scribners, 1924.

What of It? New York: Scribners, 1925.

The Love Nest and Other Stories. New York: Scribners, 1926.

The Story of a Wonder Man. New York: Scribners, 1927.

Round Up. New York: Scribners, 1929.

June Moon (with George S. Kaufman). New York: Scribners, 1930.

Lose with a Smile. New York: Scribners, 1933.

The Portable Ring Lardner, edited with introduction by Gilbert Seldes. New York: Viking Press, 1946.

Shut Up, He Explained, edited with introductions by Babette Rosmond and Henry Morgan. New York: Scribners, 1962.

The Ring Lardner Reader, edited with introduction by Maxwell Geismar. New York: Scribners, 1963.

CRITICAL AND BIOGRAPHICAL STUDIES

Elder, Donald. *Ring Lardner.* Garden City, N.Y.: Doubleday, 1956.

Fitzgerald, F. Scott. "Ring," in *The Crack Up,* edited by Edmund Wilson. New York: New Directions, 1945.

Geismar, Maxwell. *Writers in Crisis: The American Novel, 1925–40.* Boston: Houghton Mifflin, 1942. Pp. 1–36.

—*OTTO FRIEDRICH*

Sinclair Lewis

1885-1951

HARRY SINCLAIR LEWIS was the youngest of the three sons of a country doctor, Edwin J. Lewis. He was born on February 7, 1885, in the Minnesota village of Sauk Centre, a raw little town less than thirty years old. No one now knows where the name Harry came from, but the name Sinclair, which was to become famous, was the surname of a Wisconsin dentist who was Dr. Lewis' good friend. The boy's mother was an ailing woman who had to spend much of her time away from home, in the South and Southwest, and when Harry was five, she died. In a year the doctor was married again—to a good, brisk, busy woman well suited to the hard-working doctor's unbending, frugal temperament. Harry Lewis' boyhood was curiously loveless, vexatious.

He was homely, ill-coordinated, astigmatic, redheaded, a stumbling, noisy, awkward boy. He was inept at hunting and fishing, could hardly swim, was shunned in boys' games and sports, derided by his fellows and patronized by his elders. He was nearly friendless and was early given to solitary tramps about the countryside and to wide, indiscriminate reading. He yearned to be in some place both more colorful and more kindly than Sauk Centre.

When he was seventeen, his father, whose forebears had lived near New Haven, Connecticut, allowed him to enroll in Yale College after six months of necessary preparation in the Oberlin Academy. The college experience dashed his hopes for a happier life: at Yale he was again friendless and lonely, more the outsider than ever, even though a number of his professors, recognizing his lively intelligence, were good to him. In high school he had written occasional verses, and now at Yale he began to write regularly. Writing was not only a substitute for those social amenities that were denied him but also, he saw, the one means available to him whereby he might win the recognition and respect of his fellows.

His early verse and prose bore almost no resemblance at all to either the subjects or the manner for which he would ultimately become famous. The poetry was imitative, occasionally of Kipling but generally of Tennyson and Swinburne, and he was much given to medieval subjects as he conceived them. His prose was archaic and floriated and its subject matter fantastic and melodramatic. Still, in 1904, he was the only freshman at Yale to appear (with a poem called "Launcelot") in the *Yale Literary Magazine*. That poem is not without a certain imitative charm and almost certainly represents the highest poetic achievement of H. Sinclayre Lewys (as, at sixteen, he had thought of his literary persona).

LAUNCELOT

"Oft Launcelot grieves that he loveth the Queen
But oftener far that she cruel hath been."

Blow weary wind,
The golden rod scarce chiding;
Sir Launcelot is riding
By shady wood-paths pleasant
To fields of yellow corn.
He starts a whirring pheasant,
And clearly winds his horn.
The Queen's Tower gleams mid distant
    hills;
A thought like joyous sunshine thrills,
"My love grows kind."

Blow, weary wind,
O'er lakes, o'er dead swamps crying,
Amid the gray stumps sighing
While slow, and cold, and sullen,
The waves splash on the shore.
O'er wastes of bush and mullen,
Dull crows flap, evermore.
The Autumn day is chill and drear
As yon knight, thinking Guenevere
Proves most unkind.

Once this poem was accepted, the way was open for him on the *Lit*. In the following years he became a regular contributor to this and other undergraduate periodicals and in his third year the number of his contributions won him a place on the editorial staff of the *Lit*.

During two of his summers he made cattle-boat trips to England and on these trips he began to take systematic notes for fiction. One summer he returned to Sauk Centre, where excruciating boredom led him to conceive of a novel to be called *The Village Virus*. (When this novel was at last written, it was called *Main Street*.) In spite of his literary success at college, life at Yale grew increasingly exasperating for him, and at the beginning of his senior year he abruptly fled from New Haven to become a janitor and general handyman at Helicon Hall, the odd experiment in communal living that Upton Sinclair had just established near Engle-wood, New Jersey, on the Palisades. He sustained that effort for about a month.

Since in this recusant period his father was not giving him any money at all, the young man went to New York determined to live by his pen, but after several months of near starvation he left for Panama, where he hoped to find work on the canal then under construction. That failing, too, he suddenly decided to return to New Haven and finish his education at Yale. He was readmitted to the College and he was graduated in June of 1908, a year behind his class.

There followed a number of years of miscellaneous adventure all over the United States, a time in which he tried to be a newspaperman without success, and continued to try to publish without much success. Iowa, New York, San Francisco, Washington, New York again. For a brief period he lived in a newly established bohemian colony in Carmel, California, where his associates were such writers as George Sterling and Jack London. Failing to sell his own stories, Lewis sold a number of plots (from the enormous plot file that he had put together) to London for sums ranging from five to fifteen dollars, but even this munificence on the part of the older writer could hardly be expected to support the younger and more inventive writer. From the end of 1910 until the end of 1915, he worked in publishing houses in New York and on a number of periodicals. During his vacation one summer he wrote a boys' book, *Hike and the Aeroplane*, on commission for Frederick A. Stokes Company and published it under the pseudonym of Tom Graham.

More important, Lewis was working all the time on what would be his first novel, and although his friends in publishing circles discouraged him in his effort to be a serious novelist, he continued to work at it until he had what he thought was a publishable manuscript. After it was rejected by several publishers, it was accepted at last by the firm of Harper and published in February of 1914. Two months later, on April 15, Lewis was married to his first wife, a young woman named Grace Livingstone Hegger, who gave up her employment in the office of *Vogue* to establish the first Lewis ménage in the Long Island community of Port Washington. Lewis was still working in Manhattan, writing furiously at home before and after work and on commuting trains, but he was always pining for the time when he could afford to live by writing alone.

Our Mr. Wrenn had a reasonably good press but very small sales. The second novel, *The Trail of the Hawk*, published in 1915, enjoyed the same fate. At work on a third novel, Lewis found suddenly that his whole situation was altered when the *Saturday Evening Post* accepted his story called "Nature, Inc." This acceptance was quickly followed by three more, and Lewis was being paid $1000 for each story. With money in the bank for the first time in his life, he resigned his position at the Doran publishing house and in December of 1915 set out with his wife on what would be a life of wandering throughout their marriage. Traveling once more all over the United States, briefly setting up one residence and then another, he was writing literally scores of stories, almost all of them to be published in the slick periodicals, and he was also working at a number of books. The first of these, called *The Innocents*, was in fact planned as a magazine serial, and is one of the worst books he ever wrote. The next, though the first to be published as a book—both it and *The Innocents* appeared in 1917—was titled *The Job*; it is one of the best of his early books. The fifth of his novels, called *Free Air*, is a sentimental fictionalization of the Lewis trip across the

continent in a Ford, and was published in 1919. At the same time that he was finishing *Free Air*, Lewis was working at what would be *Main Street*, finished in Washington early in the summer of 1920 and published in the fall of that year. Now the apprenticeship was abruptly ended, and ended in a positive storm of vilification and applause. Suddenly Sinclair Lewis was a famous man.

When *Main Street* appeared, plunging literary America into a rare and heated controversy, it seemed that nothing like it, with its shrill indictment of village life, the middle class, provincial America, had been published before. For many years popular American fiction had been picturing village life as sweet and good, the middle class as kindly when not noble, the provinces as aglow with an innocence in sharp contrast to the cruelty and corruption of the cities. In the fifty years before 1920 there had, to be sure, been exceptions—novels a good deal more critical of village life than was the rule; but the prevailing view was that of Friendship Village, and it was this view that *Main Street* abruptly and perhaps forever ended.

Main Street seemed to those readers who had known Lewis' earlier work to be a complete rupture with everything he had done before. A look at those earlier novels now shows this not to have been the situation at all. All five works had essentially the same pattern: the impulse to escape the conventions of class or routine; flight; a partial success and a necessary compromise with convention. Realistic in detail, these novels were optimistic in tone in a way that was not generally associated with what was then thought of as the school of realism, and it was the combination of the optimistic view of human character with the body of observed social detail that critics remarked and some readers enjoyed.

There had been satirical flashes in the earlier books, if not the generally sustained and less good-tempered satire of *Main Street*, but satire nevertheless and satire directed against the same general objects. Furthermore, when those earlier novels were effective, they were so because of the body of closely observed physical detail, but it was detail more impressionistically, less massively presented than in *Main Street*. Certain character types that were to be made famous by *Main Street* had already appeared —the hypocritical bigot, the village atheist, the aspiring idealist, and so on. And the basic pattern of *Main Street* was exactly the same pattern that has already been described: a young creature is caught in a stultifying environment, clashes with that environment, flees from it, is forced to return, compromises.

Carol Kennicott, the heroine of *Main Street*, has no alternative to compromise. Her values, her yearning for a free and gracious life, had only the vaguest shape, and when she tried to put them into action in Gopher Prairie, Minnesota, she found only the most artificial and sentimental means. To some readers even then (when thousands of women were identifying themselves with her) she seemed like a rather foolish young woman, and so today she must seem to every reader. In the end, the true values are those of her husband, "Doc" Kennicott, who, for all his stolidity, is honest, hardworking, kindly, thrifty, motivated by common sense—altogether like Lewis' brother, Dr. Claude, and even rather like his father, Dr. E. J. It is Kennicott who has the last word. In the end, then, it is the middle class that triumphs and the Middle West, and the middle-brow. And so it would always be in fact in the novels of Sinclair Lewis.

It is more accurate to say that the triumph is given to the *best* qualities of the middle class and that it is its worst qualities that the novel castigates: smugness, hypocrisy, a gross materialism, moral cant. These are the qualities that Lewis' satire, even when the focus begins to blur as it does with *Dodsworth*, would continue to assail. Thus, immediately after *Main Street*, he plunged into his research in that section of American life where those qualities were most obvious and therefore most readily lampooned—the commercial world of the middle-class businessman in a medium-sized city. "Research" is the correct word if one thinks of a novelist operating in the fashion of a sociologist preparing to make a field report. It is the novel *Babbitt* that established what would henceforth be Sinclair Lewis' characteristic method of work, a method toward which he had been moving ever since his cattleboat note-taking days.

To begin, he chose a subject—not, as for most novelists, a character situation or a mere theme, but a social area that could be systematically studied and mastered. Ordinarily, this was a subclass within the middle class, a profession, or a particular problem of such a subclass. Then, armed with his notebooks, he mingled with the kind of people that his fiction would mainly concern. In Pullman cars and smokers, in the lobbies of side-street hotels, in athletic clubs, in a thousand junky streets he watched and listened, and then meticulously copied into his notebooks whole catalogues of expressions drawn from the American lingo, elaborate lists of proper names, every kind of physical detail. He drew intricately detailed maps, and maps not only of the city in which his story was set but of the houses in which his actions would take place, floor plans with furniture precisely located, streets and the kind and color of dogs that walked on them. Mastering this body of material, he would then write out a summary of his story, and from this, a much more extended "plan," as he called it, with every scene sketched in, the whole sometimes nearly as long as the book that would come from it. A first draft would then follow, usually much longer than the final version, and then a long process of revision and cutting, and at last the publishable text. Although he traveled the length and breadth of the United States in 1920 and 1921, always listening and looking with *Babbitt* in mind, it was, in fact, Cincinnati, Ohio, that provided the chief scene of his researches for this novel about a place called Zenith.

Again, *Babbitt* (1922) plunged the nation into literary controversy. Again, the novel seemed absolutely new, unlike anything that had come before it. Again, to many the assault on American virtue seemed brutal, uncompromising, and unfair. All over the United States Sinclair Lewis was denounced as a villain and a traitor, and all over the United States thousands and thousands of people bought his novel. In Europe it seemed that someone in America was finally telling the whole truth about the appalling culture of that deplorable country. A class had been defined, as it had been given the name that stays with it still. H. L. Mencken's abstraction of *boobus Americanus* had been given a body, a body that lives still in the American imagination.

Lewis' original intention in *Babbitt*, he later said, was to recount twenty-four hours in the life of his character, "from alarm clock to alarm clock." That original structural conception remains in the first seven chapters as the book stands. The remaining twenty-seven chapters are systematically planned if rather aimlessly assembled set pieces that, taken together, give us the sociology of middle-class American life. These pieces have as their topics such matters as Politics, Leisure, Club Life, Trade Association Conventions, Class Structure and Attitudes, Conventional Religion, "Crank" Religion, Labor Relations, Marriage and the Family, and such lesser topics as The Barbershop and The Speakeasy. There is no plot to contain and unite these interests, but their fragmentariness is in part overcome by the fact that George Babbitt moves through all of them in the course of his rising discontent, his rebellion, his retreat and resignation. Each of these three moods, in turn, centers in a more or less separate narrative: the first in the imprisonment of Paul Riesling after he shoots his wife; the second in Babbitt's attempt to find sympathy in Tanis Judique and "the Bunch"; the third in the pressures brought on him by the Good Citizens' League and his wife's happily coincidental emergency operation. It is not surprising that the general thematic and narrative movement, like the central figure himself, is sometimes lost to sight in the forest of marshaled mores.

Had the early optimist vanished in the Menckenian pessimist, as it seemed to so many readers in 1922 and 1923? In fact, the essential narrative pattern had not changed in *Babbitt*: the individual trapped in an environment, catching glimmerings of something more desirable beyond it, struggling to grasp them, succeeding or failing. Babbitt fails—or nearly does—with the result that the comic-satiric element here is both heightened and broadened over that of the earlier novels. Clifton Fadiman, writing later, defined the essential pattern when he wrote of Dodsworth as a man who "can neither give himself wholly over to the business of *being* a businessman nor give himself wholly over to the more difficult business of being a man. His vacillation between the part and the whole forms the basic theme of all of Sinclair Lewis's finest novels." Similarly, Frederick Hoffman suggested that there are two Babbitts, one the perfect Menckenese "boob," the other the "doubting Babbitt." A double question follows: can the doubting Babbitt conceive of the qualities that make a man as well as a businessman, that create a society as well as a mere association of "joiners"; and, can Sinclair Lewis?

The novel makes it easy enough for one to name the values that would save Zenith and Babbitt with it. They are love and friendship; kindness, tolerance, justice, and integrity; beauty; intellect. For the first two of these Babbitt has a throbbing desire if no very large capacity. Of the next four he has intimations. The seventh he can approach only in the distortions of his reveries, as in his morning dream of the "fairy child." To the last he is a total stranger. Of Lewis one may say he was much like Babbitt in the first two, with no greater capacity; that the next four constitute the core of his character and of his demand on life; of the next, that it is too readily softened by sentiment, as is Babbitt's; and of the last that on the evidence of the novels the matter remains enigmatic.

We have omitted from this list the power of observation, which, in its full sense, may depend on all the other qualities taken together and become the highest form of intuition; but in the more limited sense in which we commonly use the term in both social intercourse and literary discourse, it is this quality that differentiates Lewis from his creature. It is this quality that enabled John O'Hara, many years later, to say that "Lewis was born to write Babbitt's story. . . . All the other novelists and journalists and Babbitt himself were equally blind to Babbitt and Zenith and the United States of America until 1922."

The novel was, in fact, the first of its kind in two striking ways. American literature had a full if brief tradition of the business novel. James, Howells, London, Phillips, Herrick, Sinclair, Wharton, Dreiser, Poole, Tarkington —all these writers had been centrally concerned with the businessman; and, after James

and Howells, only Tarkington was to find in him any of the old, perdurable American virtues. Business was synonymous with ethical corruption; the world of business was savagely competitive, brutally aggressive, murderous. The motivation of the businessman was power, money, social prestige—in that order. But the businessman in almost all this fiction was the tycoon, the powerful manufacturer, the vast speculator, the fabulous financier, the monarch of enormous enterprises, the arch-individual responsible only to himself. And his concern was production.

After World War I, the tycoon may still have been the most colorful and dramatic figure in the business myth, but he was no longer the characteristic figure, and *Babbitt* discovers the difference. This is the world of the little businessman and, more particularly, of the middleman. If his morals are no better, his defections are anything but spectacular. Not in the least resembling the autocratic individualist, he is the compromising conformist. No producer himself, his success depends on public relations. He does not rule; he "joins" to be safe. He boosts and boasts with his fellows, sings and cheers in praise of the throng, derides all difference, denounces all dissent—and only to climb with the crowd. And with the supremacy of *public* relations, he abolishes human relations. All this Sinclair Lewis' novel was the first to give back to a culture that was just becoming aware that it could not tolerate what it had made of itself.

And it did it with a difference. The older novels, generally speaking, were solemn or grandly melodramatic denunciations of monstrous figures of aggressive evil. *Babbitt* was raucously satirical of a crowd of ninnies and buffoons who, if they were malicious and mean, were also ridiculous. And yet, along with all that, Babbitt himself was pathetic.

With *Babbitt*, Sinclair Lewis' extraordinary gift for satirical mimicry of American speech found a fuller and more persistent expression than in any previous work. Nowhere is it more successful than in Babbitt's address at the annual meeting of the Zenith Real Estate Board: " 'Some time I hope folks will quit handing all the credit to a lot of moth-eaten, mildewed, out-of-date, old, European dumps, and give proper credit to the famous Zenith spirit, that clean fighting determination to win Success that has made the little old Zip City celebrated in every land and clime, wherever condensed milk and paste-board cartons are known! Believe me, the world has fallen too long for these worn-out countries that aren't producing anything but bootblacks and scenery and booze, that haven't got one bathroom per hundred people, and that don't know a loose-leaf ledger from a slip-cover; and it's just about time for some Zenithite to get his back up and holler for a show-down!' " And so the stream of clotted argot and cliché floods on and on.

With this book, Sinclair Lewis seemed to most readers to have become America's leading novelist. The reviews were extravagant, and the one that seemed to mean most to Lewis himself appeared in the *New Statesman* and was written by Rebecca West. "It has that something extra, over and above," she wrote, "which makes the work of art, and it is signed in every line with the unique personality of the writer." After quoting from one of Babbitt's public speeches, she continues: "It is a bonehead Walt Whitman speaking. Stuffed like a Christmas goose as Babbitt is, with silly films, silly newspapers, silly talk, silly oratory, there has yet struck him the majestic creativeness of his own country, its miraculous power to bear and nourish without end countless multitudes of men and women. . . . But there is in these people a vitality so intense that it must eventually bolt with them and land them willy-nilly into the sphere of intelligence; and this immense commercial machine will become the instrument of their aspiration."

There were dissenting voices among the reviewers. There were those who argued that the vitality of the novel was only the aimless if "unique" vitality of the author himself, and what a critic like Gilbert Seldes, even when praising the book, was really saying was that the imaginative vitality of Sinclair Lewis failed to find any satisfactory aesthetic organization. The whole book should have been rewritten, he argued, after Lewis had taken a long look into himself. The implication was—and it was made explicit by others—that the book had no values beyond Babbitt's own, and that satire, comic and critical as it may be, must found itself on positive standards that are clearly there even if they are not stated. Some critics personalized this view by saying that Lewis himself was Babbitt, and ascribed the success of the novel to the fact that the audience that Lewis satirized recognized in the author not an enemy but an ally, not a teacher but a brother. And, indeed, many of the most loosely enthusiastic reviews that the book received came from the newspapers of those middle-sized middle-western cities that most resembled Zenith and that took pride in having served, as they thought, as the model for that modest metropolis.

If his environment is too powerful for George Babbitt, Lewis' next hero was to prove more powerful than his, and, after the preceding two novels, critics thought again that a "new" Lewis had emerged. In fact, *Arrowsmith* (1925) merely permitted the idealism that had always been present to prevail. The idealist is no longer a solitary figure, for, besides Martin Arrowsmith, there are also Gottlieb, Sondelius, Terry Wickett, and others. These are the dedicated truth seekers, the pure scientists who will not compromise with commercial standards or yield to institutional pressures. If, in the end, in order to maintain their own standards, they are forced to withdraw entirely from institutions, their standards are nevertheless victorious.

After *Babbitt*, Lewis had not intended to write a novel about the medical profession. Returning to the Middle West, he was pursuing his intermittent researches for a "labor novel" which he had had in mind ever since his youth. In Chicago he quite accidentally met a young medical research scientist recently associated with the Rockefeller Institute in New York, Paul de Kruif, and together the two discussed the possibility of a novel about the corruptions of the medical profession and of medical research. The idea seized upon Lewis' imagination. His father and brother were both doctors and two of his uncles had been doctors, and while he had already treated the type of the country doctor, he had not dealt with medical science in its grander aspects, and this subject, too, had long interested him. With de Kruif, he arranged a tour of the Caribbean, where much of the action of *Arrowsmith* was to take place, and then they proceeded to England, where Lewis, with De Kruif always at his elbow, began to write the novel. The writing of this novel probably gave him more personal satisfaction than any other that he had already published or that he was to publish. It released a latent strain of idealism that was very powerful in his character but that his other subject matter had not permitted full expression.

The other side of this idealism continued the same as before, and involved the same subjects for satire. A narrow provincialism, hypocrisy, complacency, the "security" of organizational activity, pomposity, the commercial spirit, and the ideal of cash—all these were present again. Their presentation differed not only in that their opposites were given more

substantial representation but also in that they were woven into a story that was itself more exciting than any other that Lewis had devised and in that this story included a heroine, Martin's wife, Leora, with whom everyone could sympathize, as not everyone could with Carol Kennicott.

The praise for *Arrowsmith*, except for the disgruntled remarks of a few doctors, was universal. In Evanston, Illinois, an obscure young English teacher named Bernard De Voto was able to say what the book was not: it was not urbane, sophisticated, ironical, symmetrical, concise. If it was in some ways naive, so were Hawthorne, Whitman, Mark Twain. And this is what *Arrowsmith* is—America!—in its naiveté no less than its splendor. And thus, trying to tell us what Sinclair Lewis' true quality is, the young critic, as critic, gives up; but not the enthusiastic reader: "It is the most American novel of the generation; and if it is not the best, at least it can never hereafter be out of mind when the few, diverse novels entitled to compete for such an epithet are considered. . . . It goes down to the roots of our day. It is the almost inconceivable pageant of our America. . . . And that will . . . put *Arrowsmith* safely among the permanent accomplishments of its generation—to endure with a few other great novels of America, none of them quite innocent of defect." The voice grows hoarse; it was, the young De Voto confessed within the review, "the most extravagant praise" he had ever written. And he was by no means alone but only a part of the booming chorus. It came as no surprise that this novel, unlike the controversial works that had preceded it, should command the interest of the donors of the Pulitzer Prize.

Sinclair Lewis had by this time become a public figure of such quixotic reputation that it came as no great surprise either when he declined to accept the honor. His grounds, not very well argued, were that such prizes tended to legislate taste. Whether or not he was being disingenuous, attempting to punish the Pulitzer people for not having given him the prize for *Main Street* or *Babbitt*, the fact remains that the attendant publicity was worth infinitely more to him than the prize itself or the publicity that he would have received had he accepted it. With this gesture and his next two books, he swiftly reversed the augmented reputation he had won as an idealistic novelist.

The first of these two novels was a piece of hack work, a ridiculous account of adventures in northwest Canada called *Mantrap* (1926), and the second, *Elmer Gantry* (1927), was another explosion, the most controversial of all his books, the most brutal attack on American standards.

Elmer Gantry deals with the shabby area of evangelical religion. Lewis chose Kansas City as the field for his research, and there he cultivated ministers of every denomination and faith. The result was the broadest and the most slashing satire that he was ever to write and the satire least concerned with the presentation of positive values.

Like most of Lewis' novels, *Elmer Gantry* is a loosely episodic chronicle which involves no primary conflict about which all the action is organized, in which value can achieve a complex definition, and by which at least two orders of value are dramatized. The chronicle, like *Babbitt*, breaks down into three large parts, each pretty nearly independent of the others. In each event Elmer's progress is colored and in two of them threatened by his relation with a woman, but from each Elmer emerges triumphant. The first part takes us through his Baptist education, his ordination, his first pulpit, and his escape from Lulu; the second takes us through his career as an evangelist with the fantastic Sharon Falconer; the third takes us through his experience of New Thought and his rise in Methodism, together with the decline of his marriage to Cleo and his escape from Hettie, who threatens to bring him to public ruin but who is herself routed as, in the final sentence, Elmer promises that "We shall yet make these United States a moral nation!"

It should not be supposed that the frank prominence in *Elmer Gantry* of sexual appetite—a rare enough element in a Lewis novel— or the fact that it several times threatens Elmer's otherwise unimpeded success, in any way provides the kind of dramatized counterpoint on the absence of which we are remarking, or that it in any way serves to introduce an element of human tenderness that modifies Elmer's brutality. On the contrary, it is an integral part of his inhumanity and an integral part of the inhumanity of the religious environment within which he exists. Indeed, of all the forms of relationship that the novel presents, the sexual relation is most undilutedly brutish, and it is perhaps the chief element in that animus of revulsion that motivates the author's creation of this cloacal world.

Hovering on the fringes of the plot are a few figures of good like Frank Shallard, honest clergymen of sincere religious conviction, but these figures, all minor, are never allowed to enter the action or to oppose effectively the major characters, notably Elmer Gantry himself, one of the great beasts of all literature. The minutely detailed history of Elmer Gantry involves an extraordinarily full account of every form of religious decay in American life, an account in which nothing is missing except all religion.

The world of *Elmer Gantry* is a world of total death, of social monsters without shadow. And in some ways therefore the novel gives us the purest Sinclair Lewis. More than this, one may say that, although it caused the greatest furor of all Lewis' novels at the time of publication and although it provided a script for a widely shown film in the 1960's, it remains the most neglected and perhaps most underestimated of Lewis' major works. For the subject animated in Lewis a latent strain of extravagant fantasy on the one hand and, on the other, a devastating sense of the possible poverty of human experience. The two moods, nearly opposite and yet clearly counterparts, can be readily illustrated.

The first is best observed in the phantasmagoric scene in which Sharon capitulates to Elmer before an altar where she associates herself, in a ritual invocation, with all goddesses of fertility:

" 'It is the hour! Blessed Virgin, Mother Hera, Mother Frigga, Mother Ishtar, Mother Isis, dread Mother Astarte of the weaving arms, it is thy priestess, it is she who after the blind centuries and the groping years shall make it known to the world that ye are one, and that in me are ye all revealed, and that in this revelation shall come peace and wisdom universal, the secret of the spheres and the pit of understanding. Ye who have leaned over me and on my lips pressed your immortal fingers, take this my brother to your bosoms, open his eyes, release his pinioned spirit, make him as the gods, that with me he may carry the revelation for which a thousand thousand grievous years the world has panted. . . . O mystical rose, O lily most admirable, O wondrous union; O St. Anna, Mother Immaculate, Demeter, Mother Beneficent, Lakshmi, Mother Most Shining; behold, I am his and he is yours and ye are mine!' "

The absurd extravagance of this scene is somehow emphasized by the absence in it of any honest recognition of human need or of human fulfillment. The travesty that it makes of both the sexual and the religious experience is of course to be associated with the temper of evangelistic orgy that permeates the novel.

Dramatically, however, it should be juxtaposed with such an earlier scene, as blankly homely as this one is hilariously horrible—a scene in which a deaf old retired preacher and his wife are going to bed after fifty years of marriage, and the whole of that marital experience is finally equated with the memory of an "old hoss":

" 'I would of liked to had you try your hand at politics. If I could of been, just once, to a senator's house, to a banquet or something, just once, in a nice bright red dress with gold slippers, I'd of been willing to go back to alpaca and scrubbing floors and listening to you rehearsing your sermons, out in the stable, to that old mare we had for so many years—oh, laws, how long is it she's been dead now? Must be—yes, it's twenty-seven years—

'Why is it that it's only in religion that the things you got to believe are agin all experience? Now drat it, don't you go and quote that "I believe because it *is* impossible" thing at me again! . . .

'Twenty-seven years! And we had that old hoss so long before that. My how she could kick—Busted that buggy—'

They were both asleep."

The two scenes supplement one another; they represent the extremes of the nightmare image of a world that, totally empty of human value, monstrously, and without relief, parodies the reality.

The book, to the great advantage of its sales, was immediately banned in Boston, and bans of one kind or another—from the simple refusal of public librarians to put it on their shelves, to announcements by booksellers that they would not stock it, to wholesale municipal bans—extended from Kansas City to Camden, from Boston to Glasgow. Every ban provided the publishers with the least expensive form of promotion.

News stories of every kind developed out of the publication of the book and the character of the author. The Boston *Transcript* announced that "it is neither wrong nor unjust to accuse Lewis of being one of the greatest egoists in the world today." He was invited to a lynching party in Virginia; one cleric suggested that a prison sentence of five years was clearly in order. Letters of abuse cluttered his mail.

In a resolution supporting the Anti-Saloon League of New York State, one Methodist minister declared before the annual assemblage of the New York East Conference, "The Methodist Church is cordially hated, not only by the class represented by Mr. Sinclair Lewis and the rum organizations, but also by every evil organization of every kind whatsoever," while only a few weeks later the graduating class of New York University voted Sinclair Lewis its favorite author. An item in an Ohio newspaper ran as follows: "Trouble in the home of Leo Roberts, general manager of the Roberts Coal and Supply Company, began when his wife brought home a copy of *Elmer Gantry* and he burned it as undesirable reading matter, according to Mrs. Roberts at a hearing Wednesday before Judge Bostwick of Probate Court, when Roberts was ordered to a private sanitarium for a short rest, after his wife, Mrs. Margaret Roberts, 1671 Franklin Park South, charged him with lunacy." Very soon ministers' wives were seeking divorces on the ground that their husbands were Elmer Gantrys, i.e., adulterers; and ministers themselves were demanding that colleagues too attentive to their choir singers be investigated. In less than six weeks, even the least literate of churchgoers had heard the novel denounced from the pulpit of his church.

Never has a profession cooperated so zealously with a publisher as the clergy, of all denominations and faiths, in 1927. Generally, of course, the novel was the subject of denunciation: "slime, pure slime," "sordid and cowardly," "venomous," "unprincipled," "an insult," "filthy"—these were some of the terms of abuse. The evangelist Billy Sunday called Lewis "Satan's cohort." He was not only "Mencken's minion," he was Judas. Yet here and there, quieter clerical voices suggested that, while Elmer Gantry was a monster, the novel itself was a useful tonic in a situation not entirely healthy.

Reviewers praised the novel and abused it with equal vigor. Again, thousands of people bought it. H. L. Mencken thought it one of the great satires of all time and compared Lewis with Voltaire. The novel could not have been more appropriately dedicated than it was —to Mencken, "with profound admiration."

There were to be further reversals. Lewis' first marriage had by now fallen into decay and he was wandering about Europe, alone, looking for new subject matter while the furor over *Elmer Gantry* raged at home. He found his subject matter in the story of a wealthier, more powerful, somewhat more sensitive Babbitt named Samuel Dodsworth, unhappily married, wandering about Europe and discovering a superior woman who would become his second wife. So, stumbling into Berlin, Sinclair Lewis met a superior woman, the handsome Dorothy Thompson, best-known newspaperwoman in Europe, and presently she would become his second wife.

He interrupted the writing of *Dodsworth* to expand into a book-length work a short story he had recently published in the *American Mercury*—"The Man Who Knew Coolidge"— the monologue of an idiotic, sub-Babbitt type named Lowell Schmaltz. Exercising here once more his remarkable gift for imitating the speaking American voice, he nevertheless added very little to his stature with this work.

Then, after his marriage in London on May 14, 1928, he returned to the United States with his new wife and there finished *Dodsworth* (1929). This work once more assured Lewis' readers that he was a generous man, for while it again had its share of satire, the satire was directed largely at the frenetic pretentiousness and snobbery of Dodsworth's first wife, and it presented Dodsworth himself, with all his solidly American middle-class virtues, in full sympathy. Here there was no occasion at all for controversy. And what Sinclair Lewis himself believed in, at the bottom of his blistered heart, was at last clear: a downright self-reliance, a straightforward honesty, a decent modesty, corn on the cob and apple pie.

The terms of the novel are much the same as they had always been, and the pattern is the same, of the man who glimpses a dream beyond the trivial actualities and stifling habits of his life, and who, now, can make it real. Only the emphasis had been shifted, and the object of satire drastically reversed. Whereas in earlier novels he had satirized the stuffy middle-western citizenry, with its smugness, materialism, and aggressive provinciality, and approved of the "outsiders," Carol and Paul Riesling and Martin Arrowsmith and Frank Shallard, now he satirizes the poor critic of Babbittry that he chooses to give the reader in the character of Fran Dodsworth, and approves the middle-western citizenry in the person of Sam, who has more money than Babbitt and needs, therefore, to think less about it, but who is hardly less aggressive in his own kind of provincialism.

For nearly the first time in his major novels he was handling material that was by no means new—for generations there had been novels about Americans in Europe; but what he was doing, or so it seemed, was new to him: approving the substantial middle-class, middle-western virtues, the best of Babbitt. He had,

of course, been doing this all the time and very explicitly in the early, little-read books; but after *Elmer Gantry* and *The Man Who Knew Coolidge*, it seemed a sharp reversal.

No critics observed the larger significance of *Dodsworth* in the career of Sinclair Lewis and in modern American writing. Between the end of the war in 1918 and the beginning of the Depression of the 1930's, a revolution had overtaken American life in manners and morals and all intellectual assumptions, and *Main Street, Babbitt, Arrowsmith,* and *Elmer Gantry*, whatever their aesthetic limitations, had played a major part, probably the major literary part, in this transformation. At the end of the 1920's, writers were left either in the situation of Scott Fitzgerald, trying "to hold in balance the sense of futility of effort and the sense of the necessity to struggle," or in the situation of young radicals who tried to turn their writing into social action on behalf of a hypothetical "proletariat." Only extremes of attitude presented themselves as possible: the jaded "aristocratic" attitude implied in the work of Fitzgerald (and implicit in such a school of criticism as the New Humanism, however far this school may have been from him) and the enthusiastic espousal of the revolutionary "working class" attitude exemplified by the *New Masses* and any number of "proletarian" writers. In *Dodsworth*, Lewis refused the extremes and turned back to a reassertion of those very middle-class, middlebrow, and middle-western values that the decade of the twenties seemed to have destroyed forever, and that it had most emphatically modified at least; and with those values he, who would henceforth seem to be the most old-fashioned of modern American novelists, would henceforth abide.

Yet it was the Lewis of *Babbitt* rather than the Lewis of *Dodsworth* that led the Swedish Academy, at the end of 1930, to award him, the first American writer, the Nobel Prize in literature. That event followed on the birth of Lewis' second son, Michael, to his second wife, in the middle of that year, and it was probably a considerably less expected event for him. But for some time European readers had been looking with increasing favor on American novelists, and especially on those who, like Sinclair Lewis, were critical of American culture. Other American novelists who were popular in Sweden—Jack London, Upton Sinclair, Edith Wharton, Theodore Dreiser, Sherwood Anderson—were read in much the same spirit as he was, as social critics of the same materialism and chauvinistic complacency, and with no important aesthetic discriminations to be made between them.

Under these circumstances, it is not surprising that Lewis, who was the sharpest and the most detailed critic and who yet wrote out of what seemed to be love of his country, should have come to seem the leader. He had come to seem the leader, however, of a body of literature that was in itself as exciting as any in the world, and a body of literature that, in its very criticism of American culture, demonstrated its maturity.

That criticism Lewis brought to its climax in his famous address delivered in Stockholm on December 12, 1930, and known now under the title "The American Fear of Literature." An attack on the atrophied tradition of gentility and academicism in American critical values, it announced that "Our American professors like their literature clear and cold and pure and very dead." Rather unfairly, it placed the blame on the continuing prestige of William Dean Howells (who had, in fact, been gracious to the still unknown young Lewis in their single encounter in 1916), and, defying "official" custodians of American literary culture, such as the American Academy of Arts and Letters, it praised such dissident novelists as Theodore

Dreiser and Sherwood Anderson, and brought to the attention of its European audience the names of a whole group of young American writers who were still almost entirely unknown abroad. There are fallacies as well as injustices in the address, but it was composed in an authoritative spirit that made Lewis, on that day, in that year, the spokesman—what Walt Whitman had called the "literatus"—for the literary culture of the United States.

If Sinclair Lewis' reception of the Nobel Prize was the historic event—and his spokesmanlike acceptance of it only the marker of the event—its historic import was not merely in its putting American literature on a par with any other literature in the world, but also in its acknowledging that in the world America was a power that twenty years before it had not been, and that, until now, Europe had been reluctant to concede that it was. In December 1930 Sinclair Lewis was bigger than America knew; proud as he may have been—and he was proud, above all, because he was regarded as of equal importance with three eminent scientists—he was bigger than even he himself knew, or would ever know. Or should we say that he was a smaller writer than he thought and a much larger symbol?

In Berlin early in 1931, in a fit of pique that climaxed long brooding, Lewis wrote his publisher, Alfred Harcourt, of Harcourt, Brace, and Company in New York, to tell him that their connection was severed. For a long time, he wrote Harcourt, he had felt that the firm had lost real interest in his books, and its failure to rise to the occasion of the Nobel Prize had made its indifference all too clear. With proper advertising of the event, all his novels would have leaped into soaring sales figures again, Lewis announced. Worse than that, Harcourt had done nothing, even though he had the whole European press at his disposal, to counteract the supercilious and denigrating remarks about Lewis in the American press. "If you haven't used this opportunity to push my books energetically and to support my prestige intelligently, you never will do so, because I can never give you again such a moment."

Alfred Harcourt released him from his contractual obligations without any attempt to meet his charges. He may very well have felt that the separation came at a logical time. The decade through which Harcourt, Brace, and Company had helped to make Sinclair Lewis an international reputation, and in the course of which Lewis' novels had helped to make of Harcourt, Brace, and Company a substantial firm, was over. Throughout that decade Lewis had promulgated his version of the American reality, and his effort had been brought to a climax with the great honor. But the decade was over, and Lewis' sense of reality was no longer central to American history. He would never be able to change that sense, but history had already changed and would continue to change in his time, leaving him uneasily behind. His own discomforted sense of the change and of his inability to cope with current history as confidently as he had coped with the past may very well have been the major ingredient in his dissatisfaction with his publisher. His novels would continue to make money, and there would be many more of them, but they would never again bring distinction to a publisher's list as, in a succession of five smashing titles, they had brought to Harcourt, Brace, and Company. The Nobel Prize had come to him at precisely the right moment: it was the moment at which Lewis, the serious novelist, was finished.

He was now forty-six years old and the author of twelve published novels. There were to be twenty more years and ten more novels. The beguilements of alcohol, which had for some time been a problem for him, would become an increasingly acute problem as these twenty years passed. His second marriage would fall into even more sordid decay than had his first. His first son would be killed in World War II. His second son would grow up to be a not very successful actor and would justify his own peccadilloes in adolescence and irresponsibilities in maturity by the example of the conduct of his father. Lewis, an increasingly restless man, would move from one establishment to another, from one city to another, all over the world, briefly occupying magnificent houses which, after a few months or a year or two at most, he would sell at great financial loss, when he would move on again in the hope of finding a better place. Precisely like his characters, he was always pursuing some vague and undefined glimmer of a happier place, a richer life.

How far he had moved, in these splendid establishments, from his humble beginnings in Sauk Centre! And yet there was always something bleak and unlived-in about even his most lavish houses that suggested all too clearly that the bleakness of Sauk Centre still clung to him and lived on deep within him. How far, too, his international literary reputation had removed him from those taunts and jibes that had plagued him in his youth and young manhood, and yet he felt himself still the victim of taunts and jibes, never really taken seriously as an artist, he felt, by other artists. In a kind of mounting frenzy he sought out the comforts of women much younger than he, especially young actresses, during a period when he was infatuated with writing for the stage and even took to acting himself, and finally, at the end of the 1930's and for a time in the 1940's, he did find a young actress who was willing to try to comfort him. But in some profound way he was not to be comforted or consoled, and after the young woman abandoned him to marry a man more nearly her own age, Lewis began a series of restless wanderings in Europe, and there, finally, in 1951, he was to die alone, among strangers, in Roman ostentation. But all through those maddening years of decline, he continued, with a kind of mechanical regularity and even ruthlessness, to produce his novels.

The first of these was *Ann Vickers*, published in 1933—the story of an American career woman, and already, so soon after his second marriage, shot through with all his ambiguities of feeling about the career of his new wife, which was to be phenomenally successful through all that decade and into the next. The novel attempts, through a large part of the life of a single character, to sketch in the chief interests in a whole period of American social history from before World War I into the Great Depression. For this history, Lewis drew largely on the background of his new wife's life but partly as well on that of his own earlier years —pre-war Christian socialism, feminism and settlement house work, charity organizations, liberal and radical thought, prison reform, sexual emancipation, the crisis of the Depression, careers for women, equal rights, and so on. Through it all is the recurrent theme of a woman who is trying to find herself as a woman, not only as a Great Woman, just as *Dodsworth* was the story of a man trying to find himself as a man within the Businessman.

What is probably most interesting about the novel is the author's own ambiguous feeling about his heroine—exactly the feeling that he was already developing about Dorothy Thompson. Having chosen her as the prototype of Ann Vickers, he put himself in the position of describing sympathetically qualities that he was already resenting in life. His approval of Ann's dedication to "do-good" principles is at least uneasy; he resents the liberal and radical causes that his own characterization of her committed him to approve; the satiric touches are sporadic and sprawling, settling on her, on him, on them, but never pulling these together into real satire at all. Most interesting is the portrait of Ann's

husband, a feeble fellow who is jealous of her expansiveness and prestige. Ann is rescued from this marriage by a man with red hair— Sinclair Lewis was famous for his red hair and was nicknamed "Red"—but he bears no other resemblance to Sinclair Lewis, is, rather, quite his opposite—a kind of dream figure of warm tolerance and relaxed sensuality that Lewis would have liked to be but had never been and would never be able to be.

Work of Art (1934), the next novel, was probably the first of Lewis' serious novels since *Main Street* to be completely without distinction. (By "serious" one means work that he himself took seriously.) This novel brings to a climax, certainly, his old, uneasy suspicion of intellect and art, and his deep respect for middle-class virtue, for effort. A novel about the hotel industry in America, it deals with two brothers, Myron and Ora Weagle. Myron is steady and reliable and, even as a boy, dreams of someday owning a perfect hotel. Ora is "literary" and spends his good-for-nothing days mooning in romantic fantasies and in writing verse of much the same sort as Sinclair Lewis wrote as a boy and a young man, and this portrait, a fantastic caricature of the Poet, is Lewis' belated act of exorcism. Ora grows up to be a commercial success and a hack, always self-deluded and scornful of his downright brother. But Myron is the true artist, and Lewis makes nearly his every effort analogous to an act of artistic creation. Ultimately, Myron even keeps a notebook, "what must, in exactness, be called 'The Notebook of a Poet,'" in which he jots down ideas for improving hotel management and reflections upon his experience as a hotelkeeper. Myron, too, has great success, then through the chicanery of others falls to low estate, and recovers when he concludes that no hotel can be perfect but that he can still make a "work of art" of a tourist camp in Kansas. If one wishes to learn about hotel management the novel is no doubt an admirable handbook, and no duller than a handbook; if one wishes to learn anything about art, and especially the art of the novel, there is nothing here at all. *Work of Art* is the fantasy of the perfect Rotarian. It is almost as if George F. Babbitt had suddenly produced a novel.

It was no longer the best of the middle-class character that Sinclair Lewis was praising, but the very middle of the middle. His wife, in a few years, had gained a tremendous reputation on the international scene as a political commentator, and the greater her authority grew and the brighter the glamour that clung to it, the deeper Lewis drove himself back into the defensive but pathetic aggressiveness of Sauk Centre. If he ever divorced his wife, he is reputed to have said, he would name Adolf Hitler as corespondent. But he could not have written his next novel, *It Can't Happen Here* (1935), if he had not been intimately exposed to her intense interest in international affairs, a subject the discussion of which, he continually complained, would drive him out of his wits.

At least one of Lewis' novels after *It Can't Happen Here* was to make more money for him, but no other was to cause such excitement. In this book, it seemed, he was at his greatest: denouncing the Fascist elements in American life, praising the independent spirit, holding out for freedom. In 1935 the United States was being heckled on every side by demagogues like Huey Long, and Lewis, seizing on this proliferation of the totalitarian impulse, which did seem to pose a serious threat to the democratic traditions and promises of American life, translated it into the terms of political establishment. The horror of fascism in Europe and local imitations were enough to persuade many readers that Lewis had written an impressively prophetic work.

What he had in fact written was a tour de force in which he simply documented the trans-formation of traditional American political and social customs into their opposites. Doremus Jessup, the hero, driven into his epic stance at the end of the novel, is not really very different from Lewis' next hero, Fred Cornplow, of *The Prodigal Parents* (1938). *It Can't Happen Here* elicited considerable excitement among left-wing sympathizers who could, from this novel, be assured that Lewis was not a Fascist; but *The Prodigal Parents*—a miserable novel—gave these sympathizers small comfort, for in this book Lewis defended the stuffiest middle-class attitudes against the silliest "proletarian" views.

Considered as a whole work, *It Can't Happen Here* differs from other examples of the genre in having neither the intellectual coherence of Aldous Huxley in *Brave New World* nor the persuasive vision of a nightmare future of George Orwell in *1984*. But in 1935 readers in the United States, like readers in Britain and in France (*Impossible Ici!*), were sensitive to their immediate history, and it was to the immediate possibility of that history that Lewis' novel shook their attention. Yet to have seen the novel as committing Sinclair Lewis to what was then called the United Front—the collaborative effort of all liberal and radical parties against the threat of fascism—was an error; for Lewis, while once a socialist and still a liberal of sorts, was certainly in no sense a political radical. This fact became abundantly clear in the next novel, that sad effort of *The Prodigal Parents*. This story of Fred Cornplow and his wife, Hazel, in revolt from their foolishly radical and irresponsible children, brings to a lame end, no doubt, Lewis' one-time ambition to write a novel about political idealism. Radical politics are parodied in the figure of a comic-strip Communist and through the vagaries of undergraduates whose absurd concern with the problems of labor is apparently the net result of Lewis' observation of liberal student attitudes in the United States during the 1930's, when he lived in the neighborhood of Dartmouth College. Against these feeble antagonists is set the good American, Cornplow, a stodgy bundle of received opinions, the stereotype approved.

Now, at the end of the fourth decade of the twentieth century, with the United States about to plunge into another world war and a rather different kind from the first, Sinclair Lewis was only a confused man. Retreating into the absorbing life of the theater and devoting himself to the pursuit of young actresses, he turned, not surprisingly, to frivolous subjects in a half-dozen unsuccessful plays and in his next novel. *Bethel Merriday* (1940) is a novel about a young actress. Less embarrassing than *The Prodigal Parents*, it is hardly more important as fiction. Through the education of his young heroine in summer stock and touring companies, Lewis was able to include everything that he had learned about the theater; attached to, rather than incorporated in, this handbook material is a pale romance. Learning as much as one does of the theater, one learns nothing of the impulses that drive an actor or of the kind of satisfactions that an actor finds in his profession; and while the novel at one point glances at a May and December relationship, one learns no more of Sinclair Lewis' passion for young women than for the stage.

Gideon Planish (1943), the novel that followed, seemed to promise something of a return to the old Lewis. While he apparently intended, in this satiric attack on organized philanthropy and the activities of liberal "do-gooders," a return to the savage mode of *Elmer Gantry*, he achieved in fact little more than a crude parody and none of the solidity of that earlier novel. It is a splenetic attack, arising from the narrowest channels of a provincial mind, on the efforts of the professional "intellectual," and its satire deteriorates into farce very soon after the novel gets under way. One figure in the book, Winifred Homeward, "the Talking Woman," a cartoon-like take-off of his newly divorced wife, only underlined the essential lack of seriousness that characterizes this novel. And yet, self-deluded, Sinclair Lewis was able to autograph a copy of this work with the inscription "My most serious book—therefore, naturally, not taken too seriously."

That he intended to be serious in *Gideon Planish*, at least at the outset, one cannot doubt; but it is something of a relief to turn to the next novel, *Cass Timberlane* (1945), with its much less serious subject. A novel about American marriage, it is half sentimental, half splenetic. It is his own thinly veiled love story, or rather, an extrapolation of such little love story as he had to tell; and from this situation arose his chief novelistic difficulties. Cass Timberlane is presented as forty-one years old, in love with a girl of twenty-three; but he behaves in some ways like a man of sixty, which Lewis now was, and in others like a fumbling boy of sixteen, which he also was. Cass's most remarkable quality—which goes unremarked in the novel itself—is his sexual naïveté, and when the young Jinny Marshland leaves him and enjoys an adulterous affair with his contemporary and best friend, it is not, the reader can only assume, his age that has been his problem.

The story of Cass and Jinny is treated with a kind of sentimental affection, with only the faintest overtones of irony, and its treatment marks it off very sharply from the treatment of marriage in a whole group of surrounding sketches which the novel presents under the heading of "An Assemblage of Husbands and Wives." In these often brutally conceived accounts of female willfulness, tyranny, and lechery, the recognition of the American matriarchy is as clear as the method is uncompromisingly satirical. It is as if the novelist is trying to say two things at once, that all these are American marriages in general, including his own two marriages, but that this one at the center, of Cass and Jinny, is another matter, the marriage that he would now make if he could. With the slightest change of method—that is to say, with the slightest shift in perspective on his own situation—that central marriage would become only another in the great assemblage of miserable marriages at large. But one must remember that even Lewis' best novels were not notable for their clarity of point of view or for their power of self-evaluation. Should one expect these of him at sixty, infatuated?

And so he staggered toward his end. In *Kingsblood Royal* (1947) he made his last strenuous effort to re-enter American realities by addressing himself to the problem of the black minority in American life. The book aroused some excitement as a social document but none whatever as a literary performance, and even its social usefulness, it is now clear, is minimized by Lewis' mechanical oversimplification of what is, of course, one of the most complex, as well as one of the most pressing, issues in the national life of the United States. From this attempt to deal with the immediate present, Lewis retreated into the historical past of Minnesota. *The God-Seeker* (1949) is apparently the first part of what was finally projected as a trilogy about labor in the United States. But it is a wooden, costumed performance about which even Lewis' faithful publishers despaired. And his last novel, *World So Wide*, published posthumously in 1951 (he died on January 10 of that year), is a thin attempt to write another *Dodsworth*. It is the final self-parody. As Malcolm Cowley wrote, his characters sound now "like survivors from a vanished world, like people just emerging from orphanages and prisons where they had listened for thirty years to nothing but tape recordings of Lewis novels."

As he had experienced a long and unrewarding apprenticeship before his phenomenal, ten-year success, so he suffered a long and sad decline. This beginning and this end do not make easy the problem of delivering any final literary judgment on Sinclair Lewis. The estimate of his literary contemporaries, which became so apparent at the time of the Nobel award, does not make the problem any easier.

The aggressively enlightened had, of course, almost never taken him seriously. The experimentalists and the expatriates thought of him as a commercial hack. The academic critics, whether simple literary historians like Fred L. Pattee, or dogmatic authoritarians like Professor Irving Babbitt and his followers in the New Humanism, or old-fashioned conservatives like Henry Van Dyke in the American Academy of Arts and Letters—they were united in their displeasure with the award. "Nothing [Lewis] can write can matter much now," Professor Pattee had just pontificated in *The New American Literature*, and the brilliant young liberal critic T. K. Whipple had just published his damaging estimate (one of the few genuinely critical appraisals of Lewis up to that time, and up to this) in this book called *Spokesmen*. Young radicals found Lewis politically illiterate. Older writers of no particular allegiance, like Sherwood Anderson, spoke out against him on the grounds of art. A younger writer, Ernest Hemingway, writing to a friend, called the award a filthy business whose only merit was that it had eliminated the "Dreiser menace." Dreiser held Lewis in gross and sullen contempt.

This is all rather cruel because Lewis himself was among the most generous of men in his relations with other writers. He encouraged the young and struggling with praise and with money. He habitually put the men who had chosen him as their enemy, Dreiser and Anderson, at the very head of his list of the greatest modern American writers. He recognized early the brilliant quality of the young Ernest Hemingway and he was instrumental in getting an award for the mature Hemingway as he was for getting a large cash prize for Theodore Dreiser. He in effect "discovered" Thomas Wolfe for the world when, only a year after the publication of *Look Homeward, Angel,* Lewis spoke of this book at a press conference before departing for Sweden and mentioned Wolfe again in the Nobel speech itself.

And it is quite true, of course, that even his most famous novels have crass defects. He was, in the first place, the kind of writer who found it temperamentally impossible to objectify his own anxieties, the tensions of his inner life, or even to draw upon them except in the most superficial way, in his own writing, and the writer, after all, is not different from the man who contains him. Shunning the subjective, he often fell into the sentimental. Yet there are other realities than those that pertain to the subjective life. His twenty-two novels, so uneven in quality, do share in one likeness: they are a long march all directed toward a single discovery, the "reality" of America. This aim was Lewis' inheritance as a novelist who was formed in the second decade of this century, when the discovery of the "real" America, an America beyond the chauvinistic nonsense and the merely sentimental optimism that had formed the image of an earlier generation, became the aim of nearly every writer who took himself seriously. It was a period that, however briefly, put its trust in the democratic promise of American life. For Sinclair Lewis, America was always promises, and that was why, in 1950, he could say that he loved America but did not like it, for it was still only promises, and promises that nearly everyone else had long ago given up. Sinclair Lewis had nothing else to turn to.

There is a personal as well as a cultural basis for this situation. For what were these promises? They were promises, first of all, of a society that from his beginning would have not only tolerated but treasured *him.* That is the personal basis. Generalized, it becomes an idealization of an older America, the America of the mid-nineteenth century, an America enormous and shapeless but overflowing, like a cornucopia, with the potentialities for and the constant expression of a wide, casually human freedom, the individual life lived in honest and perhaps eccentric effort (all the better for that), the social life lived in a spirit that first of all tolerates variety and individual difference. It was the ideal America of Thoreau, of Whitman, of the early Mark Twain, of the cracker barrel in the village store and of the village atheist, of the open road and the far horizon and the clear, uncluttered sweep of prairies. Like Thoreau, Whitman, and Twain, Lewis, too, could see the difference between the idealization and the actuality. It was Thoreau who wrote this indictment: "With respect to true culture and manhood, we are essentially provincial still, not metropolitan—mere Jonathans. We are provincial, because we do not find at home our standards; because we are warped and narrowed by an exclusive devotion to trade and commerce and manufacture and agriculture and the like, which are but the means, and not the ends."

Sinclair Lewis was always carrying around the works of Thoreau. When he claimed him as the major influence on his work, it could have been only this basic element in his own thought, the Thoreauvian ideal of individual freedom and native integrity, that he had in mind.

Of Thoreau, R. W. B. Lewis has written in *The American Adam* as follows: "Probably nobody of his generation had a richer sense of the potentiality for a fresh, free, and uncluttered existence; certainly no one projected the need for a ritual burning of the past in more varied and captivating metaphors. This is what *Walden* is about; it is the most searching contemporary account of the desire for a new kind of life . . . the total renunciation of the traditional, the conventional, the socially acceptable, the well-worn paths of conduct, and the total immersion in nature."

All of this, item by item, even to the last, not only appealed to Sinclair Lewis but in fact formed the positive element in his largely negative presentation of American life. And into that idealism it was not difficult to weave the more diluted optimism that he had found in the novels of the other literary figure who profoundly influenced him, H. G. Wells—the happy belief that the little man, the obscure man, the middle-class man, the outsider like the young Lewis, could break into such freedom as Thoreau envisaged. This was the motive of Lewis' life as it was of his fiction. Deep under the quixotic social conduct, and deep under the satire of social surfaces lay this ambition and this yearning.

The American defection from the American potentiality for individual freedom is the large subject of Lewis' satire. When he excoriated Americans it was because they would not be free, and he attacked all the sources by means of which they betrayed themselves into slavery: the economic system, intellectual rigidity, theological dogma, legal repression, class convention, materialism, social timidity, hypocrisy, affectation, complacency, and pomposity. These two, the individual impulse to freedom and the social impulse to restrict it, provide the bases of his plots in novel after novel. Even when he used Europe as his point of contrast, the conflict was not so much between American and European values as between the true America as Lewis saw it—that is, individual Americans true to their individuality—and the false America, or Americans who yield to val-

ues not their own or to values of less amplitude than their own should be. The result in the novels is often an apparent praise of provincialism, even of a deplorable Philistinism, but in its impulse the praise is of something much larger and of something rather noble.

But he was himself sentimental and a Philistine, and often these led him to settle for the very stolidity in American life that he flayed. "Sinclair Lewis is the most successful critic of American society," T. K. Whipple said, "because he is himself the best proof that his charges are just." If he was the village intellectual, the village atheist, the rebel, the nonconformist crank for whom the dialect, the cracker barrel, and the false whiskers served as counterpoise to the stuffed shirt in his defense of what Lloyd Morris called "the old, free, democratic, individualistic career of the middle class," he was at the same time the pontifical village banker, the successful manufacturer of automobiles, the conservative, the very middle of the middle. His trust in "culture" was equaled by his trust in "things." His respect for science was certainly greater than his respect for art. Brought up in an environment that condescended to art and reverenced success, he managed, in that America, to make a success of "art." Often and increasingly it was bad art, and the success was in many ways abrasive and self-destructive. In his novels, he loved what he lamented; in his life, he was most secure and content with the kind of people who might have been the prototypes for his own creatures.

Ten years before his death, in a mock obituary, he said of himself that he had "affected but little the work of younger writers of fiction," that his style and his conception of the novel had in no way altered the contours of the American literary tradition. One can only wonder whether he had any sense at all of how increasingly old-fashioned he came to sound, or that the generation immediately following upon his own—Fitzgerald, Hemingway, Faulkner—was in fact quite a different generation which his work could in almost no way impinge upon, that he spoke for an older American experience than theirs. But in a larger sense than is suggested by the most familiar words in our critical vocabulary, *style* and *structure, symbol* and *strategy, tone* and *tension* and *intention*, he was an extraordinary influence, the major figure, probably, in what is called the liberation of modern American literature.

He had other impressive qualities, among them the ability to create a gallery of characters who have independent life outside the novels, with all their obvious limitations—characters that live now in the American historical tradition. A number of them have become gigantic, archetypal figures that embody the major traits of their class. Lewis' novels, as a result, are perhaps the last important American novels that are primarily concerned with social class. Or are John Marquand and John O'Hara and James Gould Cozzens of his stature? If Lewis' novels often depended more heavily than theirs on the mere report of social minutiae and of the details of the American lingo and more often failed to realize that material imaginatively, they nevertheless—as Joseph Wood Krutch has said—"recorded a reign of grotesque vulgarity which but for him would have left no record of itself because no one else could have adequately recorded it."

He performed a function that has nearly gone out of American fiction, and American fiction is thinner for the loss. Many American novelists today tell us about our subjective lives, and on that subject Sinclair Lewis could hardly speak at all. Fitzgerald, Hemingway, Faulkner—they all had some sense of the tragic nature of human experience that was denied to Lewis. Lyric joy, sensuous ecstasy—to these, too, he was apparently a stranger. But he had a stridently comic gift of mimicry that many a more polished American writer does not have at all. And a vision of hot and dusty hell: the American hinterland. He gave Americans their first shuddering glimpses into a frightening reality of which until he wrote they were unaware and of which he himself may also have been unaware. As Alfred Kazin wrote: "There is indeed more significant terror of a kind in Lewis's novels than in a writer like Faulkner or the hard-boiled novelists, for it is the terror immanent in the commonplace, the terror that arises out of the repression, the meannesses, the hard jokes of the world Lewis had soaked into his pores." With that America "soaked into his pores," he could document for an enormous audience the character of a people and a class, and, without repudiating either, criticize and laugh uproariously at both. In any strict literary sense, he was not a great writer, but without his writing one cannot imagine modern American literature. No more, without his writing, could Americans today imagine themselves. His epitaph should be: *He did us good.*

Selected Bibliography

WORKS OF SINCLAIR LEWIS

Our Mr. Wrenn: The Romantic Adventures of a Gentle Man. New York: Harper, 1914.

The Trail of the Hawk: A Comedy of the Seriousness of Life. New York: Harper, 1915.

The Job: An American Novel. New York: Harper, 1917.

The Innocents: A Story for Lovers. New York: Harper, 1917.

Free Air. New York: Harcourt, Brace, and Howe, 1919.

Main Street: The Story of Carol Kennicott. New York: Harcourt, Brace, 1920.

Babbitt. New York: Harcourt, Brace, 1922.

Arrowsmith. New York: Harcourt, Brace, 1925.

Mantrap. New York: Harcourt, Brace, 1926.

Elmer Gantry. New York: Harcourt, Brace, 1927.

The Man Who Knew Coolidge: Being the Soul of Lowell Schmaltz, Constructive and Nordic Citizen. New York: Harcourt, Brace, 1928.

Dodsworth. New York: Harcourt, Brace, 1929.

Ann Vickers. New York: Doubleday, Doran, 1933.

Work of Art. New York: Doubleday, Doran, 1934.

Selected Short Stories. New York: Doubleday, Doran, 1935.

Jayhawker: A Play in Three Acts (with Lloyd Lewis). New York: Doubleday, Doran, 1935.

It Can't Happen Here. New York: Doubleday, Doran, 1935.

The Prodigal Parents. New York: Doubleday, Doran, 1938.

Bethel Merriday. New York: Doubleday, Doran, 1940.

Gideon Planish. New York: Doubleday, Doran, 1943.

Cass Timberlane: A Novel of Husbands and Wives. New York: Random House, 1945.

Kingsblood Royal. New York: Random House, 1947.

The God-Seeker. New York: Random House, 1949.

World So Wide. New York: Random House, 1951.

From Main Street to Stockholm: Letters of Sinclair Lewis, 1919–1930, edited by Harrison Smith. New York: Harcourt, Brace, 1952.

The Man from Main Street: Selected Essays and Other Writings, 1904–1950, edited by Harry E. Maule and Melville H. Cane. New York: Random House, 1953.

CRITICAL AND BIOGRAPHICAL STUDIES

Dooley, D. J. *The Art of Sinclair Lewis.* Lincoln: University of Nebraska Press, 1967.

Grebstein, Sheldon Norman. *Sinclair Lewis.* (United States Authors Series.) New York: Twayne, 1962.

Guthrie, Ramon. "Sinclair Lewis and the 'Labor Novel,'" *Proceedings* (Second Series, Number 2), American Academy of Arts and Letters. New York, 1952. (An interesting account of Lewis' attempt to write his labor novel.)

———. "The 'Labor Novel' That Sinclair Lewis Never Wrote," *New York Herald Tribune Books*, February 10, 1952. (A shorter version of the preceding.)

"Harrison, Oliver" (Harrison Smith). *Sinclair Lewis.* New York: Harcourt, Brace, 1925. (A promotion piece commissioned by Lewis' publisher.)

Lewis, Grace Hegger. *Half a Loaf.* New York: Liveright, 1931. (This novel by Lewis' first wife is a bizarre *roman à clef.*)

———. *With Love from Gracie.* New York: Harcourt, Brace, 1955. (A biographical memoir following closely *Half a Loaf.*)

Manson, Alexander (as told to Helen Camp). "The Last Days of Sinclair Lewis," *Saturday Evening Post*, 223:27, 110–12 (March 31, 1951). (An account by Lewis' last secretary, much less effective than Perry Miller's.)

Miller, Perry. "The Incorruptible Sinclair Lewis," *Atlantic*, 187:30–34 (April 1951). (A persuasively written impression of Lewis' last days in Florence.)

Schorer, Mark. *Sinclair Lewis: An American Life.* New York: McGraw-Hill, 1961; New York: Delta Books, 1963. (Contains a reliable check list of Lewis' publications.)

———, ed. *Sinclair Lewis: A Collection of Critical Essays.* (Twentieth Century Views.) Englewood Cliffs, N.J.: Prentice-Hall (Spectrum Books), 1962. (The best critical writing about Lewis is contained in this collection.)

Sherman, Stuart Pratt. *The Significance of Sinclair Lewis.* New York: Harcourt, Brace, 1922. (A promotion piece commissioned by Lewis' publishers.)

Silhol, Robert. *Les tyrans tragiques—un témoin*

pathétique de notre temps: Sinclair Lewis. Paris: Presses Universitaires de France, 1969.

Thompson, Dorothy. "Boy and Man from Sauk Centre," *Atlantic*, 206:39–48 (November 1960). (A touching piece of reminiscent speculation.)

Van Doren, Carl. *Sinclair Lewis: A Biographical Sketch*, with a bibliography by Harvey Taylor. New York: Doubleday, Doran, 1933. (A promotion piece commissioned by Lewis' publisher; the bibliography is highly unreliable.)

—*MARK SCHORER*

Jack London

1876-1916

JACK LONDON lived at a time when a dramatically new set of ideas, growing out of the theory of evolution, was changing the course of men's thinking. These ideas stimulated, frustrated, and tantalized London all his adult years. Charles Darwin and Herbert Spencer, messiahs of the new creed, became his intellectual mentors, along with Friedrich Nietzsche and Karl Marx. It might be said that London's very real private struggle with life—which he dramatized in stories so arresting and exciting that they are still read over the world—became for him an epitome of the Darwinian Struggle for Existence, his success an example of the Spencerian Survival of the Fittest.

It is not easy for people today, who have lived with accelerating change through two-thirds of the twentieth century, to grasp how revolutionary and shattering were Darwin's and Spencer's ideas. Before they burst upon the intellectual horizon it was, for example, generally held that the world had been created in precisely the year 4004 B.C. and that the various species of flora and fauna were immutable: a rose, or a horse, or a man had always been the same creature, although variations or developments *within* each kind were possible. Then came Darwin in 1859 to propose that the earth was many millions of years old and that all extant species had evolved from a com-

mon beginning in the sea at some remote moment of time. Design and order had not presided over this evolution, either; it took place through the accumulation of infinitesimal and accidental variations. Millions upon millions of individuals (in whatever species) were wasted in the struggle for existence in which the slightly superior variation managed to survive and reproduce itself. The first reaction to this great theory was outrage. Darwin was denounced from countless Christian pulpits by ministers who accused him of maintaining that man descended from monkeys—although this was one point that he did not urge in his *Origin of Species*. Even so, the implication was unmistakable, and the very foundations of religion seemed to be threatened.

If Darwin was the scientist of evolution, Herbert Spencer was its philosopher. He worked from 1860 to 1903 on the many volumes of his great *Synthetic Philosophy*, a work that undertook a new synthesis of knowledge based on a new guiding idea, which was, of course, evolution. Spencer asserted that evolution is the fundamental law of social as well as physical process: from simple and relatively uniform materials evolve increasingly complex and specialized structures. He contended that the more complex forms, whether individual creatures or social organizations, are the more stable—

and thus he saw the social struggle for existence as leading up to the ultimately perfect and stable society. The evils of child labor, poverty, unemployment, and industrial warfare which were rampant in Western Europe and America were justified because they were the means to that perfect society. The fit would survive. Every social and industrial violence, every outrage caused by competition, was beatified with an aura of destined good in the philosophy of Social Darwinism. This put the humanitarianism and idealism of the nineteenth century under a frightful strain. The blessed prospect of the perfect society springing from child labor called for specially tinted lenses.

For many, a central figure in the social struggle came to be the "superman." In his ruthless quest for power this giant among men would help along the selection of the fittest by crushing the weak and helpless. The superman so appealed to Spencerian thinking that surely he would have been invented by someone else if the German philosopher Nietzsche had not done so. In fact the term "superman" by itself had the power to inflame the imaginations of many who had never read *Thus Spake Zarathustra,* and the rugged individualist supermen that emerged in popular literature—often ferocious blond Vikings—bore small resemblance to the type of genius Nietzsche described.

At the same time the role of unbridled individualism in the evolution of society was being challenged by the philosophy of socialism. In *The Communist Manifesto* Karl Marx had called upon the workingmen of the world—the supposedly weak and helpless victims of natural selection—to unite and overthrow their exploiters and oppressors, the industrialist ruling classes. According to the followers of Marx, not the superman individualist but the socialist community of workers must be the instrument of evolutionary progress.

It was this complex of ideas, contradictions and all, that captured the strong but untutored mind of young Jack London and permeated his writing. If we look briefly at his early trials in a world of extremes in wealth and poverty, in opportunity and helplessness, we may be led to understand how he came to fight—in his private life and in his work—up and down the line between Social Darwinism and social justice, between individualism and socialism. He had the physical and intellectual powers to make him identify with the superman sweeping lesser beings out of his way in the upward climb to the perfect society; at the same time he had both the experience of privation and the capacity for sympathy to make him take up the cause of all the hapless waifs crushed under a ruthless industrial juggernaut. He was inspired by the American dream of success even while he was living among the most oppressed of outcasts.

London was the offspring of a strange union between Flora Wellman and "Professor" W. H. Chaney. Flora came of sturdy Welsh stock, but she had been stricken by typhus in her girlhood, and afterwards she was unstable if not unbalanced. Chaney was an itinerant intellectual who made all knowledge his province and apparently remembered everything he had ever read. He always denied the paternity of Jack London, but the evidence of physical appearance and intellectual quality seems to be undeniable. Irving Stone, biographer of London who made considerable study of Chaney's writings, reports that they reveal "a clear, forceful, and pleasing literary style, an authentic erudition, courage to speak his mind, a sympathy for the mass of humanity, and a desire to teach them to better themselves. His point of view is modern and progressive." Chaney believed that a proper use of astrology would enable mankind finally to improve the human condition. Flora was an ardent spiritualist, and séances were offered along with lectures on astrology and spiritualism while she and Chaney were living together, from June 1874 to June 1875. Flora wanted marriage and a child, but Chaney was too distressed by her violent temper to consider a permanent union; when she declared that she was pregnant by him and he denied responsibility, she either genuinely attempted to commit suicide or pretended to do so. In any event, Chaney was denounced and ostracized, even by his own family. Flora gave birth to a son on January 12, 1876, in San Francisco. Eight months later she married John London and named her child for him, John Griffith London.

John London went into one business after another in California. Although he was a man of character and determination, he was repeatedly ruined, sometimes by the scoundrelism of a partner or, more typically, by the irresponsible plans of Flora. Young Jack lived from hand to mouth, getting a spotty primary education and working at one job after another to help his indigent family, which finally settled in Oakland. When he was thirteen he bought a small boat and learned to sail on San Francisco Bay. A year or so later, out of school, he got a larger boat and became an expert sailor. But just when freedom seemed within his grasp, John London was injured and Jack became the mainstay of the family. He supported this crushing load by becoming an oyster pirate—one of a gang of small boat owners who raided the oyster beds in the dark of night and sold what they stole to markets and saloons in San Francisco. On his first raid he made as much money as he had been earning in three months of "legitimate" toil.

Jack had a young mistress on his oyster boat, the *Razzle Dazzle*. He also began at the age of fifteen to drink very heavily and nearly killed himself in the process. At the same time he was devouring books taken from the Oak-

land library. From oyster pirate he became a member of the State Fish Patrol, whose duty it was to arrest illegal fishermen. At seventeen he shipped on a sealing vessel, the *Sophie Sutherland*. After seven months on the Pacific he returned to California and worked about a year at common labor for miserable wages (the Panic of 1893 had caused widespread unemployment, depressing wages). London then joined the march on Washington of Kelly's Industrial Army, which planned to join forces with Coxey's Army in the East to demand government aid for the jobless. His affiliation with the Army was rather loose, for he acted as a self-appointed advance guard, arriving in town ahead of the Army and living in solid comfort for a day or so while the residents debated how to welcome (or rebuff) the main force when it appeared. The march on Washington failed, and London became a hobo. He served time in prison for vagrancy and saw the seamiest side of American life before making his way back to California.

Determined to prepare himself for better than common labor, he entered Oakland High School when he was nineteen. He published in the school magazine, made interesting friends, and through the Henry Clay Debating Society was put in touch with a widening circle of stimulating people. He had become an avowed socialist, however, and when he was thrown in jail for speaking in a park without a license he found that many of his more prosperous new acquaintances drew back. The newspapers reported on him as if he were a combination of devil and maniac. In 1896, after a summer of merciless cramming (nineteen hours a day, according to him), he passed the entrance examinations and entered the University of California. There he was popular in a small circle of students and seemed happy, but life never left London in peace. After a single semester he had to leave and go back to work to support his parents, John London's health having failed. But first he had a heroic go (fifteen hours a day) at writing, turning out stories, poetry, essays, and tracts and sending them east with his last pennies. The manuscripts all came back. Jack went to work. After some months of exhausting physical labor he borrowed a considerable sum of money from his stepsister Eliza and embarked for the Klondike in March 1897.

London came home a year later without an ounce of gold but with head and notebook full of plans for stories. It turned out to be the most valuable period of his life. He wrote like a man possessed, gaunt, hungry, twitching. This time he found success. In May, June, and July 1899 his stories and articles appeared in the *Overland Monthly, Orange Judd Farmer, Black Cat, Buffalo Express, Home Magazine, American Journal of Education,* and *The Owl.* In December the *Atlantic Monthly* accepted a long story for the princely sum of $120, and Houghton Mifflin shortly afterwards contracted to publish a volume of short stories. At the same time London was avidly reading and taking notes on the best writers in the new sciences of nature, man, and society. His dedication to the enlightenment of man and the cause of socialism was terribly earnest, and people felt his strength and his sincerity; he made many friends and impressed whomever he met. He and his mother (John London had died) moved into a large house in Oakland that became a center of social, intellectual, and roistering activities; old friends from the sea and the road rubbed elbows with writers, philosophers, anarchists, and literary highbrows.

Three critical events took place in the spring and the summer of 1900. His stories appeared in book form as *The Son of the Wolf* and won extraordinary acclaim. Editor-publisher S. S. McClure asked to become his literary sponsor

and took a steady flow of his stories for good prices; McClure also agreed to advance the young author $125 a month while he wrote his first novel. And London gave up the girl he had been courting, Mabel Applegarth, whose mother dominated her and promised to dominate the marriage, and married instead Bessie Maddern. This turned out to be a leap from the frying pan into the fire, for London's mother, the neurotic Flora, now proceeded to make home a hell as she battled with Bess for control of the premises. Moving Flora into a separate house added to London's expenses without solving the problem, for she promptly laid siege to the main house, carried the campaign to the neighbors, and went back to her old business schemes—making new debts for her son.

McClure's "salary" was stopped after October 1901 because the editor did not find London's output holding up to the quality he had expected. But still London's reputation was growing. Macmillan accepted a volume of stories about the Indians of Alaska, *Children of the Frost* (1902). He turned out two juveniles, *The Cruise of the Dazzler* (1902) and *Tales of the Fish Patrol* (1905). Lippincott published his first novel, *A Daughter of the Snows* (1902). He worked with one of his few platonic women friends, Anna Strunsky, on a volume called *The Kempton-Wace Letters* (1903), in which he took the scientific-intellectual point of view on various topics and she the romantic-aesthetic position. He set out for South Africa in 1902 to report the Boer War for the American Press Association. When he arrived in London en route to find a cable canceling the assignment, he bought himself shabby old clothes and plunged into London's East End, where humanity languished in one of its lowest depths. From his observations he wrote in the three months he was there *The People of the Abyss,* a powerful image of misery. "Year by year rural England pours in a flood of vigorous young life that perishes by the third generation. At all times four hundred and fifty thousand human creatures are dying miserably at the bottom of the social pit called London." When he landed in New York, George Brett, head of the Macmillan Comany, promptly accepted the manuscript and agreed to pay London $150 a month for two years while he wrote the novels that he was now confident about.

This was only the beginning. Home in California, he was inspired to write a dog story. What he began as a short story grew and grew until it became *The Call of the Wild.* Macmillan gave him $2000 for all rights to the book in lieu of royalties—much more than London had ever made from a book or expected to make in the near future. By 1900 standards it was more than a generous income for a year. To London, who scarcely three years before had been pleading in vain for five dollars which the *Overland Monthly* had promised him for "To the Man on Trail," it was a fortune. He was happy to accept the offer. Macmillan made a fantastic profit on the arrangement: well over two million copies of the English edition alone have been sold. Even so, it was for the best. According to Irving Stone, "No less than a hundred people a week walked through his front door, enjoyed his hospitality," and occupied his time. It was his salvation to have cash to buy a good sloop on which he could disappear for weeks at a time to write in peace. London also received a substantial sum for *The Call of the Wild* from the *Saturday Evening Post,* which serialized it.

The pattern of prodigious success and prodigious spending was now set. *The Call of the Wild* (1903) was immediately declared a classic. Serialization of *The Sea-Wolf* (1904) brought $4000 from *Century* magazine, and

the book sold forty thousand copies in advance of publication. Three weeks after publication it topped the best-seller list. These books plus *The People of the Abyss* (1903) and *War of the Classes* (1905) were on everybody's lips. Also topics of widespread interest were London's ardent preaching of socialism, his divorce from Bessie in 1905, and his marriage to Charmian Kittredge two days later. He bought a large ranch in California and planned to cruise around the world for seven years, on a ketch to be called the *Snark,* while the ranch's crops were developing. He burned his way through *Before Adam* (1906), going back to the dawn of humanity, and *The Iron Heel* (1907), jumping prophetically forward seven hundred years to a Marxist analysis of the triumph of fascism. Meanwhile he had decided to build the forty-five-foot *Snark* himself, a decision that proved the costliest of his life up to this point. He poured between $30,000 and $50,000 into a boat that was not as good as one he could have bought for $5000. He was cheated and victimized; and yet one cannot escape the impression that he created many of his own troubles. Sailing time was repeatedly put off, but finally he limped out of San Francisco Bay in a boat that had been crushed, foundered in mud, almost sunk—and was still far from finished—limped off in worse debt than ever before. The chaotic voyage lasted over two years, taking London to Hawaii, the Marquesas, Tahiti, and Australia, and among other troubles it came very close to ruining his health. Yet during the course of it he wrote a long novel, *Martin Eden* (1909), also *Adventure* (1911), and many stories. Returning to San Francisco in July 1909, his business affairs in a desperate state and his literary reputation at low ebb, he plunged into another nineteen-hour-a-day orgy of work to rehabilitate himself. He came back so strongly that by 1911 he was again earning hugely and enjoying renewed critical acclaim. And again he plunged into new buying and building.

London's landholdings increased in a few years to fifteen hundred acres; he employed more than a hundred people, with a payroll of $3000 a month. While a stone dream palace was a-building, he had a great house called Beauty Ranch reconditioned and set up as a mecca for the guests from all over the world who daily poured into the Glen Ellen station, took the wagon that met every train, and enjoyed the Master's hospitality while they contributed to his knowledge of human nature. He impressed visitors of every level as one of the most brilliant minds they had ever encountered. At the same time he was steadily writing a thousand words a day, with contracts for everything he could turn out. Earning $75,000 a year, he was never less than $25,000 in debt and often $50,000: he was panhandled by acquaintances, milked by people he had never met, cheated by friends who were handling his affairs or his money, and robbed by his employees.

A climax came in 1913 when his magnificent dream castle, called Wolf House, built over four years at a cost of perhaps $100,000, was destroyed by fire shortly before the Londons were to move into it. Someone had apparently done it deliberately—and it was uninsured. During the same year London published *The Night-Born, The Abysmal Brute, John Barleycorn, The Valley of the Moon,* and *The Scarlet Plague* (in serial form), completed *The Mutiny of the Elsinore* (1914), and began *The Star Rover* (1915). But his faith in man was shaken, his drinking increased with his debts, drought ruined his crops, disease plagued his stock, and his own health was failing.

During his last three years he became more businessman and less artist. He said to a young interviewer, "I dream of beautiful horses and fine soil. I dream of the beautiful things I own. . . . And I write for no other purpose than to add to the beauty that now belongs to me. I write a book for no other reason than to add three or four hundred acres to my magnificent estate." He was more renowned now for husbandry than for his writing; he laid plans to revitalize California stock breeding and agriculture by scientific methods. He did not care about his debts because he was sure that he was creating a self-sufficient empire at Glen Ellen where he could defy the world. Irving Stone says that he was "a modest megalomaniac, like most native Californians"! His latest biographer, Richard O'Connor, says, "He was gypped, hoodwinked, overcharged and outbargained wherever he went, but the illusion of fiscal capability would not die. Like Mark Twain, and along much the same lines, he was tempted to beat the businessmen at their own game and make himself independent of any income from writing."

But the writing still paid. In April 1914, when the United States was landing troops at Vera Cruz, he was offered $1100 a week by *Collier's* to report events in Mexico. There the pacifist-socialist revealed a changing face. He admired the American army and navy, affirmed that war was fundamental to the human condition, and took the side of American oil interests against the Mexican freedom fighters, whom he saw as simply bandits and robbers. He was roused by World War I to declare that Germany was a mad nation that should be destroyed at any cost. Disillusioned with socialism, he now resigned from the party because it blamed the war on international capitalism rather than on Germany.

Increasingly London became a man yearning for the past. His greatest literary resource was, after all, the Klondike. As it receded from the public mind, London found himself falling behind Harold Bell Wright as an entertainer and Theodore Dreiser as avant-garde. He found Charmian increasingly possessive, jealous, childish. But worst of all he was very sick: constant headaches, agonizing uremia and nephritis, rheumatism, dysentery, and excess weight—all apparently due to his heavy drinking and voracious eating. He died from an overdose of narcotics. It was not a premeditated suicide, for he had gone to bed after making plans for the morrow, but apparently an attack of uremia brought more pain than he could bear, and he took the fatal dose in order to escape. At forty he had written fifty books and piled up a burden of debt and illness that he could carry no further.

London's Klondike stories brought strong praise; he was called the successor to Poe, the equal of Kipling, a new voice rising above the prissy sentiment of the genteel tradition. The best of his stories have extraordinary power, which is generated by bold ideas, vigor and concreteness of language, and that combination of mystery and suspense that is the mark of the born storyteller. London jumps into the middle of his situation; he keeps the reader on tenterhooks by withholding facts in a way that makes him participate in the action.

One of London's earliest stories, "The White Silence," written in 1898, published in February 1899 in the *Overland Monthly*, is typical of the best. It introduces the Malemute Kid and his pal, Mason, caught two hundred miles from town in weather sixty-five degrees below zero with starving dogs and inadequate food for themselves. With them is Ruth, Mason's devoted Indian wife, carrying his child, sustained by the hope of seeing the white man's great cities. They experience the White Silence: "All movement ceases, the sky clears, the heavens are as brass; the slightest whisper seems sacri-

lege, and man becomes timid, affrighted at the sound of his own voice. Sole speck of life journeying across the ghostly wastes of a dead world, he trembles at his audacity, realizes that his is a maggot's life, nothing more." Mason is fatally injured by a falling tree. If they wait for him to die, they will all die. He insists that they go on. After a day of grim waiting, Malemute Kid sends the girl on ahead, shoots the dying man, and lashes the dogs into a wild gallop as he flees across the snow.

"To Build a Fire" (1908) describes in minutest detail a man in the same cold "The White Silence" describes, trying to build a fire to warm himself before he freezes to death. He does get a fire going, but underneath a spruce tree, and the snow falls off the tree and puts it out. Lighting it the second time is the ordeal; his toes are frozen, his fingers too numb to feel the match, and he does not quite make it. The cold rapidly closes in on him. Dreams and hallucinations flutter through his consciousness as the end comes near. The suspense builds to an intense pitch.

"Bâtard" (1902) is a rich concoction of raw elements. Bâtard is the son of a gray timber wolf and a "snarling, bickering, obscene, husky" bitch with "a genius for trickery and evil." Black Leclère buys this dog because he hates him and wants to torment him. But Bâtard had "his mother's tenacious grip on life. Nothing could kill him. He flourished under misfortune, grew fat with famine, and out of his terrible struggle for life developed a preternatural intelligence. His were the stealth and cunning of the husky, his mother, and the fierceness and valor of the wolf, his father." Dog and master are bound by a savage hatred.

In their first major encounter, the dog leaps at Leclère's throat while he sleeps; the master disdains weapons, and in the ensuing fight they almost kill each other: "It was a primordial setting and a primordial scene, such as might have been in the savage youth of the world. An open space in a dark forest, a ring of grinning wolf-dogs, and in the centre two beasts, locked in combat, snapping and snarling, raging madly about, panting, sobbing, cursing, straining, wild with passion, in a fury of murder, ripping and tearing and clawing in elemental brutishness." Still the dog does not run away, and the master does not kill him, for they are linked by their hatred. But the master torments him incredibly—and with a reason: Bâtard invokes a subconscious death impulse in Leclère. "Often the man felt that he had bucked against the very essence of life—the unconquerable essence that swept the hawk down out of the sky like a feathered thunderbolt, that drove the great gray goose across the zones, that hurled the spawning salmon through two thousand miles of boiling Yukon flood."

The climax is a masterpiece of fiendish savagery. And appalling as it is, it is also convincing. The hate lives in London's intense language; even if that language is somewhat extravagant—as it certainly is—it convinces. It shows what it was that enthralled his audience by outdoing readers' wildest dreams of adventure. Perhaps the single word to describe it is energy: the writing renders a fierce commitment to life. It was the quality that made London's personal magnetism, and it vibrated in his prose.

The three volumes of his Yukon stories that appeared in 1900–02—*The Son of the Wolf, The God of His Fathers,* and *Children of the Frost*—established his reputation. At the same time he was turning to the novel form, in which his first try produced a tangle of ideas that merits discussion. As he complained later, *A Daughter of the Snows* contains enough material for several novels. It has a lavish assortment of ideas. To begin with, London asserts determinism: people's actions are the result of forces working upon them. A man may run, "each new pressure prodding him as he goes, until he dies, and his final form will be that predestined of the many pressures." He celebrates primordialism, which is another name for atavism; it is the notion that man's adaptability depends upon his possession of primitive qualities that existed before men became highly specialized and therefore incapable of adapting to new challenges. There is also a subordination of morals to survival. The superwoman heroine of the novel, Frona Welse, glories in physical strength, obeys her own instincts, and makes them the measure of what is good: "Why should she not love the body, and without shame?" Presently, however, these physical survival values are endowed with spiritual qualities: the choice of strength is a choice of good; weakness is evil; for it is the strong who will redeem mankind.

Now a set of ideas is one thing, but dramatizing them in a plotted action is quite another. The action here involves two suitors for the hand of Frona Welse. One is Gregory St. Vincent, who has already won her heart when Vance Corliss arrives in the frozen North, straight from the effeminacies of civilization, yet already responding atavistically to the challenge of the frontier. In order to create suspense, Frona must be blinded to the cowardice and treachery of St. Vincent, and Corliss must stand by heroically silent while she manifests her goodness by her loyalty (noble because misguided) to St. Vincent. Thus the action rests upon standard Victorian pieties. The moral order triumphs when St. Vincent is providentially exposed for the base creature he is, and Frona is free to pledge her heart and hand to Corliss. In the choices that, finally, determine characterization, Frona and Corliss are chaste, loyal, morally courageous, whereas St. Vincent is ruthless, selfish, and dominated by his impulses. These qualities should make him a perfect natural man, but in fact they make him the villain.

London was at the height of his powers in 1902 when he began writing the dog story which he thought of as balancing his account of the vicious husky given in "Bâtard." London finished *The Call of the Wild* in just over a month, his prose flowing pure and sharp with the story line, free from excessive expositions of intellectual theory.

Buck, a pleasant big dog, half Scotch shepherd, half St. Bernard, was stolen from his comfortable home in California and sold. Taken to the Yukon and put into brutal service in a dog team, he quickly learned the law of club and fang, learned that to survive in these arctic wilds he would have to be stronger and more cunning than other dogs on the team. His first big step was stealing a morsel of bacon from the other dogs. In this act his comfortable old morality was rejected as "a vain thing and a handicap in the ruthless struggle for existence," where respect for others might be suicidal. Soon he began to feel some savage atavism stirring his depths, and with the aurora borealis flaming overhead he joined in the old mournful song of the huskies, "old as the breed itself—one of the first songs of the younger world in a day when songs were sad." He fought with the leader of the team and took his place.

After several journeys, Buck was sold to another owner who was going to kill him when he was rescued and cared for by John Thornton. A great love grew between Buck and Thornton, and Buck more than once saved Thornton's life in camp and on the trail. Thornton almost brought Buck back to his old self, and perhaps he would have in time. But Thornton was murdered by Indians while Buck was chasing a moose. When Buck returned to find his dead master and the slayers, he raged through the camp like a thunderbolt, killing several Indians and wounding others. Then he fled into the wilderness, eventually becoming one of a wolf pack.

The story ends with a sentence that shows London at his best, a sentence that must have flowed in triumph from a writer who had come to the end of his purest book: "When the long winter nights come on and the wolves follow their meat into the lower valleys, he may be seen running at the head of the pack through the pale moonlight or glimmering borealis, leaping gigantic above his fellows, his great throat a-bellow as he sings a song of the younger world, which is the song of the pack."

At first glance *The Call of the Wild* seems to be entirely outside any traditional society and therefore free from its tensions, but in fact the narrative reveals various sorts of relations to the patterns of such a society. The values of love and fair play are central to the story; these are traditional and even heroic values. Buck begins happy and satisfied in a setting of comfort and love. Standard justice is betrayed when he is stolen and sold into bondage, but he rises to the challenge by drawing upon qualities of courage and hardihood. These are presented as atavistic, but they are also "moral" qualities that have always been respected in Western literature. And they are given new dignity when Buck responds to the love of John Thornton: the subordination of strength and courage to kindness and love is profoundly rooted in chivalry—which comes from the deep heart of Europe. Vengeance on the "inhuman" Indians who kill Thornton is chivalric, too; it reaches back to the Crusades and beyond. So strong are these appeals, indeed, that one may feel a certain regret when Buck finally abandons human society.

Civilized man—especially American man—

lives constantly with the call of the wild, but the call is quite different from the thing itself. The call represents the yearning toward freedom and purity that is an aspect of any human involvement; but one retreats in order to return with new strength. Robert Frost, climbing his birches to get away from it all, is very explicit:

I'd like to get away from earth awhile
And then come back to it and begin over.
May no fate willfully misunderstand me
And half grant what I wish and snatch me away
Not to return. Earth's the right place for love....

If we substitute "society" for "earth" we have the same problem stated more literally. Buck represents the human qualities that are always somewhat sullied in the actual world; he represents revolt and escape; and he enacts his qualities in the story. Running at last, full-throated through the pale moonlight, exulting in his freedom and strength, he "sings a song of the younger world," which is the song of the American dream of innocence and Adamic purity, when man was fresh-minted and society had not bowed him down under its load of falsity. In this light, *The Call of the Wild* shines almost as a lyric rather than a novel. In any event, London here achieved an ideal fusion of form and subject. Since perfect escape is inhuman, it is not so extraordinary that his hero should be a dog.

Three years later London wrote *White Fang* (1906), a companion piece to *The Call of the Wild*. If in the first book he had shown a domestic dog reverting to wolf, the later one told how a wolf was domesticated. White Fang is three-fourths wolf and bred in the wild like a wolf. First he makes the "old covenant" between the wolf and man, which goes back to primitive times, by which the wolf adopts the man-god for protection and food while in turn he obeys and protects his master. White Fang's first convenant, with a harsh Indian, is based on instinct, fear, and respect, but there is no love or affection. This covenant is broken during a great famine, restored when the wolf comes back, but broken forever when the master sells him for a bottle of liquor to a man who pits him against a bulldog, for money, and is willing to see him killed. In his second covenant, to his rescuer, White Fang gives himself wholly in love. He ends in just the sort of luxurious comfort that Buck enjoyed at the beginning of his story. *White Fang* is twice as long and perhaps not as bare, tense, and gripping as *The Call of the Wild*; but it is a powerful book.

In these two stories we can see the disguised and projected expression of London's contradictory theories of individualism and socialism. Buck is the individualist who defies society and finally rejects it completely. White Fang is tamed by love and turns from a savage wolf into a loving and home-keeping dog. This is the theory, but the impact of *White Fang* is still in violence, war, and survival by prowess. Most of the book concerns White Fang's struggles with savage nature, Indians, dogs, and white men, struggles that are as harsh as those of Buck in the first story. White Fang as clearly as Buck enacts London's own myth of a man unloved by his mother, unknown to his father, reared in poverty and deprivation, yet growing stronger and craftier because of innate powers that assert themselves and enable him to survive under extreme adversity.

The conclusion is prepared for by a vivid account of the experiences that molded White Fang's heredity while he was becoming fit to survive in the jungle of life: "Hated by his kind and by mankind, indomitable, perpetually warred upon and himself waging perpetual war, his development was rapid and one-sided. . . . The code he learned was to obey the strong and to oppress the weak. . . . He became quicker of movement than the other dogs, swifter of foot, craftier, deadlier, more lithe, more lean with iron-like muscle and sinew, more enduring, more cruel, more ferocious, and more intelligent. He had to become all these things, else he would not have held his own nor survived the hostile environment in which he found himself."

It is a wolf book, in short, and if at the end the wolf is tamed by love he is still a wolf. This merely reinforces one's conviction that London's heart was in individualism rather than socialism. His lip service to the latter is a protest against his early poverty; but he does not dwell on the presumed benefits of a socialist society. He writes instead of the evils of capitalism, the brutality of the industrial world, and the need for violent revolution to destroy them. The peace in his writing is the opulent peace of the great individualist who has beaten the system single-handed and can now afford to relax and live like a lord on his baronial domain. This is the peace of White Fang after he has conquered the world of club and fang by his prowess as a fighter. Near the end of the book White Fang kills a desperate murderer bent on destroying his master's father, thus showing the great power that is his, the power that he relaxes into love and ease but still keeps ready in case there is need for it in the treacherous world.

If White Fang ends where Buck was until he was stolen and sold into bondage, the lesson is that he must be stronger and smarter than Buck if he is to maintain his comfortable retirement in baronial splendor. This was London's dream of Wolf House—built of solid stone to outlast the ages while its master enjoyed the rewards of success. London loved to be called Wolf, signed his letters "Wolf," and had his bookmarks engraved with a picture of a wolf-dog's head. He wrote of animals as if they were people—and of people as if they were animals, recognizing no essential difference between human and animal societies.

White Fang begins with two men traveling through the arctic with dog team and sled, followed by a pack of famished wolves who pick off the dogs, one by one at night, get one of the men, and almost get the other. The point of view then shifts to the wolves and stays with them. Far from being a defect, the shift shows that the struggle for survival prevails in the same terms on all levels of life, with the same need for craft, strength, and courage. It is interesting to note, in this context, that Jack London wrote *The Call of the Wild* immediately after returning from his visit to London's East End, where he had seen society in the harshest terms of dog-eat-dog. Having established himself—largely with that book—he moved toward separating himself from society, buying more land than he could afford in order to have his own self-sufficient domain. In the beginnings of this withdrawal he wrote *White Fang*, symbolically projecting the lonely wolf into his own specially chosen world of love and security.

In *The Sea-Wolf* London ventured his second bout with a superior human being, this time a superman rather than a superwoman. The story begins with Humphrey Van Weyden, a rather delicate aesthete who has not been exposed to the harsh realities, swept off a ferry crossing San Francisco Bay and presently rescued by Captain Wolf Larsen of the sealing schooner *Ghost*. Humphrey, forced to work as cabin boy, is on hand to study Wolf Larsen. He is terribly strong, totally amoral, contemptuous of civilization's slave morality. He is also something of an intellectual, close to genius, who has read the philosophers and become an avowed materialist. Humphrey finds his powers in atavism: "he is the perfect type of the primitive man, born a thousand years or generations too late and an anachronism in this culminating century of civilization. . . . He was a magnificent atavism, a man so purely primitive that he was of the type that came into the world before the development of the moral nature." Wolf is a fascinating character. He may turn from reciting poetry or expounding philosophy to kick a troublesome sailor in the stomach; he sneers at God and morals; and yet the sense of waste of his great powers compels the reader's sympathy, as it does Humphrey's. A third of the book is taken up with this exposition.

The plot begins when the *Ghost* picks up a handful of survivors from a wreck. Among them is a beautiful, delicate, genteel poetess, Maud Brewster. Humphrey, with high idealism, falls in love with her; Wolf lusts after her with heartless egotism. Humphrey can no longer be a spectator to Wolf's self-assertion. He escapes with the poetess in a small boat and through stormy seas fetches an island seal rookery in far northern waters. The lovers establish themselves chastely in adjoining cottages and prepare to lay in supplies of seal meat against the long winter. And now the dismantled *Ghost* floats into their little harbor bearing only Wolf Larsen, who has been abandoned by his crew. Humphrey could kill him, but he is inhibited by his morality and by the force of Wolf's personality. Wolf is having terrible headaches, and presently he goes blind. Humphrey sets about readying the *Ghost* to sail, but at night the blind Wolf gropes over the ship and destroys what Humphrey has done. In this suspenseful situation, while Humphrey is trying to summon the resolution to act, Wolf is stricken by paralysis—and presently dies.

The Sea-Wolf seems to turn into a different book with the appearance of Maud; the reason may be that it corresponded with a turning point in London's life. When he was halfway through writing the book, in 1903, he deserted Bess for Charmian Kittredge. Charmian, gushy, flirtatious, an intellectual chatterbox with a fine seat on a horse and an energetic social gaiety, set her traps for London and snared him. The relationship was kept secret for a long period during which the lovers exchanged volumes of fluttery, shrill, passionate letters. Charmian's style invaded Jack's style, and it was never quite the same again. Charmian is the model for Maud, "a delicate, ethereal creature, swaying and willowy, light and graceful of movement. It never seemed . . . that she walked, or, at least, walked after the ordinary manner of mortals. Hers was an extreme lithesomeness, and she moved with a certain indefinable airiness, approaching one as down might float or as a bird on noiseless wings." At about the same time, Charmian was writing to London, "Oh, you are wonderful—most wonderful of all. I saw your face grow younger under my touch. What is the matter with the world, and where do I belong. I think nowhere, if a man's heart is nowhere." And he wrote to her: "My arms are about you. I kiss you on the lips, the free frank lips I know and love. Had you been coy and fluttering, giving the lie to what you had already appeared to be by manifesting the slightest prudery or false fastidiousness, I really think I should have been utterly disgusted. 'Dear man, dear love!' I lie awake repeating those phrases over and over."

London has been roundly criticized for his treatment of Wolf Larsen. Lewis Mumford says that instead of a higher type of human being, he created "a preposterous bully . . . little more than the infantile dream of the messenger boy or the barroom tough or the nice, respectable clerk whose muscles will never quite stand up under the strain. He was the social platitude of the old West, translated into a literary epigram." London later insisted that "the hurried superman of action" was doomed because he "is antisocial in his tendencies, and in these days of our complex society and sociology he cannot be successful in his hostile aloofness. . . . he acts like an irritant in the social body." This seems to be hindsight. Wolf Larsen had to be disposed of because of the new turn the book had taken, toward romantic love.

London later told the story of such a creature more consistently. *Burning Daylight* is about a comparable (if somewhat less intellectual) frontier superbrute. At one point he rushes into the office of the corporation that is cheating him and forces the squirming capitalists at gunpoint to do him justice. Here the hero represents a natural force asserting itself against the corruption and hypocrisy of the modern world; he gains sympathy and approval. Wolf, too, is presented as despising and defying the petty viciousness of a business-ridden society and the slave morality that sustains it; but once Maud Brewster took over the novel, London did not know what to do with him. The conflict with his crew or even with his soul (in the manner of a Captain Ahab) had to be abandoned. His reappearance at the seal island, stricken with blindness and paralysis, does not dramatize the forces presented earlier with so much intensity. The original Wolf could have become involved in an exciting and significant action.

Startling subjects, a bold narrative line, and the play of new ideas constitute London's appeal. As the years went by, his personal tie with his reader became an important element as well. He recognized the need for interesting material. He was always reading, meeting new people, and taking notes by the boxful. He was a tireless observer of events, situations, and matters of intellectual novelty. His famous Wednesday evening parties, attended by a parade of bums, grifters, cranks, and intellectuals, were not merely an indulgence, for these people were a source of characters and ideas. He even bought plots from the young Sinclair Lewis to bolster flagging invention. In his search for the unusual, the attention-catching, however, he increasingly moved too far from the representative concerns of men into the realm of fantasy. Without describing his works to tedium we may profitably follow this trend through a few of his stories, all written before 1906 (and all collected in a book of that year, *Moon-Face*).

An unsettling story, which joggles the bases of the social structure, is "The Minions of Midas" (1901). A multimillionaire is blackmailed for twenty million dollars by "members of [the] intellectual proletariat" who remind him that his wealth rests on power and declare that they will kill a designated person every week until he pays the sum demanded. He does not pay, "And week by week, as certain as the rising of the sun, came the notification and death of some person . . . just as much killed by us [the millionaire and his secretary] as though we had done it with our own hands." The millionaire holds out, disbursing "at the rate of one hundred thousand per week for secret service." As the murders continue, he increases it to a quarter of a million. He offers rewards totaling ten million dollars, but the murders continue. Then the symbolism is spelled out with a most ingenious ambiguity: "As I said before," the narrator explains, "a word from him and the slaughter would have ceased. But he refused to give that word. He insisted that the integrity of society was assailed; that he was not sufficiently a coward to desert his post; and that it was manifestly just that a few should be martyred for the ultimate welfare of the many." The narrator means by "a few" the people being murdered, but the reader is forced to think of people sacrificed to make capitalism flourish—whether in sweat-shop, industrial strife, or wars. The millionaire kills himself in anguish. And now the Minions of Midas speak more explicitly in another let-ter. They declare, "We are the inevitable. We are the culmination of industrial and social wrong. We turn upon the society that has cre-ated us. We are the successful failures of the age, the scourges of a degraded civilization. . . . We meet force with force. Only the strong shall endure." Capitalism has crushed wage slaves, shot strikers; now it is a free-for-all of power against power. So bold a stroke through the foundations of society must have been disturb-ing in 1901, although subsequent history has made it comparatively feeble.

Straight out of Edgar Allan Poe comes "Moon-Face" (1902), told by a man consumed with hatred for his jolly neighbor. The nar-rator kills his neighbor's dog, burns his barn, forecloses his mortgage, and finally commits the perfect crime. It is "William Wilson" and "The Cask of Amontillado" compressed into ten lively pages. Out of Mark Twain and the other humorists comes "The Leopard Man's Story" (1903) of how the knife thrower in a circus gets revenge on the lion tamer for look-ing at his wife. He drops some snuff on the lion tamer's hair, and when at the culmination of his act the latter puts his head in the lion's mouth, the lion sneezes and bites off his head with a *crunch*.

The infatuation with language so character-istic of the period, which seems to assume that anything is funny if it is told in three times as many words as necessary, overflows in "Local Color" (1903) in the account by a philosoph-ical hobo of how he demonstrated that it would cost a town less to entertain a tramp in its best hotel than to arrest, convict, and incarcerate him for the same period. The hobo got thirty dollars for the story from a newspaper editor, put in some "local color" at the request of the

editor who was pushing a campaign against the incumbent magistrate—and got sixty days in jail when haled before said magistrate after drinking up his thirty dollars in a brawl at the hoboes' haven. The picture of the magistrate had been too vivid.

Out of Poe, again, and the humorists comes "The Shadow and the Flash" (1903), a story about two brilliant rivals who become distin-guished scientists. They compete desperately, whether for honors or women, until finally they take up the challenge of invisibility. One contends that there can be a black so black that it will be invisible because it reflects no light at all; the other seeks a chemical that will make him perfectly transparent. Both succeed, but the first when coated with his black paint has a shadow, and the second when made transparent by an injection emits a flash when-ever the sun hits him from a certain angle. They come together in a final fury and kill each other in an invisible battle.

When the situations are this bizarre, the story leads to a conflict and choice likely to be equally bizarre; and the characterization which is the product of that choice will be fantastic. The jealous geniuses of "The Shadow and the Flash" cannot be taken seriously as people. And the same is true where the character is so enveloped in mystery that we can't know what makes him tick. For example, in "Planchette" (1906) a man endowed with godlike beauty and charm refuses after four years to disclose the mystery that prevents him from marrying the girl he deeply loves, who loves him as in-tensely. Two horses try to kill him. Then at a planchette (Ouija board) session, the spirit of the girl's father, who was a cavalry officer, promises to kill him. A day or so later another horse, famous for its steadiness, suddenly leaps over a cliff, carrying the man to his death. There is no explanation in this hair-raising tale, just suspense and mystery and a rich sensual throb that is sustained between the girl and the man up to a moment before his death. The assumption that the spirit of the father had some special influence over horses is not explanation enough.

Several qualities of *The Cruise of the Snark* (articles 1906–09, book 1911) strike the reader immediately. There is, first, the evidence that London has a public to whom he speaks directly and intimately. Like Mark Twain he assumes that the smallest detail of his life will be of interest. He talks about Charmian and Roscoe Eames (Charmian's uncle and nominal navigator on the *Snark*) by their first names as if the reader shared his connections with them. He builds suspense and emotional involvement for the reader over the question of how he (London) felt about every item in the calendar of delay and fraud that marked the building of the boat. A whole chapter tells how the months crept by while he lost bet after bet on his sailing date, spent $30,000, and was frustrated at every turn. The suspense grows from his original description of the wonderful Nova Scotia deck planks, the watertight compartments, the special engine, the power windlass, and all the custom-forged fittings to his successive discoveries that the planks were not full length, the compartments leaked, the engine was not secured properly (it broke loose from its bed and was carried to Hawaii as ballast), and the windlass and fittings were inferior (the windlass broke on first trial and the fittings snapped like matches). He maintains an air of happy trust and exuberance, leaving the reader to grind his teeth over the outrages London is suffering.

One feels here the pressures on a man trying to live three or four lives at once. Love, business, sailing, and debt consume London's time and vitality while forcing him to grind out his thousand words a day even if he has nothing to say. Thus a very little fact is stretched out over page after page with humorous repetition. We are told that the *Snark* won't heave to in a high wind; then this monstrous defect is rehearsed as every sail in the locker is tried. A whole chapter quotes letters from people all over the world who volunteered for the cruise. How London mastered the mysterious art of navigation in a couple of afternoons is told, then retold.

To sustain creation from almost nothing implies a powerful talent, and the more one reads the more one is struck by London's control of the language. He can evoke sharp images, explain complex procedures, describe intricate mechanisms and processes with economy and clarity. In Hawaii he does not merely admire the Kanakas surfing; he goes into the theory of wave motion and explains it in detail: "The face of that wave may be only six feet, yet you can slide down it a quarter of a mile, or half a mile, and not reach the bottom. For, see, since a wave is only a communicated agitation or impetus, and since the water that composes a wave is changing every instant, new water is rising into the wave as fast as the wave travels. You slide down this new water, and yet remain in your old position on the wave, sliding down the still newer water that is rising and forming the wave. You slide precisely as fast as the wave travels. . . . If you still cherish the notion, while sliding, that the water is moving with you, thrust your arms into it and attempt to paddle; you will find that you have to be remarkably quick to get a stroke, for that water is dropping astern just as fast as you are rushing ahead." This passage is an epitome of London's appeal: he involves the reader in an intellectual adventure that is just difficult enough to keep him alert with the effort to understand. The rush of thought is of a piece with the rush of discovery and adventure; here it surges along with the foaming racing sea. London not only draws the reader into the intellectual theory but also makes him participate in the adventurer's first incompetent attempts to master the skill. An intimacy is established thus and maintained through the book, as London enacts the reader's romantic dreams and timid impulses.

London's heart goes out to the lepers of Molokai, and he explodes the myth of their horror and despair by showing how active and happy they are in their colony. The description of the sixty-day passage, without sight of smoke or sail, from Hawaii to the Marquesas rivals *Kon-Tiki*. At Nuka-hiva he follows Melville's footsteps into the Valley of Typee, to find those magnificent people almost exterminated by white men's diseases. The closing paragraph of this chapter, although it has one or two false notes, ends with a cadence that links it to the best of American prose: "The feast ended, we watched the moon rise over Typee. The air was like balm, faintly scented with the breath of flowers. It was a magic night, deathly still, without the slightest breeze to stir the foliage; and one caught one's breath and felt the pang that is almost hurt, so exquisite was the beauty of it. Faint and far could be heard the thin thunder of the surf upon the beach. There were no beds; and we drowsed and slept wherever we thought the floor softest. Near by, a woman panted and moaned in her sleep, and all about us the dying islanders coughed in the night."

As the party moves into the Solomons, they are overwhelmed with fever and various sores and infections; and so while the material grows richer, the ability of the author to handle it weakens. Hair-raising adventures are lost under the welter of medical detail. One wonders how the Londons survived this trip that was "all for fun." Jack in fact finally had to abandon the cruise and wound up with a long stay in an Australian hospital.

London drew heavily upon the romantic myth of himself for interest in his books. From the very first story of the Yukon, he was living violence, adventure, and triumph vicariously for the common reader. What is frankly central to the appeal of *The Cruise of the Snark* lurks in varying degrees very close to the surface in other books that his readers took as autobiography.

For London the living and writing became almost one, but it may be said that the writing really came first in the sense that it defined and directed the living. Just as the anguish of Hamlet's

If thou dids't ever hold me in thy heart,
Absent thee from felicity a while
And in this harsh world draw thy breath in pain
To tell my story

is unimaginable without the language in which it comes to us, so London's agonies had to be expressed if they were to achieve fullness and intensity. Hamlet of course lives only in the poetry. There he only is. But the same is almost true of a Jack London. He exists in his books as he writes, as he expresses, as he discovers the meanings and intensities for which he could not even yearn without language. He grows in the books and lives his evolving role between them, as the man in the flesh enacts the man in the books. London's biographers comment in surprise on the fact that he could be almost dead with thirst on the becalmed *Snark* and stagger down to the cabin to write a story about a sailor dying of thirst. But he had to write the experience before he really knew it.

The interest in *Martin Eden* is richest if we read the book to see what sort of sense London could make of the intellectual and psychological materials that he knew best in himself. The long "novel" begins with an uncouth sailor entering the luxurious home of a cultured friend (whom he has, characteristically, saved from a gang of toughs). His wide shoulders and lurching walk make a space large enough for six people seem too narrow; he breaks out into a sweat of anxiety. An amused glance from the friend "burned into him like a dagger-thrust," for "under that muscled body of his he was a mass of quivering sensibilities." The exposition proceeds to show a mind of dazzling intensity that jumps from the present event to evoke brilliant images of past experience. While he talks painfully to the friend's ethereal sister (Ruth Morse), scenes of brawls, whores, engine rooms, prisons, and wild seas surge and tumble before his mind's eye. The excitement grows in a new dimension as the frail girl responds—and is shocked by her response—to his superb body while she is horrified by his grammar.

Martin Eden is famished for knowledge, power, life—and the story plunges straight into his quest for them. He goes on to great successes, to disillusion, to suicide. But the struggles surging through the mind of the author break the confines of the single story he had to write and so confuse the characterization of the hero. London was indignant with his notices and said, "Not one blessed reviewer has discovered that this book is an attack on individualism, that Martin Eden died because he was so utter an individualist that he was unaware of the needs of others, and that, therefore, when his illusions vanished, there was nothing for him for which to live." This sentence may describe London better than his hero, for while creating his self-destructive individualist London was also creating and exploring the mystery of his own famished spirit that could never rest while it could never be satisfied, because it did not understand (and could not understand) that its trouble was rooted in his fatherless, homeless, famished childhood. And London edits his own life in ways that tell more than he could have realized. The anemic Mabel Apple-garth is transformed into a Ruth Morse who is beautiful and proud and harries Martin Eden because he is not respectably employed. Jack broke with Mabel because she could not get free from her dominant mother. Money was not the problem. Ruth breaks her engagement when Martin is reported in the press as having made a flaming socialist speech (falsely, for it was a Nietzschean attack on socialism). Bessie Maddern does not appear in the book. And Ruth evolves somewhat. Late in the story she offers to become Martin's mistress so that she can convince him of her sincerity and persuade him to marry her. This is a disguised Charmian London, who did indeed seduce Jack and then lured him away from Bessie by holding herself at a distance until he got his divorce. Charmian was five years older than Jack; Ruth is three years older than Martin.

Martin Eden turns into a daydream of prowess, wish-fulfillment, and revenge. London's own problems are transmuted into glories of beauty, strength, and intelligence pitted against supernal outrages. His face "was once as white as the underside of his arm; nor did he dream that in the world there were few pale spirits of women who could boast fairer or smoother skins than he—fairer than where he had escaped the ravages of the sun." As, fired by love, he begins to educate himself, "She detected unguessed finenesses in him . . . and was often puzzled by the strange interpretations he gave to mooted passages [in Browning's poetry]. It was beyond her to realize that, out of his experience of men and women and life, his interpretations were far more frequently correct than hers. . . . He was tortured by the exquisite beauty of the world. . . . He was drunken with unguessed power," which is not only creative but also physical, for "The old familiar blaze of health rushed out from him and struck her like a blow. It seemed to enter into her body and course through her veins in a liquid glow, and to set her quivering with its imparted strength." Inspired by her, "he spent the day in the white-hot fever of re-creating the beauty and romance that burned in him." Hints of megalomania abound, as when "he rented a typewriter, and spent a day mastering the machine"—rather in the manner that the young Mozart is said at the age of six to have picked up a violin and performed a part in his father's string quartet.

The romance with Ruth, floating on his inchoate but enraptured vision of the beauty of the world, bumps against her cultured disdain for excess—which is, however, not able to suppress her physical response to his electrifying power. "Mentally she was in a panic to shoot the bolts and drop the bars into place, while wanton instincts urged her to throw wide her portals and bid the deliciously strange visitor to enter in." She would like to kill the male in him and yet have it, too, but under her genteel control and guided into profitable and respectable channels. Consciously, however, she recoils from physical contact with a man who has lived through the imagined and unspeakable evils of a sailor's world. Finally her mother-dominated spirit gives in to her burgeoning womanhood and she discovers a passionate (but of course chaste) love for Martin, even though she remains spiritually absorbed, self-centered, uncommunicating, hoping he will give up his mad writing and get a steady job.

Martin toils on, knowing that he is Ruth's intellectual superior, as he also knows that inspiration alone is not enough and that his genius must be supported by knowledge. Now "His was deliberate creative genius, and before he began a story or poem, the thing itself was already alive in his brain, with the end in sight, and the means of realizing that end in his conscious possession." His studies led to a synthetic essay. "It was brilliant, deep, philosophical, and deliciously touched with laughter. . . . The writing of it was the culminating act of a long mental process, the drawing together of scattered threads of thought, and the final generalizing upon all the data with which his mind was burdened." Such ability and application should have been recognized, but the weeks of heroic toil went on and on, while the rejection slips accumulated and the money dwindled until Martin had nothing but potatoes to eat. He was out of his head with starvation and fever when the big letter came (not from the *Black Cat* as in London's life, but from the *White Mouse*) offering him $40 for a story.

The action of this novel drags along as Martin's intellectual explorations are spelled out, for these are used to represent the period of his apprenticeship, in place of London's own Klondike adventures, months on the road and in prison, assault on high school and university, and days at sea. The effect is to make the period of his self-education more concentrated and intense than the corresponding years of London's life, and also much more limited in activities. The debaters, socialists, and professors in Eden's life are met at Ruth Morse's home, and he is more than a match for them all, even for the most brilliant professor in the university, whose intellect he diagnoses as deficient in biological insights. "Professor Caldwell sat for a full minute, silent and fingering his watch chain. 'Do you know,' he said at last, 'I've had that same criticism passed on me once before—by a very great man, a scientist and evolutionist, Joseph Le Conte. But he is dead, and I thought to remain undetected; and now you come along and expose me.'" The rest of the upper class Martin considers parasites, but he is aligned with them because he is an avowed individualist, not, as London thought he himself was, a socialist.

He does not stay on their side, however, because he rapidly sees what shams and leeches they are. In ruthless discussions with pompous bankers and judges at the Morses' dinner table, he confutes them with facts and abuses them with eloquence. He makes one brilliant insight here into the future of American politics. " 'You persuade yourself,' " he tells the judge, 'that you believe in the competitive system and the survival of the strong, and at the same time you endorse with might and main all sorts of measures to shear the strength from the strong. . . . It's on record, your position on interstate commerce regulation, on regulation of the railway trust and Standard Oil, on the conservation of the forests, on a thousand and one restrictive measures that are nothing else than socialistic.' " These predictions, milder than the prophecy of world fascism in *The Iron Heel*, are much nearer the truth—although they are not essentially different.

Eden meets an incomparably brilliant nihilist named Brissenden, who argues that the critics, the publishers, and especially the magazines are despicable haters and destroyers of literature. Brissenden writes the greatest poem of the century ("It was a mad orgy of imagination, wassailing in the skull of a dying man who half sobbed under his breath and was quick with the wild flutter of fading heart-beats"), which he refuses to sully by publication. He begs Martin to give up his quest for wealth via the contemptible magazines: " 'Love beauty for its own sake . . . and leave the magazines alone. Back to your ships and your sea—that's my advice to you, Martin Eden. What do you want in these sick and rotten cities of men? You are cutting your throat every day you waste in them trying to prostitute beauty to the needs of magazinedom. If you got [fame] it would be poison to you. You are too simple, too elemental, and too rational, by my faith,

to prosper on such pap. . . . It is not in what you succeed in doing that you get your joy, but in the doing of it. . . . Beauty hurts you. It is an everlasting pain in you, a wound that does not heal, a knife of flame. Why should you palter with magazines?' " Brissenden expresses what Martin believes with increasing conviction, but this is very far from the real Jack London, who always wrote for the market and bragged of doing so. Martin Eden, too, studies the magazines to discover the formula of success; his later despair over the public's failure to appreciate the utter passionate beauty of his work is as phony as a three-dollar bill. London's wish-fulfillment makes Martin's motivation inconsistent, his characterization a failure.

Brissenden takes Martin to an enclave in the slums where a group of intellectuals who have renounced the bitch-goddess success and all that goes with "respectability" engage in far-ranging discussions that embrace all knowledge. The words describing the brilliance of these men are as excessive as the actual discussion is sophomoric: "He swiftly saw, no matter upon what they talked, that each man applied the correlation of knowledge and had also a deep-seated and unified conception of society and the Cosmos. . . . Never had Martin, at the Morses', heard so amazing a range of topics discussed. . . . Martin was struck by the inside knowledge they possessed. They knew what was never printed in the newspapers—the wires and strings and the hidden hands that made the puppets dance." The debate ranges Locke, Berkeley, Hume, Kant, Spencer, and Haeckel against each other through two pages of high-falutin oversimplification. It provides the perfect footnote to the statement that London was an uneducated man of genius.

At a socialist meeting, Martin brilliantly expounds the Nietzschean attack on socialist slave morality which protects the weak and prevents evolutionary development. He is reported in the papers as a socialist; Ruth breaks their engagement; he is denounced by his neighbors, his family, and the tradesmen who have given him credit. Brissenden commits suicide, leaving Martin alone and really at the end of his rope. He is in a daze of exhaustion, despair, disappointed love, and, most of all, utter disillusion with the stupidity of critics and intellectuals.

Then a long-overdue check comes, and Martin uses it to send out all his manuscripts for a final try at the market. Success! They are accepted one after another and the money comes in faster than Martin can spend it. A book of philosophy (forsooth!) causes a sensation, sells sixty thousand copies; the publisher sends a blank contract for anything he has either planned or written and responds with a check for $5000 when he writes a title on the blank line. His first and second books now top the best-seller list, week after week, "thus proving himself to be that rare genius, a critic and a creator in one." Still numb, he forgives his enemies, buys a milk farm for his kind Portuguese landlady, allows himself to be interviewed by the reporter who wrote him up as a socialist, and accumulates a fortune without writing another line.

As Martin turns the other cheek to one indignity after another (he finances the two brothers-in-law who forbade him their homes), the effect is of a childish, sulky daydream of revenge. He is an angry infant breaking his toys to spite the grownups. He broods incessantly over the fact that the work was all performed when he was a lonely outcast; now the stinking world wallows at his feet while he smiles in tight-lipped disdain. Ruth's attempt to seduce him is an ultimate abasement that lets him pour out all his disgust for "bourgeois vulgarity." But the question he keeps asking with

such tormented intensity—"And what is puzzling me is why they want me now. Surely they don't want me for myself, for myself is the same old self they did not want"—is a question to which he has known the answer all his life: they want him for his fame and his money. Anybody knows that. It's so obvious that it's not worth saying; it makes the ending painfully false; the suicide becomes an act of sulky spite, of childish pique.

Martin Eden has been considered London's best work, but I believe it is among his worst. It lacks aesthetic distance; it lacks the sense of control that comes when a writer has *made* a book. Its author is nakedly, naïvely, embarrassingly present in its situations. The best of London is to be found in the short stories, *The Call of the Wild*, and *White Fang*.

Burning Daylight (1910) is cut from the same cloth. London plays the Viking hero bearding the pigs of capitalists and making them eat crow; he is heroic as socialist and as individualist. *John Barleycorn* (1913) is an incantation, a solemn ritual of exorcism. London writes in the first person to explain the perils of drink and to tell how he conquered it. The book is wish-fulfillment, for London was far gone in alcoholism when he wrote it and was to be a physical ruin in a year or two more. The psychology of alcoholism is profoundly—if unconsciously—revealed in this book. *The Valley of the Moon* (1913) concentrates on the struggle of a young couple through the social jungle and on to where they leave society and become scientific farmers in their private valley. This book is full of Anglo-Saxon racism, a misbegotten offspring of Darwin and the notion that only a pure breed could be strong. *The Little Lady of the Big House* (1916) is all about Jack and Charmian and Wolf House. Into their Eden comes a friend from Yale who unintentionally falls in love with the heroine.

She then finds herself in love with both men. The hero insists that she make a choice freely, and the story descends into bathos; yet one cannot avoid the impression that the sentimental death of the heroine represents Jack's growing impatience with his jealous, frilly, demanding, and irresponsible wife.

London contributed greatly to one myth of the American writer, which he passed from Mark Twain on to F. Scott Fitzgerald and Ernest Hemingway. All these writers (and the line extends thinly back to Poe) tried to live several lives at once and in the attempt sacrificed their lives, their art, or their peace to the excess they attempted. London is like Mark Twain in his grandiose and disastrous business schemes. He was like Fitzgerald in alcoholism and in his involvement with a woman who took so much of his life that she invaded his art. He was like Hemingway in his boyishness, his two-fisted courage, his public display of dangerous living, and even his great capacity for friendship. Like the others, he seemed always to be in a desperate struggle with his writing, so that the extra activities might be regarded as symptoms rather than causes of their frustration.

The classic book about this problem is Van Wyck Brooks's *The Ordeal of Mark Twain.* Brooks maintains that Twain, with an incomparable genius, was frustrated by Puritanism, by frontier distrust of excellence which forced him to be a funny man, and finally by his own sellout to the Gilded Age, which disastrously compromised his art. Brooks says that Twain would have had to become a great satirist if he was to fulfill himself and defeat the Gilded Age. London, in a similar state, did become a satirist. He spent his life discovering and castigating abuses of every sort, from capitalism in all its corrupt manifestations, through organized religion, and on even to bullfighting. And he was confused and frustrated in the same way that Mark Twain was.

It may be suggested that the root of this problem is not what Brooks claims, but is, rather, the absence in America of an established society that could be taken seriously by the artist because in its manners, customs, and values he found problems about which he could write a rich and steady flow of serious novels of manners. Or perhaps one should say either the absence of such a society or the absence of a *tradition* of taking it seriously. Once a writer like London or Twain has uttered his wild assault on the stupidity of society in general, he is out of material. He must go to the Klondike, or back to the Middle Ages, or into boys' stories, or through the green hills of Africa with rod, gun, or pen, or down into the South Seas; or contrive hoaxes like *Tom Sawyer Abroad*; or bring the devil himself down to discuss what man is; or make fun of Europe; or create a popular myth of himself to exploit. With exotic subjects and intellectual protest he will have the greatest difficulty making plots that move seriously through the center of society, and therefore he will not generally be able to create characters that are representative. They will instead be burlesques, outlaws, brutes, Indians, children, or adventurers.

To make the point by way of contrast, one may look at the career of J. P. Marquand. He did find American society, with all its defects, worth his sustained and serious attention. He was able to write one long book after another dealing with various problems of that society, problems of war, business, love, and so on, that moved right through the heart of American life. Marquand has generally been considered a writer just below the first rank, but the point here is that he was always interesting, always serious, and never in the least danger of running out of materials. It is significant, in passing, that Marquand began with satires—*The Late George Apley* and

H. M. Pulham, Esq.—but abandoned this tone apparently because its burlesque note faded quickly.

Jack London never wrote a novel of manners, never took the patterns of American society seriously, never found typical problems in it with which he could wholeheartedly engage himself. His stories of the Klondike are valid because the Gold Rush was an actual experience of Americans in an actual part of the continent; the Darwinian struggle for survival was at that time a foremost preoccupation in American thought. His socialist writings are often moving because they take us into areas of misery and deprivation with which modern man is deeply concerned; but this stream soon runs into the sands, compelling the author to invent new fantasies of violence or prophecy. These elements place London in the naturalistic movement, which embraces scientific determinism, Darwinism, the Spencerian philosophy of evolution, and Marxism, all of which in some way reflect the antisupernaturalism and anti-traditionalism of a presumably scientific approach to human affairs. These all theoretically (although never in practice) renounce the free will and ethical responsibility that underlay the classic well-made novel of manners—and thus contribute to the restless search for form that has characterized the American novel since 1900.

London's special genius appears in his command of detail and pace. He knows how to produce realism and suspense by giving the minutest factual items of a situation—and how on the other hand to jump over large areas of fact and make the reader supply the information or the meaning. He can bring the most seasoned sophisticate to the edge of his chair and have him fidgeting with anxiety as a story builds toward its climax. A good introduction to London is the three-volume *Bodley Head Jack London.* Reading this collection of his best in novels and stories, one must acknowledge that that best is very good indeed.

Selected Bibliography

WORKS OF JACK LONDON

NOVELS AND COLLECTIONS OF SHORT STORIES

The Son of the Wolf, Tales of the Far North. Boston: Houghton Mifflin, 1900.

The God of His Fathers and Other Stories. New York: McClure, Phillips, 1901.

A Daughter of the Snows. Philadelphia: Lippincott, 1902.

Children of the Frost. New York: Macmillan, 1902.

The Call of the Wild. New York: Macmillan, 1903.

The Faith of Men and Other Stories. New York: Macmillan, 1904.

The Sea-Wolf. New York: Macmillan, 1904.

The Game. New York: Macmillan, 1905.

Moon-Face and Other Stories. New York: Macmillan, 1906.

White Fang. New York: Macmillan, 1906.

Before Adam. New York: Macmillan, 1906.

Love of Life and Other Stories. New York: Macmillan, 1906.

The Iron Heel. New York: Macmillan, 1907.

Martin Eden. New York: Macmillan, 1909.

Lost Face. New York: Macmillan, 1910.

Burning Daylight. New York: Macmillan, 1910.

When God Laughs and Other Stories. New York: Macmillan, 1911.

Adventure. New York: Macmillan, 1911.

South Sea Tales. New York: Macmillan, 1911.

The House of Pride and Other Tales of Hawaii. New York: Macmillan, 1912.

Smoke Bellew Tales. New York: Century, 1912.

A Son of the Sun. New York: Doubleday, Page, 1912.

The Night-Born. New York: Century, 1913.

The Abysmal Brute. New York: Century, 1913.

The Valley of the Moon. New York: Macmillan, 1913.

The Strength of the Strong. New York: Macmillan, 1914.

The Mutiny of the Elsinore. New York: Macmillan, 1914.

The Scarlet Plague. New York: Macmillan, 1915.

The Star Rover. New York: Macmillan, 1915.

The Little Lady of the Big House. New York: Macmillan, 1916.

The Turtles of Tasman. New York: Macmillan, 1916.

The Human Drift. New York: Macmillan, 1917.

The Red One. New York: Macmillan, 1918.

On the Makaloa Mat. New York: Macmillan, 1919.

Hearts of Three. New York: Macmillan, 1920.

Dutch Courage and Other Stories. New York: Macmillan, 1922.

The Assassination Bureau, Ltd. (completed by Robert L. Fish). New York: McGraw-Hill, 1963.

PLAYS

Scorn of Women. New York: Macmillan, 1906.

Theft. New York: Macmillan, 1910.

The Acorn-Planter. New York: Macmillan, 1916.

ESSAYS, TRACTS, TRAVEL, AUTOBIOGRAPHY, LETTERS

The Kempton-Wace Letters (with Anna Strunsky). New York: Macmillan, 1903.

The People of the Abyss. New York: Macmillan, 1903.

War of the Classes. New York: Macmillan, 1905.

The Road. New York: Macmillan, 1907.

Revolution and Other Essays. New York: Macmillan, 1910.

The Cruise of the Snark. New York: Macmillan, 1911.

John Barleycorn. New York: Century, 1913.

Letters from Jack London, edited by King Hendricks and Irving Shepard. New York: Odyssey Press, 1965.

JUVENILES

The Cruise of the Dazzler. New York: Century, 1902.

Tales of the Fish Patrol. New York: Macmillan, 1905.

Jerry of the Islands. New York: Macmillan, 1917.

Michael, Brother of Jerry. New York: Macmillan, 1917.

RECENT SELECTED EDITION

The Bodley Head Jack London, edited by Arthur Calder-Marshall. 3 vols. London: Bodley Head, 1963–64.

BIBLIOGRAPHY

There is no adequate bibliography for London. "A Jack London Bibliography" appears in Charmian London, *The Book of Jack London* (New York: Macmillan, 1921), II, 397–414. Bibliographical information may also be found in Joseph Gaer's *Jack London* (Monograph No. 1 of California Literary Research Project, 1934) and J. Haydock's "Jack London: A Bibliography of Criticism," *Bulletin of Bibliography,* 23:42–46 (May–August 1960).

CRITICAL AND BIOGRAPHICAL STUDIES

Feied, Frederick. *No Pie in the Sky: The Hobo as American Cultural Hero in the Works of Jack London, John Dos Passos and Jack Kerouac.* New York: Citadel Press, 1964.

Foner, Philip S. *Jack London: American Rebel.* New York: Citadel Press, 1947, 1964.

Geismar, Maxwell. *Rebels and Ancestors.* Boston: Houghton Mifflin, 1953. Pp. 139–216.

Herrick, Robert. *The Memoirs of an American Citizen.* New York: Macmillan, 1905.

James, George W. "A Study of Jack London in His Prime," *Overland Monthly,* 69:361–99 (May 1917).

Johnson, Martin. *Through the South Seas with Jack London.* New York: Dodd, Mead, 1913.

Lane, R. W. "Life and Jack London," a serial in *Sunset* extending from October 1917 to May 1918.

London, Charmian. *The Book of Jack London.* 2 vols. New York: Century, 1921.

———. *The Log of the Snark.* New York: Macmillan, 1915.

———. *Our Hawaii.* New York: Macmillan, 1917; revised edition, 1922.

London, Joan. *Jack London: An Unconventional Biography.* New York: Doubleday, 1939.

McDevitt, William. *Jack London as Poet*. San Francisco: Recorder-Sunset Press, 1947.

Mencken, H. L. *Prejudices: First Series*. New York: Knopf, 1921. Pp. 236–39.

Mumford, Lewis. *The Golden Day: A Study in American Literature and Culture*. New York: Boni and Liveright, 1926. Pp. 247–50.

Noel, Joseph. *Footloose in Arcadia: A Personal Record of Jack London, George Sterling, Ambrose Bierce*. New York: Carrick, 1940.

O'Connor, Richard. *High Jinks on the Klondike*. Indianapolis: Bobbs, Merrill, 1954.

———. *Jack London: A Biography*. Boston: Little, Brown, 1964.

Pattee, Fred L. *Side-Lights on American Literature*. New York: Century, 1922. Pp. 98–160.

Payne, Edward B. *The Soul of Jack London*. London: Rider, 1926.

Schorer, Mark. *Sinclair Lewis: An American Life*. New York: McGraw-Hill, 1961. Pp. 164–66 and *passim*.

Stone, Irving. *Sailor on Horseback*. Boston: Houghton Mifflin, 1938. (Reissued as *Jack London, Sailor on Horseback: A Biographical Novel*. New York: Doubleday, 1947).

Walcutt, Charles Child. *American Literary Naturalism, a Divided Stream*. Minneapolis: University of Minnesota Press, 1956. Pp. 87–113.

Walker, Franklin. *Jack London and the Klondike: The Genesis of an American Writer*. San Marino, Calif.: Huntington Library, 1966.

Williams, Blanche C. *Our Short Story Writers*. New York: Moffat, Yard, 1920. Pp. 256–57.

—CHARLES CHILD WALCUTT

Henry Wadsworth Longfellow

1807-1882

THE span of Henry Wadsworth Longfellow's life, from 1807 to 1882, arched over the transforming years between two American worlds. The New England of his birth was agricultural and mercantile in its economy, anchored to seaports, rivers, and farms, provincial but refined in its culture, engaged in reconciling inherited, semi-aristocratic values with the ideals of a circumscribed but dynamic republicanism; the New England of his death was shaped by post–Civil War industrialism, with its noisy railroads, smoky cities and grim mill towns, emerging class conflicts, and crumbling pieties. Of the nature of this transformation, and its real import, Longfellow was, like most of his contemporaries, only partly and at moments aware. To the issues and occurrences susceptible of judgment by his clear, unexamined moral principles or his somewhat vague but deeply religious convictions, he responded vigorously—to the "shabby" Mexican war, the antislavery movement, and the human misery caused by financial panics. The range of his interests, however, is clearer in his diaries, journals, and letters than in his poetry. Although his poetry is more frequently topical than is sometimes realized, its relation to the age's history is usually indirect: with some exceptions, events and causes served as catalysts rather than as subject matter or primary topics of the

verse. Before many contemporary developments, Longfellow could only confess his bewilderment. Always affective and associative rather than analytic and theoretic in his response to life, he could sense the reality of profound change, and its menace, but he could not criticize it. His characteristic answer was the tireless reassertion of the values cherished by the stable society of his early maturity or drawn from his own love of traditional Western culture and the experiences of his childhood and youth.

Born at Portland, Maine, on February 27, 1807, Henry was the second of eight children, descended from Wadsworths and Longfellows who had already established their families' provincial importance. His mother, Zilpah, shared his literary interests and inspired him with her own religiously motivated idealism, including a lifelong hatred of war and violence. His father, Stephen, a public-spirited lawyer, a trustee of Bowdoin College, and briefly congressman from Maine, was an efficient adviser to his son, and later provided him with financial aid as well as encouragement at the beginning of his career. Hardly second to happiness at home was the joy provided by life in a coastal city. The nearby woods and the northward sweep of primeval forest beyond them; the color and bustle of the harbor; above all, the restless Atlantic with its changing moods—these were to haunt Longfellow's imagination throughout his life and to give much of his poetry its dominant imagery. In his almost obsessive recall of time and happiness past, Arcadia lay in childhood and its geography was that of the New England coastline. His most intense poetic exercise in personal recollection is "My Lost Youth," whose familiar third stanza echoes the tone of the whole.

I remember the black wharves and the slips,
    And the sea-tides tossing free;
And Spanish sailors with bearded lips,
And the beauty and mystery of the ships,
    And the magic of the sea.
    And the voice of that wayward song
    Is singing and saying still:
    "A boy's will is the wind's will,
And the thoughts of youth are long, long
    thoughts."

In 1821, Longfellow was admitted to Bowdoin College, at Brunswick, Maine, although he did not take up residence there until his sophomore year. Inadequate as the young college was in several respects, its curriculum, modeled on Harvard's, prescribed substantial study of the classical languages, mathematics, Scripture, and the branches of philosophy, as well as briefer study of natural science. Longfellow, well prepared by Portland Academy and by his own extensive reading, readily mastered the required subjects and also took the then rare opportunity to receive part-time instruction in French. As important as his work in course was the informal education he received, especially through his membership in the Peucinian, a literary society with a well-stocked library. The reading and critical discussion of papers at its meetings sharpened Longfellow's growing desire for a literary career. This bias may have been further encouraged by a faculty member, Thomas Coggs-

well Upham, who came to Bowdoin in 1824 with a missionary zeal for the creation of a native American literature. So well did Longfellow profit from the combined influences of his collegiate years that his academic promise came to the attention of the trustees. In 1825 the new graduate was offered a just-established professorship in modern languages, with the stipulation of a period of European study—at his own expense—as preparation for the position. The offer was quickly accepted, and on May 15, 1826, Longfellow sailed from New York.

The three years in France, Spain, Italy, and Germany were touched with enchantment as Longfellow's romantic imagination responded to a past still visible in monuments and customs, and to the storied associations which were, the associationist critics maintained, the source of poetic beauty. Longfellow also laid down solid intellectual foundations, especially in Romance languages and literature, but the new task he envisaged from his steadily American perspective was essentially artistic: to help create a great national literature not by radical novelty, as the so-called "Young American" writers urged, but by transmitting to America a rich European heritage for incorporation into its own culture. His pursuit of this goal through essays, lectures, translations, and adaptations from foreign literature exacted a price: if it did not cause, it certainly intensified the bookish tendency of Longfellow's writings. It also resulted, however, in an important contribution to the increasingly important relationship between American and European literature.

Assuming his professional duties in September 1829, Longfellow discovered that he had virtually to establish a new area of studies and to provide its very materials; between 1830 and 1832 he edited or translated six texts in French, Spanish, and Italian. His labors were rewarded: his competence in basic instruction, skill as a lecturer, and courtesy to students quickly made him an influential teacher. Further, he was making a professional reputation. His translations—the book-length *Coplas de Don Jorge Manrique* appeared in 1833—attested his linguistic proficiency, in Spanish particularly; he was also publishing essays on southern European languages and literature that demonstrated scholarship. Longfellow's attention in these years was focused primarily on academic achievement; the writing of original poetry, begun before he entered Bowdoin and continued during his college days, had almost ceased after 1825, and his literary ambitions now found outlet in prose sketches of his travels interspersed with tales in the manner of Washington Irving. After an abortive beginning in serial form, the completed account was published in 1833–34 as *Outre-Mer: A Pilgrimage beyond the Sea.*

There were also nonprofessional reasons for satisfaction. After a short courtship, Longfellow was married in 1831 to Mary Storer Potter, a delicately attractive girl interested in mathematics and poetry, who made a self-effacing but effective helpmate. Yet, for all his success, Longfellow found Brunswick distressingly provincial after Europe, and energetically sought a larger public stage. This he attained in 1834, when the distinguished George Ticknor, Smith Professor of Modern Languages at Harvard College, designated Longfellow as his successor. Once more preparatory study abroad, this time in Germanic languages, seemed wise, and the Longfellows left for Europe in April 1835.

The pattern of Longfellow's life was decisively changed by the second European journey. The linguistic goals were accomplished: Longfellow added Dutch, Danish, Icelandic, Swedish, and some Finnish to his store of languages, acquired a thorough knowledge of German romantic literature, and began his lifelong reading in Goethe. It was not intellectual achievement, however, that made the period crucial, but the violent emotional experience originating in his wife's death. Mary's health had always been uncertain; now she was pregnant, and the rigors of a Scandinavian trip exhausted her. Back in Holland, she suffered a miscarriage; infection subsequently developed, and on November 29 she died. Soon after sending her body home for burial, Longfellow received news of the death of his closest friend. Suddenly, it seemed to him, life had taken on the unreality, the transiency, of a dream. Courageously, at times hectically, he pushed on with his work, haunted by loneliness and often acutely depressed.

In the spring of 1836, his spirits slightly improved, Longfellow visited the Tyrol. In July, at Interlaken, he encountered the wealthy Bostonian Nathan Appleton and his family, and with the beautiful, talented, and sensitive young Frances Appleton he fell promptly, passionately in love. In August he had to leave for America, his love unreturned; thus began an extended courtship, long unpromising and broken off by Fanny after publication of the too-autobiographical *Hyperion* in 1839. A chance meeting four years later begot a reconciliation, and on April 17, 1843, Longfellow received a note from Fanny that set him walking at top speed from Cambridge to Boston through a transfigured day, and into one of the happiest marriages on record.

The seven-year wait, however, was not spent in palely loitering. Occupying rented quarters in Brattle Street's dignified Craigie House, now maintained as a Longfellow museum, Longfellow performed with distinction his duties as Smith Professor. Although he came to detest departmental business and the drilling in fundamentals, and conducted a continuous, low-keyed quarrel with Harvard's then-conservative administrative policies, he took real delight, as did his listeners, in the delivery of his scrupulously prepared lectures. He not only gave the expected instruction in the history of European languages, but also opened to his students the world of modern German literature, of Jean Paul Richter, Schiller, and, above all, Goethe. His teaching of *Faust*, indeed, was the first such offering in an American college.

More important to his own future, he also resumed writing, the European experience having reawakened the long-dormant creative impulse. In 1839, in addition to the prose *Hyperion*, there appeared *Voices of the Night*, his first collection of poems, some of which, including the sensationally popular "A Psalm of Life," had been previously printed in magazines. *Ballads and Other Poems* followed in 1841; *Poems on Slavery*, written during his return from a brief third European trip, in 1842; and a poetic drama, *The Spanish Student*, in book form, in 1843. The renewed conflict between academic and literary ambitions was increasingly resolved in favor of the latter, until it was settled in 1854 by the cessation of teaching.

Longfellow's success was already making him a public figure, a role for which he was well suited. Striking in appearance, elegant, even dandified in dress, urbane and mildly witty, endowed with innate courtesy and a peculiarly masculine sweetness of temper, he made the very model of a New England gentleman-author, and his genuine talent for friendship rapidly wove a web of lasting relationships that embraced the obscure and the famous alike. When he and Fanny were married on July 13, 1843, his father-in-law's gift was Craigie House itself, and the young Longfellows soon gave it a wide reputation as a center of cultivated hospitality.

The years from 1843 to 1860 were Longfellow's most fruitful. Besides editing and contributing to three collections of verse, he wrote many of his best shorter poems, gathered in *The Belfry of Bruges and Other Poems* (1846) and *The Seaside and the Fireside* (1850), as well as "Paul Revere" and "The Saga of King Olaf," to be used later in *Tales of a Wayside Inn;* a novel, *Kavanagh* (1849); and his most successful long poems: *Evangeline* (1847), *The Golden Legend* (1851), *The Song of Hiawatha* (1855), and *The Courtship of Miles Standish* (1858). Many of the volumes sold in numbers and with a speed unprecedented in American publishing history.

Public acclaim mounted yearly in Europe as in America, while distinguished guests and unimportant strangers descended endlessly upon Craigie House and seriously hindered Longfellow's work. Moreover, his domestic happiness was nearly complete, shadowed only by the death of one of the six children born to the Longfellows. The single source of continuous anxiety was the national scene. Longfellow observed the sharpening prewar tensions closely and with growing concern, until the opening of hostilities left him torn between his abhorrence of slavery and his hatred of war, and dejected by public disaster.

To national tragedy was soon added personal. On July 9, 1861, Longfellow was resting on a couch in his study while, in an adjoining room, his still romantically loved wife was sealing locks of their daughters' hair in packets: a scene so Victorian as to seem a period piece. Then a spark or a drop of hot wax ignited Fanny's flimsy summer dress. Ablaze and in agony she ran to Longfellow, whose efforts to beat out the flames left him critically burned. During the night Fanny died and, while she was being buried, Longfellow lay helpless in bed, his life feared for, his sanity at first despaired of by his friends and himself. Physically he made a thorough recovery, although the circumstances of Fanny's death had a grotesque consequence; the scars on Longfellow's face made further shaving impossible, and thus was created the placid bearded image that was destined to gaze from the walls of a thousand future classrooms. Psychic recovery came more slowly, and the inner wounds never completely healed. The journals for the following months he later destroyed, but evidence of his near-despair survives in communications with his friends.

To this shattering experience Longfellow directly refers only once in all his later poetry, although knowledge of it is necessary to a full understanding of several poems, including the six sonnets prefixed to his translation of Dante, and the tone of his lyrics is pervasively affected by it. The sole direct reference is a sonnet written in 1879, when Longfellow came upon a picture of a mountain in whose ravines lay a cross-shaped deposit of snow, and found there the image of his unrelenting pain.

In the long, sleepless watches of the night,
  A gentle face—the face of one long dead—
  Looks at me from the wall, where round its
      head
  The night-lamp casts a halo of pale light.
Here in this room she died; and soul more white
  Never through martyrdom of fire was led
  To its repose; nor can in books be read
  The legend of a life more benedight.
There is a mountain in the distant West
  That, sun-defying, in its deep ravines
  Displays a cross of snow upon its side.
Such is the cross I wear upon my breast
These eighteen years, through all the changing
      scenes
And seasons, changeless since the day she died.

"The Cross of Snow" was published posthumously; like another sonnet, the "Mezzo Cammin" of 1842, it seemed to Longfellow too personal for print.

Initially forcing himself to resume writing as an escape from grief, Longfellow was soon engaged in some of his most ambitious undertakings. The three series of narrative poems constituting *Tales of a Wayside Inn* were published in 1863, 1872, and 1874 respectively; the translation of the whole of the *Divina Commedia* occupied the years from 1865 to 1867; the *New England Tragedies* appeared in 1868 and *The Divine Tragedy* in 1871, two works that were linked with *The Golden Legend* by prologue, interludes, and epilogue to make up the complete *Christus* in 1872. From 1876 to 1879 Longfellow acted as editor, in practice as editor-in-chief, of the thirty-one volumes of *Poems of Places*, which included several of his own contributions. Meantime, a but slightly diminished flow of shorter poems, including the fine sonnets, continued, filling most of six volumes: *Flower-de-Luce* (1867); *Three Books of Song* (1872); *Aftermath* (1873); *The Masque of Pandora and Other Poems* (1875); *Kéramos and Other Poems* (1878); and *Ultima Thule* (1880).

These last years were for Longfellow the years of apotheosis. The distinctions between the poet and the venerable figure of Craigie House were lost in a chorus of affectionate acclaim, in which the dissenting voices of the younger generation were drowned out. The last European journey in 1868–69 was an almost royal progress, with honorary degrees conferred by the universities of Oxford and Cambridge, to the cheers of the undergraduates, and with a reception by Queen Victoria. From the Continent, Victor Hugo saluted Longfellow as a man who brought honor to America, and at home the schoolchildren of Cambridge presented him with an armchair made from the wood of the original spreading chestnut tree. In American eyes, he was clearly the uncrowned poet laureate, and he played his part to the end. On March 12, 1882, he finished ten six-line stanzas of "The Bells of San Blas," typically celebrating with nostalgia a past of picturesque devotion when "the priest was lord of the land." On March 15, he also typically added a single-stanza counterstatement:

> O Bells of San Blas, in vain
> Ye call back the Past again!
> The Past is deaf to your prayer;
> Out of the shadows of night
> The world rolls into light;
> It is daybreak everywhere.

He had reassured himself and his readers for the last time. Nine days later, after a very brief illness, he was dead at the age of seventy-five, and the spontaneous mourning was international. Enough uncollected poems remained to provide *In the Harbor* (1882), and, in 1883, the impressive fragment of his projected poetic drama, *Michael Angelo*, was separately published. With this his art had reached its period, a fact emphasized by the substantially complete and massive edition of his works in 1886. In its eleven volumes the results of sixty-two literarily active years were assembled for the judgment of posterity.

Longfellow's prose works are, with one exception, of minor importance. *Outre-Mer* contains vivid descriptions of Western Europe in the 1820's, and reflects Longfellow's romantic sensibility in a charming manner, but its studied picturesqueness palls, and it remains inferior to the *Sketch Book* that it too obviously imitates. Longfellow's various essays and articles, important in their day, are now chiefly of historical and biographical interest. Their knowledge has been superseded, and their critical methods and point of view seem outmoded, although they still yield some appreciative insights. The one novel, *Kavanagh*, lacks the technical and imaginative unity necessary to success. Its moderately realistic representation of life in a rural New England community deserves the praise Emerson gave it, and there

are some amusingly lively scenes satiric of old-line Calvinism and of the patriotic literary theory that assumed the future greatness of American poetry as a consequence of the greatness of American scenery. The love story, however, is flat and sentimentalized, and the characters are insubstantial, save for the sensitive but ineffectual Mr. Churchill, apparently Longfellow's wry portrait of an aspect of himself. *Kavanagh*'s most serious interest perhaps lies in its reflection of the religious and cultural changes beginning to transform New England life, but this, too, suffers from the novel's episodic construction. Only in *Hyperion: A Romance* did Longfellow succeed in extended prose fiction.

Hyperion, the most autobiographical of all Longfellow's works, describes under a thin veil of fiction the personal crisis of 1835–36; by Longfellow's own account, its writing was a therapy by which he worked his way from morbidity to health. The spiritual journey, a frequent theme in his works, is imaged here in a romanticized account of the second European trip. Paul Flemming, the hero, despairing over the loss of his "dear friend," retraces Longfellow's expeditions and experiences; at Interlaken he meets and falls in love with Mary Ashburton (Frances Appleton) and is rejected by her. Finally, restored to mental health, he self-reliantly faces the future alone—a stance that his creator and original was unable to adopt. So immediately identifiable were the persons and events of *Hyperion* that "all Boston" was soon happily gossiping and being scolded by Longfellow for its narrow-minded censoriousness. Only as passing years dimmed the topical interest could *Hyperion* be read as an imaginative representation of a not simply personal but generically youthful and romantic odyssey.

Into *Hyperion* Longfellow poured the accumulations of three years. Traveler's notes, long descriptions, general reflections, anecdotes and tales, extended literary and philosophic commentaries, topics from his Harvard lectures, translations from German literature—all are crowded in, often with little explicit connection, and are set in a romantic-plush style certain to try the patience of post-romantic readers. Longfellow was then under the spell of Jean Paul Richter, whose style, in apparent chaos, mingled the serious, comic, sublime, and grotesque; it delighted in abruptly changing moods, materials, and manners, in archaic phrasing, flamboyant figurative expression, and rhapsody. In varying degree, these qualities are also in *Hyperion*, so that the first impression is of confusion and cloying whimsicality. Beneath the patchwork, however, lies a real unity of emotion and experience.

The symbolism of the central journey is developed in simple, traditional imagery. Beginning on a dark, cold, mist-shrouded December morning in the Rhine valley, the action moves, for the climactic scenes of Book IV, up into the Swiss mountains in full summer, with the sun high and strong. The past is figured throughout by darkness and the grave, and is extended to include not only Flemming's personal past but the historical past whose monuments surround him in Europe; similarly, the present is a brightness into which not only he but mankind must enter. As Flemming's enthrallment began at a grave, so deliverance comes in St. Gilgen's churchyard among the tombs. The liberating formula he finds, as Longfellow actually found it, on a tablet affixed to a tomb: "Look not mournfully into the Past. It comes not back again. Wisely improve the Present. It is thine. Go forth to meet the shadowy Future without fear, and with a manly heart."

The immediate result of this directive Flemming calls almost miraculous, but later he asks, "Can such a simple result spring only from the long and intricate process of experience?" The process of a single experience is precisely what unifies, however loosely, the widely disparate materials of *Hyperion* and revivifies its traditional imagery by providing a freshly individual context. Embodying a conflict that runs throughout Longfellow's life and poetry and displaying at length the recurrent terms and images of that conflict, as well as of its outcome, *Hyperion* forms the literary substratum of a large part of Longfellow's later work.

Outre-Mer and *Hyperion* played a significant part in making Europe's thought and art available to the American public; so, too, did Longfellow's translations of poetry, which occupy a substantial place in his canon and were produced with varying frequency throughout his career. To translation Longfellow was drawn by his personal, sometimes indiscriminate delight in European literature, as well as by the literary and linguistic challenge of the task itself and the pedagogical usefulness of the results. Spanish, Italian, and German literature furnished the most numerous originals, but there are also translations from French, Danish, Swedish, Anglo-Saxon, and Latin poetry, and even three renditions, by way of extant prose translations, of Eastern poems. The originals are qualitatively a hodgepodge of everything from sentimental trivia to Dante's *Divina Commedia*.

Accepting Goethe's belief that the translator should adopt the author's situation, mode of speaking, and peculiarities, Longfellow scrupulously attempted to minimize the unavoidable sacrifices of translation and to move as close to literal correspondence as other considerations permitted. His earlier translations take measured liberties, such as the use of "equivalent stanzas" in rendering the *Coplas de Don Jorge Manrique*; his later translations are austerely restrictive. The great test was the translation of the *Divina Commedia*. After pondering the insurmountable difficulties of Dante's *terza rima*, Longfellow decided to abandon the rhyming so that he could preserve the tercet structure and achieve literal precision. The justification of this decision is the translation itself, which, in spite of unevenness and deficiencies, reflects something of the linguistic economy and rhythmic severity of the original. Although Longfellow's rendition does not attain the semi-independent poetic value of great verse translations, it remains one of the most faithful and effective Englishings of Dante.

On the value of translation to the practicing poet, Longfellow was of divided mind. Judging from his own experience, he insisted that successful translation evidenced real creative power, and that the act of translating served as stimulus to the poet's own thought and feeling; but he also refers to the attendant dangers. Translation is, in his own words, "like running a ploughshare through the soil of one's mind; a thousand germs of thought spring up (excuse this agricultural figure), which otherwise might have lain and rotted in the ground—still it sometimes seems to me like an excuse for being lazy,—like leaning on another man's shoulder." For Longfellow, whose art was highly responsive to external suggestion, translation probably did start ideas, and it undoubtedly contributed to his notable skill in versification. Nevertheless, his preoccupation with translation, even during a period of life normally crucial in the development of independence, may indeed have encouraged a habit of leaning on other men's shoulders that partly explains the limited originality of his own subsequent poetry.

Longfellow's first published poem, "The Battle of Lovell's Pond," derivatively celebrating a skirmish whose importance was monumental-ly local, appeared in the *Portland Gazette* for November 17, 1820, over the signature "Henry." Between this and the final "Bells of San Blas" stand well over five hundred poems whose variety makes generalization pause. Ranging from such brief, pure song as "Stars of the Summer Night" to the composite *Christus,* which occupies one hundred and sixty double-columned pages in the Cambridge Edition, the poetry includes not only "ode and elegy and sonnet" in abundance, but hortatory, meditative, and imagistic lyrics; poetic dramas; and many kinds of narrative from popular ballad to epic-tinged idyll, of widely varying length and manner. The gamut of quality is almost as extended, the good poems being sometimes obscured by the disproportionately large number of bad or indifferent ones. Some lines of development can be chronologically traced, especially for the long poems, but these, with rare exception, mark tonal and emphatic changes, or shifts in predominant verse forms or genres, rather than fundamental alterations in Longfellow's major ideas or attitudes, which, although modified with time, persist in recognizable form from *Voices of the Night* to the end.

The essential characteristics, even the qualitative variance, of Longfellow's poetry are related to his humanistic although unsystematized views on art. Art, he held, is the revelation of man, and of nature only "through man." His abandonment of nature description, Longfellow explained, meant not that he loved nature less, but man more. This basically traditional attitude receives a distinctively nineteenth-century coloring from Longfellow's understanding of artistic usefulness in terms of "elevation." Poetry, he argued in his 1832 "Defence of Poetry," is an instrument for improving the condition of society and advancing the great purpose of human happiness; in America's democratic society, this implied an endorsement of literature's growing concern with the literate common man. So Longfellow's Michael Angelo, in the drama bearing his name, defines art as

> "All that embellishes and sweetens life,
>   And lifts it from the level of low cares
>   Into the purer atmosphere of beauty;
>   The faith in the Ideal . . ."

Thus poetry, even at the risk of losing itself in the "low cares," will serve to charm, to strengthen, and to teach—a formula in which many critics and poets concurred: Walt Whitman, praising Longfellow as an unrecognized master in the treatment of common occurrences, declared his evocation of the poetic quality of everyday things to be truly representative of the spirit of democracy.

That a useful muse might become too housewifely Longfellow was aware. The nature and the problems of the artistic process make a recurrent theme in his poetry, especially from the two poems "Prometheus" and "Epimetheus" of 1854 to the poems of the 1870's, *The Masque of Pandora*, "Kéramos," and *Michael Angelo*, and the problem most reflective of his own experience was that of the frustrating distance between the exaltation of original inspiration and the flatness of final achievement. Longfellow knew that the highest inspiration is Promethean, and he suspected that great art comes only from the continual isolation and the total commitment of struggling with the gods—the art of a Shakespeare or Dante, before whose accomplishment he openly confessed his own inadequacy. Yet, like many of his contemporaries, he half-feared this heroic posture as a humanly perilous one, a cutting-off of the artist from humanity's common lot, from the world of Pandora's opened box and Epimetheus' humanitarian compassion. How the initial lofty vision could without betrayal and without obscurity be made accessible and instructive to a wide audience was the puzzle. Finding no solution, Longfellow accepted without undue repining the Epimethean role of poetic concern with daily sorrows and hopes, but he was haunted by the figure of Prometheus, symbol of the daring act of imagination essential to the birth of all poetry, even that which apparently ended up in slippers at the fireside.

The major ideas underlying Longfellow's poetry are characteristically expressed in a conventional nineteenth-century terminology that invites partial misreading, partly because of subsequent changes in meaning, especially in connotation, and partly because important terms are often so inclusive as to seem indeterminate. Longfellow's constant appeal to the heart is frequently understood as the consequence of a vague, sentimental notion that the gentler emotions could resolve problems and order life, to the near-exclusion of thought. His usage, however, like that of his contemporaries, reflects an older and wider meaning of *heart*. The word refers not only to the emotions, but also to will and intuitive reason. The heart is the source of insight as well as of joy or grief; it embraces the moral sensibility that accepts or rejects truth and that acts as conscience in its unstudied response to generally self-evident laws. When Longfellow writes,

> "It is the heart, and not the brain,
>   That to the highest doth attain . . ."

his use of "heart" is close to that of the Pauline formula, in the phraseology of the Authorized Version, "with the heart man believeth to righteousness." The heart, therefore, may stand for all of man's immaterial nature, save his discursive reason, which is often signified by "brain." Moreover, in his simple division of man into body and soul, Longfellow assigned all thoughts, all feelings, all desires to the soul, not the body, which is only the instrument.

"It is the soul," he insisted, "that feels, enjoys, suffers. . . ." Thus the affections themselves are spiritual, and, directed to good ends, can properly be called "holy."

Longfellow's frame of ultimate reference is formed by his religious convictions. When he established in 1824 the first Unitarian society at Bowdoin, he was not simply revolting against the "consociation of 'old sanctities,'" as he once called the college's conservatively Congregationalist clergy, but affirming the strong personal faith that pervaded his life and writings. Like his father, Longfellow in general accepted the teaching of William Ellery Channing: that man is fundamentally good, endowed by God with reason, conscience, and an intuitive awareness of the divine; and that Christianity, the purest faith known to man, is progressing toward a full realization of its ideals in a universal church of the future. The core of man's religion is a self-sacrificial love issuing in noble actions and sentiments, and in humanitarian concern for human welfare. Not by creeds, whether Athanasian or Calvinistic, but by deeds is man judged, and his faith made effective.

For so optimistic a belief, the chief problem is that of sin and evil, and the greatest imaginative failure of Longfellow's poetry is its inability to probe life's dark or sordid aspects. The causes of failure were partly temperamental. A natural fastidiousness led Longfellow to recoil from the physical and spiritual ugliness that caused him actual pain. Although he was personally subject to periods of neurotic depression with moments of panic, he regarded these visitations as transient phenomena that raised no intellectual question about man's nature or destiny. What experience failed to provide, faith could not supply. Especially in his long poems, Longfellow represents or alludes to the malicious, fanatic, and selfish behavior men are capable of, but he suggests no deeper

cause than a defect incidental to man's present condition, reformable although not yet reformed. The chief weakness of *The Golden Legend* is therefore the characterization of Satan, who, although cast as a fallen angel, is in action only a badly behaved, treacherous superman, neither terrifying nor awe-inspiring, and almost cursorily dismissed. Somehow—and Longfellow is never deeply curious about "how's"—everything will come out all right. So, at least, his reasoning assured him. Yet his attraction to Dante, the pessimistic feeling that tinges *Christus*, and the powerful vision of final nullity in *Michael Angelo* all suggest a sensibility whose perceptions are often at variance with the formulating ideas.

Indeed, the simply held ideas by which Longfellow attempted to order experience are frequently unable to contain the strong current of feeling that is a distinctive quality of his romantic sensibility. Although he was sharply critical of what he considered the excesses and absurdities of romanticism, his own poetry is saturated with a romantic sense of life's fragility. The crumbling ruins, encroaching darkness, and vivid but fleeting visions are not fashionable accessories, but the authentic images of Longfellow's deepest emotion, as his journals testify. That human life is a dream in which the apparent solidities of time and place dissolve into insubstantial forms is a nearly obsessive theme. To Longfellow, the most powerful flow of time and consciousness is backward, from present to past, from actuality to dream, and into the magic night of communion and reminiscence that gives access to the remembered past. However tempered in expression by his almost classical restraint and social poise, the dominant mood of Longfellow's poetry is a melancholy not unlike that of Washington Irving, compounded of nostalgia, the sadness of personal loss, and the painful awareness of transcience and mortality. If there is truth in the comment that Longfellow did not face the primary facts of life and nature, one reason may be his feeling that "facts" are neither primary nor solid, but the phenomena of a dream. So pervasive is dream or reverie in Longfellow's imagination that his most effective lyric or meditative poems are likely to be built on dreamlike associations, and the felicitous "legend style," as he called it, of some of his longer works depends upon an atmosphere of dreamy distance.

When physical surfaces lose their bounds and firmness, the natural world is easily invaded by the circumambient world of spirit. From the early "Footsteps of Angels" to the late "Helen of Tyre," Longfellow's poetry is recurrently haunted by phantoms, as the planes of nature and spirit, always thought by Longfellow to be exactly correspondent, seem to converge at a visionary point somewhere between reality and unreality. Longfellow's belief in the interaction of the invisible world and the world of sense led him actually to experiment with spiritualism a few times. In practice, he found spiritualism unconvincing and unedifying, but he never lost the sense of continuity between this world and another, between the living and the dead, that makes the pervasive mysteriousness of many poems so memorable.

To withdraw into the haunted night, to surrender to nostalgia and reverie, was Longfellow's natural inclination, intensified by his domestic catastrophes and, in his later years, by loneliness. His beliefs and character, however, prohibited such a retreat: the voices of night must be answered by the voices of day, or by aspiration the dreaming night must be made holy with stars. To assert present reality and the possibility of meaningful action in it becomes the necessary countermovement against the pull of the past; it is the thrust of health against incipient morbidity. On the side

of reality are religious faith, human love, and the achievements and obligations of civilization; these are the foundations of hope and inescapable duty. Thus the longing for imaginative flight is characteristically confronted by a resolute will: this was the fundamental conflict in Longfellow's experience and, mirrored in his art, provides the only continuous tension in a poetry whose structure and language have little of that quality.

The conflict is often described rather than presented, and the resolution stated rather than achieved. Even in such simple poems, however, there is occasionally a conviction successfully communicated that seems unaccountably to be an increment from the underlying experience itself. In the once overacclaimed, now overabused "A Psalm of Life," the conflict exists chiefly as a background for the celebration of triumphant resolve, directly expressed. That this hortatory poem should have a witnessed effect denied to countless other exhortations may be due to a residual force not earned, according to the modern prescription, through the strategy of the poem itself, but subtly transmitted to it as a tone from the prior struggle and its resolution that was indeed earned, since "A Psalm of Life" springs from the same experience that produced *Hyperion*. In Longfellow's more complex didactic poems the countering assertion of hope or purpose is not always poetically successful; at times it is imposed, or inadequate to the strength of the preceding melancholy. But in the best poems it is sufficiently implied in the foregoing situation or images to be a valid climax.

The major ideas of Longfellow are clearly reflected in his poetry considered as a whole; he repeatedly makes explicit reference to them, and indulges in overt teaching based upon them. His poetry, nevertheless, is not a poetry of ideas: certainly it is not philosophic or genuinely reflective, if "reflective" implies extended analysis of experience and systematic deliberation upon it. Except occasionally and on some few subjects, notably art, Longfellow's poems are primarily meditative; they express intuitions of experience, whether personal or literary, their thought usually arising immediately from feeling and remaining closely attached to it, or interwoven with it. Habitually, there is little progressive development of idea or attitude: a poem's underlying experience is made concrete in a described object, situation, or story—an image whose significance is presented sometimes as almost a short allegorization, more often as a correspondence or connotation on another plane. Since the image, from whatever source it is drawn and however simple or complex it may be, not only determines the tone of the whole poem but is also the essential figure of the experience, Longfellow's meditative poetry is, on the whole, fundamentally metaphoric, although in many poems the lack of compression, the extended statement, and the failure to renew conventional images all dissipate metaphor's possible intensity.

Some of Longfellow's important images by their complexity, recurrence, and stability become true symbols, at times restricted or extensively modified by particular contexts, but possessing a sufficiently persistent significance throughout the poetry to express Longfellow's imaginative apprehension of life. A few symbols are based on artifacts or on artistic creation—bells, walled forts or castles, music— but most are drawn from nature. Largely traditional, they are sometimes casually used as cultural hand-me-downs; more often, however, their significance has clearly been rediscovered at a deep level of experience. The most pervasive symbols are archetypal: the darkness of haunted night, oblivion, and the past, whose chill is the coldness of the grave; the warm

light of reality, of vital energy, and, for Longfellow, of love, concentrated in the sun; water, whose flow is the motion of feeling, spirit, and time, and whose fluidity Longfellow attributes also to sky, air, and light; the stars of divine or spiritual order and, more personally, of aspiration.

Above all others are the symbols drawn from Longfellow's memory of youthful experience; his landscape of the human situation and of individual inner life is that of the Maine coastline: the sea, the nearby forest, and the narrow habitable strip between. This last, the scene of rational and civilized life, additionally provides a symbol of precarious security, the home centered in the hearth, whose warmth is the focus of human relationships and a protection against the storms without: although Longfellow's fireside scene is likely to be sentimentalized, it occasionally reflects in muted fashion the ancient image of man huddled by his saving fire. The forest, boundless and majestic, frequently wailing in the wind, embodies a primitive life somewhat ominous for civilized man. The sea is Longfellow's deepest and most inclusive symbol; no contemporary writer save Melville was more profoundly or constantly responsive to it. In Longfellow's poetry, the sea is the restless mystery of existence, and its unfathomable source; it is the energy of unconfined and subconscious life, and of liberty. In its effects, it is also paradoxical, merciful and merciless, purifying yet dangerous, at once death-giving and life-giving.

In spite of the importance of images and symbols, however, the typical movement of a poem by Longfellow is toward a formulated decision; that is, however complex the underlying feelings or situation, any tension or conflict, or any balance of opposites, is resolved by a choice amongst the possibilities or by a limiting statement of specific significance. Since the poems ordinarily do not fully present whatever struggle or turbulence there may have been in the originating experience, but only selected, usually subdued aspects of it, the resolution often appears easy or oversimplified. In the best poems, however, the concluding statement is at once a natural consequence of an imaginative prior development and an explication sufficiently complex to embrace all the possibilities.

The lyric and meditative poems, and several of the shorter narratives, are characteristically, although not exclusively, developed in distinguishable stages, moving from image to analogy or statement, or from image to analogy to statement; much more rarely, from statement to image. In a large number of the poems, the image is fully presented in one or more initial stanzas of verse paragraphs and its moral or spiritual significance set forth in the following ones, frequently with an exact correspondence in the lengths of presentation and of statement, a balance well exemplified in "Seaweed" and "The Beleaguered City." Alternatively, the statement may be a comparatively brief conclusion, or even a counterstatement of denial, revulsion, or change of direction, as in "The Bells of San Blas," rather than a climax to what has preceded it. In many poems, the movement between image and comparison or statement is continuously back and forth, the image being presented in steps, each of which is accompanied by an immediate reflection upon it. The poems that do not move by clearly defined stages may conveniently be designated as one-stage. Classification by stages, however, can be only approximate: an indicated spiritual significance, for example, may cling so closely to an image, as it does in "Sandalphon," that it seems simply to be an overtone of it.

In the one-stage poems, the presentation may be hortatory, descriptive, or narrative; it either produces a direct, uncomplicated, often emotional effect or clearly implies a further meaning without openly indicating or stating it. Into this category fall most of the short narratives and also many of the poems most appealing to modern taste, the quasi-imagistic poems that present a concentrated image with expanding overtones: "Chrysaor," "The Bells of Lynn," "Aftermath," "The Tide Rises, the Tide Falls" are representative of this group, and "The Ropewalk" is similar in its reliance on suggestion, although it employs a series of images, central and associated, rather than one image alone. A few two-stage poems are also primarily imagistic in effect, some of them, like "The Warning," developing their analogy closely in terms of the original image, others, like "Snowflakes," using their analogy actually to reinforce the image. However stimulating Longfellow's imagistic poems may be, they are nonetheless too small in number to be typical of his poetry.

The three-stage poems usually consist of initial image, analogy, and explicit statement, with attention more or less evenly distributed among them, a method that is obvious in the three stanzas of the feeble "Rainy Day," whose initial lines run "The day is cold, and dark, and dreary . . . My life is cold, and dark, and dreary . . . Be still, sad heart! and cease repining . . ." For some reason, the three-stage poems include many of Longfellow's bad and indifferent pieces; on the other hand, they also include some of the more completely satisfying meditative verses, such as "Palingenesis" and a sensitively wrought ode, "The Building of the Ship," whose oratorically eloquent, hortatory last stanza begins with the familiar "Thou, too, sail on, O Ship of State!" and makes an illogical but emotionally appropriate and powerful new application of the poem's structural analogy between the construction and launching of a ship and the progress of romantic love climaxed in marriage.

The largest number of Longfellow's shorter poems, including the sonnets and such important compositions as the brief "In the Churchyard at Cambridge" and "Jugurtha" and the lengthier "Fire of Driftwood," "My Lost Youth," and "Morituri Salutamus," are two-stage; if his imagination found any method especially congenial, it is this one, so that his notable achievement in sonnet form is not surprising.

The early two- or three-stage poems usually end in explicit declaration; after the mid-1840's there is increasing reliance on a final metaphor or symbol, as in "Autumn Within":

It is autumn; not without,
    But within me is the cold.
Youth and spring are all about;
    It is I that have grown old.

Birds are darting through the air,
    Singing, building without rest;
Life is stirring everywhere,
    Save within my lonely breast.

There is silence: the dead leaves
    Fall and rustle and are still;
Beats no flail upon the sheaves,
    Comes no murmur from the mill.

The poem is too short to be widely representative, but it bears the Longfellow impress: the quatrains observe a 2-2 rhetorical division; the lines are four-stress, in falling rhythm; the accommodations of stress and pause to meaning are minor but careful; the language is simple and the word order nearly normal, save for the deliberate departure in the concluding lines; there is a touch of showy pathos in the eighth line; the images are traditional, and, especially in the last two lines, rather "poetic" or literary. The fundamental comparison of inner states and outer seasons allows easy further comparison between seasons and thus inner states, and so moves into the suggestive final revelation of age's fruitlessness in a favorite image: the cessation of sound. In so short a poem, the procedure is abbreviated but clear. The initial image is quickly introduced in three words; its spiritual significance is explicitly stated at once; the comparison is somewhat tenuously explored, and the conclusion intensifies the comparison by shifting the images associated with autumn to the signified spiritual state. Like so many of Longfellow's good if obviously minor poems, this has a personal feeling that manages, even if barely, to come through the conventional scenery; it also has something of Longfellow's typical facility, attended, as often, by the bad and good angels of glibness and grace.

Like much nineteenth-century poetry, Longfellow's seems in retrospect leisurely, even too relaxed. The slow development of ideas, the elaboration of details, the multiplication of parallels, the explication of the already-evident are practices that destroy some of his poems and in varying combinations and degrees characterize most of them. The language, too, bears the stamp of its time in its tendency to expansive statement, its often predictable vocabulary and phraseology, and its fondness for literary diction. Like the sporadic addiction to poetically picturesque subject matter, these qualities are alien to sophisticated modern taste, although whether or to what extent they are necessarily faults is a problem of literary theory and the absoluteness of critical standards. Historically considered, the kind of poetry Longfellow wrote lay within a poetic tradition that with various adaptations served the larger part of a century, and was imaginatively satisfying to the romantic-Victorian sensibility. Within the age's literary conventions, Longfellow used language skillfully and sensitively. At its best, his language is simple and economical, natural in movement, emotionally exact in its use of words and phrases, and restrained in statement. Furthermore, Longfellow's handling of language is largely responsible for his achievement of an impressive tonal range from the formality of semi-epic narrative to the humor-seasoned easiness of the discourse of polite society. He makes the traditional poetic language, with often minimal alteration, express distinctively his own insights and feelings.

As a poet more evocative than creative of experience, Longfellow employs language with a notable awareness of the way in which it becomes charged with meaning from the inescapable situations of human life. Frequently he depends not upon connotations or overtones developed within the context of a poem, but upon a resonance provided immediately by general experience itself and renewed in the poem by allusions to the appropriate common events or situations, or by brief descriptions of them. This habit demands from the reader a supply of significance from his private store and a willingness to accept suggestive reference rather than precise control in the poem—a concession not demanded by great poetry, and by some critics austerely refused to any. It is, however, a concession habitually made to occasional poems, whose otherwise vague or flabby language may acquire exactness from setting and event. When, in "Morituri Salutamus," Longfellow recalls his audience from thoughts of friends dead and buried to

. . . these scenes frequented by our feet
When we were young, and life was fresh and
      sweet,

the last line is not vaguely sentimental, but, like the poem's title, genuinely moving because emotionally appropriate and provided with definable meaning by the situation: an aging poet addressing the dwindled number of college classmates at certainly their last reunion, held fifty years after graduation.

Like other aspects of his poetry, Longfellow's prosody is remarkable for resourcefulness and variety within traditional limits. His uncommon talent in versification and his absorption in its technical problems led to no prosodic revolution; indeed, a dangerous facility, combined with a taste for euphony, brings his verse at moments close to that of the typical Victorian "sweet singer." Within accepted bounds, however, Longfellow's versatility in rhythmical, metrical, and rhyming patterns and his constant experimentation, directed toward the creation of a unique effect for each poem, reveal a technical mastery rarely approached in American poetry. Although his prosodic variety is most obvious in the surprisingly various patterns of his stanzaic verse, it is perhaps more subtly displayed in meeting the resistance of a set form like the sonnet, where, employing the Italian pattern and almost invariably observing a strict octet-sestet division, Longfellow achieves striking rhythmic differences by ingenious handling of metrical substitution, run-on and end-stopped lines, and caesuras. In freer forms, his skill is no less evident: the extremely uneven blank verse of *The Divine Tragedy* has reflective passages in which comparative rhythmic freedom works with approximately normal word order to produce lines that sometimes collapse into prose but that occasionally attain a thoroughly natural movement barely but unmistakably tightened into poetry, as in the course of the soliloquy by Manahem the Essenian in the third part of the "First Passover":

The things that have been and shall be no
      more,
The things that are, and that hereafter shall be,
The things that might have been, and yet were
      not,
The fading twilight of great joys departed,
The daybreak of great truths as yet unrisen,

The intuition and the expectation
Of something, which, when come, is not the
    same,
But only like its forecast in men's dreams,
The longing, the delay, and the delight,
Sweeter for the delay; youth, hope, love, death,
And disappointment which is also death,
All these make up the sum of human life;
A dream within a dream, a wind at night
Howling across the desert in despair,
Seeking for something lost it cannot find.

The technical virtuosity of Longfellow's art is manifested in several accomplishments: the successful maintenance of falling rhythm in spite of English poetry's strong tendency to rising rhythm; the dexterous control of varied rhythm and free rhyming by an organization based on parallelism, balance, and alliteration; and the giving of widely varied movement to such uncomplicated verse forms as the quatrain. Even so straightforward a narrative as "Paul Revere" shows a meticulous attention to technical detail that partly accounts for the rather complex effect of an apparently simple poem. As a rule, the closer the examination of Longfellow's verse technique, the greater is the appreciation of a diversity that can succeed in the subdued four-line stanzas of his meditative poetry, in the stately hexameters of *Evangeline*, and in the jaunty tetrameter couplets of "The Rhyme of Sir Christopher."

The shorter poems of Longfellow enjoyed a contemporary popularity, in England and other countries as well as in America, that has rarely been rivaled, yet it was not these poems but his long ones on which his reputation chiefly rested, especially the long narratives: *Evangeline, Hiawatha, The Courtship of Miles Standish*, and *Tales of a Wayside Inn*. More recently the major narrative poems have been relegated to the classroom, often at a rather elementary level, in acknowledgment of Long-

fellow's ability to tell a story in them, and with the implication that he does no more. The nineteenth century knew better: when *Evangeline* was published in 1847, one English reviewer hailed it as "the first genuine Castalian fount which has burst from the soil of America!" In spite of his fanciful image, the critic was properly celebrating what was in fact the first important sustained poem by an American and was endorsing the general acclaim that made Evangeline herself a symbol of the Acadian "cause."

Like all of Longfellow's major poems, *Evangeline* was, in modern academic jargon, "well researched," and one result of Longfellow's reading was to make the poem in part a richly descriptive tour of expanses of western and southern America. The story itself, however, is an altogether simple one, whose essentials were first given to Longfellow by Hawthorne: in the dispersal of the French Acadians in 1755, two lovers, Evangeline and Gabriel, are separated, and for weary years Evangeline attempts to trace Gabriel through the settlements and wilds of the American colonies; finally, aging and losing earthly hope, she becomes a Sister of Mercy in a Philadelphia hospital, where, during a plague, the dying Gabriel is brought and the lovers are reunited just before his death. Gabriel early recedes into the background as the sought rather than seeker, and the focus of the whole poem is upon Evangeline, giving the temperamentally chivalric Longfellow full scope for the development of an idealized, simple woman of absolute fidelity, the kind of heroine most congenial to his imagination. In a realistically represented milieu Evangeline would seem too etherealized, but the deliberately legendary treatment of the story and the touch of dreamlike remoteness in the setting create an idyllic effect appropriate to the characterization. Moreover, the idealization of the heroine is closely related to the poem's meaning: Evangeline is increasingly spiritualized by the patiently endured sufferings of her nearly endless journey until she finally emerges as a saintly figure.

The journey of Evangeline and the whole story in which she moves are raised to semi-heroic proportions by Longfellow's mythologizing of his materials. Acadia is also Arcadia; the simple lives of the peasants, viewed under a summer sun, recall the Golden Age and Eden, and the murmuring pines and hemlocks color the scene with childhood innocence recalled. With expulsion and separation, a mythic pattern specifically Christian develops: the pious Evangeline is the exiled wayfarer making her dedicated journey through the world to her final renunciation of it and her entering upon the more purely spiritual pilgrimage of return to the true Arcadia of Heaven, where alone reunion can be lasting. When the two lovers at one dramatic point miss each other by the narrowest of margins, it is, as one critic has said, like the touch of God's hand reserving Evangeline for another marriage. Despite the slowness and occasional thinness of the narration, the pattern of *Evangeline* gives the poem substance and dignity.

In creating the hexameter lines of *Evangeline* Longfellow sensibly treated the problem of English hexameter as a practical one, and paid little heed to the theoretic objections that have enlivened criticism since the Renaissance. Encouraged by Goethe's example and by the experiments of Southey and Coleridge, he solved the immediate problems by using a basically dactylic line with a trochaic close and free trochaic substitution; the minimally necessary spondees he obtained by juxtaposing monosyllabic words and by coaxing the second syllable of trochees into an approximation of spondees. The resultant hexameters give *Evangeline* a slow processional movement; the longer line admits lavish introduction of concrete detail through additional modifying words, and has a pleasantly lingering effect appropriate to idyllic tone, as Longfellow apparently realized, since extended use of hexameters occurs chiefly in his idylls—*Evangeline*, *The Courtship of Miles Standish*, and "Elizabeth" in *Tales of a Wayside Inn*.

The Courtship of Miles Standish, although published eleven years later, resembles *Evangeline* in measure, in use of a legendary-historical foundation, and in pastoral coloring. The *Courtship*, however, has a vein of humor that leaves readers suspended between sentiment and amusement. The story has long since passed into folklore: how John Alden loved Priscilla Mullins but, out of friendship, wooed her in Captain Miles Standish's behalf, and how, with a false report of Standish's death, John and Priscilla married, with the captain returning just in time to assent. It is not the tale but the telling that has distinction. Longfellow moves through variations of tone with impressive assurance, from satirical humor to romance tinged with sentimentality, through sobriety and comedy alternatively.

The success of the *Courtship* lies principally in its humorous juxtaposition of two extravagant attitudes, each described in appropriate language and imagery, with each other and with common sense. One attitude is embodied in Captain Miles Standish, the hot-tempered commander of a twelve-man army, a swaggerer, a valiant man, and a student of the wars of the Hebrews, Caesar's *Commentaries*, and an artillery guide "designed for belligerent Christians"; on the other side is John Alden, sincere, hard-working, overscrupulous, compelled to disguise pleasure as duty before he can enjoy it, and fearful lest his preference of love over friendship may be "worshipping Astaroth blindly, and impious idols of Baal."

At the center is commonsensical Priscilla, quiet, loving, amused at her suitors' posturings, and busy at the spinning wheel emblematic of settled life with its civilizing domesticity.

The marriage of John and Priscilla, however humorous its preliminaries, is nevertheless, in the barely surviving Plymouth colony that is the setting, an affirmation of faith in America's future and a promise of its fruitfulness. Thus the almost lush description of the climactic bridal day is without serious incongruity set forth in images of religious ritual and of fertility, as the sun issues forth like a high priest, with the sea a laver at his feet, and Priscilla rides on a snow-white bull to her wedding while golden sunlight gleams on bunches of purple grapes. Longfellow again introduces the imagery of Eden and expulsion as he describes the land of privation and hardship lying before John and Priscilla, and adds,

But to their eyes transfigured, it seemed as the
　　Garden of Eden,
Filled with the presence of God, whose voice
　　was the sound of the ocean.

The final balance of sometimes broad humor, romantic sentiment, and gravity is a tonal achievement of no small order.

With *Hiawatha* Longfellow made his chief contribution to nineteenth-century American literature's search for a usable national past, whose necessity to the creation of a native culture was assumed from the analogy of European cultural history. America's antiquity, however, was Indian and primitively tribal, and therefore both racially and culturally alien. The pieties of nationalism nonetheless demanded that the gap between the two worlds be bridged; countless authors valiantly responded, and, with a few notable exceptions, artistically perished in the attempt. To Longfellow the whole effort seemed misdirected, since America's cultural past was essentially European, although he had been long interested in Indian lore and history, and was acquainted with such authorities on Indian life as Heckewelder and Schoolcraft. Typically, he found his own formula for relating the Indian past to the American present in a European national poem, the Finnish *Kalevala*, which suggested the use of legends linked together by the central figure of a culture hero, the creations of myth and folklore being, for the cultivated imagination, more viable than the grubby data of actual primitive living. In American terms, the Indians' passage from savagery to a low level of civilization could be treated as preparatory to the climactic arrival of high civilization represented by the white man, and poetry could thus create the continuity that history had failed to provide. One result of this plan is the weakest moment in *Hiawatha*, when the hero unreservedly recommends to his people the religion and culture of the white man, represented by the Jesuit missionaries: the abrupt transition from a legendary world to that of fictionalized history in unconvincing, as it was probably certain to be, in spite of its theoretical justification as a means of relating Indian and white civilization, the chief desideratum of the age.

Like the creators of the Noble Redman, Longfellow adapted his Indians to contemporary tastes and interests. His hero is a bowdlerized version of a mythic Algonkian chief, and Hiawatha's romance with Minnehaha is conducted by the rules of sentimental fiction. The idealization, however, is largely intended by Longfellow, as a part of the deliberately legendary atmosphere of the narration. Criticisms based on realistic assumptions, whether Emerson's mild blame or Schoolcraft's praise, were, in Longfellow's eyes, fundamentally irrelevant: Hiawatha was, he stated, a kind of "American

Prometheus," and the poem was "an Indian Edda," a recognizably poetic romance, based on ancient myths and traditions and thus to be read as an attractively colorful reflection not of Indian actuality, but of primitive imagination.

The language and versification of *Hiawatha* were designed as part of its legendary effect. The trochaic tetrameter meter, suggested by the *Kalevala* and by earlier Indian romances, has an accentuation sufficiently strong to invite easy exaggeration into singsong, an invitation readily accepted by most modern readers. In so long a poem, the conspicuous rhythm, the constant use of parallelism and repetition, the profusion of exotic Indian names, and the simple personifications all finally threaten monotony and make parody irresistible. Critical objections to *Hiawatha*'s verse can be countered only by treating the verse, according to Longfellow's intention, as a part of the primitive machinery. Thus regarded, the verse loses its apparent eccentricity and contributes a suitable effect of chant and of quaintness to the legendary atmosphere Longfellow sought to create. Unfortunately, it also heightens the sense of artifice pervasive in *Hiawatha* and perhaps inseparable from a pseudo-primitive genre.

Present-day concern with myth, legend, and folklore gives *Hiawatha* a more serious interest than it possessed in the recent past, even if the modern reader usually prefers to take his myth neat or as revitalized in current forms. The episodes of *Hiawatha* are based upon now familiar mythic patterns. Hiawatha himself, begotten by the West Wind upon the daughter of moon-descended Nokomis, is a demigod aligning himself with humanity. He teaches his people how to plant and cultivate maize, and begins to instruct them in the arts of civilization, the skills of fishing and agriculture, and the art of picture-writing. With the help of his few close companions and of the helpful animals of folklore, he slays the spirit of evil, the serpent-guarded Magician, and Pau-Puk-Keewis, the champion of the old, anarchic savagery, and finally departs for the Islands of the Blessed. From one standpoint, *Hiawatha* is a set of picturesque variations on mythic themes, and its recapitulation of a whole mythic pattern gives it in its entirety an imaginative strength greater than its incidental faults would apparently support. Its major weakness as a whole arises primarily from its literarily calculated primitivism: the sophistication of its simplicity makes it too manifestly a tour de force.

Longfellow's last major narrative work, *Tales of a Wayside Inn*, was published in three installments over an eleven-year period. The design of the work, a collection of stories in a unifying framework, recalls the *Canterbury Tales*, but Longfellow's self-confessed inability to rival Chaucer makes the Chaucerian work properly a point of reference rather than of comparison. In Longfellow's *Tales*, the stories are clearly primary, the framework a support. The setting is the Red-Horse Inn (now the reconstructed Wayside Inn) in Sudbury, Massachusetts, a hostelry well known to Longfellow and his friends. The narrators, designated by profession, avocation, nationality, or race, are all based upon actual acquaintances of Longfellow's: the Poet was Theophilus Parsons, a translator of Dante; the Musician was the Norwegian violinist Ole Bull; the Sicilian was Luigi Monti, an instructor in Harvard's modern languages department. Their individual characteristics are generalized into more or less typical ones, but there can be no satirical representation or socially or dramatically significant quarreling: the narrators form a friendly and homogeneous group. What is possible in the framework is realized—an animated running discussion of topics suggested by the tales and of points of view expressed by the tellers. In flexible tetrameter couplets, Longfellow takes the discussion from aesthetics to religion, and achieves an effect of individually colored discourse sufficient to support the tales and often interesting in itself.

Individually considered, the tales vary greatly in nature, interest, and quality. A few, like "Lady Wentworth" and "Azrael," dwindle into anecdote, and others, like "The Ballad of Carmilhan," are principally evocative of mood or of that ghostly atmosphere that Longfellow could always effectively create. Most of the stories, however, are marked by Longfellow's real narrative talent: the ability to make well-selected, continuously progressing events and vividly, if broadly, drawn characters deliver in a climactic scene some comment upon an aspect of life or a typical movement of human feeling. The accomplishment of the *Tales*, however, lies less in particular stories, as good as several of them are, than in the variety of the gathered narratives. Contrasting with each other in scene, tone, and poetic structure, and held together by the framework, the stories in juxtaposition suggest the inclusive range possible to the simple, immemorial activity of storytelling, and the way in which even traditional tales may reflect attitudes and feelings of the narrators. Many kinds of effects are embraced, from the grimness of "Torquemada" to the broad fabliau humor of "The Monk of Casal-Maggiore" or the vividness of "The Saga of King Olaf," one of the most vigorous of all Longfellow's poems, with its balladlike but well-developed dramatization of the mingled zeal and barbarism of the first Viking champions and enemies of Christianity. Moreover, a few of the tales, like "Emma and Eginhard" and "The Falcon of Ser Federigo," reflect a more realistic and tolerant assessment of human behavior than Longfellow's poetry commonly displays. The reputation of the *Tales* is unavoidably linked to the fortunes of narrative poetry, especially of straightforward narrative;

within that limited area, the *Tales* occupies a place of considerable honor.

The major irony of Longfellow's literary career was the commitment of his hopes for distinctive major achievement to the form in which he was most consistently unsuccessful, the poetic drama. From 1849 to 1872 he intermittently labored over what he regarded as "his loftier song" in "sublimer strain," as his greatest work, "the equivalent expression for the trouble and wrath of life, for its sorrow and mystery." The completed *Christus: A Mystery* consists of three parts comprising four poetic dramas, all so manifestly closet dramas that they could be properly described as dramatically organized poems. The first part is *The Divine Tragedy*, the last to be published; the second part is *The Golden Legend*, the first published; the third part, *The New England Tragedies*, consists of two dramas, *John Endicott* and *Giles Corey of the Salem Farms*. The three parts are linked by interludes and the whole *Christus* is provided with an "Introitus" and "Finale." No other works of Longfellow's had such intended scope or received such dedicated attention; and none were so disappointing in result. The twenty-odd years spent in composition, the lapse of time between publication of the parts, and the fact that each part is also a substantially self-contained work explain why the *Christus* seems partly to be an assemblage; indeed, it is surprising that the whole does achieve a loose unity which makes it more than the sum of its parts.

Longfellow's general failure in dramatic form is understandable. His talent was narrative and lyrically meditative, and he could not refrain from reliance on narration and exposition, even to the destruction of dramatic effect. The sequence and relationship of episodes and actions is basically determined, especially in the last two parts of the *Christus*, by narrative not dramatic logic and development. It is thus unfortunate that from 1849 on he increasingly looked to drama as the vehicle of his most important ideas. It is his least pretentious dramatic work, the early *Spanish Student*, that is in many respects the most successfully realized; in spite of its lack of intellectual significance, it is a colorful, pleasant comedy of intrigue, technically more proficient than the later poetic dramas. Two minor dramatic works, *Judas Maccabeus* and *The Masque of Pandora*, have interesting themes but are extremely weak in execution. Only the partly completed *Michael Angelo*, closely related to Longfellow's own life and work, and containing in a few passages some of his strongest poetry, shows an apparently emerging mastery of dramatic form in the 1870's.

The fundamental obstacle to the *Christus'* success, however, is not simply a flawed dramatic technique, but an internal conflict in the work between its ostensible intention and its meaning. Originally planned as a dramatizing of the progress of Christianity, the *Christus* loosely employs the theological virtues of faith, hope, and charity as the basis of organization, *The Divine Tragedy* expressing hope through its representation of Christ's life and mission, the *Golden Legend* depicting faith in its full medieval flowering, and the *New England Tragedies* pointing to the religious freedom of the age of charity or love. The optimism of the design is realized in some scenes and is recurrently asserted as a proposition, but it is not borne out in the *Christus'* development and accumulated feeling, which are finally somber and even pessimistic in their tendency. Longfellow's emotional recoil from several aspects of the contemporary religious scene apparently caused him to lose much of his professed hope for the future and left its mark especially on the first and third parts, the latest composed, of the *Christus*. If the last part inculcates love and tolerance at all, it does so only by exhibiting the horrors of bigotry, and the relentless power of intolerance is in fact the dominant force; in *John Endicott* a series of special providences, occurring near the conclusion, indicate divine displeasure with persecution, but the Quakers are saved only by an intervening royal mandate of that unlikely *deus ex machina*, Charles II; in the final, still grimmer *Giles Corey*, where the maliciously accused though innocent Corey is put to death by pressing, this climactic scene is followed by a hasty, excessively short speech by Cotton Mather predicting that never again will such things happen, a judgment perhaps validated by history, but certainly not by the action or tone of the drama. Furthermore, the interlude preparing for the *New England Tragedies* is a soliloquy by Martin Luther that alternates between an announcement of spiritual freedom recovered from religious tyranny and a condemnation of humanism reflecting the sectarianism and hatred most repellent to Longfellow: it is an unpromising introduction to the latest stage of an assertedly progressive historical movement.

That the *New England Tragedies* made a darkened climax Longfellow was probably aware. He originally planned a third, more confident concluding play based on the simple, pious life of Pennsylvania's Moravian sisterhood. This, however, he never wrote, and its abandonment may be explained by the actual state of his sentiments and especially by the developing mood of the *Christus* itself. The opening "Introitus" finds in the sadness of pre-Christian ages the sign of a coming Redeemer, but the "Finale" is not a celebration of redemption achieved; rather, it is a melancholy review of the Christian centuries, concluding that "the evil doth not cease." The survey is not despairing, but its limited hope is proclaimed in spite of rather than out of Christian history, and hope's realization seems indefinitely postponed: meanwhile

Poor, sad Humanity
Through all the dust and heat
Turns back with bleeding feet,
By the weary road it came. . . .

So the tracing of the human condition comes nearly full circle back to the "Introitus," and is saved from cyclical completion only by Longfellow's characteristic emphasis upon the persistence of the ideal and the possibility of individual Christian action.

Perhaps the most successful part of *Christus* is the *Golden Legend*, which, in spite of an elementary plot, an unmedievally melancholy hero, and a sentimentalized heroine, effectively profits from Longfellow's knowledge of the Middle Ages. Although the deepest intellectual and spiritual life of the medieval world is not mirrored here, the varied contrasts and conflicts of the medieval surface, as well as the immediately underlying crosscurrents, are colorfully represented through skillfully shifted scenes presented in a freely handled answerable verse. An acid portrayal of Goliardic friars is set against a simple, reverentially composed nativity play, and the satiric presentations of wrangling scholastics and of a sensational preacher are placed in a sympathetically imagined background of ringing bells and chanting pilgrims. So picturesquely drawn are the diverse actions of a world where "the will is feeble and passion strong," but where everything is seen in a transcendent light, that the effect is of a pageant arranged by religious and historical feeling, almost rich enough to conceal the weaknesses of the dramatic core.

The Divine Tragedy, composed in three "Passovers" or acts, with an "Introitus" and an epilogue, is based, often closely, on the Biblical account of Christ's life. The faults are many and obvious, ranging from insubstantial scenes to timidity in handling the text of the Bible, but in centering the action upon the effects of divine love and human response to it, Longfellow achieves some genuine thematic and dramatic development. Each "Passover" concentrates upon one aspect of Christus' expanding mission: upon the casting out of demons, which is the ejection of irrationality and fear; the curing of blindness, which is the dispelling of ignorance; and sacrifice, the perilous commitment of love. Recurrent themes and images, and frequent cross references, make the action less episodic than it at first appears to be, and an interpretative chorus is provided by Manahem the Essenian. Above all, a basic unity is found in Longfellow's preoccupation with that most persistent and personal of his themes, the problem of dream and reality. The fear expressed throughout *The Divine Tragedy* is that life is a delusive dream within a dream, and Christus the visionary of an unreal kingdom. The act of faith thus becomes primarily an assertion of reality, its validity being finally confirmed by the appearance of the risen Christus. Yet the haunting fear is too powerfully expressed to be completely dissolved even by an apparently victorious conclusion.

The study of Longfellow's poetic reputation is perhaps more relevant to the history of criticism than to the evaluation of his art. His most literate contemporaries delivered varying decisions, some finding the poetry seriously deficient, others praising it without reservation, most setting a very high value on the best poems while pointing out the weakness of others. It was popular acclaim, hailing the man as much as the poet, that elevated Longfellow to a position no sober critical judgment could sanction. With the emergence of modern literature and the literary wars it evoked, the defenders of the new order found it necessary and not unpleasant to counter the hostility of presumably Victorian attitudes by attacking Victorian ideals and achievements. In America, Longfellow, in his popular canonization, offered himself as the surest target for an assault on the nineteenth century; at the nadir, one influential critic advanced the proposition that Longfellow's poetry has no iota of the poetic character. Later, however, as the early twentieth-century revolution itself receded into the past, it became possible for Longfellow to share in the general revaluation of Victorian literature. To this more objective examination, dating especially from Odell Shepard's reserved but often acute essay prefixed to his selective edition of Longfellow's poems, many studies have contributed, including such full-length ones as Lawrance Thompson's reassessment of the young Longfellow's experience, Edward Wagenknecht's two important and sympathetic interpretations of Longfellow as person and author, Newton Arvin's uniquely valuable analysis of the poetry as a whole, and Cecil Williams' placing of Longfellow in the American literary tradition. From this continuing reconsideration has come a clear view of the many limitations of Longfellow's talent, but also a new respect for his accomplishment within them.

Selected Bibliography

WORKS OF HENRY WADSWORTH LONGFELLOW

Coplas de Don Jorge Manrique, Translated from the Spanish . . . Boston: Allen and Ticknor, 1833.

Outre-Mer: A Pilgrimage beyond the Sea. 2 vols. Boston: Hilliard, Gray (Vol. I); Lilly, Wait (Vol. II), 1833–34.

Hyperion: A Romance. 2 vols. New York: S. Colman, 1839.

Voices of the Night. Cambridge, Mass.: J. Owen, 1839.

Ballads and Other Poems. Cambridge, Mass.: J. Owen, 1841.

Poems on Slavery. Cambridge, Mass.: J. Owen, 1842.

The Spanish Student, A Play in Three Acts. Cambridge, Mass.: J. Owen, 1843.

The Poets and Poetry of Europe, with Introductions and Biographical Notices by Henry Wadsworth Longfellow. Philadelphia: Carey and Hart, 1845.

The Belfry of Bruges and Other Poems. Cambridge, Mass.: J. Owen, 1846.

Evangeline, a Tale of Acadie. Boston: Ticknor, 1847.

Kavanagh, a Tale. Boston: Ticknor, Reed, and Fields, 1849.

The Seaside and the Fireside. Boston: Ticknor, Reed, and Fields, 1850.

The Golden Legend. Boston: Ticknor, Reed, and Fields, 1851.

The Song of Hiawatha. Boston: Ticknor and Fields, 1855.

Drift Wood, A Collection of Essays. Boston: Ticknor and Fields, 1857.

The Courtship of Miles Standish and Other Poems. Boston: Ticknor and Fields, 1858.

Tales of a Wayside Inn. Boston: Ticknor and Fields, 1863.

The Divine Comedy of Dante Alighieri, Translated by Henry Wadsworth Longfellow. 3 vols. Boston: Ticknor and Fields, 1865–67.

Flower-de-Luce. Boston: Ticknor and Fields, 1867.

The New England Tragedies. Boston: Ticknor and Fields, 1868. (Privately printed, 1867.)

The Divine Tragedy. Boston: Osgood, 1871.

Christus: A Mystery. 3 vols. Boston: Osgood, 1872.

Three Books of Song. Boston: Osgood, 1872.

Aftermath. Boston: Osgood, 1873.

The Hanging of the Crane. Boston: Mifflin, 1874.

The Masque of Pandora and Other Poems. Boston: Osgood, 1875.

Kéramos and Other Poems. Boston: Houghton, Osgood, 1878.

Ultima Thule. Boston: Houghton Mifflin, 1880.

In the Harbor. Boston: Houghton Mifflin, 1882.

Michael Angelo. London: Houghton Mifflin, 1883.

SELECTED AND COLLECTED EDITIONS

Complete Works, edited by Horace E. Scudder. Riverside Edition. 11 vols. Boston: Houghton Mifflin, 1886. (Reprinted in Standard Library Edition, with *Life* by Samuel Longfellow and illustrations. 14 vols. Boston: Houghton Mifflin, 1891. Reprinted also in Craigie Edition, with illustrations. 11 vols. Boston: Houghton Mifflin, 1904.)

Complete Poetical Works, edited by Horace E. Scudder. Cambridge Edition. Boston: Houghton Mifflin, 1893. (Reprinted in Household Edition, with illustrations. Boston: Houghton Mifflin, 1902.)

Longfellow's Boyhood Poems, edited by George T. Little. Saratoga Springs, N.Y.: Ray W. Pettengill, 1925.

Henry Wadsworth Longfellow: Representative Selections, edited by Odell Shepard. American Writers Series. New York: American Book, 1934.

Kavanagh, a Tale, edited by Jean Downey. Masterworks of Literature Series. New Haven, Conn.: College and University Press, 1965.

LETTERS

Letters of Henry Wadsworth Longfellow, edited by Andrew Hilen. Vol. I, 1814–36; Vol. II, 1837–43; other volumes in progress. New York: Oxford University Press, 1966–.

BIBLIOGRAPHIES

Dana, H. W. L. "Henry Wadsworth Longfellow," in Vol. II of the *Cambridge History of American Literature*. 4 vols. New York: G. P. Putnam's Sons, 1917.

Livingston, Luther S. *A Bibliography of the First Editions in Book Form of the Writings of Henry Wadsworth Longfellow*. New York: Privately printed, 1908.

CRITICAL AND BIOGRAPHICAL STUDIES

Arms, George T. "Longfellow," in *The Fields Were Green*. Stanford, Calif.: Stanford University Press, 1948.

Arvin, Newton. *Longfellow: His Life and Work.* Boston: Little, Brown, 1963.

Austin, George L. *Henry Wadsworth Longfellow: His Life, His Works, His Friendships.* Boston: Lee and Shepard, 1883.

Gorman, Herbert. *A Victorian American, Henry Wadsworth Longfellow.* New York: Doran, 1926.

Hatfield, James T. *New Light on Longfellow, with Special Reference to His Relations with Germany.* Boston: Houghton Mifflin, 1933.

Hawthorne, Manning, and Henry Dana. *The Origin and Development of Longfellow's "Evangeline."* Portland, Maine: Anthoensen Press, 1947.

Higginson, Thomas W. *Henry Wadsworth Longfellow.* American Men of Letters Series. Boston: Houghton Mifflin, 1902.

Hilen, Andrew. *Longfellow and Scandinavia.* New Haven, Conn.: Yale University Press, 1947.

Johnson, Carl L. *Professor Longfellow of Harvard.* Eugene: University of Oregon Press, 1944.

Jones, Howard M. "Longfellow," in *American Writers on American Literature*, edited by John Macy. New York: Liveright, 1931.

Longfellow, Samuel. *Life of Henry Wadsworth Longfellow.* 2 vols. Boston: Ticknor, 1886.

———. *Final Memorials of Henry Wadsworth Longfellow.* Boston: Ticknor, 1887.

Martin, Ernest. *L'Evangeline de Longfellow et la suite merveilleuse d'un poème.* Paris: Librairie Hachette, 1936.

More, Paul Elmer. "The Centenary of Longfellow," in *Shelburne Essays, Fifth Series.* Boston: Houghton Mifflin, 1908.

Morin, Paul. *Les Sources de l'oeuvre de Henry Wadsworth Longfellow.* Paris: Emile Larose, 1913.

O'Neil, Rev. Joseph E., S.J. "Poet of the Feeling Heart," in *American Classics Reconsidered*, edited by Rev. Harold C. Gardiner, S.J. New York: Scribners, 1958.

Scudder, Horace E. "Longfellow and His Art," in *Men and Books.* Boston: Houghton Mifflin, 1887.

Thompson, Lawrance. *Young Longfellow, 1807–1843.* New York: Macmillan, 1938.

Van Schaick, John, Jr. *The Characters in "Tales*

of a Wayside Inn." Boston: Universalist Publishing House, 1939.

Wagenknecht, Edward. *Longfellow: A Full-Length Portrait*. New York: Longmans, Green, 1955.

_____. *Mrs. Longfellow: Selected Letters and Journals of Fanny Appleton*. New York: Longmans, Green, 1956.

_____. *Henry Wadsworth Longfellow: Portrait of an American Humanist*. New York: Oxford University Press, 1966.

Whitman, Iris. *Longfellow and Spain*. New York: Instituto de las Españas en los Estados Unidos, 1927.

Williams, Cecil B. *Henry Wadsworth Longfellow*. New York: Twayne, 1964.

Williams, Stanley T. "Longfellow," in Vol. II of *The Spanish Background of American Literature*. 2 vols. New Haven, Conn.: Yale University Press, 1955.

—EDWARD L. HIRSH

Amy Lowell

1874-1925

BECAUSE April 1915 was to see the publication of an anthology, *Some Imagist Poets*, sponsored by Amy Lowell, that energetic lady journeyed to New York City at the end of March to attend a meeting of the Poetry Society of America. She had been promised five minutes at the end of the program during which to explain and illustrate this new Imagist poetry which had begun to attract notice in America some two years earlier. She did not overrun her time. But as soon as she had finished, excited auditors jumped up and, despite the society's rule that addresses by guests were not to be discussed, denounced Miss Lowell's advocacy with fury.

Whatever the status of Imagism (and after only a few years its limitations became apparent even to Miss Lowell), one thing was clear: Miss Lowell was news. In fact, literarily speaking, she was at the center of the news. And there, or near it, so far as the United States was concerned, she remained for the rest of her life. At first, her public readings or lectures not infrequently evoked the kind of hostility evinced by the Poetry Society. But she was indomitable and, for the most part, indefatigable. Gradually, her quickness in repartee, her skill as a reader, the colloquial ease of her lectures, and, no doubt in some measure, the audience's consciousness that she was a Lowell won her

hearers to enthusiastic receptiveness, so that her letters often speak of crowded halls, extra chairs being carried in, and would-be listeners unable to get admission even as standees. Her poems appeared in (some of the editors might have said "were propelled into" would more accurately characterize the situation) the leading American magazines. She wrote reviews promoting the poetry of others, and sometimes dictated an editor's choice of a reviewer for one of her own books. She gave money to needy poets and poetry magazines. Poetry continued to be news; and in the United States no name emerged oftener in connection with this news than Amy Lowell's. A final accolade unfortunately came shortly after her death: her *What's O'Clock?*, published posthumously, was awarded in 1926 the Pulitzer Prize for the best volume of verse by an American author appearing in 1925.

Miss Lowell naturally hoped that her own works would enjoy an enduring fame. At times she was even confident, for "failure" was not a word in the vocabulary of the Lowell tradition. In her *A Critical Fable*, of which the authorship was at first concealed, she wrote of herself:

The future's her goose and I dare say she'll
    wing it,

Though the triumph will need her own power
    to sing it.
Although I'm no prophet, I'll hazard a guess
She'll be rated by time as more rather than less.

A *Complete Poetical Works*, comprising all the books of her poems issued in and after her lifetime, is in print, though this is actually not completely "complete": eleven longish poems about World War I, intended for publication under the title *Phantasms of War*, remain scattered in the periodicals where they appeared. But all except one of the separate books of her poems are out of print, and this is a pity. For they were all designed to follow as closely as possible the format of the first edition of Keats's *Lamia*. This choice exhibited perfect taste. The binding is unpretentiously pleasing; the type is agreeable to the eye; the books are easy to hold in the hand or to slip into the pocket; and all of them together bestow a graceful uniformity on a library shelf. Moreover, the *Complete Poetical Works* lacks the prefaces in which Miss Lowell expounded her ideas about Imagism, vers libre, and polyphonic prose. Only the explanations introductory to the book of translations from Chinese, *Fir-Flower Tablets*, have been retained. And as a kind of codicil to neglect, the *Selected Poems* edited in 1928 by Professor John Livingston Lowes is likewise unavailable.

In prose, both by and about Miss Lowell, she has fared better. Her own books of prose, including the interesting *Poetry and Poets*, a selection of prose articles assembled posthumously, are in print—and the opinion has been hazarded by a fellow poet, Horace Gregory, that "her nearest approach to a revelation of whatever she thought or felt is in her prose." S. Foster Damon's biography, coming ten years after her death, is available as a voluminous source of information about her activities. And in 1958 it was supplemented by Horace Greg-

ory's *Amy Lowell: Portrait of the Poet in Her Time*. Yet critical commentary in this country has virtually ceased. A lone exception is a ten-page essay by Winfield Townley Scott, "Amy Lowell of Brookline, Mass.," which, revised from earlier versions, was printed as recently as 1961 in his volume of essays, *Exiles and Fabrications*. This essay is notable for its just perceptiveness. Perhaps Mr. Scott was responding to a kind of challenge, for he records that a publisher said to him ten years after her death, "Who the hell wants to read about Amy Lowell?"

The best seller—and some of Miss Lowell's books were indeed such—that in its day wins universal critical acclaim and ten years later is forgotten is unhappily a frequent enough phenomenon. Was Miss Lowell merely one more example? If so, all that need be said about her has already been said by others. Actually, her status is much more complex. No single formula sums it up. For she must be assessed not only by the legacy of verse and prose criticism she has left. Distinguishable from her role as author, though of course related to this, was her role as Public Literary Personage. Her salience as such is hardly contestable. She may have originated less than she supposed; but at the crowded carrefour where all literary ways met, there was Miss Lowell, directing the traffic. And even in her private life, she was no less a personage. Almost as soon as her verse was in print, she herself began to be wafted abroad on the tongues of men as a legend. No matter if some details of the legend were verifiable as fact. Collectively, they stimulated wonder; and where wonder is aroused, legend is just around the corner.

How was Miss Lowell able to achieve so speedily what one might call a para-literary eminence? Her surname is an obvious clue. Through her father she was descended from the able and wealthy family after whom the city of Lowell, Massachusetts, was named. Through her mother she was descended from the no less able and almost as wealthy Lawrence family, after whom the city of Lawrence, Massachusetts, was named. Born in 1874, the youngest among five children, she was not the only one of them to win fame. The younger of her two brothers, Abbott Lawrence Lowell, became president of Harvard; the elder, Percival Lowell, turning his chief attention to astronomy when nearly forty, founded the Lowell Observatory at Flagstaff, Arizona. It was from this post of vantage that he observed the hitherto undiscerned canals in the planet Mars. Later planetary specialists have been inclined to ascribe these appearances to inorganic phenomena unduly regularized by Percival Lowell's imaginative enthusiasm. More immediately relevant to literature were his ten years spent as a young man in the Orient, chiefly in Japan, for these gave him the material for two books, *Chosön* and *The Soul of the Far East*. It was his letters and knickknacks sent to his youngest sister that aroused her interest in Oriental culture, years before any idea of besting Ezra Pound or Witter Bynner as transmitters of the exotic East could have entered her head.

Notable, too, was the house which was Miss Lowell's home throughout her life: Sevenels, in Brookline, Massachusetts, so named by Amy's father not because of any resemblance to any House of the Seven Gables (there was no such resemblance), but because after Amy's birth the house sheltered seven Lowells. Nowadays engulfed by residential urbanism, the house as Miss Lowell knew it was set in an estate of some nine and a half acres, comprising a meadow, a grove, stables with the horses Amy loved to drive, lawns, terraces, a vegetable garden, a fruit garden, shrubbery, and especially gardens of flowers bordering the walks, festooning the arbors, massed in glow-

ing beds. Nobody acquainted with Miss Lowell's poems can have failed to notice, as a dominant motif in her verse, flowers, whether listed kaleidoscopically in their daytime brilliance or depicted in their muted expectancy in the moonlight. When in 1913 Pound requested Miss Lowell's "In a Garden" for his anthology *Des Imagistes*, his choice admitted the possibility of a coincidence in taste between two poets who soon were contending for leadership of the Imagists. But Pound could hardly have hit upon a poem more representative of the center of Miss Lowell's memories.

After her parents' death, Miss Lowell in 1900 became mistress of Sevenels. Moreover, she was independently wealthy, and could live as she chose. Her regimen—rational enough when measured by her aims—seemed so eccentric to the outside world that it was bruited as a legend. She awoke about three of an afternoon; and her domestic establishment, hushed until that moment, simultaneously shifted into high gear. She frequently invited guests for dinner. These, if arriving at Sevenels on foot, would be met at the entrance of the estate by a manservant detailed to escort them to the front door, lest Miss Lowell's Old English sheepdogs, ranging freely about the grounds, bear away portions of the guests' clothing as trophies. Dinner, of a hearty old-fashioned kind, would be served at eight o'clock. Mrs. Ada Dwyer Russell, Miss Lowell's companion from about 1914 until Miss Lowell's death, acted as hostess until Miss Lowell herself appeared—usually not until the roast had gone back to the kitchen. But conversation enlivened the pause while Miss Lowell caught up with the rest. After dinner everyone gathered about the great fireplace in the library, the guests being provided with heavy towels to spread in their laps as a protection against the demonstrative affection which was the indoor mood of the sheepdogs. (These became a casualty to food rationing during World War I, and were replaced by a single cat, Winky, who makes an appearance in several of Miss Lowell's poems.) Just after midnight the guests would be ushered out, in time for those who were walking to catch the last streetcar for Boston at the bottom of the hill.

Now that entertainment had ended—and there remains abundant testimony to the intellectual vigor, the excitement, and the charm of Miss Lowell's conversation—work could begin. In an armchair before the fire of four-foot logs split to four-inch diameter so that she could replenish them herself, she wrote. A cold supper awaited her on a near table, and she might continue writing until toast and coffee from the household's breakfast was at hand. More often she ceased at dawn, leaving a pile of manuscript for her two secretaries to type out during the day, while the discarded drafts she had tossed on the floor were swept up and burned. Climbing to her childhood's room on the top floor, she would prepare in her characteristically leisurely way for sleep in the huge bed with its sixteen pillows—that bed in which, Professor Damon reports, gossip had it that "one afternoon she had been seen . . . smoking a hookah and writing under an umbrella to keep the sun off." Very possibly so, for was not an awesome ingredient of the Lowell legend the fact that the sister of the president of Harvard *smoked*?—and this at a time when women's smoking was condemned in American society. To be sure, Miss Lowell seldom smoked outside Sevenels, and the "big black cigars" were invented by the horrified popular imagination; actually she smoked a small, pale brand of Manila cigar, not robust enough for male tastes. Yet to Bostonians the habit seemed somehow, well, incendiary.

Bizarre as her schedule might seem, it was nevertheless sensible because it was convenient. She had chosen a vocation requiring intense and prolonged mental effort. Two great enemies of such effort are interruption and noise. What aspiring author, unblessed with a spouse to fend off intrusion, would not pray to be delivered from the roar of the vacuum cleaner and the pan-clattering of the cook, from the clamor of perambulating lawn mowers and the honk of interminable autos, from the unwelcome visitor and—malign demon of the household!—the ever inopportune telephone? Many a writer amid his labors has turned night into day, if his finances permitted him to turn his day into night. Miss Lowell could afford to pay for her immunity. To achieve insulation, Marcel Proust inhabited a room with cork-lined walls; Miss Lowell's insulation was the night. Similarly reasonable was her preference for cigars. Her nerves, she felt, needed to be soothed; and cigarettes, then just beginning their popularity, furnished too few puffs in their transit from match to ashtray. Cigars were less distracting.

Miss Lowell might seem blessed with every material advantage for which one could wish. But, just as in many a familiar folktale, among the good fairies who showered blessings on her cradle, there was one wicked fairy indeed. The result began to manifest itself in her girlhood. Never tall, by the time she was a debutante she was already stout. (At the private school for girls she attended in Boston, she had been cast for the part of Tony Lumpkin in Goldsmith's *She Stoops to Conquer*, but her parents forbade her to act in a male part.) Miss Lowell's appearance in her adult years is often summarized in the remark that when she stood, she seemed as broad as she was tall. Her great overweight resulted from a glandular imbalance that the medical science of her time lacked means to control. Inevitably, this handicap penalized her in all sorts of ways. It made her specially vulnerable to muscular strains: a mishap while she was driving near her summer home in Dublin, New Hampshire, in 1916 led to a hernia which, in spite of repeated operations, persisted through the rest of her life and caused her much distress. In her bedroom, the mirrors and other bright objects were swathed in black, and whenever she traveled, all hotel rooms she occupied underwent the same alteration. Whether she would have married, had her appearance been less unusual, is uncertain. In her early twenties, she had accepted a proposal of marriage from a young Bostonian with whom she was in love. But he became involved in some way elsewhere, so that the commitment had to be canceled. At any rate, Miss Lowell seems to have put wifehood out of her mind.

Her physical abnormality may bear the responsibility for barring her from a career she might otherwise have chosen, and for which she was perhaps even more fitted than for that of poet. She had, it is true, embarked on writing in her childhood; a small pamphlet containing a few brief stories by her had been sold at a charity bazaar. And after her graduation from school she tried—unsuccessfully in her own opinion—her hand at novels, short stories, and plays. Note that last word—plays. She enjoyed attending the theater, and as late as 1919 took a leading role in an amateur performance of Wilde's *Ideal Husband*, performed on a stage set up in the library at Sevenels. In 1913 she translated Rostand's *Pierrot Qui Pleure et Pierrot Qui Rit*, a comedy with accompanying music, and in 1914, Wekerlin's operetta *La Latière de Trianon*: both these were intended for charity performances. As Professor Damon puts the matter, "It was a commonplace remark in Boston that if Amy Lowell had been beautiful, she would have been a great actress. . . . On the lecture platform, without scenery, costumes, or even gestures, she could make the public forget her size, and follow the drama solely from her

voice. . . . her clear soprano blurred no word but varied continually according to the content." With her acute sense of theatrical effectiveness, her shrewdness in judging people, her ambition, and, not least of all, her money, she might well have become, as actress-playwright-director and even producer, a very great lady of the theater indeed.

It was, then, singularly appropriate that her determination to become a poet was generated, not by her response to the poetry of the written word, but by her response to the enchantment of a great actress. Miss Lowell had seen Eleonora Duse during her American tours of 1893 and 1896; now, in 1902, Duse was again in Boston, appearing in plays by D'Annunzio. Miss Lowell saw her again, went home, and the same evening wrote a tribute to Duse in seventy-one lines of blank verse—her first attempt at verse since she was in her mid-teens, and she was now twenty-eight. Crude as was this effusion—it was published in *Poetry* for August 1923 in a series of childhood poems by youthful aspirants—Miss Lowell regarded her evening's experience in the theater as apocalyptic. As she put the matter in a letter to a friend some twenty years later, "it revealed me to myself" and "I found out where my true function lay."

For the next ten years Miss Lowell devoted herself to the study of poetry. She did not rush into print; the first periodical contribution recorded in the list of her publications to be found in Damon's biography is dated 1910; and her first book, *A Dome of Many-Coloured Glass*, did not appear until October 1912.

Unfortunately, Miss Lowell's studies were too largely grounded on a model that was nearly eighty years out of date. Before her school days in Boston were over, she had come across, in her father's library, a book by Leigh Hunt, the English minor essayist, critic, journalist, and poet who had died in 1859 at the age of seventy-four. This book was Hunt's *Imagination and Fancy; or, Selections from the English Poets, illustrative of those first requisites of their art; with markings of the best passages, critical notices of the writers, and an essay in answer to the question 'What is Poetry?'* The selections, interspersed with Hunt's comments, ranged from Chaucer to poets of Hunt's own day. His answer to the question "What is Poetry?" derives from Coleridge; it is a vulgarization of Coleridge's distinction between imagination and fancy. For Hunt, imagination is a "perception of sympathies in the nature of things"; and fancy is "a sporting with their resemblance, real or supposed." Both are manifested by the poet's choice of similes and metaphors; the distinction is simply that imagination operates with tragic, or at least serious, materials, whereas fancy operates with materials comic or trivial. The presence of imagination in poetry is attested by a concomitant presence of what Hunt calls "music," by which he means chiefly an agreeable smoothness of versification. As for the critic, he best served his calling by liking as many kinds of things as he could, and by writing about these as enthusiastically as possible. Judgment is dissolved into taste. And Hunt's taste as connoisseur, when not seduced by the siren sentimentality, was better than his own poetry might suggest. Amy Lowell testified that his book was the best schoolbook of poetry she had discovered. And in one respect she owed it a great deal. It was this book that introduced her to the poetry of Keats.

Less fortunate was the bias which Miss Lowell's choice of a mentor gave to her own efforts. The title of her first book, a phrase from the often-quoted finale of Shelley's elegy in memory of Keats, *Adonais*, is reflected in, or perhaps was suggested by, the shortest poem in the book, "Fragment."

What is poetry? Is it a mosaic
　Of coloured stones which curiously are
　　　wrought
　Into a pattern? Rather glass that's taught
By patient labour any hue to take
And glowing with a sumptuous splendor, make
　Beauty a thing of awe; where sunbeams
　　　caught,
　Transmuted fall in sheafs of rainbows
　　　caught,
With storied meaning for religion's sake.

Yet such a poem as "To Elizabeth Ward Perkins" in this same book makes clear the fact that Miss Lowell had abandoned the traditional Christian faith in which she had been christened at Trinity Church. Nor does "sumptuous splendor" in any way characterize the verses she had assembled: some lyrics of sentiment, some jejune moralizing elicited from undistinctive landscapes, a few tributes to Oriental artifacts, twenty-eight sonnets in a huddle, a tribute to the Boston Athenaeum, and last, but scarcely least, eight "Verses for Children." Miss Lowell later wished that the book, save for fewer than a dozen poems, might disappear from print. Of the three poems she specially favored—"Before the Altar" (the opening poem), "Behind a Wall," and "The Road to Avignon" ("The last, I admit, is old-fashioned, but I think it is rather good of its kind" she said in a letter eight years later)—Lowes retained the first two in his *Selected Poems* and added two sonnets, "The Fruit Garden Path" and the deplorable "To John Keats," of which the first line runs "Great master! Boyish, sympathetic man!" Reviews of the book were dismissive. Even Louis Untermeyer, later one of the author's friends, whose "Memoir" prefaces the "complete" poetry, ended his review by saying that Miss Lowell's *Dome*, "to be brief, in spite of its lifeless classicism, can never rouse one's anger. But, to be briefer still, it cannot rouse one at all." No more than eighty copies were sold during the first year.

Miss Lowell was depressed, but being of Puritan stock, she was not deterred. Soon, a lucky chance opened to her a new avenue to explore. In the January 1913 issue of *Poetry* she read some poems signed "H.D., *Imagiste*" and (in her own words) realized "Why I, too, am an *Imagiste!*" In the March issue appeared some discussion of Imagism by Ezra Pound, writing from London. Miss Lowell decided to go at once to what might be the source of a rejuvenation for poetry, her own as well as others'. By the summer, she was on shipboard bound for England with a companion. On a second trip the following summer, she was accompanied by her noted maroon automobile and one of her two maroon-liveried chauffeurs. After all, it could do no harm to let the English, too, know that a Lowell is a Lowell is a Lowell.

In London she learned that Ezra Pound a year earlier had joined with the American poet Hilda Doolittle ("H.D.") and the British poet Richard Aldington, later Miss Doolittle's husband, in asserting three principles that needed to be re-emphasized in the writing of poetry. These were, as Pound has worded them in "A Stray Document,"

1. Direct treatment of the "thing" whether subjective or objective.

2. To use absolutely no word that does not contribute to the presentation.

3. As regarding rhythm: to compose in the sequence of the musical phrase, not in the sequence of a metronome.

It was Pound who devised for this creed the term "Imagisme," the final "e" perhaps being a charm to ward off British insularity.

It was not long before the contact between Pound's urge to initiate and Miss Lowell's impulse to organize effervesced into a struggle for domination of the group of writers who in varying degrees had become affiliated with the new movement. (Certainly, D. H. Lawrence, both in profession and in practice, was farthest away from the center.) But soon, circumstances separated Pound and Miss Lowell. World War I broke out, and Miss Lowell returned to America, having cannily dispatched her car and chauffeur thither by an earlier boat. Pound, on the other hand, characteristically lost interest in the movement as soon as it showed symptoms of becoming established, and his restlessness propelled him into launching a newer movement, Vorticism. How this differed doctrinally from Imagisme never became clear, but unlike the earlier movement, it enlisted practitioners of the other arts.

Miss Lowell by no means returned to Boston empty-handed. She had enlisted the support of six poets: the English Richard Aldington, F. S. Flint, Ford Madox Hueffer (who later changed his surname to Ford), and D. H. Lawrence; and the Americans H.D. and John Gould Fletcher. She had acquired a new confidence in her own career, for she had acquired a new set of principles which emphasized, she felt, those elements in poetry most suited to her own abilities. Indeed, she became in a way the custodian of the Imagist creed (she discarded the final "e" as irrelevant in America), which her group of Imagists—chiefly Aldington—elaborated into six principles, as follows:

1. To use the language of common speech, but to employ always the *exact* word, not the nearly-exact, nor the merely decorative word.

2. To create new rhythms—as the expression of new moods—and not to copy old rhythms, which merely echo old moods. We do not insist upon "free verse" as the only method

of writing poetry. We fight for it as for a principle of liberty. We believe that the individuality of a poet may often be better expressed in free-verse than in conventional forms. In poetry a new cadence means a new idea.

3. To allow absolute freedom in the choice of subject. It is not good art to write badly about aeroplanes and automobiles, nor is it necessarily bad art to write well about the past. We believe passionately in the artistic value of modern life, but we wish to point out that there is nothing so uninspiring nor so old-fashioned as an aeroplane of the year 1911.

4. To present an image (hence the name: "Imagist"). We are not a school of painters, but we believe that poetry should render particulars exactly and not deal in vague generalities, however magnificent and sonorous. It is for this reason that we oppose the cosmic poet, who seems to us to shirk the real difficulties of his art.

5. To produce poetry that is hard and clear, never blurred nor indefinite.

6. Finally, most of us believe that concentration is of the very essence of poetry.

In *Some Imagist Poets* (1915), in which this creed appears, it is preceded by the declaration that "These principles are not new; they have fallen into desuetude. They are the essentials of all great poetry, indeed, of all great literature."

Sword Blades and Poppy Seed, published in the autumn of 1914, disclosed the fact that in the two years just past Miss Lowell had learned more than she had in the previous ten. Although about three-fourths of the book consisted of poems in meter, the best poems were those in vers libre, a mode of writing verse on which she commented in a preface. To the French term "vers libre," which had already won acceptance in English, she preferred the term "unrhymed cadence" for several reasons.

It connotes the fact that the basis of this species of writing is, as she termed it, "organic," varying with the rhythms of breathing. And it connotes the intermediate patterning of such writing: less regular than metrical verse, but exhibiting, more pronouncedly than prose, the occurrence of stresses and of what she called a "curve," by which she seemed to mean a greater premonition of an appropriate ending in any beginning. Yet in spite of the flexibility and "subtlety" of cadenced verse, she insisted that "it is constructed upon mathematical and absolute laws of balance and time."

Moreover, for three poems dealing with thwarted love Miss Lowell chose "polyphonic prose," which she described more fully in the preface to a later volume, *Can Grande's Castle*. Miss Lowell states there that it was from compositions by the French poet Paul Fort, in which passages in regular verse—mostly the French alexandrine or hexameter—were interspersed with passages in prose, that she derived her concept of a form that should be more varied, that is to say, more "polyphonic," in its uses of poetic devices than any hitherto attempted. Yet to avoid giving the impression of a typographical medley, the visual form would be prose. To achieve melody and richness, any of the traditional devices of poetry might be used: rhyme, assonance, alliteration, and what she called "return"—"the recurrence of a dominant thought or image." But all these were to be used irregularly and at moments not dictated by any set scheme of expectations. Of course, without a basic unifying principle of some kind polyphonic prose would not be a form at all but merely a concatenation; its variations, however surprising, could have no significance. The most usual basic form in English verse for large-scale compositions has been iambic pentameter verse. This, however, Miss Lowell felt was accentually too insistent to lend itself to agreeable variations; and she finally decided her basis should be "The long, flowing cadence of oratorical prose." She admits that some readers may be puzzled to find the label "prose" affixed to a form intended to be distinguished from prose, but regards the difficulty as one imposed by the exigencies of the printed page. Warning her readers not to allow their previous metrical habits to betray them into stressing such devices as rhymes when these catch their eye, she declares that her audiences have found no difficulty in responding adequately to polyphonic prose when this has been read aloud with intelligence. She hails it as, "in a sense, an orchestral form"; moreover, as a form of which the chief fundamental principle is "an insistence on the absolute adequacy of the manner of a passage to the thought it embodies. Taste is therefore its determining factor; taste and a rhythmic ear." An admirable summation—but in what way distinctive? Of how much memorable verse can this much *not* be said?

Vers libre or free verse is of course in no degree synonymous with Imagism. The latter is a species of doctrine and practice connected with the referential content of verse; the former is a species of doctrine and practice connected with the phonetic structure of verse. But the two were often concomitant. Amy Lowell believed herself to be a practitioner of Imagism; she certainly *was* a practitioner of free verse. It was this auditory aspect of her evangel that evoked the most passionate controversy. And, as her discussions of her technical innovations exemplify, an auditory concern was conspicuous in Miss Lowell's own consciousness. Whenever a reader encounters difficulty with her poetry in print, she recommends that he read it aloud, or hear it read. She stresses her conviction that her audiences find no difficulty in responding to her poems. It is of course a commonplace remark that poetry arose as a communication from a voice to an ear; and its fundamental principles remain those of an art in and of sound. But the spread of visual means of communicating language has complicated and subtilized poetry so markedly that for much poetry, a hearing alone is insufficient for an adequate response. And insofar as an ear listens, it is nowadays often not the physical ear, but an interiorized ear, the ear of the auditory imagination. Miss Lowell's emphasis on poet as minstrel, however much by chance it augured a future of radio and television, was in its literary result a reaffirmation of a tradition of the past, and tended to exclude from her verse, save only occasionally, the more or less clearly indicated overtones of meaning and undertones of preconception characteristic of poetry of first importance today.

From Miss Lowell's prose in her explanatory prefaces, and of course elsewhere, several others of her traits can be adduced. For one thing, her innovations are not indicative of a salient originality. Though she acquired a considerable skill in verse technique, her novelties were, as she acknowledges in her account of "polyphonic prose," developments of what she had found in other writers. For another thing, allied to her enthusiasm for new poets and poetries was a decided tendency to overstate. She declares that the laws governing free-verse cadences are "absolute" and "mathematical." Yet nowhere does she provide any definitions of these laws, any criteria with respect to which absoluteness might be established. Unless indeed her discussion amounts to saying that such cadences must absolutely accord with the taste of the poet who devises them—and this individualistic kind of absoluteness, being perceptible only to God and the poet, is no absoluteness at all for the poet's audience. As for the "mathematical" laws, neither in phrase nor in formula are these ever disclosed. Finally, a trait that is perhaps the compensatory obverse of her occasional excess of dogmatism: her prose is mostly eminently readable. It may lack profundity or seductiveness, but it is fluent, self-confident, and literately colloquial. Some of her terminology remains imprecise; it never becomes certain, for example, just how much or how little she means by her term "return." But her syntax is hardly ever baffling, though sometimes careless. Her prose seems cogent—especially to readers whose knowledge of the matters she discusses is no more extensive than was her own.

As for Imagism, it is easy to see why Miss Lowell was attracted to it, beyond the simple fact that she perceived it was the "coming thing," and she had a keen nose for the scent of the near future. (This, by the bye, is no discreditable attribute; it is often a necessity for even a brief fame in times of rapid change.) Miss Lowell, like other energetic people who are also intelligent, was a good noticer. Such people can bestow an at least fleeting glance on, can perceive the objective "thereness" of, throngs of particular items without being confused or swamped. In Miss Lowell, this ability was specialized visually: she could see and note in rapid sequence flowers, birds, *objets d'art*, people; somewhat more diffused targets of attention like weather and seasons (for the observation of which New England offers exceptional opportunities); and above all, lights, shadows, and colors. Indeed, Miss Lowell's fondness for colors was almost obsessive; she wove lists of them into her verse at any provocation. For instance, in the first ten lines of "The Captured Goddess," in Miss Lowell's second book, five colors are mentioned, and another is implied in "moonbeams."

Over the housetops,
Above the rotating chimney-pots,
I have seen a shiver of amethyst,
And blue and cinnamon have flickered

A moment,
At the far end of a dusty street.

Through sheeted rain
Has come a lustre of crimson,
And I have watched moonbeams
Hushed by a film of palest green.

Yet although Amy Lowell was accounted leader of the Imagist movement after Pound withdrew, and rewarded those who acknowledged her leadership by sponsoring in 1915, 1916, and 1917 three anthologies, all under the title *Some Imagist Poets*, in which their work could appear, it is questionable whether she is best described as an Imagist poet. Ezra Pound certainly thought not; he derisively termed her views and verse "Amygism." A distinguishing feature of Imagism as originally propounded was brevity. The genesis of an Imagist poem was to be the presentation of an image—usually, though not necessarily, visual —not depicted with all the details appropriate to it, nor even with all the constituents ordinarily thought of as essential to it. Rather, it was to be identified through some one of its features or aspects. This single focus would oftenest be conveyed, however, through a comparison or allusion to something else. By virtue of this comparison, a new insight into the nature of the originating image would be communicated. Furthermore, the comparison might confer upon the image a status in some wider realm of reference—nature, life, love, time, eternity—but, again, often by implication from a compact mention, though the derivative image might be somewhat more discursive. (Ezra Pound has spoken of this mode of generating a poem as "a form of superposition.")

The well-known "Oread" by H.D., who among all the Imagists best and most indisputably exemplified Imagist theory, illustrates "superposition."

Whirl up, sea—
whirl your pointed pines,
splash your great pines
on our rocks,
hurl your green over us,
cover us with your pools of fir.

Because the poem's title—"Oread"—designates a nymph of the mountains, one may assign primacy to the image of clustering masses of evergreen trees among the rocks. This is what is *seen*. However, this image is "placed" in the entire pageant of life by being regarded as the result of surges of the sea hurling themselves upon the land. The connection is visually valid, because the sea is commonly experienced as dark green; and it is conceptually valid, because the sea was, so paleontologists assert, the womb in which life on our planet originated. It would of course be feasible to analyze this poem in a contrary direction, taking the sea as what is seen first—the first line of the poem is devoted to it—and taking the trees as the derivative, parochial in the way the mind of an oread might naturally be. Still, a duality remains in the imagery.

More characteristic of Miss Lowell's imagination is, to choose a poem of equivalent length, "July Midnight," from a later book, *Pictures of the Floating World.*

Fireflies flicker in the tops of trees,
Flicker in the lower branches,
Skim along the ground.
Over the moon-white lilies
Is a flashing and ceasing of small,
lemon-green stars.
As you lean against me,
Moon-white,
The air all about you
Is slit, and pricked, and pointed with
sparkles of lemon-green flame

Starting out of a background of vague,
blue trees.

Here, obviously, what is *seen* is depicted in considerably more detail. Not only are the fireflies assigned diverse locations—high aloft, about head-high, and on the ground—but they are mentioned in conjunction with two backgrounds—"moon-white lilies" and "vague, blue trees"—thus enabling Miss Lowell to play colors against one another, as she is so fond of doing. Moreover, the air is "slit, and pricked, and pointed" with firefly sparkles. Perhaps "slit" presents a flash that traverses a short distance, and "pricked" one that seems stationary; but if so, what does "pointed" add? It is not to be charged against Miss Lowell that here, as in many of her brief nature pieces, the secondary image that confers an extension of meaning on the primary image is simply "you," assimilated into the picture by being "moon-white." Yet the point (the dedicatee) of such poems is mostly left to the reader's goodwill for acceptance, not being present to the reader's imagination distinguishably from the scene the poet intends as a tribute. The interest of the poem is limited to the scene described.

From this sample of Miss Lowell's "Imagism" can be inferred what more extensive quotation would confirm, namely, that although Imagism was congenial to her penchant for noticing her surroundings, the Imagist stress on conciseness was quite antipathetic to her temperament. Whatever Miss Lowell's virtues, succinctness, except sometimes in repartee, was not among them. Her energy and enthusiasm impelled her to write on, often beyond the limit that a more careful artist would set for himself. She was lavish in her use of repetition as a means of coherence and emphasis. (Perhaps this repetitiveness was in part the meaning of her term "return.") As her confidence in her own powers increased, so did the number of longer poems in her books. Besides, and most important, allied to her rapport with audiences was her fondness for one of the oldest means of holding an audience's attention—the telling of stories. There had been but two in her first book, of no consequence. In her second book, counting dramatic monologues as narratives, there are ten.

And of several diverse kinds. Ordinarily, one thinks of Imagism as the contrary of the Symbolist movement that arose in France in the latter half of the nineteenth century. Imagism typically begins with the thing seen, and finds for it a significance. Symbolism begins with a significance, and finds for it an embodiment in an image. This "significance" may be a conviction or attitude or mood definite enough to be expressed as an assertion; but more characteristically, it is so subtle or elusive as to seem inexpressible with any exactness apart from the particular embodiment given to it in the poem. Miss Lowell was by no means a Symbolist in the more narrowly technical sense; yet a half-dozen or so of her poems can be found in the whole range of her work that similarly elude dogmatic analysis. The frequently anthologized "Meeting-House Hill" is one such poem. Another is the narrative "The Book of Hours of Sister Clotilde" in her second book. Sister Clotilde, illuminating a book of hours, could not find the right color for the Virgin Mary's robe, until she saw in the convent garden an iridescent snake. Seizing the snake, she was bitten, and saved from death only by the timely intervention of the gardener; but she had found the hue she sought. The poem leaves the implication of the story undetermined.

Of the three poems in the same book written in polyphonic prose—all three, incidentally, dealing with love thwarted, by the loved one's narcissism, or adultery, or abandonment

by her lover—the first of these, "The Basket," is embodied in a sequence of vividly hallucinatory images which, however determinate their general import, are severally ambiguous. Another trio can be formed of poems, dissimilar in setting and pace, that are alike in leading the hero to suicide through his absorption in the pursuit of an ideal: "The Great Adventure of Max Breuck," "Clear, with Light Variable Winds," and "The Shadow." Five of the poems are dramatic monologues, among which the most striking, or at least hectic, is "After Hearing a Waltz by Bartók." As the speaker whirls in the dance, he is overcome by a delirium in which the corpse of the rival he has murdered seems to clutch him in a strangling grasp. Some readers may discern in this poem authentic reverberations of Bartók; others will hear (no doubt, tuned up a bit) the accents of Robert Browning in, say, "Porphyria's Lover." More importantly, the poem exemplifies an enduring fondness of Miss Lowell's for the exotic, whether of locale, décor, or deed, possibly by way of counterpoint to the decorums of Brookline. She liked to spice a book with occasional episodes of gruesome events in Gothic surroundings, rather Poesque or Grand Guignol in flavor.

Like most poets who write any considerable amount of poetry, Miss Lowell uses symbolism in a less specialized sense of the term—that is, events or images may carry a significance that is quite definite; it may even be commented on didactically. The first poem in *Sword Blades and Poppy Seed*, which gives its title to the whole, is one such. The narrator, a young man, is accosted by an old man with "strange eyes flashing through the haze." The two go to the old man's abode, which contains a shop stocked oddly with numerous small boxes and phials appropriate to an apothecary's, and with stabbing, slashing, and cutting weapons and implements. The old man is finally identified as "Ephraim Bard, Dealer in Words"; the contents of the shop are explained by the fact that "All books are either dreams or swords,/ You can cut, or you can drug, with words." For payment for any of his wares, old Ephraim will accept nothing less than the young man's whole life. With this bargain tacitly achieved, the two part. It is odd that of the two categories into which this book is parceled, Miss Lowell has assigned all her narratives to the second: "Poppy Seed." Can she have been willing to rank herself, as narrative poet, among successors of William Morris, as another "idle singer of an empty day"? At any rate, the success in the United States of her book (it was hardly noticed in England) confirmed her in her determination to be a poet, and collections of her own verse appeared thenceforth in quick succession.

She adopted a tactic of alternating books of longish narrative and descriptive poems with books made up mostly of brief lyrics, though she composed both sorts concurrently. Her next book of poems, *Men, Women and Ghosts*, published in 1916, was one of the former sort. Of its thirty poems about half were in free verse, a third in rhymed meter, and a sixth in polyphonic prose. Among the twelve poems dealing with wars, past or present (five were evoked by World War I, then in progress), four, collectively called "Bronze Tablets," presented anecdotal scenes during the Napoleonic period, though Napoleon himself is hardly more than glimpsed. Like her friend Thomas Hardy, Miss Lowell was drawn to an era in which all Europe was dominated by the figure of a single man: one whom she admired, not as a genius in warfare, but as a leader who set in motion currents of new ideas and aims. And she believed that his adversaries were more harmful than he. Of the eight poems dealing with love or passion, all but one are told from the woman's point of view. The eerie excep-

tion, "The Cross-Roads," narrates the attempts of a suicide buried at a crossroads to re-emerge when the woman he has loved passes by above. "Above" here is not, however, in Gothic Europe, but in New England; "Edgarstown" and "Tilbury" (instead of the actual Tisbury) might suggest Martha's Vineyard.

Four more narratives grouped under the title "The Overgrown Pasture" continue this turning to New England not only for stories, but for what Miss Lowell took to be New England rural dialect as well. When challenged about its accuracy, she maintained she had compared it with the speech in the books of Alice Brown, presumably a phonologically unimpeachable source. She criticized Robert Frost for *not* using dialect in his New England scenes. But the movement of Frost's verse, suggesting rapid burts of straightforward syntax punctuated by pauses for breath and for thinking ahead, sounds more authentic than "jest" and "oughter." In print such renderings all too easily suggest an author who is condescending to his characters. In another less objectionable way Miss Lowell emphasized the fact that she was a poet of the ear, which needs time to listen in, and not of the eye only, which can see in the Imagistic moment. In "The Cremona Violin" the story is presented in rhyme royal, but the concert is conveyed in a variety of verse media, so as to suggest varying effects produced by the violin. And she claimed that her "Stravinsky's Three Pieces 'Grotesques,' for String Quartet" had elicited from several musicians the comment that the "movement" of the music was "accurately given."

D. H. Lawrence, the most discerning and candid among the young writers whom Miss Lowell's wealth enabled her to succor in difficulties, preferred this to her earlier books, liking best in it the closing group, "Towns in Colour"; these record Imagistic details in sequences that produce a cinematic effect, whereas the typical Imagist poem arrests sight at a particular moment. Most readers were most impressed by the first poem in the book, Miss Lowell's oftenest anthologized poem, "Patterns." Here an Englishwoman of noble rank, walking in her garden arrayed in the elaborately stiffened costume of Queen Anne's days, is handed a message revealing that the Duke, her husband-soon-to-be, has been killed in battle. Repressing signs of her agitation, she continues her walk until, at the end of the poem, her vision of her loss, now that her lover has perished "In a pattern called a war," vents itself in the cry "Christ! What are patterns for?" On a first reading this poem usually strikes a reader forcibly. But with repeated readings, the elaborately stylized setting seems no longer appropriately summarized by an outburst in an idiom too contemporary with our own probable feelings to suit its generating episode. We may even be tempted to use the exclamation to delve psychoanalytically into Amy Lowell's own life.

Miss Lowell thought of polyphonic prose as an "orchestral form." In her next volume of poetry, appearing two years later, in 1918, she gave it orchestral scope. *Can Grande's Castle,* so named from the refuge where Dante labored at his vision, contains only four poems, written throughout in polyphonic prose. The longest, "The Bronze Horses," paints the scenes witnessed successively in Rome, Constantinople, and Venice through the centuries by the four bronze horses that now adorn the façade of St. Mark's Cathedral in Venice; the closing scene is an Austrian air raid early in World War I. "Sea-Blue and Blood-Red" weaves chiaroscuro scenes in Italy, Egypt, England, and at Trafalgar, to invest with glamour Lord Nelson and his mistress, Lady Emma Hamilton. The motif "red" is contributed not only by blood, but by the flare of Vesuvius. "Guns as Keys; and the Great Gate Swings" depicts alternately Commodore Perry's expedition on its way to force open the ports of Japan to international trade, and the ineffectual efforts of the Japanese to discover in their traditional usages any means of repelling the incursion. The shortest of the four, "Hedge Island," is a descriptive paean to the mail and stage coaches which before the advent of railways were the arteries of national life radiating from London as from a heart.

It is hardly possible to exhibit this genre of writing through brief quotation. Even the texture is distorted, varying as this does from impasto scene-painting to snapshotted action. The following brief excerpt lifted at random samples both in miniature:

"The lady shrugs her shoulders. 'These fishermen are very droll. What do the *canaglia* know about love. Breeding, yes, that is certainly their affair, but love! *Più presto,* Giuseppe. How the sun burns!' Rock over the streaked lagoon, gondola, pock the blue strips with white, shock purple shadows through the silver strata, set blocks of iris cannoning against gold. This is the rainbow over which we are floating, and the heart-shaped city behind us is a reliquary of old ivory laid upon azure silk."

Miss Lowell's command of cadence and color, and her ability to sustain animation, are amazing. But to be amazed so prolongedly results at last in exhausted stupefaction. The experience is akin to traversing interminable corridors adorned with tapestries whose patterns are intricate, insistent, and finally incapacitating.

In 1919 *Pictures of the Floating World* appeared, comprising the short lyrics Miss Lowell had written since her second book: poems on nature (two of her best garden poems, "Madonna of the Evening Flowers" and "The Garden by Moonlight" among them), love, poetic creativeness, a few on war. The chief new accent in this book appeared in its first two sections, "Lacquer Prints" and "Chinoiseries." As already noted, Amy Lowell's interest in Japan had been aroused in her youth by her brother Percival. By 1919 the vogue of the Imagists was waning, to judge by the lessening popularity of the yearly anthologies. On the other hand, an interest in Japanese poetry had become apparent in France as early as 1905, and had been greatly stimulated by Marcel Revon's influential anthology of Japanese literature in 1910. Not that Miss Lowell was a mere camp follower; she aspired to be at least a division commander. But she had a keen sense of where, at any given moment, were to be found the campaigns likely to be productive in the immediate future.

The "Lacquer Prints" were mostly adaptations of the Japanese haiku, which *Webster's Seventh New Collegiate Dictionary* defines as "a fixed lyric form of Japanese origin consisting of three short unrhymed lines of five, seven, and five syllables that are typically epigrammatic or suggestive." Obviously, this species of poem would aid Miss Lowell to preserve the Imagistic conciseness she usually exceeded, and it encouraged free verse as the medium for its translation. The haiku can record an impression of nature as viewed by a serene observer, as in "Proportion":

> In the sky there is a moon and stars,
> And in my garden there are yellow moths
> Fluttering about a white azalea bush.

Or it can record nature transfused with a personal concern of the beholder, as in "The Fisherman's Wife":

> When I am alone,
> The wind in the pine-trees
> Is like the shuffling of waves
> Upon the wooden sides of a boat.

Poems of these dimensions, encountered in small groups, say, not more than a half-dozen, capture attention by the felicity of their separateness. But when encountered in assemblies of fifty or more, they are likely to register in consciousness as a swarm, in which each mote as soon as seen is submerged among the others. The title of the whole book is a translation of the Japanese *ukiyo-e*, of which the basic significance is that "the world of the senses" (pictured in such art) is "illusory and evanescent," in comparison with the beatified world attained through renunciation of all desire. But did Miss Lowell know, one wonders, whether derived, specialized meanings of the phrase include not only "the world of everyday commonplaceness," but also "the world of pursuers of pleasure such as actors and courtesans," and "the world of erotic experience"?

In the preface to her next book, *Legends*, which was published in 1921, Miss Lowell asserted that the narratives in this collection were intended to carry a freight of meaning greater than she had hitherto essayed. She sketches in miniature an anthropology. Man's civilization is the accumulation of man's knowledge of how he can best thrive with his fellows on his planet. As man moves toward such understanding, he becomes conscious, first, of innumerable curiosities; then, as he prospers, of knowledge that satisfies those curiosities. At this stage, he becomes aware of a desire to impart to others what he has learned. He does so, first and typically, by embodying his knowledge in stories. Such stories are what we call legends—Miss Lowell's choice of a term; folklorists today mostly prefer the term "myths" for what Miss Lowell has in mind. Such legends seem durably significant to later ages because the legends contain truth—no doubt provisional because intuitive, but often justified when later summoned to the bar of science, with its rigorous demand for proof. Of the eleven poems in the book, seven comply with the terms of this description; three are merely narratives enshrining superstitions, and one is a dramatic lyric. Since the weight of a legend as conceived by Miss Lowell resided in its freight of archetypal truth about the enduring human situation, and not in the details of the narrative which transported this freight, she did not attempt to follow the form of a particular legend as she came across this in her extensive reading in folklore and anthropology. She abridged, expanded, combined, altered, in whatever way would enforce what she took to be the basic import of a legend, though she did not attempt to modernize; she tried to preserve the prehistoric flavor of her narratives. A new interest of Miss Lowell's comes to the fore in her choice of material. She identifies the provenance of her poems as, for two, New England; for one, England; for three, Europe; for one, China; for two, North America; for one, Yucatán; and for one, Peru. The last four are all drawn from the lore of aborigines of the New World, including the poem she thought the best one, the North American "Many Swans," the tale of the Indian brave who possessed himself of the ultimate gift, the sun itself, and thereupon destroyed every community in which he sought refuge from his loneliness.

Fir-Flower Tablets, which appeared in December of the same year, exhibited Miss Lowell in the role of member of a two-party team of translators from the Chinese. She knew no Chinese, but becoming acquainted with Mrs. Florence Ayscough, daughter of a Canadian father and an American mother, who had been born and had lived much of her life in China and had interested herself in the scholarly study of Chinese literature, Miss Lowell decided that an ideal means of translating poetry from one language to another utterly dissimilar language would be a collaboration between a scholar commanding the language being translated from and a poet expert in the language being translated into. As Miss Lowell has explained the collaborators' procedure, Mrs. Ayscough supplied Miss Lowell with the text of each poem transliterated into the Roman alphabet, to acquaint Miss Lowell with the sound and rhyme scheme of the poem. Opposite each word she then put all its relevant dictionary meanings. To these she added, wherever a need seemed evident, an analysis of connotations of the Chinese word, such as might arise from the meaning of constituent written elements from which the sign had been compounded. Lastly, Mrs. Ayscough furnished Miss Lowell with a connected prose paraphrase of the meaning of the Chinese text, together with whatever notes—on matters "historical, mythological, geographical, and technical"—the elucidation of the poem might require. The substance of many of these notes has been included in the collected edition of Miss Lowell's poems, and retains a variegatedly antiquarian charm.

As might be expected whenever nonacademicians traverse territories appropriated by academic explorers, this anthology was attacked by Sinologues, who impugned the correctness of some of Mrs. Ayscough's renderings, and depreciated the extent of her knowledge of the history of Chinese literature. As for Amy Lowell's share in the enterprise, Arthur Waley, universally admitted to be the most eminent translator from Chinese and Japanese in the twentieth century, stated that "Miss Lowell succeeds best in the reflective and narrative poems. Her rendering of Tu Fu's 'House Unroofed by the Gale' is splendid. In the purely lyrical poems she fails." Since three-fifths of the poems are translations from the predominantly lyrical Li T'ai-po, Waley's approval was hardly copious. On the other hand, the American polylingual poet Kenneth Rexroth, who has himself translated admirably directly from Chinese, has in a bibliography listed *Fir-Flower Tablets* as "Very good" (and in the same list, ranks a later book by Mrs. Ayscough, *Tu Fu*, as "Excellent"). Therefore Miss Lowell has not lacked competent defenders. What these translations certainly do illustrate is the fact that, here as so often, Amy Lowell's timing of an enterprise depended partly on considerations extrinsic to the enterprise itself. Ezra Pound, it was admitted by everyone, including Miss Lowell, had with his *Cathay*, published in London in 1915, been superbly successful in his transpositions into English of originals written in a language of which he had no knowledge. Miss Lowell wished to try her powers against his. When she heard that Witter Bynner, with whom her relations were not always cordial, was intending a volume of translations from Chinese, she resolved to get her book out first. And she did. Bynner's *The Jade Mountain* appeared in 1929. She beat him by nearly eight years.

Postponing consideration of her next book, *A Critical Fable*, more interesting for its critical judgments than for its verse, one overpasses her death to notice her last three books. *What's O'Clock?*, *East Wind*, and *Ballads for Sale*, which appeared in 1925, 1926, and 1927, respectively. The first was a gathering of short poems; the second, a last book of longer narratives, thirteen in all; and the third (unlike the preceding two, not prepared by Miss Lowell herself) was, despite its title, a collection of lyrics and brief tributes to persons and places, assembled by Miss Lowell's companion, Mrs. Russell, to whom the corpus of Miss Lowell's poetry had been dedicated. These books do not call here for special comment, since they exemplify no new experiments or interests. Miss Lowell's adventuring was finished. Yet *What's O'Clock?* showed no falling-off in quality; indeed, in it came "Lilacs" and "Meeting-House Hill," two of her best and most frequently anthologized poems. The New England psychological and even supernatural oddities recounted in *East Wind*—Miss Lowell's last entry in an amicable race with Robert Frost, whose fame in America was initiated by her laudatory review of *North of Boston* in 1915—are entertaining exhibits of the eccentric or the marvelous, though their characters do not engage the reader's sympathies, as do those in Frost's poems. And even the *Ballads* contains a poem—"On Looking at a Copy of Alice Meynell's Poems, Given Me, Years Ago, by a Friend"—that deserves inclusion whenever Miss Lowell is anthologized; for it is her most nearly unflawed utterance of a deep personal emotion.

Upon this greying page you wrote
A whispered greeting, long ago.
Faint pencil-marks run to and fro
Scoring the lines I loved to quote.

A sea-shore of white, shoaling sand,
Blue creeks zigzagging through marsh-grasses,
Sand pipers, and a wind which passes
Cloudily silent up the land.

. . . .

Silent the sea, the earth, the sky,
And in my heart a silent weeping.
Who has not sown can know no reaping!
Bitter conclusion and no lie.

. . . .

How strange that tumult, looking back.
The ink is pale, the letters fade.
The verses seem to be well made,
But I have lived the almanac.

And you are dead these drifted years,
How many I forget. And she
Who wrote the book, her tragedy
Long since dried up its scalding tears.

. . . .

I've recollected both of you,
But I shall recollect no more.

Between us I must shut the door.
The living have so much to do.

Almost inadvertently, perhaps, one new motif has been given utterance in the late poetry of these books: the motif of self-distrust. Has, after all, the poetic labor of years achieved no music more memorable than sounding brass and tinkling cymbals? "Footing up a Total" in *What's O'Clock?* energetically conjures up this doubt—and does not allay it. It reappears less memorably, but more briefly, in "Still Life: Moonlight Striking upon a Chess-Board" in the final book, of which the last four lines ruefully surmise that

I might have been a poet, but where is the
    adventure to explode me into flame.
Cousin Moon, our kinship is curiously
    demonstrated,
For I, too, am a bright, cold corpse
Perpetually circling above a living world.

But "perpetually"? No. The course of events could have been read as symbolic of an ending. The year before Miss Lowell's death, Eleonora Duse, on tour in America, died. *What's O'Clock?* contains six sonnets addressed to her, and two more poems "To Eleonora Duse" are in *Ballads for Sale*. It was the sight of Duse's eloquent art that had first inspired Amy Lowell to make an art her career. One might almost say that Fate now signaled "Finis."

Miss Lowell's books of prose recall us to 1915, the year in which *Six French Poets* appeared. She had been exploring French poetry for at least seven years, and her Imagist-hunting voyages to London acquainted her with Pound's French enthusiasms. Pound asserted that the three most important French poets of recent date were Laforgue, Corbière, and Rimbaud, and that "since Rimbaud, no poet in France had hit upon anything fundamental." But Miss Lowell was of another opinion, and

decided to introduce through lectures to the American public six Symbolist poets—Emile Verhaeren, Albert Samain, Rémy de Gourmont, Henri de Régnier, Francis Jammes, and Paul Fort—more recent than Pound's trio (either because they were born later or lived longer) and relatively unknown in America.

René Taupin in his often-cited book on the influence of French Symbolism on American poetry from 1910 to 1920 has treated Miss Lowell's book severely. He asserts that some of her critical comments are bizarre; that those which are not bizarre had all been enunciated earlier by other critics; that she presented her authors "d'une façon assimilable aux plus mediocres esprits" (that is, in such a way as to be understood by persons of mediocre intelligence; did M. Taupin say this from firsthand experience of American women's clubs?); and finally, that the greater number of Miss Lowell's "citations" (the word in French means "quotations" as well as citations in the English sense) had been "borrowed from the anthology of Van Bever and Léautaud." M. Taupin's charges, however, should not be accepted without scrutiny. For example, the matter of borrowed quotations: even were the charge true, Miss Lowell's numerous quotations of entire poems could hardly have come from a more respectable source, for Van Bever and Léautaud's anthology of modern French poetry was accepted in her day by all competent judges as the best book of its kind; it was used and praised by Pound. But what are the facts? The French anthology in the 1913 edition likely to have been used by Miss Lowell includes sixteen poems by Verhaeren; of the nine Verhaeren poems Miss Lowell quotes entire, only one appears in the anthology. One more trial sounding: this edition of the French anthology contains nineteen poems by de Régnier; of the twenty-six de Régnier poems quoted by Miss Lowell either entire or extendedly, only three appear in the French anthology. M. Taupin's "la plupart"—the greater part—is unsupported by any evidence.

The faults that can be urged against Miss Lowell's undertaking are mainly two. She seems here, as sometimes elsewhere, to envisage the course of literary history as following an evolutionary cycle, if "evolutionary" is given its popular optimistic interpretation: what comes later is more developed, more self-aware, in short, *better,* simply because it is later. And this interpretation reinforced her natural tendency to exaggeration. Here, indeed, MM. Van Bever and Léautaud may have influenced her, for these gentlemen begin their comments on de Régnier by hailing him as "the premier and most celebrated of 'the poets of today,' " the title phrase of their anthology. This praise points in the direction of, but goes less far than, Miss Lowell's salutatory sentence in her essay: "Henri de Régnier is universally considered the greatest of the *Symboliste* poets." Which is nonsense. For what Miss Lowell took to be the crest of a wave was in fact a trough; her six were lesser poets than Mallarmé, Verlaine, and Pound's trio who preceded them, and than the more variegated and vigorous talents that have emerged since the days of Apollinaire. Because of the homage of Pound and T. S. Eliot, Rémy de Gourmont has been known to writers in English, but as critic, not as poet. In a recent one-volume history of French literature written by Professor Louis Cazamian, Verhaeren, a sort of Belgian Whitman who foresaw the evils generated by urbanization, gets a page; but the rest of Miss Lowell's group get but a third of a paragraph apiece except for Fort, who gets half a paragraph, presumably because, born in 1872, he went on living until 1960.

Miss Lowell's next collection of lectures, *Tendencies in Modern American Poetry,* issued in 1917, also exemplifies her optimistic evolutionism. She distinguished three stages in the development of the "New" poetry, that is, poetry of which Imagism was the clearest expression; and she offered a pair of poets as exemplars of each stage. Her first pair—Edwin Arlington Robinson and Robert Frost—were Evolutionists. That is, they evinced a new sensitiveness to reality, a new fidelity to truth; but they were hampered by their consciousness of inherited conventions and traditions whose authority they could not entirely renounce. Next came a pair of Revolutionists—Carl Sandburg and Edgar Lee Masters, who did reject inherited conventions and traditions, on behalf of the freedom of the individual human being; but they did not clear away from their poems the debris strewn about by their insurrection. And finally, in two Imagists—H.D. and John Gould Fletcher—a modernity was attained that was serenely free from vestiges of or reactions against earlier modes uncongenial to it. Miss Lowell vastly overestimated the merits of Fletcher—naturally so, for he was the kind of younger poet whose advocate she became because he suffered in his personal life from handicaps that enlisted her sympathy. The other poets she estimated with considerable shrewdness, and they wrote to her in friendly response except for Masters, who was furious at being bracketed with Sandburg.

However, this book was superseded by Miss Lowell herself when, five years later, in 1922, she perpetrated her hoax, *A Critical Fable.* Her great-grandfather was half brother to the father of James Russell Lowell. Amy Lowell had met her famous relative in her girlhood. She became tired of explaining to people that she was not his granddaughter; and as her own ambitions flourished, she came to feel that his reputation was an obstacle to her own. But she was willing to turn his example to her own account; and her poem, in its slapdash meter, jocosely libertarian rhyming, and general jauntiness, surveyed the work of her poetic contemporaries as her cousin in his poem of the same name had surveyed his. Besides the six American poets of her earlier book, she now in bantering vein sketched Vachel Lindsay, Conrad Aiken, Grace Hazard and Hilda Conkling, Alfred Kreymborg, Louis and Jean Untermeyer, Ezra Pound, T. S. Eliot, William Rose Benét, Maxwell Bodenheim, Edna St. Vincent Millay, and Wallace Stevens, whose work was just beginning to appear. The hoax consisted in the fact that not only did this poem appear anonymously, but Miss Lowell denied authorship of it, and took pains to fasten suspicion on another person, Leonard Bacon, a professor of English who had some note as a writer of satirical verse. This maneuver involved her in what might in a male writer have been called plain lying; in a lady, perhaps the phrase "decorative fiction" will do. A year and three months after publication, the true authorship became known in America. Miss Lowell had included the *Fable* in listing her works for the British *Who's Who*.

A chief fault of the *Fable* is its initial prolixity; the machinery of the fable—a conversation between a young man strolling in Cambridge beside the Charles and an elderly stranger who stops just short of declaring himself to be the revenant J.R.L.—is too long in getting under way. The elderly auditor is amazed to learn that the twentieth century ranks Poe and Whitman highest among American poets of the nineteenth, with Emily Dickinson not far behind. Miss Lowell was obviously abreast of the trends in American literary scholarship. In her judgment of her contemporaries she was more open to objection—as what critic is not? Even famous critics are lucky if their score in predicting the future runs much above fifty per cent. They are great because of the ideas they bring to bear in arriving at their judgments, both when these are confirmed and when they are rejected by the future. Miss Lowell scored, for instance, in perceiving straightway the importance of Wallace Stevens. On the other hand, she had serious doubts about the eminence of Eliot. But mention of him gave her a chance to play off him and Pound against each other.

> Eliot's mind is perpetually fixed and alert;
> Pound goes off anywhere, anyhow, like a squirt.
> . . . .
> Eliot's learning was won at a very great price;
> What Pound calls his learning he got in a trice.
> Eliot knows what he knows, though he cannot
>   digest it;
> Pound knows nothing at all, but has frequently
>   guessed it.
> Eliot builds up his essays by a process
>   of massing;
> Pound's are mostly hot air, what the vulgar
>   call 'gassing.'

Thus Miss Lowell rattles on about the two, with happy hits and perhaps no less happy misses. Edmund Wilson, whose opinion in this matter is worth more than most people's, thought highly enough of Miss Lowell's *Fable* to include it entire in his anthology of writings important in the history of American critical taste, *The Shock of Recognition*.

When Miss Lowell's biography, *John Keats*, was published in February of 1925, she had achieved the book into which she had put her most intense and prolonged efforts, her deepest interests, and probably what became her chief ambition. She might well have been satisfied with a posthumous fame as the outstanding Keats scholar of the twentieth century. Toward this end, ever since buying the entire Rowfant Library Keats collection in 1905 after the death of its previous owner, she devoted an increasing amount of time and money, finally assembling what she perhaps correctly regarded as the largest and best collection of Keats manuscript materials in private hands. As a sample—by no means exceptional—of its quality, she owned Keats's holograph manuscript of *The Eve of Saint Agnes*. In factual matters, she made some mistakes, but she made some new discoveries and corrected some prevalent errors. She aimed to furnish almost a day-to-day record of Keats's whereabouts and activities; and she characterized judiciously those with whom he had dealings of whatever sort. In doing so, Miss Lowell rendered one notable service. Beginning with some of Keats's own closest friends, a tradition had grown up of depreciating Fanny Brawne as incapable by nature of valuing Keats at his true worth; and her behavior was construed in unfavorable ways. Miss Lowell stoutly defended her; and it is probably this book that began the current higher estimate of Fanny Brawne.

Yet this biography is not without serious faults. Its eleven hundred pages testify to Miss Lowell's verbosity. And there was an overplus also of emotional involvement in her attitude toward her subject. Not that she omitted all adverse criticism. She submitted Keats's poems to the kind of inspection a conscientious college-educated mother might bestow on the first literary efforts of a gifted but undertrained son. But this motherly attitude was carried over into every aspect of Keats's life. He had, it was true, written letters to Fanny Brawne difficult to justify from the pen of a rational man. To Miss Lowell, the explanation was simply disease and despair. When Keats was himself, he was not merely a superb poet; he was a clean-living, upright young man who could have passed indistinguishably among the best young men of Boston, had he been Amy's son. To be sure, this portrait is not the reverse of the truth, but it is far less interesting than the whole truth.

Some familiarity with the mores of London during the Regency—from 1811 to 1820—illuminates certain aspects of Keats better than any approximation to Bostonian notions.

Fate, too, dealt hardly with Miss Lowell for undertaking so capacious a project. Her labors for several years in preparing the book exhausted her, and most certainly facilitated, if they could not exactly be said to cause, the cerebral hemorrhage that on May 12, 1925, brought about her death within a couple of hours. Then, cresting a flood of other publications, the 1960's have seen the publication of three Keats books of first-rate importance, by W. J. Bate, Aileen Ward, and Robert Gittings, respectively—the first superior to Miss Lowell's in stylistic analysis; the second, in psychological insight; and the third, in discovery of new facts that introduce fresh nuances into our view of Keats's life. Miss Lowell's biography will long remain a book for research students to consult; but it has already been superseded for the general reader.

Now, finally, what remains of lasting importance from Miss Lowell's many years of arduous and intelligent industry devoted to what she would no doubt see as a "cause": poetry?

In the first place, until the time of her death she held so prominent—one might even say "commanding"—a position among people in America interested in poetry during the second and third decades of the twentieth century that she cannot be left out of any history of American poetry in her time. To do so would not be equivalent to leaving out Hamlet from the play *Hamlet*; but it would be equivalent to the absence, from a performance of that play by a new company, of the stage manager. In the next place, some half-dozen of her shorter poems deserve inclusion in any anthology of the American poetry of the first half of the twentieth century. But, more extensively, she deserves to be kept in print in a selected edition of more generous scope than Professor Lowes's selection, now out of print. He had little room for her narrative poems. Many of these—especially tales macabre in theme or grotesque in personages—are interesting on a first and even a second reading; and of how many books can this much not be said! Moreover, a selected edition ample enough to illustrate all the kinds of her work would in itself be an anthology illustrative of what was going on in American poetry during her career. She had a keen sense for whatever was beginning to be noticed, and a genuine interest in it, which usually issued in her own attempt to produce some of it. Her work is thus a mirror of her time.

But in saying that, one indicates a great limitation. The poet of major genius does not try to keep up with his times. He in some measure *appropriates* them. The dates of his flourishing become his dates. He may give his name to an age: the Age of Wordsworth, the Age of—Eliot? Period histories of American literature are unlikely to bear the title "The Age of Amy Lowell." Fate has even played her a trick in the matter of her more restricted ambition—to be the best poet among the Lowells. It is no longer a question of whether she took first honors away from James Russell Lowell. For a third Lowell, great-grandnephew of James Russell, and distant cousin of Amy, is now in the running. Most watchers would bet on Robert Lowell to win.

Perhaps as Miss Lowell lies at rest in the Mount Auburn Cemetery in Cambridge, her best trophy is a success of a rather different sort. D. H. Lawrence, as might be expected, came out with the essential point, in a letter he wrote to Miss Lowell in November 1914: "I wish one saw more of your genuine strong, sound self in this book *Sword Blades and Poppy Seed*, full of common sense & kindness and the restrained, almost bitter Puritan passion. . . . how much nicer, finer, bigger you are, intrinsically, than your poetry is." Amy Lowell was not easy to live with, in the same household. People much wealthier than their associates seldom are, for they assume, perhaps unconsciously, that they are entitled to two votes to everybody else's one. Yet the more one learns about Amy Lowell's life and enterprises, the more one comes to admire and even, quite heartily, to like her.

Selected Bibliography

WORKS OF AMY LOWELL

SEPARATE WORKS OF POETRY
A Dome of Many-Coloured Glass. Boston: Houghton Mifflin, 1912.
Sword Blades and Poppy Seed. New York: Macmillan, 1914.
Men, Women and Ghosts. New York: Macmillan, 1916.
Can Grande's Castle. New York: Macmillan, 1918.
Pictures of the Floating World. New York: Macmillan, 1919.
Legends. Boston: Houghton Mifflin, 1921.
Fir-Flower Tablets. Boston: Houghton Mifflin, 1921.
A Critical Fable. Boston: Houghton Mifflin, 1922.
What's O'Clock? Boston: Houghton Mifflin, 1925.
East Wind. Boston: Houghton Mifflin, 1926.
Ballads for Sale. Boston: Houghton Mifflin, 1927.

SELECTED AND COLLECTED EDITIONS OF POETRY
Selected Poems, edited by John Livingston Lowes. Boston: Houghton Mifflin, 1928.
Complete Poetical Works, with an introduction by Louis Untermeyer. Boston: Houghton Mifflin, 1955.

A Shard of Silence: Selected Poems of Amy Lowell, edited by G. R. Ruihley. New York: Twayne, 1957.

PROSE

Six French Poets. New York: Macmillan, 1915.

Tendencies in Modern American Poetry. New York: Macmillan, 1917.

John Keats. 2 vols. Boston: Houghton Mifflin, 1925.

Poetry and Poets. Boston: Houghton Mifflin, 1930.

CORRESPONDENCE

Lowell, Amy, and Florence Ayscough. *Correspondence of a Friendship,* edited with a preface by Harley Farnsworth MacNair. Chicago: University of Chicago Press, 1945.

BIBLIOGRAPHY

The third or bibliographical volume of the three-volume edition of Robert E. Spiller, Willard Thorp, Thomas H. Johnson, Henry Seidel Canby, and Richard M. Ludwig's *Literary History of the United States* (New York: Macmillan, 1963), together with a supplementary volume of more recent bibliographical entries, contains the best listing of periodical articles on Amy Lowell.

CRITICAL AND BIOGRAPHICAL STUDIES

Aiken, Conrad. *A Reviewer's ABC: Collected Criticism from 1916 to the Present.* New York: Greenwich Editions (Meridian), 1958. (Now published under the title *Collected Criticism.* New York: Oxford University Press.)

————. *Scepticisms: Notes on Contemporary Poetry.* New York: Knopf, 1919.

Aldington, Richard. *Life for Life's Sake: A Book of Reminiscences.* New York: Viking Press, 1941.

Boynton, Percy H. *Some Contemporary Poets.* Chicago: University of Chicago Press, 1924.

Brooks, Van Wyck. *New England: Indian Summer, 1865–1915.* New York: Dutton, 1940.

Bryher, Winifred. *Amy Lowell: A Critical Appreciation.* 2nd edition. London: Eyre and Spottiswoode, 1918.

Coffman, Stanley K., Jr. *Imagism: A Chapter for the History of Modern Poetry.* Norman: University of Oklahoma Press, 1951.

Damon, S. Foster. *Amy Lowell: A Chronicle, with Extracts from Her Correspondence.* Boston: Houghton Mifflin, 1935.

Greenslet, Ferris. *The Lowells and Their Seven Worlds.* Boston: Houghton Mifflin, 1946.

Gregory, Horace. *Amy Lowell: Portrait of the Poet in Her Time.* New York: Nelson, 1958.

———— and Marya Zaturenska. *A History of American Poetry, 1900–1940.* New York: Harcourt, Brace, 1946.

Hughes, Glenn. *Imagism and the Imagists: A Study in Modern Poetry.* Stanford, Calif.: Stanford University Press, 1931.

Lowes, John L. *Essays in Appreciation.* Boston: Houghton Mifflin, 1936.

Monroe, Harriet. *Poets and Their Art.* New edition revised and enlarged. New York: Macmillan, 1932.

Scott, Winfield Townley. "Amy Lowell of Brookline, Mass.," in *Exiles and Fabrications.* New York: Doubleday, 1961.

Sergeant, Elizabeth Shepley. *Fire under the Andes: A Group of North American Portraits.* New York: Knopf, 1927.

Taupin, René. *L'influence du symbolisme français sur la poésie américaine (de 1910 à 1920).* Paris: Champion, 1929.

Untermeyer, Louis. *Modern American Poetry.* New and enlarged edition. New York: Harcourt, Brace & World, 1962.

Waggoner, Hyatt H. *American Poets: From the Puritans to the Present.* Boston: Houghton Mifflin, 1968.

—F. CUDWORTH FLINT

Robert Lowell

1917-

*F*OR all the horrors of this age, and for all the attractions of others . . . I'd rather be alive now than at any other time I know of. This age is mine, and I want very much to be a part of it," Robert Lowell remarked in 1965. Though deeply, irredeemably, involved in the present, Lowell characteristically approaches the present through the perspective of the past. This is hardly surprising. Born on March 1, 1917, into a family whose history was mingled with New England's, Lowell was personally obliged to acknowledge the importance of his lineage and forced to recognize the influence on him of what he inherited. The first woman to step off the *Mayflower* was one of Lowell's ancestors; another was twice elected governor of Plymouth. The earliest Lowell in America, Percival, became a merchant in Massachusetts in 1639. John Lowell served in the provincial and federal congresses and founded Boston's first United States Bank. Other distinguished Lowells included the builder of the Lowell cotton mills, the founders of the Lowell Institute and the Lowell Observatory, and two poets, James Russell Lowell and Amy Lowell. Rebels against tradition, yet forebears of traditions, the Lowells were energetic, curious, and inventive—but also conservative; individualistic—but also formal and ceremonious.

In Robert Lowell these paradoxes would be sharpened into a poetry equally remarkable for a sense of the apocalyptic present and a knowledge of past history, for force and control, for richness and restraint. Under the pressure of such a system of contraries, Lowell's poetic manner has changed drastically during the last thirty years. His earliest verse was characterized by a tone of baroque exaltation —for instance, in "The Drunken Fisherman" (1944):

> Wallowing in this bloody sty,
> I cast for fish that pleased my eye
> (Truly Jehovah's bow suspends
> No pots of gold to weight its ends);
> Only the blood-mouthed rainbow trout
> Rose to my bait. They flopped about
> My canvas creel until the moth
> Corrupted its unstable cloth.

> A calendar to tell the day;
> A handkerchief to wave away
> The gnats; a couch unstuffed with storm
> Pouching a bottle in one arm;
> A whiskey bottle full of worms;
> And bedroom slacks: are these fit terms
> To mete the worm whose molten rage
> Boils in the belly of old age?

By the sixties, Lowell's poetry had experienced many modifications. No longer oratorical and less pointedly symbolic, it might be dramatic— as in "The Drinker" (1964):

The man is killing time—there's nothing else.
No help now from the fifth of Bourbon
chucked helter-skelter into the river,
even its cork sucked under.

Stubbed before-breakfast cigarettes
burn bull's-eyes on the bedside table;
a plastic tumbler of alka seltzer
champagnes in the bathroom.

No help from his body, the whale's
warm-hearted blubber, foundering down
leagues of ocean, gasping whiteness.
The barbed hooks fester. The lines snap tight.

Or intensely personal, even confessional—as in "Fourth of July in Maine" (1967):

We watch the logs fall. Fire once gone,
we're done for: we escape the sun,
rising and setting, a red coal,
until it cinders like the soul.
Great ash and sun of freedom, give
us this day the warmth to live,
and face the household fire. We turn
our backs, and feel the whiskey burn.

Despite such striking external shifts, all of Lowell's work exhibits the same preoccupations. His basic subject has always been the fate of selfhood in time, and his basic method the examination of the convergence in man of past history and present circumstance. Much that seems contradictory in Lowell's development becomes clear when we understand that he imaginatively projects a system of tensions and contrasts which is designed to express both his will to believe and his capacity for doubt, his necessary reverence toward man or God as well as his inevitable irreverence toward the universe. Like the skeptical satirists of the Renaissance or the encyclopedists of the seventeenth and eighteenth centuries—Montaigne, Burton, Rabelais, Diderot—Lowell is essentially an ironist, interested in enigma rather than in certitude, in awareness more than in knowledge. The critic of Lowell, then, must trace out the stages and varieties of his development in order to show the unity of his work and describe the nature of his achievement.

Robert Lowell's youth was characterized, he has said, by "the anarchy of my adolescent war on my parents." His mother "did not have the self-assurance for wide human experience; she needed to feel liked, admired, surrounded by the approved and familiar." As for his father, "By the time he graduated from Annapolis . . . he had reached, perhaps, his final mental possibilities. He was deep—not with profundity, but with the dumb depth of one who trusted in statistics and was dubious of personal experience." For the "morose and solitary" young Robert, "hurting others was as necessary as breathing." Since he was uncertain of his own identity he concluded that his heritage was not precisely the one he wanted and that he would need to reshape it if he were ever to accept it.

It was in poetry that he sought principles upon which to base an education, and to define himself and his vocation. Around the age of seventeen he wrote a metrical epic about the Crusades which he showed to Robert Frost. ("You have no compression," Frost said.) Richard Eberhart, who was then on the faculty of Lowell's prep school, St. Mark's, remembers that Lowell brought him about sixty poems, "shyly placing [them] on my desk when I was not there." These included "Madonna," Lowell's first published poem ("Celestial were her robes:/ Her hands were made divine;/ But the Virgin's face was silvery bright/ Like the holy light: Which from God's throne/ Is said to shine"), "Jericho," "New England," "Death," "Easter, an Ode," "Jonah," and "Phocion." Written in difficult Latin forms, these poems mixed Catholic with Puritan materials ("When Cotton Mather wrestled with the fiends from Hell"), bewailed the conflict between the poet and society ("Most wretched men/ Are cradled into poetry by wrong"), and emphasized mystical awareness ("A sight of something after death/ Bright Angels dropping from the sky"). Eberhart remembers that "a heavy driving force and surd of prose which would bind the lyric flow in strict forms" were already evident in them.

At Harvard between 1935 and 1937, Lowell attempted to find "new life in his art" and shed "his other life." He rebelled against the pedantry of the Harvard English Department and scorned the *Advocate*—which refused to print his violent poems. He put Leonardo and Rembrandt prints on his walls and Beethoven on his phonograph, and collected "soiled metrical treatises . . . full of glorious things: rising rhythm, falling rhythm, feet with Greek names." Aided by these, he "rolled out Spenserian stanzas on Job and Jonah surrounded by recently seen Nantucket scenery. Everything I did was grand, ungrammatical and had a timeless, hackneyed quality." In 1937 his discovery of William Carlos Williams' work unsettled his convictions about the necessity for exotic meters, intricate style, and elaborate diction and left him still longing for guidance, while rebelling against the negative identities which America, his parents, Harvard, and Boston tradition threatened to impose upon him.

At this crucial moment he defined himself through another series of writers. On the strength of a casual invitation from Ford Madox Ford, he drove to Monteagle, Tennessee, to visit him at the house of Allen Tate and Caroline Gordon. Ford had not yet arrived. But Tate immediately offered himself as friend, magisterial teacher, and literary father —exactly what Lowell was seeking. "Stately yet bohemian, leisurely yet dedicated," Tate learnedly maneuvered Lowell through the English, Greek, and Latin classics, while "blasting" most "slipshod" modern poets. His unequivocal declaration that "a good poem had nothing to do with exalted feelings" convinced Lowell that a poem "was simply a piece of craftsmanship, an intelligible or cognitive object," and that he might master its techniques. After completing the Harvard term, Lowell returned to Monteagle. With "keen, idealistic, adolescent heedlessness," he camped for three months on Tate's lawn and sweated out a series of "grimly unromantic poems—organized, hard and classical as a cabinet."

That fall, with Tate's encouragement, Lowell transferred to Kenyon College, where John Crowe Ransom set the self-consciously Aristotelian, anti-Romantic, ceremonious, and politically orthodox intellectual tone. Lowell was to be permanently affected by the influences exerted on him at this time—Ransom's New Critical emphasis on wit and paradox, Tate's "attempt to make poetry much more formal . . . to write in meters but to make the meters look hard and make them hard to write," contemplative religious literature, Hart Crane, the classics, and criticism like William Empson's *Seven Types of Ambiguity*. Attempting to synthesize all these, he found each poem he wrote "was more difficult than the one before, and had more ambiguities." To make matters more difficult, Lowell was experiencing a spiritual crisis which ended in his rejection of the secularistic accommodations of his Protestant heritage and his conversion to Catholicism. His personal crisis resounded in his poems. Though regarding them as "forbidding and clotted," Ransom accepted two Lowell poems for *Kenyon Review* in 1939.

During the year following his *summa cum laude* graduation from Kenyon in 1940, Lowell and his new wife, Jean Stafford, lived with the Tates. While their wives hummed along on fiction, the two poets studied, talked, and wrote slowly; Lowell completed only a handful of poems in this year. Still, the creative energies released by Lowell's education, conversion, marriage, and poetic apprenticeship finally took form in a slim first volume, *Land of Unlikeness* (1944).

Strengthened by what Tate called "a memory of the spiritual dignity of man," Lowell writes in this book as an avowed Christian, with T. S. Eliot and G. M. Hopkins as his conscious models. Reviewing Eliot's *Four Quartets* in 1943, he argued that *"union with God is somewhere in sight in all poetry."* A 1944 "Note" on Hopkins shows Lowell interested in the way Hopkins' "unique personality and holiness" flowered in poetry. Certainly, much of the turbulence of Lowell's early poetry comes from his conscious struggle to approach Christian perfection. "According to Catholic theology," he wrote, "perfection demands a *substantial transformation* which is called first 'sanctifying' grace and then beatitude, it involves the co-working of grace and free will." His effort to order his language and perfect his verse was analogous (as he saw it) to the discipline of contemplation, the achieved aesthetic experience of a poem analogous to spiritual illumination. But Lowell's way with poetry would be neither Hopkins' nor Eliot's. In the American romantic tradition, he not only merged poetry with religion but equated both with culture, and thus attempted to be oratorical and satirical, exalted and apocalyptic, visionary and prophetic, idealistic and pessimistic, hortatory and violent. Yearning for a civilization in which men bear a likeness to God, he finds in the modern world only St. Augustine's *regio dissimilitudinis*—capitalism, war, secularized consciousness.

Lowell had learned much from his soiled metrical treatises—most of all from Bridges' *Study of Milton's Prosody*. His poetic techniques in *Land of Unlikeness* are carefully calculated to convey strain and tension. "There is not," R. P. Blackmur commented, "a loving metre in the book." The use of thud-meter with sporadic substitution and hard, short run-over lines, often with strong caesuras immediately preceding the final stress, clogs the rhythms and hints at an agonized consciousness, able only to stab itself into language. Short, heavily stressed lines and jangling rhymes shatter the harmony, as if mellifluousness were a disease which threatened to infect him. Strained verbs call attention to the harshness of being. Repetition is the basis of his style: repeated symbols (instead of narrative development), serious puns, frequent allusions, parallelism, formal recurrence, lack of transitions, and repeated assonantal and alliterative sound devices all suggest astonished concentration on the same matter, taken up from different aspects. In losing his perception of his eternal soul's likeness to God, man is lost in time. "The Park Street Cemetery" begins the volume; "Leviathan," an apocalyptic poem of the future, ends it. Between them is a senseless present. Secular man cannot see that he is the "ruined farmer" Cain, that the Charles River is the Acheron, that war renews Christ's crucifixion, that King Philip's severed head is John the Baptist's, that the Puritans are Dracos. Such equivalences, literally understood, were basic to Lowell's imaginative conviction that history is reiteration. They necessarily kept his poems from developing: there are no climaxes in them, only the momentary shutting down of vision.

"The Boston Nativity" typifies Lowell's effects and themes. A child stillborn on Christmas Eve parallels Christ, whose redemption of man is also abortive since men at the "spun world's hub" celebrate a secular Christmas, forgetting their likeness to God and their kinship to Christ. "Progress can't pay/For burial," the poet admonishes this Christ/child.

Child, the Mayflower rots
In your poor bred-out stock. Brave mould,
    here all
The Mathers, Eliots and Endicots
    Brew their own gall. . . .

He concludes by symbolizing in this child the apocalyptic anti-Christ whose nativity—World War II—signalizes the consummation of this civilization: "Soon the Leviathan/Will spout American."

"The Park Street Cemetery," "On the Eve of the Immaculate Conception, 1942," and "Christ for Sale" are similar. There may be hope, the poets suggests in the last—"Us still our Savior's mangled mouth may kiss/Although beauticians plaster us with mud"—but only for the kiss of death, the boon of extinction. The true analogue for these poems is not mystic contemplation, but the desperation of Tashtego's last in *Moby Dick*—spiking the sky-hawk to the mast and so taking down a form of divinity with the damned *Pequod*. Lowell is fully aware of its many echoes in his concluding "Leviathan":

Great Commonwealth, roll onward, roll
On blood, and when the ocean monsters fling
    Out the satanic sting,
Or like an octopus constrict my soul,
Go down with colors flying for the King.

Although Lowell retained ten poems from *Land of Unlikeness* for *Lord Weary's Castle*

(1946), he dropped the outraged, Christian poems that Tate pointed to as the core of *Land of Unlikeness*, and kept only those which could be rewritten with dramatic and elegiac points of view. *Lord Weary's Castle* studies the dulled consciousness of modern man, weary of morality and responsibility, indifferent to crime, numb to punishment, ungrateful and purposeless. Like the Lord Wearie of the ballad, man has neglected the payment due Lambkin, Christ, the architect of his salvation. The prophet of conscience, who had taken the epigraph for *Land of Unlikeness* from St. Bernard's sermon on the Song of Songs, shifted to the poet of consciousness, who found in a traditional ballad and a humanistic use of Christian myth vehicles to express the new concerns of his imagination.

These are best indicated by Lowell's revisions of the earlier "Christmas Eve in the Time of War: A Capitalist Meditates by a Civil War Monument." "Tonight," the capitalist bitterly remarks in the original version, "the venery of capital/Hangs the bare Christ-child on a tree of gold"; hysterical, he cries "for Santa Claus and Hamilton/To break the price-controller's strangle-hold." At the conclusion, the avenging Christ answers his bawling:

"I bring no peace, I bring the sword," Christ
    said,
"My nakedness was fingered and defiled."
But woe unto the rich that are with child.

Thoroughly rewritten, reduced from five to three stanzas, and retitled "Christmas Eve under Hooker's Statue," the *Lord Weary's Castle* version dramatizes man's historic infidelity to himself in war and usury. An anonymous speaker compares the Civil War to his own disillusion; both his nation and he have been stung by knowledge. He is answered not by an apocalyptic Christ, but by Herman Melville—and not the Melville of *Moby Dick*, but of

Battle-Pieces, a book ruled by conciliation and forgiveness. Thus Lowell hints at a stage beyond vengeance, a promise of reconciliation.

"All wars are boyish," Herman Melville said;
But we are old, our fields are running wild:
Till Christ again turn wanderer and child.

Awakened to the dramatic possibilities of restoration, Lowell can end his poems climactically instead of catastrophically. Irony had resulted from his earlier method of contrasting doubt and faith, affirmation and rejection, synthesis and disintegration: now their interaction results in drama.

The first poem in *Lord Weary's Castle*, "The Exile's Return," announces and defines the principles of this shift. At the end of *Land of Unlikeness* Lowell had pointed to the consequences of man's disobedience: "When Israel turned from God's wise fellowship,/He sent us Canaan or Exile." But the exile has returned. He can, Lowell suggests in Shelleyan imagery of the seasons, have spring, a return from exile, by enduring the winter of his death. Lord Weary's destroyed castle—specifically the broken buildings and "torn-up tilestones" of occupied Germany—might be rebuilt. But man is still "unseasoned," unchanged. Lowell's symbol for contemporary man in "The Exile's Return" is Thomas Mann's Tonio Kröger, torn between nineteenth-century serenity and twentieth-century Armageddon. Thus, the poet, pointing hesitantly toward a revivification of European Christianity ("already lily-stands/ Burgeon the risen Rhineland, and a rough/ Cathedral lifts its eye"), considers man's renewal unlikely. *"Voi ch'entrate*, and your life is in your hands," he ambiguously concludes.

"The Exile's Return" is Lowell's inscription to the hell of his volume. Subsequent poems poise man in the Purgatorio of his indecision. "The year/The nineteen-hundred forty-fifth of grace," he writes in the second poem ("The Holy Innocents"), "Lumbers with losses up the clinkered hill/Of our purgation." "Colloquy in Black Rock," which follows, dramatizes the dialects of indecision central to the first two poems. In its first and second sestets, locating the poem in an industrial section of Bridgeport, Connecticut, Lowell parallels the technological "jack-hammer" hell of machine-society to the frenzied human heart beating jackhammer-like toward death, breaking down into elemental "Black Mud." But the quatrain connecting these sestets, alluding to "the martyre Stephen, who was stoned to death," reminds the reader that Lowell took his epigraph for *Lord Weary's Castle* from the Secret of the Mass for St. Stephen, the first martyr for his faith. The second quatrain develops this theme: even though Stephen "was broken down to blood," his heart was the "House of our Savior" and his death a "ransom," salvation. Resolved to mud, man might escape the mire of flesh; then, mud "Flies from his hunching wings and beak—my heart,/The blue kingfisher dives on you in fire." Although this final image recalls the "dove descending" of *Little Gidding* and Hopkins' "The Windhover," it provides a violent, and successful, epiphany. By developing ordered moral connections between the Black Rock of civilization (hell), the Black Mud of death (purgatory), and the blue kingfisher-Christ (salvation), Lowell created an image of salvation as powerful as his images of destruction. The poem which investigates their connections coheres and develops.

Asked to comment on his poetry, Lowell said he was "essentially in agreement" with Randall Jarrell's review of *Lord Weary's Castle*. Lowell's poems, Jarrell argued, "understand the world as a sort of conflict of opposites": there is "the cake of custom," the realm of inertia, complacence, and necessity, everything that blinds or binds: "the Old Law, imperialism, militarism, capitalism, Calvinism,

Authority, the Father, the 'proper Bostonians,' the rich . . .''; against this grinds "everything that is free or open, that grows or is willing to change." Lowell's earliest poems moved toward the closed world—from unfulfilled possibility to the necessity of apocalypse. Now he moves them from necessity toward intimations of liberation.

The major poem of the second mode is "The Quaker Graveyard in Nantucket." New England's whaling industry, based on the greedy exploitation of nature; Ahab's arrogant vengeance in *Moby Dick;* modern war, resulting in the death at sea of Lowell's cousin Warren Winslow; and modern politics, Hobbes's Leviathan, the state, are all analogues of each other. Constricting human possibility, all hint at the way that modern men prey on each other and point to the "promised end" described in *King Lear* as the result of violations of the cosmic order.

Sections I to V of the poem are generally pervaded by images of the closed world, all that is wrecked and destroyed—Winslow himself, the shipwreck described in Thoreau's *Cape Cod*, the doomed *Pequod*, and, at last, secular America. But in this poem Lowell works from the apocalyptic to the elegiac tradition—the obvious model for his prosody, themes, and organization coming from Milton's "Lycidas." Like Milton, Lowell asserts that disaster can be averted and the moral order restored through Christ. The apocalyptic analogies are balanced by a redemptive series: the design of Creation announced in Genesis; Quaker traditions of pacifism; the traditional symbolization of Christ as a whale, "IS, the whited monster"; Father Mapple's warnings in *Moby Dick* about the neglect of gospel duty; St. Matthew's claim (12:40) that Jonah's imprisonment in the whale's belly for three days prophesied Christ's resurrection; the Jewish mystical tradition that (as summa-

rized in Jessie L. Weston's *From Ritual to Romance*), "at the end of the world, Messias will catch the great Fish Leviathan, and divide its flesh as food among the faithful"; and, at last, the Virgin's shrine at Walsingham, destroyed in the Reformation and recently restored. By section VI, these suggest a cosmic arc of liberation, the promised end of salvation—for Winslow and "the world [that] shall come to Walsingham" to contemplate the Unknowable "expressionless/Face" standing above the world of profane action. At first associated with the closed world, Winslow is finally identified with the liberating re-creation. Lowell's last line, "The Lord survives the rainbow of His will," alludes to God's covenant with Noah after the flood wiped away a corrupt world, as well as to Shelley's famous conclusion to "Adonais." Like Keats, trampled to fragments in life, Winslow is transfigured in the image of the rainbow, the "dome of many-colored glass" of a renewed genesis and covenant with man. The self—of Winslow or of the poet who meditates on his death—is defined by its absorption into suprapersonal structures of behavior and belief.

Elsewhere in the volume Lowell employs the opposite method—defining the ego by its separation from coherent spiritual guides. In poems of this mode, he mixes psychological, naturalistic, and clinical with phantasmagoric images and perspectives. "I lean heavily to the rational, but am devoted to surrealism," he has said. The utterly rational man, he implies, can be described only by surrealist techniques; the self locked in itself is nightmarish, and makes surrealism "a natural way to write our fictions."

The major poem of this mode is "Between the Porch and the Altar." Its contemporary hero "thinks the past/Is settled. It is honest to hold fast/Merely to what one sees with one's own eyes." For past affirmations of social, political, or religious communities, he has only "awed contempt." Separated from these, he has only a lost self talking and dreaming itself into existence, and he must conclude: "Never to have lived is best." The final section of the poem is his death fantasy. At a Boston nightclub called "The Altar" he and his mistress watch an ice-skating floor show. Driving home, he dreams he has an automobile accident near a church where his funeral mass is being performed. Self-contained, his existence has had no meaning except the numbed agony of self-consciousness; his birth and death are one wheel of fire—"The bier and baby-carriage where I burn."

Yet, submerged in his unconscious reflections, dreams, and memories are suprapersonal archetypes by which the hero might have been more than a Meredith and enter ancient passion even through modern love. The title of the poem is derived from Joel 2:17, the epistle read in the Mass on Ash Wednesday, and hints at the whole of sacred history between genesis (the Porch) and apocalypse (the Altar). The fall of Adam is re-created in the speaker's failure. Images of idols, serpents, and dragons writhe in his mind from Ezekiel and Revelation. Even his dream that he has raced "through seven red-lights" is a phantasmagoric overflow of his suppressed guilt over committing the seven deadly sins. Unable to acknowledge these beliefs, which torment him into guilty nightmare, the speaker is tragic, his poem a drama of consciousness.

The major modes of *Lord Weary's Castle* are (1) the definition of the individual through suprapersonal structures and (2) the dramatization of the self's terrifying alienation from these through the divorce of observation from feeling and of sensibility from culture. "In Memory of Arthur Winslow" combines these modes. In a well-defined theological tradition of New England writing—Mrs. Stowe's *The Minister's Wooing* is an earlier example—this poem, a meditation on Winslow's death outside the religious community, raises basic questions concerning the relation between belief and salvation. Winslow, section I suggests, is conducted "Beyond Charles River to the Acheron" and hell (a greater Boston) by "longshoreman Charon," damned because he had no faith. He contrasts to earlier New England's "Pilgrim Makers," in whose lives politics were united with belief in God's Holy Will for his people in America. In the family cemetery where Winslow is buried (section II), the tombstones of the early settlers "are yellow," "sunken landmarks," echoing unheeded "what our fathers preached." Their faith had made the Pilgrims "point their wooden steeples lest the Word be dumb"; now, dwarfed pines (instead of steeples), "the first selectman of Dunbarton," a "preacher's mouthings," and a dying sun symbolize the dwarfed civilization (the "shell of our stark culture") of which Winslow has been a part. He "must have hankered for our family's craft," Lowell writes in III. But lacking his ancestors' sense of permanency, he has not attached himself to anything permanent. His modern "craft" substitutes capitalistic for communitarian accomplishments and allows him to lose in Boston real-estate speculations the gold hosed out from Colorado.

In section IV, "A Prayer for My Grandfather to Our Lady," the poet defines his own permanent attachments. He will not unsay his judgments of the "painted idols" adored by his grandfather, but he musters the faith to pray for him: "Mother, run to the chalice, and bring back/Blood on your finger-tips for Lazarus who was poor." His prayer is a collage of his two modes. Imitating the stanzaic form of Matthew Arnold's "The Scholar Gypsy" and recalling the "sea of faith" in "Dover Beach," Lowell symbolizes in Winslow the closed world, "Beached/On . . . dry flats of fishy real estate," sterile even at the edge of the sea. But the poet is in the sea striking for shore. Denouncing modern degradation, he yet achieves a dramatic ecstasy of awareness; and mediating between the closed and open worlds, he speaks for himself.

Lord Weary's Castle brought Lowell, barely thirty, a Pulitzer Prize, praise from T. S. Eliot, Conrad Aiken, William Carlos Williams, and George Santayana, and appointment as the consultant in poetry at the Library of Congress. His third volume, *The Mills of the Kavanaughs* (1951), showed further development of his technical range. Having explored Puritan and Catholic Christian humanism in his first two books, he now gave up orthodox affiliation with any church and proceeded to use Western civilization and his personal crisis as material for his poetry. This new work showed the increasing influence of Ransom rather than Tate; of narrative poets like Chaucer, Dryden, Milton, Browning, Hardy, E. A. Robinson, and Conrad Aiken rather than of the metaphysicals or Hart Crane; and of prose writers like Henry Adams, James, Tolstoi, Chekhov, and Faulkner. Earlier, Lowell's language had been characterized by its tension, a straining to push to and beyond the capacities of language. In *The Mills of the Kavanaughs* he moved toward the language of urbanity, where the strain exists in the sensibility and consists in the attempt to conceal the strain which periodically leaps through the conversational surface. Lowell reined his tendency toward generalization and accusation and developed single-mindedly his talent for complex plots, conversational ease, and vivid characters. While his verse shows a marked decrease in religious fervor it correspondingly increases in sensuous observation, interest in sexual passion, preoccupation with individual yearning and frustration, and emphasis on particularized character.

Love and morality are the central themes of *The Mills of the Kavanaughs*. The speaker of each of the seven poems has experienced a crisis of belief which arises from his involvement with morality and love. In "Falling Asleep over the Aeneid" an old man dreams that at the funeral of Pallas he is Aeneas. He remembers that years before, his aunt called him away from reading the *Aeneid*—" 'Boy, it's late./Vergil must keep the Sabbath' "—to prepare for his Uncle Charles's funeral, attended by "Phillips Brooks and Grant," the cultural and military heroes of the American Civil War. The *Aeneid* and the Civil War merged in the boy's mind and affected his life. Now the old man, missing church for Vergil and using his uncle's sword for a crutch, comes to understand the meaning of his uncle's death as a heroic aspect of American history by redreaming it through the perspective of the Roman epic of man and nation. Though Lowell's technique is borrowed from *Sweeney Agonistes*, his old man achieves stature denied to Sweeney by asserting the power of memory over habit and of perspective over the present. Though outwardly pathetic, the old man himself is a hero in emphasizing, like Vergil, the enduring powers of morality and love and celebrating them imaginatively.

Lowell's longest consecutive poem, "The Mills of the Kavanaughs" brings cultural memory together with psychological analysis through the mode of drama. Based on the principles of mythic literature that Eliot defined in reviewing *Ulysses*, the poem manipulates "a continuous parallel between contemporaneity and antiquity," as "a way of controlling, or ordering, of giving a shape and significance to the intense panorama of fertility and anarchy which is contemporary history." Anne Kavanaugh, suddenly faced with a crisis of memory and self, plays solitaire with the Douay Bible as her partner and "dummy" opponent. But, irresistibly, she finds her analogue not so much in Christian myth as in Ovid's account of Persephone in

Metamorphosis, V. Four-parted, in imitation of Persephone's circle of seasons, her reverie details her life in relation to her husband's. Beginning in spring, when she meets Harry (stanzas 1–7), and continuing through the summer of their courtship (8–15), the autumn of marriage (16–22), and the winter of Harry's manic depression and suspicion (23–38), her recollections join myth and fact in daydreams and nightmares. Harry, the Demeter-Pluto to her Persephone, turns "whatever brought one gladness to the grave."

As characters in his poems find secular stability through suprapersonal forms of belief, myth, or meditation, so perhaps Lowell himself turned to drama as a way of achieving poetic objectivity and personal stability during the breakup of his first marriage. His crisis of self prompted him to portray people at critical moments. That he did not yet dare express personal emotions directly, but concealed them in myth and dramatic monologue, prompted W. C. Williams to complain that he preferred "a poet of broader range of feeling" than that shown in *The Mills of the Kavanaughs*.

Still, this volume points directly to Lowell's development in his subsequent work, in which three strains predominate: (1) imitations, disconnected from the mythic method, however "repoeticized" (as in *Imitations*, 1961, and *The Voyage and Other Versions of Poems by Baudelaire*, 1968); (2) drama, associated either with the mode of imitation (as in *Phaedra*, 1961, and *Prometheus Bound*, 1969) or with Lowell's efforts to dramatize the history of culture (as in *The Old Glory*, 1965); and (3) poems exploring the central character of the poet himself (as in *Life Studies*, 1959, *For the Union Dead*, 1964, and *Near the Ocean*, 1967).

An important influence on *The Mills of the Kavanaughs* was Chaucer, whom Lowell called "our one English poet to tell stories in a clear, distinguished, witty, absorbing style." For Lowell, Chaucer provided not only an example of narrative clarity; Chaucer's contemporaries called him the "great translatour" in recognition of the skill with which he freely rendered foreign tales into English poetry. Already interested in translation, Lowell in the fifties began seriously to write what he would call "imitations," repoetizations of European authors. This work was not published until 1961, however. In the fall of 1949 Lowell went with his second wife, Elizabeth Hardwick, to teach at the Writer's Workshop of the University of Iowa and promptly announced a course called "Five Poets in Translation" (Rimbaud, Baudelaire, Valéry, Rilke, Horace), soon adding others to these (Foscolo, Leopardi, Vigny, Musset, Verlaine, Mallarmé, Gautier, and Hugo). Inevitably led to study the heritage of these poets, he next offered a "Greek Poetry Workshop" in Homer (his favorite poet) and Pindar. His critical method, as recalled by one of his Iowa undergraduates, is illuminating. After reading a poem in the original and loosely translating it, he proceeded to commentary: "He would describe a phrase in terms of another phrase, another poet, a group of people, a feeling, a myth, a novel, a philosophy, a country. . . . He would compare and contrast, describe." Such teaching, followed by three years' residence in Europe, led to Lowell's imitations. Imitation became his way of discovering himself in poetic tradition. But he also regarded the act of translation as an act of culture—the retrieval or the preservation of a heritage of sense and sensibility, for the sake of contemporary life. He said that because "no [earlier] translator [had] had the gifts or the luck to bring Racine into our culture," he attempted to translate *Phèdre*, a play adapted by Racine from Euripides' *Hippolytus*. By doing so, he hoped, some of the concerns shared by classical and enlightenment culture would be made available to modern men. He also claims contemporary relevance for his rendering of *Prometheus Bound*: "I think my own concerns and worries and those of the time seep in." As Americans have often learned their Americanism abroad, Lowell sharpened his American vision through classical and European poetry. Williams had warned Lowell not to remain in Europe. His imitations brought him back by showing him how best to possess Europe as an American.

Lowell rewrote, shortened, lengthened, or otherwise altered others' poems with Jamesian boldness, as if revising his own earlier work according to his mature perspective, designing *Imitations* to be read as a sequence of original poems. Finding "something equivalent to the fire and finish of [the] originals" involved, Lowell remarked, "considerable re-writing." Stressing the unity of his selections by rendering all in the same style, he also ordered them in a continuous sequence which breaks chronology in order to repeat and interweave themes. Not at all an eclectic collection of European poems, *Imitations* resembles many modern long poems based on the principle of "Song of Myself" in developing through a sequence of insights, investigations, images, and observations.

In *Imitations* a single mode of the imagination predominates: the poet confronts and understands himself through engagement with all that is not-the-self—others' selves, as in "For Anna Akmatova"; historical objects, as in "A Roman Sarcophagus"; other poets, as in the Gautier elegies; myth, as in "Helen." But the self confronts itself chiefly through what Lowell calls the "mania" in man and physical nature. The first poem is Lowell's description (from Homer) of the killing of Lykaon by Achilles. "Sing for me, Muse," he begins, "the mania of Achilles." Rich in the imagination of atrocity, the speech of Achilles is indeed manic. In his last poem (Rilke's "Pigeons," dedicated to Hannah Arendt, who has written of the manias of modern man) Lowell reminds us of the persistence in modern times of the ancient Achillean way, closing the volume with an image of mania's eternal return:

Over non-existence arches the all-being—
thence the ball thrown almost out of bounds
stings the hand with the momentum of its
    drop—
body and gravity,
miraculously multiplied by its mania to return.

A meditation on historical circularity, then, *Imitations* begins with Achilles' manic joy in irrationality and violence and shows man repeating his madness. The Trojan War provides Lowell's main symbols—in the first and last poems, in Sappho ("Helen forgot her husband and dear children"), Villon ("Helen has paid this debt—no one who dies dies well"), Heine ("That fellow in Homer's book was quite right"), Valéry (the poem "Helen"), and Pasternak ("Summer . . . hears the god's Homeric laughter"). Troy, of course, merely represents man's ever-present mania for violence.

But equally strong and as omnipresent is man's impulse toward boredom. Indeed, though violence and ennui seem to be opposites, they are really, Lowell suggests, but the two faces of the single mania of the human condition, the alternating poles between which human activity runs. Sappho ("to have lived is better than to live!") and Montale ("even your ennui is a whirlwind") both hint at this relatedness, directly treated in Lowell's imitation of Baudelaire's "To the Reader": "Among the vermin, jackals, panthers, lice,/gorillas and tarantulas" driving man, his central impulse, Lowell writes, "makes no gestures, never beats its breast,/yet it would murder for a moment's rest,/and willingly annihilate the earth./It's BOREDOM." Atrocity and ennui, the manias which Lowell orchestrates in his sequence, combine at the book's center in Rimbaud's "The Poet at Seven": "What he liked best were dark things:/ . . . dizziness, mania, revulsions, pity!" Other recurrent themes, concerning the melancholy state of existence, old age and death, and endeavor and frustration, provide a dark background for these even darker main themes.

Certainly, what Lowell called "the dark . . . against the grain" stands out in *Imitations*; but blind mania is not the unabated concern of the book. In *Prometheus Bound* his hero declares that "Zeus has consented to let [man] live, miserable, dying, though equal to the gods in thought." This distinction between a blank, unremitting universe and man's consciousness runs through *Imitations*. The artist's confrontation of human atrocity in himself and others, and the self-consciousness which, in consequence, he may turn ito art as a heritage for others—this alone prevents history from being merely a sequence of manias. The light against the grain in Lowell's series is the growth of sensibility. Lowell constructs a myth by using other poets and their poems as characters and themes; those he imitates as well as the contemporaries to whom he dedicates his imitations—Williams, Eliot, William Meredith, and Stanley Kunitz—are characters in this cultural myth. His poems are testaments of the consciousness which artists have achieved in the "troubled depths" of atrocity and indifference.

His imitations, Lowell said, were guided by his sense of "what my authors might have done if they were writing their poems now and in America." *The Old Glory,* his dramatic trilogy, is a forceful restoration, on native grounds, of Hawthorne and Melville, who perceived in the 1850's the development of national dilemmas which have culminated disastrously in the present. The mania for authority pervading American culture connects the separate plays of *The*

Old Glory. Ideals are inevitably compromised by becoming institutionalized; their triumphs include the promise of their defeats; fearing, yet wishing, their own destruction, men hold power through oppression, even while knowing that this must bring their downfall. In Lowell's first play, *Endecott and the Red Cross*, two versions of authority collide through Blackstone and Morton. Blackstone argues for a hierarchical world in which "Our kingdom is a pyramid,/Charles Stuart stands at the top. Below him,/his subjects descend uniformly and harmoniously/ down to the lowest farmer." "That's your theory," replies Morton, who represents the commercial values of the merchant class. "I have mine for this country./ Lords and college men are needed in England. I'm needed here." Holding the power to establish either Blackstone's political or Morton's commercial authoritarianism on American soil, Endecott, the governor of Puritan Salem, inclines toward both; wavering, feeling himself a "suit of empty armor," and knowing that he must betray one part of himself whatever he does, he determines to establish Puritan Theocracy—the authority of God—and to expunge both Blackstone and Morton.

The result is foreseeable. By the Revolutionary period, when *My Kinsman, Major Molineux* takes place, Puritanism has become decadent through power and Blackstone's and Morton's authoritarianisms are once again in conflict. Molineux, representative of the King, a later Blackstone, has gained power; but he is once again opposed by the commercial spirit of Morton, represented by the democratic Man in Periwig, who cries: "I have/ authority, authority!" When political power leads to oppression, democratic commercialism seems to promise freedom. Molineux is ousted and his kinsman, Robin, the central figure in the play, remains in the commercial town of Boston. "It's strange/ to be here on our own—and free," he says. But already sensing the impermanence of freedom, he also asks uneasily: "Where will it take us to?" Inevitably, as *Benito Cereno* shows, in democracy different forms of authority and oppression are instituted. Convinced that in his "icy dignity" a captain is the opposite of a slave, Captain Amasa Delano loves hierarchy of all kinds and re-creates Blackstone's pyramidal world on his ship. *"A good master deserves good servants!"* he declares. His name, he thinks, has "some saving/ Italian or Spanish virtue in it"; he tells his mate: "We need inferiors, Perkins,/ more manners, more docility, no one has an inferior mind in America."

Delano is a later Endecott whose democracy is compromised by his power. Lowell wrote *Benito Cereno*, he said, "to show my horror of slavery and violence." Though Delano can kill Babu, the trilogy shows that the exercise of power is the doom of authority. "The future is with us," the slave cries before he is killed; and Delano answers, as he shoots, "This is your future." Their future—our own time—is different from what either could envision, yet both are right: Endecott, the revelers of Merry Mount, Robin, his brother, the citizens of Boston, Delano, Perkins, and Babu are all innocents spun about by their involvement in history. "America's is the Ahab story of having to murder evil: and you may murder all the good with it if it gets desperate enough to struggle," Lowell has written. "God help me," Delano moans, "nothing's solid." What *is* solid, *The Old Glory* shows, is the mania for power in history and the inevitability of its corruption through the "occult connection" between idealism and violence.

Lowell's poetic and dramatic imitations constituted only one of the developments in his work in the fifties and sixties. For a time after completing *The Mills of the Kavanaughs*, Lowell seemed unable to write original poems —his imagination seemed clogged. Dissatisfied with his "distant, symbol-ridden, and willfully difficult" manner, he felt that all his work had the same "stiff, humorless and even impenetrable surface." A number of factors were important in the unbinding of his imagination. His imitations freed him from too narrow a concentration on America by prodding him to discover in his own voice the equivalent to the voices of earlier, non-American poets. Settling in Boston in 1954 with a view toward rediscovering some roots, he made a start on a prose autobiography. He became interested in psychoanalysis, particularly in Freud. Now, "Freud seemed the only religious teacher" to him. He began giving poetry readings, and "more and more [he says] I found that I was simplifying my poems. If I had a Latin quotation I'd translate it into English. If adding a couple of syllables in a line made it clearer I'd add them." His readings loosened his tight, difficult forms; and his interest in autobiography and self encouraged respect for prose ("less cut off from life than poetry is") and diminished his interest in highly rhetorical poetry. In short, he became interested in the discovery, the invention, and the definition of his self; and he attempted to incorporate into his work the contemporary forms, myths, and metaphors which describe the individual imagination.

The result was *Life Studies*, published in 1959. Believing that personal experience alone guarantees truth, many modern poets have written autobiography. But Lowell's confessional poetry derives less from alienation than from an understanding of the destiny of personality in culture. Terrorization of individual man, he knows, has been continuous in the history of society; but culture sometimes nourishes the best achievements of the self. Involved in both, he renders the interconnected realities of personality and culture without simplifying or distorting either. Modernizing

Thoreau through Freud, Lowell writes letters from the distant land of self to kindred selves. Even his most painfully personal poems have public dimensions and (as confessions) imply a listener—the analytic faculty of the poet's imagination overhearing the secrets of his personality. The New Englander and the Viennese Jew are Lowell's distant kindred, and their sharply different cultures the mixed audience he assumes.

Lowell gave *Life Studies* coherence through carefully structuring his book into four parts. In the first poem, "Beyond the Alps," he describes his meditations during a train trip from Rome to Paris; concluding that he will leave "the City of God where it belongs" to take up citizenship in the City of Man, he announces the point of view from which the volume is organized. Through commentary on economics, politics, and militarism, the next three poems in Part One explore the societal context for human activity outside the City of God. The remaining three parts investigate the consolations given to the sensibility willingly exiled in the City of Man. Human responsiveness—to humor and guilt, memory and remorse, consciousness and conscience—in short, receptivity to experience, still remains. "91 Revere Street," an autobiographical prose fragment, shows Lowell in the process of revivifying his own responsiveness by remembering its origins in his youth. Reviving Henry James's concept of autobiography in *A Small Boy and Others*, he first gives an account of the solitary "small boy," then of the "others" through whom he further defines himself and grows to manhood. He implies that a childhood constituted as his was led him to the discovery of artistic sensibility and made it inevitable that he become a poet. Appropriately, then, "91 Revere Street" is followed by four poems exploring varieties of aesthetic impulses. "Ford Madox Ford," "For George Santayana," "To Delmore

Schwartz," and "Words for Hart Crane" suggestively parallel the first four poems of the volume and explore what satisfaction art opens to men having to do without faith though "divorced" from the "whale-fat" of corrupted social life. These form a dramatic interlude equipping the man of experience with intimations about how to make experience meaningful, a substitute for the lost life of the City of God, through art.

The synthesis of experience and art is tested in the fifteen confessional poems of Part Four, "Life Studies." Section I of this part, consisting of eleven poems, continues the reminiscential materials of "91 Revere Street." But now the poems imply connections between the poet in the present and his accounts of his past. This is obvious by the ninth poem, "During Fever," when Lowell refers to his own child, his "daughter in fever." In the next two poems, "Waking in the Blue" and "Home after Three Months Away," Lowell defines his present dilemmas as the result of his heritage and writes about himself, "frizzled, stale and small." In contrast to his first three volumes, where experience grates against the perception of it, in *Life Studies* Lowell is unwilling and unable to locate value through the absolutes of the City of God and accepts the City of Man as the single context for the content of human experience.

This shift of context is stressed in "My Last Afternoon with Uncle Devereux Winslow," a poem designed to remind the reader of "In Memory of Arthur Winslow." Both are four-parted; and, as the earlier poem is followed in *Land of Unlikeness* by a coda ("Winter in Dunbarton"), "My Last Afternoon" precedes "Dunbarton," an account of the burial place of Devereux Winslow. As before, Lowell hints at the vacuity, spiritual hollowness, and pretensions of his ancestors. But he also adopts the perspective of the Jamesian small boy, to whom "Nowhere was anywhere after a summer/ at my Grandfather's farm"; the boy's puzzled and sympathetic point of view prevails. Certainly, as F. W. Dupee wrote of *Life Studies*, "The book abounds in second-class Lowells, in mothers who were unequal to their pretensions when alive and to their black and gold coffins when dead"; but the poems as critically observe the boy, "who had chronic asthma, chronic truculence, and got himself expelled from the public gardens. Lowell's often merciless anatomy of his parents is matched by his merciless account of himself." Like his Victorian ancestors, whom he can now accept with their unmitigable faults, the poet is on a journey—toward the acceptance of his own faults, and so of himself as their inheritor. Thus in *Life Studies* there is no gritting between the poet and his experience. Both are criticized, understood, and accepted from the same perspective.

"My Last Afternoon" epitomizes Lowell's synthesis of material experience with art, its images paralleling the four basic elements with kinds of art. Section I combines images of earth ("One of my hands was cool on a pile/ of black earth, the other warm/ on a pile of lime") and the fertility of the earth ("oranges, lemons, mint, and peppermints") with images of literature ("A pastel-pale Huckleberry Finn"). Section II develops this order by naming water ("Distorting drops of water") and expanding the plastic imagery of section I in references to sculpture: the boy speaks of the "Olympian/ poise of my models" and sees himself as a "stuffed toucan." Moving upward in the elements in section III, he looks "Up in the air," and also portrays his Great Aunt Sarah and the "soundless" music which he practices on a dummy piano. Deepening his perception of the connections between nature and art in this section, he summarizes his earlier images —of earthly fertility and literature ("trouble-

some snacks and Tauchnitz classics"), of water ("by the lakeview window," "a thirsty eye"), of statuary ("naked Greek statues draped with purple") and the bird ("risen like the phoenix").

All these are focused on section IV, as, combining nature with art, the poet prepares to face the otherwise meaningless early death of Devereux Winslow. While the fourth element of fire ("a barrage of smoke-clouds") is hinted at, and another form of art, posters and photographs, is introduced, the important movement of the imagery in section IV is its aesthetic synthesis of the boy's metaphoric experience; he has achieved perspectives whereby to view death as an aspect of natural and artistic order. His heightened sense of the connections between experience and art allows the poet to become simultaneous with his own childhood and assert "I wasn't a child at all." The child who experienced the death and the adult artist are united. At the end of the poem, he returns to the earth, meaningful in terms of the whole ordered cycle of creation.

He was dying of the incurable Hodgkin's dis-
    ease. . . .
My hands were warm, then cool, on the piles
of earth and lime,
a black pile and a white pile. . . .
Come winter,
Uncle Devereux would blend to one color.

The four poems in the second section of "Life Studies" unify the volume by closely paralleling the four which began it. Since secularism, economics, politics, militarism, and insanity—public and private madness—have assumed personal meaning through the revelations and identifications of the intervening poems, the poet renders them through his own experiences, rather than those of Marie de Médicis, President Eisenhower, or a mad Negro soldier. Having delineated experience through symbols external to his own experience, Lowell made himself his central symbol and so passed (as he remarked of "Skunk Hour") "way beyond symbols into reality." "I want the reader of my poems to say, this is true," he declared in an interview. "I want him to believe he is getting the *real* Robert Lowell."

The authentic Lowell dominates "Skunk Hour," where he writes of the crisis of self which led to the mental derangements and hospitalization dramatized earlier in *Life Studies*. Here he investigates the principles by which the ill mind moves—tentatively, and through art—back to health. Hinting in his title at the formalized Chinese calendar, Lowell suggests that he too will have his hour of truth—new awareness. Stanzas 1–4 center on the paradoxical association of role-playing with death: in the aged "hermit/ heiress"; in the gaily dressed summer millionaire who has either died or become bankrupt; and in the Maine landscape, whose ruddy autumn barely conceals the white death of approaching winter. Masks have less and less efficacy to hide the dead hollows beneath them. The portrait of the decorator in stanza 4 outrightly names him "our fairy"; and though he laments that "there is no money in his work,/ he'd rather marry," the feminine rhyme (fairy/ marry) strikes through the mask. Human corruption— through solitude, fraudulence, and trivialization—is vividly portrayed in this first half of the poem. The second half focuses on the poet, himself implicated in the masquerading "ill-spirit" he observes in others. How can he avoid the corruption that he sees? And if he responds intensely to it, how can he preserve himself from despondency and madness, the derangements in his heritage?

"We poets in our youth begin in sadness;/ thereof in the end come despondency and madness," Lowell had given Delmore Schwartz to say in Part Three of *Life Studies*. Schwartz cannot be a Wordsworth to Lowell's Coleridge;

though "resolution" and "independence" might preserve him at the end of "Skunk Hour," Lowell is obliged to write odes to dejection before lyrics of affirmation. He defines his emotional crisis, then, by references to a variety of familiar passages describing spiritual disaster: St. John of the Cross's Dark Night of the Soul ("One dark night"), Christ's crucifixion ("the hill's skull"), Lear's confusion on the heath ("My mind's not right"), and Satan's self-condemnation at the prospect of Eden in Book IV of *Paradise Lost* ("I myself am hell;/ nobody's here"). His sense of tradition does not save him —it simply gives him a way of understanding (and so for a moment controlling) his personal crisis, an aspect of the general human madness.

That the leap which his mind takes toward restoration occurs in the sole run-on stanza conveys vividly the mental rush necessary to revivify the disordered mind before self-disgust extinguishes it. The available image ("only skunks") which he almost hopelessly seizes upon for support turns out to possess extraordinary power as a symbol for naturalness, passion ("eyes' red fire"), fertility, and persistence—human qualities which the poet must revive in himself. Not the literature of disaster, but the primitive nature religion of the racial unconscious provides his symbols— the column and the pail, the "wedge-head" and the "cup"—reminders (from *The Golden Bough*) of continuing fertility. "Skunk Hour," in short, describes a poet who has moved from contemplation of the hermit-mother "in her dotage" to the skunk-mother in her prime, from a decadent human world to individual revitalization. Lowell began *Life Studies* by pointing to the journey he would take. In "Skunk Hour" he is still traveling. He has gone beyond Paris, the City of Man, to himself, in Maine. Often set adrift, and through the shipwreck of his absolutes made "frizzled, stale and small," he ascends in this last poem "the hill's skull" for one more crucifixion. But by finding in the mother skunk a way to express the possibility of vitality, he stands at the end "on top/ of our back steps." The steps of his own house are all the Alps or Golgotha he will have; for he has shown through the volume that the City of Man—of society and of self—will suffice. Now, like the skunk, he "will not scare." Instead, as in a symposium Lowell said of his composition of this poem, he survives his "strange journey . . . clinging to spars, enough floating matter to save [him], though faithless."

After the completion of *Life Studies* Lowell felt emptied of self, uninterested in individuality. "Something not to be said again was said," he wrote to M. L. Rosenthal. "I feel drained, and know nothing except that the next outpouring will have to be unimaginably different—an altered style, more impersonal matter, a new main artery of emphasis and inspiration." At the Boston Arts Festival in 1960, Lowell remarked: "When I finished *Life Studies* I was left hanging on a question mark. . . . I don't know whether it is a death rope or a lifeline." It remained for him to join the modes of *Imitations* and *Life Studies* by investigating simultaneously the sense that self makes out of the history it hoards and the culture that draws back the self which would be lost through fleeing it. The possibilities of this synthesis provide the "new main artery of emphasis and inspiration" of *For the Union Dead* and *Near the Ocean.*

In *For the Union Dead* old poems are revived, previous themes are reinvigorated, the vatic utterance of his earliest manner and the confessional tone of his most recent are recalled. It is not so much a coming to grips with a new poetry as a completion of all that was implied in the earlier. The parallels with previous volumes are innumerable: "Water" recalls "The Quaker Graveyard" and "The North Sea Undertaker's Complaint," and (in its scene and situation) "Skunk Hour." "The Old Flame" rewrites the marriage sequence of *The Mills of the Kavanaughs* in personal terms, and recalls such *Life Studies* poems as "Man and Wife" and " 'To Speak of Woe That Is in Marriage.' " "Memories of West Street and Lepke" ("These are the tranquillized *Fifties*,/ and I am forty") is updated by "Middle Age" ("At forty-five,/ what next, what next?"). "Grandparents" of *Life Studies* ("They're all gone into a world of light") is generalized both in "The Scream" and in "Those before Us." "The Public Garden," "Beyond the Alps," and "Epigram" are revisions of poems which appeared first in *The Mills of the Kavanaughs*, *Life Studies*, and *Imitations.* "The Drinker" secularizes "The Drunken Fisherman." "Salem," which presented the half-unconscious meditations of an old seaman concerning the past glory and present decay of the port, had alluded to the "Custom House" section of *The Scarlet Letter*; in "Hawthorne" Lowell treats his source directly. As a description of Hawthorne himself he goes on to incorporate into the poem Hawthorne's portrait of Septimius Felton and to gloss it with his own comment on the imaginative mode he shares with Hawthorne, who, he says, broods on "the true/ and insignificant." In "Jonathan Edwards in Western Massachusetts" and "Fall 1961" he repeats the same process, openly recalling two earlier poems, "Mr. Edwards and the Spider" and "After the Surprising Conversions." Most strikingly recollective is "Soft Wood," another in the series of Winslow elegies. Its opening metaphor ("Sometimes I have supposed seals/ must live as long as the Scholar Gypsy") alludes directly to the stanzaic form of "In Memory of Arthur Winslow." But like other recent work, the new poem relies on ironic balances and self-identification with tragedy. "Soft Wood" is perhaps Lowell's first poem in which the chief values are the mixed, but triumphant, human values of weakness, "a wincing of the will," a bending to the wind "forever," mortality and compromise, sensitivity, and endurance.

The Americans about whom Lowell writes in the title poem gave up everything to serve the state. Resembling poems like Tate's "Ode to the Confederate Dead" and James Russell Lowell's "Ode Recited at the Harvard Commemoration," "For the Union Dead" elegizes the war dead through a succession of apparently unrelated "views"—the Old South Boston Aquarium, the construction of a garage under Boston Common, Augustus Saint-Gaudens' memorial relief of Colonel Robert Gould Shaw leading his black regiment, and an advertisement in a store window. Each becomes an apocalyptic analogue of the other, each a monstrous emblem of man's self-destructiveness. The central image of the poem derives from Albany's remark in *King Lear*: "It will come./ Humanity must perforce prey on itself,/ Like monsters of the deep." The aquarium is closed and its fish tanks are dry; breathing is cut off, life suffocated. The steam shovels digging the garage resemble monstrous metal fish, yellow dinosaurs; and the fence around the construction site is a cage hardly protecting the city from these rough apocalyptic beasts. The shaking Boston Statehouse is encircled by girders, and the Shaw monument is unceremoniously "propped by a plank splint against the garage's earthquake." Compounding catastrophic signs, on Boylston Street, "a commercial photograph/ shows Hiroshima boiling/ over a Mosler Safe." The state demands servility; no longer confined to the aquarium, its underworld is loosed upon the world: "Everywhere,/ giant finned cars nose forward like fish;/ a savage servility/ slides by on grease." *For the Union Dead* seems destined to conclude as *Lord Weary's Castle* did, with the poet declaring himself "a red arrow on this graph/ of Revelations," pointing a livid finger

to the day of wrath, when man consumes himself through the inhumanity of the Leviathan state he has created to protect and nourish him.

But *Life Studies* had made a difference; even while terror accumulates about the emblems of final darkness, the poet's memory is not extinguished by the apocalypse of the state. He is in touch with the energy of true primitivity: "I often sigh still/ for the dark downward and vegetating kingdom/ of the fish and reptile." And he can restore, if not the Shaw monument, the more important recollection of what energies for human rights might still be symbolized by Shaw "and his bell-cheeked Negro infantry." Shaw can be a "compass-needle" pointing to a kind of human integrity which the state might extinguish, but whose importance it cannot alter. The millennial "ditch is nearer"; yet Shaw, who "waits/ for the blessèd break" of the political bubble which drifts from the mouth of Leviathan, points to an alternative mode of political life. Enduring in the aquarium of memory, Shaw's monument reminds the poet of a life of service; his decision "to choose life and die" freed his life from the state. The poet, similarly, though hedged by apocalypse, can assert his own "blessèd break" with the state through a poetic career. This poem concludes a volume which summarizes that career by refocusing and revising the themes and emblems of his earlier work.

In *Near the Ocean* Lowell emphasizes invention over memory and makes striking combinations and juxtapositions of his central themes—the horrors and attractions of antiquity, of Western civilization, of nineteenth-century New England, and of his own age. Between Rome and America Lowell makes deft connections; both have the same imperial urge for dissipation and extinction. The sea extending from Europe to America is the ocean of his title, America is as near the ocean as

Rome, and the Roman disease of power has washed over the American land. Juvenal's Romans know the terrors of night, where "each shadow hides a knife or spear"; while Lowell interrupts his night thoughts in "Central Park" to observe of the present: "We beg delinquents for our life./ Behind each bush, perhaps a knife." Lowell's Romans are characterized (by way of Horace, Juvenal, Dante, and Gongora) as vain, envious, greedy, and lustful; their power is the fountain of their disgrace, their possessions the wellsprings of their unhappiness; their military triumphs the reason for their defeat; their desires reservoirs for the numbing of desire. From their greatness issues the chief horror—the insignificance of glory, the triumph of the quotidian: "what was firm has fled. What once/ was fugitive maintains its permanence."

The same is true of the America described in "Waking Early Sunday Morning." Its subject is the degradation of the Pilgrim hopes for a Promised Land, and its form, consisting of eight-line stanzas of octosyllabic couplets, is that of a typical New England hymn. The poet stirs just before dawn; possessed by a sublime dream of freedom, he imagines himself a chinook salmon breaking loose from the sea to clear a waterfall—an Adamic man. But the dawn brings "blackout," domestic data that keep his mind from maintaining this imaginative intensity: the objects that possess his waking imagination are "serene in their neutrality." Lowell's reference to Wallace Stevens' "Sunday Morning" is self-deprecative; and fragments recalling romantic intensities available imaginatively to Wordsworth, Masefield, Whitman, and Homer mock the poet's inability to humanize nature or to naturalize the mind.

His meditation (stanzas 6–7) on the dream of the "City on a Hill" in America—as expressed in Puritanism ("they sing of peace, and preach despair") and in Transcendentalism ("Better dressed and stacking birch")—is interrupted by a recollection of Baudelaire's poem of despair "Anywhere Out of This World." Obliteration of the spirit is the only release in this post-Baudelairean world. Instead of going to church, then, the poet explores the woodshed of his imagination for "its dregs and dreck."

The "dregs and dreck" of the Puritan dream were revivified in America through the Federalist dream of the democratic republic. In stanzas 9–13 the poet extends his meditation to the contemporary consequences of that dream; recalling the decay of Israel and Rome into militarism, he finds in America as well only "Hammering military splendor,/ top-heavy Goliath in full armor," restlessness, excess, self-deception, and "ghost-written rhetoric." Again, he cries: "anywhere, but somewhere else." The Adamic dream of the individual, the Promised Land of America, and the dream of democracy have all been betrayed. Lowell's final stanza is a hymn whose theme is the poet's inability to sustain or create new hymns:

> Pity the planet, all joy gone
> from this sweet volcanic cone;
> peace to our children when they fall
> in small war on the heels of small
> war—until the end of time
> to police the earth, a ghost
> orbiting forever lost
> in our monotonous sublime.

What remains for the poet who has been made aware of the degradation of his democratic dogmas is his continuing ability to perceive (even to pity) the planet, to discover individual objects worth observing and naming, and to give them permanence through memory, and so preserve the self by its attachment to itself through things. The permanence of mind is the subject of "Fourth of July in Maine," another elegy on Harriet Winslow, where Lowell makes his cousin an emblem of the "genius" of memory. Although all the transcendental dreams—of personal freedom (she is "ten years paralyzed"), of religion ("not trusting in the afterlife"), and of politics (she dies in Washington, D.C.)—escaped her, she avoided the disasters which accompany them; she has the permanence of memory, of the transient, of the gentle. From writing poems in which his ancestors are emblems of all that is wrong with the past, Lowell found in her an emblem of what may be right about the future, and took Harriet Winslow as the genius for his own child, "mistress of/ your tireless sedentary love."

In 1943 Lowell, "a fire-breathing Catholic C.O.," had been sentenced to a year and a day for refusing to serve in World War II. After attempting to enlist earlier, he contended that now the Allies were fighting as ruthlessly as their opponents. In a published letter to President Roosevelt he reminded the President that he was "an American, whose family traditions, like your own, have always found their fulfillment in maintaining, through responsible participation in both civil and military services, our country's freedom and honor." From 1943 to the present, Lowell has been concerned with the relations between politics, society, and the individual. Active in civil-rights and antiwar protests, he refused an invitation from President Johnson in 1965 to appear at a White House arts festival, since "every serious artist knows that he cannot enjoy public celebration without making subtle public commitments." Somewhat later, introducing Soviet poet Andrei Voznesensky to a large Town Hall audience, he said: "This is indiscreet, but both our countries, I think, have really terrible governments. But we do the best we can with them." Lowell's continuing concern with the rela-

tions between politics, society, and individual conscience is the subject of *Notebook 1967–68* (1969), a volume designed, he says, "as one poem, jagged in pattern." Its "plot" consists of the daily accumulations of memory, as chance events, which might drive the poet out of himself, instead bring his submerged thoughts, half-thoughts, and unanswered puzzles into sharp focus and allow him, through meditation on them, to reach the partial answers and tentative solutions possible on that day. "Famished for human chances," he will not turn away from the daily dates of his culture—but he is also faithful to himself and asserts of events only what he can truly know or feel of and through them. As a man participating in culture, he experiences its daily flux; as a poet so participating, he derives from the experience of culture and self the tentative, but objective, perception of value upon which a civilization can be based or an individual preserved. Through poetic form he saves the unsavable.

Notebook 1967–68 is unified through the development, restatement, and repetition of several themes and concerns: (1) growing, a theme embodied particularly in poems on Lowell's daughter, Harriet; (2) the relation between the past—what one grows from—and the present that one daily grows into (this theme leads Lowell to reflect on his childhood); (3) the contexts of growing: history (of Lowell's ancestors, of America, and of Europe), politics, and consciousness; (4) concern with the poet's personal history; (5) achievement of an uneasy, but joyful, acceptance of the dark side of history, politics, and modern life, so that even the apocalyptic poem "Dies Irae" can be subtitled "A Hope" (he ultimately asserts in "Mexico," 5: "I am learning to live in history"); (6) a willing involvement of himself with the tragedies of family, society, other persons, and self. What defenses are there against age and change and death, Lowell asks early in his poem (in "Long Summer," 11)—"Who can help us from our nothing to the all,/ we aging downstream faster than a scepter can check?" His own right to involvement, hard-won in the book, provides the answer.

These themes develop within the general framework of the moving seasons. The poem begins in midsummer with "Harriet" and Lowell's reflection on growing. But the autumnal, Indian summer mood soon enters. Saying "we asked to linger on past fall in Eden," he moves from the innocence of growing to the state, "past fall," of experiencing other, adult concerns. Poems on "Aunt Sarah" and "My Grandfather," autumnal Victorians, and those, like "Munich, 1938" and "October and November," on modern degradation dominate this season's meditations. He recalls his own youth in "Harvard" and "In the Forties." The coming of winter inevitably leads him to pursue the theme of his growing to his present situation—as writer ("Writers"), as teacher ("Blizzard in Cambridge"), and as traveler ("Lines from Israel"). "Infirmity," he can at last declare (in "Mexico," 10) is "a food the flesh must swallow,/ feeding our minds."

April and the approach of spring turns his mind to "shining remembrance"—of Harriet ("Words of a Young Girl"), who continues to grow, of women friends ("Mania"), and of historical personages whose power was more benevolent than others introduced earlier—Roland, Bishop Berkeley, and F. O. Matthiessen. Exhausted by winter, he finds a kind of rebirth in April and places his "New Year's Eve 1968" at this point, as the poem moves, through difficulty, upward. He affirms this restoration by revising, in the direction of acceptance, two poems from *For the Union Dead*, "Night-Sweat" and "Caligula," and one from *Near the Ocean*, "For Theodore Roethke: 1908–1963." Because he has experienced authentically the

pain emphasized earlier, he can forcefully reject nihilism ("The Nihilist as Hero").

"Circles" introduces the expected return to summer. Several poems on Harriet and Lowell's wife appear as he moves toward passionate involvement with other people: his wife and child, his "family chronicle" ("Sound Mind, Sound Body"), and politics ("The Races"). Lowell has insisted, "It is harder to be a good man than a good poet." Understanding life as the supreme art, even in poems on writers (like Tate and Berryman) Lowell emphasizes their personal struggles. He has grown through art to life: instead of the book of a century ("Growth"), he writes the notebook of a year. "Summer" comes at last to complete the circle—of the seasons, and of his changing mind. To express the new birth of energy which he has experienced, he writes of his possible reincarnations—as a seal ("If we must live again, not us; we might/ go into seals") and again as a poet ("Some other August,/ the easy seal might say, 'I could not sleep/ last night; suddenly I could write my name' ").

Affirming such imaginative energies, he can write a series of codas—"Close the Book," "Half a Century Gone," and "Obit"—ending in a vision of his personal death and his fierce continuance in eternal return, through involvement in life.

I'm for and with myself in my otherness,
in the eternal return of earth's fairer children,
the lily, the rose, the sun on dusk and brick,
the loved, the lover, and their fear of life,
their unconquered flux, insensate oneness, their
    painful "it was . . ."
After loving you so much, can I forget
you for eternity, and have no other choice?

His passionate involvement in what continues, continues him.

Notebook 1967–68 illustrates Lowell's refusal to repeat himself, his insistence on development. "Somehow [I] never wrote something to go back to," he writes in "Reading Myself." He has moved with his culture. Like earlier New England poets, he first developed his sensibility in opposition; but unlike them, he has been forced by the rapid changes in American life repeatedly to reconstitute his principles of opposition, and thus always to define freshly his relation to his fellows. He has developed three basic directions for his work: a critique of public action and attitude in America; a critique of the state of the individual ego; and a sense of the historical, religious, mythological, and literary contexts which provide perspectives whereby to understand the possibilities of public or private life at any time. As his society has shifted during the last twenty-five years, Lowell has emphasized various combinations of these.

During the mid-forties, while Americans were confident, Lowell's poetry boiled with apocalyptic despair and condemnation of the diseases which infected Americans. During the late forties and early fifties, the era of the "silent generation," Lowell's poetry was rhetorical and extravagant. While Americans wished to consolidate minor triumphs, Lowell's verse suggested that success of an ordinary kind was impossible and undesirable.

By the late fifties, disillusioned with war and international involvements, Americans sought various escapes from self-consciousness and the powerhouse of history. In *Life Studies* and *Imitations* Lowell faced himself and America's European heritage directly. Increasingly, in the sixties, a sense of alienation and collective disaster darkened the American mind. Lowell well described the attitude: "We're burning, we're decaying, we're in mid-century. . . . Genocide has stunned us; we have a curious

dread it will be repeated." Americans had arrived at his earlier despair. But in *The Old Glory, Prometheus Bound*, and *For the Union Dead* Lowell was emphasizing the continuities of culture and the inevitable involvement of the private self with public concerns.

While Americans in the late sixties began stressing immediate social reform without correcting the roots of social ills, Lowell stressed the values of contemplation, a quiet faith amid public clamor, and intelligence in *Near the Ocean* and *Notebook 1967–68*. Even justice, he showed, can become a dogma and murder itself. "We must bend, not break," he says. Where Americans have understood new moral incoherence, he has seen new moral possibilities. He has defined the four major contemporary problems as "how to join equality to excellence, how to join liberty to justice, how to avoid destroying or being destroyed by nuclear power, and how to complete the emancipation of the slaves." As a radical he has identified these, as a conservative declared them "almost insoluble"; as a liberal he has worked to solve them and written poems describing a state of widened consciousness which might encourage solutions; and as a traditionalist, he has identified similar dilemmas in Roman history and nineteenth-century America, in the careers of Plutarch's heroes and Abraham Lincoln. He has kept his mind flexible and contradictory, allowing the half-truths of any position to support and absorb its opposite. An account of his career is a history of how he has allowed his contradictions to seep into his poetry as the society to which he is responding changes.

His work, in short, has been a mirror to his culture, supplying society with elements for advance. He has criticized the poets of his generation whose "writings seem divorced from culture." Culture, he came to see, provides the necessary background for art: neither, without the other, can endure. Constantly updating old poems for inclusion in new volumes, he moves with culture and refuses to let society catch up with him. "One side of me," he has said, "is a conventional liberal, concerned with causes, agitated about peace and justice and equality. . . . My other side is deeply conservative, wanting to get at the roots of things, wanting to slow down the whole modern progress of mechanization and dehumanization, knowing that liberalism can be a form of death too." He has been able to combine these tendencies intricately and to employ his imaginative powers to locate and express permanent aspects of mind which his civilization has temporarily forgotten or rejected. "One feels," he said in criticism of Wallace Stevens, ". . . that a man is able to be an imagination and the imagination able to be disinterested and urbane only because it is supported by industrial slaves. Perhaps if there are platonists, there must always be slaves." Lowell has refused to be a Platonist, an imagination, and has insisted on being a *man* of imagination. Serving and leading his culture by opening, through his work, the lines along which it might evolve, he has built a career like those of Jonson, Dryden, Goethe, Howells, and James. His power as a poet derives from his understanding that, like these writers, he can be a man of letters only insofar as he can remain a man among men.

Selected Bibliography

WORKS OF
ROBERT LOWELL

POETRY

Land of Unlikeness. Cummington, Mass.: Cummington Press, 1944.

Lord Weary's Castle. New York: Harcourt, Brace, 1946.

The Mills of the Kavanaughs. New York: Harcourt, Brace, 1951.

Life Studies. New York: Farrar, Straus and Cudahy, 1959.

Imitations. New York: Farrar, Straus and Cudahy, 1961.

For the Union Dead. New York: Farrar, Straus and Giroux, 1964.

Near the Ocean. New York: Farrar, Straus and Giroux, 1967.

The Voyage and Other Versions of Poems by Baudelaire. New York: Farrar, Straus and Giroux, 1968.

Notebook 1967–68. New York: Farrar, Straus and Giroux, 1969; second printing, revised, 1969.

PLAYS

Phaedra, in *Phaedra and Figaro*, translated by Robert Lowell and Jacques Barzun. New York: Farrar, Straus and Cudahy, 1961.

The Old Glory. New York: Farrar, Straus and Giroux, 1965; revised edition, 1968.

Prometheus Bound. New York: Farrar, Straus and Giroux, 1969.

PROSE

"Four Quartets," *Sewanee Review*, 51:432–35 (1943).

"A Note" [on Hopkins], *Kenyon Review*, 6:583–86 (1944).

"The Verses of Thomas Merton," *Commonweal*, 42:240–42 (1945).

"Imagination and Reality," *Nation*, 164:400–02 (1947).

"Thomas, Bishop, and Williams," *Sewanee Review*, 55:493–503 (1947).

"Paterson II," *Nation*, 166:692–94 (1948).

"John Ransom's Conversation," *Sewanee Review*, 56:374–77 (1948).

"Prose Genius in Verse," *Kenyon Review*, 15:619–25 (1953).

"Visiting the Tates," *Sewanee Review*, 67:557–59 (1959).

"I. A. Richards as a Poet," *Encounter*, 14:77–78 (February 1960).

"Yvor Winters: A Tribute," *Poetry*, 98:40–42 (April 1961).

"William Carlos Williams," *Hudson Review*, 14: 530–36 (1961–62).

"Randall Jarrell," in *Randall Jarrell, 1914–1965*, edited by Robert Lowell, Peter Taylor, and Robert Penn Warren. New York: Farrar, Straus and Giroux, 1967.

CRITICAL STUDIES

Alvarez, A. "A Talk with Robert Lowell," *Encounter*, 24:39–43 (February 1965).

Cambon, Glauco. "Robert Lowell: History as Eschatology," in *The Inclusive Flame: Studies in American Poetry*. Bloomington: Indiana University Press, 1963.

Eberhart, Richard. "Four Poets," *Sewanee Review,* 60:327–31 (1947).

Ehrenpreis, Irvin. "The Age of Lowell," in *American Poetry*. New York: St. Martin's Press, 1965.

Hochman, Baruch. "Robert Lowell's *The Old Glory*," *Tulane Drama Review*, 11:127–38 (Summer 1967).

Kunitz, Stanley. "Talk with Robert Lowell," *New York Times Book Review*, October 4, 1964, pp. 34–36, 38–39.

Martz, William J. *The Achievement of Robert Lowell*. Glenview, Ill.: Scott, Foresman, 1966.

Mazzaro, Jerome. *The Poetic Themes of Robert Lowell*. Ann Arbor: University of Michigan Press, 1965.

Mills, Ralph J., Jr. *Contemporary American Poetry*. New York: Random House, 1965.

Parkinson, Thomas, ed. *Robert Lowell: A Collection of Critical Essays*. Englewood Cliffs, N.J.: Prentice-Hall, 1968.

Perloff, Marjorie. "Death by Water: The Winslow Elegies of Robert Lowell," *ELH*, 34:116–40 (1967).

Ricks, Christopher. "The Three Lives of Robert Lowell," *New Statesman*, 69:496–97 (March 26, 1965).

Rosenthal, M. L. *The New Poets: American and British Poetry since World War II*. New York: Oxford University Press, 1967.

Seidel, Frederick. "An Interview," *The Paris Review Interviews, Second Series*, edited by Malcolm Cowley. New York: Viking Press, 1963.

Staples, H. B. *Robert Lowell*. New York: Farrar, Straus and Cudahy, 1962.

Waggoner, Hyatt H. *American Poets from the Puritans to the Present*. Boston: Houghton Mifflin, 1968.

Wilbur, Richard, and others. "On Robert Lowell's 'Skunk Hour,'" in *The Contemporary Poet as Artist and Critic*, edited by Anthony Ostroff. Boston and Toronto: Little, Brown, 1964.

Woodson, Thomas. "Robert Lowell's 'Hawthorne,' Yvor Winters and the American Literary Tradition," *American Quarterly*, 19:575–82 (1967).

—*JAY MARTIN*

Mary McCarthy

1912-

MARY McCarthy has so far written six novels, as well as eleven books of other kinds, and though all the novels are not equally successful, each has so much life and truth, and is written in a prose so spare, vigorous, and natural, and yet at the same time so witty, graceful, and, in a certain way, poetic, that it becomes a matter for wonder that she is not generally named among the finest American novelists of her period. She is much admired, of course, and has achieved a best seller, but that is not the same thing. The reason, I think, is that she is a sort of neoclassicist in a country of romantics. The sprightliness and detachment of her prose, her preference for sense over sensibility, her satirical eye for the hidden ego in our intellectual pretensions are qualities we are not comfortable with in this country. They may amuse, but they also antagonize. And they don't, among all our heaven-storming Titans, seem Important. At any rate, whatever the reason, the qualities and meanings that lie beneath her sparkling surface tend, even by admiring critics, to be misconceived. Her novels have been called "essayistic," for instance—designed to persuade us of ideas rather than to present living characters and felt experiences. And their subject is often supposed to be a supercilious, zestfully destructive view of people she dislikes, a view unredeemed by any examples of the humanly admirable— except in the heroines who represent herself. These charges are so common, in fact, that it may be useful to begin with a preliminary answer to each.

As to the first, though she has written mainly about her own class of American intellectuals, people who try to live by ideas or to give the appearance of doing so, and has therefore naturally admitted the play of ideas into her stories, her chief concerns have always been psychological, emotional, and above all, moral, the concerns of the novelist. Whenever her characters express ideas, something of more urgent human interest is also going on, whether they know it or not. And though her novels, like most of those which are nowadays taken seriously, are meaningfully organized, it is no simple polemical formula that turns out to be their meaning. It is, rather, the kind of vision, precisely the novelist's, which moves us, which enlarges our sympathies, and which brings us closer to a complex reality. The fact is, if one remembers her novels freshly at all, it is surely characters and not ideas which their titles bring first to mind —the man in the Brooks Brothers shirt, Macdougal Macdermott, Will Taub, Henry Mulcahy, Domna Rejnev, Miles Murphy, Warren Coe, the girls in "the group" and certain of their men and their parents. In novels these days, Miss McCarthy has complained, "there are hardly any people," only "sensibility" and "sensation," but her own have been an exception. Moreover, though she is of course right in noting the enormous difference between her art and that of the novelist she says she would most like to resemble, Tolstoi, yet her admiration for the godlike realist is reflected at least in the way her intentions are always buried deep inside a flesh of vividly rendered particulars. The concrete world of her people, their tics of behavior, their ways of talking—a precise notation of these gives her work throughout the special authority of the visible and the audible. Indeed, her eye for the particular qualities of things makes half the charm of her style, where it adds to the more sober virtues deriving from her intelligence and honesty a flashing witty poetry of metaphor.

As for that other notion, that she is a heartless satirist whose chief interest is to demonstrate her own superiority to the silliness of her victims—this is just as mistaken. While she does make characters out of people she regards as morally weak or ugly or dangerous, and makes them with a bold thrust toward grotesque extremes that recalls another writer she admires, Dickens, the norms of sense or decency which such people violate are equally vivid in her novels. We see these norms both in the passionate indignation between her lines and in the large number of her characters who cannot live without struggling toward them or becoming their champions. In fact, it is precisely one of her distinctions that she has succeeded in creating good people—even out of twentieth-century intellectuals!—who are at once convincing and attractive. (Her Domna Rejnev is a delightful young woman.) It should be added, however, that the characters she values are not necessarily intellectuals. On the contrary, they may be, like Warren Coe, the kind of people at whom her clever, learned heroines tend to smile. And we must add also, what is equally true and equally unnoticed by the run of her critics, that the heroine who represents herself is often, for all her cleverness, the character most roughly treated by the ironical author. If she ends by coming out all right, it is with a rightness reached after much agonizing error, and itself riddled with imperfections sadly accepted.

Amid the currently fashionable criticism of fiction, a kind which concentrates so hard on technique or symbols that it often bypasses what technique and symbols are intended to serve, Miss McCarthy's ideas on the subject can be liberatingly sensible. Here (from "Settling the Colonel's Hash" in *On the Contrary*) is a remark that may be taken as an introduction to the present study:

"It is now considered very old-fashioned and tasteless to speak of an author's 'philosophy of life' as something that can be harvested from his work. Actually, most of the great authors did have a 'philosophy of life' which they were eager to communicate to the public; this was one of their motives for writing. And to disentangle a moral philosophy from a work that evidently contains one is far less damaging to the author's purpose and the integrity of his art than to violate his imagery by symbol-hunting, as though reading a novel were a sort of paper-chase.

"The images of a novel or a story belong, as it were, to a family, very closely knit and inseparable from each other; the parent 'idea' of a story or a novel generates events and images all bearing a strong family resemblance. And to understand a story or a novel, you must look for the parent 'idea,' which is usually in plain view, if you read quite carefully and literally what the author says."

The same thing is surely true of the serious writer's total oeuvre: all his works will, for the same reason, show this family resemblance. Since Miss McCarthy, in spite of the abundant social reality in her novels, is as autobiographical a novelist as Fitzgerald or Hemingway, we can best approach the "parent idea" underlying her career by beginning with her life. And the first point to make is that it has been a life blessed—and cursed—with an unusual amount of freedom. Orphaned at six, she was taken care of for years by coldly cruel guardians and later by grandparents who were kind but detached. Doris Grumbach tells us that a former Vassar classmate, now a psychiatrist, remembers that at college Mary McCarthy was " 'aloof, independent, irrelevant . . . lonely,' seemingly rootless because she, unlike most of the others, had no real family she had to please. 'She appeared to be much freer than we were and this fascinated and frightened us.' " Such freedom resembles, it is true, the freedom to think and do as they wish that many clever young people of our time claim as a right, but for the orphaned Mary McCarthy it was a condition more serious than a bright student's pose. She was really free, and had to experience what this meant in her deepest nature. And the kind of freedom that comes from having no family to please—is it not a freedom from those pressures, loyalties, urgencies of feeling that, though they hamper us, also give us a sense of who we are, of what is real, of what is right? To lack such direction can mean one is at the mercy of merely plausible ideas on such matters, ideas which decent people hope to choose according to their truth, of course, but which, amid the multiple "truths" life offers, even the best of us are in danger of choosing with our vanity, or our fear, or our lust. To be directed by external authority has its own dangers; these are the dangers of freedom.

Her work is about the painful mixed blessing of freedom for her kind of people—for in-

tellectuals—and in particular, about how hard it has been for intellectuals in our time to behave decently and humanly. For to be free and clever has often meant only to be able to escape from difficult, limiting reality into the realm of flattering abstractions. And yet—for I have said that to speak of what she dislikes is to speak of only half her subject—if she shows what makes her kind go wrong, she shows just as vividly what makes them go right. She shows that sometimes, even in intellectuals free to please themselves, there arises a love for reality that is greater than love of self. This development, because it means that the self must be willing to suffer for something it values more than its own ease, can be one of the moving and beautiful events of a human life—it can be heroic. At any rate, the conflict between these two tendencies of the mind is at the center of all Miss McCarthy's novels. Because this conflict is her own, her reports on it have the variety, complexity, and intensity of personal experience. But because the freedom to live by ideas, ideas which may lead away from the real as well as toward it, is what distinguishes the whole class of twentieth-century intellectuals, her tales of the troubled Mary McCarthy heroine have developed naturally into social satire.

The exquisitely written *Memories of a Catholic Girlhood* (1957) reveals how deeply rooted Miss McCarthy's stories are in her own life. She tells us that she was born in Seattle in 1912 to a Protestant mother, whose own mother was Jewish and who accepted her husband's religion, and a Catholic father. The mother was beautiful. The father was a partial invalid, irresponsible as a breadwinner, but handsome, charming, a delight to his children with his stories and presents. When she was six both parents died in one week from flu. The rich McCarthy grandparents, whose Catholicism was a "sour and baleful doctrine in which old hates and rancors had been stewing for generations, with ignorance proudly stirring the pot," placed her and her three brothers in a house as poor as their own was luxurious and under the guardianship of a couple of Dickensian monsters, a great-aunt and a German-American husband. The theme of the first chapters of *Memories* is injustice, and Miss McCarthy describes the needless poverty, the ugliness, the sadistic, self-righteous beatings with an unaccustomed, if controlled, intensity of rage and pity.

At the age of eleven she was rescued and taken to Seattle by her other grandfather, also rich, but a model of the Protestant virtues. To cite qualities she later found he shared with Julius Caesar, Grandfather Preston was "just, laconic, severe, magnanimous, detached." She was no longer wretched, but she remained an outsider—in her new home, whose moral standards were oppressively high; in the Catholic convent school she went to first, where she lost her faith; later in a public school, among the school "hearties"; finally in an Episcopal boarding school, where she was set apart by her "brilliance" and her independence. And here, at sixteen, she underwent experiences which, as described in the chapter of *Memories* called "The Figures in the Clock," clearly foreshadow the characteristic moral vision, and even the organizing "conflicts," of the fiction to come.

In this chapter it is a conflict between the wicked conspirator Catiline and Julius Caesar. Acting the part of Catiline in a play written by her Latin teacher, she made a sensation by reading her lines so as to *vindicate* the rebel, to champion his self-willed brilliance—and thereby her own—against mere dull law and order. Shortly after this, however, a strange thing happened. Under the guidance of Miss Gowrie (the fictitious name she gives her teacher), the girl fell in love with Julius Caesar! "The sensa-

tion was utterly confounding. All my previous crushes had been products of my will, constructs of my personal convention, or projections of myself, the way Catiline was. This came from without and seized me . . . the first piercing contact with an impersonal reality happened to me through Caesar." She and her teacher loved that mind "immersed in practical life as in some ingenious detective novel, that wished always to show you how anything was done and under what disadvantages . . . the spirit of justice and scientific inquiry that reigned over the *Commentaries*." "Justice, good will, moderation, and *uncommon fidelity*," why, she asks, quoting Caesar's praise of a conquered Gaul loyal to himself, "should these substantives of virtue have stirred the Seminary's Catiline? At the time I was sublimely unaware that my fortifications had been breached, that the forces of law and order were pacifying the city while the rebel standard still waved on the ramparts."

What she loved in Caesar hints not only at the moral values in the novels to come, but at their art—their way with details and their way with sentences. But we are not done with the meaning of this rich chapter. Another insight alternates with the first "like the two little wooden weather figures in a German clock, one of which steps out as the other swings back into the works, in response to atmospheric pressures." The "good Gaul" whose loyalty to Caesar she and Miss Gowrie admired was after all a "quisling," traitorously loyal to his people's conqueror. Later, when "bad Gauls" merged in her mind with those who resisted Hitler, she was angry with her Latin teacher for having steered her wrong. But then, later still, it came to her that it had been Miss Gowrie who had seen to it that her Catiline costume was especially gorgeous—she has at last "an eerie sense that Miss Gowrie, unsuspected by me, was my co-conspirator." It appears that for her teacher too that preference for Caesar, for "impersonal reality" and law and order over the lawless ego, was haunted by the contradictory possibility that the ego can have a self-justifying beauty, or that law and order, with changes in "atmospheric pressure," that is, in the context, may serve error, and the self-asserting individual be in the right. And in her note to the chapter Miss McCarthy tells us that this conflict is rooted in her inheritance. "Caesar, of course, was my [Preston] grandfather . . . Catiline was my McCarthy ancestors. . . . To my surprise, I chose Caesar and the rule of law. This does not mean that the seesaw between these two opposed forces terminated; one might say, in fact, that it only began during my last years in the Seminary when I recognized the beauty of an ablative absolute and of a rigorous code of conduct."

A word about her life after the Seminary. For a summer she studied acting; then, from 1929 to 1933, she attended Vassar College. In 1933 she married the actor and unsuccessful playwright Harold Johnsrud, and began to write reviews for the *New Republic* and the *Nation*. Her essay "My Confession" tells how at this time she was drawn into political controversy by her indignation at the smug dishonesty of American Communists and especially by their defense of the "Moscow trials," in which the exiled Trotsky was being discredited by an elaborate structure of lies. In 1936, her marriage dissolved, she lived in Greenwich Village, wrote reviews, and worked for an art dealer. A year later she began to write a monthly "Theater Chronicle" for the recently revived *Partisan Review*. In these essays there was much good sense and some affected and excessive rigidity of principle, as she herself admits in a preface to the book *Sights and Spectacles* (1956) in which they were later collected. In 1938 she married the critic Edmund Wilson. The marriage ended

after seven years, but he was the father of her only child, Reuel, and it was at Wilson's suggestion that she began to write fiction. Her first story, "Cruel and Barbarous Treatment," became the opening chapter of *The Company She Keeps*. For two years she was a college teacher—at Bard in 1945–46 and at Sarah Lawrence in 1948–49—and her history since then, aside from her marriage to Bowden Broadwater, which lasted from 1946 to 1961, and to James West in 1961, is mainly the history of her books.

In 1956, along with *Sights and Spectacles*, she published the first of two works on Italian cities, *Venice Observed*, and in 1959 the second, *The Stones of Florence*. Each book is an account of the city's history, architecture, art, and people. The first is the slighter, the more personal and anecdotal, the second the more sober and scholarly, and at the same time the more passionate: The art and architecture of Florence moved her intensely. This latter book, in fact, is surprisingly readable for so scholarly a work, and the reason is only in part the lively, taut, and elegant style. Even more important is her clear concern throughout with the "human interest" of the history and the art.

In 1962 the essays she had been writing since 1946 on a variety of subjects were collected in the volume *On the Contrary*. These differ in quality. Most valuable are her contributions to the political debates of the time—on the Moscow trials, on McCarthyism, on Communists in the schools—and her essays on fiction and drama, "Settling the Colonel's Hash," "The Fact in Fiction," "Characters in Fiction," and "The American Realist Playwrights." Of the latter group it is enough to say here that they constitute, by implication, a defense of the kind of art she herself has practiced. This is a realistic art, which gives us what might usefully be called *samples* of reality rather than *symbols* of it. (She herself speaks of "natural symbolism.") For the reader to do justice to such work, he needs to be alert rather to human matters—the psychological or moral meaning of actions or tones—than to literary allusions and strategies.

We are now ready for the novels, on which her permanent reputation will surely rest. The first of these, *The Company She Keeps* (1942), consists of six chapters published originally as stories in magazines. In a very interesting and useful *Paris Review* interview, Miss McCarthy has said that though she had originally intended them as separate stories, "about halfway through I began to think of them as a kind of unified story. The same character kept reappearing, and so on. I decided finally to call it a novel in that it does in a sense tell *a* story, one story." The reappearing character is Margaret Sargent, of whom we learn at the end that she was the daughter of a tolerant, intelligent Protestant father and a beautiful Catholic mother, and was brought up as a Catholic, after her mother's early death, by a vulgar and bigoted Catholic aunt. Not only has Miss McCarthy given her heroine a background substantially like her own; she has told us herself that the stories are all autobiographical except one, "Portrait of the Intellectual as a Yale Man." In fact, the book is remarkable for the honesty of its self-exposure, an exposure which dares to include the ignoble and the humiliating and which shows a kind of reckless passion for the truth that is to remain an important element of her talent.

This passion for the truth not only provides the motive power behind the self-exposure in these tales. It turns out to be their underlying subject as well. The author has suggested, and it has been repeated by many critics, that the "one story" of the book is that of the heroine's vain search, amid her many identities, for some real identity underlying them all. But this search seems actually to be less important

than her moral development, a development of which the ultimate goal is not to know what she is but to behave as an adult should. What we mainly watch as her story unfolds is Miss Sargent's increasingly desperate struggle, against all the temptations to falsehood in the intellectual life of her time, to stop lying and to live by the truth.

She begins far enough from any truth. In the first chapter, "Cruel and Barbarous Treatment," which is not so much a story as a witty satire on nameless generalized types and their typical behavior, she is a married "Woman with a Secret" delighting in an affair with a "Young Man" chiefly because it "was an opportunity, unparalleled in her experience, for exercising feelings of superiority over others." Play-acting irresponsibly with life's realities, she reduces them to fashionable clichés that minister to her vanity. The second chapter, "Rogue's Gallery," in which Miss Sargent works for a rogue who runs an art gallery and appears as a naïve, good-natured foil for her colorful con man of a boss, seems a mere exercise in the Dickensian picturesque. But in the third the book's deeper story continues: the heroine's play-acting is complicated by an opposing impulse. "The Man in the Brooks Brothers Shirt" is an account of how Miss Sargent, now seen in the role of poised, sophisticated New York intellectual, is drawn into an affair with a businessman on a cross-country train trip because she enjoys playing that role before such an audience. And yet, showing off an advance copy of a new book, she wonders uneasily "if her whole way of life had been assumed for purposes of ostentation." When the man speaks shrewdly about her past, she leans forward. "Perhaps at last she had found him, the one she kept looking for, the one who could tell her what she was really like. . . . If she once knew, she had no doubt that she could behave perfectly." Then there is her horrified shame, when she awakens in his compartment, at the drunken sex of the night before which she gradually remembers. (This is the first of those cool "shocking" notations of the unattractive particulars of "romantic" episodes for which Miss McCarthy has won a certain notoriety, though far from being exploitations of sex, they seem expressions of a puritanical disgust.) Finally, she becomes aware of a reluctance to leave the man, who, falling in love with her, had changed in her eyes from the vulgar businessman type to an actual and attractive person; and at this "a pang of joy went through her as she examined her own sorrow and found it to be real." The affair dies away after the trip, and the story ends with both falling back into the stereotypes from which they had briefly emerged, but Margaret Sargent has acquired substance as a character with the disclosure that she is divided, like the rest of us, and that the hunger of her intellectual's vanity is opposed by a hunger for reality.

In "The Genial Host" we see this new Miss Sargent again. She is now the dinner guest of one Pflaumen, who is shown as having repressed both his natural tendency to fat and hairiness and his natural personality of a Jewish paterfamilias to become the elegant familiar and host of clever, fashionable, successful people. Moreover, this reality-avoider collects his guests for their "allegorical possibilities," that is, for the chic intellectual positions to which they have sacrificed their own reality. Thus, Margaret, hotly defending Trotsky against the party's Stalinist, and delighted at the effect she is making, is horrified to note that Pflaumen is beaming at her for performing as expected, while the party's one honest man, a poor young Jewish lawyer, is applauding ironically. The story ends in another capitulation: she dare not yet rebel against Pflaumen and the falsenesses by which she sings for her suppers, she

is still too "poor, loverless, lonely." But in the next, "Portrait of the Intellectual as a Yale Man," though she is still in need, she has ceased to capitulate.

This story is mainly about the Yale Man, who, though naïve and second-rate, has been welcomed onto the Stalinist-dominated weekly magazine the *Liberal* because he comes as a healthy, happy, clean-cut, average American, a type rare among them. This was a time—the thirties—when out of loyalty to the ideal of communism a large proportion of the intellectual establishment had accepted so many of the lies and brutalities of the Stalin dictatorship that they had lost the sense of the relevance to politics, and even to life, of the ordinary decencies. Such people lied in defense of the Communist party's shifts in policy or vilified the opposition rather than debate with it, and did both with a sincere feeling of virtue. Jim Barnett, the Yale Man, is not one of these; he tries to be honest, but he is able to make a living as a radical political commentator only because his shallowness is precisely suited to the intellectual climate of this milieu, from which the Stalinists have largely excluded reality.

Margaret Sargent was put into this story, says Miss McCarthy, "because she had to be in it," that is, for the sake of the unity of the book to come, but her role turns out to be crucial, for she is there as an eruption of integrity into that world of blur and lies. Now when she defends Trotsky, it is among Stalinist editors who can fire her from the magazine job she needs. "You had to admire her courage," Jim thinks, "for undertaking something that cost her so much." Even her way of taking Jim for a lover is significantly different from her past behavior. She submits to this married man's sudden overpowering lust—and perhaps to her own as well—with a "disconsolate smile"—no play-acting here. Jim quits his job indignantly when she is fired, and in this time of proud excitement, he gets an idea for an important book. But the effort to write the book and to live on that moral peak is really beyond his means. He gives up both, gets a handsome job on the conservative magazine *Destiny*, and though he continues to send checks to the American Civil Liberties Union, he grows increasingly impatient with opinionated unsuccessful left-wing intellectuals. And for Margaret he comes to feel a kind of hatred. Pathetic though she is in her "too tense" clinging to her truth, in her unsuccess, she is somehow triumphant. In the story's beautifully written last pages she haunts him as a reminder of the dead illusion of his youth, the illusion that he could be free of "the cage of his own nature" and better than himself.

In the last story, "Ghostly Father, I Confess," after five years of an unhappy second marriage to an architect apparently congenial but really authoritarian and unimaginative, Margaret is spending an hour on a psychoanalyst's couch. She has been sent by her husband, who is fed up with the way she uses her "wonderful scruples as an excuse for acting like a bitch." And now, though she disapproves of psychoanalysis, whose conclusions can never be proved wrong since all disagreement is mere resistance, and considers her doctor a limited man, she finds herself drawn into an agonizing search for the cause of her misery and bad behavior, for it is also a search for the "meaning" that will redeem her life from "gibberish." The story is crammed with the up-welling, emotion-charged facts of her life —from the childhood passed between her father's rationalism and her aunt's vulgarities to the second marriage, in which she feels herself suffocating amid such stylish middle-class culture-objects as "her white pots of ivy, her Venetian blinds, her open copy of a novel by Kafka . . . each in its own patina of social

anxiety." Miss McCarthy seems to have thrown boldly into the story the confusion of her own life. Yet it moves with a nightmarish coherence amid the chaos, and, in fact, what she understands at the end makes the story a unity and a fitting conclusion to the book's whole development.

The story is about the pressure on Margaret Sargent to accept the life of the intellectually sophisticated middle class which she detests. And for that life she is now to be made fit by a mode of "therapy" which is presented as the most insidious of all its ways of avoiding reality. The object of the therapy is to perform a "perfectly simple little operation." First the consciousness is put to sleep by "the sweet, optimistic laughing-gas of science (you are not bad, you are merely unhappy . . . poor Hitler is a paranoiac, and that dirty fornication in a hotel room, why, that, dear Miss Sargent, is a 'relationship')." Then the doctor cuts out "the festering conscience, which was of no use to you at all, and was only making you suffer." But to have a conscience is to remain aware of what is outside one's wishes, and to prefer the truth, however painful, over lies, however gratifying. Under the pressure of the idea that she is unhappy merely because she is ill, "her own sense of truth was weakening. This and her wonderful scruples were all she had in the world, and they were slipping away." And it is this that makes her most miserable. She can't behave as she should, but not to know when she does evil, and not to mind, is to lose her grip on reality and to shrink from a healthy adult into an invaild or a child.

The story ends with an apparent inconclusiveness that is really, as I have said, a sufficient conclusion, both to the story and the book. She is almost persuaded by her doctor that she can be good and free and strong inside her marriage, which is to say, that all can yet be well at no painful cost, when she remembers a dream she had begun to tell him earlier. In this dream she had enabled herself to accept the embraces of a Nazi type by pretending that he was really rather Byronic. As she walks away from the doctor's office, feeling the hateful expected tug of an attraction to him, she suddenly understands the dream. It has told her that all will *not* be well, that unable to love herself except through the love of men, she will again seek a new love to rescue her from past failures and will again snatch at it blindly and perhaps unscrupulously. But though in the dream she pretended the Nazi was a Byron, "she could still detect her own frauds. At the end of the dream, her eyes were closed, but the inner eye had remained alert. . . . 'Oh my God,' she said . . . 'do not let them take this away from me. If the flesh must be blind, let the spirit see. Preserve me in disunity.' "

Thus is completed the "one story" of Margaret Sargent. Beginning as a manipulator and falsifier of reality, she is now its true lover, who would rather suffer than pretend and whose suffering, because it means the clarity of mind to see the truth and the courage to face it, is the measure of a new dignity.

It is no doubt true, as Elizabeth Hardwick has suggested, that all such "frank" confession is in part self-exculpation. But Miss McCarthy's frankness in confessing weakness and error in this book seems to earn her the right to move on, for a completer truth indeed, to the virtues of her defects. At any rate, the portrait of Margaret Sargent carries conviction, and her struggle toward honesty has a permanent relevance to our experience.

Certain themes in the first book are repeated in *Cast a Cold Eye* (1950), a collection of four stories and three early versions of chapters of her *Memories*. In "The Weeds" is treated somberly, and in "The Friend of the Family" with bitter humor, the sort of marriage seen in "Ghostly Father." It is the marriage that destroys the individual's integrity, his troublesome loyalty to the truth of his own nature. "The Old Men," less successful than the other two but interesting for its meanings, tells how a young man who has long been uncertain of his own identity comes to feel that the self is no more than a *"point du départ"* for "impersonations," and that reality, the actual, is "pornography" and to be avoided. At this, "blithe and ready to live, selfishly and inconsiderately," he sings out the Yeats epitaph which gives the book its title, and shortly afterwards, as if for want of any reason to live, he abruptly dies. It thus appears that the "cold eye" which reviewers have generally supposed the author meant as her own is meant in fact to describe what she most reprobates, that indifference to what is outside the self which deprives the self of reality and makes life pointless.

Miss McCarthy has defended *The Oasis* (1949) from the charge that it is not a novel by insisting that it was not intended to be, that it is a *conte philosophique*. This explains its lack of action, for instead of plot we have slight episodes explored for their large meanings and characters revealed less by what they do than in long satirical descriptions. But it cannot eliminate the sense that the tale's developments, which ought after all to arise by an inner necessity, are sometimes arbitrarily asserted, as if to get things moving. And yet the reminder of an elegant eighteenth-century prose form does point to qualities that will keep the tale, in spite of its imperfections, interesting for a long time. The satirical descriptions do not merely imitate but genuinely duplicate the qualities of eighteenth-century prose masters—the psychological insight, the general wisdom, the witty, epigrammatic, gracefully balanced sentences.

The Oasis is the story of a group of New York intellectuals—based apparently on well-known friends of the author, but to the rest of us quite recognizable as contemporary types—

who, shortly after World War II, form a colony called Utopia in the Taconic Mountains of New York State. The colonists fall mainly into two factions. The "purists" hope the colony will illustrate "certain notions of justice, freedom, and sociability" derived from their Founder, a saintly Italian anarchist lost in "a darkened city of Europe." This group is led by Macdougal Macdermott, a man who rightly senses that he does not naturally belong to "that world of the spirit" which he yearns to enter, but who, "ten years before . . . had made the leap into faith and sacrificed $20,000 a year and a secure career as a paid journalist for the intangible values that eluded his empirical grasp. He had moved down town into Bohemia, painted his walls indigo, dropped the use of capital letters and the practice of wearing a vest" and become the editor of a "libertarian magazine." The "realists," on the other hand, have come only for a holiday from the pressures of real life. They look upon "conspicuous goodness" like the Founder's as a "form of simple-mindedness on a par with vegetarianism, and would have refused admission to Heaven on the ground that it was full of greenhorns and cranks." Moreover, they find absurd the assumption of "human freedom" which underlies all that the purists believe, for they are inheritors of Marxian "scientific socialism," and though they had discarded the dialectic and repudiated the Russian Revolution, "the right of a human being to *think* that he could resist history, environment, class structure, psychic conditioning was something they denied him with all the ferocity of their own pent-up natures and disappointed hopes." And since "ideological supremacy" has become "essential to their existence," they look forward with pleasure to the colony's failure. They do, however, wish it to fail convincingly, of its own foolishness, and this seduces them into unusually good behavior. Soon Will Taub,

their leader, finds that he participates "in the forms of equity with increasing confidence, and though of course he did not take any of it *seriously*, his heavy and rather lowering nature performed the unaccustomed libertarian movements with a feeling of real sprightliness and wondering self-admiration, as if he had been learning to dance."

In Will Taub we have the first full-fledged example of the enemy in Miss McCarthy's world, the Other to all that she values. He is one who is at home only in the realm of ideas, who is flat-footed in his behavior with children, women—in all non-intellectual relations—who feels pain at the very word "Jew" because "his Jewishness [was] a thing about himself which he was powerless to alter and which seemed to reduce him therefore to a curious dependency on the given." And this rejection of the "given," the real, on behalf of a world of ideas where he can reign supreme involves too a rejection of moral responsibility. It is for the realists a felt oddity in Utopia that "here they were answerable for their deeds to someone and not simply to an historical process." And Taub is even capable, like the later Henry Mulcahy, of beginning to believe his own lie (that an embarrassingly cowardly reaction of his is due to former police persecution) in order to maintain his cherished supremacy.

These two characters, and Joe Lockman, the go-getting businessman who comes to Utopia determined to get more spiritual profit out of it than anyone else, are the tale's most vivid portraits. But it is a fourth, Katy Norell, to whom its chief events tend to happen and out of whose responses its meanings emerge. Katy, a teacher of Greek, suffers from "a strong will and a weak character," an awkward compulsion to tell the truth even when it aggravates her problems, and a readiness to feel guilty when things go wrong. Though it was her "instinctive opinion . . . that the past could be

altered and actions, like words, 'taken back,' "
her husband's disgust with her, on one occasion
when it seems serious, gives her a frightening
glimpse of life "as a black chain of consequence, in which nothing was lost, forgot, forgiven, redeemed, in which the past was permanent and the present slipping away from
her." This character, weak but scrupulous, who
wishes life were easy but can't shut out the
perception that it is hard, is, of course, a sister
of Margaret Sargent as well as of the later
Martha Sinnott, though, unlike the others, she
pays for representing her author's inner life by
being one of the less vivid characters in her
book. But it is out of her inner contradictions
that the book's closing insights come. These
insights are initiated by the last of several challenges to the colony's "sociability"—the stealing of their strawberries by some rough inter-
lopers, whom Katy herself, frightened when her
pleading is answered with threatening gestures,
demands be ejected by force. Taub taunts her
with her contradiction, her yielding to "human
nature," and at this, lulled or liberated by the
dinner wine, she begins to understand. They
did wrong, she thinks, to cling to the strawberries without needing them—it was only the
idea of the strawberries they really cared about.
They had let "mental images" possess them as
the idea of sex dominates the mind in pornography. But the mind should stick to its own objects, "love, formal beauty, virtue"; they should
not have tried to make real things dance to
the mind's tune. And this is only a small example of their fundamental error. As the tale
draws to an end, she realizes that Utopia is
going to fail because of their wish to "*embody*
virtue.*" If they had been content to manufacture, not virtue, but furniture, it might have
survived.

It is a rueful, if not tragic, conclusion. To
replace the stubborn complexity of people and
society with ideas is the mistake of both parties
in Utopia. The cynics who insist that our behavior is determined by history and the "idealists" who believe so easily that man can be
what he wishes to be are shown to be equally
removed from the life we actually live. And
yet those like Katy Norell, who see through this
error, who feel and suffer life up close, are
better off, if at all, only because it is better to
understand. For their superiority consists
mainly in desiring a virtue they know they can
never attain.

"And search for truth amid the groves of
academe"—this quotation from Horace prefaces Miss McCarthy's next novel. The search
for truth, and the human defects that hinder it,
we have seen to be her permanent subject. Now
again the private concern becomes a way of
understanding the large public matters that her
life has brought before her: this time the political liberalism of the "witch-hunting" era of
Joseph McCarthy (the 1950's) when the reactionary right, not the Communist left, frightened or confused intellectuals into self-betrayal;
and progressive education, with its own less
obvious hindrances to the search for truth. But
The Groves of Academe (1952) is her first real
or completely successful novel because now, for
the first time, she has found a setting, characters, and a plot that dramatize both her private
and her public subjects in one lively story.
With this novel, moreover, her resemblance to
Jane Austen, already evident in the irony,
sanity, and grace of her prose, and the combination of moral concern and tough intelligence in her approach to people, grows even
more striking. She gives us now, in that same
prose, a group of characters vividly and comically idiosyncratic, with a wonderful comic
villain in the center. She gives us a plot which
evolves with perfect illuminating logic from
the moral qualities of the characters. And she
gives us the peculiarly Austenish pleasure of
watching good, intelligent, and articulate peo-

ple work their way through much painful error to the relief of shared understanding.

The plot is a most ingenious stroke of wit. Its humor is based on the fact that where in the outside, non-intellectual world it had become dangerous in this period to have once been a Communist, in the world of liberal intellectuals a man persecuted for a Communist past had become almost a holy martyr and entitled to defense. Miss McCarthy's joke is that when the incompetent, irresponsible (though learned and brilliant) Henry Mulcahy is about to be let go by the liberal president of Jocelyn College, he is able to win the support of his colleagues by pretending to have *been* a Communist. The joke reaches its climax when an old anarchist acquaintance of Mulcahy's is interrogated by President Hoar and a faculty committee about whether their colleague really had this claim on their respect and protection, and the anarchist, who "sings," betrays the shocking secret that Mulcahy's Communist past had been a lie. Upon which, in an explosion of topsy-turvyness, Mulcahy comes raging to Hoar like the righteous victim of a witch-hunt, and using the secret investigation as evidence that the president has betrayed his liberal principles, forces *him* to resign.

It is a pity to tell the punch line of such a story, but the fault is less grave than it might be because the fun here lies in the characters and in the fine detail by which they and their world are kept always very much alive. Most of all the story belongs to the magnificently repulsive Henry Mulcahy, in whom the kind of intellectual dishonor which we have already begun to recognize as Miss McCarthy's chief target is carried to breathtaking extremes. It is moreover a special triumph of the book that she has shown us this comic monster from the inside (she calls the technique "ventriloquism," as George Henry Lewes once wrote of Jane Austen's "dramatic ventriloquism"), mimicking

his mode of thought so fully and felicitously that it is impossible, for all his excesses, not to recognize him as real.

In Henry Mulcahy, a pear-shaped, soft-bellied father of four, Ph.D., contributor to serious magazines, Guggenheim Fellow, etc., the intellectual's besetting sins—his lust for supremacy and his preference for flattering ideas over mere facts—undergo a marvelous efflorescence. He not only identifies himself with Joyce, Kafka, and other "sacred untouchables of the modern martyrology"; he comes to regard disloyalty to himself as "apostasy," and the dismayed Domna Rejnev discovers that "behind Joyce . . . is the identification with Christ." At the same time his great lie is to him the work of an artist, who creates out of life's raw material "a figurative truth more true than the data of reality." (Remembering vaguely that he had once heard the phrase "heart murmur" used of someone in his family, he is soon exclaiming to himself—sincerely!— that he holds Hoar "personally responsible for the life of his wife and/or son.") And, when the defeated president finally asks him, "Are you a conscious liar or a self-deluded hypocrite?" Mulcahy replies, "A Cretan says, all Cretans are liars." Having thus put in question the very possibility of finding truth, he frankly declares, "I'm not concerned with truth. . . . I'm concerned with justice."

The faculty for whom Mulcahy has thus set a special problem in truth-seeking are all sharply realized, but those who share the center of the stage with Mulcahy are two teachers who are most different from him, and who bring what Miss McCarthy honors as effectively to life as he re-creates what she despises. Domna Rejnev and John Bentkoop are also intellectuals but to them the truth matters more than their own success and comfort. In Miss Rejnev, beautiful twenty-three-year-old daughter of Russian émigrés, whose "finely cut, mobile nostrils quivered during a banal conversation as though, literally, seeking air," and who, in a crisis, asks herself "What would Tolstoy say?" this intellectual passion is endearingly childlike in its ardor and even in its vanity. The ardor we see when she hears of Mulcahy's "persecution": "Her strange, intent eyes were shining; she tossed her head angrily and the dark, clean hair bobbed; she clicked her pocket-lighter and drew in on a cigarette. 'This cannot be permitted to happen,' she declared quickly, amid puffs of smoke. 'One simply refuses it and tells Maynard Hoar so.' She jumped up, knocking a book off the desk, and seized her polo coat from the coatrack. 'I shall do it myself at once to set an example.' "

And we see the vanity when she warmly praises Mulcahy's learning to silent colleagues out of her pleasure in honoring excellence. "She rather enjoyed the idea that she was sufficiently spendthrift (that is, sufficiently rich in resources)." But this pride is so far from the smug confidence of the self-worshipers that a colleague lets her pour out a passionate argument without interrupting "because he knew her to be honest and presumed that therefore, before she had finished, a doubt would suddenly dart out of her like a mouse from its hole." Sure enough, it is her agonizing recognition not only that she had been wrong about Mulcahy, but that she had been seduced into pretending not to know defects in him which she did know, into a sort of lying, that is to be her climactic experience in the book.

The deep, the metaphysical opposition between Mulcahy's kind and hers emerges during a painful dinner at the Mulcahy home when Domna suddenly learns she has been defending a liar. Uneasy, he tries to recoup by suggesting that, being handsome, she is a "monist," but that unattractive people like himself "know that appearances are fickle. We look to somebody else to discover our imperishable essence." And he asks her if she could love a leper, meaning, as she understands, himself. "If you mean a moral leper, no," she says. "Fair without and foul within has no charm for me. Nor the reverse, for that matter. . . . People whose inside contradicts their outside . . . have neither essence nor existence." Mulcahy, in short, can feel virtuous when he does evil and entitled to loyalty even by those whom he betrays because he believes instinctively in a sort of dualism according to which the concrete world, where actions have consequences and entail responsibilities, can be regarded as mere "appearance"—of secondary importance beside those abstractions (Norine Schmittlapp of *The Group* will call them "intangibles") which his ego can manipulate. The others are like Domna—or like Virginia Bentkoop, who, in a charming touch, though "she had met Domna only once, at a college lecture . . . divined correctly that her feet were wet." They are people who notice and respect the actualities of the world.

This, however, is a progressive college, and these are liberals of the fifties, and the combination has guaranteed Mulcahy's triumph. For, as the novel has also been suggesting, and as one teacher puts it at the end, progressive education means a concern with "faith and individual salvation"—that is, the student's inner quality is considered to be more important than his demonstrated mastery, through hard work, of real subject matter. This has a sinister resemblance to Mulcahy's self-defense that "appearance"—the mere concrete facts of what one is and does—is somehow less important than one's invisible "essence." And it is a view that is plainly akin to the tendency of many liberals of the era to separate "justice," in the words of Mulcahy again, from "truth," to consider scruples that interfered with work for a "good cause" mere ivory tower pedantry. Not that Miss McCarthy fails to make clear that the progressive college and its liberal faculty are right and attractive in many ways, and create a world in which good things can grow as well as bad. But her story makes it even clearer that there is no safety in good intentions when their pursuit requires us to ignore the truth.

Because *The Groves of Academe* is about college teachers, much of its drama comes to us in the clash of explicit ideas amid explicit descriptions of the college world and its intellectual character. For some readers this may sometimes clog or confuse the otherwise lively story. There can be no such objection to *A Charmed Life* (1955), for though this novel is equally rich in meaning, its meaning is more centrally human and expressed more completely by the rushing story alone. And the style, having to argue and explain less, having only to serve the urgent events and emotions, seems lighter, swifter, and richer in Miss McCarthy's characteristic poetry.

Perhaps too the novel is her best so far, the most poignant and powerful under the usual ironic control, because she has here found a subject which dramatizes the conflict among her own most cherished values—that "seesaw" between the demands of the self and those of "impersonal reality"—and which therefore taps her own strongest feelings. This conflict is foreshadowed in a new twist given to her familiar heroine. Martha Sinnott is another woman of mind, another lover of that "impersonal reality," but an element in the type hitherto regarded as only a source of difficulty is now permitted to present fully its own case. For this very clever and learned young playwright is also a woman, as her husband tells us, with "an obstinate childish heart," one to whom reality speaks a "little language" and who cannot bear that it ever utter, in her marriage, what is not true and beautiful and good. She not only insists that life conform to her dream,

but, to make it conform, she dares to act as if, in the words of Katy Norell in her weakness, "the past could be altered and actions, like words, 'taken back.'" Miss McCarthy herself tells us that the novel is about "doubt," and it is true that the doubt which, among contemporary intellectuals, automatically dogs every dream and every piety is important in the story. But even more important is the "obstinate childish heart" by which the doubt is opposed. It is her heroine's "romanticism" that is now this "neoclassic" novelist's subject, and it is that romanticism's tormenting ambiguity which gives the story its wealth of meaning and its almost desperate intensity.

The romantic demand which Martha Sinnott (her last name suggests the McCarthy heroine's usual vain wish) makes upon life acquires a special urgency as the story opens because she has, to finish a play, come back with her second husband to the same Cape Cod town where she had once lived with her first—that is, to a place where her new love and new hope are in danger. New Leeds is dangerous for two reasons. First, because it is a contemporary bohemia, full of artists and intellectuals who live in a state of freedom from tradition, convention, morality, and regular work. These are people who are always divorcing and remarrying, sinking into alcoholism or fighting it, falling down flights of stairs or into wells, and who yet seem to bear a charmed life—nothing seems to hurt them. The reason for this grows clear when Martha, in a moment of near hysteria, cries out that though the New Leedsian will never "admit to knowing anything, until it's been proved," and though he is always setting himself free to do as he pleases by demanding, "Explain to me why not. Give me one reason why not," the fact is, "you don't really doubt. You just ask questions, like a machine. . . . Nobody is really curious because nobody cares what the truth is." The New

Leedsian's life is charmed into unreality by his moral indifference. Nothing really matters to him and so nothing can really hurt him. And that she is right to fear this moral casualness emerges when her husband goes out of town for a night and she is brought together by a friend—for the fun of it—with her ex-husband, Miles Murphy.

Miles is the second danger she fears. He is not quite a typical New Leedsian, since he is capable of disciplined study and work (he is a writer and a psychologist). But he shares with the others their moral qualities. He is unscrupulous, and can cheat not only an insurance company but also a friend. And he is brutally self-regarding and self-assertive: Martha had never been able to resist his utter inability to doubt himself.

The promise in all this is fulfilled when Miles takes her home from the party. After a struggle in which she yields partly to force but even more to the pressure of Miles's conviction that it isn't worth fighting—there is no "reason why not"—she lets him have her. One reason soon appears. Shortly afterward she finds herself pregnant. And though for the ordinary New Leedsian this would not have mattered, since her husband need never know what happened, for Martha it matters to the point of anguish. She cannot bear to have a child of whose paternity she must always be in doubt, or who might give the awful Miles a claim on her, and she cannot bear to base her life with John upon a lie. She decides to have an abortion. And it is in her struggle to determine whether this is right or wrong that we come upon that ambiguity already mentioned.

Such a way of making everything beautiful again has, to begin with, an unsettling resemblance to the ordinary New Leedsian's tendency to evade the consequences of his mistakes, to shirk responsibility. And yet the romantic dream need not always be self-indulgent fantasy. It may be the faith—the religion—which directs and ennobles our lives. In fact, Martha's inner struggle is sometimes described in religious terms. During one terrible night she is besieged and tempted by the devil himself, and at her blackest hour she finds rising to her lips the cry, "Father, let this cup pass from me." *Her* devil, of course, is a New Leedsian. "The medieval temptations, with all the allures of gluttony and concupiscence could not, Martha thought, have been half so trying as the sheer dentist-drill boredom of listening to the arguments of the devil as a modern quasi-intellectual." He utters now all the bright ideas of contemporary sophistication, and his object is to convince her that her vision of the good cannot stand up under rational cross-examination. (In the voice of the psychologist Miles the devil whispers that she doesn't really want a baby and is merely seizing this pretext to get rid of it.)

Her dream is thus opposed by the devil because it is a dream of living for what is right and not for what is merely pleasant. Indeed, among her weapons, as she struggles, is a sense of how the right makes itself known that would have won the approval of the author of *Pilgrim's Progress*. It is worth quoting for its bold recapitulation of an unfashionable morality, as well as for its prose.

"Yet all the while the moral part of Martha knew that she would have to have an abortion because all her inclinations were the other way. The hardest course was the right one; in her experience, this was an almost invariable law. If her nature shrank from the task, if it hid and cried piteously for mercy, that was a sign that she was in the presence of the ethical. She knew this also from the fact that she felt no need to seek advice; what anyone else would do under the circumstances had no bearing. The moral part of her seemed to square its shoulders dissociating itself from the mass of weakness that remained. It was almost a social question, she observed with wan interest: the moral part of her would stop speaking if she did not do what it commanded. But how, she cried out, weeping. How am I to do it, all by myself? There was no answer. The rest of her, the low part, apparently, was supposed to devise the methods. The lawgiver was impractical, a real lady, disdaining to soil its hands, leaving the details to its servants. Martha could have laughed aloud, except for the pride and awe she felt in the acquaintance. She would not have guessed she had so much integrity. In the midst of her squirming and anguish, there was a sensation of pleased surprise."

Thus the past-canceling abortion, which might well have seemed a New Leedsian act, takes on the character of an act of moral heroism, of faith.

Having won the inner battle, she gets the external help she needs from the artist Warren Coe. Warren, a beautifully realized comic character who listens with enormous respect to the "deep" talk of people like Martha and seems created to be her butt, turns out to be her very counterpart in what matters most. What he is and what the others are and, indeed, what the whole story is about is suggested in a delightful discussion of Racine's *Bérénice*, which is read aloud at that fateful New Leeds party. This play, in which the newly crowned emperor Titus must renounce forever his beloved Hebrew queen because a Roman may not marry a foreign monarch, is a tragedy about the conflict between love and duty. And though Miles and Martha came together at first like brilliant equals among ordinary people, it soon appears that it is Warren and not Miles whose ideas she shares. Miles thinks "love is for boys and women," at which Martha raises her brows and Warren, hearing his wife blandly agree, declares, "I could eat that *rug*." When Warren wants to give a hypothetical man who likes to murder old women a reason not to, Martha sympathizes with his wish for universal principles superior to the self, but Miles thinks we do what we can get away with. "The electric chair . . . that's the reason we give him," he tells Warren, and then adds a remark for which one is tempted to forgive him all his crimes: "For you, it's an academic question. If you don't want to murder old women, let it go at that. Don't worry about the other fellow. Live selfishly." The play itself illuminates Martha's position by contrast. It is Racine's view that one can't live the moral life and have one's heart's desire as well. But Martha wants honor *and* she wants her love, she wants both together again as if her one lapse had never occurred; and in the world of Mary McCarthy, as well as of Racine, such a wish has to be vain.

As Martha is driving home from the Coes' with Warren's loan for the abortion in her pocketbook, her husband, who thinks her recent preoccupation has been due to her worry about buying him a proper Christmas present, leaves a note in her typewriter: "Martha, I love you, but life is serious. You must not spend any money on Christmas." And in this moving touch we are surely intended to see that John is not as mistaken in the nature of her errand as he appears on the surface. She does want to buy him a present, and she is buying him something only an "obstinate childish heart," impatient of adult seriousness, would dare to fix on. Moreover, she turns out to be childishly extravagant too—she pays with her life. She is killed in a head-on collision with another car. This death has been called arbitrary, but it is, with a sort of playfulness, given roots in the tale. The other car is driven by a woman who significantly resembles Martha, a woman with a past, a writer, an intellectual, and a "cautionary example of everything Martha was trying not to be," and she is driving—of course—on the wrong side of the road. It is clearly because Martha has been such a woman that she is now at the woman's mercy. With this death, the real, with its chain of ineluctable consequences, asserts its dominion over her romantic dream.

And yet—is Martha only another New Leedsian after all? Obviously, she is not—she bears no charmed life. The saving difference is that she cares, "cares about the truth," and cares enough—Miss McCarthy tells us this in the *Paris Review*—to "put up a real stake." We read near the end, "The past *could* be undone, in certain conditions. It could be bought back, paid for by suffering. That is, it could be redeemed." In fact, what makes her happy in her last moments is the conviction that she is earning back, by means of her suffering, the right to her husband's trust, that whether or not she later tells him what she has done, her ordeal would restore "truth between them again," and "it would be all right." It is apparently thus, and thus alone, that the romantic's "obstinate childish heart" can be reconciled, in the world of Mary McCarthy, with her implacable devotion to "impersonal reality."

The Group (1963) was Miss McCarthy's first best seller, but to many critics it was an embarrassing failure. There were two main objections to the book. The first was that it exhibited a descent, surprising in so "intellectual" a writer, to the preoccupations and the language of women's magazines. The second was that its characters were "dummies," all alike and all created merely to be "humiliated." Now it is true that the success of the book is not uniform throughout, but to speak of that kind of "descent" was possible only to those who took literally what was intended as irony, who ascribed to the author preoccupations and language of which the whole point is that they testify to the limitations of the characters. (Miss McCarthy herself has said that the novel is "as far as I can go in ventriloquism," and that almost all of it is enclosed in "invisible quotation marks.") And that same inattention to significant detail probably accounts for the failure to notice that the novel's many characters are, in fact, sharply distinct from each other. The truth is, *The Group* differs from her early work mainly in its scope. Where each previous novel had been about some problem of a committed intellectual (though her heroines did indeed yearn toward the more centrally human), *The Group* is about the characteristic attitudes and life patterns of a whole social class, as shown in the loves, jobs, marriages, and housekeeping, as well as the clichés of thought and language, of a group of more or less ordinary girls.

To this one must immediately add, however, that the girls in her group *are* upper-middle-class college graduates of the thirties, which is to say they belong to a species one of whose main characteristics is a pride in keeping up with advanced ideas. In fact, these girls are a suitable subject for their author because their chief problem is another version of Miss McCarthy's permanent problem: the danger to the emotional and moral life, when the guidance of family ties and traditions has disappeared, of the freedom to live by ideas. Miss McCarthy has said the novel is about "the loss of faith in progress." This must refer to the author's own loss of such faith, since the characters who have it keep it to the end; it might be more exact to say that the novel shows the poisonous effects of that faith—of the confidence of most of these ordinary girls that they know better how to manage their lives than people ever knew before. In general, their troubles result from the fact that they are cut off by their advanced ideas from the realities of life and their own nature; less up-to-date, they might well have been better and happier people.

The novel consists of chapters written from

the viewpoint and in the language of the chief members of a group of Vassar friends (class of '33) and what unifies their varied, interweaving histories is the story of one of them, Kay Strong. It is at Kay's marriage to Harald Petersen in 1933 that we first meet them, at her funeral seven years later that we see them together for the last time, and it is mainly because of her, her parties, and her often grotesquely pitiful troubles, that the girls keep coming together during the years between. A sketch of what the girls are like and of what they represent should make clear both the qualities and the meaning of the novel.

Kay seems at times an oddly confused conception. Miss McCarthy apparently began by thinking of her as another "sister" to Margaret Sargent; at least, her college personality and her life seem clearly autobiographical. An attractive girl, she came to Vassar from out West, dominated her college friends with her crushing analytical cleverness, was interested in the theater, married a would-be playwright whose bullying made her miserable, longed to be admired and was often awkwardly honest. But the girl whose troubles we now follow— this later Kay quite convincing and alive— lacks any kind of intellectual distinction or even interests and could not conceivably dominate anyone. In fact, her tragedy is precisely that she is a childlike creature, "a stranger and a sojourner" in this time and place, and pathetically driven by a snobbish longing for "nice" things, who depends for her ideas and for her prospects of acquiring identity, self-respect, admiration on a husband who totally fails her. This husband is another of Miss McCarthy's fine monsters of egoism. A second-rate talent whose ambition is due mainly to jealousy of the rich and the successful and whose cheap brilliance is used for self-display, self-exculpation, or the sadistic pleasure of exercising his power over his vulnerable wife, he is shaped to be the perfect frustration of her needs. He denies, for instance, with his ill-bred, outsider's contempt for all tradition, Kay's need for traditional elegance in the home and at the table. Some funny and horrible moments come from their warring ideas of a proper meal.

Priss and Libby are simpler, less interesting types. The first is mousy and stammering, loves neatness and order, and is easily mastered by tidy theories and confident men. Seeing a stain on a friend's dress, she mentally applies Energine ("her neat little soul scrubbed away"), and it is she who is the book's ardent New Deal Democrat, eager to make society too conform to an ideal of the reasonable. (Her pediatrician husband is an anti-Roosevelt Republican, but he is infatuated with his own new deal in the form of up-to-date theories of infant care, theories he forces on his screaming baby and equally suffering wife with inhuman rigidity.) Libby, on the other hand, is not interested in bettering the world but in rising in it, her need to be the envied heroine of every encounter so frantic that she is incapable of even thinking the truth, and her chattering mouth seems to Polly like a "running wound."

With Dottie we come to a more original creation. Dottie is a shy, humorless, literal-minded girl, who is most at home in cozy chats with "Mother" and whose shyness conceals a great power of love, sexual and emotional. Her story is a tragicomedy in which a girl clearly made to be happy with old-fashioned romance and marriage but ready to behave as the new epoch thinks right is coolly and efficiently deflowered and then sent to be fitted for a pessary by a lover who doesn't even kiss her, let alone pretend that the "affair" has anything to do with love. (Docile little student of the *Zeitgeist* though she is, that omitted kiss does bother her.) Later, in one of the novel's wittiest and most touching scenes it is her *mother* who, with a timidly "bold" respect for love which is already out of date, presses Dottie to seek out that first lover. Dottie, scorning those old attitudes (and her own emotions), insists on going through with a practical marriage.

In Norine Schmittlapp Blake, occasional mistress of Kay's husband, Miss McCarthy gives us another example of that perversion of the life of the mind to which clever people are liable—this time as it appears among ordinary college graduates. Her mind and her talk are wholly given up to advanced ideas—her very apartment, painted black as Macdermott's was painted indigo, is a "dogmatic lair," all its furnishings "pontificating . . . articles of belief." She is so quick to display her superior progressiveness that it is she who announces near the end the change from one epoch and style of intellectual cliché to another by declaring that of course "no first-rate mind can accept the concept of progress any more." As before in Miss McCarthy's work, the reason for such a love of "ideas" is an inability to see, let alone to value, real things, an inability that is almost literally a blindness. This was foreshadowed in college, where she declared that a Cézanne still life (which the coldly knowing Lakey called "the formal arrangement of shapes") presented "the spirit of the apples." That phrase, with its implied scorn for the concrete, becomes her *Leitmotif,* and we find her later feeling pleasantly superior to people like the sensible Helena, who seems to shrink from "imponderables" and "intangibles." (It is part of the same indictment that her husband, Putnam, is a fund-raiser and publicist for labor organizations—that is, not a real laborer at anything, but a manipulator of notions and "images" for causes that entitle him to feel virtuous even if he lies—and that he is impotent.) Not only is Norine's apartment so filthy that poor Helena experiences an awkward block when she goes to her bathroom; her preference for lofty "intangibles" over mere

realities enables her to feel superior in virtue while she is up to her neck in moral nastiness. This is carried to a comic climax when Helena asks her pointedly where Kay had been while Norine and Kay's husband were, as Norine put it, with her fine intellectual disdain for middle-class euphemisms, "fornicating" on her couch. " 'Kay [a Macy's employee] was working,' said Norine. 'The stores don't observe Lincoln's Birthday. They cash in on the fact that the other wage slaves get the day off. It's a big white-collar shopping spree. When do you think a forty-eight-hour-week stenographer gets a chance to buy herself a dress? Unless she goes without her lunch? Probably you've never thought.' "

This extreme example of the mode of life and thought Miss McCarthy detests evokes, in one of the novel's best scenes, a wonderful explosion of the other mode by which she has always opposed it. It is Helena who explodes, the rich girl to whose parents Miss McCarthy gave her own Protestant grandfather's wealth and his passion for education, and whose encyclopedic knowledge and many accomplishments have left her wry, unassertive, good-natured—passionate about nothing but the truth. The simple concreteness of what she says when at last she can stomach Norine's falseness and ugliness no more, though it is intended literally, is also intended as samples of larger things, and her outburst is worth quoting at length because it is so funny and true and because it can be taken as implying the fundamental McCarthy creed.

" '. . . if I were a socialist, I would try to be a good person. . . . You say your husband can't sleep with you because you're a "good woman." . . . Tell him what you do with Harald. . . . That ought to get his pecker up. And have him take a look at this apartment. And at the ring around your neck. If a man slept with you, you'd leave a ring around him. Like your bathtub. . . . I'd get some toilet paper. There isn't any in the bathroom. And some Clorox for the garbage pail and the toilet bowl. And boil out that dishcloth or get a new one. . . . I'd unchain the dog and take him for a walk. And while I was at it, I'd change his name.' 'You don't like Nietzsche?' 'No,' said Helena, dryly. 'I'd call him something like Rover.' Norine gave her terse laugh. 'I get it,' she said appreciatively. 'God, Helena, you're wonderful! Go on. Should I give him a bath to christen him?' Helena considered. 'Not in this weather. He might catch cold. Take a bath yourself, instead . . . And buy some real food —not in cans. If it's only hamburger and fresh vegetables and oranges.' Norine nodded. 'Fine. But now tell me something more basic.' . . . 'I'd paint this room another color.' . . . 'Is that what you'd call basic?' she demanded. 'Certainly,' said Helena. 'You don't want people to think you're a fascist, do you?' she added, with guile. 'God, you're dead right,' said Norine. 'I guess I'm too close to these things. . . . Next?' 'I'd take some real books out of the library.' 'What do you mean, "real books"?' said Norine, with a wary glance at her shelves. [Earlier we had been told that these shelves contained "few full-size books, except for Marx's *Capital,* Pareto, Spengler, *Ten Days That Shook the World, Axel's Castle,* and Lincoln Steffens," all trademarks, as it were, of the radical intellectuals of the time.] 'Literature,' retorted Helena. 'Jane Austen. George Eliot. Flaubert. Lady Murasaki. Dickens. Shakespeare. Sophocles. Aristophanes. Swift.' 'But those aren't seminal,' said Norine, frowning. 'So much the better,' said Helena. . . . 'Is that all?' said Norine. Helena shook her head. Her eyes met Norine's. 'I'd stop seeing Harald,' she said."

Two members of the group remain to be mentioned, aside from fat comfortable Pokey, who is most valuable for bringing into the story her funny parents, absolutely stupefied with their wealth and self-importance, and their even funnier butler, Hatton, whose mastery of his profession entitles him to a self-importance greater, if possible, than that of his employers. These other two rank with Helena among the characters respected by their author, and with them the novel comes to an end.

Helena, Lakey, and Polly have Miss McCarthy's respect because, like other characters she has valued, they are honest, incapable of hurting or using others for their own advantage, and attentive to what is outside themselves— they notice things. But they differ significantly too. In Helena and Lakey intellectual development has crippled ordinary humanity. Helena is so enormously cultivated, so utterly knowing, that she is incapable of passion—except, as I've said, for the truth. She is cool, virginal, she even looks like a boy rather than a woman —charming to talk to, in short, but not a girl to marry. In Lakey it is her sensibility that has suffered the crippling overdevelopment. She is aware of failures of tact or artistic taste to the point, at times, of torture. It is fitting that she becomes an expatriate, spending years as a rich student and connoisseur of art in Europe, and that, though her exquisite refinement is housed, appropriately enough, in a person of exquisite beauty, she too turns out to be a girl one doesn't marry. She startles her friends by returning from Europe with a woman lover, as if, for the most scrupulous feminine sensibility, the male is too gross. This is not shown as a degradation. She is now obviously attractive as a human being, able to wince at her past snobberies, and so on. But she is also obviously incomplete. Polly Andrews alone is all that a woman ought to be, and this may be why she is referred to several times as a creature out of a fairy tale.

Polly seems, in fact, to be an audacious embodiment of a McCarthy daydream, the author's "ideal," the sort of person the little daughter of her gay invalid father and beautiful mother might have become if her hair were long and golden, if her parents had lived, and if her happy childhood had fulfilled itself, after the inevitable fairy tale trials, in a properly happy ending. For Polly's childhood too was delightful with games and presents. Her father too—one of Miss McCarthy's most successful comic creations—is a gay, fun-dispensing invalid. (He is a manic-depressive.) In her poor apartment house, Polly seems to her first lover "a girl in a story book—a fairy tale. A girl with long fair hair who lives in a special room surrounded by kindly dwarfs." What is this fairy tale creature like? She takes pleasure in the work of the kitchen, and even the laundry, she makes her own Christmas presents, she is happy and generous in love, she has a sense of humor—in short, she has the gift of being able to live enjoyably in the real world. Then, as we have found before, this openness to the real has a moral dimension. She is not only honest and morally conscientious—often to comic and troublesome extremes—she is a nurse: her profession is to help people. When she decides to marry a handsome doctor, her chief praise of him is that he is "good." (An oddly foreign word to people in her world—her mother says, "I suppose you mean he's a bit of an idealist.") And yet—her Jim is a psychiatrist. But no, this turns out to be only a spell put on him by the evil spirits of the *Zeitgeist*. He took up psychiatry, he explains, under the mistaken impression that it was a science, but he is changing to research. He will study "brain chemistry"—that is, the reader of Mary McCarthy will by now understand, he will give up the delusive freedom of psychiatry, a freedom to deal masterfully in untestable ideas, and work instead with concrete "impersonal" realities. Polly marries this good man, and taking her father to stay with them—to

the horror of all their up-to-date friends—they live happily, for all we know, ever after.

As I have said, *The Group* is not perfectly successful. A defect of its method is that characters whose human importance is comparatively trifling (Libby) or who are of mainly sociological interest (Priss) are treated as fully as those who engage the author more deeply; with such characters, though they are often amusing, the narrative urgency slackens. And there are Polly's two lovers, who seem created only to make points with or to serve the plot. Nevertheless, the book is mainly a pleasure to read. The pleasure comes from the characters (most of them), so pathetic and comic, so true, in their struggle to live up to their advanced ideas or to cling to reality amid the general falsenesses; from the continuous vivifying detail of their setting, appearance, tone, and gesture; and from the sheer quantity of people and experiences the story brings to life.

Miss McCarthy has published five books since *The Group*, a collection of three articles, plus a chapter of "Solutions," called *Vietnam* (1967). This book followed a trip to Vietnam and is a report of her impressions of the war which, for eight years, the United States had been waging in that country, a war some Americans regard as a righteous crusade against communism and others as an unwarranted, arrogant, and brutal intervention in another country's internal affairs. The book expresses the latter point of view, and gives for it an appalling and convincing mass of evidence. This is not the place to comment on her position. But what is relevant here is the intensity of her involvement in this great public tragedy, and of her insistence that it must be regarded as a moral problem, to be solved by doing not what is "practical" but what is right. "Either it is *morally* wrong for the United States to bomb a small and virtually defenseless country or it is not," she tells us, "and a student picketing the Pentagon is just as great an expert in that realm, to say the least, as Dean Rusk or Joseph Alsop." Reading this sentence—and indeed the whole book—one wonders if it is only Domna Rejnev who asks herself the question "What would Tolstoy say?"

Such undercutting of complicated authoritative theorizing by a return to the human realities which the theories obscure is, we have seen, the primary action of Miss McCarthy's mind. It is in this sense that she is a "realist," and this is why realism, which it is nowadays fashionable to consider a worked-out vein, has shown in her fiction undiminished possibilities of intelligence, feeling, wit, and grace. She herself remarks in the *Paris Review* that she can't help "a sort of distortion, a sort of writing on the bias, seeing things with a swerve and a swoop, a sort of extravagance." But though, like any serious artist, she selects her own kind of data to serve her own vision, her stories are surely offered as true examples of the experience of our time. That "swerve and swoop" are only the wit, play, and poetry in her manner of reporting what she has seen, and these qualities are not more important in her work than her accuracy. Like the "philosophy of life" it expresses, her art comes from her loyalty to the life we actually live, her pleasure in the concrete particulars of people and the world, her refusal to be seduced away from them by ideas, however fashionable or however flattering. She is, in fact, one of several current novelists and critics—Saul Bellow, with his boisterous insistence on the life of feeling, is one; Lionel Trilling, with his critique of what he calls the "second environment," that cozy conformist world of received ideas inhabited by so many "nonconformists," is another—who write out of impatience with their own class of intellectuals. Different though they are in so many ways (Bellow, for instance, is quite as "romantic" as Miss McCarthy is

"neoclassic"), they stand together against the intellectual's tendency to value chic ideas more than the human experience or the human ends they are supposed to serve, or, worse still, to conceal from themselves, with the help of such ideas, realities they prefer not to see.

As for the contempt thought by many to be her sole motive power, the cutting satire supposed to be her main quality, these, as I have tried to make clear, are by-products of something more fundamental. They come not from an intellectual's superciliousness but from an intellectual's hunger for the ordinary decencies and delights of life. When she strikes out, it is precisely at the kind of people who think cleverness is better. What has given Miss McCarthy's work its deepest interest is that, for all her "brilliance," she knows very well how little the mind's accomplishments may be worth in the face of life's agonizing difficulties, and that before the non-intellectual virtues—kindness, honesty, conscientiousness, the ability to take pleasure in people and the world—she lowers willingly her formidable weapons.

During the four years since 1968, when the above was written, Miss McCarthy has published four more books. Two of them continue her examination of the monstrous American destruction of Vietnam: *Hanoi* (1968), about her visit to the capital of North Vietnam, and the bravery and suffering of its people; and *Medina* (1972), about the trial and acquittal of the officer in charge of the 1968 mission into the village of My Lai which resulted in a massacre of unarmed civilians by American soldiers. (Captain Calley, who actually led the mission, had already been found guilty.) The other books are *The Writing on the Wall* (1970), a collection of essays, chiefly on literary subjects, written between 1962 and 1969; and the novel *Birds of America* (1971).

The last two books confirm one's sense that

she belongs among those especially interesting writers who are always offering a personal vision, but whose self-exploration becomes more and more a way of understanding the world. For many of the essays, though devoted to other writers, turn out to be about her own deepest preoccupations. And the idea in her previous novels that "freedom for her kind of people—for intellectuals" has often led only to "escape from difficult, limiting reality into the realm of flattering abstraction" has become in both books a frankly gloomy vision of the whole drift of contemporary civilization.

The three most recent essays in *The Writing on the Wall*—on Ivy Compton-Burnett, Orwell, and Nature—are full of what might almost be notes for *Birds of America*. Compton-Burnett is seen to be obsessed by the ambiguities and contradictions in "two insistent words . . . : Nature and Equality." Orwell is shown as a man who felt "obliged to believe in progress," but who loved "some simpler form of life" and "hated the technology he counted on to liberate the majority." And in "One Touch of Nature" she finds that Nature has ceased to determine values, but "has become subject to opinion" and "is no longer the human home." *Birds of America* is, in fact, a rich study of the contradictions within and between those two ideas, Nature and Equality, which we have dreamed we can bring together, and of how the latter, given irresistible power by technology, is destroying the values associated with the former. The contradictions are brought to life in the relationship of nineteen-year-old Peter Levi and his much divorced artist (harpsichordist) mother, Rosamund Brown, who, though the story and its point of view are his, remains a sort of loved and opposed other self throughout.

Peter and his mother have returned to Rocky Port, Massachusetts, for the 1964 summer holiday preceding his junior year abroad, and the story begins with his memory of their first visit four years earlier, the happiest time of his life. In that earlier period he was "deeply in love with his mother," and he also loved Nature, which meant then the New England countryside and above all its wild birds. Of his mother we see chiefly what she can share with Peter—her delight in the pleasures and customs of her childhood and of an earlier, simpler America, and in particular, in cooking real food. Since she is "a hopeless romantic" who "turned everything into a game," she decides to cook only American recipes from an old Fanny Farmer cookbook, and nothing that has been "naturalized" less than a hundred years. The story is in part the funny spectacle of her difficulties as she struggles to cook the old recipes with the proper ingredients and utensils in a town whose shops "get no call" for such things any more, and of Peter's "mature" irony at a childish intensity and lack of logic he really enjoys. But it is also about the pleasure they take in their food, their walks, their games. And above all, it is the story of their love, the love of two people who "notice things" with exceptional sensitivity and hence are always scrupulously just both for and against each other and themselves, and of the playful delicacies by which they express, or conceal, their feelings. When the flashback ends and we return to the 1964 Rocky Port, we find it buried four years deeper under the "improvements" of technology. The mother's struggle for old-time reality in the kitchen has grown a bit frenzied: she wants "fowl" rather than fryers because they're cheaper and "economy is contact with reality. I love reality, Peter. I hope you will too"—but spends gallons of gas hunting for real jelly glasses. Peter, less simply "in love" and more aware of the outside world—civil rights workers vanishing in Mississippi—begins to wonder if she isn't "making too much of the minutiae." He has become, moreover, a devotee of the ethics of Kant, whose categorical imperative—perform no action whose principle you would not accept as a universal law—is his supreme commandment, and so is uneasy about the aristocratic refinement of taste by which his artist-mother instinctively decides what is good and right. The rest of the novel, though its tone stays mostly light or ironic, draws out for Peter the increasingly painful implications of the battle these two fought with Rocky Port, each other, and themselves.

The absurd idea of some reviewers, resembling a kind of tone deafness, that Peter is a "prig," without "passions or contradictions," and Rosamund is an "overcultivated cipher," seems to rest on the assumption that passion must be sexual—or at least noisy—and that characters with intelligence, wit, and learning, especially if their manners are reserved, must be unreal. But "the mightiest of the passions," as Shaw's Jack Tanner declares, is "moral passion." And what chiefly characterizes Peter and his mother, what makes them funny and touching, is the unremitting intensity of their moral concern, their way of seeing moral issues in minutiae. As for contradictions, it is precisely Peter's inner tug-of-war that is the point of his story. And this keeps it alive as fiction even when "story" of the usual kind is, in varying degrees, abandoned.

The adverse reviews say the novel turns into an "essay" and imply that its fictional vitality disappears. Now, it is true that except in these first two chapters, another in the middle, and the last, the book is not a conventional realistic novel: what we are given of characters and their relationships is mainly what can serve a development in ideas, and the wide and witty application of the ideas certainly makes for a good deal of the fun. But if "essay" means a kind of writing in which the author merely announces her own worked-out conclusions,

then all the chapters, even that of Peter's long philosophic letter to his mother, are clearly something else, and this a something else which retains precisely the reality peculiar to fiction. For fiction restores reality to ideas by giving up the pretense that they exist apart from particular persons in particular situations and that they are static. In *Birds of America* all the ideas emerge from the mental life of *Peter,* whom we have come to know in non-intellectual ways as well; in her mimicry of idiom, tone, and personal style Miss McCarthy is as amusingly accurate with this American boy of the 1960's as she has been with so many other characters. Moreover, his mental life is a constant struggle among ideas that actively contend with each other. In short, the novel gives us ideas in their living state. For, as Gide's Edouard affirms so passionately, ideas "live; they fight; they perish like men." Edouard admits that "ideas exist only because of men; but that's what's so pathetic; they live at their expense."

So Peter's encounter in a train to Paris with some Midwest American schoolmarms, as kind and neighborly as they are naïve and vulgar, becomes a squirming inner battle between the taste, intellect, and need for privacy he shares with his mother and his American egalitarian sense of justice. So, though his letter to his mother begins by rejecting her ethics of "taste" as those of a "snob," it goes on to tell of a battle he fights to keep clean the public toilet of his Paris lodgings which others leave disgustingly filthy, a battle which leads him to a devastating possibility: "Could humanity be divided into people who noticed and people who didn't? If so there was no common world." And later it is his own reactionary tendencies that are jolted. After smiling at an elderly Italian's old-fashioned faith in the power of American technology to free men from slavery and want, he is reminded that the picturesque

European simplicities he prefers are only the way slavery and want look to the comfortable outsider—Mistrust the picturesque, the man says. It stinks.

The climax of this conflict occurs in the next to last chapter when Peter argues in the Sistine Chapel with the novel's chief spokesman for contemporary American civilization, his sociologist faculty adviser. This man, named with Dickensian appropriateness Mr. Small, had earlier reduced Peter's complex dissatisfactions to neurotic symptoms easy to "explain" and advise. He now has a foundation grant to study the flight patterns of the new, and mainly American, flying creature, the tourist. Not only does Small defend against Peter's "elitist" objections both American capitalism and the technology by which, at some temporary cost here and there, it spreads the good things of life more and more widely; he also demonstrates the new "anti-elitist" trend in American education in his belief that the great frescoes are really in essence abstractions —Norine Schmittlapp's "intangibles"—accessible to all with the right feelings. To him Peter's insistence that they say something in a language which a little education would illuminate is only the old business of shutting out the "disadvantaged." Finally, he tries to share their lunch check equally, though he in fact ate more than Peter, and then, with the "warmth" of the new "with-it" teacher, gives Peter a farewell hug to show their differences don't matter, a neat illustration of that blurring of distinguishing particulars some egalitarians call justice—or love.

The last chapter is again pure—and poignant—fiction. It depicts a series of betrayals. First, Peter finds sleeping on his lodging stairs one cold winter night a stinking, drink-stupefied woman, a *clocharde,* waiting for him "like a big package with his name on it: Peter Levi,

Esq., Noted Humanitarian." Taking her to his room for a night's shelter, he experiences all the little self-betrayals generated by moral actions that make one's flesh crawl: if one doesn't act, one feels guilty, but if one does, one feels hypocritical, for no action is ever enough to silence the inner critic. Then President Johnson betrays his election promises to keep America out of war by bombing North Vietnam; when Peter goes to the zoo for comfort in his horror and despair, an angry swan wounds the bird-lover with a beak dripping with polluted water; in a hospital afterwards technology almost kills him with penicillin, to which he is allergic; and finally his mother tells him she will play in Poland for the U.S. State Department because "it's only music." He knows he can reawaken her moral common sense, but the fact that he should need to destroys her authority for him forever—a small sample of the current division between the generations in America. And the book ends with a brief but tellingly described dream visit by Kant, who announces gravely that, not God, whom men have long managed without, but "Nature is dead."

This bold statement of the book's "message" in its last line, far from flattening the closing emotional effect, oddly intensifies it. We feel an earnestness in the author that drives her to abandon the usual coyness of fiction. Still, summing up, as it does, the rich complexity of the book's theme, the statement is really mysterious. It may therefore be worthwhile to conclude by suggesting a little of what it means.

Nature, because it has seemed out of the reach of the ego-driven human will or of shifting private opinion, has been a guide, a determiner of value, a basis for ethical assumptions we can hold in common. But nature is actually the realm of minute particulars, and every real relationship to these must also be minutely particular; that is, it is the realm of differences and inequalities, both in things and in our ability to notice, appreciate, and possess them. For this reason, if men are to share equally in all life's goods, these goods must be stripped of the particulars which limit their accessibility. They must be "processed" into easily reproducible and portable (also inexact and tasteless) approximations of the real thing—and this applies to the products of mind as well as to those of Nature. Nor is it only those two kinds of products that make for inequality and call for such "processing." There are also the particulars of custom and tradition that have evolved out of the history of nations, neighborhoods, families. These give us our unique childhoods, the sources and objects of our emotional life, our identity, but they do keep us apart; equality therefore demands that such uniqueness be replaced by a generalized humanity we can share. In a single sentence, the pursuit of equality is an attempt to live by an idea, and therefore, however "self-evident," beautiful, and irresistible the idea, it is a constant flight from reality. Hence the quotation which serves as a motto for the book: ". . . to attempt to embody the Idea in an example, as one might embody the wise man in a novel, is unseemly . . . for our natural limitations, which persistently interfere with the perfection of the Idea, forbid all illusion about such an attempt. . . ."

Actually, in spite of her Kant's concern to distinguish Nature's death from the death of God announced by Nietzsche, they are very much alike, and the loss here registered by Miss McCarthy has a fundamental similarity to the loss of religious faith. For her Nature (also capitalized) seems to be only the line to which God has lately retreated; both serve, in Arnold's phrase, as that reality not ourselves which makes for righteousness. And what

Miss McCarthy is saying is that, with the growing power of technology, there is no longer any reality not ourselves. The ego-serving manipulation of reality which she has always detested in intellectuals (including herself) turns out to have been only her personal near-at-hand example of the process of technology as it serves the idea of equality. This is an idea she cannot of course reject, but neither can she help seeing that that process replaces the realities of Nature (and of our "second nature," custom) with convenient and comparatively shallow abstractions, i.e., cuts us off from something greater than ourselves, and that more and more it is taking command of the world.

A sad conclusion. And though many of us refuse to give up a sort of animal faith in the power of human creativity to save us yet again, the pessimism of this profound and moving novel is certainly an appropriate response to the world we now inhabit.

Selected Bibliography

WORKS OF MARY McCARTHY

FICTION

The Company She Keeps. New York: Simon and Schuster, 1942.

The Oasis. New York: Random House, 1949.

Cast a Cold Eye. New York: Harcourt, Brace & World, 1950.

The Groves of Academe. New York: Harcourt, Brace & World, 1952.

A Charmed Life. New York: Harcourt, Brace & World, 1955.

The Group. New York: Harcourt, Brace & World, 1963.

"The Hounds of Summer," *New Yorker,* 30:47–50 (September 14, 1963).

Birds of America. New York: Harcourt Brace Jovanovich, 1971.

NONFICTION

Sights and Spectacles: 1937–1956. New York: Farrar, Straus, 1956.

Venice Observed. New York: Reynal, 1956.

Memories of a Catholic Girlhood. New York: Harcourt, Brace & World, 1957.

The Stones of Florence. New York: Harcourt, Brace & World, 1959.

On the Contrary: Articles of Belief, 1946–1961. New York: Noonday Press, 1962.

"General Macbeth," *Harper's*, 224:35–39 (June 1962).

"J. D. Salinger's Closed Circuit," *Harper's*, 205: 46–48 (October 1962).

Mary McCarthy's Theatre Chronicles, 1937–1962. New York: Noonday Press, 1963.

"On Madame Bovary," *Partisan Review*, 31:174–88 (Spring 1964).

"The Inventions of I. Compton-Burnett." *Encounter*, 27:19–31 (November 1966).

Vietnam. New York: Harcourt, Brace & World, 1967.

Hanoi. New York: Harcourt, Brace & World, 1968.

The Writing on the Wall and Literary Essays. New York: Harcourt, Brace & World, 1970.

Medina. New York: Harcourt Brace Jovanovich, 1972.

BIBLIOGRAPHIES

Goldman, Sherli Evens. *Mary McCarthy: A Bibliography*. New York: Harcourt, Brace & World, 1968.

CRITICAL AND
BIOGRAPHICAL STUDIES

Auchincloss, Louis. "Mary McCarthy," in *Pioneers and Caretakers*. Minneapolis: University of Minnesota Press, 1965.

Brower, Brock. "Mary McCarthyism," *Esquire*, 58:62–67, 113 (July 1962).

Grumbach, Doris. *The Company She Kept*. New York: Coward-McCann, 1967.

Hardwick, Elizabeth. "Mary McCarthy," in *A View of My Own: Essays in Literature and Society*. New York: Noonday Press, 1963.

Kazin, Alfred. *Starting Out in the Thirties*. Boston: Little, Brown, 1965. Pp. 155 ff.

Mailer, Norman. "The Case against McCarthy: A Review of *The Group,*" in *Cannibals and Christians*. New York: Dial Press, 1966.

McKenzie, Barbara. *Mary McCarthy*. New York: Twayne, 1966.

Niebuhr, Elisabeth. "The Art of Fiction XXVII," *Paris Review*, 27:58–94 (Winter–Spring 1962).

—IRVIN STOCK

Carson McCullers

1917-1967

SINCE Carson McCullers' gifts as a novelist are essentially celebratory and elegiac, it is appropriate that the simple facts of her life should evoke both wonder and melancholy. She was born Lula Carson Smith in Columbus, Georgia, on February 19, 1917, of French Huguenot and Irish ancestry. Lamar Smith, her father, had come a few years earlier from Society Hill, Alabama; her mother, Marguerite Waters, had been born in Dublin, Georgia.

From an early age, Carson was recognized as an odd, lonely girl of uncommon talents and her parents tried to be especially sensitive to her needs. When, at five, she revealed a passion for music, her father bought a piano; when, at fifteen, she first began to shape plays and stories, he came home one day with a typewriter. To both the piano and the typewriter she devoted an unusual amount of energy. As she was later to recall: "[In childhood] my main interest had been music and my ambition was to be a concert pianist. My first effort at writing was a play. At that phase my idol was Eugene O'Neill and this first masterpiece was thick with incest, lunacy, and murder. The first scene was laid in a graveyard and the last was a catafalque. I tried to put it on in the family sitting room, but only my mother and my eleven-year-old sister would cooperate. . . . After that I dashed off a few more plays, a

novel, and some rather queer poetry that nobody could make out, including the author." Among those vanished adolescent works were "A Reed of Pan," a novel about a musician seduced by jazz; and "Fire of Life," a two-character verse play in which Christ debates with Nietzsche.

Supported by funds from the sale of a valued family ring, Carson at eighteen traveled to New York to attend the Juilliard School of Music. Almost immediately her dream dissolved. A girl from Columbus, with whom she had agreed to room in Manhattan, claimed to have lost all the tuition money on the subway, and Carson was forced to work instead of study. She did, however, register for creative writing courses at Columbia and New York University, and during the next year she worked feverishly at fiction and dutifully at a half-dozen part-time jobs. Just before her twentieth birthday, "Wunderkind," the tale of a prodigy's failure, appeared under her maiden name in the December 1936 issue of *Story* magazine. The following autumn, she married a young Georgian named Reeves McCullers.

During her stay in New York, Mrs. McCullers suffered a recurrence of a childhood ailment that was to exercise so powerful and poignant an influence on her life. She had always been a frail girl, but after having experienced a severe attack of rheumatic fever in the winter of 1936–37, she began her third decade in a vulnerable state of health. For the next thirty years, pneumonia, heart disease, and a savage series of paralytic strokes were to become the frightful facts of daily life, tests for her spirit to survive.

In the two years following their marriage, the McCullerses lived happily in Charlotte, North Carolina, where Reeves worked as a credit manager and Carson blocked out a novel originally called *The Mute*. At the suggestion of Sylvia Chatfield Bates, her New York writing teacher, Mrs. McCullers used an outline of the work in progress to apply for a Houghton Mifflin Fiction Fellowship. She won praise, $1500, and a contract. After the editors changed the title to *The Heart Is a Lonely Hunter*, the book appeared in June 1940 to generally enthusiastic reviews. Most critics praised the work as a formidable achievement in its own right, but the age of the author was too startling a fact to minimize. For a twenty-two-year-old girl to probe at such length the passionate idealism of a half-dozen adult characters was an astonishing act of imaginative sympathy.

At the time of her sudden fame, Mrs. McCullers was already at work on *Reflections in a Golden Eye*, a story of infidelity, murder, and perversion at an army base in the South. When it appeared in February 1941, the critical response was chilly. Most reviewers found it an unpalatable and self-consciously bizarre performance, deficient in just those qualities of psychological intuition that made the first novel so memorable. In his severity, Hubert Creekmore is typical: "the characters are all somewhat hermetically sealed in the pigeonholes of their neuroses. None of them reacts on the others. . . . You watch them go through their paces like a series of parallel dots and the experience is barren."

The disappointment at the reception of the new novel was matched by a private misfortune. In 1940 the McCullerses quarreled and agreed to divorce; and for the next five years Mrs. McCullers lived for short periods of time in Columbus and Saratoga Springs, but mostly amidst a legendary gathering of artists and writers called February House at Seven Middagh Street in Brooklyn Heights, New York. At the time of her marital troubles, her friend George Davis, the editor of *Mademoiselle*, had suggested renting an old brownstone house as the site for an experiment in cooperative living. Before long they were joined by the poets W. H. Auden, Louis MacNeice, and Chester Kallman; the novelists Paul and Jane Bowles, Christopher Isherwood, and Richard Wright; the designer Oliver Smith, the composer Benjamin Britten, and the tenor Peter Pears. During the war years, a visitor to the house might find any one of the transient charter members, or such guests as Aaron Copeland playing the piano, Denis de Rougemont talking to Salvador Dali, or Pavel Tchelitchew decorating the walls with a mural. Domestic details were managed by Auden, Mrs. McCullers, or Gypsy Rose Lee.

For a twenty-three-year-old girl from Georgia, Seven Middagh Street provided unusually spirited company and singular material for novels and stories. A strutting hunchback who came each evening to a bar near the Brooklyn Navy Yard now lives in "The Ballad of the Sad Café," and a New York fire engine played a role in the birth of Frankie Addams. After meditating for weeks on the disjointed elements in a story of an adolescent girl, Mrs. McCullers heard a siren just outside the house. Following Gypsy Rose Lee out the door, she was oddly inspired to shout: "Frankie is in love with her brother and his bride and wants to become a member of the wedding."

The early 1940's proved to be Mrs. McCullers' most productive period. "A Tree, a Rock, a Cloud" was chosen for the *O. Henry Memorial Award Prize Stories* in 1942, and "The Ballad of the Sad Café" for Martha Foley's *Best American Short Stories* two years later. Meanwhile, encouraged by fellowships from the Guggenheim Foundation and the American Academy of Arts and Letters, she had been working steadily on *The Member of the Wedding*. Even her personal life seemed momentarily to stabilize: her recently widowed mother bought a house in Nyack, New York, into which Carson was later to move; and she began once again to correspond with Reeves when he was wounded fighting in Europe. Shortly after his return to the United States in February 1945, they were married for a second time.

For the next three years, Mrs. McCullers fought against failing health and tried to find a producer for the dramatic version of *The Member of the Wedding*, which had been published as a novel in 1946. In Paris, the summer of 1947, a stroke impaired the vision of her right eye; and that autumn still another stroke left her partially paralyzed on one side of her body. Although recuperation at the American Hospital in Paris and the Columbia Presbyterian Hospital in New York was disheartingly slow, the decade was to end on a triumphant note. On the night of June 5, 1950, *The Member of the Wedding* opened at the Empire Theatre in New York to the extravagant praise of the audience and newspaper critics. In the *World-Telegram*, William Hawkins spoke for the majority: "I have never before heard what happened last night at the curtain calls for *Member of the Wedding* when hundreds cried out as if with one voice for Ethel Waters and Julie Harris." The next year, the play won both the Donaldson Award and the prize of the Drama Critics Circle, and after running for 501 performances it was filmed by Stanley Kramer.

On the crest of this popular and critical success, Houghton Mifflin published Mrs. McCullers' three novels and seven stories in an omnibus volume. Reviewing the British edition the next year, V. S. Pritchett called its author "a genius . . . and the most remarkable novelist to come out of America for a generation." At thirty-four, Mrs. McCullers was, in Gore Vidal's recollection, "*the* young writer" of the period, "an American legend from the beginning." Even critics like Edmund Wilson and Diana Trilling, while expressing serious reservations about her talent, were likely to talk of her youth and the undeniably rich promise of her future. If, Joseph Frank wrote, Mrs. McCullers could, like Dostoevski, place her characters in a situation where their grotesqueness takes on symbolic value, "American literature may find itself with a really important writer on its hands."

From this point on, however, the life story of Carson McCullers becomes the history of declining health and talent. The promise, which in the 1940's was on everybody's lips, was never fulfilled. In 1951, she and her husband bought a house at Bachvillers, near Paris, where they lived on and off for two years; but domestic calamity made much of the interlude a nightmare. Reeves drank heavily, took drugs, and fell into fits of wild, almost maniacal abusiveness. Mrs. McCullers, desperate, returned alone to Nyack and soon learned that Reeves had committed suicide in Paris. Other personal disasters weakened her resistance: the death in 1954 of a favorite aunt was followed a few months later by the loss of her mother. Given the severity of the stresses under which she labored, the play and the novel Mrs. McCullers published in 1958 and 1961 were triumphs of stoicism but, unhappily, failures of art. *The Square Root of Wonderful*, a maladroit comedy of manners, closed after forty-five performances in New York; and

Clock without Hands, an ambitious, long-studied novel about race, is devoid of both energy and plausible social observation. But despite these disappointments, her earlier work continued to be widely read and appreciated; each of the first four volumes sold more than a half-million copies in hard- and soft-covered editions and adaptors were eager to translate her books into other media. Edward Albee dramatized "The Ballad of the Sad Café" in 1963; John Houston cast Marlon Brando and Elizabeth Taylor in a film of *Reflections in a Golden Eye* (1967); and Robert Ellis Miller directed Alan Arkin and Sondra Locke in *The Heart Is a Lonely Hunter* (1968).

Against the physical afflictions of her last decade, Mrs. McCullers responded with admirable gallantry and spirit. A heart attack, breast cancer, paralysis, pneumonia, and a bone-crushing fall occurred in terrible succession from 1958 to 1964, and yet she traveled, received guests, and worked fitfully on unfinished manuscripts. In August 1967 she was felled by still another stroke and lapsed into a coma from which she never regained full consciousness. She died on September 29, 1967.

Any reader who wishes to determine the characteristic strengths and limitations of Carson McCullers as a writer could do no better than to begin with *The Heart Is a Lonely Hunter*. Not only is this first novel an admirably complete introduction to her themes and subject matter, but it raises in a complex and provocative way the major critical issues posed by all her important work. The scene is the deep South; the characters are estranged and disadvantaged; and the theme is loneliness and the inevitable frustrations of love.

When the book opens, John Singer and Spiros Antonapoulos, two deaf-mutes, have been joined for ten years in a close but enigmatic friendship. The active and quick-witted Singer has been entirely infatuated with his impassive and feeble-minded friend. Although most of the other people in this depressed factory town are isolated, the two mutes never seem lonely at all. Singer gives; his friend receives; and each seems absorbed in his role as lover and beloved. But suddenly Antonapoulos becomes mysteriously ill and a social menace, stealing silverware, jostling strangers, urinating in public places. Despite his distress and passionate concern, Singer can do nothing; the deranged Greek is packed off to an asylum two hundred miles away. At this point, still very early in the story, Singer involuntarily enters the life of the community by renting a room in the Kelly house and taking his meals at the New York Café.

During the course of the next few months, Singer unwittingly becomes the focal point of the lives of four other people, who, visiting his room, see in him a mysterious figure to complete their own obsessive but fragmentary dreams. For Mick Kelly, a twelve-year-old tomboy with a blossoming gift for music, Singer's imagined harmony of spirit brings Mozart to mind. To the crusading Negro doctor Benedict Copeland, the mute symbolizes an all-too-rare instance of white compassion. For Jake Blount, a haggard radical agitator with a greater gift for talk than action, Singer is divine because he listens. For Biff Brannon, the café owner who self-consciously observes the human pageant, Singer is a fit subject for contemplation because of the attention paid to him by others. None of these dreamers knows of Singer's love for Antonapoulos; nor are they aware of the bewilderment with which he observes their interest in him. When Antonapoulos dies, Singer commits suicide, and the disciples are left to ponder and to grieve.

From the opening pages of *The Heart Is a Lonely Hunter* one is aware that this strange and absorbing story is designed to be read both as a realistic tale of a half-dozen displaced southerners and as a generalized parable on the nature of human illusion and love. And, at the start at least, each level operates satisfactorily with the other. All the carefully observed details needed to authenticate the mutes are present. Antonapoulos, fat and slovenly, works in a fruit store; Singer, tall and immaculately dressed, engraves silver for a local jeweler. Their routine is carefully set, odd perhaps in its regularity, but entirely credible: they play at chess, and go once a week to the library, to the movies, and to a local photography store. As we move on, characters read *Popular Mechanics* and write letters to Jeanette Mac-Donald; they sing "Love's Old Sweet Song" and "K-K-K-Katie," smoke Target tobacco and speak of Joe Louis and Man Mountain Dean. Behind the exotic Georgian passion play stand Chamberlain, Munich, and the Danzig Corridor, and when Mrs. McCullers stops to describe a character from the viewpoint of Biff Brannon, she writes with the specificity familiar in traditional realistic fiction.

Yet along with the virtues of specification go the vaguer promptings of allegory. The symmetrical obsessions of Singer's four admirers quickly make him a special case, more interesting as a catalyst than as a complex human being; and soon afterwards the admirers themselves take on generalized significance: the adolescent, the idealistic Negro, the failed reformer, the philosophical student of human affairs. Through the passion with which each constructs the god he needs, he bears ironical witness to the many and wayward forms of human mythmaking.

For the first one hundred pages of *The Heart Is a Lonely Hunter*, Mrs. McCullers is able to persuade us that contemporary reality and legendary story are one; but soon afterwards her technique falters and the novel becomes increasingly unsatisfactory both as document and

as myth. On the literal level the difficulties center on implausible psychology and faulty observation of character. Biff Brannon is introduced as a man with a rare gift for disinterested observation and described in such a way as to suggest that he should function as Mrs. McCullers' *raisonneur*, the one person to make objective sense of the action. As a café owner, he can see more of the drama than anyone else and he is sympathetic to a wide range of emotional grotesques; as a male with a strong feminine strain, he is able to temper the chill of analysis with the warmth of an intuitive compassion. Following the presentation of Singer, Biff is the first of the main characters to be introduced, and his reflections form the coda that brings the novel to an end.

Throughout the early pages, Biff is described as thoughtful, inquisitive, and alert; whenever something happens, he is often the first, perhaps the only, person to notice. As the pattern of the action evolves, however, Biff is of little use beyond his ability to tell us things we have already established on our own. Sometimes, his vaunted insight is merely banal: "By nature all people are of both sexes. So that marriage and the bed is not all by any means. The proof? Real youth and old age. Because often old men's voices grow high and reedy and they take on a mincing walk." But most often his discoveries are posed in terms of coils, puzzles, unanswered questions; after rubbing his nose, narrowing his eyes, fixing his stare, he is most likely to come up with this: "How Singer had been before was not important. The thing that mattered was the way Blount and Mick made of him a sort of homemade God. Owing to the fact he was a mute they were able to give him all the qualities they wanted him to have. Yet. But how could such a strange thing come about? And why?"

It is just "how it came about" and "why" that Biff is never able to tell us, and—on many of the more important matters—neither can Mrs. McCullers. In this respect, the fundamental weakness of *The Heart Is a Lonely Hunter* is that past midpoint, the central theme (men make strange gods in their own image) is not so much developed as embroidered by still another fancy but no more enlightening illustration.

Related to this inadequacy is Mrs. McCullers' failure to establish a satisfactory relationship between the various idealizations of Singer and what actually happens to each dreamer in the novel. A number of commentators have insisted that the forlorn fate of each character at the end of the book is prompted by Singer's suicide. When the Kelly family is pressed by poverty, Mick quits school to work in the dime store, her musical promise thwarted. Copeland, devastated by the bestial white torture of his prisoner son, goes in broken health to live with relatives who ignore his message. But these events are not causally related to Singer's death. The Kelly family is impoverished because of damages they must pay to the mother of a child their son injured, and Mick took the dime store job while Singer was still alive; in fact, he approved the choice. Copeland is shattered not by anything related to Singer, but by impotence, frozen incomprehension, and the obvious failure of his dream.

There is a growing sense, toward the close of the novel, that the death of God is anticlimactic, or perhaps even beside the point. The dreamers would have been doomed to frustration had the mute never lived, and the kind of fierce inevitability that so beautifully links a Kurtz to a Marlow, a Clarissa to a Lovelace, or Ahab to his own white whale does not bind the characters to Singer in *The Heart Is a Lonely Hunter.*

On a realistic level there are other small problems as well. Several of the episodes in the middle section of the novel are either irrelevant or gratuitous to the main lines of the action (I am thinking of the shooting of Baby Wilson, Blount's encounter with the crazed evangelist, the riot at the amusement park; but others could be mentioned). Occasionally, characters are given dialogue so preposterous that it would bring high color to the face of a Victorian melodramatist: Copeland, who reads Spinoza and Shakespeare, says "Pshaw and double pshaw" when goaded into anger. Several times in the novel people express frustration and rage by hitting their heads against walls, fists against tables, thighs against stones. And, finally, climactic scenes collapse because the writer is too busy establishing lofty poetic meaning to notice the absurdity of a literal image. Here, for instance, is Biff's final recognition on the last page of the book: "Between the two worlds he was suspended. He saw that he was looking at his own face in the counter glass before him. Sweat glistened on his temples and his face was contorted. One eye was opened wider than the other. The left eye delved narrowly into the past while the right gazed wide and affrighted into a future of blackness, error, and ruin. And he was suspended between radiance and darkness. Between bitter irony and faith." Like the legendary student who wrote of Petrarch standing with one foot in the Renaissance while with the other he spanned the Middle Ages, Mrs. McCullers has forgotten the classic rule: specify first; signify later.

When one remembers, however, that *The Heart Is a Lonely Hunter* is the work of a twenty-two-year-old girl, the realistic lapses are understandable; they could easily be corrected by more careful observation and growth. But the failures on the level of fable are more troublesome because they point to an ambivalence that was a permanent feature of Mrs. McCullers' sensibility. There existed in her nature a continuing conflict between her nearer and her further vision, between her desire to document the world and a desire to give it evocative poetic significance. Like Edward Albee (who—in Philip Roth's fine phrase —was "born Maupassant but wished to be Plato") she seemed to waver in her own evaluation of her gifts, and sometimes would express contradictory allegiances almost in the same breath. The most remarkable and revealing example of this occurs in a set of notes on writing, "The Flowering Dream," published in *Esquire* in 1959. First, she tells an anecdote that confirms her existence on a plane beyond mundane reality: "What to know and what not to know? John Brown, from the American Embassy, was here to visit, and he pointed his long forefinger and said, 'I admire you, Carson, for your ignorance.' I said, 'Why?' He asked, 'When was the Battle of Hastings, and what was it about?' . . . I said, 'John, I don't think I care much.' He said, 'That's what I mean. You don't clutter your mind with the facts of life.'" But then, two paragraphs later, comes this expression of the ultimate supremacy of living facts in fiction: "Every day, I read the *New York Daily News*, and very soberly. It is interesting to know the name of the lover's lane where the stabbing took place, and the circumstances which the *New York Times* never reports. In that unsolved murder in Staten Island, it is interesting to know that the doctor and his wife, when they were stabbed, were wearing Mormon nightgowns, three-quarter length. Lizzie Borden's breakfast, on the sweltering summer day she killed her father, was mutton soup. Always details provoke more ideas than any generality could furnish. When Christ was pierced in His *left side*, it is more moving and evocative than if He were just pierced."

The trouble with the symbolism of *The Heart Is a Lonely Hunter* begins with Mrs. McCullers' inability to decide whether Singer is pierced on his left side, just pierced, or never pierced at all. The characters themselves are rarely in doubt. For Mick Kelly, the thought of God conjures up an image of Mr. Singer with a long white sheet around him, and she whispers: "Lord forgiveth me, for I knoweth not what I do." Preparing her lesson for the Sunday school, Alice Brannon chooses the text "All men seek for Thee"; and a moment later, reflecting on the gathering of the disciples, her husband thinks of the mute. Gradually, however, the correspondences become rather murky. Copeland's daughter, Portia, claims that Singer's shirts are as white as if John the Baptist wore them; and as the plot thickens, the mute becomes poignantly and comically all things to all men: a Jew to the Hebrews, a Turk to the Turks, a wizard to the ignorant. Obviously, Mrs. McCullers wants us to see Singer as an ironic God figure, a product of mass wish-fulfillment; but even an ironic symbol runs the danger of becoming too indiscriminately resonant. Part of the problem stems from Mrs. McCullers' flawed control over the implications of the symbol itself. Usually, the insistence on Singer's religious nature is made by one of his blinded admirers, but sometimes the objective narrator seems to confirm their romantic obsessions. Singer, Mrs. McCullers writes, has "the look of peace that is seen most often in those who are very wise or very sorrowful." And finally, the mute is thirty-three when he dies, a detail chosen not by Blount or Mick Kelly, but by the author.

Some of the same uneasiness must greet the frequent assertion that *The Heart Is a Lonely Hunter* is an allegory about fascism. Although Mrs. McCullers has given this reading her guarded blessing, its origin is difficult to pinpoint. I suspect, however, that it may have grown from the casual remark of Clifton Fadiman, who—in his early notice—confessed to seeing signs of a myth of fascist and antifascist forces in the human soul. Yet, even if we recall Mrs. McCullers' cautious disclaimer ("the word is used here in its very broadest terms . . . the spiritual rather than the political side of that phenomenon") the analogy has no roots in the narrative. In what sense does Singer actively tyrannize anyone; who is being regimented, and to what degree? Can Christ and Hitler live comfortably within the confines of the same myth?

What we have here, I think, is early evidence of Mrs. McCullers' susceptibility to portent, her tendency to glide irresistibly toward any beckoning abstraction so long as it is somber, suggestive, and poetic. She never wrote a book that was not to some degree weakened by this inclination, and only once (in "The Ballad of the Sad Café") was she able to put dark fancy to the service of a compelling and powerful literal truth. In *The Member of the Wedding*, her finest achievement, there is less aberrant symbolizing than in any of her other works.

Yet even after all the damaging charges have been made, *The Heart Is a Lonely Hunter* remains what it was in 1940: "a queer sad book that sticks in the mind." The original design is brilliant enough not to be wholly dimmed by the failure of the performance. If the inflated myth finally collapses, the sense of small-town meanness holds up. Few books of the 1930's communicate as well the stagnancy of life in a depressed textile community and the inevitable frustration for those who try to stir free from it. "Find an octopus and put socks on it," says Blount in a phrase that sums up a generation. If the solemnity of the novel palls, the flashes of shrewd country humor remain bright: the antics of Grandpa Copeland and his ancient mule Lee Jackson; the fancies of Bubber Kelly, who prefers fairy tales that have something to eat in them. If Brannon and Copeland seem flat, Mick Kelly is about as

round as a twelve-year-old can be. Laughter has always been the finest defense against pretentiousness, and in her treatment of several minor characters and of Mick herself, Mrs. McCullers reveals an affectionate gaiety that provides wholesome leavening for the pessimism so pervasive in this first novel.

The portrait of Mick Kelly is a charming evocation of the sensitivity and thickness, the exuberance and boredom, the ease of flight and quickness of descent that mark a familiar period in early adolescence. Like so many characters in Mrs. McCullers' books, Mick is defined by the extremity of her isolation and the fever of her fantasy life. Although she wants desperately to connect with other people, she cultivates those qualities of talent and personality that might bring her increased separateness as well as applause. Excitement keeps her imagination at boiling point. To escape the squalor of her slum environment, she climbs a ladder to the roof of a house being built nearby and sits reflecting on the possibilities of celebrity and fortune. In her inventor's phase, she hopes to market radios the size of green peas that people could stick in their ears and to provide flying machines to fit comfortably on a voyager's back. During her heroic period, she expresses her desires in murals of natural and human catastrophe, "Town Burning," or "Sea Gull with Back Broken in Storm." In her interlude as a composer, she hopes to rival Mozart in symphony and song, but since her family cannot afford an instrument, she tries to make a violin out of a broken ukulele. Her tunes, dissonant and intense, carry titles like "Africa," "The Snowstorm," "A Big Fight." The magniloquent but unfinished "This Thing I Want, I Know Not What" is her masterpiece.

As the conflict worsens between the world and her imagination, Mick constructs her most elaborate and personal defense: "She sat down on the steps and laid her head on her knees. She went into the inside room. With her it was like there was two places—the inside room and the outside room. School and the family and the things that happened every day were in the outside room. Mister Singer was in both rooms. Foreign countries and plans and music were in the inside room. The songs she thought about were there. And the symphony." A moment later, Mrs. McCullers conveys the transparent frailty of her defense with the sentence: "'Spareribs stuck his dirty hand up to her eyes because she had been staring off at space. She slapped him."

Although Mick is irrepressibly creative, she is by no means free from an egotism strident enough to injure others. When her brother accidently shoots Baby Wilson, she torments him with visions of Sing Sing and hellfire; and we are told earlier that she had continually hit him whenever she noticed his hands in his pants, so that now he never "peed normal like other kids" but with his hands behind him. Although Mick is a virtuoso of escape, her artistry is rarely effective, and at the end of the novel she feels the disquiet of being barred from the inside room. She does, however, manage to express a qualified affirmation, which—in its vernacular familiarity—is one of the most convincing moments of celebration in the novel:

"But maybe it would be true about the piano and turn out O.K. Maybe she would get a chance soon. Else what the hell good had it all been—the way she felt about music and the plans she had made in the inside room? It had to be some good if anything made sense. . . .

"All right!

"O.K.!

"Some good."

Part of Mick's appeal rests in her indomitability, and it is this sense of a human being refusing to accept meanness that Mrs. McCullers is able to celebrate so skillfully. Singer talking blissfully with his hands to an incomprehending Antonapoulos; the feuding Kelly family joined for a short while in loyalty and love; the weary Copeland hearing "rich, dark sounds" from the pages of Spinoza—these are moments of beauty as well as pathos. Rage, anger, and indignation are often in this story the other side of love, for Mrs. McCullers—like Keats—believed that a street fight is ugly, but the energies displayed can be beautiful.

No such beauty exists in *Reflections in a Golden Eye*, the most pompous and disagreeable of all her books. Almost as if to spite those critics who complained of the squalor of her subject matter, Mrs. McCullers created a swamp where no light shines and no people live. In 1941, when the novel first appeared, reviewers intensified their earlier objections to the morbidity of her materials: perversion, voyeurism, mutilation, and murder; but now, three decades and many a Gothic novel later, the objection is not to the luridness of the subject but, rather, to lack of artistry in Mrs. McCullers' treatment. *Reflections in a Golden Eye* is a muddled, pretentious book that promises to illuminate shadowy places of the human psyche, but manages only to exploit them.

The scene is an army camp in the deep South during the late 1930's, and the characters (to quote the best line in the book) are "two officers, a soldier, two women, a Filipino, and a horse." One officer is Captain Penderton, a tightly repressed latent homosexual, infatuated with his wife's lovers; the other is Major Langdon, an easygoing charmboy who bedded the lusty Leonora Penderton in a blackberry patch two hours after their first meeting. The soldier, a moronic *naïf* named Williams, sees Mrs. Penderton framed nude in a window and begins tiptoeing into her bedroom to worship her while she sleeps. The other woman, Alison

Langdon, frail and neurasthenic, has recently clipped off her nipples with a garden shears, and now finds solace in the company of a prancing houseboy, Anacleto. The horse, Firebird, is tended by Williams, adored by Leonora, and despised by her husband. After a series of violent, inconclusive adventures, Penderton is drawn in love and hate toward the silent Williams; but when he finds that the private has eyes only for his wife, he murders him.

After such action, what explanation but fantasy? And recently a number of critics have argued that *Reflections in a Golden Eye* is not supposed to be read literally but, rather, as a deliberately extravagant symbolic prose poem, true not to the real world but to the vagaries of abnormal psychology. In its charity, however, this argument ignores the fact that the novel never establishes credible connections with any world, literal or fantastic, and that its understanding of human pathology is misty to the point of meaninglessness. As often happens in Mrs. McCullers' weakest books, the fatal devils are an overriding ambition and something less than full clarity of intention. Her basic subject is clear enough: the ravages of dammed-up sexual energies; but in a desire to marry Faulkner to Flaubert and D. H. Lawrence, she takes three mutually contradictory attitudes toward her subject matter. First, as an objective narrator, she introduces the action in a detached and formal manner: short sentences, sculptured paragraphs, a poised monotonic response to everything miraculous and mundane. Designed to establish the verisimilitude of the story, this style depends on a great many details drawn from a firsthand experience of army life—matters of rank, architecture, armor, and so on. Existing simultaneously with the reporter is a satirist, whose aim is to demolish everyone in sight for the assorted vices of pride, moral vacancy, and

self-deceit. Leonora is shown to be so dim-witted that the demands of writing a thank-you note reduce her to nervous exhaustion; her husband, a storehouse of technical information, cannot put two facts together to make an idea, and is entirely blind to the most obvious of his own physiological impulses; the mindless Major Langdon orders his life on the premise that only two things matter: "to be a good animal and to serve my country"; and young Williams, when driven to the point of action, finds "the vaporish impressions within him condensed to a thought." The third voice in the novel belongs to a mythopoeic explorer who sees in this grotesque domestic drama a monumental conflict of will against instinct, the artificial against the natural, and death against life.

The journalist and the satirist do their work only too well. By concentrating on the facts of the physical and social scene, Mrs. McCullers makes it impossible for us not to ask that her human beings remain plausible; but by insisting that the people are pathological types, and by damning them with such relentless sarcasm, she makes it difficult for us to care for their inhumanities. There is excessive malice, too, in the mockery. Usually, satire achieves force by aiming at targets that represent some universal yet remedial failing (the self-interest of politicians, the heartlessness of society women, the greed of bankers); but Mrs. McCullers' satire deals with perverse emotional failures of which the characters themselves are unaware, or about which they can do nothing (Penderton's unconscious desire for a handsome young primitive, Williams' witlessness, and so on).

It is, however, only when the poet takes over that Mrs. McCullers reveals the full inadequacy of her conception, since she has neither the language nor the depth of insight to give the sordid drama the elemental force of myth. Different as they are, the voices of the realist, the satirist, and the mythmaker can exist compatibly in a single work (*St. Mawr* and *Heart of Darkness* are modern examples) but in Lawrence and Conrad the ordinary people are free agents and the narrator's analysis of their situation is weighty enough to give them a significance beyond the realm of the natural. In Mrs. McCullers' book, the people are caricatures and the narrator's commentary is a triumph of adjectives over analysis, reminiscent of the worst in Poe rather than the best in Lawrence. Penderton and Williams continually move in states between stupor and somnambulism, experiencing rootless terror and dark, unspeakable desires. When the captain is near the private, he suffers "a curious lapse of sensory impressions" and finds himself "unable to see or hear properly"; and Williams often stands silent staring ominously into space "in the attitude of one who listens to a call from a long distance." Unfortunately, the call never comes through for Williams, or for the reader; the menace remains obscure and Mrs. McCullers' promptings stir only laughter and disbelief.

In the last analysis, *Reflections in a Golden Eye* provides no genuine insight into sexual pathologies, but merely an arbitrary series of gaudy, melodramatic episodes that shock without illuminating and never coalesce into larger patterns of action or meaning. Penderton may drop a kitten into a freezing mailbox, but his sadism seems less significant than his stupidity. Williams, standing over the sleeping body of Leonora, finishes her half-eaten piece of chicken; we may remember the gesture, but not the true nature of the man who made it. When Alison sees the soldier hiding in the shadows of the Penderton house, she feels "an eerie shock," closes her eyes, and counts "by sevens to two hundred and eighty." People counting by seven to two hundred and eighty—this is a useful image to describe what goes on in *Reflections in a Golden Eye*—are strange, oddly

provocative, but not very enlightening about human character and conduct.

"The Ballad of the Sad Café" is a good deal more rewarding. Instead of trying to compete with writers of much greater psychological awareness and architectonic skill, Mrs. McCullers here wisely moves in a limited area more suited to her talents—the alien, elemental world of legend and romance. Like all good ballads, her story is urgent, atmospheric, and primitive, and yet, in its melodramatic swiftness and simplicity, tells us more things memorable about human life than all the devious sophisticated posturings of *Reflections in a Golden Eye*.

In the background are the physical facts of life that count for so much in the ballad world: a dingy southern town cut off from the accommodations of civilized society, boundaries of swamps and cold black pinewood, weather that is raw in winter and white with the glare of heat in summer. Only those who must come here: the tax collector to bother the rich; an investigator to refuse credit to Ryan, the weaver; a lost traveler to find his way back to his destination. Decayed buildings lean in imminent collapse and intimations of mortality are everywhere. The moon makes "dim, twisted shadows on the blossoming peach trees," and the odor of sweet spring grass mingles with the warm, sour smell of a nearby lagoon. Strangers arrive suddenly, often at night, and they have intimate ties with the twilight world of animals. The hunchback's hands are like "dirty sparrow claws," and he perches on a railing the way "a sick bird huddles on a telephone wire," to "grieve publicly." Much depends on the cycle of the seasons and the climactic events of the plot often have their effective climatic correspondences. Autumn begins with cool days of a "clean bright sweetness," but when the villain comes home from prison, the weather turns sticky, sultry, and rotten. A month before the famous wrestling match that brings the story to a close, snow falls for the first time in living memory.

The boldness and precision with which she creates the sense of a town estranged from the rest of the world is the first of Mrs. McCullers' successes in "The Ballad of the Sad Café." Unlike those narrators in the earlier novels who move uneasily from realism to myth and back again, the invented voice in this story has an obvious authority and grace. Beginning simply in the present, she tells us that things are dismal now but once upon a time there was gaiety and color in the human landscape. No attempt is made to mask the calamitous outcome; ruin is announced at the start; our interest will be entirely in how it was accomplished. Since she is confident in her grasp of the moment and the milieu, Mrs. McCullers assumes a relaxed, colloquial style, punctuating the narrative with phrases like "time must pass" and "so do not forget."

Knowing that her gruesome story might, if too solemnly told, seem wildly melodramatic, she skillfully uses folk humor to sweeten the Gothic tale. When the shambling, toothless Merlie Ryan spreads the rumor that Amelia has murdered the newly arrived Lymon, Mrs. McCullers casually reports: "It was a fierce and sickly tale the town built up that day. In it were all the things which cause the heart to shiver—a hunchback, a midnight burial in the swamp, the dragging of Miss Amelia through the streets of the town . . ." But then, moments later, she parades her little peacock proudly down the stairs. Throughout the narrative, understatement and playfulness humanize the actors and make their behavior seem less morbid. Often, in dialogue, they use an idiom full of the comic hyperbole so common in country speech. Amelia claims to have slept as soundly as if she were drowned in axle grease, and when she is dizzy with apprehension and love, the neighbors speak of her being "well on her way . . . up fools' hill," and they can't wait to see how the affair will turn out.

It turns out badly. "The Ballad of the Sad Café" is the story of Miss Amelia Evans, a quirky amazon who sells feed, guano, and domestic staples in the town's only thriving store. Tall, dark, and unapproachable in a rough, masculine way, Amelia is an uncompromising merchant with a passion for vindictive lawsuits and a beneficent witch doctor with a genuine desire to ease human pain. Both her business acumen and her healing powers are legendary; what she shrewdly extracts in trade she gives back in the free and effective dispensation of a hundred different cures. Since her liquors relieve melancholy, her foods hunger, and her folk remedies pain, this perverse cross between Ceres, Bacchus, and the neighborhood medicine man is the one indispensable person in town.

That the hard-fisted Amelia has the living touch is demonstrated at the arrival of a sniveling hunchbacked dwarf who asks for food and shelter. His worth, he claims, is based on the urgency of kinship, and his weird unraveling of cousins, half sisters, and third husbands is a neat parody of the mysterious genealogical links in ballad and romance. Miss Amelia immediately acknowledges the tie, lightly touches his hump, and offers him liquor, dinner, and a bed. Soon, Cousin Lymon is installed in Amelia's sanctuary, sharing rooms rarely seen by living eyes, and a bizarre relationship, very much like love, transforms them both. As lover, she becomes softened, graceful, communicative, eager to extend the rewards of companionship to others; he, the beloved, becomes proud, perky, aristocratic. Even the townspeople benefit. The liquor that Miss Amelia used to dispense on her doorstep is now served inside, and gradually the store evolves into a café featuring the exotic hunchback and some palatable food and drink. Warmth, affectionate fellowship, "a certain gaiety and grace of behavior," momentarily replace suspicion, loneliness, egotism, and rough-hewn malice—the rigorous truths of the world outside. Niggardly Amelia puts free crackers on the counter, customers share their liquor, and the flourishing café provides the one bright page in the history of this melancholy town.

Unhappily, the festive interlude lasts only six years before the sins of the past exact their tribute and the catastrophe announced at the start is set in motion. Some years before the appearance of Lymon, the young Amelia had been married for ten stormy days to Marvin Macy. Handsome, mercurial, vicious, and cunning, Macy had been a most notable young scoundrel, the demon lover of every "soft-eyed" young girl in town. Miraculously enough, *he* had fallen passionately in love with the haggard Amelia and became her long-suffering romantic knight. As a disdainful mistress, Amelia needed little instruction; after their marriage, she rejected his advances, sold his presents, and battered his face with her punches. Macy, disconsolate and swearing vengeance, ran off to a life of crime and an eventual stretch in the Atlanta penitentiary. Afterwards, Miss Amelia cut up his Klansman's robe to cover her tobacco plants.

Once Macy reappears in town, the tempo quickens and everyone prepares for the inevitable confrontations of the two epic antagonists. Most of the wise money is on Amelia, for she had beaten more than her weight several times before. The twist, however, in this tale is provided by Cousin Lymon, who completes the eccentric triangle of love relationships by falling desperately for the roguish Macy. This time it is Amelia's turn to suffer at the hands of a capricious beloved. While Lymon slavishly follows the scornful Macy about

town, she becomes increasingly distraught at the turn in his affections; but nothing can be done. Lymon announces that Macy will move in with them and Amelia comes to the mournful recognition that "once you have lived with another . . . it is better to take in your mortal enemy than face the terror of living alone."

Step by step, Amelia and Macy prepare for the hand-to-hand combat that everyone knows must come. On the second of February, when a bloody-breasted hawk gives the signal by flying over Amelia's house, all the townspeople move as spectators toward the café. At seven o'clock, the two contestants begin to pound one another with hundreds of bone-cracking blows. After a savage half-hour, when boxing has turned to wrestling, Amelia puts her triumphant hands to the throat of her fallen adversary; but with astonishing swiftness, Cousin Lymon flies at her back, pulls her off, and gives the victory to Macy. That night, to celebrate their triumph, the two men smash up Amelia's property and disappear. In the months that follow, Amelia lets the café and her healing practice fall into ruin, and she eventually becomes a recluse. The town returns to its desolate, mechanical ways; "the soul rots with boredom"; and the tale ends with the swelling song of a chain gang.

Much of what is permanently haunting in this grotesque little story is the product of Mrs. McCullers' easy relationship with the properties of the ballad world. Experience heightened far beyond the realm of plausibility is given a valid, poetic truth by the propriety of those conventions that make the miraculous seem oddly real. Dreams, superstitions, omens, numbers, musical motifs, all operate here to provide an authentic atmosphere for this perverse triangle of passion, and to make the inexplicable longings of the characters seem like dark elemental forces in the natural world. Enigmatic melodies are heard in the night: wild, high voices singing songs that never end. Macy, the demon lover, plays the guitar, and when he sings the tunes glide "slowly from his throat like eels." As a doctor, Amelia depends on a stunning variety of secret herbs; her Kroup Kure, made from whiskey, rock candy, and an unnamed third power, is a wonder drug, while her liquor has been known to bring up messages from the bottom of the human soul. When she guards the low fire of her ritual still, Amelia likes to untie knots in rope, and in her parlor cabinet she keeps an acorn and two small stones. The acorn she picked from the ground the day her father died, and the stones had once been removed from her kidney. If she wants Lymon to come along to Cheehaw, she asks him seven times, and when he continually refuses, she draws a heavy line with a stick around the barbecue pit and orders him not to trespass that limit. Naturally, when the time must be set for the epic fight, seven o'clock is chosen. Miss Amelia is not the only character to be given a powerful armory of signs and talismans. Lymon sits regularly on a sack of guano and is rarely without his snuffbox. Years earlier, Macy had courted his love with a bunch of swamp flowers, a sack of chitterlings, and a silver ring; and when he returns from prison the neighbors fear him as more dangerous than ever because while put away, he "must have learned the method of laying charms." Always called devilish, Macy never sweats, not even in August, and that—Mrs. McCullers reminds us—is surely "a sign worth pondering."

By relying so heavily on charms and rituals, the characters emphasize the fated, irrational quality of so many of their decisive acts. Like most works in its traditional genre, "The Ballad of the Sad Café" illustrates the consequences of moral choice but does not probe it; analysis is less vital than the starkness of dramatic presentation. Yet an evocative atmosphere and a strong story line would not in themselves ensure success if the illustration were not thematically absorbing as well. The richly patterned, sinister dance in which Macy, Amelia, and Lymon play at different times the roles of lover and beloved dramatizes the wayward nature of human passion and the irreconcilable antagonism inherent in every love relationship.

At one point in his poem "Prayer for My Daughter," William Butler Yeats, speaking of the splendid contrariety with which females choose their lovers, describes how beautiful women sometimes eat "a crazy salad with their meat." "The Ballad of the Sad Café" is about the "crazy salad" of every man: ugly and beautiful, heiress and outlaw, dwarf and amazon—they all choose love objects in ways that demonstrate that passion is the most permanent and amazing of all the human mysteries. In the McCullers world, the lover occupies the highest seat in the pantheon, for he has the restlessness and imagination to wish to break free from the constrictive prison of ego and connect with another person. His choices are often arbitrary and improbable, but once made he worships them with a constancy that can only inspire amazement. Everyone wants to be a lover because the lover is the archetypal creative spirit: dreamer, quester, romantic idealist. If love compels, it can also soften. When Macy is smitten with Amelia, he becomes improved in civility; and Amelia's passion for Lymon not only refines her temperament and reduces her lawsuits, but also results in the establishment of the café. Product of her love, the café is the symbol of the ability of human affection to create intimacy and delight where only barrenness existed before. Yet, if love can sweeten and refine, it can also leave the lover defenseless. Having created the beloved in the image of his own desperate desire, the lover is open to rebuff and betrayal, for he tempts the one permanent quality of any beloved—his cruelty. In "The Ballad of the Sad Café," the beloved is a static figure, chosen by someone else. Easily resentful of being considered a token, he is also quick to recognize the assailability of his admirer and the extent of his own manipulative powers.

In Mrs. McCullers' triangle, each character is revealed successively in the roles of lover and beloved. In his suit of Amelia, Macy is meek with longing and easily swayed by others; he saves his wages, abandons fornication, and goes regularly to church. But in response to Amelia's chilling rejection, he becomes more brutally antisocial than he had ever been before. On his return to town, cast as his wife's revenger and Lymon's beloved, he alternates between abusiveness and complete indifference, calling the sullen dwarf "Brokeback" at one moment and ignoring him the next. Like Macy, Lymon is also violently contradictory in both roles. Admired by Amelia, he gains forceful self-assurance, but also learns to exercise the hateful tyranny of a spoiled child. Finicky, boastful, self-absorbed, he becomes wildly obsessive in his demands for personal gratification. Yet when he falls for Macy, his reversal is perhaps even more disagreeable. Obsessed now by his desire to attract Macy's attention, he flaps his ears and mopes about pathetically like a small dog sick for love.

The most memorable metamorphosis, however, is experienced by Amelia. Chosen by Macy at nineteen, she spits in contempt and strikes out fiercely at every opportunity. Hard-hearted, peremptory, and self-sufficient, she does not let her rage affect her capacity to turn a deal in her own favor, and she quickly strips her husband of everything he owns. At thirty, however, when she chooses Lymon, a remarkable change occurs. The rudest misanthrope in town turns genial, even cheerful, moving easily among people, sharing her

liquor, forgetting to bolt the door at night. Instead of overalls and swampboots, she occasionally dons a soft red dress, and as she rubs Lymon twice a day with pot liquor to give him strength, her hatred of physicality relaxes. Suddenly nostalgic about the past, she turns candid about the present, confiding in the dwarf about trade secrets and the size of her bank account. As lover for the first time in her life, Amelia takes emotional risks by putting herself in a position of extreme vulnerability. Staring at Lymon, she has the fascinating expression of "pain, perplexity, and uncertain joy"—the lonesome look of the lover. When she learns that Macy may return, she—in her pride—miscalculates Lymon's fickleness and her own power over his life; and after his affection is alienated, she becomes frightfully distracted, pursuing those contradictory courses that lead to her downfall.

Because she has the capacity to change and the energy to pursue her awakened desire for companionship, Amelia turns from a harridan evoking awe to a woman worthy of compassion. By learning to love she has become more human—more tender, gracious, amiable, perceptive; but also more obviously exposed to the inevitable stings of loneliness, betrayal, and suffering. As healer, hostess, and lover, she is —despite her rudeness and suspicion—a force for good in the community, and the destruction of her dream is a cause for genuine mourning. "The Ballad of the Sad Café" is an elegy for Amelia Evans, and it has all the brooding eloquence and eccentricity to stand as a fitting tribute to that very peculiar lady.

Although "The Ballad of the Sad Café" is by far the best of Mrs. McCullers' excursions into the grotesque, it is not without reminders of the penumbral insistence that mars her worst work. Too much is occasionally made of dark nights of the soul and of things going on there that only God can understand. Because the things that go on in *The Member of the Wedding* are available to everyone and are recorded with vivacity by an artist who understands them, it is the best of all her books.

Like a number of other carefully patterned modern novels *(Nostromo, A Passage to India, To the Lighthouse, The Sun Also Rises), The Member of the Wedding* is divided into three parts to call special attention to the rhythmical quality of the action. In Hemingway's book, for instance, a false sense of movement is established by having Brett go off with Robert Cohn at the close of the first part and with Pedro Romero at the close of the second. Part III, however, ends as it should with Brett and Jake, sterile as ever, sitting in a stationary taxi. In Mrs. McCullers' book, the rhythm—different but equally self-conscious—follows the familiar journey of adolescent initiation: the stirrings of dissatisfaction, jubilant hope founded on misplaced idealism, and disillusionment accompanied by a new wisdom about the limits of human life.

In Part I, we are introduced to the world of Frankie Addams, a tall, gawky, motherless, twelve-year-old tomboy with cropped hair and the scars of wildness decorating her feet. Ever since April, Frankie has been in the press of a vague but powerful discontent, and now—in the heat of August—she approaches her first serious teen-age crisis. As Diana Trilling has remarked, summer is the most disquieting time of the child's year because the end of school throws him back "so completely on his own incoherent resources"; and Frankie validates this observation both by the range of her resources and by the charming extremity of her incoherence. Often she is an agile, quick-witted girl, her language able to reveal the quality of her mind and sensibility. Thinking of her brother and Janice, his fiancée, she can coin the phrase "they are the we of me"; and she has the wit to dramatize her passion for "hopping-

john" (a mixture of peas and rice) by asking her cousin to wave a plate under her nose when she lies in her coffin, for if a breath of life is left her she will sit up and eat. At the edge of adolescence, however, she doesn't quite know what she is going to say until she says it, and she continually falls back on words like "curious," "queer," "puzzling," and on such affected literary borrowings as "I am sick unto death." Her main complaint is separateness; she is "an unjoined person" and "a member of nothing in the world."

Since Frankie now feels far more than she is able to express, Mrs. McCullers wisely uses a narrative technique similar to the Jamesian point of view in *The Ambassadors*, following the girl around, reporting what she does and sees, but speaking of her only in the author's third-person voice. Thus, she is able to achieve sympathy and a certain distance, to convey the vivid, poetic, but essentially unformed quality of Frankie's fantasy life. And Frankie is nothing if not a fantast. In the heat of the Georgia summer, she dreams and writes little plays about polar bears and igloos, and when she puts seashells to her ear, she has no trouble hearing tides in the Gulf of Mexico. Thinking of the warmth and conviviality of family life, she imagines people around a hearth talking with "woven voices." And in her finest performance, she sits with eyes half-closed at the kitchen table conjuring up the wedding of Jarvis and Janice in a snow-covered, silent church—the bride and groom with luminous blankness where their faces should be.

The first part of *The Member of the Wedding* fills in the details of this fine portrait of twelve going on thirteen: the blend of prescience and infantilism; the edginess, indecision, continual bluster; the brooding inarticulateness mixed with the wackiest kind of exactitude. Although Frankie cannot describe her convulsive feelings about life, she has figured out with frightful precision that if her present growth continues she will be just over nine feet tall at her eighteenth birthday. By turns solemn and giddy, she does anything that impulse drives her to do, but whatever she does is always wrong and not at all what she actually would like to do. In the most effective instance of this muddle, she picks up a knife to have something to hold on to, but soon flings it across the kitchen to scare the bewildered cook and to demonstrate her claim to be the finest knife thrower in town. (Amusingly enough, this point was transformed in the stage version, when—to keep Julie Harris from having to perform as a virtuoso every night—Mrs. McCullers had the knife miss the beam and Frankie exclaim: "I *used* to be the best knife thrower in town.")

A significant part of our response to Frankie is complicated and controlled by the setting in which she is placed and the people with whom she has to deal. The kitchen in the ramshackle house at 124 Grove Street, where most of the action takes place, is a stale, ugly square room decorated fitfully with the odd drawings of children. In the background, a radio, crossing several stations, blends war reports with advertisements and the music of a honky-tonk band. In the foreground is the imposing figure of Berenice Sadie Brown. At thirty-five or thereabouts (she is described as cagey about her age in the novel, and as forty-five in the play), Berenice gives off an air of power and tranquillity. Short, broad-shouldered, and very black, she speaks with a slow, measured cadence that suggests a wisdom painstakingly earned; and her stock of folk sayings ("it is a known truth that gray-eyed people are jealous," "I believe the sun has fried your brains") reveals both an earthy common sense and a gift for high-flown metaphorical language. For much of the novel, Berenice's clarity and bluntness serve as a genial check on Frankie's

foggy romanticism, and she spends a good deal of her time calling the girl back to the things of the real world. This mild, yet affectionate antagonism between Frankie and Berenice is the source of some of the most delicate comedy in the novel, and Mrs. McCullers' steady gift for recording its turns and counterturns is an index to her mastery of these homely materials.

Yet Berenice would not be so memorable a character if she did not also embody in her own personality a complementary response to realism, for she is a woman with a profound romantic strain that has not been extinguished by those very disappointments on which her most mature stoicism is based. The physical sign of Berenice's fascination is her false eye, the glittering blue counterpart of her real eye, which is melancholy and dark. That this black woman should want a bright blue eye is a mystery to Frankie but not to us, for it symbolizes her powerful desire to break free from the fated conditions of her birth and social position. The moral sign of Berenice's exoticism is implicit in the history of her four marriages, a story that she tells with the leisure and formulaic vividness of an ancient bard. When she sits in the dreary Addams kitchen and begins the narrative that Frankie has heard countless times before, she seems to the girl "a colored queen unwinding a bolt of cloth of gold." The first husband had been Ludie Freeman, a brickmason with whom she lived happily for nine passionate years, and when he died suddenly in November 1931, she embarked on an unconscious voyage to find his equal in other, less satisfactory, men. Ludie had been a handsome fellow with only one touch of ugliness—a bruised and disfigured thumb. One day, half a year after his death, Berenice was astounded to see a replica of that thumb on a man sitting next to her at church. Transfixed by the sign, she married Jamie Beale, who soon turned out to be alcoholic and worthless. Henry Johnson, the third husband, was also created in the image of the beloved Ludie. He had bought the dead man's coat at a second-hand clothing store and hypnotized Berenice by the familiarity of the fine figure he made. But poor Johnson, lacking his share of good sense, began to dream of eating while asleep, and after he swallowed a swatch of the bed sheet, Berenice felt compelled to try her luck elsewhere. The fourth husband, Willis Rhodes, gouged out her eye, stole her furniture, and ended up in jail, but his resemblance to Ludie never quite comes clear, since Berenice insists that the tale is not fit for adolescent ears.

Because of Berenice's legendary history, Frankie's response to her is properly double. She is fascinated by the shining blue eye and by thoughts of marital melodrama, but she is suspicious of Berenice's hard-won, untheatrical stoicism. After Berenice presses a gaudy dress that she had previously ridiculed, Frankie "would have liked for her expression to be split into two parts, so that one eye stared at Berenice in an accusing way, and the other eye thanked her with a grateful look. But the human face does not divide like this, and the two expressions canceled out each other." This combination of hostility and admiration is also revealed in Frankie's response to the kitchen itself, and to the third member of its daily triumvirate, her little cousin John Henry. The ritual of the kitchen—the protracted dinners, the ragged card games, the repetitious, rhythmical conversation—is comforting and disquieting; and the room itself (in the words of Gerald Weales) is both a sanctuary and a prison. The droll and elfin John Henry may be able to draw Picasso-like profiles of the telephone man, with one eye measured just above the nose and another just below; but the harsh reality of the kitchen is less than gentle with his dreams. He makes a wonderful, original

biscuit man, with a little grinning raisin mouth, but when it comes out of the oven it looks just like any biscuit man ever made by a child, the fine, eccentric work of John Henry having been baked out. The boy, still an innocent six-year-old sensualist, stares through his glasses, wipes the biscuit man with a napkin, and butters his left foot. For Frankie, however, the kitchen is more threatening. Although she recognizes the genuine warmth and protection to be found there (the way human voices can "bloom like flowers"), she instinctively realizes that her final destiny is elsewhere. If Berenice takes her pleasure mainly in the past, and John Henry entirely in the present, then Frankie must place her fondest hopes on the promise of the future; and at the close of Part I she makes her triumphant announcement that she will become a member of her brother's wedding.

The opening pages of Part II (in which Mrs. McCullers describes the joy of a girl who seems to be walking just outside paradise) is one of the finest examples of her powers as a celebratory novelist. By inventing a bold conceit and then convincing us of its inevitability and aptness, she effectively dramatizes the paradoxical freedom to be found in human solidarity. Inspired by her new sense of belonging, Frankie finds the day before the wedding magical and unique because the familiar, not the unexpected, strikes her "with a strange surprise." To communicate this "twisted sense of the astonishing," Mrs. McCullers relies heavily on a series of fresh metaphors that catch Frankie's bright new perception of her ordinary world. In the old days, Frankie was like Uncle Charles's blindered mule, moving laboriously in the same deadening circle, lingering on street corners, browsing at the dime store, passing time at the local movie; but now—rechristened F. Jasmine—she is an exotic animal set free to wander in places she has never seen before. When F.

Jasmine wakes up on this unforgettable Saturday morning, she feels as if "her brother and the bride had slept . . . on the bottom of her heart," and she immediately thinks of the Sunday wedding. Forgoing her usual outfit of mismatched clothing, she enhances a neat pink dress with lipstick and a new perfume. Downstairs at breakfast, she gives another demonstration of the benevolent powers of human connection. Exhilarated by the thought of her role at the wedding, she is able for the first time to understand the mundane ritual of her father's life. Watching him across the kitchen, she breaks free from the prison of her ego, and feels a new tenderness for this bluff, good-hearted widower. Mrs. McCullers, realistic and anxious to avoid sentimentality, has Frankie's expression of love throttled by her father's demand for a monkey wrench and screwdriver.

Once wandering through town, F. Jasmine feels the quickness and enthusiasm of a voyager in an enchanted land. For the first time in her life, the shouts of neighborhood children have an ineffable sweetness, and she feels a heightened sensitivity to every passing object and human being. In this new state of gladness, her perceptions are of an almost visionary intensity. When an old colored man glances at her from atop a wagon, she feels a vibrant sense of connection and can immediately conjure up a mental image of his home and his field. Like the Ancient Mariner obsessed with a story he must share with others, F. Jasmine is compelled to tell people about the wedding; but instead of interrupting a marriage feast with a morbid tale, she amuses passers-by with a sweet one. To her first listener, a sullen Portuguese café owner, she begins the narrative like "a circus dog" breaking through a paper hoop; and later, spilling her story to an old lady sweeping a porch, she discovers that the tale has "an end and a beginning, a shape like a song." Starting like a march tune, it

softens to a dreamy melody that slows her footsteps to a wander. Over drinks with a soldier, her aural hallucinations turn visual again, and she suddenly sees herself walking with her brother and his bride "beneath a cold Alaskan sky, along the sea where green ice waves lay frozen and folded on the shore." When they climb a glacier, friends call in Alaskan their "JA" names. A few minutes later, on the way home, she sees Janice and Jarvis again in a startling burst of light, but when the brightness fades, the reality turns out to be two colored boys standing in an alley.

The early morning bliss that F. Jasmine feels at no longer being separate from herself and from other people is powerful but temporary, and in the remainder of Part II the facts of the ordinary world gradually reassert themselves. As soon as she returns home, "the afternoon was like the center of the cake that Berenice had baked last Monday, a cake which failed"; and in several long and revealing conversations, Berenice's blunt but eloquent common sense punctures F. Jasmine's romantic pretensions. But the girl keeps dodging past the truth, and when she finds it hard to argue with the obvious facts, she slides off with "You wait and see," or some equally transparent evasion.

The rhythm established in the middle section of *The Member of the Wedding* depends on F. Jasmine's incorrigible gift for flight and Berenice's unerring ability to bring her spinning back down to the ground. F. Jasmine, anxious to leave her childish identity behind her, argues that a person can change his nature by changing his name, but Berenice insists that things are always accumulating around one's name, and that "We all of us somehow caught. We born this way or that way and we don't know why. But we caught anyhow. I born Berenice. You born Frankie. John Henry born John Henry. And maybe we wants to widen and bust free. But no matter what we do we still caught. Me is me and you is you and he is he. We each one of us somehow caught all by ourself."

F. Jasmine's proud refusal to accept the accuracy of Berenice's simple equation "me is me" is carried into the third section of the novel and adds dramatic force to her eventual disillusionment. Just as the opening pages of Part II show Mrs. McCullers in her best celebratory voice, so the closing pages of the book reveal her ability to mourn for maturity as well as to praise it. At the beginning of Part III, the wedding ("unmanaged as a nightmare") is described in a half-dozen paragraphs and the remaining thirty pages deal with the accommodations of a girl now called Frances. At first, in the full flush of her disappointment, she is tearful and wickedly misanthropic, but after a comically abortive attempt to run away from home, she begins gradually to realize the childishness of her earlier dreams. Between herself and all the places she had so loftily dreamed of visiting, "there was a space like an enormous canyon she could not hope to bridge or cross. . . . She was back to the fear of the summertime, the old feelings that the world was separate from herself." Now, having parted with her fantasies, she begins to compromise like most other thirteen-year-old girls. She becomes close friends with Mary Littlejohn (whom she ridiculed when she was Frankie), reads Tennyson, and plans at sixteen to take a leisurely trip around the world. Frances is a good deal more reasonable than F. Jasmine, but not altogether more attractive. In her pompous way, she corrects Berenice's diction; and in her preoccupation with Mary Littlejohn, she forgets the recently dead John Henry and seems unconcerned that Berenice will no longer work for the family. Without her spectacular and sparkling dreams, with her days filled with school and friendship, Frances seems just a bit too much like everyone else.

The Member of the Wedding is Mrs. McCullers' best book because it remains complete in itself—a small but undeniably affecting story of adolescent joy and frustration. The plot, limited to a few days in the life of a twelve-year-old girl, is more skillfully managed than the elaborate murder story in *Reflections in a Golden Eye,* or the haunting but ultimately mechanical quest pattern in *The Heart Is a Lonely Hunter.* The characters carry great conviction because Mrs. McCullers is wholly in command of their limited psychologies, and does not strain to suggest that they are darkly symbolic of more than themselves. Tonally, the novel is one of the few sentimental comedies to escape the charge of being maudlin; stylistically, it is the freshest and most inventive of her novels and stories.

In his survey *Fiction of the Forties,* Chester Eisinger has traced the main flaw in *The Member of the Wedding* to "its focus on the child's self-centered world in which the macrocosm plays no part." But this, I think, is precisely the source of its strength. Throughout this essay, I have argued that Mrs. McCullers is fundamentally a master of bright and melancholy moods, a lyricist, not a philosopher, an observer of maimed characters, not of contaminated cultures. That she writes best of uncomplicated people in fairly straightforward narrative forms is proven positively by *The Member of the Wedding* and "The Ballad of the Sad Café," and negatively by the failure of her last full-length work of fiction. Published in 1961, after ten years of painful composition, *Clock without Hands* tries to link the existential crisis of a man doomed by cancer to the sociological crisis of the South poisoned by racial strife. But because Mrs. McCullers was ill and working against her natural grain, the novel is deficient in both psychological intuition and cultural analysis.

The man condemned to die of leukemia is a forty-year-old druggist named J. T. Malone, whose final year in Milan, Georgia, 1953–54, provides the novel with its time scheme and organizational frame. Running parallel to Malone's story is the history of the town's leading family, the Clanes. At eighty-five, the former congressman Judge Fox Clane is a racist, voluptuary, and praiser of his own past; while his grandson Jester is a solemn adolescent of muddled but progressive inclinations. Both Clanes are haunted by the memory of the Judge's son and Jester's father, John, who committed suicide after the unsuccessful defense of a Negro accused of murdering the husband of a white woman with whom he had been intimate. For the Judge, the suicide represents a mysterious act of personal spite; for Jester, it is a puzzle he must solve in order to establish his own identity. An important clue to the puzzle is a blue-eyed Negro, Sherman Pew, a sullen poseur who insults white men but lives slavishly by the standards of bourgeois advertising. Jester, anxious to practice brotherhood, befriends Sherman; the Judge, aware that the boy is the illegitimate son of the Negro and the white woman, hires him as his secretary. The climax of the novel occurs when Sherman, stumbling on the truth about his ignominious origins, commits a series of outrages against the white community, drinking at a restricted fountain, watering the Judge's insulin injections, murdering Jester's dog, and renting a house in the white section of town. A vigilante committee meets, but Malone, drawing the assassin's ballot, refuses to carry out the challenge from fear for his immortal soul. In his place, a mill foreman, Sammy Lank, proudly heaves two bombs through Sherman's window. Afterwards, at the point of murdering Sammy

in vengeance, Jester learns not to be ruled by the lust for violence, and lets his hostage go. As the book ends, the Supreme Court announces school desegregation, Jester prepares to become a lawyer, Judge Clane tumbles into senility, and Malone quietly dies.

To anyone who remembers the daring symbolic design of *The Heart Is a Lonely Hunter*, the measured suspense in "The Ballad of the Sad Café," or the shrewd sense of motivation in *The Member of the Wedding, Clock without Hands* must come as an unhappy reminder of a talent no longer at full strength. In none of her earlier books is the plot so clumsily managed, the pacing so tedious, the people so vacant, the symbolism so ineffectively contrived.

Take Malone, for example. At the start of the novel, he is the epitome of the common man, drab in thought, hesitant in action. When first given the death sentence, he refuses to face the truth, and looks for consolation in religion, mystery stories, and afternoon naps; but gradually, he wakes up to the emptiness of his entire life. It is here, however, that his creator fails him. Instead of providing Malone with heightened awareness and a language in which to express it, Mrs. McCullers continues to describe his dread as "amorphous" and his terror as "something awful and incomprehensible." If Malone has little credibility as an existential hero, Fox Clane and Sherman have even less as actors in a drama of racial conflict. Sodden with the worst illusions of the antebellum South, and anxious "to defend his womankind against the black and alien invader," the Judge at the start is a vigorous comic caricature. But by the third chapter, his endless ranting against TVA, FHA, FDR, Bolsheviks in government, and Negresses at the Lincoln Memorial becomes tiresome and easy to predict. In the light of his obvious political cunning, his plan to redeem Confederate money is entirely implausible; and his final collapse, during which he chants the Gettysburg Address on the radio, is preposterous. Sherman, too, is given a set of contradictory emotions that never seem to live convincingly under the same skin. Most often he is swaggering, truculent, and comically gullible, insulting Jester with infantile obscenities or drinking Lord Calvert's whiskey in hopes of becoming a "Man of Distinction." When the Judge tells the boy about his scheme to restore the financial health of the South, Sherman's lips and nostrils flutter, and he fiercely smashes the old man's fountain pen. Yet, a moment later, after the Judge speaks of "polarities," Sherman writes the word down and thinks how he is "benefitting from the Judge's vocabulary if nothing else." Given these absurdities, it is impossible to believe in Sherman's role as the defiant young Negro breaking community barriers by renting a house.

For these lifeless and improbable characters, Mrs. McCullers seems to have had a symbolic intention. In a letter, written while the book was still in manuscript, she spoke of Malone's white blood cells crowding out the dark as "peculiarly a symbol of the South." That Fox Clane is supposed to be "the South regenerate," Malone "the South finding its conscience at 11:59," and Sherman a variety of the "social fantasy choking" the entire region was noticed by the book's earliest reviewers; but neither they nor most later readers found any part of the symbolism convincing.

Although *Clock without Hands* is a disappointment, it can—if viewed properly as an object lesson—direct us back to Mrs. McCullers' earlier works and help us to see their virtues more clearly. In the past decade, a number of critics have sometimes taken her intentions in her weakest novels as a measure of her performance, and have evoked the names of Tolstoi, Proust, and Faulkner to describe the range and quality of her achievement. Yet "The Ballad of the Sad Café" and *The Member of the Wedding* (the stories that will most likely last) demand comparison not with books by the prolific masters of European literature, but with works by three fine writers of a more moderate level of accomplishment: Eudora Welty, Katherine Anne Porter, and Flannery O'Connor. Like Carson McCullers, these contemporaries have, by exploring the lives of isolated grotesques in twilight corners of the American South, produced a small body of fiction marked by eccentric originality, artistic finish, and a bleak poetic effect. Although Mrs. McCullers may eventually rank fourth in this distinguished quartet, she belongs by disposition and the solidity of her accomplishment in their company.

Selected Bibliography

WORKS OF CARSON McCULLERS

SHORT STORIES
"Wunderkind," *Story*, 9:61–73 (December 1936).
"The Jockey," *Mademoiselle*, 17:15–16 (August 23, 1941).
"Madame Zilensky and the King of Finland," *New Yorker*, 17:15–18 (December 20, 1941).
"A Tree, a Rock, a Cloud," *Harper's Bazaar*, 76:50 ff. (November 1942).
"The Ballad of the Sad Café," *Harper's Bazaar*, 77:72 ff. (November 1943).
"The Sojourner," *Mademoiselle*, 31:90 ff. (May 1950).
"A Domestic Dilemma," *New York Post Magazine* (September 16, 1951), p. 10.
"The Haunted Boy," *Botteghe Oscure*, 16:264–78 (1955); and *Mademoiselle*, 42:134 ff. (November 1955).
"Who Has Seen the Wind?" *Mademoiselle*, 43:156 ff. (September 1956).
"Sucker," *Saturday Evening Post*, 236:68–71

(September 28, 1963). An early story printed for the first time.

"The March," *Redbook* , 128:64–65, 114–23 (March 1967).

NOVELS

The Heart Is a Lonely Hunter. Boston: Houghton Mifflin, 1940.

Reflections in a Golden Eye. Boston: Houghton Mifflin, 1941.

The Member of the Wedding. Boston: Houghton Mifflin, 1946.

Clock without Hands. Boston: Houghton Mifflin, 1961.

REMINISCENCES AND AUTOBIOGRAPHY

"Brooklyn Is My Neighborhood," *Vogue,* 97:62 ff. (March 1, 1941).

"We Carried Our Banners; We Were Pacifists, Too," *Vogue,* 97:42–43 (July 15, 1941).

"How I Began to Write," *Mademoiselle,* 27:191 ff. (September 1948).

"Home for Christmas," *Mademoiselle,* 30:53 ff. (December 1949).

"The Vision Shared," *Theatre Arts,* 34:28–30 (April 1950). (Autobiography.)

"The Discovery of Christmas," *Mademoiselle,* 38:54 ff. (December 1953).

"A Child's View of Christmas," *Redbook,* 28:30 (December 1961).

SKETCHES AND OTHER PROSE

"Look Homeward Americans," *Vogue,* 96:74–75 (December 1, 1940).

"Night Watch over Freedom," *Vogue,* 97:29 (January 1, 1941). (Patriotic tribute.)

"Correspondence" (Letter of Manoel Garcia), *New Yorker,* 18:36 (February 7, 1942). (Fictional exchange.)

"Art and Mr. Mahoney," *Mademoiselle,* 28:120 ff. (February 1949).

"The Flowering Dream: Notes on Writing," *Esquire,* 52:162–64 (December 1959).

"The Dark Brilliance of Edward Albee," *Harper's Bazaar,* 97:98–99 (January 1963).

"Isak Dinesen: In Praise of Radiance," *Saturday Review,* 46:28, 63 (March 16, 1963).

"Hospital Christmas Eve." *McCall's,* 95:96–97 (December 1967).

POEMS

"The Mortgaged Heart," *New Directions,* 10:509 (1948).

"The Dual Angel," *Botteghe Oscure,* 9:213–18 (1952) and *Mademoiselle,* 35:54 ff. (July 1952).

"When We Are Lost," *Voices,* 149:12 (December 1952).

"Stone Is Not Stone," *Mademoiselle,* 45:43 (July 1957).

Sweet as a Pickle and Clean as a Pig. Poems. Boston: Houghton Mifflin, 1964. (Children's verses.)

PLAYS

The Member of the Wedding. New York: New Directions, 1951.

The Square Root of Wonderful. Boston: Houghton Mifflin, 1958.

COLLECTED EDITIONS

The Ballad of the Sad Café. Boston: Houghton Mifflin, 1951. (Contains "The Ballad of the Sad Café," "Wunderkind," "The Jockey," "Madame Zilensky and the King of Finland," "The Sojourner," "A Domestic Dilemma," "A Tree, a Rock, a Cloud," *The Heart Is a Lonely Hunter, Reflections in a Golden Eye,* and *The Member of the Wedding.*)

The Mortgaged Heart. Boston: Houghton Mifflin, 1971. (Previously uncollected writings.)

BIBLIOGRAPHIES

Stewart, Stanley. "Carson McCullers, 1940–1956: A Selected Checklist," *Bulletin of Bibliography,* 22:182–85 (April 1959).

Phillips, Robert S. "Carson McCullers: 1956–1964: A Selected Checklist," *Bulletin of Bibliography,* 24:113–16 (September–December 1964).

CRITICAL STUDIES

Baldanza, Frank. "Plato in Dixie," *Georgia Review,* 12:151–67 (1958).

Eisinger, Chester E. *Fiction of the Forties.* Chicago: University of Chicago Press, 1963. Pp. 243–58.

Emerson, Donald. "The Ambiguities of *Clock without Hands,*" *Wisconsin Studies in Contemporary Literature,* 3:15–28 (Fall 1962).

Evans, Oliver. *The Ballad of Carson McCullers.* New York: Coward McCann, 1966.

Felheim, Melvin. "Eudora Welty and Carson Mc-Cullers," *Contemporary American Novelists,* edited by Harry Moore. Carbondale: Southern Illinois University Press, 1964. Pp. 41–53.

Hassan, Ihab. *Radical Innocence.* Princeton, N.J.: Princeton University Press, 1961. Pp. 205–29.

"Human Isolation," *Times Literary Supplement* (London), 52:460 (July 17, 1960).

Kohler, Dayton. "Carson McCullers: Variations on a Theme," *College English,* 13:1–8 (October 1951).

Phillips, Robert. "The Gothic Architecture of *The Member of the Wedding,*" *Renascence,* 16:59–72 (Winter 1964).

Pritchett, V. S. "Books in General," *New Statesman and Nation,* 44:137–38 (August 2, 1952).

Schorer, Mark. "McCullers and Capote: Basic Patterns," in *The Creative Present,* edited by N. Balakian and C. Simmons. New York: Doubleday, 1963. Pp. 79–109.

Smith, Simeon M. "Carson McCullers: A Critical Introduction." Unpublished dissertation, University of Pennsylvania, 1964.

Vickery, John. "Carson McCullers: A Map of Love," *Wisconsin Studies in Contemporary Literature,* 1:14–24 (1960).

Weales, Gerald. *American Drama since World War II.* New York: Harcourt, Brace & World, 1962. Pp. 176–79.

—LAWRENCE GRAVER